Handbook of
Feminist Research

Second Edition

This book is dedicated to my sister Georgia Geraghty
& in loving memory of my sister Janet Green Fisher

With much admiration to feminist researchers who pursue subjugated
knowledge in the service of social justice and transformation
for women and other oppressed groups

Handbook of
Feminist Research

Theory and Praxis

Second Edition

Edited by
Sharlene Nagy Hesse-Biber
Boston College

Los Angeles | London | New Delhi
Singapore | Washington DC

Culture & Demographics

SAGE

Los Angeles | London | New Delhi
Singapore | Washington DC

FOR INFORMATION:

SAGE Publications, Inc.
2455 Teller Road
Thousand Oaks, California 91320
E-mail: order@sagepub.com

SAGE Publications Ltd.
1 Oliver's Yard
55 City Road
London EC1Y 1SP
United Kingdom

SAGE Publications India Pvt. Ltd.
B 1/I 1 Mohan Cooperative Industrial Area
Mathura Road, New Delhi 110 044
India

SAGE Publications Asia-Pacific Pte. Ltd.
33 Pekin Street #02-01
Far East Square
Singapore 048763

Acquisitions Editor: Vicki Knight
Associate Editor: Lauren Habib
Editorial Assistant: Kalie Koscielak
Production Editor: Astrid Virding
Copy Editors: Karen E. Taylor and
                Gillian Dickens
Typesetter: C&M Digitals (P) Ltd.
Proofreader: Scott Oney
Indexer: Will Ragsdale
Cover Designer: Candice Harman
Marketing Manager: Helen Salmon
Permissions Editor: Adele Hutchinson

Printed in the United States of America

Library of Congress Cataloging-in-Publication Data

Handbook of feminist research : theory and praxis / Sharlene Nagy Hesse-Biber, editor. — 2nd ed.

p. cm.
Includes bibliographical references and index.

ISBN 978-1-4129-8059-3 (cloth : alk. paper)

1. Women—Research—Methodology. 2. Women's studies—Methodology. 3. Social sciences—Research—Methodology. 4. Feminist theory. I. Hesse-Biber, Sharlene Nagy.

HQ1180.H35 2012
305.42072—dc23   2011032016

This book is printed on acid-free paper.

15 10 9 8 7 6 5 4 3 2

CONTENTS

PREFACE

The second edition of the *Handbook of Feminist Research: Theory and Praxis* presents both a theoretical and a practical approach to conducting social science research on, for, and about women. The primary goal of the *Handbook* is to enable readers to develop an understanding of feminist research by introducing a range of feminist epistemologies, methodologies, and methods that have had a significant impact on feminist research practice and women's studies scholarship.

As a teacher at the Graduate Consortium in Women's Studies at Radcliffe College in the mid-1990s, I co-taught a course titled "Feminist Perspectives in Research: Interdisciplinary Practice in the Study of Gender." I came to appreciate the importance of taking an interdisciplinary approach to the study and teaching of feminist perspectives on theory and methods. The mission of the Graduate Consortium in Women's Studies, which began in 1992, was to bring faculty from various disciplines to "discuss ways of consolidating and increasing the availability of feminist research and teaching across the disciplines and across institutions" (Hesse-Biber, Gilmartin, & Lydenberg, 1999, p. 5).

The first edition of the *Handbook* materialized after many years of my own involvement as a teacher of undergraduate and graduate research methods courses: I found that the topic of feminist research was too often neglected in standard research methods books. Distinctly breaking from that tradition, the first edition of the *Handbook* had as its goal the establishment and legitimization of new feminist perspectives on the theory and practice of research. This second edition of the *Handbook* builds on these goals by expanding the base of scholarship with several new chapters on the place of feminism in the natural sciences, social work, the health sciences, and environmental studies. It extends the scholarship related to the intersections of race, class, gender, and globalization by including a new chapter that explores issues of gender identity, a chapter that considers, among other things, transgender, transsexualism, and the queering of gender identities in the research process.

All chapters retained from the first edition of the *Handbook* have been expanded and updated with the most current scholarship, including scholarship on the role that new technologies play in the feminist research process across the disciplines. We have continued to stress the tight link between feminist research and social change and transformation.

WHAT'S NEW IN THE SECOND EDITION?

We continue to reach out to two primary constituencies. The first is researchers, practitioners, and students within and outside the academy, people who conduct a variety of research projects and who are interested in consulting "cutting-edge" research methods and gaining insights into the overall research process. This group also includes policy makers and activists who are interested in how to conduct research for social change. The second edition's audience continues to include academic researchers who, it is hoped, will use the *Handbook* in their research scholarship as well as in their courses, at the upper-undergraduate and graduate levels, as a main or supplementary text.

The second edition of the *Handbook* also includes a range of new research and teaching resources for both these readership groups and provides a list of websites as well as journal references that are specifically geared to each chapter's content. In addition, the second edition has an enhanced pedagogical feature at the end of each chapter: a set of key discussion questions intended as a praxis application for the ideas and concepts contained in that chapter.

The Second Edition's Structure

The second edition's overall structure has become more focused on theory and praxis and is now divided into three sections that represent, respectively, broader perspectives and research frameworks; feminist praxis; and deeper issues and insights in praxis and pedagogy. Each chapter in this edition has also been restructured to include research case studies, so as to provide readers with step-by-step praxis examples for conducting their own research projects.

Part I, "Feminist Perspectives on Knowledge Building," traces the historical rise of feminist research and begins with the early link of feminist epistemologies and perspectives within the research process. We trace the contours of early feminist inquiry and introduce the reader to the history, and historical debates, of and within feminist scholarship. We explore the androcentrism (male bias) in traditional research projects and the alternative set of questions feminist researchers bring to the research endeavor. We explore the political process of knowledge building by introducing the reader to the link between knowledge, authority, representation, and power relations.

The chapters in Part I introduce the unique knowledge frameworks feminists offer to enhance our understanding of social reality. We explore some of the range of issues and questions feminists have addressed, the emphasis of feminist epistemologies and methodologies on understanding the diversity of women's experiences, and feminism's commitment to the empowerment of women and other oppressed groups.

We examine a broad spectrum of the most important feminist perspectives, and we take an in-depth look at how a given methodology intersects with epistemology and method to produce a set of research practices. The *Handbook*'s overall thesis is that any given feminist perspective does not preclude the use of specific methods but serves to guide how a given method is practiced in the research process. Each feminist perspective is distinct but sometimes shares elements with other perspectives. We discuss the similarities and differences across the spectrum of feminist perspectives on knowledge building.

Part II of the *Handbook*, "Feminist Research Praxis," examines how feminist researchers utilize a range of research methods in the service of feminist perspectives. Feminist researchers use a range of qualitative and quantitative methods as well as mixed methods and multimethods, and this section examines the unique characteristics feminist researchers bring to the practice of feminist research because they maintain a tight link between their theoretical perspectives and methods practices.

This section includes three new chapters. Deboleena Roy's chapter, "Feminist Approaches to Inquiry in the Natural Sciences: Practices for the Lab," tackles how feminist researchers go about their work within a natural science laboratory setting. She notes the importance of being reflexive about the range of ethical conundrums that are contained within practicing the scientific method. Roy suggests the importance of infusing laboratory research with a sense of "playfulness" and what she terms a "feeling around" in the pursuit of feminist laboratory knowledge building, an approach that privileges a reaching out to other scientists in order to build a community of "togetherness" among researchers.

Stéphanie Wahab, Ben Anderson-Nathe, and Christina Gringeri's new chapter, "Joining the Conversation: Social Work Contributions to Feminist Research," provides exemplary case studies of the practice of feminist research within a social work setting. Wahab and her colleagues suggest that social work's history of being grounded in praxis, ethics, and reflection can contribute to feminist knowledge building. In turn, social work's engagement with feminist theory may help to disrupt the assumptions of knowledge contained in social work practice.

Kristen Intemann's new chapter, "Putting Feminist Research Principles Into Practice," suggests that the research principles of feminist praxis can benefit scientific research. Intemann proposes that scientific communities need to tend to issues of difference in the scientific research process by including diverse researchers (in terms of experiences, social positions, and values). This diversity will serve to enhance a critical reflection on scientific research praxis with the goals of enhancing the perspective of the marginalized and working toward a multiplicity of conceptual models.

Part III of the *Handbook*, "Feminist Issues and Insights in Practice and Pedagogy," examines some of the current tensions within feminist research and knowledge building and discusses a range of strategies for positioning feminist research within the dominant research paradigms and emerging research practices. Part III also tackles the conceptualization of difference and its practice as well as how feminist researchers can develop an empowered feminist community of scholars across transnational space. In addition, Part III focuses on issues within the practice of feminist pedagogy, and it includes a discussion of how feminists can or should convey the range of women's studies scholarship so as to differentiate this scholarship from the charge that it conveys only ideology, not knowledge.

A new chapter added to this section is Katherine Johnson's contribution, "Transgender, Transsexualism, and the Queering of Gender Identities: Debates for Feminist Research." Johnson examines some of the core issues of contention within queer studies with the goal of identifying those theoretical perspectives that have particular relevance to feminist researchers. Johnson argues that feminist researchers need to be cognizant of the range of identity positions with regard to gender identities. Johnson encourages feminist researchers to explore definitions, terminology, and areas for coalitions in order to promote the crossing of identity borders. Johnson's work analyzes the dialogues between feminism and transgender, transsexual, and queer studies and looks at how the fields may work together to produce more robust research.

As Sharlene Hesse-Biber and Abigail Brooks's introduction to this section reminds us, "There is no *one* feminist viewpoint that defines feminist inquiry." Rather, "feminists continue to engage in and dialogue across a range of diverse approaches to theory, praxis, and pedagogy" (Hesse-Biber & Brooks, Chapter 24, this volume).

OVERALL RESEARCH AND PEDAGOGICAL GOALS OF THE SECOND EDITION

The overall goal of the second edition of the *Handbook* continues to be that of providing a set of clearly defined research concepts that are devoid of as much technical language as possible, recognizing that our audience also includes students and others new to the field. The second edition of the *Handbook* continues to engage readers with cutting-edge debates in the field and to explore practical applications and issues for those whose research affects social policy and social change.

For academics, the *Handbook* reflects the most current thinking about feminist research emerging within and across the disciplines and geographical regions. For professors and students who will use this *Handbook* in their courses, the theoretical content (e.g., concepts and ideas) presented continues to be well grounded with the inclusion of specific hands-on research examples from the research literature. The second edition of the *Handbook* reflects a diversity of scholarship with respect to race, class, sexual orientation, and geographic region (e.g., developed and developing societies). For practitioners and activists, the content reflects the ongoing power relationships in which research is practiced; especially relevant to this group is the expanded content of those chapters that discuss feminist praxis issues.

The second edition of the *Handbook* also expands on the wealth of interdisciplinary understandings of feminist research praxis that is grounded in a tight link between epistemology, methodology, and method. My hope is that the second edition of this *Handbook* will provide researchers with the tools for excavating subjugated knowledge on women's lives and the lives of other marginalized groups in order to achieve feminist goals of empowerment and social change.

—Sharlene Nagy Hesse-Biber

ACKNOWLEDGMENTS

This *Handbook* would not be possible without the assistance and support of many members within the feminist community. First, I want to express a heartfelt thank-you to the authors of this *Handbook* for providing stellar, state-of-the-art chapters.

I want to thank especially Alicia Johnson (Boston College class of 2011) and former Boston College undergraduates Natalie Horbachevsky (Boston College class of 2009) and Hilary Flowers (Boston College class of 2010) for their invaluable editorial assistance and outstanding general academic support toward the completion of the second edition of the *Handbook*.

The *Handbook* would not be possible without the vision, wisdom, and support of my editor, Vicki Knight. Her editorial expertise and guidance were invaluable.

I want to express my love and deepest appreciation to my family, in particular to my daughters Julia Ariel and Sarah Alexandra, for their patience, love, and forbearance. I especially value the friendship, love, and support of my husband, Michael Peter Biber, MD.

I dedicate this *Handbook* to all whose knowledge remains subjugated, and I hope this *Handbook* serves as a stepping-stone to emancipation for those who seek to gather new perspectives on the knowledge-building process and who seek to use new research tools and refashion old ones—and may it serve as a place that will nurture as well as encourage dialogue about our differences.

I also dedicate this volume to my dearest sister, Janet Green Fisher, whose youthful life was cut short by breast cancer. Her humor, courage, love, and compassion continue to sustain and inspire those whose lives she touched. In addition, I want to thank my extended family—my mother, Helene Stockert, as well as my sister, Georgia Geraghty, and brother, Charles Nagy.

Last, I want to thank my wonderful Portuguese water dog, Zoli. He reminds me of the importance of play in our lives and keeps me connected to things outside my work.

—Sharlene Nagy Hesse-Biber

Boston College

Chestnut Hill, Massachusetts

ABOUT THE EDITOR

Sharlene Nagy Hesse-Biber, PhD University of Michigan, is Professor of Sociology and Director of the Women's and Gender Studies Program at Boston College. Her monograph, *Am I Thin Enough Yet?* (Oxford, 1996), was selected as one of *Choice* magazine's best academic books for 1996. She is author of *The Cult of Thinness* (Oxford, 2007) and *Mixed Methods Research: Merging Theory With Practice* (Guilford Publications, 2010). She is the coauthor of *Working Women in America* (Oxford, 2005) and *The Practice of Qualitative Research* (Sage, 2006; 2011). She is the coeditor of *Approaches to Qualitative Research* (Oxford, 2004), *Feminist Perspectives on Social Research* (Oxford, 2004), *Emergent Methods in Social Research* (Sage, 2006), and *The Handbook of Emergent Methods* (Guilford, 2008). She is also the editor of *The Handbook of Feminist Research* (Sage, 2007), an AESA Critics' Choice Award winner and selected as one of *Choice* magazine's outstanding academic titles for 2007, and coauthor of *Feminist Research Practice: A Primer* (Sage, 2007; second edition forthcoming, 2012). She is editor of *The Handbook of Emergent Technologies in Social Research* (Oxford, 2011). She is codeveloper of HyperRESEARCH, a software tool for analyzing qualitative data, and Hyper TRANSCRIBE, a transcription software tool (www.researchware.com).

ABOUT THE CONTRIBUTORS

Ben Anderson-Nathe holds master's degrees in social work and public policy and a doctorate in youth studies from the University of Minnesota. He has worked with youth in out-of-home care environments (foster and group care), community mental health, homeless and street youth centers, religious institutions, and GLBT services. His areas of research and practice are youth work and youth development, sexuality, social justice and anti-oppressive practice, and the application of interpretive research methods to practice environments. He is currently Assistant Professor in the Child and Family Studies program at Portland State University's School of Social Work and coeditor of *Child & Youth Services*.

Kum-Kum Bhavnani is Professor of Sociology at the University of California at Santa Barbara, having arrived there in 1991. She is the author and coeditor of a number of books and articles on "race" and feminisms; methodologies; and women, culture, and development. Before joining the UC Santa Barbara faculty, she studied and worked in the UK: her undergraduate degree is from Bristol, her MA from Nottingham, and her PhD from King's College, Cambridge (1988). She is also a filmmaker. Her first film was *The Shape of Water* narrated by Susan Sarandon (2006: www.theshapeofwatermovie. com), and her second film is *Nothing Like Chocolate* (forthcoming, 2011: www.nothing likechocolate.com).

Sharon Brisolara (PhD) is a program evaluator who is founder and owner of Evaluation Solutions, an evaluation organization operating in Northern California. Her areas of expertise include feminist evaluation, participatory evaluation, qualitative methodology, and mixed method studies. She is an active member of the American Evaluation Association, the Feminist Evaluation Topical Interest Group (TIG), and the Public Engagement Priority Action Team. Dr. Brisolara coedited *Feminist Evaluation: Explorations and Experiences: New Directions for Evaluation* (2002) with Dr. Denise Seigart and has written and presented in various forums on feminist evaluation and feminist theory. She is currently collaborating with Dr. Denise Seigart, and Dr. Saumitra Sengupta on an edited volume, *Feminist Evaluation and Research: Advances in Understanding and Implementation,* to be published by Guilford Press in 2012.

Abigail Brooks enjoys teaching in the Women's and Gender Studies Program and in the Sociology Department at Boston College, where she also received her doctorate in sociology in 2008. Her current book project draws from in-depth interviews to examine women's attitudes and experiences of growing older in an increasingly normalized culture of cosmetic anti-aging intervention in the United States.

Jennifer Castellow is a doctoral student in Clinical-Community Psychology at the University of South Carolina in Columbia. Her specialties include homelessness, disaster, and community mental health. She is active in community work involving substance abuse among people experiencing homelessness. She also collaborates with a local drug and alcohol treatment facility to develop and implement a program designed to address the needs of pregnant, substance-abusing women. Her current research employs a mixed-method, intersectional analysis to observe how the response to disaster elicits community action and can temporarily relieve negative stereotypes associated with homelessness. In so doing, disasters can provide a unique opportunity to imagine and to implement innovative programs to address housing needs.

Debjani Chakravarty is pursuing her doctoral studies in the Women and Gender Studies Program at Arizona State University. Her research interests span transnational feminisms, gender and citizenship, feminist jurisprudence, feminist epistemology, and cyberfeminism. Debjani has a master's and an M.Phil in sociology from the University of Pune, India. Her work is informed by feminist, postcolonial, and critical neo-Marxian theories, as well as by her experience as a journalist and social worker in India and her hybrid social location as a feminist academic in spaces of intellectual and social engagements in the global South and global North. Her dissertation project interrogates the discourse of transnational feminisms in India and the United States.

Kathy Charmaz is Professor of Sociology and Director of the Faculty Writing Program at Sonoma State University. She teaches in the areas of social psychology, classical sociological theory, medical sociology, and qualitative methods and works with faculty to advance their scholarly writing. She has written, coauthored, or coedited nine books including *Good Days, Bad Days: The Self in Chronic Illness and Time*, a recipient of the Distinguished Book Award from the Pacific Sociological Association and the Charles Horton Cooley Award from the Society for the Study of Symbolic Interaction. Her 2006 book, *Constructing Grounded Theory: A Practical Guide Through Qualitative Analysis*, received a Critic's Choice Award from the American Educational Society and has been translated into Chinese, Japanese, Polish, and Portuguese. Among her most recent writings are two multiauthored books, *Five Ways of Doing Qualitative Analysis: Phenomenological Psychology, Grounded Theory, Discourse Analysis, Narrative Research, and*

Intuitive Inquiry (2011) and *Developing Grounded Theory: The Second Generation* (2009). Professor Charmaz has received the Feminist Mentors Award and George Herbert Mead Award for Lifetime Achievement from the Society for the Study of Symbolic Interaction. She has served as president of the Pacific Sociological Association; vice-president of Alpha Kappa Delta, the international sociological honorary society; and editor of *Symbolic Interaction*, and she has just completed her term as president of the Society for the Study of Symbolic Interaction. Professor Charmaz gives frequent workshops on grounded theory methods and writing for publication to faculty, researchers, and doctoral students around the globe.

Adele E. Clarke is currently Professor of Sociology and Adjunct Professor of History of Health Sciences at the University of California, San Francisco. Her research has centered on studies of science, technology, and medicine, especially reproductive sciences and contraceptive technologies. Her book *Disciplining Reproduction* won the Basker Award and the Fleck Award. Her coedited book *The Right Tools for the Job: At Work in Twentieth Century Life Sciences* (Princeton University Press, 1992) was translated into French. Her publications on women's health include the coedited *Women's Health: Differences and Complexities* (Ohio State University Press, 1997) and *Revisioning Women, Health, and Healing: Feminist, Cultural and Technoscience Perspectives* (Routledge, 1999). On research methods, her *Situational Analysis: Grounded Theory After the Postmodern Turn* (Sage, 2005) won the Cooley Award and has been translated into German (Wiesbaden: VS Verlag für Sozialwissenschaften, 2012). Framing grounded theory methods developments historically, Clarke also coauthored *Developing Grounded Theory: The Second Generation* (Left Coast Press, 2009). Working in the sociology of health and illness field, she recently coedited *Biomedicalization: Technoscience and Transformations of Health and Illness in the U.S.* (Duke, 2010). Clarke is also coeditor of the journal *BioSocieties* and on the board of the international periodical *East Asian Science, Technology, and Society*. Her current projects center on methods, reproductive technologies in transnational travels vis-à-vis biocapital and biolabor, and the politics of "anticipation" as a dominant orientation of value, affect, and truth production in the contemporary moment.

Elizabeth R. Cole is a professor of women's studies and psychology at the University of Michigan, USA, where she has taught since 2000. Her research aims to bring feminist theory on intersectionality to social science research on race, class, and gender.

Judith A. Cook is Professor of Psychiatry at the University of Illinois at Chicago (UIC), Department of Psychiatry. She received her PhD in sociology from The Ohio State University and completed an NIMH postdoctoral training program in clinical research training at the University of Chicago. Currently she directs the Center on Mental Health Services Research and Policy (CMHSRP) that houses a federally funded center and a number of research and evaluation studies. The UIC Center on Psychiatric Disability and Co-Occurring Medical Conditions is funded for five years to conduct research that identifies health disparities, promotes delivery of evidence-based care, and empowers people to pursue health goals as part of their recovery from serious mental illness. Dr. Cook served as an expert consultant on employment and income supports for the president's New Freedom Commission on Mental Health, and she authored a report from its subcommittee entitled "Employment and Income Supports for People With Mental Illness." She consults with a variety of federal agencies including the U.S. Department of Labor, the Government Accountability Office, the Social Security Administration, the Health and Human Services Office of the Inspector General, the Veteran's Administration, the National Institute of Mental Health, the U.S. Department of Education, and the White House.

Bronwyn Davies is a professorial fellow at Melbourne University and works as an independent scholar. She is well known for her work on gender, literacy, children's play, and classroom research and for her writing on post-structuralist theory. More recently, she has been working on a critique of neoliberalism as it impacts on subjectivities at work and at school, the relations between pedagogy and place, and a Deleuzian approach to collaborative writing. Details of her books and other publications can be found at bronwyndavies.com.au. Her most recent collaborative books include *Pedagogical Encounters* (2009) and *Deleuze and Collaborative Writing: An Immanent Plane of Composition* (2001), both published by Peter Lang.

Marjorie L. DeVault is Professor of Sociology at Syracuse University. Her research has explored women's "invisible work" in the household and family and in the historically female field of dietetics and nutrition education. Trained in the Chicago-school fieldwork tradition and deeply influenced by the feminism of the 1970s, she has written extensively on qualitative and feminist methodologies and contributed to the development of institutional ethnography as a "sociology for people." She is the author of *Feeding the Family: The Social Organization of Caring as Gendered Work* (1991) and *Liberating Method: Feminism and Social Research* (1999) and editor of *People at Work: Life, Power and Social Inclusion in the New Economy* (2008).

Bonnie Thornton Dill is Dean of the College of Arts and Humanities and Professor of Women's Studies at the University of Maryland, where she served as chair of the Women's Studies Department and founding director of the Consortium on Race, Gender, and Ethnicity. Her research focuses on intersections of race, class, and gender with an emphasis on African American women and families. Dill's scholarship has been reprinted in numerous collections and edited volumes. Her recent coedited collection (with Ruth E. Zambrana) entitled *Emerging Intersections: Race, Class, and Gender in Theory, Policy, and Practice* was published by Rutgers University Press in 2009. Dill has won a number of prestigious awards, including two for mentoring: one from Sociologists for Women in Society and a second from the University System of Maryland Regents. She also received the Jessie Bernard Award and the Distinguished Contributions to Teaching Award, both given by the American Sociological Association. She is currently president of the National Women's Studies Association and served as vice president of the American Sociological Association from 2005 through 2008. In 2009–2010 she was a visiting professor in the Department of Sociology at Princeton University.

Mary Margaret Fonow is Professor of Women and Gender Studies and Director of the School of Social Transformation at Arizona State University. Her research areas include transnational labor activism, union feminism, and feminist methodology. She is the author of *Union Women: Forging Feminism in the United Steelworkers of America* (2003), coauthor with Suzanne Franzway of *Making Feminist Politics: Transnational Alliances Between Women and Labor* (University of Illinois Press, 2011), and coeditor with Suzanne Franzway and Val Moghadam of *Making Globalization Work for Women: Social Rights and Trade Union Leadership* (forthcoming in 2011, SUNY Press). Her current work focuses on sexuality, labor unions, and economic justice.

Susanne Gannon is Associate Professor in the School of Education at the University of Western Sydney, Australia. She teaches in the Master of Teaching (Secondary) and convenes the Master of Education (Leadership). She is coeditor with Bronwyn Davies of *Doing Collective Biography* (2006) and *Pedagogical Encounters* (2009). She has written articles pertaining to gender that have been published in various journals, including the *International Journal for Qualitative Studies in Education*; *Feminism and Psychology*; *Gender and Education*; *Gender, Work & Organization*; *Sex Education*; *Crime, Media, Culture*; *Qualitative Inquiry*; *Learning, Media and Technology*; *thirdspace*; and *Outskirts*. Her research examines gendered and racialized subjectivities, youth, textuality, creativity and writing, and questions of place through the methodologies of collective biography, narrative, ethnography, and poetic and fictive writing. She also conducts visual and media analysis from a cultural studies perspective, and she makes particular use of feminist post-structural theories in her work.

Christina Gringeri is Associate Professor in the College of Social Work at the University of Utah. She teaches in the areas of social policy, health policy, qualitative research methods, and theoretical perspectives for MSW and doctoral students; she enjoys guiding and supporting doctoral students in their research process, as well as learning and working with students enrolled in the summer Study Abroad Program in Mexico. In her research, she focuses on the social support networks of low-income women, work and poverty in rural areas, international service learning, and, most recently, examinations of qualitative and feminist research in social work. Dr. Gringeri has been a member of the Editorial Board of *Affilia: Journal of Women and Social Work* since 2002, has served as column editor for Women Creating Change, and currently serves as Book Review Editor for the journal.

Glenda Gross is a PhD candidate in sociology at Syracuse University. She also has an MA in sociology and has a certificate of advanced studies (CAS) in women's and gender studies at Syracuse University. Her research and teaching interests include feminist methodologies; feminist theories; structural inequalities related to race, gender, class, and sexuality; studies in the social organization of knowledge; institutional ethnography; and antiracist feminist pedagogies. Her current research examines the social organization of antiracist feminist educators' work in academe.

Yuri Han is a doctoral student in Adult Education and Human Resource Development at the University of Georgia. She received her MA in Counseling Psychology from Ewha Women's University in Seoul, Korea. Her main interest is in qualitative research methodology in organizational contexts.

Sandra Harding is a professor in the Department of Education at UCLA, where she also teaches in the Women's Studies Department. She is the author or editor of 15 books and special issues of journals including *The Feminist Standpoint Theory Reader* (2004) and *The Postcolonial Science and Technology Studies Reader* (2011). She directed the UCLA Center for the Study of Women from 1996 to 2000 and coedited *Signs: Journal of Women in Culture and Society from* 2000 to 2005.

Mary Hawkesworth is Professor of Political Science and Women's and Gender Studies at Rutgers University. Her teaching and research interests include feminist theory, women and politics, contemporary political philosophy, the philosophy of science, and social policy. Her major works include *Political Worlds of Women:*

Activism, Advocacy and Governance in the 21st Century (Perseus, 2011); *War and Terror: Feminist Perspectives* (University of Chicago Press, 2008); *Globalization and Feminist Activism* (Rowman and Littlefield, 2006); *Feminist Inquiry: From Political Conviction to Methodological Innovation* (Rutgers University Press, 2006); *Women, Democracy, and Globalization in North America* (Palgrave, 2006); *The Encyclopedia of Government and Politics* (Routledge, 1992, 2004); *Beyond Oppression: Feminist Theory and Political Strategy* (Continuum Press, 1990); and *Theoretical Issues in Policy Analysis* (State University of New York Press, 1988). She is currently serving as the editor of *Signs: Journal of Women in Culture and Society*.

Rachel M. Hershberg is a PhD candidate in applied developmental psychology at Boston College and an American Association of University Women Dissertation Fellowship recipient. She has also completed a Certificate in Human Rights and International Justice, and, for the past four years, she has been part of the Post-Deportation Human Rights Project, an interdisciplinary participatory and action research project of the Center for Human Rights and International Justice at Boston College.

Catherine E. Hundleby is an associate professor of philosophy, cross-appointed with the Women's Studies Program, and a fellow of the Centre for Research in Reasoning, Argumentation, and Rhetoric at the University of Windsor, Canada, and she is co-president of the Association for Feminist Epistemologies, Methodologies, Metaphysics and Science Studies. Hundleby works on feminist epistemology from both the standpoint and empiricist perspectives, and argues that these approaches are complementary ("Where Standpoint Stands Now," *Women & Politics*, 1997). Her background is in feminist philosophy of science, and her current research develops a feminist approach to argumentation theory and informal logic. Hundleby's articles appear in journals across the disciplines, including *Informal Logic*, *Hypatia*, *Social Epistemology*, and the *International Feminist Journal of Politics*. In 2010, she coedited with Phyllis Rooney two special journal issues in feminist epistemology: "Just Reason," an issue of *Studies in Social Justice*, and "Reasoning for Change," an issue of *Informal Logic*.

Kristen Intemann is an associate professor of philosophy at Montana State University. Her main areas of specialization are feminist philosophy of science and research ethics. Her current work examines the ways in which ethical and political values can enhance scientific research without undermining objectivity, as well as the implications this has for our conceptions of bias and impartiality. She has published in both philosophy and science journals including *Philosophy of Science*, *Biology & Philosophy*, *Hypatia*, *Science & Education*, *Nature*, *The FASEB Journal*, and *The European Journal of Epidemiology*.

Toby Epstein Jayaratne received her PhD in developmental psychology from the University of Michigan and is currently an assistant research scientist in the Department of Health Behavior and Health Education (School of Public Health) at the University of Michigan. Originally trained in survey research at the Institute for Social Research (University of Michigan), Dr. Jayaratne has directed or coordinated several large survey research projects. She is currently the principal investigator on a study funded by the National Institutes of Health that examines the effects of Americans' genetic explanations of diabetes on preventive attitudes and behaviors. Dr. Jayaratne previously served as principal investigator for a national study exploring the lay public's genetic explanations for a range of human traits, such as intelligence, sexual orientation, and violence and for perceived gender, class, and race differences. She has also written several articles on issues central to feminist methodology.

Katherine Johnson is Principal Lecturer in Psychology in the School of Applied Social Science. Her research interests are in interdisciplinary gender and sexuality studies, critical and community psychology, and qualitative research methods. She has written about transsexual and transgender embodiment and lesbian, gay, bisexual, and trans mental health. Her current research draws on visual methodologies and participatory action research in order to reflect on the relationship between personal and social transformations. She is coeditor of *Community Psychology and the Socio-Economics of Mental Distress: International Perspectives* (2012, with Carl Walker and Liz Cunningham) and is completing a single authored book on *Sexualities* for Polity Press (forthcoming, 2013).

Debra Renee Kaufman is the founder and current director of Women's Studies at Northeastern University, where she is a Matthews Distinguished University Professor and Professor of Sociology. Among her award-nominated and -selected books are *Achievement and Women* (honorable mention, C.W. Mills Award), *Rachel's Daughters: Newly Orthodox Jewish Women* (nominated for three awards), and an invited guest-edited edition of *Contemporary Jewry* entitled "Women and the Holocaust." She has numerous published articles on feminist theories and methodologies. Her commitment to feminist scholarship is evident in her published articles and chapters on post-Holocaust Jewish identity politics and her forthcoming book, *Post Holocaust Identity and an Ever-Dying People: Contemporary Narratives.* She is currently researching intergenerational ties among adult Jewish daughters and their mothers.

Noretta Koertge is Professor Emerita of History and Philosophy of Science at Indiana University, where she continues to teach in the Hutton Honors College. Dr. Koertge taught chemistry before studying philosophy at the University of London during the heyday of Popper and Lakatos. Her research deals principally with theories of scientific inquiry, including the history of methodology; special issues in the social sciences; and the role of ethical considerations. Koertge is a fellow of the American Association for the Advancement of Science and past editor of both the journal *Philosophy of Science* and *The New Dictionary of Scientific Biography.*

Marla H. Kohlman is currently Associate Professor and Chair of the Department of Sociology at Kenyon College. She holds a PhD in sociology from the University of Maryland, a JD from the Washington College of Law at The American University, and an MS in law and justice from the School of Public Affairs at The American University. Prior to teaching at Kenyon, Dr. Kohlman was an attorney practicing in Maryland and Washington, D.C. She has recently published a comparative study of race and gender differences in the reporting of sexual harassment across the military sectors of the U.S. Department of Defense, a project partially funded by a 2006–2007 AAUW Educational Foundation Fellowship. She is currently working on a study investigating the negotiation of work and family dynamics by attorneys across the United States and another project entitled *Notions of Family: Intersectional Perspectives* to be published as a volume of the *Advances in Gender Research* series in 2012.

Rachel Lewis is a graduate student in the English department of Northeastern University, where she teaches "College Writing" and consults with students in the writing center. She was previously a middle and high school teacher of math and science. Her academic interests include critical and feminist pedagogy, composition studies, and modern literature. She was a recipient of both the Charles J. Hoff Scholarship and the 1941 Humanitarian Award while an undergraduate at the University of Massachusetts–Amherst in recognition of her efforts to join academic scholarship in the humanities with social activism.

M. Brinton Lykes is Professor of Community-Cultural Psychology, Associate Director of the Center for Human Rights and International Justice, and Chair of the Department of Counseling and Applied Developmental and Educational Psychology at Boston College, USA. She works with survivors of war and gross violations of human rights, using the creative arts and participatory action research methodologies to analyze the causes and document the effects of violence and develop programs that aspire to rethread social relations and transform social inequalities underlying structural injustices. Her feminist-infused activist scholarship has been published in refereed journals, edited volumes, research handbooks, and organizational newsletters; she is coeditor of three books and coauthor, with the Association of Maya Ixil Women–New Dawn, of *Voces e Imágenes: Mujeres Mayas Ixiles de Chajul/Voices and Images: Maya Ixil Women of Chajul.* Her current interdisciplinary participatory and action research focuses on migration and post-deportation human rights violations and their effects for women and children, with a particular focus on transnational identities and "mixed families" (in Boston and New Bedford, Massachusetts; Providence, Rhode Island; and Zacualpa, Guatemala);

health disparities and antiracist, cross-community women's leadership (in post-Katrina New Orleans, Louisiana); and women's struggles for justice, healing, and reparations (Guatemala). She is a cofounder and participant in the Boston Women's Fund and the Ignacio Martín-Baró Fund for Mental Health and Human Rights. She is also a member of the board of directors of Women's Rights International and Impunity Watch. Her website is www2.bc.edu/~lykes/

Sarah Maddison is an Australian Research Council Future Fellow in the Faculty of Arts and Social Sciences at the University of New South Wales (Sydney, Australia). She has published widely in the areas of young women and feminist activism, social movements, Indigenous politics, nongovernment organizations and democracy. Her books include *Activist Wisdom* (2006), *Silencing Dissent* (2007), *Black Politics* (2009), and *Beyond White Guilt* (2011). She has also coauthored, with Emma Partridge, the gender and sexuality audit reports for the Democratic Audit of Australia (2007).

Cris Mayo is associate professor in gender and women's studies and educational policy studies at the University of Illinois at Urbana-Champaign. Her publications in queer studies and philosophy of education include *Disputing the Subject of Sex: Sexuality and Public School Controversies* (Rowman and Littlefield, 2004, 2007) as well as articles in *Educational Theory*, *Philosophy of Education*, *Review of Research in Education*, and *Sexuality Research and Social Policy*.

Jennifer Bickham Mendez is Associate Professor of Sociology at The College of William & Mary. Her areas of research include migration, social movements, and gender in the global economy. She is the author of *From the Revolution to the Maquiladoras: Gender, Labor, and Globalization in Nicaragua* (2005, Duke University Press), a cowinner of the 2008 Book of the Year Award from the Political Economy of the World System Section of the American Sociological Association. She has published articles in journals such as *Gender & Society*, *Mobilization*, *Identities: Global Studies in Culture and Power*, and *Social Problems*. Her current work focuses on Latino/a migrants in Williamsburg, Virginia. Recently, her article

coauthored with Natalia Deeb-Sossa, "Enforcing Borders in the Nuevo South: Gender and Migration in Williamsburg, Virginia and The Research Triangle, North Carolina," was awarded the Outstanding Article Award from the Sex and Gender Section of the American Sociological Association. Currently, she and coeditor Nancy Naples are compiling an edited collection that features work on social movements, border enforcement, and cross-border organizing.

Kathi N. Miner received her PhD in psychology and women's studies from the University of Michigan and is currently an assistant professor of psychology and women's and gender studies at Texas A&M University. Her research investigates the link between interpersonal mistreatment in organizations and occupational health. Most of her work has focused on incivility, harassment, and discrimination in work settings and how being a target or observer of these mistreatments affects employees' psychological, physical, and job-related well-being. She is especially interested in the degree to which individuals from low-status social groups (for example, groups based on gender, race, and sexual orientation) are disproportionately targets of mistreatment.

Daphne Patai was born in Jerusalem and immigrated to the United States as a child. She is a Professor of Brazilian Literature at the University of Massachusetts Amherst, where she also teaches literary theory and utopian fiction. A recipient of fellowships from the Guggenheim Foundation, the National Endowment for the Humanities, and the National Humanities Center, she is the author and editor of more than a dozen books, including *Brazilian Women Speak: Contemporary Life Stories* (1988), *Women's Words: The Feminist Practice of Oral History* (coedited with Sherna Berger Gluck, 1991), *Professing Feminism: Education and Indoctrination in Women's Studies* (coauthored with Noretta Koertge; new, enlarged edition, 2003), and *Theory's Empire: An Anthology of Dissent* (coedited with Will H. Corral, 2005). Her most recent books are *What Price Utopia? Essays on Ideological Policing, Feminism, and Academic Affairs* (2008) and *História oral, feminismo, e política: Ensaios* (Brazil, 2010).

Amanda Pesonen received her MS in industrial-organizational psychology from Texas A&M University. Her research domain includes interpersonal mistreatment in organizations with a focus on workplace incivility. Specifically, she is interested in how mistreatment applies to women and other marginalized groups in society, as well as in how it affects job-related outcomes and physical and psychological well-being. Additionally, she is interested in the impact of large-scale societal events on the development of social identities and the subsequent consequences for interpersonal relationships at work.

Deborah Piatelli is a visiting assistant professor of sociology and faculty coordinator of the AHANA Community Research Program at Boston College, where she teaches courses in research methodology, race relations, and social change, and offers a community-based research and social policy seminar. She is the author of *Stories of Inclusion? Power, Privilege, and Difference in a Peace and Justice Network* (Lexington Books, 2009).

Wanda S. Pillow is jointly appointed in the Department of Education, Culture, and Society and the Gender Studies Program at the University of Utah, where she teaches courses in qualitative methodology, feminist theories, and gender, race, and sexuality studies. She has published several pieces on methodology, including a critical 2003 article on reflexivity in *The International Journal of Qualitative Studies in Education* and a coedited book entitled *Working the Ruins/Feminist Poststructural Research in Education* (2000). Her research focuses on the intersections of gender, race, and sexuality in educational policy and cultural studies. Her book *Unfit Subjects/ Educational Policy and the Teen Mother* (2003) offers a definitive historical analysis of the construction of the teen mother, and she remains active in research on the educational rights of pregnant or mothering students. Her most recent work takes up historical and present-day representations of Sacajawea and York of the Lewis and Clark expedition, and it includes a 2007 *Hypatia* article, "Searching for Sacajawea."

Judith Preissle is the 2001 Distinguished Aderhold Professor for the College of Education at the University of Georgia where she has taught since 1975. She is an affiliate faculty member in the Institute for Women's Studies, who honored her with the 2006 Women's Studies Faculty Award. As an interdisciplinary scholar, she works across several areas: qualitative research methods and design, the anthropology of education, and gender, ethnic, and immigration studies. Recently she has been studying ethics and the philosophy of social science. She is the coauthor of *Ethnography and Qualitative Design in Educational Research* (1984, 1993), translated into Spanish in 1988, and coeditor of *The Handbook of Qualitative Research in Education* (1992). Her most recent book, coauthored with Xue Lan Rong, is the second edition of *Educating Immigrant Students* (2009). In addition to numerous book chapters, she has authored articles appearing in such journals as the *American Educational Research Journal,* the *Anthropology of Education Quarterly,* the *Journal of Contemporary Ethnography,* the *Review of Educational Research,* the *Educational Researcher,* the *International Journal of Qualitative Studies in Education,* and *The Elementary School Journal.* She e-manages QUALRS-L (Qualitative Research for the Human Sciences), established in 1991 and the oldest such forum online, and QualPage, a webpage on qualitative research. She founded the qualitative research program at the University of Georgia that now offers a graduate certificate program. In 2009, she was awarded Fellow of the American Educational Research Association.

Diane Reay is a Professor of Education in the Faculty of Education, University of Cambridge, with particular interests in social justice issues in education, Pierre Bourdieu's social theory, feminist methodologies, and cultural analyses of social class. She has written widely on social inequalities in education, focusing on intersections of gender, race, and class. Her most recent book, *White Middle Class Identities and Urban Schooling* (with Gill Crozier and David James, 2011), examines how the English white middle classes manage to maintain their educational advantages when sending their children to multiethnic, predominantly working-class urban comprehensive schools.

Judith Roof is the William Shakespeare Chair in English at Rice University. She is the author of five books, including most recently, *The Poetics of DNA*, and the editor or coeditor of four collections, including *Who Can Speak? Authority and Critical Identity*. She writes about a broad range of subjects in 20th-century literature, drama, film and media, critical and feminist theory, and studies in sexuality.

Sue V. Rosser currently serves as Provost at San Francisco State University, where she is also a professor of sociology and of women's studies. From 1999 to 2009, she was Dean of Liberal Arts at Georgia Tech, where she held the Ivan Allen Dean's Chair of Liberal Arts and Technology and was a professor of public policy and of history, technology, and society. Author of 12 books, she has also published more than 130 journal articles on women, science, technology, and health.

Deboleena Roy is Associate Professor of Women's Studies and Neuroscience and Behavioral Biology. She received her PhD in neuroendocrinology and molecular biology in 2001 from the Institute of Medical Science at the University of Toronto. In her doctoral work, she examined the effects of estrogen and melatonin on the gene expression and cell signaling mechanisms in gonadotropin-releasing hormone (GnRH) neurons of the hypothalamus. The focus of her current research and scholarship in feminist science studies is to bridge feminist critiques of science with transformations in the processes of scientific knowledge production. Her teaching focuses on integrating biology and women's studies and addressing issues of gender, race, and class in science education. She has published her work in journals such as *Hypatia: A Journal of Feminist Philosophy*, *Australian Feminist Studies*, *Rhizomes: Cultural Studies of Emerging Knowledge*, the *American Journal of Bioethics*, *Neuroethics*, *Endocrinology*, *Neuroendocrinology*, and the *Journal of Biological Chemistry*. Roy was a faculty research fellow at the Clayman Institute for Gender Research at Stanford University from September 2008 to June 2009. While at the institute, she developed a project in feminist neuroethics and is currently working on a manuscript entitled "Mapping Gender, Hormones, and Neurons: Feminist Configurations in the Neurosciences." She recently received a grant from the National Academies Keck Futures Initiative to develop a training program that instructs graduate students in biomedicine, bioengineering, and bioethics on the ethical and social implications of synthetic biology research. The program will also develop participatory research practices to address the need for critical engagement with nontraditional stakeholders.

Denise Seigart received her PhD in human service studies/program evaluation from Cornell University in 1999. She is an active member of the American Evaluation Association and has served as chair and program chair of the Feminist Issues in Evaluation Topical Interest Group. In collaboration with Dr. Sharon Brisolara, Dr. Seigart edited *Feminist Evaluation: Explorations and Experiences: New Directions for Evaluation*, a critical work regarding feminist evaluation, which was published in December 2002. She is currently working on articles discussing the results of a feminist evaluation of school-based health care conducted during a 2008–2009 sabbatical in Australia and Canada. Dr. Seigart is Associate Dean of Nursing Education at Stevenson University.

Frances Shaw is a doctoral student in the School of Social Sciences and International Studies at the University of New South Wales. She is currently writing her dissertation on the political significance of feminist discourse in Australian blog networks, discursive activism in online spaces, and the impact of online communities on political identity. Taking a feminist, grounded theory approach, she has followed Australian feminist blogs over a long period and held semi-structured interviews with a variety of bloggers and other community participants. Some of the main themes of her inquiry include the application of social movement theory to online activism, public spheres and private spaces online, affective involvement in online communities, and gendered aspects of online communication. She has responsibility for the discursive legacy component of the Mapping the Australian Women's Movement project, an Australian Research Council project led by Marian Sawer and Sarah Maddison.

Abigail J. Stewart is the Sandra Schwarz Tangri Professor of Psychology and Women's Studies at the University of Michigan, director of the UM ADVANCE Program, and associate dean of the Rackham Graduate School. She is the former director of both the Women's Studies Program (1989–1995) and the Institute for Research on Women and Gender (1995–2002), and she held the position of Associate Dean for Academic Affairs in the College of Literature, Science, and the Arts at the University of Michigan (2002–2004). She was on the faculty at Boston University from 1975 through 1987 and was the founding director of the Henry A. Murray Research Center of Radcliffe College (1978–1980). She holds degrees from Wesleyan University (BA), the London School of Economics (MS), and Harvard University (PhD). Her contributions to the University of Michigan have been recognized by awards, including (in 2000) the Henry Russel Lectureship and a Distinguished University Professorship. She has also received external awards, including the Henry Murray Award (in personality psychology) and the Carolyn Wood Sherif Award (in the psychology of women) from the American Psychological Association. Dr. Stewart has published many scholarly articles and several books, focusing on the psychology of women's lives, personality, and adaptation to personal and social changes. Her current research, which combines qualitative and quantitative methods, includes comparative analyses of longitudinal studies of educated women's lives and personalities; a collaborative study of race, gender, and generation in the graduates of a Midwest high school; and research and interventions on gender, race, and sexuality as they affect people's careers in science and technology.

Molly Talcott is an assistant professor of sociology and Latin American studies at California State University, Los Angeles. As an interdisciplinary teacher and scholar-activist, she researches "race" and racism, gender, labor, and human rights in the Americas. Her work has been published in *Signs: Journal of Women in Culture and Society* (2004), in *Critical Globalization Studies* (2005, Routledge, with Kum-Kum Bhavnani and John Foran), and in *Social Change, Resistance, and Social Practices* (2010, Brill). She serves on the editorial boards of *Gender & Society* and *Societies Without Borders*. She is coeditor (with

Dana Collins, Sylvanna Falcón, and Sharmila Lodhia) of the 2010 special issue of the *International Feminist Journal of Politics,* "New Directions in Feminism and Human Rights."

Stéphanie Wahab is an Associate Professor at Portland State University's School of Social Work, where she teaches in the master's and doctorate programs. Her areas of specialization include intimate partner violence, commercial sex work, anti-oppressive practice and research, and critical and constructivist inquiry. Her scholarly projects typically revolve around the intersections of privilege, oppression, gender, sexuality, cultures, and relationships. Dr. Wahab currently serves as an editorial board member of *Affilia: Journal of Women and Social Work.*

Lynn Weber is Professor of Psychology and Women's and Gender Studies at the University of South Carolina, where she directed the Women's and Gender Studies Program for 11 years, from 1996 to 2007. Her initial work on social class, resulting in *The American Perception of Class* (with Reeve Vanneman, 1987), and her work as cofounder and then director of the Center for Research on Women at the University of Memphis led her to pioneer in the study of intersectionality. In 2010, Oxford University Press published the second edition of *Understanding Race, Class, Gender, and Sexuality: A Conceptual Framework,* the first text to present a conceptual framework for intersectional analysis. In addition to her leadership in advancing the conceptual foundations of intersectionality, she has applied its insights to health disparities and women's health, disaster displacement and recovery, social mobility, and classroom pedagogy. Weber's current research examines inequalities in the recovery from Hurricane Katrina among communities on the Mississippi Gulf Coast and in the experiences of people displaced to Columbia, South Carolina. In conjunction with a national research network, she recently completed a book, *Displaced: Life in the Katrina Diaspora,* coedited with Lori Peek, forthcoming from the University of Texas Press. Recent publications on health disparities and intersectionality include "Race, Ethnicity, and Health: An Intersectional Approach" in the *Handbook of the Sociology of Racial and Ethnic Relations* and "Reconstructing the Landscape of Health Disparities Research: Promoting Dialogue and Collaboration Between the Feminist Intersectional and Positivist Biomedical Traditions" in *Race, Class, Gender and Health.*

Diane L. Wolf is Professor of Sociology at the University of California Davis and author of *Beyond Anne Frank: Hidden Children and Jewish Families in Holland* (2007, University of California Press) and *Factory Daughters* (1992, University of California Press). She also edited *Feminist Dilemmas in Fieldwork* (1996, Westview). Her current work is a collaboration with Yen Le Espiritu on memory, trauma, and identity among children of Vietnamese refugees and of Holocaust survivors.

Alison Wylie is Professor of Philosophy and Anthropology at the University of Washington. She is a philosopher of science who works on philosophical issues raised by archaeological practice and by feminist research in the social sciences: ideals of objectivity, the role of contextual values in research practice, and models of evidential reasoning. Her publications include *Thinking From Things: Essays in the Philosophy of Archaeology* (2002); edited volumes such as *Value-Free Science?* (2007, with Kincaid and Dupré), *Epistemic Diversity and Dissent* (special issue of *Episteme*, 2006), and *Feminist Science Studies* (*Hypatia*, 2004); and essays that appear in *Feminist Epistemology and Philosophy of Science* (2011), *How Well Do Facts Travel?* (2010), *The Ethics of Cultural Appropriation* (2009), *Agnatology* (2008), *Evaluating Multiple Narratives* (2007), and *Science and Other Cultures* (2003). She is currently working on a monograph, *Standpoint Matters, in Feminist Philosophy of Science.*

Lauren Zurbrügg received her MS in industrial-organizational psychology from Texas A&M University. Her research interests include processes of marginalization and empowerment for women and minorities in organizations and, specifically, how experiences of mistreatment impact the health and occupational outcomes of these individuals. Her current projects utilize survey, experimental, and cross-cultural research methods to investigate these topics.

INTRODUCTION

1

FEMINIST RESEARCH

Exploring, Interrogating, and Transforming the Interconnections of Epistemology, Methodology, and Method

SHARLENE NAGY HESSE-BIBER

FEMINIST VOICES AND VISIONS ACROSS THE CENTURIES

This *Handbook* begins with voices, visions, and experiences of feminist activists, scholars, and researchers, speaking to us across the decades of the 19th, 20th, and 21st centuries. They provide a legacy of feminist research, praxis, and activism. There lies within these voices a feminist consciousness that opens up intellectual and emotional spaces for all women to articulate their relations to one another and the wider society—spaces where the personal transforms into the political.

> I do earnestly desire to arouse the women of the North to a realizing sense of the condition of two millions of women at the South, still in bondage, suffering what I suffered, and most of them far worse. I want to add my testimony to that of abler pens to convince the people of the Free States what Slavery really is. Only by experience can anyone realize how deep, and dark, and foul is that pit of abominations. May the blessing of God rest on this imperfect effort in behalf of my persecuted people! (Harriet Jacobs, 1861/1987, pp. 1–2)

Harriet Jacobs calls for the alignment of women across their racial, class, and geographical differences to fight the abomination of slavery. Through her words, Jacobs demonstrates how the concrete lived experience is a key place from which to build knowledge and foment social change.

> It was thus that I found myself walking with extreme rapidity across a grass plot. Instantly a man's figure rose to intercept me. Nor did I at first

Author's Note: Much appreciation and gratitude to Alicia Johnson, Hilary Flowers, Abigail Brooks, and Deborah Piatelli, who contributed their academic insights and skillful editing and editorial advice.

understand that the gesticulations of a curious-looking object, in a cut-away coat and evening shirt, were aimed at me. His face expressed horror and indignation. Instinct rather than reason came to my help: he was a Beadle; I was a woman. Thus was the turf; there was the path. Only the Fellows and Scholars are allowed here; the gravel is the place for me. (Virginia Woolf, 1929, p. 258)

Thus humanity is male and man defines woman not in herself but as relative to him; she is not regarded as an autonomous being. . . . For him she is sex—absolute sex, no less. She is defined and differentiated with reference to man and not he with reference to her; she is the incidental, the inessential as opposed to the essential. He is the Subject, he is the Absolute—she is the Other. (Simone de Beauvoir, 1952, pp. xviii, xxiii)

The problem lay buried, unspoken, for many years in the minds of American women. It was a strange stirring, a sense of dissatisfaction, a yearning that women suffered in the middle of the twentieth century in the United States. Each suburban wife struggled with it alone. . . . she was afraid to ask even of herself the silent question—"Is this all?" For over fifteen years there was no word of this yearning in the millions of words written about women, for women, in all the columns, books, and articles by experts telling women their role was to seek fulfillment as wives and mothers. . . . We can no longer ignore within women that voice that says: "I want something more than my husband and my children and my home." (Betty Friedan, 1963, pp. 15, 32)

Virginia Woolf, Simone de Beauvoir, and Betty Friedan, speaking many decades later, express their deep feelings of exclusion from the dominant avenues of knowledge building, seeing their own experiences, concerns, and worth diminished and invalidated by the dominant powers of their society.

In some ways, the origins of feminist research's epistemological and methodological focus draws on these insights and struggles; feminist empiricism, standpoint theories, postmodernism, and transnational perspectives all recognize the importance of women's lived experiences to the goal of unearthing subjugated knowledge. Each perspective forges links between feminism, activism, and the academy and women's everyday lives.

Women [were] largely excluded from the work of producing the forms of thought and the images and symbols in which thought is expressed and ordered. . . . The circle of men whose writing and talk was significant to each other extends backwards in time as far as our records reach. What men were doing was relevant to men, was written by men about men for men. Men listened . . . to what one another said. (Dorothy Smith, 1978, p. 281)

Feminist perspectives also carry messages of empowerment that challenge the encircling of knowledge claims by those who occupy privileged positions. Feminist thinking and practice require taking steps from the "margins to the center" while eliminating boundaries that privilege dominant forms of knowledge building, boundaries that mark who can be a knower and what can be known. For Virginia Woolf, it is the demarcation between the "turf" and the "path"; for Simone de Beauvoir, it is the line between the "inessential" and the "essential"; and for Dorothy Smith, it is the path that encircles dominant knowledge, where women's lived experiences lie outside its circumference or huddled at the margins.

Working right at the limits of several categories and approaches means that one is neither entirely inside or outside. One has to push one's work as far as one can go: to the borderlines, where one never stops, walking on the edges, incurring constantly the risk of falling off one side or the other side of the limit while undoing, redoing, modifying this limit. (Trinh T. Minh-ha, 1991, p. 218)

To engage in feminist theory and praxis means to challenge knowledge that excludes, while seeming to include—assuming that when we speak of the generic term *men*, we also mean women, as though what is true for dominant groups must also be true for women and other oppressed groups. Feminists ask "new" questions that place women's lives and those of "other" marginalized groups at the center of social inquiry. Feminist research *disrupts* traditional ways of knowing to create rich new meanings, a process that Trinh (1991) terms becoming "both/and"—insider and outsider—taking on a multitude of different standpoints and negotiating these identities simultaneously.

The history of research from many indigenous perspectives is so deeply embedded in colonization that it has been regarded as a tool only of colonization and not as a potential tool for self-determination and development. For indigenous peoples, research has a significance that is embedded in our history as natives under the gaze of Western science and colonialism. (Linda Tuhiwai Smith, 2005, p. 87)

Feminists bob and weave their threads of understanding, listening to the experiences of "the other/s" as legitimate knowledge. Feminist research is mindful of hierarchies of power and authority in the research process, hierarchies that are so well described by Linda Tuhiwai Smith (2005), including those power differentials that lie within research practices that can reinforce the status quo, creating divisions between colonizer and colonized.

I continue to be amazed that there is so much feminist writing produced and yet so little feminist theory that strives to speak to women, men and children about ways we might transform our lives via a conversion to feminist practice. (bell hooks, 1994, pp. 70–71)

Advocating the mere tolerance of difference between women is the grossest reformism. It is a total denial of the creative function of difference in our lives. Difference must be not merely tolerated, but seen as a fund of necessary polarities between which our creativity can spark like a dialectic. Only then does the necessity for interdependency become unthreatening. Only within that interdependency of different strengths, acknowledged and equal, can the power to seek new ways of being in the world generate, as well as the courage and sustenance to act where there are no charters. (Audre Lorde, 1996, p. 159)

The quotations used in this chapter contain a quality of agency that challenges dominant discourses of knowledge building, urging women to live and invite in differences, to embrace the creativity and knowledge building that lies within the tensions of difference. Difference matters. Author bell hooks (1994) implores feminists to root their scholarship in "transformative politics and practice," pointing out that

"in this capitalist culture, feminism and feminist theory are fast becoming a commodity that only the privileged can afford" (p. 71). Audre Lorde (1996) provides a path to empowerment by urging an embrace of difference through an "interdependency of different strengths, acknowledged and equal" (p. 159).

The tensions between opposing theories and political stances vitalize the feminist dialogue. But it may only be combined with respect, partial understanding, love, and friendship that keeps us together in the long run. So mujeres think about the carnalas you want to be in your space, those whose spaces you want to have overlapping yours. (Gloria Anzaldúa, 1990, p. 229)

Indeed, it is our acknowledgment and appreciation of difference that sustains our ability to navigate uncharted terrain toward meaningful social change. Gloria Anzaldúa (1990) employs a "sandbar" metaphor to capture traversals of the difference divide:

Being a sandbar means getting a breather from being a perpetual bridge without having to withdraw completely. The high tides and low tides of your life are factors which help decide whether or where you're a sandbar today, tomorrow. . . . A sandbar is more fluid and shifts locations, allowing for more mobility and more freedom. Of course there are sandbars called shoals, where boats run amuck. (p. 224)

Although Anzaldúa now envisions herself turning into a sandbar, her own stance on difference fluctuates between a "persistent ridge," a "drawbridge," or even "an island." For Anzaldúa (1990), traversing the difference divide becomes a process—with its own range of connections and disconnections as "each option comes with its own dangers" (p. 224).

Feminist research shares some common angles of vision that are "connected in principle to feminist struggle" (Joey Sprague & Mark Zimmerman, 1993, p. 266), often with the intent to change the basic structures of oppression. But there is no single feminist epistemology or methodology. Instead, multiple feminist lenses wake us up to layers of sexist, racist, homophobic, and colonialist points of view. Some lenses provide radical insights into knowledge building that upend traditional epistemologies and methodologies, offering more complex understandings and solutions toward reclaiming subjugated knowledge.

Feminists engage both the theory and practice of research—beginning with the formulation of the research question and ending with the reporting of research findings. Feminist research encompasses the full range of knowledge building that includes epistemology, methodology, and method. An *epistemology* is "a theory of knowledge" (Sandra Harding, 1987b, p. 3) that delineates a set of assumptions about the social world—who can be a knower and what can be known. These assumptions influence the decisions a researcher makes, including what to study (based on what *can* be studied) and how to conduct a study. A *methodology* is "a theory of how research is done or should proceed" (p. 3). A *method* is "a technique for (or way of proceeding in) gathering evidence" (p. 2). Very often, the term *method* is used as an umbrella term to refer to these three different components of the research process, which can make the use of the term somewhat confusing.

Feminist research takes many twists and turns as a mode of social inquiry. In this introduction, we provide a brief overview of some of the "critical moments" in the legacy of feminist theory and praxis. We take up the dialogues surrounding issues of epistemology, methodology, and method. Feminist research begins with questioning and critiquing androcentric bias within the disciplines, challenging traditional researchers to include gender as a category of analysis. Subsequently, through this shift in perspective, we can observe the beginnings of an overall challenge to the scientific method itself and the emergence of new paradigms of thinking about basic foundational questions: What is Truth? Who can be a knower? What can be known?

FEMINIST RESEARCHERS CHALLENGE ANDROCENTRIC BIAS ACROSS THE DISCIPLINES

In the 1960s through to the 1980s, feminist scholars and researchers called attention to examples of androcentric bias within the sciences and social sciences. These feminist scholars and researchers, known as feminist empiricists, embarked on projects to "correct" these biases by adding women into research samples and asking new questions that enabled women's experiences and perspectives to gain a hearing. Margrit Eichler and Jeanne Lapointe's (1985) research primer, *On the Treatment of the Sexes in Research*, provides a critique of empirical research as well as a checklist for the inclusion of gender as a category of analysis in social research. Their work provides many important nuggets of advice concerning what *not* to do (p. 9). These include the following:

- Treating Western sex roles as universal
- Transforming statistical differences into innate differences
- Translating difference as inferiority

Feminist empiricist researchers did much to "deconstruct" what they perceived as errors, or examples of androcentrism, across a range of academic disciplines and professional fields. Feminist empiricists' insights into androcentrism, and their goal of eradicating sexist research, cascaded across the disciplines of psychology, philosophy, history, sociology, education, and anthropology, as well as the fields of law, medicine, language, and communication. The 1970s and 1980s saw the publication of many groundbreaking anthologies critical of androcentric research. In 1975, Marcia Millman and Rosabeth Moss Kanter coedited the volume *Another Voice: Feminist Perspectives on Social Life and Social Science*. In their editorial introduction, they compare traditional knowledge building with the story of "The Emperor's New Clothes." They note,

> Everyone knows the story about the Emperor and his fine clothes; although the townspeople persuaded themselves that the Emperor was elegantly costumed, a child, possessing an unspoiled vision, showed the citizenry that the Emperor was really naked. . . . The story also reminds us that collective delusions can be undone by introducing fresh perspectives. (p. vii)

Sociologists Millman and Kanter (1975) criticize the androcentric bias of sociology by noting how sociology uses certain "field-defining models" that prevent the asking of new questions. They note, for example, that the Weberian concept of rationality, used to understand an individual's motivations and social organization, "defines out of existence, from the start, the equally important element of emotion in social life and structure" (p. ix). Their edited volume presents a range of new feminist perspectives on the social reality to "reassess the basic theories, paradigms, substantive concerns, and methodologies of sociology and the social sciences to see what changes are needed to make social theory and research reflect the multitude of both female and male realities and interests" (p. viii). The works in this volume also point out how sociology emphasizes the "public sphere" of society and "leaves out the private, supportive, informal, local social structures in which women participate most frequently" (p. xi). A stark example of this comes from a research article in their volume by Arlie Hochschild (1975), "The Sociology of Feeling and Emotion: Selected Possibilities." Hochschild demonstrates how the frequency of specific emotions is not distributed evenly across social structures. She explores the gendered, raced, and classed aspects of emotional expression. She notes, for example, that anger tends to flow down the social structure, while love flows up the social hierarchy. In effect, those at the bottom of the social ladder become "the complaint clerks of society, and . . . for the dwellers at the top, the world is more often experienced as a benign place" (p. 296). She notes in particular the role of gender in emotional expression whereby women "receive not only their husband's frustration displaced from the office to home, but also the anger of other women who are dissimilarly displaced upon" (p. 296). In a later work, Hochschild (1983), a prime mover in establishing the field known as "the sociology of emotions," demonstrates how emotions are often co-opted for commercial benefit. For example, those women employed in female-dominated clerical, service, and sales occupations often find that "emotional work" is a part of their job in addition to their more formal job description. They are expected to keep things functioning smoothly by managing the emotional climate at work—by smiling and comporting an upbeat and friendly demeanor.

Dale Spender's (1981) anthology *Men's Studies Modified: The Impact of Feminism on the Academic Disciplines* focuses on gender and knowledge building across the disciplines. Spender notes,

> Most of the knowledge produced in our society has been produced by men. . . . They have created men's studies (the academic curriculum), for, by not acknowledging that they are presenting only the explanation of men, they have "passed off" this knowledge as human knowledge. (p. 1)

In writing this volume, Spender hoped to draw attention to cutting-edge research across the disciplines that began to "alter the power configurations in the construction of knowledge in society" (p. 8).

Many anthologies quickly followed, including Sandra Harding's (1987a) edited volume, *Feminism and Methodology*. In the preface to this volume, Harding raises a central issue, namely, "Is there a unique feminist method of inquiry?" She suggests that at the heart of feminist inquiry are the emergent questions and issues that feminists raise about the social reality and the practices of traditional research. She asserts,

> A closer examination of the full range of feminist social analyses reveals that often it is not exactly alternative methods that are responsible for what is significant about this research. Instead, we can see in this work alternative origins of problematics, explanatory hypotheses and evidence, alternative purposes of inquiry, and a new prescription for the appropriate relationship between the inquirer and his/her subject of inquiry. (p. vii)

If we look inside Harding's volume, we find several articles that interrogate the relationship between gender and the social sciences. Carolyn Wood Sherif's (1987) article calls attention to androcentric research being conducted in the field of psychology. Sherif begins her analysis of bias by quoting Naomi Weisstein's thesis of the 1960s that "psychology has nothing to say about what women are really like, what they need and what they want, essentially because psychology does not know" (p. 38). In seeking to raise the status of their discipline, psychologists began to emulate the theories and practices of the more prestigious hard sciences. This reliance on biological and physical science models of inquiry invariably led to biased theories about women and gender. Bonnie Thornton Dill's (1987) article in this same volume points to the tendency of researchers, including some feminist researchers, to generalize women's social situation, leaving out differences of race, class, and cultural context. She uses the example of "femininity" and explains how the concept has been dominated by images of white middle- and upper-middle-class conceptions of womanhood. She provides alternative frameworks for analyzing the concept by taking women's race, class, and cultural context-bound differences into account. Joan Kelly-Gadol's (1987) article in Harding's edited volume provides a critique of the androcentrism of historical method by illustrating the myriad ways in which feminist research questions historical work. Kelly-Gadol focuses on historians' use of field-defining concepts such as "periodization," a particular set of events historians chose to focus on (usually those activities men were engaged in, such as diplomatic and constitutional history, as well as political, economic, and cultural history). She troubles the concept of periodization by including gender as a category of analysis that opens the possibility of asking new questions: Was the period called *the Renaissance* beneficial for women? Although the Renaissance brought dramatic changes in social and cultural life that benefited many men, a growing division between private and public life meant that most women, even those of the upper class, experienced increasing segregation from men and a loss of power and freedom in the public sphere. Kelly-Gadol's vision of including women in history challenges the fundamental way historians visualize historical periods. In addition, our understanding of social change also shifts when we conceive of women as *agents* of historical change. Kelly-Gadol does not include a specific discussion of other differences such as race, class, and sexual preference in her vision of historical method. However, by decentering white male concerns and activities as the central focal point of historical inquiry and by making sex a category fundamental to historical analysis, she (and others) paved the way for alternative viewpoints to reconfigure the historical landscape. Including sex as a category of

analysis also provides historians with a more complex understanding of history's influence on both sexes.

Nancy Tuana's edited volume *Feminism & Science* (1989a) contains a range of readings that critique the gendered nature of the sciences. In the preface to her volume, Tuana notes, "Although feminists were not the first to reject the traditional image of science, we were the first to carefully explore the myriad ways in which sexist biases affected the nature and practice of science" (p. xi). Nancy Tuana's own research article in this volume reveals the extent to which "scientists work within and through the worldview of their time" (1989b, p. 147). Tuana examines theories of reproduction from Aristotle to the preformationists and shows how these theories justify women's inferiority. She notes, "Aristotle set the basic orientation for the next 2000 years of embryological thought . . . the gender/science system is woven tightly into the fabric of science" (p. 169).

Emily Martin's (1987) monograph *The Woman in the Body*, published around the same time as Nancy Tuana's book, also provides a feminist analysis of science, but through an examination of medical discourse. Martin exposes the range of sex-biased assumptions embedded within reproductive medical texts that serve to disempower women and compares these images to women's perceptions of their reproductive lives. She discovers that medical texts employ an image of birth as "production," with the uterus likened to a "machine." Within this framework, menstruation and menopause become "failed production." Martin also finds that white middle-class women are most apt to accept these dominant images. Like Tuana's work, Martin's research underscores the androcentrism embedded in scientific literature and research and demonstrates the extent to which the "hard" sciences exist within value-laden social contexts that affect their practices and findings.

TURN TOWARD FEMINIST EPISTEMOLOGIES AND METHODOLOGIES

Although we have barely touched on the range of contributions of feminist scholarship, it is clear that the decades of the 1970s and 1980s contributed to the deconstruction of traditional knowledge frameworks—taken-for-granted knowledge across several disciplines. In contrast to this endeavor, the 1980s and 1990s saw feminists launching other important challenges to knowledge building, starting with a basic foundational question:

- What is the nature of the social reality?

Positivism is a traditional research paradigm based on "the scientific method," a form of knowledge building in which "there is only *one* logic of science, to which any intellectual activity aspiring to the title of 'science' should follow" (Russell Keat & John Urry, quoted in Lawrence Neuman, 2000, p. 66). Positivism's model of inquiry is based on logic and empiricism. It holds out a specific epistemology of knowing—that truth lies "out there" in the social reality waiting to be discovered, if only the scientist is "objective" and "value free" in the pursuit of knowledge building. It posits "causal relationships" between variables that depend on the testing of specific hypotheses deduced from a general theory. The goal is to generalize research findings to a wider population and even to find causal laws that predict human behavior. Positivists present their results in the form of quantified patterns of behaviors reported in the form of statistical results. Early on, the social sciences (e.g., sociology and psychology) wanted to establish themselves as "scientific" in consort with the natural sciences (e.g., biology and chemistry). Auguste Comte (1798–1857), known as the father of French positivism, sought to incorporate the primary tenets of positivism into the discipline of sociology. Comte envisioned knowledge building passing through the "law of three stages": the "theological" or "fictitious" stage, characterized by beliefs in the supernatural; the "metaphysical" or "abstract" stage, a transitional state of knowledge building in which nature and its abstract forces are at work; and, finally, the "positivist" or "scientific" stage, the pinnacle of knowledge, through which we seek to uncover the laws that govern social behavior (Comte, 1896/2000, p. 27).

Émile Durkheim (1858–1917) also aspired to make sociology more scientific. In *The Rules of Sociological Method*, Durkheim (1895/1938) asserts that the discipline of sociology can create the same objective conditions that exist in the natural sciences. He codifies positivism by providing social scientists with specific rules and guidelines that will enable them to conduct value-free research, to separate facts from values, and to discover what he terms "social facts"—facts that "have an independent existence outside the individual consciousness" (p. 20). According to Durkheim, discarding sensation (feelings, values, and emotion) is an imperative aspect of knowledge building:

> It is a rule in the natural sciences to discard those data of sensation that are too subjective, in order to retain exclusively those presenting a sufficient degree of objectivity. Thus the physicist substitutes, for the vague impressions of temperature and electricity, the visual registrations of the thermometer or the electrometer. The sociologist must take the same precautions. (p. 44)

Feminist researchers do not necessarily embrace or eschew the practice of a positivist mode of inquiry. Some feminist researchers warn that the practice of positivism can lead to "bad science." This idea was the very motivation of *feminist empiricists* who urged scholars and researchers across the disciplines to be mindful of who is *left out* of research models' generalized claims and to tend to issues of difference in the research process (see, e.g., the preceding critique of androcentrism and Hundleby, Chapter 2, this volume). Other feminist scholars and researchers have critiqued positivism's tendency toward dualisms—between quantitative and qualitative research, between the subject and object of research, and between rationality and emotion. Sprague and Zimmerman (1993) argue, for example, that by setting up a subject-object split, whereby the researcher is removed from the research process and placed on a different plane, the practice of positivism promotes a hierarchy between the researcher and the researched that mimics patriarchy. Sprague and Zimmerman also challenge the positivist exclusion of emotions and values from the research process and call for an integration of quantitative and qualitative research.

On the other hand, positivism per se is not the enemy of all feminist inquiry; rather, the adversary is how positivist principles of practice are deployed in some mainstream research projects. Some feminist researchers see positivism as having merit, especially as it adds validity to feminist research projects. Feminist empiricists continue to draw on positivist traditions (see in this volume Miner, Jayaratne, Pesonen, & Zurbrügg; Rosser; and Cole & Stewart). Additionally, some research questions may call forth a positivistic framework, especially if the goal of the research project requires the testing of a specific research hypothesis across a broad spectrum of data with the aim of generalizing findings to a wider population. Some feminist social policy advocates have also argued for its inclusion. For example, Roberta Spalter-Roth and Heidi Hartmann (1996), in their social policy work on women and welfare, call for the "strategic" use of a quantitative paradigm in conjunction with a qualitative one to "heighten consciousness and to provide credible numbers that can help advocates to mobilize political support" (p. 221).

Finally, sociologist Janet Saltzman Chafetz (1999) objects to the confounding of positivism with such terms as "instrument of social control" and "masculine knowledge building." She attributes these misrepresentations to the confusion surrounding the meaning of the term:

> In part this has happened because of the erroneous confusion of this term with the kind of mindless empiricism that has marked so much sociological research. I believe that theory development and well-crafted, theoretically oriented research go hand-in-hand, and that this is in fact what "positivism" is all about. (p. 327)

According to Saltzman Chafetz (1999), there is "nothing in the view that patterned behaviors and processes exist, can be measured, and can be explained in substantial measure cross-culturally and pan-historically that automatically denigrates or controls people" (pp. 327–328). Instead, Saltzman Chafetz sees the positivistic perspective working for feminist ends.

Feminist empiricism made important contributions toward uncovering androcentric bias in social research by encouraging the practice of "good" science. A more radical set of feminist epistemologies and methodologies was to come,

as feminist researchers began to interrogate, disrupt, modify, and, at times, radically challenge existing ways of knowing within and across their disciplines, creating a shift in the tectonic plates of mainstream knowledge building. Beginning with a critique of positivism's concept of scientific objectivity—and from the idea of a "value-free" science with its stress on the detachment of the researcher from the researched—the feminist movement toward alternative epistemologies began to take shape. Feminists went to the heart of some basic foundational questions, namely, who can know? What can be known?

Instead of working to improve the accuracy, objectivity, and universality of mainstream research by including women, feminists started to challenge the viability and utility of concepts like objectivity and universality altogether. Knowledge is achieved not through "correcting" mainstream research studies by adding women, but through paying attention to the specificity and uniqueness of women's lives and experiences.

Donna Haraway (1988), Sandra Harding (1993), and Kum-Kum Bhavnani (1993) argue, for example, that objectivity needs to be transformed into "feminist objectivity." Donna Haraway defines feminist objectivity as "situated knowledges": *knowledge and truth are partial, situated, subjective, power imbued, and relational.* The denial of values, biases, and politics is seen as unrealistic and undesirable (see also Bhavnani, 1993, p. 96; Harding, 1993, p. 49). Historian Joan Scott (1999) disputes the positivist notion of a one-to-one correspondence between experience and social reality. Instead, she asserts, experience is shaped by one's particular context—by specific circumstances, conditions, values, and relations of power, each influencing how one articulates "experience." Scott ushered in a "linguistic turn" in our understanding of social reality by pointing out how experience is discursively constructed by dominant ideological structures. Tracing the discourse surrounding experience provides a method for examining the underlying mechanisms of oppression within society that, in fact, may provide new avenues of resistance and transformation.

In addition to valuing women's unique and situated experiences as knowledge (Gloria

Bowles & Renate Duelli-Klein, 1983; Smith, 1987, 1990; Liz Stanley & Sue Wise, 1983), some feminists make the case for validating the importance of emotions and values as a critical lens in research endeavors (Alison Jaggar, 1997; Sprague & Zimmerman, 1993). Alison Jaggar recognizes emotion as a central aspect of knowledge building. According to Jaggar (1997), it is unrealistic to assume emotions and values do not surface during the research process. Our emotions, in fact, are an integral part of why a given topic or set of research questions is studied and how it is studied. The positivistic dualism between the rational and the emotional becomes a false dichotomy:

> Values and emotions enter into the science of the past and the present not only on the level of scientific practice but also on the metascientific level, as answers to various questions: What is Science? How should it be practiced? And what is the status of scientific investigation versus nonscientific modes of enquiry? (p. 393)

Sandra Harding's (1993) concept of "*strong objectivity*" is a specific example of how to practice the basic premise of "feminist objectivity." Harding critiques the traditional, or positivist, concept of objectivity because its focus resides only on the "context of justification" in the research process—how the research is carried out and making sure that the researcher's values and attitudes do not enter into this process. What is left out of consideration is the extent to which values and attitudes of the researcher also enter into the "context of discovery," that part of the research process that asks questions and formulates specific research hypotheses. Donna Haraway (1988) characterizes this positivist tendency as the "god trick," and notes that it is "that mode of seeing that pretends to offer a vision that is from everywhere and nowhere, equally and fully" (p. 584). By contrast, Harding (1993) argues that throughout the research process, subjective judgments on the part of the researcher are always made "in the selection of problems, the formation of hypotheses, the design of research (including the organization of research communities), the collection of data, the interpretation and sorting of data, decisions about when to stop research,

the way results of research are reported, and so on." And to practice strong objectivity requires all researchers to self-reflect on what values, attitudes, and agenda they bring to the research process—strong objectivity means that "the subjects of knowledge be placed on the same critical causal plane as the objects of knowledge" (p. 69). How do a researcher's own history and positionality influence, for example, the questions she or he asks? It is in the practice of strong self-reflexivity that the researcher becomes more objective.

Feminist philosopher Lorraine Code (1991), in her book *What Can She Know? Feminist Theory and the Construction of Knowledge*, offers yet another viewpoint regarding positivism's "objectivity" claim. She argues for a "mitigated relativism" that avoids charges of "objectivism" and "relativism."

> I prefer to characterize the position I advocate as a *mitigated relativism*, however, or the freedom it offers from the homogenizing effects of traditional objectivism, in which differences, discrepancies, and deviations are smoothed out for the sake of achieving a unified theory. With its commitment to difference, critical relativism is able to resist reductivism and to accommodate divergent perspectives. Mitigated in its constraints by "the facts" of material objects and social/political artifacts, yet ready to account for the mechanisms of power (in a Foucauldian sense) and prejudice (in a Gadamerian sense) that produce knowledge of these facts, and committed to the self-critical stance that its mitigation requires, such relativism is a resourceful epistemological position. (pp. 320–321)

By disclosing their values, attitudes, and biases in their approaches to particular research questions and by engaging in strong reflexivity throughout the research process, feminist researchers can actually improve the objectivity of research. Feminists have forged new epistemologies of knowledge by incorporating women's lived experiences, emotions, and feelings into the knowledge-building process. We now turn to take a more in-depth look at the branch of feminist epistemology that centers on women's experience as a primary source of knowledge.

FEMINIST STANDPOINT EPISTEMOLOGY: FEMINIST RESEARCH GROUNDED IN THE EXPERIENCE OF THE OPPRESSED

Feminist standpoint epistemology borrows from the Marxist and Hegelian idea that individuals' daily activities or material and lived experiences structure their understanding of the social world. Karl Marx viewed knowledge as historically constructed and relative because it is based on a given "mode of production." Elites (owners of the "means of production") shape knowledge and ideology to justify social inequality. For both Marx and Hegel, the master's perspective is partial and distorted, whereas the worker/slave's is more complete because the worker/slave must comprehend his or her own world and that of the master—the worker/slave must know both worlds to survive. Feminist standpoint scholars argue that it is a woman's oppressed location within society that provides fuller insights into society as a whole; women have access to an enhanced and more nuanced understanding of social reality than men do precisely because of their structurally oppressed location vis-à-vis the dominant group, or men. Dorothy Smith (1987), an early proponent of the standpoint perspective, stresses the necessity of starting research from women's lives: taking into account women's everyday experiences through paying particular attention to and finding and analyzing the gaps that occur when women try to fit their lives into the dominant culture's way of conceptualizing women's situation. By looking at the difference between the two perspectives, the researcher gains a more complex and theoretically richer set of explanations of the lives of the oppressors and the oppressed.

Early critics of standpoint epistemology argued that it collapses all women's experiences into a single defining experience and pays little attention to the diversity of women's lives, especially to the varied experiences of those women who differ by race, class, sexual preference, and so on. Still others raised questions such as the following: If knowledge starts out from the oppressed, how does one ascertain who is the most oppressed? Feminist standpoint scholars and researchers have responded to these concerns, and standpoint epistemology has undergone many different iterations over time. The concept of multiple standpoints has been introduced. Later versions of standpoint are open to comparing and understanding the interlocking relationships between racism, sexism, heterosexism, and class oppression as additional starting points into understanding the social reality (see Harding, Chapter 3, this volume; Wylie, Chapter 26, this volume). The current dialogue (Harding, 2004), ongoing development, and diversity of approaches to feminist standpoint epistemology notwithstanding, by calling attention to women's lived experiences of oppression as the starting point for building knowledge, feminist standpoint scholars and researchers provided a new way to answer two epistemological questions: Who can know? and What can be known?

FEMINIST EPISTEMOLOGIES AND METHODOLOGIES: THE CHALLENGE AND POSSIBILITIES OF THE POSTMODERN TURN

We can think of postmodernism as a theoretical paradigm that serves as an "umbrella term" for a variety of perspectives from critical theory to post-structural theory to postmodern theories. What creates unity among these perspectives is their concern for highlighting the importance of researching difference—there is an emphasis on including the "other" in the process of research (Hesse-Biber, Leavy, & Yaiser, 2004, p. 18). The perspectives contained within this umbrella term call for, in a range of degrees, the transformative practices of research that lead toward both challenging dominant forms of knowledge building and empowering subjected understandings. But there is also variation and contestation among and between perspectives within this umbrella term. For example, critical theory is especially cognizant of the role that power plays in producing hegemonic knowledge. Critical theorists seek to expose dominant power relationships and knowledge that oppress with the goal of "critical emancipation"—creating an environment in which oppressed groups "gain the power to control their own lives in solidarity with a justice-oriented community" (see Joe Kincheloe & Peter McLaren, 2000, p. 282). However, some might consider critical theory's emphasis on emancipation to be inconsistent with the tendency of postmodern and post-structural theories to deconstruct dominant discourse. These variations in postmodern perspectives are compared and contrasted in more detail in Gannon and Davies (Chapter 4, this volume). Gannon and Davies point out how labels such as postmodernism, post-structuralism, and critical theory are often confusing, and how practitioners of these perspectives don't always agree on what these terms mean. They note,

> These frameworks are, however, quite slippery and hard to pin down. . . . There is, then, no orderly, agreed upon, and internally consistent set of ideas that sits obediently under each of these headings. But each of them, along with the disputed ground between them, has produced new ideas that have helped feminists break loose from previously taken-for-granted assumptions. (p. 65)

In *Feminist Perspectives on Social Research* (2004), Patricia Leavy, Michelle Yaiser, and I point out the affinity of postmodernism with feminist research pursuits. We note that postmodernism's emphasis on bringing the "other" into the research process

> meshes well with the general currents within the feminist project itself. Feminists from all traditions have always been concerned with including women in their research in order to rectify the historic reliance on men as research subjects. This is a general feminist concern. (Hesse-Biber et al., 2004, p. 18)

In addition, postmodernism's emphasis on the empowerment of oppressed groups is congruent with feminists' emphasis on social change and social justice. This congruence is also particularly the case with postmodern feminists, including postcolonial feminists who seek to explore "political cultural resistance to hierarchical modes of structuring social life by being attentive to the dynamics of power and knowledge" (Hesse-Biber et al., 2004, p. 18). Although postmodern and post-structural perspectives invigorate feminist theory and praxis, there is also a tendency for them to destabilize it (Barrett & Phillips, 1992). For example, post-structural theorists have challenged essentialist categories: women, sex, gender, and the body. Michèle Barrett and Ann Phillips (1992), in *Destablizing Theory: Contemporary Feminist Debates*, note,

> The fear now expressed by many feminists is that the changing theoretical fashions will lead us towards abdicating the goal of accurate and systematic knowledge; and that in legitimate critique of some of the earlier assumptions, we may stray too far from feminism's original project. (p. 6)

Christina Gilmartin, Robin Lydenberg, and I point out in our book *Feminist Approaches to Theory and Methodology* (Hesse-Biber, Gilmartin, & Lydenberg, 1999) how the destabilizing of these binary categories served to polarize feminist theory:

> French feminists like Hélène Cixous and Catherine Clément (1986), Luce Irigaray (1991), and Julia Kristeva (1986) were accused by social constructionists of biological essentialism, of establishing the female body and maternity as foundational and symbolic sources of woman's psychic and sexual difference. . . . post-structuralist critics, like Judith Butler, expose even the materiality of the body as "already gendered, already constructed." Extending her argument that gender and sex are the result of the "ritualized repetition" of certain behaviors designed to render the body either "intelligible" (normative, heterosexual) or abject (unthinkable, homosexual), Judith Butler asserts that the body itself is "forcibly produced" by power and discourse (Butler, 1993, p. xi). (Hesse-Biber et al., 1999, p. 4)

The challenge for feminism is to dialogue around these tensions and to be open to different points of view. Gannon and Davies (this volume) examine the opportunities that open up for feminist theory and research when the postmodern meets the feminist terrain of theory and praxis.

FEMINIST EPISTEMOLOGIES AND METHODOLOGIES: THE TURN TOWARD DIFFERENCE IN FEMINIST THEORY AND PRACTICE

The positivist paradigm assumes the viability of the *value-neutral and objective* researcher, who can obtain generalized findings or universal truths. Based on these assumptions, positivism has very specific answers to epistemological questions. Certain types of "knowledge" are not considered scientific knowledge, certain ways of obtaining knowledge are not valid, and certain people may not posses knowledge. Because positivism was the dominant paradigm in social science for many years, certain people, knowledge, and methods have been excluded from social science research. These "others" and the knowledge they possess are not considered valid or valuable.

Feminists initiated their critique of positivism by (1) calling attention to the fact that women had been left out of much mainstream research and (2) valuing the perspectives, feelings, and lived experiences of women as knowledge. In the 1980s and 1990s, however, some feminists warned against the tendency to reduce all women to one category with shared characteristics. Yes, it was important to give voice to women who had been left out of mainstream research models and to recognize women's life stories as knowledge. But which women's stories were being told—whose life experiences were included, and whose were left out? Through feminism's interaction with postcolonialism, post-structuralism, and postmodernism, there occurred a turn toward difference research. Feminists became increasingly conscious of the diversity of women's experiences. They argued against the idea of one essential experience of women and began to recognize a plurality of women's lived experiences.

Feminist research on difference stressed issues of difference regarding race, class, and gender. Feminists of color critiqued the failure of early feminist research to explore the important interconnections among categories of difference in terms of gender, ethnicity, and class (see, e.g., Anzaldúa, 1987; hooks, 1990; Mohanty, 1988). As Hirsch and Keller (1990) observed, "Feminists of color have revealed to white middle-class feminists the extent of their own racism" (p. 379). Sociologist Patricia Hill Collins (1990) stresses the significance of black feminist thought—"the ideas produced by Black women that clarify a standpoint of and for Black women" (p. 37). Listening to the experiences of the "other" leads to a more complete understanding of knowledge. Black women, argues Collins, are "outsiders within." To navigate socially within white society, black women have to cope with the rules of the privileged white world, but, at the same time, they are constantly aware of their marginalized position in terms of their race and gender. In contrast, sociological insiders, because of their privileged positionality, are "in no position to notice the specific anomalies apparent to Afro-American women, because these same sociological insiders produced them" (p. 53). Along with this epistemology, Patricia Hill Collins develops a "matrix of domination" framework for conceptualizing difference along a range of interlocking inequalities of race, class, and gender. These factors affect each other and are socially constructed. It is only through collectively examining the intricately connected matrix of difference that we can truly understand a given individual's life experience. Feminists of color challenged and changed white feminist scholarly research and the conceptualization of feminist standpoint epistemology by asking this question: Which women? For example, Patricia Hill Collins's conception of "standpoint" as relational, and including multiple systems of oppression, forced white feminists to examine white privilege as an element of oppression (see McIntosh, 1995).

Bonnie Thornton Dill and Marla Kohlman (Chapter 8, this volume) expand and elaborate on the early work of scholars like Hill Collins with a focus on analyzing the interconnections of differences among race, class, and gender. They employ the term *intersectionality* to "[emphasize] the interlocking effects of race, class, gender, and sexuality, highlighting the ways in which categories of identity and structures of inequality are mutually constituted and defy separation into discrete categories of analysis." Their chapter traces the impact of diversity on disciplinary and interdisciplinary scholarship over the past several decades and charts some future directions for knowledge building that embody a vision of intersectionality within academic institutions.

FEMINIST EPISTEMOLOGIES AND METHODOLOGIES: THE TURN TOWARD GLOBALIZATION

Feminist scholars and researchers continue to engage issues of difference across gender, ethnicity, and class. As Bonnie Thornton Dill (1987) reminds us, "Our analysis must include critical accounts of women's situation in every race, class, and culture—we must work to provide resources so that every woman can define problematics, generate concepts and theories" (Dill, 1987, p. 97). In the first decade of the 21st century, feminists expanded their focus on difference to include issues of sexual preference and disability, as well as nationality and geographical region. There is also a growing awareness among feminist researchers of the importance of women's experiences in a global context with respect to issues of imperialism, colonialism, and national identity (see the chapters in this volume by Bhavnani & Talcott, Mendez & Wolf, and Dill & Kohlman). Frequently, analyses that incorporate race, class, and gender differences ignore the diversity among women with regard to their particular geographical or cultural placement across the globe.

- How do we conceptualize and study difference in a global context?
- What research frameworks serve to empower and promote social change for women?

Feminists doing international research, who attempt to speak for "the other/s" in a global context, should be particularly mindful of the inherent power dynamics in doing so. In what sense does the researcher give voice to the other, and to what extent is that privilege one that is taken for granted by "the other/s"? Postcolonial feminist Gayatri Chakravorty Spivak (1990) notes:

On the other side of the international division of labor, the subject of exploitation cannot know and speak the text of female exploitation even if the absurdity of the nonrepresenting intellectual making space for them to speak is achieved. The woman is doubly in shadow. (p. 894)

Historian Deniz Kandiyoti (1999) discusses the tendency of some Western feminist researchers to "universalize" disciplinary concepts, ignoring the ethnocentrism that lies deep within constructs such as patriarchy. Kandiyoti also calls for the employment of a historical-comparative lens to strengthen our understanding of the cross-cultural context of conceptual meaning across Western and non-Western societies (Mohanty, 1988).

Feminists working in a global context call for a heightened attention to power and difference. But what about the potential for women to come together across difference and to forge social change? Some feminist researchers call for employing a type of "strategic essentialism" in their research projects (Spivak, 1994). Susan Bordo (1990) encourages the strategic use of essentialism for women to promote their political agenda (see also Spivak, 1990, p. 10). She argues that "too relentless a focus on historical heterogeneity . . . can obscure the transhistorical hierarchical patterns of white, male privilege that have informed the creation of the Western intellectual tradition" (Bordo, 1990, p. 149). Chandra Talpade Mohanty (1999) also employs the strategic use of essentialism, using three case studies of third world women involved in the global division of labor. Mohanty shows how ideologies of domesticity, femininity, and race are employed by capitalists to socially construct the "domesticated woman worker"—the dominant perception of women as "dependent housewives" allows the capitalist to pay them low wages. By having women identify with each other as "women" and through their shared material interests as "workers," they are able to overcome differences of nationality, race, and social class. These identifications across difference provide a rethinking of third world woman as agents rather than victims. Mohanty argues for political solidarity among women workers as a potential "revolutionary basis for struggles against capitalist re-colonization" (see also Hesse-Biber, 2002).

Locating the intersections where women's differences cross is a way that some feminists have begun to research difference in a global context and to empower women's voices. Kum-Kum Bhavnani and Molly Talcott (Chapter 7, this volume) suggest the need to look for *interconnections* between women, and they do not believe that using an "intersecting" metaphor works well to empower women's lives. In fact, the concept of an "intersection" implies the image of a crossroad, whereby those who meet are coming from and going to a given destination, which is defined by the route that these roads take. This metaphor does not provide a way for a new road to be charted. A race-d/gender-ed person stands at the crossroad (that point where race and gender routes intersect), yet, as Bhavnani and Talcott note,

> A crossroads metaphor . . . directs the gaze to the intersections of the roads and the directions in which they travel and meet. . . . This matters because, if we are not only to analyze the world but to change it, then the easiest way to imagine the shifts in the relationships between race/ethnicity and gender is to imagine the roads being moved to form new intersections.

They suggest that a more empowering metaphor might be to think of these roads as

> *interconnections that configure* [which] connotes more movement and fluidity than lies in the metaphor of intersection, as well as offering a way of thinking about how not only race and gender but also nation, sexuality, and wealth all interconnect, configure, and reshape each other.

Much of the theorizing and many research studies on the concerns of women in a global context, however, remain fragmented. Black feminists, third world feminists, and global, postcolonial, or transnational feminists often remain uninformed about each other's theories, perspectives, and research (see Mendez & Wolf, Chapter 31, this volume). What remains a challenge for feminist research is the creation of links between these strands of knowledge building so as to gather a more complex understanding of the workings of racism, imperialism, and neocolonialism across historical and cultural contexts. What are the models of knowledge building that will allow feminist researchers to study these interconnections? To do this requires an understanding of how feminists carry out their research practices and of what overarching principles guide their work.

The journey we have only briefly outlined thus far opens a window into feminist thinking on issues of epistemology and methodology. Feminists have employed new ways of thinking and have modified our understanding of the nature of the social world—providing new questions and angles of vision by which to understand women's issues and concerns. Feminist epistemology and methodology directly affect feminist praxis.

FEMINIST PRAXIS: A SYNERGISTIC PERSPECTIVE ON THE PRACTICE OF FEMINIST RESEARCH

Feminist praxis refers to the varied ways feminist research proceeds. Feminist perspectives challenge the traditional research paradigm of positivism, which assumes a unified truth with the idea of testing out hypotheses. There is little room for the exploration of personal feelings and experiences, given the strict observance of objectivity as a basic tenet of positivism. Yet, as we have seen, new theoretical contributions from feminist standpoint theory (Harding, Chapter 3, this volume; Wylie, Chapter 26, this volume), postcolonial theory (Bhavnani & Talcott, Chapter 7, this volume; Mohanty, 1999), and postmodernism (Gannon & Davies, Chapter 4, this volume), for example, ask *new* questions that call forth getting at subjugated knowledge, particularly as this relates to issues of difference. Early on, feminists saw the need to make a radical break in positivism's traditional research paradigm. Helen Roberts's (1981) edited volume *Doing Feminist Research* asks the question "What is feminist research?" Roberts's pathbreaking volume puts a feminist sociological lens onto the research process and notes, "The accounts in this collection point to the theoretical, methodological, practical and ethical issues raised in projects where the investigator has adopted, or has at least become aware of, a feminist perspective" (p. 2). Ann Oakley's (1981) now classic article "Interviewing Women: A Contradiction in Terms?" in Roberts's volume, demonstrates the importance of breaking down the hierarchical power relationship between the interviewer and the researched that she views as characteristic of a positivist research paradigm and antithetical to the view of women as agents of social change with their own set of experiences. She argues that interviewing is "not a one-way process where the interviewer elicits and receives, but does not give information" (p. 30).

Liz Stanley and Sue Wise's (1983) visionary volume *Breaking Out: Feminist Consciousness and Feminist Research* calls for feminist researchers to "upgrade the personal as an object of study." They argue for a "naturalist" as opposed to a "positivistic model" of research to study women's experiences, or what they term "feminist consciousness," in which "feeling and experience" are the primary guideposts for feminist research (p. 178). For Stanley and Wise, there is no demarcation between "doing feminism" and "doing feminist research." Patti Lather's (1991) book *Getting Smart: Feminist Research and Pedagogy Within/In the Postmodern* takes up the issue of power in research and teaching practices. She combines insights from feminism and postmodernism with the goal of "emancipatory" knowledge building, during which the researcher and researched cocreate meaning through "reciprocity and negotiation." She is interested in what research designs, teaching practices, and curricula produce "liberatory knowledge" and "empower" the researched and the pedagogical process.

Other works on the intersection of feminism and methods quickly followed and span the next several decades. Some of the most notable volumes, to name only a few, are Patricia Hill Collins's (1990) *Black Feminist Thought: Knowledge, Consciousness, and the Politics of Empowerment*; Joyce McCarl Nielson's (1990) *Feminist Research Methods: Exemplary Readings in the Social Science*s; bell hooks's (1990) *Yearning: Race, Gender, and Cultural Politics*; Liz Stanley's (1990) *Feminist Praxis: Research, Theory, and Epistemology in Feminist Sociology*; Mary Margaret Fonow and Judith A. Cook's (1991) *Beyond Methodology: Feminist Scholarship as Lived Research*; Sherna Berger Gluck and Daphne Patai's (1991) *Women's Words: The Feminist Practice of Oral History*; Shulamit Reinharz's (1992) *Feminist Methods in Social Research*; Mary Maynard and June Purvis's (1994) *Researching Women's Lives From a Feminist Perspective*; Sandra Burt and Lorraine Code's (1995) *Changing Methods: Feminists Transforming Practice*; Diane L. Wolf's (1996) *Feminist Dilemmas in Fieldwork*; Louise Lamphere, Helena Ragone, and Patricia Zavella's (1997) *Situated Lives: Gender and Culture in Everyday Life*; Marjorie L. DeVault's (1999) *Liberating Method: Feminism and Social Research*; Linda Tuhiwai Smith's (1999) *Decolonizing Methodologies: Research and Indigenous Peoples*; Elizabeth A. St. Pierre and Wanda S. Pillow's (2000) *Working the Ruins: Feminist Poststructural Theory and Methods in Education*; and Nancy A. Naples's (2003) *Feminism and Method: Ethnography, Discourse Analysis,*

and Activist Research. Each volume highlights how feminist researchers create a tight link between the elements of the research process—epistemology, methodology, and method. We see this linkage unfolding by looking at how feminists engage with the research process—starting with the research questions they devise, how research methods are practiced, and the special attention given to issues of power, authority, reflexivity, ethics, and difference in the practice, writing, and reading of feminist research.

In all these volumes, feminist epistemologies and methodologies inform research practices. A feminist empiricist perspective on knowledge building informs the practice of survey methods by interrogating the male bias of some survey questions as well as the power differentials between the researcher and researched in the survey interview. A feminist standpoint epistemology questions whether the research sample and research questions of a particular method are responsive to issues of difference and whether the findings are interpreted in a way that includes the experiences of marginalized populations. Increasingly, feminists are tweaking old methods and inventing new methods to get at women's experience. We see this most vividly in how feminists practice interview methods. In Marjorie DeVault's (1999) volume as well as in her coauthored chapter with Glenda Gross, "Feminist Qualitative Interviewing: Experience, Talk, and Knowledge" (Chapter 11, this volume), there is an awareness of the importance of listening during the interview process:

> One of feminism's central claims is that women's perspectives have often been silenced or ignored; as a result, feminist researchers have been interested in listening for gaps and absences in women's talk, and in considering what meanings might lie beyond explicit speech. (p. 217)

By listening through the gaps in talking and by attending to what is not stated, but present—such as the hidden meanings of terms like "you know?"—DeVault suggests one can get at "subjugated knowledge." What each of these books also demonstrates is that feminists use a range of methods, and some even employ multiple methods within the same, concurrent, or follow-up research projects, to answer complex and often novel questions. Feminist research, then, can be qualitative or quantitative or a combination of both.

Shulamit Reinharz (1992), in her classic text *Feminist Methods in Social Research*, notes that "feminism supplies the perspective and the disciplines supply the method. The feminist researcher exists at their intersection" (p. 243). Although feminist research is multiple, complex, quantitative, and qualitative, nevertheless, if we were to examine *inductively* the range of research studies and topics cited in these works and within this volume, which are by no means exhaustive of the population of feminist research, we could discern some common principles of feminist research praxis.

Feminists Ask New Questions That Often Get at Subjugated Knowledge

The women's movement of the 1960s, as well as increasing globalization, forged new feminist theoretical perspectives (see Part I of this *Handbook*). Feminist standpoint theory (Harding, Chapter 3, this volume; Wylie, Chapter 26, this volume), postcolonialism (Bhavnani & Talcott, Chapter 7, this volume; Mendez & Wolf, Chapter 31, this volume), postmodernism, ethnic studies, queer studies, critical theory, and critical race theory (Gannon & Davies, Chapter 4, this volume) serve to upend traditional knowledge by asking new questions that expose the power dynamics of knowledge building. "Subjugated" knowledge is unearthed and issues of race, class, sexuality, nationality, and gender are taken into account. These types of questions are different from those questions feminist empiricists ask in that they go beyond correcting gender bias in dominant research studies. In asking new questions, feminist research maintains a close link between epistemology, methodology, and methods.

Feminist Praxis Takes Up Issues of Power, Authority, Ethics, and Reflexivity

Feminist praxis builds on the understanding of difference and translates these insights by emphasizing the importance of taking issues of power, authority, ethics, and reflexivity into the practice of social research. Feminist researchers are particularly keen on getting at issues of power and authority in the research process, from question formulation to carrying out and writing up research findings (see Roof, Chapter 25, this volume). Focusing on our positionality within the research process helps to break down the idea that research is the "view from nowhere."

Feminist research practitioners pay attention to reflexivity, a process whereby researchers recognize, examine, and understand how their social background, location, and assumptions affect their research practice. Practicing reflexivity also includes paying attention to the specific ways in which our own agendas affect the research at all points in the research process—from the selection of the research problem to the selection of method and ways in which we analyze and interpret our findings (see Hesse-Biber & Piatelli, Chapter 27, this volume). Hesse-Biber and Leckenby's (2004) work on the importance of self-reflexivity on the part of the researcher notes,

> Feminist researchers are continually and cyclically interrogating their locations as both researcher and as feminist. They engage the boundaries of their multiple identities and multiple research aims through conscientious reflection. This engagement with their identities and roles impacts the earliest stages of research design. Much of feminist research design is marked by an openness to the shifting contexts and fluid intentions of the research questions. (p. 211)

Ethical discussions usually remain detached from a discussion of the research process; some researchers consider this aspect of research an afterthought. Yet, the ethical standpoint or *moral integrity* of the researcher is a critically important aspect of ensuring that the research process and a researcher's findings are "trustworthy" and valid. The term "ethics" derives from the Greek word "ethos," which means "character." A feminist ethical perspective provides insights into how ethical issues enter into the selection of a research problem, how one conducts research, the design of one's study, one's sampling procedure, and the responsibility toward research participants. Feminist ethical issues also come into play in deciding what research findings get published (see Preissle & Han, Chapter 28, this volume).

Feminist Researchers Often Work at the Margins of Their Disciplines

Feminist research, while breaking out of the traditional circle of knowledge building, remains on the margins of discussion within mainstream methods texts. In 1962, Thomas Kuhn published *The Structure of Scientific Revolutions*, in which he argued that science is enmeshed in a particular mode of thinking—a paradigm or worldview—that tends to dominate a given field of science. Those insiders who practice within a reigning paradigm do get recognition and gain legitimacy for their work through a range of institutional structures—from promotions and tenure committees within the academy and mainstream journals within their field to monetary rewards from granting agencies and foundations. For feminist epistemologies and methodologies to gain greater recognition and rewards in and outside the academy and to harness these gains into social policy changes for women, feminists must work at multiple levels. Work must be done within and outside the circle to ensure that women's scholarship is recognized and rewarded as legitimate scholarship within their disciplines and within the social policy initiatives of funding agencies:

> Feminist researchers may need to be strategic about their mission and goals concerning how to organize as a research movement toward social change for women. Issues of difference in the research process need to be carefully addressed as this discussion proceeds. Issues dealing with power and control both within the research process and discussions of differences and similarities among different/competing feminist epistemologies and methodologies would be productive and energetic beginnings toward raising the consciousness of the feminist research communities. (Hesse-Biber & Leckenby, 2004, p. 225)

Feminist Research Seeks Social Change and Social Transformation

Sandra Harding (1991) speaks of "emancipation" as one important goal of feminist research; knowledge building in pursuit of this goal does not lean in the direction of the dominant groups but instead toward democratic ends (Hesse-Biber and Leckenby, 2004, p. 221). As the articles in this *Handbook* demonstrate, most feminist researchers seek to connect their research to social transformation and social change on behalf of women and other oppressed groups. Patti Lather (1991) notes that feminist researchers "consciously use . . . research to help participants understand and change their situations" (p. 226).

We begin the *Handbook* with a historical grounding in the diverse range of theoretical and epistemic perspectives that make up the history of feminist engagement with research. We provide an overview of historical contributions of feminists to the knowledge-building process.

Part I. Feminist Perspectives on Knowledge Building

This section traces the historical rise of feminist research and begins with the early links between feminist theory and research practice. We trace the contours of early feminist inquiry and introduce the reader to the history of, and historical debates within, feminist scholarship. This section also explores the political process of knowledge building by introducing the reader to the links between knowledge and power relations. Several questions guide our selection of theoretical and research articles for this section:

- How have feminist scholars redefined traditional paradigms in the social sciences and humanities?
- What new theoretical and research models guide their work?

In this section, we will explore the nature of methodologies, frameworks, and presumptions dominant within the social sciences and humanities. We will point out what we think are the critical turning points in feminist research: "adding women and stirring," feminist standpoint theory, the inclusion of difference, and the debates surrounding method, methodology, and epistemology. Feminist research endeavors often began by pointing out the androcentrism in the sciences. This research approach is often referred to as feminist empiricism, as we shall see in philosopher Catherine Hundleby's chapter "Feminist Empiricism." Here, she explores the specific challenges feminists pose for traditional models of knowledge building. She investigates the concept of "objectivity" in the research process and how some feminist researchers have developed alternatives to traditional objectivity. Feminist empiricists work within a positivistic model of knowledge building with the goal of creating "better" science. This better and more objective science is achieved through the application of more rigorous practices, incorporating difference into the research process, and more strictly following the basic tenets of positivism.

Sandra Harding's article, "Feminist Standpoints," looks at the origins of standpoint theories, which grew out of feminist activism of the 1960s and 1970s, and examines the antipositivist "histories, sociologies, and philosophies of science" emerging in Europe and the United States. Harding provides us with a history of the development of the standpoint perspective, which begins with research questions (methodologies) rooted in women's lives—their everyday existence. Drawing on the Marxist theory of the master-slave relationship, Nancy Hartsock (1983), for example, argues that, because of women's location within the sexual division of labor and because of their experience of oppression, women have greater insights as researchers into the lives of other women. Dorothy Smith (1987) stresses the importance of creating knowledge based upon the standpoint and experience of women. In this volume, Harding also takes up the critiques against a standpoint perspective. Some critics are uncomfortable with giving up positivism's claim of universal truth. If, as standpoint theory suggests, there are multiple subjectivities, won't this perspective lead to chaos? Others charge that standpoint theory is too essentialist and Eurocentric in that it distills all women's experience into a single vision (Western, white women's).

The following five chapters address a range of issues, including understanding the diversity of women's experiences and the feminist commitment to the empowerment of women and other oppressed groups. Susanne Gannon and Bronwyn Davies (Chapter 4, this volume) discuss postmodern, post-structural, and critical perspectives regarding cultural theory. They look at how some feminist theorists, such as Butler, Grosz, and Briadotti (as cited in Gannon & Davies, this volume) incorporate the insights

of these perspectives into their own theoretical work and research. Gannon and Davies also illuminate several feminist critiques of these perspectives, such as relativism, a lack of a political vision, and a tendency to reinforce the status quo.

Aiding Mary Hawkesworth's exploration of feminist epistemology (Chapter 5, this volume) are analyses of feminist methodology. Working through notions of objectivity and truth in terms of the feminist critiques that have been raised against them, Hawkesworth considers their implications for feminist research. Feminist empiricists, standpoint theorists, postmodernists, science studies scholars, and those who are interested in the "posthuman" have all thought through objectivity and truth and developed their possibilities within feminist research projects.

Kum-Kum Bhavnani and Molly Talcott (Chapter 7, this volume) are specifically concerned with the emergence of the visibility and audibility of women's experience in feminist research. Using a global feminist ethnographic approach, Bhavnani and Talcott ask, "Which women's lives are being analyzed, interrogated, and even evaluated?" Accounts of difference, this chapter argues, should be reconceptualized and broadened within a global context. By pointing to studies on women and development, Bhavnani and Talcott emphasize the importance of transnationality and the utility of a global perspective in examinations of oppression. Feminist researchers are better able to approach the full range of women's experience by widening their field of inquiry to include global perspectives.

Elizabeth Anderson's and other feminist researchers' and scholars' claim that "gender . . . ought to influence our conceptions of knowledge" is controversial (2011; cited in Koertge, Chapter 6, this volume), and Noretta Koertge (Chapter 6, this volume) argues that gendering epistemology may not always be beneficial to feminist research. Taking into account the influence of gender on inquiry and challenging the works of Andrea Nye, Sandra Harding, and Helen Longino, all of whom conclude that a feminist epistemology is necessary, Koertge warns against gendered epistemology.

Bonnie Thornton Dill and Marla Kohlman (Chapter 8, this volume) offer an account of intersectionality as a conceptual tool within feminist theory and practice. For research that sets out to look at, for example, intersections of race, class, gender, and sexuality within identity, intersectionality is particularly appropriate because it assumes difference and recognizes that such concepts are mutually constitutive and inseparable. Intersectionality as a conceptual model has provoked debates about its theory and practice, and this chapter seeks to both trace the development of intersectionality and speak to its future in feminist research.

Feminist perspectives on knowledge building have pushed against the dominant circles of knowledge, cautious about re-creating hegemonic knowledge of the past, sometimes stumbling, but committed to pushing past the boundaries of traditional knowledge. Feminists do not always agree on the specific paths to travel, and there remain significant tensions among feminists concerning how best to research and represent women's issues and concerns, as well as how to confront the power dynamics that continue to reinforce hegemonic forces that serve the status quo. What is clearly needed from examining the range of perspectives feminists offer onto the landscape of knowledge building is a dialogue among feminists. Where are the points of agreement? Disagreement? How can we foster a more transdisciplinary approach to knowledge building? How do we construct a climate where feminist theorists and researchers listen to each other? How tolerant are feminists of each other's points of view? These are the issues that we address in Part I of this *Handbook*.

Part II. Feminist Research Praxis

Part II of this *Handbook* debates the issue of whether or not there is a unique feminist method. What makes a method feminist? What are the unique characteristics feminists bring to the practice of this method? What are the strengths and challenges in practicing feminist research? What is gained and what is risked? This section looks at how feminists use a range of research methods in both conventional and unconventional research studies. Many feminist research projects have used survey methods and quantitative data analysis—two traditionally androcentric methods—to produce very women-centered results. Methods such as intensive interviewing, the collection of oral histories, and qualitative data analysis are often labeled feminist methods

by traditional sociologists; however, these methods have been tweaked and modified in various ways to uncover women's issues and concerns. The labeling of certain methods as traditional or feminist by social scientists and the use of specific methods by feminist researchers are the focus of Part II.

This section also stresses the idea that feminist researchers come from a variety of epistemological positions. Feminist researchers use multiple tools to gain access to and understanding of the world around them and may use multiple methods within the same study. The selections chosen for this section are not exhaustive of all feminist research or all the methods feminists use. These selections do, however, provide a broad context within which to examine feminist research. Deborah Piatelli and I provide a detailed introduction and theoretical and research context for Part II in our chapter, "The Synergistic Praxis of Theory and Method."

Part II starts off with a look at ethnographic methods, as Wanda S. Pillow and Cris Mayo (Chapter 10, this volume) put forth the history and development of feminist ethnography in order to locate their examples of feminist ethnographic research. Issues of definition and method in terms of women's lives remain at the forefront of Pillow and Mayo's presentation of feminist ethnographic research. In addition to promoting the challenging practice of feminist ethnography, this chapter accounts for its current status and its future in research endeavors.

The interview has been used frequently by feminist research as a way for researchers and participants to work together to illuminate experience. Marjorie L. DeVault and Glenda Gross (Chapter 11, this volume) discuss the complexity of the interview encounter and how the interview has been implemented in feminist research projects. Specifically paying attention to how identity, social location, reflexivity, and active listening operate in the interview, DeVault and Gross suggest ways of engaging in ethical, collaborative interviews. Ethicality is significant in this chapter, as DeVault and Gross emphasize the accountability and responsibility of the interviewer to the participants and to social change.

Structurally different from the interview, the survey can play an important role in feminist research projects. In their chapter regarding quantitative data, Kathi Miner, Toby Epstein

Jayaratne, Amanda Pesonen, and Lauren Zurbrügg (Chapter 12, this volume) point to the survey as offering useful applications to feminist research. The history and criticisms of survey research are presented, as are the influences of feminism on survey practices. Miner et al. flesh out the survey method and how feminist perspectives may be best applied to survey research.

The fact that the scientific community has come to accept that its practices are biased by values (gender being only one) is evidence, for Sue Rosser (Chapter 13, this volume), of feminism's contribution to the areas of science, technology, and medicine. Rosser explores the impact of feminist theories on different stages of the scientific method. To illustrate feminism's effects on scientific practice, she highlights theories that have incorporated feminist viewpoints to modify their experimental methods.

According to Sharon Brisolara and Denise Seigart (Chapter 14, this volume), feminist evaluation is still an emerging and developing model within feminist research. In order to understand feminist evaluation fully, these authors single out and highlight contributions to research projects that use multiple theoretical models. Among its possibilities for feminist research projects, evaluation research can allow for new questions to arise regarding its aims, methods, and results by paying attention to, for example, its ethics and possible biases.

Deboleena Roy (Chapter 15, this volume) delves into the development of feminist research practices within the natural sciences as influenced by feminist engagements with ontological and ethical questions. The feminist researcher should, as this chapter argues, consider questions of ethics and ontology while practicing the scientific method. Proposing the inclusions of "playfulness" and "feeling around" in feminist research, Roy suggests that the feminist laboratory researcher may work to connect himself or herself with the research at hand and with other researchers.

Not only looking at participatory action research (PAR) in terms of feminist usage in recent research, Brinton Lykes and Rachel Hershberg (Chapter 16, this volume) also summarize the origins of this research method, which is a resource for critical inquiry in working toward improving social systems and ameliorating social inequalities. PAR is deeply bound up with issues of

relationships between coresearchers, processes of reflection, and change for communities and policy. PAR is manifested in many different ways, and Lykes and Hershberg analyze work that is characteristic of feminist PAR while identifying its limitations and possibilities.

The combination of qualitative and quantitative methods has emerged in research praxis, and Elizabeth Cole and Abigail Stewart (Chapter 17, this volume) discuss how such combinations contribute to feminist research. They identify various ways of mixing methods in order to demonstrate the many possibilities of combining qualitative and quantitative methods and to emphasize how widely such combinations may be applied. Cole and Stewart propose that feminist research may benefit from the use of both qualitative and quantitative approaches.

Situational analysis, an extension of grounded theory, brings notions of post-structuralism to feminist theories in order to highlight difference and power. Adele Clarke (Chapter 18, this volume) expands upon the definition of grounded theory and emphasizes its intrinsic links to feminist theory. Clarke shows how grounded theory's ties to feminism have been transformed from implicit to explicit by feminist research projects, and then she shows how situational analysis, similarly, is feminist.

Social movement research, Sarah Maddison and Frances Shaw (Chapter 19, this volume) believe, can benefit from further connections to feminist epistemology and methodology. While feminist social movement scholars have brought a gendered focus to social movement scholarship and theory, research on collective identity can further incorporate feminist standpoints in order to reconfigure its analytic method, and Maddison and Shaw use a case study to show the intersection of feminism and social movement research.

Lynn Weber and Jenn Castellow (Chapter 20, this volume) present, first, feminist research bent on working against health disparities and then, strategies for better locating feminist intersectional health research in dialogues around health science and public policy. Looking at recent scholarship that refines feminist critiques of health science research and policy and at developments in feminist health theory and practice, Weber and Castellow examine the contributions and influences of feminist research on health science practices and policies. Studies relating to recent health developments (e.g., the HPV vaccine and the Patient Protection and Affordable Care Act of 2010) help to show how feminist engagement with health-related policies and practices are able to draw attention to power hierarchies within social relationships.

Dialogues about feminist research within the social sciences have also failed to include social work, argue Stéphanie Wahab, Ben Anderson-Nathe, and Christina Gringeri (Chapter 21, this volume). Drawing attention to examples of feminist research within the realm of social work, Wahab et al. suggest that social work praxis may beneficially influence feminist research projects in the social sciences generally. Further, a social work engagement with feminist theory may help to disrupt the assumptions of knowledge that social work often makes.

By closely looking at writing practices within feminist research reports, Kathy Charmaz (Chapter 22, this volume) is able to answer questions about the construction of feminist research writings and about the strategies that feminist researchers employ in their written reports. Carefully reading feminist research reports is significant, Charmaz argues, because the writing strategies employed contain the researchers' views and values. Certain writing patterns, used consciously or not on the part of the writers, contain specific meanings and judgments, and so the process of writing itself becomes central to the conveying of research data. Charmaz reinforces the importance of written method and concludes by offering advice on the writing process.

Specifically using climate change research as an example, Kristen Intemann (Chapter 23, this volume) argues that research principles praised by feminist science scholarship can benefit scientific research. Intemann proposes that scientific communities should include diverse researchers (in terms of experiences, social positions, and values), allow for critical reflection on the chosen methodology and methods, assume the perspective of the marginalized, and work toward a multiplicity of conceptual models.

Part III. Feminist Issues and Insights in Practice and Pedagogy

Judith Roof's chapter, "Authority and Representation in Feminist Research," provides a historical context for looking at how feminist researchers have framed issues of power and authority and argues that feminists are "trading between the authority of science and the power of experience." In particular, she notes the tensions between "the impersonal practices of generalization and the more problematic questions of rhetoric and representation" (Roof, Chapter 25, this volume).

Alison Wylie (Chapter 26, this volume) is concerned with how scientific practices are carried out by feminists. Carefully noting the fact that the credibility of a scientific research project may be damaged or compromised by an explicit feminist approach, Wylie believes that a reconfiguration of standpoint theory may offer a way out of this problem. Wylie provides an overview of specific practices that will combat this challenge to credibility and affirms that feminist theory and scientific research can coexist to produce generative research projects.

Judith Preissle and Yuri Han's chapter, "Feminist Research Ethics," examines feminist challenges to traditional Western approaches to ethics. They conceptualize feminist ethics as an "ethics of care" and discuss the implications of a feminist ethical approach for the practice of social research. What are the specific ethical practices feminist researchers employ across the research process? Preissle and Han note that a feminist perspective on ethics is a double-edged endeavor, which will "likely generate as many issues as they may help either avoid or address. This is particularly evident in trading a detached, distant, and hierarchical stance for an intimate, close, and equitable position. Distance and intimacy create their own problems" (Preissle & Han, Chapter 28, this volume).

The relationship between feminism and transgender, transsexual, and queer studies is elucidated in Katherine Johnson's chapter (Chapter 29, this volume). Central debates within queer studies are set forth in order to identify theoretical points that have particular relevance to feminist researchers. Feminist research, Johnson argues, should adopt practices that take into account a variety of identity positions. Exploring definitions, terminology, and areas for coalitions to emerge across identity borders, for example, Johnson looks both at the dialogues between feminism and transgender, transsexual, and queer studies and at how the fields may work together to produce better research.

Deborah Piatelli and my chapter (Chapter 27, this volume) stresses the need for a holistic approach to the process of reflexivity that runs "from the formulation of the research problem, to the shifting positionalities of the researcher and participants, through interpretation and writing." We provide specific research examples and strategies for implementing "holistic reflexivity" in the research process.

Attention to difference is often found in feminist research. Diane Reay (Chapter 30, this volume) looks at how feminist research addresses difference and how difference affects research praxis. Reay provides examples of how differences are navigated and handled by drawing on research that accounts for differences such as social class, ethnicity, political commitment, sexuality, and age. This chapter also puts forth research practices that may be successful at incorporating feminist theory.

Jennifer Bickham Mendez and Diane Wolf (Chapter 31, this volume) question how feminist research can better account for globalization. Mendez and Wolf suggest that global considerations may allow for the reconfiguration of analytical categories and models and may also allow for productive change in research practice. Awareness of the global community may enable researchers to better understand certain forms of women's oppression in globalized power structures and, furthermore, provides the opportunity for feminist researchers to forge transnational research bonds. Feminist dialogue and research, Mendez and Wolf believe, will be expanded and enriched by a consideration of globalization.

An experiential account of feminist pedagogy is offered by Debra Kaufman and Rachel Lewis (Chapter 32, this volume), who analyze the ways in which their feminist perspectives have influenced their methods of teaching in the classroom. Kaufman and Lewis demonstrate how classroom learning may benefit from the use of feminist theory, as they view the classroom as a space in which knowledge across disciplines can be decentered and reworked. Approaching questions of knowledge production within the classroom illuminates the hierarchical structures that position knowledge. Kaufman and Lewis conclude with the possibilities for incorporating feminist perspectives in academia as well as the possible dangers of doing so.

With similar interests in the role of feminism in teaching, Daphne Patai (Chapter 33, this volume) asks what it means to apply the term "feminism" to research and pedagogical practices. She views feminist politics as possibly incongruous with teaching and research. Teaching, for Patai, requires a perspective different than that offered by feminism, which introduces a political project. Patai's chapter troubles the links between knowledge and politics.

The intersection of feminism and teaching again arises in Debjani Chakravarty, Judith A. Cook, and Mary Margaret Fonow's chapter (Chapter 34, this volume). In order to develop and distribute feminist methodology, it must be taught. Training in feminist research methodology should teach a feminist researcher to create and execute a research project while considering its multiple and varied effects (e.g., ethical, social, transnational, political). Feminist research, this chapter argues, has always held the workings of power structures as a central focus, but new to feminist research are trends of technological development and the expansion of feminist methodology into other realms.

Abigail Brooks and I provide a fuller context and discussion of these articles in the introductory chapter to Part III, "Challenges and Strategies in Feminist Knowledge Building, Pedagogy, and Praxis."

CONCLUSION

It is my hope that this *Handbook* provides you with a set of unique knowledge frameworks to enhance your understanding of the social world, especially the range of women's lived experiences. The *Handbook* contributors explore a range of feminist issues, themes, and questions including a commitment to the empowerment of women and other oppressed groups. Although the *Handbook* is by no means exhaustive, its authors take an in-depth look at a broad spectrum of some of the most important feminist perspectives on how a given methodology intersects with epistemology and method to produce a set of research practices. Our thesis is that any given feminist perspective does not preclude the use of specific methods but serves to guide how a given method is practiced. Whereas each perspective is distinct, they sometimes share elements with other perspectives.

The ground underneath the theory and practice of feminist research is ever evolving, and it is the shifting of these tectonic plates of knowledge that provides an opportunity for what Teresa de Lauretis (1988) suggests as "not merely an expansion or reconfiguration of boundaries, but a qualitative shift in political and historical consciousness" (pp. 138–139).

REFERENCES

Anzaldúa, Gloria. (1987). *Borderlands/La frontera: The new mestiza.* San Francisco: Spinsters/Aunt Lute.

Anzaldúa, Gloria. (1990). *Bridge, drawbridge, sandbar or island.* In Lisa Albrecht & Rose M. Brewer (Eds.), *Bridges of power: Women's multicultural alliances* (pp. 216–231). Philadelphia: New Society Publishers.

Barrett, Michèle, & Phillips, Anne. (1992). *Destabilizing theory: Contemporary feminist debates.* Stanford, CA: Stanford University Press.

Bhavnani, Kum-Kum. (1993). Tracing the contours: Feminist research and feminist objectivity. *Women's Studies International Forum, 16,* 95–104.

Bordo, Susan. (1990). Feminism, postmodernism, and gender-skepticism. In Linda Nicholson (Ed.), *Feminism/postmodernism* (pp. 133–156). London: Routledge.

Bowles, Gloria, & Duelli-Klein, Renate D. (Eds.). (1983). *Theories of women's studies.* London: Routledge & Kegan Paul.

Burt, Sandra, & Code, Lorraine. (Eds.). (1995). *Changing methods: Feminists transforming practice.* Peterborough, ON: Broadview Press.

Butler, Judith. (1993). *Bodies that matter: On the discursive limits of "sex."* New York: Routledge.

Chafetz, Janet Saltzman. (1999). Some thoughts by an unrepentant "positivist" who considers herself a feminist nonetheless. In Sharlene Hesse-Biber, Christine Gilmartin, & Robin Lydenberg (Eds.), *Feminist approaches to theory and methodology* (pp. 320–329). New York: Oxford University Press.

Cixous, Hélène, & Clément, Catherine. (1986). *The newly born woman.* Minneapolis: University of Minnesota Press.

Code, Lorraine. (1991). *What can she know? Feminist theory and the construction of knowledge.* Ithaca, NY: Cornell University Press.

Collins, Patricia Hill. (1990). *Black feminist thought: Knowledge, consciousness, and the politics of empowerment.* New York: Routledge.

Comte, Auguste. (2000). *The positive philosophy of Auguste Comte* (Vol. 1, Harriet Martineau, Trans.). Kitchener, ON: Batoche Books. (Original work published 1896)

de Beauvoir, Simone. (1952). *The second sex.* New York: Vintage Books.

de Lauretis, Teresa. (1988). Displacing hegemonic discourses: Reflections on feminist theory in the 1980s. *Inscriptions, 3*(4), 127–145.

DeVault, Marjorie L. (1999). *Liberating method: Feminism and social research.* Philadelphia: Temple University Press.

Dill, Bonnie Thornton. (1987). The dialectics of black womanhood. In Sandra Harding (Ed.), *Feminism and methodology* (pp. 97–108). Bloomington: Indiana University Press.

Durkheim, Émile. (1938). *The rules of sociological method.* Glencoe, IL: Free Press. (Original work published 1895)

Eichler, Margrit, & Lapointe, Jeanne. (1985). *On the treatment of the sexes in research.* Ottawa, ON: Social Sciences and Humanities Council.

Fonow, Mary Margaret, & Cook, Judith A. (Eds.). (1991). *Beyond methodology: Feminist scholarship as lived research.* Bloomington: Indiana University Press.

Friedan, Betty. (1963). *The feminine mystique.* New York: W. W. Norton.

Gluck, Sherna Berger, & Patai, Daphne. (Eds.). (1991). *Women's words: The feminist practice of oral history.* New York: Routledge.

Haraway, Donna. (1988). Situated knowledges: The science question in feminism and the privilege of partial perspective. *Feminist Studies, 14*(13), 575–599.

Harding, Sandra. (Ed.). (1987a). *Feminism and methodology.* Bloomington: Indiana University Press.

Harding, Sandra. (1987b). Introduction. In Sandra Harding (Ed.), *Feminism and methodology* (pp. 1–14). Bloomington: Indiana University Press.

Harding, Sandra. (1991). *Whose science, whose knowledge? Thinking from women's lives.* Ithaca: Cornell University Press.

Harding, Sandra. (1993). Rethinking standpoint epistemology: What is "strong objectivity"? In Linda Alcoff & Elizabeth Potter (Eds.), *Feminist epistemologies* (pp. 49–82). New York: Routledge.

Harding, Sandra. (Ed.). (2004). *The feminist stand-point theory reader: Intellectual and political controversies.* New York: Routledge.

Hartsock, Nancy. (1983). The feminist standpoint: Developing the ground for a specifically feminist historical materialism. In Sandra Harding & Merrill Hintikka (Eds.), *Discovering reality* (pp. 283–310). Dordrecht, The Netherlands: Kluwer Academic.

Hesse-Biber, Sharlene. (2002). Feminism and interdisciplinarity. In JoAnn DiGeorgio-Lutz (Ed.), *Women in higher education* (pp. 57–66). Westport, CT: Praeger.

Hesse-Biber, Sharlene, Gilmartin, Christina, & Lydenberg, Robin. (Eds.). (1999). *Feminist approaches to theory and methodology: An interdisciplinary reader.* New York: Oxford University Press.

Hesse-Biber, Sharlene Nagy, Leavy, Patricia, & Yaiser, Michelle L. (2004). Feminist approaches to research as a process: Reconceptualizing epistemology, methodology, and method. In Sharlene Nagy Hesse-Biber & Michelle L. Yaiser (Eds.), *Feminist perspectives on social research* (pp. 3–26). New York: Oxford University Press.

Hesse-Biber, Sharlene Nagy, & Leckenby, Denise. (2004). How feminists practice social research. In Sharlene Nagy Hesse-Biber & Michelle L. Yaiser (Eds.), *Feminist perspectives on social research* (pp. 209–226). New York: Oxford University Press.

Hirsch, Marianna, & Keller, Evelyn Fox. (1990). Practicing conflict in feminist theory. In Marianne Hirsch & Evelyn Fox Keller (Eds.), *Conflicts in feminism* (pp. 370–385). New York: Routledge.

Hochschild, Arlie Russell. (1975). The sociology of feeling and emotion: Selected possibilities. In Marcia Millman & Rosabeth Moss Kanter (Eds.), *Another voice: Feminist perspectives on social life and social science* (pp. 280–307). New York: Anchor Press/Doubleday.

Hochschild, Arlie Russell. (1983). *The managed heart: Commercialization of human feeling.* Berkeley: University of California Press.

hooks, bell. (1990). *Yearning: Race, gender, and cultural politics.* Boston: South End Press.

hooks, bell. (1994). *Teaching to transgress: Education as the practice of freedom.* New York: Routledge.

Irigaray, Luce. (1991). In M. Whitford (Ed.), *The Irigaray reader.* Cambridge, MA: Blackwell.

Jacobs, Harriet A. (1987). *Incidents in the life of a slave girl, written by herself.* Cambridge, MA: Harvard University Press. (Original work published 1861)

Jaggar, Alison. (1997). Love and knowledge: Emotion in feminist epistemology. In Diana Tietjens Meyers (Ed.), *Feminist social thought: A reader* (pp. 385–405). New York: Routledge.

Kandiyoti, Deniz. (1999). Islam and patriarchy: A comparative perspective. In Sharlene Hesse-Biber, Christina Gilmartin, & Robin Lydenberg (Eds.), *Feminist approaches to theory and methodology: An interdisciplinary reader* (pp. 236–256). New York: Oxford University Press.

Kelly-Gadol, Joan. (1987). The social relation of the sexes: Methodological implications of women's history. In Sandra Harding (Ed.), *Feminism and methodology* (pp. 15–28). Bloomington: Indiana University Press.

Kincheloe, Joe L., & McLaren, Peter. (2000). Rethinking critical theory and qualitative research. In Norman K. Denzin & Yvonna S. Lincoln (Eds.), *Handbook of qualitative research* (2nd ed., pp. 279–313). Thousand Oaks, CA: Sage.

Kuhn, Thomas. (1962). *The structure of scientific revolutions.* Chicago: University of Chicago Press.

Lamphere, Louise, Ragone, Helena, & Zavella, Patricia. (Eds.). (1997). *Situated lives: Gender and culture in everyday life.* New York: Routledge.

Lather, Patty. (1991). *Getting smart: Feminist research and pedagogy within/in the postmodern.* New York: Routledge.

Lorde, Audre. (1996). The master's tools will never dismantle the master's house. In Audre Lorde (Ed.), *The Audre Lorde compendium: Essays, speeches and journals* (pp. 158–171). London: Harper Collins.

Martin, Emily. (1987). *The woman in the body: A cultural analysis of reproduction.* Boston: Beacon Press.

Maynard, Mary, & Purvis, June. (Eds.). (1994). *Researching women's lives from a feminist perspective.* London: Taylor & Francis.

McIntosh, Patricia. (1995). White privilege and male privilege: A personal account of coming to see correspondences through work in women's studies. In Margaret Andersen & Patricia Hill Collins (Eds.), *Race, class, and gender: An anthology* (pp. 76–86). Belmont, CA: Wadsworth.

Millman, Marcia, & Kanter, Rosabeth Moss. (Eds.). (1975). *Another voice: Feminist perspectives on social life and social science.* New York: Anchor Press/Doubleday.

Mohanty, Chandra. (1988). Under Western eyes: Feminist scholarship and colonial discourses. *Feminist Review, 30,* 61–88.

Mohanty, Chandra. (1999). Women workers and capitalist scripts: Ideologies of domination, common interests, and the politics of solidarity. In Sharlene Hesse-Biber, Christine Gilmartin, & Robin Lydenberg (Eds.), *Feminist approaches to theory and methodology* (pp. 362–388). New York: Oxford University Press.

Naples, Nancy A. (2003). *Feminism and method: Ethnography, discourse analysis, and activist research.* New York: Routledge.

Neuman, W. Lawrence. (2000). *Social research methods.* Boston: Allyn & Bacon.

Nielson, Joyce McCarl. (Ed.). (1990). *Feminist research methods: Exemplary readings in the social sciences.* Boulder, CO: Westview Press.

Oakley, Ann. (1981). Interviewing women: A contradiction in terms. In H. Roberts (Ed.), *Doing feminist research* (pp. 30–61). London: Routledge & Kegan Paul.

Reinharz, Shulamit. (1992). *Feminist methods in social research.* New York: Oxford University Press.

Roberts, Helen. (Ed.). (1981). *Doing feminist research.* London: Routeledge & Kegan Paul.

Scott, Joan. (1999). The evidence of experience. In Christine Gilmartin & Robin Lydenberg (Eds.), *Feminist approaches to theory and methodology* (pp. 79–99). New York: Oxford University Press.

Sherif, Carolyn Wood. (1987). Bias in psychology. In Sandra Harding (Ed.), *Feminism and methodology* (pp. 37–56). Bloomington: Indiana University Press.

Smith, Dorothy E. (1978). A peculiar eclipsing: Women's exclusion from man's culture. *Women's Studies International Quarterly, 1*(4), 281–296.

Smith, Dorothy E. (1987). *The everyday world as problematic: A feminist sociology.* Boston: Northeastern University Press.

Smith, Dorothy E. (1990). *The conceptual practices of power: A feminist sociology of knowledge.* Boston: Northeastern University Press.

Smith, Linda Tuhiwai. (1999). *Decolonizing methodologies: Research and indigenous peoples.* London: Zed Books.

Smith, Linda Tuhiwai. (2005). On tricky ground: Researching the native in the age of uncertainty. In Norman K. Denzin & Yvonna S. Lincoln (Eds.), *The SAGE handbook of qualitative research* (3rd ed., pp. 85–107). Thousand Oaks, CA: Sage.

Spalter-Roth, Roberta, & Hartmann, Heidi. (1996). Small happiness: The feminist struggle to integrate social research with social activism. In Heidi Gottfried (Ed.), *Feminism and social change: Bridging theory and practice* (pp. 206–224). Urbana: University of Illinois Press.

Spender, Dale. (Ed.). (1981). *Men's studies modified: The impact of feminism on the academic disciplines.* Oxford, UK: Pergamon Press.

Spivak, Gayatri Chakravorty. (1990). *The postcolonial critic: Interviews, strategies, dialogue.* New York: Routledge.

Spivak, Gayatri Chakravoty. (1994). Can the subaltern speak? In Patrick Williams & Laura Chrismen (Eds.), *Colonial discourse and postcolonial theory: A reader* (pp. 66–111). New York: Columbia University Press.

Sprague, Joey, & Zimmerman, Mark. (1993). Overcoming dualisms: A feminist agenda for sociological methodology. In Paula England (Ed.), *Theory on gender/feminism on theory* (pp. 255–280). New York: Aldine DeGruyter.

St. Pierre, Elizabeth, & Pillow, Wanda S. (Eds.). (2000). *Working the ruins: Feminist poststructural theory and methods in education.* New York: Routledge.

Stanley, Liz. (Ed). (1990). *Feminist praxis: Research, theory, and epistemology in feminist sociology.* London: Routledge.

Stanley, Liz, & Wise, Sue. (1983). *Breaking out: Feminist consciousness and feminist research.* London: Routledge & Kegan Paul.

Trinh, T. Minh-ha. (1991). *Framer framed.* New York: Routledge.

Tuana, Nancy. (Ed.). (1989a). *Feminism & science.* Bloomington: Indiana University Press.

Tuana, Nancy. (1989b). The weaker seed: The sexist bias of reproductive theory. In Nancy Tuana (Ed.), *Feminism & Science* (pp. 147–171). Bloomington: Indiana University Press.

Wolf, Diane L. (Ed.). (1996). *Feminist dilemmas in fieldwork.* Boulder, CO: Westview Press.

Woolf, Virginia. (1929). *A room of one's own.* New York: Harcourt Brace Jovanovich.

PART I

FEMINIST PERSPECTIVES ON KNOWLEDGE BUILDING

2

FEMINIST EMPIRICISM

Catherine E. Hundleby

Feminist empiricism draws in various ways on the philosophical tradition of empiricism, which can be defined as epistemology that gives primary importance to knowledge based on experience. Feminist demands for attention to women's experiences suggest that empiricism can be a promising resource for developing a feminist account of knowledge. Yet feminists also value empiricism's purchase on science and the empiricist view that knowers' abilities depend on their experiences and their experiential histories, including socialization and psychological development.

This chapter explores the attractions of empiricism for feminists. Feminist empiricist analysis ranges from broad considerations about popular understandings to technical analysis of narrowly defined scientific fields. Whatever the scope, feminist reworkings of empiricism have two central themes. The first theme is the interplay among values in knowledge, especially connecting traditionally recognized empirical values, such as evidence and objectivity, with moral and political values. The interplay of these values undermines the traditional association of empirical knowledge with individual knowers, and the separation of individual knowledge from the politics of communities, by suggesting that the knower is not an isolated person. In this way, contesting the nature or locus of the knower and

developing new accounts of *agency* in knowledge emerges as the second theme in feminist empiricism.

Most feminist empiricists employ the methodology for developing epistemology known as naturalized or naturalist epistemology. Naturalism is controversial, but it welcomes disputation, takes up new resources for epistemology on an ongoing basis, and encourages multiple approaches to the evaluation of knowledge. This pluralism undercuts naturalism's and empiricism's conservative tendencies and imbues current formulations of empiricism with radical potential.

Feminist Attraction to Empiricism

Empiricism traces in the philosophy of the global North as far back as Aristotle,[1] but it is classically associated with the 18th-century British philosophers, John Locke, George Berkeley, and David Hume. Most recently the noteworthy empiricists include the logical empiricists as well as Willard Van Orman Quine and his naturalist followers. All empiricists emphasize the role of sensory experience in knowledge—evidence, data, and facts—and downplay the role of innate ideas and inborn mental capacities, which rationalists have historically championed. Science provides especially good examples of empirical knowledge, and most feminist empiricists focus on the types of knowledge produced by science. Although feminists substantially revise empiricism, the traditional association remains attractive because of its rhetorical power to engage practicing scientists and academic philosophers. The naturalist form of empiricism also insists on attention to the social and physical embodiment of knowledge that concerns feminists.

Empiricism's concern with identifying and making the most of the strengths of science provides feminists with a useful point of departure for theorizing about knowledge. Many of the early 20th-century logical empiricists aimed to develop a science that would serve social purposes, including sociopolitical emancipation of various sorts; and so the goal of an emancipatory science is part of the empiricist heritage (Okruhlik, 2003). Attention to the strengths of science supports the development of feminist "successor science projects" (Harding, 1986). Feminist experiences as scientists and feminist analyses of scientific problems orient most feminist empiricist analysis. Yet some feminist empiricists consider knowledge in a wider domain that includes everyday understanding and that draws on diverse sources of experience (Code, 2006a). The experiences from which we gain knowledge do not all arise from scientific methodology and may even include reading fiction (Code, 2006b). This broad view of experience is congruent with Quine's expansive notion of science that includes the experiential knowledge of people with no special training (Haack, 1993; Nelson, 1990).

Representing progressive concerns and liberatory values in empiricist terms is rhetorically powerful, providing persuasive force and thus strategic advantage that eludes more explicitly progressive or revolutionary theories. Scientists and Anglo-American philosophers of science tend to conceive of science in empiricist terms, and the public understanding of science follows suit. In both these rarefied and commonplace contexts, using the terminology of "facts" (Code, 2006a), "evidence" (Nelson, 1993), and "objectivity" (Longino, 1990) provides a valuable discursive authority.

Because of empiricism's historical centrality to the philosophy of science in the global North,

feminist empiricism is analogous to liberal feminism. Both revise traditionally accepted approaches to the problems at hand: empiricist approaches to scientific knowledge and liberal approaches to democratic politics, respectively.[2] The political mainstream and the culture of science give less currency to more contested socialist, post-structuralist, and post-colonial theoretical orientations (Harding, 1989). Yet traditional rhetoric can convey radical ideas, and, when it does, it can be far more powerful than the more obviously revolutionary approaches. Therefore, a radical future can emerge from feminist empiricism just as Zillah Eisenstein argued it does from liberal feminism (Harding, 1986; Tuana, 1992).

The rhetorical advantage can be strategically essential because it allows feminists to transform the power of science.

> The point of feminist science criticism must, in the end, be to change science, and changing science requires changing the practices of scientists. Hence, scientists must be brought into the dialogue. Since scientists are empiricists, that dialogue will have to make room, at least in the beginning, for empiricists and for, at least as a topic of discussion, empiricism. (Nelson, 1990, pp. 6–7)

Appealing to the traditional empirical valuation of experience and logic provides a strategic advantage for feminism. Yet, feminists must rework empiricism and our understanding of what constitutes scientific standards in order to account for the role of sociopolitical values, as must the not-specifically feminist promoters of the empiricist tradition.

Many feminist epistemologists gain inspiration from a late 20th-century development of empiricism known as "naturalized" or "naturalist" epistemology. Naturalists' attention to the situation of human physical and cultural embodiment abandons abstract ideals of knowledge that assume an omniscient god's-eye view of values or ideals, such as knowledge and justice, and provides a concrete account of epistemic agency—*who* knows. The same approaches that naturalists reject on empiricist grounds feminists reject for being implicitly masculine: disassociating ideal understanding from the material realities of human existence excludes or at best further marginalizes typical or traditional women's ways of engaging the world in the global North and conflicts with the dominant ideals of femininity. Women's experience and knowledge claims gain credibility from their grounding in material and empirical resources for understanding. Naturalism suggests that new ways to address and redress the traditional Western discounting of these forms of understanding can be found in scientific and historical accounts of knowledge (Hundleby, 2002).

Thus, feminist epistemologists, whether or not they consider themselves naturalists or even empiricists, probably demonstrate most thoroughly the use of empirical data to scrutinize science, which is the method of philosophical epistemology that naturalists recommend. Feminist naturalists especially—like any naturalists—appropriate science to provide accounts of knowledge; however, as Phyllis Rooney (2003) argues, feminist naturalism extends to reflexive examinations of the underlying motivations and worldviews of the social and individual cognitive sciences. Background assumptions—about the nature of gender as a dimension for investigating knowledge, for instance—are not merely noted but subject to challenge (Rooney, 2003, p. 226).

THE SPECTRUM OF FEMINIST EMPIRICIST ANALYSIS

Scientific knowledge is popularly considered to be the best of human empirical inquiry, the most systematic and responsible way to make sense of experience. Yet feminist responsibility requires attention to how sexism, racism, and other forms of oppression manifest in scientific understanding, in the very context of scientific theories and claims. Sexism appears, for instance, in cellular biology, as part of accounts of fertilization familiar to knowers with no more science knowledge than they received in grade-school sex education. A more technical area shows that sexism can deeply undermine a whole field of study: the evolutionary study of the female orgasm evinces androcentrism, in Elisabeth Lloyd's analysis (2005). Resisting sexism that can be identified as part of accepted standards of inquiry does not require abandoning all accepted methods. However, it does require questioning how these methods operate in specified contexts, from broadly cultural to narrowly academic domains.

In both academic microbiology and sex education for children and adolescents, the portrayed relationship between egg and sperm in the process of fertilization reflects androcentrism and other sexist values and is often treated as a fairy-tale romantic courtship. Images of the egg or ovum range from whoring to dutiful wifehood (The Biology and Gender Study Group, 1988) and even to hunted prey (Martin, 1991). At the same time, the sperm appears as a victorious hero reminiscent of characters in the *Odyssey* or the *Aeneid* (The Biology and Gender Study Group, 1988). Even using the term "fertilization" to name the process that can be more accurately described as "cellular fusion" assumes an asymmetry in activity (Longino, 1997). These models attribute to the male sperm cell an active role that invokes social norms of masculinity and attribute to the female ovum a passive role. Both genderings receive reinforcement from explicitly gendered imagery and go far beyond the very limited "sex" we can attribute to a single cell.[3]

The feminist empiricist response to sexism in the content of science is to scrutinize the interplay among metaphors, values, and evidence: "think through a particular field and try to understand just what its unstated and fundamental assumptions are and how they influence the course of inquiry" (Longino, 1987, p. 62). It is not to demand that the egg's activity be conceived in aggressive terms, which would only play into stereotypes of femme fatales and devouring mothers. Even equalitarian metaphors may be problematic insofar as they encourage us to anthropomorphize cells, argues Emily Martin (1991):

Although the scientific convention is to call such metaphors "dead," they are not so much dead as sleeping, hidden within the scientific content of texts—and all the more powerful for it. Waking up such metaphors, by becoming aware of when we are projecting cultural imagery onto what we study, will improve our ability to investigate and understand nature. Waking up such metaphors, by becoming aware of their implications, will rob them of their power to naturalize our social conventions about gender. (p. 501)

For instance, we must beware how anthropomorphizing gametes attributes intentionality—purposes and feelings—to the egg and sperm. Intervening in defense of such nominal "persons" on the basis of metaphorical understanding might include technological and legal interventions against the will or interest of the very *real* people who produce these cells (Martin, 1991). A range of social and moral views, and actions that science informs, can become loaded with undesirable social assumptions and projected ideals.

By contrast with the breadth and variability in sexist presentations of fertilization, Lloyd (2005) identifies two specific assumptions in the evolutionary science of the female orgasm: androcentrism and adaptationism. Androcentrism is being male centered or, more specifically in the case of sexuality, assuming that females are like males (pp. 1–2), and adaptationism is "commitment to finding adaptive explanations of a trait" (p. 14). The assumption that males are standard or ideal is evident in every available evolutionary account of the female orgasm, in all of the 21 accounts that Lloyd studies, and the assumption that all traits are adaptations is present in 20 of these. Each of the 21 theories fails to apply methodological, logical, and evidential standards with which their researchers are perfectly familiar and which they otherwise accept (pp. 17–18, 221–222). Adhering to these standards would prevent the ubiquitous mismatching of the hypotheses with the available evidence, a disconnect that reflects androcentrism and adaptationism (p. 20). In studies of the female orgasm, *bad* science has been science as usual.

Whereas the feminist empiricist analysis of fertilization directly addresses social complexity and scrutinizes political implications, Lloyd's analysis is much more constrained, restricted to analyzing the methodological inadequacies of this particular field. She "leaves undeveloped some of the most interesting issues, including the social significance of the science of orgasm, the adequacy and limitation of sexology data in the description of orgasm, and the role of feminist approaches to science beyond merely controlling for sexist bias" (Meynell, 2007, p. 219). The contrast illustrates Sandra Harding's distinction between "sophisticated" and "spontaneous"

or "naïve" feminist empiricism. Whereas Lloyd's study exemplifies spontaneous feminist empiricism by focusing narrowly on standards of testing, most feminist empiricists—more "sophisticatedly"—attend to the *dynamics* between theory generation and theory testing, and so to the generation of testing standards and their cultural impact.[4]

Deferring to existing scientific practices to weed out sexism is a strategy defended by Sharyn Clough (2003). She argues that feminists should attend to the local empirical standards of specific sciences and debates and avoid vain attempts to specify the general roles that values have in science. To ask general questions about epistemological justification and to seek a universal epistemology opens the door to questions that lead to global skepticism or universal doubt. We will be unable to claim knowledge of any kind if we demand one theory of knowledge to cover all types of understanding should we fail to develop one that succeeds.

Clough's rejection of broad conceptions of knowledge is fairly unique, but many feminist empiricists agree with her on the value of localized strategies. Helen Longino (1987), in her classic article "Can There Be a Feminist science?" advises inquirers to refrain from attempting to anticipate the ultimate shape of feminist science:

> Accountability [to feminist concerns] does not demand a radical break with the science one has learned and practiced. The development of a "new" science involves a more dialectical evolution and more continuity with established science than the familiar language of scientific revolutions implies. (Longino, 1987, p. 61)

What remains is to "do science as a feminist": employ the methods and methodologies that help to address the feminist concerns relevant to that particular area of inquiry. Code (2008) also advises modest goals:

> Reconsider the value of the small: of small projects that speak specifically from a careful understanding to and about the precise circumstances of a particular species, community, group, or society, and are understood well enough to make such speaking responsibly knowledgeable. (p. 199)

Such localized engagement of feminist concerns raises profound challenges to the way that epistemology and empiricism have operated in the past.

THEMES IN FEMINIST EMPIRICISM

Feminist revisions of empiricism focus on two related themes: epistemic values and epistemic agency. First, sociopolitical values have cognitive or epistemic implications and help to warrant beliefs and theories, argue feminist empiricists. Defying the traditional distinction between epistemic and political values raises questions for feminist empiricists about the significance of communities for knowledge. For some feminist empiricists, not the individual person but instead the community is the locus of knowledge. For all, the agent or the knowing subject is no longer the isolated abstract individual that was identified in earlier epistemologies of the global North, a challenge that provides the second theme in feminist empiricism.

What Do We Want? Epistemic and Political Values

Feminist empiricist analysis considers the interplay among various forms of values or theoretical virtues: empirical values, such as predictive accuracy or testability; other epistemic values, such as simplicity; and non-epistemic values, from subjective or personal values to moral or ethical values and more broadly political or cultural values. In this section, I will explain the standardly recognized empirical and epistemic values and the arguments by feminist empiricists that they are not sufficient to eliminate the political content of scientific theory. Considering the interplay of non-epistemic with epistemic values not only explains observations of sexism in science but also suggests various roles that feminist values might take in science. There is little agreement regarding how scientists and knowers more generally should integrate feminist values as part of their methods of inquiry. Yet the feminist critiques of science have provided ample evidence that feminist practice and values improve scientific knowledge.

The most generally accepted of the cognitive or epistemological values has been *truth*, which

carries realist metaphysical assumptions of an independent exterior world or at least a representationalist view of mind. To avoid such metaphysical implications, most empiricist philosophers of science follow Quine and Thomas Kuhn (1977), who speak instead of truth about *empirical adequacy*, which includes predictive accuracy and retrodictive accuracy (explaining past observations). Likewise, *facticity*, *rationality*, *evidence*, and *objectivity* are values that provide standards for scientific testing and evaluation. The operation of these general epistemological values is the central concern for feminist empiricists, a project that complements feminist standpoint theorists' concern with heuristics and the generation of ideas.[5]

Many feminist and not specifically feminist empiricists (explicitly Longino and Miriam Solomon) hope to steer a middle course between traditional empiricism and the social constructivism of the Strong Programme in the sociology of science that is sometimes read into early Kuhn (1962). The logical empiricists recognized that political matters and social and subjective inspiration affect how theories are generated. Yet they argued that processes of testing or of rational theory choice using distinctly epistemic values eliminate those influences and distinguish views with purely epistemological authority.

Contemporary empiricists, whether or not they identify as feminist, maintain that general epistemic values such as evidence or rationality are manifested or articulated in scientific practice in the form of the following more specific qualities of theories or beliefs: ontological simplicity (Ockham's razor), modesty, internal coherence, external consistency (including theoretical conservatism), predictability, explanatory power (also described as unifying power, generality, or breadth of scope), testability (also described as refutability or predictive accuracy), and theoretical fruitfulness (or fertility). Thus, following Quine and Thomas Kuhn, values receive general acceptance from (mainstream) empiricist philosophy of science.

Whichever of the cognitive values make up the basis for scientific evaluation, the list is never exhaustive for contemporary empiricists, nor can the individual values be applied in a straightforward algorithmic manner. Rarely do we find consensus among theorists about which values are important or how to apply them, or even how to weigh them against each other. Theoretical fertility or productivity, for instance, can be interpreted in different ways by different investigators and in the context of different research programs—we may ask "fruitful for what?" Also, fruitfulness may be weighted in various ways relative to the other cognitive values (Rooney, 1993), as both Kuhn and Quine recognize. For instance, the detailed focus necessary for an accurate account clearly conflicts with the applicability of that account to a range of phenomena in a range of situations that constitutes breadth of scope (Longino, 1997).

Feminists differ from other contemporary empiricists in arguing that how we identify, interpret, and weigh cognitive values also reflects political commitments (whether we realize this or not). "Responsibility and accountability requirements join verifiability high on the epistemic agenda as epistemic and moral-political issues coalesce and as statements of fact take on a less self-evidently factual demeanour" (Code, 2006a, p. 128). Scientific method and rational theory choice—articulated in terms of predictive success, observation independence, and explanatory power, by Richmond Campbell (1997, pp. 25–27)—are not sufficient to eliminate sociopolitical influences.

> [T]here are standards of rational acceptability that are independent of particular interests and values but . . . satisfaction of these standards by a theory or hypothesis does not guarantee that the theory or hypothesis in question is value- or interest-free. (Longino, 1990, p. 12)

Consider how gender roles influence cellular biology and androcentrism influences evolutionary biology, as I described previously, and how racism has informed the study of intelligence (Gould, 1996). Such non-epistemological values from the context of theory generation remain present in those theories that succeed.

Testing only shows a claim to be epistemically superior among the available contending theories, so the process can *entrench* sociopolitical values in scientific practice, as Kathleen Okruhlik argues:

> If [the available] theories have been generated by males operating in a deeply sexist culture, then it is likely that they will all be contaminated by sexism.

Non-sexist rivals will never even be generated. Hence the theory which is selected by the canons of scientific appraisal will simply be the best of the sexist rivals; and the very *content* of science will be sexist, no matter how rigorously we apply objective standards of assessment in the context of justification. In fact, the best of the sexist theories will emerge more and more highly *confirmed* after successive tests. (Okruhlik, 1994, pp. 34–35)

Social ideology and sociopolitical values play as substantial a role as "stereotypically scientific issues of evidence and logic" in scientific knowledge (Longino, 1990, p. 3). Both science in general or "as usual" and particular cases of incompetent or "bad" science involve more than purely cognitive or logical concerns.

A more complicated example of the intermingling of political with epistemic values is Longino's feminist defense of a social-cognitive model over the linear-hormonal, or "biological determinist," model for gendered differences in human physical and cognitive behavior. No purely cognitive or epistemic decision between the two models seems available according to Longino's original (1990) analysis, but the values of theoretical unification and simplicity that support the linear-hormonal model cannot be viewed only in cognitive terms. Part of the constitutive force of "simplicity" in this model is due to the operation of gender dimorphism as part of the motivation for the very understanding of biological determinism itself, although gender dimorphism is biologically contested (Rooney, 1993, p. 18). Gender dimorphism, which is assuming that bodies take two distinctly gendered forms, offers the valued "simplicity" in this case because of its resonance with existing social hierarchies; so it seemed rationally preferable because it was socially preferred.

Likewise feminist interests support certain cognitive values over others, and empiricism can support the role of feminist politics in good scientific practice (Campbell, 1998). Yet, feminist empiricists do not advocate any specific methodologies, and some refuse to search for definitive general criteria for evaluating the content of knowledge, even specifically scientific knowledge. Instead of viewing science as a product, Longino urges that we treat it as a practice, that feminist science is not an abstract ideal but a matter of "doing science as a feminist" (Longino, 1990, p. 188). "We can . . . fashion and favor research programs that are consistent with the values and commitments we express in the rest of our lives" (Longino, 1990, p. 191).

The feminist critiques of science have revealed certain patterns in valuation, a constellation of theoretical values that Longino has started to catalog (1997). Like the traditional empirical values, the feminist set begins with empirical adequacy or accuracy. This accepted epistemic value supports a specifically feminist value: "to reveal both gender in the phenomena and gender bias in the accounting of them" (Longino, 1997, p. 45). The value of *revealing gender* is served by *novelty*, *ontological heterogeneity*, and *mutuality of interaction* in the content of theories and research programs. These values are neither uniquely nor intrinsically feminist, which holds also for values of concern to feminists that are not (or are only distantly) connected to empirical adequacy: *applying science to meet current human needs*, such as those traditionally ministered by women, and *diffusing scientific power* by encouraging general access and participation in science (Longino, 1997, pp. 50–51). The feminist values may complement the more standard set or provide alternatives. For instance, ontological heterogeneity conflicts with an ontological interpretation of (standardly valued) simplicity.

The necessity for sociopolitical values in science implies that nastier—sexist, racist, and so forth—sociopolitical values could be justified and are part of not just bad science but science as usual. Criticizing the role of such values makes it difficult to support a positive role for feminist values in knowledge, a problem described by Louise Antony as the "bias paradox."[6] Yet some political values, such as feminism, can be revealed to better support empirical adequacy than others. "Doing science as a feminist" has produced any number of novel and empirically successful theories. Early feminist critiques of science led, for instance, to recognizing the activity of the ovum and to developing the "woman-the-gatherer" hypothesis in anthropology that has proved more successful than the previous "man-the-hunter" alternative (Longino & Doell, 1983). This pattern provides *evidence* of the empirical adequacy of at least some feminist values in one field at a particular point in its development.

The success of multiple feminist critiques of science indicates that feminism has a general empirical adequacy, at least at this point in the progress of science. The empirical advantage is due, at least in part, to feminist attention to the role of values, especially political values, in science; these are not generally recognized components of epistemology or methodology. "Political critique of accepted epistemic values helps reveal existing incoherences in our cognitive practices and suggests remedial options" (Hundleby, 2002, p. 263). A broader base for criticism becomes available, as does a broader horizon for action, because we consider science to be part of the larger community.

A certain number of feminist empiricists, notably Lynn Hankinson Nelson, stress that the operation of science subjects political values to ordinary standards of criticism by which people can dismiss them. Naturalists such as Nelson use scientific understandings of human knowers to account for knowledge, but the standards draw from Quine's broad notion of science, which incorporates the richness of commonsense reasoning that can be used as a basis for criticism (Nelson, 1990). Perhaps the most general value that requires attention from naturalists is the value of human survival (Code, 1996) because that value underpins human nature according to evolutionary biology. The moral and sociopolitical values dismissed by Quine for being the result of natural selection are vindicated by those origins, according to Nelson. She argues that their evolutionary success provides scientific reason to consider the values cognitively *good*: they meet the common practical needs of societies and of humanity (Nelson, 1990, p. 133). We may use these same standards to evaluate which moral and sociopolitical values have empirical value.

Because it reconfigures the role of bias in science, there is no need to distinguish between good and bad bias in Miriam Solomon's "social empiricism" (2001). She replaces the traditional epistemological distinction between epistemic or rational ("cold") and non-epistemic or biasing ("hot") factors in how scientists decide among theories with an account of *empirical* and *non-empirical* decision *vectors*. Empirical decision vectors include salience of data, availability of data, egocentric bias toward one's own data (non-cognitive—but driven by data!), and preference for a theory that generates novel predictions. Non-empirical decision vectors include ideology, pride, conservativeness, radicalism, elegance, competitiveness, and peer pressure; the list goes on and so includes much more than the sociopolitical values addressed by other feminist empiricists. Solomon argues that all sorts of personal and social values can be part of the motivation behind states of science that are justified. It is the appropriate *social distribution* of decision vectors that makes a scientific decision rational, not whether any particular vectors are present. The only relevant distinction among values is whether they are empirical.

Solomon bucks intuition and argues that dissent—and not consensus—is the scientific norm, in the sense of being the more common and general state of science. *Rational* dissent occurs under the following circumstances:

1. All theories under consideration have some empirical success (explain some observations).

2. All empirical vectors are distributed proportionately to the empirical success of each theory (productive scientific methods fall under theories proportional to their empirical success).

3. The nonempirical vectors are equally distributed.

Dissent occurs more frequently than consensus partly because only a very specific configuration of the decision vectors can justify consensus.[7] Forming consensus is only appropriate when all the empirical success supports one theory, making it a *limiting case* of dissent.

Thus Solomon, like Nelson, maintains that we can assess the scientific significance of moral and sociopolitical values. Such an assessment will only proceed in the long term, however.

> Epistemic practices at their best proceed according to (interim) standards derived from collaborative efforts to produce the best possible investigations, descriptions, and understandings, where "best" includes an ongoing self-reflexive and negotiative commitment to determining and trying out norms and standards, and evaluating their effectiveness and failures. (Code, 2008, p. 194)

While we wait for more evidence to come in, we have some reason to favor feminist values.

"Doing science as a feminist" is thus an open-ended practice.

Who Knows? Epistemic Agency

Traditional empiricists viewed the agent of knowledge as an individual person who has the same sorts of rational capabilities as other persons, a laudably equalitarian account but one that masks real differences among knowers. Individual people have different resources for understanding in accordance with their social location, their socialization, and their developmental history. Addressing these variables requires a more social account of the epistemic agent, and feminist empiricists disagree about what that account should be; they even consider that different models of epistemic agency provide the desired purchase on different projects of inquiry (Code, 2006a).

Feminists have transformed the empiricist concept of the knowing subject through various forms of attention to how individuals depend on communities for knowledge. I will present their accounts beginning with the most individualistic and proceeding through degrees of sociality toward the most communal account, and then to one that disrupts feminist dependence on the notion of community. To start, the traditional view of individuals as agents of knowledge as revised by Heidi Grasswick (2004) becomes *individuals-in-communities*. More radically, granting central roles to the community in which individuals are only secondary participants and not direct agents, Longino and Nelson argue that the practices of people coordinated in their communal relationships allow individual experiences to become significant. Communal processes qualify individual beliefs as *objective* according to Longino (1990), and coherence with communal standards qualifies individual observations as *evidence* according to Nelson (1990). In Solomon's "social empiricism" (2001), individuals fall completely out of the picture of scientific knowledge, because scientific *rationality* only occurs in relationships among competing theories, and so only at the level of communities. The strength and role of communities in knowledge remains highly contested, leading Lorraine Code (1996, 2006a) instead to adopt a more flexible concept of *society* to account for the social nature of knowledge.

Grasswick (2004) rejects the traditional view of the atomistic, self-sufficient individual but argues that recognizing the (relational, dependent) individual as the agent of knowledge remains necessary to make sense of the possibility of dissent and of how epistemic standards become challenged (p. 97). A dynamic model of epistemic agency becomes possible when we identify agents as individuals-in-communities.

Although Grasswick's location of epistemic agency in individual persons is traditional, her notion of the individual as socially dependent is transformative. Gone are assumptions that the knower has a given set of capacities for reasoning because, with Code (1991), Grasswick insists that cognitive capacities are shaped by psychological development and socialization. "Individual knowers become epistemically differentiated along the lines of their communal histories and memberships" (Grasswick, 2004, p. 102). With Code again, Grasswick emphasizes the need for trust between people and our dependence on systems of authority. Yet Grasswick's focus on communities goes beyond Code's concern with interdependence by giving communities a critical role in the development and support of individual understanding.

Grasswick (2004) insists that communities provide "standards of evidence and bodies of evidence" (p. 96) and that they prioritize some epistemic values over others (p. 104), as Longino (1990, 2004) and Nelson (1990) have also argued. However, Grasswick addresses how individuals are each involved in multiple communities that are conflicting, overlapping, and vague, a complication that Longino and Nelson barely acknowledge. They set aside the complexities of communities to focus on how a community can operate to provide objectivity and evidence for beliefs.

Longino (1990) argues that critical discursive communities grant objectivity to the beliefs of individuals by constraining individual values. "Individual values are held in check not by a methodology but by social values" (p. 102). Scientific practice is independent of individual aims, except that individuals may work toward building the appropriate communities, which are those that engage a maximal number of different points of view. Longino's social standard for assessing the objectivity of scientific discourse involves four criteria for critical interpersonal engagement. An objective community has the following: (1) avenues for the expression and diffusion of criticism; (2) uptake of, and response to, criticism; (3) public standards by reference to which theories and so forth are assessed; and, (4) equality of intellectual authority (Longino, 1990, 1993). Communities that meet these criteria, to the *extent* that they meet the criteria, produce objective views that individuals may hold.

As inquirers, we choose, at least to a certain extent, the cultures in which we participate, so, as feminists, we can choose to whom we are accountable, which community will guide our beliefs; we can even choose combinations of communities. "The feminist scientist is responsive to the ideals of a political community as well as to some subset of the standards endorsed in her or his scientific community" (Longino, 1990, p. 192). Longino's advice to choose a feminist community does not entail adopting any particular methodology. Nevertheless "doing science as a feminist" requires interpreting empirical adequacy in terms of the concerns of one's chosen community, as described in the previous section on epistemic values.

Similarly, for Nelson, individuals acquire their scientific values from communities, but, for her, the community plays a more comprehensive role. The communal quality of the standards necessary for a person to be said to know any particular thing entails that some community to which that person belongs must be the first and foremost agent of knowledge. Individual people do not have knowledge or evidence at all except insofar as each participates in knowing communities. Background beliefs and standards—for example, regarding the techniques for collecting evidence and how to make inferences from data—that we share with other people provide support in varying degrees for our theories.

Nelson's communal view of knowledge follows from her argument that sociopolitical criteria are among our tools for justifying knowledge claims, again as outlined in the previous section. The importance of sociopolitical values suggests that community is the primary epistemic agent, which also is borne out by some commonsense observations. If any one member of a community knows something, then some other member could also know it—in this limited sense we may be interchangeable. "Acceptable answers to the question 'Who knows?' include 'Everyone,' 'All of *us*,' 'Lots of people,' 'Many of us,' but only very problematically 'Only me'" (Nelson, 1990, p. 255). Yet, "we know" doesn't mean "I and you and . . . you," the "we" formed from people that each of us knows. Especially in "big science," which brings together people with vastly different skills who complete separate portions of calculation and experimentation, no one participant understands it all. So it seems that "we" must know before any "I" can begin to understand.

Methodologically, for Solomon, as individuals we cannot expect nor should we desire to be free from bias, even to a degree, though we should aim to pursue theories that have empirical success. We can address the role of nonempirical decision vectors *only* in social terms. For individuals to recognize, assess, and redistribute the nonempirical vectors in order to justify the state of science requires a range of techniques.

> [T]he identification of decision vectors and improvement of their distribution . . . typically require expertise, and, often, multidisciplinary knowledge and skills. The critical training required to identify presuppositions about gender, for example, is quite different from the psychological training and methods required to detect cognitive bias. And the statistical techniques needed to assess the role of birth order are quite different from scientific and philosophical knowledge of theoretical constraints such as simplicity. (Solomon, 2001, p. 140)

Thus, for Solomon, methodological considerations must be both socially dispersed (as in Nelson's account) and multidisciplinary in order to reveal imbalances in political values and other nonempirical decision vectors.

Solomon's naturalist demand for empirical evidence to support epistemological evaluations restrains her endorsement of Longino's recommendation (her fourth criterion for critical engagement) that we should join or develop egalitarian communities for the sake of improving our investigations. Solomon admits that such social democratization may benefit the identification of political decision vectors. Yet, at best, only political decision vectors might receive improved attention, and we remain without evidence of even that.

Among feminist empiricists, Code stands out for resisting commitment to any particular formulation of the epistemic agent and for recognizing sources of agency aside from individuals-in-communities and human communities that include our relationship with the biological and ecological environment. Although Code treats as fundamental the mutual dependence among individuals by suggesting that knowers are "second persons," a concept borrowed from Annette Baier (2002), Code's account resists any reference to communities. She recognizes that knowledge also develops in smaller and more fluid social contexts—in a "society" that remains less clearly defined and correspondingly more flexible than a community. Code suggests that we engage in "imaginaries" (a notion borrowed from Cornelius Castoriadis). *Instituted imaginaries* provide coherence among individual understandings, and *instituting imaginaries* question the social structure and make new meanings possible (Code, 2006a, pp. 30–31).

Imaginaries are "habitats" that provide "places to know," Code (2006a) argues, in two senses: as places from which we can begin inquiry and as places that we must come to understand if we are to be responsible knowers. Learning about the contexts in which we know is central to the methodology of most feminist empiricism, and it is integral to naturalized or naturalist epistemology. Naturalism treats knowers as part of nature, as subject to empirical investigation, and thus seeks to use empirical evidence especially from science to enrich and strengthen epistemological theorizing.

FEMINIST NATURALISM

Naturalized epistemologists begin with the assumption that people actually have knowledge and hence with an implicit rejection of global skepticism, the worry that knowledge is not at all possible. The means for rejecting skepticism, according to Quine, is to use our science itself to provide the explanation of how some beliefs are justified, or warranted, over others. Final answers regarding standards for inquiry are not the goal, however, for thoroughgoing naturalists. Such concerns risk begging the question about the assumptions underpinning the sciences of cognition and ignoring the ways that scientific investigation continues to develop. Instead, jumping straight in to work with scientific findings provides a constructive "looping effect" as systems of epistemic valuation are continuously informed by empirical developments (Fellows, 2010).

The relevant sciences for Quine are the sciences of individual cognition, behaviorism, and neuroscience that some feminist naturalists also take up (Antony, 2003; Duran, 1993). Even for Quine, further forms of science may shed light on how people's experiences can justify their beliefs, and thus his reformed empiricism complements Kuhn's historicism (Hundleby, 2002). Making use of all of our available resources to scrutinize our understandings reflects naturalism's inspiration by the 18th-century empiricism of David Hume, which Baier (2002) argues has a distinctly social cast that suits it for feminism (pp. 46–50).

As part of the process of naturalizing epistemology, feminists critically analyze the methodologies and basic concepts of the contemporary cognitive sciences that inform their naturalism— whether the sciences of individual psychology favored by Quine or the Kuhnian and post-Kuhnian social studies of knowledge. Feminist naturalists recognize that the scientific resources for epistemology themselves are subject to *improvement*. After all, science is open-ended in several different ways due to the open-endedness of the future, natural human ingenuity and creativity, and even the concepts we create (Rooney, 2003, pp. 218–219). The feminist treatment of the scientific resources for theorizing about knowledge as dynamic produces "a *verb-sense* of epistemology, . . . a sense of *doing* epistemology, of *reflecting* in a systematic way on knowledge and knowing while drawing ongoing critical attention to particular kinds of motivating concerns, questions, and methods in the way one does epistemology" (p. 207, emphasis original). This reflexive development of empirical standards contrasts with the usual epistemological pursuit of a "final" view, epistemology as a noun: for example, coherentism, positivism, empiricism. Such static treatments of knowledge become dynamic and defeasible in feminist hands, subject to challenge and change over time. In the context of transforming claims about what counts as knowledge, what remains continuous

and distinctive in feminist epistemology, and in feminist naturalism especially, is ongoing information by feminism and by science, even as these change over time (Rooney, 2003).

CONTROVERSIES ABOUT
FEMINIST EMPIRICISM

Feminist empiricism rarely receives complimentary treatment in overviews of feminist epistemologies and science studies, in large part because it has been misunderstood. The theoretical conservativeness of empiricism does not entail a political conservativeness. The most potentially regressive approach to feminist empiricism may be naturalism because it defers to scientific input, which inevitably reflects the status quo. Yet the reflexive revolutionary spirit of naturalism challenges even its own empiricist precepts.

The Conservative Quality of Empiricism

Naturalism may seem to resist progress in several different ways. Some concerns involve the critical weakness of naturalism and the patriarchal content of the science it relies on. Another concern is that empirical understanding, naturalized or not, can never be sufficient for political analysis. Feminist naturalists account for the fact that there are always prior epistemologies and other existing influences on the ways that we evaluate beliefs, and they demand continuous scrutiny of these value systems as concrete constitutive circumstances for all our inquiries.

Relying on science, as naturalists do, seems to at least limit and perhaps exclude the possibility of establishing new ideals for human reasoning, not only because science may employ regressive politics but also because formulating ideals is not the job of science—it's the job of philosophy. At best, science describes only people's success with respect to accepted ideals, without interrogating those standards, deferring to existing standards in a way that discourages some feminist empiricists, including Longino (1993), from naturalism. Further, naturalism's tendency toward scientism—deference to scientific evaluations—may be inherently quietist, suppressing dispute. In practice, many of the central tenets of science are beyond scrutiny, even though in some ideal forms science may be self-revising (Linker, 2003).

The patriarchal social system produces almost all of the science available that might provide empirical standards for evaluating knowledge claims. As a practical political resource, science has a history of resisting social explanations for gendered differences and seeking instead accounts based on biology that portray the differences as relatively immutable. The tendency in the scientific study of knowledge to accept gender as given and ahistorical seems to be especially strong when women's capacities have been judged to be inferior. Consider that some significant gendered differences have been found with spatial ability, but the differences are so small as to be easily explained by differences in socialization. Yet researchers persist in looking for biological reasons for gendered differences in understanding (Fausto-Sterling, 1985, 1992), such that cognitive science seems bent on justifying women's low social status. Psychologists resolutely search for differences, even when empirical results consistently reveal gender parity in verbal ability.

For such reasons, taking up scientific accounts of gender can be regressive and epistemologically dubious, especially when it comes to cognition. For instance, scientific accounts of cognition support claims made by Jane Duran (2001) that women benefit from an especially "relational" view of themselves and the world.[8] Duran seems to be among the most thoroughgoing of feminist naturalisms because she engages deeply in empirical research in both cognitive science (1993) and contemporary cultural studies (2001). However, that depth is at the expense of considering other empirical factors, including socialization, that reveal how gender dichotomies in cognition can be symptoms of oppression. It ignores a competing account that has more thorough empirical support, the evidence that women are socialized to participate in and even facilitate their oppression.

Adherence to the empiricist tradition also can be used to rule out the relevance of social liberation movements to fostering advances in science (Harding, 1986, pp. 25–26). Thus, empiricism's future can seem to be radical only insofar as its internal conflicts spark a move away from the empiricism itself. As Maureen Linker argues (2003), empirical evidence seems to have little impact on the normative correction of many forms of human knowledge, such as those assessed in terms of logical, linguistic, and moral truths.

Yet, feminist empiricism involves accounting for the relationship between values traditionally considered to be noncognitive—including social liberation and morality—and their cognitive counterparts, such as empirical adequacy. "Experience," the key concept in empiricism, is a very broad and complex notion for feminist empiricists that extends beyond and complicates simple sensory experience. Cultural resources, including some rudimentary prior epistemology, inform any empirical knowledge. Our studies in psychology and the history of science, for instance, cannot move ahead without some notion of what needs examination, without a functional ontology, an account of the nature of the world that shows how meaningful inquiry can be possible. Cognitive scientists generally assume (1) that knowledge takes the form of discrete propositional beliefs regarding isolated statements of fact (e.g., "the breadbox is larger than the teacup"), (2) that individuals are the agents of knowledge, and (3) that science is the best example of knowledge. However, "stipulation . . . simply begs the question against more robust forms of naturalizing epistemology where questions about the cognitive demarcation and delineation of beliefs are open to question" (Rooney, 2003, p. 216). No scientific authority absolves the need to scrutinize background concepts and values, whether they include the sexism of cognitive science or the empirical adequacy of psychoanalysis.

Background epistemologies belong to the communal resources that Nelson argues are necessary for individual knowledge of any kind. Yet her picture of communities as prior to individual knowledge seems to entail that what can be known is static and that individual knowledge is passive. So Edrie Sobstyl (2004) argues that science and common sense are in constant flux, and in dynamic interaction with individual experience.

This creates opportunities for knowledge to grow and change. . . . The fact that women alter their behavior in order to avoid being targets of sexual assault shows that they recognize the prevailing beliefs of a patriarchal community. But the fact that women *resist* such constraints on their behavior and demand freedom from sexual predation shows that our common sense and gendered social and political experiences have a concrete impact on what we know. It is not helpful to say that this resistance is entirely derived from the community, because our community has not been particularly willing to warrant such ideals. (p. 131)

Thus Sobstyl argues that we can revise and complete Nelson's holism by allowing for a symmetrical relationship between embodied individuals and communities rather than by giving absolute priority to communities. Individual knowledge may be derived from communal knowledge, as Nelson argues, or it may be situated in or interdependent with communal knowledge in the way that Grasswick and Sobstyl suggest.

There are many reasons to believe that the program of naturalizing epistemology will change substantially in the future. To begin with, naturalizing epistemology is a project currently in its very early stages. Even those who are sympathetic to naturalism or describe themselves as naturalists are "slow to renounce the old modes of legitimation" (Roth, 2003, p. 296), and what the new scientific modes are, exactly, remains unclear. In addition, the development of naturalism has been slow because naturalists have had to spend a good deal of their time defending the importance and viability of naturalist techniques (Rooney, 2003).

Naturalism is a continuous process, and new ways of viewing knowledge constantly emerge from the open texture of science, as Rooney (2003) argues.

At the very least, I maintain, naturalists must have a . . . verb-sense of science—that is, [of] science as a diversity of dynamic disciplines, the concepts, questions, and findings of which are continually being modified in relation to changing conditions, including the changing conditions of empirical investigation and the changing social and political worlds within which such investigation is situated. (pp. 218–219)

New scientific tools may emerge merely because science progresses in addressing people's changing concerns and because science may respond to new questions that we have about knowledge, including feminist questions.

Naturalism Supporting Rationalism

The self-critical impulse in naturalist epistemology takes the general form of requiring empiricism to be based itself on empirical investigation. The scientific evidence concerning human inquiry thus could turn out to support a nonempiricist view of knowledge, to make available "genuinely novel and transformative philosophical strategies" that explain how bias can play a positive role in reasoning (Antony, 2003, p. 142). Indeed, some evidence supports the rationalist view of mind, harking back to René Descartes, that people have native intellectual capacities, such as for language, and that, in this way, one's ability to know is independent of one's past experience (Antony, 2003).

On the basis of her rationalist (but naturalistically supported) view that knowers rely on innate mental capacities, Antony adopts the further rationalist view that knowers are interchangeable, which most feminists find objectionable because it denies the impact on knowledge of developmental history, social situation, and different forms of embodiment. Moreover, the bodies that do play a role in Antony's work and that provide one's perspective on the world do not have "bias" in the usual sense that differentiates individuals. The forms of prejudgment that are properly called biases at best are merely analogous to the shared cognitive dispositions that can make our bodies seem interchangeable.

Yet, Antony's argument demonstrates that changes in scientific accounts of cognition could, in principle, undermine the traditional empiricist view of the mind and the entailed epistemology (Campbell, 1998, p. 33). Such a turnabout is possible because developing scientific perspectives on knowledge is an ongoing activity, and this is a further reason to view naturalism in a "verb-sense" (Rooney, 2003). One may practice epistemological naturalism continuously, and ongoing naturalist revision entails that feminist empiricists may find themselves engaging in quite different forms of theorizing than that with which they started. Naturalizing is never complete because epistemology is never *finally*, *ultimately* naturalized.

Empiricism remains, at the moment and for the foreseeable future, a viable starting place or background epistemology for naturalist methods. Antony's argument does not succeed in its attempt to turn naturalism toward rationalism. Admittedly, a rationalist view of the mind—for example, the view of Descartes or Noam Chomsky—might reflect some evidence better than the behaviorism that Quine favored. Even Quine considers behaviorist psychology useful only for individuating belief states. Behaviorism is not sufficient support for epistemology because behaviors are neither the same as beliefs nor sufficient to explain them—a task for which he suggests biology, especially neurophysiology (Nelson, 1990, pp. 126–128).

Naturalist explanation must also account for the impact of different social situations and different bodies with various levels and forms of cognitive development (Code, 2006a), something only promised by Anthony's rationalism and not delivered. These nonbehavioral factors affect neurophysiology, including language development (Nelson, 1990, pp. 286–287), and so have implications not only for Quinean empiricism but also for any rationalism that is accountable to empirical evidence. The need to address how the social world impacts evidence inspired Quine's argument for naturalism (Nelson, 1990, p. 288; Quine, 1960). Therefore, to ignore social influences, as Antony's rationalist move does, is to depart from the basic spirit of naturalism rather than to defeat it on its own terms.

CONCLUSION

Employing empiricism provides feminists with valuable purchase in the dominant culture and access to the power of scientific resources. These advantages imbue empiricism with a radical potential that both critics of feminist empiricism (Harding, 1986) and defenders of it (Campbell, 1998; Nelson, 1990) recognize to include strategic rhetoric and to go far beyond rhetorical significance. Further, supporters argue that feminist naturalism demonstrates the radical future of feminist empiricism because it holds all the strengths of the early alternative approaches known as feminist standpoint theory and feminist postmodernism. Feminist naturalism, specifically, provides clear grounds for evaluating not only beliefs but also values and practices that include political views (Tuana, 1992). The broad scope of naturalist critique allows Antony

to find in it potential support for rationalism, showing that, not only in principle but also in practice, naturalism has revolutionary potential.

Naturalism's open-endedness suggests further that feminist empiricism may be mutually complementary with other feminist epistemologies, and encourages treating epistemological choices as provisional, according to the problem at hand, rather than as definitive. Looking to "small" places in Code's ecological manner requires a dynamic sensitivity, strategizing as *activists*:

> Choos[e] . . . points of concentration, of focus; discern . . . the gaps where intervention and contestation have the best hopes of entering, and work . . . to ensure that their effects will spread . . . [A]ctivists, both singly and collectively, have to know a lot just to see what might be possible and may have to develop strategic compromises to be able to work toward sometimes distant and often unstable goals. (Code, 2008, p. 201)

Methodologies may be taken up as guerrilla strategies based on shared oppositional consciousness that "operates like the clutch of an automobile: the mechanism that permits the driver to select, engage, and disengage gears in a system for the transmission of power" (Sandoval, 1991, p. 14). This U.S. third world feminist strategy identified by Chela Sandoval encourages flexibility in taking up the competing political tactics of liberal, Marxist, radical, and socialist feminism, and it denies the need to commit to a final strategy. Likewise, shifting among empiricist and other methodologies keeps inquirers free from the stagnation of any static epistemology. So feminist empiricism continues its radical progression by transforming from a hegemonic strategy into a "processual relationship" (Sandoval, 1991, p. 24) with only tentative "places to know" (Code, 2006a).

Although Code's account most clearly supports recognizing as provisional the naturalist employment of empiricism or of any other epistemology, her view resonates with other forms of feminist empiricism. Consider that because different methodologies and epistemologies, including rationalism, have some empirical support, Solomon would advise methodological dissent. Keeping different options at hand also serves Rooney's "verb-sense" of epistemology that recognizes the open-endedness of human inquiry. Finally, this pluralism can be expressed without assuming naturalism: Longino's (1990, 2004) requirement of ongoing critical engagement among divergent perspectives can apply to feminist epistemologies and methodologies as much as it does to science itself:

> The feminist interventions I imagine will be local (i.e., specific to a particular area of research), they may not be exclusive (i.e., different feminist perspectives may be represented in theorizing), and they will be in some way continuous with existing scientific work. (Longino, 1987, p. 62)

There is no one feminist empiricism, but many feminist empiricisms, an epistemological plurality that can be justified—both politically and epistemologically and from an individual and a community level—according to the various views of feminist empiricists.

Discussion Questions

1. How might a feminist empiricist view of *evidence* or *objectivity* apply beyond the domain of science to everyday knowledge? Consider how a feminist empiricist would shop for groceries or plant a garden.

2. How might scientists apply Code's view of *ecological thinking*?

   a. Grasswick's notion of knowers as individuals-in-communities may be a helpful starting point. How might a scientist present herself as an individual-in-communities? How might social scientists view their subjects as individuals-in-communities? Will this vary with the level at which we recognize societies or communities?

   b. What other aspects of scientists and subjects of study must we address to achieve ecological thinking? Is this different for different fields of inquiry?

3. What do you think are the particular strengths and weaknesses of feminist empiricism? Why might it be useful to distinguish feminist empiricism from other feminist epistemologies in some contexts but not in others? Social contexts? Historical contexts? Geographical contexts? Regarding some knowers but not others? Different bodies?

4. Might the different epistemologies work better in addressing different forms of research? Different methodologies? Different disciplines? Different research topics?

Online Resources

The Thinking Meat Project—Explaining Female Orgasm: An Interview With Elisabeth Lloyd

http://thinkingmeat.com/newsblog/?page_id=1201

The Stanford Encyclopedia of Philosophy

http://plato.stanford.edu/

This open-source encyclopedia features articles by experts in specific fields that are periodically updated.

- Anderson, E., Feminist epistemology and philosophy of science, March 16, 2011, http://plato.stanford.edu/entries/feminism-epistemology/

- Fehr, C., Feminist philosophy of biology, *June 22, 2011, forthcoming,* Fall 2011 edition, http://plato.stanford.edu/entries/feminist-philosophy-biology/

  Many feminist empiricists, especially Fausto-Sterling, Lloyd, and Longino, have made important contributions to the philosophy of biology.

- Garry, A., Analytic feminism, April 29, 2004, http://plato.stanford.edu/entries/femapproach-analytic/

  Feminist empiricism can be viewed as the epistemological wing of analytic feminism, given that empiricism has been the central epistemology and essential to the prevalence of the "analytic" approach in 20th-century Anglo-American philosophy.

- Stanford, K., Underdetermination of scientific theory, August 12, 2009, http://plato.stanford.edu/entries/scientific-underdetermination/index.html

  This theory associated with Quine's naturalism explains the interrelation of epistemic and non-epistemic values for many feminist empiricists.

- Whipps, J., Pragmatist feminism, July 9, 2010, http://plato.stanford.edu/entries/femapproach-pragmatism/

Feminist empiricists engage with pragmatist philosophy primarily through the works of Quine, but other feminists engage different elements and authors in the pragmatist tradition.

Relevant Journals

Hypatia: A Journal of Feminist Philosophy

Signs: Journal of Women in Culture and Society

Social Epistemology: A Journal of Knowledge, Culture, and Policy

NOTES

1. Speaking broadly of the global North is not to deny the variability within this historical culture, and is a somewhat artificial description, but it helps to track connections among the various manifestations and implications of European colonization and contemporary capitalism.

2. The connections between empiricism and liberalism may be deeper than a mere analogy, as Steven Shapin and Simon Schaffer suggest in *Leviathan and the Air-Pump* (1989).

3. Although social gender and biological sex are deeply integrated, distinguishing them is valuable for addressing the more flexible social and political influences. Furthermore, the sex of an organism as a whole has no necessary or sufficient connection with an aspect or portion of the body. Not even chromosomes or genitalia sex a body.

4. Lloyd's failure to consider such implications led to some misunderstanding of the intentions behind her research, which she has remedied in follow-up articles by addressing its ramifications for women's sexuality. See the interview with Lloyd listed in the "Online Resources" section of this chapter.

5. Practices of testing and evaluation as well as the standards of factuality, evidence, and objectivity are part of the "context of justification" in traditional empiricism, providing epistemic justification or warrant. By contrast, heuristics and theory generation that concern standpoint theorists are considered part of the "context of discovery."

6. Harding (1986) similarly criticized early or "spontaneous" forms of feminist empiricism for maintaining that social values both matter and do not matter in science.

7. When there is consensus, dissent approaches zero, and the conditions (1) through (3) are met as follows:

1. One theory has *all* the empirical successes (explains all the different observations);
2. *All* the empirical vectors support that theory (productive scientific methods all fall under the theory).
3. With maintained consensus, nonempirical decision vectors *all* begin to support the one theory.

8. Duran bases her view of the feminine self on object-relations theory, which generally falls under feminist standpoint theory (Harding, 1986), but she aims to develop a naturalist version.

REFERENCES

Antony, L. M. (2003). Quine as feminist: The radical import of naturalized epistemology. In L. H. Hankinson Nelson & J. Nelson (Eds.), *Feminist interpretations of W. V. Quine* (pp. 95–149). University Park: The Pennsylvania State University Press.

Baier, A. (2002). Hume: The reflective women's epistemologist? In L. Antony & C. Witt (Eds.), *A Mind of One's Own* (2nd ed., pp. 38–52). Boulder, CO: Westview Press.

The Biology and Gender Study Group. (1988). The importance of feminist critique for contemporary cell biology. *Hypatia, 3*(1), 172–187.

Campbell, R. (1998). *Illusions of paradox: A feminist naturalized epistemology.* New York: Rowman & Littlefield.

Clough, S. (2003). *Beyond epistemology: A pragmatist approach to feminist science studies.* Lanham, MD: Rowman & Littlefield.

Code, L. (1991). *What can she know? Feminist theory and the construction of knowledge.* Ithaca: Cornell University Press.

Code, L. (1995). *Rhetorical spaces: Essays on gendered locations.* New York: Routledge.

Code, L. (1996). What is natural about epistemology naturalized? *American Philosophical Quarterly, 33*(1), 1–22.

Code, L. (2006a). *Ecological thinking: The politics of epistemic location.* New York: Oxford University Press.

Code, L. (2006b). Skepticism and the lure of ambiguity. *Hypatia, 21*(3), 222–228.

Code, L. (2008). Thinking about "ecological thinking." *Hypatia, 23*(1), 187–203.

Daston, L. (1992). Objectivity and the escape from perspective. *Social Studies of Science, 22*, 597–618.

Duran, J. (1993). *Knowledge in context.* New York: Rowman & Littlefield.

Duran, J. (2001). *Worlds of knowing: Global feminist epistemologies.* New York: Routledge.

Fausto-Sterling, A. (1985). *Myths of gender: Biological theories about men and women.* New York: Basic Books.

Fausto-Sterling, A. (1992). *Myths of gender: Biological theories about men and women* (2nd ed.). New York: Basic Books.

Fellows, J. (2010, June 28). The looping effects of objectivity. Paper presented at *Feminism, Science & Values*, a meeting of the International Association of Women Philosophers, University of Western Ontario, London, ON.

Goldenberg, M. (2010, June 26). Resituating evidence in feminist science studies. Paper presented at *Feminism, Science & Values*, a meeting of the International Association of Women Philosophers, University of Western Ontario, London, ON.

Gould, S. J. (1996). *The mismeasure of man* (Rev. ed.). New York: W. W. Norton & Company.

Grasswick, H. E. (2004). Individuals-in-communities: The search for a feminist model of epistemic subjects. *Hypatia, 19*(3), 85–120.

Haack, S. (1993). The two faces of Quine's naturalism. *Synthese, 94*, 335–356.

Harding, S. (1986). *The science question in feminism.* Ithaca, NY: Cornell University Press.

Harding, S. (1989). How the women's movement benefits science: Two views. *Women's Studies International Forum, 12*(3), 271–283.

Harding, S. (1991). *Whose science? Whose knowledge? Thinking from women's lives.* New York: Routledge.

Hundleby, C. (2002). The open end: Social naturalism, feminist values, and the integrity of epistemology. *Social Epistemology, 16*(3), 251–265.

Kuhn, T. (1962). *The structure of scientific revolutions.* Chicago: University of Chicago Press.

Kuhn, T. (1977). *The essential tension.* Chicago: University of Chicago Press.

Linker, M. (2003). A case for responsibly rationalized feminist epistemology. In L. H. Hankinson Nelson & J. Nelson (Eds.), *Feminist interpretations of Quine* (pp. 153–171). University Park: The Pennsylvania State University Press.

Lloyd, E. A. (2005). *The case of the female orgasm: Bias in the science of evolution.* Cambridge, MA: Harvard University Press.

Longino, H. E. (1987). Can there be a feminist science? *Hypatia, 2*(3), 51–64.

Longino, H. E. (1990). *Science as social knowledge: Values and objectivity in scientific inquiry.* Princeton, NJ: Princeton University Press.

Longino, H. E. (1993). Subjects, power and knowledge: Description and prescription in feminist philosophies of science. In Linda Alcoff & Elizabeth Potter (Eds.), *Feminist epistemologies* (pp. 101–120). New York: Routledge.

Longino, H. E. (1997). Cognitive and non-cognitive values in science: Rethinking the dichotomy. In L. H. Hankinson Nelson & J. Nelson (Eds.), *Feminism, science, and the philosophy of science* (pp. 39–58). Boston: Kluwer.

Longino, H. E. (2001). *The fate of knowledge.* Princeton, NJ: Princeton University Press.

Longino, H. E. (2004). How values can be good for science. In P. Machamer & G. Wolters (Eds.), *Science, values, and objectivity* (pp. 127–142). Pittsburgh: University of Pittsburgh Press.

Longino, H. E., & Doell, R. (1983). Body, bias, and behavior: A comparative analysis of reasoning in two areas of biological science. *Signs: Journal of Women in Culture and Society, 9*(2), 206–227.

Martin, E. (1991). The egg and the sperm: How science has constructed a romance based on stereotypical male-female roles. *Signs: Journal of Women in Culture and Society, 16*(3), 485–501.

McCaughey, M. (1993). Redirecting feminist critiques of science. *Hypatia, 8*(4), 72–84.

Meynell, L. (2007). Review of "The case of the female orgasm: Bias in the science of evolution" by Elisabeth Lloyd. *Hypatia, 22*(3), 218–222.

Nelson, L. H. (1990). *Who knows: From Quine to a feminist empiricism.* Philadelphia: Temple University Press.

Nelson, L. H. (1993). A question of evidence. *Hypatia, 8*(2), 172–189.

Nelson, L. H. (2000). Empiricism. In A. M. Jaggar & I. M. Young (Eds.), *A companion to feminist philosophy* (pp. 30–38). Malden, MA: Blackwell.

Nelson, L. H., & Nelson, J. (1995). Feminist values and cognitive virtues. *PSA 1994: Proceedings of the Biennial Meeting of the Philosophy of Science Association, 2*, 120–129.

Nelson, L. H., & Nelson, J. (2003). Introduction. In L. H. Hankinson Nelson & J. Nelson (Eds.), *Feminist interpretations of Quine* (pp. 1–55). University Park: The Pennsylvania State University Press.

Okruhlik, K. (1994). Gender and the biological sciences. *Biology & society: Reflections on methodology* (Suppl. 20 of the *Canadian Journal of Philosophy*), 21–42.

Okruhlik, K. (2003). Logical empiricism, feminism, and Neurath's auxiliary motive. *Hypatia, 19*(1), 48–72.

Quine, W. V. O. (1960). *Word and object.* Cambridge, MA: MIT Press.

Quine, W. V. O. (1969). *Ontological relativity and other essays.* New York: Columbia University Press.

Rooney, P. (1993). On values in science: Is the epistemic/non-epistemic distinction useful? *PSA 1992: Proceedings of the Biennial Meeting of the Philosophy of Science Association, 1,* 13–22.

Rooney, P. (2003). Feminist epistemology and naturalized epistemology: An uneasy alliance. In L. H. Hankinson Nelson & J. Nelson (Eds.), *Feminist interpretations of Quine* (pp. 205–239). University Park: The Pennsylvania State University Press.

Roth, P. (2003). Feminism and naturalism: If asked for theories, just say "no." In L. H. Hankinson Nelson & J. Nelson (Eds.), *Feminist interpretations of Quine* (pp. 269–305). University Park: The Pennsylvania State University Press.

Sandoval, C. (1991). U.S. third-world feminism: The theory and method of oppositional consciousness in the postmodern world. *Genders, 10,* 1–24.

Shapin, S., & Schaffer, S. (1989). *Leviathan and the air-pump.* Princeton, NJ: Princeton University Press.

Sobstyl, E. (2004). Re-radicalizing Nelson's feminist empiricism. *Hypatia, 19*(1), 119–141.

Solomon, M. (2001). *Social empiricism.* Cambridge, MA: MIT Press.

Tuana, N. (1992). The radical future of feminist empiricism. *Hypatia, 7*(1), 100–113.

Tuana, N. (1995). The values of science: Empiricism from a feminist perspective. *Synthese, 104,* 441–461.

3

FEMINIST STANDPOINTS

Sandra Harding

Origins[1]

Feminist standpoint theories are deeply indebted to the women's political movements of the 1960s and 1970s and also to the antipositivist histories, sociologies, and philosophies of science then emerging in Europe and the United States. Canadian sociologist Dorothy Smith (1987, 1990a, 1990b, 1999) and then U.S. political philosopher Nancy Hartsock (1983/2003) argued that existing relations between politics and the production of knowledge were far from the scientifically and socially progressive ones claimed by research disciplines or by the economic, legal, medical, health, education, welfare, scientific, and other institutions that made public policies based on such research. When it came to accounting for gender relations, the prevailing philosophies of science and the research projects they legitimated were politically regressive, philosophically weak, and scientifically less than maximally effective. British sociologist of science Hilary Rose (1983), philosopher Alison Jaggar (1983), historian of science Donna Haraway (1978, 1981), and Harding (1983/2003) had all also contributed to the development of standpoint accounts by 1983. By now, three readers on standpoint theory have appeared (Campbell & Manicom, 1995; Harding, 2004a; Kenney & Kinsella, 1997).

Many clusters of essays debating the strengths and limitations of such methodologies have appeared in journals.[2] Most important, standpoint methodology is now routinely used in every social science discipline as well as in those disciplines in which the objects of study can have both social and natural features, such as medical, environmental, and archaeological research. Moreover, as we shall see, one can now recognize the standpoint "logic of research" in every other social justice movement's knowledge-production processes.

Evidence for standpoint claims initially appeared in the documentation of sexist and androcentric results of research in biology and the social sciences. Standpoint theorists analyzed causes of the gaps between the actual knowledge and power relations and those desired by women's movements. They reflected on causes of the successes of feminist research in the social sciences and biology, which seemed to violate norms for "good research." Such work led to prescriptions in some of these writings for how to produce empirically and theoretically more successful research. These writers focused also on how standpoint approaches to research could empower oppressed groups. Moreover, they argued that it was precisely the guidance of such research by feminist political goals that enabled the production of empirically better supported

knowledge claims. Epistemic and scientific successes were possible because certain kinds of
"good politics" in themselves had the potential
to advance the growth of scientific knowledge:
some kinds of politics could be productive of
knowledge.

This feminist argument drew on older
sources. Marx and Engels had argued for a pro-
letarian standpoint. How the class system actually worked could not be detected if one started
off thought from the activities of beneficiaries
of that system, such as factory owners and the
bankers who invested in industries. Instead, one
should start off from the lives of the workers.
Only from such a standpoint could one accurately explain how it was that misery accumulated in the workers' lives as wealth accumulated
in the lives of factory owners. Marx and Engels's
accounts of how class hierarchy works followed
this prescription. The Hungarian theorist Georg
Lukács developed the Marxian standpoint arguments further in the 1930s and 1940s. But they
were plagued with apparently unsolvable problems and abandoned by Marxist social scientists
and philosophers. Fredric Jameson points out
that it was not until the work of feminist theorists that the fruitful logic of Marxian arguments
was again pursued to produce the kinds of accurate and comprehensive knowledge that could
provide resources for oppressed groups.[3] Jameson
argues that the feminist work solved problems
the Marxian tradition had not through its bold
challenge to the natural sciences and its innovative account of how an oppressed group could
come to consciousness "for itself," not just as
the object of the gaze of others (Jameson, 1988;
Lukács, 1923/1971).[4]

Yet this "logic of inquiry" has other sources
in which such a legacy is not directly visible.
Moreover, echoes of its themes appear in other
writings. The sociologists cite also powerful
themes in Mannheim (1936/1954), Merton
(1972), and Simmel (1921) about the resources
provided by the "stranger's" social position.
Collins (1986, 1991) develops this into the "outsider within" position of disciplinary researchers
from marginalized social groups, such as Black
woman sociologists. In such a contradictory
social location as an insider in one respect and
an outsider in others, a researcher can learn to
detect aspects of social relations not accessible

by those who are only outsiders or only insiders.[5]
The writings of Paulo Freire (1970) and the participatory action researchers also echo standpoint themes (McTaggart, 1997; Maguire, 1987;
Petras & Porpora, 1993). Other feminist writers
at least partially independently developed standpoint arguments. From a perspective in post-
Kuhnian science and technology studies and the
history of primatology, Donna Haraway (1981,
1991) demonstrated the social situatedness of the
field of primatology and engaged with standpoint authors on their ambivalence toward their
own insistence on the situatedness of knowledge. Thomas Kuhn's project "to display the
historical integrity of ... science in its own
time," as he famously said (1962/1970, p. 1),
opened the way for thinking about the "historical
integrity" (the "fit") of social and natural science
conceptual frameworks, methods, and practices
with the gender relations of their particular historical moment. Sara Ruddick (1989/2004)
looked at the institution of mothering from the
standpoint of everyday mothering concerns, and
bell hooks (1990) argued that the very marginalization of Black people's lives created "a space
of radical openness" from which race relations
could be seen in a kind of clarity unavailable
from the perspective of those who, intentionally
or not, benefit from white supremacy.

Meanwhile, a standpoint logic can now be
seen to structure much recent work in multicultural and postcolonial studies, as well as in their
science and technology studies movements.
Twenty-five years of these studies have revealed
how Western natural sciences and technologies,
no less than those from other cultures, are local
knowledge systems, coproduced along with
their particular kinds of social relations. This
coproductionist argument fully acknowledges
that Western sciences are far more powerful in
many respects than other cultures' knowledge
systems even though they are no more autonomous from their social orders than are the sciences of other cultures. Western sciences have a
"historical integrity" with powerful global
social relations of their eras that they, in turn,
helped to constitute and maintain (Harding,
1998, 2008; Hess, 1995; Selin, 2008; see also
Jasanoff, 2004, 2005).

What was this abandoned "logic of inquiry"
that the feminist standpoint theorists took up?

A STANDPOINT LOGIC OF INQUIRY

Feminist theorists argued that sexist and andro-centric understandings of gender relations appeared even in the most abstract conceptual practices as well as in more obvious ways. They noted, as had Marx himself, that the social relations between women and men in significant respects resembled those between workers and their bosses: gender and class relations had parallel structures. Men as heads of households exploited women's reproductive and productive labor, intentionally or not. They benefited as men, as well as in the capacity of some of them as managers, administrators, designers of dominant institutions, and capitalists, from the perception that male control of women's bodies was natural. They benefited also from the conceptualization of women's unpaid domestic labor as an extension of women's "natures" or as "done for love" and from the discrimination against and exploitation of women's work in wage labor, conceptualized as reasonable since women were first and foremost mothers, not wage workers. The domestic and the wage-labor exploitation of women were causally linked, for misuse in each domain undermined women's power in the other. Such exploitation, domination, and oppression were legitimated through the conceptual frameworks of research disciplines as well as of the social institutions that such research disciplines served.

Many feminist sociologists, political scientists, legal theorists, anthropologists, psychologists, economists, and biologists were participants in the emerging women's movements. They began to provide accounts of how gender relations were articulated, not only in explicit claims about women and men and their supposedly appropriate social roles but also in the apparently value-neutral abstract conceptual frameworks of the dominant institutions and of the disciplines that serviced them. They began to look at the "conceptual practices of power," in Dorothy Smith's (1990a) phrase. They did so, it was argued, by starting off research from women's concerns and practices in everyday life rather than from the concerns of those institutions and disciplines. For example, Carol Gilligan's (1982) analyses started off thinking about the absence in moral theory of attention to the distinctive kinds of moral decisions women faced as mothers and caretakers. Moral theory elevated to the highest ethical categories only the kinds of decisions that men made as managers, administrators, lawyers, and the like—decision making from which women had long been excluded. Why was it that the most influential authors on morality and moral development (such as Kant, Freud, Piaget, Rawls, and Kohlberg, as well as religious traditions) could not perceive the kinds of moral decisions with which women were faced as also exemplifying the highest categories of moral thought?

Similarly, Catherine MacKinnon (1982, 1983) identified how what counted in courts and police stations as rape and what counted as objectivity had a distressingly close fit with only men's conceptions of such matters—conceptions that reasonably arose from men's kinds of social experiences with women and in institutionalized public thinking, such as in law courts. Thus, these researchers and scholars began their projects not from the dominant conceptual frameworks of their disciplines and institutions but rather from women's everyday lives. They did so in order to reveal and challenge dominant institutional understandings of women, men, and the social relations between them. Note that while they began their projects from women's lives, they went on to "study up": to critically reveal the principles and practices of dominant institutions, including research disciplines. Conventional ethnographies of women's lives can be useful to standpoint projects, but the latter insist on looking at how women's lives are constrained and directed by the assumptions and practices of dominant institutions, including research disciplines. (See Smith, 2005, for a standpoint version of ethnography.)

Natural and social science disciplines lacked both the will and the effective mechanisms to examine critically how their own conceptual frameworks served hierarchical power relations in the larger society. A major problem was that the traditional philosophy of science held that the "context of discovery" should be left free of methodological controls. Yet this stance blocked from critical scrutiny a major route for the entrance of social values and interests into the research process. Of course, some such values and interests, namely those that differed between researchers, would be detected by subsequent methodological controls. But those that were shared by virtually an entire research community and the larger society, as has been characteristic of androcentric, white supremacist, and Eurocentric values, for instance, could not be detected by standard research methods. If the community of qualified researchers and critics systematically excludes, for example, any women of color, and if the larger culture is stratified by race and gender and lacks powerful critiques of this stratification, it is not plausible to imagine that racist and sexist interests and values would be identified within a community of scientists composed entirely of people who benefit—intentionally or not—from institutionalized racism and sexism. The restriction of scientific method to the part of research that follows a design approved by disciplinary standards reinforces the conventional belief that the truly scientific part of knowledge seeking occurs only in the so-called context of justification, where hypotheses that are "interesting" to the discipline are tested in discipline-approved ways. Untouched by such methods are those values and interests entrenched in the discipline-approved statement of what problem is to be researched and in the concepts favored in the hypotheses that are to be tested. Recent histories of science are full of cases in which broad social assumptions stood little chance of identification or elimination through the very best research procedures of the day. Consider, for example, biological and medical research assumptions about women's supposedly inferior and sexualized bodies and agricultural, military, or industrial research's assumptions about the supposed robustness of natural environments.

Such "objectivism" operationalizes the notion of objectivity in a much too narrow way to permit the achievement of the value-free research that is supposed to be its outcome. Scientific method could come into play only in the "context of justification," after researchers had selected the social or natural phenomena to be examined, had identified what they saw as problematic about them, had chosen the hypotheses and concepts they favored to examine such problems, and had designed a research process. It was only in the research design that the methods of research were specified; obviously these could

not exercise any control over the processes that led up to their very designation, a point to which we return (Harding, 1993). In directing research to start off not from the dominant disciplinary conceptual frameworks but rather from the lives of oppressed peoples, standpoint theory in effect extended the benefits of methodological controls back to the beginning of research so as to include the "context of discovery." It makes a difference to "what we know" whose questions get to count as ones worth pursuing and how these questions are to be conceptualized and research designed to answer them. This is not to say that standpoint theory is more practical than theoretical, but rather that it starts from the everyday to critically reevaluate the adequacy of prevailing theory found in research disciplines as well as in the dominant social institutions that such research tends to serve (intentionally or not)—it "studies up."

But objectivism also conceptualizes the desired value neutrality of objectivity too broadly. It is operationalized too narrowly in one way and too broadly in another. Objectivists claim that objectivity requires the elimination of all social values and interests from the research process and the results of research. It is clear, however, that not all social values and interests have the same bad effects upon the results of research. Democracy-advancing values, such as feminist concerns for social justice, have systematically (though not invariably) generated less partial and distorted beliefs than those typically held by the dominant social institutions and the research disciplines upon which such institutions depend for knowledge of nature and social relations. To be sure, some values, interests, and other cultural influences can block the growth of knowledge. Yet some other aspects of cultures and their social relations evidently are productive of knowledge.

Articulating the "logic" of standpoint research in terms of such conventional scientific goals as good method and the objectivity of research enables the strengths of this approach to be grasped more clearly. In starting off inquiry from women's lives, feminist research projects appeared to violate the norms of good research in the disciplines in several ways. They failed to respect the rule that protected the "context of discovery" from the possibility of methodological controls. They were claimed to be importing into research feminist political agendas when they revealed the androcentric commitments of highly regarded social theories and empirical studies and the norms that guided them. Since most of these researchers were women who began asking research questions from lives which were at least something like their own, they were perceived to fail to respect the importance of impartiality, separation, and distance in the researcher's relation to the researched—a challenge which, mysteriously, men did not seem to think arose when they started off thinking about the world from lives like their own. Moreover, they proposed something that appeared outrageous to conventional philosophies of science, namely that the purportedly culturally neutral conceptual frameworks of research disciplines, including standards for objectivity and good method, were not in fact culturally neutral. Yet, in spite of such violations of research norms, it was hard to deny that substantive feminist research in the social sciences and biology that did start off from women's lives often produced empirically more accurate and theoretically more comprehensive accounts of nature and social life, as an inspection of any feminist introduction to the issues of a discipline will reveal. Indeed, the achievements of such substantive research tended to be systematically ignored by critics of standpoint epistemology and the philosophy of science.

How was this kind of apparently illicit feminist research practice to be understood? Standpoint epistemology seemed to provide resources that traditional epistemologies lacked for responding thoughtfully to such a question. Several central themes in the standpoint accounts provide a fuller picture of such resources.[6] First, how societies are structured has epistemological consequences. Knowledge and power are internally linked; they co-constitute and co-maintain each other. What people do—what kinds of interactions they have in social relations and relations to the natural world—both enables and limits what they can know.[7] Yet what people typically can "do" depends in part upon their locations in social structures—whether or not they are assigned the work of taking care of children and people's bodies and the spaces they inhabit or of administering large agencies, corporations, or research institutes. Material life

both enables and limits what people can come to know about themselves and the worlds around them. So the social structures of societies provide a kind of laboratory within which we can explore how different kinds of assigned or chosen activities enable some insights and block others.

Second, when material life is hierarchically organized, as in societies structured by hierarchical class, gender, race, ethnic, or other relations of oppression and discrimination, the understandings of such relations that are available to "rulers" and "ruled" will tend to be opposed in certain respects. The understandings available to the dominant group tend to support the legitimacy of its dominating position, while the understandings available to the dominated tend to delegitimate such domination (Hartsock, 1983/2003, p. 287). The slave owner can see his slaves' actions only as (unwilled) "behavior" caused by their inferior nature or obedience to the master's will: he commands and they obey. To judge by the slave owners' miserable treatment of slaves, the latter do not appear to be fully human to their masters. However, following around the slaves in their everyday lives, an observer from outside the master-slave relationship could see slaves' purportedly natural laziness as the only kind of political protest that they reasonably think they can get away with, or their smiling at the master as a subterfuge to obscure that they are secretly planning to run away or perhaps even kill him. The observer can see them struggling to make their own human history in conditions not of their choosing. Similarly, the women's movement of the 1970s revealed how women's work was both socially necessary and exploited labor, not just an expression of their natural inclinations or only a "labor of love," as men and public institutions saw it. To take another example, feminists pointed out that women never "asked for" or "deserved" rape or physical violence, contrary to the view of their abusers and the legal system. Rather, as MacKinnon (1982) argued, "the state is male" in its insistence to regard as objective and rational a perception of violence against women that could look reasonable only from the perspective of men's position in the social relations between the genders. Feminists revealed many more inversions and, from the standpoint of women's lives, perverse understandings of nature and social relations in the conceptual frameworks of dominant institutions.

Thus, third, the oppressors' false and perverse perceptions are nevertheless made "real" and operative, for all are forced to live in social structures and institutions designed to serve the oppressors' understandings of self and society. These hierarchical structures and institutions engage in conceptual practices that solidify and disseminate as natural, inevitable, and desirable their continued power. Social and natural sciences play an important role in developing and maintaining such ideologies, intentionally or not.[8] If women are not permitted training in Latin, logic, science, or public speaking, they will appear less rational than their brothers. If they are discouraged from physical exercise and sports, they will appear naturally weaker than their brothers. If they are not permitted legal or other training in sound argument, they will appear less capable of reasoned moral judgments in the eyes of legal systems and religious institutions. If they are encouraged to pitch their voices at the high end of their natural register and always to smile or look pleasant, while their brothers are encouraged to pitch their voices at the low end of their natural register and in public appearances to look serious or even on occasion angry, women speakers will appear less authoritative. Dominant social relations can make real many aspects of the worlds they desire.

Fourth, consequently, it takes both science and politics to see the world "behind," "beneath," or "from outside" the oppressors' institutionalized vision. Of course, no one's understanding can completely escape its historical moment; that was the positivist dream that standpoint approaches deny. All understanding is socially located or situated. Yet the success of standpoint research requires only a degree of freedom from the dominant understanding, not complete freedom from it. And it requires collective effort. Thus a standpoint is an achievement, not an ascription. Women do not automatically have access to a standpoint of women or a feminist standpoint. Such a standpoint must be struggled for against the apparent realities made to appear natural and obvious by dominant institutions, and against the ongoing political disempowerment of oppressed groups. Dominant groups do not want revealed either the falsity or the unjust political consequences of their material and conceptual practices. They usually do not know that their assumptions are false (that slaves are fully human, that poverty is not necessary, that men are not the only desirable model of the ideal human) and do not want to confront the claim that unjust political conditions are the consequence of their views and practices. It takes "strong objectivity" methods to locate the practices of power that appear only in the apparently abstract, value-neutral conceptual frameworks favored by dominant social institutions and the disciplines that service them (Harding, 1993, 2004a). Importantly, the standpoint claim is that these political struggles, which are necessary to reveal such institutional and disciplinary practices, are themselves systematically knowledge producing.

Standpoint theory is part of post-Marxian critical theories that regard ideology critique as crucial to the growth of knowledge and to liberation. The causes of the conditions of the lives of the oppressed cannot be detected by only observing those lives. Instead, one must critically examine how the Supreme Court, Pentagon, transnational corporations, and welfare, health, and educational systems "think" in order to understand why women, racial minorities, and the poor in the United States have only the limited life choices that are available to them. Because the maintenance and legitimacy of these institutions depend on the services of research disciplines, one must critically examine the conceptual frameworks of sociology, economics, and other social (and natural) sciences to understand the thinking of dominant institutions.

Fifth, the achievement of a standpoint brings the possibility of liberation. An oppressed group must become a group "for itself," not just "in itself"—as others observe it—in order for it to see the importance of engaging in political and scientific struggles to see the world from the perspective of its own lives. Women have always been an identifiable category for social thought. They have been an object conceptualized from outside the group, namely from the perspective of men. But it took women's movements for women to recognize their shared interests and transform themselves into groups "for women"—defining themselves, their lives, their needs, and desires for themselves. They learned together to recognize that it was not just "their man" (father, husband, boss) who was mean or misbehaving.

Rather, cultural meanings and institutional practices encouraged and legitimated men's treatment of women in such ways at home, in workplaces, and in public life. Women's movements created a group consciousness (or, rather, many different group consciousnesses in different groups of women) in those that participated in them (and many who only watched). This consciousness enabled feminist struggles and then further feminist perceptions. As Fredric Jameson puts the point, feminist standpoint theorists opened "a space of a different kind for polemics about the epistemological priority of the experience of various groups or collectivities (most immediately, in this case, the experience of women as opposed to the experience of the industrial working class)" (Jameson, in Harding, 2004a, p. 144). Similarly, it took civil rights struggles and Black nationalist movements of the 1960s to mobilize African Americans into collective political actions that could, it was hoped, end racial inequities. The Chicano/a movement developed to mobilize Mexican Americans to a group consciousness capable of advancing an end to the injustices visited upon them. The lesbian and gay pride movement as well as the disability movement had a similar goal and effect. New group consciousnesses were created through these processes, consciousnesses that could produce new understandings of social relations, past and present.

Let us turn directly to consider standpoint theory as a philosophy of method—a methodology. In particular, let us consider it as a counter to the charge that social research intrinsically is structured in a way that ensures that it will replicate the "colonial relation." Whatever the social inequalities researcher and researched bring to a social research project, this charge goes, the research process itself increases the oppression of the already oppressed peoples who are usually its topics of research. Standpoint theorists have tried to design a research process that itself provides resources for oppressed peoples.

AGAINST INTRINSICALLY "COLONIAL" RESEARCH PROCESSES

Researchers often bring to research situations a higher social status than those they study. There is a long history of men studying women, professional researchers studying poor people, whites studying Blacks, Westerners studying people in third world countries, and heterosexuals studying "sexual deviants." In addition to this source of inequality between researcher and researched, the structurally designated relation between the researcher and the researched appears to be intrinsically socially unequal, even a "colonial" relation. Of course, feminists are certainly not the first group to be concerned about the intellectual and political effects of this structural inequality in the research situation itself (Blauner & Wellman, 1973).

Conventionally, it is the researcher, influenced by the assumptions of her discipline and her culture—not to mention of her potential funders—who decides on what social conditions, peoples, events, or processes the research project will focus and how it will be organized, conducted, interpreted, and, to a large extent, disseminated. With the assistance of peer review committees, she decides which social situations to study; what is problematic about them; which hypothesis to pursue; upon which concepts and background literatures to rely; what constitutes an appropriate research design, including the choice of methods; how to interpret, sort, analyze, and write up data into evidence; and how and to whom the results of research will be disseminated (to the extent that she can control this last). Conventionally, the researched are allotted little say in this process. Through self-discipline plus rigorous attention to disciplinary research rules, the researcher is to secure her own disinterest, impartiality, and distance from the concerns of those she studies—control of the research process is to belong entirely to her, the researcher. If this were not the case, according to conventional thinking, the project would not be sufficiently objective and scientific and would produce unreliable results.

Yet emancipatory movements have two kinds of reasons to criticize this level of researchers' control of research. One is political. It is the behaviors of the less powerful—workers, union activists, militaries, prisoners, students, potential consumers, women, welfare users, voters, already economically and politically disadvantaged races and classes, plus colonized groups (or those that the United States or England or France intended to colonize)—that the institutions funding social research have wanted to discover how to manage more effectively for their own purposes. Thus, whatever disempowerment the researched bring to the research project is added to because of the further disempowerment occasioned by research that is designed to enable powerful social institutions to manage them and their lives more effectively. Reflection on such disempowerment illuminates also reasons for the resistance dominant groups have to becoming the object of study of social scientists. "Studying up" is politically offensive to those studied.

However, the other reason is scientific: the disempowerment of the researched in the research process (as well as outside it) tends to nourish distorted accounts of their beliefs and behaviors. Left to their own devices, researchers, like the rest of us, will tend to impose on what they observe and how they interpret it the conceptual frameworks valued in their cultures and disciplines, which all too often are those valued by the already powerful groups in the larger society. Moreover, as is well known, such a colonial situation simultaneously nourishes distorted accounts of the "colonizers"—of the researchers themselves and the social groups to which they belong and that their work services. The dominant groups' perverse understandings of themselves, too, are reinforced by research that further disempowers the groups likely to be most critical of their dominance. The purportedly natural talents and abilities, good intentions, moral virtue, intelligence, and rightful authority of the dominant groups appear far less impressive from the standpoint of the lives of those they dominate.

This is not to imply that researchers do not seek to block such conceptual impositions. The histories of ethnography, sociology, and other disciplines show constant attempts to control the cultural impulses of inquirers—attempts that have been successful in many respects. Nor is it to imply that all such imposed conceptual frameworks are unreliable; many are valuable, as noted earlier, since "the stranger" often can detect patterns and causes of behavior that are difficult for "the natives" to see. Rather, the issue is that even the most well-intentioned researchers lack some of the resources that the researched possess—resources that can be used critically to evaluate the researchers' own taken-for-granted conceptual frameworks. This is the case regardless of the relative social status of researcher and researched. However, the chance that the researchers' conceptual frameworks are unreliable increases the greater the difference in social power between the observers and the observed. So the disempowerment of already politically disadvantaged research subjects tends not only to further disempower them but also to produce "bad science"—or, rather, false results from what is generally considered to be "good science" (L.T. Smith, 1999).

How can the kind of disempowering and distorting power of the researcher, apparently inherent in the research process, be blocked to prevent such colonization of research? How can this be accomplished without losing the valuable "powers of the stranger"?

Futile Strategies

First of all, the futility of several widely practiced strategies requires recognition. For example, it should be recognized that the social statuses that the researcher and researched bring to research processes are, for the most part, permanent. No amount of empathy, careful listening, or "going native," valuable as such strategies may be for various reasons, will erase the fact that the Western, white, masculine, university-educated, or international-agency-funded researcher is going to leave the research process with no less than the economic, political, and cultural resources with which he or she arrived. And the researched will leave with, for the most part, whatever such resources they brought to the research process. Of course, conventional research processes frequently do enlarge the vision of the researcher and the researched, inviting self-reflection and in other ways contributing to the ongoing personal growth of both. Yet the fundamental economic, political, and social structural inequalities that positioned the researcher and the researched in their social relation initially will not be changed by the research process alone (Blauner & Wellman, 1973). Whether the dissemination part of the process contributes to improving the social status of the researched is another matter. Clearly strategic dissemination is important, though, of course, never completely in the control of the researcher.

Another inevitably unsuccessful strategy for equalizing the power between researcher and researched—a strategy that young (and, alas, not so young) researchers attempt—is for the researcher to try to acknowledge her own social status by "confessing" it to the reader: "I, the author, am a woman of European descent, a middle-class academic, trained as a philosopher, who has lived all her life in the United States." Some such information can be useful to the reader, but for the researcher to stop her analysis of her social location here, with just the confession, is to leave all the work up to the reader. It is the reader who must figure out just how such a location has shaped the disciplinary and other conceptual frameworks used, the questions asked, how they are pursued, and so forth. Moreover, such a strategy makes the familiar and faulty assumption of individualistic liberalism—an assumption related to Rousseau's social contract and commonly made in modern Western society—that individuals are capable of voluntarily identifying all of the relevant cultural assumptions that shape their research practices. Yet Marx, Freud, and historians have taught us how self-deluding that assumption is. Of course, we should all attempt to identify such assumptions. Our research is more powerful when we can recognize how its questions and assumptions are shaped by our particular location in society and in history. However, we must also be aware that therapy and historical analysis (perhaps even social science itself) would have little work to do if each of us were that rational and prescient! Humility about the universal validity of our knowledge claims is usually an appropriate attitude.

Yet another futile strategy researchers attempt, or at least think their methods courses have directed them to pursue, is to try to forgo any theoretical or conceptual input into the research process itself. Researchers sometimes think the most useful procedure they can undertake is simply to "record the voices" of their subjects. Critics (and even misguided defenders) of standpoint approaches have often thought that this was the standpoint project. To be sure, there are good reasons to want to record the voices of all kinds of subjects. Moreover, it is valuable to recommend that researchers try to set aside their own assumptions about their objects of study when approaching a research situation, whether or not it is familiar. However,

to restrict research to just such assumption-free transcription of "voices" would be to reduce the researcher to a kind of (inevitably inaccurate) transcription machine. Instead, researchers must strategize about how to use their expertise and resources to conceptualize and articulate social relations in both the categories articulated by the groups studied and also in, paradoxically, the kinds of disciplinary and institutional languages that can be heard by public policy makers and the disciplines and institutions upon which they depend. Standpoint research aims to have effects on disciplinary priorities and practices and on public policy.[9]

So what contributions can standpoint approaches make to block the inherently colonial relations of social research? And how do they raise new philosophic and scientific questions that conventional philosophies of science ignored or disallowed? The research process can be divided into four sites where such "colonial" relations between the observer and the observed can flourish. The first is the selection of the research problem and the design of the research project: the "context of discovery." The second is the conduct of the research—the way the particular research design is carried out in fieldwork, survey, interview, observational, archival, and/or quantitative work. The third is the writing up of the research findings—the interpretation and theorization of the data. The last is the dissemination of these findings, whether dissemination procedures are intended or not by the researcher. Standpoint methodology is valuable in every part of research. Here I focus on the first stage because it is standpoint theories that have made a distinctive contribution to methodology in insisting that this stage can valuably be brought under the control of research methods, contrary to conventional disciplinary assumptions.

The Context of Discovery: Whose Questions?

Standpoint approaches innovatively recommend that the "context of discovery" be brought under methodological controls. The dominant group's values and interests perhaps most powerfully shape research projects at this stage of inquiry in ways identified earlier. Yet it is only the "context of justification" that is regarded as legitimately controllable by method. The "logic" of scientific research does indeed begin with bold conjectures, yet the sciences have designed their methods to focus only on the process of seeking the severe refutations of primarily those hypotheses that manage to get thought up by people who can get research funded. Not everyone's "bold conjectures" are counted as equally valuable when it comes to sponsoring and funding research projects. Yet in fields where research is expensive, it is only hypotheses favored by funders that reach the starting line to face the trials of attempted refutation. The issues oppressed groups do or might want to pursue frequently seem outlandish—outside "the realm of the true"—to conventional researchers. Consider, for example, the resistance to considering these feminist proposals: that it is social arrangements, not biological traits, that account for men's greater achievements in mathematics and the sciences (Fausto-Sterling, 1994); that assumptions underlying the dominant economic theory, political philosophy, and international relations are not universally valid but rather are distinctively gendered (Tickner, 2001); or that what counts as rationality and objectivity in U.S. judicial systems and philosophies of science similarly is also distinctively gendered (Jaggar, 1989; Lloyd, 1984). Thus a new question arises: which are the politically and scientifically valuable and which the problematic ways to bring the context of discovery under methodological controls? Pursuing such a question deploys a stronger kind of reflexivity—a robust attempt to evaluate critically the selection of research problems and their conceptual frameworks and methods.

One justification for seeking out standpoints available from the lives of oppressed peoples is thus that such understandings balance and can serve as important critical views on the values and interests of the funders and sponsors of research and the professional communities whose disciplinary values and interests have shaped the standards for what counts as "good research." Because feminist researchers are both trained into such communities and also members of at least one oppressed group, they are in a particularly good position to locate such critical standpoints. Of course, as members of professional communities, they are also in a

privileged group (whatever their class, race, or ethnicity of origin), so they have often designed research projects that start off from women's lives different from their own. The point here is not to rank oppressions but rather to seek analyses that take account of the kinds of oppression that can produce valuable insights in a particular research context. The kinds of starting points for research (that is, standpoints) useful in studying obstacles to women's leadership in international organizations will probably be different from those important for understanding the needs of women in U.S. prisons or of women refugees in Eastern Europe.

But how can useful standpoints be identified? Recollect that, contrary to conventional methodological prescriptions, standpoint methods are politically engaged. They are not dispassionate, disinterested, distanced, or value free. It takes politics as well as science to see beneath, behind, or through the institutional rules and practices that have been designed to serve primarily the already most economically and politically advantaged groups. Standpoint methods recognize that some kinds of passions, interests, values, and politics advance the growth of knowledge and other kinds block or limit it. Politics can be productive of the growth of knowledge as well as an obstacle to it, as, to be sure, they often are. Which such political engagements promote and which limit the growth of knowledge? The hypothesis made plausible by standpoint analyses is that vigorous commitments to pro-democratic inclusiveness, fairness, and accountability to the "worst off" can also advance the growth of knowledge. Such commitments do not automatically do so, but neither should they automatically be excluded from playing a possibly productive role in research processes.

Thus, such considerations require reevaluation of the conventional conception of objectivity, which requires maximizing value neutrality. Attempting to maximize value neutrality can block the deployment of politics that increase the inclusiveness, fairness, and accountability of research. If research is to be accountable only to disciplinary conceptual frameworks and methodological requirements that, in fact, often service ruling institutions but not the "ruled," more of such research will succeed in further entrenching these ruling conceptual frameworks and increasing the gap between the "haves" and the "have nots." The solution here is not to abandon the project of maximizing objectivity but rather to aim for a kind of objectivity that can identify and work against the values and interests shared by dominant institutions and the research communities that serve them. One proposal for such a standard has been named "strong objectivity" (Harding, 1993).

STRONG OBJECTIVITY

There is no single, fixed, eternal meaning of "objectivity." Indeed, historians have shown how it is an essentially contested concept. In modern societies, it is persistently a site for controversies over conflicting knowledge claims (Daston & Galison, 2007; Novick, 1988; Proctor, 1991). It also has no fixed referent. Objectivity, or the capacity for it, has been attributed to individuals or groups of them, knowledge communities, the results of research, and methods of research. The last of these is our focus here. Historians point out that claims to objectivity sometimes are used to advance and sometimes to retard the growth of knowledge. Such claims have been made both on behalf of and against democratic research tendencies.

Maximizing objectivity has usually been taken to require maximizing the social neutrality of research methods. This is how the goal of objectivity is "operationalized," as philosophers of science used to put the point. Good methods are supposed to be able to identify the social values, interests, and assumptions that researchers bring to the research process. If a different researcher or research group repeats the procedures first used to support a claim and if this person or group comes up with different research results, the cause of this difference may well be found in the values, interests, and assumptions that each individual or group brings to the research. This procedure—of different scientists or groups of them repeating each other's observations— works relatively well to detect those values, interests, and assumptions that differ between individual researchers or research teams. But, when social values, interests, and assumptions are shared by all or virtually all the researchers in a given field or even in a discipline, or by most people in the larger society, as has been the case for androcentrism, white supremacy, Eurocentrism, bourgeois values, and heterosexism, repeating observations within such a field, discipline, or society is in itself unlikely to bring into focus such shared social commitments. Starting off research from "outside" such a field, discipline, or society—even from just a little bit outside, such as on the margins—can enable the detection of the dominant values, interests, and assumptions in existing knowledge claims. Of course, one can never completely get "outside" one's cultural group to float freely, completely above historical and cultural specificity, as the conventional epistemologies and philosophies of science have assumed. One cannot perform the "God trick" of seeing everywhere from no particular social location at all, as Donna Haraway (1991) put the point. But finding or creating even just a little critical distance from "the normal" can be sufficient to enable new critical perspectives to come to light. Thus, standpoint theory enables us to see that the conventional notion of objectivity has been too narrow, or too weak, to achieve its goals.

However, in another respect, this notion has been too broadly understood to maximize the objectivity of research. The value-neutrality requirement has called for eliminating all social values, interests, and assumptions from the research process. Yet standpoint theorists (and other postcolonial and science studies scholars) have argued that some such values, interests, and assumptions can be productive of knowledge. In at least many contexts, feminist social commitments have contributed to the recognition of regularities of nature and social relations that were not before detected or documented. To be sure, social commitments can often block the growth of knowledge. But at least some kinds of democratic or social justice ones offer resources for expanding our knowledge.

Thus, standpoint approaches call for "strong objectivity" to replace the only weak and excessively broad "objectivist" notion characteristic of mainstream methodology and within the philosophy of science. The intrinsically "colonial" character of the research process can be diminished through requiring such stronger standards for maximizing the objectivity of research.[10]

Let us turn now to consider responses to criticisms of standpoint theory and its methodology.

RESPONSES TO CRITICISMS

Of course, conventional rationalists, empiricists, and positivists have not been happy with standpoint theory. Thoughtful feminists, too, have worried about the loss of conventional standards for objectivity, rationality, and good method (Hekman, 1997; Walby, 2001). However, one can acknowledge that the assumptions and claims of those philosophies of science looked reasonable and desirable in older social worlds but insist that we need to be skeptical about them in our very different world. We need philosophies of research that enable the growth of knowledge today, when it is not the institutions and practices of feudalism, monarchy, the Catholic Church, or the early European industrial order that shape the production of the kinds of knowledge the powerful want. In our world, those older philosophies and the social and intellectual institutions and practices established to counter such once-powerful forces have become part of our problem. Yet standpoint approaches do not abandon the value of strong standards for objectivity, rationality, and good method. Instead, they transform and strengthen these standards so that they can function effectively in today's research contexts.

Do standpoint methodologies automatically privilege "women's ways of knowing," as some critics have charged (Grant, 1987)? It is true that all feminisms value the role of women's experiences in the production of knowledge, though just what such experiences are, how they should be interpreted, and how they should be "processed" to achieve the status of knowledge are valuably contested issues. Historians and psychiatrists continually demonstrate to us that our everyday experiences look different from the perspectives of later eras and others' points of view. In therapists' offices, we frequently change our minds about just what we did experience, and the pleasures of mystery novels (not to mention of gossip) frequently depend upon surprising revisions of what we thought we saw or heard. Of course, experience is not itself public, authenticated knowledge, for the latter requires kinds of critical reflection and collective legitimation that are not characteristic of women's or anyone else's experiences in themselves. As noted earlier, standpoint knowledge requires both collective intellectual and political struggles (Hartsock, 2004). Indeed, feminist development of standpoint theory opened the way for new "polemics" about the role of collective experience in the production of knowledge (Jameson, 1988).

Do standpoint projects commit a damaging methodological and epistemological relativism? The best response is to point out that they argue for a "principled relativism" that is not damaging at all (Jameson, 1988). Nothing is damaging to the production of reliable knowledge in the kind of "social situatedness" that is used to critically examine dominant institutions and ideologies or discourses in standpoint projects. Critics here conflate the reliability of a knowledge claim with the intentions or purposes for producing it. All knowledge—positivist no less than feminist—is distinctively socially situated in ways that "get into" the content of knowledge claims and of standards for good research. All knowledge is "relative" to particular social conditions that don't exist everywhere, at every historical moment, or for all groups in any particular society. Almost half a century of postpositivist histories, sociologies, and ethnographies of science have demonstrated how scientific knowledge is always co-constituted with the forms of social relations of the sponsoring society (Jasanoff, 2004, 2005). Yet not "anything goes" for standpoint methodologies. Rather, these use such particular historical conditions to produce more reliable and comprehensive accounts of nature and social relations. Standpoint theory demands stronger standards for empirical reliability, comprehensiveness, consistency, and other regulative ideals of research as well as for such philosophic ideals as objectivity, rationality, and good method. Moreover, the fact that these research projects could be considered "mission-directed," in that they are intended to improve women's control over the conditions of their lives, does not differentiate them from the vast amount of sound scientific research produced to advance the missions of corporations, states, militaries, or medical or environmental institutions that also intend their research to improve the lives of particular groups of people. Yet no one complains that military, medical, or environmental researchers are engaged in damagingly relativist projects. So, to answer the question in the questioner's terms, standpoint methodologies do not either commit or embrace a damaging relativism.

Another criticism has focused on the practice of essentializing "women's lives," which can be found in some standpoint and other feminist accounts (not to mention in the standard sexist and androcentric, and often racist and class-biased, mainstream accounts of women's intelligence, morality, strength, social roles, biologically determined destinies, etc.). To be sure, some standpoint writings have generalized from the lives only of women like the accounts' authors, falsely assuming an intrinsic "essence" to womanliness (and to manliness). They have thereby ignored and made invisible important differences in the conditions of women (and of men) in different ethnicities, races, classes, and other social and cultural contexts. However, this kind of no-longer-tolerable error is not itself a part of standpoint theory, as one can see by contemplating the theory's eloquent developments in the work, for example, of Patricia Hill Collins, bell hooks, Gloria Anzaldúa, and other women of color. Indeed, whether or not articulated in the language of standpoint theory, similar epistemologies and methodologies have arisen in virtually every other social justice movement of recent decades. "Things look different from the perspective of our lives," they say. Thus antiracist, postcolonial, disability, and lesbian, gay, and queer theories each make standpoint arguments in defense of the kinds of knowledge production needed and desired to better empower their constituents.[11]

Two more disputes deserve brief mention. Yes, standpoint theory is indeed useful for the natural sciences, though it was initially developed primarily with a focus on social science research. Yet, as was demonstrated in the work of feminist and antiracist researchers working on biology, the environment, and even physics, starting off from the lives of disadvantaged groups can indeed stimulate new questions about the "natural world" and how we come to know it (Rose, 1983; Fausto-Sterling, 1994; Seager, 2003; Traweek, 1988). Finally, there have been continuing debates over whether standpoint theory

is fundamentally a modern or postmodern research project. "Both" seems the soundest response. (See, e.g., Harding, 2004a.)

TRANSFORMATIONS

I have been alluding to some changes in how standpoint methodologies have been conceptualized and used since their emergence in the feminist writings of the 1970s and 1980s. Four of the most important of these changes can be summarized in the following ways. First, their dissemination has vastly increased as researchers have taken them up in different social and natural science research contexts. Standpoint methodologies are now widely used in all social science disciplines, and even in biology and other disciplines that often must address their objects of research through both natural and social science resources (such as medical and environmental research, engineering, architecture, and urban planning). And their "logic of research" can now be recognized as a central feature of knowledge projects in every social justice movement around the globe.

Second, as the use of these methodologies has expanded, so, too, has their controversiality. They do indeed engage with some of the most fundamental social anxieties confronting states and cultures around the globe today. One such issue is the high value they place on women's (or feminist) experiences as the starting point for thinking about concerns considered "not women's business," such as economic and political relations. They legitimate women's experiences as scientifically valuable. Yet these gender concerns turn out to be just one example of the social justice inequities that have shaped how a standpoint "logic of inquiry" can be heard in debates and discussions around the globe. Standpoint methodologies legitimate the distinctive questions, perspectives, and even moral and political demands arising from each and every group treated inequitably. Thus, standpoint projects are unlikely to lose their controversial character as long as such inequalities persist.

However, in the third place, it has become clear that standpoint methodologies take on their own distinctive "local" characters as they are used to challenge the dominant forms that such inequality takes in different disciplines, cultures, and colonial histories, to mention just three such kinds of "local" research contexts. For example, the concerns of standpoint methodologies in philosophy, sociology, and political science are significantly different as the theorists seek to raise standpoint issues within ongoing disciplinary concerns. (See, for example, the differences between such concerns in the three readers mentioned in the first section of this chapter.) We must speak of standpoint methodologies or epistemologies in the plural, even as we can identify their shared distinctive "logic of research."

Finally, it has become clear to many observers that well-intentioned members of dominant social groups can play important roles in advancing standpoint knowledge. For example, male feminists can educate themselves about the realities of women's lives and then use standpoint methodologies to start off their own original feminist research projects from women's lives (e.g., Digby, 1997; Harding, 1997). And many postcolonial scholars who are themselves members of formerly colonizing groups have made important contributions to postcolonial theory by starting off their analyses from the lives of the colonized or formerly colonized. Of course, members of dominant groups have not had the everyday experiences of oppressed groups and so may be less sensitive to subtle forms of discrimination. Yet researchers, regardless of their history of everyday experience, routinely ask others to give them feedback on their research projects—from beginning to end, if they are wise. And collaborative research between academics and, for example, indigenous peoples has become widespread in some fields such as anthropology. To be sure, research on oppressed groups by members of their oppressor group remains highly contentious for those who do take standpoints to be restricted to identity projects focused on the standpoint created by the researchers' own social group. However, no one can "fly off the face of the earth" and understand the world with the insights later historians can bring to such a project. So such a restriction seems to makes no sense. A Black feminist standpoint must be created initially by Black women, but the rest of us would be intellectually and morally remiss not to start off our own thoughts about dominant social institutions from the lives of Black women, too, as revealed in their own accounts.

CONCLUSION

In their almost three-decade history, standpoint theories have learned to make intellectual use of economic, social, psychological, and cultural inequalities and heterogeneities. Bringing into focus accounts of nature and social relations as these emerge from the lives of many different subjugated groups broadens the horizons of our understanding of how nature and social relations work in different social contexts. As we have noted, it is not that these subjugated understandings are automatically the best ones on sound empirical and theoretical grounds, but usually they are. Additionally, they can lead to the identification of undetected problematic or interesting natural and social phenomena, suggest different hypotheses and conceptual frameworks for investigating them, suggest different lines of evidence and challenges to favored evidence practices, uncover unnoticed cultural tendencies in the writing up of data, and make strong arguments for dissemination practices that benefit the least advantaged social groups. Moreover, investigating questions of importance to disadvantaged groups, instead of only those of importance to corporations, states, militaries, and other "ruling" groups, enables these disadvantaged groups to gain greater control over the conditions of their lives.

The ideal conditions for producing reliable knowledge require genuinely democratic societies in which inequality has already disappeared and no group is or can legitimately be silenced through formal or informal means. All citizens, then, could be equally articulate and effective in the selection of problems to research, the specification of what is problematic about them, the selection of a conceptual framework and methods of research, and so on. Of course, we do not have such a situation and are unlikely ever to attain it. My point—and the argument of standpoint theorists—is that standpoint epistemologies, philosophies of science, sociologies of knowledge, methodologies, and their political resources can help move toward such a goal.

One contribution standpoint theory can offer to such struggles is to help those of us who do occupy relatively powerful social locations to see ourselves and our conceptual practices as others see both.

Noted previously are some of the main reasons that standpoint theory remains contentious. Another source of debate between standpoint theorists from different disciplines arises from the often highly successful efforts to enter standpoint arguments into prevailing disciplinary debates. Of course, these are quite different in, for example, sociology, political philosophy, and the philosophy of science, as noted already.[12] All too often, researchers and scholars from one discipline seem completely unaware of the lively disputes occurring in a neighboring discipline. We can appreciate the multiple and complex relations that standpoint approaches to research have to disciplinarity. They can reasonably appear to be multidisciplinary, as they draw on the insights of several disciplines; antidisciplinary, as they criticize the "complicity with power" of disciplinary conceptual frameworks; transdisciplinary, as they follow a "logic" of research that has proved fruitful in many disciplines; and, paradoxically, deeply disciplinary as they attempt to make space in disciplinary conceptual frameworks for addressing issues important to women and other disadvantaged groups.

After all this controversy, what is significant is that standpoint theory appears not only to have survived but also to be flourishing anew after almost four decades of lively debate about and within it. It is by now so widely used in the social sciences and biology that it would be surprising to find any more big debates at professional meetings or in the journals of these disciplines over what it is and how to use it. That does not mean that everyone loves it. Yet, disturbing though virtually everyone may find one or another of its claims and projects, standpoint theory apparently is destined to persist at least for a while as a seductively volatile site for reflection and debate about persistent research dilemmas as well as contemporary social and political anxieties more generally. For those of us who hold that sciences and their societies co-constitute and coproduce each other, standpoint methodologies provide a compelling model for how to use these concepts as actors' (agents') categories, not just as analytic categories (Jasanoff, 2004).[13] We can try to transform our sciences to model the kinds of larger social relations we want to bring into existence, and vice versa.

Discussion Questions

1. What should a standpoint methodology do? How does it differ from an ethnography? How does Dorothy Smith's institutional ethnography differ from more conventional ethnographies?

2. How are conventional attempts to maximize objectivity conceptualized too narrowly? In what respect are they conceptualized too broadly?

3. How could one legitimately reject the charge that standpoint research is dangerously relativist?

4. How does standpoint methodology provide a transdisciplinary "logic of research"?

5. Describe examples of existing research projects that use a standpoint methodology to study issues about class, race, ethnicity, postcoloniality, sexuality, or disability.

Online Resources

The Feminist Theory Website

http://www.cddc.vt.edu/feminism/enin.html

This website is a scholarly research resource on feminist theory with an emphasis on different national, ethnic, and global feminisms.

The Theory Project: Sandra Harding

http://lilt.ilstu.edu/theory/authors/harding.htm

The Theory Project provides an audio interview with Sandra Harding (and a written summary) on the topic of standpoint theory.

Relevant Journals

Gender & Society

Hypatia: A Feminist Journal of Philosophy

Sociological Theory

NOTES

1. Parts of this chapter borrow from earlier versions of Harding (2003).

2. For examples, see Hekman (1997), with responses by Collins, Hartsock, Smith, and Harding in the same issue; Walby (2001), with responses by Harding and by Sprague in the same issue; and, most recently, essays from two American Philosophical Association programs that appear in *Hypatia* 2008 (vol. 23, no. 4) and 2009 (vol. 24, no. 4).

3. Jameson's examples were the work of Hartsock, Jaggar, and Harding.

4. Hartsock (1983/2003), Jaggar (1983), and Pels (2004) also review the Marxian history of this approach.

5. Representatives of similar researcher positions appear in Anzaldúa's (1987) "borderlands" consciousness, hooks's (1983) "theory from margin to center," and Dorothy Smith's (1987) "bifurcated consciousness" of the woman sociology graduate student. W. E. B. Dubois's "double consciousness" of African Americans is one precursor of this kind of positioning.

6. These themes are expressed here in a form that is closest to Hartsock's (1983/2003) account.

7. Note that this theme echoes standard beliefs about the effectiveness of scientific methods: Which interactions with, or kinds of observations of, natural and social worlds are pursued both enables and limits what one can know.

8. I use the term *ideology* here to mean systems of false interested beliefs, not just of any interested beliefs.

9. This is as good a place as any to point out that standpoint research uses both qualitative and quantitative methods, since the resources of each often can usefully inform the other in any kind of social science research project. Moreover, one should keep in mind that standpoint methodologies are also shaping research projects in such fields as medical, environmental, archaeological, engineering, and biotechnological research where the objects of study can have both social and natural properties (as, of course, the objects of social research always also do).

10. Other influential feminist revisions of the notion of objectivity may be found in the work of two physicists, Evelyn Fox Keller (1983/2003) and Karen Barad (2007).

11. See, for example, Walter Mignolo's (2000) account of the importance of using the lens (methodology?) of "colonial difference" to understand the history of colonial effects on Latin Americans. In an earlier book (Mignolo, 1995), he referred to this as the standpoint of Latin Americans, citing Anzaldúa (1987).

12. Compare, for example, the Campbell and Manicom (1995) reader focused on sociologist Dorothy Smith's work and the Kenney and Kinsella (1997) reader focused on political philosopher Nancy Hartsock's work.

13. See Jasanoff's own first two chapters for illuminating overviews of historical and sociological studies demonstrating that sciences and their social orders do indeed bring each other into existence: they co-constitute or coproduce each other.

REFERENCES

Anzaldúa, Gloria. (1987). *Borderlands/La frontera.* San Francisco: Spinsters/Aunt Lute.

Barad, Karen. (2007). *Meeting the universe halfway: Quantum physics and the entanglement of matter and meaning.* Durham, NC: Duke University Press.

Barker, Drucilla. (2005). Beyond women and economics: Rereading women's work. *Signs: Journal of Women in Culture and Society, 30*(4), 2189–2209.

Barker, Drucilla, & Feiner, Susan F. (2005). *Liberating economics: Feminist perspectives on families, work, and globalization.* Ann Arbor: University of Michigan Press.

Blauner, Robert, & Wellman, David. (1973). Toward the decolonization of social research. In Joyce A. Ladner (Ed.), *The death of white sociology* (pp. 310–330). New York: Random House.

Campbell, Marie, & Manicom, Ann. (Eds.). (1995). *Knowledge, experience, and ruling relations: Studies in the social organization of knowledge.* Toronto: University of Toronto Press.

Collins, Patricia Hill. (1986). Learning from the outsider within: The sociological significance of black feminist thought. *Social Problems, 33*(6), S14–S32. (Reprinted in Harding, 2004a)

Collins, Patricia Hill. (1991). *Black feminist thought: Knowledge, consciousness, and the politics of empowerment.* New York: Routledge.

Cooke, Bill, & Kothari, Uma. (Eds.). (2001). *Participation: The new tyranny?* New York: Zed Press.

Daston, Lorraine, & Galison, Peter. (2007). *Objectivity.* New York: Zone Books.

Digby, Tom. (Ed.). (1997). *Men doing feminism.* New York: Routledge.

Di Stefano, Christine. (1990). Dilemmas of difference. In Linda J. Nicholson (Ed.), *Feminism/postmodernism* (pp. 63–82). New York: Routledge.

Fausto-Sterling, Anne. (1994). *Myths of gender: Biological theories about women and men.* New York: Basic Books.

Flax, Jane. (1990). Postmodernism and gender relations in feminist theory. In Linda J. Nicholson (Ed.), *Feminism/postmodernism* (pp. 39–62). New York: Routledge.

Freire, Paulo. (1970). *Pedagogy of the oppressed.* New York: Herder & Herder.

Gilligan, Carol. (1982). *In a different voice: Psychological theory and women's development.* Cambridge, MA: Harvard University Press.

Grant, Judith. (1987). I feel, therefore I am: A critique of female experience as the basis for a feminist epistemology. *Women and Politics, 7*(3), 99–114.

Gross, Paul R., & Levitt, Norman. (1994). *Higher superstition: The academic left and its quarrels with science.* Baltimore: Johns Hopkins University Press.

Hacking, Ian. 1983. *Representing and intervening.* Cambridge, UK: Cambridge University Press.

Haraway, Donna. (1978). Animal sociology and a natural economy of the body politic, Parts 1 and 2. *Signs: Journal of Women in Culture and Society, 4*(1), 21–36; 37–60.

Haraway, Donna. (1981). In the beginning was the word: The genesis of biological theory. *Signs: Journal of Women in Culture and Society, 6*(3), 469–481.

Haraway, Donna. (1989). *Primate visions: Gender, race, and nature in the world of modern science.* New York: Routledge.

Haraway, Donna. (1991). Situated knowledges: The science question in feminism and the privilege of partial perspectives. In Donna Haraway, *Simians, cyborgs, and women* (pp. 183–202). New York: Routledge. (Reprinted in Harding, 2004a)

Harding, Sandra. (1986). *The science question in feminism.* Ithaca, NY: Cornell University Press.

Harding, Sandra (Ed.). (1987). *Feminism and methodology: Social science issues.* Bloomington: Indiana University Press.

Harding, Sandra. (1991). *Whose science? Whose knowledge? Thinking from women's lives.* Ithaca, NY: Cornell University Press.

Harding, Sandra. (1993). Rethinking standpoint epistemology. In L. Alcoff & E. Potter (Eds.), *Feminist epistemologies* (pp. 49–82). New York: Routledge. (Excerpted in Harding, 2004a)

Harding, Sandra. (1997). Can men be the subjects of feminist thought? In Tom Digby (Ed.), *Men doing feminism* (pp. 171–195). New York: Routledge.

Harding, Sandra. (1998). *Is science multicultural? Postcolonialisms, feminisms, and epistemologies.* Bloomington: Indiana University Press.

Harding, Sandra. (2003). How standpoint methodology informs philosophy of social science. In Stephen P. Turner & Paul A. Roth (Eds.), *The Blackwell guide to the philosophy of the social sciences* (pp. 291–310). New York: Blackwell.

Harding, Sandra. (2003). Why has the sex/gender system become visible only now? In Sandra Harding & Merrill B. Hintikka (Eds.), *Discovering reality: Feminist perspectives on epistemology, metaphysics, methodology, and philosophy of science* (pp. 311–324). Dordrecht, The Netherlands: Kluwer Academic Publishers. (Original work published 1983)

Harding, Sandra. (Ed.). (2004a). *The feminist standpoint theory reader: Intellectual and political controversies.* New York: Routledge.

Harding, Sandra. (2004b). Introduction: Standpoint theory as a site of political, philosophic, and scientific debate. In Sandra Harding (Ed.), *The feminist standpoint theory reader: Intellectual and political controversies* (pp. 1–16). New York: Routledge.

Harding, Sandra. (2008). *Sciences from below: Feminisms, postcolonialities, and modernities.* Durham: Duke University Press.

Harding, Sandra. (2009). Postcolonial and feminist science and technology studies: Convergences and dissonances. *Postcolonial Studies, 12*(4), 401–421.

Hartsock, Nancy. (1987). Rethinking modernism: Minority vs. majority theories. *Cultural Critique, 7,* 187–206.

Hartsock, Nancy. (1998). The feminist standpoint revisited. In Nancy Hartsock, *The feminist standpoint revisited and other essays* (pp. 227–248). Boulder, CO: Westview Press.

Hartsock, Nancy. (2003). The feminist standpoint: Developing the ground for a specifically feminist historical materialism. In Sandra Harding & Merrill Hintikka (Eds.), *Discovering reality* (pp. 283–310). Dordrecht, The Netherlands: Reidel/Kluwer. (Original work published 1983)

Hartsock, Nancy. (2004). The feminist standpoint: Developing the ground for a specifically feminist historical materialism. In Sandra Harding (Ed.), *The feminist standpoint theory reader: Intellectual and political controversies* (pp. 35–54). New York: Routledge.

Hekman, Susan. (1997). Truth and method: Feminist standpoint theory revisited. *Signs: Journal of Women in Culture and Society, 22*(2), 341–365. (See also responses by Patricia Hill Collins, Sandra Harding, Nancy Hartsock, and Dorothy Smith, as well as Hekman's reply, in the same issue, pp. 367–402; Reprinted in Harding, 2004a)

Hess, David J. (1995). *Science and technology in a multicultural world: The cultural politics of facts and artifacts.* New York: Columbia University Press.

Hirschmann, Nancy. (1997). Feminist standpoint as postmodern strategy. In Sally J. Kenney & Helen Kinsella (Eds.), *Politics and feminist standpoint theories* (pp. 73–92). New York: The Haworth Press, Inc. (Reprinted in Harding, 2004a)

hooks, bell. (1983). *Feminist theory: From margin to center.* Boston: South End Press.

hooks, bell. (1990). Choosing the margin as a space of radical openness. In bell hooks, *Yearning: Race, gender, and cultural politics* (pp. 145–153). Boston: South End Press.

Jaggar, Alison. (1983). Feminist politics and epistemology: Justifying feminist theory. In Alison Jaggar, *Feminist politics and human nature* (pp. 353–394). Totowa, NJ: Rowman and Allenheld. (Excerpted in Harding, 2004a)

Jaggar, Alison. (1989). Love and knowledge: Emotion in feminist epistemology. In Alison Jaggar & Susan Bordo (Eds.), *Gender/body/knowledge: Feminist reconstructions of being and knowing,* (pp. 145–171). New Brunswick, NJ: Rutgers University Press.

Jameson, Fredric. (1988). "History and class consciousness" as an unfinished project. *Rethinking Marxism, 1,* 49–72. (Excerpted and revised in Harding, 2004a)

Jasanoff, Sheila. (Ed.). (2004). *States of knowledge: The co-production of science and social order.* New York: Routledge.

Jasanoff, Sheila. (2005). *Designs on nature: Science and democracy in Europe and the United States.* Princeton, NJ: Princeton University Press.

Keller, Evelyn Fox. (2003). Gender and science. In Sandra Harding & Merrill Hintikka (Eds.), *Discovering reality: Feminist perspectives on epistemology, metaphysics, methodology, and philosophy of science* (pp. 187–206). Dordrecht, The Netherlands: Kluwer. (Original work published 1983)

Kenney, Sally J., & Kinsella, Helen. (Eds.). (1997). *Politics and feminist standpoint theories.* New York: The Haworth Press, Inc. (Published simultaneously as a special issue of *Women & Politics, 18*[3])

Kesby, Mike. (2005). Retheorizing empowerment-through-participation as a performance in space: Beyond tyranny to transformation. *Signs: Journal of Women in Culture and Society, 30*(4), 2037–2065.

Kuhn, Thomas S. (1970). *The structure of scientific revolutions* (2nd ed.). Chicago: University of Chicago Press. (Original work published 1962)

Lakatos, Imre, & Musgrave, Alan. (Eds.). (1970). *Criticism and the growth of knowledge.* New York: Cambridge University Press.

Lloyd, Genevieve. (1984). *The man of reason: "Male" and "female" in Western philosophy.* Minneapolis: University of Minnesota Press.

Lukács, Georg. (1971). *History and class consciousness* (Rodney Livingstone, Trans.). Cambridge: MIT Press. (Original work published 1923)

MacKinnon, Catherine A. (1982). Feminism, Marxism, method, and the state: An agenda for theory. *Signs: Journal of Women in Culture and Society, 7*(3), 515–544.

MacKinnon, Catherine A. (1983). Feminism, Marxism, method, and the state: Toward feminist jurisprudence. *Signs: Journal of Women in Culture and Society, 8*(4), 635–658.

Maguire, Patricia. (1987). *Doing participatory research: A feminist approach.* Amherst, MA: The Center for International Education, University of Massachusetts.

Mannheim, Karl. (1954). *Ideology and utopia: An introduction to the sociology of knowledge.* New York: Harcourt, Brace & Co. (Original work published 1936)

McTaggart, Robin. (Ed.). (1997). *Participatory action research: International contexts and consequences.* Albany: State University of New York Press.

Merton, Robert. (1972). Insiders and outsiders: A chapter in the sociology of knowledge. *American Journal of Sociology, 78*(1), 9–47.

Mignolo, Walter. (1995) *The darker side of the Renaissance: Literacy, territoriality, and colonization.* Ann Arbor: University of Michigan Press.

Mignolo, Walter. (2000). *Local histories/global designs: Coloniality, subaltern knowledges, and border thinking.* Princeton, NJ: Princeton University Press.

Needham, Joseph. (1969). *The grand titration: Science and society in east and west.* Toronto: University of Toronto Press.

Novick, Peter. (1988). *That noble dream: The "objectivity question" and the American historical profession.* Cambridge, UK: Cambridge University Press.

Pels, Dick. (2004). Strange standpoints, or how to define the situation for situated knowledge. In Sandra Harding (Ed.), *The feminist standpoint theory reader* (pp. 273–290). New York: Routledge.

Petras, E. M., & Porpora, D. V. (1993). Participatory research: Three models and an analysis. *The American Sociologist, 23*(1), 107–126.

Proctor, Robert. (1991). *Value-free science? Purity and power in modern knowledge.* Cambridge, MA: Harvard University Press.

Reiter (Rapp), Rayna. (1975). *Toward an anthropology of women.* New York: Monthly Review Press.

Rose, Hilary. (1983). Hand, brain, and heart: A feminist epistemology for the natural sciences. *Signs: Journal of Women in Culture and Society, 9*(1), 73–90.

Rouse, Joseph. (2004). Feminism and the social construction of scientific knowledge. In Sandra Harding (Ed.), *The feminist standpoint theory reader* (pp. 353–374). New York: Routledge.

Ruddick, Sara. (2004). Maternal thinking as a feminist standpoint. In Sandra Harding (Ed.), *The feminist standpoint theory reader* (pp. 161–168). New York: Routledge. (Original work published 1989)

Sachs, Wolfgang. (Ed.). (1992). *The development dictionary: A guide to knowledge as power.* Atlantic Highlands, NJ: Zed Press.

Seager, Joni. (2003). Rachel Carson died of breast cancer: The coming of age of feminist environmentalism. *Signs: Journal of Women in Culture and Society, 28*(3), 945–972.

Selin, Helaine. (Ed.). (2008). *Encyclopedia of the history of science, technology, and medicine in non-Western cultures* (2nd ed.). Dordrecht, The Netherlands: Kluwer.

Simmel, Georg. (1921). The sociological significance of the "stranger." In Robert E. Park & Ernest W. Burgess (Eds.), *Introduction to the science of sociology.* Chicago: University of Chicago Press.

Smith, Dorothy E. (1987). *The everyday world as problematic: A sociology for women.* Boston: Northeastern University Press.

Smith, Dorothy E. (1990a). *The conceptual practices of power: A feminist sociology of knowledge.* Boston: Northeastern University Press.

Smith, Dorothy E. (1990b). *Texts, facts, and femininity: Exploring the relations of ruling.* New York: Routledge.

Smith, Dorothy E. (1999). *Writing the social: Critique, theory, and investigations.* Toronto: University of Toronto Press.

Smith, Dorothy E. (2005). *Institutional ethnography: A sociology for people.* Lanham, MD: Rowman and Littlefield.

Smith, Linda Tuhiwahi. (1999). *Decolonizing methodologies: Research and indigenous peoples.* New York: Zed Press.

Tickner, J. Ann. (2001). *Gendering world politics: Issues and approaches in the post-cold war era.* New York: Columbia University Press.

Traweek, Sharon. (1988). *Beamtimes and life times.* Cambridge, MA: MIT Press.

Walby, Sylvia. (2001). Against epistemological chasms: The science question in feminism revisited. *Signs: Journal of Women in Culture and Society, 26*(2), 485–510. (See also responses in the same issue by Joey Sprague and Sandra Harding, as well as Walby's reply, pp. 511–540)

Weeks, Kathi. (1998). *Constituting feminist subjects.* Ithaca, NY: Cornell University Press.

Wylie, Alison. (2004). Why standpoint matters. In Sandra Harding (Ed.), *The feminist standpoint theory reader* (pp. 339–352). New York: Routledge. (Original work published 2003)

4

POSTMODERN, POST-STRUCTURAL, AND CRITICAL THEORIES

Susanne Gannon and Bronwyn Davies

Principles of Postmodern, Post-Structural, and Critical Theories

In this chapter, we explore, both separately and together, the emergence of postmodern, post-structural, and critical theories as they have been taken up in feminist research. These three theoretical positions are vital to feminism in that they offer radical strategies for bringing about change. These frameworks are, however, quite slippery and hard to pin down, not the least because they are, in some times and some places, used as if they were interchangeable. At other times and in other places, one will be used to clarify what the other is not. There is, then, no orderly, agreed upon, and internally consistent set of ideas that sits obediently under each of these headings. But each one of them, along with the disputed ground between them, has produced new ideas that have helped feminists break loose from previously taken-for-granted assumptions about issues such as subjectivity, performativity, politics, and language.

We will begin, then, by outlining what these three approaches have in common and then, in a later section, separate them out to see how they take up their own particular approach, sometimes in common and sometimes in opposition. In the latter part of the chapter, we elaborate feminist research strategies, including deconstructive writing practices and collective biography, that have emerged within these post-positivist paradigms.

In the early 1990s, in the United States, Judith Butler found that postmodernism was often characterized as a monster by scholars who wanted to hold onto the familiar, common-sense set of assumptions that underpinned their research, assumptions that postmodernism was actively putting under erasure.[1] Postmodernism targeted for demolition the centrality of the individualized human subject, the dominance of rationality as a mode of knowing, and the realist claim that language can adequately describe the real world. The opponents of postmodernism tried, in Butler's words, "to shore up the primary premises, to establish in advance that any theory of politics requires a subject, needs from the start to presume its subject, the referentiality of language, the integrity of the institutional description it provides" (Butler, 1992, p. 3). In that time and place "the postmodern" was taken to be inclusive of poststructuralism and, in some cases, of critical theory. It's a complicated story.

In what follows, we will explore some of the commonalities and oppositionalities and attempt to sketch a map that makes visible some of the ideas and practices that emerge separately and collectively within these three frameworks. We will extract a set of principles that broadly characterize the field that sets them apart from more familiar understandings of research and the social world. Our account of these perspectives is not written from a distance. It is not informed by a positivist ideal of objectivity nor written as if each theory can (or even should) be pinned down once and for all. Every definition creates exclusions that might be contested, and, as long as the ideas are alive in people's work, they will be changing. We will, with this caveat on categorizing, begin by mapping the principles that make a coherent story of the interconnections between postmodern, post-structural, and critical theories as they are taken up by feminist researchers.

Theoretical paradigms can, generally, be mapped in terms of their understanding of what it is that research aims to do. Different paradigms open different questions and analytical endeavors. In Lather's (1991) account, the earlier forms of research, characterized as positivist and interpretive, aimed to "predict" and "understand" (p. 7). To this end, they adopted a naturalistic or realist approach in which the researcher was understood as separate from the research, and the social world was independent of the researcher's gaze. This is in marked contrast to later work that aims to "emancipate." Emancipatory research sets out to make a difference to the social world and to emancipate subordinated groups from oppressive versions of reality. The "critical theory" signaled in our title maintains this commitment to emancipation, along with neo-Marxist and praxis-oriented social research. In contrast to the paradigms located before the deconstructivist break, "post theories," including postmodern and post-structural theory, work to trouble "all major

epistemological, ontological, and methodological concepts" (Lather, 2007, p. 164). While feminist paradigms emerged with emancipatory intentions, they have, as we will show, exceeded this original placement and moved to incorporate deconstruction (Lather, 2007). These deconstructive movements will be the main topic of this chapter and include a careful comparison to critical theory. Our account is not offered as a grand narrative of the progress of feminist theory from one approach to another. Such grand narratives exclude other ways of seeing, privilege accounts from those with power, and promote falsely linear versions of history. *It is a first principle, then, of critical, post-structural, and postmodern approaches to feminism that objectivity must be carefully rethought. An account, from these perspectives, is always situated. It is an account from somewhere, and some time, and some one, written for some purpose and with a particular audience in mind. It is always therefore a partial and particular account, an account that has its own power to produce new ways of seeing and that should always be open to contestation.* In this view of feminism, we do not rely on objective truth but on "being accountable for what and how we have the power to see" (Castor, 1991, p. 64).

In this section, we outline some further principles of deconstructive work and discuss how feminists have taken these up in their research. We will also point out how, and on what grounds, some feminists have been alarmed by the effects of deconstructive thinking on emancipatory feminist action and research and writing practices.

This chapter—and indeed the practices of the research to be discussed here—can be read as a simultaneous and constant weaving and unweaving of how we think and what we do and say in feminist research. *This is a second principle. Particular attention must be paid to the mode of writing, to the discursive strategies through which particular versions of the world are accomplished, especially in the present moment of writing.* In the figure of the weaver, simultaneously weaving and unweaving who she is, we ask you to consider the stuff of her weaving as the discursive threads of what is possible (nameable, seeable, doable, speakable, writeable) at any particular moment in time and place—and from a particular situated position. Feminist writers such as Laurel Richardson (1997) and

Trinh T. Minh-ha (1989, 1991, 1992) draw attention to the weft and weave of research texts and the subjectivities realized within them. Acute reflexivity—especially at the very moment of writing—is necessary for researchers working within critical, postmodern, and post-structural frameworks. By this we do not mean a reflexivity that examines the self of the researcher, but one that examines the language being used and its effects (Davies et al., 2004).

A further principle of these theoretical frameworks has to do with questions of power, emancipation, freedom, and agency. *Our third principle is that relations of power are understood as established and maintained through discourse and through positions taken up and made possible within particular discourses* (Davies & Harré, 2000; Davies, 2008b). Power is seen as complex and unstable. Agency, resistance, "freedom," and emancipation are always contingent and limited. These concepts are treated differently within critical, postmodern, and post-structural theories: indeed, their different takes on power, freedom, and agency act as distinguishing features between them, as we will show in the next section.

One aspect of discourse that has received a great deal of attention is its taken-for-granted use of binary categories. *A fourth principle is that we must be aware of binary categories with their capacity to limit and constrain how we think and what we imagine to be possible.* These binary categories—such as man/woman and good/evil—are implicated in dividing and constraining the world in ways that may be violent in their effects, positioning those categorized as belonging in subordinate categories, for example, as inferior. The discursive naturalizing and normalizing of the categories makes their membership, along with their characteristics, appear to be inevitable.

Despite the apparent orderliness of binary thought, categories tend to slip around and to glue themselves onto other binaries, conflating one with another. For example, "feminist" may be conflated with "woman" (and, conversely, "not-feminist" with "man"). The conflation of "not-feminist" with misogyny or patriarchy is a further binary move. Some of the binaries found glued to each other in Western traditions of mythology, and that continue to inform our

cultures and social practices, bind male with knowledge and female with ignorance, male with reason and female with emotion, and so on (Wilshire, 1989).

While critical feminism seeks to emancipate people within subordinated categories, postmodern and post-structural feminisms search for ways to disrupt the grip that binaries have on thought and on identity. Disruptive strategies include deconstructive writing that draws not only on rational argument but also on poetic writing, on fiction, on music, and on the performing arts (Speedy, 2008). Sometimes it rewrites figures from the past (e.g., Cixous, 1991; Clément, 1989). Through play with language and alternative forms of narrative and representation, such writing can blur the gender binaries, making a deconstructive move from either/or to both/and, disrupting, deconstructing, troubling the clichés and stereotypes of everyday thought and practice in which we are enmeshed.

It is here that we run into one of the deepest divisions within the approaches we are writing about in this chapter. The disruptive, deconstructive work on everyday binary categories may be read by those working within the critical framework to have destroyed the categories and thus made them unusable for the work of emancipation. But the "deconstructive" work is not "destruction." Butler (2004a), for example, suggests that calling terms into question doesn't mean debunking them but leads, rather, to their revitalization and the possibility of using them to do quite different work. The terms and the categories that post-structuralist and postmodernist feminists wish to deconstruct are nonetheless powerful categories that have a great deal of political purchase. In drawing attention to their constitutive power, a deconstructive approach does not foreclose the use of categories on behalf of those who are subordinated by them. In a double move that is characteristic of deconstructive writing, post-structuralist feminists continue to use particular categories, such as *woman* or *feminist*, but work to destabilize some of the categories' certainties. We can put them "*sous rature*" or "under erasure," following Derrida (1976), perhaps using a textual reminder—woman, feminist—to stand as a reminder that we both need the concept and are wary of some of its dangers. *A fifth and important principle of thought is this deep skepticism toward assumed truths and taken-for-granted knowledges, as they are generated through language, combined with a pragmatic understanding of the power of those categories to effect powerful positionalities and actions within the social world.*

Deconstructive approaches to feminism eschew simple recipes and actions in favor of a complex and continuous reflection on the ways in which subjectivities, realities, and desires are established and maintained. But these approaches do not prevent action. Feminists are capable of working within multiple discourses, depending on the social and interactive contexts in which they find themselves, on the particular moment in history, and on the particular task at hand. By making discourse and discursive practices visible, deconstructive approaches undermine the power of dominant discourses, making their messages less self-evident, less able to create normative frameworks inside of which choice is radically reduced. Whereas critical feminism is up-front about confronting existing power structures and practices, deconstructive approaches are busy shifting the ground in such a way that what previously seemed normal and natural becomes unthinkable.

Critical Theory, Postmodernism, and Post-Structuralism: Their Emergence and Interconnections

Critical Theory

Many post-structural and postmodern feminist writers began as critical theorists and maintain a strong critical edge in their writing (e.g., Haug et al., 1987; Henriques, Hollway, Urwin, Venn, & Walkerdine, 1984/1998; Lather, 1991, 2007; Walkerdine, 1990). Critical theory, as a formal description of a particular mode of research and analysis, first emerged in the Frankfurt School of social research in Germany in the 1920s and 1930s through the work of Adorno, Horkheimer, and, later, Marcuse and Habermas. These philosopher-sociologists rejected fixed notions of hierarchies of social domination. They disrupted disciplinary authority by critiquing the supposedly objective "view from nowhere" of a positivist social science that had been modeled on the natural sciences and had emerged from Enlightenment beliefs in universal reason and objective thought. They developed a

reflexive and critical social inquiry that saw social scientific knowledge itself as implicated in complex modes of production and regimes of truth. In so doing, they historicized and contextualized social science for the first time. Their work highlighted the logocentrism of Western rationalist and liberal humanist thought and questioned the belief that reason is universal, disinterested, and dispassionate and can set us free. However, they did not abandon the tenets of Enlightenment thought—the belief in reason and the rational subject. Rather than dismantle them, they reconstructed them as sociocultural forms. In contrast to some of their successors, they resisted the lure of relativism and remained committed to the belief that truth is possible and can ground social action. For the social theorists of the Frankfurt School, emancipation was part of the goal. This aspect of their work has threaded through into the liberatory discourses of contemporary critical theory.

Critical theorists continue to be influential in qualitative research in diverse disciplinary and geographic locations. Current critical theory utilizes discourses of equity, inclusion, and social justice that are familiar and compatible with feminist agendas. Lincoln and Denzin (2003) note that

> the critique and concern of the critical theorists has been an effort to design a pedagogy of resistance within communities of difference. The pedagogy of resistance, of taking back "voice," of reclaiming narrative for one's own rather than adapting to the narratives of a dominant majority . . . [aims at] overturning oppression and achieving social justice through empowerment of the marginalized, the poor, the nameless, the voiceless. (pp. 625–626)

Grand claims are made for the potential of critical theories to change the world. Kincheloe and McLaren (2003), for instance, claim that they produce "dangerous knowledge, the kind of information and insight that upsets institutions and threatens to overturn sovereign regimes of truth" (p. 433). They characterize the current "criticalist" as any researcher who believes

> that all thought is fundamentally mediated by power relations that are social and historically constituted; that facts can never be isolated from the domain of values or removed from some form

of ideological inscription; that the relationship between concept and object and between signifier and signified is never stable or fixed and is often mediated by social relations of capitalist production and consumption; that language is central to the formation of subjectivity . . . ; that certain groups in any society . . . are privileged over others. (Kincheloe & McLaren, 2005, p. 304)

This description could also include many theorists who are called postmodern/post-structuralist. With language like "ideological" and "social relations of capitalist production and consumption," the authors also reference traces of Marxism in current critical theory. However, their claim that "institutions" and "sovereign regimes of truth" might be overturned implies a more rigid and hierarchical conception of power and its operations than that to be found in post-structural theory (e.g., Foucault, 1980; Butler, 1997b).

Although few feminists overtly cling to the founding fathers of critical theory, many of us have much sympathy with these positions, particularly in our longing for emancipatory agendas. Indeed, recent critical theory is sometimes called new left theory or neo-Marxism, and it informs critical race theory, critical multiculturalism, critical psychology, critical feminist theory, and critical pedagogy. In *Getting Smart: Feminist Research and Pedagogy With/in the Postmodern* (1991), Lather's early synthesis of feminist and critical pedagogies, she articulates her indebtedness to critical theory and her continuing affinity with its emancipatory objectives, but she critiques aspects of critical theory from a postmodern perspective. Although it can also be claimed that critical theory has "largely mutated into post-structuralism" (Boler, 2000, p. 362), authors and areas of study that thematize the "critical" tend to insist that, unlike those working with postmodern and post-structural approaches, the outcome they envisage is "real" social change, with the implication that this must entail subjects who have sufficient agency to change the world.

As we will argue later, these agendas are not as absent from the work of postmodern and post-structural feminists as some critical theorists claim, though the concept of agency is carefully revised by these feminists as a "radically conditioned" form of agency (Butler, 1997b, p. 15). In Judith Butler's view, for example, the social subject is a site of ambivalence where power acts to constitute these subjects (who might elsewhere be called "individuals") in certain limiting ways but where, at the same time and through the same effects of power, possibilities to act (albeit constrained and limited) also emerge. Critical theorists are committed to a more straightforward concept of emancipation, and of the freedom of individuals to strive toward it, as a necessary and permanent possibility. Power tends to be seen within critical theory as oppressive and unilinear, thus mobilizing the binaries of dominator and oppressor. Power is enacted by certain groups upon other groups, and emancipatory potential lies in the radical overturning of those hierarchical relations of power.

Two prominent feminist exponents of critical theory have been philosophers Seyla Benhabib and Nancy Fraser. In *Feminist Contentions* (Benhabib, Butler, Cornell, & Fraser, 1995), they defend the tenets of critical social feminist theory against the effects of post-structuralism. Benhabib and Fraser see value in some postmodernist ideas, but they are wary of theories that they see as radical and dangerously relativist. Benhabib grounds her critique in three principles that she argues must not be abandoned by feminism and that, she claims, are weakened within a deconstructive approach. First, *feminists must be able to assume an autonomous feminist subject who remains capable of self-reflection and agency*. Second, she argues that large-scale narratives have their purposes, and *feminists need to maintain some distance from the social contexts they critique in order to develop objective perspectives and contribute to new narratives*. Third, she insists that *utopian ideals, abandoned by postmodernism, are necessary for feminist ethics and social and political activism* (Benhabib, 1995, p. 30).

Fraser is less resistant than Benhabib to postmodern feminism. She argues that feminism can benefit from the incorporation of "weak" versions of postmodern ideas but that feminist work must enable political action (Fraser, 1995a, 1995b). Benhabib and Fraser both acknowledge some of the contributions of postmodernism to feminism, including the constitutive effects of language and the rejection of abstract (and masculine) universal reason. Their commitment remains, however, with critical theory, which they read as enabling emancipatory political action in a way that (they claim) postmodernism does not. The goal of critical theorists, they say, is not only to interpret social life but to transform it. This transformation, like any theory of liberation, they argue, is dependent on a notion of subjectivity that allows some agency and that incorporates possibilities for choice and for freedom to act in the world.

Within postmodern and post-structural approaches to feminist research, in contrast, "liberation" is made problematic because one can never stand outside of discourse—agency is always radically conditioned by the positions made available to the acting, agentic subject; and subjectivity is always also subjection to the available ways of being. Further, the fact that post-structural and postmodern feminisms regard absolute moral or ethical truth claims with a measure of skepticism does not prevent them from passionate attachments to ethical and transformative practice (Davies & Gannon, 2006, 2009). Nevertheless, critical theorists are wary of postmodernism and post-structuralism because of the obstacles they see in such positions for political, social, and economic transformation. If critiquing the foundations of radical thought and activism leads to their collapse, then how are we to move on? How might we, they ask, effect change in the world? How might we work with the "ruins" of what we had and knew (St. Pierre & Pillow, 2000)?

Critical feminist accusations of ethical paralysis and apoliticism as the inevitable consequences of post-structuralist thought are common, but they rest on an assumption that criticism and transformation are binary, irreconcilable opposites that cannot work together in a both/and kind of way. In such feminist dismissals of post-structuralism, deconstructive criticism is allied with "theory," transformation with "praxis," and each side of the pair is positioned as oppositional, that is, as mutually exclusive. Michel Foucault (2000a) argued in contrast that (post-structural) critique and transformation are necessarily implicated in each other's operations; indeed, that radical transformation can only emerge from radical critique. The project for any critical theory, he argued, is to make it possible to think differently, and thus to open the possibility for acting differently: this does not mean to make different choices among the already known, already imagined, but to think against the grain of the already known and to open up lines of action not embedded in current thought. In this sense, critical theory, post-structural theory, and postmodern theory can work together rather than in antagonism with each other.

Postmodern Theory

The terms "postmodern" and "post-structural" have at times been used interchangeably in the United States, both terms signaling a "crisis of confidence in Western conceptual systems" (Lather, 1991, p. 159). Postmodernism is "an American term" (St. Pierre, 2004, p. 348) that has been used in diverse arenas of social and cultural life and that was, in the early 1990s, inclusive of post-structuralism. In architecture and the arts in general, postmodern aesthetics are marked by the collapse of distinctions between high and popular culture, by self-referential reflexivity, by irony, parody, pastiche, appropriation, and surprising juxtapositions of images and ideas. In a recent anthology of postmodernism, Bertens and Natoli (2002) trace three aggregations of this "protean" term: first, as a set of literary and artistic practices; second, as "a set of philosophical traditions centered on the rejection of realist epistemology and the Enlightenment project" mostly associated with French post-structural thought (p. xii); and, third, as neoliberalism—"an aggressive, entrepreneurial capitalism" (p. xv).

This linking of postmodernism with economics means that it sometimes stands as a synonym for "post-Fordist," "late," or "fast" capitalism, signaling the rise of Western consumer culture, multinationalism, and the globalization of corporate culture, capital, and labor. Neoliberal approaches to management emphasizing the flexibility of workforces and workplaces—thus the instability of subjects and of the relations of power and knowledge within which subjects are located—might be seen to be underpinned by these versions of postmodern culture. Regardless of the context or ideological intent, discourses that deploy postmodernism "seek to distance us from and make us skeptical about beliefs concerning truth, knowledge, power, history, self, and language that are often taken for granted within and serve as legitimations for contemporary Western culture" (Flax, 1990, p. 29).

In its very naming, "postmodernism" is produced both in opposition to and as a continuation of some aspects of modernism. Although gurus of postmodernity, like Lyotard (1984) and Bauman (2004), have claimed that postmodernity is very modernist, postmodernity is more usually characterized as replacing modernity, which was the era of social and cultural life and aesthetics that spanned the latter half of the twentieth century in the West. Modernity—emerging from the Enlightenment overturning of church and king as the origins of truth—validates reason, logic, and universal truth as the foundation for action in the world. The emancipatory impulses of liberal humanism and Marxism, both of which have influenced feminist movements, are rooted in the modernist project. Critique of the institutions and social practices that routinely excluded women became possible because of modernist thought.

Yet many feminists have noted that the tenets of modernism have not been friendly to women. They argue that the modernist subject—able to act autonomously in the world, with actions driven by scientific, objective knowledge and by will—is always already a masculine subject, an individual subject more or less separate from the social world and free to act upon it. As Hekman (1990) notes, the feminist position on modernism/postmodernism is "anomalous" (p. 2). Modernism is part of our Western conceptual legacy and, as the humanist ideals of social justice and equity that remain important for feminism emerge from modernism, its vocabulary and politics continue, inevitably, to work through us (St. Pierre, 2000b, p. 478). Nevertheless, both feminists and postmodernists have been critical of the modernist project, and these critiques signaled a shift toward different conceptions of the subject and of society and its signifying systems. Postmodernists argue that knowledge is contextual, historically situated, and discursively produced; that subjects are constituted within networks of power and knowledge. Yet postmodernism, like feminism, is not uncontested. Bauman (2004) explains why he gave up the term:

"The postmodern" was flawed from the beginning: all disclaimers notwithstanding, it did suggest that modernity was over. . . . In time, more flaws became clearer to me—I'll mention but two of them. One was, so to speak, objective: "postmodern" barred the much needed break or rupture. . . . "Postmodern thinking" could not but adhere to the "modernity

grid." . . . The second was subjective. I prefer to select my bedfellows and affinities myself. Ascription to the "postmodernist" camp grew more and more unsavory and unpalatable by the day as the "postmodern" writings went further and further astray and "postmodernism" came to mean, more than anything else, singing praise of the brave new world of ultimate liberation rather than subjecting it to critical scrutiny. (p. 18)

Foucault (1998) also drew attention to categorical problems when he asked, "What are we calling postmodernity? I'm not up to date" (p. 447). He continued, "I've never clearly understood what was meant in France by the word 'modernity.' . . . I do not grasp clearly what that might mean, though the word itself is unimportant; we can always use any arbitrary label" (p. 448). He goes on, nevertheless, to name the "recasting of the subject" as the central problem that allied those who had been working in what might be called postmodern theory up to that time. Of his own work he says,

the goal of my work during the last twenty years . . . has not been to analyze the phenomena of power, nor to elaborate the foundations of such an analysis. My objective, instead, has been to create a history of the different modes by which, in our culture, human beings are made subjects. (Foucault, 2000b, p. 326)

It is this task of re-situating the human subject—not as the central heroic and active agent who shapes her own destiny but as the subject who is constituted through particular discourses in particular historical moments—that is central to the postmodern approach to research. Butler also traces the splits and contradictions that are elided by the abstract collective noun "postmodernism." Like Foucault and Bauman, Butler (1992) rejects the name: "I don't know about the term "postmodern" but . . . [I know that] power pervades the very conceptual apparatus that seeks to negotiate its terms, including the subject position of the critic" (p. 6). Again, "I don't know what postmodernism is, but I do have some sense of what it might mean to subject notions of the body and materiality to a deconstructive critique" (Butler, 1992, p. 17).

Although categories are useful in academic work, and we use them and are here engaged in their perpetuation, we are less concerned with policing their borders than with exploring the work that might be done with ideas emanating from these modes of thought. The semantic puzzles prompted by namings of theoretical positions—and the seductions of theoretical progress narratives and successor regimes— have led us to a moment when we are faced with an array of descriptors including "post-post-modern theory," "posthumanist theory," "post-feminist theory," and even "post-theory theory" (Lather, 2007, p. 164). Rather than becoming entangled in these confabulations, and having alerted readers to some of the problems with such labels, we go on to explore in more detail "post-structuralism" and what that might be said to entail. Because many feminist authors who originally used the term "postmodern" have since left the term behind and moved toward the descriptor "post-structural," we will devote the remainder of part two to an exploration of post-structural theory and the concepts that have been taken up within it by feminist researchers.

Post-Structural Theory

Although the postmodern label was initially used to cover both the postmodern and the post-structural, at least in the United States, the term "post-structural" has subsequently become more common. Post-structural theory took a discursive turn and an ontological turn. It recognized the constitutive power of discourse, particularly as introduced through the work of Michel Foucault in which discourses are seen to "articulate what we think, say, and do" and to be historically con-tingent (Foucault, 1997b, p. 315). Post-structural theory turns to discourse as the primary site for analysis. This reflects a deep skepticism of realist social scientific approaches that claim to describe real worlds, which are taken to exist indepen-dently of researchers' observations and their subjects. Post-structuralism troubles the individ-ualism of humanist approaches, seeing the humanist individual as a (sometimes) troubling and fictional accomplishment of social and dis-cursive practices (Davies & Gannon, 2006, 2011). In this sense, post-structuralism (in marked contrast to postmodernism) might be seen as the antithesis of global capitalism's and neoliberal-ism's emphasis on the individual.

Humanist psychology and some aspects of psychoanalysis are among the meta-narratives that have been brought into question by post-structuralism, though many feminist post-structural researchers find aspects of psychoanalysis use-ful (e.g., Butler, 1997b, 2004b; Flax, 1990, 1993; Grosz, 1994b; Walkerdine, 1990), seeing it as necessary for theorizing desire and the changes individual subjects must engage in to bring about new patterns of desire and thus new ways of being. In its attention to language and desire, post-structuralism has been the para-digm that came to be associated with French feminist literary theorists Cixous (1981, 1986, 1991) and Kristeva (1981).

In its turn to ontology, and to a Bergsonian creative evolution (Bergson, 1911/1998), post-structural theory has returned to the subject of the body and its embeddedness and co-implication in a material universe (Davies & Gannon, 2009). Buchanan and Lambert (2005) explore the new concepts generated by Deleuze for rethinking ourselves spatially. Wilson (2004) takes this work in a feminist direction, and, working at the fore-front of this ontological turn, she deconstructs the human/nonhuman binary, pointing out that we limit our evolutionary capacity if we accept human as the dominant term, separated from and superior to other ontological systems. Feminism, in this turn, takes up the significant task of re-envisaging our past and future relations to the environment, and to each other, not as individu-alistic agents separate from the world but as beings co-implicated with others.

Post-structuralism does not provide a set of practices that might be taken up and ossified as a "method." Methodologies themselves are made strange as "thinking technologies" that are also, always, subject to critical scrutiny (Haraway, 2000). Post-structuralism promotes close textual analysis as a central strategy, but the idea of a text encompasses far more than conventional written or spoken data. It allows for macro-texts such as "capitalism" (or Marxism, humanism, feminism, postmodernism), and it allows for more familiar "micro-level" texts such as interview transcripts or literary texts. Strategies for post-structural analysis have nomadic tendencies and cross over disciplinary boundaries. Texts go beyond the conventional perceptions of literary or linguistic texts to include bodies in space, spaces without bodies, and texts comprised of nonlinguistic semiotic systems.

In post-structural research, the shift of the interpretive focus is from language as a tool for describing real worlds to discourse, as constitutive of those worlds. There are no "right" research methods that will produce a reality that lies outside of the texts produced in the research process because reality does not preexist the discursive and constitutive work that is of interest to post-structural writers. This insight is important for feminist researchers in that it makes visible the historical, cultural, social, and discursive patterns through which current oppressive or dominant realities are held in place. What might have been taken for granted as natural, even essential to the human condition, and therefore unable to be questioned in any systematic way, is no longer taken to be inevitable, no longer left invisible. The desires to demarcate and defend borders, to acquire ever more material goods, to be with people who are the same as us and avoid those who are different, for example, are not inevitable desires. Instead, the structures and practices of everyday life are opened to scrutiny. Inevitabilities are reviewed as constituted realities (which have the possibility within themselves of their own reconstitution or collapse). In its focus on discourse and discursive and regulatory practices, post-structural analysis seeks to transcend the individual-social divide and to find the ways in which the social worlds we inhabit, and the possibilities for existence within them, are actively spoken into existence by individuals and collectives. The individual, in this way of thinking, is not separate from the social landscape but co-implicated with it (Davies, 2000b; Wilson, 2004). The individual subject is itself deconstructed, removed from the center of thinking and knowing, and a broader sense of continuous collective "differenciation" is established (Davies & Gannon, 2009).

An enduring focus of feminist post-structural theorizing is on the processes of *subjectification* and the discursive regimes through which we become gendered subjects. In this way, it breaks with theoretical frameworks in which gender and sexuality are understood as inevitable, as *determined* through social structures, cognition, or biology. It rejects the essentialism that attributes the experiences of women to "an underlying essence of womanness, an essence contained in bodies and expressed in culture," or that universalizes women's experiences (Ferguson, 1993, p. 81). It also breaks with theoretical frameworks that define *power* as that which is held in hierarchical and institutional frameworks by certain groups and individuals (Foucault, 1980). The question for post-structural feminism, then, becomes that of *agency* and what possibilities there are for action.

Post-structural agency does not presume freedom from discursive constitution and regulation of subjects (Davies, 2000a, 2000b) but rather lies, first, in the capacity to recognize discursive constitution as historically specific and socially regulated through particular games of truth. As such, it can be called into question and changed. Agency lies, second, not in imagining a world external to being and setting out as an individual to bring that imagined possibility into existence but in seeing that thought is already happening in the world, evolutionary and creative thought, that can be mobilized and pushed further in a continual unfolding of difference or differentiation (Davies & Gannon, 2009).

Post-Structural Concepts

Discourses are complex interconnected webs of being, thinking, and acting. They are in constant flux and often contradictory. They are always located on temporal and spatial axes; thus, they are historically and culturally specific. We are always already constituted within discourse, and discourses operate on and in us simultaneously through constituting desires and modes of reasoning. The concept of discourse is used by post-structural thinkers to bring language into the material world where what can be understood and what can be said and done is seen as historically, socially, culturally, and materially constituted. The range of possible ways of thinking are encompassed within (in)finite discursive practices. Discourse "can never be just linguistic since it organizes a way of thinking into a way of acting in the world" (St. Pierre, 2000b, p. 485). There is no pre-discursive rational self, existing outside of or apart from discourse.

The concept of discourse serves to denaturalize what seems "natural" and to interrupt essentialist thought. It links together "power, knowledge, institutions, intellectuals, the control of populations, and the modern state as these intersect in the functions of systems of thought" (Bové, 1990, pp. 54–55). Influential discourses related to femininity, heterosexuality, fertility, and maternity have structured the conditions of women's lives. Feminists have worked to reform these discourses. In common with postmodernists, post-structuralists are suspicious of successor regimes and victory narratives. They prefer to trace how a certain mode of thought became possible at a particular juncture, and how it became a dominant discourse or regime of truth that can itself be subjected to retracings and retellings.

Discourses do not circulate in abstract realms but reach into the very "matter" of bodies, shaping desires and intimate modes of being in the world (Butler, 1993). In post-structuralism, the subject, constituted through discourse, is the pivot of operations of power.

In contrast to the humanist individualistic and essentialist version of identity, post-structuralism proposes a *subjectivity* that is not the property of any one of us but that is "precarious, contradictory, and in process, constantly being reconstituted in discourse each time we speak" (Weedon, 1987/1997, p. 32). Some feminists have worried that the idea of doing away with the subject (i.e., the individualized, essentialized subject) would mean an abandoning of the possibility of agency and so of social change. Theorizing agency has thus become one of the most important tasks for feminists working within post-structural perspectives (Butler, 1997b; Davies, 2000a). Butler (1992) argues that subjection is a precondition of agency, because we do not exist independent of the possible modes of thinking and being made available to us. Subjectivity is an ongoing construction taking place through an ongoing process of subjectification, in which one is subjected to available regimes of truth and regulatory frameworks and, at the same time and through the same processes, becomes an active subject. As we are imbricated within discourse, we become complicit in our own subjection, simultaneously seeking submission and mastery (Butler, 1997b). However, the subject remains opaque to herself, and the operations of subjectivity are never "translucent"; indeed, it is our "unknowingness" about

the conditions that make our lives possible that is integral to our constitution as human subjects (Butler, in Davies, 2008a, p. 9).

Both radical and liberal feminisms relied on a humanist conception of the individual subject as separate from and outside of language, as autonomous and capable of rationality. However, as individualism and realism have been opened up to question by critical theory and the wider effects of postmodern and post-structural thinking, many of the strong claims made from within liberal feminist and radical feminist frameworks have been opened to scrutiny and cannot be seen as absolute certainties.

The question of the ongoing formation of the subject in everyday practices draws attention to the post-structuralist concepts of *power/ knowledge*. Foucault (2000b) attended very closely to the micro-practices of power relations and their effects in the creation of subjects:

> This form of power that applies itself to immediate everyday life categorizes the individual, marks him by his own individuality, attaches him to his own identity, imposes a law of truth on him that he must recognize and others have to recognize in him. It is a form of power that makes individuals subjects. There are two meanings of the word "subject": subject to someone else by control and dependence, and tied to his own identity by a conscience or self-knowledge. Both meanings suggest a form of power that subjugates and makes subject to. (p. 331)

Power is not hierarchical, but it proceeds in every direction at once: it is capillary. It is not a possession that we have (or do not have), nor can we deploy it to oppress (or to liberate) ourselves or others. Power is productive rather than oppressive, productive of subjects and of nets of domination and subjection within which subjects are always in motion. Subjects are constituted within power relations: they are neither prior to nor apart from them, nor can they be delivered from them. The rational, autonomous subject of some critical theory is a subject generated by a masculinist discourse. Foucault talks more often about power relations, that is, about how power is operationalized in interactions between individuals and institutions, than about power as something apart from or prior to the discursive regimes within which power is in continual circulation. Indeed, we are always within relations of power, as we are always within discourse.

In his work on power, beginning with his early work on asylums and prisons through to his later work on the care of the self, Foucault explored how the disciplinary power exercised in institutions became part of the humanist subject. Disciplinary power shifted from something brought upon the individual, from outside the self, to a form of power relations taken up and internalized by individuals as their own responsibility. Similarly, women have sometimes been seen within feminism as complicit in their own oppression, though those feminisms assumed that once "false consciousness" was revealed, women would be free. Within post-structuralist conceptions of power, and the knowledge that power produces, there is no freedom from power relations, nor is there any place outside discourse. But just as within discourse we might find the possibilities for deploying new discourses, power relations also contain their own possibilities for resistance, albeit resistance that is "local, unpredictable, and constant" (St. Pierre, 2000b, p. 492).

The concept of power in Foucault's (2000c) work then circles back, inevitably, to the concept of discourse, which he developed in his early work as he struggled to analyze power and its operations:

> The way power was exercised—concretely and in detail—with its specificity, its techniques and tactics, was something that no one attempted to ascertain; they contented themselves with denouncing it in a polemical or global fashion . . . the mechanics of power in themselves were never analyzed. This task could only begin after 1968, that is to say, on the basis of daily struggles at grass-roots levels, among those whose fight was located in the fine meshes of the web of power. This is where the concrete nature of power became visible. (p. 117)

The concrete nature of power is materialized in women's desires, in their bodies, and in social relations and institutional structures, and these areas remain the focus of much feminist post-structural research (Davies, 2000a, 2000b; Davies & Gannon, 2006, 2011; St. Pierre & Pillow, 2000).

Foucault's work provides concepts with which we might think differently through what we still call "data" (though that term belongs squarely in positivist regimes of thought), that is about the *truth games* within which disciplinary and other knowledge is produced and reified. He provides us with a "tool-box" of strategies: *archaeology, genealogy,* and *technologies of the self*. Rather than distinct methods for analysis, these are intertwined modes of thought that make possible particular inquiries into games of truth, as sets of possibilities that we might take up as they are useful to us. Foucault's initial strategy of *archaeology* studies the conditions of possibility through which disciplinary knowledge is formed and becomes sedimented. It looks at discursive formations, at historical archives; it searches for subjugated knowledges. Archaeology interrogates the edifices of the disciplines, tracing how knowledge has come to define a particular domain and to underpin its associated regimes of truth. Foucault (1984) was interested in the modes of transformation of discursive practices, and his strategy of *genealogy* is directed at interrogating knowledge and power relations particularly as they operate at the level of the body, where the body is the object of the operations and technologies of power. The body is understood as

> the inscribed surface of events (traced by language and dissolved by ideas), the locus of a dissociated self (adopting the illusion of a substantial unity), and a volume in perpetual disintegration. Genealogy, as an analysis of descent, is thus situated within the articulation of the body and history. (p. 83)

Foucault (1984) talks about genealogy as "gray, meticulous, and patiently documentary" (p. 76). It has been taken up by researchers in many different ways—including as a contemporary catchall phrase for any sort of historical analysis—so how the subject is treated within genealogical studies differs greatly. For feminists, genealogy enables "a view 'from afar' that makes our most precious values, thoughts, and ideas appear strange," thus prompting "different modes of thought and with them different modes of thinking" (Bell, 2007, p. 61).

Although we sketch out some component parts of what Foucault called his "little tool-boxes" (Foucault, cited in Mills, 2003, p. 7), it is important to note that Foucault was not dog-matic. His whole corpus was dedicated to the dismantling of dogma, of received and sedi-mented "truth." This included others' use of his own work: "[a] discourse is a reality which can be transformed infinitely . . . he who writes has not the right to give orders as to the use of his writings" (Foucault, cited in Carrette, 1999, p. 111). Mills (2003) suggests "we should draw on his work as a resource for thinking, without slav-ish adherence, and we should be very aware of Foucault's weaknesses and blind spots" (p. 7). Deleuze argued that we should see Foucault not as a guru but as someone whose work might be useful in our everyday lives (Deleuze, 1988). Both Foucault's and Deleuze's work provide new ways of thinking for feminists to work with. Both provide creative ways of making visible the cracks and fissures of dominant discourses and the contradictory detail of the everyday, and they present opportunities for feminists to multiply and enable alternative discourses. The potent pleasures for feminists in post-structural decon-structive work lie in the potential for finding the means to undo sedimented truths through which they might otherwise be held captive.

Post-Structural Analytic and Textual Strategies

Deconstruction

The term *deconstruction* has also migrated into populist discourse, but, more precisely, it emerged from the work of Jacques Derrida. His analytic strategies work into the inconsistencies and weaknesses in meaning that are inherent within any text. Deconstruction was rapidly popularized in American literary studies partly because of its complementarity with the work of the Yale New Critics (Royle, 2000, p. 5). Meaning is to be found within the text, for literary decon-structionists, but that meaning will always be multiple, shifting, deferred. The text can be provoked to reveal its own contradictions and (im)possibilities through deconstructive analysis. Deconstruction does not produce definitive new readings of a text but is oriented toward the con-tinuous deferral and displacement of meaning, what Derrida calls *différance* (1976). Derrida's work began from the linguist Saussure's sepa-ration of the signified (the concept) from the

signifiers (the words representing the concept). Derrida argued that the relationship between word and meaning is arbitrary. Rather than being fixed or transcendental, meaning emerges in spe-cific temporal and discursive contexts. As we suggested in the first section of this chapter, deconstruction pays particular attention to detect-ing and displacing binary pairs, opening up the space in between. In its narrowest application, deconstruction is a strategy for identifying and disrupting binary pairs. As Royle (2000) describes it, this form "took hold (like a virus or parasite)" and could be "stupidly formalistic" (p. 5). McQuillan (2001) defines deconstruction as "an act of reading which allows the other to speak," that is, as a practice that resists closure, a "situa-tion or event of reading" rather than a method applied to a text (p. 6). Derrida prefers to con-sider "deconstructions," and he stresses that it has "never named a project, a method, or a system" (Derrida & Ewald, 1995, p. 283). Although Derrida's work can be usefully applied to specific texts, which may be its most common applica-tion, deconstruction is applicable to social institu-tions and discursive regimes that exceed a single text or set of texts. Deconstruction as it is useful for feminist post-structural research can be applied as an everyday, everywhere practice, something we might use in our lives, something active that might help us "make sense" of lived experience but that is most likely to trouble our sense-making, even to reach "into the bare bones" of what we see ourselves to be (Lenz-Taguchi, 2004).

Whatever its object or its scope, or its par-ticular strategy, deconstructive work aims to unfix meaning so that it remains incessantly at play, mobile, fluid, unable to come to rest or ossify into any rigid structures of meaning. Derridean deconstruction opens language to *dif-férance*, a principle that captures both "differ-ence" and "deferral." Deconstruction attends to the spectral logic of absences that haunt texts. It is productive and inventive, concerned with excess and ceaseless iteration. It "opens a pas-sageway, it marches ahead and leaves a trail" (Derrida, 1989, p. 42), and the trails crisscross to create new trails and surprising openings and closings. Deconstruction can, perhaps, be any-thing: "And indeed, one starts laughing, and I'm tempted to add 'deconstruction and me, and me, and me' . . . to parody the parody of a famous

French song—'50 million Chinese and me and me and me'" (Derrida, 2000, p. 283). Parody, as a strategy for defamiliarizing and deconstructing language, is one of numerous strategies that Derrida and those who have found his work useful have taken up in order to dislodge the fixity of meaning in a text (see Kamuf, 1981; Spivak, 1976). Gayatri Spivak (1976), translator of *Of Grammatology*, describes the difficulties of capturing his work in language:

> The movement of "difference-itself," precariously saved by its resident "contradiction" has many nicknames: trace, différance, reserve, supplement, dissemination, hymen, . . . and so on. They form a chain where each may be substituted for the other, but not exactly (of course, even two uses of the same word would not be exactly the same): "no concept overlaps with any other." . . . Each substitution is also a displacement and carries a metaphoric change. (p. lxx)

Although Derrida has used particular figures to work as "hinges"—as analytic devices to double and displace meaning—in particular texts under analysis, the figures available to feminist researchers for this sort of work are limited only by our imaginations and the texts we take up. Along with Spivak (2000), who has used deconstruction to take on the field of cultural studies, literary theorists Diane Elam and Peggy Kamuf have found Derridean strategies particularly fruitful for deconstructing "feminism" (Elam, 2000), "sexual difference" (Elam, 1994), "love" (Kamuf, 2000a), and "critique" itself (Kamuf, 2000b). Yet deconstruction as an analytic approach exceeds its origins, and its originator. Judith Butler, for instance, makes only passing reference to Derrida in the articulation of her radically deconstructive theory of gender performativity (1990, 1993, 1997a, 2004b).

Rhizoanalysis and Nomadism

The rhizoanalytic work of Deleuze and Guattari (1972, 1980/1987) has also been of great interest to feminists working with post-structural concepts. In contrast with the linear, systematic branching of tree roots, the rhizome is a secret, unseen, underground, creeping, multiplying growth that can strangle the tree/root of conventional thought, which "plots a point,

fixes an order" from beneath (Deleuze & Guattari, 1980/1987, p. 7). Rhizomatic plants, such as heliconias, are knobbly, unpredictable, unstable, vigorous, prolific, extending in multiple directions at once, moving underground, splitting off and springing up anew in unexpected places. Thought modeled on the rhizome links unexpected texts and events to make surprising new connections and unpredictable, unreplicable insights. Such analysis is also concerned with the dissolution of the transcendental and unitary rational subject, of he who "knows." Deleuze and Guattari modeled many strategies—cartography, rhizomatic analysis, assemblages, figurations, becomings, flows, and intensities—that have been taken up and extended in interesting and provocative work by feminists (Braidotti, 1991, 1994, 2002; Grosz, 1994a, 1994b; St. Pierre, 1997a, 1997b, 1997c). Concepts such as "bodies without organs" (BwOs), a reconception of the corporeal as rhizomatic, that is, as "nonstratified, unformed, intense matter" (Deleuze & Guattari, 1980/1987, p. 153), have been both vehemently rejected by feminists concerned about the perceived erasure of the materiality of embodied experience and taken up by other feminists as productive ways to rethink female corporeality and materiality.

Rosi Braidotti, Donna Haraway, and Elizabeth Grosz were early and influential feminists who sought new ways of thinking through Deleuze and Guattari. Braidotti (1994, 2002) has used the figuration of the nomad to generate a feminist nomadic subjectivity that emphasizes "flows of connection" and "becomings" that rely on "affinities and the capacity both to sustain and generate inter-connectedness" (Braidotti, 2002, p. 8). The feminist nomadic subject "critiques liberal individualism and promotes instead the positivity of multiple connections" (Braidotti, 2002, p. 266). The sort of feminist subjectivity that Braidotti (2002) theorizes emerges from an "empathic proximity and intensive interconnectedness" (p. 8) rather than from any independent, separate, or narcissistic mode of being human. Subjectivity is always already a "socially mediated process" (Braidotti, 2002, p. 7).

Haraway's cyborg is a sort of unsentimental Deleuzean BwO, neither girl nor woman, human nor animal, nature nor culture, corporeal nor technological but a composite of all of them, becoming all of them (Haraway, 1991). Yet the cyborg is a material and political figure as well, representing the human exploitation of underpaid workers, the invisible underclass of white capitalist production. Haraway brings Deleuzian thought together with an update of Foucault's conception of biopower, showing that "contemporary power does not work by normalized heterogeneity any more but rather by networking, communication redesigns, and by multiple interconnections" (Braidotti, 2002, p. 242).

Deconstructive Writing

The feminists that we have discussed thus far take up these new concepts creatively, but, for the most part, their writing remains clearly on the side of theory. Other feminist writers take the deconstructive challenge into radical play with form and genre, defying binaries that organize writing into either analytical or creative writing and disregarding categories such as theory, prose, poetry, drama, and film. Critical, postmodern, and particularly post-structural theories bring with them a hypervigilance to the politics, effects, and rhetorical tropes of language. A text is never innocent but is constitutive of certain truths and exclusive of others, and thus must always be placed under interrogation. Language, within post-structural thinking, is constitutive and multiple. The writers whose work we explore in the following paragraphs push language to the brink, using its creative possibilities to do highly original feminist textual work that is authorized by postmodern/post-structural paradigms.

Writing itself is a method of inquiry rather than a transparent medium for re-presenting data (Richardson, 1997). Richardson re-presents interview transcripts and other research "data" in poetic form, shifting the epistemological and ontological terrain in the process. With Richardson, Elizabeth St. Pierre theorizes writing as a "nomadic" practice, as a Deleuzian "line of flight" that asks this question: *"What else might writing do except mean?"* (St. Pierre, in Richardson & St. Pierre, 2005, p. 969). With this shift, writing is no longer "a tracing of thought already thought" but a provocation to *différance* (St. Pierre, in Richardson & St. Pierre, 2005, p. 967). Clare Colebrook (2000), influenced by Deleuze, suggests that, in reading such

writing, we might abandon the urge to interpret meaning and aim instead to "inhabit a text, set up shop, follow its movements, trace its steps and discover it as a field of singularities (effects that cannot be subordinated to some pre-given identity of meaning)" (p. 3).

Trinh T. Minh-ha is a filmmaker whose writing has been particularly important for postcolonial and feminist post-structural scholars. Her films problematize the Eurocentric ethnographic gaze on the Other as "native" and as "woman," and her writing enacts a textual practice in which Otherness is retained and given voice. Writing itself is the site of theorizing, and of interrogating theory through displacement and the disintegration of the subject who writes, of the reader, and of writing itself. Trinh (1989) claims a "hyphenated" textual space, a space where writing is both one thing and another, as the site for women's writing: "So where do you go from here? where do I go? and where does a committed woman writer go? Finding a voice, searching for words and sentences: say something, one thing, or no thing; tie/untie, read/unread" (p. 20). Her writing brings together theory and fiction, analysis and creativity. Trinh (1992) develops a "politics of form," "the irrespectful mixing of theoretical, militant and poetical modes of writing" (p. 154). She provokes a collision where "theorizing and practices of representation [are brought] into the same space each to bring the other into crisis" (Clough, 1994, p. 118). Trinh refuses the separation of theoretical and creative linguistic practice. Her work plays with the aesthetics and effects of language and is simultaneously intensely and provocatively political. Her play with language has serious intent as it draws attention to and deconstructs representations of women, "natives," and "others" (Trinh, 1989).

Hélène Cixous, likewise, works in another highly original textual location. Although she has been positioned for English readers as a theorist, she refuses that name. She writes fiction, criticism, psychoanalysis, and philosophy "without enclosing herself in any of them" (Conley, 1991, p. 12) and often within the same texts. Cixous' explication and practice of *écriture féminine*, of a feminine writing that exceeds the phallogocentrism of rational thought, has influenced diverse feminists, including Trinh

(Cixous, 1981, 1986), and has come to be associated with post-structural feminist thinking. *Écriture féminine* is a practice of writing that Cixous says "will never be able to be theorized, enclosed, coded, which does not mean it does not exist" (Cixous, 1986, p. 92). Cixous' work is also at the same time radically conceptual. She writes dense, enigmatic, intensely lyrical texts of desire and of loss that might be understood as texts of bliss (Barthes, 1975). Her writing shimmers with "signifiers that flash with a thousand meanings" (Cixous, 1991, p. 46). It pays careful attention to the possibilities of language and is sensitive to the multiplicity and excess of language. Like Trinh, she shows that the simple truth (if such a thing can be said to exist) is neither desirable nor possible. She attends to other sources of language beyond the conscious, beyond reason. She locates her imagery and understanding of the corporeal effects of language in dreams, in the unconscious, and in what she calls *"zones in(terre)conscious"* (Cixous & Calle-Gruber, 1997, p. 88). Cixous (1991) reads her body as a text. The approach to bodily inscription in her work locates writing within the body, as the source of language. The body, for her, always mediates every experience and is itself the ultimate text.

Bodies are texts of lives and can be written within an embodied writing practice of *écriture féminine*. It was in theater that Cixous found the medium in which the writer, as ego, could let go and make space for the multiplicity of the other: "In the theatre one can only work with a self that has almost evaporated, that has transformed itself into space" (Cixous, cited in Sellers, 1996, p. xiv). In the space of theater, the writer must imagine and create and *be* everyone. She can encounter and inscribe the other, and, in writing the other, she puts herself under erasure. It is in writing for theater that the self will "consent to erase itself and to make space, to become, not the hero of the scene, but the scene itself: the site, the occasion of the other" (Cixous, in Sellers, 1996, p. xv). She sees her writing for theater as a critical component of her scholarly practice and as the place where an ethics of writing becomes possible. For Cixous, more broadly, an ethics of writing could be characterized as a "poet*h*ics" within which writing is a "conjunction of poetry and philosophy" or a form of

"thinking-writing" beyond the textual and conceptual conventions of realism (Cixous & Calle-Gruber, 1997, p. 79).

The writers in this section have been inspirational in our own writing, provoking us to develop a post-structural practice of autoethnography (Gannon, 2006) and to (re)work data as fiction, drama, and poetry in a range of feminist textual interventions (Davies, 2000a, 2000b, 2009; Gannon, 2004a, 2004b, 2005). This approach is not exclusive to feminism but can be traced through other postpositivist paradigms. For feminism, it can contribute to the disruption of a binary of academia and the wider world and open feminist scholarship to multiple audiences and sites. It can turn feminist scholars to their research again and again as they reread and rework data to draw out nuances and complexities, to recognize and work further into impasses rather than generalize across them (as Richardson describes with her poem "Louisa May's Story of Her Life," 1997). Attention to embodied knowledge and bodily inscription has been particularly evident in feminist work of this sort.

Our methodology of collective biography provides an example of an approach to feminist research that is directed at developing deconstructive writing and research practices. Collective biography recognizes discursive effects, incorporates bodily knowledge and affect, and aims to move beyond an individualized version of the subject toward subjects-in-relation, subjects-in-process (Davies & Gannon, 2006, 2009, 2011). In collective biography, memory becomes the site for theorizing. The process of collective biography becomes a means to read/write embodied selves and to use that reading/writing to produce material with which we can explore how it is that we become subjects and go on becoming subjects. The doubled action of dwelling in particular moments of being and moving toward new possibilities of seeing and of being is reflected in the term "mo(ve)ments" to stress that opportunities for agency, for ways of moving into different discursive frameworks, open and close in unexpected liminal spaces. Thus, collective biography shifts analysis of lived experience from individual biography toward collective readings and the deconstruction of discursive regimes.

The work we discuss in this section disrupts language, pushing at the boundaries of understanding so that multiple meanings can be provoked and multiple readings invited. This is achieved through a politics of form that disrespects generic integrity and disciplinary boundaries and through attention to affective and bodily knowledges.

CONTROVERSIES, GAPS, AND POSSIBILITIES

The intersection of feminist and post-structural theories has been a vehemently contested and productive site. Although some readings of the debates suggest that post-structuralism has closed off possibilities for feminist work, vigorous new fields have emerged from this collision. In this final section of the chapter, we will further delineate some of the criticisms of these paradigms, and we will outline some of the emerging responses to these in recent feminist research.

Many of the accusations with which post-structural and postmodernist work have habitually been charged by feminists hinge on their apparent *relativism*, explicitly their rejection of fixed truths and certainties. In contrast, researchers who locate their work as "critical theory," who claim emancipatory agendas and privilege praxis over (or alongside) theory, have not generally been subjected to this critique. Accusations of relativism work along various axes in critiques of post-structural theorizing. Each axis rests on a binary way of thinking that asserts particular possibilities and impossibilities entailed in post-structuralism.

Relativism and Social Action

The first axis relates to *action*. The history of the feminist movement, as "women's liberation," was characterized by individual and collective action directed at political and social change. The relativism of post-structural feminism is seen by some critics as incapable of provoking any action to improve the lives of women. If "women" as a coherent category has been deconstructed and "power" is seen as a capillary and localized operation, then how and where can feminists work to improve social worlds? Critics suggest that social theory that does not foreground radical social action and that problematizes agency is

suspect for feminist purposes. This position is evident in some critiques of postmodern and post-structural feminism, critiques that see the focus on discourse as inconsistent with an orientation to social change. Waugh, for example, parodies this attention to language: "Rather than searching for scientific proof or metaphysical certainty, or a structural analysis of economic or social inequality, we should now recognise that the way to understand and to change our world is through the artificial mutation and manipulation of vocabularies" (Waugh, 1998, p. 183). Not surprisingly, she goes on to claim that (her version of) what she calls a "strong" postmodern position "raises enormous difficulties for any emancipatory collective movement concerned with profound economic and social inequalities" (Waugh, 1998, p. 183). This "emancipatory collective movement" stands in for "feminism" in the sentence and in her argument. Differences between and within feminism(s) are elided in order to allow feminism—as a collective movement—to right the wrongs of patriarchy. Feminism is equated with and defined by its action orientation, much as an orientation to praxis and social transformation is definitive of Marxist, socialist, and critical theories. The argument rests on a set of binary oppositions whereby postmodernism and post-structuralism are set on one side of a binary against feminism, and the former are associated primarily with language and the latter with action. Each side of the binary excludes the other, and is defined by that exclusion.

From this angle, deconstructive paradigms are seen to be forever and necessarily precluded from social action. As we have previewed in our earlier discussions of Foucault, Derrida, and Butler, we do not see this to be the case. The problem, rather, lies in how we might bring postmodernism and post-structuralism, with all that they entail (including a deconstructive stance toward language and the social world), together with the action orientation of feminism. The radical contingencies of subjectivity and agency in post-structuralism may seem problematic, but, as Butler (2004b) argues, although "agency is riven with paradox [this] does not mean it is impossible. It means only that paradox is the condition of its possibility" (p. 3).

Of course, the dismissal of postmodern and post-structural thought from the arena of "action" relies on the definitions of social activism and of emancipation that are used. Critics assert that social action is underpinned by grand narratives (such as the relentless oppression of women by patriarchy), narratives that imply large-scale social action as the ideal goal for feminists (see, for example, Waugh, 1998; Tong, 1998). We do not see this as the only possibility. Although it does not provide broad or simple answers to social problems, post-structural critique does enable close analysis of the operations of power. It enables us to examine how power operates to construct our desires, our thoughts, and our ways of being in the world—our subjectivities—in ways that can make us (un)consciously complicit in our own and others' oppression. By drawing attention to discourse and its constitutive force, its capacity to normalize and naturalize the subordination of some and the dominance of others, it enables us to transform how we think, making what seemed obvious and unquestionable no longer acceptable, no longer desirable, no longer thinkable. It thus opens us up to the not yet known, and to what Bergson (1911/1998) calls creative evolution.

Post-structural analysis of subjectification—that is, how power works on bodies to produce us as subjects—enables individuals and groups to undertake close readings of lived experience. With subjectification, we focus on the *processes* through which the subject is produced. The post-structural research and writing strategy of collective biography that we have developed from the memory-work of Haug and her collective (1987) works at this level to map the operations of power on bodies (Davies, 1994, 2000b; Davies & Gannon, 2006, 2009, 2011).

As critics such as Waugh have noted, the dislodging of habitual ways of thinking and being that underpins post-structural work also entails the dislodging of fixed notions of the subject. This abandonment of the stable subject as the foundation for agency is seen as detrimental to action, as potentially paralyzing for feminists. However, the contrary has been the case for feminists, such as those cited in this chapter, who work with post-structuralist notions of the subject. Social change cannot be held apart from transformation that becomes possible at the levels of individuals and groups. Yet the social/personal transformation that might be possible is

an ongoing and continuous process of self and societal critique and engagement rather than a step forward in a linear progress narrative toward something we might recognize as "emancipation" into which we might relax with satisfaction as though we had achieved the social changes we desired. The achievements of second wave liberal feminism have been remarkably fragile in the face of neoconservative discursive regimes. We do not see that an interest in deconstructive philosophies of the subject should be positioned as helping or hindering our participation in large-scale social activism, nor as limiting our search for social justice in all the arenas of our lives. It can be claimed that poststructuralists, rather than being apolitical, "are to the far left of the spectrum" as they "build genealogical approaches that clash with the dogma of historical materialism" and emphasize the "continuous 'becoming' that is the social, political, and personal pursuit of radical change and transformation" (Braidotti, 2000, p. 717). Thus, the claims we (and others) make about our projects, the language we (and others) use, and the actions we (and others) take will be subjected to rigorous and continual reflexive examination rather than accepted as taken-for-granted truths or emancipatory programs.

Relativism and Ethics

Another axis for critiques of postmodern and post-structural theories rests on the question of *ethics*. Although these paradigms—like any theoretical models—are not in themselves "ethical" or "unethical," they do question the absolutist foundations of any system of ethics. This is the work that postmodern and post-structural researchers set out to do. In humanist philosophy, ethics operates as an appeal to autonomous, rational subjects who are able to act impartially, to choose their actions. Rather than relying on an autonomous subject or promoting any set of absolute rules, approaches to an ethical position within a post-structural framework shift to analyses of relationality and the forms of thought and action that are made possible in any particular context. Multiple readings of a particular event might elaborate different discursive effects and operations within that event. As feminists take up and further post-structural interrogations of these concepts, inventive and radical work becomes possible. Early feminist work in this field theorized an ethics that was based on "mothering" and was characterized by "caring and interpersonal relations" (see McNay, 1992, p. 93). In this framework, characterized by the work of Carol Gilligan (1982), questions of right behavior are relativized within a network of relationships and responsibilities, but they tend to rest on ahistorical and acultural essentialist notions of the feminine that are incompatible with the anti-foundationalism of post-structural thinking. The work of reconfiguring ethics for feminists within post-structuralism does not take up a moralistic position that prescribes correct behavior and judges both self and other for falling short.

Foucault differentiates between morals—prescriptive codes of moral behavior that are externally imposed (though they may be taken up as our own desires)—and the ethical projects of the self upon the self (Foucault, 1985). Rather than a revelation (or an imposition) of right thought, post-structural conceptions of ethics imply that we must engage constantly in the project of "self-reflection, self-knowledge, self-examination . . . the decipherment of the self by oneself, . . . the transformations that one seeks to accomplish with oneself as object" (Foucault, 1985, p. 29).

Bennington (2000), discussing Derrida's ethics, also differentiates between ethics and duty:

> Simply following one's duty, looking up the appropriate action in a book of laws or rules, as it were, is anything but ethical—at best this is an *administration* of rights and duties, a *bureaucracy* of ethics. In this sense an ethical act worthy of its name is always *inventive*, and inventive not at all in the interests of expressing the "subjective" freedom of the agent, but in response and responsibility to the other. (p. 68)

Rather than post-structural thought having abandoned ethical practice, Derrida's work locates it within social relations: "the other has a radical prior claim on me, or even allows 'me' to exist as essentially . . . [responsible] to and for the other. I do not exist first, and then encounter the other: rather the (always singular) other calls me into being as always already responsible for him" (Bennington, 2000, p. 69).

Deleuze also distinguishes between morality and ethics. He opposes the kind of morality that argues from an idealized essence or from a form of categorization that presumes to judge and find wanting those who cannot realize this imposed essence in its perfection:

> Morality is the system of judgment. Of double judgment, you judge yourself and you are judged. Those who have the taste for morality are those who have the taste for judgment. Judging always implies an authority superior to Being, it always implies something superior to an ontology. . . . In an ethics it is completely different, you do not judge. . . . Somebody says or does something, you do not relate it to values. You ask yourself how is that possible? How is this possible in an internal way? In other words, you relate the thing or the statement to the mode of existence that it implies, that it envelops in itself. How must it be in order to say that? Which manner of Being does this imply? You seek the enveloped modes of existence, and not the transcendent values. It is the operation of immanence. (Deleuze, 1980, ¶ 15–16)

Thinking through Deleuze, Braidotti (2002) reconceptualizes the self as "a relay-point for many sets of intensive intersections and encounters with multiple others," a self that "can envisage forms of resistance and political agency that are multilayered and complex . . . an empirical transcendental site of becoming . . . [that] actively desires processes of metamorphosis of the self, society, and its modes of cultural representation . . . [that] results in a radical new ethics of enfleshed, sustainable subjects" (p. 75). Thus "becoming is to do with emptying out the self, opening it to possible encounters with the 'outside'" (Braidotti, 2006, p. 145). Such an encounter "propels the self out of the black hole of its atomized isolation" and also confirms its "singularity" as the subject "receives and recomposes itself around the onrush of data and affects" (Braidotti, 2006, p. 145). The ethical subject is traced through the assemblages she construes as "becoming-world," "becoming-ethical," and "becoming-animal" (Braidotti, 2006). Within this paradigm, life-sustaining ethical and political work is not contingent on essentialist notions of human subjects but, rather, is more possible and more urgent when human subjects are reconceived as multilayered and non-unitary entities.

Yet other recent figurations of ethics within post-structuralism draw on a range of theorists (such as Butler, Deleuze, Nancy, and Levinas) to foreground performativity and relationality. Bell (2007), for example, notes that it is difficult "to imagine everything as composition, set in relation, to imagine even oneself as constituted *over* the relation with the other" (p. 121). In this approach, "'the subject' is coextensive with his or her outside" and "the locus of effects of his or her surroundings" (p. 11). Interiority is an effect rather than a fact as "[o]ne cannot opt out of the assemblages within which one operates, for one is tied in a myriad of ways to their processes of construction" (Bell, 2007, p. 123).

The ethical subject emergent in Butler's recent work is formed in response "to the address and query of another": "I am implicated in a relation to the other before whom and to whom I speak. . . . I come into being as a reflexive subject" (Butler, 2008, p. 25). Furthermore, "my very formation implicates the other in me . . . part of what I am is the enigmatic traces of others" (Butler, 2004a, p. 46). In her work on ethics and subjectivity, Butler (2004a) examines the conditions of possibility that make certain lives seem more or less intelligible and more or less viable. It is this vulnerability of the other and their precariousness that "operates to produce a struggle for me, and establishes this struggle at the heart of ethics" (Butler, 2004a, p. 135).

Butler has been influenced in part by Italian feminist Cavarero (2000, 2005), who, using Levinas, Nancy, and Arendt, emphasizes the singularity and particularity of the other in encounter. Ahmed (2000), too, influenced by a similar configuration of theorists, elaborates the responsibility for the other as the very condition of possibility for the subject that is entailed in such a relational approach to ethics. The approach to feminist ethics that is emerging in these works does not rely on an essentialist conception of womanhood or femininity, nor does it rest upon notions of the subject as discrete and independent rational identity. Rather, it is contingent on post-structural notions of the subject as fluid, dispersed, and

multilayered, yet—because of this radical openness to the other—capable of ethical accountability and response.

Corporeality/Materiality

Another ongoing criticism of the feminist theories surveyed in this chapter has been that they valorize discourse at the expense of the carnal body. How can postmodern or post-structural theory account for the corporeal enfleshed events that impact women's lives? Although for Foucault (1984) "the body is the inscribed surface of events" (p. 83), it is feminist post-structuralists who have brought the corporeal, sexed body into post-structural theory. This can be a risky strategy for post-structural work in that sex, gender, and desire are simultaneously put under erasure and troubled by deconstructive work. We would argue that the fleshy body is neither separate from nor inferior to the ontological post-structural body. As Butler points out, "discourses do actually live in bodies. They lodge in bodies; bodies in fact carry discourses as part of their own lifeblood" (quoted in Meijer & Prins, 1998, p. 282). She rejects the binary opposition between discursive construction and the lived body in part by emphasizing the "fundamentally dramatic"; the body is not "merely matter but a continual and incessant *materializing* of possibilities. One is not simply a body, but, in some very key sense, one does one's body" (Butler, 1997a, p. 404). At the same time, the performativity of the body is contingent on the recognition and intelligibility of that performance by others (Butler, 2004a, 2004b).

Some of the most sophisticated and subtle post-structuralist work has consistently come from feminists rethinking the body. For example, Susan Bordo (1993/2003) uses Foucauldian language and ideas to refine her readings of bodies as carriers of culture, and she has a particular interest in the effects of consumer capital in Western culture on women's bodies. Vicki Kirby (1991, 1997, 2008) interrogates essentialist thinking and further disrupts the nature/culture binary as she theorizes the material body at the (as the) scene of writing. Elizabeth Grosz in particular has been influential in her theorizing of a corporeal feminism.

Grosz (1994b) has argued that there has been "a conceptual blind spot" in both philosophy and feminism and that feminism is "complicit in the misogyny that characterizes Western reason" by uncritically adopting philosophical assumptions about the implicitly masculine rational body of Enlightenment thought (p. 3). The female body is abject and expelled from (male) normativity as "unruly, disruptive, in need of direction and judgment" (Grosz, 1994b, p. 3). The universal body has, Grosz (1994b) suggests, always functioned as "a veiled representation and projection of a masculine which takes itself as the unquestioned norm, the ideal representative without any idea of the violence that this representational positioning does to its others" (p. 188). Prior to this work, feminist philosophy had generally been "uninterested in or unconvinced about the relevance of refocusing on bodies in accounts of subjectivity" (p. vii). Grosz (1994b) demonstrated that corporeal interventions into theory—across the mind/body split—could bring theory toward new and productive horizons as "[b]odies have all the explanatory power of minds" (p. vii). In her most recent work, Grosz (2005, 2008) has continued to radically rethink what has been impossible to think. She focuses on temporality and indeterminacy, striving for a "politics of surprise," so feminist politics might look "to what is beyond current comprehension and struggle, to becoming unrecognizable, becoming other, becoming artistic" (Grosz, 2005, p. 5). Her critique of corporeality in theory sees her breaking open concepts that are usually seen as unchanging, such as "the real," "being," "materiality," and "nature," opening them to their "immaterial or extramaterial virtualities or becomings, to the temporal forces of endless change . . . to history, biology, culture, sexuality" (Grosz, 2005, p. 5). She is interested in excess and in exploring what Merleau-Ponty called "wild being," including "the substance of the world, the nature of materiality, the composition of the body, the ingredients of subjectivity, and their relations to the material universe" (Grosz, 2005, p. 114).

This work is characteristic of what is claimed as a new "material turn" in feminist thought, whose authors claim to build on post-structural work by accomplishing a radical deconstruction of what they insist is a persistent "material/discursive dichotomy" (Alaimo & Hekman, 2008, p. 6). Grosz, Kirby, and Bordo have been associated with this turn alongside feminists working in science and technology studies. This move recognizes an inevitable interconnectedness, which means that "discourses have material consequences that require ethical responses" (Alaimo & Hekman, 2008, p. 7).

Despite claims that post-structural concepts elide the body, work which foregrounds and simultaneously deconstructs the body as the foundation for knowledge can be found throughout much critical and post-structurally oriented feminist research. The work of Haug and her group (1987), using memories of lived experience to unpack how the female body is materially inscribed by discourses of appropriate feminine deportment, demonstrates how critical theory can be held to account by female corporeality. In our own adaptations of this work (Davies, 1994; Davies & Gannon, 2006, 2009, 2011), we generate texts of the body in order to expand post-structural theory in directions that are amenable to feminist readings of bodies and the world. Lather and Smithies (1997) conduct post-structurally inflected ethnographic research in a community of women who are HIV positive, producing a textual mosaic that is concerned to retain "the weight and density" of the women and to resist the allure of the "comfort text" by using a range of disruptive textual strategies to trouble any easy reading (Lather, 2001, p. 212). Sedgwick (1999) takes what she calls an "adventure in applied deconstruction" in writing of her own experience with breast cancer within a post-structural analytical framework. Acknowledging the astonishment that some readers might have at the possibility "[t]hat deconstruction can offer critical resources of thought for survival under duress," Sedgwick (1999) responds that she encountered breast cancer "as someone who needed all the cognitive skills she could get," including "some good and relevant ones from my deconstructive training" (p. 156).

At the ethnographic coalface, many feminist researchers working with girls and women use corporeal feminism and post-structural approaches to think their data differently. In turn their work, theoretically informed and politically oriented, feeds back into theory. A sampling of recent feminist ethnographic research shows how post-structural thought interrogates the fleshy subjectivities of girls and women. Working with preteens, Gonick (2003) analyzes the discourses and practices of feminine sexuality, embodiment, desire, and relationship to others through which these girls imaginatively and corporeally construct femininity. Pillow (2004) takes up the body as a "deconstructive practice" in her study of pregnant teenage mothers and schooling. In a study of Danish university students, Søndergaard (2002) examines enactments of desire in the "signs on the body" inscribed by sexual/romantic storylines. Each of these empirical investigations thinks back into theory from enfleshed female bodies. Rather than arguing that the body is elided from deconstructive work, we suggest that feminist appropriations of critical, postmodern, and post-structural theories tend to foreground the body and make use of it as the volatile, unstable, and inventive ground for theorizing around the discursive production of sexed, corporeal subjects.

CONCLUSION

In closing, we would like to reiterate the strengths of feminist postmodern, post-structuralist, and critical discourses. Rather than conceive of this work as nihilistic, excessively relativist, amoral, or apolitical, we hold that post-structural thought opens us to creative evolution, to the "not-yet-known" (Davies, 2010). When dominant discourses that hold us in place and lock us into sedimented ways of thinking and being are dislodged, we might shift into other—more hopeful and often more radical—modes of thought and existence. We might argue, in contrast to the implications of the critics, that feminism and critical, postmodern, or post-structural paradigms have much in common to begin with in that they share a "hermeneutics of suspicion" (Braidotti, 2002, p. 68). Additionally, we would stress that we do not intend to locate critical, postmodern, and post-structural theories as successor regimes within a history of feminist ideas. Rather than abandoning discourses emanating from liberal or radical feminisms—those allied with humanist Enlightenment ideals—we would hold onto what we can that can be worked with in the "ruins" of such thought (St. Pierre & Pillow, 2000). There are many discourses of feminism in circulation, and we need, at times, to deploy them all. We cannot completely abandon discourses, such as

humanism, that have shaped how we know and live in the world (Foucault, 1997d; St. Pierre, 2000b). Rather than rejecting them, we need to become adept at mobilizing these discourses alongside and with(in) a post-structural, post-positivist skepticism, aiming to think different, even contradictory, thoughts—simultaneously. Taking up the post-structuralist dissolution of the subject as our project, we posit that what feminist post-structuralism allows for is a "new" subject of feminism, a subject that is "not *W*oman as the complementary and specular other of man but rather a complex and multi-layered embodied subject who has taken her distance from the institution of femininity . . . a subject-in-process" (Braidotti, 2002, p. 11).

How might we conclude this chapter on postmodern, post-structural, and critical theory and their (sometimes) uneasy relation to feminism? Early in this chapter, we introduced the figure of the woman weaver, engaged in the constant and simultaneous processes of weaving and unweaving herself in the discursive texts of the wor(l)d. This figure recalls Penelope, the wife of Odysseus, from Greek mythology, who, for 20 years, wove in daylight and unpicked her work by moonlight. Through this tactic she was able to fend off the suitors who would replace the missing king in her bed and on the throne. Resolution of her work—completion of the text/tapestry she wove—was stalled, deferred, postponed, undone. In the endless iteration of her daily and nightly work, she came to it each time anew. Each time, no doubt, it changed. She changed. The threads would fade and thin and twist, as did her fingers. One day the light would draw to her attention a tiny part of the design that might be better. Another day the particular blue of the sky or the dark of clouds or her own longings would provoke a subtle variation. The themes of the work would change as time passed or in response to the company she kept. There may have been as many versions as there were days. Penelope is usually read as the quintessential devoted wife; indeed, her story is shaped by her responsibility to this other, her husband. But she managed the estates and the nation in his absence. She was trapped in a patriarchal system, the wife whose only likely option was a change in husbands, a woman trapped in a tale told by a man. Not even a central character. Yet she found—at least for a time—the possibility to make something her own, something new, something that was not an answer, not freedom, not escape, not truth, but a way to live in the time and place where she found herself, a way to live that had integrity, that was hers.

Discussion Questions

1. How is the "subject" constituted within post-positivist feminisms?

2. What are the key principles shared by critical, postmodern, and post-structural theories?

3. Describe some of the implications of postmodern and post-structural theories for feminists.

4. How would you define deconstruction? How do deconstructive practices affect academic writing?

5. How do postmodern and post-structural feminists approach corporeality and materiality?

6. In your view, could postpositivist paradigms be understood as postfeminist?

Online Resources

Women's Studies Resources: Feminist Theory

http://bailiwick.lib.uiowa.edu/wstudies/theory.html

This website links together many of the feminist theorists whose work is discussed in this chapter, including Cixous and Butler.

Relevant Journals

Australian Feminist Studies

Differences: A Journal of Feminist Cultural Studies

European Journal of Women's Studies

Feminist Theory

Gender and Education

Outskirts: Feminisms Along the Edge

Signs: Journal of Women in Culture and Society

Thirdspace: A Journal of Feminist Theory and Culture

Women's Studies International Forum

Note

1. Butler's influential paper "Contingent Foundations" appeared as part of a philosophical symposium or an "extended conversation" about feminism and postmodernism, held in 1990 in Philadelphia between Judith Butler, Drucilla Cornell, and Nancy Fraser. These papers were published together in Butler and Scott (1992), *Feminists Theorize the Political,* and again, with additional material from Seyla Benhabib and an introduction by Linda Nicholson, as *Feminist Contentions* in 1995. As Nicholson (1995) notes, disagreements about the meaning and usefulness of the term "postmodernism" characterized the exchange from the beginning: the "ontological status of the term postmodernism is highly vague: the term functions variously as an historical characterization, a theoretical position, a description of an aesthetic practice and a type of social theory" (p. 4). Butler's contention in the symposium was that rather than worrying about its definition, we focus on the "political consequences of using the term" and ask "what effects attend its use" (quoted in Nicholson, 1995, p. 4).

References

Ahmed, S. (2000). *Strange encounters: Embodied others in post-coloniality*. London: Routledge.

Alaimo, S., & Hekman, S. (Eds.). (2008). *Material feminisms*. Bloomington: Indiana University Press.

Barthes, R. (1975). *The pleasure of the text* (R. Miller, Trans.). New York: The Noonday Press.

Bauman, Z. (2004). Liquid sociality. In N. Gane (Ed.), *The future of social theory* (pp. 17–46). London: Continuum.

Bell, V. (2007). *Culture and performance: The challenge of ethics, politics and feminist theory.* Oxford, UK: Berg.

Benhabib, S. (1995). Feminism and postmodernism. In S. Benhabib, J. Butler, D. Cornell, & N. Fraser, *Feminist contentions: A philosophical exchange* (pp. 17–34). New York: Routledge.

Benhabib, S., Butler, J., Cornell, D., & Fraser, N. (1995). *Feminist contentions: A philosophical exchange.* New York: Routledge.

Bennington, G. (2000). Deconstruction and ethics. In N. Royle (Ed.), *Deconstructions: A user's guide* (pp. 64–82). New York: Palgrave.

Bergson, H. (1998). *Creative evolution* (A. Mitchell, Trans.). Mineola, NY: Dover Publications Inc. (Original work published 1911)

Bertens, H., & Natoli, J. (Eds.). (2002). *Postmodernism: The key figures*. Martens, MA: Blackwell.

Boler, M. (2000). An epoch of difference: Hearing voices in the 90s. *Educational Theory, 50*(3), 357–381.

Bordo, S. (2003). *Unbearable weight: Feminism, Western culture and the body*. Berkeley: University of California Press. (Original work published 1993)

Bové, P. A. (1990). Discourse. In F. Lentriccia & T. McLaughlin (Eds.), *Critical terms for literary study* (pp. 50–65). Chicago: University of Chicago Press.

Braidotti, R. (1991). *Patterns of dissonance*. New York: Routledge.

Braidotti, R. (1994). *Nomadic subjects*. New York: Columbia University Press.

Braidotti, R. (2000). The way we were: Some post-structuralist memoirs. *Women's Studies International Forum, 23*(6), 715–728.

Braidotti, R. (2002). *Metamorphoses: Towards a materialist theory of becoming*. Cambridge, UK: Polity Press.

Braidotti, R. (2006). *Transpositions: On nomadic ethics*. Cambridge, UK: Polity Press.

Buchanan, I., & Lambert, G. (2005). *Deleuze and space*. Edinburgh: Edinburgh University Press.

Butler, J. (1990). *Gender trouble: Feminism and the subversion of identity*. New York: Routledge.

Butler, J. (1992). Contingent foundations. In J. Butler & J. W. Scott (Eds.), *Feminists theorize the political* (pp. 3–21). New York: Routledge.

Butler, J. (1993). *Bodies that matter: On the discursive limits of sex*. New York: Routledge.

Butler, J. (1995). For a careful reading. In S. Benhabib, J. Butler, D. Cornell, & N. Fraser, *Feminist contentions: A philosophical exchange* (pp. 127–144). New York: Routledge.

Butler, J. (1997a). Performative acts and gender constitution: An essay in phenomenology and feminist theory. In K. Conboy, N. Medina, & S. Stanbury (Eds.), *Writing on the body: Female embodiment and feminist theory* (pp. 401–417). New York: Columbia University Press.

Butler, J. (1997b). *The psychic life of power: Theories in subjection*. Stanford, CA: Stanford University Press.

Butler, J. (2003). [Interview with] Judith Butler. In G. A. Olsen & L. Worsham (Eds.), *Critical intellectuals on writing* (pp. 42–52). Albany: State University of New York.

Butler, J. (2004a). *Precarious life: The powers of mourning and violence*. London: Verso.

Butler, J. (2004b). *Undoing gender*. New York: Routledge.

Butler, J. (2008). An account of oneself. In B. Davies (Ed.), *Judith Butler in conversation: Analyzing the texts and talk of everyday life* (pp. 19–38). New York: Routledge.

Butler, J., & Scott, J. W. (Eds.). (1992). *Feminists theorize the political*. New York: Routledge.

Carrette, J. R. (Ed.). (1999). *Religion and culture*. New York: Routledge.

Castor, L. (1991). Did she or didn't she? The discourse of scandal in the 1988 U.S. presidential campaign. *Genders, 12,* 62–76.

Cavarero, A. (2000). *Relating narratives: Storytelling and selfhood*. London: Routledge.

Cavarero, A. (2005). *For more than one voice: Towards a philosophy of vocal expression*. Stanford, CA: Stanford University Press.

Cixous, H. (1981). The laugh of the medusa. In E. Marks & I. de Courtivron (Eds.), *New French feminisms: An introduction* (pp. 245–264). Brighton: The Harvester Press.

Cixous, H. (1986). Sorties: Out and out: Attacks/ways out/forays (B. Wing, Trans.). In H. Cixous & C. Clément (Eds.), *The newly born woman* (pp. 63–134). Manchester, UK: Manchester University Press.

Cixous, H. (1991). *"Coming to writing" and other essays* (S. Cornell, D. Jenson, A. Liddle, & S. Sellers, Trans.). Cambridge, MA: Harvard University Press.

Cixous, H., & Calle-Gruber, M. (1997). *Rootprints: Memory and life writing*. London: Routledge.

Cixous, H., & Derrida, J. (2001). *Veils: Cultural memory in the present* (G. Bennington, Trans.). Stanford, CA: Stanford University Press.

Clément, C. (1989). *Opera or the undoing of women* (B. Wing, Trans.). Minneapolis: University of Minnesota Press.

Clough, P. T. (1994). *Feminist thought: Desire, power, and academic discourse*. Cambridge, MA: Blackwell Publishers.

Colebrook, C. (2000). Introduction. In I. Buchanan & C. Colebrook (Eds.), *Deleuze and feminist theory* (pp. 1–17). Edinburgh: University of Edinburgh Press.

Colebrook, C. (2002). *Understanding Deleuze*. Crow's Nest, N.S.W.: Allen & Unwin.

Conley, V. A. (1991). *Hélène Cixous: Writing the feminine*. Lincoln: University of Nebraska Press.

Davies, B. (1994). *Poststructuralist theory and classroom practice*. Geelong, Australia: Deakin University Press.

Davies, B. (2000a). *A body of writing*. Walnut Creek, CA: AltaMira Press.

Davies, B. (2000b). *(In)scribing body/landscape relations*. Walnut Creek, CA: AltaMira Press.

Davies, B. (2003). *Shards of glass: Children reading and writing beyond gendered identities* (2nd ed.). Cresskill, NJ: Hampton Press. (Original work published 1993)

Davies, B. (Ed.). (2008a). *Judith Butler in conversation: Analyzing the texts and talk of everyday life*. New York: Routledge.

Davies, B. (2008b). Re-thinking "behaviour" in terms of positioning and the ethics of responsibility. In A. M. Phelan & J. Sumsion (Eds.), *Critical readings in teacher education: Provoking absences* (pp. 173–186). Rotterdam: Sense Publishers.

Davies, B. (2009). Life in Kings Cross: A play of voices. In A. Jackson & L. Mazzei (Eds.), *Voice in qualitative inquiry: Challenging conventional, interpretive, and critical conceptions in qualitative research* (pp. 197–220). New York: Routledge.

Davies, B. (2010). The struggle between the individualised subject of phenomenology and the multiplicities of the poststructuralist subject: The problem of agency. *Reconceptualizing Educational Research Methodology, 1*(1), 54–68.

Davies, B., Browne, J., Gannon, S., Honan, E., Laws, C., Mueller-Rockstroh, B., & Bendix Petersen, E. (2004). The ambivalent practices of reflexivity. *Qualitative Inquiry, 10*(2), 360–390.

Davies, B., & Gannon, S. (Eds.). (2006). *Doing collective biography: Investigating the production of subjectivity*. Berkshire, UK: Open University Press/McGraw Hill.

Davies, B., & Gannon, S. (Eds.). (2009). *Pedagogical encounters*. New York: Peter Lang.

Davies, B., & Gannon, S. (2011). Feminism/poststructuralism. In C. Lewin & B. Somekh (Eds.), *Theory and methods in social research* (pp. 312–319). London: Sage.

Davies, B., & Harré, R. (2000). Positioning: The discursive production of selves. In B. Davies, *A body of writing* (pp. 87–106). Walnut Creek, CA: AltaMira Press.

Deleuze, G. (1980). Cours Vincennes: Ontologie-Ethique 21/12/1980. *Les cours de Gilles Deleuze*. Retrieved May 27, 2011, from http://www.webdeleuze.com/php/texte.php?cle=190&groupe=Spinoza&langue=2

Deleuze, G. (1988). *Foucault*. London: The Athlone Press.

Deleuze, G., & Guattari, F. (1972). *Anti-Oedipus: Capitalism and schizophrenia*. London: The Athlone Press.

Deleuze, G., & Guattari, F. (1987). *A thousand plateaus: Capitalism and schizophrenia*. London: The Athlone Press. (Original work published 1980)

Derrida, J. (1976). *Of grammatology* (G. Spivak, Trans.). Baltimore, MD: Johns Hopkins University Press.

Derrida, J. (1978). *Spurs: Nietzsche's styles/Éperons: les styles de Nietzsche* (B. Harlow, Trans.). Chicago: University of Chicago Press.

Derrida, J. (1989). Psyche: Inventions of the other (C. Porter, Trans.). In L. Waters & W. Godzich (Eds.), *Reading de Man reading* (pp. 25–65). Minneapolis: University of Minnesota Press.

Derrida, J. (2000). Et cetera. In N. Royle (Ed.), *Deconstructions: A user's guide* (pp. 282–305). New York: Palgrave.

Derrida, J., & Ewald, F. (1995). A certain "madness" must watch over thinking. *Educational Theory, 45*(3), 273–291.

Elam, D. (1994). *Feminism and deconstruction: Ms. en abyme*. London: Routledge.

Elam, D. (2000). Deconstruction and feminism. In N. Royle (Ed.), *Deconstructions: A user's guide* (pp. 83–104). Basingstoke, UK: Palgrave.

Ferguson, K. E. (1993). *The man question: Visions of subjectivity in feminist theory*. Berkeley: University of California Press.

Flax, J. (1990). *Thinking fragments: Psychoanalysis, feminism, and postmodernism in the contemporary West*. Berkeley: University of California Press.

Flax, J. (1993). *Disputed subjects: Essays on psychoanalysis, politics, and philosophy*. New York: Routledge.

Foucault, M. (1978). *The history of sexuality: Vol. 1. An introduction* (R. Hurley, Trans.). London: Penguin.

Foucault, M. (1980). *Power/knowledge: Selected interviews and other writings*. Brighton, UK: The Harvester Press.

Foucault, M. (1984). Nietzsche, genealogy, history. In P. Rabinow (Ed.), *The Foucault reader* (pp. 76–120). New York: Pantheon.

Foucault, M. (1985). *The history of sexuality: Vol. 2. The use of pleasure* (R. Hurley, Trans.). London: Penguin.

Foucault, M. (1997a). The ethics of the concern for the self as a practice of freedom (P. Aranov & D. McGrawth, Trans.). In P. Rabinow (Ed.), *Essential works of Foucault (1954–1984): Vol. 1. Ethics* (pp. 281–301). London: Penguin.

Foucault, M. (1997b). On the genealogy of ethics: An overview of work in progress. In P. Rabinow (Ed.), *Essential works of Foucault (1954–1984): Vol. 1. Ethics* (pp. 253–280). London: Penguin.

Foucault, M. (1997c). Technologies of the self. In P. Rabinow (Ed.), *Essential works of Foucault (1954–1984): Vol. 1. Ethics* (pp. 223–252). London: Penguin.

Foucault, M. (1997d). What is enlightenment? In P. Rabinow (Ed.), *Essential works of Foucault (1954–1984): Vol. 1. Ethics* (pp. 253–280). London: Penguin.

Foucault, M. (1998). Structuralism and poststructuralism. In P. Rabinow (Ed.), *Essential works of Foucault (1954–1984): Vol. 2. Aesthetics, method, and epistemology* (pp. 433–458). New York: The New Press.

Foucault, M. (1999). About the beginnings of the hermeneutics of the self (T. Keenan & M. Blasius, Trans.). In J. R. Carrette (Ed.), *Religion and culture* (pp. 158–181). New York: Routledge.

Foucault, M. (2000a). "So is it important to think?" In J. D. Faubion (Ed.), *Essential works of Foucault (1954–1984): Vol. 3. Power* (pp. 454–458). New York: The New Press.

Foucault, M. (2000b). The subject and power. In J. D. Faubion (Ed.), *Essential works of Foucault (1954–1984): Vol. 3. Power* (pp. 326–348). New York: The New Press.

Foucault, M. (2000c). Truth and power. In J. D. Faubion (Ed.), *Essential works of Foucault (1954–1984): Vol. 3. Power* (pp. 111–133). New York: The New Press.

Foucault, M. (2000d). What is called punishing? In J. D. Faubion (Ed.), *Essential works of Foucault (1954–1984): Vol. 3. Power* (pp. 382–393). New York: The New Press.

Fraser, N. (1995a). False antitheses. In S. Benhabib, J. Butler, D. Cornell, & N. Fraser, *Feminist contentions: A philosophical exchange* (pp. 59–74). New York: Routledge.

Fraser, N. (1995b). Pragmatism, feminism, and the linguistic turn. In S. Benhabib, J. Butler, D. Cornell, & N. Fraser, *Feminist contentions: A philosophical exchange* (pp. 157–172). New York: Routledge.

Gannon, S. (2004a). Crossing "Boundaries" with the collective girl: A poetic intervention into sex education. *Sex Education, 4*(1), 81–99.

Gannon, S. (2004b). Out/performing in the academy: Writing "The Breast Project." *International Journal of Qualitative Studies in Education, 17*(1), 65–81.

Gannon, S. (2005). "The tumbler": Writing an/other in fiction and ethnography. *Qualitative Inquiry, 11,* 622–627.

Gannon, S. (2006). The (im)possibilities of writing the self: French poststructural theory and auto-ethnography. *Cultural Studies ↔ Critical Methodologies, 6*(4), 474–495.

Gilligan, C. (1982). *In a different voice: Psychological theory and women's development.* Cambridge, MA: Harvard University Press.

Gonick, M. (2003). *Between femininities: Ambivalence, identity, and the education of girls.* Albany, NY: SUNY Press.

Grosz, E. (1990). *Jacques Lacan: A feminist introduction.* Sydney, Australia: Allen and Unwin.

Grosz, E. (1994a). A thousand tiny sexes: Feminism and rhizomatics. In C. V. Boundas & D. Olkowski (Eds.), *Gilles Deleuze and the theatre of philosophy* (pp. 187–210). London: Routledge.

Grosz, E. (1994b). *Volatile bodies: Towards a corporeal feminism.* Bloomington: Indiana University Press.

Grosz, E. (1995). *Space, time, and perversion: Essays on the politics of bodies.* Sydney, Australia: Allen and Unwin.

Grosz, E. (2005). *Time travels: Feminism, nature, power.* Durham, NC: Duke University Press.

Grosz, E. (2008). Darwin and feminism: Preliminary investigations for a possible alliance. In S. Alaimo & S. Hekman (Eds.), *Material feminisms* (pp. 23–51). Bloomington: Indiana University Press.

Haraway, D. (1988). Situated knowledges: The science question in feminism and the privilege of partial perspective. *Feminist Studies, 14*(3), 575–599.

Haraway, D. (1991). *Simians, cyborgs, and women: The reinvention of nature.* New York: Routledge.

Haraway, D. (2000). There are always more things going on than you thought! Methodologies as thinking technologies. *Kvinder, Køn & Forskning, 4,* 52–60.

Haug, F., Andresen, S., Bünz-Elfferding, A., Hauser, K., Lang, U., Laudan, M., et al. (1987). *Female sexualization: A collective work of memory* (E. Carter, Trans.). London: Verso.

Hekman, S. J. (1990). *Gender and knowledge: Elements of a postmodern feminism.* Boston: Northeastern University Press.

Henriques, J., Hollway, W., Urwin, C., Venn, C., & Walkerdine, V. (1998). *Changing the subject: Psychology, social regulation, and subjectivity* (2nd ed.). London: Methuen. (First edition published 1984)

Irigaray, L. (1977). *Ce sexe qui n'en est pas un* [This sex which is not one]. Paris: Minuit.

Kamuf, P. (Ed.). (1981). *A Derrida reader: Between the blinds.* New York: Columbia University Press.

Kamuf, P. (2000a). Deconstruction and love. In N. Royle (Ed.), *Deconstructions: A user's guide* (pp. 151–170). New York: Palgrave.

Kamuf, P. (2000b). The ghosts of critique and deconstruction. In M. McQuillan (Ed.), *Deconstruction: A reader* (pp. 198–216). Edinburgh: Edinburgh University Press.

Kincheloe, J., & McLaren, P. (2003). Rethinking critical theory and qualitative research. In N. K. Denzin & Y. S. Lincoln (Eds.), *The landscape of qualitative research* (2nd ed., pp. 433–488). Thousand Oaks, CA: Sage.

Kincheloe, J., & McLaren, P. (2005). Rethinking critical theory and qualitative research. In N. K. Denzin & Y. S. Lincoln (Eds.), *The SAGE handbook of qualitative research* (3rd ed., pp. 303–342). Thousand Oaks, CA: Sage.

Kirby, V. (1991). Corporeal habits: Addressing essentialism differently. *Hypatia, 6*(3), 4–24.

Kirby, V. (1997). *Telling flesh: The substance of the corporeal.* New York: Routledge.

Kirby, V. (2008). Natural convers(at)ions: Or, what if culture was really nature all along? In S. Alaimo & S. Hekman (Eds.), *Material feminisms* (pp. 214–236). Bloomington: Indiana University Press.

Kristeva, J. (1981). Women's time (A. Jardine and H. Blake, Trans.). *Signs: Journal of Women in Culture and Society, 7*(1), 13–35.

Lather, P. (1991). *Getting smart: Feminist research and pedagogy with/in the postmodern.* New York: Routledge.

Lather, P. (1996). Troubling clarity: The politics of accessible language. *Harvard Educational Review, 66*(3), 525–545.

Lather, P. (1998). Critical pedagogy and its complicities: A praxis of stuck places. *Educational Theory, 48*(4), 487–497.

Lather, P. (2001). Postbook: Working the ruins of feminist ethnography. *Signs: Journal of Women in Culture and Society, 27*(1), 199–227.

Lather, P. (2007). *Getting lost: Feminist efforts toward a double(d) science.* Albany, NY: SUNY Press.

Lather, P., & Smithies, C. (1997). *Troubling the angels: Women living with HIV/AIDS.* Boulder, CO: Westview/HarperCollins.

Lenz-Taguchi, H. (2004). *In på bara benet* [Into the bare bones. Introduction to feminist poststructuralism.] Stockholm: HLS Förlag.

Lincoln, Y. S., & Denzin, N. K. (2003). The seventh moment: Out of the past. In N. K. Denzin & Y. S. Lincoln (Eds.), *The landscape of qualitative research* (2nd ed., pp. 611–640). Thousand Oaks, CA: Sage.

Lyotard, J. F. (1984). *The postmodern condition.* Manchester, UK: Manchester University Press.

McNay, L. (1992). *Foucault and feminism.* Cambridge, MA: Polity Press.

McQuillan, M. (2001). *Deconstruction: A reader.* New York: Routledge.

Meijer, I. C., & Prins, B. (1998). How bodies come to matter: An interview with Judith Butler. *Signs: Journal of Women in Culture and Society, 23*(2), 275–286.

Mills, S. (2003). *Michel Foucault.* London: Routledge.

Nicholson, L. (Ed.). (1990). *Feminism/postmodernism.* New York: Routledge.

Nicholson, L. (1995). Introduction. In S. Benhabib, J. Butler, D. Cornell, & N. Fraser, *Feminist contentions: A philosophical exchange* (pp. 1–16). New York: Routledge

Pillow, W. (2004). *Unfit subjects: Educational policy and the teen mother.* New York: Routledge Falmer.

Richardson, L. (1997). *Fields of play: Constructing an academic life.* New Brunswick, NJ: Rutgers University Press.

Richardson, L., & St. Pierre, E. A. (2005). Writing: A method of inquiry. In N. K. Denzin & Y. S. Lincoln (Eds.), *The SAGE handbook of qualitative research* (pp. 959–978). Thousand Oaks, CA: Sage.

Royle, N. (2000). What is deconstruction? In N. Royle (Ed.), *Deconstructions: A user's guide* (pp. 1–13). New York: Palgrave.

Scott, J. (1992). Experience. In J. Butler & J. W. Scott, *Feminists theorize the political* (pp. 22–40). New York: Routledge.

Sedgwick, E. Kosofky. (1999). Breast cancer: An adventure in applied deconstruction. In J. Price & M. Shildrick (Eds.), *Feminist theory and the body: A reader* (pp. 153–156). New York: Routledge.

Sellers, S. (1996). *Hélène Cixous: Authorship, autobiography, and love.* Cambridge, MA: Polity Press.

Søndergaard, D. M. (2002). Poststructuralist approaches to empirical analysis. *International Journal of Qualitative Studies in Education, 15*(2), 187–204.

Speedy, J. (2008). *Narrative inquiry and psychotherapy.* Houndmills, UK: Palgrave Macmillan.

Spivak, G. C. (1976). Translator's preface. In J. Derrida (Ed.), *Of grammatology.* Baltimore, MD: Johns Hopkins University Press.

Spivak, G. C. (2000). Deconstruction and cultural studies: Arguments for a deconstructive cultural studies. In N. Royle (Ed.), *Deconstructions: A user's guide* (pp. 14–43). New York: Palgrave.

St. Pierre, E. A. (1997a). Circling the text: Nomadic writing practices. *Qualitative Inquiry, 3*(4), 403–417.

St. Pierre, E. A. (1997b). An introduction to figurations: A poststructural practice of inquiry. *Qualitative Studies in Education, 10*(3), 279–284.

St. Pierre, E. A. (1997c). Methodology in the fold and the irruption of data. *Qualitative Studies in Education, 10*(2), 175–189.

St. Pierre, E. (2000a). The call for intelligibility. *Educational Researcher, 29*(5), 25–28.

St. Pierre, E. (2000b). Poststructural feminism in education: An overview. *Qualitative Studies in Education, 13*(5), 477–515.

St. Pierre, E. A. (2004). Care of the self: The subject and freedom. In B. Baker & K. Heyning (Eds.), *Dangerous coagulations? The use of Foucault in the study of education* (pp. 325–358). New York: Peter Lang.

St. Pierre, E. A., & Pillow, W. S. (Eds.). (2000). *Working the ruins: Feminist poststructural theory and methods in education.* New York: Routledge.

Tong, R. (1998). *Feminist thought: A more comprehensive introduction* (2nd ed.). Boulder, CO: Westview Press.

Trinh, T. Minh-ha. (1989). *Woman, native, other.* Bloomington: University of Indiana Press.

Trinh, T. Minh-ha. (1991). *When the moon waxes red.* New York: Routledge.

Trinh, T. Min-ha. (1992). *Framer framed.* New York: Routledge.

Walkerdine, V. (1990). *Schoolgirl fictions.* London: Verso.

Waugh, P. (1998). Postmodernism and feminism. In S. Jackson & J. Jones (Eds.), *Contemporary feminist theories* (pp. 177–193). New York: New York University Press.

Weedon, C. (1997). *Feminist practice and poststructuralist theory* (2nd ed.). Cambridge, MA: Blackwell. (First edition published in 1987)

Wilshire, D. (1989). The uses of myth, image, and the female body in revisioning knowledge. In A. M. Jagger & S. R. Borno (Eds.), *Gender/body/knowledge: Feminist reconstructions of being and knowing* (pp. 92–114). New Brunswick, NJ: Rutgers University Press.

Wilson, E. A. (2004). *Psychosomatic: Feminism and the neurological body.* Durham, NC: Duke University Press.

5

TRUTH AND TRUTHS IN FEMINIST KNOWLEDGE PRODUCTION

Mary Hawkesworth

The project of feminist theory is to write a new encyclopedia. Its title: The World, According to Women.

—Frye (1993, p. 104)

By situating feminist scholarship in the tradition of the radical eighteenth-century French *encyclopédistes,* whose objective was to systematize all human knowledge, Marilyn Frye illuminates the enormity of the task of feminist inquiry: to develop an account of the world that places women's lives, experiences, and perspectives at the center of analysis and, in so doing, corrects the distorted, biased, and erroneous accounts advanced by men. By suggesting that scholarship by men has gotten things wrong and that scholarship that starts from women's lives will get them right, Frye acknowledges that the quest for truth lies at the heart of the feminist project. She also invokes a conception of truth tied to the philosophical enterprise first developed in ancient Greece. Truth is understood as *alethia,* that

which remains when all error is purged. Thus Frye construes feminist scholarship as a maieutic art, a form of inquiry that begins with claims that are widely accepted, subjects them to critical scrutiny, and demonstrates defects in their assertions.

Feminist scholarship has grown exponentially over the past four decades, transforming knowledge in the humanities, social sciences, and natural sciences. Cutting across the divisions of knowledge that structure contemporary universities, feminist inquiry has been characterized as oppositional research because it challenges the right of the powerful to define realities across these diverse disciplines (DeVault, 1999, p. 1). To interrogate the dominant paradigms in their disciplines, feminist scholars have to develop expertise in the modes of analysis, investigation, and interpretation accredited within their fields. Thus any account of "truth" in feminist research practices must be attuned to commonalities and diversities, explicating that which feminist scholars share in common, as well as the points of divergence and disagreement across complex modes of intellectual life. This chapter will begin with an exploration of the assumptions about knowledge production shared by feminist scholars and then probe a range of debates about the nature of truth and the possibilities for discerning truth in feminist research.

FEMINIST METHODOLOGY

French philosopher Michèle Le Doeuff (1991) has defined a feminist as "a woman who does not leave others to think for her" (p. 29). Interrogating accepted beliefs, challenging shared assumptions, and reframing research questions are characteristic of feminist inquiry regardless of specialization. Feminist scholars have taken issue with dominant disciplinary approaches to knowledge production. They have contested androcentric "ways to truth" that universalize the experiences of a fraction of the human population. They have challenged the power dynamics structuring exclusionary academic practices that have enabled unwarranted generalizations to remain unchallenged for centuries or indeed millennia. They have sought to identify and develop alternative research practices that further feminist goals of social transformation.

To probe the common dynamics of diverse feminist research practices, scholars interested in the philosophy and sociology of inquiry have initiated debates about "feminist methodology," exploring ideas about the theories of knowledge, strategies of inquiry, and standards of evidence appropriate to the production of feminist knowledge. Noting the enormous range of feminist research, many scholars who have written on the question of feminist methodology have taken an inclusive approach, describing the variety of methods feminists have deployed and tracing connections between the specific methods and kinds of research questions they are particularly suited to answer (DeVault, 1999; Fonow & Cook, 1991; Hesse-Biber, Gilmartin, & Lydenberg, 1999; Hesse-Biber & Leavy, 2004; Oakley, 2000; Reinharz, 1992; Windance Twine & Warren, 2000; Wolf, 1996). The range of questions and the scope of feminist research are extensive. Archaeological, autobiographical, biographical, biological, case-study, causal, comparative, cultural, dialectical, deconstructive, demographic, discursive, econometric, ethnographic, experimental, genealogical, geographical, gynocritical, hermeneutic, historical, institutional, intertextual, legal, materialist, narrative, phenomenological, philosophical, primatological, psychoanalytic, psychological, semiotic, statistical, structural, survey, teleological, theoretical, and textual analysis have all been deployed successfully by feminist scholars across a range of disciplines. Although such an enumeration highlights the breadth of feminist inquiry, it does not resolve the question of how feminist appropriations of these diverse methods are distinctive.

Thinking about methodology in a slightly different way, then, might help to illuminate common dimensions of feminist inquiry amidst this diversity. Etymologically, the term "methodology" arises from the conjunction of three Greek concepts: *meta, hodos,* and *logos.* When used as a prefix in archaic Greek, *meta* typically implied "sharing," "action in common," or "pursuit or quest." *Hodos* was usually translated as "way," but when combined with *logos,* which was variously translated as "account," "explanation," or "truth," *hodos* suggested a very particular way to truth about the essence of reality (Wolin, 1981). Bringing the three Greek terms together opens possibilities for a variety of interpretations of methodology: "a shared quest for the way to truth," "a shared account of truth," or "the way a group legitimates knowledge claims."

The Greek roots of the term are particularly helpful in laying the groundwork for an exploration of the distinctive aspects of feminist methodology, for the etymology makes clear that methodologies are group specific and, as such, political. The appropriate methodology for any particular inquiry is a matter of contestation as scholars often disagree about the "way to truth." Strategies that are accredited as legitimate means to acquire truth gain their force from decisions of particular humans; thus, there is a power element in the accreditation of knowledge. Power is never the only factor involved, but neither is it a negligible factor.

Like all methodologies, then, feminist research is informed by a politics. But unlike methodologies developed in accordance with positivist assumptions about knowledge production, which explicitly deny any political dimension to "scientific" inquiry, feminist research acknowledges that particular political convictions inspire its existence. As a political movement, feminism seeks to eliminate male domination in all of its various manifestations. Knowledge production is a rich terrain for feminist engagement, for the authoritative accounts of the world accredited by academic disciplines, whether in the humanities, social sciences, or natural sciences, have profound effects on women's lives. "What constitutes feminist work is a framework that challenges existing androcentric or partial constructions of women's lives" (Geiger, 1990, p. 169).

In an effort to explicate how feminist principles could contribute to academic research, Adrienne Rich (2003) noted suggestively that "a politicized life ought to sharpen both the senses and the memory" (p. 454). Feminist convictions attune scholars to power dynamics that structure women's lives, which can generate challenges to dominant accounts and new questions for research. "It is the political commitment that feminists bring to diverse fields that motivates them to focus attention on lines of evidence others have not sought out or thought important; to discern patterns others have ignored; to question androcentric or sexist framework assumptions that have gone unnoticed or unchallenged; and, sometimes, to significantly reframe the research agenda of their discipline in light of different questions or an expanded repertoire of explanatory hypotheses" (Wylie, 2003, p. 38).

In recognizing the effect of the researcher's values upon the logic of discovery, feminist research has a great deal in common with a postpositivist philosophy of science. There is another dimension of feminist scholarship, however, that goes well beyond claims concerning the value-laden origins of research. Feminist scholarship suggests that a particular politics embedded in the research process improves the quality of analysis, heightens objectivity, and enhances the sophistication of research findings. Far from being a source of bias and distortion, feminist convictions and principles are deemed an asset to research. In the words of Linda Nochlin (1971/1988): "Natural assumptions must be questioned and the mythic basis of so much so-called fact brought to light. And it is here that

the very position of women as an acknowledged outsider, the maverick 'she' instead of the presumably neutral 'one'—in reality the white-male position accepted as natural, or the hidden 'he' as the subject of all scholarly predicates—is a decided advantage, rather than merely a hindrance or a subjective distortion" (p. 145).

Positivist conceptions of science, Kantian conceptions of moral reasoning, and the tenets of new criticism within literary theory insist upon neutrality or impartiality as central to objectivity. By contrast, feminist scholarship suggests that a commitment to struggle against coercive hierarchies linked to gender, race, and sexuality; to promote women's freedom and empowerment; and to revolt against institutions, practices, values, and knowledge systems that subordinate and denigrate women enhances the truth content and deepens the insights of feminist accounts of the world. Despite its diverse disciplinary and interdisciplinary settings, feminist scholarship involves "disidentification" from some of the guiding precepts of positivism, such as value neutrality, and from norms of distanced, dispassionate research and the quest for universal explanations characteristic of many disciplines. The justification for feminist scholars' disidentification emerged in the context of their sustained engagement with dominant conceptions of objectivity.

POSITIVIST AND FEMINIST CONCEPTIONS OF OBJECTIVITY

Objectivity has been a regulative ideal in philosophical and scientific investigations, ethical and judicial deliberations, and bureaucratic practices. Objectivity gains its purchase within these diverse domains on the basis of specific promises. In the context of philosophical and scientific investigations, for example, an objective account implies a grasp of the actual qualities and relations of objects as they exist independent of the inquirer's thoughts and desires regarding them (Cunningham, 1973). Objectivity, then, promises to free us from distortion, bias, and error in intellectual inquiry, to provide a path to truth that transcends the fallibility of individual knowers.

Feminist critiques of objectivity have been triggered by breach of promise. Feminist scholars have demonstrated that observations, beliefs, theories, methods of inquiry, and institutional practices routinely labeled "objective" fall far short of the norm. A significant proportion of feminist scholarship involves detailed refutations of erroneous claims about women produced in conformity with prevailing disciplinary standards of objectivity. The pervasiveness of the mistakes about the nature of women and their roles in history, politics, and society and the imperviousness of mistaken views to refutation have led some feminist scholars to examine the conception of objectivity accredited within positivist conceptions of knowledge production.

Positivism

The term *positivism* was first coined by the French sociologist Auguste Comte, who suggested that scientific understanding operates in the realm of the "positive," which denotes "real" or "actual" existence. By eschewing the metaphysical and theological and relying solely upon observable facts and the relations that hold among observed phenomena, scientific inquiry could discover the "laws" governing empirical events. Within the field of the philosophy of science, logical positivism was elaborated in the 1920s by the members of the Vienna Circle, who further restricted the possibilities for valid knowledge by elaborating the *verification criterion of meaning,* which stipulated that a contingent proposition is meaningful if and only if it can be empirically verified, that is, if there is an empirical method for deciding if the proposition is true or false. While the logical positivists sought to explicate methodological concepts in formal, logical terms, empirical researchers within the natural sciences and the social sciences drew upon positivist precepts to legitimate particular methodological techniques to generate objective knowledge. Chief among these were the fact/value dichotomy and hypothetico-deductive model of scientific inquiry. According to positivist precepts, differentiating between factual claims and evaluative judgments is the first step in the scientific process, which culminates in the vindication of empirical propositions as objective

representations of the world. Categorizing claims as empirical, that is, as statements that can be verified by sensory inspection, and separating them from those that are normative are crucial preconditions for the acquisition of valid knowledge. Together, they demarcate the range of propositions amenable to scientific investigation. Induction, a method of knowledge acquisition grounded upon the systematic observation of particulars as the foundation for empirical generalizations, was taken to provide the key to scientific investigations.

Within the positivist framework, the task of science was understood to be the inductive discovery of regularities existing in the external world. Scientific research sought to organize in economical fashion those regularities that experience presents in order to facilitate explanation and prediction. To promote this objective, positivists endorsed and employed a technical vocabulary, clearly differentiating facts (empirically verifiable propositions) and hypotheses (empirically verifiable propositions asserting the existence of relationships among observed phenomena) from laws (empirically confirmed propositions asserting an invariable sequence or association among observed phenomena) and theories (interrelated systems of laws possessing explanatory power). Moreover, the positivist logic of scientific inquiry dictated a specific sequence of activities as definitive to "the scientific method."

According to the positivist model, the scientific method began with the carefully controlled, neutral observation of empirical events. Sustained observation over time would enable the regularities or patterns of relationships in observed events to be revealed and thereby provide for the formulation of hypotheses. Once formulated, hypotheses were to be subjected to systematic empirical tests. Those hypotheses that received external confirmation through this process of rigorous testing could be elevated to the status of scientific laws. Once identified, scientific laws provided the foundation for scientific explanation, which, according to the precepts of the "covering law model," consisted in demonstrating that the event(s) to be explained could have been expected, given certain initial conditions (C_1, C_2, C_3, ...) and the general laws of the field (L_1, L_2, L_3, ...).

Within the framework of the positivist conception of science, the discovery of scientific laws also provided the foundation for prediction that consisted in demonstrating that an event would occur given the future occurrence of certain initial conditions and the operation of the general laws of the field. Under the covering law model, then, explanation and prediction have the same logical form. Only the time factor differs: explanation pertains to past events; prediction pertains to future events. Positivists were also committed to the principle of the "unity of science," that is, to the belief that the logic of scientific inquiry was the same for all fields. Whether natural phenomena or social phenomena were the objects of study, the method for acquiring valid knowledge and the requirements for explanation and prediction remained the same. Once a science had progressed sufficiently to accumulate a body of scientific laws organized in a coherent system of theories, it could be said to have achieved a stage of "maturity" that made explanation and prediction possible. Although the logic of mature science remained inductive with respect to the generation of new knowledge, the logic of scientific explanation was deductive. Under the covering law model, causal explanation, the demonstration of the necessary and sufficient conditions of an event, involved the deductive subsumption of particular observations under a general law. In addition, deduction also played a central role in efforts to explain laws and theories: the explanation of a law involved its deductive subsumption under a theory; and explanation of one theory involved its deductive subsumption under wider theories.

Critiques of Positivism

The primary postulates of positivism have been subjected to rigorous and devastating critiques (Popper, 1959, 1972a, 1972b). Neither the logic of induction nor the verification criterion of meaning can accomplish positivist objectives; neither can guarantee the acquisition of truth. The inductive method is incapable of guaranteeing the validity of scientific knowledge owing to the "problem of induction" (Hume, 1739/1975, 1748/1927). Because empirical events are contingent (i.e., because the future can always be different from the past), generalizations based upon limited observations are necessarily incomplete and, as such, highly fallible. For this reason, inductive generalizations cannot be presumed to be true. Nor can "confirmation" or "verification" of such generalizations by reference to additional cases provide proof of their universal validity, because the notion of universal validity invokes all future, as well as all past and present, occurrences of a phenomenon. Yet no matter how many confirming instances of a phenomenon can be found in the past or in the present, these can never alter the logical possibility that the future could be different, that the future could disprove an inductively derived empirical generalization. Thus, a demonstration of the truth of an empirical generalization must turn upon the identification of a "necessary connection" establishing a causal relation among observed phenomena.

Unfortunately, the notion of necessary connection also encounters serious problems. If the notion of necessity invoked is logical necessity, then the empirical nature of science is jeopardized. If, on the other hand, positivism appeals to an empirical demonstration of necessity, it falls foul of the standard established by the verification criterion of meaning, for the "necessity" required as proof of any causal claim cannot be empirically observed. As Hume pointed out, empirical observation reveals "constant conjunction" (a "correlation," in the language of contemporary social science); it does not and cannot reveal necessary connection. As a positivist logic of scientific inquiry, then, induction encounters two serious problems: it is incapable of providing validation for the truth of its generalizations, and it is internally inconsistent, for any attempt to demonstrate the validity of a causal claim invokes a conception of necessary connection that violates the verification criterion of meaning.

The positivist conception of the scientific method also rests upon a flawed psychology of perception. In suggesting that the scientific method commences with "neutral" observation, positivists invoke a conception of "manifest truth," which attempts to reduce the problem of the validity of knowledge to an appeal to the authority of the source of that knowledge (for example, "the facts 'speak' for themselves").

The belief that the unmediated apprehension of the "given" by a passive or receptive observer is possible, however, misconstrues both the nature of perception and the nature of the world. The human mind is not passive but active; it does not merely receive an image of the given but rather imposes order upon the external world through a process of selection, interpretation, and imagination. Observation is always linguistically and culturally mediated. It involves the creative imposition of expectations, anticipations, and conjectures upon external events.

Scientific observation, too, is necessarily theory laden. It begins not from "nothing," nor from the "neutral" perception of given relations, but rather from immersion in a scientific tradition that provides frames of reference or conceptual schemes that organize reality and shape the problems for further investigation. To grasp the role of theory in structuring scientific observation, however, requires a revised conception of "theory." Contrary to the positivist notion that theory is the result of observation, the result of systematization of a series of inductive generalizations, the result of the accumulation of an interrelated set of scientific laws, theory is logically prior to the observation of any similarities or regularities in the world; indeed, theory is precisely that which makes the identification of regularities possible. Moreover, scientific theories involve risk to an extent that is altogether incompatible with the positivist view of theories as summaries of empirical generalizations. Scientific theories involve risky predictions of things that have never been seen and hence cannot be deduced logically from observation statements. Theories structure scientific observation in a manner altogether incompatible with the positivist requirement of neutral perception, and they involve unobservable propositions that violate the verification criterion of meaning: abstract theoretical entities cannot be verified by reference to empirical observation.

That theoretical propositions violate the verification criterion is not in itself damning, for the verification criterion can be impugned on a number of grounds. As a mechanism for the validation of empirical generalizations, the verification criterion fails because of the problem of induction. As a scientific principle for the demarcation of the "meaningful" from the "meaningless," the verification criterion is self-referentially destructive. In repudiating all that is not empirically verifiable as nonsense, the verification criterion repudiates itself, for it is not a statement derived from empirical observation nor is it a tautology. Rigid adherence to the verification criterion, then, would mandate that it be rejected as metaphysical nonsense. Thus, the positivist conflation of that which is not amenable to empirical observation with nonsense simply will not withstand scrutiny. Much (including the verification criterion itself) that cannot be empirically verified can be understood, and all that can be understood is meaningful.

Critical Rationalism

As an alternative to the defective positivist conception of science, Karl Popper (1959, 1972a, 1972b) advanced "critical rationalism." In this view, scientific theories are bold conjectures that scientists impose upon the world. Drawing insights from manifold sources in order to solve particular problems, scientific theories involve abstract and unobservable propositions that predict what may happen as well as what may not happen. Thus, scientific theories generate predictions that are incompatible with certain possible results of observation; that is, they "prohibit" certain occurrences by proclaiming that some things could not happen. As such, scientific theories put the world to the test and demand a reply. Precisely because scientific theories identify a range of conditions that must hold, a series of events that must occur, and a set of occurrences that are in principle impossible, they can clash with observation; they are empirically testable. Although no number of confirming instances can ever prove a theory to be true due to the problem of induction, one disconfirming instance is sufficient to disprove a theory. If scientific laws are construed as statements of prohibitions, forbidding the occurrence of certain empirical events, then they can be refuted definitively by the occurrence of one such event. Thus, according to Popper, "falsification" provides a mechanism by which scientists can test their conjectures against reality and learn from their mistakes.

Falsification also provides the core of Popper's revised conception of the scientific method.

According to the "hypothetico-deductive model," the scientist always begins with a problem. To resolve the problem, the scientist generates a theory, a conjecture or hypothesis, that can be tested by deducing its empirical consequences and measuring them against the world. Once the logical implications of a theory have been deduced and converted into predictions concerning empirical events, the task of science is falsification. In putting theories to the test of experience, scientists seek to falsify predictions, for that alone enables them to learn from their mistakes. The rationality of science is embodied in the method of trial and error, a method that allows error to be purged through the elimination of false theories.

In mandating that all scientific theories be tested, in stipulating that the goal of science is the falsification of erroneous views, the criterion of falsifiability provides a means by which to reconcile the fallibility of human knowers with a conception of objective knowledge. The validity of scientific claims does not turn on a demand for an impossible neutrality on the part of individual scientists; on the equally impossible requirement that all prejudice, bias, prejudgment, expectation, or value be purged from the process of observation; or on the implausible assumption that the truth is manifest. The adequacy of scientific theories is judged in concrete problem contexts in terms of a theory's ability to solve problems and withstand increasingly difficult empirical tests. Those theories that withstand multiple intersubjective efforts to falsify them are "corroborated," identified as "laws" that, with varying degrees of verisimilitude, capture the structure of reality; for that reason, these theories are tentatively accepted as "true." But, in keeping with the critical attitude of science, even the strongest corroboration for a theory is not accepted as conclusive proof, for Popperian critical rationalism posits that truth lies beyond human reach. As a regulative ideal that guides scientific activity, truth may be approximated, but it can never be established by human authority. Nevertheless, error can be objectively identified. Thus, informed by a conception of truth as

a regulative ideal and operating in accordance with the requirements of the criterion of falsifiability, science can progress by the incremental correction of errors and the gradual accretion of objective, problem-solving knowledge.

Although Popper subjected many of the central tenets of logical positivism to systematic critique, his conception of "critical rationalism" shares sufficient ground with positivist approaches to the philosophy of science that it is typically considered to be a qualified modification of, rather than a comprehensive alternative to, positivism (Stockman, 1983). Indeed, Popper's conception of the hypothetico-deductive model has been depicted as the "orthodox" positivist conception of scientific theory (Moon, 1975, pp. 143–187). Both positivist and Popperian approaches to science share a belief in the centrality of logical deduction to scientific analysis; both conceive scientific theories to be deductively related systems of propositions; both accept a deductive account of scientific explanation; both treat explanation and prediction as equivalent concepts; and both are committed to a conception of scientific progress dependent upon the use of the hypothetico-deductive method of testing scientific claims (Brown, 1977, pp. 65–75; Stockman, 1983, p. 76). In addition, both positivist and Popperian conceptions of science are committed to the correspondence theory of truth, which holds that a statement (proposition, idea, thought, belief, opinion) is true if that to which it refers (corresponds) exists; that is, a proposition is true if and only if its central claim corresponds with the facts. Thus, both positivist and Popperian approaches also accept the corollary assumption that the objectivity of science ultimately rests upon an appeal to the facts. Both are committed to the institutionalization of the fact/value dichotomy in order to establish the determinate ground of science. Both accept that, once safely ensconced within the bounds of the empirical realm, science is grounded upon a sufficiently firm foundation to provide for the accumulation of knowledge, the progressive elimination of error, and the gradual accretion of useful solutions to technical problems. And, although Popper suggested that reason could be brought to bear upon evaluative questions, he accepted the fundamental positivist principle that, ultimately, value choices rested upon non-rational factors.

Feminist Critiques of Positivist Approaches

Ruth Berman (1989) identified three core assumptions of objectivity within positivist approaches to scientific inquiry: "that a rational method of investigation, the scientific method, exists, which can be utilized regardless of social context or the phenomenon being investigated; that any 'good,' well-trained, honest scientist can apply this well-defined, neutral method to the object being investigated and obtain objective, unbiased data; and that the 'facts (data) are the facts'; the results reported are 'hard,' immutable, and unaffected by personal concerns" (pp. 236–237). Numerous feminist scholars have taken issue with each of these assumptions.

In contrast to broad construals of the scientific method in terms of formulating, testing, and falsifying hypotheses, feminist scholars have pointed out that "science has many methods," all of which are discipline specific and most of which are closely linked to the nature of the phenomenon under study (Fee, 1983; Harding, 1986; Longino, 1990, 2002). Moreover, whether the specific method of investigation involves induction, deduction, or controlled experimentation, no method can guarantee the validity of its results. The attainment of truth cannot be assured by adherence to a simple procedural formula. Thus, conceptions of objectivity that turn on adherence to an appropriate disciplinary method are seriously defective. Nor can positivists save the belief that the scientific method guarantees the objectivity of results by appealing to replicability. Intersubjective testing and confirmation cannot be taken as reliable tokens of truthfulness because, as the history of scientific and philosophical claims about women so clearly demonstrates, conventional misogyny sustains verifications of erroneous views (Ruth, 1981). Multiple investigators deploying identical techniques may produce the same conclusions, but such intersubjective consensus cannot attest to the veracity of the claims.

It could, of course, be argued that adherence to an invariant scientific method is not a criterion of objectivity in science but that belief in such a method is an artifact of certain reconstructions of science characteristic of the philosophy of science. What is central to scientific objectivity is the neutrality of precise methods within the various scientific disciplines. Adherence to a neutral, public methodology devised to control for the idiosyncrasies of the individual inquirer produces credible scientific results. In response to this kind of claim, many feminist scholars have devoted a good deal of attention to the examination of methodological "neutrality" in the natural and social sciences. Their investigations have revealed extensive androcentrism in diverse scientific methods manifested in the selection of scientific problems deemed worthy of investigation, research design, definition of key terms and concepts, decisions concerning relevant evidence and counterexamples, data collection and analysis, interpretations of results, and assessments of practical falsifications (Bleier, 1979, 1984; Eichler, 1980; Fausto-Sterling, 1985; Hubbard, Hennifin, & Fried, 1982; Stanley & Wise, 1983; Westkott, 1979). Contrary to claims of neutrality, scientific research is riddled with sexism, which renders women invisible, ignores women's concerns, precludes elicitation of certain kinds of information about women, reproduces gender stereotypes in the operationalization of terms, denies that gender might serve as an explanatory variable in any instance, and reverts to functionalist explanations that accredit the status quo (Benston, 1982; Farganis, 1989; Kelly, Ronan, & Cawley, 1987; Vickers, 1982). Sandra Harding has suggested that not only are the concepts, methods, and conclusions of inquiry permeated by androcentrism, but sexism also influences the recruitment of personnel in science and the evaluation of the significance of scientists' research. "If women are systematically excluded from the design and management of science and their work devalued, then it appears that neither the assignment of status to persons within science nor the assessment of the value of the results of inquiry is, or is intended to be, value-neutral, objective, socially impartial" (Harding, 1986, p. 67). And Margaret Benston (1982) has concluded that "present science practices a kind of 'pseudo-objectivity' where because they are not taken explicitly into account, subjective factors are uncontrolled and unaccounted for" (p. 59).

If the disciplinary techniques devised to investigate the natural and social worlds are value permeated rather than value neutral, then perhaps the best hope for objectivity lies in the attitude of the investigator. Berman's reference to any "honest scientist" reflects the belief that the critical, nondogmatic, skeptical stance of scientists themselves can serve as a guarantor of objectivity. In disciplinary discussions of objectivity, it is not uncommon to find a peculiar displacement. In the absence of a neutral method, descriptions of the qualities of "objective knowledge" are offered as clues to the appropriate means to its attainment. Disinterestedness, dispassionateness, detachment, impersonality, and universality have been put forward as elements of model deportment for researchers on the assumption that, if the inquirer emulates the qualities attributed to objective knowledge, then the results of inquiry will be imbued with those characteristics. Feminist investigations have raised logical and empirical objections to this construal of objectivity as well. Logically, displacing the characteristics of objective knowledge onto the attitudes of "objective" inquirers can no more guarantee the attainment of truth than can a clearly elucidated research method. Empirically, there are good reasons to doubt that scientists conform to these model traits. In contrast to systematic skepticism, many scientists not only never question popular gender stereotypes but also incorporate culturally specific gender roles in their hypotheses about various animal species, cellular organisms, and social systems (Fausto-Sterling, 1985; Haraway, 1989; Martin, 1990; Strum & Fedigan, 2000). Claims of detachment, disinterest, distance, and universality merely serve as mechanisms for male hegemony, substituting certain men's perspectives for the "view from nowhere" (Nagel, 1986).

Like many postpositivist critics, feminist scholars have pointed out that the norms of value neutrality, whether pertaining to methods of inquiry or the attitudes of inquirers, seriously misconstrue the nature of cognition, creating a false dichotomy between emotion and rationality, overlooking the theoretical presuppositions that shape perception and interpretation, masking individual creativity, and concealing the politics of disciplinary practices (Grant, 1993; Hawkesworth, 1989, 2006; Jaggar, 1989; Longino, 1990, 2002). They have also pointed out that the continuing invocation of conceptions of objectivity rooted in erroneous notions of value neutrality can have pernicious consequences. "Commonly, women's perceptions of social reality have been denied, suppressed, or invalidated, and women have been labeled 'deviant' or 'sick' if they have refused to accept some dominant definition of their situation. Commonly, too, theories have been put forward in the name of 'science' or 'objectivity' which have not only denied or distorted female experience but have also served to rationalise and legitimate male control over women" (Grimshaw, 1986, p. 83).

Several feminist scholars have suggested that, rather than producing accurate depictions of natural and social worlds, allegedly objective scientific inquiry has produced propaganda that serves the purposes of social control (Harding, 1986, p. 67). Scientifically accredited "facts" are not the hard, incontrovertible, immutable givens they are purported to be; rather, they are ideological fragments that promote male dominance (Fox Keller, 1985; Mies, 1984). Rather than capturing things as they are, appeals to objectivity "bolster the epistemic authority of the currently dominant groups, composed largely of white men, and discredit the observations and claims of the currently subordinate groups including, of course, the observations and claims of many people of color and women" (Jaggar, 1989, p. 158). From this view, dominant conceptions of objectivity serve "as a potent agent for maintaining current power relationships and women's subordination" precisely because they accord authority to androcentric claims, not merely by masking their bias but by certifying their "neutrality" (Berman, 1989, p. 224).

Feminist scholarship across the disciplines has revealed that misogyny routinely blinds "objective" investigators. In addressing the "Woman Question," philosophers and scientists often ignore or violate the methodological constraints of their fields, generate contradictory claims about women that undermine the internal consistency of their arguments about human beings, and fail to notice that the hypotheses they advance about women are inadequately warranted. The frequency with which such problems arise in the context of "objective" modes of inquiry implies both that existing strictures of objectivity are insufficient to attain truth and that there are serious deficiencies in the dominant conceptions of objectivity.

Feminist scholarship offers a critique of dominant, disciplinary conceptions of objectivity, a critique that illuminates the role of social values in cognition and that has important implications beyond investigations in which women are the objects of inquiry. It has already been noted that feminists have identified a number of faulty inferences that can explain how investigators committed to objective inquiry and acting in good faith can generate erroneous claims. The assumptions that emulation of the qualities of objective knowledge can assure its attainment and that adherence to specific research techniques can guarantee the validity of results both reflect mistakes about the requirements of objectivity. Although they arise in different problem contexts, both also manifest an erroneous understanding of the social constitution of knowledge and its implications for objective inquiry.

Conceptions of objectivity premised upon the self-purging of bias, value, or emotion and those dependent upon intersubjective correction for the elimination of error both imply that the fundamental threat to objectivity is idiosyncrasy. Both share the Baconian view of subjectivity as an obscuring, "enchanted glass, full of superstition and imposture, if it be not delivered and reduced" (Bacon, 1861, p. 276). Both locate the chief obstacle to the acquisition of truth within the individual researcher. Thus the techniques of objective inquiry, whether conceived in terms of acts of pure intellect or intersubjective emendation, are designed to protect against "the capacity of the knower to bestow false inner projections on the outer world of things" (Bordo, 1987, p. 51).

The feminist discovery of persistent patterns of sexist error in "objective" inquiry suggests that the target of the various corrective strategies has been mislocated. The conviction that the central problem of objectivity lies with the emotional and perceptual quirks of the subjective self that distort, confuse, and interfere with the objective apprehension of phenomena neglects the social dimensions of inner consciousness. Situating the issue of objectivity in a contest between the inner self and external reality masks the social constitution of subjectivity. The recurrence of a profound degree of sexism that filters perceptions, mediates philosophical arguments, structures research hypotheses, and "stabilizes inquiry by providing assumptions that highlight certain kinds of observations and experiments in light of which data are taken as evidence for hypotheses" indicates a remarkable uniformity in the kinds of distortion that impede the acquisition of truth (Longino, 1990, p. 99). Such uniformity challenges the myth of radical idiosyncrasy. One need not be committed to the full implications of Foucault's view of subjectivity as normalizing practice to accept the feminist argument that even one's innermost consciousness is culturally freighted.

If social values incorporated within individual consciousness present an important obstacle to objective knowledge, then norms of objectivity that blind the individual to the role of social values or assure the individual that intersubjective consensus is a sufficient indicator of objectivity will fail to produce objective accounts of the world. For, if certain social values structure self-conceptions as well as individual perceptions of the social and natural worlds, then neither isolated acts of pure intellect nor intersubjective testing will suffice to identify them. On the contrary, the belief that subjectivity is the fundamental obstacle to objectivity will preclude detailed investigations of the shared assumptions and observations that inform intersubjectively verified theories. Rather than being perceived as a potential source of error, values such as sexism and racism that are widely held will escape critical reflection. Their very popularity will be taken to certify their validity, thereby truncating further inquiry into their merits.

Feminist scholars have illuminated the numerous points at which social values infiltrate discourses on women. Helen Longino (1990, 2002) has drawn upon these insights to develop an account of objectivity that can coexist with a clear understanding of the social and cultural construction of science. Longino identifies the crucial role played by social values in framing research questions, characterizing the objects of inquiry, accrediting forms of explanation, demarcating credible evidence, structuring modes of argumentation, and reducing a discipline's vulnerability to maverick claims. The point of Longino's investigation is not to demonstrate the impossibility of objectivity but rather to illuminate the complexity of attaining it. Only heightened awareness of the multiple sources of error and the complexity of problems of knowledge can sustain adequate strategies to achieve objectivity. And only repudiation of naive faith that adherence to a simple method can guarantee the acquisition of truth can help cultivate the sophistication essential to objective inquiry.

At the heart of this feminist conception of objectivity is the idea of cognition as a human practice, a conception that recognizes the complex interaction among traditional assumptions, social norms, theoretical conceptions, disciplinary strictures, linguistic possibilities, emotional dispositions, and creative impositions in every act of cognition. Operating in the context of cognition as complex social practice, the quest for objectivity entails the cultivation of the intellect. To track the multiple sources of error in a specific field of inquiry requires far more than intellectual engagement within a narrow sphere of specialization. Sensitivity to distortion and bias presupposes an intellect informed by the systematic study of a chosen field, familiar with the strengths and weaknesses of a wide range of methodological tools, and sufficiently knowledgeable across disciplines to analyze the role of social values in constituting the research object (Alcoff, 2000; Hawkesworth, 1989; Longino, 2002).

A capacity for critical reflection is central to this feminist conception of objectivity, but it is not the sole requirement. Intersubjectivity also plays a key role. "A method of inquiry is objective to the extent that it permits transformative criticism" (Longino, 1990, p. 75). The point of intersubjectivity within this framework is not to confirm shared assumptions about what is normal, natural, or real but rather to subject precisely what seems least problematic to critical scrutiny. Awareness of the role of social values in naturalizing oppressive practices leads feminists to emphasize the importance of critical

intersubjectivity in probing the tacit assumptions and foundational beliefs of various disciplines.

If objective inquiry is dependent upon the systematic probing of precisely that which appears unproblematic, then who does the probing may be a matter of central concern to those committed to objective inquiry. For what is taken as given, what appears to be natural, what seems to fall outside the legitimate field of investigation may be related to the gender, race, class, and historical situatedness of the investigator. Feminist scholars have argued that the attainment of objectivity by means of probing and sophisticated intersubjective critique has implications that transcend the quest for an appropriate intellectual procedure. Convinced that "methodological constraints are inadequate to the task of ruling values out of scientific inquiry," feminists have argued that objectivity demands inclusivity (Longino, 1990, p. 15). Objective inquiry cannot be attained within the preserve of privilege—whether it be the privilege of whites, the middle class, or men. The feminist argument for the inclusion of women and people of color within academic disciplines can thus be understood in terms of the demands of objectivity. To the extent that social values mediate perception and explanation, exclusionary practices can only help insulate questionable assumptions from scrutiny. A commitment to objectivity conceived as sophisticated intersubjective critique embraces diversity as a means. More and different "guides to the labyrinths of reality" (Stimpson, 1991) may help us to confront the contentious assumptions most deeply entrenched in our conceptual apparatus. The inclusion of people from different social backgrounds, different cultures, different linguistic communities, and different genders within science and philosophy cannot guarantee, but it might foster, a sustained critique of problematic assumptions long entrenched in the academic disciplines (Alcoff, 2000).

A feminist conception of objectivity does not offer an authoritative technique that can guarantee the production of truth. In lieu of a simple method, it calls for the cultivation of sound intellectual judgment. It demands a level of sophistication that can be cultivated only by sustained study across an array of disciplines. It presupposes a reconceptualization of the relation between inner self and external world. Moreover, it demands the expansion of the scientific and philosophical communities to encompass formerly excluded groups. Thus, this feminist conception of objectivity cannot be easily attained. It remains at odds with the excessive specialization of contemporary academic training and with the naive conviction that truth lies in the application of an accredited method. Moreover, it challenges efforts to preserve white, middle-class, and male hegemony in philosophy, science, and society at large. Although it goes against the grain of many dominant trends, this feminist conception of objectivity holds great potential. Its strength lies in its capacity to foster the benign aspirations and objectives of objectivity when traditional conceptions have failed.

CONTEXTUALIZING TRUTH CLAIMS: FEMINIST ANTI-FOUNDATIONALISM

Feminist scholarship across a wide range of disciplines involves a break with traditional assumptions about the possibility and necessity of value neutrality in research. It is also characterized by a rejection of "foundationalism," the notion that there is an absolute ground for truth claims, whether that ground is understood in terms of the rational capacity to comprehend things as they are, systematic powers of observation that afford an unmediated grasp of existence, or a synoptic view "from everywhere and nowhere, equally and fully" that Donna Haraway (1988, p. 586) characterized as the "god trick." Critiques of foundationalism have emphasized that the belief in a permanent, ahistorical, Archimedean point that can provide a certain ground for knowledge claims is incompatible with an understanding of cognition as a human practice. They have suggested that the belief that particular techniques of rational analysis can escape finitude and fallibility and grasp the totality of being misconstrues both the nature of subjective intellection and the nature of the objective world (Code, 1991; Hawkesworth, 1989; Tanesini, 1999).

Standard critiques of foundationalism question the adequacy of deductive and inductive logic as the ground of objective knowledge. To challenge rationalists' confidence in the power of logical deduction as a method for securing the truth about the empirical world, critics typically point out that the truth of syllogistic reasoning is altogether dependent upon the established truth of the syllogism's major and minor premises. Yet, when one moves from relations of ideas governed by logical necessity to a world of contingency, the "established truth" of major and minor premises is precisely what is at issue. Thus, rather than providing an impeccable foundation for truth claims, deduction confronts the intractable problems of infinite regress, the vicious circle, or the arbitrary suspension of the principle of sufficient reason through appeals to intuition or self-evidence (Albert, 1985; Hume, 1748/1927).

Attacks on induction have been equally shattering. It has been repeatedly pointed out that inductive generalizations, however scrupulous and systematic, founder on a host of problems: observation generates correlations that cannot prove causation and conclusions derived from incomplete evidence sustain probability claims but do not produce incontestable truth (Albert, 1985; Popper, 1972a). Moreover, where rationalism tends to overestimate the power of theoretical speculation, empiricism errs in the opposite extreme by underestimating the role of theory in shaping perception and structuring comprehension. Thus, as noted previously, the "objectivity" of the positivist project turns upon the deployment of an untenable dichotomy between "facts" and "values"—a dichotomy that misconstrues the nature of perception, fails to comprehend the theoretical constitution of facticity, and uncritically disseminates the "myth of the given" (Sellars, 1963).

As an alternative to conceptions of knowledge that depend upon the existence of an unmediated reality that can be grasped directly by observation or intellection, anti-foundationalists suggest a conception of cognition as a human practice. In this view, "knowing" presupposes involvement in a social process replete with rules of compliance, norms of assessment, and standards of excellence that are humanly created. Although humans aspire to unmediated knowledge of the world, the nature of perception precludes such direct access. The only possible access is through theory-laden conventions that organize and structure observation by according meanings to observed events, bestowing relevance and significance upon phenomena, indicating strategies for problem solving, and identifying methods by which to test the validity of proposed solutions. Knowledge, then, is a convention rooted in the practical judgments of a community of fallible inquirers who struggle to resolve theory-dependent problems under specific historical conditions. In contrast to the correspondence theory of truth, which assumes that it is possible to measure claims about reality against what actually exists, the conception of cognition as a human practice relies upon a coherence theory of truth premised on the recognition that all human knowledge depends upon theoretical presuppositions whose congruence with external reality cannot be established conclusively by reason or experience.

Acquisition of knowledge occurs in the context of socialization and enculturation to determinate traditions that provide the conceptual frameworks through which the world is viewed. As sedimentations of conventional attempts to comprehend the world correctly, cognitive practices afford the individual not only a set of accredited techniques for grasping the truth of existence but also a "natural attitude," an attitude of "suspended doubt" with respect to a wide range of issues based upon the conviction that one understands how the world works. In establishing what will be taken as normal, natural, real, reasonable, expected, and sane, theoretical presuppositions camouflage their contributions to cognition and mask their operation upon the understanding. Because the theoretical presuppositions that structure cognition operate at the tacit level, it is difficult to isolate and illuminate the full range of presuppositions informing cognitive practices. Moreover, any attempt to elucidate presuppositions must operate within a "hermeneutic circle": any attempt to examine or to challenge certain assumptions or expectations must occur within the frame of reference established by mutually reinforcing presuppositions. That certain presuppositions must remain fixed if others are to be subjected to systematic critique does not imply that individuals are prisoners trapped within the cognitive framework acquired through socialization (Bernstein, 1983). Critical reflection upon and abandonment of certain theoretical presuppositions is possible

within the hermeneutic circle; but the goal of transparency, of the unmediated grasp of things as they are, is not, for no investigation, no matter how critical, can escape the fundamental conditions of human cognition.

Thus, the conception of cognition as a human practice challenges the possibility of unmediated knowledge of the world, as well as notions such as "brute facts," the "immediately given," "theory-free research," "neutral observation language," and "self-evident truths"—all of which suggest that possibility. Because cognition is always theoretically mediated, the world captured in human knowledge and designated as "empirical" is itself theoretically constituted. Divergent cognitive practices rooted in conventions such as common sense, religion, science, philosophy, and the arts construe the empirical realm differently, identifying and emphasizing various dimensions and accrediting different forms of evidence, criteria of meaning, standards of explanation, and tokens of truthfulness. Such an understanding of the theoretical constitution of the empirical realm in the context of specific cognitive practices requires a reformulation of the notion of "facts." A "fact" is a theoretically constituted proposition, supported by theoretically mediated evidence, and put forward as part of a theoretical formulation of reality. A "fact" is a contestable component of a theoretically constituted order of things.

A coherence theory of truth accepts that the world is richer than theories devised to grasp it; it accepts that theories are underdetermined by "facts" and, consequently, that there can always be alternative and competing theoretical explanations of particular events. It does not, however, imply the relativist conclusion that all theoretical interpretations are equal. That there can be no appeal to neutral, theory-independent facts to adjudicate between competing theoretical interpretations does not mean that there is no rational way of making and warranting critical evaluative judgments concerning alternative views. Indeed, presupposition theorists have pointed out that the belief that the absence of independent evidence *necessarily* entails relativism is itself dependent upon a positivist commitment to the verification criterion of meaning. Only if one starts from the assumption that the sole test for the validity of a proposition lies in its measurement against the empirically "given" does it follow that, in the absence of the "given," no rational judgments can be made concerning the validity of particular claims (Bernstein, 1983, p. 92; Brown, 1977, pp. 93–94; Gunnell, 1986, pp. 66–68; Stockman, 1983, pp. 79–101).

Once the "myth of the given" (Sellars, 1963, p. 164) has been abandoned and once the belief that the absence of one invariant empirical test for the truth of a theory implies the absence of all criteria for evaluative judgment has been repudiated, it becomes possible to recognize that there are rational grounds for assessing the merits of alternative theoretical interpretations. To comprehend the nature of such assessments, one must acknowledge that, although theoretical presuppositions structure the perception of events, they do not create perceptions out of nothing. Theoretical interpretations are "world-guided" (Williams, 1985, p. 140). They involve both the pre-understanding brought to an event by an individual perceiver and the stimuli in the external (or internal) world that instigate the process of cognition. Because of this dual source of theoretical interpretations, objects can be characterized in many different ways, "but it does not follow that a given object can be seen in any way at all or that all descriptions are equal" (Brown, 1977, p. 93). The stimuli that trigger interpretation limit the class of plausible characterizations without dictating one absolute description.

Assessment of alternative theoretical interpretations involves deliberation, a rational activity that requires that imagination and judgment be deployed in the consideration of the range of evidence and arguments that can be advanced in support of various positions. The reasons offered in support of alternative views marshal evidence, organize data, apply various criteria of explanation, address multiple levels of analysis with varying degrees of abstraction, and employ divergent strategies of argumentation. This range of reasons offers a rich field for deliberation and assessment. It provides an opportunity for the exercise of judgment and ensures that, when scientists reject a theory, they do so because they believe they can demonstrate that the reasons offered in support of that theory are deficient. That the reasons advanced to sustain the rejection of one theory do not constitute absolute proof of the validity of an alternative

theory is simply a testament to human fallibility. Admission that the cumulative weight of current evidence and compelling argument cannot protect scientific judgments against future developments, which may warrant the repudiation of those theories currently accepted, is altogether consonant with the recognition of the finitude of human rationality and the contingency of empirical relations.

The recognition that all cognition is theory-laden has also generated a critique of many traditional assumptions about the subject or self that undergird rationalist, empiricist, and materialist conceptions of knowing. Conceptions of the "innocent eye," the "passive observer," and the mind as a "tabula rasa" have been severely challenged (Brown, 1977; Stockman, 1983). The notion of transparency—the belief that the individual knower can identify all of his or her prejudices and purge them in order to greet an unobstructed reality—has been rendered suspect. Conceptions of the atomistic self who experiences the world independent of all social influences, of the unalienated self who exists as a potentiality awaiting expression, and of the unified self who can grasp the totality of being have been thoroughly contested (Benhabib, 1986). The very idea of the "subject" has been castigated for incorporating assumptions about the "logic of identity" that posit knowers as undifferentiated, anonymous, and general, possessing a vision independent of all identifiable perspectives (Megill, 1985; Young, 1986). Indeed, the conception of the knowing subject has been faulted for failing to grasp that, rather than being the source of truth, the subject is the product of particular regimes of truth (Foucault, 1980).

In addition to challenging notions of an unmediated reality and a transparent subject/self, the conception of cognition as a human practice also takes issue with accounts of reason that privilege one particular mode of rationality while denigrating all others. Attempts to reduce the practice of knowing to monadic conceptions of reason fail to grasp the complexity of the interaction between traditional assumptions, social norms, theoretical conceptions, disciplinary strictures, linguistic possibilities, emotional dispositions, and creative impositions in every act of cognition. Approaches to cognition as a human practice emphasize the expansiveness of rationality and the irreducible plurality of its manifestations within diverse traditions. Perception, intuition, conceptualization, inference, representation, reflection, imagination, remembrance, conjecture, rationalization, argumentation, justification, contemplation, ratiocination, speculation, meditation, validation, deliberation—even a partial listing of the many dimensions of knowing suggests that it is a grave error to attempt to reduce this multiplicity to a unitary model. The resources of intellection are more profitably considered in their complexity, for what is involved in knowing is heavily dependent upon what questions are asked, what kind of knowledge is sought, and the context in which cognition is undertaken (Cavell, 1979).

The conception of cognition as a human practice suggests that feminist critique is situated within established traditions of cognition even as it calls those traditions into question. Defects in traditional accounts of knowledge engender critical feminist reflection that relies upon a range of traditional analytical techniques to criticize the limitations of received views. Thus, feminists must deal deftly with the traditions that serve both as targets of criticism and as sources of norms and analytic techniques essential to the critical project. The conception of cognition as a human practice also suggests that feminist analysis can itself be understood as a rich and varied tradition. To understand the specific conceptions of truth operative in feminist research practices, then, would require careful consideration of the diverse cognitive practices that already structure feminist inquiry. Questions concerning the subject of inquiry, the level of analysis, the degree of abstraction, the type of explanation, the standards of evidence, the criteria of evaluation, the tropes of discourse, and the strategies of argumentation deployed within feminist investigations of concrete problems would be necessary to develop a full account of the competing conceptions of truth operative within specific modes of feminist inquiry.

AREAS OF CONTESTATION IN FEMINIST DEBATES ABOUT TRUTH

Although commitments to value-critical research, anti-foundationalism, and plurality characterize feminist inquiry, there remains a good deal of contestation among feminist scholars concerning the nature of truth and the possibility of attaining it. In a path-breaking work that launched the field of feminist epistemology, Sandra Harding (1986) mapped conflicting conceptions of truth that distinguished three approaches to feminist scholarship: feminist empiricism, feminist standpoint theory, and feminist postmodernism. Although the parameters of these approaches have been the subject of rich and productive debate over the past two decades, the distinctions Harding identified help to illuminate central points of contention in contemporary feminist accounts of truth.

Feminist Empiricism

Empiricism is an old and rich epistemological tradition that dates at least to Aristotle. Many versions of empiricism suggest that the senses can generate reliable knowledge concerning facts and values as well as concerning material and immaterial reality. Although versions of empiricism dating from the nineteenth century severely constricted what the senses can know, as the previous discussion of positivism makes clear, postpositivist versions of empiricism are attuned to the value-ladenness of perception, the theoretical constitution of facticity, and the underdetermination of theory by evidence.

Contemporary feminist empiricism accepts the insights of postpositivism while also incorporating the tenets of philosophical realism (which posits the existence of the world independent of the human knower) and empiricist assumptions about the primacy of the senses as the source of all knowledge about the world (Longino, 1990; Nelson, 1990; Oakley, 2000; Walby, 2001; Wylie, 2003). Feminist empiricists emphasize the complexity and diversity of empirical strategies of knowledge production and note that conflict, contestation, argument, and disagreement are both central to and productive for the practices of scientific inquiry. For it is through such intersubjective contestations that truth claims are adjudicated.

Feminist empiricists suggest that systematic inquiry to "unbury" the data of women's lives is crucial, precisely because women have so often been omitted from scientific studies. Through empirical investigation, feminist scholars seek to discover and articulate patterns in women's experiences, judge the strength and scope of these patterns, locate particularity and deviations from these patterns, and attempt to understand the patterns and variations from them in all their complexity (Frye, 1993, p. 108). Keenly attuned to the problems of bias and distortion that result from inadequate evidence and overgeneralization, feminist scholars have been remarkably innovative in devising concepts and research strategies to describe and explain dimensions of women's realities that encompass questions of embodied existence, health, divisions of labor and power, structures of inequality, violence, reproduction, and mothering.

Within the frame of feminist empiricism, scholars working with specific methods have identified different tokens of truthfulness. Ethnographers, for example, generate "thick descriptions," detailed descriptions of a particular mode of life that attempt to situate social practices within the cultural norms and values of a particular group (Geertz, 1994). To test the validity of their accounts, ethnographers often appeal to the judgment of the group being studied, presenting their analysis to their research subjects to see if they find the account adequate to their understanding of their cultural practices (Wolf, 1996). Feminist sociologists interested in analyzing the interaction of multiple forms of structured inequality, such as race, class, and gender in particular regions of the United States, have developed sophisticated quantitative techniques to investigate multiple groups, examine the relations among them, control for a range of interaction effects, and produce systematic comparisons that help to identify dimensions and causes of inequality (McCall, 2001). To heighten the validity of their causal claims, some feminist scholars in the social sciences and the biomedical sciences use experimental methods that allow sustained observation under controlled conditions. Randomized controlled trials, which investigate the causal effects of particular interventions, such as the effects of tamoxifen on breast cancer or the effects of increased welfare payments on the work incentives of the poor, involve the comparison of particular groups of randomly selected research subjects in order to isolate particular cause-effect relations while controlling for the effects of chance (Oakley, 2000). Recognizing that the specific method of empirical inquiry chosen in a particular research context depends on the specific research question they seek to answer, feminist empiricists concur in their judgment that these diverse methods can generate reliable knowledge about the world. Working within an anti-foundationalist frame, feminist empiricists investigate a rich and complex array of issues, generating truths of critical importance to the health, livelihoods, and well-being of women in the contemporary world.

Feminist Standpoint Theories

Drawing upon historical materialism's insight that social being determines consciousness, feminist standpoint theories reject the notion of an "unmediated truth," arguing that knowledge is always mediated by a host of factors related to an individual's particular position in a determinate sociopolitical formation at a specific point in history. For example, language, nationality, class, race, and gender necessarily structure the individual's understanding of reality and hence inform knowledge claims. Although they repudiate the possibility of an unmediated truth, feminist standpoint epistemologies do not reject the notion of truth altogether. On the contrary, they argue that, while certain social positions (e.g., the oppressor's) produce distorted ideological views of reality, other social positions (e.g., the oppressed) can pierce ideological obfuscations and generate a more comprehensive understanding of the world (Collins, 1990; Hartsock, 1983; Sandoval, 2000; Smith, 1979).

Although some early proponents of standpoint theory seemed to suggest that the "standpoint of women" could be explained in terms of particular facets of women's lives, such as the unification of manual, mental, and emotional capacities in women's traditional activities; the sensuous, concrete, and relational character of women's labor in the production of use values and in reproduction; or the multiple oppressions experienced by women that generate collective struggles against the prevailing social order, these accounts were criticized for falling prey to essentialist assumptions about women that failed to recognize hierarchical structures of difference among women. They also presupposed too simple a relation between oppression and truth, suggesting that certain forms of adversity afford epistemic privilege, which could free the oppressed from confusion, error, distortion, contradiction, and fallibility (Grant, 1993; Hawkesworth, 1989; Hekman, 1997; Longino, 1993).

Over the past two decades, more sophisticated and nuanced accounts of standpoint theory have been developed, which scrupulously avoid "essentialist definition[s] of the social categories or collectivities in terms of which epistemically relevant standpoints are characterized. . . . [and] any thesis of automatic epistemic privilege . . . any claim that those who occupy particular standpoints (usually subdominant, oppressed, marginal standpoints) automatically know more, or know better, by virtue of their social, political location" (Wylie, 2003, p. 28). Within this frame, feminist scholars deploy a conception of standpoint in order to investigate "how power relations inflect knowledge; what systematic limitations are imposed by the social location of different classes or collectivities, or groups of knowers; and what features of location or strategies of criticism and inquiry are conducive to understanding this structured epistemic partiality" (Wylie, 2003, p. 31). Thus, proponents of standpoint inquiry acknowledge that it is "an empirical question exactly what historical processes created hierarchically structured relations of inequality and what material conditions, what sociopolitical structures and symbolic or psychological mechanisms, maintain them in the present" (Wylie, 2003, p. 29).

Standpoint theory in this construal serves as an analytical tool, a heuristic device that illuminates areas of inquiry, frames questions for investigation, and identifies puzzles in need of solution and problems in need of exploration and clarification. Standpoint theory also provides concepts and hypotheses to guide research (Hawkesworth, 1999, 2006). Accepting plurality as an inherent characteristic of the human condition, inquiry guided by standpoint theory recognizes that scholars must attend to the views of people in markedly different social locations. Investigation of multiple interpretations of the same phenomenon helps to illuminate the theoretical assumptions that frame and accredit the constitution of facticity within each account. To analyze and compare competing claims, the researcher must engage questions concerning the adequacy, internal consistency, and explanatory power of alternate accounts as a way to adjudicate the truth of competing interpretations.

Concerns with ideological distortion and ideology critique have been central to projects that involve standpoint analysis. While conceptions of ideology are themselves a subject of contestation, proponents of standpoint theory agree that ideologies involve systems of representation and material practices that structure beliefs and that legitimate systemic inequalities. By advocating modes of research that challenge dominant ideologies, proponents of standpoint theory suggest that feminist knowledge production can do more than describe and explain the empirical world; it can contribute to human emancipation, generating insights that can enable people to free themselves from ideological distortion and various modes of domination. Thus, the conception of truth embedded in feminist standpoint theory links claims about existing structures of inequality to modes of critical reflection that can empower people to transform existing social relations.

Feminist Postmodernism

Informed by a Nietzschean conception of perspectivism, feminist postmodernism rejects the very possibility of a truth about reality. Feminist postmodernists use the "situatedness" of each finite observer in a particular sociopolitical historical context to challenge the plausibility of claims that any perspective on the world could escape partiality. Extrapolating from the disparate conditions that shape individual identities, they raise grave suspicions about totalizing notions of human consciousness or the human condition. In addition, feminist postmodernists emphasize that knowledge is the result of invention, the imposition of form upon the world, rather than the discovery of something pre-given, some "natural order of being." As an alternative to the futile quest for an authoritative truth to ground feminist theory, feminist postmodernists advocate a profound skepticism regarding universal (or universalizing) claims about the existence, nature, and powers of reason (Flax, 1986, 1987; Hekman, 1992; Yeatman, 1994). Rather than succumb to the authoritarian impulses of the "will to truth," they urge instead the development of a commitment to plurality, multivocality, and the play of difference (Nicholson, 1990).

Discussions of the situatedness of knowers suggest that the claims of every knower reflect a particular perspective shaped by social, cultural, political, and personal factors and that the perspective of each knower contains blind spots, tacit presuppositions, and prejudgments of which the individual is unaware (Buker, 1990; Moi, 1990). The partiality of individual perspectives in turn suggests that every claim about the world, "every account can be shown to have left something out of the description of its object and to have put something in which others regard as nonessential" (White, 1978, p. 3). Recognition of the selectivity of cognitive accounts, in terms of conscious and unconscious omission and supplementation, has led some postmodern thinkers to characterize the world in literary terms, to emphasize the fictive elements of "fact," the narrative elements of all discourse—literary, scientific, historical, social, political—and the nebulousness of the distinction between text and reality. The move to "intertextuality" suggests that the world be treated as text, as a play of signifiers with no determinate meaning, as a system of signs whose meaning is hidden and diffuse, as a discourse that resists decoding because of the infinite power of language to conceal and obfuscate. Postmodernist discourses emphasize the human capacity to misunderstand, to universalize the particular and the idiosyncratic, to privilege the ethnocentric, and to conflate truth with those prejudices that advantage the knower. Indeed, postmodernist insights counsel the abandonment of the very notion of truth because it is a hegemonic and, hence, destructive illusion.

Feminist postmodernists call attention to the hubris of scientific reason and the manifold ways in which scientism sustains authoritarian tendencies. By merging the horizons of philosophical and literary discourses, feminist postmodernists loosen the disciplinary strictures of both traditions and produce creative deconstructions of the tacit assumptions that sustain a variety of unreflective beliefs. By taking discourse—structures of statements, concepts, categories, and beliefs that are specific to particular sociohistorical formations—as its primary object of analysis, postmodernists seek to heighten our understanding of the integral relations between power and knowledge and the means by which particular power/knowledge constellations constitute us as subjects in a determinate order of things (Scott, 1988, 1992).

Two analytic techniques have been central to postmodern feminist inquiry, deconstruction and genealogy. Both seek to disrupt widely accepted understandings of the world by denaturalizing categories, destabilizing meaning, unmasking the "will to truth" that informs particular discursive formations, and exposing the operation of power in knowledge production itself. Deconstruction is a method of discursive analysis developed by French philosopher Jacques Derrida (1979, 1980, 1981a, 1981b), which challenges the idea that language merely describes or represents what exists, suggesting instead that language is constitutive of reality. Within this framework, meaning is created through implicit and explicit contrasts structured by language. Binaries, such as man/woman, define terms by creating oppositions that are hierarchically ordered and that privilege the first term, insinuating that priority implies primacy and that the residual term is derivative or inferior. As an analytical technique, deconstruction involves the interrogation of binaries, examining how meaning is constrained, how mistaken assumptions of homogeneity inform each term of the binary, and how the binary form exudes the faulty notion that it exhausts the full range of categorical possibilities.

Informed by the works of Nietzsche (1969) and Foucault (1977), genealogy is a unique form of critique premised on the assumption that taken-for-granted objects, ideas, values, events, and institutions have been constituted contingently, discursively, practically. Described as diagnostic histories of the present, genealogies seek to undermine the self-evidences of the present and to open possibilities for the enhancement of life. Unlike traditional techniques of historical analysis, genealogy rejects any search for origins, notions of progress or unilinear development, and assumptions concerning definitive causes and unbroken continuity. Genealogy's unit of analysis is not "the past" as it was lived (which is taken to be unknowable) but the historical record, the arbitrary assemblage of documents and narratives with which people make sense of their pasts. Following Nietzsche, genealogists problematize such established discourses, insisting that historical narratives are framed by questions that reflect the preoccupations and concerns of the writers. Thus, the genealogist attempts to identify the conditions under which particular discourses arise, illuminate multiplicity and randomness at the point of emergence, interrogate the interests that inform the narrative, and question the values that sustain the discursive formation. In an effort to trace complexity and disparity, genealogists begin their analysis with particularity, chance, disjuncture, and accidents, dredging up forgotten documents and apparently insignificant details in order to re-create forgotten historical and practical conditions for contemporary existence. In seeking to reveal the arbitrariness of what appears "natural" and "necessary," the genealogist aspires to open possibilities by disrupting dominant discourses, stimulating reflection on and resistance against what is taken for granted about the world and about ourselves. In this sense, genealogical narratives are oriented toward the enhancement of life because they seek to release us from the strictures of the past and orient us toward the possibilities for innovation and invention. Postmodernists caution, however, that all new discursive formations produce new power/knowledge constellations.

While proponents of postmodern feminist modes of analysis explicitly challenge the legitimacy of all truth claims, some scholars have pointed out that the modes of critique they embrace presuppose the possibility of evaluating the comparative merits of various forms of knowledge (Walby, 2001). Thus, their analytic practices suggest implicit criteria for assessing "better, not merely different" knowledge claims. Indeed, the assertion that postmodern research strategies are appropriate for the analysis of the will to power in knowledge production can itself be interpreted as a claim to truth about the nature of intellectual inquiry and the analytic techniques best suited to engage that reality.

From Feminist Science Studies to the Posthuman

Although several noted scientists, such as Ruth Bleier, Evelyn Fox Keller, Ann Fausto-Sterling, and Ruth Hubbard, have contributed mightily to feminist critiques of science, feminist scientists working in the STEM disciplines (science, technology, engineering, and math) continue to experience major barriers to the incorporation of feminist insights about knowledge production into their research. As Sandra Harding (1986) pointed out decades ago, the conviction that the logic of scientific discovery is *sui generis,* governed exclusively by concerns internal to particular scientific fields, remains a fundamental obstacle to acknowledging the validity of feminist claims concerning the politics of scientific knowledge. To succeed as scientists within mainstream disciplines, feminists must work within the established paradigms of their fields, deploying feminist arguments largely to advocate for equity and diversity within science. An epistemic gulf continues to separate most feminist scientists from the flourishing field of feminist science studies.

As an interdisciplinary endeavor, feminist science studies have developed through the work of feminist historians of science, philosophers of science, sociologists of science, and cultural studies scholars. Feminist technoscience studies examine the social and political implications and formations in science and technology and encompass an extensive intellectual agenda that ranges from reproductive and genetic technologies, regenerative medicine, tissue engineering, stem cell research, therapeutic cloning, and the human genome project to cybernetics, information technology, and technology-assisted knowledge production enabled by mobile media, global positioning systems (GPS), and the open platforms of Web 2.0. In the words of Katherine Hayles (1999), the unifying motif in these studies is tied to the complex ways in which these diverse fields are culturally freighted: "Culture circulates through science no less than science circulates through culture. The heart that keeps this circulatory system flowing is narrative—narratives about culture, narratives within culture, narratives about science, narratives within science" (pp. 21–22).

Some feminist science studies scholars explore the manifold ways in which analytical categories, systems of classification, methodological approaches, and explanatory frameworks are raced, gendered, and classed (Fujimura, 2006, 2008; Koenig, Lee, & Richardson, 2008; Milam, forthcoming), illuminating how culturally specific assumptions structure scientifically accredited knowledge.

Others investigate how new media, which enable virtual and mixed reality spaces, challenge established assumptions about truth and complicate knowledge production (Balsamo, 1996). Camera-equipped cell phones, mobile recording devices, social network games, online open-source tools such as blogging, Google maps along with analog resources such as sketch maps, mobile media in conjunction with GPS, and the open platforms of Web 2.0 expand ways of knowing and the kinds of evidence that can be adduced to support knowledge claims. Parallel realities, mediated representations, sound maps, installations that integrate radio and other communications technology, and visual tags to create digital community histories, which encompass diverse local perspectives, raise questions about the "object" of investigation and the appropriate criteria for assessing truth claims. The emergence of new modes of hybridity, through the design of international annotation systems that enable globally dispersed individuals to contribute to the construction of narrative and visual archives by adding content and annotating texts and images, creates new modes of transnational cultural production that raise fundamental questions about the nature of authorship, the stability of cultural objects, and the integrity of "a work"—concerns that have been central to discussions of the ontology of art. New technologies enable the creation of parallel realities, which may distance the individual from immediate physical experiences or reconstruct space through media applications that alter sensory stabilization, thereby challenging sensation and perception, faculties central to empiricist accounts of knowledge.

Feminist technoscience also takes up questions concerning the nature of materiality, the prospects for "dematerialization," and the relation of materialization and dematerialization to embodiment and to knowledge claims about bodies, memories, pleasures, and sexualities (Barad, 1998; Brodribb, 1992; Butler, 1993; Haraway, 1990). As computers and informatics push the boundaries of a thoroughly disembodied artificial intelligence while embodied persons create multiple virtual selves, the Cartesian subject seems to have been supplanted by a "discursive, roaming subjectivity, unhinged

from the body" (Burfoot, 2003, p. 47). Feminist discussions of cyborgs blur the boundaries between the "enacted body," present on one side of a computer screen, and the "represented body," produced through verbal and semiotic markers in an electronic environment, while emphasizing that the overlay between the enacted and represented bodies is a contingent production (Hayles, 1999, 2005; Miller, forthcoming). Discussions of the cyborg stress that the contingent relation between enacted and represented bodies is technologically mediated in ways integral to the production of "identity," thereby dispelling any notion that there might be a natural relation between mind and matter. Within this frame, "materiality is the site where information patterns exert control over form and function" (Hayles, 2003, p. 136). Regenerative medicine, tissue engineering, stem cell research, and therapeutic cloning provide powerful examples of this new mode of materiality. Within this domain of "'biomedia' . . . information produces a body purified of errors. The body is not only regenerated but actually redesigned by its informatting with informational codes" (Hayles, 2003, p. 136). When changing a code changes the body, the parameters for truth, once tethered to a stable physical universe, become unmoored.

As one emblem of the "posthuman," the cyborg signals a return to a pragmatic conception of truth, with a twist. Western philosophers from Aristotle and Hobbes to Dewey have theorized domains in which a pragmatic conception of truth seems most appropriate. In the realm of human practice, where particular goals such as obtaining peace or establishing justice guide collective endeavors, "what works" in achieving those ends seems an ample index of truth. In these classic formulations, however, humans determined the ends they sought and exercised their judgment in deciding which strategies "worked." In the mediated world of posthuman technoscience, however, it is not clear whether human, artificial, or cybernetic intelligence determines the ends and assesses the adequacy of the means used to achieve them.

Questions concerning the nature of "words" and their relation to "things" have been central to both correspondence theories and coherence theories of truth. Both approaches presuppose that language is a uniquely human invention and that truth is intimately related to the referential or constitutive possibilities of language, respectively. Feminist science studies scholars (Hayles, 2005; Miller, forthcoming) are exploring a conceptualization of language as "machine code," which calls into question the anthropocentric presuppositions of conceptions of truth that accord the knowing human subject the power either to determine whether particular words correspond to things that exist in the world or to interpret the meanings and scope of constitutive discourses. With the shift to the "posthuman," the radical decentering of the human subject has important implications for understandings of language and the relationship between words and things, speakers and the spoken, intentionality and outcomes. As Ruth Miller (forthcoming, p. 25) has pointed out, linguistic activity need no longer be construed as a specifically human property. Contemporary science posits language as a property characteristic of galaxies, neurons, cells, viruses, plants, glaciers, computers, and cybernetic systems. Operating at the systems level, language does not confer recognition or bolster subjective existence. On the contrary, language can be understood as a code that is executable—that operates on a system or environment by generating change or "mutation." It "operates but does not communicate . . . executes rather than transmitting messages, sorts information rather than producing knowledge, and alters environments rather than engaging in the epistemic violence of subject formation" (Miller, forthcoming, pp. 3, 6–7). No longer tethered to embodiment or agency, "nonhuman linguistic activity" operates in human and nonhuman domains, including computational, virtual, political, ecological, and environmental systems and networks. Reconfigured in a computational mode, language becomes "fractal as well as physical"—a web of proliferating meaningless messages operating as nothing more than nodes on a mechanical and informational network.

Grounded in a theory of information developed in the 20th century, this conception of speech separates information from meaning. Information is defined as a mathematical function that depends solely on the distribution of message elements, independent of whether a message has any meaning for a receiver. As a random or accidental transmission, each articulation comes as a surprise, follows no pattern, yet transmits new information. Within a systems frame, production of information is a good in itself, independent of what it means. Indeed, "machine code" suggests that communication need not be related to speakers, listeners, message content, or even the interaction among speakers, listeners, or messages; instead, it relates to the system, field, or environment that speakers, listeners, and messages produce (Miller, forthcoming, p. 31).

Privileging networks, systems, and fields over content, sender, and receiver, this conception of computer language also eschews conceptions of cause and effect associated with liberal humanism. When machine code "executes," it produces environmental and systemic change. Computer code is "performative" in that it causes changes in machine behavior and, through networked ports and other interfaces, initiates other changes through the transmission and execution of code. In contrast to referential and constitutive conceptions of language, language qua machine code does not separate subject from object. It embraces possibilities of fusion, simultaneity, nonlinearity, accident, and chaos, wholly at odds with theories of human agency and the sovereign speaking subject. According to Miller, "machine code is simultaneously language, speech, writing, and execution; simultaneously [a] physical, mechanical, electronic, environmental, ecological, and 'natural' thing. . . . Code is context" that cannot be decontexualized (Miller, forthcoming, pp. 67, 69).

Although some feminist science studies scholars enthusiastically embrace the analytical potential of the shift to the posthuman, others have been less sanguine about these prospects. Annette Burfoot (2003) has defended "human remains," cautioning against the unsavory raced and gendered consequences of an uncritical appropriation of the posthuman. Indeed, Burfoot suggests that contemporary technoscience, like so many theories advanced over the course of Western intellectual history, construes the body as atomized, degendered, and nonhuman. As formulated in technoscience, posthumanism "reifies the objectification of the body" and "denies its formative role," while "affirming its irreducible atomic matter" (Burfoot, 2003, p. 98).

She questions technoscience's fetishized focus on the body as components (reproductive cells, uteri, genes, gametes), which reduces the life-giving qualities of the body to mechanized and malleable but mute forms, such as DNA (p. 49). When the level of analysis is shifted from the human to the molecular or cellular, meaning is no longer processed through words but through the composition and editing of actual human components (cells, genes, gametes). The bodies subsequently reassembled operate within a highly abstracted molecular concept of matter beyond bodily sensation and peculiarly devoid of sex or race (Miller, forthcoming, p. 70). The atomization of human bodies necessarily denies the significance of race and gender, precisely because these social markers of difference do not permeate all cellular or molecular formations. From a feminist perspective, the erasure of hierarchies of difference by such a shift in analytical frames may seem a suspicious sleight of hand that continues a long history of denying the political significance of raced-gendered embodiment as a system of oppression. Burfoot suggests that technoscientific discourses often replicate the gendered hierarchies that were established by privileging form over matter. Where Plato and Aristotle used form as an essentially masculine construct to vindicate male privilege in all domains of life, technoscience accords superiority to biomedical culture and the cunning of informatics to vindicate the right of science to control and intervene in the material world for the sake of progress or reform (Miller, forthcoming, p. 62).

Conclusion

Despite continuing contestation about the best strategies for feminist knowledge production, feminist scholarship has made huge strides over the past 40 years. Theoretical developments within discipline-based and interdisciplinary women's and gender studies have been rich and profound. Feminist scholars have developed systematic critiques of androcentric bias in theoretical assumptions, interpretive strategies, genres, styles of representation, rhetoric of inquiry, problem selection, standards of evidence, models of explanation, research design, data collection, analyses of results, narrative strategies, and discursive formations. Attuned to the damage done by false universals, biological determinism, essentialism, a colonizing gaze, heteronormativity, and insensitivity to race, class, ethnicity, disability, nationality, and other critical markers of difference, feminist scholars have developed multiple epistemic communities to interrogate disciplinary and interdisciplinary knowledge production.

Feminist scholars have struggled over the past 40 years to learn lessons from our own mistakes, omissions, distortions, and myopias, calling into question the most basic categories of analysis, including "woman," "gender," "race," and "nation." We have developed analytical tools to help frame new research questions by problematizing the given and denaturalizing the taken-for-granted. Attuned to ambiguity and indeterminacy and committed to an ethics of freedom, feminist scholarship does not posit essential gender opposition or invariant modes of domination and subordination but rather attends to the specificity of particular situations. Troubling both false universals and confining stereotypes, this mode of analysis tracks complex operations of power by resisting overgeneralization, recognizing the roots of particular judgments, and actively engaging multiple theoretical frames and cultural perspectives. Grounded in particularity and attentive to specificity, feminist scholarship pays tribute to the singularity of events, cultural formations, and lives, while investigating possible patterns and cross-case resonances. Feminist research in this frame involves reflective comparisons and judgments that illuminate the visible and the invisible—modes of embodiment, facets of desire, dynamics of social existence, categories that structure perception and action, intended and unintended consequences of action and inaction, macro and micro structures that constrain.

By interrogating processes of representation, racialization, gendering, and heterosexualization, feminist scholars illuminate dimensions of social, cultural, political, economic, scientific, national, and transnational life that go undetected in mainstream discourses. They create ways of comprehending the politics of difference, which refuse essentialism while also refusing to reduce processes of racialization and gendering to questions of embodiment. They document the manifold ways in which hierarchies of difference are produced, sustained, challenged, and transformed through knowledge production and regimes of visuality, as well as through economic restructuring, the practices of international governmental and financial institutions, and the laws, norms, and policies of nation-states, communities, workplaces, and households.

Feminist knowledge production has raised and continues to raise powerful challenges to established disciplines in the humanities, social sciences, and natural sciences.

It has also demonstrated that the numerous obstacles to women's full participation in social, political, economic, and intellectual life are humanly created and hence susceptible to alteration. In providing sophisticated and detailed analyses of concrete situations, feminists have dispelled distortions and mystifications that abound in malestream thought.

Based on a thorough recognition of the fallibility of human inquiry and the fluidity of life in a world of contingencies, feminists need not claim universal, ahistorical validity for their analyses. They need not assert that theirs is the only or the final word on complex questions. In the absence of claims of universal validity, feminist accounts derive their justificatory force from their capacity to illuminate existing social relations, demonstrate the deficiencies of alternative interpretations, and debunk opposing views. Precisely because feminists move beyond texts to confront the world, they can provide concrete reasons in specific contexts for the superiority of their accounts. Such claims to superiority are derived from the ability to demonstrate point by point the deficiencies of alternative explanations. At their best, feminist analyses engage both the critical intellect and the world; they surpass androcentric accounts because, in their systematicity, more is examined and less is assumed.

Discussion Questions

1. What are the central differences between positivist and postpositivist claims about knowledge?

2. In what sense do feminist empiricism, feminist standpoint theory, and feminist postmodernism share postpositivist epistemic commitments?

3. How does a shift to the "posthuman" complicate conceptions of truth?

4. How does the object of analysis vary in research strategies advanced by feminist empiricists, feminist standpoint theorists, feminist postmodernists, and feminist posthumanists?

5. Please identify a range of research questions that are

   a. best suited to empirical investigation,

   b. best addressed by standpoint approaches, and

   c. best approached with postmodern analytic techniques.

Online Resources

PhilPapers: Feminist Epistemology

http://philpapers.org/browse/feminist-epistemology

An annotated bibliography of philosophical scholarship on feminist epistemology is regularly updated in this online resource for research in philosophy.

Stanford Encyclopedia of Philosophy: Feminist Social Epistemology

http://plato.stanford.edu/entries/feminist-social-epistemology/

Elizabeth Anderson provides a helpful introduction to the key concepts in feminist epistemology and philosophy of science in this essay in the online *Stanford Encyclopedia of Philosophy.*

Internet Encyclopedia of Philosophy: Feminist Epistemology

http://www.iep.utm.edu/fem-epis/

Marianne Janack provides an overview of the emergence of the field of feminist epistemology and its relations to various approaches within the discipline of philosophy in this essay in the *Internet Encyclopedia of Philosophy.*

Feminist Research Methods: Papers

http://www.kvinfo.su.se/femmet09/papers.htm

Papers presented at a 2009 international conference entitled Feminist Research Methods, held at Stockholm University, include essays from a wide array of disciplines in the humanities and social sciences.

Relevant Journals

Feminist Theory

Hypatia

Philosophical Topic

Signs: Journal of Women in Culture and Society

Social Epistemology

REFERENCES

Albert, Hans. (1985). *Treatise on critical reason* (Mary Varney Rorty, Trans.). Princeton, NJ: Princeton University Press.

Alcoff, Linda. (2000). On judging epistemic credibility: Is social identity relevant. In Naomi Zack (Ed.), *Women of color and philosophy* (pp. 235–262). Malden, MA: Blackwell.

Bacon, Francis. (1861). *Advancement of learning: Book II*. In James Spedding & Robert Ellis (Eds.), *The Works of Francis Bacon* (Vol. 6, pp. 171–412). Boston: Taggard and Thompson.

Balsamo, Anne. (1996). *Technologies of the gendered body: Reading cyborg women*. Durham, NC: Duke University Press.

Barad, Karen. (1998). Getting real: Technoscientific practices and the materialization of reality. *Differences, 10*(2), 87–128.

Benhabib, Seyla. (1986). *Critique, norm, and Utopia*. New York: Columbia University Press.

Benston, Margaret. (1982). Feminism and the critique of scientific method. In G. Finn & A. Miles (Eds.), *Feminism in Canada* (pp. 47–66). Montreal: Black Rose Books.

Berman, Ruth. (1989). From Aristotle's dualism to materialist dialectics: Feminist transformation of science and society. In A. Jaggar & S. Bordo (Eds.), *Gender/body/knowledge*. New Brunswick, NJ: Rutgers University Press.

Bernstein, Richard. (1983). *Beyond objectivism and relativism: Science hermeneutics and praxis*. Philadelphia: University of Pennsylvania Press.

Bleier, Ruth. (1979). Social and political bias in science. In E. Tobach & B. Rosoff (Eds.), *Genes and gender* (Vol. 2, pp. 49–69). New York: Gordian Press.

Bleier, Ruth. (1984). *Science and gender: A critique of biology and its theories on women*. New York: Pergamon.

Bordo, Susan. (1987). *The flight to objectivity*. Albany, NY: SUNY Press.

Brodribb, Somer. (1992). *Nothing matters: A feminist critique of postmodernism*. North Melbourne, Australia: Spinifex.

Brown, H. (1977). *Perception, theory, and commitment: The new philosophy of science*. Chicago: Precedent Publishing Company.

Buker, Eloise. (1990). Feminist social theory and hermeneutics: An empowering dialectic? *Social Epistemology, 4*(1), 23–39.

Burfoot, Annette. (2003). Human remains: Identity politics in the face of biotechnology. *Cultural critique, 53*, 47–71.

Butler, Judith. (1993). *Bodies that matter: On the discursive limits of sex*. New York: Routledge.

Cavell, Stanley. (1979). *The claim of reason: Wittgenstein, skepticism, morality, and tragedy*. New York: Oxford University Press.

Code, Lorraine. (1991). *What can she know?* Ithaca, NY: Cornell University Press.

Collins, Patricia Hill. (1990). *Black feminist thought*. New York: Routledge.

Cunningham, Frank. (1973). *Objectivity in social science*. Toronto: University of Toronto Press.

Derrida, Jacques. (1979). *Spurs/Eperons*. Chicago: University of Chicago Press.

Derrida, Jacques. (1980). *The archaeology of the frivolous*. Pittsburgh: Duquesne University Press.

Derrida, Jacques. (1981a). *Dissemination*. Chicago: University of Chicago Press.

Derrida, Jacques. (1981b). *Positions*. Chicago: University of Chicago Press.

DeVault, Marjorie. (1999). *Liberating method: Feminism and social research*. Philadelphia: Temple University Press.

Eichler, Margaret. (1980). *The double standard: A feminist critique of social science*. New York: St. Martins Press.

Farganis, Sondra. (1989). Feminism and the reconstruction of social science. In Alison Jaggar & Susan Bordo (Eds.), *Gender/body/knowledge* (pp. 207–223). New Brunswick, NJ: Rutgers University Press.

Fausto-Sterling, Ann. (1985). *Myths of gender*. New York: Basic Books.

Fee, Elizabeth. (1983). Women's nature and scientific objectivity. In Marian Lowe & Ruth Hubbard (Eds.), *Women's nature: Rationalizations of inequality* (pp. 9–28). New York: Pergamon.

Flax, Jane. (1986). Gender as a social problem: In and for feminist theory. *American Studies/Amerika Studien, 31*(2), 193–213.

Flax, Jane. (1987). Postmodernism and gender relations in feminist theory. *Signs: Journal of Women in Culture and Society, 12*(4), 621–643.

Fonow, Mary Margaret, & Cook, Judith A. (Eds.). (1991). *Beyond methodology: Feminist scholarship as lived research.* Bloomington: Indiana University Press.

Foucault, Michel. (1977). *Discipline and punish.* New York: Vintage Books.

Foucault, Michel. (1980). *The history of sexuality.* New York: Vintage Books.

Fox Keller, Evelyn. (1985). *Reflections on gender and science.* New Haven, CT: Yale University Press.

Frye, Marilyn. (1993). The possibility of feminist theory. In Alison Jaggar & Paula Rothenberg (Eds.), *Feminist frameworks* (3rd ed., pp. 103–112). Boston: McGraw Hill.

Fujimura, Joan. (2006). "Sex genes": A critical sociomaterial approach to the politics and molecular genetics of sex determination. *Signs: Journal of Women in Culture and Society, 32*(1), 49–82.

Fujimura, Joan. (2008). Race, genetics, and disease: Questions of evidence, matters of consequence. *Social Studies of Science, 38*(5), 643–656.

Geertz, Clifford. (1994). Thick description: Toward an interpretive theory of culture. In Michael Martin & Lee C. McIntyre (Eds.), *Readings in the philosophy of social science* (pp. 213–232). Cambridge, MA: MIT Press.

Geiger, Susan. (1990). What's so feminist about women's oral history. *Journal of Women's History, 2*(1), 169–182.

Grant, Judith. (1993). *Fundamental feminism: Contesting the core concepts of feminist theory.* New York: Routledge.

Grimshaw, Jean. (1986). *Philosophy and feminist thinking.* Minneapolis: University of Minnesota Press.

Gunnell, John. (1986). *Between philosophy and politics.* Amherst: University of Massachusetts Press.

Haraway, Donna. (1988). Situated knowledges: The science question in feminism and the privilege of partial perspective. *Feminist Studies, 14*(3), 575–599.

Haraway, Donna. (1989). *Primate visions.* New York: Routledge.

Haraway, Donna. (1990). *Simians, cyborgs, and women: The reinvention of nature.* London: Routledge.

Harding, Sandra. (1986). *The science question in feminism.* Ithaca, NY: Cornell University Press.

Harding, Sandra. (1993). Rethinking standpoint epistemology: What is strong objectivity. In Linda Alcoff (Ed.), *Feminist epistemologies* (pp. 49–82). New York: Routledge.

Hartsock, Nancy. (1983). The feminist standpoint: Developing the ground for a specifically feminist historical materialism. In Sandra Harding & Merrill Hintikka (Eds.), *Discovering reality: Feminist perspectives on epistemology, metaphysics, methodology, and philosophy of science* (pp. 283–310). Boston: Reidel.

Hawkesworth, Mary. (1989). Knowers, knowing, known: Feminist theory and claims of truth. *Signs: Journal of Women in Culture and Society, 14*(3), 533–557.

Hawkesworth, Mary. (1999). Analyzing backlash: Feminist standpoint theory as analytical tool. *Women's Studies International Forum, 22*(2), 135–155.

Hawkesworth, Mary. (2006). *Feminist inquiry: From political conviction to methodological innovation.* New Brunswick, NJ: Rutgers University Press.

Hayles, N. Katherine. (1999). *How we became posthuman: Virtual bodies in cybernetics, literature, and informatics.* Chicago: University of Chicago Press.

Hayles, N. Katherine. (2003). Afterword: The human in the posthuman. *Cultural Critique, 53*, 134–137.

Hayles, N. Katherine. (2005). *My mother was a computer: Digital subjects and literary texts.* Chicago: University of Chicago Press.

Hekman, Susan. (1986). The feminization of epistemology. *Women and Politics, 7*(3), 65–83.

Hekman, Susan. (1992). *Gender and knowledge.* Boston: Northeastern University Press.

Hekman, Susan. (1997). Truth and method: Feminist standpoint theory revisited. *Signs: Journal of Women in Culture and Society, 22*(2), 341–365.

Hesse-Biber, Sharlene, Gilmartin, Christina, & Lydenberg, Robin. (1999). *Feminist approaches to theory and methodology: An interdisciplinary reader.* New York: Oxford University Press.

Hesse-Biber, Sharlene, & Leavy, Patricia. (2004). *Approaches to qualitative research.* New York: Oxford University Press.

Hubbard, Ruth, Hennifin, M. S., & Fried, Barbara. (1982). *Biological woman: The convenient myth.* Cambridge, MA: Schenkman.

Hume, David. (1927). *An enquiry concerning human understanding* (L. A. Selby-Bigge, Ed.). Oxford, UK: Clarendon Press. (Original work published 1748)

Hume, David. (1975). *A treatise of human nature* (L. A. Selby-Bigge & P. H. Nidditch, Eds.). Oxford, UK: Clarendon Press. (Original work published 1739)

Jaggar, Alison. (1989). Love and knowledge: Emotion in feminist epistemology. In Alison Jaggar & Susan Bordo (Eds.), *Gender/body/knowledge* (pp. 145–171). New Brunswick, NJ: Rutgers University Press.

Kelly, Rita, Ronan, Bernard, & Cawley, Margaret. (1987). Liberal positivistic epistemology and research on women and politics. *Women and Politics, 7*(3), 11–27.

Koenig, Barbara A., Lee, Sandra Soo-Jin, & Richardson, Sarah S. (2008). *Revisiting race in a genomic age.* New Brunswick, NJ: Rutgers University Press.

Lakatos, Imre. (1970). Falsification and the methodology of scientific research programmes. In Imre Lakatos & Alan Musgrave (Eds.), *Criticism and the growth of knowledge* (pp. 91–196). Cambridge, UK: Cambridge University Press.

Le Doeuff, Michèle. (1991). *Hipparchia's choice: An essay concerning women, philosophy, etc.* (Trista Selous, Trans.). Oxford, UK: Blackwell.

Longino, Helen. (1990). *Science as social knowledge.* Princeton, NJ: Princeton University Press.

Longino, Helen. (1993). Feminist standpoint theory and the problems of knowledge. *Signs: Journal of Women in Culture and Society, 19*(1), 201–212.

Longino, Helen. (2002). *The fate of knowledge.* Princeton, NJ: Princeton University Press.

Martin, Emily. (1990). The egg and sperm: How science has constructed a romance based on stereotypical male and female roles. *Signs: Journal of Women in Culture and Society, 16*(3), 485–501.

McCall, Leslie. (2001). *Complex inequality: Gender, race, and class in the new economy.* New York: Routledge.

Megill, Allan. (1985). *Prophets of extremity: Nietzsche, Heidegger, Foucault, Derrida.* Berkeley: University of California Press.

Mies, Maria. (1984). Toward a methodology for feminist research. In Edith Hoshino Altbach, Jeanette Clausen, Dagmar Schultz, & Naomi Stephan (Eds.), *German feminism: Readings in politics and literature* (pp. 357–366). Albany, NY: SUNY Press.

Milam, Erika. (forthcoming). Gender across the human-animal boundary: Making males aggressive and females coy. *Signs: Journal of Women in Culture and Society.*

Miller, Ruth A. (forthcoming). *Seven stories of threatening speech: Women's suffrage meets machine code.* Ann Arbor: University of Michigan Press.

Moi, Toril. (1990). *Sexual/textual politics.* New York: Methuen.

Moon, D. (1975). The logic of political inquiry: A synthesis of opposed perspectives. In F. Greenstein & N. Polsby (Eds.), *Handbook of political science* (Vol. 1, pp. 3–32). Reading, MA: Addison-Wesley.

Nagel, Thomas. (1986). *The view from nowhere.* New York: Oxford University Press.

Nelson, Lyn. (1990). *Who knows: From Quine to a feminist empiricism.* Philadelphia: Temple University Press.

Nicholson, Linda. (1990). *Feminism/postmodernism.* New York: Routledge.

Nietzsche, Friedrich. (1969). *On the genealogy of morals* (Walter Kaufman, Trans.). New York: Vintage Books.

Nochlin, Linda. (1988). Why have there been no great women artists? *Women, art, and power and other essays* (pp. 145–178). New York: Harper & Row. (Original work published 1971 in *Art News, 69*(9)).

Oakley, Ann. (2000). *Experiments in knowing: Gender and method in the social sciences.* New York: The New Press.

Popper, Karl. (1959). *The logic of scientific discovery.* New York: Basic Books.

Popper, Karl. (1972a). *Conjectures and refutations* (4th rev. ed.). London: Routledge and Kegan Paul.

Popper, Karl. (1972b). *Objective knowledge: An evolutionary approach.* Oxford, UK: Clarendon Press.

Reinharz, Shulamit. (1992). *Feminist methods in social research.* New York: Oxford University Press.

Rich, Adrienne. (2003). Notes toward a politics of location. In Carole R. McCann & Seung-Kyung Kim (Eds.), *Feminist theory reader: Local and global perspectives* (pp. 447–459). New York: Routledge.

Ruth, Sheila. (1981). Methodocracy, misogyny, and bad faith: The response of philosophy. In Dale Spender (Ed.), *Men's studies modified: The impact of feminism on the academic disciplines* (pp. 43–53). Oxford, UK: Pergamon Press.

Sandoval, Chela. (2000). *Methodology of the oppressed.* Minneapolis: University of Minnesota Press.

Scott, Joan. (1988). Deconstructing the equality vs. difference debate: Or the uses of poststructuralist theory for feminism. *Feminist Studies, 14*(1), 575–599.

Scott, Joan. (1992). Experience. In Judith Butler & Joan Wallach Scott (Eds.), *Feminists theorize the political* (pp. 22–40). New York: Routledge.

Sellars, Wilfred. (1963). *Science, perception, and reality.* New York: Humanities Press.

Smith, Dorothy. (1979). A sociology for women. In Julia Ann Sherman & Evelyn Torton Beck (Eds.), *The prism of sex: Essays in the sociology of knowledge* (pp. 137–187). Madison: University of Wisconsin Press.

Stanley, Liz, & Wise, Susan. (1983). *Breaking out: Feminist consciousness and feminist research.* London: Routledge and Kegan Paul.

Stimpson, Catharine. (1991, January 31). *On cultural democracy and the republic of letters.* Phi Beta Kappa Lecture, University of Louisville, Louisville, KY.

Stockman, N. (1983). *Anti-positivist theories of science: Critical rationalism, critical theory, and scientific realism.* Dordrecht, The Netherlands: D. Reidel.

Strum, Shirley, & Fedigan, Linda. (2000). *Primate encounters: Models of science, gender, and society.* Chicago: University of Chicago Press.

Tanesini, Allesandra. (1999). *An introduction to feminist epistemologies.* Malden, MA: Blackwell.

Vickers, Jill M. (1982). Memoirs of an ontological exile: The methodological rebellions of feminist research. In Geraldine Finn & Angela Miles

(Eds.), *Feminism in Canada* (pp. 27–46). Montreal: Black Rose Books.

Walby, Sylvia. (2001). Against epistemological caverns: The science question in feminism revisited. *Signs: Journal of Women in Culture and Society, 26*(2), 486–509.

Westkott, Marcia. (1979). Feminist criticism of the social sciences. *Harvard Educational Review, 49*, 422–430.

White, Hayden. (1978). *Tropics of discourse.* Baltimore: Johns Hopkins University Press.

Williams, Bernard. (1985). *Ethics and the limits of philosophy.* Cambridge, MA: Harvard University Press.

Windance Twine, Frances, & Warren, Jonathan W. (2000). *Racing research, researching race.* New York: NYU Press.

Wolf, Diane. (1996). *Feminist dilemmas in fieldwork.* Boulder, CO: Westview Press.

Wolin, Sheldon. (1981). Max Weber: Legitimation, method, and the politics of theory. *Political Theory, 9*(3), 401–424.

Wylie, Alison. (2003). Why standpoint matters. In Robert Figueroa & Sandra Harding (Eds.), *Science and other cultures: Issues in philosophies of science and technology* (pp. 26–48). New York: Routledge.

Ycatman, Anna. (1994). *Postmodern revisionings of the political.* New York: Routledge.

Young, Iris. (1986). Impartiality and the civic public: Some implications of feminist critiques of moral and political theory. *Praxis International, 5*(4), 381–401.

Young, Iris. (1987). The ideal of community and the politics of difference. *Social Theory and Practice, 12*(1), 1–26.

6

CRITICAL PERSPECTIVES ON FEMINIST EPISTEMOLOGY

NORETTA KOERTGE

In a useful encyclopedia article on feminist epistemology, Elizabeth Anderson (2011) writes, "Feminist epistemology and philosophy of science studies the ways in which gender does and *ought to* [italics added] influence our conceptions of knowledge, the knowing subject, and practices of inquiry and justification" (p. 1). Thanks in large part to the contributions of people working in women's studies, the claim that gender *does* influence inquiry is no longer surprising. However, the normative claim that gender *ought to* play a role in our best epistemic practices is extremely controversial. In a short essay, one cannot hope to survey the variety of epistemic approaches that label themselves as feminist. What I will do instead is critically discuss three important examples of feminist theorizing taken from the works of Andrea Nye, Sandra Harding, and Helen Longino. Each believes that dominant knowledge practices disadvantage women, so a feminist epistemology is needed. My conclusion, however, will be that trying to gender epistemology can actually be detrimental to women.

FROM IDENTITY POLITICS TO FEMINIST EPISTEMOLOGY

Mainstream philosophical approaches to the nature of knowledge propose *universally* applicable criteria for good evidence and good arguments, which would not refer to gender, race, class, or creed. To understand the roots of and motivation for a feminist approach to epistemology, we need to survey the social context in which it arose. We will then evaluate it.

The late 1960s saw the rise in America of what came to be called "identity politics"—the attempt to analyze political issues and organize groups to act politically along the lines of race (black power), gender (women's liberation), and sexual orientation (gay liberation). What happened in the 1970s was the establishment of various new "studies" programs in universities across the United States.

Women's studies (WOST) initiatives were enormously successful. Like African American studies programs and the less numerous gay (later queer) studies courses, these projects had an explicit double agenda: They were to foster new directions in research and teaching, but they were also to promote political activism. In WOST, there was a popular slogan that appeared in official mission statements: "Women's studies is the academic arm of the women's movement."

Thus, issues of political expediency could legitimately be invoked at every stage: who should be hired (was a PhD necessary, or could experience as an activist be equally relevant?); how should curriculum requirements be set (would interning at a battered women's shelter count for academic credit?); and how should essay prizes be awarded (what if the writing was good but the woman seemed not to be an active feminist?).[1] The weight awarded to such political considerations varied greatly between universities and, over time, within universities, but these factors have never been ruled completely irrelevant within a women's studies program. The issue of how much a given academic decision should be shaped according to what was perceived as good for the movement has always been a live one.

WOST programs and departments self-consciously set out to effect a revolution in scholarship as well. At first, people simply set out to study *women*—their lives, past and present; their biological, psychological, and sociological development in various cultures; and how they talk, think, worship, and otherwise conduct their lives. Here, the emphasis was on filling in the gaps and noting how dominant narratives, theories, or models would have to be changed if women were to be included.

But, very quickly, the focus shifted to gender—and the new mantra became "RCG," the study of race, class, and gender. Some programs renamed themselves "gender studies," and their research came to include the study of the social construction of "maleness" (how males define themselves in part out of fear of being thought female) and "whiteness" (how part of white identity can be a sense of relief at not being like people of color)—and how each of these constructions varies by class.

Because most feminist scholars were trained in the humanities, they relied heavily on evidence from "texts" and—here is the connection to postmodernism—learned to read "silences" when there was no overt mention of RCG in

their sources. Like Sherlock Holmes, who found great significance in the dog who failed to bark in the night, they deconstructed references to race, gender, and class when they were found and recorded absences when they were not.

This distinction between bias against women (leaving unquestioned the criteria of excellence) and bias against gendered attributes (thus advocating a change in the criteria themselves) is important to remember when we turn to feminist epistemology. Early on, WOST had developed models of "women's ways of knowing" and theories of feminist pedagogy (for further discussion, see Patai & Koertge, 2003, chap. 7). Put in a nutshell, what these approaches tended to do was to affirm various stereotypes about female mentality and valorize them. Women supposedly responded well to noncompetitive, cooperative learning situations with a "guide by the side" instead of a "sage on the stage." They liked to learn experientially, not through abstract analysis. They wanted their knowledge to be concretely applicable and used for humane purposes.

But if such an account of female cognition is in any way close to being correct, we immediately see a strong clash between so-called women's ways of knowing and traditional accounts of reasoning in logic, mathematics, and science. Feminists were quick to conclude not only that the standard pedagogical approaches to these subjects were gender biased in a way that posed barriers for students but also that there was something inherently flawed about the disciplines themselves. A striking example of this kind of feminist critique is Andrea Nye's (1990) commentary on deductive logic, which is often assumed to lie at the very core of rationality. It will illustrate nicely both the rhetorical appeal of such feminist attacks on traditional epistemology and what I will argue are the regressive political effects.

Is Logic an Instrument of Patriarchal Oppression?

Logic is the systematic study of patterns of correct inference. The first treatise on logic is Aristotle's (1964) *Prior Analytics,* written around 350 BCE, and there are remarkable similarities between the way he presented his theory of valid arguments and the way logic is still taught today. He analyzes the *form* of various inferences and then illustrates them with concrete examples. He begins with very simple cases:

> If no B is A, neither can any A be B; e.g., if no pleasure is good, no good will be pleasure.
>
> If some B is not A, it does not follow that some A is not B. By way of illustration let B stand for animal and A for man: not every animal is a man, but every man is an animal. (p. 5)

Aristotle's exposition of syllogistic reasoning was at the center of what came to be called the *Organon*, the instrument of demonstrative reasoning, and logic was an honored member of the trivium, which functioned as the "core curriculum" throughout the Middle Ages and is still influential today. At my university, beginning logic is strongly advised even for undergraduates majoring in nursing, physical therapy, and social work. As was the case with claims made about studying Latin, it is very difficult to provide compelling evidence for the salutary influence of the study of logic on human reasoning in ordinary life situations, but it clearly does help students do well on the Graduate Record Exam and the Law School Admission Test.

For this reason alone, one might well expect feminists to urge women students to take logic courses and to point out that it is not just women students who find logic difficult. Unfortunately, the predominant feminist response has been to attack logic and other traditional canons of rationality as sexist. We will look at two separate lines of critique: one dealing with the way logic is taught, the other directed at the discipline itself.

Logic textbooks are full of exercises that give the student practice in translating strings of ordinary English sentences into logical notation and then appraising the formal correctness of the inferences they illustrate. Many of the examples are now classics, such as the syllogism "All men are mortal; Socrates is a man; so, Socrates is mortal." But there is also a tradition among textbook writers of generating witty examples that are intended to keep students awake as they work their way through Venn diagrams, truth tables, or natural deduction schemata. So, for example, the exercises in Lewis Carroll's famous 19th-century logic book include whimsical sentences such as these:

> No lizard needs a hairbrush. (Carroll, 1958, p. 130)

> My dreams are all about Bath-buns. (p. 120)

As the last example about Bath buns (British breakfast rolls) illustrates, these little student exercises provide us with glimpses of both the author's psychology and contemporary popular culture.

Post–World War II American logic texts also reflect the concerns of the time, but now gender roles have become a major topic of interest. Copi's (1979) exercises include the following:

> A communist is either a fool or a knave. (p. 77)

> The United Nations will become more responsible or there will be a third world war. (p. 11)

> If any husband is unsuccessful then if some wives are ambitious he will be unhappy. (p. 89)

> All popular girls are good conversationalists. (p. 159)

> All successful executives are intelligent men. (p. 134)

> All tenors are either overweight or effeminate. (p. 83)

A similar pattern is found in other well-respected books of the period. Women or girls do not figure at all in most of the exercises, and, when they do appear, they are almost always in passive, trivial, or demeaning roles:

> Single women are decorous only if they are chaperoned. (Kalish & Montague, 1964, p. 98)

> Women without husbands are unhappy unless they have paramours. (Kalish & Montague, 1964, p. 98)

> Simone de Beauvoir is not a great writer. (Suppes, 1957, p. 107)

> If either red-heads are lovely or blondes do not have freckles, then logic is confusing. (Suppes, 1957, p. 18)

There is no question that the exercises employed in these logic books reinforced traditional sexual stereotypes. Whether this fact played a significant role in deterring women from the study of logic is less clear. As the last example above reminds us, many students, male and female, find logic confusing, boring, or difficult. What we can conclude, however, is that, in America today, thanks to the success of the women's movement, students are now sensitized to gender stereotypes and tend to find sentences such as "every girl loves a sailor" every bit as inappropriate. And more recent books, such as the fifth edition of Kahane's (1986) *Logic and Philosophy*, portray women and men in a wider variety of roles:

Art watched "General Hospital," but Betsy didn't. (p. 33)

And in Kahane's dialogue about the Liar's Paradox (a common logical problem), it is Bonny who says, "I know," and provides the proof, whereas Charlie says things like "Maybe yes, maybe no" and "I don't know why" (p. 193).

Although women students are not well-served by being encouraged to melt down at the first sight of a sexist syllogism, there is no reason for distracting them by using a barrage of examples that they or any other group of students find insulting. And as this brief survey of the change in textbooks over time suggests, authors are responding to these concerns. I wish I could end the story of the feminist critique of logic on this happy note. Unfortunately, however, some feminists have claimed that not just the homework exercises but also the very enterprise of characterizing the formal structure of logical inference cannot be separated from sexism, racism, and totalitarianism.

Conflict between rationalists and romantics—those who would rely on reason and those who would privilege feelings, respectively—predates feminism, but feminists have added some new arguments and lots of new anger to the debate. Nye's (1990) *Words of Power*, published in Routledge's Thinking Gender series, provides a good example of a radical feminist critique of rationalism and logic. Because it is more clearly written and argued than most, it is worth examining in some detail.

Nye begins with a story about the feelings she had in her logic class: how there was only one other woman in her class, how she was too unsure of herself to raise her hand in class, and how difficult it was to think in the way required. When confronted with the example "Jones ate fish with ice cream and died," Nye, who had come to the subject of philosophy with a background in literature, finds her mind wandering off into speculation about why Jones ate such a bizarre dish and why death was the consequence. The difficulty she experienced in representing the structure of the sentence with p's and q's raised a troubling question in Nye's mind: "Is it because I, as a woman, had a different kind of mind, incapable of abstraction and therefore of theorizing, [*sic*] is it because I was too 'emotional'?" (p. 2).

Many women have had such doubts. The liberal feminist reply is an analysis of how logical pedagogical styles as well as societal gender stereotypes make women feel alienated from logic. Nye's response is to put the shoe of blame on the other foot. She argues that, given its historical development from the time of the Greeks, logic, as we know it today, is not only alienated from women but also has been and continues to be a weapon of women's oppression.

Nye's first complaint is a familiar one to logic teachers: by requiring that sentences be formalized, logicians strip away nuances and metaphorical meanings. As Nye puts it, "The philosopher who combs the tangles from language must also be a butcher who trims away the fleshy fat of ordinary talk to leave the bare bones of truth" (p. 33). Nye believes that training in logic makes us focus too much on *what* is said instead of on *who* said it or *why*. As an example, she cites the success of the Willie Horton ad in the 1988 Bush-Dukakis campaign. Nye believes that listeners behaved too much like logicians in their processing of the commercials; that is, they concentrated too much on the arguments about parole policies and too little on the emotional impact of the pictures. (Needless to say, a logician would immediately point out the existence of what are technically called "hidden lemmas" (unstated assumptions) in the

Willie Horton argument and conclude that the listeners were not being logical enough!)

Nye's second objection is directed at Aristotle's law of the excluded middle, a favorite target of feminists who see it as the basis of patriarchal dualistic thinking. The law of the excluded middle simply says that everything is either A or not A. It would be a contradiction to say of something that it is at once A and not A. But Nye (1990) argues that this logic does not apply to "ambiguous bodily individuals who so often both are and are not what we desire of them" (p. 51). Many lay criticisms of the law of the excluded middle are based on a crude confusion between contraries and contradictories. The classic law does *not* claim that everything is either black or white and that there are no shades of gray. What it *does* say is that everything is either black or not-black, white or not-white, gray or not-gray. Aristotle's logic does not rule out the possibility of intersex identity, lukewarm baths, or wars that end with no victor.

However, logicians themselves have had many interesting discussions about all of Aristotle's laws of negation. Some are worried about the proper analysis of intrinsically vague terms, such as *city* (how big must a town be before it counts as a city?), and they have developed a formal analysis in terms of what are called *fuzzy sets*. Others have resisted the idea that every sentence is either true or false and have experimented with so-called three-valued logics. Philosophers of science have tried to develop a measure of "verisimilitude" that would permit us to say of two false sentences that one has a higher truth content than the other. Logic has more resources and more flexibility than are dreamt of in most feminist philosophy.

We now come to Nye's original criticism of logic, one based on an unusual reading of its history, starting with the Greeks, progressing through the Middle Ages, and then jumping to the early 20th century. Nye (1990) proudly owns up to committing the genetic fallacy and arguing ad hominem (p. 174) because she believes that the historical context in which a theory develops and the character of the person who originates it *are* relevant to the evaluation of the truth of that view. (The standard logician's response is that such historical and psychological factors may well be relevant to our understanding of *what* the person was trying to say and their motives in saying it but are totally irrelevant to whether the view is well argued.)

So when Nye describes Aristotle's syllogism, she also describes his theory of reproduction, according to which the active male semen impresses its form on passive female matter, and his doctrine of the "natural slave," as if both were somehow relevant to our evaluation of his system of logic. We learn not only of Abelard's struggle to reconcile Stoic logic with Aristotelianism but also of his dialectical assault on Heloise. And it is claimed (I confess I couldn't follow the argument) that the racist sentiments in Frege's private diary are somehow relevant to his approach to mathematical logic.

Nye (1990) finds even more damning the uses to which logic was put. Thus, she claims, as logical discourse came to be admired in Hellenic law courts or public forums, those who did not follow the prescribed modes were disenfranchised: "Logic rendered them all speechless, unable to voice their reservations and scruples, unable to validate or refute what had been said from their own experiences. And it was this dazzlement and this silencing that logic was *meant* [italics added] to create" (p. 79).

The book culminates by positing a link between Frege, a giant of early 20th-century logic, and Hitler:

> Hitler . . . guided by sentiments not unlike the ones expressed in Frege's diary, worked out the master-logic of National Socialism. . . . National Socialist thought like Frege's, did not concern itself with empirical content. . . . No personal experience could negate [its] . . . body of truth. . . . The applications of logic to action that Frege had promised came readily to hand. If Jews are a mongrel race, they must be exterminated. "A thought like a hammer" [Frege's phrase] demanded instant obedience to the dictates of logic. (Nye, 1990, p. 169)

Nye's feminist reading of the history of logic ends with these words: "Logic in its final perfection is insane" (p. 171).

But are her interpretations of sources at all plausible? If we go back to Frege's own essay, we find little solace for the authoritarian. Frege (1977) begins his final paragraph this way:

> How does a thought act? By being grasped and taken to be true. . . . If, for example, I grasp the thought we express by the theorem of Pythagoras, the consequence may be that I recognize it to be true, and further that I apply it in making a decision. (pp. 28–29)

Frege has thus focused on the individual thinker and how one's judgments of truth may influence one's actions. He then goes on to describe how thoughts are passed on to others.

> The influence of man on man is brought about for the most part by thoughts. People communicate thoughts. . . . Could the great events of world history have come about without the communication of thoughts? And yet we are inclined to regard thoughts as unactual, because they appear to do nothing in relation to events, whereas thinking, judging, stating, understanding, in general doing things, are affairs that concern men. How very different the actuality of a hammer appears, compared with that of a thought! (p. 29)

Nye would have us believe that this essay about the reality of ideas and their influences on the lives of individuals who judge them to be true should be read as a recipe for brainwashing and extermination camps. It is, of course, impossible to refute a "reading." But perhaps the quotations I have displayed might prompt some readers to read Frege for themselves. The question of the historical use and misuse of the tools of logical analysis and inference is an interesting and legitimate one, and I found much of what Nye said about Greek and medieval law thought provoking. But let us not omit the liberating moments in history. Let us also trace the connections between John Stuart Mill's *System of Logic* and the way he argues in *On Liberty* and note the influences of rationalist philosophers of the Enlightenment on the writers of the United States' Bill of Rights. Let us tell our women students who admire Adrienne Rich's *Dream of a Common Language* that Leibniz and

d'Alembert had a related dream and discuss the similarities and differences.

And, most important of all, let us stress the use of logic as an instrument of criticism. Nye is correct in saying that logic can be used as a hammer—if you accept these premises, then by God (and by modus ponens) you've got to accept these logical consequences. But *modus tollens* is a rule of logic too, and it states that if a logically correct argument leads to a false conclusion, then by God (or by Goddess!) something is wrong with the premises. Here, logic is acting like a tiny sharp needle—the discovery of one little falsehood or inconsistency can discredit an enormous deductive system. For example, the religious argument that the so-called morning-after birth control pill should be outlawed because the soul enters the embryo at conception can be skewered by pointing out that the splitting of the zygote to form the embryos of identical twins typically happens 3 or 4 days after conception. So unless one is willing to say that twins somehow share a soul, it follows that ensoulment must happen after conception. Thus, this particular religious argument falls apart. Logic is an invaluable tool for groups of people who have little physical or economic strength but do have sharp wits and a rigorous mind.

Let us now turn to some representative feminist critiques of traditional canons of scientific reasoning.

Feminist Incursions Into the Philosophy of Science: Resonances With Post-Kuhnian Concerns

Just as Nye argued that traditional logic was damaging to women, some feminists claimed that, if more women were ever to take part in science, then science itself had to change. To quote a National Science Foundation report by Sue V. Rosser (1993), science had to become more "female-friendly." She called for less emphasis on dissecting frogs and controlled experiments and more fieldwork and science-for-the-people projects (see Patai & Koertge, 2003, chap. 12).

During the 1980s, there began a vast array of feminist critiques of science, many of them originating from people who had little knowledge of either science or its history. And their goal sometimes appeared to be to dismantle the authority of and support for science. But influential work was also done by people who had classical training in various branches of what we now call science studies, and, in these cases, the authors wanted to understand science better and perhaps improve its efficiency, as well as promote feminist political goals. In the sections that follow, I will concentrate on the works of two noted feminist philosophers of science, Sandra Harding and Helen Longino.[2]

As long as one focused on issues of *women* in science, there was no tradition within the philosophy of science that would make it plausible that one would turn up anything of particular philosophical relevance. The whole point of the scientific method is to render the personal characteristics of the scientist irrelevant. But when we switch to talk of *gender* and science, the feminist program looks more promising.[3] In what is sometimes called the "historical" approach to the philosophy of science (an approach that pays a great deal of attention to actual examples of past—and present—scientific practice), there had been a lot of interest in documenting the role of what is loosely called "metaphysics" in the development of science. If prescientific conceptions of the nature of matter influenced the development of early chemistry and mythological ideas about the cosmos influenced early astronomy, then even nonfeminists would expect gender ideology to have an influence on the development of scientific accounts of reproduction in biology, theories about the relationship between males and females in anthropology, theories about the family in sociology, models of child development in psychology, and hypotheses within a myriad of other investigations in the social sciences.

Cases of gender roles influencing scientific theories were, in fact, easy to find; a classic example is Aristotle's account of the passive female egg, which supplied the inert matter, and the active male sperm, which supplied the form. But it was not at all clear what moral should be drawn from such case studies. Philosophers of science from the so-called historical school following Kuhn were interested in questions about

discovery, pursuit, and how long metaphysically based preconceptions continued to play a role as evidence was collected, as well as questions about the incommensurability between conceptual schemes, and so on. And here the cases of the apparent influence of ideas about gender seemed completely unremarkable, especially because mistaken ideas that arose from gender stereotypes were removed and corrected through the normal internal criticism characteristic of the scientific approach.

Those who were specifically interested in gender for other reasons were hoping to draw other morals—that the influence of gender ideology was especially ubiquitous and especially powerful. But even in the history of reproduction that case was surprisingly difficult to make. Just as physicists oscillated between atomistic and continuum theories of matter or wrestled with wave versus particle conceptions in the field of optics, so biologists sometimes flirted with accounts that gave the *egg* pride of place over the sperm. Were we to say that 17th- and 18th-century preformationist and ovular accounts of embryology flourished at a period when patriarchy had somehow lost its grip?

Nevertheless, there developed a kind of urban legend about gender and the history of reproduction that even found its way into *Newsweek*.[4] It goes roughly like this: Positivism said that science was not influenced by ideology, but feminists have revolutionized our understanding of how science works. For centuries, scientists thought the egg was passive, and it was the sperm that actively went courting and eventually penetrated the egg. But now (the implication being that this happened after the rise of feminism in the mid-20th century), scientists are realizing that the egg also has a say and actively envelopes the sperm of its choice. But the most that such a feminist research program, no matter how successful, could show was that societal ideas about sex and gender have some sort of impact (we could argue about how much) on the scientific study of subject matter having to do with sex and gender (which admittedly covered a pretty wide domain). But what about physics? And chemistry, and geology? What could gender feminism possibly say about them?

Here some feminist scholars took a quasi-Freudian approach to gender and found influences everywhere, as in Luce Irigaray's attempt to argue that the history of hydrodynamics was influenced, and impeded, by male scientists' fear of soft, yielding fluids and their fixation on models employing rigid bodies.[5] Using a similar approach, one could plunk for a steady state cosmology, arguing that some of the appeal of the big bang theory was its masculinist associations. However, the most interesting and sophisticated move was to see whether there might be something distinctively gendered about research methodology itself.

Women's studies scholars had already done biographical research on women scientists; feminist philosophers now started looking for distinctive, gender-related features of the way these women approached science. Some of the results were interesting additions to the history of science, but their philosophical significance was less clear. Barbara McClintock may indeed have had a "feeling for the organism" and been good at imagining jumping genes, but Albert Einstein (who now turns out to be a right old chauvinist pig) had a "nose for problems" and relied on *Fingerspitzengefühl* while visualizing rides on light rays. As more histories of antireductionist and antimechanistic approaches to science, including 19th-century romantic science and *Naturphilosophie*, were written, it became obvious that the leaders of such movements showed few signs of being protofeminists. There may indeed be some interesting variations in approaches to science—one often speaks of "lumpers" versus "splitters," Aristotelians versus Platonists, algebraic versus geometric methods, top-down versus bottom-up approaches to problem solving—but none of these mapped onto masculine versus feminine.

Do RCG Groups Have a Privileged Standpoint?

Sandra Harding (1991) proposed a more sophisticated and interesting approach to studying gender and science, which she called "standpoint epistemology"—what you see, what you find important, and how you understand the world depends on your "standpoint."[6] Just as Marx claimed that the standpoint of the proletariat is privileged on economic matters and Hegel argued that sometimes slaves have a clearer picture of what's really going on than do their masters, so, Harding argues, women and other oppressed groups have distinctive viewpoints to contribute to science. Thus, she calls for what she terms *strong objectivity*: If present science is distorted by the predominance of male perspectives, would not science become more objective by the deliberate inclusion of views from the standpoint of women, minorities, workers, and any other group that is underrepresented in today's scientific community?

A familiar example that appears to support Harding's thesis is the work of primatologist Jane Goodall, who is noted for her studies of the social organization of chimpanzees. On the face of it, much of her success appears to be attributable to her female standpoint: She exhibited exquisite patience (a stereotypical female virtue) in observing her chimpanzees. (Or was it doggedness, an attribute with other gender connotations?) And, true, she did focus in on the roles of females and the nature of family relationships, thus perhaps reflecting her "standpoint" as a woman.

But Goodall also documented aggression, murder, and even cannibalism among her beloved chimps. Does being prepared to notice cannibalism also reflect a gendered "standpoint"? Or was she just a careful scientist? Yet what about her empathy with her subjects and her intense commitment to saving their habitat? How can one look at her face on CNN and not see her female-gendered perspective shining through?

Don't get me wrong—to me, Jane Goodall is a saint—a much better role model than Mother Teresa—but how different is her standpoint from that of Jacques Cousteau, who also did naturalistic fieldwork, observed all sorts of new behaviors of the great white shark, and formed the Cousteau Society to save the oceans, all the while exhibiting a typical Gallic chauvinist flair?

But even if one could document that females bring a distinctive perspective to scientific inquiry, postpositivist philosophers of science have a blasé reply: We all know (following Kuhn) that disciplinary commitments influence science and that other perspectives may well play a role in the formative stages, but then, as evidence piles up, these extraneous influences disappear. Either the distinctive approach stands up to severe tests, or it doesn't. To revise a common aphorism, Man—or Woman—proposes, but Nature disposes.

It is all too easy to assume that certain standpoints have privileged access to the truth. I am reminded of what people used to say about simplicity—surely God would not allow the true picture of the universe to be so complex that we could not understand it. Similarly, one might believe that a goddess would not design a universe that could be accurately described by sociobiology or a world in which there were socially relevant kinds of genetic influences on intelligence, ability in mathematics, or tendencies to commit violent crimes. If one were to adopt such an article of faith, then, just as people used to take simplicity as an indicator of truth, one would now take political progressiveness as an indicator of empirical adequacy.

Let me sum up by noting that Harding's call for the inclusion of a plurality of viewpoints is surely a good idea. Science thrives on the competition among a variety of approaches to solving the problems at hand. And in applied science it becomes especially important to seek input from the users who will actually be working with the innovation. Too often, those who would export technology to developing countries have made terrible blunders that could have been avoided if they had worked more closely with people on the ground.

But it would be dubious epistemological advice to recommend that people construct their beliefs on the basis of a particular standpoint, whether it be the one they were born into or one that they deliberately constructed on the basis of identity politics. Early feminism urged women to trust their own experience and feelings. This may have been good therapeutic advice for certain individuals who had been brainwashed by authoritarian religions and families. But the whole purpose of education is to supersede provincialism. Too often, feminist pedagogy encourages treating the standpoint of one's own race, class, or gender group as privileged or as a badge of identity. Participants in the Midwest

division of the Society for Women in Philosophy (SWIP) often begin papers by declaring a standpoint—"speaking as a Chicana lesbian mother."[7] But if we are interested in scientific knowledge, a standpoint based on identity is at best a starting point!

SHOULD POLITICAL COMMITMENTS PLAY A ROLE IN EPISTEMOLOGY?

Helen Longino offers an epistemological approach that diverts attention from the mental processes of the individual knower and instead looks at the shared epistemic values of the scientific community, for example, standards such as empirical adequacy, simplicity, and explanatory power.[8] She then argues that the space of scientific hypotheses would be enriched if one looked seriously at theories that conformed to desiderata exemplified in the work of feminist scientists and commentators. These include *novelty* (a deliberate break with the approaches prevalent in the male-dominated history of science), *ontological heterogeneity* (resistance to models that gloss over individual differences), *complexity of relationship* (recognition of the importance of interactions), and *applicability to current human needs* (Longino, 1995). Longino also suggests methods of improving the ways in which scientific hypotheses are discussed and evaluated, which I will not summarize here.

Note that, as I have described it thus far, Longino's epistemology is *feminist* in only a rather sophisticated (perhaps I should say attenuated) sense. No longer are we trying to attribute to women special ways of knowing, such as intuitive or qualitative or holistic. Nor are we trying to describe gendered differences in knowing—one is not claiming that there is something masculinist about liking the big bang theory or the mechanics of billiard balls. Rather, it seems to me, Longino is making a historical point about the inspiration for her epistemology. Currently, feminists have been at the forefront in criticizing certain approaches to anthropology, biology, and psychology. Longino has extracted from these critiques a list of values that she believes are different from those embedded in mainstream science. She then proposes that science would be enriched by actively pursuing hypotheses that score well on the values that she extracted from the writings of feminists.

The issue of the presumptively feminist status of such values is perhaps less important than their intrinsic merits. Let's look at them briefly in turn. *Novelty* is a value touted by all would-be scientific revolutionaries. In some cases, it leads to progress—if epicycles seem to be multiplying without end, then maybe it's time to look beyond Ptolemaic astronomy. But every crank theory ever proposed also measures up well on the novelty scale.

The usefulness of encouraging *ontological heterogeneity* also depends on circumstances: Many scientific breakthroughs actually result in unification and thus in a reduction of heterogeneity—we now know that organic compounds do not require a vital force for their synthesis; they obey the same laws as inorganic compounds. But, in other cases, more ontological heterogeneity *is* needed. One thinks of the introduction of new fundamental particles—a neutron is not just a combo of the familiar proton and electron; it is a different kind of particle. Similar reservations arise with Longino's preference for hypotheses that try to describe the *complexity of relationships*. There are generally methodological advantages to starting out with simple models that emphasize the most salient factors, even if they don't always capture details of the phenomena. A familiar example is the ideal gas law, which was later refined by van der Waals, who took into account the forces between molecules.

As for *applicability to current human needs*, since the time of Bacon both scientists and funding agencies have shared this value. Where it gets tricky is in prioritizing needs and guessing which lines of research are most likely to pan out. Applying this criterion is also complicated by the fact that so-called basic or pure research often later turns out to be exceedingly useful in improving the human condition. I once heard a talk that tried to analyze the research leading to the birth control pill into steps that were mission directed and steps that had been taken with no such purpose in mind. What was striking to me was that the story of the birth control pill was not, as I expected, a tale that began with scattered pure research that was followed by an intense period of applied or development activity. Rather, there was a continuous interjection of, and reliance on, research results that had no intentional connection to the quest for a pill. In this case, too much emphasis on Longino's norm of applicability to human needs would probably have slowed the development of a method of birth control that has had an enormous liberating effect on women.

Leaving aside the issue of what we should make of Longino's list of proposed new epistemic values, we can surely agree with her point that they might inspire new approaches to current scientific problems, and she is certainly right to argue that a free-ranging debate that paid respectful attention to a plurality of viewpoints would certainly be of *epistemic* benefit to science (no matter how conservative our conception of scientific inquiry might be). Because women's perspectives have historically been neglected, including them would be one obvious way of diversifying the pool of hypotheses that would then be scrutinized by scientists in their search for good scientific theories. But Longino goes on to make remarks that are consistent with the radical proposal that we should include the likely political repercussions of a scientific research program as a relevant factor in our internal evaluations of it.

Longino's stance vis-à-vis this proposal is very unclear because her discussion of theories she dislikes (e.g., man-the-hunter and linear-hormonal models) describes their empirical flaws as well as their purported political infelicities. Perhaps Longino is simply reminding us of type II statistical error and urging us to adopt a precautionary strategy: If a theory is likely to have bad social consequences, we should be especially cautious about basing policy on it. Traditional philosophy of science readily admits the important role of social values in the context of the application of scientific results. It is more controversial to suggest that we rule out certain kinds of research problems simply because we are afraid of what we may find—certainly Alfred Kinsey would have objected.

But Longino also seems to be suggesting that we add political progressiveness to the traditional list of cognitive virtues that are used to evaluate scientific hypotheses. If that is her intent, then she is indeed proposing a radical feminist account of scientific rationality, one that puts a specific political agenda right at the justificatory heart of the search for knowledge. Let us briefly document what Longino says on this issue. (Her precise view is not easy to ascertain.) We will then go on to criticize the position that feminists might easily take away from reading Longino.

Longino's (1990) book, *Science as Social Knowledge: Values and Objectivity in Scientific Inquiry*, contrasts what she calls constitutive and contextual values. Constitutive values include empirical adequacy, accuracy, breadth, and predictive power; contextual values are those current in the social and cultural environment in which science operates at a given time and place (p. 4). Traditional normative accounts of the development of science would caution us to keep contextual values out of our appraisals of the epistemic merits of scientific hypotheses. Longino's social epistemology finds this prophylactic approach both unrealistic and undesirable: "The idea of a value-free science is not just empty but pernicious" (p. 191).

Her own positive account of the proper role of contextual values is not clearly spelled out. But the following quotations provide some hints: "When faced with a conflict between these commitments and a particular model of brain-behavior relationships we allow the political commitments to guide the choice" (Longino, 1990, pp. 190–191). How exactly are political commitments supposed to guide the choice between competing theories? Since Longino considers herself to be an empiricist, Anderson (2004) finds the concerns of critics such as me to be baseless. After all, Longino lists empirical adequacy as a core constitutive value for science. So wouldn't whatever emphasis she places on other values in the end be trumped by how well the theory is supported by evidence? Yet one of the distinctive features of Longino's epistemology is her emphasis on a variety of other values, and as Anderson (2004) herself reports,

> Feminist epistemologists have also sometimes used the term "context of justification" to refer to more than the process of determining the truth or

warrant of theories. Theories are evaluated with respect to all of the goals for which they were constructed. (¶ 10)[9]

Longino (1990) ends her chapter on "Science and Ideology" as follows (my comments are interspersed between sentences that were contiguous in the original): "The theory which is the product of the most inclusive scientific community is better, other things being equal, than that which is the product of the most exclusive" (p. 214). The things that must be equal presumably include how well the theory measures up to constitutive values, such as empirical adequacy.

But then Longino (1990) continues, "It [the theory] is better not as measured against some independently accessible reality but better as measured against the cognitive needs of a genuinely democratic community" (p. 214). Here we see contextual values being brought into play—the more that theories conform to the needs of a community, the better they are, other things being equal. We may be taken aback when we recall that Nazi Germany had a cognitive need for theories of Aryan superiority and that the Kansas school board has a need for research showing the inadequacy of neo-Darwinism. Longino, however, insists that science only needs to appraise theories in response to the cognitive needs of *genuinely democratic* communities.

She concludes, "This suggests that the problem of developing a new science is the problem of creating a new social and political reality" (Longino, 1990, p. 214). Here we have a stirring call for feminist action—by improving society, we will make possible an improved science. Yet Longino's proposal raises all the concerns that go along with utopian dreams. Even if one cedes for the sake of argument that incorporating political values into science would be okay in a "genuine" democracy, nothing follows about whether it is wise to let a society's cognitive needs play a role in theory appraisal within an imperfect democracy. Is the promise of research on adult stem cells as contrasted with embryonic stem cells to be influenced by what today's society wants to be the case? Or to pick examples that would appear to satisfy more progressive cognitive needs: Should we judge the scientific reliability of climate change models partly in terms of our nation's energy policy?

I think not. From the early days of the Royal Society, scientists have realized that it is much more difficult to reach consensus about religious and political matters than it is to agree on the empirical adequacy and explanatory power of competing scientific accounts. Not only are our wishes about how we want the world to be completely irrelevant to the way the world actually is, but making scientific appraisals dependent on political agendas is impractical. The one thing you can be sure of in a genuine democracy is that science policy about futuristic science agendas will be highly contested and subject to change. Science can help society improve itself by providing feedback on the viability of various scenarios. As we have seen with NASA in recent years, when a science program tries too hard to accommodate contextual values, its rockets may not work!

CONCLUSION

So where do matters stand today regarding feminist perspectives on scientific reasoning, logic, and theories of rationality? And what should we expect in the future? Anderson (2011) describes feminist epistemology as follows: "The central concept of feminist epistemology is that of a situated knower, and hence of situated knowledge: knowledge that reflects the particular perspectives of the subject. Feminist philosophers are interested in how gender situates knowing subjects" (¶ 2). In this definition, although gender is important, *situating* knowledge claims is what's really essential to feminist epistemology. Let's evaluate these two features, starting with the emphasis on gender.

The previously described critiques of three examples of feminist epistemology illustrate both the promises and weaknesses of the program of always using gender as a lens for understanding belief systems in general and science in particular. To give a topical example, we cannot hope to understand the political impact of Sarah Palin and the reception of her ideas without including a thorough analysis of her clever juxtaposition of seemingly incongruous gender stereotypes. Yet such an analysis must be supplemented with considerations of geography and frontier culture, religion and party politics, race-based fears and distrust of expertise—gender serves at best as a starting point.

An interesting example of how ideas about gender figure in the development of science is found in my colleague Elisabeth Lloyd's prize-winning book *The Case of the Female Orgasm: Bias in the Science of Evolution.* One can hardly imagine a more fertile source of gendered assumptions than debates about the female sexual response. Nevertheless, the most recalcitrant obstacle to scientific understanding in this particular case turns out to be the evolutionary doctrine of adaptationism, not sexual politics. As the subtitle reminds us, the scientific norms that are properly brought to bear when evaluating theories of the orgasm are the non-gendered norms that we depend on to transform beliefs into knowledge, and they are independent of the political progressiveness of those beliefs.

Let us agree that gender is often a salient factor in so-called situated knowledge. But should epistemology be limited to an investigation of *situated* knowledge? I grant that the prevalent view of science in the humanities today definitely centers on the social situation of the person or persons making the claims. This approach reflects the impact of feminist philosophical research, reinforced by the writings of postmodernists and social constructionists coming out of literature and cultural studies (for a thoroughgoing critique, see Koertge, 1998b; Parsons, 2003). Thus one asks, "Who would benefit if the claim were accepted, who funded the research, and who has the power to set the research agenda?" Looking at the social context can help us understand how knowledge claims arise and evolve, but there are other, more important epistemological questions to be asked. How severely has the claim been tested? Is there a variety of evidence supporting the claim? Is it logically consistent with other well-tested claims?

Since the time of the scientific revolution, philosophers and scientists have searched for methods of turning situated knowledge claims into *universal* knowledge, propositions that hold true in all situations. These methods work by deliberately trying to eliminate the effects of personal perspectives. So, for example, sometimes one can use double-blind tests. Quantitative measurements may replace subjective judgments in some cases. Statistical methods can help assess the extent of experimental error and the accuracy of results. Scientific institutions look for ways to improve the process of peer review and prevent conflicts of interest.

More recently, cognitive psychologists and behavioral economists have documented some of the sources of systematic error in the judgments of individuals who are not working in a scientific setting, and there are even popular self-help books that tell us about confirmation bias, anchoring, and the fallacy of ignoring base rates. Awareness of such factors helps us not only to improve our own belief bank but also to identify errors in what other people say.

The subset of feminist philosophers who identify themselves as empiricists will quickly reply that they do not neglect the importance of traditional epistemic norms, while reminding us of complications such as the underdetermination of theory by evidence and the theory-ladenness of observation. But, in the end, even a feminist empiricist sometimes has to decide which is more important, feminist commitments or empiricism? More worrisome are the feminist epistemologists who belittle traditional epistemic goals (see Haack, 2008, on confusions about the value of seeking true propositions). Anderson's (2011) encyclopedia article points out that some feminist philosophers are now making a distinction between "feminist science" and "doing science as a feminist"—and recommending the latter. This is a hopeful sign, although I think the ultimate goal would be to simply have "feminists doing science."

We can find a parallel tripartite distinction in the current debates about the compatibility of evolutionary theory and Christianity. Some say true Christians should only engage in "creationist science," in which biological findings are always interpreted in accord with scripture; the results include claims about dinosaurs being on Noah's ark. Recently, people such as Michael Behe could be described as "doing science as a Christian," to echo Anderson's distinction. His arguments about the irreducible complexity of bacterial flagellum gain most of their plausibility from his convictions about the operation of intelligent design, but are, in principle, open to rebuttals from mainstream biologists. Then there is a third category of biologists such as Kenneth Miller and Francis Collins, who are simply "Christians doing science." Their religious beliefs may never be visible in their scientific work, although these beliefs may influence their views on ethical issues, but such scientists play an extremely valuable role in helping Christians understand and feel comfortable with scientific results. Scientists who are feminists can play a comparable role in reducing the alienation of women and minorities from science.

Thanks to feminist concerns about the just treatment of women and other underappreciated groups, women are increasingly visible and influential in every aspect of our society. But one area where they continue to be seriously underrepresented is natural science. At first, the response of many feminist epistemologists was to claim that the norms of science were antithetical to women's ways of knowing. It was even implied that women who liked math or abstract physical theories were somehow not genuine feminists (see Koertge, 1998a, and Pattatucci, 1998). Unfortunately, such views are still influential is schools of education and affect science pedagogy (see Pinnick, 2008b).

Thoughtful feminist epistemologists do not intend their writings to discourage would-be women scientists or make educated laywomen cynical about the value of science. Quite the contrary. Yet the rhetorical style so characteristic of early feminist writings persists. A philosophy of science text published even in 2009 says the following on its book cover: "*The Gender of Science* explores the claim that modern Western science is masculine, and that its masculinity helps to perpetuate a society biased in favor of men" (Kourany, 2009).

But even a cursory look at the science section of newspapers or magazines shows successful women doing science—barriers are increasingly a relic of the past and should not be exaggerated. And it is simply not true to say that these women's studies in astronomy, biology, chemistry, dynamics, or ecology perpetuate male bias. We now need to celebrate the opportunities for women to work in all areas of science and to validate the third role described above—feminists who are simply doing science. And as feminist insights on gender and the influence of one's social situation on beliefs continue to be recognized, some day there will no longer be any need for feminist epistemology—there will simply be feminists doing epistemology.

Discussion Questions

1. Logic looks at the formal structure of sentences and arguments. In what sorts of situations might a feminist object to the use of logical analysis? How might a feminist find logical analysis useful?

2. Feminist philosophers sometimes seem to find the concept of truth unhelpful. ("The notion of truth—whatever that is—definitely takes the hindmost," and "Truth—whatever that is—will not set you free" [quoted in Haack, 2008].) Others say that to combat false claims about women's intellectual capabilities and other issues, progressives need to talk about whether such propositions are true or false. For each of the following disputes, comment on whether the concept of truth would be useful and, if so, how to utilize it.

   a. A says, " Strawberry ice cream is better than chocolate." B says, "No, chocolate is better."

   b. A says, "You were really flirting with Robin last night." B says, "No I wasn't. I was just being friendly."

   c. A says, "Based on the evidence we've presented, Your Honor, I submit that my client was sexually harassed by her supervisor." B says, "Your Honor, the defense has shown that the supervisor's actions were ordinary informal displays of office camaraderie and were neither sexual nor harassing."

   d. A says, "You are the biological father of the child, so you should pay child support." B says, "No way. I bet there are lots of liaisons who could be the father. I'm convinced it wasn't me."

3. Feminists have sometimes claimed that "modern Western science is masculine." It's true that there are more male than female scientists, but the claim goes beyond numbers. Discuss and evaluate possible interpretations of the claim, using each of the following examples as a starting point:

   a. Western science tends to prefer quantitative studies to qualitative ones.

   b. In science today, there are more biologists than physicists.

   c. Research scientists put in long hours in the laboratory, and it often takes longer than expected to get positive results.

   d. Scientists in universities generally have to compete for funding.

   e. The results of modern Western science have led to labor-saving devices and advances in medicine, but also to more lethal weapons systems.

4. Greek philosophers distinguished between *episteme* (knowledge) and *doxa* (commonly held beliefs). It was important for orators and politicians to study *doxa* so they could better understand the perspectives of their audience. The goal of philosophers, on the other hand, was *episteme,* knowledge that was independent of perspective and in principle shared by all. Consider the following claim: "Feminist philosophers may call themselves epistemologists, but their emphasis on gender and situation might seem to indicate that what they are really analyzing is closer to what the Greeks called *doxa*." Do you agree or disagree? Or are feminist philosophers doing a mixture of each, or something quite different?

Online Resources

Stanford Encyclopedia of Philosophy

http://plato.stanford.edu/

Articles are authored by reputable philosophers. One can search by either topic (e.g., standpoint epistemology) or name (e.g., Harding).

The Complete Dictionary of Scientific Biography

http://www.gale.cengage.com/ndsb/

This fully searchable e-version of the 26-volume *Dictionary of Scientific Biography* is available through major libraries. It is an authoritative resource on scientists and natural philosophers ranging from antiquity to the recently deceased (e.g., Rosalind Franklin, who played an underappreciated role in the discovery of DNA).

PhilSci Archive

http://philsci-archive.pitt.edu/

A collection of self-posted preprints of articles in the philosophy of science intended to expedite current philosophical discussions (e.g., feminist approaches to science education).

Relevant Journals

British Journal for the Philosophy of Science

Hypatia: A Journal of Feminist Philosophy

Perspectives on Science

Philosophy of Science

Philosophy of the Social Sciences

NOTES

1. For a fuller discussion of the climate in early women's studies programs, see Patai and Koertge (2003).

2. For a broader critical survey of feminist epistemological views, see Pinnick, Koertge, and Almeder (2003). Anderson's (2011) encyclopedia article provides a useful taxonomy of competing feminist epistemologies and extensive references to sympathetic feminist commentaries.

3. A former colleague of mine reports that one day he realized he needed a new file folder, one labeled "Gender and Science," to accompany his "Women and Science" offprints. It was only then that he realized the philosophical relevance of feminist commentaries on science.

4. For an amusing account of the history of the sperm-egg saga, see "Bashful Eggs, Macho Sperm, and Tonypandy" (Koertge, 1998b, chap. 4).

5. This approach was further developed by Katherine Hayles. For a critical analysis, see "An Engineer Dissects Two Case Studies: Hayles on Fluid Mechanics, and MacKenzie on Statistics," in Koertge (1998b, chap. 5).

6. Sandra Harding, now Professor of Social Sciences and Comparative Education at UCLA, made notable contributions to the traditional philosophy of science early in her career (see Harding, 1976). But she is best known for her work on feminist and postcolonialist critiques of science. Her standpoint epistemology

has received a good deal of critical attention. For a good introduction to the issues, see Parsons (2003), which provides excerpts from Harding's own writings and then comments on them.

7. For more on feminist philosophy organizations, see Patai and Koertge (2003, p. 209).

8. Longino is a distinguished philosopher of science at Stanford who draws inspiration from current feminist perspectives. For a good introduction to her epistemology, see the interview posted at http://philosophy.stanford.edu/departmental-information/undergraduate-program/the-dualist-undergraduate-journal/archives/vol10/.

9. See the review of Pinnick et al. (2003) posted on her Web site: www-personal.umich.edu/~eandersn.

REFERENCES

Anderson, Elizabeth. (2004). How not to criticize feminist epistemology: A review of *Scrutinizing Feminist Epistemology*. Retrieved June 2, 2011, from http://www-personal.umich.edu/~eandersn/hownotreview.html

Anderson, Elizabeth. (2011, March 16). Feminist epistemology and philosophy of science. In *Stanford encyclopedia of philosophy*. Retrieved May 31, 2011, from http://plato.stanford.edu/entries/feminism-epistemology/

Aristotle. (1964). *Prior and posterior analytics* (John Warrington, Trans.). London: J. M. Dent & Sons.

Carroll, Lewis. (1958). *Symbolic logic and the game of logic.* New York: Dover.

Copi, Irving M. (1979). *Symbolic logic* (5th ed.). New York: Macmillan.

Frege, Gottlob. (1977). *Logical investigations* (P. T. Geach & R. H. Stoothoff, Trans.). Bristol, UK: Western Printing Services.

Gross, Paul R. (1998). Bashful eggs, macho sperm, and tonypandy. In N. Koertge (Ed.), *A house built on sand: Exposing postmodernist myths about science* (pp. 59–70). New York: Oxford University Press.

Haack, Susan. (1998). *Manifesto of a passionate moderate.* Chicago: University of Chicago Press.

Haack, Susan. (2008). The whole truth and nothing but the truth. *Midwest Studies in Philosophy, 32,* 20–35.

Harding, Sandra. (Ed.). (1976). *Can theories be refuted? Essays on the Duhem-Quine thesis.* Dordrecht, The Netherlands: Reidel.

Harding, Sandra. (1991). *Whose science? Whose knowledge? Thinking from women's lives.* Ithaca, NY: Cornell University Press.

Kahane, Howard. (1986). *Logic and philosophy: A modern introduction* (5th ed.). Belmont, CA: Wadsworth.

Kalish, Donald, & Montague, Richard. (1964). *Logic: Techniques of formal reasoning.* New York: Harcout, Brace & World.

Koertge, Noretta. (1998a). Feminism: A mixed blessing to women in science. In A. M. Pattatucci (Ed.), *Women in science: Meeting career challenges* (pp. 189–202). Thousand Oaks, CA: Sage

Koertge, Noretta. (Ed.). (1998b). *A house built on sand: Exposing postmodernist myths about science.* New York: Oxford University Press.

Koertge, Noretta. (2004). How might we put gender politics into science? *Philosophy of Science, 71,* 868–879.

Kourany, Janet A. (1998). *Scientific knowledge: Basic issues in the philosophy of science* (2nd ed.). Belmont, CA: Wadsworth.

Kourany, Janet A. (2009). *The gender of science.* Upper Saddle River, NJ: Prentice Hall.

Longino, Helen E. (1990). *Science as social knowledge: Values and objectivity in scientific inquiry.* Princeton, NJ: Princeton University Press.

Longino, Helen E. (1995). Gender, politics, and the theoretical virtues. *Synthese, 104,* 383–397.

Longino, Helen E. (2001). *The fate of knowledge.* Princeton, NJ: Princeton University Press.

Nye, Andrea. (1990). *Words of power: A feminist reading of the history of logic.* New York: Routledge.

Parsons, Keith. (Ed.). (2003). *The science wars: Debating scientific knowledge and technology.* Amherst, NY: Prometheus Books.

Patai, Daphne, & Koertge, Noretta. (2003). *Professing feminism: Education and indoctrination in women's studies.* Lanham, MD: Lexington Books.

Pattatucci, Angela M. (1998). *Women in science: Meeting career challenges.* Thousand Oaks, CA: Sage.

Pinnick, Cassandra L. (2008a). The feminist approach to philosophy of science. In S. Psillos & M. Curd (Eds.), *The Routledge companion to philosophy of science.* New York: Routledge.

Pinnick, Cassandra L. (2008b). Science education for women: Situated cognition, feminist standpoint theory, and the status of women in science. *Science & Education: Women, Science Education, and Feminist Theory, 17*(10), 1055–1063.

Pinnick, Cassandra L., Koertge, Noretta, & Almeder, Robert F. (Eds.). (2003). *Scrutinizing feminist epistemology: An examination of gender in science.* New Brunswick, NJ: Rutgers University Press.

Rosser, Sue V. (1993). Female-friendly science: Including women in curricular content and pedagogy in science. *Journal of General Education, 42,* 191–220.

Suppes, Patrick. (1957). *Introduction to logic* (J. L. Kelly & P. R. Halmos, Eds.). Princeton, NJ: D. Van Nostrand.

7

INTERCONNECTIONS AND CONFIGURATIONS

Toward a Global Feminist Ethnography

Kum-Kum Bhavnani and Molly Talcott

A frequently encountered puzzle for feminist scholarship is whether feminism can ever be more than critique. Although it is clear that the work of critique is important in and of itself, it is also the case that feminist scholarship illuminates, through a reflection on empirical work, the real-life implications of feminist critique. This is a key reason that, in the late 1980s and into the 1990s, feminist scholars wrote so extensively on feminist epistemology, methods, and methodology—to discover what might (and might not) constitute feminist research (e.g., Behar, 1993; Bhavnani, 1993; Code, 1991; Harding, 1991; Lather, 1991; Longino, 1993; Nicholson, 1994; Reinharz, 1992; Smith, 1990; Stacey, 1988; Stanley & Wise, 1990; Trujillo, 1991). In these attempts at definition and specification, much thought went into delineating the criteria and enumerating what the range of approaches to feminist research could include. Such discussions were not without their detractors, among them feminist scholars. For example, Evelyn Fox Keller (1996) asks if there is a conflict between a commitment to feminism and a commitment to science. She suggests that when critiques of objectivity emerge from feminist work, the results of such critiques are that science is seen as a pure social product and the rigors of "science then dissolve into ideology, and objectivity loses all intrinsic meaning" (p. 31). Many disagree with Fox Keller's approach to objectivity, and, in what follows, we discuss the classic essay by Donna Haraway (1988) that offers the possibility of moving beyond the apparent binary put forward by Fox Keller (1996) between feminist and other forms of science.

As a quick summary, feminist scholars tend to agree that scholarship rooted in feminist epistemologies is characterized by a critique of positivist philosophies of science and discussions as to whether the subjects of feminist research are exclusively women (e.g., many suggest that feminist research does include research on men and masculinity, even when conducted by men); whether the researchers have to be exclusively women; and, perhaps the greatest conundrum of all, how to talk about the category "woman" given its embeddedness in, and impetus for, all discussions of difference as they are expressed through power inequalities. Such puzzles have been thoughtfully tackled by Mary Maynard (1994), who poses the question of how feminist scholars, as well as others working in different disciplinary areas who engage issues of race/ethnicity, racism, nation, sexuality, class, and difference in their writings, might ground notions of difference in empirical work (e.g., Bhavnani, 1993, 2001a; Collins, 1990; duCille, 1999; Freeman, 2001; James, 1998; Lewis, 1996; Moore, 1994; Narayan, 1997; Pajaczkowska & Young, 2000; Spelman, 1997). More recently, some have turned their attention to the dilemmas in conducting feminist research (e.g., Twine & Warren, 2000). What is agreed on, among all of this, is that feminist approaches contribute to documenting the visibility of women's lives and making women's voices audible, with the goal, also, of offering a critique of some forms of social science research and, of course, of social structures (Adair, 2008; Cabezas, 2009; Guenther, 2009; Kang, 2010; Tellez, 2008).

Visibility and audibility have many layers to them. For example, Hammonds (1995), in her discussion of black female queer sexualities, points out that while visibility is often a goal of much feminist research, what is often not attended to are the consequences of such visibility. She writes, "Visibility in and of itself does not . . . challenge the structure of power and domination, symbolic and material, that determines what can and cannot be seen" (p. 143). Gillian Rose (1997) has also noted the dangers of not seeing difference. She does this by discussing the "myth of community"—a myth because, she argues, the overused concept of community leads to a denial of difference (see also Joseph, 2002). Her suggestion for remedying this myth is that feminist scholars build a "politics of voice and translation" in empirical research. It now becomes clear that feminist research is not simply about visibility but is simultaneously about *how* those voices and lives are represented (Lewis, 1996) and what critical and feminist objectivity can be, in practice.

There seems to be little to disagree with so far. Yet this agreement is also in need of much refinement—which women's lives are being analyzed, interrogated, and even evaluated?

In which parts of the world? Which aspects of their lives? Which voices? Who edits the documentation? And, indeed, are there any continuities in the lived experiences of women across class, region, nation, sexuality, and race/ethnicity? Our argument will be that feminist ethnographies (or narrative approaches to research) that pay attention to the axes of inequality listed previously, as well as to regional and national locations, offer the possibility of glimpsing where and how the continuities and discontinuities in women's lives might speak to each other. We suggest that in doing this they are able to help in working through why we still draw on the category "woman" when we are so aware of its limitations and possibilities for masking power inequalities among women (examples of such scholarship include Aggarwal, 2000; Castillo, Gomez, & Delgado, 1999; Degiuli, 2007; Harding, 2008; Kang, 2010; Kempadoo, 1999; Nnaemeka, 2001; Puar, 1998; Puri, 2002; Robertson, 2000; Smith, 2002; Willoughby-Herard 2010).

In some of the more interesting discussions on difference (e.g., Crenshaw, 1989), attention is paid to the intersection of points of difference along axes of inequality. Difference is imagined as being synonymous with such axes of inequality, and examples are offered to show how axes of difference/inequality are not discrete from each other but intersect each other. Audre Lorde is one such person who, in herself and in her work, embodies difference in a number of ways. I myself have argued that these interconnections must form the focus of feminist analysis.[1] In 1997, I wrote that the task of feminist work, inside and outside the academy, "should be to concentrate on how 'race,' class, ethnicity, and sexuality shape and influence each other, alongside gender" (Bhavnani, 1997, p. 46).

To further develop this attempt to refine contemporary feminist thinking, I addressed the notion of interconnections along axes of difference/inequality at the United Nations World Conference Against Racism (Bhavnani, 2001b). I suggested that to conceptualize the linkages of difference as intersections, as one views road intersections, tends toward constituting the subject only as a victim rather than as, simultaneously, an agent. I argue this because a discourse of intersectionality that draws on a crossroads metaphor—for example, race and gender intersecting at a crossroads with the race-d/gender-ed person standing at the meeting point of those crossroads—directs the gaze to the intersections of the roads and the directions in which they travel and meet. This emphasis can lead to losing sight of the whole person, a human being with desires, motivations, and fears, that is, as someone with agency, who stands at those crossroads. This matters because, if we are not only to analyze the world but to change it, then the easiest way to imagine the shifts in the relationships between race/ethnicity and gender is to imagine the roads being moved to form new intersections. In this way, the person at the crossroads is seen from a different angle, and, in addition, her or his own perspective/view/gaze of the crossroads also shifts.

However, in such a metaphor, the person who is standing at the intersection does nothing—it is just that the roads are shifted. That is why we suggest that a more agentic way of thinking about inequalities might be as "interconnections" that configure each other—because *interconnections that configure* connotes more movement and fluidity than lies in the metaphor of intersection, as well as offering a way of thinking about how not only race and gender but also nation, sexuality, and wealth all interconnect, configure, and reshape each other. The concept of interconnections that configure each other also connotes a notion of active engagement, with a consequent attribution of agency to the subjects of the configurations. From this standpoint, the term *intersectionality* is too static and too close to losing sight of the agency of human beings, hence our preference for the concept of configurations as distinct from intersections.

In the past two decades, feminist scholars have also been analyzing how to understand projects of development and global processes more accurately and have demonstrated that a feminist approach allows a clearer vision of the impact of these projects and processes on people's actual lives (e.g., Antrobus, 2004; Beneria, 2003; Bhavnani, Foran, & Talcott, 2005; Enloe, 2004; Mayo, 2005; Moghadam, 2005; Peterson, 2003; Poster, 2002; Tsing, 2004). Often, work on development, global processes, neoliberalism, and the gendered consequences of such processes (especially when focused on the

third world) is necessarily replete with statistical information that some might consider to be "objective" in a positivistic sense. Yet it is crucial that, at the same time, if we are to engage with issues in the third world *qua* feminists, that is, as issues that are best understood from the point of view of the *lived experiences* of the poor, we must seek to integrate our notions of objectivity into that engagement so that we are able to consider all levels of analysis. For example, Diane Wolf's seminal edited collection *Feminist Dilemmas in Fieldwork* (Wolf, 1996), written in the last decade of the twentieth century, contains discussions based mostly on research conducted with women outside the third world to exemplify the philosophical, epistemological, and political dilemmas raised for feminists in conducting our research. Other research examples include Jasbir Puar's (1998) consideration of the meanings of transnational sexualities in her book chapter; Kamala Kempadoo's (1999) important book on sex work, based on her research in the Caribbean; and Carla Freeman's (1999) work on work, identities, and women.

The issue is, how do feminist scholars conduct research that is global in its approach while remaining feminist in its epistemology? Ethnographic research is one obvious way of conducting this type of research. There are many discussions as to whether feminist research is *by definition* ethnographic in its orientation. We will not take up that debate here. Rather, we sketch out what a global feminist ethnography might look like.

Ethnography

A chapter in a handbook of this sort is not the place in which to lay out the variety of discussions on ethnography—its origins (see, e.g., Asad, 1973; Clifford, 1988), whether ethnography is necessarily a liberatory approach, or, indeed, from the perspective of the positivist social scientist, whether ethnography offers anything more than anecdotal and, therefore, non-reliable data. What we want to do is to see what it is that ethnographic research can offer and, in so doing, suggest how feminist global ethnography might lead us to see the world through a different set of lenses.

George Marcus (1998) argues that the ethnographer is a midwife who is able, through words, to help give birth to what is happening in the lives of the oppressed. Beverley Skeggs (1994) has proposed that ethnography is, in itself, "a theory of the research process," and I have suggested that it is the power inequalities in the conduct of ethnographies that open up possibilities for seeing the world in a new and different way (Bhavnani, 1993): ethnography as midwife, ethnography as theory, ethnography as offering new lenses. But what is it that we look at with ethnography, and what is it that we wish to analyze?

In the past decade, we, along with coauthors, have been working on a new paradigm we call Women, Culture, Development (WCD) (e.g., Chua, Bhavnani, & Foran, 2000; Bhavnani, Foran, & Kurian, 2003; Bhavnani et al., 2005; Bhavnani, Foran, Kurian, & Munshi, 2009). This paradigm focuses on women in the third world and was initiated from our research, teaching, and writing about development, which here may be thought of as planned social transformation. As a footnote, we suggest that a WCD approach offers substantive, theoretical, and methodological insights across many arenas, not only development (e.g., Bhavnani & Chua, 2000). In what follows, we offer a brief summary of WCD with an emphasis on its methodological implications.

WCD argues that it is crucial in the 21st century to attend to how third world development since the 1950s has failed in its goals of ameliorating poverty (at the time of writing, 2.8 billion people are living on less than $2 per day) and offering chances for human beings to extend themselves beyond the day-to-day practices of their lives—to develop their creativity. We argue that this failure is due to overly economistic assumptions on the part of development theories and policies. Further, we demonstrate that this failure of development also lies in the exclusion of women from projects of development or in viewing women either as wives and mothers or as laborers. For example, the United Nations' Millennium Development Goals discuss girls' education (and we know who is responsible for sending girls to school in a household) and women's employment in the section on gender equality (as well as in the sections on women's and political power), and both issues are discussed in a separate section on maternal health. That is, women's roles and responsibilities are seen through the lens of labor or through the lens of mother, but not both simultaneously.

We develop our paradigm by building on the work of feminist scholars of the past four decades, so we start from the familiar feminist argument that any bifurcation of women's lives means that women's reproductive and productive contributions are not integrated with each other. We argue, therefore, that it is not development policies, projects, and theories that make women invisible; rather, the visibility of women within conventional development policies and theories does not shed light on their lives in all the wonderful complexity of the following interconnected configurations: production integrated with reproduction, the lived experience of women, and their agency. We suggest that a focus on women need not exclude men but is simply one starting point that is then able to illuminate the circumstances of all people's lives, including men's lives. We argue that to focus on women within development in this way offers prospects for seeing the lives of people as more tangled and therefore as richer than has hitherto been suggested. Thus, the WCD paradigm applies to both women and men. For example, Ming-Yan Lai (2009) shows how the theatrical performances of the Filipina maids in Hong Kong, performances that are integral to their everyday lives and that integrate their relationships in Hong Kong with their social networks in the Philippines, also impact their whole households in the Philippines, where remittances are sent with great regularity.

The methodological consequences of such an approach are what concern us here. To tease out the relationship between production and reproduction, to ensure that the agency of people is captured, and to engage with the tangle of the interconnected configurations of axes of inequality—all these research goals require that we conduct our empirical research by interrogating the actual lived experience of people. It is this requirement that forms, nowadays, for us, the basis of feminist research. Yet the interrogation of lived experience through global feminist ethnography requires that we step back and reflect upon the epistemological underpinnings of this approach, to which we now turn. Kum-Kum Bhavnani has written about such epistemological underpinnings, and we consider next her 1993 "Tracing the Contours" article, in which she offers a means for working with philosophical notions in an empirical way.

RETRACING THE CONTOURS

More than 10 years ago, I wrote "Tracing the Contours" (Bhavnani, 1993), in which I spelled out some implications of the argument that all knowledge is historically contingent and, therefore, that the processes of knowledge production are situated. In that article, I wondered if it was possible to identify the criteria that could delineate feminist objectivity and how those criteria could be put into practice by feminist scholars who conduct empirical research.

My argument emerged after I read Donna Haraway's (1988) "Situated Knowledges" article, in which she points to scientists' partiality—"being answerable for what we see"—and scientists' positioning—"limited location"—as key markers for maintaining feminist objectivity (p. 583). In being explicit as to how she is using *situated* in the title of her essay, she presents the brilliant argument that partiality is not only offered in contrast to prevailing visions of objectivity that promise "a transcendence . . . of all limits and responsibility" (p. 582) but also that the particularities of knowledge production do not lie in the characteristics of individuals. Rather, knowledge production is "about communities, not about isolated individuals" (p. 590).

Our understanding is that the idea of situated knowledges is not "reflexivity." At times, to be reflexive, researchers note their racial/ethnic identity, sex/gender, sexuality, age, class, and ability (i.e., biographical aspects of themselves are listed and presented as essential and unchanging factors). This presentation may then be followed either by a discussion of research that claims objectivity is possible as a transcendent vision or that describes research as if it were the analysis of this one individual, whose social context and intellectual biographies have totally determined the outcome of the research.

Thus, other individuals who list their social context and intellectual biographies may also be able to conduct the same research, and it is implied that this approach is equally valid to the previous research. I have referred to this as "absolute relativism" (Bhavnani, 1993), a notion that Alcoff and Potter (1993) name as "extreme relativism." It was my discomfort with reflexivity as personal biography and my unease with absolute relativism that led me to wonder how to work with Haraway's (1988) elements of accountability, positionality, and partiality. I asked this question: "What are the principles that flow from these elements and that, in turn, indicate the criteria according to which research can be defined as 'feminist'?"

Based on my 1980s empirical work with working class youth in England (Bhavnani, 1991), I suggested that Haraway's (1988) notion of being answerable for what we see—accountability—can be engaged in empirical research through the idea of reinscription. Accountability is often discussed as accountability to an individual or to one constituency. I took the view that there are many constituencies to which all academic researchers are accountable, and a key element in feminist research is that researchers be aware of these varied constituencies to which they are accountable—for example, their discipline, their institution and academic colleagues, and the idea of rigorous scientific research, intellectual integrity, and academic freedom in research, as well as, of course, being accountable to the people with whom the research is being conducted. The last constituency is a place where the feminist researcher, in order to be accountable, is publicly aware of the prevailing images of the research group and examines whether her own research reinscribes the group into dominant stereotypes. For example, if a study focuses on South Asian women and portrays the women merely as victims of patriarchal cultures, then that research only reinscribes the women into dominant representations of South Asian women, and so may not be thought of as feminist. This is because this reinscription undermines a fundamental tenet of feminist approaches—that of *comprehending* why things are the way they are (Are the women passive in their social contexts? Are they critical of the power inequalities? How do they express agency, autonomy, and resistance?) and not merely describing them in terms of essential categories. I am not suggesting here that feminist research adopt a romantic approach. What I am saying is that an empirical study that claims feminist philosophy as its basis must be accountable to a notion of feminism that *interrogates* prevailing representations rather than only reproducing them.

Haraway (1988) also discusses the significance of positionality for feminist objectivity. She suggests that it is the researcher's knowledge of her own "limited location" that creates objectivity. In other words, knowing the limitations of one's structural position as a researcher contributes to objective research because, again, there is no "god trick" (which Haraway explains is like "seeing everything from nowhere" [p. 582]). I took this idea and suggested that, for research to be feminist, the researcher, aware of what this limited location implies, has to analyze the micro-politics of the research situation—that is, feminist researchers must explore, in public, what power dynamics come into play and when, how they shift, and what their consequences might be in the many different parts of their research.

Finally, Haraway (1988) argues that partiality of vision is the third element in being objective in the sense that objectivity is about a "particular and specific embodiment . . . [not a] false vision promising transcendence of all limits and responsibilities" (p. 580). She urges an explicit partiality of vision not for its own sake "but for the sake of the connections and unexpected openings [that] situated knowledges make possible" (p. 590). I argued that to ensure a partiality of vision did not mean a partiality of theorizing (a caution presented by Haraway, 1988) but an *active engagement with difference.* I therefore proposed that all research examine difference within its empirical work and try to tease out some of the interconnected configurations of difference. Haraway's notion of situated knowledges, complemented by non-reinscription, accountability, and engagement with difference are all critical elements in the global ethnographies of the 21st century, although each needs further probing and development.

After rereading Haraway's work and "Tracing the Contours," I now understand that it is not only accountability, partiality, and positionality that can be translated into ideas for empirical research. If I am honest, in 1990 (when I started to write "Tracing the Contours"), the idea of unexpected openings and connections also resonated with me. This was a period when I was at the point of completing my book manuscript (Bhavnani, 1991), and it was therefore a time when I was intellectually confident that scholarly research must (I use the imperative here with deliberation) offer innovative and dynamic ways of seeing the world. I did not, however, 20 years ago, know how to take unexpected openings and connections further. Now, having taught feminist epistemologies to some wonderful classes of graduate students at the University of California at Santa Barbara in the past decade—who inevitably develop thought-provoking discussions—I am able to grapple with the idea of contradictions, linkages, and unexpected connections and to see how interconnections and configurations are central to such work. Next, we discuss the work of a newer generation of scholars whose work *starts* with these notions in mind.

Feminist Global Ethnography and WCD: Three Examples

The studies we discuss in this section are based on the WCD paradigm, more or less explicitly, and include a wide variety of intellectual, epistemological, and political issues.

Partial Vision—Condom Matters and Social Inequalities: Inquiries Into Commodity Production, Distribution, and Advocacy Processes

Peter Chua's (2001) multisited ethnography focuses on condoms as commodities in a global context. His work examines the production, distribution, consumption, and advocacy of condoms. His far-reaching fieldwork, which included interviews and archival analysis, was undertaken at four sites—Bangkok, Manila, Delhi, and San Francisco—and his goal was to understand how social processes in these regions both inform and influence each other and are simultaneously shaped by global and local impulses.

Chua (2001) offers three types of conclusions from his research. First, he suggests that one can see how the production of condoms affects the lives of those who make them as well as of those who do and those who do not use them. For example, one part of his dissertation follows the racial, economic, and cultural transformations in Dothan, Alabama—a southern black-white Christian town, which has two multinational condom factories and is "the condom production capital of the world." He not only examines the labor process in his analysis but also broadens his examination by investigating simultaneously the industrial waste created by condom manufacture and the social and medical consequences of these waste products for the workers and the communities in which they live.

Chua's (2001) second main conclusion is in regard to the social marketing of contraceptives, condoms in particular; he focuses on the marketing strategies developed to ensure that condoms are used. He analyzes the behaviorist strategies that underlie condom education and argues that the reason such education is often unsuccessful in achieving behavioral change—a lack of success that is often puzzling for many health educators and policymakers—is that it pays little or no attention to the agency of target groups or to the fluidity of the identities of the target groups. He arrives at this conclusion through his extensive interviewing of many groups of condom users and advocates.

Chua's (2001) final conclusion interrogates how and why condoms are distributed as part of development aid through, for example, the United States Agency for International Development (USAID). In so doing, he notes that a major assumption underlying all such aid is that third world women and *all* gay men are seen as the cause of almost all social problems that are health related. In addition, by analyzing the linkages between condom distribution and condom advocacy, Chua demonstrates how international agreements that contain clauses on condoms as aid strongly influence, and at times determine, how third world nation-states organize their social welfare and health systems.

In sum, Peter Chua (2001) teases out how global neoliberalism, sexualities, labor processes, privatization, ethnicity, and immigration are not merely discrete processes that shape contemporary understandings of a commodity such as the condom but are also processes that are intimately imbricated within each other. What is so excitingly innovative about Chua's work is that he does not simply reiterate the existence of the interconnections but, rather, because of the specific focus of his study on condoms—partiality of vision—he is able to *specify* the ways in which these interconnections configure each other and, therefore, how they operate. He achieves this specificity by drawing on comparative perspectives and research data collection and analysis techniques: Chua's research is not only geographically comparative but also comparative in terms of its labor process analysis, its critique of behavioral social marketing techniques, the interviews, and its institutional analysis. Because he juxtaposes and links incommensurate sites such as condom production in Alabama and condom advocacy in Thailand, Chua offers us a window into the ways in which condoms are actually used and commodified by constituencies as seemingly disparate as USAID, advocacy groups in India, truck drivers in Zimbabwe, and the workers who make condoms in Alabama. In other words, Chua documents how a vision of one commodity, the condom, leads to a range of visions about many aspects of health around the world.

Limited Location—Laboring Districts, Pleasuring Sites: Hospitality, "Gay" Life, and the Production of Urban Sexual Space in Manila

Dana Collins (2002) interrogates current work on sex tourism by exploring male-to-male sex tourism in her ethnography of gay men's lives in the Malate and Ermita districts in Manila, the Philippines—a research project informed by sociology, cultural studies, feminist analysis, and political economy.

In this research, Collins (2002) examined gay districts that are also tourist districts in Manila. She conducted an ethnography of gay life in Malate and Ermita, with a view to specifying the interconnections among gay life, tourism, urban space, and globalization. For this ethnography, she combined sociological and anthropological methods—that is, she kept detailed and numerous field notes and "hung out" in appropriate places, while simultaneously collecting documents from a number of sources, including the Philippine government, the Internet, and local libraries, as well as a number of leaflets from community groups who work and reside in the two neighborhoods. In addition, her informal and formal interviews were with gay hosts in the Malate and Ermita districts; male tourists from outside the Philippines; local activists; and the business owners who run cafes, bars, restaurants, and clubs for gay men.

From this extensive ethnographic research, Collins (2002) concluded that gay sexuality is performed differently in the Philippines compared with its performance in countries of the North and the West, and she documents these differences. However, because she explored many sources of data, her research was not confined to performance alone. As Collins pointed to differences in performativity, she also noted that, despite the 1990s state clampdown on "immorality" in these districts, gay bars, cafes, and clubs were thriving due to the simultaneous attempts by the Philippine state to revitalize business in Malate and Ermita. She probed this contradiction—between a clampdown on "immorality" and the desirability of having gay businesses help develop a run-down area. In doing so, she suggested that, because Malate and Ermita are viewed as "open" and "Bohemian" areas of Manila—characteristics that are desirable precisely because they embrace and sidestep discussions of immorality—they form the underpinnings for commercialization and gentrification, particularly with an eye to tourist development. Thus, the categorization of a district as open and Bohemian, combined with the state's desire to revitalize entrepreneurship, has led to an increase in gay social venues. Furthermore, because Malate is a complex mixture of Spanish, North American, and Asian influences, gay life is explicitly configured by a range of racialized ethnicities that Collins makes key in her work.

In addition to looking at gay life in the context of ethnicity, commercialization, space, and globalization, Dana Collins's (2002) work also explores class relationships. She does this by comparing the clientele of two key gay bars—Piggy's (the bar that is viewed as the "hustler" bar by many) and Joy (a more subdued bar)—to

see how class shapes and is shaped by the friendships that develop in these two sites. The way in which she has read the discursive patterns of behaviors in these bars is instructive. For example, her work shows that tourist men often talk about their fear of being "ripped off" (e.g., cheated out of their money) by call boys in Piggy's and try to avoid being "taken for a ride" in this way. However, it is clear that these same men do not go to other bars to distance themselves from the call boys in Piggy's, despite their stated fears. She came to this insight because call boys in Piggy's told her about their long-term and long-distance relationships with gay men living outside the Philippines, men whom the hosts had met when they came as tourists. That is, the call boys are sought out as gay hosts for the tourists despite the latter's fears of being ripped off or hustled.

This study is significant because it does not start from a heterosexual approach to sex tourism and sex work (see also Cabezas, 2009, for a feminist global ethnographic example of heterosexual sex/"affective" work). It is doubly significant because Dana Collins (2002) examines how the structures of urban space affect the very sex work they house. In other words, the limited location of her work (Malate and Ermita in Manila) has actually permitted her to make unexpected connections and thus see how larger theoretical approaches to "gay," "place," and "space" can be reconfigured.

Unexpected Connections—Forest Politics, Gendered Subjects: Local Knowledge and the Negotiated Meanings of Development in Rural Dominican Republic

With a theoretical emphasis on local knowledges, Light Carruyo (2002, 2007) argues that discourses of environmental conservation and economic development strategies developed by the Dominican state have focused on rescue—in this case, the rescue of the forest in the Dominican Republic from peasant subsistence practices. The state attends to this rescue with an eye to encouraging peasants to enter the Dominican economy as "productive citizens." From her fieldwork conducted in La Ciénaga, a rural community located on the edge of the Armando Bermúdez

National Park in the Cordillera Central, Light Carruyo shows how the state and discourses of environmental conservation have *jointly* created a category of rural citizenship—mediated through legislation, military force, and, more recently, development projects—that undermines both local subsistence practices and understandings of masculinity and womanhood. Her argument is persuasively documented through interviews, field notes, historical and institutional analysis, and archival material, as well as through her participation in a training for ecotourism guides. Her work also innovates by laying out what might be thought of as "webs of interest" (Carruyo, 2005, personal communication) among forest politics, tourism and nation building, and microenterprise to suggest how definitions of citizenship, development, and women are both created and contested in the Dominican Republic.

Carruyo (2002, 2007) began the research by studying local-level, grassroots development strategies in a small town—La Ciénaga—and examining the accomplishments of the community organization Asociación Nueva Esperanza, whose leadership is made up of poor women. She argues that notions of "progress" in La Ciénaga are defined by residents through their own relationship to conservation strategies, the presence of tourists in the region, and the possibilities for setting up microenterprise ventures.

By analyzing her interviews in a profoundly organic manner—that is, she looked at and specified the words each interviewee spoke, the discourses and contexts within which each spoke, and the interviewee's specific relationship to the issue being spoken about, as well as to other people in the community—Carruyo (2002, 2007) interweaves discussions of development strategies with the politics of forest conservation to demonstrate that these webs of interest are interconnected, dynamic, and configured by each other. This means that they can allow, for example, definitions of development to move away from being solely about access to cash and toward notions of development as well-being. An analysis of locally based social movements that challenge some of the tenets of globalizing processes is an important part of her work—and she grounds these discussions by critically examining what "local knowledges" might mean, in all their romantic and contradictory connotations.

Because local voices are often unexpected and complex, Carruyo (2002, 2007) demonstrates that it is necessary to specify the links between historically crafted identities and current development as they exist in the lived practices of local peoples. It then becomes possible to imagine well-being as a process that emerges from local knowledge rather than as a condition that results from rescue. Finally, she complicates her timely narrative so that what one sees is not merely a recitation of facts but an engaging analysis of how and why trees are so important in the history, present, and sociology of this country—a series of unexpected connections from which she draws some wonderful insights into the actions of the state as well as into people's lived experience of their community.

These examples of global ethnographies rely on WCD as a starting point for their empirical and theoretical bases. Other global ethnographers, while being WCD-influenced, have also taken the political implications of WCD and renewed those ideas into discussing human rights issues in their research.

The "Human Rights Turn" Within Feminist Global Ethnography: Three Examples

Earlier, we discussed the idea that central to feminist research is an investigation of how the interconnections of "race," gender, class, ethnicity, nation, and sexuality (re)configure each other to produce both inequalities and agentic subjects struggling to transform such inequalities. We have argued that global feminist ethnography is a method that is particularly suited to these objectives when researching "the global-local nexus" (Fine, Tuck, & Zeller-Berkman, 2008).

How feminists conduct global ethnography—that is, which transnational discourses, sites, and experiences we trace—is of course situated in the political, cultural, and material conditions of the historical moment in which an ethnography is produced. In the current period, globally circulated and locally contextualized discourses of "human rights," while not new, are increasing in power and influence (Coomaraswamy, 2002; Hesford & Kozol, 2005; Newdick, 2005; Philipose, 2008; Schulman, 2004; Smith, 2008). Feminist researchers working at global-local nexuses are thus developing a body of work that reflects a growing concern with interrogating what we are calling "the human rights turn" occurring within both global society and feminist research (see, e.g., Collins, Falcón, Lodhia, & Talcott, 2010, 2011). In response to the massive failures of "development" we discussed earlier, as well as the failure of socialist discourses to become hegemonic (Bhavnani et al., 2005), women and men across the world—from within community assemblies to the United Nations—are invoking, contesting, and reshaping "human rights" logics in order to reimagine social justice and (to analogize Carruyo, 2007) a holistic form of "well-being" across differences and inequalities.

Feminist global ethnography, then, is increasingly concerned with interrogating and mapping the various discourses and policies connected to human rights, including both those that reproduce elite, dominant, and imperialist or racist representations of women (see Fernandes, 2005; Newdick, 2005; Speed & Collier, 2000) and those that point to new openings for feminist transformation within human rights work, to which we now turn.

WCD Meets the Human Rights Turn: Feminist Global Ethnography on the "Social Life of Rights"

One study that exemplifies "the human rights turn" within feminist global ethnography, as it intersects with a WCD perspective, is my own work that centers on pan-ethnic indigenous women's and girls' organizing across Southern Mexico (Talcott, 2008; Talcott, 2010). In this ethnographic study, heavily influenced by critical feminist methodology (Bhavnani, 1993) and the WCD paradigm (e.g., Chua et al., 2000; Bhavnani et al., 2003; Bhavnani et al., 2005; Bhavnani et al., 2009), I conducted fieldwork to analyze how women and youth living in rural and majority-indigenous regions of Southern Mexico contest elite development agendas and reimagine and expand what encompasses "human rights."

Central to my study's methodology was my adoption of the role of the researcher-witness (Fernandes, 2003) as well as grounded theory.

Hesse-Biber and Leavy have likened grounded theory building to a "dynamic dance routine" in which "there is no one right dance, no set routine to follow. One must be open to discovery" (2006, p. 76). Grounded theory construction, we argue, also disrupts the colonizing dichotomy between "knower" and "known," as it requires the researcher ("the knower" of all) to listen to research participants and reformulate the study's questions, aims, and scope accordingly. It is therefore possible to shift authorship in the direction of a more collective, albeit still power-laden, process.

It was this process of combining grounded theory with witnessing (Fernandes, 2003) that enabled me to recognize the growing importance and shifting meanings of human rights discourses—that is, the "social life of rights" (Speed & Collier, 2000)—among pan-ethnic Southern Mexican activists. As I spent time conducting fieldwork and interviews (2005–2007) with members of the AMAP (Alianza Mexicana por la Autodeterminación de los Pueblos) coalition about their resistance to privatizing development projects, I was able to discern how women, men, and youth are leveraging the growing moral and political power of human rights and remolding this amorphous idea in pursuit of what I have called "radical, redistributive, and pluralist" ends—ends not reliant on neoliberal human rights logics that uncritically embrace capitalism, state power, and the inequities they both produce (see also Newdick, 2005; Speed, 2007). Young indigenous women and men, for example, are drawing upon human rights languages in order to carve spaces for themselves: they are creating community radio stations and using the airwaves to argue for—and to enact directly—many different forms of social change, which include the restoration of their native languages, the embrace of sexual rights, and resistance against state and transnational capitalist development projects that lead to dispossession and migration within their communities. In what began as an investigation about "development," I encountered people who wanted to tell me about their experiences with the power of radio transmitters, unwelcome intrauterine devices, small-scale popular education workshops, and, especially for women, surviving the violent imprints of patriarchy, racism, and poverty on their lives. The many women and youth who shared their lives with me asserted their own knowledges about, and desires for, distinct forms of "development" that valorize human rights and human dignity, *la vida digna.* My findings suggest that "human rights" is not a static set of foregone legal conclusions but a vibrant terrain of struggle in which women and girls consciously participate in order to contest patriarchy, racism, and ageism within Mexican society at large, as well as within their own communities and within their political coalitions. I was only able to perceive this "human rights turn" occurring at the grass roots by virtue of my adoption of a WCD approach—a feminist global ethnographic praxis that centers the lived experience and agency of indigenous women and girls living in rural Southern Mexico, thus revealing the emerging interconnections among culture, development, women's resistance, and human rights.

Transnationalism, International Law, and Feminist Human Rights Campaigns

Although debates remain vigorous among feminists about the potential problems presented by an essentialist "women's rights are human rights" legal discourse (see our earlier mention on "women" as a unitary category), many argue, from an ethnographic perspective, for the importance of human rights projects, including, but not limited to, international laws. Feminist ethnographers and analysts, faced with the choice of dismissing human rights discourses altogether (as Western, imperialist, patriarchal, etc.; see Esteva & Prakash, 1998; Chow, 2002) or examining the possibilities these can present for catalyzing social change, increasingly sit "firmly (and squeamishly) in the latter camp" (Fine et al., 2008, p. 171).

Feminist scholarly dis-ease (i.e., Fine et al.'s "squeamishness") with the state and with the (ab)uses of international law are well founded, given the long-standing and widespread relationships between states, nationalisms, and the oppressions of women. However, feminist global ethnography, as seen in the work of Sharmila Lodhia (2009, 2010a, 2010b), demonstrates the importance of critical engagements with international law and human rights in light of the contradictions produced by nation-state-based laws that fail to secure women's rights in an era of transnationalism, migration, and gendered diasporas.

Lodhia combines multisited fieldwork and archival research in India and the United States to investigate how feminist antiviolence activists working in both national contexts are grappling with the challenges presented by the "reconfiguration of citizenship and the reterritorialization of power in a transnational age" (Lodhia, 2010b, p. 161). Lodhia's pathbreaking work on the shifting interconnections between gender, migration, and violence examines, for instance, how women of the Indian diaspora grapple with not only intimate violence but also the growing phenomenon of "transnational abandonment."

Lodhia finds that multiple scenarios are emerging: in one case, a woman marries a nonresident Indian (NRI, a legal status) in the United States, and her husband disappears, leaving her with no "legal" status of her own; in another, Indian women are forced or tricked into returning to their home country and deserted; and, in a third scenario known as the "holiday bride" case, an NRI man marries a woman from India, promises to bring her to the United States, yet never does. Lodhia's research finds that men are able to leverage their own transnational mobility and power to file divorce papers, petition for custody, or evade child support payments in the jurisdiction that most likely favors their interests. Women, whom Lodhia names "brides without borders" (2010b), are less able to effectively contest these actions because of financial and travel constraints as well as the failure of laws to support their human rights, for example, freedom of movement and freedom from violence. In Lodhia's feminist global ethnography, she "follows the women." She traces the "NRI bride" within and through multiple sites. In doing so, she argues that "existing legal theory . . . resists meaningful engagement with the altered jurisdictions globalization has produced" (2010a) and the ways in which such effects are racialized and gendered. Through her careful analysis of the contradictions produced by migration, gender, racialization, and violence (including both domestic violence and abandonment), Lodhia generates a persuasive argument for the importance of feminist engagement with legal structures—on both national and transnational scales.

Interconnections Among Grassroots and UN-Level Antiracist Feminisms in the Global South and North

The research of Sylvanna Falcón, whose starting point is feminist participation at the 2001 UN World Conference Against Racism in Durban, South Africa (2006, 2008, 2009), offers some insights into the theoretical and empirical value of the human rights turn within feminist global ethnography. Falcón's multisited ethnographic work traces how antiracist feminists across the Americas (living in Canada, Peru, Mexico, and the United States) engage with human rights discourses both at United Nations meetings and "at home" within their grassroots organizing practices. For the women of Falcón's study, appealing to human rights conventions is a proactive way to hold their governments accountable for the interconnected forms of economic exploitation and gendered racism they face as women of color (of both the global North and South); in becoming human rights activists, they are able to integrate and reconfigure their identities and struggles for racial and gender justice (Falcón, 2008).

Falcón's study finds not only that feminists of color are reconfiguring United Nations discourses of human rights (and challenging their governments' lack of implementation of UN conventions) but also that the work they do within such spaces transnationalizes and reconfigures their own lenses of analysis. Her ethnographic research, which has involved attendance at meetings from Durban to Geneva and interviews with a number of UN officials as well as with many grassroots feminist activists, demonstrates the ways in which women are engaged in a political struggle that begins from their interconnections and that clearly seeks a reconfiguration of society. In addition, Falcón's work (2009) demonstrates how U.S. racial justice activists have recognized, through their participation with the UN Committee to Eliminate Racial Discrimination, that domestic civil rights paradigms leaving U.S. exceptionalism or nationalism intact

are no longer adequate lenses through which to understand and enact their movements. Falcón's ethnographic work moves us past the impasse between (often U.S.-based) "race, class, gender" studies and "transnational feminist" studies by showing the interconnections between feminist work, racial justice work, and the transnational sites of struggle in which these projects interact and reshape one another. She does this by using methods of feminist global ethnography: by traversing both elite and grassroots sites of antiracist feminist struggle across both the global North and South, Falcón is able to analyze how each site is infused by, and reshapes, the other.

Emerging Methods: Digital Feminist Ethnography, Convergences, and New Intersubjectivities?

Before concluding, we wish to emphasize the fluidity, exploration, and situatedness that characterize the diverse projects of feminist global ethnography. As an approach that explores, documents, and analyzes shifting configurations of power and resistance grounded in material conditions and cultural practices, feminist global ethnography continues to shift and expand in new directions. Endemic to feminist methodology is the practice of exploring and embracing "emergent methods," that is, of being open to "coming at things differently" (Hesse-Biber & Leavy, 2006, p. 376).

Feminist global ethnographers, for example, are devising innovative approaches to research in response to the increasingly digital, virtual, and mobile moment that the world now inhabits. Yet what does it mean to inhabit a virtual, digital field? How does the rise of the virtual field impact feminist ethnographic analyses of identity, representation, power relations, and agency? Where, for feminist ethnographers, is "the field" located, if it is no longer necessarily a material site or web of physical locales? Although this latter question of the boundaries between "the field" and "not the field" has long been wrestled over by ethnographers, the contemporary digital moment adds new layers of complexity to these questions.

Gendered, racialized, class-based, and transnational configurations of power and resistance within digital/virtual fields warrant continued feminist ethnographic research. As Zacharias and Arthurs (2007) argue, "these spaces invite a new kind of gender mapping that pays attention to the digital ecology and to the gendering of this digital ecology, as well as to the emergence of new digital selves that symbolize the historic moments of national and global transitions" (p. 203). On the one hand, feminist researchers have found that girls and women can experience empowerment through their virtual activities. For example, in her research on "mobile girls" in Korea, Yeran Kim (2007) finds that girls and young women are able to contest patriarchal and generational hierarchies (which favor adult men) by sharing their personal narratives through digital technologies that enable the formation of social participatory networks. In doing so, "mobile girls" in Korea are increasingly able to reshape popular culture and resist their historical erasure from the public sphere of society.

Moreover, Kim (2007) makes an important methodological contribution to feminist global ethnography. She writes that the digital moment allows ethnographers to reimagine fieldwork practices and knowledge production. In particular, Kim (2007) argues for a practice of "ethnographic convergence," which she describes as "a methodology in which the informant's lived experience and reflective language and the researchers' analytic discourse are intertwined in the reconstruction of social knowledge" (p. 207). The new openings presented by the digital/virtual moment call on feminist global ethnographers to rethink and reshape research practices in new ways that deepen long-standing feminist practices of participatory action research (Fine et al., 2008), witnessing (Fernandes, 2003), and deep listening (Keating, 2007).

The arrival of the digital/virtual moment also embodies the pervasive inequalities and contradictions that we, feminist global ethnographers, analyze. The idea of "the digital divide"—including its gender dimensions—is becoming central to global development discourses. As digital access and literacy become ever more crucial to participation in transnational and local civil society and social movements, even feminist global

ethnographers who are not researching digital ecologies *per se* find it increasingly important to keep an ethnographic eye on the digital/virtual dimension of "the field." For example, Jennifer Bickham Mendez (2008) notes that global gender, racial, and class inequalities continue to shape the digital divide in ways that are more complex than the oft-noted global North-South divide (p. 146). She cites her work with a coalition of faculty, staff, and students at her university (in Virginia, USA). The coalition was organizing in favor of a living wage for custodial workers and housekeeping staff, whose lack of e-mail access excluded them from full participation in the movement, exemplifying a local case of the digital divide (Mendez, 2008).

As feminist global ethnographers develop new approaches to comprehending the digital/virtual moment such as Kim's (2007) practice of "ethnographic convergence," it is vital to interrogate, also, the local and global dimensions of the digital divide in many types of feminist global ethnographic projects (as seen, for example, in Mendez's research, 2008).

It is also possible to utilize software to analyze qualitative data, which can save many hours of work spent peering at the transcripts seeking patterns in the discourses of interviewees, although I (KKB) must confess I do not like to use such software as it can take the "human" element of research away from the study. What we mean by this is that excellent qualitative research has to rely on the researcher's experience of the topic, intimate knowledge of the geographical region, and similar aspects of actual familiarity with research subjects and their contexts, and it is that human knowledge and intuition that an overreliance on software can destroy. Of course, each one complements the other. But, in real life, when a piece of software offers patterns that are interesting for the study, and researchers are up against deadlines, the time-consuming and intense human work can often be left "for later" and, sometimes, never returned to. There are other cautions. Notions of surveillance, the ability for others to obtain research results from computers without the researcher's knowledge, and the accountability of the researchers to their interviewees as well as to the many constituencies discussed earlier in this chapter start to become more porous and, therefore, more permeable. It is not enough to lock one's research data away in a fireproof safe and know that the integrity of the research is maintained. Thus, although computers are critical to all our research, we are also aware of some of the limitations that ensue from their use.

CONCLUSION

A feminist global ethnography is now in the making. The work of the emerging scholars we discuss suggests its promise. We can discern some of the contours of feminist global ethnography through their engagement with partiality of vision, limited location, and unexpected connections—Haraway's concepts for creating objectivity without the "god trick"—as they are refracted through the lens of transnational feminisms. The creative, and simultaneously rigorous, empirical studies of Light Carruyo (2002, 2007), Peter Chua (2001), and Dana Collins (2002) ground these ideas in lived experiences and structures of feeling, showing the affinity of global feminist ethnography with the insights of WCD. Because global feminist ethnography draws on the everyday experiences of people and examines those experiences in the light of structural contexts, it is *the* method that is most in line with WCD approaches. These approaches emphasize agency, integration of production and reproduction, and everyday life practices as methods of comprehending how people and why people live their lives in the way they do. Furthermore, WCD is based on understanding the structural influences that need to be more closely examined to ensure that people are able to live their lives without poverty and in dignity.

Moreover, the research conducted by Falcón (2008, 2009), Lodhia (2009, 2010a, 2010b), and myself (Talcott, 2008) demonstrates an emerging focus within feminist global ethnography: the turn to human rights. As transnational feminist scholars have noted, human rights discourses embody strategic (Coomaraswamy, 2002), polemical (Correa & Petchesky, 2003), and radical (Schulman, 2004) potential for understanding and transforming injustices, a goal to which feminist researchers are committed. However, feminist researchers also caution against essentialism and

"human rights fundamentalism" (Smith, 2008), that is to say, the practice of essentializing the idea of human rights, which in some cases has led to an uncritical acceptance among liberal feminists of imperial and neoliberal applications of human rights discourses (Fernandes, 2005). One way feminists have avoided human rights fundamentalism is not only to analyze the social life of rights (Speed & Collier, 2000; Talcott, 2008) but also to examine human rights as cultural representations through a feminist analytical lens (Hesford & Kozol, 2005; Schaffer & Smith, 2004).

For these reasons, it is critical that global feminist ethnographers continue to interrogate the interconnections between women's agency and the cultural politics of development and human rights and, moreover, how each is reshaping the other. We can do so by continuing to explore—through partial perspectives—how to "come at things differently" (Hesse-Biber & Leavy, 2006) and reconceptualize "the field" as a shifting network of material and virtual sites.

Through the interconnected configurations that help us see how inequalities are shaped and resistances are actively forged, these new approaches to ethnography offer us a glimpse into the possibilities of a world in which scholarship and people's lives and dreams speak more directly with each other across material, cultural, and virtual realms.

Discussion Questions

1. How might feminist scholars conduct research that is global in its approach while remaining feminist in its epistemology? To whom are global feminist ethnographers accountable?

2. How might feminist researchers ground complex experiences shaped by "race" and racism, nation, sexuality, class, and gender in studies that capture the texture of women's increasingly global lives?

3. Can a "Women, Culture, Development" (WCD) approach to ethnography enable feminists to produce nuanced studies of oppression, agency, and resistance, while retaining the conceptual category "woman"?

4. In what ways might a focus on feminism, anti-racism, and human rights logics deepen the

practice of global feminist ethnography? How do global feminist ethnographies of human rights help to illuminate women's agency and practices of resistance?

5. What political and ethical dilemmas does the use of qualitative analysis software raise for global feminist ethnographers? How does the use of this software shape or limit the intimacy with which researchers can analyze, narrate, and represent people's lives?

Online Resources

Women, Culture & Development Program

http://www.global.ucsb.edu/programs/wcd/wcd.html

This site describes UC Santa Barbara's WCD Program (chaired by Kum-Kum Bhavnani), which is part of the Global & International Studies Program.

Sociologists Without Borders

http://www.sociologistswithoutborders.org/

This is the website of a transnational association of sociologists committed to the following principles: that all people have equal rights to political freedoms and legal protections, to socioeconomic security, to self-determination, and to their personality. That is, old or young, regardless of where they live, their faith, and whether they are male or female, gay or straight, and regardless of their skin color, they have the same universal rights, including their rights to their own particular cultures. Sociólogos Sin Fronteras (SSF) also promotes an understanding that collective goods, including a sustainable environment, cannot be privatized.

Methodspace

http://www.methodspace.com/

This global online discussion forum on research methods aims to connect the research community.

Relevant Journals

Feminist Africa

Feminist Formations

Feminist Review

Feminist Studies

Gender & Society

International Feminist Journal of Politics

Journal of Contemporary Ethnography

Meridians: Feminism, Race, Transnationalism

Signs: Journal of Women in Culture and Society

Social Politics

Societies Without Borders

Women's Studies International Forum

Note

1. The theoretical and methodological work of one of us, Kum-Kum Bhavnani, is central to our discussion of global feminist ethnography in this chapter. As such, we will at times write in the singular first person (using "I") and when doing so, we indicate which of us is "speaking" at each instance. At other points, we write in the plural, as "we."

References

Adair, Vivyan C. (2008). The missing story of ourselves: Poor women, power and the politics of feminist representation. *NWSA Journal, 20*(1), 1–25.

Aggarwal, Ravina. (2000). Point of departure: Feminist locations and the politics of travel in India. *Feminist Studies, 26*(3), 535–562.

Alcoff, Linda, & Potter, Elizabeth. (Eds.). (1993). Introduction: When feminisms intersect epistemology. In Linda Alcoff & Elizabeth Potter (Eds.), *Feminist epistemologies* (pp. 1–14). New York: Routledge.

Antrobus, Peggy. (2004). *The global women's movement: Origins, issues and strategies.* London: Zed Press.

Asad, Talal. (Ed.). (1973). *Anthropology and the colonial encounter.* New York: Humanities Press.

Behar, Ruth. (1993). *Translated woman: Crossing the border with Esperanza's story.* Boston: Beacon Press.

Beneria, Lourdes. (2003). *Gender, development and globalization: Economics as if people mattered.* New York: Routledge.

Bhavnani, Kum-Kum. (1991). *Talking politics: A psychological framing for views from youth in Britain.* Cambridge, UK: Cambridge University Press.

Bhavnani, Kum-Kum. (1993). Tracing the contours: Feminist research and feminist objectivity. *Women's Studies International Forum, 16*(2), 95–104.

Bhavnani, Kum-Kum. (1997). Women's studies and its interconnections with "race," ethnicity and sexuality. In Diane Richardson & Victoria Robinson (Eds.), *Thinking feminist* (pp. 27–48). New York: New York University Press.

Bhavnani, Kum-Kum. (Ed.). (2001a). *Feminism and "race."* Oxford, UK: Oxford University Press.

Bhavnani, Kum-Kum. (2001b, September). *Race, women, public policy: Reflections and analysis.* Paper presented at the United Nations World Conference Against Racism, Xenophobia and Related Intolerance, Durban.

Bhavnani, Kum-Kum, & Chua, Peter. (2000). From critical psychology to critical development studies. *International Journal of Critical Psychology, 1*(1), 62–78.

Bhavnani, Kum-Kum, Foran, John, & Kurian, Priya. (2003). *Feminist futures: Re-imagining women, culture, development.* London: Zed Press.

Bhavnani, Kum-Kum, Foran, John, Kurian, Priya, & Munshi, Debashish. (Eds.). (2009). *On the edges of development: Critical interventions.* New York: Routledge.

Bhavnani, Kum-Kum, Foran, John, & Talcott, Molly. (2005). The red, the green, the black and the purple: Reclaiming development, resisting globalization. In Richard Appelbaum & William I. Robinson (Eds.), *Critical globalization studies* (pp. 323–332). New York: Routledge.

Cabezas, Amalia L. (2009). *Economies of desire: Sex and tourism in Cuba and the Dominican Republic.* Philadelphia: Temple University Press.

Carruyo, Light. (2002). *Forest politics, gendered subjects: Local knowledge and the negotiated meanings of development in rural Dominican Republic.* Unpublished doctoral dissertation, Department of Sociology, University of California, Santa Barbara.

Carruyo, Light. (2007). *Producing knowledge, protecting forests: Rural encounters with gender, ecotourism, and international aid in the Dominican Republic.* University Park, PA: Penn State University Press.

Castillo, Debra A., Gomez, Maria Gudelia Rangel, & Delgado, Bonnie. (1999). Border lives: Prostitute women in Tijuana. *Signs: Journal of Women in Culture and Society, 24*(21), 387–422.

Chew, Huibin Amelia. (2008). What's left? After "imperial feminist" hijackings. In Robin L. Riley, Chandra Talpade Mohanty, & Minnie Bruce Pratt (Eds.), *Feminism and war: Confronting US imperialism* (pp. 75–90). London and New York: Zed Books.

Chow, Rey. (2002). *The protestant ethnic and the spirit of capitalism.* New York: Columbia University Press.

Chua, Peter. (2001). *Condom matters and social inequalities: Inquiries into commodity production, exchange, and advocacy practices.* Unpublished doctoral dissertation, Department of Sociology, University of California, Santa Barbara.

Chua, Peter, Bhavnani, Kum-Kum, & Foran, John. (2000). Women, culture, development: A new paradigm for development studies? *Ethnic and Racial Studies, 23*(5), 820–841.

Clifford, Jim. (1988). *The predicament of culture: Twentieth century ethnography, literature, and art.* Cambridge, MA: Harvard University Press.

Code, Lorraine. (1991). *What can she know?* Ithaca, NY: Cornell University Press.

Collins, Dana. (2002). *Laboring districts, pleasuring sites: Hospitality, "gay" life, and the production of urban sexual space in Manila.* Unpublished doctoral dissertation, Department of Sociology, University of California, Santa Barbara.

Collins, Dana, Falcón, Sylvanna, Lodhia, Sharmila, & Talcott, Molly. (2010). New directions in feminism and human rights: An introduction. *International Feminist Journal of Politics, 12*(3–4), 298–318.

Collins, Dana, Falcón, Sylvanna, Lodhia, Sharmila, & Talcott, Molly. (2011). *New directions in feminism and human rights.* New York: Routledge.

Collins, Patricia Hill. (1990). *Black feminist thought: Knowledge, consciousness, and the politics of empowerment.* Boston: Unwin Hyman.

Coomaraswamy, Radhika. (2002). Are women's rights universal? Re-engaging the local. *Meridians, 3*(1), 1–18.

Correa, S., & Petchesky, R. (2003). Reproductive and sexual rights: A feminist perspective. In C. McCann & S. Kim (Eds.), *Feminist theory reader* (pp. 88–102). New York: Routledge.

Crenshaw, Kimberle. (1989). Demarginalizing the intersection of race and sex: A black feminist critique of antidiscrimination doctrine, feminist theory, and antiracist politics. In *Feminism in the law: Theory, practice, and criticism* (pp. 139–167). Chicago: University of Chicago Law School.

Degiuli, Francesca. (2007). A job with no boundaries: Home eldercare work in Italy. *European Journal of Women's Studies, 14*(3), 193–207.

duCille, Ann. (1999). Black Barbie and the deep play of difference. In Morag Schiach (Ed.), *Feminism and cultural studies* (pp. 106–132). Oxford, UK: Oxford University Press.

Enloe, Cynthia. (2004). *The curious feminist: Searching for women in a new age of empire.* Berkeley: University of California Press.

Esteva, Gustvo, & Prakash, Maduh Suri. (1998). *Grassroots post-modernism: Remaking the soil of cultures.* New York: St. Martin's Press.

Falcón, Sylvanna M. (2006). *Where are the women? Transnational feminist interventions at the United Nations World Conference Against Racism.* Unpublished doctoral dissertation, University of California, Santa Barbara.

Falcón, Sylvanna M. (2008). *Mestiza* double consciousness: The voices of Afro-Peruvian women on gendered racism. *Gender & Society, 22*(5), 660–680.

Falcón, Sylvanna M. (2009). Invoking human rights and transnational activism in racial justice struggles at home: U.S. antiracist activists and the UN Committee to Eliminate Racial Discrimination. *Societies Without Borders, 4,* 295–316.

Fernandes, Leela. (2003). *Transforming feminist practice.* San Francisco: Aunt Lute Books.

Fernandes, Leela. (2005). The boundaries of terror: Feminism, human rights and the politics of global crisis. In Wendy S. Hesford & Wendy Kozol (Eds.), *Just advocacy? Women's human rights, transnational feminisms, and the politics of representation* (pp. 56–74). New Brunswick, NJ: Rutgers University Press.

Fine, Michelle, Tuck, Eve, & Zeller-Berkman, Sarah. (2008). Do you believe in Geneva? Methods and ethics at the global-local nexus. In Norman K. Denzin, Yvonna S. Lincoln, & Linda Tuhiwai Smith (Eds.), *Handbook of critical and indigenous methodologies* (pp. 157–180). Thousand Oaks, CA: Sage.

Fox Keller, Evelyn. (1996). Feminism and science. In Evelyn Fox Keller & Helen E. Longino (Eds.), *Feminism and science* (pp. 28–40). Oxford, UK: Oxford University Press.

Freeman, Carla. (1999). *High tech and high heels in the global economy: Women, work, and pink-collar*

identities in the Caribbean. Durham, NC: Duke University Press.

Freeman, Carla. (2001). Is local:global as feminine: masculine? Rethinking the gender of globalization. *Signs, 26*(4), 1007–1038.

Guenther, Katja M. (2009). The politics of names: Rethinking the methodological and ethical significance of naming people, organizations, and places. *Qualitative Research, 9*(4), 411–421.

Hammonds, Evelynn. (1995). Black (w)holes and the geometry of black female sexuality. *Differences, 6*(2–3), 126–145.

Haraway, Donna. (1988). Situated knowledges: The science question in feminism and the privilege of partial perspective. *Feminist Studies, 14*(3), 575–600.

Harding, Sandra. (1991). *Whose science? Whose knowledge?* Ithaca, NY: Cornell University Press.

Harding, Sandra. (2008). *Sciences from below: Feminisms, postcolonialities, and modernities.* Durham, NC: Duke University Press.

Hesford, Wendy S., & Kozol, Wendy. (Eds.). (2005). *Just advocacy? Women's human rights, transnational feminisms and the politics of representation.* New Brunswick, NJ: Rutgers University Press.

Hesse-Biber, Sharlene Nagy, & Leavy, Patricia Lina. (2006). *The practice of qualitative research.* Thousand Oaks, CA: Sage.

James, Stanlie. (1998). Shades of othering: Reflections on female circumcision/genital mutilation. *Signs: Journal of Women in Culture and Society, 23*(4), 1031–1048.

Joseph, Miranda. (2002). *Against the romance of community.* Minneapolis: University of Minnesota Press.

Kang, Miliann. (2010). *The managed hand: Race, gender, and the body in beauty service work.* Berkeley and Los Angeles: University of California Press.

Keating, AnaLouise. (2007). *Teaching transformation: Transcultural classroom dialogues.* New York: Palgrave MacMillan.

Kempadoo, K. (Ed.). (1999). *Sun, sex, and gold: Tourism and sex work in the Caribbean.* Lanham, MD: Rowman & Littlefield.

Kim, Yeran. (2007). An ethnographer meets the mobile girl. *Feminist Media Studies, 7*(2), 204–209.

Lai, Ming-Yan. (2009). OFW tales, or globalization discourses and development. In Kum-Kum Bhavnani, John Foran, Priya Kurian, & Debashish Munshi (Eds.), *On the edges of development: Critical interventions* (pp. 192–215). New York: Routledge.

Lather, Patricia. (1991). *Getting smart: Feminist research and pedagogy with/in the postmodern.* New York: Routledge.

Lewis, Reina. (1996). *Gendering orientalism.* London: Routledge.

Lodhia, Sharmila. (2009). Legal Frankensteins and monstrous women: Judicial narratives of the "family in crisis." *Meridians: Feminism, Race, Transnationalism, 9*(2), 102–129.

Lodhia, Sharmila. (2010a). Brides without borders: New topographies of violence and the future of law in an era of transnational citizen-subjects. *Columbia Journal of Gender and Law, 19*(3), 703–746.

Lodhia, Sharmila. (2010b). Constructing an imperfect citizen-subject: Globalization, national "security," and violence against South Asian women. *Women's Studies Quarterly, 38,* 161–177.

Longino, Helen. (1993). Feminist standpoint theory and the problems of knowledge. *Signs: Journal of Women in Culture and Society, 19*(1), 201–212.

Marcus, George E. (1998). *Ethnography through thick and thin.* Princeton, NJ: Princeton University Press.

Maynard, Mary. (1994). "Race," gender and the concept of difference in feminist thought. In H. Afshar & M. Maynard (Eds.), *The dynamics of "race" and gender: Some feminist interventions* (pp. 9–25). London: Taylor & Francis.

Mayo, Marjorie. (2005). *Global citizens: Social movements and the challenge of globalization.* New York: Zed Press.

Mendez, Jennifer Bickham. (2008). Globalizing scholar activism: Opportunities and dilemmas through a feminist lens. In C. R. Hale (Ed.), *Engaging contradictions: Theory, politics, and methods of activist scholarship* (pp. 136–163). Berkeley: University of California Press.

Moghadam, Valentine. (2005). *Globalizing woman: Transnational feminist networks.* Baltimore: Johns Hopkins University Press.

Moore, Henrietta. (1994). *A passion for difference.* Bloomington: Indiana University Press.

Narayan, Uma. (1997). *Dislocating cultures: Identities, traditions and third world feminism.* New York: Routledge.

Newdick, Vivian. (2005). The indigenous woman as victim of her culture in neoliberal Mexico. *Cultural Dynamics, 17*(1), 73–92.

Nicholson, Linda. (1994). Interpreting gender. *Signs: Journal of Women in Culture and Society, 20*(1), 79–105.

Nnaemeka, Obioma. (2001). If female circumcision did not exist, Western feminism would invent it. In Susan Perry & Celeste Schenk (Eds.), *Eye to eye: Women practicing development across cultures* (pp. 171–189). New York: Zed Books.

Pajaczkowska, Clare, & Young, Lola. (2000). Racism, representation, psychoanalysis. In E. Ann Kaplan (Ed.), *Feminism and film* (pp. 356–374). Oxford, UK: Oxford University Press.

Peterson, V. Spike. (2003). *A critical rewriting of global political economy.* London: Routledge.

Philipose, Elizabeth. (2008). Decolonizing the racial grammar of international law. In Robin L. Riley, Chandra Talpade Mohanty, & Minnie Bruce Pratt (Eds.), *Feminism and war: Confronting U.S. imperialism* (pp. 103–116). London and New York: Zed Books.

Poster, Winifred R. (2002). Racialism, sexuality, and masculinity: Gendering "global ethnography" of the workplace. *Social Politics, 9*(1), 126–158.

Puar, Jasbir. (1998). Transnational sexualities: South Asian (trans)nation(alism)s and queer diasporas. In David L. Eng & Alice Y. Hom (Eds.), *Queer in Asian America* (pp. 405–422). Philadelphia: Temple University Press.

Puri, Jyoti. (2002). Concerning *Kamasutras:* Challenging narratives of history and sexuality. *Signs: Journal of Women in Culture and Society, 27*(3), 603–639.

Reinharz, Shulamit. (1992). *Feminist methods in social research.* New York: Oxford University Press.

Robertson, Jennifer. (2000). Dying to tell: Sexuality and suicide in imperial Japan. In Cindy Patton & Benigno Sanchez-Eppler (Eds.), *Queer diasporas* (pp. 38–70). Durham, NC: Duke University Press.

Rose, Gillian. (1997). Performing inoperative community: The space and the resistance of some community arts projects. In Steve Pile & Michael Keith (Eds.), *Geographies of resistance* (pp. 184–202). London: Routledge.

Schaffer, Kay, & Smith, Sidonie. (2004). *Human rights and narrated lives: The ethics of recognition.* New York: Palgrave Macmillan.

Schulman, Barbara. (2004). Effective organizing in terrible times: The strategic value of human rights for transnational anti-racist feminisms. *Meridians: Feminism, Race, Transnationalism, 4*(2), 102–108.

Skeggs, Beverley. (1994). Situating the production of feminist ethnography. In Mary Maynard &

June Purvis (Eds.), *Researching women's lives from a feminist perspective* (pp. 72–92). London: Taylor & Francis.

Smith, Andrea. (2002). Better dead than pregnant: The colonization of native women's reproductive health. In Jael Silliman & Annanya Bhattacharjee (Eds.), *Policing the national body: Race, gender, and criminalization* (pp. 123–146). Cambridge, MA: South End Press.

Smith, Andrea. (2008). Human rights and social-justice organizing in the United States. *Radical History Review, 101*, 211–219.

Smith, Dorothy E. (1990). *Texts, facts, and femininity: Exploring the relations of ruling.* London: Routledge.

Speed, Shannon. (2007). *Rights in rebellion: Indigenous struggle and human rights in Chiapas.* Stanford, CA: Stanford University Press.

Speed, Shannon, & Collier, Jane. (2000). Limiting indigenous autonomy in Chiapas, Mexico: The state government's use of human rights. *Human Rights Quarterly, 22*, 877–905.

Spelman, Elizabeth V. (1997). *Fruits of sorrow.* Boston: Beacon Press.

Stacey, Judith. (1988). Can there be a feminist ethnography? *Women's Studies International Forum, 11*(1), 21–27.

Stanley, Liz, & Wise, Sue. (1990). Method, methodology, and epistemology in feminist research processes. In Liz Stanley (Ed.), *Feminist praxis: Research, theory, and epistemology in feminist sociology* (pp. 20–60). London: Routledge.

Talcott, Molly. (2008). *Claiming dignity, reconfiguring rights: Gender, youth, and indigenous-led organizing in southern México.* Unpublished doctoral dissertation, Department of Sociology, University of California, Santa Barbara.

Talcott, Molly. (2010). As neoliberal crises persist, indigenous-led movements resist: Examining the current social and political-economic conjuncture in southern Mexico. In Richard A. Dello Buono and David Fasenfest (Eds.), *Social change, resistance, and social practices* (pp. 131–148). Leiden and Boston: Brill Publishers.

Tellez, Michelle. (2008). Community of struggle: Gender, violence, and resistance on the U.S.–Mexico border. *Gender & Society, 22*(5), 545–567.

Trujillo, Carla. (1991). *Chicana lesbians: The girls our mothers warned us about.* Berkeley, CA: Third Woman Press.

Tsing, Anna. (2004). *Friction: An ethnography of global connection.* Princeton, NJ: Princeton University Press.

Twine, France Winddance, & Warren, Jonathan. (Eds.). (2000). *Race-ing research: Methodological and ethical dilemmas in critical race studies.* London: Routledge.

Willoughby-Herard, Tiffany. (2010). "I'll give you something to cry about": The intra-racial violence of uplift feminism in the Carnegie Poor White Study volume, *The Mother and Daughter of the Poor Family. South African Review of Sociology, 41*(1), 78–103.

Wolf, Diane L. (Ed.). (1996). Situating feminist dilemmas in fieldwork. In Diane L. Wolf (Ed.), *Feminist dilemmas in fieldwork* (pp. 1–55). Boulder, CO: Westview Press.

Zacharias, Usha, & Arthurs, Jane. (2007). Introduction: Feminist ethnographers in digital ecologies. *Feminist Media Studies, 7*(2), 203–204.

8

INTERSECTIONALITY

A Transformative Paradigm
in Feminist Theory and Social Justice

BONNIE THORNTON DILL AND MARLA H. KOHLMAN

As a Black scholar writing about women's issues in the mid-1980s, Thornton Dill joined with several colleagues in calling for a feminist theoretical paradigm that would expose the disconnect between experience and theory in the often untold stories of women of color and those without economic privilege (Baca Zinn, Cannon, Dill, & Higginbotham, 1986). They understood that feminist theory was quite limited without the purposeful integration of the notion of difference, beginning with race, ethnicity, class, and culture. They also understood that the integration of race and class into the gendered discourses extant at that time would change the nature of feminist discourse in important and powerful ways.

More than two decades later, one of the first things students learn in women's studies classes is how to look at women's and men's lives through multiple lenses. The concept of *intersectionality* has been a key factor in this transition. This conceptual tool has become integral to both theory and research endeavors, as it emphasizes the interlocking effects of race, class, gender, and sexuality, highlighting the ways in which categories of identity and structures of inequality are mutually constituted and defy separation into discrete categories of analysis. Intersectionality provides a unique lens of study that does not question difference; rather, it assumes that differential experiences of common events are to be expected.

As scholars producing intersectional work began to apply their insights to institutional dynamics, they began to speak and write about the challenges and opportunities that exist within and through the academy and the labor market, and in law and public policy. Thus, intersectional scholarship is engaged in transforming both theory and practice across disciplinary divides, offering a wide range of methodological approaches to the study of multiple, complex social relations. In her widely cited 2005 article, "The Complexity of Intersectionality," sociologist Leslie McCall states that "intersectionality is the most important theoretical contribution that women's studies, in conjunction with related fields, has made so far" (p. 1771).

In this chapter, we are charged with mapping the developments in intersectional theorizing and institutional transformation in the past decade while also offering our views on the future of intersectionality for feminist theory and methodology.

Roots and History

Intersectional scholarship emerged as an amalgamation of aspects of women's studies and race and ethnic studies. Its foundations are in the scholarly tradition that began in the 19th century with Black women such as Sojourner Truth, Maria Stewart, and Anna Julia Cooper and men like W. E. B. DuBois—intellectuals who first articulated the unique challenges of Black women facing the multiple and simultaneous effects of race, gender, and class. What distinguished this early work on Black women was that it argued forcefully and passionately that the lives of African American women could not be understood through a unidimensional analysis focusing exclusively on either race or gender.

Intersectional scholarship, as we know it today, fused this knowledge from race and ethnic studies with aspects of women's studies and refined it in the debates and discourse that informed the civil and women's rights activism of the 1960s and 1970s. Before that time, women's studies emphasized the importance of gender and sexism while Black and Latino studies focused on race and racism as experienced within these respective communities. Each field sought to interrogate historical patterns of subordination and domination, asserting that we live in a society that is organized around complex and layered sets of inequalities. For example, the research of Teresa Amott and Julie Matthaei (1991, 1996) applied this emerging mode of analysis and demonstrated how oppression was experienced differently by racial-ethnic groups, and men and women within these groups, as participants within the U.S. labor market over time. Moreover, they used their research to make a strong argument about the mutual constitution of inequalities.

The essentially economic nature of early racial-ethnic oppression in the United States makes it difficult to isolate whether peoples of color were subordinated in the U.S. economy because of their race-ethnicity or their economic class. Whites displaced American Indians and Mexicans to obtain their land. Whites imported Africans to work as slaves and Asians to work as contract laborers. Puerto Ricans and Filipinas/os were victims of further U.S. expansionism. Race-ethnicity and class intertwined in the patterns of displacement from land, genocide, forced labor, and recruitment from the seventeenth through the twentieth centuries. While it is impossible, in our minds, to determine which came first in these instances—race-ethnicity or class—it is clear that they were intertwined and inseparable. (Amott & Matthaei, 1991, p. 19)

Categories of race/ethnicity, class, and gender were defined as major markers and controllers of oppression in the earliest discussions of intersectionality, with limited attention given to other categories such as sexuality, nation, age, disability, and religion, which have been discussed in more recent years. One result of this historical trajectory is a perspective asserting that individuals and groups can simultaneously experience oppression and privilege. Mere recognition of this history is not sufficient to form a complete understanding of the extensive ranges of "structures and experiences produced by intersecting forms of race and gender": neither does it ensure proper acknowledgment of the "interlocking inequalities, what Patricia Hill Collins calls the 'matrix of domination'" (Baca Zinn & Dill, 1996, p. 326).

Collins explains that "the matrix of domination is structured on several levels. People experience and resist oppression on three levels: the level of personal biography; the group or community level of cultural context created by race, class, and gender; and the systemic level of social institutions" (Collins, 1990, p. 227). Collins distinguishes her conceptualization of interlocking theories, or oppressions, from the traditional additive models of oppression found in much traditional feminist theory, which place

emphasis on quantification and categorization . . . in conjunction with the belief that either/or categories must be ranked. The search for certainty of this sort requires that one side of a dichotomy be privileged while the other side is denigrated. Privilege becomes defined in relation to its other.

Replacing additive models of oppression with interlocking ones creates possibilities for new paradigms. The significance of seeing race, class, and gender as interlocking systems of oppression is that such an approach fosters a paradigmatic shift of thinking inclusively about other oppressions, such as age, sexual orientation, religion, and ethnicity . . . [This type of analysis also] opens up possibilities for a both/and conceptual stance, one in which all groups possess varying amounts of penalty and privilege in one historically created system. In this system, for example, white women are penalized by their gender but privileged by their race. Depending on the context, an individual may be an oppressor, a member of an oppressed group, or simultaneously oppressor and oppressed. (Collins, 1990, p. 225)

By noting the ways in which men and women occupy variant positions of power and privilege across race, space, and time, intersectionality has refashioned several of the basic premises that have guided feminist theory as it evolved following the 1950s. Many have explicitly recognized that the prototypical model for feminist theory post-1950s was based on the lives of White women whose experiences as wives, daughters, and mothers were to be strictly differentiated from the experience of Black women as informed by historical precedent. "Judged by the evolving nineteenth century ideology of femininity, which emphasized women's roles as nurturing mothers and gentle companions and housekeepers for their husbands, Black women were practically anomalies" (Davis, 1981, p. 5). Indeed, "one cannot assume, as have many feminist theorists and activists, that all women have had the same experience of gender oppression—or that they will be on the same side of a struggle, not even when some women define that struggle as 'feminist' . . . [F]or peoples of color, having children and maintaining families have been an essential part of the struggle against racist oppression. [Thus, it is not surprising that] many women of color have rejected the white

women's movement's view of the family as the center of 'women's oppression'" (Amott & Matthaei, 1991, pp. 16–17), which many find to be the decisive message of books regarded as pivotal foundations of the second wave of the feminist movement such as *The Feminine Mystique* by Betty Friedan or *Of Woman Born* by Adrienne Rich. We do not mean to imply, either, that all women of color would renounce the accounts offered in the pages of these books. We offer these textual examples as evidence that intersectional scholarship has been able to highlight the myriad ways in which the experiences of some White women and women of color differ in the nuances of the maintenance of family. More specifically, these differences are to be found within the inextricable lines of racial ethnicity and gender that were influential in the fomentation of a feminist consciousness for some women that was both distinct from and dependent upon the experiences of other women.

Indeed, the family has been for many women of color a sort of "haven in a heartless world" of racism that provides the needed support to fight against oppression of many types (Dill, 1979; hooks, 1984). Drawing on the work of a number of the pioneering Black feminist intersectional scholars, Landry (2000) argues in his book on Black middle-class women that this support enabled Black women to produce a new ideology of womanhood that permitted the formation of the modern dual-career and dual-earner family. This model of womanhood rejected the notion that "outside work was detrimental to [Black women's roles] as wives and mothers" (Landry, 2000, p. 73). Indeed, Black women of the late 19th and early 20th centuries realized that "their membership in the paid labor force was critical to achieving true equality with men" (p. 74) in the larger U.S. society in a way that was not available to White women under the cult of true womanhood that constrained them to the exclusive domains of hearth and home. Women of color, having always been regarded as a source of labor in the United States, were never the beneficiaries of this ideology of protectionism and were not, therefore, hampered from developing an ideology that saw beyond the dictates of traditional feminist principles based in the experience of gender subordination perceived as endemic to all women (see, for example, Davis, 1972).

Winifred Breines (2006) provides an interesting reflection on the role and relationship of early intersectional thinking that promoted an understanding of mutually constituted structures of difference and inequality in feminist experiences. As she argues in *The Trouble Between Us: An Uneasy History of White and Black Women in the Feminist Movement*,

> In the development of the feminist movement, one of the most dramatic political shifts was from a desire to overcome difference to its promotion. Integration or interracialsim as a goal migrated toward difference and an embrace of identity that precluded togetherness. This was a disturbing process but, in retrospect, probably inevitable. Postwar young people, especially whites, knew very little about racism and sexism. They had to separate to learn who they were in the race, class, and gender terms constructed by American society. . . . Just as identity politics divided the society that created such politics in the first place, they divided the movements. (Breines, 2006, p. 16)

Breines (2006) concludes her text on the differences that emerged between Black and White women in the feminist movement with words from several young feminists, one of whom contends that "unlike second wave feminism, which has operated from a monolithic center, multiplicity offers the power of existing insidiously and simultaneously everywhere. 'Women' as a primary identity category has ceased to be the entry point for much young activist work" (p. 196). Breines (2006) follows this with the admonition that young feminists have come to this knowledge having read the experiences of those who struggled before them: "They may not be aware of it, but the racial learning curve that began in the early 1960s continues among younger—and older—feminists in the twenty-first century" (p. 199). Similar to the project embarked upon by Breines, the research and writing of feminist scholars of color continues the tradition of theorizing the experience of women of color who have been ignored in the scholarship on both

race and gender. These scholars have produced landmark studies based on lived experience at the intersections of race, gender, ethnicity, class, and sexuality.[1]

Growth and Dissemination: Emerging Inquiries and Controversies

As an approach to creating knowledge that has its roots in analyses of the lived experiences of women of color—women whose scholarly and social justice work reveals how aspects of identity and social relations are shaped by the simultaneous operation of multiple systems of power—intersectional scholarship is interdisciplinary in nature and focuses on how structures of difference combine to create a feminist praxis that is new and distinct from the social, cultural, and artistic forms emphasized in traditional feminist paradigms that focus primarily upon contrasting the experiences of women in society to those of men. Intersectionality is intellectually transformative not only because it centers the experiences of people of color and locates its analysis within systems of ideological, political, institutional, and economic power as they are shaped by historical patterns of race, class, gender, sexuality, nation, ethnicity, and age but also because it provides a platform for uniting different kinds of praxis in the pursuit of social justice: analysis, theorizing, education, advocacy, and policy development.

The people who engage with this work do so out of strong commitments to diversity, multiculturalism, and human rights, combined with a desire to create a more equitable society that recognizes, validates, and celebrates difference. The social justice agenda of this scholarship is crucial to its utility in fomenting theory and praxis specifically designed for analyzing inequalities of power and privilege, and, consequently, intersectionality is of interest to persons outside the academy who share concerns that underlie this scholarship. As Catherine MacKinnon contends, "What is important about intersectionality is what it is doing in our world, how it is traveling around the world and being used in defense of human rights, not just what it says" (MacKinnon, 2010).

The intellectual vibrancy within and around intersectional theory is yielding new frontiers of knowledge production that include, but are not limited to, scholarship on identity and the applicability of intersectionality to groups in other social locations or in multiple social locations simultaneously (Browne & Misra, 2003; Henderson & Tickamyer, 2009; Kohlman, 2010a). Discussions about methodologies, language, and images most accurately convey the complexities of these interrelationships. For example, the development of the queer of color critique (Ferguson, 2003; Johnson & Henderson, 2005) as an intervention into sexuality studies establishes race and ethnicity as critical dimensions of queer studies, scholarship on globalization and international human rights moves intersectionality beyond the U.S. context (Davis, 2008; Knapp, 2005; Mohanty, 2003; Yuval-Davis, 2006), and work that continues explicitly to link theory and practice provides an analytical foundation for social justice and critical resistance. Within each of these topics, there are disagreements about approach and perspective, which we explicitly address in what follows, and the debates and discussions contribute to the vibrancy of the topic and thus to advancing this scholarship and producing knowledge that illuminates the many factors that shape processes of experiencing multiple identities and social locations.

Because the contemporary growth of intersectionality as a theoretical approach is relatively recent and has developed in a number of different fields, future growth is largely defined by the trajectory of current debates and inquiries. This chapter identifies some of these important debates, particularly with regard to sexualities/ queer studies, globalization and transnationalism, methodologies, and new ways of linking theory and practice in academe, law, and policy.

Sexuality/Queer Studies

An intersectional approach emphasizing multiple dimensions of identity and their relationship to systems of power has been an important part of sexuality and queer studies and has been used to reveal the heterosexism of institutions, broaden understandings of gender, expose the artificiality of presumed sex differences, and expand knowledge of sexual desire (Ingraham, 2005). At the same time, sexuality studies have been critiqued by scholars of color for using

intersectionality primarily as a methodological tool that fails to address the ways in which race, ethnicity, and culture structure the experience of sexual identity and the politics of sexuality in U.S. and international contexts. These scholars specifically argue that, by largely ignoring race and failing to incorporate the insights of intersectional analysis with regard to race and racialization into its larger theoretical frame, this field of study has continued to perpetuate the commodification of sexuality as normatively White and heterosexual.

Correctives to this are found in the work of such scholars as historian John D'Emilio (2003), whose book on the life of labor and civil rights activist Bayard Rustin examines the complex ways race, gender, and sexuality intersected in Rustin's life and affected key strategies and actions of the civil rights movement. Rustin is now widely known to have been the organizer of the March on Washington in 1963 and the architect of much of Martin Luther King, Jr.'s strategy of nonviolence. It was Rustin who learned, from an early age, of the teachings of Gandhi while also being raised according to Quaker, or the Society of Friends, religious doctrine and practice. Because of the widespread homophobia in the United States at that time in history, Rustin remained closeted and behind the scenes. He and those with whom he worked understood that, because Rustin was a gay Black man and social activist, his sexual practices could easily be used to attack the movement. The analytical lens of intersectionality immediately exposes the multiplicative and interlocking power dynamics Rustin was forced to contend with in order to be a part of the civil rights struggle while simultaneously being silenced because of his sexual orientation.

Another scholar, Roderick Ferguson, in his book *Aberrations in Black: Toward a Queer of Color Critique* (2003), develops what he calls "queer of color analysis" that reveals the interconnections among sexuality, economic inequality, and race not only in the history of U.S. labor but within various forms of knowledge production. His book lays out the historical role sociology has played in labeling African American culture as deviant, and, by carefully highlighting this process, Ferguson reveals how identity is inextricably linked to power, political representation, and the ever-shifting power dynamics of identity politics.

Additionally, in their book, *Black Queer Studies: A Critical Anthology,* E. Patrick Johnson and Mae Henderson (2005) provide a useful analysis that illuminates the significant limitations of the theoretical modalities espoused in both queer studies and Black studies by presenting a thoughtful discussion of the "multiple subjectivities" incorporated within analyses of each group. More specifically, they question the effectiveness of queer studies in addressing issues of public policy that have had a direct impact on gays, lesbians, bisexuals, and transgendered people of color. They argue, in effect, that it is more useful to pursue the intersectional project of Black queer studies and the queer of color critique in order to theorize sexuality in a manner that is fully inclusive of the ways race, class, and gender mutually shape and are shaped by each other. Johnson and Henderson (2005) state that "*Black Queer Studies* serves as a critical intervention in the discourses of Black studies and queer studies" with the object "to build a bridge and negotiate a space of inquiry between these two liberatory and interrogatory discourses" (p. 1). They point out that both fields emerged from political movements and strategies that focused primarily on only one dimension of selfhood, and each erased difference and the mutually constituted nature of identity that shapes lived experience.

Doug Meyer's (2008) work, "Interpreting and Experiencing Anti-queer Violence," is another example of intersectional scholarship that challenges classical definitions of race, ethnicity, and nationality while also repositioning debates about identity politics in the United States. He specifically notes that his interviews provided evidence that

> some queer people highlighted the importance of gender and sexuality in structuring their experiences of violence; others argued that their violent experiences could not be reduced to two aspects of their identity. These comments were particularly common among queer people of color. Many queer people of color highlighted the role of racism, as well as homophobia and sexism, in structuring their violent experiences. (Meyer, 2008, p. 269)

Meyer's research reveals the ways in which cultural notions of race, gender, and sexuality intersect to determine the experience of hate crimes directed toward queer people.

Nevertheless, work in the area of queer studies may still need to be attentive to concerns raised by matters such as shifts in language usage and terminology, from "gay" to "queer" or, as Ferguson suggests, a "queer color of analysis." This connotative shift has not been accomplished without controversy. As Rhonda M. Williams suggested in 1998, although queer is seen as a "necessarily expansive impulse, we must understand how it still also reflects and, in some cases, might blur the complexities of sexual orientations and racial politics among Black gays and lesbians" (Harper et al., quoted in Williams, 1998, p. 154). For example, this blurring Williams references may lead to the erasure of the experiences of transgender or intersexed individuals who have been actively involved in the struggle over equal marriage rights for couples regardless of their gendered identities. Johnson and Henderson (2005) note that the authors in their collection "question the effectiveness of queer studies in addressing issues of public policy that have had a direct impact on gays, lesbians, bisexuals, and transgendered people of color" (p. 7). The intersectional project of Black queer studies and the queer of color critique is to theorize sexuality in a manner that is fully inclusive of the ways race, class, and gender mutually shape and are shaped by each other. At the same time, queer of color studies also challenge intersectionality scholarship to theorize race and racialization in a manner that is more fully inclusive of sexuality as a dimension of inequality, a point also argued by Patricia Hill Collins in *Black Sexual Politics* (2004).

Transnationalism(s)

Work that examines international and global perspectives is another area that advances this scholarship. For example, work examining the social constructions of race within a transnational context, along with work on African, Latino, Asian, and other diasporic groups, is seen as developing important new insights, not only for understanding the world outside the

United States but for understanding the U.S. context as well. Chela Sandoval's (2004) transnational approach to feminist theory stands in opposition to feminism as a clear, monolithic political agenda and requires us to define feminist praxis by identifying current situations of power with which we are faced and, only then, to self-consciously select the ideological form best suited to push against that form of power's current configurations. This approach is most useful because of the focus on identifying oneself in relation to others as a meaningful process of self-examination that requires more commitment to the development of pragmatic feminist theory.

The outsourcing of goods and services and the development of labor markets outside the United States have contributed to a dispersion of labor markets, the relocation of U.S. workers, and the displacement and replacement of low-wage workers. For example, benefits information on Temporary Assistance for Needy Families (TANF) has been outsourced to workers in India (Hu-Dehart, 2007). Public policy decisions such as these disproportionately impact poor women and women of color in the United States who, if working, are often working in low-wage jobs in competitive industries. For African American and Latino women recipients of TANF, who are the least likely to obtain training or a position that would lead to economic self-sufficiency, as Jones-DeWeever, Dill, and Schram (2009) found, such strategies are deeply ironic. The search for cheap labor across transnational markets exploits the labor of poor third world women from the global South at the same time that it increases economic vulnerability and limits options and opportunities for economic self-sufficiency and social mobility for women of color in the United States. Further, drawing on data presented in several studies described in the paper, they argue that, for those women who remain TANF recipients, the ability to access information on benefits is decreased by a "provider group" that is unfamiliar with the U.S. social and political context and is less likely to be linguistically appropriate to the recipients of the service.

Chandra Mohanty (2003) uses the terms "feminist solidarity" and "comparative feminist studies" to describe intersectional scholarship as a project "based on the premise that the local and the global are not defined in terms of physical geography or territory but exist simultaneously and constitute each other" (p. 242). She argues that, in addition to conceptualizing identity in multiple categories, it helps to foreground ideas of nationhood and citizenship that may in turn be used to elucidate the position of women of color throughout the United States and in international contexts. Evelyn Nakano Glenn (2002), in her book *Unequal Freedom*, demonstrates the illuminative quality of intersectional analysis with regard to citizenship, race, and gender in the U.S. context, and Rhacel Parreñas (2001) illustrates the global ramifications of intersection theory in her work on Filipina domestic workers in the United States and abroad. Theorizing about third world/southern women done in the framework of comparative women's studies, then, has had the result of making power and inequality visible and bringing attention "to the micropolitics of context, subjectivity, and struggle as well as to the macropolitics of global economic and political systems and processes" (Mohanty, 2003, p. 223). This scholarship is advancing our knowledge of how political structures, U.S. hegemony, and geographic space and place shape definitions and roles of gender and sexuality.

Linking Theory and Practice

Because intersectional knowledge is grounded in the everyday lives of people of diverse backgrounds, it is seen as an important tool linking theory with practice. Intersectional work can validate the lives and histories of persons and subgroups previously ignored or marginalized, and it is used to help empower communities and the people in them. Professors Barbara Ransby, Elsa Barkley-Brown, and Deborah King, whose paid newspaper ads applied an intersectional analysis to the vilification of Anita Hill and Clarence Thomas's distorted use of the concept of lynching during his Supreme Court confirmation hearings, present an early and classic example of this intersectional work. Signed by over sixteen hundred African American women scholars, the statement offered an interpretation of those events that went beyond the singular focus on sexual harassment, which had become the overriding concern of many White feminists, and the concurrent racial victimization narrative evoked by Clarence Thomas's "high-tech lynching" claim. It applied intersectional ideas to illustrate that constructs of race and gender intersected in the treatment of Anita Hill to demean and discredit her in a way that was consistent with the historical pattern of treatment of Black women who speak out on sexual matters or publicly criticize Black men. The statement, published in the *New York Times* and six African American newspapers, offered a perspective on the case that had been totally omitted from public discourse and debate. It challenged Americans to reckon with the fact that, as Kohlman (2010b) argues, there was no true recognition of the intersections of experience from which Hill emerged as she was forced to wage this battle. Instead, the most simplistic notions of feminist theory and praxis—ones that focused on gender only—resulted in initially championing her cause as feminist, even as many ignored the racist narrative that was used to delegitimize the experiences she recounted. As Kimberle Crenshaw has argued,

> America simply stumbled into the place where African-American women live, a political vacuum of erasure and contradiction maintained by the almost routine polarization of "blacks and women" into separate and competing political camps. . . . Because she was situated within two fundamental hierarchies of social power, the central disadvantage that Hill faced was the lack of available and widely comprehended narratives to communicate the reality of her experience as a black woman to the world. (Crenshaw, 1992, pp. 403–404)

Perhaps as a result of this earlier experience with the media and the American public, a much more assertive, confident, and fully integrated (raced *and* gendered) Anita Hill emerged in the wake of publicity surrounding the release of Clarence Thomas's memoir (2007) and his statement that Hill had been "a mediocre employee who was used by political opponents to make claims she had been sexually harassed" (Sherman, 2007, ¶ 1). On October 2, 2007, Anita Hill published an op-ed in the *New York Times,* emphatically stating, "I will not stand by and allow him, in his anger, to reinvent me" (¶ 4). Anita Hill, at this point in history, clearly exemplifies many of the qualities she was given credit for espousing in the early 1990s. Her words and actions now, however, are self-determined, borne of her own will and reflective of an intersectional presence that the American public was able to disregard completely almost 20 years ago. This is in stark contrast to the testimony elicited from her during the confrontational legal process of the Senate Judiciary Committee hearings, her inability to effectively respond as she might have wished within the organizational framework of that legal setting, and much of the media discourse that followed (Kohlman, 2010b).

Methodological Concerns

Debates around methodologies center on the concern of remaining grounded in the questions, struggles, and experiences of particular communities that generate an intersectional perspective. At the same time, methodological debates about intersectionality often extend this approach to identify common themes and points of connection between specific social locations and broader social patterns. Stated somewhat differently: How do we benefit from comparisons and interrelationships without negating or undermining the complex and particular character of each group, system of oppression, or culture? Answers to this question are embedded in discussions about the language and metaphors that most effectively convey the concept of intersectionality as well as in debates about the use of qualitative and historical versus quantitative research methodologies.

Central to the discussion of language have been disputes about the adequacies and limitations of the term "intersectionality" and the metaphors associated with it. Scholars working with these ideas continue to seek ways to overcome an image that suggests that these dimensions of inequality, such as race, class, and gender, are separable and distinct and that it is only at certain points that they overlap or intersect with one another. This concern was specifically articulated by Deborah King in 1988 when she called for a model of analysis permitting recognition of the "multiple jeopardy" constituted by the interactive oppressions that circumscribe the lives of Black women and defy separation into discrete categories of analysis. The modifier "multiple" refers not only to several simultaneous oppressions but to the multiplicative relationships among them as well (King, 1988, p. 47). It is now widely recognized that intersectionality is more than a car crash at the nexus of a set of separate roads (Crenshaw, 1989). Instead, it is well understood that these systems of power are mutually constituted (Weber, 2009) such that there is no point at which race is not simultaneously classed and gendered or gender is not simultaneously raced and classed. How to capture this complexity in a single term or image has been an ongoing conversation.

Recent work by Ivy Ken (2007) provides a useful overview of a number of the conceptual images in use: that is, the notion of "intersecting versus interlocking" inequalities, which has been expressed in metaphors such as crossing roads or a matrix or the importance of locating oppressions within "systems versus structures versus institutions." She then moves on to analyze the limitations of these analytical approaches and suggests aspects of intersectionality that remain unexplained. She further proposes an innovative and promising approach to thinking about these ideas using the processes of producing, using, experiencing, and digesting sugar as a metaphor for describing, discussing, and theorizing intersectionality (Ken, 2008). For example, she addresses the importance of context-specific relationships in understanding how race, class, and gender oppression is "produced, what people and institutions do with it once they have it in their hands, what it feels like to experience it, and how it then comes to shape us" (Ken, 2008, p. 154). Ken argues that the relationships among sources of oppression, like race, class, and gender, start with production—every aspect of race, class, and gender has been and is produced under particular social, historical, political, cultural, and economic conditions.

Given the intersectional argument that race, class, gender, and other axes of inequality are always intertwined, co-constructed, and simultaneous (Weber, 2009), questions and debates have arisen about how quantitative approaches that rely on the analysis of separate and distinct variables can account for such interactivity. Two issues frame this debate. The first is the idea that these axes of inequality are not simply characteristics of individuals to be used as variables, isolated from the particular histories, social relations, and institutional contexts that produced them (Amott & Matthaei, 1996; Stacey & Thorne, cited in Harnois, 2009). The second is the task of developing quantitative approaches that address and reveal the overlapping differences present in intersectional analyses in a way that will yield important, generalizable results.

The work of Leslie McCall (2001, 2005) with regard to race, class, and gender in different types of labor markets has been particularly important in efforts to rethink the use of quantitative tools so that they can reveal the differential ways race, class, and gender interact within different social contexts. Her *Signs* article (2005) has been an important tool in efforts to provide empirical evidence of the value of intersectional analysis in the quantitative social sciences. Specifically, McCall applies an intersectional approach to an examination of the impact of economic restructuring on wage inequalities (see also Hancock, 2008; Simien, 2007; Valentine, 2007). To do this, she studies the effect of multiple factors on different racial/ethnic, class, and gender groups and on the relationships both within and between those groups in different regional economies. What she finds is that the patterns are not the same: that a single economic environment may create advantages for some in a group and disadvantages for others in the same group relative to other groups, thus making some environments more appropriate for one set of social policies while a different set may be more appropriate for another. She states: "different contexts reveal different configurations of inequality [and] no single dimension of overall inequality can adequately describe the full structure of multiple, intersecting, and conflicting dimensions of inequality" (McCall, 2005, p. 1791).

Kohlman (2006, 2010a) has utilized intersection theory to illustrate how the experiences of men and women who report having experienced sexual harassment in the U.S. labor market differ because of the interaction of several forces of oppression that influence behavior simultaneously. She employs quantitative methods to illustrate successfully that it is both possible and imperative to deconstruct commonly used additive models of analysis, which mask the intersectional effects shaping the experiences of those embedded within them. Catharine Harnois (2005, 2009), by applying multiracial feminist theory in the design of a quantitative analysis of women's paths to feminism, has both revealed and offered meaningful explanations for variations among women by race and ethnicity, differences within racial-ethnic categories that had not been thought to exist.

Because empirical findings from quantitative analyses dominate the social sciences, are seen as authoritative and generalizable, and often provide the documentation upon which social policy is built, quantitative research that demonstrates the importance of intersectionality offers the opportunity to expand the framework's applicability and impact. The danger, however, is that these axes of inequality may be read as a reductive analysis of the interaction of a set of individual characteristics, thus diluting the power and full meaning of the experiential theory these interactions have been constructed to illustrate. Quantitative methodologies, when read in conjunction with findings produced from the qualitative studies that continue to dominate research within the intersectional paradigm, provide analytic frames that complement, apply, and extend the impact and understanding of intersectionality.

It is also important to note that debates about methodology are not limited to a quantitative versus qualitative discussion, but, rather, embrace the idea that we must continue to explore and expand the approaches we use to address an even broader range of questions that can be generated by this scholarship. These should include applied and theoretical and interdisciplinary and transversal modes of inquiry, among others. Interdisciplinary research must embrace multiple methodological approaches to capture the complexities and nuances in the lives of individuals and the experiences of groups of people (see also Hancock, 2007). A key criterion is to avoid essentializing people's experiences by burying intragroup diversity within isolated analytical categories.

Legal scholar Francisco Valdes offers a viable solution for avoiding this type of essentialization within legal jurisprudence by conceiving

of intersectionality as occurring at the intersections of legal doctrine, legal theory, and social life. In his analysis, theoretical intersectionality reflects the specific configurations of social life rather than legal doctrine, while doctrinal intersectionality is dependent upon the law itself as it is manifest in the adjudication of cases. He notes that judges, when confronted with a case that is intersectional in nature, often ignore those portions of a legal claim that fall under legal categories protected by Title VII legislation and the resulting judicial precedent established by case law (e.g., sex, race, age, or national origin) and, thereby, push the entire claim into unprotected categories (e.g., sexual orientation). In advancing this argument, Valdes identifies several categories of intersectionality that have been problematized in legal cases and therefore have been either acknowledged and then discussed, dismissed as untenable, or not recognized at all. He then posits that the gap to be found between theoretical intersectionality (lived experience) and doctrinal intersectionality (legal recognition and adjudication) is a map of the dysfunctions within the law. Valdes argues that by specifically taking note of the distinctions between doctrinal intersectionality and theoretical intersectionality, we should be able to formulate a meaningful legal praxis for addressing the range of experiences within the "gap" between the two. We can then move toward addressing the reductive impulses of juridical consideration in law. Such praxis would also provide a powerful tool for scholars to effectively identify the concepts within law and social policy that require redress in the name of social justice (Valdes, 2010).

KNOWLEDGE PRODUCTION AND INSTITUTIONAL TRANSFORMATION: IDENTITY, LAW, AND HIGHER EDUCATION

The production of knowledge is an academic enterprise and has been controlled and contained within predominantly White, elite, and middle-to upper-class institutional structures. Within this context, research is ostensibly guided by normative roadmaps, which are presumed to be neutral or objective theoretical frameworks and methodologies, but, in actuality, many aspects of these roadmaps are built upon assumptions that are subjective and convey particular images of various population groups. The culture of science, which rests upon claims of neutrality, empiricism, and positivist thinking, maintains invisible structural arrangements that perpetuate patterns of inequality. Thus, the meaning and interpretation of the numerous studies on race, ethnicity, and poverty that appear under terms such as disparity and social gradient must be unveiled with respect to the systems of power and inequality that structure the processes of knowledge production in the sciences and social sciences and that often work against changes in public policy.

The research of Valdes and others doing intersectional theory in law and policy powerfully illustrates, then, that intersectional theory and praxis is, to a large extent, about identity and the ways in which identity politics have been the subject of considerable scholarly and popular debate over the past two decades. While these political realities remain contested and much debated, extant social constructions and academic discourses about intersectionality will continue to illuminate the nature of both individual and group identities in this area. The concept of intersectionality as it relates to identity should help us understand the multidimensional ways people experience life—how people see themselves, and how they are treated by others—while also providing a particularly useful lens for examining categorical treatments of race, gender, and sexuality. This is not to say, however, that intersectionality can be reduced to a theoretical or methodological conversation about competing identity structures (Ribet, 2010). To be most useful, this interrogation must take place not only on the individual level but also at the macro level, examining how economic, political, institutional, and ideological structures construct, perpetuate, and reify group identities.

In the discourse surrounding identity, it is the tension between intersectionality as a tool for illuminating group identities that are not essentialist and individual identities that are not so fragmentary as to be meaningless that provides the energy to move the concept forward to the future. As a point of fact, one central premise of intersectionality as a paradigm of analysis is that one cannot separate a single portion of

one's identity from the rest. Arguing from this perspective, Adrien Wing (1997) asserts that one cannot see individuals

> as merely the sum of separate parts that can be added together or subtracted from, until a white male or female stands before you. The actuality of our layered experience is *multiplicative.* Multiply each of my parts together, $1 \times 1 \times 1 \times 1 \times 1$, and you still have one indivisible being. If you divide one of these parts from one you still have *one.* (p. 31)

Recognizing this fine distinction, Davis (2008) correctly cites several studies framing the controversy as to "whether intersectionality should be conceptualized as a crossroad (Crenshaw, 1991), as 'axes' of difference (Yuval-Davis, 2006) or as a dynamic process (Staunæs, 2003)" (p. 68).

At the individual level, then, identity studies continue to call attention to dimensions of difference that have been largely unexplored and ignored. Among promising aspects of identity studies has been the growth and expansion of studies of race and ethnicity that examine processes of racialization for groups other than Blacks and Whites in the United States. For example, the article "On Being a White Person of Color: Using Autoethnography to Understand Puerto Ricans' Racialization," by Salvador Vidal-Ortiz (2004), provides an example of the ways identity studies have been productively enhanced through the inclusion of concepts of nation and nationality. Vidal-Ortiz (2004) challenges classical definitions of race, ethnicity, and nationality while also repositioning debates about identity politics in the United States. He argues that an alternative racialization process occurs when Puerto Ricans represent themselves while living in the United States, as opposed to when they do the same while living on the island. By studying the impact of more than one racialization system, he shows how categories of analysis like gender, class, and sexuality may be mobilized differently depending on an individual's own geopolitical location.

Intersectional work emerging predominantly from the social sciences and humanities is an alternative mode of knowledge production that seeks to validate the lives and stories of previously ignored groups of people and is used to help empower communities and the people in them. The production of knowledge to address real-life social issues and problems and the application and use of this knowledge to solve problems of inequality have been fundamental to the intersectional project of promoting social justice.

The necessary links between theory and social justice that enable institutional transformation have been demonstrated quite effectively in the work of critical race theorists (CRT). Arguments in CRT scholarship include analyses of White privilege as structured throughout the legal system and other sociopolitical structures, as well as the examination of civil rights law that operates through "race-neutral" principles to sustain White dominance. Linking theory, policy, and practice is the principal focus of the field of critical legal theory (CLT), and this is exemplified in the work of the CLT scholars Kimberle Crenshaw and Luke Harris, cofounders of the African American Policy Forum (AAPF). The AAPF is recognized as one of the leading organizations in the field of race and gender equality, sponsoring research that explores affirmative action policies that are both global and domestic.

Two spin-offs of CLT that also extend theory on race and racialization beyond Black and White are LatCrit theory and Asian Pacific American critical race theory. Stefancic (1997) argues that Latina/o critical theory, although relatively unknown, has been around for a long time but is only recently increasing in visibility. LatCrit theory (Latina & Latino Critical Legal Theory, Inc., 2011) calls attention to the way in which conventional, and even critical, approaches to race and civil rights ignore the problems and special situations of Latina/o people—including bilingualism, immigration reform, the binary black-white structure of existing race remedies law, and much more (Stefancic, 1997, p. 1510). The invisibility of Latina/o issues is evident in multiple fields including health education and child welfare, as noted by the research of Zambrana and Logie (2000), and citizenship status, as noted by the research of Mary Romero (2008) on immigration raids and the attendant effects on mixed-status families.

LatCrit is a national organization of law professors and students whose members seek to use critical race theory to develop new conceptions of justice by actively engaging in what they term "anti-essential community building." Linking theory and practice, especially in work that brings together scholarly analysis with community organizing, is seen as a vital dimension of this scholarship, one that grows out of its roots in lived experience and is directed toward its goal of social justice. Recognizing that the knowledge produced in the field of law affects structures of power in society, LatCrit seeks to focus its analytical lens on policies and areas of the law that have previously been overlooked. No single community, LatCrit scholars argue, can produce a theory about intergroup justice without connections to other groups, and yet every single social justice movement has had a problem with essentialism, giving primacy to some aspects of its identity while ignoring others that intersect with and reform that primary identity (Delgado-Bernal, 2002). As a result, LatCrit seeks quite consciously to present Latino/a identity as a multifaceted, intersectional reality. Latinas/os, they argue, are Black, White, Asian, gay, and straight and speak many different languages and have many different nationalities, requiring that we stop categorizing Latinas/os as a one-dimensional monolithic entity. The term "anti-essentialism" has particular meaning for them because the work of LatCrit is primarily focused on incorporating issues of identity, hybridity, anti-essentialism, and liberation into the analysis of law and in legal institutions, discourse, and process. But also, as with other groups, the need to break apart the global category "Latina/o" into its many important differences is an attempt to hold the shared experiences and the factors that divide and differentiate in productive tension. For example, many will recognize this as a similar debate advanced against the term "Hispanic" in the late 1970s, recognizing that Latinas/os as an ethnic group were classified as White up until 1980, although their historic mistreatment had been documented by Chicano scholars (Almaguer, 1994).

Asian Pacific American critical (APACrit) theory focuses on the intersecting formations of race, gender, nation, citizenship, and immigration. APACrit frames analyses of social inequalities and poses possibilities of social justice that take into central account contentious national identity processes. Foregrounding formations of "Asian America" reveal critical race theory's limitations, particularly its constricted focus on the black-white binary and its lack of attention to issues of immigration and citizenship. Additionally, APACrit scholarship approaches formations as simultaneously raced and "nationed" within the context of border maintenance, national security, immigration laws and policies, racial profiling, sexual harassment laws, hate speech, and the nation-form's identity project. By foregrounding experiences of Asian American women and men and critiquing cultural representations of racial-sexual policing, APACrit also examines identity formations as simultaneously gendered, sexualized, raced, classed, and "nationed."

Since the mid-1990s, APACrit has continued to grow and expand as interdisciplinary scholarship committed to social justice. Gotanda (1995) is one of the first CRT scholars to place issues in Asian American studies and CRT in conversation. He challenges legal liberalism's presumption that identity formations rest outside the law, such that the Japanese American internment, for example, is understood in legal liberalism as a result of bad decisions and misunderstandings and certainly not as the result of broader structural inequalities in society and the legal system. As a politically productive challenge to legal liberalism, Matsuda (1996) proposes "outsider jurisprudence" that considers the histories and experiences of marginalized groups, including immigrants and those positioned outside the national identity. Chang and Aoki (1997) argue that CRT scholarship centers the immigrant in analyses of the social construction of borders, race, and national identity. Cho (1997) analyzes sexual harassment cases involving Asian Pacific American (APA) women university faculty members and calls for a change in how the law conceives of harassment. Due to the confluence of race and gender stereotypes shaped by immigration laws and cultural representations, APA women are constructed as the model minority female—as especially vulnerable to "racialized (hetero)sexual harassment" (Cho, 1997). Finally APACrit has moved into the post-9/11 world with Volpp's (2002) examination of the racialization of "Middle Eastern, Arab, or Muslim" people as terrorists and their disidentification as citizens. The formation of this new identity category is shaped by structures and ideologies of citizenship, nation, and identity. Some significant foci of APACrit are the shifting nature and definitions of citizenship, the exclusionary and discriminatory practices of immigration laws, and the standardization of APA groups as foils for real Americans (Jen, 2008).

Postmodernism has also been a major factor in reshaping identity studies—challenging it to move beyond its early "essentialist" tendencies to more complex and nuanced notions of the meaning, nature, and construction of both individual and group identities. Critiques of "identity politics" have come from many sectors: for example, from parts of the political right that perceive it as a form of balkanization of U.S. culture, from sectors of the political left that see it as a way of undermining class solidarity, and from postmodernist theory that sees it as an attempt to codify a continually shifting and contested set of ideological categories (Moya, 2002). To some extent, this critique stems from a conflict between two conceptualizations of identity—one that focuses on identity as a personal struggle taking place in the tension between the individual and the "groups" in which that individual holds membership and another that sees identity as part of a system of power and inequality in which certain categories and individuals within them receive unmerited rewards and benefits. These debates also reflect a split between theory and lived experience, between abstract ideas and political realities. As Martin Duberman (2001) astutely pointed out in an earlier column in *In These Times*,

> Many minority intellectuals are troubled about the inability of overarching categories or labels to represent accurately the complexities and sometimes overlapping identities of individual lives. We are also uncomfortable referring to "communities" as if they were homogeneous units rather than the hothouses of contradiction they actually are. We're concerned, too, about the inadequacy of efforts to create bridges between marginalized people. Yet we hold on to a group identity, despite its insufficiencies, because for most non-mainstream people it's the closest we have ever gotten to having a political home—and voice. (¶ 17–18)

The meanings and complexities of language and the images used to capture the insights and knowledge that intersectional analyses have produced continue to be central concerns for intersectional theory. Questions of language are compounded by the multiple intellectual domains in which this work is being generated and discussed. Each field approaches these issues through its own specific lens and specialized vocabulary. This process yields new insights and interdisciplinary ways of viewing the world, yet it readily lends itself to misinterpretation and miscommunication across disciplinary lines within and outside of academic spaces. Intersectional scholars must think carefully about whether or not there are ways to negotiate this tension so that intersectional scholarship provides greater clarity with regard to some of the most central concerns at issue—for example, what is social justice?—while allowing room for the vibrancy and messiness that interdisciplinary ideas necessarily generate.

Patricia Hill Collins suggests that we need debates that will clarify what is meant by social justice, and, at the same time, we must attend to the important work of providing a framework broad enough to accommodate people's different locations within these debates (Patricia Hill Collins, personal communication, 2001). She finds herself wanting to return to language with long historical roots that resonate for people outside the academy. For example, she prefers the notion of racism to that of race because, she argues, racism is a term that people recognize as politicized—one in which notions of power and inequality are embedded. It is also a term that is not limited to the U.S. context. Additionally, intersectional scholars can facilitate these discussions by seeking to explicate with even greater specificity the differences in form, structure, and impact of the different dimensions of inequality. Gender, for example, creates distinctions (male, female, etc.) that are structured to interact in intimate ways in social institutions (families) while race creates distinctions (Black, White, etc.) that are often structured into separate and unequal institutions (ghettos, Jim Crow segregation). Examining these kinds of similarities and distinctions will provide considerable richness and nuance to the field in the future.

Embedded in discussions of identity are debates about authenticity and representation as they concern national, international, and global affairs. These concerns are raised not only in the scholarship but also in the hiring, tenure, and promotion of faculty. Among these debates is the issue of who studies whom and who speaks for whom—that is, who represents the "authentic" voice or voices of a particular community or communities. Questions of speaking for and writing about "the other" have been central to the development of this scholarship.

Faculties and departments where there is a growing emphasis on scholarly questions related to race and ethnicity often face a limited supply of faculty of color and, therefore, often find themselves grappling with these issues in hiring decisions and in those attendant to reappointment, promotion, and tenure. Once hired, faculty of color most often come to realize that they are expected to "represent" people of color as a kind of "spokesperson," in a variety of service capacities, none of which are incorporated fully into their compensation or tenure evaluations. Even departments and institutions with good intentions of making race, ethnicity, and difference central to their work rely heavily on a very small number of scholars of color who are personally committed to institutional change (Baez, 2000). This is a process that faculty members must traverse carefully, ensuring that they are sensitive to the needs of the institutions where they are employed, the needs of the students they serve, and their own personal comfort and commitment to social justice work. In addition, institutions need to make a stronger commitment to providing a climate in which scholars of color can grow and flourish. This means not only training and recruiting more scholars of color but working hard to support and maintain them in the distinctively "ivory" tower of higher education.

It is worth noting, however, that scholars on an academic career track continue to find it particularly challenging to engage in theory-practice connections. Many do this work on their own time because, as in most academic locations, they will not get credit for the practical or applied side of their work. Social justice work is not as well regarded nor as well rewarded as academic publishing, and junior scholars are often warned against "widening their focus" beyond the traditional requirements for tenure. In addition, this work takes a sustained investment of time and personal energy to ensure that one maintains one's focus on social justice and outcomes that impact the lives of everyday people. These scholars must conceive of the challenges enumerated previously not as obstacles but as roadmaps illuminating the pedagogy that grows out of the lived experience of people from disadvantaged social, political, and economic locations; therefore, research must be conducted in such a way that it is neither intrusive nor exploitive of the community on which it is focused. Developing these linkages between scholarship and praxis takes an inordinate amount of time and requires the nurturing necessary to ensure some benefit to local communities. In short, these projects should benefit the community as much as, or perhaps even more than, the individual researcher or team. Although the concept of the "engaged university" offers some acknowledgement of this kind of work, it will require continuous effort to move engaged scholarship closer to the center of university missions.

Intersectional work primarily takes place in institutional settings composed of scholars and practitioners dedicated to bringing about change, and, given this, the primary agenda for utilizing this theory must be in creating and discovering previously unlooked-for analyses and histories. Using an intersectional framework means more interdisciplinary work will be focused on the historical and geographical context of events, attitudes, and cultures—and on work that is meant to transform rigid boundaries between existing institutional structures (Weber, 2009).

For a variety of educational, social, economic, and political reasons, colleges and universities are increasingly working to develop programming and public images that highlight diversity. Most often, this notion of diversity focuses on improving human relations throughout the campus by increasing awareness, acceptance, understanding, and appreciation of human differences. Rarely does it focus on the inequalities of power and resources embedded in these differences because this would require more confrontation and redirection of the very diversity initiatives

being proposed than most institutions are willing to sponsor. Perhaps because of this institutional dilemma, it is even more rare that the expertise of intersection scholars is seen as central to this interdisciplinary enterprise. The push for diversity and multiculturalism coincides with a push toward a more business-centered and entrepreneurial academy, rising tuition and fees, reduced state and federal support, and increasing student debt. By its own definition, intersectional scholarship must be produced in pursuit of social justice that purposefully interrogates how power infiltrates the research and funding processes. Intersectional work often engages with off-campus communities and integrates nonacademic voices and experiences into its findings. The results aim to fuel changes in unjust practices across a wide variety of dimensions of social and political life.

CONCLUSION

In 1979, Audre Lorde stood before an audience at a conference devoted to Simone de Beauvoir's book *The Second Sex* in New York City and spoke these words:

> Those of us who stand outside the circle of this society's definition of acceptable women; those of us who have been forged in the crucibles of difference—those of us who are poor, who are lesbians, who are Black, who are older—know that *survival is not an academic skill.* It is learning how to stand alone, unpopular and sometimes reviled, and how to make common cause with those others identified as outside the structures in order to define and seek a world in which we all can flourish. It is learning how to take our differences and make them strengths. (Lorde, 1984, p. 112)

More than three decades later, Lorde's clear mandate for social justice resonates at the very core of what intersectionality was, is, and must continue to be in order to serve the aims of those individuals who have found themselves to be situated in different social locations around the margins of feminist debates and inquiries. Just as Lorde called for feminists to turn difference into strengths, the theoretical paradigm of intersectionality has provided a voice and a vision to scholars seeking to make visible the interlocking structures of inequality to be found within the academic and everyday concerns that shape both our livelihoods and our experiences of the world.

Intersectionality has traveled a long distance, and, indeed, we recognize that it has taken many forms across academic disciplines and life histories. Intersectionality has now reached the point where it may be regarded as a member of the theoretical cannon taught in courses on law, social sciences, and the humanities. Intersectionality has, thus, increased in strength and, perhaps alternatively, suffered significant dilution in application as often happens when any theoretical tool is either misinterpreted or misapplied. As to the evidence of intersection theory's increasing strength, we know that intersectionality has been the practice of Black feminist scholars for generations; in that respect, this paradigm is not at all new. It has just been a long time coming into its own, and now, having been newly embraced as a powerful tool of social justice, social thought, and social activism by a larger population of feminist researchers, it has become more visible than ever before.

As to the evidence of its misapplication, we caution scholars to be mindful of what we consider to be "strong intersectionality" and "weak intersectionality." "Strong intersectionality" may be found in theoretical and methodological rubrics that seek to analyze institutions and identities *in relation to one another.* That is, "strong intersectionality" seeks to ascertain how phenomena are mutually constituted and interdependent, how we must understand one phenomenon in deference to understanding another. On the other hand, "weak intersectionality" explores differences without any true analysis. That is to say, "weak intersectionality" ignores the very mandate called for by Audre Lorde and seeks to explore no more than how we are different. "Weak intersectionality" eschews the difficult dialogue(s) of how our differences have come to be—or how our differences might become axes of strength, fortification, and a renewed vision of how our world has been—and continues, instead, to be socially constructed by a theory and methodology that

seeks only occasionally to question difference, without arriving at a deep and abiding understanding of how our differences are continuing to evolve.

Part of the proliferation of "weak intersectionality" may be found in the interdisciplinary narratives advancing the argument that this paradigmatic tool operates in different ways in different institutional spaces. This argument is also reminiscent of the contention that intersectional theory has been individualized within separate fields of knowledge. We can only reply to such arguments by, first, acknowledging that intersectionality has developed disparately within different spheres of knowledge because of the way in which intersectional theorizing is applied across disciplinary fields. For example, some might encounter intersectionality as a concrete reality that hinders effective litigation under the law because whole people are literally required to split their identity(ies) in order to be properly recognized in a court of law. But when this same legal phenomena is read and discussed in the social sciences or humanities, the scholars at issue might study it as a structural impediment or analytic frame that defies discrete analysis. That being said, this dilemma has the very real potential of diverting one's attention away from the theoretical imperative of intersectionality as source of illumination and understanding to one that distorts and misrepresents lived experiences of the law, social norms, and social justice.

But we also recognize, as a second proposition, that intersectionality has developed differently across spheres of knowledge because of the differing experiences and privileges we enjoy as scholars and everyday citizens of the world. We noted previously, for example, that intersectionality has benefited tremendously from differing methodological applications and transnational discourses, even as we remain steadfast in our contention that this paradigm was born of the experiences of Black women in the United States that could not be properly understood using the unidimensional lens of race or of gender in academic and legal discourses.

Having established the foregoing premises of "strong intersectionality" and "weak intersectionality," we now see intersectional theorizing developing into a paradigm of analysis that defies separation into distinct fields of knowledge because of its explanatory power as a theoretical tool that does not require tweaking "to make it fit," so to speak. This is because the primacy of the basic core principles of intersectionality—that is, mutually constituted interdependence; interlocking oppressions and privileges; multiple experiences of race, gender, sexuality, and so forth—are now more widely recognized as such and scholars are more apt to hold one another to these basic rules of application, whatever methodology is employed. In fact, the debates occurring within intersectional scholarship today reflect the growth and maturation of this approach and provide the opportunity to begin, as Lynn Weber says, to "harvest lessons learned" (as cited in Dill & Zambrana, 2009, p. 287).

Among the lessons learned and knowledge produced is a broader and more in-depth understanding of the notion of race, racial formation, and racial projects. Another is a broader understanding of the concept of nation and of notions of citizenship both in the United States and globally. Concepts such as situated knowledge (Lorde), oppositional consciousness (Sandoval), and strategic essentialism (Hurtado) offer ways to theorize about difference and diversity. A third lesson is the knowledge that there is no single category (race, class, ethnicity, gender, nation, or sexuality) that can explain human experience without reference to other categories. Thus we have and will need to continue to develop more nuanced and complex understandings of identity and more fluid notions of gender, race, sexuality, and class. The work relies heavily on a more expanded sense of the concept of social construction and rests much of its analysis on the principle of the social construction of difference. Organista (2007) contests the dominant culture's imperialism and resistance to discussion of human differences within and across cultures and calls for a discussion of difference "beyond the kind of defensive and superficial hyperbole that leaves social oppression unchallenged" (p. 101). And, although the scholarship still struggles with the pull to establish either a hierarchy of difference or a

list that includes all forms of social differentiation, both of which are antithetical to the specific objectives of intersectionality, a body of knowledge is being produced that provides a basis for understanding the various histories and organizations of these categories of inequality. This evolving body of knowledge is helping us better understand what differences render inequalities and how to resist reductionist impulses. As a theoretical paradigm,[2] intersectionality is unique in its versatility and ability to produce new knowledge. We remain optimistic about the future of intersectionality, particularly if this scholarship respects its crucial commitments to laying bare the roots of power and inequality, while continuing to pursue an activist agenda of social justice.

Discussion Questions

1. What are the historical and theoretical origins of intersectionality?

2. How is intersectionality distinct from other theoretical paradigms explaining inequality?

3. What has been the impact of intersectional theorizing on developments in transnational feminisms, sexuality studies, and legal policy?

4. How has the experience of Black women been instrumental in the articulation of intersectionality?

5. What does it mean to be "essentialized"? Have you ever had this experience? What are the practical implications of essentialism—positive and negative? Can intersectional theory be considered an essentialist concept? Why and/or why not?

6. Describe some of the ways our legal system reflects the concepts inherent in intersectionality. What other societal institutions reflect most of these concepts?

Online Resources

African American Policy Forum

http://aapf.org/

The African American Policy Forum works to bridge the gap between scholarly research and public discourse related to inequality, discrimination, and injustice. The AAPF seeks to build bridges between academic, activist, and policy-making sectors in order to advance a more inclusive and robust public discourse on the challenge of achieving equity within and across diverse communities.

University of California, Berkeley, Center for Race & Gender

http://crg.berkeley.edu/

The Center for Race & Gender (CRG) is an interdisciplinary research center at the University of California, Berkeley that fosters explorations of race and gender, and their intersections.

Consortium on Race, Gender and Ethnicity

http://www.crge.umd.edu

The Consortium on Race, Gender and Ethnicity (CRGE) at the University of Maryland is an interdisciplinary research center that promotes intersectional scholarship through original research, mentoring, and collaboration. CRGE's work explores the intersections of race, gender, ethnicity, and other dimensions of inequality as they shape the construction and representation of identities, behavior, and complex social relations.

Center for Women's Global Leadership at Rutgers, The State University of New Jersey: Background Briefing on Intersectionality

http://www.cwgl.rutgers.edu/globalcenter/policy/bkgdbrfintersec.html

This page provides information about the issue of intersectional discrimination as it has been recognized by the human rights system of the United Nations.

Relevant Journals

Advances in Feminist Research

Feminist Studies

Gender & Society

Meridians

Race, Gender and Class

Signs: Journal of Women in Culture and Society

NOTES

1. This list is not meant to be exclusive or exhaustive but a reflection of the breadth of early intersectional scholarship: Patricia Hill Collins (1990), Kimberlé Crenshaw (1989), Gloria Anzaldúa (1987), Maxine Baca Zinn and Bonnie Dill (1996), Audre Lorde (1984), Angela Y. Davis (1981), Cherríe Moraga (1983), Chela Sandoval (1991), Chandra Talpade Mohanty (1988), and bell hooks (1984).

2. In 1998, Collins referred to intersectionality as an "emerging paradigm." In 2007, Hancock argues it has become a normative and empirical paradigm.

REFERENCES

Almaguer, T. (1994). *Racial fault lines: The historical origins of white supremacy in California.* Los Angeles: University of California Press.

Amott, T. L., & Matthaei, J. A. (1991). *Race, gender and work.* Boston: South End Press.

Amott, T. L., & Matthaei, J. A. (1996). *Race, gender and work* (New ed.). Boston: South End Press.

Anzaldúa, G. (1987). *La Frontera/Borderlands: The new Mestiza.* San Francisco: Aunt Lute Books.

Baca Zinn, M., Cannon, L. W., Dill, B. T., & Higginbotham, E. (1986). The costs of exclusionary practices in women's studies. *Signs: Journal of Women in Culture and Society, 11*, 290–303.

Baca Zinn, M., & Dill, B. T. (1996). Theorizing difference from multi-racial feminism. *Feminist Studies, 22*(2), 321–331.

Baez, Benjamin. (2000). Race-related service and faculty of color: Conceptualizing critical agency in academe. *Higher Education, 39*, 363–391.

Breines, W. (2006). *The trouble between us: An uneasy history of white and black women in the feminist movement.* New York: Oxford University Press.

Browne, I., & Misra, J. (2003). The intersection of gender and race in the labor market. *Annual Review of Sociology, 29*, 487–513.

Chang, R. S., & Aoki, K. (1997). Centering the immigrant in the international imagination. *California Law Review, 85*, 1395.

Cho, S. K. (1997). Converging stereotypes in racialized sexual harassment: Where the model minority meets Suzie Wong. *Journal of Gender, Race & Justice, 1*, 177–211.

Collins, P. H. (1990). *Black feminist thought: Knowledge, consciousness, and the politics of empowerment.* Boston: Unwin Hyman.

Collins, P. H. (1998). *Fighting words: Black women and the search for justice.* Minneapolis: University of Minnesota.

Collins, P. H. (2004). *Black sexual politics.* New York: Routledge.

Crenshaw, K. (1989). Demarginalizing the intersection of race and sex: A black feminist of antidiscrimination doctrine, feminist theory, and antiracist politics. *University of Chicago Legal Forum,* 139–167.

Crenshaw, K. (1991). Mapping the margins: Intersectionality, identity politics, and violence against women of color. *Stanford Law Review, 43,* 1241–1299.

Crenshaw, K. (1992). Whose story is it, anyway? Feminist and antiracist appropriations of Anita Hill. In T. Morrison (Ed.), *Race-ing justice, engendering power: Essays on Anita Hill, Clarence Thomas, and the construction of social reality* (pp. 402–440). New York: Pantheon Books.

Davis, A. Y. (1972). Reflections on the black woman's role in the community of slaves. *The Massachusetts Review, 13*(1/2), 81–100.

Davis, A. Y. (1981). *Women, race, and class.* New York: Random House.

Davis, K. (2008). Intersectionality as buzzword: A sociology of science perspective on what makes a feminist theory successful. *Feminist Theory, 9*(1), 67–85.

Delgado Bernal, D. (2002). Critical race theory, Latino critical theory, and critical raced-gendered epistemologies: Recognizing students of color as holders and creators of knowledge. *Qualitative Inquiry, 8*(1), 105–126.

D'Emilio, J. (2003). *Lost prophet: The life and times of Bayard Rustin.* New York: Free Press.

Dill, B. T. (1979). The dialectics of black womanhood. *Signs: Journal of Women in Culture and Society, 4*(3), 543–555.

Dill, B. T., & Zambrana, R. E. (2009). *Emerging intersections: Race, class, and gender in theory, policy, and practice.* New Brunswick, NJ: Rutgers University Press.

Duberman, M. (2001, July 9). In defense of identity politics. *In These Times, 25*(16). Retrieved June 2, 2011, from http://www.inthesetimes.com/issue/25/16/duberman2516.html

Ferguson, R. A. (2003). *Aberrations in black: Toward a queer of color critique.* Minneapolis: University of Minnesota Press.

Glenn, E. N. (2002). *Unequal freedom: How race and gender shaped American citizenship and labor.* Cambridge, MA: Harvard University Press.

Gotanda, N. (1995). Critical legal studies, critical race theory, and Asian American studies. *Amerasia Journal, 21,* 127–135.

Hancock, A. M. (2007). When multiplication doesn't equal quick addition: Examining intersectionality as a research paradigm. *Perspectives on Politics, 5*(1), 63–79.

Hancock, A. M. (2008). Intersectionality as a normative and empirical paradigm. *Politics & Gender, 3*(2), 248–254.

Harnois, C. E. (2005). Different paths to different feminisms? Bridging multiracial feminist theory and quantitative sociological gender research. *Gender & Society, 19*(6), 809–828.

Harnois, C. E. (2009). Imagining a "feminist revolution": Can multiracial feminism revolutionize quantitative social science research? In M. T. Berger & K. Guidroz (Eds.), *The intersectional approach: Transforming the academy through race, class, and gender* (pp. 157–172). Chapel Hill, NC: UNC Press.

Harper, P., Cerullo, M., & White, E. F. (1993). Multi/queer/culture. *Radical America, 24*(4), 27–37.

Henderson, D., & Tickamyer, A. (2009). Staggered inequalities in access to higher education by gender, race, and ethnicity. In B. T. Dill & R. E. Zambrana (Eds.), *Emerging intersections: Race, class, and gender in theory, policy, and practice* (pp. 50–72). New Brunswick, NJ: Rutgers University Press.

Hill, A. (2007, October 2). The smear this time [Op-ed]. *New York Times,* p. A25.

hooks, b. (1984). *Feminist theory: From margin to center.* Cambridge, MA: South End Press.

Hu-Dehart, E. (2007). Surviving globalization: Immigrant women workers in late capitalist America. In S. Harley (Ed.), *Women's labor in the global economy* (pp. 85–103). New Brunswick, NJ: Rutgers University Press.

Hurtado, A. (1996). *The color of privilege.* Ann Arbor: University of Michigan Press.

Ingraham, Chrys. (Ed.). (2005). *Thinking straight: The power, the promise, and the paradox of heterosexuality.* New York: Routledge.

Jen, C. (2008). *Technoscientific race-nation-gender formations in public health discourses*. Unpublished doctoral dissertation, University of Maryland, College Park.

Johnson, E. P., & Henderson, M. G. (Eds.). (2005). *Black queer studies: A critical anthology*. Durham, NC: Duke University Press.

Jones-DeWeever, Avis, Dill, Bonnie Thornton, & Schram, Sanford F. (2009). Racial, ethnic, and gender disparities in the workforce, education and training under welfare reform. In Bonnie Thornton Dill & Ruth E. Zambrana (Eds.), *Emerging intersections: Race, class and gender in theory, policy and practice* (pp. 150–179). New Brunswick, NJ: Rutgers University Press.

Ken, Ivy. (2007). Race-class-gender theory: An image(ry) problem. *Gender Issues, 24*, 1–20.

Ken, Ivy. (2008). Beyond the intersection: A new culinary metaphor for race-class-gender studies. *Sociological Theory, 26*(2), 152–172.

King, D. (1988). Multiple jeopardy, multiple consciousness: The context of a black feminist ideology. *Signs: Journal of Women in Culture and Society, 14*(1), 42–72.

Klein, J. T., & Newell, W. H. (1998). Advancing interdisciplinary studies. In W. H. Newell (Ed.), *Interdisciplinarity: Essays from the literature* (pp. 3–22). New York: College Entrance Examination Board.

Knapp, G. A. (2005). Race, class, gender: Reclaiming baggage in fast-travelling theories. *European Journal of Women's Studies, 12*(3), 249–265.

Kohlman, M. H. (2006). Intersection theory: A more elucidating paradigm of quantitative analysis. *Race, Gender & Class, 13*, 42–59.

Kohlman, M. H. (2010a). Race, rank and gender: The determinants of sexual harassment for men and women of color in the military. In V. Demos & M. Segal (Vol. Eds.), *Advances in gender research: Vol. 14. Interactions and intersections of gendered bodies at work, at home, and at play* (pp. 65–94). Boston: Elsevier.

Kohlman, M. H. (2010b). Spotlight: Anita Hill, feminist praxis today and yesterday. In Karen O'Connor (Ed.), *Gender and women's leadership: A reference handbook* (Vol. 1, pp. 204–208). Thousand Oaks, CA: Sage.

Landry, Bart. (2000). *Black working wives: Pioneers of the American family revolution*. Berkeley: University of California Press.

Latina & Latino Critical Legal Theory, Inc. (2011). *LatCrit*. Retrieved June 2, 2011, from the University of Connecticut, Puerto Rican and Latino Studies Institute website: http://www.latcrit.org/

Lorde, A. (1984). *Sister outsider*. Freedom, CA: The Crossing Press.

MacKinnon, C. (2010, March 11). *Panelist remarks on "Rounding intersectionality: Critical foundations and contested trajectories."* Paper presented at the 4th Annual Critical Race Studies Symposium—Intersectionality: Challenging Theory, Reframing Politics, Transforming Movements, UCLA School of Law, Los Angeles, CA.

Matsuda, M. J. (1996). *Where is your body: And other essays on race, gender, and the law*. Boston: Beacon Press.

McCall, L. (2001). *Complex inequality: Gender, class, and race in the new economy*. New York: Routledge.

McCall, L. (2005). The complexity of intersectionality. *Signs: Journal of Women in Culture and Society, 30*(3), 1771–1800.

Meyer, D. (2008). Interpreting and experiencing anti-queer violence: Race, class, and gender differences among LGBT hate crime victims. *Race, Gender, and Class, 15*(3/4), 262–282.

Mohanty, C. T. (1988). Under western eyes: Feminist scholarship and colonial discourses. *Feminist Review, 30*, 61–88.

Mohanty, C. T. (2003). *Feminism without borders*. Durham, NC: Duke University Press.

Moraga, C. (1983). *Loving in the war years*. Boston: South End Press.

Moya, P. (2002). *Learning from experience: Minority identities, multicultural struggles*. Berkeley: University of California Press.

National Academy of Sciences. (2005). *Facilitating interdisciplinary research*. Washington, DC: National Academies Press.

Organista, C. K. (2007). *Solving Latino psychosocial and health problems: Theory, practice, and populations*. Hoboken, NJ: John Wiley & Sons, Inc.

Parreñas, Rhacel. (2001). *Servants of globalization: Women, migration, and domestic work*. Stanford, CA: Stanford University Press.

Ribet, B. (2010, March 11). *Panelist remarks on "Intersectional research and practice."* Paper presented at the 4th Annual Critical Race Studies Symposium—Intersectionality:

Challenging Theory, Reframing Politics, Transforming Movements, UCLA School of Law, Los Angeles, CA.

Romero, M. (2008). The inclusion of citizenship status in intersectionality: What immigration raids tells us about mixed-status families, the state and assimilation. *International Journal of Sociology of the Family, 34*(2), 131–152.

Sandoval, C. (1991). U.S. third world feminism: The theory and method of oppositional consciousness in the postmodern world. *Genders, 10,* 1–24.

Sandoval, C. (2004). U.S. third world feminism: The theory and method of differential oppositional consciousness. In S. Harding (Ed.), *The feminist standpoint reader* (pp. 195–209). New York: Routledge.

Sherman, M. (2007, September 29). Justice Thomas writes autobiography. *NewsOK*. Retrieved June 4, 2011, from http://newsok.com/justice-thomas-writes-autobiography/article/3137013

Simien, E. (2007). Doing intersectionality research: From conceptual issues to practical examples. *Politics and Gender, 3*(2), 264–271.

Staunæs, D. (2003). Where have all the subjects gone? Bringing together the concepts of intersectionality and subjectification. *Nora, 11*(2), 101–110.

Stefancic, J. (1997). Latino and Latina critical theory: An annotated bibliography. *California Law Review, 85,* 1509–1584.

Valdes, F. (2010, March 13). *Panelist remarks on "Intersectionality by design: Epistemologies, disciplines, and discourse."* Paper presented at the 4th Annual Critical Race Studies Symposium—Intersectionality: Challenging Theory, Reframing Politics, Transforming Movements, UCLA School of Law, Los Angeles, CA.

Valentine, G. (2007). Theorizing and researching intersectionality: A challenge for feminist geography. *Professional Geographer, 59,* 10–21.

Vidal-Ortiz, S. (2004). On being a white person of color: Using autoethnography to understand Puerto Ricans' racialization. *Qualitative Sociology, 27*(2), 179–203.

Volpp, L. (2002). Critical race studies: The citizen and the terrorist. *UCLA Law Review, 49,* 1575–1600.

Weber, Lynn. (2009). *Understanding race, class, gender, and sexuality: An intersectional framework* (2nd ed.). New York: Oxford.

Williams, R. M. (1998). Living at the crossroads: Explorations in race, nationality, sexuality, and gender. In W. Lubiano (Ed.), *The house that race built* (pp. 136–156). New York: Vintage.

Wing, A. K. (Ed.). (1997). Brief reflections toward a multiplicative theory and praxis of being. In A. K. Wing (Ed.), *Critical race feminism: A reader* (pp. 27–34). New York: New York University Press.

Yuval-Davis, N. (2006). Intersectionality and feminist politics. *The European Journal of Women's Studies, 13*(3), 193–210.

Zambrana, R. E., & Logie, L. A. (2000). Latino child health: Need for inclusion in U.S. national discourse. *American Journal of Public Health, 90*(12), 1827–1833.

PART II

FEMINIST RESEARCH PRAXIS

9

THE SYNERGISTIC PRACTICE OF THEORY AND METHOD

SHARLENE NAGY HESSE-BIBER AND DEBORAH PIATELLI

In the introduction to *Feminism and Methodology*, Sandra Harding (1987) asked, "Is there a distinctive feminist method of inquiry?" (p. 1). Harding responded "no" and instead discussed the contributions of feminism to the practice of research, calling attention to the interrelatedness of epistemology, methodology, and method. Methods are simply research techniques, tools that get at the research problem, whereas epistemology shapes our research questions and the theories we hold about the social world. Methodology can be thought of as a bridge between epistemology and method, shaping *how* we approach and conduct research. Whether one's epistemology is rooted in empiricism, standpoint theory, postmodernism, or postcolonial critique, a feminist methodology challenges status quo forms of research by linking theory and method in a synergistic relationship that brings epistemology, methodology, and method into dynamic interaction across the research process. A feminist methodology can enhance the development of new methods tools that, in turn, can offer new

angles of vision, reshaping both our research questions and the way we build knowledge.

Feminist scholars have long argued that conventional science operates within a male-dominated paradigm (Harding, 1991, 1993; Hartsock, 1998; Reinharz, 1992; Smith, 1987). The scientific model of research subscribes to the tenets of verification, generalization, objectivity, value neutrality, and the unity of science or the belief that the logic of scientific inquiry is the same for all fields. Feminists have challenged these principles and argued that they are rooted in a historical, positivist, androcentric paradigm that produces biased research and supports an objective, hierarchical approach to knowledge building (Harding, 1986, 1991, 1993; Hartsock, 1998; Longino, 1990; Oakley, 1998; Reinharz, 1992; Smith, 1987). In Part II of this book, Sue Rosser, in her chapter "The Link Between Feminist Theory and Methods in Experimental Research," discusses how, historically, this model has produced flawed research by focusing only on male-centered problems; omitting females in experimental research, both as researchers and as subjects; and interpreting data in a patriarchal context. Moreover, this model has made neutral and universal scientific claims based on distorted data. Through the lens of several feminist perspectives, Rosser cites a number of examples and shows how feminist research has challenged "science as usual" (Harding, 1991) and produced less biased and more valid scientific research. Rosser demonstrates how the scientific model has been challenged across disciplines in the natural, physical, and social sciences and, to some degree, in engineering—specifically through the "choice and definition of problems chosen, approaches used, and theories and conclusions drawn from the research." For instance, by placing women in the center of analysis, feminist experimental research has made groundbreaking discoveries related to many health-related problems such as cardiovascular disease, various cancers, and AIDS. Hence, feminists have called for a decentering of the white male subject in research, allowing for a multiplicity of voices and diverse research issues to be brought to the forefront—producing more complete and trustworthy research.

Feminists not only question androcentric bias; they critique the hierarchical, deductive approach to knowledge building often found in conventional models of research. These approaches are laden with power and treat knowledge as something to be discovered rather than created (Collins, 2000; Haraway, 1991; Harding, 1991; Hartsock, 1998; Reinharz, 1992; Smith, 1987). Feminist researchers call attention to the partiality, fluidity, and situatedness of knowledge and seek new ways to approach knowledge building. *Who* can know, *what* can be known, and *how* we can construct the most authentic view of the social world are at the center of feminist concerns. Feminists advocate positioning the researcher "in the same critical plane" as their participants (Harding, 1987, p. 184) and rejecting the separation of object and subject, and they call for more participatory, reflexive approaches to knowledge construction. Knowledge building becomes a relational process rather than an objective product, a process that demands critical self-reflection, dialogue, and interaction (Collins, 2000; DeVault, 1990; Mies, 1983). This relational process

requires the researcher to make continuous shifts and negotiations in positionality and a commitment to address power imbalances along the entire research process, engaging participants in the telling and interpreting of their own lives and experiences (DeVault, 1990; Reinharz, 1992; Smith, 1987; Wolf, 1996). Dorothy Smith (1974, 1987, 1999) has written at length on the inadequacies of the scientific model in studying "the social," because research questions have negated the problems of women and marginalized people, thereby silencing their voices and experiences from public discourse. Most important to Smith is the failure of conventional research to place people's experiences at the center of its inquiry rather than appropriating experience to advance its own theoretical frameworks. Although feminists advocate the privileging of lived experience, they also acknowledge that experience is relational and mediated and that all knowledge claims must be interrogated and decentered (Collins, 2000; Haraway, 1991; Harding, 1991; Smith, 1987, 1999). Through continuous reflection about how biography and the historical and social context shape the research process, both the researcher and the participants integrate their situatedness into the process of knowledge building. This integration requires an active and collaborative rather than a passive role on the part of the researcher.

An inductive approach to knowledge building is the essence of grounded theory. Grounded theory as a mode of analysis emerged in the mid-1960s as a response to a myriad of critiques of qualitative research (Charmaz, 1995, 2000). Rather than taking a deductive approach to knowledge building in which researchers impose theories on the data, grounded theory turns interpretation and analysis on its head by generating theory from, rather than imposing theory on, the lives and experiences of those we research. Most important, grounded theory revitalized the importance of the interplay between theory and method, data collection and analysis, which conventional modes of research neglected (Charmaz, 1995, 2000; Coffey & Atkinson, 1996; Glaser & Strauss, 1967; Strauss & Corbin, 2000). In her chapter "Feminism, Grounded Theory, and Situational Analysis Revisited," Adele Clarke draws our attention to the implicit feminist assumptions of grounded theory: namely, it draws on and is grounded in the voices of participants and their experiences, values and acknowledges the multiplicity of interpretation and meaning, and facilitates the interaction and reflexivity of the researcher with the data. Clarke highlights the work of a number of feminist researchers who have made grounded theory more explicitly feminist. By choosing research topics that place gender at the center of analysis, feminist researchers are able to uncover silenced discourse and generate better knowledge that displaces inadequate theories and false stereotypes about women's lives.

In the spirit of grounded theory, the themes in this chapter were derived inductively by examining the writings in Part II. When reading the chapters in this section, we found that, although the contributors come from a variety of disciplines and hold varying epistemologies, they do share a common ground in terms of what constitutes a feminist perspective to research. A feminist perspective to research offers new angles of vision that can create opportunities for raising new questions, engaging in new kinds of relationships, discovering innovative research techniques, and organizing different kinds of social relations. The research questions feminists ask are often rooted in issues of social justice, social change, and social policy for women and other marginalized groups. By raising new questions, feminists push the boundaries on traditional theoretical paradigms and conventional methodological techniques and create spaces for innovative knowledge building and research practice. By focusing on the lives and experiences of those who are often silenced in public discourse, a feminist perspective can illuminate new ways of knowing that can challenge conventional assumptions that shape social policy and our lives.

The authors in this section attempt to initiate dialogue across disciplines, epistemologies, and methodologies to facilitate more inclusive and egalitarian research practices and processes. Through their writings, they demonstrate how they, as feminist researchers, challenge conventional views on power and knowledge as they select research questions; engage their participants; choose, invent, and practice research

techniques; and address social inequality. By engaging feminism and challenging status quo approaches to research, the authors in this *Handbook* demonstrate the synergistic relationship between epistemology, methodology, and method and bring subjugated knowledge into the forefront of public discourse.

FEMINIST PERSPECTIVES ON THE RESEARCH PROCESS

Asking New Questions That Challenge Power

The chapters in this section of the *Handbook* provide an array of insights into how a feminist perspective to research allows one to see features of the world that remain invisible to conventional research. Starting from the lives of marginalized people can provide new angles of vision and reveal new research questions (Collins, 2000; Harding, 1991; Smith, 1987). Focusing on marginalized knowledge has long been a priority within feminist discourse. Brinton Lykes and Rachel Hershberg, in their chapter "Participatory Action Research and Feminisms: Social Inequalities and Transformative Praxis," discuss the impact feminism has had on generating new forms of participatory and action research—"feminist-infused action and participatory research." Although conventional participatory action research prioritizes local knowledges, fosters empowerment, and furthers the transformation of social structures that promote inequality, Lykes and Hershberg argue that, traditionally, it has "failed to either include women as independent actors in their local projects or to problematize gender oppression and heterosexism." Sharon Brisolara and Denise Seigart, in their chapter "Feminist Evaluation Research," present a similar argument regarding conventional approaches to evaluation research. For these women, research is a political project. For Lykes and Hershberg, a feminist-infused action research approach addresses the absence of women and other marginalized people in traditional studies, values the multiplicity of experience and knowledge, and reinforces the strengths that vulnerable populations bring to social change work in their communities. By placing the focus on women and marginalized communities, this research approach raises new questions, brings silenced voices into public discourse, and facilitates social change. One of the many examples that Lykes and Hershberg offer of how feminist-infused action research uncovers and brings forth subjugated knowledge in a project is the research that Lykes and her colleague Jean Williams conducted in collaboration with Mayan women. Lykes and Williams worked in partnership with these women on a project documenting the history of violence this community had suffered over long periods of war. Weaving in multiple voices, this "collective history," written by and about the experiences of violence on women, has challenged conventional assumptions about who gets to write history and how it is documented and told. This project has also raised new questions about the impact of war on women. Moreover, through the process of telling, these women were able to reflect on and find ways to overcome barriers of difference and oppression in their community.

For Brisolara and Seigart, evaluation research that focuses on the concerns of underrepresented stakeholders, such as women and people of color, can raise new questions for the field around the purposes, processes, and outcomes of the evaluation project—questions concerning positionality, bias, plurality, and ethics. In their piece, Brisolara and Seigart offer an example of a feminist evaluation that demonstrates how feminist researchers were able to draw attention to the inadequacy of theories that correlate poverty with self-esteem issues and ignore the structural inequalities that contribute to the low self-esteem of many women. By engaging women in the evaluation, these researchers uncovered new lines of inquiry around the needs of poor women, such as family planning and affordable housing. Although they have produced exemplary works, both Lykes and Hershberg and Brisolara and Seigart point to the difficulties in *naming* this work feminist. Their concerns around this issue, along with those of other authors, are discussed in the latter section of this chapter.

Bringing a gendered lens to research and examining the ways in which gender is constructed and reconstructed within relations of power is emphasized in Wanda Pillow and Cris Mayo's chapter, "Feminist Ethnography: Histories, Challenges, and Possibilities." Pillow and Mayo argue that feminist ethnography, unlike conventional forms, uncovers new knowledge by "studying the lived experiences of gender and its intersectionalities" and then building theory from these lived experiences. Feminist ethnographies look at "what is missing, what is passed over, and what is avoided." By applying a gendered lens and interrogating the "continued interplay of race [class, sexuality] and gender in the structure of power," these ethnographies raise new questions about both conventional and unconventional topics.

Everyday experience as an entry point for investigation is emphasized in many of the writings in this section, for instance in Sarah Maddison and Frances Shaw's chapter, "Feminist Perspectives on Social Movement Research." Drawing parallels between feminist standpoint theory and the study of the processes of collective identity formation, Maddison and Shaw discuss their approach to research, which "begins by acknowledging and privileging an activist standpoint." In their work with two submerged networks of contemporary young feminist activists in Australia, Maddison and Shaw privilege the activist standpoint by giving activists "a voice in articulating their commitment, highlighting their strategic and fluid engagement with a differential consciousness, and revealing the processes by which they construct their collective identities." Like other feminist social movement scholars, Maddison and Shaw critique certain theoretical approaches to social movement research that have failed to acknowledge not only gender but also its intersection with other identities such as race, class, and ethnicity. By placing these concerns at the center of social analyses, researchers can attend to unresolved questions and better contribute to advancing the aims of social activists. Using a constructivist approach, Maddison and Shaw consider their participants' multiple standpoints and the impact their approach has on both creating and sustaining a collective understanding of *who they are.* Their analysis focuses not on the product of collective identity but rather on the process of how these women construct and reconstruct understandings of themselves and their place in the contemporary Australian women's movement.

Engaging in Collaborative Relationships

Raising new questions can bring feminist researchers into dialogue with new conversational partners. By focusing on inequalities that lead to social injustices, feminists are often drawn to working with vulnerable populations (Lather & Smithies, 1997), while others choose to *study up* and strive to uncover the hidden discourse of privileged populations and how it shapes daily social interaction (Frankenberg, 1993). Although relationships become more complicated as one ventures into conversations across multiple differences, the project of deconstructing power relations within the research context is important in all researcher and participant relationships. Feminists have long questioned the canon of objectivity and argued that a detached relationship exercises control and power over the participants and can run the risk of exploitation and abuse (Reinharz, 1992; Smith, 1987; Wolf, 1992). To minimize harm and control over both the process and the product, feminists have devised innovative research strategies that cultivate collaboration and emphasize reflexivity to make visible and lessen the power inherent in the research process.

At the root of feminist inquiry is attention to power and *how* knowledge is built. Feminist research takes people as active, knowing subjects rather than as passive objects of study. Knowledge is produced and mediated through lived experience and communicated through interaction in the form of face-to-face encounters, textual discourse, or visual media. Tapping into lived experience is the key to feminist inquiry and requires innovative practices in developing relationships and building knowledge. Through collaborative, reflexive practices, researchers and participants work to eliminate hierarchies of knowledge construction, and marginalized knowers are able to name themselves, speak for themselves, and construct a better

understanding of the structures and forces that influence their experience (Dodson, 1998). The power of a feminist perspective is that it enables us to bring into view how our everyday lives are affected by social institutions and uncover possibilities for change (Smith, 1987). A feminist perspective argues that, without empathic, interpersonal relationships, researchers will be unable to gain insight into the meaning people give to their lives (Collins, 2000; DeVault, 1990). Through collaborative inquiry and reflexive knowledge building, researchers can deconstruct hierarchical relationships and produce research that is useful and meaningful to participants and the larger society.

Embracing a participatory research strategy is the epitome of collaborative inquiry. Participatory inquiry incorporates collaboration across the research process from the development of the research question, to the conduct of research, through the interpretation and treatment of the data. In their respective chapters, Brisolara and Seigart and Lykes and Hershberg emphasize how collaborative inquiry holds the potential to shift positionalities, moving research participants from objects of study to agents over the research process. The role of the researcher is engaging and interactive, working with participants to promote dialogue, foster relationships, and collectively develop greater understanding about the social structures that oppress people on a daily basis. Other authors, such as Maddison and Shaw, discuss in their respective chapters how they bring collaborative practices into their research processes by placing their subjects at the center of their inquiries, generating their research questions directly from participants' lived experience.

Integral to this collaborative process is a commitment to reflexive knowledge building. Polyvocality is central to a feminist understanding of how knowledge is built. Feminists of color have drawn our attention to the multiplicity of knowledge and have asked us to consider the cultural, social, national, racial, and gendered composition of historically different and specific forms of knowledge. These situated knowledges are partial knowledges located in a particular time and space, the knowledges of specific cultures and peoples. These knowledges express a multiple reality; they are not fixed but are ever changing. They are both critical of and vulnerable to the dominant culture, both separated from it as well as opposed to it but also contained within it. Reflexive knowledge building occurs through the dialogical practice of sharing with others and considering the relationality between varying positionalities. Reflexive knowledge building requires the interrogation of social biographies and historical context, an examination of the intersectionality of privilege and power, and the decentering of knowledge claims around interpretation and representation. Stéphanie Wahab, Ben Anderson-Nathe, and Christina Gringeri, in their chapter "Joining the Conversation: Social Work Contributions to Feminist Research," show the connections of participatory research, reflexivity, and praxis between feminist and social work research. They look at the ways both fields overlap and the future opportunities for a combined field of feminist social work research. As social work is "concerned with the interactive and reflexive relationship between research, theories, practice, and social action," so feminist theory and methodology can further develop these principles, while social work, in turn, provides a field in which to execute feminist participatory action research as well as to "deconstruct taken-for-granted binary assumptions."

Listening, interacting, sharing, and translating are some of the techniques feminists have developed to foster greater connectedness, understanding, and self-empowerment (DeVault, 1990; Mies, 1983; Oakley, 1981; Smith, 1987). Marjorie DeVault and Glenda Gross, in their chapter "Feminist Qualitative Interviewing: Experience, Talk, and Knowledge," note that a feminist approach to interviewing can lessen power dynamics and create research that is more accountable and applicable to participants' lives. Sustained engagement in the field, personal disclosure on the part of the researcher, and contextualizing discourse are some of the ways feminist researchers have attempted to deconstruct power imbalances and allow for greater trust and rapport. Similarly, a feminist-infused participatory and action research approach problematizes both the researcher's and the participants' positionalities and how they interact within the context of the research project. Lykes and Hershberg draw attention to the many ways feminist researchers "work the hyphen" (Fine, 1998) by "challenging static, boundaried notions of 'insider' and 'outsider,'" clarifying "the mediated nature of all knowledge construction," and exemplifying "'ways of knowing' that are frequently absent from mainstream, top-down theory building" (Lykes & Hershberg, Chapter 16, this volume, p. 352).

Deboleena Roy (Chapter 15, this volume) analyzes how feminist research practices within the natural sciences were especially influenced by feminist engagements with ontological and ethical questions. Roy argues that feminist researchers must consider questions of ethics and ontology in the praxis of the scientific method. She proposes the inclusion of "playfulness" and "feeling around" in feminist research. Roy stresses the importance of feminist scientists need to be connected to the wider feminist community. She suggests that the feminist laboratory researchers engage in the practice of "reflexivity" that provides a research strategy of enabling the researcher to engage with the research at hand and with other researchers.

Innovating Research Techniques

By generating new questions and exploring new forms of knowledge, have feminists radically altered the terrain of research methods? A feminist perspective can transform the most conventional of methodological techniques. Feminists have criticized traditional quantitative research on various grounds, and many have called for the dissolution of the dualism of quantitative and qualitative methods in an effort to build an emancipatory social science. They have agreed that quantitative methods can be useful but say that they are in need of reformulation to avoid bias and the objectification of research participants, reduce the hierarchical nature of research relationships, and eliminate the reproduction of dominance (DeVault, 1999; Eichler, 1997; Harding, 1987, 1991; Jayaratne & Stewart, 1991; Mertens, 2003; Oakley, 1998; Sprague & Zimmerman, 1993; Stanley & Wise, 1993). Kathi Miner, Toby Jayaratne, Amanda Pesonen, and Lauren Zurbrügg, in their chapter "Using Survey Research as a Quantitative Method for Feminist Social Change," and Elizabeth Cole and Abigail Stewart, in

"Narratives and Numbers: Feminist Multiple Methods Research," discuss how traditional *quantitative* methods have been influenced by the feminist perspective. Because feminists are more likely to focus on questions relevant to social change and ensure that vulnerable voices are translated and represented accurately, Miner et al. argue that a feminist perspective can uniquely contribute to the survey process in the development of research questions and in the interpretation of findings. Several examples of survey research that reflect a feminist perspective are discussed, illustrating the transformative potential of the survey method in supporting social change. By proposing new lines of inquiry and examining data through multiple theoretical and social lenses, a feminist perspective to survey research can advocate for women and marginalized groups in the areas of education, legislation, and public policy.

Cole and Stewart address the dilemmas of combining quantitative and qualitative methods in a single study and demonstrate how quantitative methods can support, contextualize, or broaden data analyses and research questions. Moreover, in the hands of feminists, quantitative methods and analyses have been used to study different levels of inquiry; increase the researcher's potential for insight, understanding, and knowledge building; and, most important, influence public policy. Through their presentation of seven different models of integrating *narratives and numbers*, Cole and Stewart demonstrate how the principles of polyvocality, contextualization, authenticity of voice, and commitment to improving the lives of women and marginalized people—all of which are inherent in a feminist perspective—influence how quantitative methods are collected, interpreted, and applied.

Several chapters in this section illustrate how feminist researchers have also transformed conventional *qualitative* methods as well as generated new forms of methodological inquiry, such as institutional ethnography, feminist-infused participatory and action research, and feminist evaluation research. Marjorie DeVault and Glenda Gross discuss the necessary augmentations feminists have made to the practice of interviewing in order to excavate meaning and experience. DeVault and Gross explore the idea of "radical, active listening" as a key component of feminist interviewing. Radical, active listening involves a fully engaged relationship, whereby the researcher listens for gaps and silences and considers "what meanings might lie beyond explicit speech." Being an active listener is being attentive to "the complexity of human talk," the pauses and patterns of speech and emotion that appear in everyday talk and the placement of this talk within a historical and situational context. Radical, active listening helps create "knowledge that challenges rather than supports ruling regimes." While Lykes and Hershberg use conventional methods, such as focus groups and observation, their feminist orientations influence the practice of these techniques. Attention to consciousness-raising and to avoiding exploitation and decontextualization shape their interactions and their conversations with participants. When crossing boundaries of culture, language, and difference, feminists are required to invent new techniques to excavate experience and foster greater understandings. Lykes and Hershberg use more creative techniques such as photography, drawings, storytelling, and drama to engage a diverse array of participants.

Emergent methods are not solely restricted to data collection techniques. Clarke offers her "postmodern extension of grounded theory," which she calls "situational analysis." Similar to institutional ethnography, situational analysis uses mapping techniques to uncover the connections between material reality and discourse. Situational analysis builds on grounded theory in that it takes "the situation of inquiry itself" as the problematic versus "the main social processes—human action." In other words, situational analysis seeks to make the connections and disconnections visible between discursive positions and actors across time and space to uncover the voices of "implicated actors" (actors who are left out of public discourse on issues that affect their lives), and it reveals the ways in which public discourse and social policy are shaped by the more privileged and powerful in society.

Lykes and Hershberg draw not only on conventional forms but also on nuanced forms of interpretive processes to re-present data. For instance, in community-based research, researchers often seek out and cultivate relationships with "cultural interpreters" to assist in the difficult process of translating experiential meaning and ensuring that indigenous knowledge is appropriately represented. These "interpreters" or "translators" become "the experts" because the researcher takes a back stage in the interpretive process. Pillow and Mayo not only support active engagement by participants in the interpretative phase as well as throughout the research process, but also draw attention to the political implications of choosing to write in the voice of oneself or "the other." In their chapter, Pillow and Mayo offer many examples of how feminists are grappling with this issue and creating innovative strategies and styles for representing narratives. Similarly, Kathy Charmaz, in "Writing Feminist Research," explores not what feminists study and write but how they write it. Her chapter serves as both a theoretical background in feminist writing and a provider of practical advice to researchers. Charmaz explores how feminist researchers actually go about integrating their personal experiences and perspectives into the writing process and asks in what ways personal experience and perspective shape feminist texts. By sharing their own personal experiences and perspectives with readers, Charmaz argues, authors may actually improve the credibility of their research.

Fostering Social Justice and Social Change

Feminist research is committed to challenging power and oppression and producing research that is useful and contributes to social justice. It provides space for the exploration of broader questions of social justice because of the ways in which feminists have sought to address multiple forms of structural inequality, such as race, ethnicity, class, and sexuality, as well as gender. Research is political work, and knowledge building is aimed toward empowerment, action, and, ultimately, social transformation. Feminist research creates democratic spaces within the research process for cultivating solidarity and action. Feminist research "goes beyond documenting what is to proposing an alternative and imaginative vision of what should be" (Maguire, 1987, p. 104). For some, like Lykes and Hershberg, this work translates into full,

participatory studies that value local knowledge systems and support collective, community-based solutions to systems of inequality and oppression. For others, inquiry begins with people's everyday lives and experiences, reaches out and beyond the local to reveal the social processes that organize experience, and then comes back full circle to the origin of inquiry—to expand local knowledge with a view toward change. Or for social movement researchers such as Maddison and Shaw, inquiry begins as they place the voices of activists at the center of research and provide space for the development of tools and strategies that can support social change. And for many others, such as Brisolara and Seigart, this work generates research that influences public discourse and challenges conventional assumptions that shape social policy. While diverse in approaches and aims, feminists are socially engaged, committed activists in their own disciplines and in society at large.

In "Putting Feminist Research Principles Into Practice," Kristen Intemann looks at the ability of feminist research to influence the particular case of climate change studies, exploring the places at which scientific objectivity and social justice can meet. She argues that "an objective research community is one that is *responsible or fair* in representing phenomena, building models, interpreting data, adopting value judgments, making policy recommendations." Climate change is a particular area in which feminist researchers have the opportunity to see how environmental change and policy impact marginalized populations. Similarly, Lynn Weber and Jennifer Castellow's chapter, "Feminist Research and Activism to Promote Health Equity," stresses the importance of the "scholarship-activism connection" in conducting feminist research. They suggest three specific ways in which feminist scholars and researchers can strengthen the connection between research and social justice in any field: (1) making a stronger critique against "status quo research and policy," bringing into focus the globalizing structures that influence social policy research and debates; (2) making some specific improvements on how we theorize and practice research by focusing on what she terms the "intersections" between differences within and among groups and by utilizing a range of methods across the quantitative-qualitative divide; and (3) building links and coalitions across different activist groups to promote social change.

THE POLITICS OF PRACTICING A FEMINIST PERSPECTIVE IN RESEARCH

Are there risks in labeling your project "feminist?" While DeVault and Gross find that feminist research is a well-accepted approach in their discipline, feminist researchers sometimes encounter challenges in getting their work published or in obtaining funding. "Calling an evaluation a feminist evaluation is a political act," and Brisolara and Seigart argue that feminist evaluation researchers continue to have to defend their research on the grounds of positivist ideals such as objectivity, generalizablity, and value-free bias. In many disciplines, feminist research continues to be criticized for its action and advocacy agenda, its attention to emotionality and participatory methods. Brisolara and Seigart state that funders do not want to be "construed as too radical" and worry about "maintaining a particular image in the community" so as not to jeopardize future financial support by more conservative donors. Funders sometimes choose concerns that more closely match their needs than the needs of the community. This raises important ethical questions about who has control over the research project, process, and outcomes. DeVault and Gross and Pillow and Mayo caution researchers not only to consider the danger of "appropriation" and how material is disseminated and interpreted by various audiences but also to consider whether the data serve the population involved in the study. Although, in most cases, the researcher has the ultimate authority over how and what data are collected, processed, and distributed, researchers can undertake reflexive practices to share interpretive authority with participants so as to ensure better representation. However, as Pillow and Mayo point out, reflexivity cannot eliminate authority and privilege because "there is no resolution to the problem of speaking for others" (Richardson, 1997, p. 58). Recognizing and balancing the tension between writing for and writing with is a measure of accountable and reflexive research.

Risks to the researcher are not the only concerns in embarking on a feminist research project. It is the very bonds between the researcher and the researched that are created in collaborative inquiry that can present dilemmas for feminist researchers (Lal, 1996; Stacey, 1991; Wasserfall, 1993). Examining one's social privileges and biases, overcoming cultural and language barriers, and shifting the center of power from researcher to community are some of the many tasks of the reflexive researcher. Lykes and Hershberg warn that researchers who engage in close, interactive relationships should be aware of the potential for participants to feel misunderstood, disappointed, or exploited if the research effort fails to meet their expectations. It requires great effort on the part of the researcher to continuously find ways to examine reflexively her or his positionality, relationships, and the research process to ensure that confidentiality and trust are upheld.

Feminist research, although gaining recognition in some disciplines, still remains at the margins of mainstream research. Debates continue as to the legitimacy of feminist research that is deemed "too subjective" or "not scientific." What is not recognized fully is that getting at subjugated knowledge oftentimes requires going beyond traditional methods and reaching out across the quantitative and qualitative divide, as well as across our own disciplinary boundaries. Feminist researchers embrace the full terrain of research techniques, incorporate new disciplinary tools in their work, and, as needed, forge emergent tools to gain a fuller picture of reality. To move feminist research from the "margins to the center," feminist scholars must push on the boundaries of what is considered legitimate (read: positivistic only) research. This will require the creation of a feminist research community of knowledge building that has as one of its goals the legitimizing of women's scholarship and research. As part of this process of community building, there also needs to be an internal dialogue, not debate, among the different and sometimes competing feminist epistemologies and methodologies. Where are the differences and similarities within this community? How do feminists deal with difference across their range of epistemologies and methodologies? What are the most productive ways to raise the consciousness of the feminist research community as a whole in creating a viable force for contending with dominant research structures (see also Hesse-Biber & Leckenby, 2004)? This is the challenge we take up in this *Handbook*.

REFERENCES

Campbell, Marie, & Gregor, Frances. (2002). *Mapping social relations: A primer in doing institutional ethnography.* Aurora, ON: Garamond.

Campbell, Marie, & Manicom, Ann. (Eds.). (1995). *Knowledge, experience, and ruling relations: Studies in the social organization of knowledge.* Toronto, ON: University of Toronto Press.

Charmaz, Kathy. (1995). Grounded theory. In Jonathan Smith, Rom Harre, & L. Van Langenhove (Eds.), *Rethinking methods in psychology* (pp. 27–49). Thousand Oaks, CA: Sage.

Charmaz, Kathy. (2000). Grounded theory: Objectivist and constructivist methods. In NormanK. Denzin & Yvonna S. Lincoln (Eds.), *Handbook of qualitative research* (pp. 509–535). Thousand Oaks, CA: Sage.

Coffey, Amanda, & Atkinson, Paul. (1996). *Making sense of qualitative data: Complimentary research strategies.* Thousand Oaks, CA: Sage.

Collins, Patricia Hill. (2000). *Black feminist thought* (2nd ed.). New York: Routledge.

DeVault, Marjorie L. (1990). Talking and listening from women's standpoint. *Social Problems, 37,* 96–116.

DeVault, Marjorie L. (1999). *Liberating method: Feminism and social research.* Philadelphia: Temple University Press.

DeVault, Marjorie L., & McCoy, Liza. (2002). Institutional ethnography: Using interviews to investigate ruling relations. In Jaber Gubrium & James Holstein (Eds.), *Handbook of interview research* (pp. 751–776). Thousand Oaks, CA: Sage.

Dodson, Lisa. (1998). *Don't call us out of name: The untold lives of women and girls in poor America.* Boston: Beacon Press.

Eichler, Margrit. (1997). Feminist methodology. *Current Sociology, 45,* 9–36.

Fine, Michelle. (1998). Working the hyphens: Reinventing self and other in qualitative research. In Norman K. Denzin & Yvonna S. Lincoln

(Eds.), *The landscape of qualitative research* (pp. 130–155). Thousand Oaks, CA: Sage.

Frankenberg, R. (1993). *White women, race matters: The social construction of whiteness.* Minneapolis: University of Minnesota Press.

Glaser, Barney G., & Strauss, Anselm L. (1967). *The discovery of grounded theory: Strategies for qualitative research.* Chicago: Aldine.

Haraway, Donna. (1991). *Simians, cyborgs, and women.* New York: Routledge.

Harding, Sandra. (1986). *The science question.* New York: Cornell Press.

Harding, Sandra. (1987). *Feminism and methodology.* Bloomington: Indiana University Press.

Harding, Sandra. (1991). *Whose science, whose knowledge? Thinking from women's lives.* New York: Cornell Press.

Harding, Sandra. (Ed.). (1993). Rethinking standpoint epistemology: What is strong objectivity? In Linda Alcoff & Elizabeth Potter (Eds.), *Feminist epistemologies* (pp. 49–82). New York: Routledge.

Hartsock, Nancy. (1998). *The feminist standpoint revisited.* Boulder, CO: Westview.

Hesse-Biber, Sharlene Nagy, & Leckenby, Denise. (2004). How feminists practice social research. In Sharlene Nagy Hesse-Biber & Michelle L. Yaiser (Eds.), *Feminist perspectives on social research* (pp. 209–226). New York: Oxford University Press.

Jayaratne, Toby Epstein, & Stewart, Abigail J. (1991). Quantitative and qualitative methods in the social sciences: Current feminist issues and practical strategies. In Mary Margaret Fonow & Judith A. Cook (Eds.), *Beyond methodology* (pp. 85–106). Bloomington: Indiana University Press.

Lal, Jayati. (1996). Situating locations: The politics of self, identity, and other in living and writing the text. In Diane Wolf (Ed.), *Feminist dilemmas in fieldwork* (pp. 185–214). Boulder, CO: Westview.

Lather, Peggy, & Smithies, Chris. (1997). *Troubling the angels: Women living with HIV/AIDS.* Boulder, CO: Westview.

Longino, Helen. (1990). *Science as social knowledge: Values and objectivity in scientific inquiry.* Princeton, NJ: Princeton University Press.

Maguire, Patricia. (1987). *Doing participatory research.* Amherst: University of Massachusetts.

Mertens, Donna M. (2003). Mixed methods and the politics of human research: The transformative-emancipatory perspective. In Abbas Tashakkori

& Charles Teddlie (Eds.), *Handbook of mixed methods in social and behavioral research* (pp. 297–319). Thousand Oaks, CA: Sage.

Mies, Maria. (1983). Towards a methodology for a feminist research. In Gloria Bowles & Renate Duelli Klien (Eds.), *Theories of women's studies* (pp. 173–191). Boston: Routledge.

Oakley, Ann. (1981). Interviewing women: A contradiction in terms. In Helen Roberts (Ed.), *Doing feminist research* (pp. 30–61). London: Routledge & Kegan Paul.

Oakley, Ann. (1998). Gender, methodology and people's way of knowing: Some problems with feminism and the paradigm debate in social science. *Sociology, 32*(4), 707–731.

Reinharz, Shulamit. (1992). *Feminist methods in social research.* New York: Oxford University Press.

Richardson, Laurel. (1997). *Fields of play (constructing an academic life).* New Brunswick, NJ: Rutgers University Press.

Smith, Dorothy. (1974). Women's perspective as a radical critique of sociology. *Sociological Inquiry, 44,* 7–13.

Smith, Dorothy. (1987). *The everyday world as problematic: A feminist sociology.* Boston: Northeastern University Press.

Smith, Dorothy. (1999). *Writing the social: Critique, theory, and investigations.* Toronto, ON: University of Toronto Press.

Smith, Dorothy. (2002). Institutional ethnography. In Tim May (Ed.), *Qualitative methods in action* (pp. 150–161). Thousand Oaks, CA: Sage.

Smith, George W. (1990). Political activist as ethnographer. *Social Problems, 37*(4), 629–648.

Sprague, Joey, & Zimmerman, Mary K. (1993). Overcoming dualisms: A feminist agenda for sociological methodology. In Paula England (Ed.), *Theory on gender* (pp. 255–280). New York: Aldine de Gruyter.

Stacey, Judith. (1991). Can there be a feminist ethnography? In Daphne Patai & Sherna B. Gluck (Eds.), *Women's words: The feminist practice of oral history* (pp. 111–120). New York: Routledge.

Stanley, Liz, & Wise, Sue. (1993). *Breaking out again: Feminist ontology and epistemology.* New York: Routledge.

Strauss, Anselm, & Corbin, Juliet. (2000). Grounded theory methodology: An overview. In Norman K. Denzin & Yvonna S. Lincoln (Eds.), *Handbook of qualitative research* (pp. 273–285). Thousand Oaks, CA: Sage.

Wasserfall, Rahel R. (1993). Reflexivity, feminism, and difference. *Qualitative Sociology, 16*(1), 23–50.

Wolf, Diane. (1996). Situating feminist dilemmas in fieldwork. In Diane Wolf (Ed.), *Feminist dilemmas in fieldwork* (pp. 1–55). Boulder, CO: Westview.

Wolf, Margery. (1992). *A thrice told tale: Feminism, postmodernism, and ethnographic responsibility.* Stanford, CA: Stanford University Press.

10

FEMINIST ETHNOGRAPHY

Histories, Challenges, and Possibilities

Wanda S. Pillow and Cris Mayo

What is feminist ethnography? If ethnography is understood as a written account of culture based upon observation or participant observation within the field, that is, in the place or context that culture occurs, is feminist ethnography then research about women's culture? Women's lives and issues? And is feminist ethnography performed only by women? Or only applicable to women?

Although the emergence of feminist ethnography can be traced as a response to a lack of early ethnographic work on women's lives or to what many women scholars saw as misrepresentations of women's lives, in this chapter, we argue that feminist ethnography has had a significant and broad impact on the field of ethnography across disciplines including anthropology, communications, education, and sociology. This impact has influenced how ethnographers think about research relations in the field; practices of data collection, analysis, and writing; ethical considerations; and the purposes of research. We make this claim at an interesting moment for feminism and feminist theory, a moment when the merits and utility of feminism are challenged.

Indeed, some have declared that feminism is obsolete while others feel that feminism is irrelevant or too problematic in today's world. Is feminism relevant? Does gender matter? Even those who respond to these questions affirmatively acknowledge that feminism and particularly what is presented as a Western feminist movement have come under heated debate and attacks—from within, for its own essentialism, nationalism, perpetuation of race and class inequities, and generational differences, and from without, for its role in the national decline of moral values and the breakdown of societal structures, including the "traditional" two-parent, male-headed household family unit. Further, many question the viability of feminism in today's increasingly global world asking how feminism is possible when we acknowledge that there are such differences among women. How does feminism hold up as a theoretical and political theory for women when the category of "woman" is necessarily complex in order to take into account the range of experiences of women? How can there be a feminism that accounts for the myriad ways women experience being "woman" differently across varying cultures and histories and across markers of race, class, sexuality, and language?

187

Calls for feminism to be attentive to intersections of race, class, ethnicity, sexuality, disability, and gender have been around since feminism's beginnings, though certainly not always well manifested in dominant feminist groups. However, if we are not to retain feminism for its usefulness in naming and identifying the unique experiences of women, then what are we saying? While the challenges facing feminism in theory and praxis seem overwhelming, are we ready or able to *not* talk about gender? As Zillah Eisenstein (1994) succinctly states, "however differentiated gender may be, gender oppression exists" (p. 8), and, until gender ceases to matter, feminism is necessary, and, correspondingly, feminist research, including feminist ethnography, is necessary.

Thus, as we think about what it means to do feminist research, we work out of a feminism that entails a complex examination of the identity positions and community and cultural associations that structure the lives of variously gendered people. Understanding how gender is constituted differently and differently understood and experienced according to context offers insights into social, political, familial, and religious structures and discourses and into how power is embedded in our daily lived experiences. As feminists, we also understand that, while gender bias continues, in all its varied forms, so too gender advocacy needs to continue. In our examination of feminist methods of ethnography, we draw on an understanding that all forms of oppression operate simultaneously and that, in order to address gender bias, all forms of bias must also be examined and challenged. We also understand that the intersectionality of identity means that women of color or of nondominant sexuality or with disabilities will experience gender as outsiders within, simultaneously understanding their gendered identity but also knowing that gender is imbricated in all other forms of identity.

Here, then, we use the term "feminist" with an acknowledgment of its troublesome history and usages, because we need it. At present feminism and feminist theory remains the only lens that specifically names and is reflexive about the politics and problematics of gender and that offers a means of analysis of the complicated

ways gender, race, sexuality, class, and embodiment are distinct yet intertwined in dominant structures of power. While holding on to the term "feminist" to describe trends in feminist research, here specifically ethnography, we assume that such research attends to the processes and problems entailed by the concept of gender, foregrounding, for example, questions such as these: How do we keep open the question not of what gender is but of how it operates? How do we remain attentive to the complex interactions of identities that constitute gender? How do we understand gender as not necessarily existing in "appropriate" bodies?

Thus, the feminist theory we speak of in this chapter is a feminism that recognizes the existence of a "racialized patriarchy" and points to the "continued interplay of race [and class and sexuality] and gender in the structure of power" (Eisenstein, 1994, p. 3). As Patricia Hill Collins (1990) explains it,

> Intersectionality . . . highlights how African American women and other social groups are positioned within unjust power relations, but it does so in a way that introduces added complexity to formerly race-, class-, and gender-only approaches to social phenomena. The fluidity that accompanies intersectionality does not mean that groups themselves disappear, to be replaced instead by decontextualized, unique individuals whose personal complexity makes group-based identities and politics that emerge from group constructions impossible. Instead, the fluidity of boundaries operates as a new lens that potentially deepens understanding of how the actual mechanisms of institutional power can change dramatically even while they reproduce long-standing group inequalities of race, class, and gender. (p. 68)

While we argue that ethnography needs to be attentive to intersectionality and processes of gender constitution, we also emphasize that identity categories continue to have meaning for people, even as they critically understand how those categories operate. In other words, there are aspects of ascribed identities that are pushed on groups and are oppressive, but there are other aspects of those identities that are useful to the groups themselves and may even be opposed to oppression. Further, when we think about inter-sectionality, we stress that all aspects of identity and community are not similarly arrayed along a leveled list: in a racist context, race will have more weight of meaning, experience, and poli-tics; in a homophobic context, sexuality may trump gender, even though we might see that homophobia is constituted through gender bias.

Highlighting feminism's and feminist theo-ry's necessary intersectionality both histori-cally and at present, we explore the arena of feminist ethnography considering what makes feminist ethnography unique. Is there a femi-nist ethnography? What does it mean to call ethnography "feminist"? What does a feminist ethnography look like? Does feminist ethnog-raphy study different issues or study issues differently? Who can do feminist ethnography? We ask the reader to keep these questions in mind when reading the remainder of this chap-ter.[1] These questions provide a basis for con-sidering how feminist ethnography operates across what we here characterize as four stages of doing research:

- choosing,
- doing,
- analyzing and writing, and
- endings.[2]

Utilizing reflective notes and experiences from one of the authors' ethnographic research, we explore what is uniquely *feminist* across each of these stages.[3]

In order to situate the discussion of the stages and data examples, we begin with a brief over-view of the history, shifts, and debates in femi-nist ethnography and then take up these shifts and debates within each of the stages previously delineated. We conclude with consideration of where feminist ethnography is now poised and where it might be heading. As this chapter makes evident, it is one thing to say one will do a feminist ethnography and another to actually do it. We hope that the challenges involved in actually doing feminist ethnography are ones that will be taken up by those readers who are engaging with feminist theory and research and those who believe they will themselves be doing feminist ethnography.

Introducing Feminist Ethnography

Defining what feminist research is cannot be separated from feminist theory's ontology and epistemology. Even the brief overview pre-sented here of feminist ethnography's history reveals that issues that were key to feminist research in the 1970s—including relationships with subjects and the politics of representation, reflexivity, and power—remain pertinent and foremost today. When we consider how and why it is that these issues have remained press-ing for feminist researchers, it is helpful to return to Sandra Harding's (1987) question, "Is there a feminist method?" Harding's response to this question is "no." Rather, she argues that, although methods (the way we collect our data, i.e., observations, interviews, surveys) are lim-ited in scope (there are only so many tools we can use to collect our data), our methodologies (lens of doing our research) and epistemologies (our knowledge bases) are multiple. Feminism thus provides a methodological and epistemo-logical lens for *the doing* of research methods.

There may not be distinct feminist methods, then, but there are feminist methodologies and epistemologies that impact our use of methods. That is, the method may be changed or altered by the lens the researcher approaches the meth-ods with, as in the case of, for example, femi-nist interviewing. In short, how we do our methods is impacted by feminist methodologies and epistemologies, and which methodologies and epistemologies we use matters when we do research (Pillow, 2003b). This is an acknowl-edgement that what we study, analyze, and write and how we study, analyze, and write are integrally connected to our methodological and theoretical lens.[4]

Shulamit Reinharz (1992) provides an excel-lent and thorough overview of feminist research in the social sciences in which she states that feminist theory and research are about "ques-tions of identity (what are feminist research methods?) and of *difference* (what is the differ-ence between feminist research methods and other research methods; how do feminist research methods differ from one another?)" (p. 3). Reinharz reviews a variety of methods feminist researchers use and how their use is altered by feminist theory and practice. Or, if we use Harding's definitions, Reinharz considers how methods of research are changed by encounters with feminist methodologies and epistemologies. Reinharz notes that research methods are always conducted within and against past and present methods, and she includes a review of feminist uses of interviewing, ethnography, oral history, content analysis, case studies, action research, survey and statistical research, and mixed or multiple methods. Reinharz's review and Harding's negative response to the question of whether there is a feminist method widen the arena of what are typically thought of as feminist methods. Whereas early feminist researchers argued that interviewing is the only method of feminist research, Reinharz and Harding make the case that feminists may engage in and use multiple methods for their research. What is important is *how* research is conducted and to what purpose.

For example, feminist research, according to Reinharz, is

1. focused upon analyzing and understanding gender within the context of lived experiences,

2. committed to social change, and

3. committed to challenging thinking about researcher subjectivity and the relationship between the researcher and the researched.

Applying Reinharz's characterization of feminist research in general to ethnography identifies several trends in feminist ethnography and alternatives to traditional ethnographic methods. First, however, in order for us to understand the relationship between feminist theory and ethnography, it is helpful to review the climate in which the work of feminist ethnography has been conducted.

Similar to waves of feminist thought and action (Nicholson, 1997), feminist ethnography has developed and changed through key shifts in social theory and political social action. Further, the field and arena of qualitative research and ethnography as a whole has impacted thinking about feminist ethnography. For instance, Denzin and Lincoln (2008) identify what they describe as "eight moments" of qualitative research, delineating a history of key

shifts, key "moments," in the arena of qualitative research, including ethnography. These moments include the traditional, modernist, blurred genres, crisis of representation, and postmodern periods, with post-experimental, methodologically contested present and future moments representing the sixth, seventh, and eighth moments.

In Denzin and Lincoln's model, feminist research and ethnography rises in importance in the third moment of blurred genres, a moment that "blurs" lines between the humanities and social sciences and science and ethnography. Feminist research is also integral to the fourth moment, which is marked by a perceived crisis of representation in qualitative research and ethnography—a moment that calls into question the ability of the researcher to represent and raises critical questions about researcher authority, identity, and the ethics of representation. This moment is highlighted by attentiveness, which some find paralyzing, to the politics of the gaze in ethnographic research. Who is researching whom, why, and how became integral to ethnographic writings in this period and led to a rise of researcher confessionals and practices of reflexivity in ethnographic writing. Questions of representation and practices of reflexivity are integral to feminist ethnography in which attention to the specificities of identity and power relations are primary to the research.

Similarly, feminist research and ethnography have been integral to shifts and debates within what Denzin and Lincoln describe as the postmodern and future moments of research. As is apparent in the previous description of feminist research, feminist ethnography begins from a different place than traditional ethnography, a place that questions the power, authority, and subjectivity of the researcher as it questions the purposes of the research (Oakley, 1981). Feminist ethnography has thus often initiated and impacted new ways of thinking about the doing of research and ethnographic writing. The specific contributions and questions raised by feminist ethnographers in postmodern research and future moments of research are raised at the end of this chapter, but it is important to highlight again here that consistent across feminist ethnography is a focus upon gender and its intersectionalities as central to the praxis and theory of research. This emphasis is evident precisely because a history of ethnographic traditions left out, ignored, or essentialized gender, both in terms of those who produce feminist ethnography and in terms of the study of gender.

The absence of feminist productions of ethnography was made apparent by a 1986 volume, *Writing Culture: The Poetics and Politics of Ethnography*, edited by two well-known anthropologists, James Clifford and George Marcus. *Writing Culture* signaled a crisis in representation in ethnographic writing and called for a new self-awareness within the discipline, but the volume excluded and ignored feminist ethnographic writing, including only one feminist writer, a literary critic, not an ethnographer. Although it called for a "new ethnography" that would investigate and make visible power and truth relations through the writing of ethnographies that are more dialogical, experimental, and reflexive, *Writing Culture* did not acknowledge the work and contributions of feminist writers to this agenda. Justifying this exclusion, Clifford declared that the absence of feminist writing in the volume was because those women anthropologists whom he determined had made contributions to ethnographic writing "had not done so on feminist grounds," while feminist ethnographers who had worked to challenge the canon of ethnography had not "produced either unconventional forms of writing or a developed reflection on ethnographic textuality as such" (Clifford & Marcus, 1986, pp. 21–22).

As Ruth Behar and Deborah Gordon (1995) note, "To be a woman writing culture became a contradiction in terms: women who write experimentally are not feminist enough, while women who write as feminists write in ignorance of the textual theory that underpins their own texts" (p. 5). Further, Behar and Gordon note that the "innovative" practices written of in *Writing Culture*—reflexivity, use of personal voice, attention to the textuality of the written text— were "undermined when used by women" yet "given the seal of approval in men's ethnographic accounts" (p. 4). Behar and Gordon's 1995 edited volume, *Women Writing Culture*, can be read as a feminist response to *Writing Culture* and was dramatically influenced by the initial 1981 publication of *This Bridge Called*

My Back, edited by Cherríe Moraga and Gloria Anzaldúa (1983). *This Bridge* challenged and opened up what feminist issues, subjects, and writings are, and, as Behar and Gordon state, "*This Bridge* thrust a different kind of arrow into the heart of feminist anthropology—it made us rethink the ways in which First World women had unself-consciously created a cultural other in their images of 'Third World' or 'minority' women" (p. 6). In this way, Behar and Gordon point out that feminist ethnography was forced to "come home," to focus upon its own assumptions, its own agendas. *This Bridge* further signified a shift and a crisis for ethnography and feminist ethnography, a questioning of who has the right to write culture for whom, a grappling with what it means to write and to write ethnography from a "native" perspective. The issues, questions, and crisis raised by *Writing Culture*, *Women Writing Culture*, and *This Bridge* have shaped feminist ethnography, and the challenges raised in these publications remain key to ethnography today.

As the previous brief review has demonstrated, anthropology has had a tense relationship with feminist productions of ethnography, sometimes ignoring or dismissing them. The ethnographic study of gender is also a history of absences, tensions, and shifts. For example, the 1960s and 1970s experienced a growing momentum of interest in the study of cultural perspectives in education. This new perspective, often termed the "new sociology," worked against traditional positivistic education theory and questioned the accepted hierarchical structure of knowledge (Acker, 1992). The work of both Freire (1970) and Willis (1977) helped focus emphasis on studying the "underprivileged" and working class. While such theorists introduced issues of patriarchy and agency, gender differences were not considered of major importance and therefore were not explicitly explored. When gender was included as a unit of analysis, it was often as an add-on to a list of other social indicators. Much of the existing research on women centered on a "female as deficit" model—research that studied women from the perspective of men as the norm.

Feminist research seeking to refute the prevailing "woman as deficit" model placed women at the center, emphasized the "personal as political," and sought to improve the situation of women by giving voice to women's experiences and focusing on women's own interpretations of their experiences (Belenky, Clinchy, Goldberger, & Tarule, 1986; Gilligan, 1982; Leck, 1987; Statham, Richardson, & Cook, 1991). This research worked from and further reinforced the necessity of feminist theory and practice and sought to identify "women's ways of knowing"—finding, naming, and reclaiming common characteristics across women's experiences and ways of being. Much of this research affirmed and "proved" what was already believed about women—that women are, for example, more relational, more empathetic in their relationships with others, personal or professional. However, feminist theorists soon found that such markers of womanhood could continue to oppress women (e.g., if women are innately more caring, then they are best suited for careers in the caring professions and not for technical or tactical careers). Facing this problem, a new wave of feminist researchers sought to resist binary, essentialized notions of understanding gender while still placing women at the center of their research. For example, Barrie Thorne's research complicated the recovery of "women's ways of knowing" by showing the processes by which "children act, resist, rework, and create" gender (Thorne, 1993, p. 3). By shifting from an analysis that assumes the salience of gender to one that examines the where and when of gender salience, Thorne gives us a way to understand when gender is open to contestation, when it recedes from importance, and when it is a crucial site for meaning making.

This shift from the purpose of feminist research being to identify a set of characteristics common to the category of women to research that seeks to understand gender as performative and further understand this performativity as altered by intersections with race, sexuality, class, and embodiment has led to a wealth of feminist ethnography exploring and rethinking the intersections of gender, race, class, and embodiment (Alexander, 2006; Davies, 1989; Evans-Winters, 2005; Miranda, 2003; Moraga, 1997; Patai, 1988; Valenzuela, 1999; Walkerdine, 1990). Further, the roles, responsibilities, and possibilities of feminist research have been

closely examined and rethought under postmodern thought and global feminisms (Lather, 2007; St. Pierre & Pillow, 2000; Visweswaran, 2010).

Most recently, feminist research and ethnography have provided key contributions as the boundaries of research have expanded and been challenged by technological advances and opportunities (Gajjala, 2004). As ethnography ventures into cyberspace, renewed questions about identities, power, subjectivity, research relations, and ethics are emphasized. New media and relatively older technologies like photography, tape recording, and film continue to raise dilemmas as well as enhance possibilities for feminist ethnography. As Pink (2007) explains, shifting ethnography into the visual continues the project of ethnography as narrative, as well as further linking ethnography and cultural studies in order "to explore how all types of material, intangible, spoken, preformed narrative and discourses are interwoven with and made meaningful in relation to social relationships, practices, and individual experiences" (p. 7). Although not all visual ethnography is feminist, some have been challenged by feminist and poststructural theory to address forms of representation as text and narrative to be critiqued through the lens of race, class, region, gender, sexuality, and other normative conventions.

Access to new technologies also complicates a feminist analysis of the use of new technologies and digital ethnographic methods. For instance, Murthy (2008) lauds the potential for new media to bring in marginalized voices but cautions, too, that access to new technologies continues to be defined by a digital divide shaped by racism, classism, and sexism (p. 837). Gender relations, too, define hierarchies of access (Pink, 2007), and the cyberspace ethnographer faces key questions of identity and relations. For instance, how does one study gender in cyberspace? Does gender have meaning in online communities and virtual gaming, and, if so, how and when? And in such spaces, how should the researcher situate his or her own gender identities?

These examples and questions reflect a continued attentiveness to methodology in feminist ethnography. Despite shifts in moments or waves of feminist research and ethnography and despite new sites of location and production of ethnography, the characteristics of feminist research that Reinharz describes remain prevalent and present in current ethnographic practices and writings. Recall that what is key across feminist research and feminist ethnography is a commitment to studying the "lived experiences" of gender and its intersectionalities, resulting in theory that is built from these lived experiences, whether these experiences are textual, embodied, or virtual. This changed relationship with research, in addition to a commitment to doing research responsibly and doing research that will be beneficial for women, breaks down binaries between theory and praxis, researcher and researched, objectivity and subjectivity. The importance of such challenges to the dualities of research will become apparent as we turn to a discussion of the unique purposes and practices of feminist ethnography through four stages of research: choosing, doing, analysis and writing, and endings. Specifically, issues of representation, voice, and power as manifested in the interplay of research relationships and reflexivity are situated as key across all of the presented stages of ethnography.

PURPOSES AND PRACTICES OF FEMINIST ETHNOGRAPHY: CHOOSING

The first decision the ethnographer faces is what to research, which raises questions of what is or is not a feminist topic. Can any issue be studied as a feminist ethnography? The previous discussion of the common characteristics of feminist research and the necessary intersectionality of feminist research situates the topic of the research perhaps as less important than how one approaches and does research. So we could imaginably conceive of a feminist ethnography of corporate leadership or of social constructions of gender in fraternities or of gendered relations in small-town farm communities.

Yet, despite the idea that any topic or issue can be a feminist issue of study, initially, most feminist ethnographers were or are doing what may be thought of as "women's work"—asking and investigating questions about what is typically and normatively assigned as being women's issues (e.g., domestic issues; sexuality; pregnancy, birth, child rearing and mothering; learning styles; communication styles). This work has

been and remains necessary because of the lack of ethnographic work addressing the lived realities of women's lives. Additionally, this work begins to fill in the gaps and silences surrounding women's lives and experiences and to challenge current conceptualizations and theories.

As noted, however, while early feminist theory and ethnography focused on reclaiming women's voices and stories, present-day feminist research focuses on making visible the experiences of women and, at the same time, rethinking these experiences through critical analyses of gendered power relations. Feminist ethnography pays attention to gender, working through and validating a "female feminist specificity" (Leach, 1997, p. 337) while simultaneously "interrupt(ing) a singular version" of identity (MacLure, 1997, p. 316). In this way, feminist ethnographies have also expanded the sites and locations of research, the topics of research, and who performs research. Consider, for example, how studies of masculinity and queer or gay identities have been influenced by feminist theory and practice. What would ethnographies of masculinity look like without feminist theory's deep analysis of gender, social relations, and power?

Fonow and Cook (1991) note that key to feminist ethnography is a "tendency to use already given situations both as the focus of investigation and as a means of collecting data" (p. 11). Fonow and Cook argue that feminist approaches to research are thus necessarily more creative, spontaneous, and open to improvisation, stumbling across the unexpected and being willing to follow where the unexpected leads. Such an approach yields research with a focus on the everyday world, on the lived experiences and private spaces close at hand to us as researchers, and it often results in the researcher feeling as if the research found her or him as opposed to feeling that she or he chose the research.

Researching in this way often means that the research will be changed from what the researcher expected (Delgado-Gaitan, 1993; Pillow, 2004) and has also resulted in an opening for researchers to study what is close to them, in terms of identity or interest, and to discuss their own roles and subjectivity in such research. Historically, it was not viewed as valid to study a topic "too close" to one's identity or interest; being too similar to one's research was assumed to invalidate the research. Feminist research challenged this mode of thinking, pointing out how much under such a model goes unresearched, unwritten. Now it is quite common to find that researchers are studying subjects like themselves, and, indeed, we may be facing the opposite problem now in terms of expecting that we now have to look like our research (Pillow, 2003a, 2003b).

Researchers who study community or identity groups they "come from," "belong to," or "identify with" are often referred to as "outsiders/within" (Collins, 1991; Johnson-Bailey, 1999)—researchers who seemingly have access to a setting or subjects because of their own identity (e.g., an African American woman interviewing African American teen girls or a lesbian woman interviewing other lesbian women) or because of their own shared experiences (an adult teen mother interviewing a young teen mother). While such researchers often refer to and utilize what Delgado-Bernal (1998) terms a shared "cultural intuition," these researchers also note the unique challenges and limits of doing research on one's own identity or community. For example, Sofia Villenas (1996, 2000) critically reflects on her role as a researcher of Latina mothers, noting that although her own identity as a Latina mother should have seemingly situated her as an "insider," her role as a graduate student and her access to the privilege and power associated with access to higher education situated her as an outsider and colonizer of these women.

The lived status as outsiders/within also, however, provides a unique lens of analysis. Ethnographers who find themselves to be "insiders/outsiders" or "outsiders/within" in their research face unique, conflicting, and productive issues; the issues faced by all researchers—issues of relationships, reciprocity, representation, and power—are heightened in research settings where one identifies with or is perceived to be a part of the research site or subjects (Chaudhry, 2000; Delgado-Bernal, 1998; Kondo, 1990; Villenas, 2000; Visweswaran, 1994). For example, it is likely Villenas's own understandings and lived experiences as a racialized Latina/Chicana that allow her to gain the level of critically reflexive insight that she brings to her work. The writings of women who experience and live under and with the intersections of the simultaneous oppression of race, gender, class, and sexuality lend vital understandings of political reality and provide vital theoretical lenses of analysis for feminist ethnography (Anzaldúa, 1987; Collins, 1990; Davis, 1981; hooks, 1981, 1984; Lorde, 1984; Moraga & Anzaldúa, 1983; Smith, 1983; Walker, 1974). How researchers change and are changed when faced with these conditions is further addressed later in this chapter. Regardless of whether we choose our research or feel that our research chooses us, the choosing of research is closely related to how we actually "do" feminist ethnographic research.

PURPOSES AND PRACTICES OF FEMINIST ETHNOGRAPHY: DOING

Is there something uniquely different that occurs when one is doing feminist ethnography? Recall that Reinharz (1992) and Fonow and Cook (1991) note that commitment to action/change and attention to relationships with subjects are key to feminist research. Further, practices of reflexivity—of researchers reflecting, critically examining, and exploring the nature of the research process—are key to feminist methodology. In this section, we focus upon these two issues—relationships and reflexivity—considering the contributions and practices of feminist theory to the doing of feminist ethnography.

What does it mean to have a "feminist" relationship with research subjects? Although feminist theory would suggest that feminist research should be reciprocal, another response to this question is that thinking, reflecting, and writing about relationships with subjects is a feminist task. In other words, attention to and concern about relationships with subjects—including concerns about issues of reciprocity, representation, and voice—comprise a uniquely feminist approach. Writing about and sharing how ethnographers experience their research and how ethnographers do their work—with all of the good and the bad—operate against naming the relational aspects of research as illogical or invalid and make visible the questions, complexities, and processes of doing research. Fortunately, several feminist ethnographers have taken up this task, exploring the complexities of their own and their subjects' identities and positionings (Abu-Lughod, 1992; Chaudhry, 2000; Delgado-Gaitain, 1993; Kondo, 1990; Trinh, 1991; Villenas, 1996, 2000; Visweswaran, 1994, 2010).

Reading the work of these feminist ethnographers reveals that there is not one response to what a feminist relationship with research subjects should be, as feminist ethnography may range from the researcher being an observer, a participant observer, or a full collaborator. Finding a balance as an observer-participant—when to wear the researcher hat and when to become involved by giving your opinion, providing help, or actively leading a project—is difficult and specific to each research context. Further, working within successful or unsuccessful relationships with subjects is not something that can be taught, instructed, rehearsed, or measured—rather, the relationships must be experienced, and we may often find we are unprepared for what we experience in the research setting.

For example, Delgado-Gaitan (1993) discusses how she became more involved with her research subjects than she ever imagined or ever thought was "right." As Delgado-Gaitan entered her research setting, she found that her research protocol did not fit the needs of the subjects she met. The longer she was in the field, the more the design and intent of her study became less important and shifted according to the subjects' needs. For Delgado-Gaitan, these shifts were impossible to avoid—she came to feel that, ethically, she had to change her research as she questioned her privilege and the doing of her research over the explicit needs of the people she was studying. Delgado-Gaitan further notes that, as much as the research question and process changed, she too was changed by the changing nature of her research. Her relationships to subjects, her relationships to research, and her relationships to methods were all impacted and changed by the changing of the research. Delgado-Gaitan's experiences acknowledge that research relationships can be reciprocal and not simply one way, that, indeed, the researcher may find herself more "changed" by the research than are the subjects themselves.

Yet how much involvement with subjects is too much? What is ethical here? As we move from research to advocacy, are we still doing research? In the midst of working with Latina/o parents seeking work with school personnel to improve the educational conditions for their children, one of the authors of this chapter, Cris Mayo, and colleagues began attending parent-teacher conferences at the request of parents (Mayo, Candela, Matusov, & Smith, 2008). Initially, we were engaged in taking field notes and engaging in discussions with parents and children afterward, but, as school personnel began to use disrespectful language, we increasingly engaged with parents directly before meetings, making sure that our interventions were discussed ahead of time and responded to parental concerns.

As our experience with parents grew and we learned from experienced parents to watch for particular maneuvers from school personnel (e.g., principals who couldn't be found at the scheduled time of the meeting, teachers who would only address weaknesses of students, personnel who refused to make appointments that didn't involve parents' missing work), parents and researchers all knew how to forestall the problems encountered in other meetings. In other words, our collaboration and education about advocacy from parents enabled us to change the character of our research setting as well as to ensure that positive outcomes for children were part of our research goal. Rather than taking detailed notes of school disrespect of Latina/o parents and students, we worked together with parents to prevent it. At the same time, we also recognized that it was largely our presence as researchers that was effecting the change.

While race, ethnicity, and language issues were the dominant vectors of oppression and disrespect, there were also gendered components to the schools' relationship with the students. Teachers tended to criticize young Latinas for having too many friends or spending too much time with their cousins. Essentially, girls were characterized as too social or too family oriented to take school seriously. In contrast, Latino boys were accused by teachers of being violent or too disrespectful of teachers' authority to be good students. As a result of these distinctions, boys' failure was considered to be a problem that needed intervention from school personnel (special classes, expulsion, and programs for students at risk), whereas girls' failure was largely ignored. In one case, a Latina's ability to pass as male further complicated all of the overlapping biases we had encountered, and parents began important conversations on the need to respect all genders and sexualities in their community, a situation made easier because parents perceived a linkage between their issues with the school and the school's homophobic/transphobic response to the problems the passing girl was having. The reciprocity between researchers and researched, then, opened all of our understandings to the complexity of the research situation and also pushed us to be sure that our research had a positive effect on the school experiences of the children involved.

In addition to researchers who note how their research focus and emphasis are changed according to the relational needs of those in the research setting, a review of feminist ethnography also identifies a concerted focus upon methodology—the hows and whys of the research. Many feminist ethnographers engage in continual negotiations of and explicit reflections about power relations and the specific ways gender and power work in our research. Such authors engage in a continual reflexive critique of their own gaze. This works to "draw into view unarticulated assumptions and expectations that operate silently within one's theories," and Ferguson (1993) goes on to argue that "poking around and prodding within" our theories and our positionalities are "significant feminist tasks" (p. ix).

For instance, in Mayo's research on gaystraight alliances, it became less than clear exactly who was gay and who was straight in these groups (Mayo, 2005, 2007). As researchers somewhat used to particular generationally specific definitions of sexual orientation, visits to school dances troubled our understandings of what counts as gayness or straightness. Having noted that we saw no more than the usual same-gender flirting and slow dancing, we wondered what the usual amount of same-gender attraction was. The research question began to shift from "Who are queer people in high school and what kinds of spaces do they make?" to "How straight are 'straight' girls?" On the one hand, we found substantial same-gender flirting among girls but not as much among boys (and most of the boys doing same-gender flirting were out as young gay men already).

On the other hand, we also found a lack of imagination about what it would be like to be a young queer person—some of the same girls flirting with one another had no sense of same-sex attraction as a possibility prior to high school and no clear idea about how young queer people might organize their lives in the face of "default" heterosexuality. In other words, although student activities challenged our understandings of the relationship between straightness and queerness, the girls nonetheless evinced a lack of understanding of the queer experiences of coming out, forming oppositional communities, being in the closet, and so on.

Part of feminist research, then, is looking at what is missing, what is passed over, and what is avoided. In a gay-straight alliance beginning to discuss sexualities, we observed a young black woman attempt to raise race as an issue for the group to consider. First she suggested a T-shirt design that would advocate for diversity. A white group member, citing her anger at an administrative attempt to change the group's name from "gay-straight alliance" to "diversity club," argued it would be against the group's decision to decide its own name. The next time the black young woman suggested that the group think about race was in a suggestion that members also attend an alliance that discussed African American culture and literature. She was met with silence. Although the group had just been sharing racial and ethnic family stories, she was the only African American engaged in the conversation and the only person whose comment went unanswered.

What is the role and responsibility of the researcher in this situation? Should the researcher intervene and direct conversation or allow the "natural" group dynamics to continue? Again, there is no one right feminist response to such questions. Feminist researchers have written about both the necessity and the dangers of being involved in proactive ways in the research setting (Fonow & Cook, 1991; Stacey, 1988). Reflexivity, then, becomes necessary as a way to think through the problems of attempting to do feminist research. Feminist reflexivity is not only about investigating the power embedded in one's research but also about doing research differently. The need to do research differently arises from the ethical and political problems and questions raised by feminists about traditional research methods (Oakley, 1981). These questions include how to be a nonexploitative researcher, how to produce research that is useful and empowering to women, and how to make research that is linked with political action. Feminist research points out that there are multiple places for reflexivity to work and work differently in the research process, and we discuss reflexivity further under the following section.

Purposes and Practices of Feminist Ethnography: Analyzing and Writing

Is there a feminist method of analyzing data? Of writing? Analyzing data cannot be separate from data collection and writing. Feminists have claimed that writing and choosing how to tell the stories of our research are political acts as well as places of responsibility—as we code, theme, and imagine our data, we are, in essence, writing and constructing our text. As Richardson (1997) explains, "Deciding on my narrative voice was more than a literary and theoretical problem. It was a political issue" (p. 21).

A review of ethnographies finds that feminist researchers are paying attention to *how* they write as well as to what they write. *Women Writing Culture* makes apparent the "particular challenges that ethnographic writing has posed for women authors" (Behar & Gordon, 1995, p. 12), and, since that publication, many women writers have taken up these challenges and explored and experimented with a variety of writing and narrative styles as well as with a variety of textual styles. Ranging from ethnography written as fiction, poetry, or plays to texts that are interrupted with split texts and visual elements to disrupt the eye and mind, these works seek not simply to perform something different but also to attempt to "better understand the politics of representation, how different narrative strategies may be authorized at specific moments in history by complex negotiations of community, identity, and accountability" (Visweswaran, 1994, p. 15).

Writers are pushing the edges and boundaries of what ethnographic writing is, looks like, and yields: Michele Fine (1991) provides her reader with story-like thick descriptions at the introduction of her ethnography *Framing Dropouts*; Laurel Richardson (1997) writes of her research as "fields of play" (but she also turns the phrase to "play the field"); Kamala Visweswaran (1994) makes the nuances of her writing visible in her texts to expose the politics of representation and the impossibilities of representation; Patti Lather and Chris Smithies (1997) embrace the split text interspersed with angel artifacts in their book on women living with HIV/AIDS; St. Pierre (1997) writes of being a nomadic armchair ethnographer and shares her "sensual and dream data" with the reader; and James Sanders (1999) writes his data as a play with characters, backdrops, sound effects, and props. In a different vein, reading some ethnographies can leave readers feeling that they have learned more about the researcher than the subjects or topic at hand. For example, in Ruth Linden's (1992) and Dorinne Kondo's (1990) work, we learn as much about these women as researchers as we do about their subjects. Some ethnographies become ethnographies of the self (Moraga, 1997), while other ethnographers explore their own hybridity and identities in the writing of their research (Abu-Lughod, 1992; Chaudhry, 2000; Villenas, 1996; Visweswaran, 1994).

Yet it is not simply textual styles or formats that mark certain ethnographic writing as feminist but rather the methodology behind the method. As Visweswaran (1994) reminds us, "fiction, as we know, is political" (p. 15). Further, no textual experimentation removes the fact that we are writing "about"—whether it is about others or ourselves or ourselves and others. As Richardson (1997) argues, "Whoever writes for/about/of whatever is using authority and privilege," and there is "no resolution to the problem of speaking for others" even in the speaking of ourselves (p. 58).

One way feminist ethnographers approach issues of representation, authority, and power in their research is reflexivity. According to Anderson (1989), reflexivity involves a dialectical process consisting of the researcher's constructs, the informants' commonsense constructs, the research data, the researcher's ideological biases, and the structural and historical forces that shaped the social construction under study. Denzin (1997) identifies five differing types of reflexivity in qualitative research: methodological, intertextual, standpoint, queer, and feminist reflexivity (pp. 218–223). Fonow and Cook (1991) define the "role of reflexivity as a source of insight," discussing reflexivity as the "tendency . . . to reflect upon, examine critically, and explore analytically the nature of the research process" (p. 2). While reflexivity necessarily occurs through the research process, it is particularly integral to feminist practices of writing ethnography.

Pillow (2003a), however, cautions against using reflexivity as simply a validated strategy to ensure "better data" and better ethnographic accounts. She traces how, as reflexivity has moved into the mainstream of ethnography, it is often utilized as a tool to demonstrate the validity and truthfulness of research instead of committing to, as Fonow and Cook describe, critical analysis of the "nature of the research process." Reviewing four practices of reflexivity that can be problematic—reflexivity as recognition of self, reflexivity as recognition of other, reflexivity as truth and reflexivity as transcendence—Pillow argues for what she calls a "reflexivity of discomfort." Reflexivity of discomfort makes the work of reflexivity visible and interrupts the ethnographer's desire to know, to name, and to claim, asserting that not knowing is often as powerful as knowing.

Reflexive accounts by "native" ethnographers have further challenged processes of writing ethnography. As *This Bridge* powerfully made apparent, analysis and writing are often changed when produced by those who were once or remain the colonized and those who were once or remain the objects of the ethnographic gaze. Villenas (2000) explores the complexities of doing feminist ethnography in this way:

> As a Xicana and indigenous woman, I cannot escape my own experiences of marginalization and dislocation . . . at the same time, I cannot escape the privilege afforded to me as a university professor. Yet precisely because we are not the same "we" anthropologists, our interrogations, revelations, and vulnerabilities in a feminist praxis generate intriguing insights and creations. (pp. 75–76)

Ethnographers like Villenas and Visweswaran note that "insider" status is never truly insider, yet they are also not "insiders" when it comes to the historical production of knowledge in the academy and to the construction of ethnographic writing. The tension that exists when those who were or are objects of the gaze not only return but rewrite this gaze is central to feminist research and feminist ethnography and changes the types of conversations, discussions, and theories produced in ethnographic texts.

These relationships are brought to bear even more intensely in feminist visual or performance ethnography. For example, consider the making of a video ethnography or a theater play production. Feminist ethnographers have turned to such media and venues as a means to further interrupt researcher-researched relationships, make visible research relations and methodologies, and provide a more engaged way to "give voice" and represent ethnographic subjects and subjectivites, as well as to reach wider audiences. Yet wider circulation of media can disseminate information about participatory projects detailing gender bias and resilience even as those projects point to key tensions in such participation: Does participation and reflection permeate all stages of the production of the project? At a certain point, does a participatory project become a single-director or single-producer documentary? How do resources gained through the circulation of the product improve the communities in which the initial research collaboration occurred?

In a review of *Born Into Brothels* (Kauffman & Briski, 2004), Roth notes that the questions raised by participatory projects using media are "a mirror for anthropology, in which the best intentions and attempts at participation are generally shaped into a final product by a single, privileged author" (Roth, 2010). As Pink (2007) puts it, "Gendered and economic power relations implied by images and image production have an inevitable influence on how images and technologies can be used in ethnographic research" (pp. 24–25). Visual ethnographies also raise questions of interpretation that face traditional written ethnographic accounts.

How much context should the visual ethnography make explicit? How can the feminist ethnographer present the data or the story line in a way to interrupt too easy consumption by the audience? How can the feminist ethnographer tell the difficult story, the tragic story, without collapsing into binary victim-victory narratives (e.g., the ethnographic subject as simply and only victim of circumstances or structural inequities vs. the ethnographic subject as victorious, achieving and overcoming overwhelming odds)? In his review of *Kabul Transit*, Bill Nichols (2010) marks this difficulty: in the absence of context and background information, video ethnography provides a "tapestry of moments" that places interpretation too confidently into "the observer's lap," thus potentially disengaging "the fraught cross-cultural issues brought on by massive drug trafficking, war, terrorism, extremists, and corruption along with class, gender, and status differences . . . [and making] the ethnographic pay off from *Kabul Transit* less than the situation invites" (p. 149).

Simply writing or representing in some "new" or visual way does not rescue us from the deeply complex methodological issues of power, voice, subjectivity, writing, and representation in ethnographic research. While we are eagerly awaiting the ethnographic dissertation that is written as a multimodal, multivoiced, mobile text, feminist ethnography reminds us it is *how* and *why* we would do that work that takes precedence and creates meaning. If an author or researcher simply pours data into an existing analytical or writing format, the work feels artificial, forced, and lacking in impact. Feminist ethnography is based upon the precept that an analysis occurs in the format or style that it does because the author or researcher cannot do otherwise—cannot think without the theories utilized.

Accomplishing this relationship between analysis and presentation is easier said than done, and our experience is that many ethnography students and researchers do not allow adequate time for this stage. A lack of time results in the "poured data" effect. Those who take the time and are inspired by the questions and challenges of their research engage with the tenets and complexities of doing the intersectional work of feminist ethnography. Magnet (2007) notes that research seemingly intent upon using images and content to encourage viewers to shift away from forms of interpretation reliant on the male gaze are unable to disrupt normative forms of viewing because they lack sustained engagement with race and queerness.

"Sustained engagement" with the methodological and theoretical implications of feminist ethnography yields the potential for what Patti Lather (2007) calls "naked methodology," an exposed methodology of an "effort to articulate methodology out of practice" (p. ix). Working from the "limits of representation," Lather challenges feminist ethnography to question "how research-based knowledge remains possible after so much questioning of the very ground of science" (p. viii). What then do analysis and representation look like when the limits of research have been exposed? Whether feminist ethnographic work is textual, visual, performative, or cyber-based, this question can both shape and distort where data analysis and writing take us.

PURPOSES AND PRACTICES OF FEMINIST ETHNOGRAPHY: ENDINGS

Given how feminist researchers engage in their research—with attention to relationships, reciprocity, representation, and voice—how does one "end" the research? When is our research concluded—when we leave the field; when we write; or when we complete the article, dissertation, or book? Perhaps, given feminist ethnography's attention to methodology, we do not ever leave our research; perhaps it is never ended as we continue to reflect on our actions and interpretations. Thus the question becomes *can* rather than *how does* one end research?

These questions have both pragmatic and methodological/theoretical implications, and an overview of feminist ethnographies finds many researchers struggling with these questions (Evans-Winters, 2005; Fay, 2007; Fine, 1991; Kondo, 1990; Miranda, 2003; Visweswaran, 1994; Villenas, 2000; Ward, 1999). Making the often invisible and taken-for-granted process of completing one's fieldwork visible as an ethical and methodological issue arising from feminist understandings of power, relationships, and responsibility in qualitative research is a feminist act.

Thus, an overview of ethnographies that talk about "endings" will provide examples ranging from the continuing of relationships with subjects past the "official" research timeline to closure with the provision of some service or product to those who were subjects, and most researchers remark that ending research is as complex and problematic as the doing of it. And what if we remain part of the community, virtually or otherwise—how does the researcher then negotiate her or his role? Is there a way to "end" research responsibly? There is not a set answer to this question—each researcher needs to find her or his own way through the process of endings. The endings will be based on how one was "doing" research: how connected and involved the researcher was with subjects in the research, how the researcher presented herself or himself, and what roles, if any, the researcher has in the research field.

However, this focus on endings should not overinflate the role and importance of the researcher. Although the researcher may feel deeply embedded in and a part of the research setting, the fact is that this place and people were operating without the researcher before she or he arrived and will continue to function afterward without the researcher. As Rosalie Wax (1971) found, not even an extended length of time in the field can be an assumption of intimacy. After publishing a book based on her and her husband's many years living in and studying an American Indian community, Wax was informed that the consensus among the community readers of her book was that "if we had known this was the kind of book those white people were going to write, we would *really* have talked to you" (p. 248).

Thus, while we can talk about practices of responsible ethnographic endings (easing out of the researcher relationship over time, providing continued support as desired by subjects, sharing writing with subjects or cowriting with subjects, producing visual or performative ethnographies), what again remain key are the researcher's own awareness and reflexivity about power relations in the research setting and the researcher's own acknowledgment of her or his own positionalities in the research and research setting.

Conclusion

What is the state and place of feminist ethnography today? Where are the possible futures of feminist ethnography? Some of the most interesting work in feminist ethnography is situated, as Patti Lather (1997) states, "in a feminist poststructural problematic of accountability to stories that belong to others . . . [and] how to tell such stories in a way that attends to the crisis of representation" (p. 286). Lather (1997), echoing Judith Stacey, finds that feminist researchers are working out of and with "the ruins of feminist ethnography" (p. 286). That is, they are working out of the ruins of interpretive and postmodern turns that no longer allow us to situate feminist ethnography as "innocent in its desire to give voice to the voiceless" (Lather, 1997, p. 286). Feminist researchers take on the methodological and epistemological paradoxes of "knowing through not knowing, knowing both too little and too much" (Lather, 1997, p. 286), and they attempt to address Kamala Visweswaran's (1994) question, "How does one act knowing what one does" (p. 80)?

Further, as Visweswaran notes, "With the loss of ethnographic authority, the subjects about whom we write now write back, and in so doing pose us as anthropological fictions" (p. 9). Such critiques have led some to question whether there can be, is, or even should be such a thing as feminist ethnography (Abu-Lughod, 1990; Stacey, 1988; Visweswaran, 1994). While some feminist researchers have been loath to attend the critiques postmodernism in particular raises for feminist theorists and doggedly stick to telling *the* feminist story and capturing the essence of their subjects' voices, other feminist researchers have found that there is much work to do among the ruins. As Judith Butler (1993) points out, this failure, this ruin of our theories and methodologies produces a site from which to ask different sorts of questions, to examine closely and expose the structures and discourses of concepts such as humanism, reason, truth, and a linear unfolding of history, and, in so doing, open contested possibilities. Lather (1997), reading Butler, further points out that "terms understood as no longer fulfilling their promise do not become useless. On the contrary, their very failures become provisional grounds, and new uses are derived" (p. 300).

For example, Visweswaran (1994) turns to a "feminist practice invested in decolonizing" and "one that rests on the recognition of certain impossibilities" (p. 13). The "impossibility" that must be deconstructed, decolonized, and acknowledged is, in this case, representation of the subject, in what Visweswaran refers to as a "refusal of subject." Taking up what has been central to feminist theory and practice—centering of female subjectivity—and now reworking that category of subjectivity as a refusal is a move to both retain the subject and yet acknowledge the problems with any attempt to claim, or know, the subject. This, then, is a feminist subject who cannot be contained by a researcher or writer who actively and reflexively "refuses" to contain her.

The promises and challenges of virtual, cyber, and visual feminist ethnography promise to take these questions further. As the subjects of our ethnographies become more "mobile," more nubile in the flexing of intersections of identities and social relations, what does it mean for our methods to also become more mobile (Fay, 2007; Ward, 1999)? How do virtual realities challenge conceptualizations of gender, belonging, community, home, and work? And how and where does gender matter in these spaces?

Perhaps, then, future feminist ethnographers will continue their commitment to uncovering, revealing, or responding to inequities in theory and practice, and we will continue to analyze and deconstruct our own research, discursive, and textual practices while at the same time finding ways to think, write, and live with unknowability. This does not mean that we stop asking questions; rather, we ask questions differently. If, as Jane Flax (1987) states, the "fundamental purpose" of feminism remains to analyze "how we think, or do not think, or avoid thinking about gender" (p. 626), then feminist ethnography remains a ripe vehicle for doing and unpacking this thinking in all of its intricacies, intersectionalities, hybridities, nuances, and ruins.

Discussion Questions

1. How do the authors define feminism and feminist theory? Why has the term "feminist" had a troubled past and present?

2. Is there a feminist method? If not, why not? And what does this mean for feminist ethnography?

3. What does feminist ethnography question and challenge about traditional ethnography?

4. What is the role of subjectivity in feminist ethnography? How do feminist ethnographers think about and write with subjectivity?

5. What is the role of reflexivity in feminist ethnography?

Online Resources

The Making of "Covered," A Documentary About Women and Tattoos, Directed by Beverly Yuen Thompson

http://www.youtube.com/watch?v=bfoVbGgHbz8

This video presentation recorded at the Broadcast Education Association conference (Las Vegas, April 2010) provides insight into the challenges of introducing visual media into ethnographic research.

Institutional Ethnography

http://www.youtube.com/watch?v=1RI2KEy9NDw

This talk by Professor Dorothy Smith, eminent feminist ethnographer, profiles her influential book *Institutional Ethnography: A Sociology for People* (2005).

Founders Day Honoree Patricia Zavella

http://www.youtube.com/watch?v=0SNs-ksMw4U

By describing the work and career of Professor Patricia Zavella, the UC Santa Cruz's Honored Faculty Research Lecturer of 2008, this video offers an informative look at the history and shifts within ethnography and at the potential for ethnography to be utilized for social, community, and policy change.

Relevant Journals

Gender & Society

International Journal of Qualitative Studies in Education

Qualitative Inquiry

Notes

1. For further discussion and exploration of these questions, see Abu-Lughod (1990); Collins (1990); Ferguson (1993); hooks (1984); Jardine and

Smith (1987); Johnson-Bailey (1999); Lingard and Douglas (1999); Mohanty, Russo, and Torres (1991); Moraga and Anzaldúa (1983); Nicholson (1990); Paker, Dehyle, and Villenas (1999); Patai (1991); Porter (1992); Pillow (2002); Reinharz (1992); St. Pierre & Pillow (2000).

2. The organization of this chapter through these "stages" of research is not an assumption that the process of research is easily experienced as stages. We recognize that the stages of research cross over into and impact each other. See Van Maanen (1989).

3. The data stories used in this chapter are from Cris Mayo's research with a Latino/a parental involvement project and her research on gay-straight alliances in public schools.

4. For discussions of how feminist theory impacts methodology, see Collins (1990), Fine (1994), Fonow and Cook (1991), Lather (1991), and Reinharz (1992). Certainly researchers may use multiple theoretical lenses, including feminism and postmodernism, feminism and race theory, and feminist and queer theory (see Collins, 1990; Johnson-Bailey, 1999; Lather, 1991; Nicholson, 1990; Sanders, 1999; St. Pierre & Pillow, 2000; Walkerdine, 1990). While, in this chapter, we are not advocating for a particular approach, we assume, as does Harding, that all feminist research is about social critique.

References

Abu-Lughod, L. (1990). Can there be a feminist ethnography? *Women and Performance: A Journal of Feminist Theory, 5*(1), 7–27.

Abu-Lughod, L. (1992). *Writing women's worlds: Bedouin stories.* Berkeley: University of California Press.

Acker, J. (1992). Gendered institutions: From sex roles to gendered institutions. *Contemporary Sociology, 21*, 565–569.

Alexander, B. K. (2006). *Performing black masculinity: Race, culture, and queer identity.* Lanham, MD: AltaMira Press.

Anderson, G. (1989). Critical ethnography in education: Origins, current status, and new directions. *Review of Educational Research, 59*(3), 249–270.

Anzaldúa, G. (1987). *Borderlands: The new mestiza=La frontera.* San Francisco: Aunt Lute Books.

Behar, R., & Gordon, D. (Eds.). (1995). *Women writing culture.* Berkeley: University of California Press.

Belenky, M., Clinchy, B., Goldberger, N., & Tarule, J. (1986). *Women's ways of knowing.* New York: Basic Books.

Chaudhry, L. N. (2000). Researching "my people," researching myself: Fragments of a reflexive tale. In E. St. Pierre & W. Pillow (Eds.), *Working the ruins/Feminist poststructural theory and methods in education* (pp. 96–113). New York: Routledge Press.

Clifford, J., & Marcus, G. (Eds). (1986). *Writing culture: The poetics and politics of ethnography.* Berkeley: University of California Press.

Clough, P. T. (1992). *The end(s) of ethnography: From realism to social criticism.* Thousand Oaks, CA: Sage.

Collins, P. H. (1990). *Black feminist thought: Knowledge, consciousness, and the politics of empowerment.* London: Harper Collins Academic.

Collins, P. H. (1991). Learning from the outsider within: The sociological significance of Black feminist thought. In M. Fonow & J. Cook (Eds.), *Beyond methodology: Feminist scholarship as lived research* (pp. 35–59). Bloomington: Indiana University Press.

Davies, B. (1989). *Frogs and snails and feminist tales: Preschool children.* St. Leonards, Australia: Allen & Unwin.

Davis, A. (1981). *Women, race, and class.* New York: Random House.

Delgado Bernal, D. (1998). Using a Chicana feminist epistemology in educational research. *Harvard Educational Review, 68*(4), 555–582.

Delgado-Gaitan, C. (1993). Researching change and changing the researcher. *Harvard Educational Review, 63*(4), 389–411.

Denzin, N. (1997). *Interpretive ethnography: Ethnographic practices for the 21st century.* Thousand Oaks, CA: Sage.

Denzin, N., & Lincoln, Y. (2008). *Collecting and interpreting qualitative materials.* Thousand Oaks, CA: Sage.

Edwards, D., Whitmore, G., & Zulfacar, M. (Directors). (2006). *Kabul Transit.* Kabul: Bullfrog Films.

Eisenstein, Z. (1994). *The color of gender: Reimaging democracy.* Berkeley: University of California Press.

Evans-Winters, V. (2005). *Teaching black girls: Resiliency in urban classrooms.* New York: Peter Lang Publishing.

Fay, M. (2007). Mobile subjects, mobile methods: Doing virtual ethnography in a feminist online network. *Forum: Qualitative Social Research, 8*(3). Retrieved June 2, 2011, from http://nbn-resolving.de/urn:nbn:de:0114-fqs0703141

Ferguson, K. (1993). *The man question: Visions of subjectivity in feminist theory.* Berkeley: University of California Press.

Fine, M. (1991). *Framing dropouts: Notes on the politics of an urban high school.* Albany: State University of New York Press.

Fine, M. (1994). Dis-tance and other stances: Negotiations of power inside feminist research. In A. Gitlen (Ed.), *Power and method* (pp. 13–35). New York: Routledge.

Flax, J. (1987). Postmodernism and gender relations in feminist theory. *Signs: Journal of Women in Culture and Society, 12*(4), 621–643.

Fonow, M. M., & Cook, J. (Eds.) (1991). *Beyond methodology: Feminist scholarship as lived research.* Bloomington: Indiana University Press.

Freire, P. (1970). *Pedagogy of the oppressed.* New York: Herder and Herder.

Gajjala, R. (2004). *Cyber selves: Feminist ethnographies of South Asian women.* Lanham, MD: AltaMira Press.

Gilligan, C. (1982). *In a different voice: Psychological theory and women's development.* Cambridge, MA: Harvard University Press.

Harding, S. (1987). Introduction: Is there a feminist method? In S. Harding (Ed.), *Feminism and methodology* (pp. 1–14). Bloomington: Indiana University Press.

Hey, V. (1997). *The company she keeps: An ethnography of girls' friendships.* Buckingham, UK: Open University Press.

hooks, b. (1981). *Ain't I a woman: Black women and feminism.* Boston: South End Press.

hooks, b. (1984). *Feminist theory: From margin to center.* Boston: South End Press.

Jardine, A., & Smith, P. (Eds). (1987). *Men in feminism.* New York: Routledge.

Johnson-Bailey, J. (1999). The ties that bind and the shackles that separate: Race, gender, class, and color in a research process. *The International Journal of Qualitative Studies in Education, 12*(6), 659–670.

Kauffman, R., & Briski, Z. (Directors). (2004). *Born into brothels.* New York: THINKFilm.

Kondo, D. (1990). *Crafting selves.* Chicago: University of Chicago Press.

Lather, P. (1991). *Getting smart: Feminist research and pedagogy with/in the postmodern.* New York: Routledge.

Lather, P. (2000). Drawing the lines at angels: Working the ruins of feminist ethnography. In E. St. Pierre & W. Pillow (Eds.), *Working the ruins: Feminist poststructural theory and methods in education* (pp. 284–311). New York: Routledge Press.

Lather, P. (2007). *Getting lost: Feminist efforts toward a double(d) science.* New York: SUNY.

Lather, P., & Smithies, C. (1997). *Troubling the angels: Women living with HIV/AIDS.* Boulder, CO: Westview Press.

Leach, M. (1997). Feminist figurations: Gossip as a counterdiscourse. *International Journal of Qualitative Studies in Education, 10*(3), 333–347.

Leck, G. M. (1987). Feminist pedagogy, liberation theory, and the traditional schooling paradigm. *Educational Theory, 37*(3), 343–354.

Linden, R. (1992). *Making stories, making selves: Feminist reflections on the Holocaust.* Columbus: Ohio State University Press.

Lingard, B., & Douglas, P. (1999). *Men engaging feminism.* Philadelphia: Open University Press.

Lorde, A. (1984). *Sister outsider.* Trumansburg, NY: The Crossing Press.

MacLure, M. (1997). Eccentric subject, impossible object: A poststructural reading of Hannah Cullwick. *International Journal of Qualitative Studies in Education, 10*(3), 315–332.

Magnet, S. (2007). Feminist sexualities, race and the Internet: An investigation of suicidegirls.com. *New Media & Society, 9*(4), 577–602.

Mayo, C. (2005). *Complex subjectivity in student associational groups: How straight are the straight girls in GSAs?* Paper presented at the Wisconsin Center for Educational Research, University of Wisconsin at Madison.

Mayo, C. (2007). *Disputing the subject of sex: Sexuality and public school controversies.* Lanham, MD: Rowman & Littlefield

Mayo, C., Candela, M. A., Matusov, E., & Smith, M. (2008). Families and schools apart: University experience to assist Latina/o parents' activism.

In F. Peterman (Ed.), *Partnering to prepare urban teachers: A call to activism* (pp. 103–132). New York: Peter Lang.

Miranda, M. K. (2003). *Homegirls in the public sphere.* Austin: University of Texas Press.

Mohanty, C. T., Russo, A., & Torres, L. (Eds.). (1991). *Third world women and the politics of feminism.* Bloomington: Indiana University Press.

Moraga, C. (1997). *Waiting in the wings: Portrait of a queer motherhood.* Ithaca, NY: Firebrand Books.

Moraga, C., & Anzaldúa, G. (Eds). (1983). *This bridge called my back: Writings by radical women of color.* New York: Kitchen Table, Women of Color Press.

Murthy, D. (2008). Digital ethnography: An examination of the use of new tools for social research. *Sociology, 42*(5), 837–855.

Nichols, B. (2010). *Kabul transit* [Review]. *American Anthropologist, 112,* 149.

Nicholson, L. (Ed.). (1990). *Feminism/postmodernism.* New York: Routledge.

Nicholson, L. (Ed.). (1997). *The second wave: A reader in feminist theory.* New York: Routledge.

Oakley, A. (1981). Interviewing women: A contradiction in terms? In H. Roberts (Ed.), *Doing feminist research* (pp. 30–62). London: Routledge.

Parker, L., Dehyle, D., & Villenas, S. (Eds.). (1999). *Race is . . . race isn't: Critical race theory and qualitative studies in education.* Boulder, CO: Westview Press.

Patai, D. (1988). Constructing a self: A Brazilian life story. *Feminist Studies, 14,* 143–160.

Patai, D. (1991). U.S. academic women and third world feminism: Is ethical research possible? In S. Gluck & D. Paita (Eds.), *Women's words* (pp. 137–154). New York: Routledge.

Pillow, W. S. (2002). When a man does feminism should he dress in drag? *International Journal of Qualitative Studies in Education, 15*(5), 545–554.

Pillow, W. S. (2003a). Confession, catharsis, or cure: The use of reflexivity as methodological power in qualitative research. *International Journal of Qualitative Studies in Education, 16*(2), 175–196.

Pillow, W. S. (2003b). Race-based methodologies: Multicultural methods or epistemological shifts? In G. Lopez & L. Parker (Eds.), *Interrogating racism in qualitative research methodology.* New York: Peter Lang.

Pillow, W. S. (2004). *Unfit bodies: Educational policy and the teen mother.* New York: Routledge Press.

Pink, S. (2007). *Doing visual ethnography* (2nd ed.). London: Sage.

Porter, D. (Ed.). (1992). *Between men and feminism.* New York: Routledge.

Reinharz, S. (1992). *Feminist methods in social research.* New York: Oxford University Press.

Richardson, L. (1994). Writing: A method of inquiry. In N. K. Denzin & Y. S. Lincoln (Eds.), *Handbook of qualitative research* (pp. 516–529). Thousand Oaks, CA: Sage.

Richardson, L. (1997). *Fields of play (constructing an academic life).* New Brunswick, NJ: Rutgers University Press.

Roth, J. H. (2010). *Born into brothels* [Review]. *American Anthropologist, 112*(1), 151.

Sanders, J. (1999). Dissertation as performance [Art script] (Take Three). *International Journal of Qualitative Studies in Education, 12*(5), 541–562.

Smith, B. (1983). *Home girls: A black feminist anthology.* New York: Kitchen Table, Women of Color Press.

Stacey, J. (1988). Can there be a feminist ethnography? *Women's Studies International Forum, 11*(1), 21–27.

Statham, A., Richardson, L., & Cook, J. A. (1991). *Gender and university teaching: A negotiated difference.* Albany: State University of New York Press.

St. Pierre, E. (1997). Nomadic inquiry in the smooth space of the field: A preface. *International Journal of Qualitative Studies in Education, 10*(3), 365–383.

St. Pierre, E., & Pillow, W. (Eds). (2000). *Working the ruins: Feminist poststructural theory and methods in education.* New York: Routledge.

Thorne, B. (1993). *Gender play/girls and boys in school.* New Brunswick, NJ: Rutgers University Press.

Trinh, T. Minh-ha. (1989). *Women, native, other.* London & New York: Routledge.

Trinh, T. Minh-ha. (1991). *When the moon waxes red: Representation, gender, and cultural politics.* New York: Routledge.

Valenzuela, A. (1999). *Subtractive schooling: U.S. Mexican youth and the politics of caring.* New York: SUNY.

Van Maanen, J. (1989). *Tales of the field: On writing ethnography.* Chicago: University of Chicago Press.

Villenas, S. (1996). The colonizer/colonized Chicana ethnographer: Identity, marginalization, and co-optation in the field. *Harvard Educational Review, 66,* 711–731.

Villenas, S. (2000). This ethnography called my back: Writings of the exotic gaze, "othering" Latina, and recuperating Xicanisma. In E. St. Pierre & W. Pillow (Eds.), *Working the ruins: Feminist poststructural theory and methods in education* (pp. 74–95). New York: Routledge Press.

Visweswaran, K. (1994). *Fictions of feminist ethnography.* Minneapolis: University of Minnesota Press.

Visweswaran, K. (2010). *Un/common cultures: Racism and the rearticulaton of cultural difference.* Durham, NC: Duke University Press.

Walker, A. (1974). *In search of our mothers' gardens.* New York: Harcourt Brace Jovanovich.

Walkerdine, V. (1990). *Schoolgirl fictions.* New York: Verso.

Ward, K. (1999). The cyber-ethnographic (re)construction of two feminist online communities. *Sociological Research Online, 4*(1). Retrieved June 15, 2011, from http://www.socresonline.org.uk/4/1/ward.html

Wax, R. H. (1971). *Doing fieldwork: Warnings and advice.* Chicago: University of Chicago Press.

Willis, P. (1977). *Learning to labour.* Farnborough, UK: Saxon House.

11

FEMINIST QUALITATIVE INTERVIEWING

Experience, Talk, and Knowledge

Marjorie L. DeVault and Glenda Gross

The simple thing to say is that interview research is research conducted by talking with people. It involves gathering informants' reports and stories, learning about their perspectives, and giving them voice in academic and other public discourse. Talking with others is a fundamental human activity, and research talk simply systematizes that activity.

This simple view, however appealing, neglects the fascinating complexity of human talk—the flexibility and productive powers of language; the subtle shades of meaning conveyed through the nuances of speech, gesture, and expression; issues of translation; the ineluctable locatedness of any moment or stretch of talk; the specialized vocabularies of particular settings and groups; the organizing effects of format and genre; the injuries and uses of silence; the challenges inherent in listening; and so on. The simple view also neglects the dynamics of power involved in any empirical research: the hierarchical, often charged relations between researcher and informants, the politics of interpretation and representation, and the social consequences of making claims on the basis of science. Add to this picture a political commitment to feminism, and one begins to see the terrain of feminist interview research.

Much qualitative and feminist research has been based on a relatively straightforward commitment to collecting and representing the perspectives of informants, and those projects have often had powerfully liberatory effects. Drawing on the political traditions of testimony and consciousness-raising and the research traditions of life-history and open-ended interviewing, feminists have brought forward a wealth of previously untold stories—those of marginalized peoples and also those that the more privileged may have kept hidden, awaiting a receptive audience (or a skillful interlocutor). But another essential aspect of feminist interview research interrogates the challenges of communication and the inherent contradictions in the desire to give voice to others. This strand of thinking has produced a variety of feminist studies that use interview data in complex and nuanced ways, often to explore language and discourse itself.

Feminist scholars operate reflexively and relationally, so we begin by considering our own intellectual biographies and contexts and our relations with each other and the concerns of this chapter. We are feminist scholars of different generations—Marj coming to feminism and the early days of women's studies in the mid-1970s and Glenda entering well-established fields of feminist sociology and women's studies in the late 1990s. When Marj took "Introduction to Women's Studies" in Madison, Wisconsin, in 1975, there was a dearth of feminist writing in the academy; texts for the course included the Bible and the novels of writers like D. H. Lawrence—works awaiting our critique. At that time, talking together about sexual harassment or lesbianism was startlingly illuminating. By the time Glenda took a first women's studies course in upstate New York, we had textbooks and readers, which drew upon a rich feminist literature, as well as official policies and procedures on sexual harassment. When Marj began a study of housework, as a graduate student in the early 1980s, she had to justify focusing interviews on such a "trivial" matter; yet she was inspired by a lively political literature, including that from a "wages for housework" movement. When Glenda formulated her doctoral research project in 2001, she set out to interview "feminist pedagogues," a group who had come into existence as a result of two decades of feminist theory and practice; yet her interest in their practice arose in part from the ways their practice was organized by a conservative response to academic feminism.

These histories and our reflections on the politics of feminism, especially the institutionalization of this politics in the academy, form the backdrop for our approach here. We recognize Sandra Harding's (1987) distinction between "methods" (i.e., particular research tools and practices), "methodology" (theorizing about research practices and their implications for people and communities), and "epistemology" (the study of how one comes to know); we would suggest that feminist researchers have mostly used standard methods and that distinctive feminist insights have come in our strategic theorizing about the research process and knowledge production more generally. We see that

feminist research has become an established enterprise and that "feminist interviewing" is widely accepted and taught as an approach any scholar should know and appreciate. Yet we worry that the label may travel more easily than the politics, and we yearn for ways to renew continually the political force of feminist scholarship. These observations frame our approach to this chapter. In keeping with the aims of a handbook, we hope to provide guidance for new and experienced researchers conducting feminist interview research; at the same time, our understanding of feminism leads us away from any settled codification of tools and techniques.

ARTICULATING A CONCEPTION OF FEMINIST METHODOLOGY

Researchers who claim the label *feminist* for their methodological projects must be prepared to reply to questions about the meaning and distinctiveness of "feminist" methodology and research. Because interviewing always has, to some degree, the quality of "going to the people" (Taylor & Bogdan, 1998)—who may be in various positions of power or powerlessness—this definitional task is especially important for scholars who wish to claim a distinctiveness for feminist interview methodology. The range and variety of feminist theories in the social sciences are beyond the scope of our discussion here; for the purposes of this chapter, we define feminism broadly as a set of practices and perspectives that affirms differences among women and promotes women's interests, health, and safety, locally and abroad. It is a diverse and differentiated social and scholarly movement, but, for most adherents, it includes the aspiration to live and act in ways that embody feminist thought and promote justice and the well-being of all women. This formulation reflects our desire to contribute to an inclusive and multicultural feminism, and it draws on lessons we have learned from the scholarly work of "women of color feminists" such as Patricia Hill Collins (1990), María Lugones (1990), and many others.

We would also characterize feminism, along with other social justice projects (Collins, 1998), as activity that crosses the (blurred) boundaries between academic and other activist sites. Feminist and other critical academics continually draw on the insights produced by activism outside the university; we also can sometimes create relatively protected space for the development and dissemination of activist perspectives. Sometimes, feminist researchers are engaged in activism, either in or outside the academy. Scholars may also, at times, co-opt activist ideas, "taming" them for wider consumption, and we wish to keep those risks in mind. While the academy can be a "space for imagining opposition, for producing multiple subjectivities that are capable of critical thinking and resistant action against the institution itself," it is also "an institutional structure that is part of capitalist relations of rule within the nation state as well as internationally" (Mohanty, quoted in Dua & Trotz, 2002, p. 74). So, as feminists in the academy, we feel it is important to emphasize the importance of grassroots organizing, as well as political teaching and research work, in bringing about change.

There has been a rich conversation taking place among feminists in the academy about the connections between feminist theorizing, our practice as researchers or educators, and the implications of that practice for people's daily lives. Feminists' internal critiques have dismantled the notion of "woman" as the unified and foundational subject of feminism. Arguing that women are diversely situated in history, culture, and class; that genders are multiple; and that gender itself is a discursive production, theorists of gender and sexuality (and of the intersections of both with race, class, ability, and nation) now resist any simple reliance on this categorical identity. These theoretical developments, however, have proceeded unevenly through the disciplines. In those fields tied more closely to positivist epistemologies, scholars continue to treat gender as a relatively unproblematic variable (though with increasing attention to how it is crosscut by other identities), and those in applied fields and working in activist community settings (women's shelters, women's prisons, women's entrepreneurship programs, for instance) may find that their fields of activity remain tied to cultural and political assumptions about gender, even as

scholars subject those assumptions to an increasingly sophisticated critique.

Given this context, feminist interview researchers face two challenges. The first is to construct a rationale for labeling research feminist without reproducing the false homogenization and separations of historical feminisms. That is, we need to be cognizant of the differences that exist among women and be sure that, when we speak on behalf of women, we are not really speaking only on behalf of some women (e.g., North American, Anglo, able-bodied, middle-class women). We need to locate the "historically specific differences and similarities between women in diverse and asymmetrical relations" so that we are able to create "alternative histories, identities, and possibilities for alliances" (Kaplan, 1994, p. 139). The history of feminism, much like any history, is characterized by conflict, struggle, and resistance. And feminism owes much of its history to the political organizing of women of color, poor women, lesbian women, and women with disabilities. The work of these groups of women was instrumental in dismantling the idea that all women are the same and positioned evenly in the social landscape. Thus, we argue that researchers must adapt new theorizations of feminism so that they serve empirical projects— understood in our discussion quite broadly as projects in which researchers engage with others (in the flesh or less directly) to produce new knowledge. In other words, researchers need to take up the writings of feminist theorists, learn from those writings, and consider their implications for research practices.

In addition, feminist methodologists are continually responding to new developments in the world we investigate, and our research approaches must evolve in order to allow us to explore new terrain as it opens up. For example, the increasing importance of global economic restructuring and transnational practices, at all levels, have led feminist researchers to develop distinctive strategies for data collection and analysis. Similarly, the increasing scope and significance of online interaction offer researchers new sites, communities, and modes of communication to explore—and call for new approaches to interview-based research.

Aspects of Interview Research

With this background in mind, we will explore the central idea of qualitative interviewing, that knowledge can be produced in structured encounters organized around "telling about experience." We consider feminist thinking about how to organize and conduct such encounters and then discuss several aspects of interview research with which feminists have been especially concerned: active listening; the opportunities afforded by a focus on language, narrative, and discourse; interviewing ethics and the risks of "discursive colonization" (Mohanty, 1991); and feminist strategies for transnational and online research. We conclude with a discussion of the accountability of the feminist interviewer to research participants and other audiences and the importance of continual reflection on the intellectual and institutional context in which we do scholarship. Our approach is broadly "postpositivist": that is, we reject the idea that social realities are simply "there" for researchers to find. Instead, we understand the social contexts of people's lives as historically situated and constituted through people's activities, and we consider the research process itself as an integral aspect of the construction of knowledge about society.

Although we identify a number of practices that (in our view) make interview research feminist, we would also suggest that these are never matters solely related to collecting, analyzing, or presenting data. Instead, they are modes of thought and action that continually inform these mutually constitutive stages of the research process. In the next section, we begin with a brief historical account of feminist strategies for interview research; our intention is to highlight the ways in which feminist scholarship has emerged from its activist foundations and to recognize not only the ways in which feminist thinking has advanced over time but also its indebtedness to (and continuities with) early formulations.

Telling About "Experience"

Various forms of interviewing have long been used to bring people's experiences forward and make those experiences visible in more public discussions, and such projects have often been conducted with the aim of social reform. In the progressive era, British and U.S. social reformers conducted "social surveys" in immigrant neighborhoods and racially segregated communities. Beatrice and Sidney Webb, Jane Addams and the women of Hull House, and African American researchers and reformers such as W. E. B. Dubois and Zora Neale Hurston all spent time meeting and talking with people in such communities, and they recorded those encounters systematically to bring neglected voices into a civic conversation. Interviews are not always conducted with marginalized peoples, of course—interviews are now also used to explore the lives and actions of the powerful (e.g., Conti & O'Neil, 2007), to display or uncover our experiences of "ourselves" (e.g., DaCosta, 2007), and to map discursive contexts and "regimes" of ruling (e.g., Griffith & Smith, 2005). Interviewing has also become a central element in such regimes—the way we get jobs, apply for social assistance, talk through the media, prove that we are good parents, and so on. Indeed, interviews have become so central to contemporary life and governance that Gubrium and Holstein (2002) suggest that we live in an "interview society." Still, the traditions of research interviewing have been strongly linked to social justice concerns and projects and to the idea of bringing forward neglected voices—and these traditions continue to be especially important for feminist projects.

The practice of open-ended, semistructured interviewing favored by feminist researchers is discussed in every textbook of qualitative research methods and many general methods texts in the social sciences; recent editions of such texts generally include attention to feminist research and writing about interviewing (e.g., Bogdan & Biklen, 1998; Esterberg, 2002; Hesse-Biber & Leavy, 2010; May, 2002; Taylor & Bogdan, 1998; Warren & Karner, 2005). There are also a number of excellent book-length treatments of social science interviewing (e.g., Gubrium & Holstein, 2002; Kvale & Brinkmann, 2009; Seidman, 2006; Weiss, 1994; for focus groups, see Morgan, 1997, and Stewart, Shamdasani, & Rook, 2007; for narrative approaches, see Riessman, 2008). We recommend these to feminist researchers as useful sources for basic background and technique. In the 1970s and early 1980s, as women's studies and feminist research in the disciplines began to develop, feminist scholars took up these methods enthusiastically and also began to fashion distinctively feminist ways of conducting interview research.

The notion of "experience" was central to the resurgence of Western feminist activism in the 1960s and 1970s: The insights of the women's movement of that period came from women's collective talk, which was emerging from women's wartime participation in work and labor union settings, the state and federal women's commissions of the time, and the civil rights and antiwar movements, as well as in structured consciousness-raising groups. The practice of feminist consciousness-raising was borrowed (via civil rights and other radical organizing of the time) from the revolutionary Chinese practice of "speaking bitterness," a grassroots method for empowering peasant communities (Hinton, 1966; see also McLaren, 2000). Kathie Sarachild's (1978) talks to radical groups, Pamela Allen's (1973) booklet, and the statement of the Combahee River Collective (1982) outline U.S. feminist adaptations of this practice. In a sense, women who were part of these developments were "interviewing" themselves and others like them and then working together to make sense of experiences that were both "personal" and "political" (Hainisch, 1970, cited in Mansbridge, 1995, p. 28).

Looking back, we can see that these efforts were sometimes flawed by a failure to work out the broader politics of the "personal"; that is, the institutions, processes, and interactions shaping women's experiences were sometimes overlooked, and the unequal relations among different groups of women were often unaddressed. Still, these were conversations that allowed groups of women to begin theorizing their relations to one another and to introduce into public discussion ideas such as "sexism," "battering," and "woman identification." Even now, the insights that continue to enrich feminist theory often come from groups still marginalized in feminist discourse—for example, transgender people, feminists with disabilities, immigrant women,

and those in refugee communities. Their struggles to tell their stories can still push the boundaries of our thinking about gender, race, sexuality, and power.

Feminist theorists and researchers of the 1970s and 1980s followed the early activists in their reliance on experience. Feminist theorists urged scholars to "start thought" there or to "begin with experience" (Harding, 1991; Smith, 1987) and to rely on "the authority of experience" (Diamond & Edwards, 1977), and researchers embraced interviewing as a method of making experience hearable and subjecting it to systematic analysis. These moves were radical for the time because they suggested locating authority and "truth" somewhere other than in the received wisdom of the Euro- and androcentric disciplines—in the realities of Black women's lives, for instance, or in detailed historical analyses of struggle, resistance, and everyday living. They produced studies that told "truths" about women's lives, in contrast to the often distorted representations produced in scholarly networks made up of predominantly white or Anglo, middle- to upper-class men. African American feminists produced interview studies that portrayed Black women as strong and competent in the face of oppression, writing against sexist scholarship of the era that charged Black women with responsibility for the supposed "flaws" of African American families. Joyce Ladner (1971), for example, used interviewing and participant observation to produce an influential sympathetic study of African American teenaged girls living in poverty, *Tomorrow's Tomorrow*, and Inez Smith Reid (1972), responding to a call for information about "militant" women, wrote instead about *"Together" Black Women*. Ann Oakley (1974) and Helena Lopata (1971), in Britain and the United States, respectively, interviewed working women and middle-class women about housework and their lives as housewives—exploring the contours of the "problem with no name" (Friedan, 1963). Pauline Bart (1971) interviewed midlife Jewish women hospitalized for depression when their children left home and produced an account of their situation that located the problem in the culturally constructed mothering role that engulfed them rather than in their "over-involvement." Such studies used women's stories in a collective project of ideological critique. These scholars set women's own words against the ideological constructions of a racist and "sexist society" (Gornick & Moran, 1971): African American women's words against cultural stereotypes, middle-class women's words against the culture's simultaneous romanticization and trivialization of household labor, and depressed women's own stories against individualizing psychiatric diagnoses of their pain.

As these studies went forward, feminist researchers became more attentive to the dynamics of the interview process and began to write about distinctively feminist issues and approaches to interviewing. Ann Oakley's (1981) classic article, "Interviewing Women: A Contradiction in Terms," challenged the prevailing "rules" of distanced objectivity in social research. Oakley argued that the social science pretense of neutrality (the requirement, for example, that a woman interviewing other women about pregnancy should feign ignorance of the subject in order not to contaminate the data) was in conflict with the principles of feminism. Feminists began to conceptualize the interview as an encounter between women with common interests, who would share knowledge. They also wrote reflexively, looking critically at their attempts to involve participants in the research, considering how they heard and interpreted the women's accounts, and acknowledging their own concerns echoing through their analyses (Acker, Barry, & Esseveld, 1983).

This approach began to trouble the idea that women's stories were straightforwardly a source of truth and suggested that interview researchers must develop interactive methods that allow them to challenge and explore contradictory accounts (Gorelick, 1989). Dorothy Smith (1987) developed the idea that one would discover "lines of fault" in women's experience because their activities and perspectives are tied both to an everyday world of mundane caring and support work and also to a more ideologically structured realm in which those everyday concerns are relatively invisible. Her method of inquiry— "institutional ethnography" (discussed in more detail following this section)—was built on the notion that women could report on their everyday work, and the researcher could examine their reports and map the lines of fault they reveal.

Historian Joan Scott's (1991) landmark article "The Evidence of Experience" crystallized these observations about women's "own stories" and opened a series of debates about the relation of experience and language, debates that continue to the present. She argued that "experience" is always discursively structured, and her argument presented a fundamental challenge to historians and empirical social science researchers who took as their charge finding out "what happened." Scott (1992) suggested that to understand experience as natural, inherent, or "uncontestable evidence" is too simple (p. 24). Such a naturalist view takes for granted categories like "man, woman, black, white, heterosexual, or homosexual by treating them as given characteristics of individuals" and ignores the constructed and historically situated character of any experience (p. 27). "Questions about . . . how subjects are constituted as different in the first place, about how one's vision is structured— about language (or discourse) and history—are left aside" (p. 25). Instead of telling what happened, researchers should examine the discourses at play and the subject "positions" constructed by those discourses. One might, for example, conduct a kind of Foucauldian genealogical study (tracing the historical emergence of various categories and representations with an interest in how they organize consciousness and social institutions (see, e.g., Foucault, 1977, 1978) or use people's accounts of experience to investigate how such discursive formations appear in their talk, but it would be naive to take their accounts as straightforward reports of some "actual" experience.

Feminist researchers continue to explore and debate the implications of these ideas. Some have suggested that they signal the impossibility of any representation of others that is untainted by the researcher's own need and desire (Clough, 1992) and have moved toward analyses that "perform" those needs and desires as they shape an empirical investigation (Orr, 2006). But other scholars have been reluctant to abandon some grounding notion of experience (Alcoff, Hames-Garcia, Mohanty, & Moya, 2006; Moya, 2002), emphasizing experience as a "resource for critical reflection" (Stone-Mediatore, 1998, p. 121). Moreover, Shari Stone-Mediatore (2003) notes that "despite academic critiques of experience, many social struggles, from welfare rights campaigns to fair trade coalitions . . . continue to rely on stories of experience to bring public attention to their concerns" (p. 1). Certainly, these debates have produced more sophisticated understandings of experience. Smith (1999, chap. 6), for example, in an essay on "Telling the Truth After Postmodernism," makes an argument that recognizes and draws upon the central ideas of post-structuralist theory and also preserves the significance of embodied existence. She points to the groundedness of language in social interaction; in her approach, language is critically important, but it cannot be separated from activity.

For interview researchers, we believe that these theoretical perspectives point to the necessity for a critical approach to informants' accounts. A critical approach does not have to be a dismissive or "debunking" approach; indeed, we have tried to illustrate in this section the potential uses of interview studies founded on a relatively straightforward notion of experiential authority. But the strongest feminist research brings along with that idea a complementary awareness that researchers are always working with accounts constructed linguistically. We argue that interview researchers need to recognize that experience recounted is always emergent in the moment, that telling requires a listener and that the listening shapes the account as well as the telling. Furthermore, both telling and listening are shaped by discursive histories (so that fragments of many other tellings are carried in any embodied conversation). In the next section, we consider relations between teller and listener in the feminist interview.

Conditions and Conduct of the Interview

Interview researchers have long been concerned with the identities and social locations of parties to the interview, worrying that differences will produce failures of rapport that limit disclosure and that similarities may lead to "over-rapport" and bias. Standard practice has typically involved "matching" interviewer and interviewees to the extent possible; especially in large-scale survey and collaborative research, team members may divide interviewing labor so

as to achieve this kind of fit between researcher and participants. Feminist researchers share these concerns and practices, but they have developed more complex, more thoroughly reflexive views of identity and its effects in the interview. Much feminist research has been conducted by women researchers with women participants (though, recently, feminists have turned more often than in the past to interviews with men—a trend we discuss below). Typically, feminist researchers have been committed to finding and acknowledging common ground with participants. That commitment, we suggest, has—perhaps unexpectedly—helped to bring differences into view because feminist researchers have explored and debated what actually happens when women interview women.

White feminists' early writings on interview research often began with the assumption of an automatically direct and comfortable relationship between the feminist researcher and her woman interviewee (as did Black feminist writers in their research with Black women). However, close attention to the dynamics of interviews, as they actually happen, brought more complex formulations. Catherine Kohler Riessman's (1987) influential article "When Gender Is Not Enough" marked a turning point in reflexive analysis of interview data. Riessman discussed her initial assumption that she would find common ground with women interviewees and then critiqued that too-simple desire by rereading interview material she appeared to have misunderstood in the moment of interviewing. Her article continues to provide a useful model because it not only cautions researchers against taking rapport for granted but also illustrates a strategy for working analytically with the awkward moments of difficulty in talking with others.

Women of color were quick to take up these ideas: Josephine Beoku-Betts (1994) wrote about similar challenges related to differences among women of African descent, and Patricia Zavella (1993) analyzed how her own Mexican American identity was crosscut by other dimensions (age, education, marital and family status) so that her relation to informants who shared her racial or ethnic identity was nuanced and constantly shifting. These insights continue to guide thought about relations in the field as feminist researchers explore new sites and work across increasingly varied identities. Verta Taylor and Leila Rupp (2005), for example, found "complex gender and sexual dynamics at play" in their research on drag queens:

> Ironically, we realized that being women and lesbians facilitated rather than hampered our entrée into the world of the drag queens. . . . We were also keenly aware that the ways in which we were different from the drag queens contributed to a continually shifting balance of power between them as men and the stars of the show and us as the tellers of their stories. (p. 2115)

Despite a preponderance of research by women with women, feminist researchers have not wanted to be limited to "cozy" interviews with participants who are comfortably similar; some have wanted to conduct research on and with men or with women who have had very different experiences and points of view. These projects are challenging in various ways. Meera Sehgal (2009), for example, who conducted fieldwork among women of India's Hindu right, identifies herself as a feminist "researching up—studying dangerous groups that have more power than she has" (p. 329), and she discusses her decision to veil aspects of her identity for her own safety. Rather than trying to level power relations, as many feminist researchers advocate, she found it advantageous to downplay her own knowledge and status, presenting herself as relatively inexperienced, so that movement participants saw her as unthreatening (and perhaps a potential convert). In order to learn from those she disagrees with, she located herself as a listener, as Kathleen Blee has done in her research on women of the Ku Klux Klan and in contemporary hate groups (Blee, 1991, 2002). Lois Presser (2009) addresses similar issues in the context of her interviews with men imprisoned for violent crimes. At times, Presser (2009) presented herself as "sympathetic to the men's claims of being misunderstood and mistreated" to keep the interview running smoothly, even though her sympathy was not genuine (p. 268).

Caroline Gatrell (2006), argues that it may often be important to include men as participants in feminist studies. Although she acknowledges the complexity of cross-gender interviewing, she found it useful to include men in her study of employed mothers in the UK, and she reports that male participants in her study were "just as cooperative and articulate as women" (Gatrell, 2006, p. 237). Interviewing men seems to be especially challenging when research participants are committed to masculinist projects. Terry Arendell (1997) reports that interviewing men about their divorce was more challenging than her previous research with women. The men who participated in her study responded in various ways to the interview situation, but they often tried to take charge of the situation, challenge the terms of the study, assert a masculinist superiority, and so on. Her account displays some men's remarkably explicit readings of her—they chastised her, as if she were the former wife; assumed from her interest in the topic that she was angry and bitter; and addressed her as "one of those feminists." She points out, however, that telling such stories and thus opening these encounters to "analytic scrutiny" allow researchers to examine the dynamics of gender in the research relation.

Such dynamics were even stronger for Jocelyn Elise Crowley (2007), who discusses the various ways that participants in research on a father's rights group attempted to take control and assert authority not only during but also before and after the interviews she conducted. Crowley does not self-identify as a feminist researcher, and, indeed, her account suggests that she might not have gained access if she had. Before agreeing to participate, many of her interviewees interrogated her about her beliefs and commitments, and she learned that some of them had conducted extensive research into her background and previous publications (which, incidentally, is easier for potential respondents in the age of Internet searching than in the past). We also do not know if Crowley identifies as a feminist, despite the fact that (like her potential interviewees) we looked for clues before including her work in this chapter. Rather than attempt to pin down her beliefs, we suggest here that some researchers may decide that they must forego explicit commitment to a political stance in order to engage some topics.

In these studies, men's readings of the research are particularly obvious, but we would add that research participants no doubt always make assumptions about the interviewer, and feminist researchers would be wise to consider those assumptions and their effects, even when they are not so evident. For example, informants may assume that the interviewer does not care about the informant, despite a shared gender status, or assume—particularly if the interviewer and informant are positioned differently with respect to race, gender, ability, sexuality, or age—that the interviewer will judge or misunderstand the informant.

There is relatively little writing on disability issues in feminist research, no doubt in part because people with disabilities have been so absent, until quite recently, from most of the disciplines. Yet ability structures interview encounters in powerful ways. Communication difficulties make it less likely that some will even be included in research, leading some disability advocates to argue for a "right to be researched" (Robert Bogdan, personal communication, 2005). When people with disabilities are included, able-bodied researchers may rely on false assumptions or slip too easily into stereotypical ways of thinking about their lives and capacities. Most scholarship on interviewing presumes an able-bodied researcher and is geared toward an able-bodied audience. Interview techniques are designed with particular verbal and cognitive capacities in mind, and they assume a relatively easy back and forth between interviewer and interviewee. As a result, researchers who interview elderly people with cognitive difficulties, or people with sensory, intellectual, or other impairments, for example, must adjust styles of interviewing and, in most cases, must plan on spending more time with each participant in order to produce useful data (Jones, 2007; Walmsley, 1995).

Melissa Jones (2007), for example, adapted the idea of life history interviewing in a process she calls "supportive autobiographical ethnography" in order to record the perspectives of three young women with intellectual disabilities who were enrolled in a segregated school program. She met with the participants throughout the school year, recording their accounts of their lives, and supplementing those accounts with material from her observations of their lives at school. Then she assembled the information in first-person stories that she shared

with the participants and revised as they requested. In becoming a "coauthor" of the stories, she took some interpretive authority but also provided the young women a venue in which they could share their perspectives without struggling against the expressive difficulties and judgments that permeated their school lives. Walmsley (1995) also discusses adaptations for research participants with learning disabilities, and Temple and Young (2004) address translation issues, focusing on research with Deaf participants and the power relations inherent in any cross-language project. Recognition and discussion of the additional work researchers studying people with disabilities carry out is missing from most scholarship related to interviewing and feminist research.

For feminist (and other) interviewers, we suggest that debates about who can research what (and which researchers should interview which participants) raise important issues but ultimately reveal that the more important question is how to organize interviews so as to produce more truly collaborative encounters, whatever the identities and commitments of participants. One strategy feminists have adopted is based on the basic fieldwork principle of sustained immersion; for example, Jones's (2007) coauthorship strategy, discussed previously, involves interviewing over a considerable period of time and allows the researcher and participants to revisit and revise the narratives they produce together. Projects based on life history interviewing, such as Ruth Behar's (1993) classic work with her Mexican informant Esperanza, usually involve sustained contact over long periods of time. Behar's account of her relationship with Esperanza provides illuminating details about the give and take of their research relations—on both emotional and material levels. Her text *Translated Woman* uses a collage technique that combines reporting on the interviews with "confessional" and autobiographical writing to display reflexively how the data were produced and analyzed over time.

A somewhat different strategy of immersion might involve seeking data in multiple ways, as in Christine Bigby's (2000) study of older women with developmental or intellectual disabilities. Recognizing that some of the women might not be able to provide all the information she wished to collect (and discovering that a few women were willing to participate in the study but couldn't or didn't want to be interviewed), Bigby sought additional information about each woman's situation from relatives, advocates, social workers, and other caregivers. Through these strategies, she was able to produce case studies that included the women's own perspectives and filled out their stories with supplementary information from others. This approach has the drawback of relying on others to interpret for people with disabilities, but it carries the benefit of allowing the researcher to explore experiences and issues that would otherwise be neglected.

Another dimension of reflexive interviewing that characterizes feminist interview traditions involves strategic disclosure on the part of the interviewer, whether that means sharing personal information or a willingness to reveal research interests and political commitments. Rosalind Edwards (1990), for example, suggests that white researchers interviewing Black participants should address racial identities and issues explicitly. She found that the best rapport with participants in her study came not when she asserted their similarities as women but rather when she acknowledged explicitly that her own social location differed from that of the interviewees. Marianne Paget (1983) argues that interviewing can produce a "science of subjectivity"—that is, a rigorous account of another's perspective. She thinks of the interview as a "search procedure"—a process of seeking meanings together. She suggests that the researcher share with the interviewee the concerns that animate the research, so the conversation can unfold as a collaborative moment of making knowledge. Her discussion illustrates that kind of sharing and unfolding with excerpts from her interview with a woman artist.

In some projects, it may be appropriate not only to share thoughts but also to press informants, challenging their taken-for-granted constructions. Sometimes, such a strategy might run through a set of interviews, as in Ruth Frankenberg's (1993) study of white women's racism. Frankenberg asked open-ended questions, but, given the relatively subtle ways that racism may be expressed (especially in a culture of "color-evasiveness"), she sought throughout the interviews to intervene "dialogically" in ways that would open up discussion of race and racism. In other instances, challenges to informants' taken-for-granted constructions may be more improvisational, arising in a moment of listening. For example, after several working-class informants had rejected feminism, saying in support of their position things such as "I want my husband to open the car door and light my cigarette," Lillian Rubin (1976) thought to ask one of them about the last time her husband had done that. Her interviewee, a bit taken aback, had to laugh and admit that she didn't even smoke (pp. 131–132). The moment is enlightening because it shows how this woman's perspective on feminism was rooted in cultural discourses of that period as well as in her experience.

In the conduct of any interview research, feminists attempt to maintain a reflexive awareness that research relations are never simple encounters, innocent of identities and lines of power. Rather, they are always embedded in and shaped by cultural constructions of similarity, difference, and significance. When Susan Chase (1995) interviewed women school superintendents with her research collaborator Colleen Bell, for example, they realized that the position of these powerful women shaped even the questions it was possible to ask. It was reasonable to ask them to spend time in research on their careers and achievements, but they likely would not have agreed to spend time answering questions about hobbies. Chase's book *Ambiguous Empowerment* remains an extremely useful source for feminist researchers because it illustrates how constructions of similarity and difference influence every aspect of the interview project: shaping the questions researchers ask and don't ask, the ease or difficulty of recruiting informants, the kinds of rapport that develop in the encounter, and the lenses through which researchers produce and analyze interview data.

The enlarged space that feminist thinking now allows for reflexive interpretation is evident in Raewyn Connell's 2010 analysis of a life history interview conducted 20 years earlier, in the late 1980s. While recruiting participants for a study of men's lives and masculinities, Connell was contacted by a male-to-female transsexual who wished to tell her story of masculinity, so people might come to know (in her words) "that transsexuals are just normal people, and for some unknown reason, physiological, psychological, whatever, have changed to a woman" (Connell, 2010, p. 15). Connell, who was at the time trying her best "to live as a man" (p. 4), felt a complex mix of empathy and tension during the interview, and could not decide at the time what to do with it. Later, however, following her own transition, she presents the story on its own terms (recognizing, of course, that we must always wonder if we succeed in that endeavor). She also discusses the interpretive and ethical dilemma it poses. On the one hand, the researcher wishes to honor the participant's request—to show that the interviewee is a "normal" person and to present her view of a gendered world. On the other hand, Connell expresses her own ambivalence about the gender politics of the participant's story and understanding of that world. She points out that, although transsexuality may be deeply transgressive, it is also the case that "to *operate* this revolutionary possibility, many transsexual women and many of their doctors have relied on deeply conservative gender schemata" (p. 18). When researchers are willing to reveal such personal involvements and how they affect what is at stake in the conduct and analysis of interviews, they make possible this kind of layered interpretation of the stories participants tell.

It is our impression that feminist ideas about reflexivity have traveled through the disciplines more successfully than any other feminist insights. We have observed that most scholars in the social sciences now recognize the ways that a researcher's background and commitments can influence his or her thought, and it is no longer unusual for audiences to demand some accounting of the researcher's personal stake in a project. We attribute the successful dissemination of this feminist idea to the clarity and strength with which feminist scholars have spoken of the androcentric and ethnocentric biases that so often mark research conducted as if "from nowhere." And we attribute that clarity and strength to feminists' passionate and engaged desire for scholarly coalitions that will produce research that can speak to women in many different locations and circumstances.

The desire for an inclusivity that acknowledges and values difference has also led feminist thinkers to key insights about the challenges of listening to others. Listening actively and well is such an important part of the conduct of interviews that we treat it in a separate section.

Listening

> Listening can be a radical activity. . . . For any listener, at risk are not only a sense of self, place and society, but also knowledge of one's own complicity with oppression. (Lester C. Olson, 1998, p. 448)

Listening is not as simple as it sounds, and failures of listening are often part of our interactions with others. Active listening means more than just physically hearing or reading; rather, it is a fully engaged practice that involves not only taking in information via speech, written words, or signs but also actively processing it. It means allowing that information to affect you, baffle you, haunt you, make you uncomfortable, and take you on unexpected detours—"away from abstract . . . bloodless, professionalized questions," toward peoples, knowledges, and experiences that have been disavowed, overlooked, and forgotten (Gordon, 1997, p. 40).

Antiracist feminists have long theorized the transformative potential of active listening. Audre Lorde (1984), for instance, has written on the troubling consequences of Anglo women's inability to listen actively to women of color's experiences with racism, (hetero)sexism, and economic exploitation. When white women excuse their dismissal of the concerns of women of color because these concerns are expressed with anger, she argues, the possibilities for meaningful, systemic change are significantly weakened. Lorde acknowledges that "the history of white women who are unable to hear Black women's words, or to maintain dialogue with [Black women], is long and discouraging" (p. 66). Still, she hopes more and more white women will hold themselves accountable to recognize the various forms of violence and oppression that characterize the realities and experiences of women of color.

As Bernice Johnson Reagon (1983) explains in "Coalition Politics: Turning the Century," moving outside one's cozy "barred room" into situations or spaces that are uncomfortable is not easy, but it is certainly necessary if any coalition work is to be successful. Active listening, she suggests, is about survival. "There is no chance that you can survive by staying *inside* the barred room" (Reagon, 1983, p. 358). Feminist researchers should continue to learn from these activist writings and seek insights from contemporary activist projects (see, for example, INCITE!, 2006; Naples & Desai, 2002; Tripp & Ferree, 2006). If we wish to create knowledge that challenges rather than supports ruling regimes, we must constantly be attentive to histories, experiences, and perspectives that are unnoticed, unfamiliar, or too easily neglected or misrepresented.

A researcher's practice of listening affects the data and knowledge she or he produces. Feminist researchers who take the work of active listening for granted risk producing work that reinforces dominant perspectives. For instance, a researcher who enters a research encounter assuming she or he is a naturally good listener, without consciously acknowledging the work that active listening entails, may end up hearing only what she or he wants or expects to hear. Furthermore, although it may seem plausible to assume that our status as women or feminists prevents us from reproducing power relations during and after an interview, such an assumption is problematic. As researchers, we must be cognizant of the fact that feminists may be divided by relations of power and privilege. Listening may require that we acknowledge the ignorance our own privileges may have produced before we can hear what others wish to tell us.

It is difficult, of course, to know from published reports about a researcher's practice of listening, but some feminist scholars have written in ways that open a window onto listening as an element of interview research. DeVault (1990), for example, in "Talking and Listening From Women's Standpoint," adopts an analytic approach influenced by ethnomethodology that entails close examination of the interview talk—a kind of textual representation of listening, constructed retrospectively. She suggests that this kind of approach allows the researcher to attend to silences and difficulties of communication produced by the lines of fault in women's lives. Noticing when women speak haltingly, or circuitously, for instance, can provide an opening for

analysis of a misfit between women's own experiential perspectives and the languages or ideological constructions of their cultures. Amy Best (2003) adopts a related approach to "hear" and bring forward the ways that she and the participants in her study were producing "whiteness" as they managed and negotiated their racial identities through their interview talk.

Some researchers bring forward particular instances of listening (often highlighting difficulties) and discuss what these reveal. Alison Griffith and Dorothy Smith (2005), for example, report noticing the discomfort they experienced as they interviewed mothers about their children's schooling. Recognizing that some of the mothers' reports elicited intense guilt about their own mothering, they developed an analysis of a mothering discourse that produces such feelings. Similarly, Sari Knopp Biklen (1995) reports on a series of interviews with an African American schoolteacher in which she wanted to focus on the teacher's professional work, while her informant seemed to want to share talk about their children and family lives. In retrospect, and noticing that they were the only two "working mothers" of young children in the school, Biklen believes she failed to hear the woman's attempt to share perspectives with someone in a similar circumstance.

Listening may also become an explicit topic when it is especially challenging. Rebecca Klatch (1987), who interviewed "right-wing women," describes her "non-argumentative approach": "If asked, of course I would state my own doubts or disagreements, but generally I defined my own role entirely in terms of listening and absorbing the other world view" (p. 17). In Kathleen Blee's (1991) study, based on oral history interviews with women who had been members of the white-supremacist Ku Klux Klan in Indiana during the 1920s, listening carefully allowed her to identify a cultural background she shared with the women she had been "prepared to hate and fear" and thus to see that the Klan of the 1920s expressed a racism that was exaggerated but not unrelated to the white culture of its time and place.

One of feminism's central claims is that women's perspectives have often been silenced or ignored; as a result, feminist researchers have been interested in listening for gaps and absences in women's talk, and in considering what meanings might lie beyond explicit speech. DeVault (1990, 1996) attempts this kind of analysis through close attention to speech, focusing interpretation on the moments when speech seems to falter. Wendy Luttrell (1997), who conducted life-story interviews with working-class women about their experiences with schooling, reflects not only on the content of the interviews but on moments when she believes she caught unspoken meanings in her exchanges with informants (see, e.g., pp. 16–17). In a more recent project (Luttrell, 2003), she worked with African American teens continuing their schooling during pregnancy. The young women had to confront negative social stereotypes in talking about themselves, and Luttrell developed an innovative methodology to explore their self-perspectives: The girls made collage art pieces, and Luttrell interviewed them, as a group, about the images they had chosen for these representations.

Some experiences are more obdurate, and feminist researchers must sometimes be content simply to point toward silences. R. Ruth Linden (1993), for example, in a reflexive analysis of Holocaust survivors' attempts to narrate their experiences, draws on Hannah Arendt's notion of unassimilable "sheer happenings." She suggests that gaps and silences in their narratives may point to events they experience as simply so horrific that they cannot be narrativized.

Another intriguing example comes from Rannveig Traustadóttir's (2000) ethnographic study of the friendship between two young women, one with an intellectual disability and the other a "typical" student preparing for a career in special education. Traustadóttir spends time with the two girls, interviewing them informally along the way; she also conducts more formal interviews with the young student but cannot elicit a clear statement of the other girl's perspective through formal interviewing. Despite this silence, the researcher provides a tentative interpretation of the disabled girl's (possibly) increasing dissatisfaction with the relationship, "read" through clues that Traustadóttir could observe in her behavior. As in Bigby's (2000) study (discussed earlier), there are risks of misinterpretation in such a strategy, but we would suggest that the value of bringing forward, however tentatively, a perspective that might otherwise simply fall out

of view outweighs those risks. We assume, of course, that researchers' readings of informants' views in such cases will be based on extensive and systematic observation, as well as on knowledge about informants' circumstances and contexts. We also recommend that such "readings" be put forward "lightly" (DeVault, 1996), with explicit acknowledgement that readers should consider alternative interpretations.

In summary, we argue that, if feminist researchers are interested in creating knowledge that is *for* rather than *about* the people they study, then they must be active listeners. Like the playful "world" traveler that María Lugones (1990) imagines, the active listener must interrogate her or his deep-seated assumptions about various worlds and her or his arrogant perceptions of others in those worlds. Both playful "world" traveling and active listening operate as means to identify with and love people living in alternate, unfamiliar worlds without (ab)using them. We have learned what it means to be active listeners not only from second wave feminists in the social sciences but also from women of color like Audre Lorde and others whose writings and edited collections continue to call to our attention and nourish us with stories of oppression, resistance, and survival (Alexander, Albrecht, Day, & Segrest, 2003; Anzaldúa & Keating, 2002; INCITE!, 2006). These writers and writings fuel many feminists' investigations of the social world. They remind feminist researchers to be self-reflective and critical of deeply disciplined research practices by offering "imaginative access to what is, for some, an unimaginable experience" (Code, 2001, p. 273). The insights of women of color feminists and Anglo feminists continue to cultivate the transformation of scholars from arrogant perceivers to empathetic, decolonizing researchers and to foreground the importance of active listening in all stages of the research process.

Structures of Talk and Discourse

Perhaps because of the significance of listening, feminist researchers have been especially attentive to one recent trend in interview research, which involves a heightened attention to the structures and organization of language, talk, and discourse. Since the mid-1980s, scholars have been developing an interdisciplinary stream of thought focused on narrative and representation, sometimes referred to as a linguistic or narrative "turn" (Behar & Gordon, 1995; Clifford & Marcus, 1986). One central idea is that narratives are fundamental to identity and to the ways that people make sense of their worlds. People are constantly telling stories, to themselves and to others. Elliot Mishler's (1986) influential book on interviewing pointed to the pervasiveness of stories in most interview data. He suggested that conventional approaches to analysis, which extract thematic bits of those stories, are likely to disrupt the coherence of informants' perspectives. By contrast, looking at longer stretches of talk (referred to by some as "discourse analysis") and assessing especially the stories people tell and how they tell them (typically labeled "narrative analysis") can offer distinctive possibilities for maintaining the coherence of a person's perspective.

Feminist scholars such as Catherine Kohler Riessman (2008) and Susan Bell (1999) have developed these insights and applied them in studies of women's experiences of divorce, infertility, and reproductive health. Some studies of this sort focus extensively on the structures of people's stories, so the content of their talk becomes secondary, but feminists using narrative analysis generally want to examine the structures of storytelling in order to enhance their interpretation of women's reports. Riessman's (1987, 2008) analyses of the form of a Latina interviewee's story (1987), for example, and of Indian women's accounts of infertility (2008) provide both interpretive readings that allow her to explore the accounts and a way for her to hear more fully what is being said. First readings of surface content are deepened through layered analysis of repeated themes, metaphors, and styles of narration.

Another important idea is that how stories are told is not just an individual matter; people's stories are shaped by the formats available to them and reflect the perspectives and values of their communities. Thus, a narrative may be a place to see human agency in play with social structures, expressive activity that is shaped by its social context (Maynes, Pierce, & Laslett, 2008). The narrative turn brought a new consciousness of such issues to the practice of oral

history and life history interviewing, and feminist scholars began to write much more reflexively about how such interviews are negotiated between the parties and how the researcher produces a representation of the encounter (Gluck & Patai, 1991; Personal Narratives Group, 1989). Judy Long's (1999) book *Telling Women's Lives* provides a theoretical and epistemological discussion of these issues, formulating an interpretive prism of sorts with four facets: subject, narrator, reader, and text. Like Maynes, Pierce, and Laslett (2008), she includes in her discussion not only life history interview studies but also the production of biography and autobiography. These theorists explore the intersections of gender with genre, in other words, the ways that typical or expected narratives may constrain what women can easily tell (and what listeners or readers can easily grasp) about their experience—and these perspectives may fruitfully complement more empirically grounded analyses of the narratives provided in research interviews.

Dorothy Smith's (1987) development of a "sociology for women," based on a mode of inquiry she calls "institutional ethnography" (Smith, 2005), provides a method explicitly focused on the ideological practices of "ruling" that shape women's experiences and how they recount them (in interviews and elsewhere). Smith has formulated institutional ethnography as a "feminist method" arising from the change in women's consciousness associated with the women's movement of the 1970s; more broadly, she sees it as a "sociology for people" or "alternative sociology." Her writing about the approach touches on much more than just interview research. However, interviews are often quite important in feminist institutional ethnographies (see DeVault & McCoy, 2002), and Smith's writings on the theoretical foundations of her approach have broad implications for interview research of many sorts.

Briefly, institutional ethnography takes up some "standpoint" as a point of entry to inquiry. Interviews are often used to explore activities of a particular group and to produce a full picture of their experiences at that point of entry. However, the researcher is committed to looking beyond local experience. The next step in the research is to examine local activities to see how they are connected with or "hooked into" activities occurring elsewhere. This "hooking in" or alignment is typically accomplished in contemporary societies through various texts, such as time cards and job descriptions, mission statements and strategic plans, databases and the statistics compiled from them, media portrayals and the conceptual framings they employ, and so on. These texts allow for coordinated action in the complex and interlocking institutional formations that organize contemporary societies, putting in place "ruling relations" that reach into people's daily (and nightly) activity.

The "problematic" or question posed in this kind of study is how a particular piece of "everyday life" is organized, extra-locally. Often, institutional ethnographers find that organizational practices produce difficulties in everyday life because institutional ideologies fragment "what's actually happening" for the person. It may be, for example, that only part of a battered woman's story is written up in the police report (Pence, 2001) or that only part of what the clerical or health care worker does is recognized in her job description (Rankin & Campbell, 2006; Reimer, 1995). Thus, only part of that experience is accountable in other places—in the sentencing or probation hearing, for example, or in the calculation of wages, promotion and managerial policy, or assessments of the quality of hospital care.

Smith (1987, 1990a, 1990b, 1999) has developed these ideas in a series of essays on women's perspective as a critique of conventional sociology and on text-mediated social organization and what she calls "conceptual practices of power." Many of her arguments rest on a distinction between "primary narratives"—told by an embodied narrator from an experiential point of view—and various institutional narratives produced from the "raw materials" of primary storytelling. For example, she has written about how a single observer's account of a political demonstration compares with the official account, delivered in the voice of the authorities; how a woman's behavior is worked up by acquaintances as "mental illness"; how a death becomes an officially warranted "suicide"; or how Virginia Woolf's state of mind before she killed herself is read as insanity. The logic of these essays suggests an approach to interview data based on the idea that one can find social

organization "in talk." At some points, people will narrate what they do, specifically and straightforwardly; a researcher can encourage that kind of reporting through the questions she or he asks. At other points, the interviewee's talk will draw upon institutional categories and concepts, as when teachers refer to "ADHD kids" or make reference to organizational texts, such as grade-specific curricula or the "IEP" (or individualized education plan) used in U.S. schools to spell out accommodations to be made for students identified as having disabilities. The institutional ethnographer can use both kinds of talk to explore the textual "leap" from experience to "documentary reality"—that is, how the organization "works up" the activities of teachers and students and how the coordinative texts of the educational system recruit them into relations they may not intend.

Researchers using this approach often conduct interviews with people working in several different sites rather than designing studies limited to one particular group. Because institutional ethnographers are seeking connections across sites, their research designs focus on translocal "regimes" of social organization. Once the researcher has identified significant texts, she may want to interview those who produce or work with those texts. Ellen Pence's (2001) "audit" studies of the processing of domestic violence cases, for example, involve extensive interviews with 911 operators, police dispatchers and responding officers, advocates, judges, and probation officers. Each participant contributes a locally grounded piece of the "processing" picture, and seeing how each works with a particular case shows how a woman's experience gets transformed as it becomes a "case." In addition, institutional ethnographers often combine interviewing with textual analysis, as Kamini Maraj Grahame (1998) does in a study of a feminist community organization's "outreach" to women of color and Rosamund Stooke (2003, 2004) does in her study of the gendered work of children's librarians. In recent work, Paul Luken and Suzanne Vaughan (2005, 2006) collected older women's accounts of their housing histories and then showed how their stories (and presumably, the work they did to create homes for their families) were shaped by commercial and public health discourses of their era. More on this approach can be found in Campbell and Gregor's (2002) "primer," Smith (2005, 2006), and DeVault and McCoy's (2002) discussion focused specifically on interview research.

RECENT DEVELOPMENTS IN INTERVIEW RESEARCH

Our discussion has begun with the historical foundations of feminist interview research and traced its development in relation to its social and intellectual context; we see both continuity and significant changes, as feminists have generated new conversations. In this section, we discuss two lines of methodological thinking—focused on transnational and online research—that have developed from significant (and interrelated) social changes: the increasing reach and significance of a global economy and the extraordinary development and spread of electronic technologies and the Internet.

Interviewing in Global and Transnational Research

For some time, feminist anthropologists have been developing "multisited" approaches that involve interviewing designed to investigate cultural discourses. Emily Martin (1994), for instance, interviewed scientists and lay people to explore the common social metaphors that appear in their talk. Catherine Lutz and Jane Collins (1993) used observation and interviewing to examine the production of *National Geographic* images; then they interviewed lay readers about how they saw those images. Behar's (1993) life history text (discussed previously) addresses the politics of border crossing in research by Anglo-European academics in other parts of the world. The increasing complexity of border transactions—as both people and products migrate across national boundaries—has encouraged researchers to seek ways of mapping and analyzing those transactions, as in studies of the global assembly line (Salzinger, 2003) or in "commodity chain" analysis (Freidberg, 2001). Arlie Russell Hochschild (2003), for example, adapted the commodity chain idea in order to highlight transnational flows of "care workers" who

migrate to provide domestic, child-care, and health services for more privileged families in other parts of the world. Similarly, Western feminists' increasing consciousness of their reliance on low-wage garment workers elsewhere has stimulated both activism on behalf of those workers and research meant to document and support that activism (Brooks, 2007; Harrington, 2005).

Studying transnational social relations and processes requires feminist ethnographers to research multiple sites of activity. Their unit of analysis is not a single site, but rather "flows of cultural products, people, and commodities across national borders and spaces, including the social relations that transcend borders" (Mendez, 2009, p. 69; and see Gille & Ó Riain, 2002). In one recent study, Marie Campbell and Kathy Teghtsoonian (2010) adopted the institutional ethnography approach to examine relations of "global governance" and the organization of gender, as these phenomena manifest in the work of international and local NGOs engaged in development work in Kyrgyzstan. Beginning from their awareness of how critical international funding is for NGOs working on women's issues in such locations, they consider the development of principles of "aid effectiveness" by the Organization for Economic Cooperation and Development (OECD). Their analysis considers how such principles were adopted by the Dutch aid organization funding work in Kyrgyzstan and how they were taken up (or not) in specific local projects. The project involved interviews with aid and development workers not only in Kyrgyzstan and the Netherlands but also in international organizations such as the United Nations and the OECD, where the conceptual frameworks of aid effectiveness are being developed and applied.

These kinds of projects allow researchers to move "between public and private spheres of activity, from official to 'subaltern' informal contexts—and in a very literal sense from one place to another" (Lauser, 2008, p. 87). However, conducting interviews in multiple sites introduces a variety of practical challenges. These include the negotiation of sufficient funding, finding time for necessary relationship building and follow-up, and managing communication in situations of linguistic complexity. In addition to these practical problems, Jennifer Bickham Mendez (2009) discusses "three sets of challenges to feminist research that a global approach has presented, complicated, or intensified: 'power differentials,' 'researcher as insider/outsider,' and the 'dangers' of 'accountability and ethical' issues" (p. 68).

Mendez (2009) explores the impact of global economic processes on the Working and Unemployed Women's Movement, "María Elena Cuadra" (MEC), in Nicaragua and the Program for Integral Community Health (PICH) in Williamsburg, Virginia. These organizations are similar in that they both "facilitate poor women's access to resources and services," but they are very different in terms of their location, "orientations, structures, and visions" (p. 76). As both an ethnographer and a participant in these organizations, Mendez notes that people's perceptions of her and the power relations between her and others varied considerably within and between these organizations. For example, Mendez states, "Local and global power differentials shaped my relationship with MEC, giving rise to a complicated position that would shift between 'insider/ *cooperante*' and 'outsider/foreigner'" (p. 83). In Williamsburg, Mendez's "position with PICH vacillated between 'insider,' a community partner and ally, and an 'outsider,' potentially a rule enforcer or whistle blower" (p. 86). As in other kinds of feminist research, "insider" and "outsider" are not mutually exclusive categories. Mendez suggested that the challenges and benefits wrought from being an "insider" and "outsider" are further complicated in feminist studies addressing global processes that are not confined to one locale; as one moves from site to site, "differences of culture, nationality, and place-based identities shape definitions of social membership" (p. 86).

Researching multiple sites also means researchers must be accountable to multiple, intersecting communities and groups. Inevitably, since various communities are located unevenly in the global landscape in terms of power and resources, the varied interests and concerns of these communities may conflict. For example, as someone actively involved with PICH's efforts, Mendez was exposed to information that could have negatively affected the immigrant women and their families. She had to think creatively about ways to guarantee "accountability where there are diverse, sometimes conflicting,

interests" (p. 90). Similarly, Christy Harrington (2005) studied the Fiji garment industry because she was interested in improving the work lives of Fiji garment workers. Although her allegiance was first and foremost with the garment workers, she felt constrained by the ethical obligation to protect the interests of the factory owners who allowed her to conduct the research.

Alison Mountz and her colleagues (Mountz, Miyares, Wright, & Bailey, 2003), drawing on the principles and challenges of a feminist methodological discourse, offer a perspective on the distinctive challenges of team research in a transnational project on the political activities of Salvadorans in New Jersey. Despite the team's "democratic ground rules" (p. 33), members found that their research was complicated not only by their multiple research sites but also by differences of gender, geography, and methodological knowledge. And despite their initial commitment to combining survey and qualitative interviewing, they encountered tensions—both within the team and between researchers and community members—related to participant recruitment, standardization and storytelling, and the emotional challenges of work in communities with a history of violence for participants and the interviewer. Their discussion of their collective "methodological becoming" provides an unusually frank presentation of these challenges. We expect that transnational topics will continue to engage feminist researchers, and we look forward to a methodological literature that will explore its characteristic and distinctively feminist challenges.

Online Interviewing

The rapid development in recent years of computer and information technology, the worldwide web, and social networking spaces offers new possibilities and challenges for interviewing and may ultimately bring significant changes in how we understand the interview. It is amusing now to read accounts from the early days of these developments—not so long ago—when researchers might brag about writing on their new personal computers; these accounts reveal how quickly these technologies are changing the work processes of social researchers. A lively methodological literature explores the potential for online technologies to enhance our research on offline topics and also to offer new topics for investigation. Many writers refer to the work of Mann and Stewart (2001) as an early but still key source in the area; with respect specifically to interviewing, see also O'Connor et al. (2008) and Kasmer and Xie (2008), who provide a comparative overview of face-to-face, telephone, e-mail, and instant message (IM) interviewing.

Even researchers who intend to conduct face-to-face interviews may now recruit participants and follow up with them later via e-mail, IM, or text; rely on e-mail lists or discussion groups to solicit participation; and locate individual participants or groups and organizations of interest through web searching or recruitment in social networking spaces. The convenience of these modes of communication could lead to an overreliance on Internet contacts, however. Thus, we suggest that researchers always be aware of the advantages and potential downsides of online and more direct recruitment procedures. Digital recorders and software packages designed for qualitative analysis have become standard equipment, and some researchers are experimenting with voice recognition and transcription software (though there is still no technological substitute for the labor of producing high-quality interview data). Even the best voice recognition software can only be "trained" to reproduce a single voice, so it cannot automatically transform interview tapes into text; however, some researchers recommend a process of listening to tapes and then voicing the material for reproduction. Although this strategy bypasses a good deal of typing, it still requires careful listening and assiduous checking to ensure accuracy. Furthermore, it will not suffice if the researcher aims to produce a transcript that preserves nonlexical details of talk, such as hesitation, intonation, and the like (though, of course, these features could be added later to a preliminary transcript produced with voice recognition software).

Like other qualitative researchers, feminists are experimenting with the possibilities of online data collection. (Quantitative researchers have also begun to mount surveys through online platforms; these technologies may also support the distribution and analysis of open-ended interview questions, but not the extended, indepth, improvisational back and forth of the classic qualitative interview.) Given the feminist commitment to inclusive research, one major concern is whether and how online research methods either facilitate or inhibit participation. Feminists adopting Internet methods should be conscious of the "digital divide," a term coined to refer to social disparities in people's access to and ability to derive benefit from Internet technologies. Researchers should always thoughtfully assess whether our reliance on these technologies may have the effect of excluding some potential participants in our research—or, more insidiously, may affect our conceptualization of the research topic and scope. Still, some researchers believe that online methods may open up opportunities for participation. Matthews and Cramer (2008), for example, argue that Internet technologies may enhance research conducted on and with "hidden populations," drawing on their studies of gay, lesbian, bisexual, and transgender (GLBT) communities. They suggest that chat rooms or other kinds of Internet group sites may be used to find and recruit participants and also that a researcher-created web group might be used for follow-up and to collect participant feedback on the project and its findings. They also discuss videoconferencing as an alternative to face-to-face interviewing. These techniques allow the researcher to extend the geographical range of the project, and they may also alleviate some of the worries that "hidden population" participants might have about self-disclosure to a stranger.

Similarly, Moloney et al. (2004) used Internet data collection to facilitate the participation of midlife women in a study of perimenopausal migraine headaches, thereby connecting with a group of women who, in previous research, had found it difficult to schedule time for in-person focus groups. The research team developed project-specific discussion boards in order to elicit the kind of narrative data that might come from focus group interviewing, with the researcher periodically posting questions to begin new discussion "threads." Despite the advantages of their approach, they warn that such uses of technology come with a steep "learning curve" (p. 80); in addition, the flexibility of the approach for participants brings with it a requirement that the researchers monitor the project site very regularly and be ready to respond to inevitable technical difficulties. This team also found that online interviewing diminished the kind of "engagement" that both participants and they as feminist researchers hoped to achieve (Moloney et al., 2004, pp. 81–82). This group of researchers also discusses some exclusions that seemed related to access to technology, and Matthews and Cramer (2008) point out that any deployment of online technology must take into account issues of website accessibility for people with disabilities. These discussions echo Nicola Illingworth's (2001) caution that researchers should not think of online research as an "easy option."

Illingworth (2001) turned to Internet methods in a project on involuntary childlessness when her initial attempts to recruit participants through a fertility clinic were rebuffed by institutional gatekeepers. Instead, she recruited participants through Internet discussion groups on the topic and then distributed questionnaires and conducted more open-ended e-mail interviews. She found that some participants appreciated the anonymity of computer-mediated communication. Some indicated that they might not have agreed to participate within a clinic context or would have been reluctant to express unhappiness with their treatment there. She also suggests that the relative distance between researcher and participant may have the effect of diminishing power differentials (presumably because participants have more control over their participation). Illingworth believes that her e-mail interviews were effective and offered the advantages of increased disclosure, ease of access, and ready-made transcripts. However, in addition to the potential for participant exclusion, which was also noted by other researchers, she discusses "the virtual interview as a disembodied experience," pointing out that e-mail exchanges lack the contextual cues and linguistic nuance of face-to-face conversation. She found that she often needed to conduct second and third exchanges with participants in order to be certain she understood their remarks. As another counter to the disembodiment of the virtual interview, she used self-disclosure of her own identities in order to encourage participants

to reciprocate. She suggests as well that e-mail interviewing complicates the process of leaving the field, as participants continued to contact her well beyond the period in which she was collecting data.

Feminists have also found that online worlds offer new sites and communities to investigate. For example, Michaela Fay (2007) conducted "cyber ethnographic research" on an international web-based network of feminist academics that developed as a complement and follow-up to a three-month, women-only postgraduate program on technology that was convened in Germany in 2000. Noting feminists' increasing interest in the contemporary "mobilities" of everyday lives, she set out to explore what happened when "a corporeal, on-site community was meant to become a virtual one—a networked web of attachments and connections" (Fay, 2007, ¶ 19). Given the dispersed character of the field of her research, she found that she had to address a variety of methodological questions, "some conceptual, some mundane and practical" (¶ 32). Although she began conventionally, with face-to-face interviews, Fay found that, because the participants were members of a highly mobile, international "globalised elite," web-based methods were more appropriate (¶ 35). She started by sending the network a preliminary list of open-ended questions and then sent more focused queries based on participants' first responses. She found that many participants understood the network as a space of "belonging" or even a kind of "home"— results that reinforced her sense of the potential significance of online ethnography, at least for this group. But she remained concerned about ethical issues in the research, wondering whether she could justify observing the network as a participant when only some members had given explicit permission. She also points out that online communities such as this one are less stable than most offline communities; early in the research, the group was concerned about whether the network could be adequately funded and maintained over time.

Other online studies explore the activities of smaller groups that are more directly tied to online worlds. Rosalind Hanmer (2003) took advantage of an Internet fan club focused on the television series *Zena Warrior Princess* to explore the ways that some lesbian viewers respond to the show. Some audiences have found a "lesbian subtext" in the series—that is, hints of same-sex desire between characters—and some fans have established web spaces devoted to promoting and discussing that idea. Like most other Internet researchers, Hanmer began by observing the group's chat space and then contacted several key members to ask for an introduction to the group, taking care to introduce herself and her research clearly and completely. However, she points out that a researcher following such a procedure must continue to reiterate the purposes and ethical safeguards of the research, making sure that each participant understands and agrees. She cautions that patience is often required, as the researcher waits for participants to respond, deals with technical issues, and works with the time delays of instant messaging. Her research became more successful over time as she relaxed and adopted more flexible approaches to contact with participants. She concludes that social networking sites may offer not only opportunities for "online performance" that enacts and displays new strategies of resistance to hegemonic discourses but also rich opportunities for research.

Online researchers must make provisions to safeguard data, both to avoid the destruction or loss of data and also to protect participants' privacy. Standard ethical procedures apply to online research but may require distinctive adaptations. For example, researchers must negotiate provisions for obtaining documentation of consent with ethics boards that typically ask for signed consent forms, and they should inform participants if e-mail correspondence is retained for some period of time by the service provider. Clare Madge (2007) argues that Internet researchers should engage with ethics boards not only in order to formulate procedural guidelines but also to ensure that an Internet ethics discourse will be characterized by the flexibility and reflexivity required if it is to be workable and useful.

As noted, the growth of online research methods may eventually raise questions about the character and definition of an interview. The Moloney et al. (2004) study of headaches, discussed previously, used discussion board thread starters to simulate open-ended focus group questions, but surely people's contributions to the discussion board—composed on a keyboard, at home, and on a schedule quite different from that of a face-to-face group discussion—may be quite unlike what they would have said in the moment, face to face. Many researchers have begun to collect data from Internet chat rooms and listserv discussions, but are the data comparable to accounts that might be produced in face-to-face interviews? These are questions that Internet researchers will no doubt continue to explore and discuss.

ETHICS OF INTERVIEW RESEARCH

> What analytical and strategic knowledges and conceptual tools do we need to not relive the violence of our inherited histories? (Chandra Talpade Mohanty, 2003, p. 187)

Beyond Institutional Ethics

All qualitative researchers are, of course, bound by the codes of ethics of their disciplines: Those conducting interviews are required to secure informed consent from participants, to conduct the interview in ways that are sensitive to participants' concerns and feelings, and to protect the identity of interviewees by using pseudonyms and, if necessary, changing some details when representing them in research reports. The costs of participation in the research, for informants, are to be weighed against the potential benefits of the research for participants and others. Feminist researchers, acutely aware of the harms produced by generations of male-centered research that distorted women's realities, have set themselves an even higher ethical standard. In some cases, they have challenged disciplinary codes of ethics.

A group of feminist scholars who called themselves the Nebraska Feminist Collective (1983), for example, developed an early statement of feminist research ethics, arguing that, from a feminist point of view, ethical conduct is not just a procedural matter but also involves the substance of the research—questions asked and interpretations of findings—and, ultimately, allegiance. They insisted on an allegiance to women first, even if that sometimes puts feminist researchers in conflict with their disciplinary standards. Confidentiality, for instance, does not always seem to serve feminist goals. Linden (1993), for one, suggests that such practices are not appropriate for her participants, whose survival through the Holocaust is itself a testimony. Given their history and its meaning, assigning pseudonyms (or worse, numbers) to these people, in the name of protection, may seem more like another erasure of their existence. Such discussions have encouraged feminist researchers to be flexible about confidentiality and to negotiate procedures for identifying participants individually, respecting each participant's wishes.

As research ethics review has become increasingly institutionalized, many qualitative researchers have shared with feminists the sense that routinizing ethical review can work against the inductive, improvisational character of qualitative research. As the ethics review becomes a "fact" of institutional life, however, some feminist researchers argue for an engagement with ethics review processes that will bring feminist insights into those processes and also preserve space for feminist research. Christine Halse and Anne Honey (2005), for example, recount a prolonged process of negotiation with an Australian ethics board in which they struggled to maintain their feminist commitments and also gain approval for their project. One issue, in their study of girls' own views of their struggles with eating disorders, was the question of how to define the group of participants; the ethics board expected that a medical diagnosis could define the group, while Halse and Honey wished to include participants who might define themselves in ways that differed from the experts' opinions. The discussion provides a model for a productive stance on ethics that respects institutional requirements and still introduces into the ethics process the distinctive commitments and insights of a feminist ethics.

As feminists have become increasingly concerned with building knowledge inclusive of all perspectives and attentive to differences of power and privilege among women, they have also developed constructions of ethics that address how interview material is used—issues of "appropriation." The question here is whether the interview is a one-way or reciprocal exchange: When the participant offers up her story, does the researcher simply take it and disappear? To what use does she put the data—does it serve only the researcher's career or also people in the informant's group or community? These concerns might perhaps be construed in the "cost-benefit" terms of the ethical review board, but these institutionalized procedures have not historically emphasized such concerns, focusing instead on rights and harms as individual matters. Feminist constructions of research ethics are sharpened by an acute sensitivity to a "matrix of domination" (Collins, 1990) within which research is conducted and by an awareness of collective interests in researchers' representations.

Feminist theorists have contributed to methodologists' heightened sense of the stakes in research ethics. Calling attention to the politics of any representation, they remind us that the participants in our scientific investigations must be understood as "subjects in their own right," instead of being made "into mere bearers of unexplained categories" who have no existence outside those categories (Lazreg, 1988, p. 94). Instead, our interviewees should be acknowledged as agents actively located in history—as makers of the worlds around them rather than as mere victims of an overarching patriarchy.

Antiracist feminists, particularly women of color, have critiqued and continue to challenge knowledge that presumes to be outside history, beyond the contexts and workings of actual people (Collins, 2000; Mohanty, 2003; Narayan, 1997). These writers suggest that Western feminists' analyses of the experiences of third world women are often problematic because they are organized around the assumption that third world women are victims of backward, uncivilized traditions and cultures (the same assumption that has been used to justify the violent colonization and appropriation of seemingly untamed bodies and territories in the past and that continues to justify imperialist efforts today).

For instance, Uma Narayan (1997) has argued that white Western feminist representations of *sati* as an uncivilized Indian practice replicate what she terms a "colonialist stance toward Third-World cultures" and communities (p. 43). These representations suggest that "Third-World contexts are uniform and monolithic spaces with no important internal cultural differentiations, complexities, and variations" and falsely homogenize Indian women as victims of their culture (p. 50). Representations emanating from this "colonialist stance," she argues, erase the work and agency of women and others involved in the transformation of their worlds, legitimize "problematic economic and political interventions," and stifle transnational feminist coalitions and cross-cultural communities of resistance (p. 126).

Practically, such critiques suggest that, too often, well-meaning feminist researchers embark on projects involving other women without a thorough and grounded knowledge of their contexts and the histories that have produced those contexts. They suggest that feminist researchers should carefully think through the purpose of interviewing, that they must study and learn as much as possible before approaching others. In particular, feminist researchers should avoid using interviews—especially with women in vulnerable or marginalized social locations—as a way to learn things that could be gleaned from available sources. Doing this preparatory work is one way that researchers can display respect for the time, effort, and, often, pain involved in sharing experiences. Lynet Uttal (1990) argues that only by doing such "homework" (p. 44) will the process of inclusion of women of color in feminist scholarship avoid reproducing unequal relationships.

Another strategy for preventing discursive colonization (Mohanty, 2003) is to analyze and present interview material with an eye to its historical context. What is often lacking in colonizing social scientific analyses is a presentation of women research participants as agents active in transforming their surroundings and shaping their experiences. Says Marnia Lazreg (1988), "To take intersubjectivity into consideration when studying Algerian women or other Third World women means seeing their lives as meaningful, coherent, and understandable instead of being infused 'by us' [the West] with doom and sorrow" (p. 98). Often, such a goal may be achieved by combining interview data with other kinds of material, as in Lisa Law's (1997) study of women's entry into sex work in the Philippines; setting these women's stories against the political-economic history of U.S. military presence and the state sponsorship of tourism, she challenges conventional, dichotomous thinking

about choice or coercion, agency, and structure. Studies of paid domestic workers in the United States and elsewhere (e.g., Chang, 2000; Hondagneu-Sotelo, 2001; Parreñas, 2001; Rollins, 1985; Romero, 1992) have also fruitfully set women's accounts of that work within a broader historical context.

It is also useful to be mindful of women interviewees as agents in their own lives. Sometimes, feminist researchers accomplish this goal by seeking out women who are challenging oppressive conditions, either individually or collectively. Two volumes that present such studies—some based on interview research—are Kimberly Springer's (1999) *Still Lifting, Still Climbing,* which includes studies of African American women's activism, and Nancy Naples and Manisha Desai's (2002) collection *Women's Activism and Globalization* on the activist efforts of transnational feminist organizations. In other studies, treating women as agents is more a matter of how the researcher interprets their struggles. For example, Ellen Scott, Andrew London, and Nancy Myers (2002) look searchingly at interview accounts from welfare-reliant women in the recent period of U.S. welfare "reform" and find that, as benefits are withdrawn, some of them are drawn into "dangerous dependencies" on violent partners. Despite these women's circumstances, the researchers do not see them only as vulnerable victims but rather treat their actions as decisions they make about how to survive.

Finally, feminist interview researchers often strive to share or negotiate interpretive authority with research participants. Ultimately, the researcher makes decisions about producing the final text, but feminists have involved interviewees in decision making about representation in various ways, primarily by asking for commentary on developing analyses or feedback on representational decisions. Although such practices parallel qualitative researchers' traditional reliance on "member checks," the feminist emphasis is not only on "getting it right" but also on the politics of representation. Some feminists adopt participatory research methods to share research decision making more fully (Campbell, Copeland, & Tate, 1998; Naples, 1996), but their discussions frequently point to practical barriers and often question whether full sharing is always desirable.

Feminist theorists have shown us that texts produce and carry ideology (Bannerji, 1995a; Clough, 1992; Smith, 1999), and the research texts we produce do so no less than the texts we critique. Thus, we urge interview researchers to devote more attention to the reception and uses of interview research, an area that has been less fully explored than the conduct of interviews. We turn to this topic in the next and final section of our discussion.

Accountability

Feminist interview research is often characterized by a desire to make change or produce material results. That is to say, most feminist researchers aim to do more than merely stimulate contemplation about women's status locally and abroad. The challenge, then, is to make the knowledge produced through interviewing applicable to the worlds that women live in. Some interview studies are designed so as to lead to quite specific modifications of institutional practice. For example, Ellen Pence's (2001) institutional audits of domestic violence case processing are designed to discover how changes in institutional practice might enhance women's safety. Pence works with a team of community responders and finds that they not only have the expert knowledge of those actually doing the work of processing but are often quite interested in discussing modifications of their practice.

In other projects, researchers develop ways of disseminating information gleaned from interviews to nonacademic audiences who might have a use for it. After interviewing paid domestic workers in Los Angeles, Pierrette Hondagneu-Sotelo (2001) worked with an advocacy organization to produce materials about the rights of these workers and how they might address exploitative situations, distributing them in an accessible graphic format modeled after the culturally familiar *novela*. Some feminist researchers have adopted the "photovoice" methodology, which involves asking participants to photograph aspects of their lives; interviews then focus on their explanations and interpretations of the images. These projects generally involve not only academic publication, but

some kind of more public presentation of the images, typically in the participants' own communities. Examples include Lisa Frohmann's (2005) work with survivors of domestic violence on "framing safety" and Wendy Luttrell's work with elementary school children, including many from immigrant families. Luttrell found that her fifth- and sixth-grade participants were often eager to portray their mothers as smart, resourceful women—a portrait at odds with the way they felt school personnel saw their families—and exhibits within their school have allowed them to assert their own perspectives, on this and other matters.

Marie Campbell's research team drew material from their interviews of people with disabilities, home health care workers, and agency administrators to develop a board game that simulated some of the challenges facing all of those involved. After concluding the analytic phase of their research, Campbell and her colleagues used the game in various settings to raise consciousness of systemic issues and to stimulate discussion about improving service delivery (Campbell, personal communication, 2001). It is important to note that these explicit efforts at social change require a phase of activity not typically considered part of the research process; these researchers not only speak and write about what they have learned from others but also commit time and energy to activities that will carry research results beyond the academy. Such efforts are relatively rare because they are not so consistently rewarded as more academic forms of disseminating results.

Another goal shared by many feminist researchers is that of producing "relational knowledge"—that is, showing how the varied circumstances of women (and others) are related through the web of social organization that connects us all. It's not only our status as "women" that matters; doing the work of understanding and mapping the unequal, uneven, complex relationships between women—locally and abroad—and our relationships to the histories of colonialisms, patriarchies, imperialisms, and racisms is essential to any liberatory feminist project (Grewal & Kaplan, 2000; Mohanty, 2003). Power is multifaceted and complex; therefore, if our aim is to understand how power works, we need to make a concerted effort to map the relations among people's activities, resistance, experiences, struggles, histories, and nationalisms and their linkages to broader systems of global capitalism. Such mapping might entail illuminating third world women's engagement with feminism and their resistance to oppressive regimes in relation to states and histories of colonization, as Chandra Talpade Mohanty (2003) did in "Cartographies of Struggle." Or it could mean taking on a more technical approach, meticulously detailing how the everyday lives of people and the textually mediated activities of organizations and institutions are "connected into the extended relations of ruling and the economy" (Smith, 1987, p. 188). Mapping is fundamental to any project seeking to explicate relationships among groups, histories, and contexts. As a methodological tool, it brings the social (i.e., historicity, activity, and agency) back to the knowledge we produce. In our interview studies, it is our responsibility not only to report back on what our respondents said but also to locate our informants' responses in a particular historical context and to recognize each response as mediated by power relations. Our emphasis should not only be the "micropolitics of context, subjectivity, and struggle," but "the macropolitics of global economic and political systems and processes" as well (Mohanty, 2003, p. 223).

As universities and colleges become more and more corporatized, the challenges to antiracist feminism and oppositional knowledge production grow. Feminists in the academy continue working to transform dominant ways of thinking and acting, confronting processes of administration and governance designed to manage difference-affirming efforts and "dialogic spaces of dissent and transformation" (Mohanty, 2003, p. 185). Like educators elsewhere, we are also required to be more accountable to a production-oriented administrative regime; and our heightened accountability to these institutional concerns makes holding ourselves accountable to the communities and people we write about all the more difficult. Still, to succumb to the bureaucracy of the academy, to shortchange our hopes of changing the worlds around us, and to forget the brutal realities and histories of subaltern peoples is to become the colonizer we've been so adamant to critique. When we write for, rather than about, the people we study, we begin to redefine the relationship between our world and our work in the academy. We begin to reorient the knowledge we produce to attend to "the needs and interests of . . . people" rather than "the needs and interests of ruling" (Smith, 1999, p. 16). As feminist researchers, we need to use interviews to facilitate our informants' and their communities' understanding of the social world and their efforts to change it.

CONCLUSION

Interviewing is a powerful research tool for feminist researchers interested in exploring women's experiences and the contexts that organize their experiences. Interviewing is powerful in part because it involves relatively direct exchanges of views and perspectives among researchers, participants, and readers. Because those exchanges are mediated by the language and discourses that shape experience and knowledge, interviews can also be seen as occasions that put those discursive operations in view. Feminist scholars have used interviewing, in various ways, to challenge received knowledge about women's and others' lives, and we have no doubt that interviewing will continue to be significant for creative, critical feminist work.

We consider interview research as part of an "apparatus of knowledge production" that has sometimes "constructed and sustained women's oppression" (DeVault, 1999, p. 30). As Dorothy Smith (1996) argues,

> Knowledge is socially organized; its characteristic textual forms bear and replicate social relations. Hence, knowledge must be differently written and differently designed if it is to bear other social relations than those of ruling. (p. 187)

Feminist research is a process that is situated and carried out in a larger historical context. Like knowledge, it, too, is socially organized. If we acknowledge that the "cognitive domain of social science is itself a social relation" and that "knowledge is a social accomplishment," then, as social scientists, we are also responsible for continually questioning the methods we use to establish our findings and develop our analyses (Smith, 1987, p. 72).

We would also insist that, given our "historical and positional differences," there is no commonality of gender experience across "race and national lines" (Mohanty, 1990, p. 180); our experiences as women are ineluctably complex and varied. Assuming that there is a unified common experience among all women violates and ignores women's differences. Ignoring or dismissing rather than affirming women's differences produces divisions and hinders coalition efforts. Thus, while making generalizations about groups of women can be useful (particularly in the social sciences where one goal is to identify domestic and cross-cultural trends in human behavior), such generalizations can also be used to reinforce the very power structures feminists have sought to dismantle. Indeed, it was the critique of abstract, generalized forms of knowledge as lacking the complexity and contradictions that characterize women's lives that pushed feminists to acknowledge that representing others is no objective, benign process. Therefore, understanding the politics of representation is imperative to any feminist research project. We suggest that it is in continuing to work out the implications of these ideas that scholars will sustain the political force of feminist interview research.

Discussion Questions

1. How would you characterize a feminist approach to interviewing?

2. How do the identities and social locations of the interviewer and interviewee shape the interview process and data collection? What strategies have feminists used to work toward a reciprocal and collaborative, rather than a one-way, interview encounter?

3. How have discussions of feminist interviewing developed and changed over time? What continuities do you see? How has this discourse informed and been expanded by more recent feminist interviewing projects?

4. What kinds of ethical concerns characterize feminist thought? What precautions could

feminists take in conducting and writing up interview research? What additional concerns are raised in online research?

5. What responsibilities do feminist researchers have to the communities and people they study? How are these complicated by transnational or multisited research involving multiple communities with different kinds and amounts of resources and power?

6. How might feminist interview research be used to facilitate social justice and social change?

Online Resources

ESDS Qualidata Teaching Resource

http://www.esds.ac.uk/qualidata/support/inter views/feminist.asp

This website is part of a UK data archive designed for the management and sharing of research data. It includes material on feminist interviews (under the heading of "diverse interview types"), examples from a feminist interview study, and a teaching activity focused on feminist and life-history interviewing.

Exploring Online Research Methods

http://www.geog.le.ac.uk/orm/

This site, funded by the Economic and Social Research Council (ESRC) Research Methods Programme (UK) and hosted by the University of Leicester, offers online resources related to Internet research methodologies. Target audiences include public policy and corporate researchers as well as academics and graduate students.

The Maine Feminist Oral History Project, University of Maine

http://umaine.edu/womensstudies/womens-studies/general-description/

There are numerous sites devoted to oral history interviewing; this local site from the Women in the Curriculum and Women's Studies Department of the University of Maine describes an oral history project about the Spruce Run Association, one of the oldest domestic violence projects in the United States. Oral histories of the organization's work were used to create a reader's theater script, which is available on the site.

Relevant Journals

Gender & Society

Qualitative Inquiry

Sex Roles

Women's Studies International Forum

REFERENCES

Acker, Joan, Barry, Kate, & Esseveld, Joke. (1983). Objectivity and truth: Problems in doing feminist research. *Women's Studies International Forum, 6,* 423–435. (Reprinted, with an "Afterword," in *Feminism and social change*, pp. 60–87, by Heidi Gottfried, Ed., 1996, Urbana, University of Illinois Press)

Alcoff, Linda M., Hames-Garcia, Michael, Mohanty, Satya P., & Moya, Paula M. L. (Eds.). (2006). *Identity politics reconsidered.* New York: Palgrave Macmillan.

Alexander, M. Jacqui, Albrecht, Lisa, Day, Sharon, & Segrest, Mab. (Eds.). (2003). *Sing, whisper, shout, pray! Feminist visions for a just world.* Fort Bragg, CA: EdgeWork Books.

Allen, Pamela. (1973). Free space. In Anne Koedt, Ellen Levine, & Anita Rapone (Eds.), *Radical feminism* (pp. 271–279). New York: Quadrangle.

Anzaldúa, Gloria, & Keating, Analouise. (Eds.). (2002). *This bridge we call home: Radical visions for transformation.* New York: Routledge.

Arendell, Terry. (1997). Reflections on the researcher-researched relationship: A woman interviewing men. *Qualitative Sociology, 20,* 341–368.

Bannerji, Himani. (1995a). Beyond the ruling category to what actually happens: Notes on James Mill's historiography in *The history of British India.* In Marie Campbell & Ann Manicom (Eds.), *Knowledge, experience, and ruling relations: Studies in the social organization of knowledge* (pp. 49–64). Toronto: University of Toronto Press.

Bannerji, Himani. (1995b). *Thinking through: Essays on feminism, Marxism, and anti-racism.* Toronto: Women's Press.

Bart, Pauline B. (1971). Depression in middle-aged women. In Vivian Gornick & Barbara K. Moran (Eds.), *Woman in sexist society: Studies in power and powerlessness* (pp. 163–186). New York: Basic Books.

Behar, Ruth. (1993). *Translated woman: Crossing the border with Esperanza's story.* Boston: Beacon Press.

Behar, Ruth, & Gordon, Deborah A. (1995). *Women writing culture.* Berkeley: University of California Press.

Bell, Susan E. (1999). Narratives and lives: Women's health politics and the diagnosis of cancer for DES daughters. *Narrative Inquiry, 9,* 1–43.

Beoku-Betts, Josephine. (1994). When black is not enough: Doing field research among Gullah women. *NWSA Journal, 6,* 413–433.

Best, Amy. (2003). Doing race in the context of feminist interviewing: Constructing whiteness through talk. *Qualitative Inquiry, 9,* 895–914.

Bigby, Christine. (2000). Life without parents: Experiences of older women with intellectual disabilities. In Rannveig Traustadóttir & Kelley Johnson (Eds.), *Women with intellectual disabilities: Finding a place in the world* (pp. 69–85). London: Jessica Kingsley.

Biklen, Sari Knopp. (1995). *School work: Gender and the cultural construction of teaching.* New York: Teacher's College Press.

Blee, Kathleen M. (1991). *Women of the Klan: Racism and gender in the 1920s.* Berkeley: University of California Press.

Blee, Kathleen M. (2002). *Inside organized racism: Women in the hate movement.* Berkeley: University of California Press.

Bogdan, Robert C., & Biklen, Sari Knopp. (1998). *Qualitative research for education: An introduction to theory and method.* Boston: Allyn & Bacon.

Campbell, Marie, Copeland, Brenda, & Tate, Betty. (1998). Taking the standpoint of people with disabilities in research: Experiences with participation. *Canadian Journal of Rehabilitation, 12,* 95–104.

Campbell, Marie, & Gregor, Frances. (2002). *Mapping social relations: A primer in doing institutional ethnography.* Aurora, ON: Garamond.

Campbell, Marie, & Teghtsoonian, Kathy. (2010). Aid effectiveness and women's empowerment: Practices of governance in the funding of international development. *Signs: Journal of Women in Culture and Society, 36*(1), 177–201.

Chang, Grace. (2000). *Disposable domestics: Immigrant women workers in the global economy.* Cambridge, MA: South End Press.

Chase, Susan E. (1995). *Ambiguous empowerment: The work narratives of women school superintendents.* Amherst: University of Massachusetts Press.

Clifford, James, & Marcus, George E. (Eds.). (1986). *Writing culture: The poetics and politics of ethnography.* Berkeley: University of California Press.

Clough, Patricia Ticiento. (1992). *The end(s) of ethnography: From realism to social criticism.* Newbury Park, CA: Sage.

Code, Lorraine. (2001). Rational imaginings, responsible knowings: How far can you see from here? In Nancy Tuana & Sandra Morgen (Eds.), *Engendering rationalities* (pp. 261–282). Albany: State University of New York Press.

Collins, Patricia Hill. (1990). *Black feminist thought: Knowledge, consciousness, and the politics of empowerment.* Boston: Unwin Hyman.

Collins, Patricia Hill. (1998). *Fighting words: Black women and the search for justice.* Minneapolis: University of Minnesota Press.

Collins, Patricia Hill. (2000). *Black feminist thought: Knowledge, consciousness, and the politics of empowerment* (Rev. ed.). New York: Routledge.

Combahee River Collective. (1982). A black feminist statement. In Gloria T. Hull, Patricia Bell Scott, & Barbara Smith (Eds.), *All the women are white, all the blacks are men, but some of us are brave* (pp. 13–22). Old Westbury, NY: Feminist Press.

Connell, Raewyn. (2010). Two cans of paint: A transsexual life story, with reflections on gender change and history. *Sexualities, 13*(1), 3–19.

Conti, Joseph A., & O'Neil, Moira. (2007). Studying power: Qualitative methods and the global elite. *Qualitative Research, 7*(1), 63–83.

Crowley, Jocelyn E. (2007). Friend or foe? Self-expansion, stigmatized groups, and the researcher-participant relationship. *Journal of Contemporary Ethnography, 36*(6), 603–630.

DaCosta, Kimberly M. (2007). *Making multiracials: State, family, and market in the redrawing of the color line.* Stanford, CA: Stanford University Press.

Dalmiya, Vrinda, & Alcoff, Linda. (1993). Are "old wives' tales" justified? In Linda Alcoff & Elizabeth Potter (Eds.), *Feminist epistemologies* (pp. 217–244). New York: Routledge.

DeVault, Marjorie L. (1990). Talking and listening from women's standpoint: Feminist strategies for interviewing and analysis. *Social Problems, 37,* 96–116.

DeVault, Marjorie L. (1991). *Feeding the family: The social organization of caring as gendered work.* Chicago: University of Chicago Press.

DeVault, Marjorie L. (1999). *Liberating method: Feminism and social research.* Philadelphia: Temple University Press.

DeVault, Marjorie L., & McCoy, Liza. (2002). Institutional ethnography: Using interviews to investigate ruling relations. In Jaber Gubrium & James Holstein (Eds.), *Handbook of interview research* (pp. 751–776). Thousand Oaks, CA: Sage.

Diamond, Arlyn, & Edwards, Lee R. (1977). *The authority of experience: Essays in feminist criticism.* Amherst: University of Massachusetts Press.

Diamond, Timothy. (1992). *Making gray gold: Narratives of nursing home care.* Chicago: University of Chicago Press.

Dua, Ena, & Trotz, Alissa. (Eds.). (2002). Transnational pedagogy: Doing political work in women's studies: An interview with Chandra Talpade Mohanty. *Atlantis, 26*(2), 66–77.

Edwards, Rosalind. (1990). Connecting method and epistemology: A white woman interviewing black women. *Women's Studies International Forum, 13,* 477–490.

Eichler, Margrit. (1988). *Nonsexist research methods: A practical guide.* Boston: Unwin Hyman.

Esterberg, Kristin G. (2002). *Qualitative methods in social research.* Boston: McGraw-Hill.

Fay, Michaela. (2007). Mobile subjects, mobile methods: Doing virtual ethnography in a feminist online network. *Forum Qualitative Sozialforschung/ Forum: Qualitative Social Research, 8*(3). Retrieved July 1, 2011, from http://nbn-resolving.de/urn:nbn:de:0114-fqs0703141

Foucault, Michel. (1977). *Discipline and punish: The birth of the prison* (Alan Sheridan, Trans.). New York: Pantheon Books.

Foucault, Michel. (1978). *The history of sexuality* (Robert Hurley, Trans.). New York: Pantheon Books.

Frankenberg, Ruth. (1993). *White women, race matters: The social construction of whiteness.* Minneapolis: University of Minnesota Press.

Freeman, Jo. (1975). *The politics of women's liberation: A case study of an emerging social movement and its relation to the policy process.* New York: McKay.

Friedan, Betty. (1963). *The feminine mystique.* New York: Norton.

Frohmann, Lisa. (2005). The framing safety project: Photographs and narratives by battered women. *Violence Against Women, 11*(11), 1396–1419.

Gatrell, Caroline. (2006). Interviewing fathers: Feminist dilemmas in fieldwork. *Journal of Gender Studies, 15*(3), 237–251.

Gluck, Sherna Berger, & Patai, Daphne. (1991). *Women's words: The feminist practice of oral history.* New York: Routledge.

Gordon, Avery. (1997). *Ghostly matters: Haunting and the sociological imagination.* Minneapolis: University of Minnesota Press.

Gorelick, Sherry. (1989). The changer and the changed: Methodological reflections on studying Jewish feminists. In Alison M. Jaggar & Susan R. Bordo (Eds.), *Gender/body/knowledge: Feminist reconstructions of being and knowing* (pp. 336–358). New Brunswick, NJ: Rutgers University Press.

Gornick, Vivian, & Moran, Barbara K. (Eds.). (1971). *Woman in sexist society: Studies in power and powerlessness.* New York: Basic Books.

Grahame, Kamini Maraj. (1998). Feminist organizing and the politics of inclusion. *Human Studies, 21,* 377–393.

Grewal, Interpal, & Kaplan, Caren. (Eds.). (1994). *Scattered hegemonies: Postmodernity and transnational feminist practices.* Minneapolis: University of Minnesota Press.

Griffith, Alison I., & Smith, Dorothy E. (1987). Constructing cultural knowledge: Mothering as discourse. In Jane Gaskell & Arlene McLaren (Eds.), *Women in education: A Canadian perspective* (pp. 87–103). Calgary, AB: Detselig.

Griffith, Alison I., & Smith, Dorothy E. (2005). *Mothering for schooling.* New York: Routledge/Falmer Press.

Gubrium, Jaber F., & Holstein, James A. (Eds.). (2002). *Handbook of interview research: Context and method.* Thousand Oaks, CA: Sage.

Hanmer, Rosalind. (2003). Lesbian subtext talk: Experiences of the Internet chat. *International Journal of Sociology and Social Policy, 23*(1/2), 80–106.

Harding, Sandra. (1991). *Whose science? Whose knowledge: Thinking from women's lives.* Ithaca, NY: Cornell University Press.

Heilbrun, Carolyn G. (1998). *Writing a woman's life.* New York: Norton.

Hesse-Biber, Sharlene N., & Leavy, Patricia L. (2010). *The practice of qualitative research* (2nd ed.). Thousand Oaks, CA: Sage.

Hinton, William. (1966). *Fanshen: A documentary of revolution in a Chinese village.* New York: Vintage Books.

Hondagneu-Sotelo, Pierrette. (2001). *Doméstica: Immigrant workers cleaning and caring in the shadows of affluence.* Berkeley: University of California Press.

Illingworth, Nicola. (2001). The Internet matters: Exploring the use of the Internet as a research tool. *Sociological Research Online,* 6(2). Retrieved June 30, 2010, from http://www.socresonline.org.uk/6/2/illingworth.html

INCITE! Women of Color Against Violence. (Ed.). (2006). *The color of violence: The INCITE! anthology.* Cambridge, MA: South End Press.

Jones, Missy M. (2007). An ethnographic exploration of narrative methodologies to promote the voice of students with disabilities. *Journal of Ethnographic and Qualitative Research, 2*(1), 32–40.

Kaplan, Caren. (1994). The politics of location as transnational feminist critical practice. In Inderpal Grewal & Caren Kaplan (Eds.), *Scattered hegemonies: Postmodernity and transnational feminist practices* (pp. 137–152). Minneapolis: University of Minnesota Press.

Klatch, Rebecca E. (1987). *Women of the new right.* Philadelphia: Temple University Press.

Kvale, Steinar, & Brinkmann, Svend. (2009). *InterViews: Learning the craft of qualitative research interviewing.* Thousand Oaks, CA: Sage.

Ladner, Joyce A. (1971). *Tomorrow's tomorrow: The black woman.* Garden City, NY: Doubleday.

Lauser, Andrea. (2008.) Philippine Women on the Move: Marriage across Borders. *International Migration* 46(4): 85-108.

Law, Lisa. (1997). A matter of "choice": Discourses on prostitution in the Philippines. In Lenore Manderson & Margaret Jolly (Eds.), *Sites of desire, economies of pleasure: Sexualities in Asia and the Pacific* (pp. 233–261). Chicago: University of Chicago Press.

Lazreg, Marnia. (1988). Feminism and difference: The perils of writing as a woman on women in Algeria. *Feminist Studies, 14*(1), 81–107.

Linden, R. Ruth. (1993). *Making stories, making selves: Feminist reflections on the holocaust.* Columbus: Ohio University Press.

Long, Judy. (1999). *Telling women's lives: Subject/narrator/reader/text.* New York: New York University Press.

Lopata, Helena Z. (1971). *Occupation housewife.* New York: Oxford University Press.

Lorde, Audre. (1984). *Sister outsider: Essays and speeches.* Freedom, CA: Crossing Press.

Lugones, María. (1990). Playfulness, "world"-traveling, and loving perception. In Gloria Anzaldúa (Ed.), *Making face, making soul—Haciendo caras: Creative and critical perspectives by feminists of color* (pp. 390–402). San Francisco: Aunt Lute Books.

Luttrell, Wendy. (1997). *Schoolsmart and motherwise: Working-class women's identity and schooling.* New York: Routledge.

Luttrell, Wendy. (2003). *Pregnant bodies, fertile minds: Gender, race, and the schooling of pregnant teens.* New York: Routledge.

Lutz, Catherine A., & Collins, Jane L. (1993). *Reading* National Geographic. Chicago: University of Chicago Press.

Madge, Clare. (2007). Developing a geographers' agenda for online research ethics. *Progress in Human Geography, 31*(5), 654–674.

Mansbridge, Jane. (1995). What is the feminist movement? In Myra Marx Ferree & Patricia Yancey Martin (Eds.), *Feminist organizations: Harvest of the new women's movement* (pp. 27–34). Philadelphia: Temple University Press.

Martin, Emily. (1994). *Flexible bodies: The role of immunity in American culture from the days of polio to the age of AIDS.* Boston: Beacon Press.

Matthews, John, & Cramer, Elizabeth P. (2008). Using technology to enhance qualitative research with hidden populations. *The Qualitative Report, 13*(2), 301–315.

May, Tim. (2002). *Qualitative research in action.* London: Sage.

McLaren, Anne E. (2000, September 1). The grievance rhetoric of Chinese women: From lamentation to revolution. *Intersections: Gender, History and Culture in the Asian Context, 4.* Retrieved February 5, 2005, from wwwsshe.murdoch.edu.au/intersections/issue4/mclaren.html

Mishler, Elliot G. (1986). *Research interviewing: Context and narrative.* Cambridge, MA: Harvard University Press.

Mohanty, Chandra Talpade. (1990). On race and voice: Challenges for liberal education in the 1990s. *Cultural Critique, 14,* 179–208.

Mohanty, Chandra Talpade. (1991). Under Western eyes: Feminist scholarship and colonial discourses. In Chandra Talpade Mohanty, Ann Russo, & Lourdes Torres (Eds.), *Third world women and the politics of feminism* (pp. 51–80). Bloomington: Indiana University Press.

Mohanty, Chandra Talpade. (2003). *Feminism without borders: Decolonizing theory, practicing solidarity.* Durham, NC: Duke University Press.

Moloney, Margaret F., Strickland, Ora L., Dietrich, Alexa, & Myerburg, Stuart. (2004). Online data collection in women's health research: A study of perimenopausal women with migraines. *NWSA Journal, 16*(3), 70–92.

Morgan, David L. (1997). *Focus groups as qualitative research* (2nd ed.). Thousand Oaks, CA: Sage.

Mountz, Alison, Miyares, Ines M., Wright, Richard, & Bailey, A. J. (2003). Methodologically becoming: Power, knowledge and team research. *Gender, Place and Culture, 10*(1), 29–46.

Moya, Paula M. L. (2002). *Learning from experience: Minority identities, multicultural struggles.* Berkeley: University of California Press.

Naples, Nancy A., with Emily Clark. (1996). Feminist participatory research and empowerment: Going public as survivors of childhood sexual abuse. In Heidi Gottfried (Ed.), *Feminism and social change: Bridging theory and practice* (pp. 160–183). Urbana: University of Illinois Press.

Naples, Nancy A. (1998). *Grassroots warriors: Activist mothering, community work, and the war on poverty.* New York: Routledge.

Naples, Nancy A., & Desai, Manisha. (Eds.). (2002). *Women's activism and globalization: Linking local struggles and transnational politics.* New York: Routledge.

Narayan, Uma. (1997). *Dislocating cultures: Identities, traditions, and third-world feminisms.* New York: Routledge.

Nebraska Feminist Collective. (1983). A feminist ethic for social science research. *Women's Studies International Forum, 6,* 535–543.

Oakley, Ann. (1974). *The sociology of housework.* New York: Pantheon Books.

Oakley, Ann. (1981). Interviewing women: A contradiction in terms. In Helen Roberts (Ed.), *Doing feminist research* (pp. 30–61). London: Routledge and Kegan Paul.

Olson, Lester C. (1998). Liabilities of language: Audre Lorde reclaiming difference. *Quarterly Journal of Speech, 84,* 448–470.

Orr, Jackie. (2006). *Panic diaries: A genealogy of panic disorder.* Durham, NC: Duke University Press.

Paget, Marianne A. (1983). Experience and knowledge. *Human Studies, 6,* 67–90.

Parreñas, Rhacel S. (2001). *Servants of globalization: Women, migration, and domestic work.* Stanford, CA: Stanford University Press.

Pence, Ellen. (2001). Safety for battered women in a textually mediated legal system. *Studies in Cultures, Organizations and Societies, 7,* 199–229.

Personal Narratives Group. (1989). *Interpreting women's lives: Feminist theory and personal narratives.* Bloomington: Indiana University Press.

Presser, Lois. (2009). Power, safety, and ethics in cross-gendered research with violent men. In Martha K. Huggins & Marie-Louise Glebbeek (Eds.), *Women fielding danger: Negotiating ethnographic identities in field research* (pp. 251–270). Lanham, MD: Rowman & Littlefield Publishers, Inc.

Reagon, Bernice Johnson. (1983). Coalition politics: Turning the century. In Barbara Smith (Ed.), *Home girls: A black feminist anthology* (pp. 356–368). New York: Kitchen Table Press.

Reid, Inez Smith. (1972). *"Together" black women.* New York: Emerson Hall.

Reimer, Marilee. (1995). Downgrading clerical work in a textually mediated labour process. In Marie Campbell & Anne Manicom (Eds.), *Knowledge, experience, and ruling relations* (pp. 193–208). Toronto: University of Toronto Press.

Richardson, Laurel. (1997). *Fields of play: Constructing an academic life.* New Brunswick, NJ: Rutgers University Press.

Riessman, Catherine Kohler. (1987). When gender is not enough: Women interviewing women. *Gender & Society, 1,* 172–207.

Riessman, Catherine Kohler. (1990). *Divorce talk: Women and men make sense of personal relationships.* New Brunswick, NJ: Rutgers University Press.

Riessman, Catherine Kohler. (2002). Analysis of personal narratives. In Jaber Gubrium & James Holstein (Eds.), *Handbook of interview research* (pp. 695–710). Thousand Oaks, CA: Sage.

Rollins, Judith. (1985). *Between women: Domestics and their employers.* Philadelphia: Temple University Press.

Romero, Mary. (1992). *Maid in the U.S.A.* New York: Routledge.

Rosen, Ruth. (2001). *The world split open: How the modern women's movement changed America.* New York: Penguin.

Rubin, Lillian B. (1976). *Worlds of pain: Life in the working-class family.* New York: Basic Books.

Sarachild, Kathie. (1978). Consciousness-raising: A radical weapon. *Documents from the women's liberation movement: An on-LINE archival collection.* Retrieved February 5, 2005, from Duke University Libraries, Special Collections Library website: http://scriptorium.lib.duke.edu/wlm/fem/sarachild.html

Scott, Ellen K., London, Andrew S., & Myers, Nancy A. (2002). Dangerous dependencies: The intersection of welfare reform and domestic violence. *Gender & Society, 16*(6), 878–897.

Scott, Joan W. (1991). The evidence of experience. *Critical Inquiry, 17,* 773–797.

Scott, Joan W. (1992). Experience. In Judith Butler & Joan W. Scott (Eds.), *Feminists theorize the political* (pp. 22–40). New York: Routledge.

Sehgal, Meera. (2009). The veiled feminist ethnographer: Fieldwork among women of India's Hindu right. In Martha K. Huggins & Marie-Louise Glebbeek (Eds.), *Women fielding danger: Negotiating ethnographic identities in field research* (pp. 325–352). Lanham, MD: Rowman & Littlefield Publishers, Inc.

Seidman, Irving. (2006). *Interviewing as qualitative research: A guide for researchers in education and the social sciences* (3rd ed.). New York: Teachers College Press.

Smith, Dorothy. (1987). *The everyday world as problematic: A feminist sociology.* Boston: Northeastern University Press.

Smith, Dorothy. (1990a). *Conceptual practices of power: A feminist sociology of knowledge.* Boston: Northeastern University Press.

Smith, Dorothy. (1990b). *Texts, facts, and femininity: Exploring the relations of ruling.* New York: Routledge.

Smith, Dorothy. (1996). The relations of ruling: A feminist inquiry. *Studies in Cultures, Organizations and Societies, 2,* 171–190.

Smith, Dorothy. (1999). *Writing the social: Critique, theory, and investigations.* Toronto: University of Toronto Press.

Smith, Dorothy. (2005). *Institutional ethnography: A sociology for people.* Lanham, MD: AltaMira.

Smith, Dorothy. (Ed.). (2006). *Institutional ethnography as practice.* Lanham, MD: Rowman & Littlefield Publishers, Inc.

Springer, Kimberly A. (Ed.). (1999). *Still lifting, still climbing: Contemporary African American women's activism*. New York: New York University Press.

Stewart, David W., Shamdasani, Prem N., & Rook, Dennis W. (Eds.). (2007). *Focus groups: Theory and practice*. Thousand Oaks, CA: Sage.

Stone-Mediatore, Shari. (1998). Chandra Mohanty and the revaluing of "experience." *Hypatia, 13*(2), 116–134.

Stone-Mediatore, Shari. (2003). *Reading across borders: Storytelling and knowledges of resistance*. New York: Palgrave Macmillan.

Stooke, Rosamund. (2003). (Re)visioning the Ontario early years study: Almost a fairy tale—but not quite. *Journal of Curriculum Theorizing, 19*(2), 91–101.

Stooke, Rosamund. (2004). *Healthy, wealthy, and ready for school: Supporting young children's education and development in the era of the national children's agenda*. Unpublished doctoral dissertation, University of Western Ontario, London, Ontario, Canada.

Taylor, Steven J., & Bogdan, Robert. (1998). *Introduction to qualitative research methods* (3rd ed.). New York: Wiley.

Taylor, Verta, & Rupp, Leila J. (2005). When the girls are men: Negotiating gender and sexual dynamics in a study of drag queens. *Signs : Journal of Women in Culture and Society, 30*(4), 2115–2139.

Temple, Bogusia, & Young, Alys. (2004). Qualitative research and translation dilemmas. *Qualitative Research, 4*(2), 161–178.

Traustadóttir, Rannveig. (2000). Friendship: Love or work? In Rannveig Traustadóttir & Kelley Johnson (Eds.), *Women with intellectual disabilities: Finding a place in the world* (pp. 118–131). London: Jessica Kingsley.

Tripp, Aili M., & Ferree, Myra M. (2006). *Global feminism: Transnational women's activism, organizing, and human rights*. New York: New York University.

Uttal, Lynet. (1990). Inclusion without influence: The continuing tokenism of women of color. In Gloria Anzaldúa (Ed.), *Making face, making soul—Haciendo caras: Creative and critical perspectives by feminists of color* (pp. 42–45). San Francisco: Aunt Lute Books.

Walker, Gillian. (1990). *Family violence and the women's movement: The conceptual politics of struggle*. Toronto: University of Toronto Press.

Walmsley, Jan. (1995). Life history interviews with people with learning disabilities. *Oral History, 23*(1), 71–77.

Warren, Carol A. B., & Karner, Tracy X. (2005). *Discovering qualitative methods: Field research, interviews, and analysis*. Los Angeles: Roxbury.

Weiss, Robert S. (1994). *Learning from strangers: The art and method of qualitative interview studies*. New York: Free Press.

Zavella, Patricia. (1993). Feminist insider dilemmas: Constructing ethnic identity with "Chicana" informants. *Frontiers, 13*, 53–76.

12

USING SURVEY RESEARCH AS A QUANTITATIVE METHOD FOR FEMINIST SOCIAL CHANGE

Kathi N. Miner, Toby Epstein Jayaratne,
Amanda Pesonen, and Lauren Zurbrügg

The point is not merely to describe the world but also to change it.

—Sherry Gorelick (1996)

Conducting research with a feminist perspective means exploring issues of feminist relevance with an awareness of difference, social power, and scientific oppression, and acting in service of political and social activism (Hesse-Biber, Leavy, & Yaiser, 2004). Feminist research, then, is one avenue to advance social change. Like most researchers, those who engage in feminist research select from a diverse array of investigative methods and, therefore, can allow their questions, rather than one specific method, to guide their work. In this chapter, we describe one investigative method, survey research, that may be particularly applicable and beneficial for addressing many feminist research questions. Survey research generally refers to research that is conducted using questionnaires to collect data about a phenomenon of interest. The data are typically interpreted in numerical format and analyzed statistically.

Of course, the methods that feminist researchers are most apt to use are influenced by their feminist perspective and the disciplinary norms from which they come. We come to this chapter as feminists schooled in the standards of mainstream social science research and with an appreciation for the utility of survey research. At the same time, we see ourselves as social justice scholars who hold a feminist perspective and strive to use survey research as a vehicle for improving the lives of women and advancing feminist issues. In our home discipline of psychology, as well as in many other social science disciplines, the use of the survey research method is widespread. This is not to say that social scientists use only the survey research method. Indeed, social scientists use a number of different methods (e.g., experiments, case studies) to conduct their research. Moreover, many social scientists use surveys to gather qualitative data, which we describe elsewhere in this chapter. However, because most surveys are quantitative in nature, we focus on the quantitative survey research method predominately in this chapter.

Although we use survey research methods to pursue feminist goals, we acknowledge that some feminists have been critical of these methods. In brief, they argue that survey research, and especially quantitative survey research, is antithetical to feminist aims due to its historical grounding in the positivist tradition. We disagree. We argue in this chapter that survey methods are not inherently positivistic and, further, that they have the potential for concrete social change, which aligns them with feminist values. With many feminist researchers seeking new ways to extend their research into practical action and social transformation for women (however these goals are conceived), we advocate survey research as a valuable strategy for achieving these objectives, particularly through legislation and public policy reform. We contend that survey research can be one of the most effective tools for social change and can be wholly consistent with feminist goals and philosophies. Survey research is especially well-suited for influencing policy and public opinion because it allows for the sampling of a large and diverse group of individuals in a relatively quick and cost-effective manner. Consequently, we believe that survey research is one method that can both facilitate our understanding of the lived experiences of women and other marginalized groups and spawn changes in society that can impact their lives positively.

Over the past few decades, criticisms of survey research techniques have emanated not only from the feminist community (and other researchers who do work on marginalized peoples) but also from mainstream survey researchers themselves. This critique has led to discussions, usually within each of these groups, about how survey research might be improved and developed. In fact, these criticisms of and suggestions for improving survey research from the feminist and mainstream perspectives have actually been quite parallel. One objective in this chapter, therefore, is to link these two perspectives explicitly and demonstrate their compatibility. We point out how current mainstream survey researchers

and feminist survey researchers both seek one common goal: high-quality research that helps us to understand social phenomena. Such research is reliable, valid, respectful, ethical, and reported honestly. In addition, as has generally been the case for feminist researchers, many current mainstream survey researchers emphasize the importance of social change, particularly with regard to marginalized social groups.

A second objective of this chapter is to give the reader a clearer understanding of how we actually go about conducting survey research with a feminist perspective. We illustrate the survey research process by describing the major components of this method and pointing out how each is fully compatible with feminist principles, offering examples to demonstrate this correspondence. Although this chapter offers feminist scholars a general introduction to survey research, it is critical before engaging in such research to acquire a more comprehensive understanding of survey techniques. We refer the reader to several excellent sources of additional information on this topic (e.g., Dillman, Smyth, & Christian, 2008; Fowler, 2008; Groves et al., 2009; Tourangeau, Rips, & Rasinski, 2000).

OVERVIEW OF ISSUES

DEFINITIONS OF KEY CONCEPTS AND TERMS

To help the reader understand the various issues we address in this chapter, we first review a few basic concepts and terms undergirding our discussion. Following Harding (1987), the term *research methodology* refers to "a theory and analysis of how research does or should proceed" (p. 3). Feminist researchers generally employ a *feminist research methodology* in their research. That is, they believe that research should be predicated on feminist principles and the unique feminist vision of social change for the betterment of women (Hesse-Biber et al., 2004; Sprague & Zimmerman, 1993). Acker, Barry, and Esseveld (1996) described feminist methodology as encompassing three components: (1) a goal of social change for women through the production of knowledge that is for, rather than on, women;

(2) the use of methods in the attainment of this goal that are not oppressive; and (3) a continuous questioning of dominant intellectual paradigms and their developments.

In contrast to research methodology, "a *research method* is a specific technique used for gathering evidence" (Harding, 1987, p. 2). Thus, the survey research method is one technique used for acquiring information. Within this specific technique, there are a number of components including the survey design and the collection, processing, and analysis of survey data (Groves et al., 2009). A *survey* is a way of obtaining "information from (a sample of) entities for the purpose of constructing quantitative descriptors of the attributes of the larger population of which the entities are members" (Groves et al., 2009, p. 2). The quantifiers are called *statistics*, which are "summaries of observations on a set of elements" (Groves et al., 2009, p. 2). The general goal of statistics is to describe the characteristics and experiences of a population or to test specific *hypotheses* (i.e., predictions about what the data will indicate). Typically, a standardized set of questions in a survey is called a *questionnaire*. Questions can be read and answered on paper, on a computer, or over the Internet. Alternatively, when a survey is read to a respondent either over the phone or in person, it is called an *interview*. Surveys are usually administered to individual people, but survey data can be based on any source of information (e.g., organizations or media articles).

When a researcher collects such *quantitative data*, individuals' answers to questions (often in word format) are translated into numerical categories, usually predefined by the researcher and then evaluated using statistical analyses. Choosing categories a priori—before the start of data collection—is referred to as *deductive coding*. Beginning with existing theory and then developing categories a priori allows the researcher to replicate, extend, or contradict the existing state of research and theory in a given area (Boyatzis, 1998). Often, the categories defined are very narrow in scope (e.g., for race, there may only be the categories of white and nonwhite), with most researchers deciding beforehand what specific aspects of people's experiences or attitudes they will examine. In this situation, research participants have little influence on what information is subjected to analysis (Jayaratne & Stewart, 1991). Moreover, because the categories are defined beforehand, researchers assume they know enough about the phenomenon to construct relevant categories. However, not all quantitative research proceeds in this way. Sometimes researchers collect data without confining them to predetermined categories (e.g., asking race as a free-response, fill-in-the-blank question), and they later transform these responses into quantitative data (e.g., collapsing responses of "white" and "Caucasian" into the same category). Whichever data collection method is used, once the data are categorized into numerical codes, they are subject to statistical analysis based on those codes.

In contrast to quantitative data, *qualitative data* (i.e., nonnumeric data, often from semistructured or unstructured interviews) are generally evaluated through the use of themes or categories that emerge *after* data collection. This categorizing is referred to as *inductive coding*, which is useful for developing new areas of research or theory building (Joffe & Yardley, 2004). Because the themes or categories are not narrowly defined a priori by the researcher, participants often have the freedom to respond to research questions in ways that make sense to them personally. Proponents of qualitative research methods argue that this aspect of qualitative research is extremely important because participants should be able to describe their experiences as they perceive them, not through the researcher's preconceived notions about what their world is like (Marecek, Fine, & Kidder, 1997; Wallston & Grady, 1992). Additionally, because the data are analyzed in a contextual form, it allows the researcher to gain an in-depth understanding of phenomena. It is important to recognize, however, that even in the case of inductive research, it is impossible for the researcher to be completely uninfluenced by past research and theory. The researcher is not a blank slate but is actively constructing her framework through existing schema derived from exploring preexisting research and experiences. In fact, recognizing that the researcher's experiences, motivations, and field of study play an integral role in the research she chooses, the framework she utilizes, and the theory she builds upon is a key aspect of feminist methodology and its rejection of positivist objectivity (e.g., DeVault, 1999; Kirsch, 1999).

It is critical to note that there is not a particular method that is consistent with feminist values, so, rather than relying on one method, it is often useful to employ multiple methods (Hesse-Biber, 2010; Reinharz, 1992; Riger, 1992; also see Cole & Stewart, Chapter 17, this volume). Such triangulation (Jick, 1979) helps confirm that our findings are not an artifact of the specific method; consequently, we can be more confident of findings and conclusions. By using multiple methods, feminist researchers can balance the drawbacks and benefits of different approaches. Triangulation also allows interpretations about the complexities of human behavior that may not be possible with other methods. Having reviewed these key concepts and terms, we now turn to a brief history of survey research.

HISTORY OF THE SURVEY RESEARCH METHOD

The history of survey research reflects a field of inquiry that has evolved in response to social and technological change. We will briefly highlight a few of the major historical developments, but we suggest other sources (e.g., Converse, 1987; Groves et al., 2009) for more detailed coverage of this subject. The earliest and most well-known type of survey is the census, which began in the United States in 1790 and is conducted each decade by the federal government (United States Census Bureau, 1989). The census seeks to describe the characteristics (e.g., gender, race, average number of people per household) of an entire population (i.e., people in the United States). Another purpose of surveys in their early development was to gain an understanding of social problems (e.g., see Charles Booth's survey investigating the life and work of London's poor between 1886 and 1903, http://booth.lse.ac.uk/), and even feminists employed such methods at that time. For example, during the late 1800s and early 1900s, feminists trained at the University of Chicago designed surveys and developed statistical techniques to advance the social sciences and the creation of social welfare programs (Deegan, 1988, as described in Spalter-Roth & Hartmann, 1996).

This first generation of feminist survey researchers developed a system for social change (called *critical pragmatism*) that involved connecting survey data with social action. Specifically, the University of Chicago women who founded the Hull-House intellectual movement are credited with developing the method of "mapping" demographic factors in urban regions (Deegan, 1988), an early form of survey research. These feminist scholars used mapping as a research tool that allowed them to reveal to policy makers and residents alike the living conditions of those in underprivileged neighborhoods. In this way, these early feminists were able to bring about changes that improved the lives of those they surveyed (Deegan, 1988). Further, in their pursuit of social knowledge and reform, these pioneers embraced the positivist stance that strict adherence to empirical observation would reveal the true state of the world—in their case the social truths they sought to uncover. These women are considered by some to have founded the movement called *feminist empiricism*, which seeks to eliminate bias in research by stricter adherence to the scientific method. The research of the Hull-House scholars epitomizes feminist empiricism because of their avid use of the scientific method to highlight important social problems for the underprivileged.

A significant impetus for mainstream survey research development was World War II, as the federal government was interested in assessing Americans' opinions and attitudes regarding the war and other social issues (Groves et al., 2009). This period was critical in the evolution of survey research, as survey researchers began to learn the importance of question wording, data collection techniques, interviewer training, and sampling procedures (Converse, 1987; Groves et al., 2009). Since that time, opinion surveys have been conducted in the areas of journalism and market research to gain an understanding of the "typical" American's views, including preferences for political candidates in upcoming elections and for various products and services (Groves et al., 2009).

A second generation of feminist survey researchers, who received their training during the 1960s and 1970s, were, like earlier feminist researchers, committed to using surveys to advance social policy. Although they were passionate activists in the quest for social change for women (Spalter-Roth & Hartmann, 1996), this later generation was generally more cautious about accepting positivist methodology intact, as exemplified by traditional scientific investigation. Although these feminists employed the survey research method, they also acknowledged some of the limits of quantitative methods. They viewed the dominant scientific methods of their day as social constructs shaped by a patriarchal society. It was during this time that the quantitative versus qualitative research methods debate among feminists and other social science researchers came to the forefront of discussions on best practices in research. Qualitative research was seen as a way to capture women's everyday experiences and reduce the hierarchical nature of the participant-researcher relationship (Spalter-Roth & Hartmann, 1996). Although these early critiques still resonate today, they have been refined and responded to by feminist scholars in subsequent decades. This discourse resulted in the more general acceptance of survey research among many feminists (Jayaratne, 1983; Reinharz, 1992), although some are still wary about the use of quantitative methods.

Perhaps the most important development in survey research was the use of computers in the research process, starting in the 1960s (Groves et al., 2009). Survey researchers first employed computers only for statistical analyses, but computers quickly became indispensable for all aspects of the research process, including survey design, sampling, data collection, and analysis. Presently, the fastest growing area of survey research via computers is the web survey, which has participants complete a survey over the Internet with a computer; this aspect of survey research has had an enormous impact on when and where survey research can be conducted, as well as on who is able to respond to surveys.

FEMINIST CRITICISMS OF QUANTITATIVE RESEARCH AND THE SURVEY RESEARCH METHOD

Epistemological Issues

In the past few decades, scholars have addressed the epistemological groundings of quantitative research methods generally, including survey research. Discussions of these issues

have come from many disciplines, have been inherently philosophical, and have often been filled with technical jargon (Campbell & Wasco, 2000). The major criticism of quantitative survey research focuses on its roots in the tradition of positivism, which embraces a pursuit of knowledge that is objective and value free. Numerous feminist scholars (e.g., Crawford & Marecek, 1989; Haraway, 1991; Harding, 1987, 1998; Hartsock, 1998; Peplau & Conrad, 1989) argue that the ideal of objectivity and neutrality, on which the quantitative survey research method is primarily based, is necessarily masculine. Science is purported to be impersonal, unemotional, and detached—attributes that are central to the traditional construction of the male gender. The culmination is a science that is built on a foundation of masculinity and male perspectives, while femininity and female perspectives become antithetical to science. Consequently, what is considered to be objective and neutral can only be seen as masculine because these aspects are at the core of traditional masculinity. The opposite of these scientific attributes (e.g., emotionality, subjectivity, compassion) is thought to be associated with the feminine and to have no place in science. As a result, women are sometimes perceived as unobjective and are often excluded from traditional scientific discourse. Not only are women's voices stifled by traditional science in this way, but women have historically been discouraged from pursuing scientific careers because they are not seen as legitimate researchers (e.g., as unbiased investigators).

Advocates of feminist standpoint epistemology (e.g., Harding, 1987, 1998; Hartsock, 1998) argue that, in order to rectify the problems associated with conventional objectivity, we should focus on women's unique experiences because knowledge gained from conventional objectivity only represents a partial understanding of human behavior and social life. The premise of this theory is that the perspective of people in subordinated positions provides for a more complete understanding of human behavior and experiences. Because each subordinate social group is in a position that those with power do not occupy, its members come to know a world that remains invisible for those in other, more powerful groups. Therefore, each unique social position provides a perspective that people in other positions do not share. Standpoint theorists and other feminist scholars (e.g., Crawford & Marecek, 1989; Haraway, 1991; Harding, 1987, 1998; Hartsock, 1998; Peplau & Conrad, 1989) argue that, because people live in different social locations, attempting to establish general laws of behavior and experience is futile. They point out that such an approach ignores individuals' unique experiences, especially as these are influenced by the interlocking systems of gender, race, class, sexual orientation, and other social identities. Moreover, they observe that, even though the goal of traditional, mainstream science has been to determine laws that can apply to all people, women have largely been excluded as research participants. For example, it is not uncommon for research findings based exclusively on samples of men (usually white) to be used to represent the experiences of both men and women. Further, even when women are included as participants in the research, their experiences are sometimes folded into those of men, masking women's unique voice and any important differences between men and women (Crawford & Marecek, 1989) and resulting in research findings that are ultimately biased and inaccurate (even though they are often purported to be objective and applicable to all human beings).

Although many feminist scholars have criticized the notion of objectivity and neutrality, some feminist researchers have actually advocated closer adherence to the scientific method as a way of incorporating feminist principles into their research. As discussed previously, this strategy (which can be traced back to the women of the Hull-House movement) has been labeled *feminist empiricism* (Harding, 1987, 1998). In contrast to feminist standpoint theorists and those critical of positivistic research, feminist empiricists actually promote conventional objectivity and argue that male-centered bias can be eliminated from the research process *only if* the positivist principle of objectivity is rigorously upheld. For these women, the principle of objectivity is not inherently masculine and can be used to obtain truths unbiased by a gendered perspective. The beginnings of feminist empiricism can be traced as far back as Hollingworth (1914), who utilized the scientific method to attempt to convince the public that gender bias

was inaccurate (as described in McHugh & Cosgrove, 2004). However, feminist empiricists differ from traditional scientists in that they consciously examine both the *context of discovery* (i.e., the process through which researchers develop research questions) and the *context of justification* (i.e., questions, collecting data, testing hypotheses, and validating and presenting research). In other words, feminist empiricists discuss both *why* and *how* they study a particular topic; this *why* aspect of research is typically absent from traditional science. In disclosing this information, feminist empiricists generally address the decisions that influenced the design of the research, the power relations pertaining to the topic, and how they can continue to be reflexive about the research process (Hesse-Biber et al., 2004). Thus, feminist empiricists, like other feminist researchers, view their research as a holistic process, attending to the relationship between the context of discovery and the context of justification. However, feminist empiricists do not question the primary epistemological tenets of the scientific method, especially the value of conventional objectivity. It is this aspect that continues to be a factor in discussions of feminist research (Hesse-Biber, 2010) because some feminists contend that objective, bias-free research is impossible, and thus should not form a basis for inquiry.

Despite these disagreements, the current consensus among many feminist scholars is that positivism is not necessarily intrinsic to the quantitative survey research method, and, in fact, this method is frequently used by feminist social scientists (Maynard, 1994). Indeed, feminist survey researchers have integrated feminist beliefs into their research and often question the core assumptions of conventional science (Peplau & Conrad, 1989). Many have also reshaped traditional approaches to research, so these are more in line with feminist goals and values and highlight the unique benefits of survey research and quantitative methods more generally (Harding, 1987; Peplau & Conrad, 1989).

Benefits of Quantitative Methods

What are the unique benefits of quantitative methods, including survey research? Perhaps the most important benefit of such methods is that they can be helpful for understanding how particular attitudes, behaviors, or experiences are distributed or associated in a population, which can then determine the best course of action in implementing social change for women. For example, Chafetz (2004) argues that finding similarities among women is a particularly useful way to proceed in understanding and alleviating gender oppression. Although acknowledging that these commonalities "take different values in different times, places, and among subpopulations in a given time and place" (Chafetz, 2004, p. 322), she emphasizes that, unless a researcher's aim is to develop a *deep* level of understanding about a phenomenon, the process of identifying and connecting overarching patterns of experience (e.g., via survey research and the testing of quantitative models) is appropriate and necessary to examine the validity of theories about gender and advance them.

Another benefit of quantitative research methods is that they provide a vehicle for feminists to introduce issues of sexism, racism, classism, heterosexism, and other social justice concerns into mainstream discourses. Because science is built on the ideal of stringent objectivity, mainstream researchers and the general public may be uncomfortable with alternative epistemologies and may be more apt to listen to and consider valid research that is quantitative (Spalter-Roth & Hartmann, 1996). Although all research should be judged by high standards, feminist research, which may be seen by some as biased due to its advocacy for women's advancement, will likely benefit from employing methods that are perceived as objective and valid. Maynard (1994) points out that "feminist work needs to be rigorous if it is to be regarded as intellectually compelling, politically persuasive, policy-relevant, and meaningful to anyone other than feminists themselves" (p. 24). In describing her experiences as a feminist advocacy researcher, Steinberg (1996) recalls the necessity of "conducting defensible studies of publishable quality" in order to maximize the benefits her research could offer for advancing and supporting women's issues (p. 247). As Steinberg (1996) mentions, lack of "methodological rigor" can be used as an excuse to reject research findings when a topic of study or approach (such as feminist methodology) is considered politically undesirable or a challenge to the status quo.

A final benefit of quantitative methods is the use of statistics, which may facilitate disseminating findings to nonfeminists, the lay public, and policy makers. Specifically, the brevity of numerical information makes it easy to report (e.g., women earn 70 cents for every dollar men earn for comparable work) and allows greater recall and comprehension than other methods (Reinharz, 1992). This advantage of statistical research can be particularly beneficial for feminist advocates because its relative simplicity can be readily translated into policy (Jayaratne & Stewart, 1991). Because of these benefits, quantitative research methods are important in promoting a feminist agenda and have a well-founded place in the broader theory of how to do feminist research (Harding, 1987).

FEMINIST METHODOLOGY AND THE SURVEY RESEARCH PROCESS

Although mainstream and feminist survey researchers share many views about the research process, the major distinction between them is that feminist survey researchers employ a *feminist methodology* in their research. In other words, the progression of their work is based on feminist principles (e.g., doing research "for" rather than "on" women) and a feminist social change approach, which specifically focuses on advancing social justice for women as a group. This perspective is critical in influencing some, but not necessarily all, aspects of the survey research method. In line with Kelly (1978), we contend that the feminist perspective is most applicable during two specific points in the research process: the development of research questions (i.e., the context of discovery) and the interpretation of findings. These two points respectively occur at the beginning and end stages of the survey research process and can best be conceptualized as the "bookends" of that process; they hold the core of the research together (i.e., the "books") and give individual components of the research process shape, structure, and meaning.

The components of the survey research method that come after the development of research questions and before the interpretation of findings (i.e., the middle stage) involve decisions about how to implement the research, that is, choosing specific survey research techniques. According to Kelly (1978), the decisions made in this middle stage must be made so that the research can be as unbiased and impartial as possible, rather than being influenced by the perspective of the researcher. This impartiality is necessary because the primary purpose of this phase of the research is to answer the research question. The middle stage of the survey research process, then, should be the least influenced by the feminist perspective, as it is during this stage that accepted survey research protocol should be followed so that bias is minimized. Although the goal of impartiality has traditionally been considered a masculine component of science, we contend that rigorous, unbiased research protocol is not necessarily anti-feminist. As Kelly (1978) argues, "any research methodology can be feminist in the right hands" (p. 232), and the labeling of research techniques as "masculine" or "feminine" is ultimately counterproductive; rationality and objectivity are fundamentally *human* attributes and need not be exclusively associated with either masculinity or femininity.

To be clear, we are not arguing that incorporating a feminist methodology into the survey research process does not or should not affect the intermediary steps of the research but, rather, that the feminist perspective is *most* applicable during the beginning and end stages of the process. Moreover, we maintain that the progression of feminist survey research in the middle stage is not *necessarily* feminist, as all good survey research incorporates the same principles into the research process. Although we agree with Kelly's recommendation that the middle stage should be minimally guided by a feminist viewpoint, we also acknowledge and concur with the feminist criticisms that science (in any stage of the research process) cannot be *entirely* value neutral. Thus, although we contend that research is never completely impartial, we also recognize the importance of conducting research (the middle stage) in such a way as to reduce bias (error) as much as possible, whether that bias emanates from a sexist or a feminist perspective (or that of any other ideology). This approach was recently termed *strong objectivity* by Harding (2004), and, earlier, it was called

feminist objectivity by Haraway (1988). In this view, recognizing that knowledge is situated actually maximizes objectivity. In other words, researchers are better able to understand the true meaning of the information obtained by becoming aware of and acknowledging the factors that influence the research process while, at the same time, attempting to minimize such influences. Additionally, although we emphasize that the feminist perspective is most critical at the start and end of a research project, we do not mean to imply that feminist principles and values should never impact other aspects of the research. Indeed, we believe that the feminist values of inclusiveness, sensitivity, comprehensiveness, and respect are necessary elements of each phase of the research process, particularly the middle stage. However, they do not represent the feminist perspective alone; these values are shared by researchers who follow the standards of the survey research method, regardless of their overarching research orientation.

In sum, we recommend that, if the survey method is selected as a research strategy, the unique feminist perspective should be emphatically employed at the beginning (development of research questions) and end (interpretation of findings) stages of the research endeavor. All subsequent decisions during the research process, including which type of survey to use, whom to interview, how to design the survey instrument, how to collect the data, and how to prepare, analyze, and interpret data, should be based on general principles of survey research and feminist objectivity. In the next section, we present a brief overview of these components of survey research and highlight issues of particular relevance to feminist researchers.

MAJOR COMPONENTS OF SURVEY RESEARCH

RESEARCH QUESTIONS AND HYPOTHESES

The various components of the typical survey research process are presented in Figure 12.1. As illustrated, the first steps are to formulate research questions and develop hypotheses based on the analysis of previous research, theory, and, most

Figure 12.1 Major Components of Survey Research

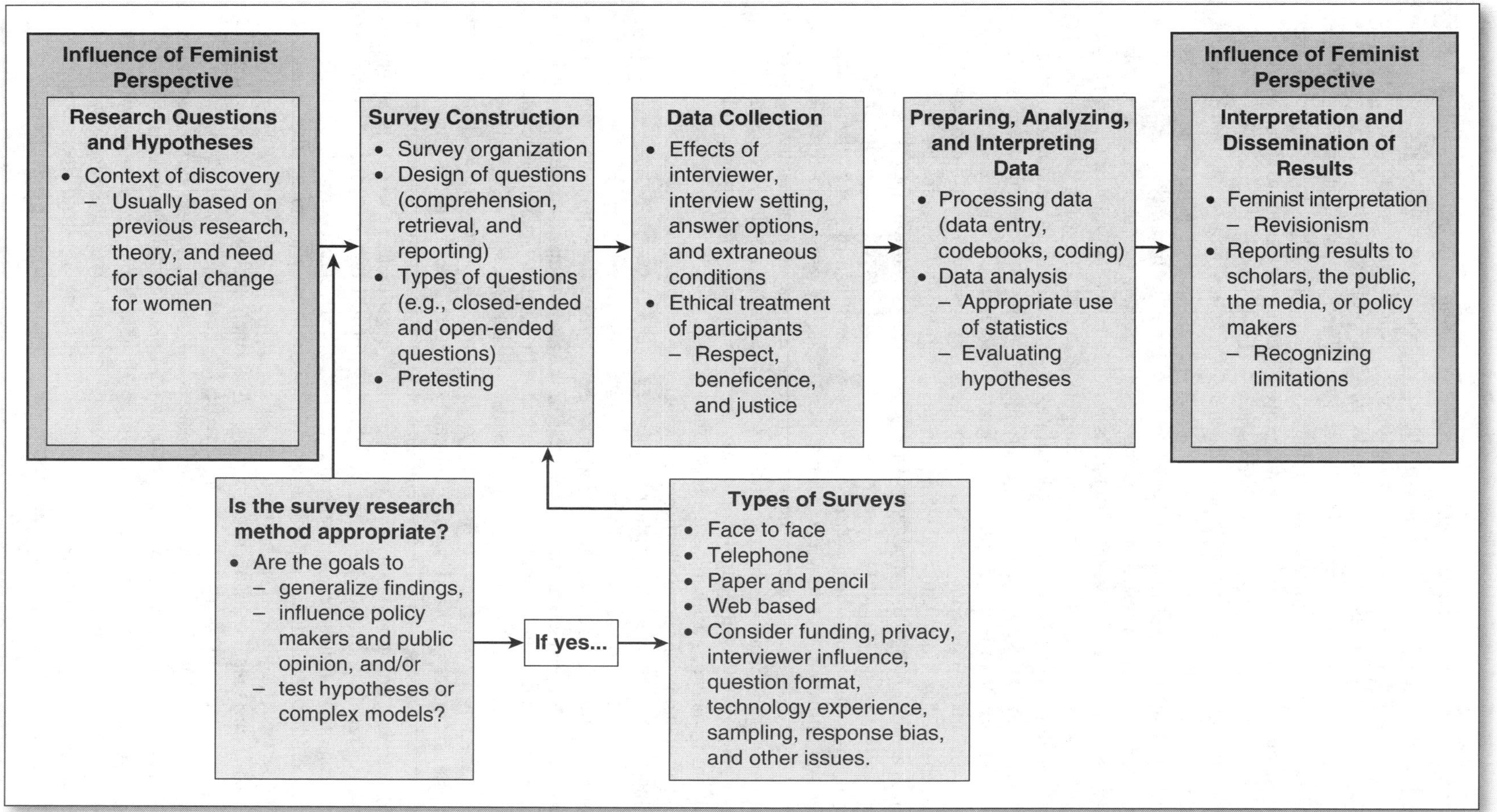

Influence of Feminist Perspective

Research Questions and Hypotheses
- Context of discovery
  – Usually based on previous research, theory, and need for social change for women

Survey Construction
- Survey organization
- Design of questions (comprehension, retrieval, and reporting)
- Types of questions (e.g., closed-ended and open-ended questions)
- Pretesting

Data Collection
- Effects of interviewer, interview setting, answer options, and extraneous conditions
- Ethical treatment of participants
  – Respect, beneficence, and justice

Preparing, Analyzing, and Interpreting Data
- Processing data (data entry, codebooks, coding)
- Data analysis
  – Appropriate use of statistics
  – Evaluating hypotheses

Influence of Feminist Perspective

Interpretation and Dissemination of Results
- Feminist interpretation
  – Revisionism
- Reporting results to scholars, the public, the media, or policy makers
  – Recognizing limitations

Is the survey research method appropriate?
- Are the goals to
  – generalize findings,
  – influence policy makers and public opinion, and/or
  – test hypotheses or complex models?

If yes...

Types of Surveys
- Face to face
- Telephone
- Paper and pencil
- Web based
- Consider funding, privacy, interviewer influence, question format, technology experience, sampling, response bias, and other issues.

important, the goal of the research (e.g., social change, policy development). The investigator then conducts the research to answer the questions and test the hypotheses. In some mainstream research, questions derive from an interest in advancing theory or extending empirical findings without direct application to solving social problems. However, feminists are more likely to ask questions and develop hypotheses in a manner such that the research findings will have direct relevance to feminist social change. For example, feminist researchers interested in decreasing violence against women might ask, "What influences this violence?" The hypotheses researchers put forth will reflect not only their knowledge of previous research (e.g., that gender roles contribute to this violence) but also their interest, as feminists, in ultimately applying the findings of the research to reduce violence toward women. In this way, a feminist perspective directly impacts the formulation of research questions as well as the way the hypotheses are articulated.

A good illustration of how the feminist perspective impacts and informs the context of discovery is the work of Schick, Zucker, and Bay-Cheng (2008), who sought to discover the relationship between adopting a feminist ideology and both condom-use self-efficacy (i.e., the ability to negotiate with one's partner for the use of a condom) and sexual satisfaction. The researchers hypothesized that the adoption of a feminist ideology would promote awareness of sexist norms and sexual liberation, which in turn would enhance sexual subjectivity and motivation (i.e., knowing what one desires and how to achieve such desires), and would ultimately predict condom-use self-efficacy and sexual satisfaction. Survey research was utilized to establish relationships among these variables[1] and promote women's sexual health and well-being through the demonstration that women's empowerment facilitates engagement in safe and satisfying sexual relationships.

It is critical to consider which specific research method to use only after the research questions and hypotheses are formulated because they will determine which method should be used. What factors influence the decision to employ the survey research method? In general, if the goal of the research is to generalize the

findings, to influence policy makers and public opinion, or to test hypotheses or complex theoretical models, the survey method may be an appropriate choice. For example, Jayaratne, Thomas, and Trautmann (2003) employed the survey method to evaluate an intervention program designed to keep middle school girls involved in science. The specific goal of the research was to determine the effectiveness of various aspects of the program among minority and nonminority girls. The survey research method was chosen for this project because it allowed the researchers to (1) gather the opinions of a large number of girls, (2) generalize the findings to all middle-school girls, (3) influence policy makers on the importance of science interventions for girls, and (4) statistically test hypotheses about outcome differences between girls who participated in the intervention and those who did not. Thus, the objectives of the study were better addressed by conducting surveys than by using other strategies. This use of survey research reflects a feminist perspective in that the information that was generated could be utilized in the development of programs to increase girls' participation in science.

TYPES OF SURVEYS

Surveys are typically categorized by how they are administered, that is, by how the data are collected. Traditional methods include face-to-face questions (asked by an interviewer in person, also termed personal interviewing), telephone questions (asked by an interviewer over the phone), and paper-and-pencil or mailed questionnaires (typically when respondents fill in answers on paper and return questionnaires to the researcher, usually by mail). Newer methods of survey administration employ computers in the data-collection process, as evidenced by the increased use of web surveys (Groves et al., 2009).

Each of these survey techniques has various benefits and drawbacks. Factors such as available funding, privacy issues, interaction between interviewer and respondent, question format, experience with technology, sampling, and response bias are all relevant aspects that should be taken into account. Many researchers employ multiple methods or combine methods to balance these factors. In some situations, the optimal type of survey will be determined by a single overriding factor, such as strict funding limitations. Below, we briefly outline some of the major advantages and disadvantages of each type of survey.

Face-to-face interviews tend to be very costly, but they allow the most direct involvement of the interviewer compared with other methods. This method is most appropriate for surveys that require extensive probing and clarification. However, when the topic of investigation is particularly sensitive, face-to-face interviews may yield data that are influenced by social desirability, because the presence of an interviewer may cause respondents to reply with answers that put them in a positive light or that they believe the interviewer prefers (see Campbell, 1982). This is important to consider when conducting research on gender, race, or sexuality, which may involve sensitive and controversial matters. However, high-quality feminist research on very sensitive issues has been conducted using such interviewing techniques. Stewart and Dottolo's (2005) research provides a good example. In their work, diverse groups of students were interviewed regarding their experiences of sexism, racism, and heterosexism in academia, and the researchers obtained quite thoughtful and honest responses. In order to encourage students to respond honestly, the interview protocol included such measures as ensuring confidentiality to participants, taking steps to avoid participants being interviewed by someone they knew (as all interviewers were students as well), and, where possible, matching participants with interviewers of the same race. These techniques were meant to eliminate perceived power differentials between the interviewer and the participant, prompting the participant to be more open about his or her experiences.

Another example is the work of Beck and Britto (2006), who developed and implemented a sensitive-issues interview protocol to help them better understand the lived experiences of family members of capital offenders, a group that has a history of trauma and negative feelings associated with the criminal justice system.

Beck and Britto (2006) emphasized the importance of showing participants support and empathy during the interviews as well as maintaining a reciprocal relationship with participants by following up with them and informing them of the impact their experiences made on others. As a result, the researchers gained valuable information about respondents' experiences from the respondents' perspectives. In short, if done respectfully and ethically (that is, in a manner that does not exploit participants nor cause them harm or undue hardship through the disclosure of sensitive information), face-to-face interviews can provide a wealth of information.

Telephone interviewing has been shown to produce results generally similar to those found with face-to-face interviewing methods (Groves & Kahn, 1979). Although telephone interviews are considerably less expensive and seem less intrusive, results can also be affected by respondent-interviewer interaction during the interview process. In recent years, the development of devices or services for screening telephone calls has resulted in lower rates of response for telephone surveys. Research shows that, in general, these lower rates have not affected the types of individuals who answer telephone surveys (Pew Research Center, 2004). However, researchers should be aware of this issue and how it might affect data collection.

Using computers to conduct surveys is quickly becoming the norm, with researchers collecting data via computers in many different situations. For example, researchers sometimes have participants complete surveys in a dedicated location (e.g., a research laboratory or office), which allows researchers to closely observe data collection. This strategy enables researchers to ensure that participants complete the entire survey and answer survey questions in the correct order and under controlled conditions (e.g., without obvious distractions). Researchers are also available to answer any questions or address any concerns participants may have while completing the survey. More commonly, researchers administer surveys via the Internet. With web-based or online surveys, participants respond to the survey via the Internet using a computer in various settings (e.g., at home, in their offices). Almost any type of research that can be done with a paper-and-pencil test can be adapted for online use (Fraley, 2004). Web-based questionnaires can include rating scales, checklists, and open and free responses (Dunn, 2008), and they can be used to collect both quantitative and qualitative data (Bryman, 2004).

There are many benefits to researchers' use of web surveys. First, such surveys are typically much less expensive than either telephone or face-to-face surveys, because the cost is mainly for software or computer programming. Second, online surveys afford participants the ease of taking a survey when and where they prefer. Because of this, samples can often be acquired more easily, as when seeking survey data from single mothers, who can take the survey when it is most convenient for them, or from sexual minorities who are concerned about anonymity (Harding & Peel, 2007). Enabling participants to take a survey at a distance from the researcher also eliminates some of the difficulties associated with honesty and social desirability bias (Dillman et al., 2008) and with acquiring random, diverse samples, which has been an issue in behavioral science research (Dunn, 2001). Third, Internet respondents tend to represent a greater range of people than is often possible with those responding to paper-and-pencil surveys. That said, individuals who have access to the Internet tend to be better educated than the average person, potentially excluding lower-income individuals, and Internet surveys may be likely to attract a more restricted audience on certain demographic variables (Dunn, 2008; Reips, 2000). These differences are likely already diminishing as the Internet becomes more commonplace and its users become more representative of the population (Vaux & Briggs, 2006). A final benefit for researchers is that responses from web surveys can often be downloaded directly from the data collection website into a database. This is not only convenient; it also reduces the measurement error associated with relying on humans to input data from paper-and-pencil surveys or from notes into a database (Groves et al., 2009).

Despite these benefits, there are also several potential disadvantages associated with web surveys. For example, there is less influence over how they are administered because respondents often fill them out in unknown circumstances. This means that there is always the possibility that an individual other than the targeted respondent is answering the questions or influencing the responses. The presence of other people can also compromise the privacy and level of honesty of respondents while they are completing the survey (Groves et al., 2009). Consequently, respondents should be instructed to complete the survey on their own without the help of others, be informed that their honest answers are the most helpful to researchers, and be told that their privacy will be protected. Additionally, there is no control over other distractions that might affect responses, such as a crying baby or a respondent having to rush through the survey if there isn't enough time. Also, because it is easy for participants to decline to participate or to terminate the survey before they have answered all the questions, lower response rates can be a problem. Therefore, it is important that online surveys be kept brief and that incentives for completing these surveys be used when possible (Dillman et al., 2008). It is also helpful to collect demographic data from participants to compare those who finished the survey with those who did not (see Knapp & Heidingsfelder, 2001). Obviously, the decision about which type of survey to employ is multifaceted, but it is significant in that it impacts all other aspects of the research and has major implications for the quality of the data collected.

SAMPLING

Sampling refers to the selection of people from a population to whom the survey will be administered (Stangor, 2004). A *population* is defined as the larger group of individuals the researcher wants to study, and a *sample* is the smaller subset of individuals that actually participates in the research. Sampling is important in survey research because it determines if it is appropriate to generalize the research findings from a sample to a population.

There are two main types of sampling techniques, probability and nonprobability. Each has its own set of advantages and disadvantages, and both are prone to sample bias. In nonprobability sampling, respondents are selected using some nonrandom procedure, such as surveying particular groups of individuals of interest. The primary benefits of nonprobability sampling are that it is relatively inexpensive and can usually generate a large sample more quickly than probability sampling strategies (Biemer & Lyberg, 2003). This sampling method can also be ideal for the preliminary tests of hypotheses before they are validated using a more representative sample. The primary disadvantage of nonprobability sampling is that it does not permit researchers to make broad generalizations about their findings.

One type of nonprobability sampling is *convenience sampling*. Convenience sampling consists of recruiting participants from places where they are easily accessible. For example, much research in feminist social psychology utilizes samples of college students (e.g., Smith & Frieze, 2003). Although convenience sampling can provide insights into the sampled population (e.g., college students), researchers who use this method of selection need to be cautious about generalizing their findings beyond the characteristics of their sample (e.g., to middle-aged individuals). This caution is necessary because, if characteristics of the sample (for example, age or level of education) are related to any of the variables of interest in the study, researchers may find different results and reach different conclusions when conducting an identical study on a different population.

A variation of convenience sampling is *snowball sampling*, in which participants invite others in their social network to join the sample. The work of Konik and Stewart (2004) provides a good example of snowball sampling. This research was rooted in the feminist goal of illuminating the psychological strengths of sexual minorities, who have often been stigmatized by both mainstream psychology and the general public. This sampling method was utilized because minority group members (i.e., sexual minorities) can be difficult to identify in the larger population. By using this sampling technique, these researchers were able to increase the number of people included in their study because participants were encouraged to recruit their friends and acquaintances to also

participate. Web surveys are particularly amenable to snowball sampling. For example, Szymanski and Owens (2009), who were also interested in the experiences of sexual minorities, utilized websites such as YahooGroups and Gayyellowpages.com to recruit participants who were sent e-mails that contained a link to an online survey. A single link to the survey website, which can be distributed among social networks, can facilitate the ease of access to the survey for interested participants. However, a major drawback of snowball sampling is that it can create systematic sources of sampling error because participants are likely to recruit others who share similar characteristics in addition to the characteristic of interest; for instance, sexual minorities may recruit other sexual minorities, but they may also recruit individuals of the same age, gender, or race, which would limit the ability to generalize the results to all sexual minorities.

Probability samples (also called random samples) are those in which every individual in a target population has a known (nonzero) chance of selection, and the selection process is random (Czaja & Blair, 1996). This sampling strategy has the distinct advantage of producing findings that can be generalized to the population of interest. Because probability sampling techniques allow the researcher to collect information from a wider spectrum of people, when compared with nonrandom techniques, the findings will be inclusive of many viewpoints. This advantage should be important to feminist researchers who are interested in information that generalizes not only to women but also to various marginalized populations (e.g., ethnic minorities, sexual minorities) that have been neglected in past research. Additionally, if the goal of the research is to inform public policy regarding women's issues, probability sampling may be preferable because such research will be more persuasive if it is generalizable. The choice of whether to use probability or nonprobability sampling, however, ultimately depends on the resources available to the researcher and the need to apply the results broadly. Researchers should carefully choose the sampling method by weighing the advantages and disadvantages associated with various sampling techniques.

SURVEY CONSTRUCTION

Survey construction addresses issues such as the length and format of the overall survey, as well as the design, order, and format of the specific questions that will be included. The main prerequisites for designing a good survey are deciding exactly what is important to *measure* (i.e., what questions will be asked) and how questions will be asked (Groves et al., 2009). For feminists, some of those decisions come during the discovery phase and should be based on what information is needed in order to evaluate the stated hypotheses. This process of translating a hypothesis into a specific, testable, and measurable procedure is called *operationalization* (Vogt, 1999), and exactly which questions are asked will depend on how concepts are operationalized.

In the beginning stage of survey construction, it can be beneficial to conduct in-depth discussions with individuals who are representative of the population of interest (e.g., focus groups). These conversations can help the researcher understand the way people talk about the issues the survey will address, so he or she can choose the appropriate vocabulary and phrasing of questions. Using this method can suggest issues, concerns, and ways of looking at the topic that the researcher has not considered (Groves et al., 2009). Thus, these discussions can be a valuable tool to gain situated knowledge about a subordinated group. For example, in their study of AIDS-related behaviors and attitudes, Quina et al. (1999) conducted focus groups with two community samples of low-educated women who gave feedback about the researchers' draft survey, its readability, length, format, and content. The women also commented on their emotional responses to the survey and their truthfulness in responding to it. This process allowed the population of interest (i.e., low-educated women) to participate in the research process and have a voice in the research; these are aspects that are central to feminist methodology.

Survey Organization

The organization of the survey, that is, the layout and format of the questions, should make the tasks of the respondent (and the interviewer when administering a telephone or face-to-face survey) as easy as possible. The survey should begin with the most general questions, and questions should flow smoothly and easily from section to section. However, because the order of questions can profoundly affect responses, the *dependent measures* (i.e., the outcome of interest) should come before the *independent measures* (i.e., the cause of interest). For example, questions about respondents' satisfaction with their job should come before questions assessing their experiences of sexual harassment because questions about sexual harassment can "prime" negative workplace experiences, which can affect their responses to all later questions on the survey. Moreover, unless there is good reason to administer different questions or survey formats to different groups of respondents (such as when a researcher wants certain subgroups of respondents to answer additional questions or to examine explicitly whether question order affects participant responses), all respondents should get the same set of questions in the same format (Fowler, 2008). Questions should also be grouped together by topic (e.g., questions about work) and by response categories (e.g., agree/disagree), so respondents have to focus on only one issue or set of response options at a time (Alreck & Settle, 1995). The survey should conclude with the most sensitive and intrusive questions, when rapport and trust are likely greatest—important components of the feminist research process.

Designing Questions

It is preferable to use measures already shown to be valid and reliable. *Valid measures* are those that actually assess what they are intended to assess; *reliable measures* consistently measure the same construct (Fowler, 2008). If such measures are not available, or their exact format is not practical, the researcher will need to design questions or adapt existing measures suited to the population of interest. One significant problem with early survey research was that measures that were validated on men were often given to women without being validated with samples of women (Eichler, 1988). Because these measures were based on the male perspective, they may not have been appropriate or meaningful for use with women, as the meaning of and responses to survey items may systematically vary by gender.

Indeed, empirical research shows that respondents can and do have different interpretations of the same questions, especially when those questions are vague or contain technical terms (Groves et al., 2009; Schwarz, Groves, & Schuman, 1998). Landrine, Klonoff, and Brown-Collins (1992) examined black and white women's interpretations of gender-related words and phrases (e.g., "I am feminine," "I am passive," and "I am assertive") and found that women associated very different meanings with the words, which influenced their responses to how well the words characterized themselves. For example, while black women defined the word *passive* as not saying what one really thinks, white women defined it as laid-back or easygoing, suggesting differences in question meaning and interpretation. Thus, when the focus of research is on any specific group of individuals, it is important, if possible, for researchers to use measures that have been validated on individuals in that group. If an existing measure has not been appropriately validated, or if the researcher is unsure of the validation history of the measure, a test of the measure's validity should be incorporated into the research. This testing may be accomplished by including measures in the survey that have known or theoretically predicted relationships (or complete non-relationships) with the new measure, so the researcher can analyze responses to the two measures statistically to ensure that they relate in the expected manner, which will support the validation of the new measure.

The major issues to address in designing questions are comprehension (the ease with which the respondent interprets and understands the question), retrieval (the degree to which the respondent can recall the information needed to answer the question), and reporting (the ability to formulate a response and put it in the required format) (Groves et al., 2009). Clearly, if questions are not understood by the respondent, retrieval and reporting will also be inaccurate. To aid in comprehension, researchers should use nontechnical, unambiguous language when designing questions. Additionally, following the principles of feminist research, they should take into account differences between various social groups (e.g., different ethnicities, social classes, or cultures) and use non-oppressive (e.g., nonsexist, nonracist) language (Eichler, 1988). To assist respondents with the retrieval of information, specifically, to help them recall behavior, the researcher can provide helpful cues, such as asking participants to think about situations occurring at a specific time and place and involving specific people (Schwarz et al., 1998). The most accurate recall occurs when a person is asked for responses to recent events; thus, it is recommended that memory of recent events be stimulated first, which may aid in the recall of more temporally distant events if necessary. Questions about attitudes, which unlike behavioral questions are more likely to be influenced by personal bias, are highly susceptible to response errors resulting from question wording and the order in which questions are presented. Some suggested strategies for handling such errors are to use more than one (or even more than a few) items to tap into one question or construct, to vary the format and wording of questions throughout a survey, and to examine responses to items independently without assuming that all items in a scale are interchangeable. Regarding reporting, because the survey format typically requires participants to respond on a scale provided by the researcher, it is important to take into account the breadth of options provided in order to gain accurate responses. Complications that may occur during the reporting stage could also be due to the desire to edit or censor one's responses, an effect that can be diminished through increased anonymity.

In short, when newly developed or revised measures are used, the psychometric properties (e.g., validity, reliability) of the measure should be evaluated to maximize feminist objectivity. Statistical corrections and controls may be applied to account for imperfect measures, but, ultimately, if a researcher finds that a measure is valid for one group but not for another, the researcher should not use the measure for the group in which it is not valid until it has been reconstructed (e.g., items have been reworded or added and removed) and validated. Furthermore, as will be discussed in the following section, utilizing a mix of closed-ended and open-ended questions can aid researchers in understanding individuals' interpretations of questions and can give voice to all participants beyond what can be understood with the use of only a structured survey measure.

Types of Questions

There are two different types of questions used in survey research: *closed-ended* questions and *open-ended* questions. Closed-ended questions present participants with a list of specific response options, while open-ended questions allow participants to provide their own answers. In survey research, open-ended questions are similar to fill-in-the-blank or short-answer questions, and closed questions are more like multiple-choice questions (Groves et al., 2009). When designing closed-ended questions, researchers should provide a broad range of response options so that they do not exclude any answers an individual might want to offer. Although closed-ended questions can limit richness and variety because they do not allow respondents to respond in their own words, they can also be beneficial because they are quicker and easier to answer, making individuals more likely to respond (Fowler, 2008). Additionally, although open-ended questions typically generate more complete and nuanced answers, they are not easily subjected to statistical analysis, so even though they may fully represent the viewpoint of a single individual, they may not accurately portray the experiences of a large group of respondents. Whether one uses closed-ended or open-ended questions, the question format should be short and specific, resulting in less error on the part of both the respondent and, in the case of survey interviews, the interviewer (Fowler, 2008). One example that illustrates the use of both open- and closed-ended questions is the work of Hester and Donovan (2009), who demonstrated in their study of same-sex domestic violence that using both types of questions can be highly valuable, especially when dealing with sensitive issues in minority populations. By using both open- and closed-ended questions, they found that respondents were better able to express nuanced aspects of their identities, which made for a richer understanding of their experience of violence in their romantic relationships.

Pretesting

After the survey is initially designed, it is important to pretest it, that is, to administer it to a small group of individuals to determine if it requires further revision. Those pretesting the survey should be similar to the individuals who will ultimately complete it but not the same people that are in the survey sample. In a pretest, the researcher typically asks individuals not only to respond to questions but also to articulate their thoughts about the wording of questions (e.g., if the questions were clear) and the overall design of the survey. This process can provide insights into interpretations of question meanings (Schwarz et al., 1998) and therefore may enhance the quality of the survey instrument. A similar technique for improving surveys prior to their administration is cognitive interviewing, in which respondents report in-depth understanding of questions (e.g., verbalize their thoughts while they are answering a question).

DATA COLLECTION

Although the term *data collection* tends to imply that respondents' opinions exist independently of how they are assessed, it is critical to recognize that the *process* of data collection is an integral part of what constitutes data (Groves et al., 2009). For example, the interviewer, the interview setting, and the answer options as well as extraneous conditions can all influence the information that is obtained. Early survey research tended to ignore the effect of some of these elements, resulting in data that were often biased in favor of the researcher's viewpoint or the prevailing social discourse. This aspect of traditional survey research was a major focus of much feminist criticism because it meant that a woman's viewpoint was frequently distorted. Researchers are more aware of such issues today. For example, Scraton, Caudwell, and Holland (2005) conducted interviews with black and Indian Hindu women soccer players to examine their unique experiences with everyday discrimination. The researchers argued that the survey interview was the ideal technique to collect data due to its ability to capture the complexity of everyday experiences of a previously uninvestigated group. However, they were also cognizant about potential problems associated with how they conducted the interviews. For example, the soccer players were interviewed by white women investigators, which could bias the interpretation of the experiences of ethnic minority respondents. Current survey techniques emphasize the value of minimizing such error effects during data collection (Groves et al., 2009) and promoting awareness of how cultural factors (e.g., ethnicity, gender, and class) and interviewer attributes impact the quality of the research. As stated previously, removing the researcher from the survey administration by conducting it over the Internet can help tremendously with such bias effects.

Ethical Treatment of Participants

Numerous aspects of the research process are subject to ethical evaluation (e.g., truthful reporting of data, giving credit to those contributing to the research), that is, the assessment of how well the research conforms to culturally accepted ethical principles. However, most discussions of research ethics have tended to focus on how the participants in research are treated by the researcher. This emphasis is likely a result of the serious abuses of research participants that have occurred in the not too distant past. Perhaps the most notorious, well-known examples are Milgram's obedience studies (Milgram, 1974) and the Tuskegee syphilis study (see Jones, 1981). Milgram led participants to believe they were administering shocks to another person for the purposes of "teaching"—a procedure that greatly distressed many of the participants. In the Tuskegee experiment, the government studied the progress of syphilis in African American males without informing these men of their disease and without treating them, despite the existence of penicillin as an effective remedy. Although these are not examples of survey research, per se, they show why an awareness of such exploitation resulted in a broad effort to prevent the mistreatment of participants in all research on human subjects.

Among the voices included in this movement to enact strict standards for the ethical treatment of research participants were those of feminist scholars. In fact, many initial feminist critiques of research targeted this particular aspect of the

research process, as exploitation of research participants conflicted with the basic humanistic values that are fundamental to feminists. These critiques often advocated decreasing or eliminating the power differential between the researcher and the researched (Du Bois, 1983; Fee, 1983). For example, Reinharz (1979) suggested that an equal relationship would likely yield information that reflects the participant's reality rather than the researcher's reality, as power differentials may not only influence participants' responses but also facilitate the development of a researcher's biased interpretation of responses. She characterized this collaboration as "non-hierarchical, non-authoritarian, non-manipulative" (p. 181), terms that reflect core feminist principles. Other feminists called for the need to redefine the process as "research with" or "research for" rather than "research on" (Stanley & Wise, 1983). As Harding (1987) explained, "the best feminist analysis . . . insists that the inquirer her/himself be placed in the same critical plane as the overt subject matter" (p. 9). Thus, feminists sought to appreciate and value research participants, rather than considering them as "objects" of study.

One result of this concern about treatment of research subjects was the establishment of institutional review boards (now commonplace in most research organizations), which set mandatory standards for the conduct of research, such as the protection of privacy and protection from harm. These standards are clearly laid out in the Belmont Report (National Commission for the Protection of Human Subjects of Biomedical Research, 1998), which specifies three principles for the conduct of research on human research participants: (1) respect for persons (informed consent and protection from the risk of harm), (2) beneficence (maximizing benefits and minimizing risks to subjects), and (3) justice (fairness in the distribution of the benefits of research and equal treatment). While these guidelines cannot guarantee that all research involving humans will follow these principles, they do go a long way in promoting such standards.

One major change resulting from these guidelines is that individuals who currently participate in research must give informed consent, that is, they must indicate that they understand the nature of their research participation and freely agree to be involved. Informed consent thus makes explicit the importance of respect for those taking part in the research. Although it is heartening that science has come so far in attempting to protect individuals who are susceptible to exploitation in the name of science, it is imperative that we, as feminists, be vigilant in maintaining and applying those safeguards, especially as we frequently engage in research for marginalized populations who may be vulnerable to exploitation. Furthermore, although these standards promote the ethical treatment of subjects, they do not eliminate the power differential between the researcher and the researched, a theme of central importance among feminists. Thinking of respondents as "collaborators" not only helps to minimize the power differential but also, as Reinharz (1979) suggests, allows us to gather information that more accurately describes the reality of respondents' lives.

Because of the rise of web surveys, it is important to consider the unique ethical implications of online research. In general, Internet research has some very tangible ethical benefits over paper-and-pencil surveys. For one, participation is fully voluntary—respondents can simply close their browser window at any time if they do not wish to participate in the survey; indeed, when administering online surveys, researchers should make this option explicit in the informed consent form. Respondents may also feel more comfortable completing a survey over the Internet because direct contact with the researcher is unnecessary. Additionally, researchers using online surveys frequently do not collect personal identifying information from participants, which helps to bolster the confidentiality of the data (although this protocol tends to be subject to the unique IRB protocols of various universities; see Fraley, 2004). At the same time, however, maintaining respondents' privacy during Internet data collection offers unique challenges because respondents may fear that people other than the researchers may be able to access their responses in cyberspace, a legitimate concern when the survey covers sensitive or controversial issues (Israel & Hay, 2006). Although Internet surveys generally do more to promote anonymity than to compromise it, it is advisable for researchers to analyze statistically the responses of individuals who complete the survey as compared with individuals who drop out

before completing all measures. If differences are found between those who finished the survey and those who did not (for example, if men were more likely than women to complete the survey), we recommend that researchers evaluate whether the steps taken to assure participants of their anonymity were adequate. Additionally, some evidence exists that the initial interaction between the researcher and the participant heavily influences the participant's decision to participate or not (see Schwarz et al., 1998); thus, participants' first impressions of the survey (e.g., e-mail invitations, informed consent forms) should be designed to assure participants immediately that their privacy will be protected and that their responses are highly valued by the researcher.

Szymanski and Owens (2009), for example, employed several strategies for protecting confidentiality in their study of sexual minority women who completed an Internet survey on heterosexism and psychological distress. One strategy they offered was to have participants access the research survey via a hypertext link rather than e-mail to ensure their anonymity. Additionally, they used a separate raffle database to track the monetary rewards or "lottery" they offered as an incentive for participation, so there was no way to connect a woman's raffle submission with her survey. Furthermore, to ensure data integrity, they used a secure server protected with a firewall to prevent tampering with data and programs and inadvertent access to the confidential information provided by research participants. Although these are excellent steps to take in order to ensure privacy, it is ultimately the researcher's task to evaluate the efficacy of such strategies, to be clear and open with participants about how their information is being protected, and to make a priority of managing data in an ethical manner. See Reips (2000) for more guidelines for ensuring the confidentiality of online data.

Preparing, Analyzing, and Interpreting Data

Processing of Data

Once the data are collected, a series of procedures are frequently required before they can be analyzed. These involve data entry (entering the raw numeric data into computer files; note that this step is unnecessary if online surveys are used or if the data are entered by an interviewer during telephone interviewing), codebook construction (variable documentation), and coding (translating nonnumeric data into numerical categories). A *codebook* is a record of the variables in the survey, and each entry includes the variable name, a number assigned to the variable (required in many statistical analysis programs), the question wording, and the numeric code value for and meaning of each of the answer options (e.g., the value of "1" could be assigned to represent "women" and "2" to represent "men" in a gender variable). Most of these procedures are routine and serve to minimize errors in the data while increasing the efficiency of the data analysis; therefore, they have little direct relevance to feminist values. One exception is when open-ended questions are coded. In this case, the interpretation and classification of responses can be influenced by the particular perspective of the coder, so coding these answers is especially relevant to the issue of feminist objectivity. In what follows, we briefly discuss the coding of open-ended responses, as these types of questions are popular among many feminist researchers. Open-ended questions are often favored among feminist researchers because they allow the individuals to respond in their own voices (Landrine et al., 1992; Marecek et al., 1997; Wallston & Grady, 1992).

Typically, answers to closed-ended questions (e.g., agree/disagree) are precoded in that each answer is associated with a particular numeric value prior to the coding process. Open-ended responses can be sorted into just a few categories, or those with short, simple answers that are clearly interpreted (e.g., employment status) can be coded in a straightforward manner by assigning a number code to each category. For more complex open-ended answers, such as political opinions expressed in participants' own words, the researcher must interpret the meaning of the response as well as assign the response to a particular numeric category. Because data in survey research are not usually reported or analyzed verbatim but rather are aggregated into categories, the interpretation and coding of those responses is significant. On the one hand, because the interpretive process can be highly subjective, applying a feminist perspective (or any other particular perspective) when coding can distort the *intended* meaning of the response (and may increase error). On the other hand, such interpretation may be seen as using a feminist lens through which to view the data and articulating a feminist viewpoint (which may otherwise be suppressed). In short, there is a fine line between highlighting a feminist standpoint within a narrative and mistakenly representing a participant's narrative. Consequently, this dialectical aspect of feminist survey research (i.e., translating open-ended data into categories for statistical analysis) is an important issue in feminist scholarship, as the researcher attempts to maintain conventional objectivity while at the same time giving voice to women or any subjugated group. To help ease this tension, the researcher can use various methods to minimize or estimate bias during coding, such as conducting extensive coder training, using more than one coder and calculating the interrater reliability of coding, obtaining feedback from the coders during the coding process, and asking for input from respondents regarding the "correct" interpretation of their words or what categories they see as emerging from the data. However, none of these methods ensures an accurate representation of the intended meaning of the response during the coding process, and thus researchers who engage in the coding of such data should consider using some combination of these methodological checks and balances along with careful reflexivity on the nature of their project to help decrease bias.

Data Analysis

As quantitative information, survey data are analyzed using a broad and complex array of statistical techniques, which are continually evolving and expanding to meet the needs of survey researchers. Given the large number of possible ways in which data can be analyzed, a subject that is covered thoroughly in statistical courses and texts (e.g., Frankfort-Nachmias & Leon-Guerrero, 2008), here we will focus on more general issues regarding both the function of statistical analysis and the appropriate use of statistics for answering the research question. In discussing the uses of statistics, we will briefly address feminist concerns that statistics are tools that objectify and distort women's voices.

Purpose of Statistical Analysis

Statistical analysis is a technique used to summarize quantitative data, that is, to aggregate individual numeric items of data. This process is generally necessary in survey research because the information that is collected cannot be easily understood, interpreted, or disseminated in its raw form, as it is often comprised of multiple elements representing the opinions or beliefs of many individuals. Without statistical analysis, determining the meaning of this information would be unwieldy and subject to a wide range of interpretations. Because statistics allow us to better understand the data, they can offer a way to more "objectively" judge various hypotheses, compared with other analytic methods (Jayaratne, 1983). For example, if two different but equally plausible strategies are proposed by feminists for persuading voters to support legislation upholding a woman's right to choose, a statistical analysis of data on voter attitudes should demonstrate which method is likely to be most effective in accomplishing this goal.

Knowing which statistical techniques should be used to answer a specific research question is a significant issue because conducting inappropriate statistical analyses can not only distort the findings of a study but also, in the worst case scenario, produce results that are opposite from those that accurately reflect the collected data. Therefore, we emphasize the importance of a comprehensive understanding of statistics before embarking on any survey research study. However, it is also critical to recognize that no matter how well one applies statistical principles during data analysis, if other aspects of the research are in violation of accepted standards, the results of the statistical analysis will be invalid; as it is commonly phrased, "garbage in, garbage out." For example, when a survey question does not capture the intended construct, then statistical procedures will produce results that are not valid in testing the hypothesis.

Statistics have been the target of feminist criticism because feminists have linked them with the quantification of subjective personal experiences, which has the potential to distort participants' responses. However, as feminist methodology has evolved, some feminist scholars (e.g., Jayaratne & Stewart, 1991) have tempered this criticism by pointing out that it is not statistics, per se, that are objectionable; rather, how they are used within the broader context of research determines whether they violate feminist principles. For example, sexist or racist theories have often been supported by supposedly objective statistical analyses (e.g., Buss, 1989; Herrnstein & Murray, 1994). Despite these misuses of statistics, the evaluation of data based on mathematical standards and statistical principles is not inherently consistent with either feminist or sexist values. We contend that, rather than seeing statistical methods as a violation of feminist values, as mentioned in earlier critiques, scholars can use statistics appropriately in feminist research and actually increase the likelihood that findings are interpreted as valid (Jayaratne, 1983; Reinharz, 1992). Because of this, we argue that the use of statistics can advance the feminist research goals of achieving social justice and change for women.

Evaluating Hypotheses Using Statistical Results

When statistical analyses are complete, researchers should use the statistical results in evaluating the hypotheses. If the research components (e.g., sampling, question wording, data analysis) are appropriately chosen and implemented, then this interpretation should be clear. However, this hypotheses evaluation stage is rarely as straightforward as it sounds. For example, it is not uncommon for statistical analyses to produce equivocal findings. Sometimes, one set of results contradicts another set. It might also be the case that the research findings appear to conflict with feminist ideals and interests. In this situation, it may be worthwhile to reevaluate the research to explore the possibility that such findings result from a deviation in accepted research protocol (e.g., misinterpretations of question wording or sampling bias). However, it may additionally be helpful to ask why a particular finding appears to conflict with feminist principles. This might lead to alternative understandings of the phenomenon of interest, ones not previously considered. For the novice feminist researcher who is likely to expect clear-cut answers, this can be frustrating. Nevertheless, because social behaviors or attitudes are subject to multiple, interacting influences, which frequently cannot be accounted for fully, our attempt to understand or predict these outcomes is inexact. For many investigators, studying complex phenomena without definitive answers is a valuable and rich part of research.

INTERPRETATION AND DISSEMINATION OF RESULTS

The final component of survey research is the interpretation and dissemination of findings. We consider the feminist perspective to be particularly applicable and necessary in this phase of the survey research process. This stage (or "bookend") can be most amenable to influencing real social change for women and other marginalized groups.

Interpretation of Results

How a researcher interprets the overall results is the culmination of the investigation in the sense that it involves the evaluation of findings as they pertain to the research question, which was articulated in the initial steps of the research process. Unlike the evaluation of the hypotheses using statistical information (a process that should follow accepted survey research practice), interpreting the meaning of the research results, as it applies to the research question, should especially be subject to a feminist perspective. Giving feminist significance to the results is a critical aspect of feminist survey research. For example, if a statistic indicates that there is a significant difference between men and women on some characteristic (such as mathematical ability), there are myriad interpretations of what that means. One could see this finding as indicating support for the "deficit hypothesis," that is, that women

are naturally inferior to men in this characteristic. Alternatively, one could interpret this difference as reflecting the oppression of women (e.g., as resulting from unequal educational experiences) and pointing to the need for social change. Therefore, the feminist meanings we give our results are what mark the research endeavor as a significant feminist enterprise.

Evaluating Findings in Relation to the Literature

The purpose of research is to advance incrementally our understanding of the interplay between human behaviors, attributes, and social conditions. In order to attain this goal, researchers must interpret overall findings as they relate to the larger body of empirical and theoretical literature. This can mean supporting previous research by presenting findings that are consistent with prevailing work or, as in the case of much feminist scholarship, that challenge the dominant paradigm. Revisionist activity (i.e., the reinterpretation of traditional, male-oriented research by infusing new findings that are consistent with feminist perspectives) has been a major function of feminist scholarship and continues to be a central aspect of feminist methodology. For example, past research has posited that there are inherent differences between men and women, differences that can explain the overrepresentation of men in positions of organizational power; however, King, Hebl, George, and Matusik (2010) emphasize that it is gender inequity in the workplace, not fundamental differences between the sexes, that prevents women from advancing at the same rate as men. Utilizing the findings of this study and others, feminist researchers are able to revise current theory on gender and correct for historical biases pertaining to women and other minority members of society.

The Dissemination of Research Findings

The final step of the entire research process can be an exceptionally gratifying part of the research journey, not only because there is anticipated closure but also because this step addresses the most fundamental goal of feminist research—to enact real-world social change for women. This step is the dissemination of findings that acts as a catalyst for social change. For feminists, the dissemination of research findings means reporting the results to scholars, the public, the media, or policy makers by linking the results back to women's lives with a clear understanding of how the findings can benefit women. As we have argued, survey research can be particularly amenable to advocating for women and other marginalized groups in public policy arenas because it is both mainstream and feminist.

An excellent example of how survey research can be applied to achieve real-world social change for women is the Supreme Court's rulings on affirmative action at the University of Michigan. In 2003, the American Psychological Association submitted an amicus curiae brief to the Supreme Court, which supported the University of Michigan's policy of race- and gender-aware admissions in higher education in two court cases (*Gratz v. Bollinger*, 2003; *Grutter v. Bollinger*, 2003). This brief drew heavily upon the work of feminist psychologist Patricia Gurin's survey research on the value of diversity in academia that demonstrated the benefits of such environments for students (as summarized in Gurin, Dey, & Hurtado, 2002). The court's decision to uphold the principle of considering race and gender in college admissions illustrates the effective use of survey data in contributing to social change efforts.

A final important aspect of disseminating results is acknowledging the limitations of the research. This is one way of employing feminist objectivity. Indeed, no research is perfect; all research includes some unintended error. Because error decreases the validity of the findings, this aspect of research must be acknowledged up front, as the results are disseminated. Specifically, it is important to indicate limitations that are likely to impact the findings or their generalizability. It is helpful when doing this to identify particular sources of error explicitly, such as those found in sampling, in measurement, or with the misspecification of the model (e.g., not including important variables in the analyses). This aspect of the research is imperative for those whose goals include feminist social change because of the possibility that this research will generate skepticism from those with a more traditional perspective. Stating the limitations of one's research lends methodological credibility to the entire research process because it diminishes the likelihood that the findings will appear as ideologically influenced, which is a major criticism some mainstream researchers have directed toward feminist research. Although it might seem counterintuitive that by admitting error the data can seem more error free, we posit that recognizing the limitations of the research causes results to appear more objective; thus, they are more likely to be accepted as valid.

CONCLUSION

Feminist research includes a multitude of methods for investigation, each of which can uniquely influence the social change effort to improve the lives of women and attain greater gender equity. In this chapter, we focused on one particular method, survey research, and the important role it can play in this endeavor. We have shown how survey research methods were utilized by early feminists as a means of improving scholarly research and effecting social change (Spalter-Roth & Hartmann, 1996). Although some of these pioneers, such as the feminist empiricists involved in the Hull-House movement, adhered to positivist notions of objectivity in research, others, such as the academic feminists of the 1960s and 1970s, sought to improve upon survey research by disconnecting from positivism and creating their own version of *feminist* objectivity within the survey research process. Today, the survey method remains an important resource within the feminist methodological toolbox, and modern feminist scholars are able to draw upon the modifications that feminists of the past and present have made to enhance this method's effectiveness in promoting the values of feminism.

We have emphasized how the survey method can be an especially useful tool for social change because it is a respected research strategy among nonfeminists and can suggest effective ways to challenge the existing power structure. Further, when conducted rigorously, survey research can provide a representative picture of the collective experiences of large groups of people. Both feminist and nonfeminist researchers who seek to understand the unique experiences of those who may often be overlooked in traditional research can use surveys to better understand the world from the perspective of marginalized and oppressed populations. Thus, while surveys may not be the most suitable option for studying individuals on a case-by-case basis, they are an excellent tool for addressing large-scale social issues. But perhaps most important, we have argued that the survey method is wholly consistent with feminist values and goals.

The perspective we have presented in this chapter derives directly from our personal experiences as feminists and as social science researchers who have employed survey methods to examine issues of significance to women and minority groups. We have seen how our work and that of other survey researchers can promote a progressive agenda and influence public opinion and legislative policy. Thus, we believe it valuable to explain the benefits of these methods to those who might be unaware of how such techniques are wholly consistent with feminist values and can be utilized to support such values. Although our work in survey research occurs primarily in the social sciences, this research strategy has application across many academic and nonacademic domains. Survey research is thus an appropriate method of study for a wide array of feminist topics that remain ripe for investigation. As feminist scholars explore the various research methods available, it is important that they select those that can best address their research goals. We hope that the survey research method, which we have outlined in this chapter, is among the many options considered.

Discussion Questions

1. How can conducting rigorous survey research help marginalized populations? As the goal of feminist research is to produce knowledge that is for, rather than on, women, how can researchers ensure that this goal is not distorted when they use survey methodology?

2. For many feminists, the positivist ideals of objectivity and neutrality are not considered exclusively masculine and in opposition to feminist principles. How are these ideals in line with femininity and the female perspective, as practiced in feminist empiricism?

3. How does feminist objectivity reconcile the goal of scientific research to be value neutral with the goal of feminist research to induce social change? How might one respond to a nonfeminist accusation that the goal of social change makes feminist research inherently biased?

4. How can researchers responsibly use statistics to aggregate data while assuring that the perspectives of all respondents are represented in inferences drawn from the data? Because statistics represent the opinions of the target population in general, how can survey researchers make sure that women's unique experiences are conveyed to the public and policy makers?

Online Resources

Resources for Feminist Research

http://www.oise.utoronto.ca/rfr/pages/internet.html

This site was created by the Ontario Institute for Studies in Education at the University of Toronto. It provides excellent resources, such as lists of online feminist journals, newspapers, feminist and queer websites, and social research search tools.

Social Psychology Network (SPN)

http://www.socialpsychology.org/methods.htm#survey

This website has a wide array of information about social psychology and social psychology methods. The link will take you to the specific section on survey methods. Studies can also be posted on this site.

The Web Center for Social Research Methods

http://www.socialresearchmethods.net/

Created by Cornell University, this website provides thorough, detailed information pertaining to research methods in the social sciences and covers a broad range of research designs and statistical tests.

American Association for Public Opinion Research

http://www.aapor.org/Home.htm

The website of the leading association for public opinion and survey research professionals, this online resource provides a list of frequently asked questions about polls and conducting survey research.

Relevant Journals

Gender & Society

Journal of Social Issues

Psychological Methods

Psychology of Women Quarterly

Sex Roles

Sociological Methods & Research

NOTE

1. A variable is any concept that can assume different values among people, such as age, gender, income, or attitudes.

REFERENCES

Acker, J., Barry, K., & Esseveld, J. (1996). Objectivity and truth: Problems in doing feminist research. In H. Gottfried (Ed.), *Feminism and social change: Bridging theory and practice* (pp. 60–87). Urbana, IL: University of Illinois Press. (Reprinted from *Women's Studies International Forum, 4*, pp. 423–435, by Elsevier Science Ltd., 1983, Oxford, England: Pergamon Press)

Alreck, P. L., & Settle, R. B. (1995). *The survey research handbook: Guidelines and strategies for conducting a survey.* Burr Ridge, IL: Irwin.

Beck, E., & Britto, S. (2006). Using feminist methods and restorative justice to interview capital offenders' family members. *Journal of Women and Social Work, 21,* 59–70.

Biemer, P. P., & Lyberg, L. E. (2003). *Introduction to survey quality.* Hoboken, NJ: Wiley.

Boyatzis, R. E. (1998). *Transforming qualitative information.* London: Sage.

Bryman, A. (2004). *Social research methods* (2nd ed.). Oxford, UK: Oxford University Press.

Buss, D. M. (1989). Sex differences in human mate preferences: Evolutionary hypotheses tested in 37 cultures. *Behavioral and Brain Sciences, 12,* 1–49.

Campbell, P. B. (1982). Racism and sexism in research. In H. Mitzel (Ed.), *Encyclopedia of educational research* (5th ed., pp. 1515–1520). New York: Free Press.

Campbell, R., & Wasco, S. M. (2000). Feminist approaches to social science: Epistemological and methodological tenets. *American Journal of Community Psychology, 28,* 733–791.

Chafetz, J. S. (2004). Some thoughts by an unrepentant "positivist" who considers herself a feminist nonetheless. In S. N. Hesse-Biber & M. L. Yaiser (Eds.), *Feminist perspectives on social research* (pp. 320–329). New York: Oxford University Press.

Converse, J. (1987). *Survey research in the United States.* Berkeley: University of California Press.

Crawford, M., & Marecek, J. (1989). Psychology reconstructs the female, 1968–1988. *Psychology of Women Quarterly, 13,* 147–165.

Czaja, R., & Blair, J. (1996). *Designing surveys: A guide to decisions and procedures.* Thousand Oaks, CA: Pine Forge Press.

Deegan, M. J. (1988). *Jane Addams and the men of the Chicago school, 1892–1918.* New Brunswick, NJ: Transaction Books.

DeVault, M. L. (1999). *Liberating method: Feminism and social research.* Philadelphia: Temple University Press.

Dillman, D. A., Smyth, J. D., & Christian, L. M. (2008). *Internet, mail, and mixed-mode surveys: The tailored design method.* New York: Wiley.

Du Bois, B. (1983). Passionate scholarship: Notes on values, knowing, and method in feminist social science. In G. Bowles & R. Duelli Klein (Eds.), *Theories of women's studies* (pp. 105–116). Boston: Routledge & Kegan Paul.

Dunn, D. S. (2001). *Statistics and data analysis for the behavioral sciences.* New York: McGraw-Hill.

Dunn, D. S. (2008). *Research methods for social psychology.* New York: Wiley.

Eichler, M. (1988). *Nonsexist research methods: A practical guide.* New York: Routledge.

Fee, E. (1983). Women's nature and scientific objectivity. In M. Lowe & R. Hubbard (Eds.),

Woman's nature: Rationalizations of inequality (pp. 9–27). New York: Pergamon.

Fowler, F. J. (2008). *Survey research methods.* Beverly Hills, CA: Sage.

Fraley, R. C. (2004). *How to conduct behavioral research over the Internet: A beginner's guide to HTML and CGI/Perl.* New York: Guilford.

Frankfort-Nachmias, C., & Leon-Guerrero, A. (2008). *Social statistics for a diverse society.* Thousand Oaks, CA: Pine Forge Press.

Gorelick, S. (1996). Contradictions of feminist methodology. In H. Gottfried (Ed.), *Feminism and social change: Bridging theory and practice* (pp. 23–45). Urbana: University of Illinois Press.

Graham, H. (1983). Do her answers fit his questions? Women and the survey method. In E. Gamarnikow, D. Morgan, J. Purvis, & D. Taylorson (Eds.), *The public and the private.* London: Heinemann.

Gratz v. Bollinger, 539 U.S. 244 (2003).

Groves, R., Fowler, F. J., Couper, M. P., Lepkowski, J. M., Singer, E., & Tourangeau, R. (2009). *Survey methodology* (2nd ed.). New York: Wiley.

Groves, R., & Kahn, R. (1979). *Surveys by telephone: A national comparison with personal interviews.* New York: Academic Press.

Grutter v. Bollinger, 539 U.S. 306 (2003).

Gurin, P., Dey, E. L., & Hurtado, S. (2002) Diversity and higher education: Theory and impact on educational outcomes. *Harvard Educational Review, 72*, 330–366.

Haraway, D. (1988). Situated knowledges: The science question in feminism and the privilege of partial perspective. *Feminist Studies, 14*, 575–599.

Haraway, D. (1991). *Simians, cyborgs, and women: The reinvention of nature.* New York: Routledge.

Harding, R., & Peel, E. (2007). Heterosexism at work: Diversity training, discrimination law, and the limits of liberal individualism. In V. Clarke & E. Peel (Eds.), *Out in psychology: Lesbian, gay, bisexual, trans and queer perspectives* (pp. 247–271). Chichester, West Sussex, UK: Wiley.

Harding, S. (1987). Introduction: Is there a feminist method? In S. Harding, (Ed.), *Feminism and methodology* (pp. 1–14). Bloomington: Indiana University Press.

Harding, S. (1998). *Is science multicultural? Postcolonialisms, feminisms, and epistemologies.* Bloomington: Indiana University Press.

Harding, S. (2004). Rethinking standpoint epistemology: What is "strong objectivity"? In S. N. Hesse-Biber & M. L. Yaiser (Eds.), *Feminist perspectives on social research* (pp. 39–64). New York: Oxford University Press.

Hartsock, N. C. M. (1998). *The feminist standpoint revisited and other essays.* Boulder, CO: Westview Press.

Herrnstein, R. J., & Murray, C. (1994). *The bell curve: Intelligence and class structure in American life.* New York: Simon and Schuster.

Hesse-Biber, S. N. (2010). *Mixed methods research: Merging theory with practice.* New York: The Guilford Press.

Hesse-Biber, S. N., Leavy, P., & Yaiser, M. L. (2004). Feminist approaches to research as a process: Reconceptualizing epistemology, methodology, and method. In S. N. Hesse-Biber & M. L. Yaiser (Eds.), *Feminist perspectives on social research* (pp. 3–26). New York: Oxford University Press.

Hester, M., & Donovan, C. (2009). Researching domestic violence in same-sex relationships—A feminist epistemological approach to survey development. *Journal of Lesbian Studies, 13*, 161–173.

Israel, M., & Hay, I. (2006). *Research ethics for social scientists.* Thousand Oaks, CA: Sage.

Jayaratne, T. E. (1983). The value of quantitative methodology for feminist research. In G. Bowles & R. Duelli Klein (Eds.), *Theories of women's studies* (pp. 140–161). Boston: Routledge & Kegan Paul.

Jayaratne, T. E., & Stewart, A. J. (1991). Quantitative and qualitative methods in the social sciences: Current feminist issues and practical strategies. In M. M. Fonow & J. A. Cook (Eds.), *Beyond methodology: Feminist scholarship as lived research* (pp. 85–106). Bloomington: Indiana University Press.

Jayaratne, T. E., Thomas, N. G., & Trautmann, M. T. (2003). An intervention program to keep girls in the science pipeline: Outcome differences by ethnic status. *Journal of Research in Science Teaching, 40*, 393–414.

Jick, T. D. (1979). Mixing qualitative and quantitative methods: Triangulation in action. *Administrative Science Quarterly, 24*, 602–610.

Joffe, H., & Yardley, L. (2004). Content and thematic analysis. In D. F. Marks & L. Yardley (Eds.), *Research methods for clinical and health psychology* (pp. 56–58). Thousand Oaks, CA: Sage.

Jones, J. (1981). *Bad blood: The Tuskegee syphilis experiment.* New York: Free Press.

Kelly, A. (1978). Feminism and research. *Women's Studies International Quarterly*, *1*, 225–232.

King, E. B., Hebl, M. R., George, J. M., & Matusik, S. F. (2010). Understanding tokenism: Antecedents and consequences of a psychological climate of gender inequity. *Journal of Management, 36*, 482–510.

Kirsch, G. E. (1999). *Ethical dilemmas in feminist research*. Albany: State University of New York Press.

Knapp, F., & Heidingsfelder, M. (2001). Drop-out analysis: Effects of the survey design. In U.-D. Reips & M. Bosnjak (Eds.), *Dimensions of Internet science* (pp. 221–230). Lengerich, Germany: Pabst Science Publishers.

Konik, J., & Stewart, A. J. (2004). Sexual identity development in the context of compulsory heterosexuality. *Journal of Personality, 72*(4), 815–844.

Landrine, H., Klonoff, E. A., & Brown-Collins, A. (1992). Cultural diversity and methodology in feminist psychology. *Psychology of Women Quarterly, 16*, 145–163.

Marecek, J., Fine, M., & Kidder, L. (1997). Working between worlds: Qualitative methods and social psychology. *Journal of Social Issues, 53*, 631–644.

Maynard, M. (1994). Methods, practice, and epistemology: The debate about feminism and research. In M. Maynard & J. Purvis (Eds.), *Researching women's lives from a feminist perspective* (pp. 10–26). Bristol, PA: Taylor & Francis Ltd.

McHugh, M. C., & Cosgrove, L. (2004). Feminist research methods: Studying women and gender. In M. A. Paludi (Ed.), *Praeger guide to the psychology of gender*. Westport, CT: Praeger Publishers.

Milgram, S. (1974). *Obedience to authority*. New York: Harper & Row.

National Commission for the Protection of Human Subjects of Biomedical Research. (1998). *The Belmont report: Ethical principles and guidelines for the protection of human subjects of research*. Retrieved June 27, 2011, from http://ohsr.od.nih.gov/guidelines/belmont.html

Peplau, L. A., & Conrad, E. (1989). Beyond nonsexist research: The perils of feminist methods in psychology. *Psychology of Women Quarterly, 13*, 379–400.

Pew Research Center. (2004, April 20). *Polls face growing resistance, but still representative survey experiment shows*. Retrieved June 27, 2011, from http://people-press.org/2004/04/20/polls-face-growing-resistance-but-still-representative/

Pratt, M. G. (2009). For the lack of a boilerplate: Tips on writing up (and reviewing) qualitative research. *Academy of Management Journal, 52*, 856–862.

Quina, K., Rose, J. S., Harlow, L. L., Morokoff, P. J., Deiter, P. J., Whitmire, L. E., Lang, M. A., & Schnoll, R. A. (1999). Focusing on participants: Feminist process model for survey modification. *Psychology of Women Quarterly, 23*, 459–493.

Reinharz, S. (1979). *On becoming a social scientist*. San Francisco: Jossey-Bass Publishers.

Reinharz, S. (1992). *Feminist methods in social research*. New York: Oxford University Press.

Reips, U. D. (2000). The Web experiment method: Advantages, disadvantages, and solutions. In M. H. Birnbaum (Ed.), *Psychological experiments on the Internet* (pp. 89–117). San Diego: Academic Press.

Riger, S. (1992). Epistemological debates, feminist voices: Science, social values, and the story of women. *American Psychologist, 47*, 730–740.

Schick, V. R., Zucker, A. N., & Bay-Cheng, L. Y. (2008). Safer, better sex through feminism: The role of feminist ideology in women's sexual well-being. *Psychology of Women Quarterly, 32*, 225–232.

Schwarz, N., Groves, R. M., & Schuman, H. (1998). Survey methods. In D. T. Gilbert, S. T. Fiske, & G. Lindzey (Eds.), *The handbook of social psychology* (Vol. 1, pp. 143–179). New York: McGraw-Hill.

Scraton, S., Caudwell, J., and Holland, S. (2005). "Bend it like Patel": Centering "race," ethnicity and gender in feminist analysis of women's football in England. *International Review for the Sociology of Sport, 40*, 71–88.

Smith, C. A., & Frieze, I. H. (2003). Examining rape empathy from the perspective of the victim and the assailant. *Journal of Applied Social Psychology, 33*, 476–498.

Spalter-Roth, R., & Hartmann, H. (1996). Small happinesses: The feminist struggle to integrate social research and social activism. In H. Gottfried (Ed.), *Feminism and social change: Bridging theory and practice* (pp. 206–224). Urbana: University of Illinois Press.

Sprague, J., & Zimmerman, M. (1993). Overcoming dualisms: A feminist agenda for sociological methodology. In P. England (Ed.), *Theory on gender/feminism on theory* (pp. 255–280). New York: Aldine De Gruyter.

Stangor, C. (2004). *Research methods for the behavioral sciences.* Boston: Houghton Mifflin.

Stanley, L., & Wise, S. (1983). *Breaking out: Feminist consciousness and feminist* research. London: Routledge & Kegan Paul.

Steinberg, R. J. (1996). Advocacy research for feminist policy objectives: Experiences with comparable worth. In H. Gottfried (Ed.), *Feminism and social change: Bridging theory and practice* (pp. 225–255). Urbana: University of Illinois Press.

Stewart, A. J., & Dottolo, A. L. (2005). Socialization to the academy: Coping with competing social identities. In G. Downey, J. Eccles, & C. Chatman (Eds.), *Navigating the future: Social identity, coping, and life tasks* (pp. 167–187). New York: Russell Sage.

Syzmanski, D. M., & Owens, G. P. (2009). Group-level coping as a moderator between heterosexism and sexism and psychological distress in sexual minority women. *Psychology of Women Quarterly, 33*, 197–205.

Tourangeau, R., Rips, L., & Rasinski, K. (2000). *The psychology of survey response.* Cambridge, UK: Cambridge University Press.

United States Census Bureau. (1989). *A century of population growth, from the first census of the United States to the twelfth, 1790–1900.* Baltimore: Genealogical Publishing Company.

Vaux, A., & Briggs, C. S. (2006). Conducting mail and Internet surveys. In F. T. L. Leong & J. T. Austin (Eds.), *The psychology of research handbook: A guide for graduate students and research assistants* (pp. 186–209). Thousand Oaks, CA: Sage.

Vogt, W. P. (1999). *Dictionary of statistics and methodology: A nontechnical guide for the social sciences.* Thousand Oaks, CA: Sage.

Wallston, B. S., & Grady, K. E. (1992). Integrating the feminist critique and the crisis in social psychology: Another look at research methods. In J. S. Bohan (Ed.), *Seldom seen, rarely heard: Women's place in psychology* (pp. 307–336). Boulder, CO: Westview Press.

13

THE LINK BETWEEN FEMINIST THEORY AND METHODS IN EXPERIMENTAL RESEARCH

SUE V. ROSSER

As feminism and women's studies continue to advance, the cross-fertilization among science, technology, medicine, and feminism has continued to blossom and bear fruit. These fields have come to accept feminist perspectives and gender analyses, and particularly their extension to experimental methods, albeit more slowly than did the humanities and social sciences. Those of us who had one foot in science and the other in women's studies worked hard to "build the two-way streets" between science and feminism, an endeavor best articulated by Anne Fausto-Sterling (1992).

A first step for feminist scientists was recognizing the possibility that androcentric bias would result from having virtually all theoretical and decision-making positions in science held by men (Keller, 1983). Not until a substantial number of women had entered the profession could this androcentrism be exposed (Rosser, 1986). As long as only a few women were scientists, they had to demonstrate or conform to the male view of the world to be successful and have their research meet the criteria for "objectivity."

The demonstration that contextual values, including gender, bias not only individuals' scientific research but also what is accepted as valid science by the entire scientific community, represents one of the major contributions that feminism has made to science (Keller, 1982, 1985). In *Feminism in Twentieth-Century Science, Technology, and Medicine* (Creager, Lunbeck, & Schiebinger, 2001), the contributing authors respond to the question of what difference feminism has made to the fields of science, technology, and medicine. They build on coeditor Londa Schiebinger's (1999) book *Has Feminism Changed Science?* In that volume, Schiebinger examines how the presence of women in traditionally male disciplines has altered scientific thinking and awareness, concluding that feminist perspectives have had little effect on mathematics and the physical sciences but more impact on biology, including medicine, archaeology, reproductive and evolutionary biology, and primatology. Although the degree and specifics of the impact of feminism on science, medicine, and technology vary from one subdiscipline to another, as the coeditors of the 2001 volume state, "Feminism connects gender to other systems that structure our lives and individual identities" (Creager et al., 2001, p. viii).

Feminisms and feminist perspectives have increased in variety and complexity over time. Since publication of the first edition of this volume, major advances in science, technology, and medicine, such as new uses of information technology (IT) and improvements in gene sequencing, have further impacted and complicated the interactions between these fields and feminist theories and methods. Some of the impacts appear positive for women and feminism, while others seem neutral or negative.

The Internet and new technologies that exploit its use such as online journal publishing, Twitter, Facebook, and other social networking tools tend to have the positive effects of expanding access to science, technology, and medicine to more individuals and beginning to level the playing field among richer and poorer institutions. Simultaneously, a negative impact may be that the revelation of detailed information about location and habits through some media may make women especially vulnerable.

Cheaper and faster gene sequencing techniques increase the emphasis upon biological determinism while opening new venues for exploring genealogical narrations and ancestry. The increasing emphasis upon technology transfer and translational research from basic science opens the door to the invention of new products, many of which will benefit women. In contrast, the percentages of women involved in creating new inventions through technology transfer remain extremely low, thus suggesting that women are excluded yet again from the leading edge of science and technology.

In this chapter, I use different feminist theories to explore feminist impact in the various stages of the scientific method—in choice and definition of problems, approaches used, and theories and conclusions drawn from the scientific research. All feminist theories place women and gender in central focus, but each theory brings a specific angle or perspective to that focus. Many feminist theories evolved to correct a deficiency in or add

a dimension missing from previous theories. The particular theories I have chosen to discuss here represent those I find most influential in understanding the impact of feminism on experimental methods in the natural, physical, and social sciences. Although feminist analyses have had greatest exploration and impact in biology and health-related fields where gender applies directly to experimental subjects and results, I will also attempt to include examples from the physical sciences, engineering, and newer technologies such as gene sequencing and IT.

LIBERAL FEMINISM

A general definition of liberal feminism is the belief that women are suppressed in contemporary society because they suffer unjust discrimination (Jaggar, 1983). Liberal feminists seek no special privileges for women and simply demand that everyone receive equal consideration without discrimination on the basis of sex.

Most scientists would assume that the implications of liberal feminism for biology and other disciplines within the sciences are that scientists should work to remove overt and covert barriers that have prevented women from entering and succeeding in science (Committee on Science, Engineering, and Public Policy [COSEPUP], 2007; National Science Foundation [NSF], 2002; Rosser, 2004; Rossiter, 1982). Although they might hold individual opinions as to whether or not women deserve equal pay for equal work, access to research resources, and equal opportunities for advancement, most scientists do not recognize that liberal feminism actually accepts positivism as a both objective and value-free theory of knowledge and belief scientists use to obtain unbiased knowledge (Jaggar, 1983).

Given the high costs of sophisticated equipment, maintaining laboratory animals and facilities, and paying the salaries of qualified technicians and researchers, little experimental research is undertaken today without governmental or foundation support. While the Internet has increased access to research results for individuals distant from major research libraries and has even allowed more scientists from less research-intensive institutions to contribute to major projects, the choice of problems for study in research is substantially determined by a national agenda that defines what is worthy of study (i.e., worth funding). Members of Congress and the individuals in theoretical and decision-making positions within medical and scientific establishments—overwhelmingly white, middle or upper class, and male—set priorities and allocate funds for research. The lack of diversity among congressional and scientific leaders may allow unintentional, undetected flaws to bias the research in terms of what we study and how we study it. Examples from research studies demonstrate that unintentional bias may be reflected in at least three stages of the application of the scientific method: (1) choice and definition of problems to be studied; (2) methods and approaches used in data gathering, including whom we choose as subjects; and (3) theories and conclusions drawn from the data.

Feminist critiques have revealed the impact of distinct gender bias in the choice and definition of health research problems. For example, many diseases that occur in both sexes have been studied in males only or with a male-as-norm approach. Cardiovascular diseases serve as a case in point. Research protocols for large-scale studies of cardiovascular diseases failed to assess gender differences (for examples, see Grobbee et al., 1990; Multiple Risk Factor Intervention Trial Research Group [MRFIT], 1990; Steering Committee of the Physicians' Health Study Group, 1989). Women were excluded from clinical trials of drugs because of fear of litigation from possible teratogenic effects on fetuses. Exclusion of women from clinical drug trials was so pervasive that a meta-analysis surveying the literature from 1960 to 1991 on clinical trials of medications used to treat acute myocardial infarction found that women were included in less than 20% of those studies (Gurwitz, Nananda, & Avorn, 1992). A study by Zucker and Beery (2011) found that many articles across all science and medical fields failed to report subject sex at all, while two-thirds of the studies that included both males and females failed to analyze the data by sex (Wald & Wu, 2010).

Using the white, middle-aged, heterosexual male as the "basic experimental subject" ignores the fact that females may respond differently to the variable tested; it also may lead to less accurate models even for many men. For example, the standard dosage of certain medications is not only inappropriate for many women and the elderly but also for most Asian men because of their smaller body size and weight. Certain surgical procedures such as angioplasty and cardiac bypass initially resulted in higher death rates for women (Kelsey et al., 1993) and Asian men and required modification for the same reason (Chinese Hospital Medical Staff & University of California School of Medicine, 1982; Lin-Fu, 1984). Studies of the use of statins to prevent cardiovascular disease revealed that, in men, stroke is the major cardiovascular event most often prevented by statin use while, in women, it is unstable angina (Mora et al., 2010).

Theories and results may also be presented in androcentric, ethnocentric, or class-biased language. When proponents of menopause hormone therapy talk about the very large number of women who stopped hormone replacement therapy after the results from the Women's Health Initiative were announced in 2002,

> They often say women are "confused" about HT. . . . We've always known that women are very capable of understanding information about their bodies and medical treatments. We knew many women stopped taking HT because they learned they had been given HT for unproven uses like preventing heart disease or Alzheimer's. (National Women's Health Network, 2010)

The choice of development of particular technologies from basic research may also reflect male priorities. Having large numbers of male engineers and creators of technologies also often results in technologies that are more useful from a male perspective (i.e., these technologies fail to address important issues for women users). The development and funding of many technologies have military origins (Barnaby, 1981; Norman, 1979), which make the civilian application of these technologies less useful for women's lives (Cockburn, 1983). Many studies have explored the overt and covert links between the military, whose origins and current directions conjoin with masculinity in our culture, and the theories for applications drawn from the research funded for the military. For example, Janet Abbate (1999) studied the origins of the Internet in ARPANET (Advanced Research Projects Agency Network), funded by the Department of Defense. The unique improvement of the Internet was that it was a network, overcoming the vulnerability to nuclear attack of the previous star configuration computer network.

In addition, men designing technology for the home frequently focus on issues less important to women users. For example, Berg's (1999) analysis of "smart houses" reveals that such houses do not include new technologies; instead, they focus on "integration, centralised control and regulation of all functions in the home. . . . Housework is no part of what this house will 'do' for you" (pp. 306–307). Knowledge of housework appears to be overlooked by the designers of smart houses. As Ruth Schwartz Cowan's (1983, 1985) work suggests, the household technologies developed in the first half of the 20th century actually increased the amount of time housewives spent on housework and reduced their role and status; they went from being the general managers of servants, maiden aunts, grandmothers, children, and others to being individuals who performed manual labor alone aided by household appliances.

Male dominance in engineering and the creative decision-making sectors of the IT workforce may result in similar bias, particularly design and user bias. Shirley Malcom (personal communication, October 1997) suggests that the air bag fiasco suffered by the U.S. auto industry serves as an excellent example of gender bias reflected in design; this fiasco would have been much less likely had a woman engineer been on the design team. Because, on the average, women tend to be smaller than men, a woman designer might have recognized that a bag designed for a larger male body would be flawed when applied to smaller individuals, killing, rather than protecting, children and smaller adults.

Although liberal feminism suggests that true equity of women in the science and technology workforce will lead to the inclusion of women in clinical trials and correct bias in design to better serve women's interests, by definition, liberal feminism does not address the potential of gender to affect "fundamentals" (i.e., Do women scientists define, approach, or discover different fundamentals such as string theory?). Liberal

feminism accepts positivism as the theory of knowledge and assumes that human beings are highly individualistic and obtain knowledge in a rational manner that may be separated from their social conditions, including conditions of race, class, and gender. Because liberal feminism reaffirms, rather than challenges, positivism, it suggests that "fundamentals" will always remain the same. Once they become aware of potential bias, both male and female scientists and engineers can correct for such biases, which previously resulted from the failure to include women and their needs and interests.

SOCIALIST FEMINISM

In contrast to liberal feminism, socialist feminism rejects individualism and positivism. Although socialist feminists argue that women's oppression predated the development of class societies, Marxist critiques form the historical precursors and foundations for socialist feminist critiques and define all knowledge, including science, as socially constructed and emerging from practical human involvement in production. Because knowledge is a productive activity of human beings and the basic categories of knowledge are shaped by human purposes and values, it cannot be objective and value free. In the early 21st-century United States, capitalism, the prevailing mode of production, determines science and technology and favors the interests of the dominant class.

Different societies construct their material worlds, including the artifacts created and used, in different ways. The culture of a certain society may use the artifacts or attach particular meanings to them differently at different times or historical periods. Thus, particular technologies and science are situated in place, time, and culture (Lerman, Oldenziel, & Mohun, 2003). The social and technological shape each other. This so-called mutual shaping at times of technological change leads to contests over social categories such as gender being reflected in new interactions with the material world (Lerman et al., 2003). Some scholars (Fox, Johnson, & Rosser, 2006) have also referred to this "mutual shaping" of the social and technological aspects as the "co-evolution of gender and technology."

Feminist scholars rightly point out that science and technology and the social shaping of technology (Wajcman, 1991; Webster, 1995) and science (Rose, 1994) have often been conceptualized in terms of men, excluding women at all levels. Socialist feminist critiques include women and place gender on equal footing with class in shaping science and technology.

Considerable research focus and dollars target diseases, such as cardiovascular disease, that are especially problematic for middle- and upper-class men in their prime earning years. Although women die from cardiovascular disease with the same frequency as men, on average, women die at later ages. Hence, until recently, most cardiovascular disease research targeted white middle-class men. Many of these studies, including the Physicians' Health Study, were flawed not only by the factors of gender and age but also by factors of race and class. Susceptibility to cardiovascular disease is known to be affected by lifestyle factors such as diet, exercise level, and stress, which are correlated with race and class. Because physicians in the United States are not representative of the overall male population with regard to lifestyle, the results may not be applicable even to most men.

Biases in the populations sampled and the choice and definition of problems raise ethical issues. Health care practitioners treat the majority of the population, which consists of females, minorities, and the elderly, based on information gathered from clinical research in which women and minorities are undersampled or not included. Bias in research thus leads to further injustice in health care diagnosis and treatment.

In contrast, significant amounts of time and money are expended on clinical research on women's bodies in connection with aspects of reproduction. Substantial clinical research has resulted in the increasing medicalization and control of pregnancy, labor, and childbirth. Feminists have critiqued the conversion of a normal, natural process controlled by women into a clinical, and often surgical, procedure controlled by men (see, for example, Ehrenreich & English, 1978; Holmes, 1981).

New reproductive technologies provide further intertwining of class and gender. Class appears to affect prices paid to egg donors. Women at U.S. universities are routinely offered more for their eggs than the $10,000 limit suggested by the American Society for Reproductive Medicine. The exact sums offered, obtained from a survey of 300 advertisements in college newspapers, vary, with a $2,000 increase in the fees advertised for potential egg donors for each 100-point difference in a university's average SAT score (Levine, 2010).

Understandings of class relations under capitalism and gender relations under patriarchy help to explain the intertwining of the military and masculinity (Enloe, 1983, 1989; MacKenzie & Wajcman, 1999), which drives much technological innovation in this country and elsewhere. These understandings also explain the choices made to develop technologies in a certain way, including engineering decisions that favor rich people over relatively less expensive technologies, such as devices for the home, that would aid many people, especially women.

Caro's (1974) work revealed that Robert Moses, the master builder of New York's roads, parks, bridges, and other public works from the 1920s to the 1970s, had overpasses built to specifications to discourage buses on parkways. White upper- and middle-class car owners could use the parkways, such as Wantagh Parkway, for commuting and for accessing recreation sites, including Jones Beach. Because the 12-foot height of public transit buses prohibited their fitting under the overpass, people of color and poor people dependent on public transit did not have access to Jones Beach (Winner, 1980).

Socialist feminist approaches also suggest why men dominate the creation of new technologies. Stephan and El-Ganainy (2007) suggest that the fact that more men than women are employed at higher ranks at Research I institutions, where most patenting occurs, accounts partially for the gender gap in patenting. Class issues enter because Research I institutions with high prestige and better salaries are dominated by men. These institutions provide more access to venture capital, geographic mobility, and scientist-directed work schedules that enable long hours and flexible timetables, which may be as critical as technological expertise for the success of start-ups.

Current intellectual property rights agreements and laws provide opportunities for choices in technology development that further exacerbate class differences by transferring technologies developed using public moneys to the private realm through patents. The decisions regarding which products are developed fall under the influence of capitalist interests in profit margins. Such intellectual property rights function as a form of privatization (Mohanty, 1997). They permit decisions about which products will be developed to occur in the private, rather than the public, realm. This results in capitalist interest in the bottom line, rather than public needs and interests, dictating which "products" are developed. In the patenting of intellectual property, rights (and profits) get transferred from the public, which paid for the research with their tax dollars, to the private company, institution, or individual who controls the patent. Socialist feminists might view this transfer from the pockets of working-class men and women, who pay the taxes to underwrite federal research, to the patent holders in the private sector, who will reap massive profits, as serving the interests of bourgeois capitalists. New technologies in computer science and engineering are often developed using federal grants (paid for by taxes). Some studies also document that women purposely avoid commercialization of their research, which they view as "selling their science" and pandering to capitalism (Rosser, 2009).

AFRICAN AMERICAN FEMINISM AND WOMANISM

African American or black feminism and womanism also reject individualism and positivism for social construction as an approach to knowledge (Collins, 1990; hooks, 1992). These theories are based on African American critiques of Eurocentric approaches to knowledge (Harding, 1998). Whereas socialism posits class as the organizing principle around which the struggle for power exists, African American critiques maintain that race is the primary oppression. African Americans critical of the scientific enterprise may view it as a function of white Eurocentric interests with the methodology a reflection of those interests.

African American feminist critiques uncover the place or role of race in combination with gender. Racism intertwines with and reinforces differing aspects of capitalism and patriarchy.

African American feminists have examined the respective intersection of race and gender to provide a more complex, comprehensive view of reality. Many African American women and other women of color are also uncomfortable with the word *feminism* because of its historical association with white women and its ignoring of racial/ethnic diversity. Womanism (Steady, 1982), critical race theory (Williams, 1991, 1998), and black feminism (Collins, 1990), although all placing race in central focus, provide slightly differing critiques. Just as their African American sisters have done, Latina, Asian American, and American Indian women and women from other racial or ethnic perspectives have developed critiques that place race/ethnicity and gender in central focus.

Just as many studies fail to report or analyze gender differences, studies also neglect to report and analyze racial/ethnic differences. A 2009 study of 97,253 women—89,259 white women and 7,994 black women—aged 50 to 79 participating in the Women's Health Initiative, focused on the possible health effects of optimism and cynical hostility in postmenopausal women. Overall, optimism decreased the risk of dying from cardiovascular causes or any other cause, while cynical hostility increased the risk of dying from cancer. Among black women, the associations were more pronounced. Among the most optimistic, black women had a 33% lower risk of death from all causes and a 44% lower risk of cancer death compared with white women's 13% and no effect on these same measures. Among the most cynical and hostile women, black women had a 62% higher risk of death from all causes, a 102% higher risk from heart disease, and a 142% higher risk of death from cancer; comparable figures for white women were 13%, 18%, and 18%, respectively (Tindle et al., 2009).

Frequently, it is difficult to determine whether women are treated disrespectfully and unethically due to their gender or whether race and class are more significant variables. From the Tuskegee syphilis experiment (1932–1972), in which the effects of untreated syphilis were studied in 399 men over a period of 40 years (Jones, 1981), it is clear that men who are black and poor may not receive appropriate treatment or information about the experiment in which they are participating. Scholars (Clarke & Olesen, 1999) now explore the extent to which gender, race, and class become complex, interlocking variables that may affect access to and quality of health care.

The popularity of the now relatively low-cost gene-sequencing techniques permits individuals to trace their genealogy and ancestry. In the PBS documentary miniseries *Faces of America*, coproducer, host, and writer Henry Louis Gates, Jr., the director of the W. E. B. DuBois Institute for African and African American Research and professor at Harvard, collaborated with genetic scientists to discover the genealogy of famous individuals. This sometimes led to revelations of shocking information, such as that Malcolm Gladwell's Jamaican maternal ancestor, a free woman of color, owned slaves of African descent. Perhaps because of the possibilities of these sorts of revelations being taken out of context and because of questions about use of ownership of such DNA, some refuse to submit to gene sequencing. For example, the Native American writer Louise Erdrich refuses to assent to genetic ancestry testing because she understands her DNA to belong to her community (Nelson, 2010).

Just as Professor Gates has collaborated with genetic scientists of differing ethnicities and races, a growing recognition has evolved of the strength and necessity for diversity on teams (Knights, 2004). Diversity in gender and race is becoming critical, along with the long-established recognition of the importance of having an engineering team representing varied intellectual and technical backgrounds for designing complex technologies. Because knowledge and consideration of the user, client, or customer are central to the technology design, a design team with racial and gender diversity coupled with surveys of demographically diverse customers will increase diversity in technology design.

African Americans and Hispanics are underrepresented in engineering and in the upper end of the technology workforce, relative to their percentage (27.3%) in the overall U.S. population (NSF, 2010). In 2007, African Americans constituted 4.6% of engineers and 9.8% of computer and mathematical scientists; 5% of engineers and 7.1% of mathematical and computer scientists identified as Hispanic (NSF, 2010, Table H-4). Although engineering has been traditionally defined as a career path for mobility

from the working to middle class, engineering is pursued by disproportionately fewer blacks and Latinos than whites. Even fewer African American women and Latinas become engineers or scientists than their male counterparts, despite the higher percentage of African American women (compared with African American men) in college.

In stark contrast, women of color are disproportionately represented in the lowest paying and highest health risk portions of the technology labor force. Studies demonstrate that women of color occupy the ghettos in the cities where the electronic assembly occurs (Hesse-Biber & Carter, 2005). Outside the technology production workforce, women of color also represent the group most likely to be replaced by technology when automation takes over the work formerly done by their hands. Although technology has not resulted in the extreme reductions in female clerical workers once feared, increasing automation has forced some women of color from higher paying assembly-line factory work into lower paying service-sector jobs (Hesse-Biber & Carter, 2005; Mitter, 1986).

ESSENTIALIST FEMINISM

African American and socialist feminist critiques emphasize race and class as sources of oppression that combine with gender in shaping and being shaped by science and technology. In contrast, essentialist feminist theory posits that all women are united by their biology, specifically their secondary sex characteristics and their reproductive systems. Frequently, essentialist feminism may extend this view of female-male distinction to include gender differences in visuospatial and verbal ability, aggression and other behaviors, and other physical and mental traits based on prenatal or pubertal hormone exposure.

The biomedical model, although too restricted for an approach to most diseases, remains especially inadequate for women's health, particularly for exploring the causes, treatments, and prevention of events such as menopause that occur as part of the life-cycle course and are influenced by both biology and a variety of social, environmental, and other factors. Until the Women's Health Initiative (WHI), very little research on women's menopausal experience existed. The WHI, launched by the National Institutes of Health (NIH) in 1991 to study cardiovascular diseases, cancers, and osteoporosis, attempted to raise the priority of women's health and provide baseline data on previously understudied causes of death in women (Pinn & LaRosa, 1992). As the baby-boom generation aged, pharmaceutical companies developed an extreme interest in capturing the market of women approaching menopause. These companies redefined menopause as a disease that required hormones to cure it and made large amounts of money by selling hormone replacement therapy (HRT) to women before, during, and after menopause. This tradition places responsibility at the level of the individual rather than society as a whole.

Using only the methods traditional to a particular discipline may result in limited approaches that fail to reveal sufficient information about the problem being explored. On July 9, 2002, the NIH announced that the hormone replacement therapy (HRT) and estrogen/progestin portion of the WHI would be stopped. The study had shown that women taking HRT had a 26% increase in breast cancer, a 41% increase in strokes, and a 200% increase in the rates of blood clots in the legs and lungs (National Women's Health Network, 2002). Subsequent studies also revealed that HRT did not improve "quality of life" issues or memory, although women taking HRT did have 37% less colon cancer and 34% fewer hip fractures.

Many women expressed outrage against the pharmaceutical companies after the announcement that the HRT portion of the Women's Health Initiative was halted (Worcester, 2009). Until the Women's Health Initiative, very little research compared the health of menopausal women who took HRT with the health of those who did not take HRT. Women wanted to know why they had been given HRT before such research had been done. The approach to HRT reveals the American health care system's focus on individual responsibility rather than on overall societal responsibility for the increasingly significant proportion of the population that consists of elderly women, who will need a disproportionately large amount of health care.

Ecofeminism, sometimes defined as a type of essentialist feminism, suggests that men, because of their biology and inability to conceive, also develop technologies to dominate, control, and exploit the natural world, women, and other peoples (Easlea, 1983). Women, in contrast, are able to give birth, which gives us less direct control over our bodies and connects us more closely with nature, other animals, and life (King, 1989; Merchant, 1979). In its most simplistic extreme form, essentialism implies that men use technologies to bring death and control to other people, women, and the environment, while (or because) women give birth and nurture life in all its forms. In his study of the discovery and development of nuclear weapons and the atomic bomb, Easlea (1983) examines the language and behavior of the scientists involved. Analyzing the aggressive sexual and birth metaphors the scientists use to describe their work, he argues that men "give birth" to science and weapons to compensate for their inability to give birth to babies.

Both ecofeminism and essentialism suggest that because of our biology, women would design different technologies and use them differently. Indeed, studies done of inventions by women and surveys of the patents obtained by women (Macdonald, 1992) suggest that many women develop technologies related to reproduction (e.g., nystatin to prevent vaginal yeast infections), secondary sex characteristics (the backless bra), or babies or children (the folding crib). An essentialist feminist theoretical approach to these invention and patent data studies implies that differences in women's, compared with men's, biology—differences such as hormone levels, menstruation, giving birth, and the ability to lactate to nourish offspring—lead to women designing different technologies and using technologies differently from men. The dearth of women currently involved in technology transfer and patenting suggests why fewer technologies and products useful to women continue to be developed.

Essentialism can be used to support either the superiority or the inferiority of women compared with men, as long as the source of difference remains rooted in biology. Essentialism was originally seen as a tool for conservatives who wished to keep women in the home and out of the workplace. Eventually, feminists reexamined essentialism from perspectives ranging from conservative to radical with a recognition that biologically based differences between the sexes might imply superiority and power for women in some arenas (Corea, 1985; Dworkin, 1983; MacKinnon, 1982, 1987; O'Brien, 1981; Rich, 1976).

EXISTENTIALIST FEMINISM

Existentialist feminism, first described by Simone de Beauvoir (1949/1989), suggests that women's "otherness" and the social construction of gender rest on society's interpretation of biological differences. Existentialists see "women's and men's lives as concretely situated" and emphasize concepts like "freedom, interpersonal relations, and experience of lived body" (Larrabee, 2000, p. 187). In contrast to essentialist feminism, existentialist feminism purports that not the biological differences themselves but the value that society assigns to biological differences between males and females has led woman to play the role of the "other" (Tong, 1989).

Demographic projections reveal that the majority of the U.S. population soon will come from the current racial "minorities"; as the baby-boom generation ages, the elderly populations, predominantly female, will increase dramatically. Perceiving the flaws in the male-as-norm approach in its applications to the "other" of women opens the door to understanding the diversities among women. Lesbians, women of color, women from non-U.S. cultures, and disabled and elderly women remain the "other" compared with white, middle-aged, heterosexual, able-bodied, U.S.-born women upon whom much of the research has been done. To rectify this dearth of research and avoid problems from failing to include the health of the majority of U.S. women, research concerning the needs of diverse women must become a central focus.

An existentialist feminism framework might be used to explain the higher frequency of inventions by women of technologies useful for menstruation, childbirth, lactation, and hormones.

In contrast to essentialism, rather than placing the emphasis for the origin of the technology on the biology itself, existentialism would suggest that the value assigned by society to women as other leads to technology. Women serve as the predominant caretakers of babies and children, perhaps because they give birth to them and nurse them. Existentialist feminism suggests that the assignment of this role, based on the biological reasons, leads to women having more experience caring for babies and children. In turn, this experience leads them to invent more technologies useful for child care, such as the baby changing stations found in public bathrooms, disposable diapers, and folding cribs (Macdonald, 1992).

In direct ways, the use of the male norm excludes women as the users of technology. Military regulations often apply Military Standard 1472 as anthropometric data in ergonomic design, and this standard suggests the use of the 95th and 5th percentile of male dimensions in designing weapons systems. Using these specifications led to the cockpits of airplanes being designed to fit the dimensions of 90% of male military recruits (Weber, 1997), which worked relatively well as long as the military was entirely male. In the case of the Joint Primary Aircraft Training System, used by both the Navy and Air Force to train pilots, the application of the standard accommodated the 5th through 95th percentile of males (90%), but only approximately the 65th through 95th percentile of females (30%). The policy decision by Secretary of Defense Les Aspin to increase the percentage of women pilots uncovered the gender bias in the cockpit design (Aspin, 1993, p. 1). Exclusion of such large numbers of women by dimensions alone made it extremely difficult to meet the military's policy goal of increasing the number of women pilots. The officers initially reacted by assuming that the technology reflected the best or only design possible and that the goal for the percentage of women pilots would have to be lowered or the number of tall women recruits would have to be increased. This initial reaction, which represented the world viewpoint of men, eventually changed (de Beauvoir, 1949/1989). When political coalitions, the Tailhook scandal, and feminist groups reinforced the policy goal, a new cockpit design emerged, which reduced the minimum sitting height from 34 to 32.8 inches, thereby increasing the percentage of eligible women (Weber, 1997, p. 239).

The Michelle R. Clayman Institute for Gender Research at Stanford University, through its gendered innovations project, seeks to bring attention to the need for changes in both technology and policy to fit the needs and requirements of women, such as a different seat belt design for pregnant women and a requirement that the new design be tested on appropriate subjects (pregnant women) before wearing the belt is required by law (Stanford University, 2011).

Frequently, designing products or technology for the needs of a particular group viewed as the "other" yields a resulting design or product that is better for the "norm" as well. For example, the curb cuts designed for wheelchairs also facilitate crossing the street for people with strollers, suitcases on wheels, and other wheeled devices. Since the number of people over 65 in the United States is predicted to double in 20 years, with those over 80 quadrupling in 40 years worldwide, we stand poised for a major demographic shift (Monaghan, 2010). Universal design to accommodate the needs of this increasingly elderly and disabled population, now defined as "other," should cater to a wider range of human capability.

PSYCHOANALYTIC FEMINISM

Evelyn Keller (1982, 1985) applied the work of Chodorow (1978) and Dinnerstein (1977) to suggest how science, populated mostly by men, has become a masculine province in its choice of experimental topics, use of male subjects for experimentation, and interpretation and theorizing from data, as well as in the practice and applications of science undertaken by the scientists. Keller suggests that, because the scientific method stresses objectivity, rationality, distance, and autonomy of the observer from the object of study (i.e., the positivist neutral observer), individuals who feel comfortable with independence, autonomy, and distance will be most likely to become scientists.

Psychoanalytic feminists have suggested that the objectivity and rationality of science are synonymous with a male approach to the physical, natural world.

The particularly reductionistic version of the biomedical model currently in vogue, in which extreme attention is drawn to genetic causes for diseases, has been critiqued by feminists as positivist and enforcing distance and autonomy between the observer and object of study. Interdisciplinary approaches might most effectively target women's health issues, for example, studying the effects of exercise level and duration on the alleviation of menstrual discomfort. Although these issues would not require high-tech or expensive drug testing as solutions, effective research would include methods from the social and natural sciences, such as interviews and case studies, which shorten the distance between the observer and the object of study.

The distant and autonomous approaches of science are reflected in medical tests that do little to connect with the realities for women susceptible to cancers such as ovarian cancer. Because symptoms typically develop after the disease has become incurable, ovarian cancer has been called a "silent killer." In a National Cancer Institute study, more than 75,000 healthy women were randomly assigned to undergo either usual care or annual CA-125 testing plus trans-vaginal ultrasound. If a woman's CA-125 testing or ultrasound was positive, she was referred to a gynecologist. After annual screening for more than four years, on average, 19.5 women had undergone surgery for each identified case of ovarian cancer; 72% of the cancers detected were already at late stage (Robb-Nicholson, 2010).

Carriers of the BRCA-1 or BRCA-2 gene mutations and women with a mother, sister, daughter, grandmother, aunt, or niece who had ovarian cancer (and thus are at high risk genetically) can benefit from CA-125 and trans-vaginal ultrasound, and most experts recommend combination screening of high-risk women with CA-125 and trans-vaginal ultrasound every six months. If they obtain a positive result, they must undergo invasive surgery. It is also recommended that high-risk women past childbearing years consider having their ovaries removed. These surgeries seem unappealing and, in themselves, appear to be high-risk solutions to many of these high-risk women. For women who are not high risk, the risk of general screening with CA-125 alone far outweighs the benefit because current screening misses half of all women with early stage cancer, due to lack of test specificity. Not surprisingly, many women find the existence of this test a distant help in making everyday health decisions (Robb-Nicholson, 2010).

A psychoanalytic feminist framework might provide the theoretical backdrop for Cockburn's (1981, 1983, 1985) work documenting the intertwining of masculinity and technology; encouraged to be independent, autonomous, and distant, male engineers and computer scientists design technologies and IT systems reflecting those characteristics. As Bødker and Greenbaum (1993) suggest, the "hard-systems" approach to computer systems development follows the positivist, linear, and technicist approach compatible with Western scientific thought. The technical capabilities, constraints of the machines, and rational data flow become the focus and driver of the technology design.

This hard-systems design approach used by developers (mostly male) of computer systems assumes separation, distance, and independence on two levels: (1) between the abstract systems development and the concrete real world of work—a separation that ignores the often circular and interconnected forces of organization, assuming that they remain linear and unaffected by other hierarchical power relations; and (2) between the developers and users: because users do not contribute to the design of the system, their needs and suggestions that might make the system function more smoothly in the real world of work are ignored. The problems caused by this abstraction, objectivity, autonomy, and separation have spawned methods such as "soft-systems" human factors approaches to solving the problems and mediating the gap. In contrast, Twitter, Facebook, and other social networking sites provide a mechanism to allow users to contribute to the design of these systems.

The gender constellation predicted by psychoanalytic feminism also becomes transparent in technology; the men who design hardware systems design them in ways reflective of their perspective on the world with which they feel comfortable. Such system designs tend to prioritize data and ignore relationships between people. Women, socialized to value connections and relationships, tend to feel uncomfortable with the hard-systems approach. As users, they find that the technology fails to aid much of the real-world work, and the design inhibits or fails to foster good teamwork and other relationships among coworkers. Because the design does not reflect their priorities and actively ignores the reality of power and gender relations, women tend to be excluded, and to exclude themselves, from hard-systems design.

Critiques of information technologies from a psychoanalytic feminist perspective raise the very interesting question of how systems design might change if more feminine values and connection became priorities. Sørenson (1992) explored whether male and female computer scientists worked differently. He found that men tended to focus on mathematical models and computer programming while women spent more time running experiments, reading scientific literature, and plotting data. After studying the technological and political values of men and women engineering students, graduate students, and junior R&D scientists at the Norwegian Institute of Technology, Sørenson found that women brought "caring values" to research in computer science. "Caring values" included empathy and rationale of responsibility. "In computer science, this means that women have a caring, other-oriented relationship to nature and to people, an integrated, more holistic and less hierarchical world-view, a less competitive way of relating to colleagues and a greater affinity to users" (Sørenson, 1992, p. 10).

The popularity of "apps," often created by users, represents another way of shortening the distance between the designers and users. Although some might view these creations as an example of Harding's "strong objectivity," this shortening of the distance between the user and the system design mimics the description of McClintock's work given by Keller (1983) in *A Feeling for the Organism*. In the shortening of the distance between the observer and the object of study, Keller describes less autonomy, independence, and separation as classic hallmarks of psychoanalytic feminism when applied to the work of women scientists.

RADICAL FEMINISM

Radical feminism, in contrast to psychoanalytic feminism and liberal feminism, rejects the possibility of a gender-free science or a science developed from a neutral, objective perspective. Because men dominate and control most institutions, politics, and knowledge in our society, all of these societal and knowledge producing systems reflect a male perspective and are effective in oppressing women. Radical feminism rejects most scientific theories, data, and experiments because they not only exclude women but also are not women centered.

The theory that radical feminism proposes (Tong, 1989) is not as well developed as some of the other feminist theories. The reasons that its theory is less developed spring fairly directly from the nature of radical feminism itself. First, it is radical in that it rejects most currently accepted ideas about scientific epistemology—what kinds of things can be known, who can be a knower, and how beliefs are legitimated as knowledge. Radical feminism also rejects the current methodology—the general structure of how theory finds its application in particular scientific disciplines. Second, unlike the feminisms previously discussed, radical feminism does not have its basis in a theory such as Marxism, positivism, psychoanalysis, or existentialism, all of which have been already developed for decades by men. Because radical feminism is based in women's experience, it rejects feminisms rooted in theories originally developed by men based on their experience and worldview. Third, the theory of radical feminism must be developed by women and based in women's experience (MacKinnon, 1987).

Because radical feminism maintains that the oppression of women is the deepest, most widespread, and historically first oppression (Jaggar & Rothenberg, 1994), women have had few opportunities to come together, understand their experiences collectively, and develop theories based on those experiences. Perhaps because of this dearth of opportunities, radical-libertarian feminists (Firestone, 1970; Rubin, 1984) view sexuality as a powerful force that society seeks to control, and they encourage women to violate sexual taboos and use artificial means to control reproduction. In contrast, radical-cultural feminists (Dworkin, 1983; Ferguson, 1984) view heterosexual relations as forms of male domination, as evidenced in pornography, prostitution, rape, and sexual harassment; these feminists encourage the elimination of patriarchal institutions and caution women regarding the use of artificial intervention in reproduction because they see "natural" reproduction as a source of power for women.

The implications of radical feminism for science and experimental methods are much more far-reaching than those of other feminist theories. Radical feminism implies rejection of much of the standard epistemology of science. Radical feminism posits that it is women, not men, who can be the knowers. Because women have been oppressed, they know more than men. They must see the world from the male perspective to survive, but their double vision from their experience as an oppressed group allows them to see more than men. However, radical feminism deviates considerably from other feminisms in its view of how beliefs are legitimated as knowledge.

Because radical feminists believe in a connection with and a conception of the world as an organized whole, they reject dualistic and hierarchical approaches. Linear conceptions of time and what is considered to be "logical" thinking in the Western traditions are frequently rejected by radical feminists. Cyclicity as a conception of time and thinking as an upward spiral seem more appropriate approaches to studying a world in which everything is connected in a process of constant change (Daly, 1978, 1984). Radical feminists view all human beings, and most particularly themselves, as connected to the living and nonliving worlds. Consequently, radical feminists view themselves as "participators" connected in the same plane with, rather than distanced from, their object of study (Jaggar, 1983). Many radical feminists also believe that, because of this connection, women can know things by relying on intuition or spiritual powers.

Some might define the work of Bratteteig (2002) and her coworkers as radical feminism because it originates from women's discourse on computer science problems and methods. Bratteteig and others insist on prioritizing the applicability of systems and putting users and developers in the same plane as collaborators in systems development. This starting from the understanding of a woman worker and her abilities and then focusing on how her professional competence can be augmented by the use of a system reflects radical feminism in that it begins with women's experience and is consistent with feminist principles. In addition, the use of instant messages and other forms of cyber communication to create rapid public protests that appear to occur spontaneously, such as the coordination of protests about the G20 summit in London that used social networking sites such as Facebook and Twitter, might be seen as representing such cyclicity (Beaumont, 2009).

In addition to the focus on women and seeking to empower women, MacKinnon (1987) adds a further criterion to radical feminism. She suggests that the consciousness-raising group provides a methodology for radical feminism. Because patriarchy pervades and dominates all institutions, ideologies, and technologies, women have difficulty placing their experiences, lives, and needs in central focus in everyday life and environments. Using their personal experiences as a basis, women meet together in communal, nonhierarchical groups to examine their experiences to determine what counts as knowledge (MacKinnon, 1987). Internet feedback sites, chat rooms, Twitter, blogs, Facebook, and other social networking sites provide a 21st-century mechanism for women to compare their personal experiences virtually without meeting in the consciousness-raising groups popular in the 1970s.

Unfortunately, Bayer Pharmaceuticals, manufacturer of the intrauterine contraceptive device (IUD) Mirena, appears to have exploited a version of the consciousness-raising group, using house parties for women identified through online communities to sell its product.

The strategy got Bayer into trouble with the Food and Drug Administration (FDA) for misrepresenting Mirena's approved uses. Bayer partnered with Mom Central (a social networking website) to identify female bloggers and solicit hostesses for house parties (Walden, 2010). Intended to provide a venue to share scripted information about Mirena, the house parties brought women together under the pretense of facilitating woman-to-woman conversations. A salesperson was secretly inserted in the group to influence attitudes and behavior, including passing along false information about the IUD's supposed benefits (Pearson, 2010).

Another aspect of hierarchy that does not mirror women's bodies or experiences appears in the organization of the specialties within medicine, which may contribute to the dearth of research and lack of focus on certain diseases such as breast cancer. The breast does not "fit" into the territory of any particular specialty. The breast fails to fit the traditional location of obstetrics or gynecology, usually considered to be about a woman's reproductive system below the waist—the ovaries, oviducts, uterus, vagina, urethra, and their associated glands; even its involvement in sexual activity has not resulted in its being claimed as the province of obstetrics or gynecology. After birth, during lactation, the breast may briefly fit under pediatrics. For palpation to detect changes or lumps, it may fall into the territory of the obstetrician or gynecologist, general practitioner, or internist during the course of a physical examination. Radiologists claim the breast for mammography screening.

Only after the breast becomes cancerous does it intersect with the territory of other specialists—the surgeon for lumpectomy or mastectomy, the pathologist for the determination of malignancy, the oncologist to oversee chemotherapy, and the radiologist who delivers radiation to kill cancerous cells. Eventually, a plastic surgeon may undertake reconstruction using implants. In brief, the breast is the territory of virtually all specialists and of none. Although the notion of a team of specialists now enjoys recognition as the favored approach for patient treatment, the typical breast cancer research project does not routinely use such a large, interdisciplinary team of researchers.

Because the organization of the NIH correlates with the medical specialties, it is not remarkable that breast cancer research has fallen through the cracks until recently. New online publications such as the *International Journal of Women's Health* (Al-Chaer, 2009–) may help to overcome this issue of silos through its interdisciplinary focus and providing access to more women.

LESBIAN SEPARATISM

Radical feminists examining information technologies might interpret the binary (0-1) foundation of computers and computing as based on the primary dichotomy or dualism of male-female. The "switchers," "controls," and "operations" language of computing fit the patriarchal mode of control. This dichotomy is reinforced by the domination of men and relative absence of women from the design process. "So, the domination of men and the absence of women from the design process is one factor which creates technologies which are closely geared to the needs of men and which are inappropriate to women's requirements" (Webster, 1995, p. 179).

To understand the complete, comprehensive influence of patriarchy and begin to imagine alternative technologies, lesbian separatism (often seen as an offshoot of radical feminism) suggests that, in a patriarchal society, women must separate entirely from men in order to understand their experiences and explore the potential of science and the impact of technologies (Frye, 1983; Hoagland, 1988). Although some lesbian separatists also now identify with queer theory, others prefer to retain a more separate stance because queer theory also embraces gay men (Butler, 1990; de Lauretis, 1991).

As women and as nonheterosexuals, lesbians are doubly distanced from the heterosexual male focus of health research and care. Although lesbians are often ignored in studies, when they are recognized, they may be categorized only as women or homosexuals, thereby lumping lesbian health issues with those of heterosexual females or male homosexuals. In fact, lesbians may be at higher risk for certain diseases such as breast and uterine cancer because many lesbians do not have children,

have higher body fat, and limit their access to regular health care checkups relative to heterosexual women because of fear of discrimination (Campbell, 1992). Very few studies have focused on lesbians as a separate population for health studies.

Some suggest the value not only of lesbian-specific research but of female-only scientific institutions. Cockburn (1983) advocates women-only organizations in information technology:

In my view, by far the most effective principle evolved to date is separate, woman-only organisation. It enables us to learn (teach each other) without being put down. Provide schoolgirls with separate facilities and the boys won't be able to grab the computer and bully the girls off the console. Provide young women with all-women courses so that they can gain the experience to make an informed choice about an engineering career. (p. 132)

The establishment of engineering at Smith College, a women's college, may provide a site where ideas, curriculum, and pedagogy in technology can be explored in an environment somewhat separate from men.

Lesbian separatism would suggest that the reason no truly feminist alternative to technology exists is that men, masculinity, and patriarchy have become completely intertwined with technology and computer systems in our society. So imagining technology from a woman-centered perspective in the absence of patriarchy becomes extremely difficult, if not impossible. Because engineering and technology development in the West and the global North foreground control—over nature, people, and machines—imagining a technology premised on cooperation and collaboration runs contrary to our image of the technology that evolved in a patriarchal, heterosexist society. Brun (1994) suggests that the creation and protection of human life should be the point of departure for technological development for women: "Women's ethics . . . is not sentimental. It is practical. It implies a concrete and holistic consideration of people's need for a sustainable environment and that basic security which is the precondition of common responsible action" (p. 79).

QUEER AND TRANSGENDER THEORIES

Queer and transgender theories, seen by some as successors to theories of radical feminism and lesbian separatism, question links between sex, gender, and sexual orientation (Butler, 1990; de Lauretis, 1991; Stryker, 1998). They raise additional challenges about the links between gender in our society and economic, racial, and dominance factors. As Judith Butler (1990, 1992, 1994) argues, the very act of defining a gender identity excludes or devalues some bodies and practices, while simultaneously obscuring the constructed character of gender identity; describing gender identity creates a norm.

When lesbians are lumped together with heterosexual women in studies of the incidence or cause of sexually transmitted diseases or other gynecological problems from which they are exempt or for which they are at low risk because they do not engage in heterosexual intercourse, both lesbians and non-lesbians suffer. Defining such studies generally as research on "women's health issues" rather than on "health issues for women engaging in heterosexual sex" leads the general population and some health-care workers to think that lesbians are at risk for diseases that they are unlikely to contract, while obscuring the true risk behavior for women engaging in heterosexual sex.

The possibility of assuming various or multiple gender identities in virtual exchanges may further complicate and obscure self, community, and knowledge creation. Researchers at the Georgia Institute of Technology developed *The Turing Game*, an online game played internationally in which individuals construct their own identities and create communities (Berman & Bruckman, 2000). This game explores the creation of these norms and how the Internet opens possibilities for identity changes or deception. The use of avatars with a different race, gender, or sexual orientation allows individuals to assume and explore different identities online. The game's creators explain their goals and methodologies in the following terms:

> Do men and women behave differently online? Can you tell who is a man and who is a woman based on how they communicate and interact with others on the Internet? Can you tell how old

someone is, or determine their race or national origin? In the online world as in the real world, these issues of personal identity affect how we relate to others. Societies are created and destroyed by these understandings and misunderstandings in the real world. Yet, as the online world becomes increasingly a part of our lives, identity in this new medium is still poorly understood. (Berman & Bruckman, 2000, p. 61)

POSTMODERN OR POST-STRUCTURAL FEMINISM

Liberal feminism suggests that women have a unified voice and can be universally addressed (Gunew, 1990). Post-structuralists (Derrida, 2000; Foucault, 1976/1978; Lacan, 1957/1977, 1973/1998) have challenged some of the fundamental assumptions about knowledge, subjectivity, and power through transforming the theory of meaning and the assumptions about subjectivity found in structural linguistics. Feminist poststructuralists (Irigaray, 1977/1985; Kristeva, 1986) critiqued the absence of women and the feminine in these assumptions.

Like post-structuralists, postmodernists (Jameson, 1981; Lyotard, 1986) question the fundamental assumptions of the Enlightenment, with postmodern feminists critiquing the absence of women. Postmodernism dissolves the universal subject, and postmodern feminism dissolves the possibility that women speak in a unified voice or that they can be universally addressed. Postmodern perspectives stress that, due to her situatedness—the result of her specific national, class, and cultural identities—the category of woman can no longer be regarded as homogeneous. Although postmodern feminists (Grosz, 1994; Irigaray, 1977/1985) see the material body as significant and a site of resistance to patriarchy, postmodern feminist theories imply that no universal health research agenda or application of technologies will be appropriate and that various women will have different reactions to science and technologies depending on their class, race, sexuality, country, and other factors.

Some have critiqued the implications of post-structural and postmodern feminism, saying that, through the dissolution or weakening of the idea of "womanness," they enable the continuance of approaches to science and technology that view each woman as a biological entity separate from her societal context. A limitation of the biomedical model with its cellular, hormonal, and genetic approaches is its tendency to center on the individual and her body, while bringing less attention to surrounding social, economic, and political factors that may contribute to disease and its progress. The incidence of breast cancer has increased about 30% in the past 25 years in western countries, according to the American Cancer Society, due, in part, to increased screening, leading to detection in earlier stages. The reduction in the use of hormone replacement therapy led breast cancer rates to decrease by 10% between 2000 and 2004. The lifetime probability of developing breast cancer in developed countries is about 4.8%; in contrast, the lifetime probability is about 1.8% in developing countries, mostly because of lifestyle and dietary differences (American Cancer Society, 2007).

Inclusion of social, psychological, and public health perspectives is needed for a more comprehensive research base to explore why poor women and women of color have higher death rates from breast cancer than middle-class, white U.S. women. Epidemiological approaches include these perspectives; they reveal factors important for disease prevention. Because "the poor, in general, have a 10 to 15 percent lower cancer survival rate regardless of race" (Altman, 1996, p. 37), research that relies on biology alone and ignores socioeconomic factors will be unlikely to uncover the best way to remove this survival differential. White, Hawaiian, and African American women have almost four times the incidence of invasive breast cancer in the United States compared with Korean, American Indian, and Vietnamese women. African American women have the highest death rate from breast cancer and are more likely to be diagnosed with a later stage of breast cancer than white women (American Cancer Society, 2007). Interdisciplinary approaches may tease apart the relative effects that more exposure to workplace and environmental carcinogens and less access to high-quality medical care, nutritious food, and decent living conditions have on the higher incidence and lower survival rates experienced by African Americans with regard to breast cancer.

As postmodern feminist theory recognizes limitations with perceiving women as a universal group, so have deeper, more complex studies of technology industries revealed the limitations of simplistic assumptions in technology designs and innovations. Although international data reveal that women in all countries, disciplines, and sectors patent at a much lower rate than their male counterparts, a study of patenting in 14 countries reveals that women in Australia (13.7%), Spain (17.5%), and New Zealand (14.0%) rank highest, while Switzerland (7.4%), Germany (5.9%), and Austria (4.5%) rank lowest (Frietsch, Haller, Vrohlings, & Grupp, 2007).

Studies focused on women in the technology workforce have tended to imply a universalist stance, assuming that all women have similar needs for uses of technology and that the employment categories and effects within technology industries affect women uniformly. Interviews with women at a major multinational company in the computer industry revealed that women in India and China working for the company expressed a strong desire to join women-only groups to increase their knowledge and access to patenting (Rosser, 2009). Similarly, the "flexibility" and "casualization" of the workforce, which telecommuting permits, may hurt wages, benefits, and long-term stability overall. Although it creates or increases the double burden for women who can mind children while working at home, some women prefer this option to no work at all.

Women may react differently to technologies, depending on their race, class, age, ability status, parental status, urban-rural location, or other factors. Coupled with the rapid and changing pace of technology, postmodern feminism suggests why universal theories fail to fit the reality of women's lives. The lack of universalism may inhibit gender-based coalitions and organizing, making it also easier to understand the political inactivity of which individuals who articulate postmodern perspectives may be accused (Butler, 1992).

Just as women's needs for technology designs differ and vary depending on class, nationality, culture, age, and other factors, the employment of women in technology industries also does not fit a universal or uniform pattern. Some groups of women have improved or lost ground in their employment in technology industries. For example, some women have benefited from programs designed to increase female representation in IT and other technology industries. These equity and access programs (based in liberal feminist theories) have benefited some professional middle-class women whose educational backgrounds position them to capitalize on better employment opportunities (Phipps, 2008).

Although relocation and temporization of work have tended to hurt employees in general and women in particular, the effects may depend on urban location. For example, closing offices in city centers and metropolitan areas has tended to hurt urban women, more likely to be of lower socioeconomic status and of color, while creating employment for women in the suburbs (Greenbaum, 1995). In contrast, the development of offshore information processing has improved employment for women in poorer countries. Information and data processing functions, once performed by women in the first world, have now been exported to low-cost economies because telecommunications and satellite technologies make this possible (Webster, 1995, p. 182).

Postcolonial Feminism

Beginning in 1947, following various campaigns of anticolonial resistance, often with an explicitly nationalist basis, many colonial empires formally dissolved, and previously colonized countries gained independence (Williams & Crissman, 1994). The continuing Western influence in these countries, particularly in the economic arena but also in the political, ideological, and military sectors, came to be called *neocolonialism* by Marxists (Williams & Crissman, 1994). Feminists have suggested that patriarchy continues to dominate in postcolonial and neocolonial life, much as it dominated colonial life.

Not surprisingly, science and technology reflect the varying complex aspects of the interrelationships among developed and developing countries in general and between the particular cultures of the colonized and colonizing countries. General themes include the underdevelopment of the southern continents by Europe and other northern continents (Harding, 2006, 2008); ignoring, obscuring, or misappropriating the earlier scientific achievements and histories of countries in southern continents; fascination with so-called indigenous science (Harding, 1998); the idea that the culture, science, and technology of the colonizer or former colonizing country remains superior to that of the colony or postcolonial country; and the insistence that developing countries must restructure their local economies to become scientifically and technologically literate and compete in a global economy (Mohanty, 1997). Both postcolonialist and feminist discourses center on otherness or "alterity." Postcolonial feminism has focused generally on issues of cultural identity, language, nationalism, and the position of women in formerly colonized countries as they have become nation-states (Mehta, 2000).

The implementation and use of reproductive technologies demonstrate quite vividly the significance of diversity among women surrounding health issues. The use of low-technology techniques, such as cesarean section, and high-technology processes, such as in vitro fertilization and rented uteri, varies within and between countries. Pressures to make women conform to the norms of the patriarchal culture and class within which they are located provide similarities for women in the use of these technologies. Different cultures, classes, races, and nationalities provide the parameters for differences of use between women within a culture and between cultures.

Although differences and complexities among cultures represent one type of diversity, class differences represent another. Women in developed countries experience more use of such technologies than women in developing countries, possibly because of socioeconomic differences. Wealthy individuals and couples often seek poorer women either in the United States or in developing countries to serve as egg donors or surrogates. The diffractions of reproductive health in modern global society define infertility as the key reproductive health problem for women of certain races and classes in developed countries, while overpopulation (and, consequently, lack of birth control) is defined as the problem for women of other races and lower socioeconomic status in developing countries.

Using observation, trial and error, and the sharing of information across generations, women in developing countries discovered methods of cleaning and cooking and feeding their families food to maximize health and minimize disease; women learned which plants held medicinal properties. Part of their indigenous scientific knowledge included the recognition of herbal remedies to enhance fertility, prevent conception, and cause abortion. The major efforts made by pharmaceutical companies to identify the plants used in traditional healing in indigenous cultures today constitute some recognition of these women's knowledge. However, just as when society credited doctors with the discovery of the herbal remedies they obtained from midwives and so-called witches in the 19th-century United States (Ehrenreich & English, 1978), the modern pharmaceutical companies award patents to the scientist who does the "work" of synthesizing the compound based on the extract from the medicinal plant, thereby defining the indigenous women's knowledge as nonscience and nonwork.

In many developing countries, cultural mores encourage the adoption of only part of the health care practices from developed countries; mores prevent the adoption of other practices. In over-populated parts of Latin America, such as the *favelas* in the *nordeste* (northeast) states of Brazil, the culture of breast-feeding has been lost because the father's provision of milk symbolizes paternity. To breast-feed her baby signifies that the woman has been abandoned by the baby's father. The adoption of some "modern" health practices such as bottle-feeding simultaneously with the non-adoption of others such as contraception demonstrate the role of culture in mediating these diffracted reproductive health practices.

Many women in the so-called third world or developing countries receive employment in technology industries or because of technological developments such as satellites that permit rapid data transmission over large geographic distances. The United States, Western Europe, and Japan house the corporate headquarters, owners, and decision makers of these global,

multinational corporations; technological developments permit these companies to roam the globe and use women in offshore, formerly colonized or developing nations as cheap sources of labor. Because new technologies transcend boundaries of time and space, they facilitate corporations in dispersing work around the globe to exploit sexual and racial labor divisions.

The IT industry especially uses subcontracted female labor in developing countries, particularly for software development. Western managements control the conduct of software development projects, relying on women from India, China, Mexico, Hungary, and Israel as programmers. Telecommunications technologies ease the transmission of specifications and completed work between the workers in developing countries and client companies in the West. Women from these developing countries are preferred as workers over those in developed countries because of their technical skills and English proficiency, relatively high rates of productivity, and relatively low costs of labor.

These examples clearly demonstrate aspects of postcolonialism in that control of the economy of developing countries remains in the hands of developed countries. They demonstrate patriarchal control because women, not men, in the developing countries become the sources of cheap labor. Language becomes an interesting feature that continues to tie former colony with colonizer. Theoretically, satellites and telecommunications transcend geographical barriers and permit any developed country to use labor in any developing country. Practically, the former ties developed between colony and colonizer, as well as the language of the colonizer learned by the colonized during the period of colonization, mean that former colonial relationships continue in the neocolonial modern world. Innovations such as Twitter permit instant brief communications to ascertain how a particular request is understood or received by workers around the world. Technologies such as the cell phone are used differently in developing as compared with developed countries. For example, in Africa, most individuals use the cell phone for banking transactions, while, in the United States, the cell phone is used for this quite infrequently.

CYBERFEMINISM

Cyberfeminism stands not only as the most recent feminist theory but also as the theory that overtly fuses modern science and technology with gender. As the name suggests, cyberfeminism explores the ways that information technologies and the Internet provide avenues to liberate (or oppress) women. The term *cyberfeminism* was first used in the early 1990s in various parts of the world (Hawthorne & Klein, 1999), with VNS Matrix, a group of Australian media-based artists, being one of the first to use the term.

The individuals who defined cyberfeminism (Hawthorne & Klein, 1999; Millar, 1998) saw the potential of the Internet and computer science technologies to level the playing field and open new avenues for job opportunities and creativity for women. They describe cyberfeminism as "a woman-centered perspective that advocates women's use of new information and communications technologies of empowerment. Some cyberfeminists see these technologies as inherently liberatory and argue that their development will lead to an end to male superiority because women are uniquely suited to life in the digital age" (Millar, 1998, p. 200).

Biomedicine fuses technology with the biological human body in the form of artificial hips, heart valves, pacemakers, and implants to deliver drugs, creating the cyborgs discussed by Donna Haraway (1997). Simultaneously, new media technologies explore the reciprocity between science and media, by which, in this age of genetics as the life code, culture may become biology. Analyses of metaphors in genome research suggest that, because researchers transpose literature onto biology, it is not possible to critique science without critiquing culture.

Haraway moves beyond investigating the use of computers to consider the sequencing of the human genome in an effort to explore how the image of the cyborg embodies the extent to which technoscience interventions have become part of us and of women's health. She uses the image of the "virtual speculum" to "open up observation into the orifices of the technoscientific body politic to address these kinds of questions about knowledge projects"

(Haraway, 1997, p. 67). As the pioneer of feminist science studies, Haraway focuses on interdependencies and interrelationships among bodies, technologies, and cultures.

But how are women scientists actually interacting within the world of the cyborg, the world that fuses the body, technology, and culture. In 1980, women represented 37% of computer science majors. The early history of computing reveals that Ada Lovelace contributed to the development of the protocomputer and Grace Hopper created the first computer language composed of words and invented virtual storage (Stanley, 1995). Women performed calculations and wired hardware for the first digital electronic computer, ENIAC (Electronic Numerical Integrator and Computer). In the late 1980s, a drastic change began to occur. The numbers of women majoring in computer science plummeted; in 2007, the percentage of U.S. women receiving computer science degrees was 18.6% (NSF, 2010). This plunge coincided with the restructuring of the capitalist system on a global scale and with the rise of financial speculation.

As Millar (1998) and other cyberfeminist critics point out, the existing elites have struggled to seize control and stabilize the commercial potential of digital technologies, as well as their research and development. Discontinuity, speed, symbolic and linguistic spectacle, and constant change characterize information technology and digital discourse. Although changing technology's instability and indeterminacy open the possibility for other changes in the social realm and power relations, it is very unclear that information technologies and cyberculture will result in such social changes.

Some critics suggest that the current information technology revolution has resulted in a rigidifying and reifying of current power relations along previously existing gender, race, and class lines. The Internet becomes a tool making women more vulnerable to men using it for ordering brides from developing countries, prostitution, cybersex, the assumption of false identities, and pornography. A woman who "Twitters" that she's having coffee at Starbucks at Dupont Circle and P makes herself vulnerable to individuals who can find her there or rob her home.

Despite their postmodern veneer of fragmentation, shifting identities, and speed, information technologies rest on the power of science and technology to emancipate humans and a faith in abstract reason. Millar (1998) defines this situation as "hypermodern," which describes the packaging of modernity power relations that are universally patriarchal, racist, and bourgeois in a postmodern discourse of discontinuity, spectacle, and speed.

This view raises the question of whether cyberfeminism is really a feminist theory. In *Cyberfeminism: Next Protocols*, the Old Boys Network (2004) claims that "CYBERFEMINISM is not simply an evolution of historical feminism created as a more adequate answer to meet the changed conditions of the Information Age" (p. 14). After describing cyberfeminism as a feminist intervention into the information age to explore how the conditions of the information age challenge the political and social conditions of feminism, the authors raise questions about the parameters of cyberfeminism. Could cyberfeminism merely represent an attempt to see information technology as the latest venue for women's liberation, much as Shulamith Firestone (1970) envisioned such liberation resulting from reproductive technologies? Although reproductive technologies have resulted in significant feminist critiques, theorizing, and discussion, no one considers them to be a feminist theory or method.

CONCLUSION

This chapter has used several feminist theoretical perspectives to examine the relationships among women, gender, science, and technology. Taken together, the spectrum of feminist theories provides different, new insights to explore these relationships. All of these perspectives have affected experimental methods by placing women in central focus. Each of the theories discussed here (and some not included) has contributed at least one new perspective or emphasis overlooked in other theories. Because many feminist theories emerged in response to critiques of a preceding theory or theories, successor theories tend to be more comprehensive and compensatory for factors or groups overlooked by previous theories.

Knowledge of the range of theories (and of the particular factors each emphasizes) allows one to better understand the context in which each may be most useful. For example, in providing testimony before Congress or other legislative bodies, a liberal feminist approach remains the theoretical venue most likely to resonate successfully with the audience because, despite the failure to pass the Equal Rights Amendment (ERA), the universal equity and access underlined in liberal feminism are acceptable and familiar to those enmeshed in our judicial and legislative systems. Although raising issues of class (socialist feminism) or race (African American feminism), particularly if the testimony centers on health care or other issues known to be affected by income or ethnicity, may be successful, using radical feminist approaches would be unlikely to work in the congressional setting.

Just as the composition of the audience and other contextual factors make different feminist theoretical approaches more useful in some settings than others, the impact of feminism on experimental methods also varies within different disciplines. Feminism appears to affect experimental methods more significantly in fields such as the social sciences and biology, where sex or gender is prominent and evident. Gender does impact the more applied areas of information technology, particularly in its uses for social networking and gene sequencing, although women appear to be less involved in technology transfer and patenting. Feminism seems to have less effect in areas of basic research in the physical sciences and mathematics.

The physical sciences and technology fields also have significantly smaller percentages of women than the biological and social sciences ((NSF, 2009), where women now receive half of undergraduate degrees. In the humanities and many areas of the social sciences, increases in the number of women have correlated with increases in emphases on women and gender in research and scholarship (Boxer, 2000; Rosser, 2002). A critical mass of women physicians was needed to push for medicine to provide increased attention to women's health (Dan & Rosser,

2003) and basic research on gendered medicine (Wald & Wu, 2010). When the percentage of women in physics, computer science, and engineering exceeds 30%, perhaps women may begin to explore the gendered nature of the questions asked and the approaches, theories, and conclusions drawn from the data in those disciplines.

In the technological and applied areas of physics, math, and the natural sciences—such as engineering, computer science, and medicine—the very powerful fusion of biology and computer science has created a new technoscience. Technoscience has facilitated sequencing the human genome and amazing advances in biomedical engineering, as well as cyberfeminism. Feminist theories must be used to place gender in central focus to evaluate critically the social and political implications of these new technosciences. Cyberfeminism reinforces the significance of linking feminist theories with research methods to critique this new fusion of feminism and technology.

Discussion Questions

1. At what levels can androcentrism bias science and technology?

2. What do all feminist theories share in common? How do the theories differ from each other?

3. Why may a particular feminist theory be more useful in some contexts than in others? Why is liberal feminism the feminist theory most compatible with the scientific method in most respects?

4. Why may using only the methods traditional to a particular discipline result in limited approaches that fail to reveal sufficient information about the problem being explored?

5. Is cyberfeminism really a feminist theory? Why or why not?

Online Resources

Committee on Women in Science, Engineering, and Medicine (CWSEM) http://sites.nationalacademies.org/PGA/cwsem/index.htm

This is a committee of the National Research Council in the United States. The mandate of

CWSEM is to coordinate, monitor, and advocate action to increase the participation of women in science, engineering, and medicine.

Women, Minorities, and Persons with Disabilities in Science and Engineering

http://www.nsf.gov/statistics/wmpd

This digest of statistical information is published by the National Science Foundation to comply with the Science and Technology Equal Opportunities Act of 1980, mandating that the NSF collect and analyze data and report to Congress on a biennial basis on the status of women and minorities in the science and engineering professions.

Women-Related WebSites in Science/Technology

http://www.research.umbc.edu/~korenman/wmst/links_sci.html

This web page, maintained by Joan Korenman, provides addresses of websites and organizations with information on this topic.

Relevant Journals

Feminist Formations (formerly the *NWSA Journal*)

Journal of Women and Minorities in Science and Engineering

Journal of Women's Health

REFERENCES

Abbate, Janet. (1999). Cold war and white heat: The origins and meanings of packet switching. In Donald MacKenzie & Judy Wacjman (Eds.), *The social shaping of technology* (2nd ed., pp. 351–371). Philadelphia: Open University Press.

Al-Chaer, Elie D. (Ed.). (2009–) *International Journal of Women's Health*. (Available from Dove Medical Press Ltd.) Retrieved May 10, 2010, from http://www.dovepress.com/international-journal-of-womens-health-journal.

Altman, Roberta. (1996). *Waking up/fighting back: The politics of breast cancer*. Boston: Little, Brown & Company.

American Cancer Society. (2007). *Global cancer facts & figures 2007*. Atlanta, GA: Author.

Armstrong, Bruce, & Doll, Richard. (1975). Environmental factors and cancer incidence and mortality in different countries, with special reference to dietary practice. *International Journal of Cancer, 15*(4), 617–631.

Aspin, Les. (1993, April). *Policy on the assignment of women in the armed forces.* Washington, DC: Department of Defense.

Barnaby, Frank. (1981). Social and economic reverberations of military research. *Impact of Science on Society, 31,* 73–83.

Beaumont, Claudine. (2009, April 1). G20: Protesters use Twitter, Facebook and social media tools to organise demonstrations. *The Telegraph.* Retrieved June 13, 2011, from http://www.telegraph.co.uk/finance/g20-summit/5090003/G20-summit-Protesters-use-Twitter-Facebook-and-social-media-tools-to-organise-demonstrations.html

Berg, Anne-Jorunn. (1999). A gendered socio-technical construction: The smart house. In Donald MacKenzie & Judy Wacjman (Eds.), *The social shaping of technology* (2nd ed., pp. 301–313). Philadelphia: Open University Press.

Berman, Joshua, & Bruckman, Amy. (2000). The Turing game: A participatory exploration of identity in online environments. In Peter Day & Doug Schuler (Eds.), *Proceedings of Directions and Implications of Advanced Computing (DIAL) 2000: Shaping the network society* (pp. 61–64). Seattle, WA: Computer Professionals for Social Responsibility.

Berman, Joshua, & Bruckman, Amy. (2001). The Turing game: Exploring identity in an online environment. *Convergence, 7*(3), 83–102.

Bødker, Susanne, & Greenbaum, Joan. (1993). Design of information systems: Things versus people. In Jenny Owen, Eileen Green, & Den Pain (Eds.), *Gendered by design: Information technology and office systems* (pp. 53–63). London: Taylor & Francis.

Boxer, Marilyn. (2000). Unruly knowledge: Women's studies and the problem of disciplinarity. *NWSA Journal, 12*(2), 119–129.

Bratteteig, Tone. (2002). Bringing gender issues to technology design. In Christiane Floyd, Govind Kelkar, Sivie Klein-Franke, Cheris Kramarae, & Cirilia Limpangog (Eds.), *Feminist challenges in the information age* (pp. 91–105). Opladen, Germany: Leske & Budrich.

Brun, E. (1994). Technology appropriate for women? In Ewa Gunnarsson & Lena Trojer (Eds.), *Feminist voices on gender, technology, and ethics.* Luleå, Sweden: Luleå University of Technology Centre for Women's Studies.

Butler, Judith. (1990). *Gender trouble: Feminism and the subversion of identity.* New York: Routledge.

Butler, Judith. (1992). Introduction. In Judith Butler & Joan W. Scott (Eds.), *Feminists theorize the political* (pp. xii–xvii). New York: Routledge.

Butler, Judith. (1994). *Bodies that matter: On the discursive limits of "sex."* New York: Routledge.

Campbell, Kristina. (1992, October 2). 1 in 3 lesbians may get breast cancer, expert theorizes. *Washington Blade,* pp. 1, 23.

Caro, Robert. (1974). *The power broker: Robert Moses and the fall of New York.* New York: Random House.

Chinese Hospital Medical Staff & University of California School of Medicine. (1982, May). *Conference on health problems related to the Chinese in America.* San Francisco: Author.

Chodorow, Nancy. (1978). *The reproduction of mothering: Psychoanalysis and the sociology of gender.* Berkeley: University of California Press.

Clarke, Adele E., & Olesen, Virginia L. (Eds.). (1999). *Revisioning women, health, and healing: Feminist, cultural, and technoscience perspectives.* New York: Routledge.

Cockburn, Cynthia. (1981). The material of male power. *Feminist Review, 9,* 41–58.

Cockburn, Cynthia. (1983). *Brothers: Male dominance and technological change.* London: Pluto Press.

Cockburn, Cynthia. (1985). *Machinery of dominance: Women, men, and technical know-how.* London: Pluto Press.

Collins, Patricia Hill. (1990). *Black feminist thought.* New York: Routledge.

Committee on Science, Engineering, and Public Policy (COSEPUP). (2007). *Beyond bias and barriers: Fulfilling the potential of women in academic science and engineering.* Washington, DC: National Academies Press.

Corea, Gena. (1985). *The mother machine: Reproductive technologies from artificial insemination to artificial wombs.* New York: Harper & Row.

Cowan, Ruth S. (1983). *More work for mother: The ironies of household technology from the open hearth to the microwave.* New York: Basic Books.

Cowan, Ruth S. (1985). The industrial revolution in the home. In Donald MacKenzie & Judy Wajcman

(Eds.), *The social shaping of technology* (pp. 181–201). Milton Keynes, UK: Open University Press. (Original work published 1976 in *Technology and Culture, 17*, 1–23)

Creager, Angela N. H., Lunbeck, Elizabeth, & Schiebinger, Londa. (Eds.). (2001). *Feminism in twentieth-century science, technology, and medicine.* Chicago: University of Chicago Press.

Daly, Mary. (1978). *Gyn/ecology: The metaethics of radical feminism.* Boston: Beacon Press.

Daly, Mary. (1984). *Pure lust: Elemental feminist philosophy.* Boston: Beacon Press.

Dan, Alice, & Rosser, Sue. (2003). Editorial. *Women's Studies Quarterly, 31*(1–2), 6–24.

de Beauvoir, Simone. (1989). *The second sex* (H. M. Parshley, Trans. & Ed.). New York: Vintage Books. (Original work published 1949)

de Lauretis, Teresa. (1991). Queer theory: Lesbian and gay sexualities. *Differences: A Journal of Feminist Cultural Studies, 3*(2), iii–xvii.

Derrida, Jacques. (2000). *Limited, Inc.* Evanston, IL: Northwestern University Press.

Dinnerstein, Dorothy. (1977). *The mermaid and the minotaur: Sexual arrangements and human malaise.* New York: Harper Colophon Books.

Dworkin, Andrea. (1983). *Right-wing women.* New York: Coward-McCann.

Easlea, Brian. (1983). *Fathering the unthinkable: Masculinity, scientists, and the nuclear arms race.* London: Pluto Press.

Ehrenreich, Barbara, & English, Deirdre. (1978). *For her own good: 150 years of the experts' advice to women.* New York: Anchor Press, Doubleday.

Enloe, Cynthia. (1983). *Does khaki become you? The militarism of women's lives.* London: Pluto Press.

Enloe, Cynthia. (1989). *Bananas, beaches, and bases.* Berkeley: University of California Press.

Fausto-Sterling, Anne. (1992). Building two-way streets: The case of feminism and science. *NWSA Journal, 4*(3), 336–349.

Ferguson, Anne. (1984). Sex wars: The debate between radical and liberation feminists. *Signs: Journal of Women in Culture and Society, 10*(1), 15–31.

Firestone, Shulamith. (1970). *The dialectic of sex.* New York: Bantam Books.

Foucault, Michel. (1978). *The history of sexuality: Vol. I. Introduction* (R. Hurley, Trans.). New York: Pantheon Books. (Original work published 1976)

Fox, Mary, Johnson, Deborah, & Rosser, Sue. (Eds.). (2006). *Women, gender, and technology.* Champaign: University of Illinois Press.

Frietsch, Rainer, Haller, Inna, Vrohlings, Melanie, & Grupp, Hariolf. (2007, October 16). Battle of the sexes? Main areas of gender-specific technological and scientific activities in industrialized countries. Paper presented at the Georgia Institute of Technology, Atlanta, GA.

Frye, Marilyn. (1983). *The politics of reality.* Trumansburg, NY: Crossing Press.

Greenbaum, Joan. (1995). *Windows on the workplace: Computers, jobs, and the organization of office work in the late twentieth century.* New York: Monthly Review Press.

Grobbee, Diederick E., Rimm, Eric B., Giovannucci, Edward, Colditz, Graham, Stampfer, Meir, & Willett, Walter. (1990). Coffee, caffeine, and cardiovascular disease in men. *New England Journal of Medicine, 323*, 1026–1032.

Grosz, Elizabeth. (1994). *Volatile bodies: Towards a corporeal feminism.* Bloomington: Indiana University Press.

Gunew, Sneja. (1990). *Feminist knowledge: Critique and construct.* New York: Routledge.

Gurwitz, Jerry H., Nananda, F. Col, & Avorn, Jerry. (1992). The exclusion of the elderly and women from clinical trials in acute myocardial infarction. *Journal of the American Medical Association, 268*(2), 1417–1422.

Haraway, Donna. (1997). *Modest_Witness@Second_Millenium. FemaleMan©_Meets_OncoMouse™: Feminism and technoscience.* New York: Routledge.

Haraway, Donna. (2008). *When species meet.* Minneapolis: University of Minnesota Press.

Harding, Sandra. (1998). *Is science multicultural? Postcolonialisms, feminisms, and epistemologies.* Bloomington: Indiana University Press.

Harding, Sandra. (2006). *Science and social inequality: Feminist and postcolonial issues.* Urbana: University of Illinois Press.

Harding, Sandra. (2008). *Sciences from below: Feminisms, postcolonialities, and modernities.* Durham, NC: Duke University Press.

Harris, Jay R., Lippman, Marc E., Veronesi, Umberto, & Willett, Walter. (1992). Breast cancer. *New England Journal of Medicine, 327*, 319–328.

Hawthorne, Susan, & Klein, Renate. (1999). *Cyberfeminism.* Melbourne, Australia: Spinifex.

Healy, Bernadine. (1991). Women's health, public welfare. *Journal of the American Medical Association, 266,* 566–568.

Hesse-Biber, Sharlene Nagy, & Carter, Gregg Lee. (2005). *Working women in America: Split dreams.* Oxford, UK: Oxford University Press.

Hoagland, Sarah L. (1988). *Lesbian ethics.* Chicago: Institute of Lesbian Studies.

Holmes, Helen B. (1981). Reproductive technologies: The birth of a women-centered analysis. In Helen B. Holmes, Betty B. Hoskins, & Michael Gross (Eds.), *The custom-made child?* (pp. 1–18). Clifton, NJ: Humana Press.

hooks, bell. (1992). *Race and representation.* London: Turnaround Press.

Irigaray, Luce. (1985). *This sex which is not one* (Catherine Porter & Carolyn Burke, Trans.). Ithaca, NY: Cornell University Press. (Original work published 1977)

Jaggar, Alison. (1983). *Feminist politics and human nature.* Totowa, NJ: Rowman & Allanheld.

Jaggar, Alison, & Rothenberg, Paula. (Eds.). (1994). *Feminist frameworks.* New York: McGraw-Hill.

Jameson, Fredric. (1981). *The political unconscious: The narrative as a socially symbolic act.* Ithaca, NY: Cornell University Press.

Jones, James H. (1981). *Bad blood: The Tuskegee syphilis experiment: A tragedy of race and medicine.* New York: Free Press.

Keller, Evelyn Fox. (1982). Feminism and science. *Signs: Journal of Women in Culture and Society, 7*(3), 589–602.

Keller, Evelyn Fox. (1983). *A feeling for the organism.* San Francisco: Freeman.

Keller, Evelyn Fox. (1985). *Reflections on gender and science.* New Haven, CT: Yale University Press.

Kelsey, Sheryl F., James, Margaret, Holubkov, Ann Lu, Holubkov, Richard, Cowley, Michael J., Detre, Katherine M., & Investigators from the National Heart, Lung, and Blood Institute Percutaneous Transluminal Coronary Angioplasty Registry. (1993). Results of percutaneous transluminal coronary angioplasty in women: 1985–1986. *Circulation, 87*(3), 720–727.

King, Ynestra. (1989). The ecology of feminism and the feminism of ecology. In Judith Plant (Ed.), *Healing the wounds: The promise of ecofeminism* (pp. 18–28). Philadelphia: New Society.

Knights, James J. (2004). Why the FBI seeks more women as special agents. *Women in Higher Education, 13*(3), 30–31.

Kristeva, Julia. (1986). *The Kristeva reader* (Toril Moi, Ed.). Oxford, UK: Blackwell.

Lacan, Jacques. (1977). The agency of the letter in the unconscious or reason since Freud. In Alan Sheridan (Trans.), *Ecrits: A selection* (pp. 146–178). New York: W. W. Norton. (Original work delivered as a lecture 1957)

Lacan, Jacques. (1998). *The four fundamental concepts of psychoanalysis.* New York: W. W. Norton. (Original work published 1973)

Larrabee, Mary Jeanne. (2000). Existential feminism. In Lorraine Code (Ed.), *Encyclopedia of feminist theories* (pp. 186–187). New York: Routledge.

Lerman, Nina, Oldenziel, Ruth, & Mohun, Arwen. (2003). *Gender & technology.* Baltimore: Johns Hopkins University Press.

Levine, Aaron. (2010). Self-regulation, compensation, and the ethical recruitment of oocyte donors. *Hastings Center Report, 40*(2), 25–36.

Lin-Fu, J. S. (1984, July/August). The need for sensitivity to Asian and Pacific Americans' health problems and concerns. *Organization of Chinese American Women Speaks,* pp. 1–2.

Longino, Helen. (1990). *Science as a social knowledge: Values and objectivity in scientific inquiry.* Princeton, NJ: Princeton University Press.

Lyotard, Jean-François. (1986). *The postmodern condition.* Manchester, UK: Manchester University Press.

Macdonald, Anne L. (1992). *Feminine ingenuity: Women and invention in America.* New York: Ballantine Books.

MacKenzie, Donald, & Wajcman, Judy. (1999). *The social shaping of technology* (2nd ed.). Milton Keynes, UK: Open University Press.

MacKinnon, Catharine. (1982). Feminism, Marxism, and the state: An agenda for theory. *Signs: Journal of Women in Culture and Society, 7*(3), 515–544.

MacKinnon, Catharine. (1987). *Feminism unmodified: Discourses on life and law.* Cambridge, MA: Harvard University Press.

Mehta, Brinda J. (2000). Postcolonial feminism. In Lorraine Code (Ed.), *Encyclopedia of feminist theories* (pp. 395–397). New York: Routledge.

Merchant, Carolyn. (1979). *The death of nature.* New York: Harper & Row.

Millar, Melanie. (1998). *Cracking the gender code: Who rules the wired world?* Toronto, ON: Second Story Press.

Mitter, Swasti. (1986). *Common fate, common bond.* London: Pluto.

Mohanty, Chandra T. (1997). Women workers and capitalist scripts: Ideologies of domination, common interests, and the politics of solidarity. In M. Jacqui Alexander & Chandra T. Mohanty (Eds.), *Feminist genealogies, colonial legacies, democratic futures* (pp. 3–29). New York: Routledge.

Monaghan, Peter. (2010, February 12). Design for disability will become the norm. *The Chronicle of Higher Education*, pp. B6–B7.

Mora, Samia, Glynn, Robert, Hsia, Judith, MacFadyen, Jean, Genest, Jacques, & Ridker, Paul. (2010). Statins for the primary prevention of cardiovascular events in women with elevated high-sensitivity C-reactive protein or dyslipidemia. *Circulation, 121*, 1069–1077.

Multiple Risk Factor Intervention Trial Research Group. (1990). Mortality rates after 10.5 years for participants in the multiple risk factor intervention trial: Findings related to a prior hypothesis of the trial. *Journal of the American Medical Association, 263*, 1795.

National Science Board. (2004). *Science and engineering indicators 2004* (Vols. 1–2, Publication No. NSBB 04-01). Arlington, VA: Author.

National Science Foundation. (2002). *Women, minorities, and persons with disabilities in science and engineering: 2002* (NSF 03-312). Arlington, VA: Author.

National Science Foundation. (2009). *Women, minorities, and persons with disabilities in science and engineering.* Retrieved May 5, 2010, from http://www.nsf.gov/statistics/wmpd

National Women's Health Network. (2002). *The truth about hormone replacement therapy: How to break free from the medical myths of menopause.* Roseville, CA: Prima Publishing.

National Women's Health Network. (2010, March/April). Women's health snapshots. *The Women's Health Activists*, p. 9.

Nelson, Alondra. (2010, March 5). Henry Louis Gates's extended family. *The Chronicle of Higher Education*, pp. B12–B13.

Norman, Colin. (1979, July 26). Global research: Who spends what? *New Scientist,* pp. 279–281.

Norwood, Chris. (1988, July). Alarming rise in deaths. *MS,* pp. 65–67.

O'Brien, Mary. (1981). *The politics of reproduction.* Boston: Routledge & Kegan Paul.

Old Boys Network. (2004). Call for contributions. In Claudia Reiche & Verena Kuni (Eds.), *Cyberfeminism: Next protocols.* Brooklyn, NY: Autonomedia.

Pearson, Cynthia. (2010). "Who are we listening to?" *The Women's Health Activist, 35*(4), 2.

Phipps, Alison. (2008). *Women in science, engineering, and technology: Three decades of UK initiatives.* Stokes on Kent, UK: Trentham Books.

Pinn, Vivian, & LaRosa, Judith. (1992). *Overview: Office of research on women's health.* Bethesda, MD: National Institutes of Health.

Rich, Adrienne. (1976). *Of woman born: Motherhood as experience.* New York: Norton.

Robb-Nicholson, Celeste. (2010). Progress on ovarian cancer screening. *Harvard Women's Health Watch, 17*(8), 1–3.

Rose, Hilary. (1994). *Love, power, and knowledge: Towards a feminist transformation of the sciences.* Bloomington: Indiana University Press.

Rosser, Sue V. (1994). *Women's health: Missing from U.S. medicine.* Bloomington: Indiana University Press.

Rosser, Sue V. (2002). Twenty-five years of NWSA: Have we built the two way streets between women's studies and women in science and technology? *NWSA Journal* [Special 25th anniversary issue], *14*(1), 103–123.

Rosser, Sue V. (2004). *The science glass ceiling: Academic women scientists and the struggle to succeed.* New York: Routledge.

Rosser, Sue V. (2009). The gender gap in patenting: Is technology transfer a feminist issue? *NWSA Journal, 21*(2), 65–84.

Rossiter, Margaret. (1982). *Women scientists in America: Struggles and strategies to 1940.* Baltimore: Johns Hopkins University Press.

Rubin, Gayle. (1984). Thinking sex: Notes for a radical theory of the politics of sexuality. In Carole S. Vance (Ed.), *Pleasure and danger: Exploring female sexuality* (pp. 267–319). Boston: Routledge & Kegan Paul.

Schiebinger, Londa. (1999). *Has feminism changed science?* Cambridge, MA: Harvard University Press.

Sørenson, Knut H. (1992). Towards a feminized technology? Gendered values in the construction of technology. *Social Studies of Science, 22*(1), 5–31.

Stanford University. (2011). *Gendered innovations.* Michelle R. Clayman Institute for Gender Research. Retrieved June 13, 2011, from http://www.stanford.edu/group/gender/Gendered Innovations/index

Stanley, Autumn. (1995). *Mothers and daughters of invention: Notes for a revised history of technology.* New Brunswick, NJ: Rutgers University Press.

Steady, Pilomena. (1982). *The black woman culturally.* Cambridge, MA: Schenkman Publishing.

Steering Committee of the Physicians' Health Study Group. (1989). Final report on the aspirin component of the ongoing physicians' health study. *New England Journal of Medicine, 321,* 129–135.

Stephan, Paula, & El-Ganainy, Asmaa. (2007). The entrepreneurial puzzle: Explaining the gender gap. *Journal of Technology Transfer, 32,* 475–487.

Stryker, S. (1998). The transgender issue: An introduction. *glq: A Journal of Lesbian and Gay Studies, 4*(2), 145–158.

Tindle, Hilary A., Chang, Yue-Fang, Kuller, Lewis H., Manson, JoAnn E., Robinson, Jennifer G., Rosal, Milagros C., Siegle, Greg J., & Matthews, Karen A. (2009). Optimism, cynical hostility, and incident coronary heart disease and mortality in the Women's Health Initiative. *Circulation, 120*(8), 656–662.

Tong, Rosemarie. (1989). *Feminist thought: A comprehensive introduction.* Boulder, CO: Westview Press.

Wajcman, Judy. (1991). *Feminism confronts technology.* University Park: Pennsylvania State University Press.

Wacjman, Judy. (2004). *Technofeminism.* Cambridge, UK: Polity.

Wald, Chelsea, & Wu, Corinna. (2010). Of mice and women: The bias in animal models. *Science, 327,* 1571–1572.

Walden, Rachel. (2010). "With friends like these. . . ." *The Women's Health Activist, 35*(4), 11.

Weber, Rachel. (1997). Manufacturing gender in commercial and military cockpit design. *Science, Technology, and Human Values, 22,* 235–253.

Webster, Juliet. (1995). *Shaping women's work: Gender, employment, and information technology.* New York: Longman.

Wickham, James, & Murray, Peter. (1987). *Women in the Irish electronic industry.* Dublin: Employment Equality Agency.

Williams, Patricia. (1991). *The alchemy of race and rights.* Cambridge, MA: Harvard University Press.

Williams, Patricia. (1998). *Seeing a color-blind future.* New York: Noonday Press.

Williams, Patrick, & Crissman, Laura. (1994). Colonial discourse and post-colonial theory: An introduction. In Patrick Williams & Laura Crissman (Eds.), *Colonial discourse and post-colonial theory* (pp. 1–20). New York: Columbia University Press.

Winner, Langdon. (1980, March 26). Do artifacts have politics? *Daedalus, 109,* 121–136.

Worcester, Nancy. (2009). Hormone replacement therapy (HRT): Getting to the heart of the politics of women's health? In Sue V. Rosser (Ed.). *Diversity and women's health.* Baltimore: Johns Hopkins University Press.

Zucker, Irving, & Beery, Annaliese K. (2011). Sex bias in neuroscience and biomedical research. *Neuroscience and Biobehavioral Reviews, 35*(3), 565–572.

14

FEMINIST EVALUATION RESEARCH

SHARON BRISOLARA AND DENISE SEIGART

THE EVALUATION ENTERPRISE

Program evaluation emerged as a professional field in the United States during the 1960s with the expansion of social programs during that period. Although evaluation is a discipline in its own right, practitioners often receive training in other fields before embarking on a career in program evaluation. Program evaluation can be described as the application of social science research methods to the assessment of "the conceptualization, design, implementation, and utility of . . . social intervention programs" (Rossi & Freeman, 1993, p. 5). Program evaluation makes use of a range of methods and draws from a range of methodologies used by social science researchers; however, a program evaluation effort tends to be more focused, concentrating as it does on a project or program for the purpose of improvement or assessing the merit or worth of an intervention.

This focus on a program distinguishes program evaluation from social research. A program can be understood as a way of constructing services to meet social needs. Conceptually, programs are "experiments with alternative futures, models for the reform of

discredited presents or extensions of favored pasts" (Kushner, 2005, p. 334). A program can be very large, such as a nutrition program implemented nationwide, or small, such as a one-day workshop. Regardless of its focus, which could be on a program's ongoing improvement or on judging whether a program should continue or not, a program evaluation is intended to inform decisions and action.

During the course of the past 20 years, evaluators have debated, often vigorously, the parameters of valid evaluation research practice. Experts in the field have developed theories, designed data collection methods, and articulated models as a result of their reflections and experience. *Models* are essentially approaches to program evaluation that espouse particular theoretical values and methodologies; a model, therefore, provides guidelines to designing and conducting evaluations and to ways of thinking about evaluation practice and utilization. A model is, at heart, a paradigm made explicit. Many evaluators choose to design their work in adherence with one or more evaluation models.

Despite the relatively short history of the profession, numerous evaluation models have been developed and have gained legitimacy. Initially, the models in use looked very similar to social research approaches. Evaluation models can differ in many respects, including in the primary purpose of evaluation activities, the role of the evaluator, and the nature of the relationship of program participants to the evaluation. Responsive evaluation, for example, is a model that focuses on determining program quality through a focus on stakeholder concerns. Stakeholders are thought to have different understandings of a program, and one of the uses of evaluation is to inform each group of stakeholders about the perspectives of other groups. Utilization evaluation as a model posits that all aspects of an evaluation, from initial discussions and design to follow-up on recommendations, should be focused on the "intended use by intended users." Theory-driven evaluation bases its assessment of a program on the theory upon which the program has been constructed, seeking not only to answer the question of whether or not a program works but also to assess the reasons that it worked the way it did (see Mathison, 2005; Patton, 1997). These are just a few of the models that have gained wide followings as well as the respect of the profession.

In the past decade, several models (which will be described in this chapter) have emerged that have challenged practitioners in the field of program evaluation by raising questions about historically accepted notions of what can be known, what is reality, what is truth, and what are the most ethical and effective ways of understanding a program, its outcomes, and dynamics? Similar to critiques occurring within the social sciences, these challenges were initially epistemological, reflecting a move away from the positivist beginnings of the profession, when scientific knowledge was thought to be the most advanced form of knowledge because it was based on sense experiences and could be verified objectively. Now, social science research and program evaluation widely accept the idea that our ability to discern "reality" is limited and that not all forms of knowledge can be positively verified. Those assuming more positivist stances are more likely than their predecessors to acknowledge limits on objectivity and validity. However, newer models posed significant ontological and methodological challenges that could not be ignored.

Among the most successful in pushing the parameters of the profession have been some forms of participatory evaluation. Transformative forms of participatory evaluation took a strong stance on the importance of participant involvement in evaluation activities, including giving participants an equal voice in design, data collection, analysis, and decisions about the use of findings. Although many viewed the purpose of evaluation as providing information to decision-makers interested in making changes, empowerment evaluation explicitly describes its purpose in evaluating as a means of fostering "improvement and self-determination." Later, the "Fourth Generation Evaluation" model challenged multiple assumptions, including the idea that program participants also react to a program based on their social-psychological constructions, an orientation influenced by critical theory and phenomenology, and ideas about what constitutes trustworthiness within evaluation work, presenting instead concepts that were very different from traditional notions of reliability, internal validity, external validity, and generalizability (see Mathison, 2005). Such models have provided fodder for what one of the field's earliest evaluation theorists termed the "contentious community of truth seekers"; at annual conferences, in scholarly journals, and on campuses vigorous debates ensued, the validity of approaches were challenged, and practitioners often took sides. Given the focused nature of evaluation practice and the fact that actions were taken based on evaluation findings can have important consequences for the people being served by and those leading programs, such questions seemed critical to many in the field. Feminist evaluation is a relatively recent challenger model that has entered the field, raising both core questions about the nature of the program evaluation enterprise and also unique questions about the nature of knowledge, the process of knowledge creation, and how to appropriately and effectively engage in program evaluation.

Feminist evaluation is an approach to evaluation that begins with the premise that gender matters. As a model, its purpose can involve judging the merit or worth of a program or contributing to program improvement. Like most current evaluation models, feminist evaluation draws from a wide range of social science methods in order to determine the effectiveness and progress of a program with an additional and sometimes greater goal of contributing to greater social justice and gender equity for those who are marginalized. Women are a particular, but not the only, population of interest. Feminist evaluation attempts to consistently apply principles of inclusivity, participation, and reflection and to remain aware of structural inequities and of the importance of working for change and embracing diverse forms of knowledge (Patton, 2002; Seigart, 2005).

Evaluation practitioners who espoused feminist beliefs were engaged in what they had begun to call feminist evaluation long before the term was recognized in the field as an emerging model. In 1995, the American Evaluation Association first provisionally included "Feminist Issues" as a topical interest group (TIG) within the association; the TIG was formally recognized as being active in 1997. There were limited papers and articles on feminist evaluation before an attempt was made in the mid-1990s to propose a *New Directions for Evaluation* volume on this model. The project initially met with resistance from reviewers and considerable requests for revisions. The original authors of the proposal, after much work on the project, enlisted new editors, and the volume was completed in 2002 (Seigart & Brisolara, 2002). Soon after, requests for the volume demonstrated a level of interest in this model that surprised both publishers and evaluators. Feminist evaluation is still in the process of development; there still exists a need to collect the experiences and results of implemented projects and to tease apart the contributions of feminist evaluation from those of other models when various models are co-implemented.

Visioning Feminism

Feminism is not any more inclined than other philosophical positions to be strictly defined or categorized. Perhaps it is even less interested in being classified, given the critique at the heart of feminist theory about the essentializing tendency of male-dominated theories and

disciplines; the caution against claiming to speak for all women, even all feminists; and the revolutionary nature of the feminist project (Fox-Genovese, 1992). Women's movements in the United States and Britain, for example, have been charged in the past with privileging the concerns and priorities of white, middle-class women. In many Latin American forms of feminism, the concerns of middle- to upper-class women who are often of European heritage have frequently been privileged. Much attention and greater resources have been given to feminist theory developed by Western scholars, many of whom are white, middle to upper class, and highly educated. Feminist evaluation draws heavily from the work of feminist researchers and theorists in a range of disciplines within and external to the social sciences and so necessarily must address these critiques and challenges.

In fact, there exist groups of women who have chosen not to identify themselves with the term *feminist*, choosing instead other names and titles to describe their particular women-centered ideological positions. This variety of concerns, priorities, and perspectives about the aims and tenets of feminist inquiry (shaped as they are by race, culture, and class) result in *feminisms*.

The fact that there are multiple feminisms, however, does not preclude a definition of some of the elements that unite these various forms. For us, feminism is a practical and ideological position arising from social and intellectual movements, a stance that deeply values and acts in keeping with women's perspectives and experiences with the greater aim of fostering greater social justice and equality. Most feminist positions acknowledge that the majority of contemporary cultures are organized around patriarchal values and institutions. A common response of feminisms is that greater equality and justice for all persons often requires greater attention to the social, economic, physical, spiritual, and political needs of women that sex and gender cannot be seen in isolation from race, ethnicity, sexual orientation or preference, culture, or socio-economic status. Among the themes that have prevailed in feminist inquiry is an interest in remedying the unfair distribution of material, political, social, cultural, and psychic rewards across individuals, a distribution that adversely affects women.

Contemporary forms of feminist inquiry contend that inquiry, and the knowledge that emerges from inquiry, should contribute to the removal or alleviation of such distortions. Feminist evaluation, then, is an evaluation-specific form of inquiry espousing methods, methodology, and theory informed by feminist theory and values in the service of greater equity for women and greater social justice for all people. Feminist evaluation also seeks to inform and guide the development of evaluation practice more broadly, with the aim of encouraging attention to the ontological and epistemological challenges raised by feminist theory and the ethical and practical implications of these challenges for the field. Central to feminist evaluation are the key feminist values that guide the questions, structure, and process of the evaluation and that require some form of action as a critical element of the evaluation project. These values are addressed in a later section of the chapter.

The Context in Which Feminist Evaluation Developed

As previously discussed, it is important to speak of feminist theory broadly, recognizing the diversity within feminist thought and acknowledging that a significant segment of feminist theory presented here has been developed in the West, even when it has been based on the experiences of women from non-Western nations. Feminist evaluation has been shaped by both feminist theory and the actions and practices of women's movements; these have iteratively influenced each other. In the section that follows, we consider some of the sociohistorical and epistemological antecedents of the contemporary feminist theory upon which feminist evaluation draws so significantly. In so doing, we employ the following descriptors: the foundations, the structure, and apertures.[1]

The Foundations

The first wave of feminism, according to some, began in the 1700s. Philosophical treatises such as *Some Reflections on Marriage* by Mary Astell (1700/1970), *Vindication of the Rights of Women* by Mary Wollstonecraft (1797/1988), and *On the Subjugation of Women* by J. S. Mills and Harriet Taylor (1868) were instrumental in creating and supporting debate and social action. Much of this action in the United States and Britain surrounded the struggle for suffrage. In the United States, the experiences of pioneer women (many of whom won the vote 50 years prior to the federal vote for women's suffrage) and of women who held leadership positions in some Protestant churches promoted a desire for and the expectation of greater participation in the political process. The Seneca Falls conference of 1848 issued a call for reform, particularly regarding access to education and property rights for married women.

This period of feminism is generally characterized as drawing heavily from liberal philosophy. Liberal feminism focused on the materially based, individualistic rights of women and on women's (individual and collective) social and political interests. The state was the primary target for women-centered appeals, and the movement held a belief in the efficacy of incremental and progressive reform as a road to social change. A key concern of participants during this stage of theoretical development was that women be treated as equals to men (Humm, 1992). Equal access to political and social rewards, in particular, was an important focus in the early 1900s. Women in Britain and the United States "won" the vote by the 1920s, but, in both countries, political participation remained limited (Bouchier, 1983). In the 1920s, women in Egypt were protesting against the veil and for women's rights. Women in many Latin American countries had been voting for years, though participation in the political process was similarly limited.

Social and economic forces temporarily assisted the feminist struggle for greater access to the labor market. The Depression, for example, resulted in an increase in labor force participation by women in lower classes, but these women were employed in lower paying service jobs. Middle-class women were pushed out of the labor force as a result. World War II saw a temporary increase in the labor force participation of women from the middle and lower classes and an increase in the participation of married women. However, these women were pushed out with the postwar return of men into the labor market (Bouchier, 1983). As a result of the temporary nature of these economic advances, suffrage remained the crowning victory and defining moment of this period.

Perhaps the earliest recognized cohorts of women social researchers whose work influenced the direction of feminist inquiry more broadly were women who undertook advanced study within various social science departments at the University of Chicago in the late 1800s and the beginning of the 20th century. While their male counterparts entered the academy, women trained in the Chicago school, as it was later known, were more likely to work within the government or private organizations, using knowledge and research as a means to encourage social reform (Fitzpatrick, 1990; Spalter-Roth & Hartmann, 1996). These women became activists in the sense that they were engaged in contemporary social issues, worked to educate the public and more specialized audiences about the nature of these issues and their relevancy and importance, and put knowledge and research in the service of reforming laws that would improve social conditions such as poverty, unemployment, unsafe working conditions, and child labor. According to Spalter-Roth, Hartmann, and others, various sociohistorical factors contributed to a move away from an interest in social reform: the onset of World War I with its accompanying social changes, the waning of the progressive movement, and a concurrent shift within an academy dominated by men and male priorities away from social action.

During this period, social science in particular was defined by positivism, the idea that there is a "Reality" or "Truth" that can be known with the appropriate methods, correctly applied. Positivists did not necessarily deny that our ability to know truth is limited, but they focused on quantitative measures and methodologies that were thought to ensure the greatest possible objectivity and validity. Both those engaged in creating these scientific methods, precepts, and procedures and the subjects of the research subsequently conducted were predominantly men,

often economically and socially privileged men. The first professionals to be involved in conducting program evaluations were trained in universities where positivism was the dominant ideology.

The Structure

Within women's movements in the United States and Great Britain, social and political changes beginning in the 1950s led to a renewed interest in activism. Technological advances in and the increased availability of contraceptive measures in the 1950s, various nationalistic movements in Latin American countries, social movements such as the civil rights and the peace movements in the United States, and the Cuban revolution provided fertile soil for the consolidation of the women's movements in many countries. In the United States, the initial involvement of women in the civil rights movement and political calls to action such as Betty Friedan's (1963) *The Feminine Mystique* led to the creation of the National Organization of Women (NOW) and other associations. In the United States, women's collective efforts became known as the women's liberation movement in the 1970s; a focus on reproductive choices drew younger women into the struggle (Humm, 1992). In Great Britain, women's struggles tended to be class-based and aligned with socialist and Marxist movements that were gaining attention within the country (Bouchier, 1983).

Women in Latin America were more likely to promote women's issues through progressive movements within the Catholic Church and as leaders of neighborhood movements aimed at securing sustenance and survival. Protests and action against the state's economic and physical aggression dominated organized women's agendas in many Latin American countries during this time. Although such movements were initially viewed by feminist theorists as reinforcing traditional roles for women, contemporary theorists now consider these movements as ones that combined women's practical and strategic concerns in ways that used patriarchal constructions as sites of resistance in which women could make social and political demands (Schirmer, 1993; Radcliffe & Westwood, 1993).

Feminism during the 1950s through the 1970s maintained an interest in material outcomes but expanded its attention to include social, psychic, political, and cultural concerns. Women's movements became more concerned with the differences that existed among groups of women and also in creating a moral solidarity from which women could collectively promote common issues of concern. The two predominant types of feminism that characterized this period are socialist feminism and radical feminism. Socialist feminism and its cousin Marxist feminism focused on women's double oppression as workers within the capitalist system and as "homemakers" and consumers responsible for the reproduction of the labor force without material compensation (Folbre, 1982). The capitalist, patriarchal state was seen as responsible for the oppression of men and women; the men and women supporting patriarchy were seen as responsible for the oppression of women within the sexual division of labor. The seeds for this analysis occur in Engels's *On the Origin of Family, Property, and the State.* Radical feminism (often used by critics as a representation of all feminism) held that men and patriarchal social structures, including the family, are responsible for women's oppression. Radical feminists promoted women's separation from men as the only assurance of independence and freedom from such injustice. Lesbian feminism during this period was closely aligned to the radical feminist movement in its focus on patriarchy as a predominant source of women's oppression (Bouchier, 1983).

Women attending U.S. graduate schools during the 1960s and 1970s, according to Spalter-Roth and Hartmann (1999), were often interested in social action and engaged in work to influence policy, legislation, and organizations in ways similar to their foremothers. Within the social sciences, women scholars and practitioners became involved in social reform-related projects but clearly focused on contemporary issues of concern to women. Spousal abuse and domestic violence, rape, divorce, and comparable worth are some examples of the policy and social issues of interest to these cohorts of women.

Variants of postpositivism became more dominant. Postpositivists held that there is no one "reality" and that methods and instruments, most notably the human instrument, are inherently fallible, yielding partial answers to our partial, fallible questions. Most postpositivist paradigms or inquiry models during this period would not abandon nor necessarily weaken the attempt to construct and implement methods and procedures that would optimize objectivity or that sought to implement research in the most valid manner possible. Feminist social scientists, however, were among the loudest voices, particularly during the 1980s and 1990s, describing science as "a social construct, its inquiries and methods shaped by relations of power, specific historical contexts, dominant ideologies, and the standpoint of the scientist" (Spalter-Roth & Hartmann, 1999, p. 336). Female social scientists increasingly began to pay attention not only to disaggregating data by sex, but also to the significance of research issues selected, the use of a range of qualitative methods, and the inclusion of women's perspectives in the design and analysis of the data. Furthermore, they were concerned with ensuring that research was being used in service of the people being researched.

Although the earliest evaluation practitioners would have been adherents of positivist frameworks, the evaluation profession consolidated during this period of heightened attention to social concerns.. Campbell and Stanley's (1963) work on quasi-experimental design and analysis was a catalyst for postpositivist thought within the field, and Weiss (1973) and Chelimsky (1987), among others, insisted on awareness of the fact that the contexts in which we work are highly political and multifaceted and that these contexts constrain our actions and shape our practice. Evaluation began to explore and consider the multiple contexts in which evaluations were implemented. These included programmatic-cultural, sociocultural, moral-ethical, and political-economic contexts (Brisolara, 1998).

Apertures

Like the attempt to describe a landscape from a fast-moving train, defining contemporary or recent trends is often a struggle for researchers. And yet, we can say that contemporary feminist-related movements have both deepened and broadened feminist research and evaluation. More recent developments have included ecofeminism, racial or cultural identity-based collectives (such as Latina or Chicana movements), and theoretical or philosophical stances (e.g., postmodernist, poststructuralist, or psychoanalytic feminism). Feminists and women's movements in recent years have also been shaped by responses to conservative backlashes in the 1980s and early 1990s, the scaling back of abortion rights, the apparent increase (or more obvious use) of rape and violence against women as an instrument of war, and the negative cultural and social effects of the global assembly line for many women workers. Feminist literary theorists have raised the importance of voice as a conceptual category. Theorists from various disciplines have revisited Freud, Foucault, Lacan, and Derrida to invite the heuristic possibilities that their works offer feminist thought. Others have urged a return to feminist theory to find inspiration and resources for understanding concepts such as power, empowerment, representation, and the like. However it may be defined in retrospect, this stage of feminist thought will be partly characterized by a search to recognize, embrace, and celebrate diversity and to recognize and promote solutions to pressing ecological concerns, that threaten the sustainability of all life forms.

Concurrent with this focus on diversity has been an interest in the best ways to address multiplicity within the research project. There has certainly been a focus on multiplicity of methods (mixed methods designs), competing values, stakeholders, and even realities within feminist and other models that have challenged traditional scientific practice (Brisolara, 1998). The idea that individuals operate from a position that is informed by and straddles multiple social identities is a key feminist concept. Our divergent identities construct each other and are inextricably linked: our sex and gender cannot be isolated from our class, age, sexual orientation or preference, and physical ability. Oppression is recognized as being structural, socially constructed, externally imposed, and both consciously and unconsciously internalized. Forms of oppression that focus on one of these identities (e.g., homophobia, classism,

ageism) inevitably oppress women who are members of these groups as well, and generally do so in a disproportional manner. At the heart of many forms of feminist inquiry and feminist evaluation lies a belief in the importance of working to overcome, to the extent possible, sexism and gender inequality, as an important strand in a web of oppressions, none of which should be ignored.

In recent decades, there has been within the social sciences and evaluation a stronger focus on action research models and participatory forms of inquiry. Some of the same social and economic forces that have shaped the development of feminist theory and movements within evaluation have influenced models that value democratic decision making and stakeholder participation; these models include democratic evaluation and stakeholder-based evaluation (Brisolara, 1998). Democratic evaluation, for example, values pluralism and places at the core of the evaluation project an awareness of the relationships of power, accountability to various stakeholders, and dissemination of knowledge to a range of stakeholders (MacDonald & Kushner, 2005). Stakeholder-based evaluation advocates for the inclusion of key stakeholder groups as well as stakeholder values in key elements of the evaluation. More recently, explicitly collaborative and participatory models that combine participation with action in evaluation have emerged and gained a significant following; among the most important participatory models are participatory evaluation (e.g., Weiss & Greene, 1992; Whitmore, 1998), morally engaged evaluation (Schwandt, 1991), empowerment evaluation (Fetterman, 2000), emancipatory and critical action research (McTaggart, 1991; Noffke, 1994), and appreciative inquiry as used in evaluation (Preskill & Catsambas, 2006). These evaluation models have provided somewhat different responses to the following questions about the evaluation process: What is the role of the evaluator? To what extent should action be a part of the evaluation enterprise? What constitutes legitimacy? These models have developed alongside feminist evaluation and have, collectively, obliged other practitioners in the field to examine their own responses to these questions. Through dialogue and debate, a greater number of models have become legitimate approaches to conducting evaluation, and existing models have been refined.

KEY FEMINIST EVALUATION CONCEPTS, EMERGING GUIDELINES, AND THEIR THEORETICAL GROUNDING

As is true of other models, feminist evaluation has emerged from theoretical developments in a number of disciplines and has been brought into evaluation in response to pressing needs within evaluation practice. Feminist evaluation makes significant contributions to the profession's growing interest in these issues: the utilization of evaluation results, the inclusion of traditionally underrepresented stakeholders in evaluations, effectively addressing pluralism, grounding evaluation practice in theory and evaluation theory in practice, and recognizing and responding to the play of power and politics in the field and within evaluation contexts in an ethically sound manner. As will be discussed later, some of the ways in which feminist evaluation accomplishes these goals is by encouraging evaluators to engage in reflexivity, being open about one's own identity when presenting findings, working to ensure that interactions with program participants occur in a way that allows for a greater balance of power in decision making, and creating real opportunities for stakeholder involvement.

As a challenger model, feminist evaluation has raised important questions for the field and presses practitioners to engage in the work of articulating responses. Some of these questions are ones to which the developers of current models cannot avoid responding. How do we respond to the fact that "objectivity" cannot be achieved? How do we position ourselves (or our work) given that the subject matter, programs, and products of our work are political in nature? Which voices are not being heard (who or what important data are missing from our work) and what does this mean for our clients (or our integrity)? If we maintain a commitment to social justice and pluralism, what is the evaluator's role vis-à-vis our primary clients, other stakeholders, and members of the larger community? How is the role of the evaluator shaped and bounded by her or his personal experiences and characteristics?

What constitutes ethical evaluation practices, particularly regarding our interaction with the people most likely affected by our work? What assumptions are we bringing to our work, and how do they affect what we "know"? Feminist evaluation offers unique responses to questions such as these and, in doing so, furthers the development of evaluation practice and theory. Other questions that feminist theory asks practitioners to investigate include the following: What is the nature of structural and gender inequities within this context? In what ways are women (men, bisexual and transgendered people, etc.) treated differently within the program, and how do their experiences and outcomes differ? In what ways do class, race, and gender combine to expand or contract possibilities for participants? In what ways should the evaluator become involved as an advocate against the injustices made apparent through the evaluation?

In our volume on feminist evaluation, we proposed six key ideas that feminist evaluators have used in selecting and designing their efforts (Sielbeck-Bowne, Brisolara, Seigart, Tischler, & Whitmore, 2002). These key concepts have been expanded since the volume was published. It has been our intention to engage in continued dialogue and discussion surrounding an articulation of guidelines that remains sensitive to developments within feminist evaluation practice. These concepts are not intended to be the definitive statement on what constitutes key feminist evaluation approaches. Rather, these ideas serve as guidelines for the creation of a feminist evaluation; these guidelines have informed the development of feminist evaluation to date and form the basis of what makes feminist evaluation unique. What follows is a summary of these key concepts. Each will be further explained in ensuing sections.

Key Feminist Evaluation Concepts

1. Feminist evaluation is, in part, a response to the fact that evaluation and research methods, institutions, and practices are all social constructs and have been strongly influenced by a dominant male and patriarchal ideology.

2. Feminist evaluation has as a central focus the gender inequities that lead to social injustice. A central moral premise is that gender inequities

are one manifestation of social injustice and are an important starting point given that gender issues have long been and are still frequently overlooked.

3. Discrimination based on gender is systemic and structural. Although it may manifest differently, it cuts across race, class, and culture and is inextricably linked to all three.

4. Evaluation is a political activity. The contexts in which evaluation operate are politicized and imbued with asymmetrical power relationships. The personal experiences, perspectives, and characteristics evaluators bring to evaluations (and with which they interact) both come from and lead to a particular political stance. Evaluation projects and their contexts are imbued with asymmetrical power relationships.

5. Knowledge is a powerful resource that serves an explicit or implicit purpose. Knowledge should be a resource of and for the people who create, hold, and share that knowledge.

6. Action and advocacy are morally and ethically appropriate responses of an engaged feminist evaluator. The purpose of knowledge is action.

7. There are multiple ways of knowing; some ways are privileged over others (e.g., within the social sciences or evaluation) by those with the power to sanction or privilege certain ways of knowing. Consequently, engaging a range of stakeholders in a participatory manner is important to feminist evaluation practice.

8. Knowledge is culturally, socially, and temporally contingent. Knowledge is also filtered through the knower.

Feminist evaluation theory has been developed within and has influenced the development of many disciplines, each of which has made unique and important contributions to feminist thought. Those scholars who engaged in the development of feminist theory and practice have generally been provided with the opportunity to refine their work in the fire of heated debates and challenges, sometimes from the sharpest critics in diverse fields. The responses, which have been open to criticism and scholarly debate since, have encouraged theoretical and methodological development outside of feminist circles. The following section describes some of the key feminist contributions from various disciplines that have influenced the creation of these feminist evaluation values. We frame this discussion in terms of our eight key concepts.

Feminist Evaluation as a Response to Postpositivist, Male-Dominated Practice. An early focus of feminist theorists[2] was to critique practices within the social and natural sciences that had been developed exclusively, or nearly exclusively, by a relatively homogeneous scientific community: predominantly white, privileged men. They challenged the appropriateness and validity of knowledge that was devoid of the input and perspectives of women and the validity of questions and priorities that reflected male middle- and upper-class concerns. Moreover, feminists charged that the experiences and concerns of women and people of color were rarely reflected in scientific work. The work of these scholars often emphasized the contributions that women's perspectives could make to knowledge acquisition and the ethical and practical issues involved with including or excluding women. For example, the testing of pharmaceuticals on men only contributed to a lack of knowledge regarding the effects of these drugs in women; however, including women in scientific trials then placed them at risk for side effects and possible harm related to the use of previously untested drugs. Research with victims of family violence has also demonstrated the necessity of giving space to the voice of women without endangering them. These scholars reminded the scientific community that methods and methodology as well as what constitutes important questions and knowledge are constantly in flux, being influenced by a number of historical, societal, and disciplinary concerns (Reinharz, 1989). The acceptance of particular methods and theories within a discipline often depend on the attention and interest that they attract from influential practitioners or funding agencies to a greater extent than their unique abilities to ferret out dynamics, relationships, or experiences.

A conservative perspective was posited by feminist empiricists who held to many tenets of positivism while critiquing misogynist bias as an important obstacle to obtaining objective knowledge (Harding, 1983; Hawkesworth, 1989). For feminist empiricists, objectivity remained a possibility once prejudice was removed; the remedies recommended were to promote more women to important positions within scientific institutions, to encourage more women to choose careers in science, and to make women the focus of more studies. Later, feminist writers working within the field of international development were quick to point out the inefficacy of an "add women and stir" approach. Such a response, they argued, merely extended the authority of the existing paradigm (Smith, 1972).

Although feminist theorists contend that there is no one truth or reality, it is possible to have, as Sandra Harding (1991) states, underlying regularities, conditions or experiences that are similar and somewhat constant within particular contexts. Bringing multiple and diverse perspectives to a social situation to bring awareness to these underlying regularities is one of the tasks of feminist inquiry (Harding, 1990). Truman draws from Harding and others in positing a feminist objectivity that is not neutral and can be achieved through the use of reflexive processes. Feminist objectivity criteria include accountability (to those being researched and to feminist values), positioning (acknowledging one's social positions and identities), and a conscious partiality of the limits of research (Bhavnani, 1993; Harding, 1992a; Truman, 2002). Such a position invites greater participation in research or evaluation dynamics and promotes democratic principles. Illuminating these underlying tendencies and the forces that constrain or promote them is one of the gifts of feminist inquiry and evaluation. As Hawkesworth has noted, "In the absence of claims of universal validity, feminist accounts derive their justificatory force from their capacity to illuminate existing social relations, to demonstrate the deficiencies of alternate interpretations, and to debunk opposing views" (1989, p. 557).

Feminist Evaluation Has as a Central Focus the Gender Inequities That Lead to Social Injustice. This, perhaps, is the central concept that distinguishes feminist evaluation from other participatory, action models. Sexism (like racism and classism) is an issue that has long affected our world, including the contexts in which we work

and the theories produced within our field. Recognizing the effects of discrimination so as to minimize them requires a concentrated and intentional focus. A woman-centered perspective is the lens through which feminist evaluators approach discrimination. As others have noted, "[b]y emphasizing the suppression of all women as women, feminists are attempting to understand the advantage and prerogative of some women by race, class, and nationality" (Fox-Genovese, 1992, p. 230). Historically, women have been adversely affected by gender equities to a greater degree than men. However, feminist evaluation is also interested in gender inequity experienced by men, who may also be feminist evaluators. As Hood and Cassaro (2002) remind us, gender is a relational concept: an identity as woman is interdependent with an identity as man. Gender cannot be abstracted; rather, it is one position that must be negotiated among other positions (Hurtado, 1996). Hood and Cassaro further highlight the attention of some feminist researchers on questions related to the definition of sex and gender categories; they question the existence of only two sexes, recognize the biological gradations from female to male that occur, acknowledge new categories that include transgendered individuals, and encourage awareness of the intersexed body (Fausto-Sterling, 1993).

Ward (2002) suggests a guideline for creating and developing feminist evaluations that are related to this concept. She suggests that we place women and their material realities at the center of evaluation planning and analysis. Ward posits that this guideline is what defines feminist evaluation and separates it from other forms of evaluation. Other feminist evaluators suggest that putting gender and the material realities of the subjects of the evaluation project at the center of evaluation planning and analysis is an alternative articulation of this guideline, one that is closer to the spirit of feminist theory. Truman's (2002) needs assessment of the sexual health needs of men who have sex with men is a clear example of a feminist evaluation project that illustrates this difference.

Discrimination Based on Gender Is Systemic and Structural. Gender discrimination is shaped and bounded by race and class; it is historically and culturally situated. For feminist evaluators, recognizing the ways in which discrimination is deeply embedded within society—how key institutions (such as churches, temples, mosques, schools, and governmental programs), popular media, and culture reinforce the dominant patriarchal paradigm—is critical. Divergent forms of oppression are related; they support and reinforce each other, as previously discussed. The stakes of continued oppression (e.g., societal and domestic violence, poverty, sexual violence as a tool of war, and addiction) are exceedingly high.

Ward (2002) suggests a corollary to this concept: understand the problem context from a feminist perspective. Understanding the structural and systemic nature of gender discrimination is, perforce, to use a feminist lens. But beyond the initial recognition, Ward reminds us not to forget the obvious: the need to center and recenter our questions and approaches within feminist thought and to clarify the feminist perspective from which activities are developed.

Evaluation and Evaluation Contexts Are Political and Imbued With Asymmetrical Power Relationships. The idea that evaluation is political is no longer a radical notion. Whether or not we explicitly address the issues of whose interests are served, what agendas are being promoted, what the consequences will be for people involved, and what or who is being neglected, our work offers a particular response, from a particular position, to these questions. For feminist evaluators, the evaluation process, the role played by the evaluator, and the products and learning that issue forth from a project are politicized expressions of feminist tenets and assumptions.

From the women's liberation movement in the 1970s came the well-known phrase "the personal is political." From a feminist scientific perspective, this phrase signified the need to value the lived experiences of women, in particular, as legitimate and important subjects of study and to recognize the importance of daily, often discounted experiences (Stanley & Wise, 1989). Writers such as these were quick to note the explicit and implicit political agendas promoted via the construction of research communities and projects. They began asking for what purposes knowledge was being generated and for whom.

Martha Mies (1991) and others began their critique by pointing out that positivist and postpositivist paradigms were political in the very claim to be "objective" and "value free." Feminist thinkers responded, in part, to criticism regarding the political nature of their work by countering that all research, all science, was political in motivation and in use. Many took the stance that the ethical choice, given this situation, was to make one's political approach apparent and to challenge existing power structures, opening these structures to greater participation by people who are not normally "heard." With time, feminist writers spent less time in countering challenges, since such debates implicitly acknowledged that the current state of affairs was the standard by which all practice should be judged, and invested greater effort in developing their own theories.

Recognizing power dynamics and the asymmetrical relationships in which power comes into play is a central theme underlying many key feminist evaluation concepts. Feminist evaluators have drawn from the work of critical theorists and others in developing a textured understanding of the power dynamics interacting within relationships, cultures, institutions, academia, and the world of science. Power differentials lead to gender inequities; the exercise of "power over others" has created systemic and structural discrimination including the legitimizing of particular scientific paradigms (such as positivist approaches and quantitative methods in the past) and certain populations (such as the more affluent or educated) or agendas (sometimes related to the search for power or acquisition). We know that power is exerted in many overt and covert ways and that powerlessness can be internalized and perpetuated by the very groups who are being oppressed. Feminist evaluators and researchers, given the nature of our work, are also keenly aware that language is a constitutive force that creates reality. It legitimizes particular evaluation practices, how we see ourselves, how others come to see us, the relationship between individuals and groups, and what is valued (Bierema & Cseh, 2003; Patton, 2002; Richardson, 1994). As Patton (2002) explains,

> The power to define is the power to control, to include and exclude. . . . This root problem is

the power of the dominant few to define what constitutes legitimate activity and real knowledge, and these dominant few not only define themselves as the inclusive kind of whatever is being defined, in this case evaluator, but also as the norm and the ideal. (p. 99)

Examples of feminist research into power issues include the work of feminist economists and those writing within the field of international development. These scholars have made great strides in understanding differential labor processes, including the sexual division of labor and the shifting role of production under structural adjustment, among other areas (see, for example, Beneria & Roldan, 1987; Hartsock, 1983; Moser, 1989). These scholars have helped promote shifts in our understanding of economic theory (Blank, 1992), exploitation within the capitalist system and within the family (Dwyer & Bruce, 1998; Folbre, 1982), individual and household economic decision making (Sen, 1990; Stitcher & Papart, 1990), and the intersection of the patriarchal state with the patriarchal family (Safa, 1995).

Centering an evaluation analysis in key gender issues, understanding the project from a feminist perspective or with a feminist lens, and engaging others as real participants in a critical and open discussion of the evaluation and related issues, particularly those that affect women, are all guidelines suggested by Ward (2002) that can be implemented in order to keep the evaluation true to its feminist ideals.

Knowledge Is an Important Resource and Should Be Used for Action. Knowledge is a powerful resource. It has immediate and long-term effects. It serves a purpose. For the feminist evaluator, it is imperative that knowledge should serve pressing human (social, political, and economic) needs and that it be used for action in the service of greater equity.

Within a feminist framework, furthermore, knowledge should be placed in service of those who have generated such knowledge: the people studied or evaluated. In particular, feminists purport that knowledge should be enacted in the service of those who are most affected by structural inequities and should shift the balance of power in favor of those currently

disadvantaged in a given context. To understand what is happening requires action because reality is a process, something that is encountered and enacted in relationship (Reason & Rowan, 1981); or, as Marx argued, reality consists of "sensuous human activity, practice" (quoted in Hartsock, 1983). Action on research or evaluation issues may occur throughout the project, is overt, and is informed by multiple perspectives through active interaction with participants and participant involvement in various stages of the evaluation. Thus, at minimum, a focus on action requires participant involvement in the formulation of key issues at hand, including the problems currently being faced to make possible such collaboration (Reinharz, 1989). What constitutes action differs by theory and model; for some, engaging in discussions with the director of a nonprofit about the importance of findings is action. To another, action is working for the changes articulated through report findings. At the heart of this urge to action is Mies's explanation: "In calling for the integration of research and science in an emancipatory process, I do not have in mind a particular action or action research model . . . [i]t is much more a matter of the reunification of life and thought, action and knowledge, change and research" (Mies, 1991, p. 68). Feminist values, social justice aims, and the needs and desires of the people involved in the projects guide action strategies, such as giving greater attention to the education of men in violence prevention efforts.

Ward (2002) suggests that feminist evaluators should exhibit a willingness to challenge the status quo. Feminist evaluators in our volume agreed that their work necessarily challenged the status quo on a number of fronts: they challenged the reigning norms in academic and other institutions, the implicit theories embedded within programs, conventional ideas of how and which methods should be implemented, what constitute appropriate evaluator roles, and contemporary ideas about the purposes of evaluation.

Multiple Ways of Knowing. The acquisition of knowledge through reason characterizes most research practices. Feminist researchers have countered that there are actually many ways of knowing and many sources of knowledge beyond rational forms; these ways and sources, outside of feminist theory, have largely been devalued. Hawkesworth (1989), for example, has mentioned "[p]erception, intuition, conceptualization, inference, representation, reflection, imagination, [and] remembrance" as being among other forms of knowing (p. 551). Writers like Hawkesworth were reacting, in part, to a division between quantitative, "objective" methods for knowing and qualitative (all other) ways of understanding reality that were deemed invalid as sources of knowledge. They advocated for an acknowledgment of the role of these other forms of knowing within research and for the importance of drawing more specifically from them in structured and unstructured ways. Emotions, intuition, and relationships themselves (interaction with other human beings, the natural world, or one's own subject matter) serve as legitimate sources of knowledge. Jane Goodall, who worked with chimpanzees, and Barbara McClintock, who worked with grains of maize, have both acknowledged the significant role that empathy, love, and affection played in deepening their understanding of their subject matter (and of their subject matter within human contexts) and in leading them to make the significant contributions that they made (in Keller, 1985). Within a rationally based view of knowledge, emotions are separated from sense. Jaggar (1989) has described emotions as intentional as well as socially constructed "ways in which we engage actively, even construct the world" (pp. 152–153). Others, espousing concerns and interests similar to those of ethnographers and anthropologists, urge feminist researchers to explicitly set aside the self as data source and instrument (Stanley & Wise, 1989).

In addition to focusing on who is generating the defining questions of science and of scientific studies, feminists began to ask who or what sorts of individuals were legitimated as "knowers." They enjoined their colleagues to consider the wisdom possessed by others not typically "sanctioned" by science as individuals capable of generating knowledge: ordinary people, nonscientists, and scientists from different racial, cultural, and socioeconomic backgrounds who possessed ideas shaped by their very different experiences in the world. Feminist social scientists rejected the idea that scientists, or feminists, could become experts in the lives of others (Stanley & Wise, 1989) and thus emphasized the importance of individuals' participation in the construction of meaning surrounding issues of significance to them. Furthermore, feminist sociologists, those within the philosophy of science, and others have criticized the tendency to usurp the knowledge of others and urged a greater emphasis on the needs, interests, and concerns of the people who are the foci of the studies conducted (Harding, 1992a). For some, this concern suggests the critical role of integrating research subjects into the research process as real participants, with the scope of their participation guided by a real understanding, on the part of both researchers and the researched, of the consequences and meaning of participation and of the study.

Another aspect of acknowledging multiple ways of knowing is the exhortation to use mixed methods in order to enhance our ability to "see" in different ways (Ward, 2002). The use of mixed methods is no longer controversial and is often simply good evaluation and research practice. Gender is not only a category of analysis, and feminist concepts and guidelines are used in the design, selection, and implementation of methods and in the analysis of data.

Knowledge Is Culturally, Socially, and Temporally Contingent. Knowledge is inevitably from a perspective, colored by the social and personal experiences and characteristics of the individual who knows. Feminist standpoint theorists posited that knowledge is always mediated by a particular (engaged and interested) position. Other feminists have been instrumental in acknowledging that knowledge is historically, culturally, and socially contingent, based on the judgments of a community of inquirers (Hawkesworth, 1989) who are, like all of us, limited in their ability to understand reality (Harding, 1991). From this perception comes the feminist concern with location and being situated. "If we begin from the world as we actually experience it, it is at least possible to see that we are located and that what we know of the other is conditional upon that location as part of a relation comprehending the other's location also" (Smith, 1987, p. 93).

Feminist researchers suggest that certain social positions, such as that of the oppressed, offer an important and useful perspective from which existing ideologies can be pierced or deconstructed (Hawkesworth, 1989).

Similarly, feminist theorists propose that it is critical for researchers and theorists to reveal their particular histories and characteristics, attitudes, and values in order for the reader to better detect any reasons that an author might favor or espouse a particular political or philosophical position. Along these lines, others urge an account of the research process and a clarification of the relationship between the researcher and the researched. There can be no dispassionate research, nor is it desirable that there be any; individuals approach research with particular interests in the questions, people, or issues involved. Indeed, the notion of objectivity criticized by feminists and others relies on a radical separation between self and the object of study, an idea based on the concept of a "separative" self (England, 1989; Keller, 1985). Many feminist theorists suggest that a subjective objectivity is more appropriate: a full, textured understanding of the pluralistic values, beliefs, and knowledge systems of others (Lather, 1991; Reason & Rowan, 1981).

To say that knowledge is situated does not mean that nothing can be known. It does mean that, in order to know something, we are obliged to recognize and explore the unique conditions and characteristics of the issue under study. We must also be clear about the particular values, experiences, and histories through which we are filtering our understanding so that we do not essentialize the people who will ultimately be affected by our work. We must allow for the critical review of our work. Another implication of this principle is that, although we can learn from our work and contribute to the knowledge that is brought to bear on similar issues, generalizability, as it is typically understood, is a concept of limited usefulness.

Ward (2002) includes within her discussion of this guideline an entreaty to ensure participant input. How participation is negotiated and in what areas are context specific. However, feminist evaluation shares a deep affinity with participatory evaluation's propositions that the subjects of research or evaluation possess critical knowledge of the issues studied as well as of the dynamics inherent within researched contexts and that subject participation and the consequences of acting, or not acting, affect findings. Not all feminist evaluators design participatory projects; however, having participant input beyond that elicited from them as the subjects of data collection is an important feminist evaluation value.

Action and Advocacy Are Morally and Ethically Appropriate Responses of an Engaged Feminist Evaluator. The role of action within feminist inquiry is predicated on an understanding of power and politics that is structural and systematic. In this chapter, knowledge has been described as an important resource in preparation for action. And the language we use and the dialogues we create are also constitutive elements of reality. Feminist evaluation is also committed to broader, more explicit action, including advocacy, if appropriate, and other forms of social action. Action typically includes the active and purposeful dissemination of findings and can include advocating for and with participants (see Ward, 2002). Feminist evaluation joins empowerment evaluation (Fetterman, 2000), diversity inclusive evaluation (Mertens, 1998), transformative participatory evaluation (see Cousins & Whitmore, 1998), and elements of democratic evaluation (House & Howe, 2000) in using critical change criteria as a means of judging the credibility of feminist evaluation and research (Patton, 2002). In striving to promote change and social justice, for example, feminist evaluators reject the idea of objectivity and bring an "explicit agenda of elucidating political, economic, and social inequalities, and in so elucidating, they critique social inequities, raise consciousness, and strive to change the balance of power in favor of those less powerful" (Patton, 2002, p. 103).

CHALLENGES TO FEMINIST EVALUATION AND THE RESULTING DEBATE

In the short term, feminist evaluators find themselves in the position of having to respond to criticism posed by evaluation practitioners and theorists not open to feminist principles; all models that have challenged the status quo have engaged in discussions surrounding these questions. Many of these challenges arise in a context of beliefs and assumptions often accepted without critical reflection that have been long held as inviolable truth, such as the idea that the researcher should position herself outside of and apart from the subjects of her research. Because feminist evaluation challenges the assumptions on which these questions are based, theorists have begun to respond to the spirit of the questions posed as understood from within a feminist inquiry perspective. Some of the most common questions raised by critics, and the feminist reframing of these issues, appear below.

Challenges to Feminist Evaluation as a Legitimate Evaluation Model

1. How does feminist evaluation ensure objectivity? Feminist reframing: What procedures and stances do we introduce to ensure that we are making the best effort to know and assess what is happening? Who is asking the questions and from what position?

2. Of what use are your findings if they are not generalizable (if they cannot be externalized) to similar situations? Feminist reframing: For whom are we producing "knowledge"? What constitutes knowledge, and how open to and aware are we of other ways of knowing?

3. Doesn't a focus on action compromise the center of evaluation practice, making of evaluation, advocacy? Feminist reframing: How (and to what extent) should an evaluator be involved in social action aimed at meeting the needs of those involved in the evaluation project? What is the role of action in evaluation practice, and how do we define action?

4. Do the action agenda and the involvement of the evaluator compromise, if not prevent, validity? Feminist reframing: What constitutes validity, and what is needed in order to create meaningful and credible results? Who is being affected by our work and in what ways? How should we orient ourselves to the cultural and social challenges of changing demographics and economic trends?

5. Does it matter whether or not an evaluation is named a feminist evaluation? When and with whom should that naming occur? How important is the naming, and in what cases should an evaluator call herself or himself a feminist evaluator?

6. In what cases and under what circumstances is a feminist evaluation possible? Desirable?

7. What expectations should we realistically have of those implementing feminist evaluations?

Challenges to the Practical Implementation of Feminist Evaluation

Challenges to feminist evaluation as a legitimate evaluation practice are largely addressed earlier in the chapter in the section on feminist theory. We discussed the use of mixed methods and participation as a means of ensuring that we are better positioned to recognize the underlying regularities that are "reality." Feminist theory encourages us to disclose who we are, to engage in self-reflexive practices and dialogue with others as we focus and refocus on key feminist concepts and guidelines. We have discussed that knowledge is primarily a resource for the people who have generated that knowledge, that there are multiple ways of knowing and forms of knowledge (including emotions and intuition, for example), and that knowledge is not only a powerful resource for action—rather, its final end is action.

However, it is important that we say a few more words about the role of action and advocacy in evaluation. Feminist evaluation, as previously mentioned, is not the only evaluation model that proposes action as an important, even necessary, element of the evaluation enterprise. Whether or not action and advocacy are appropriate roles for the evaluator is one of several contemporary debates hotly contested among evaluation professionals. Most evaluators, however, would agree that evaluation findings should be useful, that a program or organization's capacity to conduct evaluation activities and use evaluation results is a positive outcome, and that evaluators are well-positioned to facilitate how findings may be used to improve social programs.

Critics like Scriven suggest that truth and objectivity, although not understood in the same manner as they were understood under a positivist paradigm, remain critical to the evaluation enterprise and that critiques of truth and objectivity levied by empowerment models and others go too far in their distancing from these terms and from traditional evaluation practice (see Scriven, 1997). Indeed, not all feminist evaluators or participatory evaluation practitioners reframe the notion of truth and objectivity, partly for the reasons that Scriven describes but also because they need this concept to convince particular audiences of the legitimacy of their claims (Spalter-Roth & Hartmann, 1999; Truman, 2002). Scriven (1997) has spoken strongly against the idea that the evaluator should serve as an advocate; the evaluator's role is to be empiricist and logician. Few feminist evaluators, regardless of how wedded to objectivity they are, would see their role as so narrowly defined, even if they were uncomfortable with a more engaged advocacy position. Stake has written that evaluators should resist and minimize advocacy even if engaged in helping others to recognize the kinds of advocacies present. He suggests that some types of advocacy are acceptable while others are not and that key issues of concern for the profession should be any lack of rigorous debate or of holding each other to standards.

> Advocacy for educational reform, curricular remediation, and pedagogical change . . . are fundamental to our work. . . . But we seem to be moving further and further into advocacy of little-agreed-upon values. And of course we know that some advocacies are not acceptable. (Stake, 1997, p. 475)

On the other side of the fence, Stake names Jennifer Greene (1995), who has written that advocacy, like politics, is inherent in evaluation and so the decision becomes for whom we advocate and in what ways—she suggests we advocate for the program participants.

There is no one feminist evaluation position on action and advocacy. However, the continuum of feminist positions on this issue is shaped by an interest in the welfare of the individuals who are the subjects of study and in ensuring that the evaluation findings are used and correctly understood, particularly when the subjects of research face real or potential negative consequences if findings are not acted upon or are made public without specific protections of confidentiality or similar protections being secured. Feminist evaluators, in short, are interested in conducting evaluations resulting in the dissemination of findings that will be put to use in service of achieving greater social justice with respect to gender inequities. As such, many feminist evaluators would find themselves strongly aligned with Greene.

Some of the challenges to the practical implementation of feminist evaluation will be addressed in the following section. However, language is an important issue that requires attention. Patton (2002) wrote on the role of language in feminist evaluation in preparation for his article in the *New Directions for Evaluation* special issue on feminist evaluation. In a section not included in the final volume, he writes that language, like gender, matters and that, furthermore, "calling an evaluation a 'feminist evaluation' is a political act, one hopefully taken with intentionality and knowledge. However, the primary elements of feminist evaluation can be manifest in a design without attaching the feminist label." What is important to consider, he suggests, is what may be gained and what may be lost in the naming or not naming.

Among feminist evaluators, naming or not naming an evaluation "feminist" is not an easily resolved matter. For some, self-reflexive practice and disclosure require us to be up front and honest about who we are, our values, and our agendas. In such cases, a key concern may be how we present ourselves as feminists and how we present feminist evaluation—as the sole model for assessment or as one of two or more models or as supporting ideology. When a feminist evaluation can be called a feminist evaluation, it should be. However, others take the position that social change, particularly with respect to gender inequity, will not happen if we only speak to those sympathetic to and comfortable with feminist ideals. Taking this position raises many questions: Are we suggesting that a relationship must be formed before feminist evaluation can be a possibility? If the key feminist concepts are employed and other stakeholder evaluation needs and interests are met, are we accomplishing the goals of feminist evaluation? Is it more in keeping with feminist ideals to work for a greater awareness of these issues in an evaluation that uses another model as its dominant guiding force? Can such feminist concerns be advanced if we do not promote feminist evaluation as legitimate?

Feminist evaluation (similarly to participatory evaluation) has been criticized for being idealist and for promoting romantic, unrealistic notions of what the evaluator practitioner should achieve and what she or he must be. Perhaps these foci are related to the passionate nature of the proponents of feminist evaluation who are deeply committed in their personal lives to social change. Perhaps we, as evaluation practitioners, are not used to discussing personal standards outside of the ethical standards of our profession. Perhaps we would be better served by presenting expectations in more practical language. For example, instead of urging practitioners to be self-reflexive, we could speak of the methods by which other ways of knowing and awareness of biases may be documented and considered throughout the research and evaluation process. Instead of encouraging full participation in all stages of the evaluation process, we could provide guidelines related to participatory research in various circumstances and show how feminist theory helps in the selection of the level and type of participation. Similarly, we could clarify levels of action and advocacy and give guidance as to making choices between levels of involvement.

Other questions such as "how should we orient ourselves to the cultural and social challenges of changing demographics and economic trends?" are the subject of ongoing debate and dialogue. Indeed, many of the "how" questions raised by feminist evaluators and others may be answered: reflexively, in dialogue, and with a constant revisiting of the feminist guidelines and theoretical ideas we have chosen to follow.

IMPLEMENTING FEMINIST EVALUATION

The implementation of feminist evaluation, as is true of the implementation of other models, can be more challenging than the theoretical discussion. In fact, Roy (2004) has suggested that some may not be capable of working from this model:

What the feminist inquiry does . . . is to ask the scientist to uncover the social and political forces driving their research questions as well as to establish a relationship with their research subject(s). Perhaps the real problem that traditional scientists have with feminism is that they are not up to the intellectual challenge presented by the feminist inquiry. (p. 276)

Questions such as who can do feminist evaluation, when or in what circumstances can feminist evaluation be done, and what methods are appropriate within a feminist evaluation are all debated in the evaluation field. Some evaluators will argue that feminist evaluation can only be conducted by evaluators with a feminist orientation. Others will argue that feminist issues and concerns can be addressed by including feminist viewpoints in the design and implementation of studies. Although many examples of feminist research exist, few studies utilizing a feminist evaluation approach have been published to date. Examples of case studies, such as the evaluation of a woman's substance abuse program by Rebecca Beardsley and Michelle Miller, can be found in the *New Directions for Evaluation* issue edited by Seigart and Brisolara (2002).

As there is no orthodox feminism and because the guidelines that define feminist evaluation are emerging, there are multiple ways to implement feminist evaluation. In the brief discussion that follows, we address the key elements of implementation, sharing our perspective on the parameters of implementation from a feminist evaluation perspective. These elements are summarized in the following questions: Who can be a feminist evaluator, what methods are legitimate within a feminist evaluation, in what circumstances can one implement a feminist evaluation, and how are feminist evaluations implemented?

Although many evaluation practitioners would argue that women are better suited to conduct feminist evaluation given their social positions and, hence, ability to identify with gender discrimination and develop a feminist perspective, we would argue that not gender but ideology and theory are the most important criteria determining who might be a feminist evaluator. What is critical is that an evaluator is well versed in the tenets of feminist theories and familiar with a particular feminist theoretical framework, personally holds key feminist values, and actively expresses and engages these values within his or her evaluation practice. A feminist evaluator should be willing to explore and adhere to feminist values in the design, implementation, and analysis stages of evaluation; must be prepared to be self-reflexive; and must willingly disclose potential conflicts of interest, sources of privilege, and other areas where who she or he is may obfuscate or distort what participants or the subjects of the evaluation project experience or articulate. Feminist evaluators must be able and willing to engage in and reflect the lived experiences of women or other evaluation subjects.

Not only women are feminist evaluators and not only women are the subjects of feminist evaluation. Truman (2002) provides us with an example of a feminist evaluation focused on policy development that was conducted with gay and bisexual men. For the most part, the experiences of women are the focus of feminist evaluations; however, the central concern of feminist evaluation is structural, systematic discrimination that perpetuates gender inequality; in some cases, for example, those affected by such discrimination are gay men or transgendered individuals.

Earlier in the development of feminist inquiry, qualitative methods, particularly the unstructured interview, were seen as being the feminist inquiry method of choice. It is true that qualitative methods do provide a greater opportunity for the subject-based expression of lived experiences and allow for the emergence of unanticipated thoughts and understandings. However, individuals engaged in feminist evaluation have often found themselves in need of quantitative data, and most are proponents of evaluation designs that mix methods, choosing these for the same reasons that other evaluators use mixed-method designs. Ward (2002) suggests that one of the guidelines for conducting a feminist evaluation is the use of mixed methods and describes the value of using both quantitative and qualitaive methods in her analysis of an adolescent gender violence prevention program. Beardsley and Miller (2002) administered surveys that collected quantitative and qualitative information in their three-phase study of a women's substance abuse program. Bamberger and Podems (2002) discuss the value of implementing mixed-method

evaluation designs, noting that evaluations conducted in the context of international development experience several constraints but could benefit from such a mixing of methods and that new guidelines in the field recommend the use of multiple methods. Feminist evaluators concur with Harding (1983): methods are not feminist or nonfeminist. What is important is the methodology that one selects in applying particular mixed methods and the way in which methods are chosen and implemented (Hood & Cassaro, 2002; Reinharz, 1992).

It is more difficult for feminist evaluators to come to a consensus regarding in what circumstances a feminist evaluation can or should be implemented. Earlier in this chapter, we discussed when we would call an evaluation a feminist evaluation. But what are the parameters under which a feminist evaluation should be implemented, regardless of what it is called? There are many questions that arise in this regard that bear further discussion. For example, how much resistance to a feminist approach is too much resistance? To what extent should concerns about the legitimacy of the project to external agencies determine whether or not a feminist evaluation model can be used? That is, are the feminist aims of the project or of the evaluation better served by merging a feminist perspective with a more familiar evaluation model even if particular elements of the feminist evaluation must be sacrificed?

Contributors to the feminist evaluation model volume referenced earlier did not address these questions directly. However, their work provides us with some clues as to the directions feminist evaluators may take. To force a feminist evaluation model is antithetical to the nature of the feminist evaluation project, and, depending on the political context, insisting on a feminist evaluation can seriously jeopardize the feminist and other aims of the evaluation project. Bamberger and Podems (2002) note that, given the importance of cultural sensitivity to feminist evaluation and to evaluations in the international development context, rather than assuming a feminist agenda, creating a space in which a range of issues can be discussed is important. Truman (2002) writes about the importance of an evaluator's legitimacy and credibility to the audience(s) contracting the evaluation as being an important factor that helps to legitimize the evaluation model chosen. Finally, Patton (2002) reminds us that models and criteria from different evaluation frameworks are often mixed, in practice, suggesting that a feminist evaluation model can contribute significantly to an evaluation without being implemented in its "pure" form and without making feminist evaluation or feminist language the dominant criteria of the evaluation model. In the real world of evaluation, evaluators often combine compatible models in service of cultivating a better grasp of the context or subject matter or to strengthen the ability to craft findings and recommendations that speak to diverse audiences. Additionally, sometimes the principles of a model fit well with the needs of the evaluation, but the use of feminist language might be considered distracting or likely to elicit resistance that might not otherwise be present. For example, while on sabbatical in Australia, Seigart implemented an evaluation of school-based health care, utilizing many of the principles of feminist evaluation but not labeling the work as such because she was immersed in a very conservative religious community resistant to the language of feminism.

As is true of other challenger models, feminist evaluations tend to be imbued in theory but pragmatic in implementation, seeking an engaged praxis. What follows are a few guidelines that practitioners could use in making a decision about whether or not to implement feminist evaluation in a particular circumstance. The evaluator leading a feminist evaluation should either be a feminist evaluator or identify strongly with the key values of feminist evaluation. The lead evaluator should not operate in isolation, even if participatory methods are not implemented; continued dialogue and reflection should be the manner in which the lead evaluator operates in order to protect against the evaluator's biases or influence negatively affecting or skewing the results. We would suggest that an initial resistance to feminist evaluation does not preclude a feminist evaluation from emerging, through dialogue and discussion. However, strong resistance to using a feminist approach can significantly limit the effectiveness of the evaluation or any action that may occur as a result.

Feminist evaluation values would also suggest that a feminist evaluation not be implemented if the risk of doing so will be borne by participants in the project who are those ostensibly served by the program.

How feminist evaluations are implemented may vary widely; however, there are some key roles and responsibilities for feminist evaluators. Feminist evaluators should engage in dialogue with the key stakeholders of the project, immerse themselves as much as possible in the evaluation context, reflexively engage with other stakeholders and evaluators to understand and check out emerging ideas and analyses, and self-disclose (to others but also by documenting their own reflections) regarding any biases or identities that might lead to limits in perspective. Reflexivity and keeping feminist evaluation guidelines in the forefront of our work and thought can help feminist evaluators pay attention to language and the power dynamics operating within the evaluation; once observed or once such issues are raised, the feminist evaluator is called upon to work toward restoring a balance of power—sometimes among groups of subjects, sometimes between the funders and subjects or the evaluators and subjects—within the evaluation setting. Finally, it is important that the feminist evaluator keep in mind that the purposes of the evaluation are both action and the specific utilization of the evaluation findings.

CONCLUSION

Feminist evaluation, like other evaluation models, will face various challenges in the coming years. Some of those challenges are ones that will affect the profession as a whole. Technological changes bring new methods and change the ways in which we implement old methods. One simple example is the way we might design and calculate error for telephone surveys given the effect of cell phone only households, caller ID, call blocking, and the tendency to screen calls. In the United States, as well as in other countries, the current economic downturn will likely continue to affect funding for education and social programs negatively; if the past is any indication, women will disproportionally experience the negative consequences of this downturn and of its resultant increase in unemployment and restriction of aid and services. Changing demographics in the United States and increasingly diverse communities will affect not only how we do evaluation but also the methods that we choose. Increasing diversity will inevitably change the face of feminism as well as the context in which feminism operates, as more voices emerge from new arenas.

Feminist evaluation will continue to provide responses to some of the same questions that it has attempted to influence since its inception. There is a continuing debate, for example, on what the role of the evaluator should be (partner and critical friend, advocate, or objective assessor of facts), what the purpose of evaluation should be (action, use, knowledge, program improvement, accountability, or what measure of each), what practitioners think about current and emerging evaluation theories and their methods, and what can be learned from and by emerging evaluation fields in countries around the globe.

As feminist evaluation continues to develop, we see this model being implemented into new fields of interest; what has been learned through these experiences is only now coming to light. There are more feminist evaluators working in international development contexts and from within many different countries; the variety of cultural contexts and the diverse challenges that they experience will broaden our understanding. Evaluators taking on these issues are working both on how to refine practice (including strengthening methods and designs) and on refining theories and the feminist evaluation model itself. The authors of this chapter are currently engaged with others in coediting a volume of current efforts.

Given the divergent interests of its practitioners, then, feminist evaluation will continue simultaneously to push for legitimacy and to work from outside of officially sanctioned models, constantly pressing for the changes its adherents believe are needed in the field. We believe that the programs and people we serve, and the field of evaluation itself, will be richer for these contributions.

Discussion Questions

1. How much resistance to a feminist approach is too much resistance? To what extent should concerns about the legitimacy of the project to external agencies determine whether or not a feminist evaluation model should be used?

2. Reflect on an evaluation (or even a research project) that you have participated in or know about. How might the use of a feminist evaluation framework have changed the focus or results of that evaluation or project?

3. How does the application of a feminist evaluation framework affect your understanding of what constitutes valid research or evaluation work?

Online Resources

Bringing Evaluation to the Grass Roots

http://www.infed.org/evaluation/evaluation_globalization.htm

This website discusses the challenges of evaluation research in an activist setting using the case study of the protest group Mobilization for Global Justice. The author concludes with a number of suggested evaluation approaches, including feminist evaluation.

Troubling Empowerment

http://eprints.qut.edu.au/18365/

Troubling Empowerment (a doctoral thesis available for download in PDF) provides an example of the evaluation of a feminist action research project from a "transdisciplinary" approach.

Gender (and Feminist) Issues in Global Evaluation

http://www.eval.org/SummerInstitute07/Handouts/si07.podemsF.pdf

In a presentation prepared for the Macro International Inc. AEA/CDC Summer Institute, Donna Podems discusses gender frameworks and feminist evaluation in the context of international development.

Relevant Journals

American Journal of Evaluation

Canadian Journal of Program Evaluation

Evaluation and Program Planning

Evaluation Review

New Directions in Evaluation

NOTES

1. One way that the history of feminist or women's movements in the West has been organized and understood has been through the rubric of *three waves of feminism*. The development of women's involvement in and contributions to social research methods has been described as first and second generation.

2. In this section, we use feminist theorists as a convenient means of describing those scholars and practitioners who contributed directly or indirectly to the development of feminist thought, recognizing that their definition of feminism or of feminist priorities may differ significantly.

REFERENCES

Astell, M. (1970). *Some reflections on marriage.* New York: Source Books Press. (Original work published 1700)

Bamberger, M., & Podems, D. R. (2002). Feminist evaluation in the international development context. *New Directions for Evaluation, 96,* 83–96.

Beardsley, R. M., & Miller, M. H. (2002). Revisioning the process: A case study in feminist program evaluation. *New Directions for Evaluation, 96,* 57–70.

Beneria, L., & Roldan, M. (1987). *The crossroads of class and gender: Industrial homework, subcontracting, and household dynamics in Mexico City.* Chicago: University of Chicago Press.

Bhavnani, K. K. (1993). Tracing the contours: Feminist research and feminist objectivity. *Women's Studies International Forum, 16*(2), 95–104.

Bierema, L., & Cseh, M. (2003). Evaluating AHRD research using a feminist research framework. *Human Resource Development Quarterly, 14*(1), 5–26.

Blank, R. M. (1992). A female perspective on economic man? In S. Rosenberg Salk & J. Gordon-Kelter (Eds.), *Revolutions in knowledge: Feminism in the social sciences* (pp. 111–124). Boulder, CO: Westview Press.

Boston Women's Health Collective. (1998). *Our bodies, ourselves for the new century.* New York: Simon & Schuster.

Bouchier, D. (1983). *The feminist challenge: The movement for women's liberation in Britain and the United States.* London: Macmillan Press.

Brisolara, S. (1998). The history of participatory evaluation and current debates in the field. *New Directors for Evaluation, 80,* 25–41.

Campbell, D. T., & Stanley, J. C. (1963). *Experimental and quasi-experimental designs for research.* Boston: Houghton Mifflin.

Chelimsky, E. (1987). The politics of program evaluation. *Social Science and Modern Society, 25,* 24–32.

Cousins, B., & Whitmore, E. (1998). Framing participatory evaluation. In E. Whitmore (Ed.), Understanding and practicing participatory evaluation [Special issue]. *New Directions for Evaluation, 80,* 5–24.

Dwyer, D., & Bruce, J. (1998). *A home divided: Women and income in the third world.* Stanford, CA: Stanford University Press.

England, P. (1989). A feminist critique of rational choice theories: Implications for sociology. *The American Sociologist, 20*(1), 14–28.

Fausto-Sterling, A. (1993). The five sexes: Why female and male are not enough. *The Sciences, 33*(2), 20–25.

Fetterman, D. M. (2000). *Foundations of empowerment evaluation: Step by step.* Thousand Oaks, CA: Sage.

Fitzpatrick, E. (1990). *Endless crusade: Women social scientists and progressive reform.* New York: Oxford University Press.

Folbre, N. (1982). Exploitation comes home: A critique of the Marxian theory of family labour. *Cambridge Journal of Economics, 6,* 317–329.

Fox-Genovese, E. (1992). *Feminism without illusions: A critique of individualism.* Chapel Hill: The University of North Carolina Press.

Friedan, B. (1963). *The feminine mystique.* New York: Norton.

Greene, J. (1995, November 15). *Evaluators as advocates.* Paper presented at the annual meeting of the American Evaluation Association, Vancouver, BC.

Harding, S. (1983). Why has the sex/gender system become visible only now? In S. Harding & M. Hintikka (Eds.), *Discovering reality: Feminist perspectives on epistemology, metaphysics, methodology, and the philosophy of science* (pp. 311–324). Dordrecht , The Netherlands: D. Reidel.

Harding, S. (1990). Feminism, science, and the anti-Enlightenment critiques. In L. J. Nicholoson (Ed.), *Feminism/postmodernism* (pp. 83–106). New York: Routledge.

Harding, S. (1991). *Whose science? Whose knowledge?* Ithaca, NY: Cornell University Press.

Harding, S. (1992a). Re-thinking standpoint epistemology: What is "strong objectivity"? *Centennial Review, 36*(3), 437–470.

Harding, S. (1992b). *Women and knowledge: The politics of epistemology.* Lecture given at Cornell University.

Hartsock, N. (1983). The feminist standpoint: Developing a ground for a specifically feminist historical materialism. In S. Harding & M. Hintikka (Eds.), *Discovering reality: Feminist perspectives on epistemology, metaphysics, methodology, and philosophy of science* (pp. 283–310). London: D. Reidel Publishing Company.

Hawkesworth, M. E. (1989). Knowers, knowing, known: Feminist theory and the claims of truth. *Signs: Journal of Women in Culture and Society, 14*(31), 533–557.

Hood, D., & Cassaro, D. (2002). Feminist evaluation and the inclusion of difference. In D. Seigart & S. Brisolara (Eds.), Feminist evaluation: Explorations and experiences [Special issue]. *New Directions for Evaluation, 96*, 27–40.

House, E. R., & Howe, K. R. (2000). Deliberative democratic evaluation. In K. E. Ryan & L. De Stephano (Eds.), *Evaluation as a democratic process: Promoting inclusion, dialogue, and deliberation* [Special issue]. *New Directions for Evaluation, 85*, 3–12.

Humm, M. (Ed.). (1992). *Modern feminisms: Political, literary, cultural.* New York: Columbia University Press.

Hurtado, A. (1996). Strategic suspensions: Feminists of color theorize the production of knowledge. In N. R. Goldberger, J. M. Tarule, B. M. Clinchy, & B. Belenky (Eds.), *knowledge, difference, and power: Essays inspired by women's ways of knowing* (pp. 372–392). New York: Basic Books.

Jaggar, A. (1989). Love and knowledge: Emotion in feminist epistemology. In A. Jaggar & S. Bordo (Eds.), *Gender, body, knowledge* (pp. 145–169). Piscataway, NJ: Rutgers University Press.

Keller, E. F. (1985). *Reflections on gender and science.* New Haven, CT: Yale University Press.

Kushner, S. (2005). Program evaluation. In S. Mathison (Ed.), *Encyclopedia of evaluation* (pp. 334–338). Thousand Oaks, CA: Sage.

Lather, P. (1991). *Getting smart: Feminist research and pedagogy with/in the postmodern.* New York: Routledge.

MacDonald, B., & Kushner, S. (2005). Democratic evaluation. In S. Mathison (Ed.), *Encyclopedia of evaluation* (pp. 109–113). Thousand Oaks, CA: Sage.

Mathison, S. (Ed.). (2005). *Encyclopedia of evaluation.* Thousand Oaks, CA: Sage.

McTaggart, R. (1991). *Action research: A short modern history.* Geelong, Australia: Deakin University Press.

Mertens, D. M. (1998). *Research methods in education and psychology: Integrating diversity with quantitative and qualitative approaches.* Thousand Oaks, CA: Sage.

Mies, M. (1991). Women's research or feminist research? The debate surrounding feminist science and methodology (Trans. A. Spencer). In M. Fonow & J. A. Cook (Eds.), *Beyond methodology: Feminist scholarship as lived research* (pp. 60–84). Bloomington: Indiana University Press.

Mills, J. S., & Taylor, H. (1970). The subjection of women. In A. S. Rossi (Ed.), *Essays on sex equality* (pp. 123–242). Chicago: University of Chicago Press.

Moser, C. (1989). The impact of recession and adjustment policies at the micro-level: Low income women and their households in Guayaquil, Ecuador. In UNICEF, Americas and Caribbean Regional Office (Ed.), *The invisible adjustment: Poor women and the economic crisis* (Vol. 2, pp. 137–162). Santiago, Chile: UNICEF.

Noffke, S. E. (1994). Action research: Towards the next generation. *Educational Action Research, 2*, 9–21.

Patton, M. Q. (1997). *Utilization-focused evaluation* (3rd ed.). Thousand Oaks, CA: Sage.

Patton, M. Q. (2002). Feminist, yes, but is it evaluation? In D. Seigart & S. Brisolara (Eds.), Feminist evaluation: Explorations and experiences [Special issue]. *New Directions for Evaluation, 96*, 97–108.

Preskill, H., & Catsambas, T. T. (2006). *Reframing evaluation through appreciative inquiry.* Thousand Oaks, CA: Sage.

Radcliffe, S. A., & Westwood, S. (Eds.). (1993). *Viva: Women and popular protest in Latin America.* London: Routledge.

Ratcliff, K. (2002). *Women & health: Power, technology, inequality, and conflict in a gendered world.* Boston: Allyn & Bacon.

Reason, P., & Rowan, J. (Eds.). (1981). *Human inquiry: A sourcebook of new paradigm research.* New York: John Wiley and Sons.

Reinharz, S. (1989). Experiential analysis: A contribution to feminist research. In S. Bowles & R. D. Klein (Eds.), *Theories of women's studies* (pp. 162–191). London: Routledge and Kegan Paul.

Reinharz, S. (1992). *Feminist methods in social research.* New York: Oxford University Press.

Richardson, L. (1994). Writing: A method of inquiry. In N. K. Denzin and Y. S. Lincoln (Eds.), *Handbook of qualitative research* (pp. 516–529). Thousand Oaks, CA: Sage.

Rossi, P. H., & Freeman, H. E. (1993). *Evaluation: A systematic approach.* Newbury Park, CA: Sage.

Roy, D. (2004). Feminist theory in science: Working toward a practical transformation. *Hypatia, 19*(1), 255–279.

Safa, H. I. (1995). Economic restructuring and gender subordination. *Latin American Perspectives, 22*(2), 32–50.

Schirmer, J. (1993). The seeking of truth and the gendering of consciousness: The comadres of El Salvador and the CONVIGUA widows of Guatemala. In S. A. Radcliffe & S. Westwood (Eds.), *Viva: Women and popular protest in Latin America* (pp. 30–64). London: Routledge.

Schwandt, T. A. (1991). Evaluation as moral critique. *New Directions for Evaluation, 49*, 63–72.

Scriven, M. (1997). Truth and objectivity in evaluation. In E. Chelimsky & W. Shadish (Eds.), *Evaluation for the 21st century: A handbook* (pp. 477–500). Thousand Oaks, CA: Sage.

Seigart, D. (2005). Feminist evaluation. In S. Mathison (Ed.), *Encyclopedia of evaluation* (pp. 154–156). Thousand Oaks, CA: Sage.

Seigart, D., & Brisolara, S. (Eds.). (2002). Feminist evaluation: Explorations and experiences [Special issue]. *New Directions for Evaluation, 96.*

Sen, A. K. (1990). Gender and cooperative conflicts. In I. Tinker (Ed.), *Persistent inequalities: Women and world development.* Oxford, UK: Oxford University Press.

Sielbeck-Bowne, K. A., Brisolara, S., Seigart, D., Tischler, C., & Whitmore, E. (2002). Exploring feminist evaluation: The ground from which we rise. *New Directions for Evaluation, 96*, 3–8.

Smith, D. E. (1972, June). Presentation for the meeting of the American Academy for the Advancement of Science (Pacific Division), Eugene, OR.

Smith, D. E. (1987). Women's perspective as a radical critique of sociology. In S. Harding (Ed.), *Feminism and methodology* (pp. 84–96). Bloomington: Indiana University Press.

Spalter-Roth, R., & Hartmann, H. (1996). Small happinesses: The feminist struggle to integrate social research and social activism. In H. Gottfried (Ed.), *Feminism and social change: Bridging theory and practice* (pp. 206–224). Urbana: University of Illinois Press.

Spalter-Roth, R., & Hartmann, H. (1999). Small happiness: The feminist struggle to integrate social research with social activism. In S. J. Hesse-Biber, C. K. Bilmartin, & R. Lydenberg (Eds.), *Feminist approaches to theory and methodology: An interdisciplinary reader* (pp. 333–347).

Stake, R. (1997). Advocacy in evaluation: A necessary evil. In E. Chelimsky & W. Shadish (Eds.), *Evaluation for the 21st century: A handbook* (pp. 470–476). Thousand Oaks, CA: Sage.

Stanley, L., & Wise, S. (1989). "Back into the Personal" or: Our attempt to construct "feminist research." In S. Bowles & R. D. Klein (Eds.), *Theories of women's studies* (pp. 20–60). London: Routledge and Kegan Paul.

Stitcher, S., & Papart, J. L. (1990). *Women, employment, and the family in the international division of labor.* Philadelphia: Temple University Press.

Truman, C. (2002). Doing feminist evaluation with men: Achieving objectivity in a sexual health needs assessment. In D. Seigart & S. Brisolara (Eds.), Feminist evaluation: Explorations and experiences [Special issue]. *New Directions for Evaluation, 96*, 71–82.

Ward, K. (2002). Reflections of a job done: Well? In D. Seigart & S. Brisolara (Eds.), Feminist evaluation: Explorations and experiences [Special issue]. *New Directions for Evaluation, 96*, 41–56.

Weiss, C. H. (1973). Where politics and evaluation meet. *Evaluation, 1*(3), 37–45.

Weiss, H., & Greene, J. C. (1992). An empowerment partnership for family support and education programs and evaluations. *Family Science Review, 5*, 131–148.

Whitmore, E. (Ed.). (1998). Understanding and practicing participatory evaluation [Special issue]. *New Directions for Evaluation, 80.*

Wollstonecraft, M. A. (1988). *Vindication of the rights of women* (2nd ed., C. H. Poston, Ed.). New York: Norton. (Original work published 1797)

15

FEMINIST APPROACHES TO INQUIRY IN THE NATURAL SCIENCES

Practices for the Lab

Deboleena Roy

Making Connections Between Theory and Praxis

Traditional feminist critiques of science such as interrogations of the scientific method and analyses of gendered paradigms have been very helpful for the feminist scientist to reorient herself in the laboratory setting. However, recent work in feminist science studies has brought to light that these feminist theoretical contributions have not dealt closely enough with issues of ontology, that is, with theories of the nature of existence and being, particularly in the context of our relationship with the physical and biological matters of the natural world. Feminist science studies scholars, largely influenced by continental philosophy, are interested in extending questions of being, becoming, and difference to the processes of scientific inquiry.

For the feminist scientist in the natural sciences, it might be said that engagements with issues of ontology, even if not clearly articulated as such, are always hovering nearby. These engagements can be traced back to the very beginning of her inquiry, even before her arrival at a hypothesis. For instance, through the design of her research methodology, she must consider how to approach the encounter with what it is that she wishes to know. She may question her role as a feminist knower and think carefully about her relationship with what is to become the known. In fact, this kind of a reflexive inquiry into ontological issues may serve to inform her overall ethical reflections on research praxis. This chapter aims to develop a new vocabulary for these ontological and ethical practices in the laboratory setting of the natural sciences and is driven by a desire to position the

Author's Note: I would like to thank the faculty research fellows from the Michelle Clayman Institute for Gender Research at Stanford University (2008–2009) for commenting on an early version of this chapter.

knower in the same critical plane as that which becomes known. In the context of the natural sciences, issues of ontology become intertwined with issues of ethics when we realize that the "me" in a situated knowledge has always been an "us" and, particularly in the research laboratory, that this "us" includes the nonhuman as well as the inorganic. Questions of ontology may also emerge from the mundane or everyday methods (techniques and tools) that the feminist scientist requires for her inquiry. She may be aware that her techniques and tools become part of the apparatus of gathering scientific knowledge and therefore require deep reflection. A link, therefore, for the feminist scientist between theory and praxis seems logical, but, for whatever reasons, there has been a limited amount of discussion on theories of ontology and their potential influence on the development of new feminist praxes in the laboratory. In her editorial "Continental Philosophy and Bioethics," written for a special issue of the journal *Bioethical Inquiry,* Catherine Mills (2010) explains that the dearth of continental philosophy in the area of bioethics, for instance, can be attributed to the fact that "recent continental philosophy has been more concerned with ontological questions than normative ones" (p. 146). But Mills argues that the strict separation between questions of ontology and praxis is neither correct nor useful. As Mills (2010) suggests,

> Continental philosophy is often criticized, if not derided, for a perceived failure to provide normatively clear guidelines about "what should be done." Two brief responses can be given to this critique. First, it is inaccurate to imagine that ontological presuppositions do not impact upon normative resolutions; in fact, such presuppositions frame the very way in which normative questions can be posed, let alone the way in which one might respond to such questions. Second, it is short-sighted to think that Continental philosophers are not concerned with normative issues simply because they do not typically use the terminology of rights, interests and harms so central to liberal moral philosophy. A more expansive view would indicate that they are working toward the development of a new grammar and a new vocabulary of the normative . . . one that revolves

around notions of vulnerability, interdependence, embodiment, singularity, forms of life and bio-power. (p. 146)

Following cues from feminist scholars including Karen Barad, Patti Lather, Isabelle Stengers, and Donna Haraway, and drawing from the work of Gilles Delueze and Félix Guattari, this chapter examines how recent feminist engagements with questions of ontology and ethics through the notions of "intra-actions," "getting lost," "risk," and "becoming with" may influence our discussions on the development of new feminist research practices in the natural sciences. Furthermore, I will argue that, by turning to these "ontological presuppositions" that foreground this new and growing "vocabulary of the normative," the researcher may envision a new set of feminist research practices that works *with* instead of *against* more traditional forms of scientific practice.

It is perhaps important to emphasize here, in a handbook of feminist research, that although the categories of ethics, ontology, epistemology, and methodology are often separated, there are ways in which these categories cannot be easily dissected. In my own analyses of neuroscience, reproductive biology, and molecular biology research, for instance, I have been interested in understanding why certain materializations and treatments of biological molecules and organisms have taken form. Drawing from such theories and methodologies as standpoint theory, situated knowledges, agential realism, the methodology of the oppressed, and becoming molecular (Roy, 2004, 2007, 2008), I have called for feminist scientists who are working in the laboratory to learn to see the politics of why and how particular forms or representations of biological molecules and organisms are manifested over and over again. But I have also stressed the importance of bridging these critiques of biology with practical transformations in the processes of scientific knowledge production. My concern for supporting feminists in the laboratory has involved creating new practices for facing the everyday nitty-gritty technical core of scientific knowledge production in the natural sciences. However, my preference for the term "feminist practices" has not been unintentional. Much as the term *methodology* is used in this handbook to describe an overarching concept that includes the entire research process, one linking onto-logical and epistemological concerns with the design of research questions, my use of the term *practice* is meant to reflect the need for engagement with a full range of theoretical interventions that are available to the feminist scientist (Roy, 2008). These interventions can only be explored if she is simultaneously open to new modes of inquiry at the levels of episte-mology, ontology, and ethics. Once the feminist scientist finds herself in front of a lab bench, she may find that her feminist research prac-tices will begin to inform her more traditional scientific practices, and she will be motivated to ask difficult questions that typically would not have been raised in her traditional scientific training. A likely place that her feminist research practices will first lead her are to ques-tions that deeply interrogate the idea of who can be a knower and what can be known. For instance, how should she approach the object of study? How should she treat this object of study that is the other? What should she make of bio-logical and statistical differences that emerge in the measurement of this other? How will these differences influence her understanding of sub-jectivity? Alternatively, the feminist scientist working in the lab may find that questions of ontological and ethical significance may begin to emerge directly out of her repetitive and ritu-alized performances of the scientific method. If we are willing to take the time to have some joint conversations, we might realize that many scientists (feminist or not) are dealing with questions of ontology and ethics that are similar to those being raised within recent feminist sci-ence studies scholarship. With their hands-on experiences of working with live organisms and dealing with the difficulty of experimental reproducibility, biologists are accustomed to witnessing the fluidity, vulnerability, and unfixed "nature" of life. They have observed the extent of biological flux and variability, and, even though it may not be articulated as such, they are well aware of issues of ontologi-cal and ethical relevance. The question then is, How do we extend the scope of feminist research practices in the laboratory setting so that the feminist scientist can more readily open up to broader questions of ontology and ethics?

LEARNING TO READ CONTROVERSY IN THE LABORATORY

In her book *Meeting the Universe Halfway*, Karen Barad (2007) advances ontological dis-cussions in feminist science studies for the physical and natural sciences. Through her knowledge of quantum physics, she invites us to reexamine and reformulate our current feminist theoretical treatments of matter and reality. In her introduction, for instance, she shares with us the short story of an exchange between the quantum physicists Niels Bohr and Werner Heisenberg, leaving us with a powerful lesson in ontology:

> For Bohr, what is at issue is *not* that we cannot *know* both the position and momentum of a parti-cle simultaneously (as Heisenberg initially argued), but rather that particles do not *have* deter-minate values of position and momentum simulta-neously. . . . In essence, Bohr is making a point about the nature of reality, not merely our knowl-edge of it. What he is doing is calling into ques-tion an entire tradition in the history of Western metaphysics: the belief that the world is populated with individual things with their own independent sets of determinate properties. The lesson that Bohr takes from quantum physics is very deep and profound: there aren't little things wandering aim-lessly in the void that possess the complete set of properties that Newtonian physics assumes (e.g., position and momentum); rather, there is some-thing fundamental about the nature of measure-ment interactions such that, given a particular measuring apparatus, certain properties become determinate, while others are specifically excluded. Which properties become determinate is not governed by the desires or will of the experimenter but rather by the specificity of the experimental apparatus. (Barad, 2007, p. 19)

If we were to extend this idea, we might also start to recognize that the matters that we study as biologists, for example, or that we attempt to define and then regulate, do not preexist. In fact, "we" as we tend to define ourselves as scientists and knowers also may not preexist but rather, as Barad (2007) suggests, participate in the "mutual constitution of entangled agencies" (p. 33). What becomes "determinate" or known is a result of the specific interactions of an apparatus. What constitutes the apparatus includes a range of players including the knower, the tools of measurement, and discursive practices. This mutual entanglement is how Barad defines her idea of intra-action. The insights that follow from this ontological approach to matter and reality should be made to rub up against our development of new scientific practices in the natural sciences. As Mills (2010) suggests of other ontological presuppositions relevant to bioethics, Barad's "ontoepistemological framework" will also have an impact on normative resolutions in the physical and natural sciences (p. 44). For instance, Barad (2007) would have us orient ourselves to an ontological and epistemological framework whereby we become accountable for "the material nature of practices and how they come to matter" (p. 45). This sense of accountability and our role in the making of any phenomena partly describes Barad's broader idea of agential realism. Making her own entanglements between agential realism, intra-action, and objectivity, Barad (2007) further explains,

> In my agential realist account, scientific practices do not reveal what is already there; rather, what is "disclosed" is the effect of the intra-active engagements of our participation with/in and as part of the world's differential becoming. . . . What is made manifest through technoscientific practices is an expression of the objective existence of particular material phenomena. . . . Objectivity is a matter of accountability for what materializes, for what comes to be. It matters which cuts are enacted: different cuts enact different materialized becomings. (p. 361)

Barad's idea of the "agential cut" might be thought of as a momentary slice in time and space and a pause button in the apparatus of inquiry (which includes more than just the knower and what is thought to become the known). This pause allows for a "resolution of the ontological indeterminacy" and the "condition for the possibility of objectivity" (Barad, 2007, p. 175). To better illustrate Barad's notion of an agential cut and the usefulness of her onto-epistemological framework, I would like to share what I consider to be a very interesting story of technoscientific practices in the neurosciences.

Recently, scientist and Nobel laureate Linda Buck stirred up a storm of controversy when she retracted the findings from one of her own groundbreaking scientific works published in the highly acclaimed scientific journal *Nature*. Embedded within this controversy are deeper questions related to issues of ontology, epistemology, ethics, and the nature of discursive practices. Buck, who studies the olfactory systems in mammals and the mechanisms involved in odor and pheromone sensing, shared the 2004 Nobel Prize in Physiology or Medicine with Richard Axel. Working as a postdoctoral fellow in Axel's lab in the 1980s, she set out and successfully managed to identify a family of over a thousand genes that code for odor receptors (Howard Hughes Medical Institute, n.d.). Buck has since spent a very productive scientific career mapping out the neurological and molecular basis of olfaction. Her work has also revealed the interaction between olfaction and reproduction at the neuro-molecular level (Boehm, Zou, & Buck, 2005). In fact, of her many scientific accomplishments, Buck and her colleagues are known for utilizing molecular visualization techniques such as genetic tracing methods to better understand the neural circuits involved in the regulation of the olfactory system. Using transneural tracers, for instance, Buck and colleagues have shown that gonadotropin-releasing hormone (GnRH) neurons "receive pheromone signals from both odor and pheromone relays in the brain" and that "feedback loops are evident whereby GnRH neurons could influence both odor and pheromone processing" (Boehm et al., 2005, p. 683). Buck's lab was the first to have engineered transgenic mice in which GnRH neurons also expressed the transneuronal tracer barley-lectin (BL) and green fluorescent protein (GFP). By performing immunostaining of brain sections derived from these mice, Buck has been able to map the neural circuits of GnRH neurons visually.

The scientific work surrounding which the controversy has emerged, however, involved

Buck's research on the visualization of signaling from specific odorant receptors to specific clusters of neurons in the olfactory cortex (Zou, Horowitz, Montmayeur, Snapper, & Buck, 2001). In the March 2008 retraction of the original paper, Buck and her colleagues stated,

> During efforts to replicate and extend this work, we have been unable to reproduce the reported findings. Moreover, we have found inconsistencies between some of the figures and data published in the paper and the original data. We have therefore lost confidence in the reported conclusions. We regret any adverse consequences that may have resulted from the paper's publication. (Zou, Horowitz, Montmayeur, Snapper, & Buck, 2008, p. 120)

One of the reasons this retraction is so interesting and has caused such a stir is that it comes from a Nobel Prize winner—one who also happens to be a woman. Also, the retraction statement goes on to reveal that the actual experiments that have been put into question were not done by Buck herself but rather by one of the two primary authors of the article, Zhihua Zou, who was a former postdoctoral fellow in her lab. In scientific circles, the retraction of an article from a prestigious journal always makes for sensational news. Commenting on the retraction, an article entitled "How to Read a Retraction" posted in the science blog DrugMonkey (2008) suggests how strange it is to see an "author contribution" list in the retraction statement, a list that did not exist in the original article and one that outlines the exact contributions of each scientist. Basically, the "author contributions" information reveals that Zhihua Zou's work is what is under question here, and it is he who is being made to take the fall for the faulty research.

How can this event be read? The question is not so much what Buck should have done differently but what we, as feminist scientists, can see and know differently as a result of this event. If, for instance, we are to be guided by a feminist research practice that is informed by Barad's onto-epistemological framework, we might begin to ask some different questions. What are the ontological and ethical consequences that emerge from this research? What intra-active engagements have occurred? What is the nature of the discursive practices involved in this event? It is of course possible that the postdoctoral fellow somehow fudged the results. But from an agential realist (Barad, 2003, 2007) account, we would also have to ask what "effect" has been "disclosed" as a result of the intra-active engagements of Buck, her other scientific colleagues, the retraction statement, and of course, the odorant receptors and neurons of the olfactory cortex. It would appear that prior to November 2001, the intra-actions that had formed up until that point had resulted in a lack of scientific knowledge regarding the neural mechanisms of olfaction in mammals. In fact, until Buck's original work in the 1980s, the odorant receptors themselves (as we have come to know them) did not exist. After November 2001, upon the publication of their findings in the journal *Nature*, Buck and colleagues, as well as the entire scientific community that supports a system of peer review, entered into a new reality. New intra-actions between scientists, mice, the transneuronal tracer barley-lectin, and visualization techniques had disclosed a new type of biological relation, one of signaling between olfactory receptors and neurons. After March 2008, however, this knowledge was put into question and a formal retraction published in a scientific journal, thereby "dematerializing" that biological relationship that had come to be. How could this have happened? What changed?

From a traditional perspective of scientific method and objectivity, it is hard to say what happened, and perhaps pointing a finger toward the postdoctoral fellow seems like the easiest thing to do. From the perspective of Barad's agential realism, however, we might be able to imagine a new feminist praxis emerging that encourages us to raise some different possibilities for dealing with variability and flux in biology. We might suggest, for example, that the apparatus (that is, the combination of all the human, nonhuman, organic, and inorganic actors and measuring devices that went into creating the examined phenomenon) changed and thus new agential cuts were enacted. Buck claims that she is no longer able to repeat the findings of this initial experiment in her lab. But what is not readily known is that her lab moved from the time when the initial experiments were conducted. The results published in 2001 were based on work that her postdoctoral fellow had done at the Howard Hughes Medical Institute at the Harvard Medical School in Boston. Buck tried to repeat the experiment, likely with a new postdoctoral fellow, a new generation of transgenic mice, and a new water source to mix the chemical reagents needed for the experiment in her new lab in Seattle, at the Fred Hutchinson Cancer Research Center, University of Washington. Following the theoretical insights of Barad's onto-epistemological framework, the "inconsistencies" that Buck refers to in the retraction statement should in fact be read to imply much more than simply the lab notes taken by Zhihua Zou. Perhaps Buck's statement, in a way, also reveals the possibility for a new scientific approach to dealing with the variability and flux of biological matter. What we in fact may be dealing with here is a scientific experiment that can lead us to ask questions on the very nature of existence. Through the appearance and disappearance of signals between olfactory receptors and specific neurons, we may be able to see a scientific approach that moves from a theory of being that treats what it encounters in biology as fixed, to a theory of becoming that treats seriously the ideas of biological fluidity and flux. Whatever her motivations, Buck's actions do reveal to us that she is taking responsibility or "accountability for what materializes, for what comes to be" (Barad, 2007, p. 361) or not to be in this particular case. The "materiality" we are talking about here is the presence or absence of a biological signaling system involving protein receptors and neuronal cells. Buck is demonstrating the effect of a different set of technoscientific practices and intra-active engagements and thereby illustrating for us the enactment of "different materialized becomings" (Barad, 2007, p. 361) in reference to these very "real" biological matters.

I would suggest that Barad's emphasis on becoming accountable for what materializes could also be used to direct us toward a normative resolution. Indeed, the issue of accountability has long been at the heart of many ongoing conversations in feminist methodology. Barad's onto-epistemological framework, designed with accountability in mind, may however require us to reassess the direction in which some of our previous normative resolutions have progressed. First of all, if we can appreciate Barad's idea of

the "mutual constitution of entangled agencies," we may want to revisit, for instance, the ontological presuppositions entailed in our feminist discussions on the relationship between the knower and the known. We are forced to reexamine the previously untroubled and pre-given status of who counts as a knower, and what constitutes that which is to be known. Second, if it matters which cuts are enacted, it matters *how* those cuts are enacted. If it matters what is made manifest through technoscientific practices, it matters *how* something is manifested. Working within this onto-epistemological framework, then, what new normative questions can we draw upon to help us navigate our way through the many technoscientific practices available to us in the natural sciences?

I shall return to my first point regarding the relationship between the knower and the known later. Regarding my second point, I am inclined to say that the best way for the feminist scientist to begin grappling with these questions of *how* to enact such a cut is by using the technoscientific practices and tools that she already has readily available to her—in many cases the very same ones used by her nonfeminist counterparts. Perhaps the key is to keep on using the scientific method with the tools and technoscientific practices that she has at hand until a "subversive repetition" of the scientific method takes her to somewhere new (Lather, 2007, p. 33). This may also involve figuring out how to work alongside other scientists in the lab. But how do we live with the discomforts that arise from the problematic nature of the many methods, tools, and traditional scientific practices used to enact agential cuts on a daily basis? Can we draw from existing feminist praxes? In what follows, I suggest that some creative approaches to how we may chase these questions of *how* can be found through Patti Lather's recent work on "getting lost" and Isabelle Stengers's notions of "risks" and "joint perplexity."

LEARNING TO APPROACH THE QUESTION OF HOW

In her book *Getting Lost: Feminist Efforts Toward a Double(d) Science*, Patti Lather (2007) theorizes "getting lost" as a feminist methodology that also functions as a "fertile ontological space and ethical practice" (p. viii). Lather's getting lost can serve as a perfect example of how strict distinctions between ontology, ethics, epistemology, and methodology cannot easily be drawn. Lather (2007) articulates getting lost in the following way:

> At its heart, *Getting Lost* situates feminist methodology as a noninnocent arena in which to pursue questions of the conditions of science with/in the postmodern. Here we are disabused of much in articulating a place for science between an impossible certainty and an interminable deconstruction, a science of both reverence and mistrust, the science possible after our disappointments in science. Against tendencies toward the sort of successor regimes characteristic of what feminist philosopher of science, Sandra Harding (1991), terms triumphalist versions of science, this book asks how to keep feminist methodology open, alive, loose. . . . Given my interest in the science possible after the critique of science, my central argument is that there is plenty of future for feminist methodology if it can continue to put such "post" ideas to work in terms of what research means and does. (p. x)

Lather gets it. Being able to work in a laboratory and continue to raise that pipette despite our disappointments with science is indeed a crucial and challenging task for the feminist scientist. The list of disappointments is long and includes the distress caused by biological theories that have been used for deterministic ends and have contributed to the normalization of inequality, the regret over biotechnologies that have caused environmental harm and have been produced at the cost of many lives, and the frustration that can accompany the use of the scientific method. But, obviously, if she is to continue in the lab, a feminist scientist must learn how to look beyond these disappointments and continue to navigate her steps—or, as Lather puts it, learn to work within the "ruins." The feminist scientist must learn to take her disappointments with existing technological practices and look at them in a new light, as Lather (2007) suggests in her description of what she calls "Plateau 4: Working the Ruins":

> In such a time and place, terms understood as no longer fulfilling their promise do not become

useless. On the contrary, their very failures become provisional grounds, and new uses are derived. . . . To situate inquiry as a ruin/rune is to foreground the limits and necessary misfirings of a project, problematizing the researcher as "the one who knows." Placed outside of mastery and victory narratives, inquiry becomes a kind of self-wounding laboratory for discovering the rules by which truth is produced. (pp. 10–11)

Calling upon the earlier work of Judith Butler (1993), Lather (2007) continues,

> In this move, the concept of ruins is not about an epistemological skepticism taken to defeatist extremes, but rather about a working of repetition and the play of difference as the only ground we have in moving toward new practices. (p. 11)

Like Barad, Lather raises both ontological concerns in this brief statement as well as the ethical issue of accountability for "the one who knows." If the feminist scientist is to take these concerns to heart, however, and learn to work within the ruins of her discipline, *how* can she learn to turn herself willingly toward a practice of inquiry that is self-wounding? This is, as one might guess, perhaps not the easiest task to undertake, particularly in the natural sciences. But, as Lather suggests, "getting lost" is about becoming at ease with the idea of uneasiness. Learning to live with uneasiness is indeed most crucial here. Lather (2007) would have the feminist scientist see the benefits of getting lost by learning to live without absolute knowledge (p. 17) and by respecting the demand for complexity (p. 74). It may be of some benefit at this point to look back now for a moment and consider once again the story of Linda Buck— neuroscientist, Nobel laureate, and retractor of a published scientific work. Are we now able to see how feminist praxis can be used to read Buck's traditional scientific praxis in a new light? Can we learn to see how Buck herself may have "foregrounded the limits and necessary misfirings" of her project? Can we learn to read her retraction and response to the entire affair as an attempt to be "accountable to complexity"? Is Linda Buck getting lost?

The idea of moving toward new practices and finding a way toward getting lost is easier to appreciate when we recognize that the self-wounding practice Lather is advocating draws upon and is a productive engagement with the concept of difficult knowledge. As a pedagogical theory developed by Deborah Britzman (1998), "difficult knowledge" is built upon the idea that knowledge is produced in the classroom through difficult situations. Learning does not happen "naturally" on the part of students, simply by their reading a text, for example. Rather, sometimes students are made uncomfortable by what they are studying and through these "positive discomforts" are challenged to consider viewpoints that are not their own. Applying this concept to feminist theoretical and methodological discussions, Lather (2007) draws further from Britzman's work to suggest that being open to discomfiture is both principled and practical:

> There is a tendency to avoid the difficult story, to want to restore the good name of inquiry with these "new" and "better" methods. . . . Rather than heroism or rescue through some improved methodology, Britzman argues that we may be in a time and place where we are better served by ethnography if it is positioned as a means to see the need to be wounded by thought as an ethical move. (p. 8)

This openness to self-wounding is an openness to existing scientific knowledge, scientific praxes, and scientific tools that have disappointed us. But this openness also has the potential to create in us positive discomforts that will take us to a new place and help us see new ways to proceed. If the starting point for moving forward necessitates gathering up one's disappointments within a discipline, surely, if nothing else, the feminist scientist can begin to see the benefit of such an approach. There will be no shortage of places for her to begin her inquiry, and, in fact, her predicament may turn around once she begins to see how "rich in loss," as Lather (2007) would say, she is capable of becoming.

We now have some sense as to how the feminist scientist may go about enacting new agential cuts even if she has to use the traditional scientific techniques and tools that are readily available to her. The point may not be to create "new or better" methods but rather to work within the dominant tradition, in this case

the scientific method, and gain what new knowledge she can by accepting the loss that accompanies the use of this method—and by allowing herself to be wounded by her disappointments. The self-wounding that will occur because she works with the traditional technoscientific practices and tools in the natural sciences should not become paralyzing, and her disappointments should not stop her from continuing to stand in front of a lab bench. Rather, the movement that will occur from getting lost in this place of *how* may bring with it a new ethical position that neither claims to produce better knowledge than that produced by her nonfeminist peers nor chases after the ultimate "truth" (Lather, 2007, p. 76). Drawing from the work of Deleuze and Guattari, Lather (2007) further refines her description of the position of feminist scientific inquiry, which she sees as being distinct from any quest for universal truth:

> [B]ig bang theories of social change have not served women well. Here, something begins to take shape, perhaps some new "line of flight" (Deleuze and Guattari, 1987) where we are not so sure of ourselves and where we see this not knowing as our best chance for a *different sort of doing* in the name of feminist methodology. (p. 76, *emphasis added*)

As a methodology, then, at first glance getting lost may be confusing to the beginner feminist researcher in the natural sciences. We are used to following clearly labeled flow charts and nicely organized protocols. Getting lost may seem counterintuitive, and, in a way, shows us *how* to proceed without explaining exactly how. Addressing the very issue raised earlier by Catherine Mills, Lather avoids a normative program through her methodology of getting lost. As Lather (2007) says, getting lost aims to be "minimally normative" (p. 76). After years of training in a laboratory, I too am now drawn to those feminist approaches to answering these questions of *how,* which are minimally normative and much less prescriptive in their design.

Working from a similar line of flight but perhaps a different set of plateaus, I wish now to move the feminist scientist from a terrain filled with disappointments and loss to another set of productive discomforts. With the full intention of drawing on a minimally prescriptive framework,

I would like to work toward developing a feminist praxis for the natural sciences that adds an element of playfulness to getting lost. I would suggest that the feminist scientist might find some more ways to proceed with inquiry in the natural sciences by following the advice of the philosopher of science Isabelle Stengers. Stengers suggests that we need to learn how to take risks in scientific inquiry and search for moments of joint perplexity with other (more traditional) scientists. Both Lather and Stengers develop frameworks for inquiry that elicit sensory experiences, but whereas Lather's idea of getting lost is aligned with Derridean deconstruction, Stengers's conception of taking risks and discovering joint perplexities may be thought to work toward Deleuzian becomings. Both frameworks of inquiry are committed to learning to live without absolute knowledge.

I think we have to be willing to acknowledge that feminists aren't the only ones in the laboratory who have the capacity to be disappointed. Following cues from Stengers (2005) and her ecology of practices, I am interested in expanding upon how the feminist scientist might be able to work with instead of against the science that has produced her disappointments. How can the feminist scientist and her traditional scientific praxes impinge upon one another in order to take her to a new place? As Isabelle Stengers (2005) might suggest in response to this query,

> The problem for each practice is how to foster their own force, make present what causes practitioners to think and feel and act. But it is a problem which may also produce an experimental togetherness among practices, a dynamics of pragmatic learning of what works and how. This is the kind of active, fostering "milieu" that practices need in order to be able to answer challenges and experiment changes, that is, to unfold their own force. This is a social technology any diplomatic practice demands and depends upon. (p. 195)

To me, this quotation suggests that feminist scientists need to go deep into the methods and protocols of their research projects and gain an intimate knowledge of the inner workings of their experimental setups. They have to learn to recognize as many of the intra-acting players that comprise the apparatus as possible. This intimate knowledge will give them the courage to take risks and ask different questions. In her earlier text *Power and Invention*, Isabelle Stengers (1997) explains the importance of taking "risks" in order to move forward with scientific inquiry and find those moments of experimental togetherness that can turn risks into moments of joint perplexity to be shared with other scientists. This concept of risk forms the basis of an ontological and ethical framework that Stengers refers to as *cosmopolitics*. In his foreword to Stengers's book, Bruno Latour (1997) discusses the link between this notion of risk and Stengers's use of the term *cosmopolitics*:

> There are constructions where neither the world nor the word, neither the cosmos nor the scientists take any risk. These are badly constructed propositions and should be weeded out of science and society. . . . On the other hand, there exist propositions where the world and the scientists are both at risk. Those are well constructed, that is, reality constructing, reality making, and they should be included in science and society; that is, they are CC [cosmopolitically correct], no matter how politically incorrect they may appear to be. (p. xiv)

Drawing upon this passage from Latour, Sarah Kember, who works at the intersections of artificial life, biology, and cyberfeminism, suggests that "at the heart of Stengers's cosmopolitics is a philosophy in which scientific realism and social constructionism are not opposed" (Kember, 2003, p. 189). This idea is similar, in some ways, to Karen Barad's agential realism, which aims to move "beyond the well-worn debates that pit constructivism against realism" (Barad, 2007, p. 26). However, Kember (2003) goes on to state that "Stengers advocates a philosophy in which the object, the thing, the world is recognized as having something to say for itself. It is about embracing the risk which is therefore posed to science and to the scientist" (p. 89). At this point, perhaps, the ontological theories developed by Barad and Stengers part paths—in the idea of the existence of that thing in itself, followed by the idea of it having to say something for itself. Stengers's cosmopolitics also attempts to adopt a notion of "risky constructivism" (Latour, 1997, p. xiv), placing itself apart from those types of practices that promote scientific imperialism. As Steven Shaviro (2005) writes in his scholarly blog *The Pinocchio Theory,*

> She [Stengers] seeks, rather, through constructivism and the ecology of practices, to offer what might be called (following Deleuze) an entirely immanent critique, one that is situated within the very field of practices that it is seeking to change. . . . Stengers' vision, like Latour's, is radically democratic: science is not a transcending "truth" but one of many "interests" which constantly need to negotiate with one another. This can only happen if all the competing interests are taken seriously (not merely "tolerated"), and actively able to intervene with and against one another. (¶ 2)

The task for the feminist scientist, then, is not to argue for the erasure of difference or to critique traditional scientific practices in order to dismiss them. Nor is it sufficient simply to learn how to tolerate such practices. Movement must be made from seeking to secure a position of transcending "truth" to one of joint perplexity and "immanent critique." This process may involve reorienting ourselves to the matter, practices, and other scientists around us. In fact, this need for reorientation returns me to the point I raised earlier regarding accountability. The development of feminist praxes in the natural sciences depends on our ability to revisit the relationship between the knower and the known. If, as Stengers believes, we are able to picture ourselves in a location of immanent critique, we might then be able to see the formation of another kind of ethical response emerging between the incomplete knower and the incompletely known. Following Stengers, we might say that, in this plane of immanent critique and joint perplexity, all become partial knowers.

Feminist scientists can benefit from the combined vocabulary emerging from the work of Lather and Stengers. Getting lost and taking risks can be seen as feminist practices that help us to approach the question of how to deal with positive discomforts in a more productive way. A feminist approach to scientific praxis does question and interrogate the workings of a more traditional scientific model that also makes room for ethical reflection. To demonstrate the usefulness of these feminist practices, I would like to venture out into that place of the cosmos where issues of gender and sex differences have recently collided with traditional scientific praxis in neuroscience. This is certainly a terrain that is full of disappointments for the feminist scientist. I am particularly interested in the technological practices of neuroimaging. My own research in this area has revealed that this particular "possible unknown" (Haraway, 2008, p. 83) has been constructed by a large number of diverse entities. We are talking about a cosmos where some of these entities, but certainly not all, have decided, for instance, to use the intersecting space of gender and functional magnetic resonance imaging (fMRI) technology to study stereotype formation and bring forward, into a material realization, the idea that men really do see bikini-clad women as objects, much in the same way that they would view their power tools (Landau, 2009). Others have gone out of their way to bring forth a material representation that suggests that heterosexual men who are shown erotic images of women are likely to take larger financial risks (Knutson, Wimmer, Kuhnen, & Winkielman, 2008). We need, perhaps for the benefit of all parties concerned, to take a deep breath and try very hard to look for the positive discomforts that can emerge from this body of work.

How do we work among these ruins? How do we move on from getting lost in the disappointment? As I myself hesitate, I find that I am not the only one getting lost or even trying to take risks. Scientists are getting lost too— scientists such as Allan Reiss, Howard C. Robbins Professor of Psychiatry and Behavioral Sciences and Director of the Center for Interdisciplinary Brain Sciences Research (CIBSR) at Stanford University. In 2005, two articles were published out of the research conducted in Reiss's lab in the same online issue of the scientific journal *Proceedings of the National Academy of Sciences.* One article was entitled "Personality Predicts Activity in Reward and Emotional Regions Associated With Humor" (Mobbs, Hagan, Azim, Menon, & Reiss, 2005). The second article was entitled "Sex Differences in Brain Activation Elicited by Humor" (Azim, Mobbs, Jo, Menon, & Reiss, 2005). The two papers together addressed a major research focus in Reiss's lab and at the CIBSR, a focus on human resilience. In an interview for the *Stanford Report,* Reiss is quoted to have said, "The combined results of these two studies suggest that humor taps into several neural systems associated with gender or personality and helps to explain individual differences in humor appreciation" (Brandt, 2005, p. 2). As the authors explain, the first article deals with "the neural and behavioral associations between humor appreciation and the personality dimensions of introversion-extroversion and emotional stability-neuroticism" (Mobbs et al., 2005, p. 16502). It is the second article, however, on sex differences in the brain in response to humor, that seems to have garnered a great deal more publicity for Reiss.

My attention was first drawn to this particular fMRI study by an article published in the *Stanford Report* highlighting Reiss's abovementioned work. The article in the *Stanford Report* was entitled "Gender Differences Are a Laughing Matter, Study Reveals" (Brandt, 2005). At first, the play on words infuriated me. I would not have described this initial encounter as producing a positive discomfort. The study appeared to contribute to the current backlash against feminism by belittling and bringing into question the validity of the concept of gender itself. I was ready to dismiss the research. But what I came to realize after some time was that my frustration was also in part due to the cleverness of the title. Indeed, my initial reluctance or inability to move forward and get lost in this admission stopped me from seeing an opportunity for taking a risk and opening up a space for negotiation. I was unable to foreground the limits and misfirings of this work. I had to spend a great deal of time getting lost in the actual scientific research on gender, neuroscience, and laughter to realize that I could work in a productive way with this study—not by dismissing it, not by tolerating it, but rather by searching it for an opportunity of joint perplexity. Trying to work with the ruins of this study, I grabbed the title of the *Stanford Report* article from the other end, turned it around, and tweaked it to read "Study Reveals: Gender, Differences, and Laughing as Matter." The study now appealed to me. With the help of Barad's idea of intra-actions, Lather's concept of getting lost, and Stengers's notion of risk, I was able to move to

a new kind of engagement with this body of scientific work, one that allowed me to see a different possibility for the materialized becomings of gender, differences, and laughter (Barad, 2007, p. 361).

LEARNING TO APPROACH THE KNOWER AND THE KNOWN

As some readers may anticipate, no chapter on developing feminist praxes in the natural sciences would be complete without invoking the work of Donna Haraway. Her writing directs us toward some of the best kinds of getting-lost and risk-taking maneuvers that a feminist scientist can hope for. As I mentioned in the introduction to this chapter, I am interested in developing this new vocabulary of ontological and ethical gestures that the feminist scientist in the lab may find herself making. I am particularly interested in those gestures that position the feminist scientist as a knower in the same immanent plane as that which becomes known. In her latest book, *When Species Meet* (2008), Haraway develops her project on companion species relationships. Throughout the text, she asks two main questions: "(1) Whom and what do I touch when I touch my dog? and (2) How is 'becoming with' a practice of becoming worldly?" (Haraway, 2008, p. 3). Her concept of "becoming with" is complex, but it begins with the idea that to respond is to respect and that the practice of "becoming with" is to "remove the fibers of the scientist's being" (p. 23). To explicate her idea of "becoming with," Haraway (2008) first paints for us a scenario of the traditional scientist working within the framework of traditional scientific praxes; specifically, she describes the work of primatologist Barbara Smuts:

> Trained in the conventions of objective science, Smuts had been advised to be as neutral as possible, to be like a rock, to be unavailable, so that eventually the baboons would go on about their business in nature as if data-collecting humankind were not present. Good scientists were those who, learning to be invisible themselves, could see the scene of nature close up, as if through a peephole. The scientists could query but not be queried. People could ask if baboons are or are not social

subjects, or ask anything else for that matter, without any ontological risk either to themselves . . . or to their culture's dominant epistemologies. (p. 24)

Haraway goes on to explain that this traditional approach did not work for Smuts because the more she ignored the baboons, the less satisfied they were with her presence: "If she really wanted to study something other than how human beings are in the way, if she was really interested in these baboons, Smuts had to enter into, not shun, a responsive relationship" (p. 25). The practice of "becoming with" is then described as a type of dance that brings together the knower and the known in that moment of inquiry. "Becoming with" alludes to both ontological and ethical gestures that can inform how we as feminist scientists can learn to approach that relationship between the knower and the known. In fact, it goes one step further to disturb our ontological presuppositions of what constitutes a knower and the known. Haraway (2008) explains it this way:

> Instructed by Eva Hayward's fingery eyes, I remember that "becoming with" is "becoming worldly." *When Species Meet* strives to build attachment sites and tie sticky knots to bind intra-acting critters, including people, together in the kinds of response and regard that change the subject—and the object. Encounterings do not produce harmonious wholes, and smoothly preconstituted entities do not ever meet in the first place. Such things cannot touch, much less attach; there is no first place; and species, neither singular nor plural, demand another practice of reckoning. In the fashion of turtles (with their epibionts) on turtles all the way down, meetings make us who and what we are in the avid contact zones that are the world. Once "we" have met, we can never be "the same" again. (p. 287)

Haraway's practice of "becoming with" involves giving up human exceptionalism but also takes us away from making ethical gestures guided by a sense of "responsibility" toward those that are guided by the ability to respond. Haraway wants us to think about becoming "response-able" (p. 71).

It is from a parallel site of play, upon a plane of immanence, that I would like to toggle the switch a bit here and gather the effects of our growing vocabulary. In analyzing that relationship between the knower and what is to become the known, I am also interested in the ontological and ethical consequences of moving from gestures of responsibility to gestures of becoming response-able. As such, I would like to reflect more closely on what Barbara McClintock described as her approach to science; an approach that was based on developing a "feeling for the organism" (Keller, 1983). McClintock made this comment while being interviewed by Evelyn Fox Keller more than 25 years ago. It is not my intention here to attempt to channel McClintock or to get to the "real" meaning behind her statement. Rather, I would like to examine what this statement can now mean for those of us who are engaged in critical feminist science studies and who also share the insights of recent engagements with issues of ontology and ethics. As I mentioned previously, the question of ethics has been at the heart of feminist critiques of science from the very beginning and has revealed itself as a deep concern for the relationship between the knower and known. At its basis, McClintock's "feeling for the organism" is in fact about the relationship between the knower and the known. But what I want to pursue further here is the uncertainty that remains over the precise nature of that relationship and the boundaries being drawn between the knower and known. Is it a feeling "for" the organism or a "feeling" for the organism? The distinction I am trying to make here is subtle, but our attraction, our possible ontological commitment to one meaning over another has had and will continue to have deep impacts on the outcomes of the feminist praxes we develop for the natural sciences. I would like to suggest that McClintock's phrase might in fact be used to describe and examine two possible types of encounters that we can envision between the feminist scientist and the "natural world." In the first instance, the feminist scientist may learn to develop a feeling "for" the organism. Her interaction with that organism, an organism that is no longer seen as an object simply available at her disposal, is reevaluated so as to accommodate a new ethical relationship of responsibility between that scientist and the organism. This is how she becomes accountable. In attempting to develop a feeling "for" the organism, she will have to ask herself what her ethical commitment is toward that "other" organism. This type of ethical commitment may lead to separability and transcendence.

Alternatively, a "feeling" for the organism may also be interpreted as a type of feeling "around," a type of searching in motion and attentive movement or groping, a reaching toward and between always unfixed and incompletely knowable organisms in search of a response, any response—or, put differently, between and within assemblages that include the feminist scientist herself as well as that which she attempts to know. Feeling around for the organism can make us "response-able." What is at stake here, then, is the feminist scientist's orientation to an ethical, ontological, and epistemological framework that will operate in her everyday feminist practices. The ethical and ontological approaches we bring to our understanding and treatment of the relationship between the knower and known become different. What we might be referring to here is whether or not ethics precedes ontology or whether ethics *is* ontology for the feminist scientist (Smith, 2001, p. 179). Put another way, does she choose transcendence, or does she choose to remain in the plane of immanence? Is accountability about responsibility or response? Putting the question in Deleuzean terms, does the feminist scientist see her work operating in a molar/major key or in a molecular/minor key? While explaining the distinction between molar and molecular projects, Rosi Braidotti (2002) suggests that "the 'molar' line" is "that of Being, identity, fixity and *potestas* . . . and the 'molecular' line . . . that of becoming, nomadic subjectivity and *potentia*" (p. 84). My inclination is to think that the feminist scientist can develop scientific projects using either one of these approaches and that, to some extent, these projects may even operate simultaneously. I am not trying to suggest that one orientation to this framework is better than the other but rather that the type of projects that become available to the feminist scientist will differ depending on her particular orientation toward or within this framework.

I would like to propose that "feeling around" for the organism in this immanent sense can be used as a grammar or syntax that organizes the new vocabulary that is emerging from recent feminist engagements with issues of ontology and ethics. I am positing "feeling around" for the organism as a new feminist practice in the natural sciences that moves the theoretical contributions of "intra-actions," "getting lost," "risk," and "becoming with" into some form of normative resolution. Whereas "getting lost" may be thought of as a more introspective practice, feeling around invites an openness and movement of a more extroversive kind. Feeling around can be thought of as a minimally normative methodology, or as a feminist praxis in the natural sciences that opens the feminist scientist up to broader questions of ontology, ethics, and epistemology. It can be thought of as a way to connect with what we wish to know and with other scientists who also wish to know.

A New Vocabulary for Feminist Praxis

Thus far, this chapter has employed a range of feminist perspectives to envision a set of feminist research practices for the natural sciences. These theories are wide-ranging, and the line of flight or *way of thinking* that they create is not fixed and should not be seen as being singular in either impact or interpretation. In an effort to be minimally normative, this chapter has presented a flexible assemblage of feminist practices to motivate the feminist scientist to pick up and run with her own set of sensations and desires. In the last section of this chapter, I would like to follow up on some of my own desires of "feeling around" for the organism and explore a traditional scientific method that, in my opinion, is absolutely crucial in the natural sciences. Feminist scientists will recognize that learning how to read a scientific paper *closely* is indeed a much-needed feminist practice in the natural sciences. It is extremely important for the feminist scientist to learn how to read peer-reviewed scientific articles as texts and look for the possible ruins and risks entangled within these texts. By feeling around from the starting point of the text, she can begin to take risks and explore the science that remains possible after her disappointments in that science. To demonstrate how this feminist research practice might look, I would like to perform a very close reading of the gender and humor fMRI study mentioned previously and, in the process, mark as many intra-actions, ruins, risks, and opportunities for joint perplexity as I can along the way.

Reiss and his colleagues start off the scientific article on sex differences and humor by stating, "The long trip to Mars or Venus is hardly necessary to see that men and women often perceive the world differently [*Ruin 1*]" (Azim et al., 2005, p. 16496). They are right—the trip is unnecessary. But they go on to draw evidence from previous studies that have indicated that these differences in perception are "rooted in the brain's structural and functional organization [*Ruin 2*]," noting that "females have been credited with relatively more left-lateralized language and emotion processing, whereas males often tend toward right-lateralized visuospatial activity [*Intra-Action 1*]" (p. 16496). In their experiment, an event-related fMRI study was designed to better understand the sex-specific characteristics of humor-related neural networks. They suggest that their study builds on recent work attempting to find the neural basis of cognitive and affective components of humor appreciation [*Joint Perplexity 1*] (p. 16499). They assert that this has medical and clinical implications in that it helps to understand why there is a sex discrepancy when it comes to the frequency of mood disorders and why women appear to suffer from depression twice as much as men [*Intra-Action 2; Ruin 3; Risk 1*] (p. 16501). Their experimental design and results are summarized in the abstract of the article:

> Males and females share an extensive humor-response strategy as indicated by recruitment of similar brain regions. . . . Females, however, activate the left prefrontal cortex more than males, suggesting a greater degree of executive processing and language-based decoding. Females also exhibit greater activation of mesolimbic regions, including the nucleus accumbens, implying greater reward network response and possibly less reward expectation. These results indicate sex-specific differences in neural response to humor with implications for sex-based disparities in the integration of cognition and emotion. (p. 16496)

The cartoons used in the study and classified as "funny" or "unfunny" were preselected by participants described as being of similar age and background to the experimental subjects [*Intra-Action 3; Ruin 4*]. As stated in the abstract, there were many similarities found between male and female subjects. For instance, there was no significant difference between the sexes in the number of cartoons that were found to be funny. There was also no sex difference in rating how funny the humorous stimuli were on a scale of 1 to 10. The response times for rating funny cartoons were also similar between males and females. The researchers interpret these similarities to suggest that males and females "recruit a very similar coherence network when presented with funny stimuli, implying parallel cognitive correlates across sexes" (p. 16500).

However, several sex-based differences did emerge in the study. One significant difference was in the response time for females to unfunny cartoons. Interestingly, females were able to respond faster than males to cartoons that were "unfunny" [*Joint Perplexity 2*]. Second, the prefrontal cortex, an area in the brain associated with language and executive processing, seemed to light up more in the female brain. This suggested to the researchers that females make greater use of "executive functions" [*Risk 2*]. These include functions involved in coherence, working memory, mental shifting, verbal abstraction, self-directed attention, and irrelevance screening (p. 16500). When exposed to funny cartoons, female subjects also displayed more activity in a specific region of the brain associated with reward processing. The authors comment on how "surprising" this finding was to them [*Joint Perplexity 3*]. This result suggested to them that,

> surprisingly, females also demonstrate more robust recruitment of mesolimbic reward regions at the right NAcc, suggesting greater reward network activity during humor response. This small brain region has been implicated in psychological reward, including situations of self-reported happiness, monetary reward receipt, the processing of attractive faces, and cocaine-induced euphoria. . . . The correlation between unexpected reward and NAcc activation may be related to humor processing in that the more unexpected the "punch line," the greater the activity in the network as it encodes prediction error. In the present experiment, females

may expect the reward less, resulting in a large reward prediction error when the "punch line" arrives. (p. 16500)

The authors further develop the idea that females went into the study assuming that the cartoons would not be funny to also explain why their reaction time to the unfunny cartoons was much quicker than that of males [*Risk 3*]. The "lack of female expectancy [*Ruin 5*]" (p. 16500) allowed them to identify the unfunny stimuli faster. The authors end the article by once again referring to the medical and clinical significance of their work. They suggest that their study demonstrates the interaction of cognitive and affective pathways and may "help to inform the development of better diagnostic and therapeutic approaches to clinical depression [*Risk 4*]" (p. 16501). However, Reiss and colleagues (Azim et al., 2005) also end with a very powerful admission, as if casting out a net to draw in new sets of entanglements:

> Equivalent subjective amusement seems to recruit divergent processing strategies that manifest equivalent behavior, indicating either that these differences in neural processing appear without behavioral correlate, or that our behavioral assays are insensitive to more subtle dissimilarities. (p. 16501)

The authors admit that there may be more subtle dissimilarities between the sexes and that, within their experimental design, there is room for improvement, particularly in the setup of their behavioral assays [*Joint Perplexity 4*]. These kinds of admissions are usually placed in the discussion section of an article and are meant to convey methodological limitations as well as to signal the scientists' plans for future experiments. I think it is beneficial for the feminist scientist to see these admissions of limitations and directions toward future work as gestures toward joint perplexity. The feminist scientist should make sure to pause on these gestures as they can be used as opportunities to create experimental togetherness (Stengers, 2005). After reading the discussion, she can start feeling around for a new set of entanglements. At this point several questions can be brought forward. What are the ontological presuppositions that have gone into the research? How are the scientists in the paper becoming

accountable? How would a feminist scientist become accountable if she were to attempt the study? The next task would be to foreground the limitations of the study. What are the disappointments with the traditional scientific practices utilized in the study? Where are the ruins located? But she must also realize that her work is not done here—she must continue. How can she foreground the limits but then also move forward? How can she work toward creating a sense of experimental togetherness?

As I mentioned previously, feminist scientists aren't the only ones getting lost or taking risks. I have marked what I see as several of these moments in the study. These are all points of departure, places from where one can start feeling around for the organism and move forward in search of a new response. One such notable moment in the research occurs in a media podcast reporting on the findings from the study. In the podcast, Reiss can be seen and heard to literally slow down—all the way down to a pause to the point of getting lost—at several points during his commentary. The following is a transcription of an extremely interesting remark made by Reiss (2005) during the interview:

> In this study, the women participants were subjecting the cartoons to much more analytical processes and also not expecting necessarily that they would be funny. On the other hand, men, we speculate, expected perhaps all the cartoons to be funny and didn't subject them to as much analytical and language processing as the women. Now what's interesting about that is that that might have something to do [*pause*] with [*pause*] the [*long pause*] sense that men and women don't connect fully on humor.

Reiss seems to be getting lost and arrives at a loss for words, at his own ruin one might say, while trying to explain *why* differences may exist between the participants in the study. He pauses several times before taking a risk and deciding to go with a popular binary distinction in order to fill in the blanks. We can learn more by paying attention to each other's pauses. In the spirit of engagement, entanglement, creating experimental togetherness, and feeling around, I end here by offering a few thoughts on how a feminist scientist might proceed with this particular study.

Feeling Around 1: I would offer to the authors of the paper and others interested in the study that cartoons, like jokes, are often funny because they come at the expense of someone or something else. It may be important to take a closer look at how the funny and unfunny cartoons were selected in the first place. Who were the participants who selected the funniest cartoons? The paper states that they were of similar age and background to the subjects used in the experiment. Were they comprised of an equal distribution of males and females? What does a similar background mean in this case?

Feeling Around 2: We may also wonder together why both female and male subjects only found approximately 82% of the predetermined "funny" cartoons funny. Out of 30 cartoons, this translates into approximately 25 cartoons, leaving 5 cartoons that had been determined as funny to be designated, in fact, as unfunny. Did males and females find the same 5 predetermined funny cartoons to be unfunny? The paper mentions that the participants (described as "subjects" this time) were native English speakers. Were they all from similar ethnic backgrounds? Could markers such as ethnicity, race, class, or sexual orientation influence what one finds to be funny in a cartoon? Could religious, political, or other group affiliations influence what one considers funny in a cartoon?

Feeling Around 3: We may also wonder together why females in the study would have had shorter response times to unfunny cartoons. Why would the punch lines have been more unexpected in females than in males? Why would females go into the study expecting the reward from the cartoons to be less? Why would women have more highly active executive functioning capabilities, such as irrelevance screening, in response to a simple cartoon? Perhaps we should be searching for other aspects of human resilience that might be playing out here. Have women had to develop defense mechanisms against cartoons? Could it be that women are so accustomed to seeing visual imagery that is denigrating toward them, whether in the form of films, advertisements, television shows, or cartoons, that, when they are not disparaged by a cartoon, the pleasure derived from

not being derided lights up the same area of the brain as does cocaine-induced euphoria? Males went into the study with greater reward anticipation, thereby lowering the "unexpectedness" of the punch lines. Why would males go into this study already prepared to be amused? Could it be that they are accustomed to the knowledge that a cartoon's punch line will not come at their expense?

Feeling Around 4: Last, I am drawn to the idea that gender differences in humor are being studied in a lab that is dedicated to understanding human resilience. As we know, many feminists have long theorized laughter and humor as political practices (Cixous, 1981; Stengers, 2000a, 2000b). Feminists know a thing or two about resilience, and we have also learned that laughter and humor can be used in many different ways to sustain us. What might this experiment look like if it included a wider range of gender categories such as women who consider themselves butch, men who are comfortable being effeminate, and self-identified transgender individuals? What if males, females, and a wider assortment of experimental subjects were shown previously determined funny and unfunny *feminist cartoons?*

Conclusion

I would like to end by emphasizing that I extend these thoughts and questions not to dismiss the work conducted by scientists such as Reiss and his colleagues but rather as a movement toward a shared possible unknown. As Haraway (2008) states,

> Forbidding both the dream (and nightmare) of a final solution and also the fantasy of transparent and innocent communication, cosmopolitics is a practice for going on, for remaining exposed to consequences, for entangling materially with as many of the messy players as possible. (p. 106)

It is hard to know where these entanglements will take us, but I hope the theories and questions I have raised here can be read as feminist practices for moving forward in the natural sciences.

Developing feminist research practices specifically designed for the natural sciences used to feel a little bit like putting a letter into a bottle and sending it out into the sea; it was hard to predict if a feminist scientist working away quietly and diligently in a lab, without a connection to a broader feminist community, was ever going to find the research practice, let alone pick it up. Over the last few years, however, I have been delighted to see the growing number of undergraduate double majors in women's studies and biology. It will no doubt be very exciting to watch as these feminists enter the lab and start feeling their way around.

Discussion Questions

1. What is ontology, and why are questions of ontology important to the development of feminist methodologies?

2. In Lather's minimally normative practice of getting lost, why is it important for the feminist scientist to learn how to identify the ruins or disappointments in her discipline?

3. Why is it important for the feminist scientist to learn how to reach out to other scientists and build an atmosphere of experimental togetherness? How can the feminist practices of becoming accountable, getting lost, and feeling around help her toward this goal?

4. What is the distinction between transcendence and immanence? Why are immanent critique and Stengers's cosmopolitics useful as ethical and methodological guides for the feminist scientist?

Online Resources

Feminist Epistemology and Philosophy of Science

http://plato.stanford.edu/entries/feminism-epistemology/

This section of the online *Stanford Encyclopedia of Philosophy* is a great resource for the feminist scientist. It introduces newcomers to the field to the many different theoretical approaches that feminists have used to engage with scientific inquiry. There is also a short but helpful section on feminist postmodernism.

subRosa

http://www.cyberfeminism.net/

This website contains the projects and publications of the feminist collective subRosa. The collective is comprised of interdisciplinary feminist artists whose art and social activism can help us to imagine new feminist practices for the lab. The group is committed to exploring and critiquing the intersection of information and biotechnologies on women's bodies.

Relevant Journals

Australian Feminist Studies

Configurations

differences: A Journal of Feminist Cultural Studies

Frontiers: A Journal of Women's Studies

Hypatia: A Journal of Feminist Philosophy

Signs: Journal of Women in Culture and Society

REFERENCES

Azim, E., Mobbs, D., Jo, B., Menon, V., & Reiss, A. L. (2005). Sex differences in brain activation elicited by humor. *Proceedings of the National Academy of Sciences, 102*(45), 16496–16501.

Barad, K. (2003). Posthumanist performativity: Toward an understanding of how matter comes to matter. *Signs: Journal of Women in Culture and Society, 28*(3), 801–831.

Barad, K. (2007). *Meeting the universe halfway: Quantum physics and the entanglement of matter and meaning.* Durham, NC: Duke University Press.

Boehm, U., Zou, Z., & Buck, L. B. (2005). Feedback loops link odor and pheromone signaling with reproduction. *Cell, 123*, 683–695.

Braidotti, R. (2002). *Metamorphosis: Towards a materialist theory of becoming.* Cambridge, UK: Polity Press.

Brandt, M. (2005, November 7). Gender differences are a laughing matter, study reveals. *Stanford Report.* Retrieved September 1, 2007, from http://med.stanford.edu/news_releases/2005/november/humor.html

Britzman, D. (1998). *Lost subjects, contested objects: Towards a psychoanalytic inquiry of learning.* Albany: State University of New York Press.

Butler, J. (1993). Poststructuralism and postmarxism. *diacritics, 23*(4), 3–11.

Cixous, H. (1981). The laugh of the Medusa. In E. Marks & I. de Courtivron (Eds.), *New French feminisms* (pp. 245–264). New York: Schocken Books.

Deleuze, G., & Guattari, F. (1987). *A thousand plateaus: Capitalism and schizophrenia* (B. Massumi, Trans.). Minneapolis: University of Minnesota Press.

DrugMonkey. (2008, March 5). *How to read a retraction.* Retrieved May 2, 2009, from http://scienceblogs.com/drugmonkey/2008/03/how_to_read_a_retraction.php

Haraway, D. (1997). *Modest_Witness@Second_Millenium.FemaleMan©_Meets_ Oncomouse™: Feminism and technoscience.* New York: Routledge.

Haraway, D. (2008). *When species meet.* Minneapolis: University of Minnesota Press.

Harding, S. (1991). *Whose science? Whose knowledge? Thinking from women's lives.* Ithaca, NY: Cornell University Press.

Howard Hughes Medical Institute. (n.d.). *Linda B. Buck, Ph.D.* Retrieved May 1, 2009, from http://www.hhmi.org/research/investigators/buck_bio.html

Keller, E. F. (1983). *A feeling for the organism: The life and work of Barbara McClintock.* New York: W. H. Freeman and Company.

Kember, S. (2003). *Cyberfeminism and artificial life.* New York: Routledge.

Knutson, B., Wimmer, G. E., Kuhnen, C. M., & Winkielman, P. (2008). Nucleus accumbens activation mediates the influence of reward cues on financial risk taking. *Neuroreport, 19*(5), 509–513.

Landau, E. (2009, April 2). *Men see bikini-clad women as objects, psychologists say.* Retrieved February 19, 2009, from http://www.cnn.com/2009/HEALTH/02/19/women.bikinis.objects/index.html

Lather, P. (2007). *Getting lost: Feminist efforts toward a double(d) science.* Albany: State University of New York Press.

Latour, B. (1997). Foreword. In Isabelle Stengers, *Power and Invention* (pp. vii–xix). London: University of Minnesota Press.

Mills, C. (2010). Continental philosophy and bioethics [Editorial]. *Bioethical Inquiry, 7*, 145–148.

Mobbs, D., Hagan, C., Azim, E., Menon, V., & Reiss, A. L. (2005). Personality predicts activity in reward and emotional regions associated with humor. *Proceedings of the National Academy of Sciences, 102*(45), 16502–16506.

Reiss, A. (2005). *Gender differences are a laughing matter* [podcast]. Retrieved July 1, 2011, from http://med.stanford.edu/news_releases/2005/november/humor.html

Roy, D. (2004). Feminist theory in science: Working towards a practical transformation. *Hypatia: A Journal of Feminist Philosophy, 19*(1), 255–279.

Roy, D. (2007, Summer). Somatic matters: Becoming molecular in molecular biology. *Rhizomes: Cultural Studies in Emerging Knowledge, 14.* Retrieved July 1, 2011, from http://www.rhizomes.net/issue14/roy/roy.html

Roy, D. (2008). Asking different questions: Feminist practices for the natural sciences. *Hypatia: A Journal of Feminist Philosophy, 23*(4), 134–157.

Shaviro, S. (2005). Cosmopolitics. *Pinocchio theory.* Retrieved February 12, 2009, from http://www.shaviro.com/Blog/?p=401

Smith, D. (2001). The doctrine of univocity: Deleuze's ontology of immanence. In M. Bryden (Ed.), *Deleuze and religion* (pp. 167–183). New York: Routledge.

Stengers, I. (1997). *Power and invention: Situating science.* London: University of Minnesota Press.

Stengers, I. (2000a). Another look: Relearning to laugh. *Hypatia: A Journal of Feminist Philosophy, 15*(4), 41–54.

Stengers, I. (2000b). *The invention of modern science.* Minneapolis: University of Minnesota Press.

Stengers, I. (2005). Introductory notes on an ecology of practices. *Cultural Studies Review, 11*(1), 183–196.

Zou, Z., Horowitz, L. F., Montmayeur, J. P., Snapper, S., & Buck, L. B. (2001). Genetic tracing reveals a stereotyped sensory map in the olfactory cortex. *Nature, 414*, 173–179.

Zou, Z., Horowitz, L. F., Montmayeur, J. P., Snapper, S., & Buck, L. B. (2008). Retraction of "Genetic tracing reveals a stereotyped sensory map in the olfactory cortex." *Nature, 452*, 120.

16

PARTICIPATORY ACTION RESEARCH AND FEMINISMS

Social Inequalities and Transformative Praxis

M. Brinton Lykes and Rachel M. Hershberg

Community- and organization-based research projects that are conducted by local participants and university-based researchers and seek to transform social inequalities have been described as action research (AR), participatory research (PR), or participatory action research (PAR). This chapter explores research at the interface of feminisms and these participatory and action research processes and outcomes. It begins with an overview of the multiple "origin stories" of PAR, AR, and PR that frame the research processes and projects to be discussed later in the chapter. In the introduction, we situate feminist and participatory and action research as modes of praxis with shared and distinctive theoretical assumptions and applications. In the second section, we present a framework for understanding work at the interface of feminist and participatory and action research and then describe various social locations or sites wherein work at this interface has been engaged, including schools, health contexts, and local communities as well as among "people on the

move." The third section presents a current framework for organizing at this interface, which we characterize herein as "feminist-infused participatory and action research," that is, an iterative set of processes and outcomes performed in one of three ways: (1) to reposition gender, race, and class; (2) to excavate indigenous cultural knowledges and generate voices; or (3) to deploy intersectionality as an analytic tool for transformation. We present and discuss multiple examples of work that reflects each of these three iterations of feminist-infused participatory and action research. In the fourth section of the chapter, we explore the similarities and differences within and across these distinctive iterations of feminist-infused participatory and action research and discuss some design and implementation challenges facing coresearchers.[1] We offer this framework as one "pause" in the journey of a developing praxis and as a resource for thinking systematically and critically about research at the interface of feminisms and PAR, AR, and PR. We conclude the chapter with a discussion of the possibilities of creating processes and outcomes in the academy and in the community that aspire to and generate transformative praxis.

Origin Stories

Some have argued that the participatory and action research approaches to knowledge generation and social change noted above can be traced back to early Greek philosophers or to indigenous communities (see, e.g., Eikeland, 2001). Others trace their beginnings to 20th-century social scientific research, more specifically to the work of Kurt Lewin in the 1940s and the experiential learning and inquiry communities of the 1960s (see Adelman, 1993; Greenwood & Levin, 1998; Gustavsen, 2001). Moreover, action research contributed importantly to the fields of organizational behavior and development, introducing strategies for enhancing communication and cooperation as well as system changes. Lewin and his students developed such practices in industry and business (Whyte, 1991).

Adelman (1993) defined action research as "the means of systematic enquiry for all participants in the quest for greater effectiveness through democratic participation" (p. 7). Zeichner (2001) identified five major educational AR traditions in the English-speaking world and argued that some draw on emancipatory practices developed in Asia, Africa, and Latin America, extending their focus beyond the school to the local community (see also Brydon-Miller & Greenwood, 2003, for a brief historical overview). This emancipatory perspective moved well beyond Lewin's work. The latter neither critiqued broader societal structures nor analyzed "power bases that define social roles and strongly influence the process of any change" (Adelman, 1993, p. 10).

Those who live and work in Latin America, Africa, and Asia and engage in AR, PR, or PAR are more likely to trace the origin of their work to Paulo Freire (1970) or Orlando Fals-Borda (1985) and Mohammad Ansiur Rahman (Fals-Borda & Rahman, 1991). In the late 1960s and 1970s in India and Latin America, liberation educators and social change advocates were influenced by Paolo Freire's understanding of critical consciousness, that is, *conscientização*

(conscientization). These educators and community activists sought to create participatory processes that tap into and engage local knowledge systems toward emancipatory practices. Participatory rural appraisal (PRA) within the context of community development and humanitarian aid initiatives in the rural communities of Africa and Asia embraces similar values. Notably absent from this work, despite its variability and women's involvement in a wide range of community-based research, was an explicit focus on gender or women's oppression. Moreover, although PAR, AR, and PR each has a distinct "origin story," unless specifically noted, we refer to them collectively as participatory and action research in this chapter. Further, we refer to work at the interface of feminist research and PAR, AR, and PR as feminist-infused participatory and action research, unless otherwise noted.

Approximating an Understanding of PAR, AR, and PR

The seeming independence of these origin stories belies a set of overlapping values and goals as well as a set of basic assumptions about power inequalities and social oppression. Moreover, PAR, AR, and PR seek to promote collective processes of inquiry that expose the ideological, political, and social processes underlying and permeating systems of inequality. They seek to solve everyday problems and—to a greater or lesser extent—to transform the social inequalities exposed through research by facilitating and engaging in specific actions that contribute toward human well-being and a more just and equitable world. PAR, AR, and PR are approaches to research wherein collaborations or partnerships are formed between those directly affected by an issue or problem that becomes the focus of the project (often called insiders, participants, community members) and others with technical skills and formal knowledge (often called outsiders, researchers, facilitators, catalysts) that complement indigenous knowledge systems and expertise to facilitate knowledge construction, education, collaborative learning, and transformative action. PAR, AR, and PR thus emphasize the processes as well as the outcomes of research and the sharing of results within and beyond the participant communities.

PAR, AR, and PR projects seek to generate knowledge and practice that is of genuine interest to all coresearchers. Thus PAR, AR, and PR projects necessitate the development of "mutually dependent and cooperative relationships" (Martin, 1996, p. 88). Participants engaged in PAR, AR, and PR transform themselves at a very personal level, and the process typically politicizes them with respect to relationships among coresearchers and to the desired outcomes (Khanna, 1996). The generation of shared spaces wherein the various knowledge systems and skill levels of all research participants can be valued, shared, and exchanged is critical to this work. These spaces facilitate the development of shared procedures for generating, appraising, and reflecting on the data gathered during the research process. Institutional, professional, or personal interests and choices are negotiated within a primary commitment to generate knowledge and action toward addressing immediate social issues or problems.

The methodology and epistemology of participatory and action research challenge the assumptions of neutrality and objectivity that characterize much empirical social scientific and educational research. Participatory and action researchers emphasize multiple ways of knowing and involvement throughout the research process, striving for consensual validation through data collection and analysis that is formulated around local priorities. Thus, an understanding of knowledge as socially constructed within particular social, cultural, and linguistic communities characteristic of most participatory and action research has contributed to Peter Reason and Hilary Bradbury's (2008) argument that PAR, AR, and PR have embraced the mid- 20th-century postmodern linguistic and cognitive turn within social science. Despite this embrace, the problem-posing processes characteristic of AR, PR, and PAR presume that there is a reality that facilitates and constrains all social relations, confirming that participatory and action researchers accept at least the basic assumption of positivism that there is a "real" and material social world. The turn toward action, characteristic of all PAR, AR, and PR, enriches the interface of the modern and postmodern and creates a synergy that

is shared by the diversities of practice engaged by these researchers.

Feminisms and the Research Process

Although early participatory and action researchers criticized power inequalities and sought to redress social injustice, they failed to either include women as independent actors in their local projects or problematize gender oppression and heterosexism. Women and, more specifically, feminists were marginal and marginalized in the early articulations of these research processes, as well as at professional gatherings (see, e.g., Maguire, 2001, for details). Yet, at this same time, feminists were making important contributions to social movement building (see, e.g., Evans, 1979; Freeman, 1975; Friedan, 1963; Rosen, 2000) and to university-based scholarship (see, e.g., Personal Narratives Group, 1989; Roberts, 1981).

Despite the importance of this work, women of color (see, e.g., Davis, 1981; Moraga & Anzaldúa, 1983; Spelman, 1988) criticized this second wave feminism for its oversimplified and universalizing tendency to essentialize women's oppression and ignore diversities of race and social class, as well as for its failure to analyze critically racism and class oppression within and among its adherents (see, e.g., hooks, 1981, and Lorde, 1984, among many others). Women of color within the United States (Collins, 1998; hooks, 1984) and postcolonial theorists of color (Mohanty, 2003; Trinh, 1989; Williams & Chrisman, 1994) describe their work as womanist (Walker, 1983), Black feminist (see Collins, 1996), or *mujerista* (Dyrness, 2008). Each challenges the white privilege characteristic of much second wave feminist organizing and scholarship and contributes to the development of an increasingly diverse and critical theory, research, and practice.

Early contributions to an emerging field of feminist research methodology include Barbara Du Bois (1983), Sherna Gluck and Daphne Patai (1991), Sandra Harding (1986), and the Personal Narratives Group (1989). This work has been importantly complemented and extended by the work of postcolonial theorists (e.g., Sandoval, 2000) who inform contemporary theory and activist research, particularly work that crosses national, linguistic, and cultural borders (see, e.g., Mitchell & Reid-Walsh, 2002; Mohanty, 2003). Feminist research is not (only) about gender differences but critically explores social status and the participants' positionalities (see Collins, 1990; Naples, 2003; Smith, 1987, 1991); and feminist researchers focus their work on generating consciousness (their own and that of others with whom they work) about gendered oppression and how it constrains women's lives. Thus, despite its important grounding in women's experiences, this work was typically neither community-based nor focused on community-identified social problems.

In 1992 sociologist Shulamit Reinharz argued that feminism is a perspective, not a research method, identifying seven themes characteristic of feminist research, including that it is guided by feminist theory, involves an ongoing criticism of nonfeminist scholarship, may be trans- or interdisciplinary, aims to create social change, and strives to represent human diversity. Reinharz argued further for a diversity of research methods, a diversity reflected in publications over the past 20 years (see, e.g., *Feminism and Psychology* [1991–] or *Signs: Journal of Women in Culture and Society* [1975–]) and, as significantly, the first edition of this *Handbook* (Hesse-Biber, 2007).

In addition to this diversity of methods, feminists using a single research method do so from different epistemological stances or frameworks. For example, constructivist or critical theorist feminists may distribute surveys or engage other, more positivist, research methods to gain understanding of or to develop a critique of existing relations for the purposes of transforming them rather than for the purposes of explanation, prediction, or control, characteristics of more positivist and postpositivist research designs (Denzin & Lincoln, 2000). This latter incorporation of a diverse range of methods parallels a development in participatory and action research, as will be illustrated in this chapter.

More recently, feminist critical scholarship has informed contemporary feminist and participatory and action researchers. For example, Patricia Hill Collins's (1990) and Dorothy Smith's (1987, 1991) discussions of how power shapes gender relations within and across racial,

class, and sexual diversities are reflected in the work of Fine, Maguire, Lykes, McIntyre, and others who work at the interface of feminism and participatory and action research. These researchers' practices reflect the critical feminist epistemologies wherein women's work is problematized and women's agency tapped toward activism and social change. They use a diverse range of research methods to facilitate distinct processes of knowledge construction, engagement with women, political activity, and social change work. They are representative of a much wider group of feminist researchers who have contributed significantly to theory and practice within participatory and action-engaged research, thus contributing to an important interface of feminist and participatory and action research explored herein.

The remainder of this chapter will focus on women and men who engage research at this interface. In the next section, we define, and then explore, developments at the interface of feminist and participatory and action research, clarifying three distinctive iterations of these action-reflection processes and outcomes, which we offer as a possible framework for better understanding the contributions of this praxis to women's well-being and personal and social transformative change.

WORKING AT THE INTERFACE OF PARTICIPATORY AND ACTION RESEARCH AND FEMINISMS

Participatory and action research theory and practice share multiple underlying assumptions and principles with feminist and womanist social movements, research, and scholarship. Yet, despite these similarities, there has been—and, some would argue, continues to be—relatively little visibility of feminisms within PAR, AR, and PR. One example of an effort to redress this absence was a workshop convened in the summer of 2001, wherein Mary Brydon-Miller, Patricia Maguire, and Alice McIntyre invited a group of feminists who engage in action and participatory praxis to "meet at the crossroads" and critically explore the intersection of what some perceived to be overlapping circles of the feminist and action research communities. The resulting coedited volume (Brydon-Miller, Maguire, & McIntyre, 2004) explores a range of critical issues among women and men working at the interface of feminisms and PAR, AR, and PR, as well as the equally challenging dynamics between those working from the academy and those working from the community. In 2003, Cornell University brought together academic and community feminists and activists who engage action research methods to, among other things, explore the possibility that the interface of feminisms and action research might facilitate the revitalization of both, at least for those whose praxis is based in or emerges from the academy (see http://www.einaudi.cornell.edu/parfem/parfem.htm). There, Patricia Maguire argued for the importance of reenergizing and repoliticizing participatory work. She suggested that participatory and action research brings to feminist theory a challenge to act, while feminism has importantly challenged action researchers to turn their critical lens toward women's experiences of oppression and marginalization as well as to the important strengths women bring to social change work (see Fine, 1994, for similar arguments, and Patai, 1994, for a contrasting position). The diversity of sites where coresearchers engage in participatory and action research include, among others, educational and service delivery institutions, local communities (including economic and social development projects within these communities), and organizational or informal spaces. Within these arenas, there is a breadth and diversity of participatory and action research, but those projects that aspire to or actualize transformative praxis are the focus of this chapter.

Approximating an Understanding of Work at the Interface

Drawing on Maguire's work (1987, 2001, 2004), as well as on the work reviewed in this chapter, we argue that researchers who work at the interface of feminisms, participation, and activism embrace a continuous and iterative process or approach to life, an attitude toward being and doing "in the world" rather than a single research method. This approach seeks, in the first place, to foreground women who live at the intersections of oppressions and social inequalities—or privileges—due to gender, race, class, sexualities, abilities, ethnicities, languages, and other systems of oppression. As significantly, this work recognizes and values women's multiple intelligences, diverse ways of knowing, and frequently contradictory and sometimes silent or silenced voices, and it presses to develop "just enough" trust among coresearchers to initiate shared action-reflection processes. Coresearchers include girls, boys, and women and men of color, those with limited incomes or with special needs, as well as refugees, asylum seekers, and those who are undocumented. The work requires creating "safe enough" spaces that strive to be inclusive and supportive of these developing relationships; it necessitates valuing strengths, capabilities, social capital, and resiliency. Some of these efforts press beyond the inclusion of diverse voices, engaging gender as a social construct and a tool for change. They seek to be sufficiently challenging to engage us in reflective critical practices that problematize the matrices of power, privilege, and domination that circulate among us and in our social worlds. Some are grounded in feminist theory and discourse, reaching toward transformative praxis through building movements that support individual and social change.

Despite these strengths, as participatory and action research methods have become increasingly visible—in universities; in the work of governments, international organizations (e.g., the World Bank), and nongovernmental organizations; in schools and universities; and in the research literature (see, e.g., Dick, 2004, for a review)—there is a growing concern that PAR, AR, and PR risk becoming depoliticized tools that persist in marginalizing some voices, including those of women, from decision making and the exercise of power. Similar concerns have been raised repeatedly by communities of color and women vis-à-vis the theory and research generated by feminist and race theorists in the academy. More recently, Maguire has joined Frisby and Reid (Frisby, Maguire, & Reid, 2009) to argue further that feminist theories have a critical role to play in action research with transformative goals. This chapter seeks to elucidate some of this work.

Selecting Research Strategies

Methods or research strategies and resources are selected for their appropriateness to the processes already described, that is, in order to gather diverse types of information or data that serve iterative discovery, analysis, co-learning, and action processes. The participation of coresearchers with a wide range of abilities, languages, and skills demands a diversity of methods that facilitate engagement among all. Some examples of such participatory methods include focus groups; observational strategies such as ethnographic and participant observation; visual texts including collages, collective drawings, photography, and PhotoVoice (see Wang, 1999); oral histories, life stories, narratives, and testimony; embodied movement including dramatization, dramatic multiplication, and sculptures; community and asset-based mapping exercises; and, more recently, digital and other web-based communication and documentation resources. These are used individually or in combination to facilitate active engagement among all coresearchers and with others in participating groups, organizations, or communities. As significantly, researchers who enter a community or organization "from outside" its linguistic, cultural, racial, gender, sexual, or ability borders have used these methods to generate processes of discovery whereby potential participants can clarify and engage with local or traditional knowledge systems.

Strategies for appraising, reflecting on, and analyzing shared experiences used in the exemplars presented in this chapter and by others engaged in similar work include content analysis, grounded theory analysis, narrative analysis, and a range of techniques for analyzing or re-presenting collages and other visual resources. In addition to these participatory methods, techniques that require more advanced technical skills, inaccessible to some participants, are reserved for specific tasks that have been identified by all coresearchers as serving the goals of their shared work. A nonformally educated community group with no statistical experience might contract with a coresearcher or external consultant with the technical expertise when the group itself agrees that these resources will advance their goals. For example, epidemiological data about their communities have sometimes been critical to the activist goals of local HIV/AIDS groups. Large volumes of survey data may need to be reduced and interpreted to complement other knowledge sources generated by more participatory strategies. A university-based technical consultant who works at the behest of the group or community may facilitate a group's achieving its research goals. Alternatively, a university-based researcher's assertion of her or his academic expertise in the absence of a collective request may be experienced as a threat (for further discussion see http://www.incommunityresearch.org/research/paresearch.htm). These methodological considerations are important to think about when embarking on a feminist-infused participatory and action research project, as will be illustrated through reviewing an array of examples of such work in subsequent sections of this chapter.

Sites of Engagement

Work at the interface of feminisms and PAR, AR, and PR takes place in a wide array of sites and with diverse populations. Below we discuss some of these, seeking to clarify the importance of place in the design and implementation of feminist-infused participatory and action research projects.

Schools

Action research in schools emerged in the 1970s in England during the teacher-as-researcher movement that was characterized by school-based curriculum reforms. This movement was a reaction to an exclusive focus on measurable learning outcomes, and it emphasized the importance of process values as a basis for redesigning the curriculum. Since then, there has been a virtual explosion of action and participatory research processes in the English-speaking educational world (Brydon-Miller & Maguire, 2009).

PAR strategies have been used by educators in preservice and inservice teacher training with a variety of goals: to improve the quality of instruction in classrooms and whole school districts, to measure the effectiveness of curricula and instructional changes, to transform particular classroom settings and educational systems, and to develop and disseminate knowledge about issues of particular relevance to schools (see Zeichner, 2001, for a review of this literature). Educators are likely to make better decisions and engage in more effective teaching and learning practices if they engage in inquiry research about their own classroom practices. Moreover, PAR *with* students—both in school and in afterschool programs—is critical because knowing youth's perspectives *and* acting with and on behalf of young people in education increases opportunities for developing more equitable education (Brydon-Miller & Maguire, 2009). Thus, practitioner inquiry based on PAR principles encourages educators to work with community partners, families, *and* their students to explore the social, economic, and political contexts of schooling while examining the roles educators, students, and other stakeholders can play in transforming unequal educational systems and the societies that engender them (Brydon-Miller & Maguire, 2009). Most explicitly, political forms of participatory and action research in education, whether or not explicitly feminist, draw on the work of the Brazilian educator, activist, and political leader Paulo Freire (1970; see http://www.paulofreire.org/ for a review of Freire's work). Feminists working in educational contexts from a Freirean perspective have sought to develop praxis that raises consciousness about, for example, the gendered, racialized, and class-based dimensions of the achievement gap reflected in high-stakes test outcomes. This educationally focused work has been extended to include prisons, urban and rural barrios, public health initiatives, and beyond.

Health Contexts

Public health initiatives and action research methodologies converge in community-based research projects, of which there is a flourishing body in Europe, the United States, Canada, and the majority world.[2] Issues of sexual health (e.g., sexually transmitted diseases and reproductive health) as well as the health needs of women and lesbian, gay, bisexual, and transgender communities are also commonly addressed by community-based participatory research (CBPR; Minkler & Wallerstein, 2003). More recently, health practitioners and researchers have used CBPR methods to address a range of health problems

disproportionately affecting particular populations. These include, for example, diabetes and obesity (Harvey et al., 2009), multiple sclerosis, and other chronic illnesses (Allen & Hutchinson, 2009; Kralik, Koch, & Eastwood, 2003).

At least since the publication of the first edition of *Our Bodies, Ourselves* (Boston Women's Health Book Collective, 1973), women and, more particularly, feminists have criticized sexism throughout the health care delivery system, both in research and in the increasingly market-driven health care industry. Challenging women to reclaim their bodies, feminists have organized multiple actions to demand that research and practice be marshaled to create quality and accessible prevention and treatment. Health-based work at the interface of feminist and participatory and action research is informed by both Freirean pedagogy and this social movement activism.

Nurses and public health practitioners have used participatory and action research strategies to examine medical practices and the health profession critically in a variety of health care settings, from traditional, hierarchical hospitals to grassroots community health centers (see, e.g., Minkler & Wallerstein, 2003). In countries of the majority world, public health workers in conjunction with community members and with the individuals and communities affected by the problems or issues being studied have used participatory and action research processes to assess community needs and health disparities in order to implement educational initiatives regarding, for example, HIV and AIDS (see, e.g., Fournier, Mill, Kipp, & Walusimbi, 2007; Molestane et al., 2009). These initiatives discourage top-down mandates and facilitate community engagement and the development of culturally responsive strategies. Care is taken to identify implicit and explicit community communication codes that limit those with whom one can feel safe discussing issues such as HIV and AIDS. Interventions are thus grounded in an understanding of acceptable and taboo health-related topics within a community (see, e.g., Fournier et al., 2007; Welbourne, 1998). Actions focus on improving the conditions that gave rise to the health disparities and thus rendering better health services (Fournier et al., 2007). Participatory approaches are more likely to ensure that preventative or treatment interventions are sustainable in the context for which they are generated. Participatory research can also help a group or community, even one that has been historically disempowered, set goals to influence policy makers, thus equipping local residents with the power to make change (Fournier et al., 2007; Themba & Minkler, 2003).

Local Communities

In contrast to research contexts within the global North, where inquiry and action research at the interface of feminism and participatory and action research is usually based in an institution, the work within the majority world or global South is more frequently located in local communities. Many of these initiatives have been carried out as part of community economic or participatory development processes. In Latin America, the work has been and continues to be strongly influenced by Paulo Freire's liberatory pedagogy and his theories of critical consciousness and empowerment. Similar approaches that assume that knowledge generates power and that people's knowledge is central to social change emerged in parts of Asia (Fals-Borda & Rahman, 1991) and Africa (see Hope & Timmel, 1984–2000). These efforts stress the ideological, political, and economic dimensions of social relations in and through which all knowledge is generated. They frequently involve international collaborations wherein external catalysts engage with local farmers (see, e.g., Debbink & Ornelas, 1997) or cooperatives (see, e.g., Arratia & de la Maza, 1997) to improve the quality of life for residents through participatory processes that are designed to generate change.

Andrea Cornwall (1996, 1998), among others, has collaborated with local communities to develop participatory rural appraisal and action research projects with women and girls in their local communities. She (Cornwall, 2000, 2003) has elucidated many of the challenges in this work at the interface of feminism and PAR, cautioning community-based development researchers who assume women's solidarity and arguing that, in local communities, women may rather see their interests as aligned with their sons or kin. As significantly, both institutional

or structural barriers to women's participation in decision making and social constraints, including a lack of formal education, public speaking experience, or numerical presence in public spaces, conspire to limit women's protagonism in achieving significant changes to power inequalities. Many participatory projects may offer women the "tactics to grapple with" these realities but not real "strategies for change because they [these women] lack the power and agency to do so" (Cornwall, 2003, p. 1331).

People on the Move

Some of the ideas discussed already have been extended and used to deliver humanitarian aid and to undertake interventions with survivors of war and state-sponsored violence and with displaced populations; these ideas have informed collaborative approaches to rethreading social life in the context of structural economic poverty and in the wake of extreme violence (Lykes, Terre Blanche, & Hamber, 2003; Worthen, Veale, McKay, & Wessels, 2010). Moreover, contemporary local communities are increasingly established and reconstituted by immigrants and displaced populations fleeing poverty and violence. Within the United States and Europe, this latter work has focused on collaborations with refugees and undocumented migrants, many of whom have fled wars and extreme poverty in their countries of origin.

Although war has historically been fought by armed men in conflict, who were its primary victims and survivors, the majority of the victims of contemporary warfare are civilians and, increasingly, women and children. UNICEF estimates that 90% of those killed in today's wars are civilians and half of those are children; 80% of refugees from conflict are estimated to be women and children (UNICEF, 2005). Violence against women and gender inequalities in war are extreme manifestations of discrimination and gender violence under conditions of peace. In war, women, including young girls, are victims of incest, rape, pornography, battering, harassment, and sexual slavery. Members of militaries or paramilitary forces frequently rape women as part of war's booty (Swiss & Giller, 1993; Worthen et al., 2010) or, as human rights observers in the former Yugoslavia suggest, as one dimension of a strategy of ethnic cleansing (Ecumenical Women's Team Visit, 1992; Mazowiecki, 1993). The "feminization of poverty" has been a focus of extensive debate and research among feminists who have documented how hunger, joblessness, housing crises, and recent environmental catastrophes disproportionately affect women and children. Although an extensive discussion of these two literatures is beyond the scope of this chapter, we do include selected examples of work by researchers and activists seeking to better understand these realities and accompany people "on the move" as they rethread community in terror's wake.

So far, we have identified some of the underlying assumptions and epistemologies shared by those working at the interface of feminist and participatory and action research and enumerated selected methodological resources and sites for engaging with coresearchers. Next, we elaborate a developing framework, that is, a way of thinking about this work, one that seeks to (1) suggest an iterative process through which feminist-infused participatory and action research is being developed and (2) illuminate this work through exemplars. We then discuss similarities and diversities within and across the examples and clarify aspirations toward and the attendant challenges of developing transformative praxis.

THREE ITERATIONS OF FEMINIST-INFUSED PARTICIPATORY AND ACTION RESEARCH

The three iterations of feminist-infused participatory and action research discussed in this section are, arguably, representative of three moments in the development of AR, PR, and PAR as they have been infused by feminist theories of intersectionality. The distinctions between each iteration, or area of praxis, are not clear-cut; the borders are permeable. By organizing studies within these three iterations and discussing diverse sites in which women and men have enacted feminist-infused participatory and action research in these ways, we seek to affirm the diversities among these

processes and projects while challenging all researchers and activists to engage in inclusive projects that press toward challenging power inequalities through transformative actions. The first iteration, *repositioning gender, race, and class,* includes projects through which girls and boys and women and men are positioned as racialized, classed, and gendered. The work describes how girls and women struggle alongside boys and men in schools, health clinics, and local communities. Coresearchers focus on developing critical consciousness and redressing specific social inequalities within their institutional settings. The second set of projects, *excavating indigenous cultural knowledge(s) and generating voice(s),* focuses more explicitly on engendering voices, emphasizing processes that break silence and tell heretofore-untold stories while also advocating for changes in the systematic silencing of women. These projects are most frequently single-sex initiatives, with many engaging women as coparticipants and identifying and attending to indigenous knowledge systems and practices. This iteration includes the greatest number of projects as we also discuss herein the more recent feminist-infused participatory and action research projects that utilize creative mediums and new technologies to access and illuminate gendered voices. The third iteration, *deploying intersectionality as an analytic tool for transformation,* discusses projects that explicitly embrace feminist theory and discourse toward raising awareness or generating consciousness about gendered oppression. It also includes projects that focus on how gendered oppression constrains women's and men's lives and on how gender, understood as intersectionality, can be used as an analytic tool for transformation.

Repositioning Gender, Race, and Class

The projects classified in this iteration include various sites of engagement, with most located in the context of education. Each is explicitly activist but implicitly feminist, and it is because of their underlying assumptions and engaged praxis that we selected them as representative of this iteration of feminist-infused participatory and action research, that is, of PAR, AR, and PR that deploys gender, race, and class as resources for change.

Youth Engage in Educational Change

Julio Cammarota and Augustine Romero have worked since 2003 with students and educators at Cerro High School in the Tucson Unified School District to develop the Social Justice Educational Project (SJEP), an innovative curriculum serving the cultural, social, and intellectual needs of Latinas/os (Cammarota & Romero, 2010). SJEP, which reviews American history, U.S. government, Chicano studies, critical race theory, and critical pedagogy in culturally relevant ways, was designed to fulfill social science requirements for juniors and seniors while also enhancing the students' critical consciousness. Further, participating students developed PAR projects that addressed the socioeconomic conditions in their communities. Findings from their inquiry projects are presented to family members, teachers, principals, the district superintendent, school board members, and local, state and federal officials. These presentations reflect their engaged praxis, that is, their critical thinking about social and economic inequality, *and* propose actions toward redressing these injustices. One example of resistance described by Cammarota and Romero (2010) involves the students' struggle to ensure the future of the SJEP curricula through a takeover of their school district's Post-Unitary Community Forum. Moreover, the authors reported personal changes among students and educators, changes that promoted healthy positive identities, community activism, and empathy toward other students. Yet they noted that, despite these examples of individual change through participation in the SJEP curricula, institutional changes were harder to actualize.

The Graduate Center of the City University of New York is a site from which high school students have organized to challenge opportunity gaps in education (Fine et al., 2004; Torre, 2008). University researchers and a diverse group of more than 50 high school student formed a "Youth Research Community"; participated in research camps where youth learned participatory skills; were exposed to the research

and writing of critical feminist scholars, including Collins (1990), hooks (1990), and Harding (1986); and gained an understanding of critical race theories, epistemology, and research methods (Torre, 2008). Students thus explored their own and each other's perceptions of social class, race, gender, ethnicity, and opportunity (Torre, 2008; Torre & Fine, 2003). They also designed a survey, which they later administered to 9,174 youth from 15 New York and New Jersey urban and suburban districts. A team of youth and university-based coresearchers analyzed this data as well as that gathered in focus groups, observations, and archival research, and from the youth coresearchers' creative writing. Findings were presented through song, performance, and dramatization and recorded for publication as a DVD (Fine et al., 2004; Torre, 2008).

Torre (2008) discussed the ways in which the research process created "safe spaces" where youth and adults could work together "to go deeper" in their explorations and analyses of experiences of racism and oppression. Conflicts were engaged as opportunities for developing a more critical understanding of the macrostructures that create access for privileged youth—primarily white and with economic resources—and deny it to others—primarily "of color" and poor. Storying and analyzing the micro-practices of injustice in daily school and community-based experiences richly complemented structural analyses and are threaded through the multiple actions that commemorate, celebrate, and challenge U.S. educators and communities 50 years after *Brown v. Board of Education* (see Fine et al., 2004). As significantly, through this project, students defined and occupied a common space in which they could wrestle with and respond to injustices that they identified in their schools. For example, the students identified Advanced Placement classes as strategically privileging some students, while systematically oppressing others (Torre, 2008). Thus, student participants came to see that they were mutually implicated in the tracking system in U.S. schools. Spaces for working together, *nos-otras* (see Torre, 2008), facilitated the students' recognition that, despite their diverse communities of origin, each had unique or particular relationships to privilege and power, and that through PAR, they cocreated a social justice agenda (Torre, 2008). More recently, Fine and colleagues have engaged in similar processes with youth to document and contest police brutality toward urban adolescents and their "circuits of dispossession" (Fine & Ruglis, 2009).

Gender Inclusive Health Advocacy

In a gender inclusive participatory initiative involving men and women in Buwenda, Uganda, Welbourne (1998) aimed to improve HIV/AIDS prevention measures among members of the community where HIV was spreading at a significant rate. The work was framed around a "Stepping Stones" approach, wherein similar participants met in peer groups for periods of self-reflection and action planning. The peer-group meetings were periodically interchanged with "mixed sessions," at which members from different peer groups would meet together. These discussions allowed for the examination of similarities, differences, and solutions among participants. Community participants reported outcomes that included greater awareness of the causes of HIV, sustained increase in condom use, improved relations among others in the community who had learned about the workshop, increased ability to communicate positively (particularly between men and women), and a greater sense of well-being and respect for others (Welbourne, 1998).

Immigrants, Refugees, and Receiving Communities

In the last several years, participatory projects have investigated some of the challenges facing newly arrived immigrant and refugee communities in North America and Europe. These projects have focused on identifying resources through which participants can engage and transform gender, race, and social class relations in their host communities. One such project included African refugee and immigrant women in the Fargo-Moorhead areas of North Dakota and Minnesota (Okigbo, Reierson, & Stowman, 2009). Men and women from Egypt, Kenya, Liberia, and Nigeria, among other African countries, took part in workshops and discussions on integration and acculturation

processes in phase one of a three-part project. In the second phase, they were joined by African men and women professionals from their communities in participatory discussion sessions focused on identifying barriers to acculturation, such as mental health problems and depression, financial concerns, transportation problems, the U.S. educational system, loss of Africanness, and experiences of racism (Okigbo et al., 2009). In women-only groups, professionals incorporated a training and educational program that helped women participants and coresearchers identify potential solutions, including joining religious groups to facilitate carpool networks and transportation assistance to events and activities. Other proposed solutions included more interaction with native English speakers and advocating for refugee resettlement agencies to provide newly arriving immigrants and refugees with more supports over a longer period of time (Okigbo et al., 2009). In the project's third phase, participants reviewed the acculturation climate in a town similar to Fargo, wherein newly arriving immigrants and refugees had had a relatively positive and easy acculturation experience. This discussion of a "model city" enabled them to envision more solutions to their acculturation challenges. Despite these benefits and a commitment to continue the collaborations, professionals and academics lacked the resources to actualize the proposed solutions identified by PAR participants, leaving the latter disappointed by the participatory and action research endeavor. Researchers' reports of the work nonetheless affirmed that the project succeeded in creating knowledge about the acculturation experiences of newcomers and in contributing to developing networks within and across immigrant and refugee communities, professionals, and academics (Okigbo et al., 2009; see Balcazar, Garcia-Iriarte, & Suarez-Balcazar, 2009, for similar work with Colombian immigrants in Chicago).

In another project, both authors of this chapter have joined social workers, lawyers, social science and law students, and three community-based immigrant organizations in New England—as well as a community group in Guatemala—to generate knowledge about the challenges facing transnational families and migrants, with at least one undocumented family member in the context of a volatile U.S. deportation system. This participatory action and research project seeks to understand local constructions of the effects of detention and deportation on mixed-status and transnational families and to facilitate leadership development among Central American migrants. In-depth interviews (Brabeck, Lykes, & Hershberg, 2011) conducted in the first year of the project contributed important knowledge "in the immigrants' own voices," and a community survey (Brabeck & Xu, 2010) based on a wider Latino population complemented these findings to illuminate the psychosocial effects of U.S. policies on undocumented adult caretakers of U.S. citizen children here. Some described current Immigrant and Customs Enforcement (ICE) policies and practices as a "second war"; others spoke of living with a "broken heart"—both experiences referencing the civil wars they survived in their countries of origin, where many had left their first-born children with relatives as they headed North to "seek a better life" for their families. Actions articulated iteratively with the interviews include community discussions as well as the collaborative design and elaboration of the community-based and participatory "Know Your Rights Workshops," the publication of a bilingual annual report (see the Post-Deportation Human Rights Project [PDHRP] annual reports for 2009 and 2010), and the legal defense of illegally deported individuals. The workshops include participatory theater and reflection groups as resources for consciousness-raising and for critical analysis of the racialized and class hierarchies underlying and shaping anti-immigrant policy and practices. The project's ultimate goal is to advocate, in collaboration with affected families and communities, for fundamental changes that will introduce proportionality, compassion, and respect for family unity into U.S. immigration laws and bring these laws into compliance with international human rights standards.

Discussion

The action research processes briefly summarized here are deeply participatory and critically situated within and challenging of the

matrix of domination that continues to marginalize the majority of U.S. youth, rural men and women of the global South, and those "on the move" from access to educational opportunities, adequate health care, and safe and secure communities. They are also explicitly activist and, we argue, implicitly feminist (see, e.g., Fine, 1992, 1994). We situate them as exemplars of the first iteration of feminist-infused participatory and action research because, despite their press for transformative individual and institutional change and their situatedness at the intersection of gender, race, and class, they do not prioritize women's and girls' voices, opting to work with both boys and girls and men and women within cultural arrangements, nor do they explicitly problematize or embrace gender as a tool for structural change.

Excavating Indigenous Cultural Knowledge(s) and Generating Voice(s)

The second set of projects turn a more critical eye toward cultural and indigenous knowledge systems and the generation of frequently silenced gendered voices. These projects also engage creative strategies and a range of traditional and contemporary media as resources through which the subaltern speaks in varied social and community contexts. The studies reviewed here begin in communities in rural North Carolina and move through diverse sites of engagement, including with women in the majority world and in sites of violence.

Gendered Voices for Health Advocacy and Change

Several projects in rural North Carolina were designed with Latino men (Rhodes et al., 2007) and African American youth (Coker-Appiah, 2009) to address the disproportionate rate of HIV/AIDS transmission within their communities. Through seven focus groups, Latino participants (see Rhodes et al., 2007) revealed to health practitioners and researchers what they perceived to be obstacles to accessing health care for themselves and their fellow Latino community members. Participants also (1) explored how masculinity impacts their risk behaviors; (2) discussed beliefs about successful interventions for health promotion and disease prevention among similarly situated Latinos; and (3) developed and implemented HoMBReS: Hombres Manteniendo Bienestar y Relaciones Saludables (Men Maintaining Wellbeing and Healthy Relationships), a support group that aims to reduce HIV/STD exposure and transmission among Latino men and to encourage healthful behaviors and responsible and empowered decision making (Rhodes et al., 2007).

In another community-based HIV prevention intervention project, African American youth between 16 and 25 years of age participated in the design and delivery of Project GRACE with members of their rural North Carolina community (Coker-Appiah, 2009). Focus groups were sites for discussions of the greater risk of HIV/AIDS infection facing young African American men and women and boys and girls—and sites for problem solving. Recommendations included (1) early identification and targeting of youth for preventative interventions, (2) preventative interventions led by peer educators similarly situated to youth of interest, (3) recognition of social networks as a strength for youth of interest, and (4) acknowledgement that youth face pervasive barriers to attending interventions, including the fear of talking about the highly stigmatized topic of HIV/AIDS transmission (Coker-Appiah, 2009). Reports of this community-based participatory health project described neither the gender of project participants nor whether gender was engaged or problematized within the project. Despite this absence, health practitioners and researchers involved in Project GRACE responded to the research process and outcomes through actions that included the development of a youth advisory board for guiding interventions that targeted youth of color in rural North Carolina. Also, the university-community partnership that initiated Project GRACE added youth, who were previously marginalized from decision making, to its steering committee (Coker-Appiah, 2009). These two examples of CBPR projects focused on HIV/AIDS transmission and public health and attended, in varying degrees, to the voices of boys and men and girls and women of color as sites of power and participation. Significantly, youth were incorporated into sites of power and decision making in ongoing efforts to reduce HIV/AIDS in these communities of color.

In Panchmahals, a district of Gujarat in western India, Renu Khanna (1996) collaborated with SARTHI, a local volunteer organization, to develop a participatory action research project for women's health. Together, they created a space for sharing stories and studying traditional remedies for women's health. Based on these experiences, they developed self-help workshops to train women in socially embedded and gender-sensitive gynecology. Khanna (1996) identified evidence of women's empowerment and health activism at multiple levels including the intra- and interpersonal, the group, and the community. In the first instance, women moved beyond *sharam* (shame) and began to talk about their bodies. In small group discussions, they identified the characteristics of daily living that impeded or facilitated health and well-being. At the community level, participants organized for collective action, mobilizing for quality health care and addressing the health issues women of their community faced, including domestic violence (Khanna, 1996). Thus, gender was mobilized to elicit voice, excavate and critique cultural practices, and advocate for changes at individual and community levels.

Culture and Voice Through Photography and PAR

Feminist-infused participatory and action research has introduced creativity as an important resource through which girls and women, particularly those who are nonformally educated or illiterate, can record, represent, and communicate their stories. Perhaps the most widely disseminated practice in this domain draws on photography and narratives or storytelling to generate wider audiences for gendered voices and policy change (see, e.g., Allen & Hutchinson, 2009; Hergenrather, Rhodes, & Bardhoshi, 2009; Umrungi, Mitchell, Gervaise, Ubalijoro, & Kabarenzi, 2008; Wang, Burris, & Xiang, 1996). Caroline Wang and her colleagues equipped rural Chinese women with resources to identify their needs and the needs of their community (Wang et al., 1996). The inclusion of photography, a research strategy not dependent on literacy, extended opportunities for participation to a wider group of women, many of whom had heretofore been excluded from collaboration as coresearchers. Through a participatory research strategy that yoked photography and the analysis of pictures as text about women's lives, project participants developed a photo-text exhibit and book that informed local, regional, and provincial policy makers about the risks of rural labor practices to women's and children's safety and well-being (Wu et al., 1995). The work generated significant policy change, improving child care and health care in the participating provinces. Ironically, perhaps, the highly centralized and hierarchical Chinese service delivery system and sponsorship of this project by regional officials facilitated greater access to decision making and change than is typically available either to rural women or in much locally based participatory and action research.

The work of this chapter's first author and 20 Mayan women in rural Guatemala further exemplifies the power and complexities of PAR and photography as resources for women's gendered voices and social change (Women of PhotoVoice/ ADMI & Lykes, 2000). This participatory and action research project emerged from and was embedded in the work of a local women's organization that fostered economic development (through several animal husbandry projects and a revolving loan fund), education (through a community after-school program for children and a community library), leadership development, and psychosocial interventions. These aims were undertaken in the midst and wake of civil war and in a context of ongoing ethnic- and gender-based discrimination and violence (see Lykes et al., 1999, for details). Society-wide initiatives to end the war—including the 1996 Peace Accords, signed by the government and the revolutionary movements, and the initiation of two commissions to document gross violations of human rights (Commission for Historical Clarification [CEH], 1999; ODHAG, 1998)— created some of the conditions necessary for a PhotoPAR process. Incorporating aspects of the "talking pictures" methodology developed by the Chilean anthropologist Ximena Bunster (Bunster & Chaney, 1989) and Caroline Wang's photovoice work in rural China (see Wang et al., 1996), the coresearchers constructed the community's photo-texts of war, its effects, and how one small group of women were rethreading

their lives and creating alternatives for their children. All 20 Mayan women coresearchers were given point and shoot cameras and discussed using cameras and strategies for taking pictures in training workshops. After each roll was developed, each photographer picked four to six pictures she thought best represented the theme chosen for the previous month and recounted a story for each picture. Long-silenced stories of, for example, cultural practices suppressed during the war, sexual violence against women and children, and women's survival and growth through cooperative organizing were transcribed, and each photo-text was then reorganized and re-storied through group analytic participatory processes. These safe spaces were contexts for generating knowledge about and critical analyses of the structural inequalities that gave rise to Guatemala's 36-year war and the genocidal project of the military against the Maya (CEH, 1999). The project was undertaken in Spanish and Ixil and culminated in the production of a bilingual photo-essay, *Voces e Imágenes: Mujeres Mayas Ixiles de Chajul/Voices and Images: Mayan Ixil Women of Chajul* (Women of PhotoVoice/ADMI & Lykes, 2000). Coresearchers from Chajul extended their photographing and storytelling to document the experiences of women of the surrounding villages with whom they later organized women's support and educational groups. The coresearchers thus contributed to deepening knowledge about the diverse consequences of the 36-year war, both locally and in more remote contexts.

New Technologies: Interrogating Media and Gendered Voice

In addition to exemplifying the challenge of producing both feminist knowledge and action-based projects, recent feminist-infused participatory and community-based works have also problematized the means and mediums used to record, write about, represent, and communicate women's voices. Digital stories (Christiansen, 2010), film (Molestane et al., 2009), and other creative mediums have been embraced as more technologically sophisticated resources that reach wider audiences and further democratize research. These studies force the question of not only whose voice should be represented but also what ways are best for the subaltern to articulate her experience and speak on her own behalf (Brydon-Miller, 2004). Additional concerns include how women can best be understood by audiences who will "experience" their voices (Brydon-Miller, 2004) and what forms of representation will best capture the voices of participants in a feminist participatory and action research project.

Three Chicana teens collaborated with Sánchez (2009) in a PAR project in Northern California and Mexico. They developed a counter-text to that produced by schools and the mainstream media about transnational students. The coresearchers drew on knowledge excavated and generated through photography, video, interviews, and storytelling with families on both sides of the border. They illustrated a children's book that showcased their own and their families' cultural resources, indigenous knowledge or "*conocimientos,*" and pride about family background, thereby re-storying the dominant image of the migrant as criminal (Sánchez, 2009).

Young female Cape Verdeans in Boston, each of whom had lost a family member to violent death, incarceration, or deportation, collaborated with Elise Christiansen (2010) in a PAR project. The coresearchers formed a youth group within VALOR (Values Affecting Learning Our Roots), a community-based program developed by a Boston-based Cape Verdean NGO to help its members rebuild ties and process losses in the wake of widespread violence and discrimination. Through their participation in focus groups, healing circles, and multiple art projects, the girls recognized the limited resources available within their families for addressing the multiple losses of family and friends due to violence in their communities. They reported that their participation in VALOR and in the PAR process enabled them to develop a context of support through which they developed critical consciousness and agency. Drawing on their artwork, storytelling, journaling, and community photographs, each participant created a digital story that gave voice to the experiences of growing up in an urban context of poverty and violence that included the murder, incarceration, and deportation of men in their lives (Christiansen, 2010). The girls presented and performed their digital stories in community events in order to educate the wider community

through communicating their understandings of and responses to the violence in their lives. Through this PAR process, girls found their voices, developed an analysis of some of the causes of the violence in their lives, and recognized their individual and collective strength through their actions to educate and advocate for change within their community. This small project demonstrates the personally transformative power of a participatory and action research process that prioritized girls who had been marginalized within their own communities as well as by the larger community of Boston.

Based on her work among young North American female high school students, Chantal Drolet (2008) argues that digital filmmaking is an alternative form of media literacy and communication that is well suited to support young women's interest in communication and technology while also equipping them with creative and critical processes through which they can create their own scripts. Young digital filmmakers can use their stories to respond to gender biases and to convey powerful messages that will influence the public's behavior. Drolet argues that integrating digital film and other communication technologies into education positively feminizes pedagogy, assuring that young girls and women will be more engaged in their own education and in information technologies. She concludes that digital film provides young women with both the skills and the means through which their perspectives and voices can be critically developed, represented, and communicated to parents, peers, and the public at large.

Molestane and colleagues (2009) initiated a participatory and action research project in rural South Africa that turned to video as a resource for representing female voices. Similar to Drolet's work, this project sought to equip young women with the video-making skills through which they could understand their experiences and communicate their unique perspectives to peers and the wider public. Young women participants sought to reconstruct their experiences of poverty and HIV/AIDS, to reflexively analyze themselves and the challenges they encountered in an effort to identify and propose action solutions. These rural women produced a video, *It All Began With Poverty,* through which they analyzed their life experiences and envisioned possibilities for change in their families, schools, and communities. They shared this vision through video presentations to students in classrooms and in other community contexts, where they initiated in-depth discussions of poverty and its negative effects on women and their communities. Molestane et al. (2009) argued that the camera enabled rural women participants to represent poverty's negative effects, linking it to other social problems and to gender inequalities. The project demonstrated how some marginalized women creatively engaged in identifying issues that directly constrained their life options and were able to pose possible solutions from which subsequent interventions and actions would be more likely to emerge and to be effective (Molestane et al., 2009).

Another PAR project involving rural women and new technologies was initiated by Lennie (2002), who advocated for rural women in Australia to have better mastery of and access to communication technologies in order to (1) increase opportunities for them to network with other women and professionals, (2) develop business management skills, and (3) access information that would improve their qualities of life and overall levels of empowerment. To work toward these goals, Lennie facilitated an Internet-based feminist-oriented action research project in the Queensland communities between eight industry and government partners and nine rural women. Online groups, focus groups conducted via audio-conference, and diaries kept by several participants were the means of communication, relationship building, and data generation in this project. Through an evaluation of the project, Lennie found that several rural women participants reported feeling disempowered and excluded or marginalized in their online networks. Some rural participants described the professional participants as dominating online communication through multiple postings that emphasized differences in educational backgrounds, skill sets, and levels of confidence among coresearchers. Thus, this Internet-based feminist and participatory project suggests that feminist assumptions about the emancipatory effects of connecting women to one another through newer forms of communication technologies need to be embraced

with caution as such connections do not necessarily lead to closeness, particularly when they involve women differently positioned due to education, social class, and geography and when they fail to engage the women's different intersectional identities and positionalities critically (Lennie, 2002).

In reflecting on the PhotoPAR project with Mayan women (already described briefly), Lykes (2010) discusses the challenges and successes of new technologies as forms of representation and resources for transformative change. Dramatization, community mapping, and collective drawing as well as photography, interviews, and collective storytelling were engaged to facilitate Ixil and K'iche' women's definition of life problems, analysis of the causes of these problems, search for solutions, and collective actions in this PhotoPAR process. Lykes (2010) reviewed her field notes, group analyses, and multiple iterations of the photo-texts generated through the participatory and action research process, 10 years after the project's completion and the book's publication. Her secondary analysis focuses on how power circulates among insiders and outsiders in the PhotoPAR process, revealing in complex ways the intersectionality of gendered voices.

Specifically, she argues that, despite the project's goals of engaging women's diverse voices, much of the group's ethnic and religious diversity was silenced, even erased, in various photo-narratives presented in the published book. For example, Ixil and K'iche' coresearchers from ethnically and linguistically different Mayan groups were active participants, as is seen in their appearances in *traje* (traditional dress) in various photographs. Yet they neither interrogated these differences in participatory workshops in which these photographs were analyzed nor represented them in the final photo-narratives. This suggests PhotoPAR's failure to develop a social space where long-standing ethnic conflicts could be positively engaged, re-presented, or reconstituted, defying at least one of the project's transformative goals, that is, to instantiate human rights and challenge long-standing ethnic and racial discrimination (Lykes, 2010).

In another example, Lykes (2010) discusses how the destruction or rupturing of traditional religious beliefs and practices by *la violencia*[3] was a frequent topic of group discussions and evident in the collective analyses of the photographs taken in the project. However, the final published photo-narratives including these images focus more on culture, lifestyle, and identity. Through her reanalysis of published texts and unpublished field notes and project documents, Lykes traces the storylines, local negotiations, and decision making about the inclusion and exclusion of various voices in the co-construction of the final photo-narratives. She suggests that outsider university-based and urban Guatemalans' input may have implicitly facilitated an emphasis on more contemporary and universal themes, such as gender equality and human rights, marginalizing the voices of those who emphasized more traditional intersections of gender, class, or ethnic hierarchies. Despite these limitations, Lykes notes that PhotoPAR was a resource through which participants, including Mayan women and international collaborators, created a dynamic space of contention and contestation—one that allowed women who had survived horrific assaults against material, social, and cultural bodies to reclaim them and reconstitute their subjectivities, repositioning themselves as Mayan Ixil and K'iche' women and rethreading their communities.

Discussion

These studies raise important considerations about gender and feminisms. The HoMBReS project problematized masculinities and thereby fostered a questioning of how traditional gender roles constrain men's access to adequate health care. In contrast, Project GRACE embraced cultural knowledge to foster the greater engagement of African American boys and girls and men and women in the fight against HIV/AIDs transmission in their community, but it left the role of gender in this process uncontested. The SARTHI initiative in western India drew heavily on cultural codes to better understand women's marginalization, establishing gender-based women's support groups and then translating that knowledge and women's increased self-confidence to advocacy for women's health at the community level. The final set of projects embraced creativity, using the arts and new technologies as resources for elucidating cultural practices and women's voices and their positions at the intersection of ethnicity, class, and other social oppressions.

Despite their differences, each of these participatory and action research projects sought to confront social inequalities, and each identified people marginalized from access to power as potential protagonists in self-advocacy initiatives. Most projects described important outcomes through which both girls and boys and women and men voiced identity and expressed newly developing critical consciousness toward change. Attention to cultural codes that had previously silenced these participants was infused into the PhotoPAR and new technologies projects, at least several of which engaged gender as a tool for critical consciousness and change.

Yet many of the "outsider" researchers eschewed explicitly feminist or womanist discourse within the projects themselves. To risk such an approach can position the "outsider" researcher as a critic of traditional community beliefs and practices, which frequently serve as cultural capital and are, as seen in the previous examples, strengths that increase participation and can foster community actions. Despite this risk, we suggest here that a stronger emphasis on intersectionality as a critical analytic resource—either in the project's formulation or in the researcher's post-project reflections—can enhance the critical potential of participatory and action research to strengthen both participants' self-understanding of their positionalities at the interface of gender, race, class, and culture and their potential as actors who generate transformative change on their own behalf and for their communities. Feminist-infused participatory and action research projects aspire to foster an understanding of the local communities with which outsider researchers are engaged. The latter strive to deepen existing knowledge of oppression and resistance at the intersection of gender, race, social class, and culture and aim to design, with participating communities, more efficacious and clear action and advocacy plans directed toward the transformative change of systems and policies and practices related to social disparities (Reid & Frisby, 2008).

Deploying "Intersectionality" as an Analytic Tool for Transformation

As the previous two iterations illustrate, feminist-infused participatory and action research projects aspire to foster knowledge about research sites and coresearchers' experiences and local understandings while also contributing to situating this work at the intersection of gender, race, class, and culture; exploring how these social forces position coresearchers as social subjects; and examining critically constraints on them due to the institutional or structural arrangements of power. Feminist and transformative theories of knowledge construction and change, as described in the first section of this chapter, inform the selection of research sites and strategies as well as the participants with whom outsiders seek to develop coresearch. Feminist and action researchers thus seek to catalyze action-reflection processes through which coresearchers can develop efficacious and clear action and advocacy plans directed toward transformative change of individual participants, for example, consciousness raising, as well as of the systems and policies and practices that have structured and sustained social inequalities (Fals-Borda & Rahman, 1991; Lykes & Mallona, 2008; Reid & Frisby, 2008). There is also a constant and persistent attention to and respect for indigenous knowledge systems and cultural practices. Thus, much of the work already described reflects explicit participatory processes and actions for change and implicit feminist or transformative ideologies. Projects discussed in this section, which explores the third iteration of feminist-infused participatory and action research, include those that we believe succeed at generating transformative changes among participants and in institutions or systems while aspiring to mobilize intersectionality in the projects themselves and, to different degrees, within the sites in which these projects are engaged.

Schools and Universities

Andrea Dyrness (2008), an anthropologist from Trinity College, discussed the success of Madres Unidas, a group of Latina mothers who engaged in participatory action research aimed at exploring their roles in the creation of a small school in Oakland, California. Participants included five Latina immigrant mothers from the Oakland Coalition for Community Action (OCCA–a pseudonym chosen by Dyrness). They sought to understand how school reform was being defined and put into practice at their children's schools. The objectives of their project included (1) developing a critical analysis of school practices, policies, and power relations that silenced them and other parents; (2) providing a safe space for the creation of community trust and testimonials; and (3) allowing mothers to take new roles at their children's school and extend the vision of community beyond the home.

Dyrness (2008) argues that this participatory action research process incorporates critical feminist and *mujerista* epistemologies. Specifically, when mothers assembled at one mother's home, they created a unique *mujerista* or Latina "womenist" space through their use of *testimonio* (testimonials) and through the relationships they developed with *confianza* (trust). Together they explored the history of the small school and named and recorded each other's experiences, which had been suppressed as the school had framed Latino/a parents as "problems" or "bad parents" (Dyrness, 2008). Mothers reframed these negative labels that "othered" them and identified themselves as advocates for their community. Madres Unidas sought to change relationships among parents and between them and the school. To that end, mothers made presentations to the school, which included sharing their personal experiences, video recordings of their meetings, and their evaluations of both. These efforts also led the mothers to create a parent center at the school, eventually, a place wherein *mujerista* elements of *testimonio* and *confianza* could be expanded from the home of Madres Unidas participants to the school community, thus challenging teachers to reframe the role of parents and, in particular, of mothers in the school.

This project demonstrates how a feminist and *mujerista* PAR process engaged a group of low-income immigrant mothers, many of whom had limited proficiency in English, enabling them to successfully examine *and change* their children's school (Dyrness, 2008). These mothers created a new form of community through which they and other parents enacted a vision of community within their children's school (Dyrness, 2008). The mother who organized the first workshop reported that this project had given her courage. Moreover, upon conclusion of the PAR project, other Madres Unidas participants took on additional leadership roles in the school, including serving on an English Language Advisory Committee and as parent representatives on hiring committees (Dyrness, 2008). Thus, this project at the intersection of gender, race, class, and culture also centers women's voices and demonstrates how, through personal, school-based, and community change, community participants and coresearchers succeeded in designing institutional change and pressing toward social transformation. That is, they extended the borders of home to create "school-home," a site that infused *mujerista* values and transformed "community."

While the school was the site of engagement for the feminist-infused PAR project initiated by Dyrness, schools and universities have also become sites for educating a new generation of feminist and action research scholars. A web-based search reveals more than 20 courses in universities internationally. Most syllabi for courses on PAR, AR, and/or PR assign readings related to feminism or give space for critical reflection on the implications of power in the research process, including the power differentials associated with gender. The increased inclusion of feminist theories and research principles in these syllabi suggest a growing recognition of work at this interface.

Christine Sleeter, Myriam Torres, and Peggy Laughlin (2004) exemplify this pedagogy in teacher inquiry courses wherein they scaffold consciousness raising or conscientization processes for and with preservice teachers. Alice McIntyre's (1997) feminist-informed participatory action research project with a group of white, middle- and upper-middle-class university-based female student teachers documented the challenges of such pedagogy. McIntyre found that the preservice teachers who participated in a series of action-reflection workshops

developed to explore critically their experiences as white student teachers in urban schools sustained a dominant discourse that privileged "whiteness," despite having participated in this PAR project that sought to engage them in critical self-reflection about race and racism in their educational practice. McIntyre's project documented how "whiteness" is sustained and reproduced within and among those seeking change in order to better equip future teachers in disrupting and eliminating systems of discrimination and white privilege in their classrooms. McIntyre, Chatzopoulos, Politi, and Roz (2007) also engaged in a reflexive participatory and action research project with preservice teachers. The project was conducted with girls of color at Williams Elementary School in an urban Northeast community. In this project, the teachers in training who participated engaged in reflexive research that enabled them to examine how they viewed themselves, the Latina female students in the schools in which they were student teaching, and the multiple issues that affected teaching and research. Yet, despite the reliance on feminist assumptions and reflexive strategies, much of this work focused on personal transformation in the absence of any systematic efforts to realize broader educational change.

In contrast, Patricia Maguire (2004) explicitly incorporated feminist activism in an action research course she taught at the Western New Mexico University School of Education. Based on her conviction that we grow and thrive in relationship, she argued that this was a context in which as "traveling companions on a journey of how to do collaborative action research in service to social justice . . . we are challenged to take action, however imperfect. When all is said and done, feminism is about action: collective politicized action" (Maguire, 2004, pp. 131–132). The students in Maguire's course were challenged to examine critically their multiple identities and the implications that these have for their work as teachers with diverse student populations. Each student designed an action research project on site, that is, where he or she was teaching, in order to clarify where and how feminisms were implicated. The assumption underlying Maguire's pedagogical praxis is that integrating feminism and activism into action research is critical to developing its transformative potential.

Gendered Identities, Conflict, and Community Organizing

Feminists and action researchers have been engaged with local communities who are living through ongoing war and subsequent transitions. Within contemporary intrastate conflicts, ethnically based violence is a prominent dimension wherein difference is targeted for political purposes. Moreover, fear of "the other" is mobilized where there was once solidarity and community, further undermining social relationships and polarizing identities.

In Sierra Leone, Liberia, and northern Uganda, researchers worked in a PAR project with young mothers who were formerly associated with armed groups; a goal was to heal social relationships between the young mothers and their communities of origin (Worthen et al., 2010). This project incorporated empowerment and human rights approaches as means for examining how "girl-mothers" who participated in the Disarmament, Demobilization, and Reintegration (DDR) campaign in different areas of Africa experienced reintegration processes and what, in their views as participants, could be done to better support them. Focus groups as well as interviews and improvised drama and song constituted the participatory processes that also served as points for data collection. Young mothers shared experiences of being rejected by their families and communities upon returning from war and of having these communities attribute shame and promiscuity to them because of their having been sexually violated. They also reported that the PAR processes facilitated their development of coping strategies, which they then used when their families refused to take them back.

Through ongoing meetings, participating mothers decided on actions to address these challenges as well as resultant problems, including a lack of livelihood, threats to their and their children's health, stigma, and a lack of family support. Resources provided by the researchers included literacy classes and micro credit for women interested in beginning small businesses. Having developed "just enough trust" in this PAR process, members of the group focused on developing a critical understanding of their own subjective experiences and an analysis of how and why their own communities had rejected them. Researchers described a process through which the girls' strengthening relationships contributed to their self-recognition as worthy of respect and dignity, which then contributed to their initiating a process of renegotiating relationships with their communities.

Alison Crosby (2009) analyzed a workshop organized collaboratively by the Consejeria en Proyectos/Project Counseling Services (PCS), an international NGO and local Guatemalan nonprofit, and by Crosby and Lykes. This work describes an explicitly feminist and participatory transformative process of collective memory construction, psychosocial accompaniment, and the search for justice with women survivors of sexual violence in armed conflict. A participatory workshop was designed for those who accompany women survivors in Guatemala, Peru, and Colombia to (1) share their understandings of the underlying causes of sexual violence against women in war and the ways in which they approach supporting survivors, (2) examine strategies and lessons learned from past experiences, and (3) explore "best practices." It also focused on how accompaniers' sustained commitment to the work of supporting survivors individually and through women's organizations had affected advocacy and legal strategies for combating impunity toward perpetrators of violence against women in armed conflict (Crosby, 2009). Participants included women who had been targets of threats and acts of intimidation because of their advocacy efforts, as well as academic participants and advocates.

Crosby (2009) argues that the participatory workshop and the community narrative produced by the workshop's facilitators embody processes of self-discovery and of breaking silences to speak truth in a context of ongoing impunity. The experiences recounted and re-presented in the workshop clarified how feminist participatory endeavors among differently positioned women at the intersections of gender, race, social class, and culture—and against gendered, militarized violence—can provide a space of common struggle, wherein the fear and mistrust experienced by victims and others affected by gendered violence can be transformed into vulnerability toward one another, which contributes to transformative participation (Crosby, 2009).

Discussion

Similar to the projects in the first two iterations of feminist-infused participatory and action research projects, the work described here shares a concern with engaging women in raising awareness about themselves and about the social conditions that impede their well-being in educational and health care institutions, in local communities, and with women survivors of war and state-sponsored violence. The language of feminism is more explicit in most of these projects, wherein co-researchers interrogate gendered oppression and problematize gender as well as race, social class, language, and ethnicities. A problem-posing, reflexive, critical, and self-critical teaching-learning process is central to each project. Coresearchers encourage a critical examination of situated subjectivities, and reflexivity is mobilized by "outsider" researchers. These processes facilitate and sustain perspective change and individual or collective actions toward transformative change. The changes described are within and beyond institutions, changes that enable girls and women to more fully articulate their values and beliefs and incorporate and reflect their evolving cultural and gendered positions in ways that improve and transform their lives, their organizations, and their communities. Thus, this group of action-reflection processes more fully represents feminist-infused participatory and action research that engages both feminist and participatory and action research epistemologies, shared assumptions, and engaged activism.

EXPLORING SIMILARITIES AND DIFFERENCES ACROSS FEMINIST-INFUSED PARTICIPATORY AND ACTION RESEARCH

In the feminist-infused participatory and action research projects described herein, participants as coresearchers, through reflexivity and in relationship, discover the limits and constraints of their own personal and interpersonal power. Through processes of conscientization within local matrices of power and powerlessness, they contest social oppression and, sometimes, collectively mobilize resources on behalf of themselves, their families, and their communities. In what follows, we explore several processes that cut across most of the examples already presented, that is, the insider-outsider dichotomy, reflexivity, voice, and relationality. These processes both emerge from and constitute feminist-infused participatory and action research. They are defined and redefined through a dialectical and iterative process of action and reflection. As such, they are core processes through which feminist-infused participatory and action research is embodied and performed.

"Insiders" and "Outsiders"

As argued, the researcher's theories of being (ontology) and knowing (epistemology) influence who she is, the positions she assumes, the methodologies she engages during the research process, and the advocacy or actions she mobilizes. Participatory and action research challenge participants to think critically about their own identities, as well as about the ways in which the multiple identities of all participants, that is, all coresearchers, interact within the context of the research process. Some PAR researchers argue that presumed power inequities between "insiders" and "outsiders" need to be examined, critiqued, and deconstructed in all research (see, e.g., Bartunek & Louis, 1996; Fine, 1994; Merton, 1972). These scholars challenge feminist-informed participatory action researchers to stretch the boundaries of the hypothesized insider-outsider dichotomy, or, in the words of Michelle Fine (1994), "work the hyphen" (p. 31).

Many participatory and action research processes are collaborations between researchers with technical skills, who live "outside" of the community of praxis, and "insiders" or participants, who are members of the "target" community. In examining feminist methodology, Sherry Gorelick (1996) offers an important caution to all who hope to do feminist-infused participatory action research beyond their communities of origin, suggesting that the external researcher's "relationship to oppression, as either privileged or oppressed . . . is contradictory, complex, and, to some degree, up to us" (p. 40). Writing about a community-based participatory research project working with public health professionals in low-income communities of color in the United States, Chavez, Duran, Baker, Avila, and Wallerstein (2003) suggest that for "professionally trained researchers who are white or otherwise advantaged, privilege is one of the most important and difficult arenas . . . to address, as it in part defines who [the researchers] understand [themselves] to be" (p. 91).

The work of independent researcher and activist Susan Stern exemplifies some of these challenges "at the hyphen." Stern undertook a conversation-based research project in a predominantly Black suburban neighborhood near Washington, D.C., in the early 1980s, upon being appalled at the poor quality of the teaching and the low academic expectations rampant in the local elementary school in which her daughter had enrolled. As a white woman, her activism required continual conversation with other predominantly Black parents and teachers about the implications of race and racism for their collaboration. As Stern (1998) explains, "at the personal level, our different racial backgrounds threatened to maintain a barrier between us. At the social level, racial differences and race-based policies and procedures were at the core of the problem at hand—[in the] children's school" (p. 115). Although Stern was an "insider" in the school community due to her status as the parent of a student, as a white, Euro-American in an almost exclusively Black community she was an "outsider." Each of her multiple identities held different implications and challenges for her position and for the relationships she formed and the actions in which she engaged through the research process.

Stern's example demonstrates the matrix of interlocking interactions between researchers and participants that both conceal and illuminate continuities and discontinuities in participatory processes of meaning making and change. By challenging static, boundaried notions of "insider" and "outsider" or "researcher" and "participant," feminist-infused participatory and action research clarifies the mediated nature of all knowledge construction and exemplifies "ways of knowing" that are frequently absent from mainstream, top-down theory building. Further, Rahman (2004) suggests that the "desired relation between external activists and people is best expressed by the term *uglolana,* meaning 'sharpening each other,' and by a "companion concept . . . *uakana,* meaning 'to build each other.'" He suggests that these two South African Bantu terms are "the profoundest articulation of the participatory development paradigm" (p. 17). We suggest that they not only redefine the insider-outsider dialectic of coresearchers but refashion the discourse of power at the interface of feminisms and participatory and action research that seeks transformation.

Reflexivity: Self as Vehicle for Reflection and Action

Nancy Naples (2003) argues that collaboration is possible only if coresearchers can create a space of engagement where participants can assert themselves through reflective strategies and dialogic processes. She suggests that reflective strategies are tools to "make visible what is privileged as . . . data" (p. 38). Through adopting reflective strategies, feminist researchers "work to reveal the inequalities and processes of domination that shape the 'field'" (Naples, 2003, p. 38). Although Naples was referring explicitly to the ethnographic research with which she was engaged, these methodological considerations are informative for the feminist-infused participatory and action research discussed in this chapter.

Some (see, e.g., Williams & Lykes, 2003) have extended these ideas, suggesting that *reflexivity,* namely, the ways in which researchers and participants use themselves and their critical reflections about themselves to generate knowledge and collective action, rather than *reflectivity* is critical in participatory and action research processes. Through critical and self-critical reflections on one's standpoint as a participant or researcher, one accesses different kinds of knowledge about the observable processes in which one is engaged, and this, in turn, enables one to deploy one's particular "selves" within the collective process of feminist-infused participatory and action research.

For example, in 1996 Williams joined Lykes and 20 Mayan Ixil and K'iche' women in

Guatemala, all of whom were engaged in the PhotoVoice project described briefly above. They sought to collaborate with these rural women of Chajul as they storied their lives through words and photographs to, among other things, "strengthen their individual and organizational capacities and resources" (Williams & Lykes, 2003, p. 288). Upon reconvening one month after a series of successful and enthusiastic meetings through which the project had been launched and the participants had received training in the use of cameras, the Mayan coresearchers reported that only a few of them had even attempted to take photographs, despite their earlier enthusiasm for the process and commitment to do so. Williams and Lykes's (2003) disappointment and reflection on their emotional responses to the group contributed to their decision to facilitate a "participatory process of reflection and action" engaging disappointment, doubts, and self-questioning about what had happened to the women in the interlude between workshops. During this process, women were invited to role-play what had occurred when they set off to take their first photographs, and then to identify and analyze the barriers they had experienced as a way of exploring their own responses to participation. The material and psychological challenges they reported were enacted through dramatizations and reenacted through dramatic multiplication techniques (Lykes, 1994). This praxis facilitated the participants' clarification of emotional responses to taking pictures, responses that had contributed to their inaction as well as reconnected them to thoughts and feelings they had experienced as a consequence of war and organized violence.

These reflexive practices (Williams & Lykes, 2003) exemplify a process through which participant coresearchers were invited into self-reflective praxis. The project's impasse was transformed; women engaged the process as photographers while increasing in self-knowledge. Other similar participatory problem-solving processes provided a forum for the group's discussion of family and community conflicts, gender relations, and Mayan traditions, raising participants' critical awareness. Significantly, the external coresearchers became more integrated within the action research process as they better understood the powerful tool of reflexively engaging their own emotional responses to the research process and using them as entry into strengthened relationships with the participants and as resources for data generation and analysis.

Multiplicity of Voices

As argued previously, many feminist-infused participatory and action research projects have explicit or implicit goals of breaking silence, engaging diverse voices, and generating audiences to hear women's varied stories. Despite these goals, there are multiple systematic barriers to the full expression of participants' "voices" in this work. Language is one systematic barrier in some of the projects already described.

Barriers to Voicing Stories

Literal translation within and across native languages sometimes complicates the research processes. Moreover, the impossibility of communicating many culturally situated and embedded linguistic constructs and social expressions serves to dilute further the messages of participants or confuse their meanings. Questions of translation may also emphasize or reinforce existing racial dynamics.

As significantly, academic language and assumptions underlying university "culture" "often clash with the majority of people in the communities where [PAR] research is conducted" (Chavez et al., 2003, p. 89). Indeed, the divide between the communities who participate in PAR and the institutions or universities initiating these projects has been felt by many participatory action researchers. Researchers based in the academy "face many difficulties in balancing the social worlds of academia, policy makers, and the public, and the 'community'" (Cancian, 1996, p. 188). Thus, cultural interpreters and translators are frequently essential players in a community-based research process, as they bridge the gap between communities and institutions. This bridge can be particularly important when PAR is conducted across a racial divide, with communities of color, for example. Yet, as Chavez et al. (2003) note in their work with public health workers in low-income communities of color, researchers of color, who may attempt to provide this bridge, are often not the primary researchers but translators or interpreters who are recognized as less central to the research process.

Balancing the Input of Coresearchers

Qualitative research methods may help researchers establish a finer balance among their multiple roles as they are generally designed to encourage the preservation of participants' individual input and particular context more so than many de-individualizing positivist methods. What is at stake is how the "voices" of participants, that is, their lived experiences, their indigenous knowledge, their perceptions, and their words are accepted as data, and how and for what that data are appropriated. Yet, as Marecek, Fine, and Kidder (2001) note, "as researchers become witnesses, bringing their knowledge of theory and their interpretive methods to participants' stories, they . . . become active agents" (p. 34). The researcher thus becomes one of multiple influences in the research, regardless of the methods used, and, as Lykes (2010) argues, co-constructive processes may obscure or distort "insiders'" voices (Stacey, 1996, pp. 91–92).

Michele Fine (1992) cautioned strongly that the researcher who serves as a "ventriloquist," that is, who speaks over or for participants, often contributes misinformation, obscuring the respective and varied roles and voices of the participants. She urges researchers to situate themselves as facilitators of the voices of the community participants with whom they work and to create opportunities for public storytelling. The public thus both hears these stories and is held accountable to the storytellers.

Cocreating a "Third Voice"

Although an important cautionary tale, Fine's analysis implies a "self" and "other" who are independent, wherein one holds power and the "other" is less powerful or powerless. Lykes and colleagues (2003) have suggested that participatory collaborations that seek to be transformative are constitutive of a new or "third voice" through which the voices of the researcher and researched together transgress traditional representational forms. They worked with two women's groups, one in Guatemala and the other in South Africa, both of which were situated in moments of larger ongoing political struggles to overcome externally imposed repressive practices that censored the voices of marginalized communities. The authors, thus, joined historically marginalized women of color in transforming and deploying representational tools (photography and press releases) to "speak out" about experiences of political and military repression. In both cases, the group's agendas evolved over time, so that what emerged was not so much a particular account of themselves, or even the development of a particular "voice" for speaking about themselves, but an unfolding process—for the groups and for the researchers who accompanied them—of becoming active players in the postmodern, mediated world of self-representational politics and social struggle (Lykes et al., 2003).

Although many projects continue to describe themselves as processes wherein outsider researchers "give voice" to the "voiceless" or marginalized, we suggest here that feminist-infused participatory and action research seeks to interrogate and contest these ideas by problematizing voice and transforming the binaries of power and powerlessness, voice and voicelessness, situating the work within representational and transformational politics.

Research Relationality: Building and Sustaining Relationships

Establishing collaborative research relationships is central to many qualitative approaches to research and is a basic goal of critical theorist and constructivist feminist researchers. Researchers committed to democratic participation and emancipation seek to raise individual and collective awareness of oppressive practices in the world and to organize for change. Feminist-infused participatory and action research is, thus, built upon the development of relationships; it is through relationships that participants are transformed (McIntyre & Lykes, 2004). Hierarchical research models are antithetical to this value system.

Human beings undergoing a shared process of personal and collective change through feminist-infused participatory and action research naturally form bonds and attachments. McIntyre and Lykes (2004) argue, on the basis of years of collaboration with women in the North of Ireland and in Guatemala, respectively, that personal relationships constructed over time through participatory action research and collaborative activism stretch the boundaries of the presumed dichotomy between researchers and participants. They suggest that friendships formed through long-term commitments may be more accurately descriptive of feminist-infused participatory and action research. Indeed, it has been argued here that such bonds are the stuff of transformation.

However, the practical requirements of those bonds beyond the boundaries and goals of the participatory or action research process raise challenging questions for researchers. Although a bond may exist among researchers and participants, developing that bond into a working friendship, requiring continual, mutual self-disclosure, reciprocity, and sustainability, may not be an appropriate or productive extension of the experience of the research process. Some researchers have found that the expectations of reciprocity in feminist participatory or action research limit them. For example, in reevaluating a 1983 qualitative study of all white, mostly middle-class women "at the end of their intense period of mothering," Acker, Barry, and Esseveld (1996) reflected on the burden that they as researchers experienced in not being able to meet the expectations of friendship that participants developed during the project. In addition, they felt that a female interviewee who compared herself to one of the external researchers of the same age, who was also a recent mother, saw herself negatively, which contributed to this participant's self-censoring, a process that might not have occurred in a traditionally hierarchical research relationship (Acker et al., 1996).

Participants' expectations of relationality within feminist-infused participatory and action research are frequently intertwined with issues of researcher self-disclosure. Reflecting on a feminist participatory research project educating immigrant women in Canada regarding their legal rights, Susan McDonald (2003) urged that external researchers fully consider the implications of self-disclosure prior to embarking upon a feminist-infused research project, opining that

they hold a level of responsibility to attend to participant needs for "appropriate support" (identified as emotional and logistical support, among other forms). Patricia Maguire (1987) discussed similar challenges in her feminist action research among Native American survivors of domestic abuse.

Due, in part, to the complexities involved, the richness of these experiences and their contextualized natures defy formulas and require fluidity and ongoing negotiation. A research conversation between and among coresearchers and communities requires interconnected and overlapping dialogue, wherein the relationships themselves are interrogated and the roles of difference and power at work on both interpersonal and larger systems levels are explored.

Discussion

Although not all-inclusive, these four processes—insider-outsider dynamics, reflexivity, voices, and relationality—are, as argued previously, core processes within and defining of feminist-infused participatory and action research. We suggest here ways in which they have been articulated by researchers toward pressing for transformative change in individuals, institutions, and communities. In the final section of the chapter, we explore transformative praxis—and the challenges faced by feminist-infused participatory and action researchers who seek to actualize it.

TOWARD THE POSSIBILITY OF TRANSFORMATIVE PRAXIS

Feminist-infused participatory and action research is, as argued here, a set of theoretical and methodological orientations, processes, and outcomes whereby researchers and groups of women, men, and children engage in cross-community knowledge construction and action. They are also, at least in part, focused on redressing inequality and facilitating social change. Such claims do not negate the potential contribution to solving social problems claimed by those who engage in more traditional, hierarchical, and positivist research. For example, Cancian (1996) argues that survey research by demographers and sociologists regarding the widening income gap between the rich and poor in the United States had an impact on legislators' and voters' willingness to redistribute resources within the United States in the mid-1990s (pp. 202–203).

However, in contrast to positivist and post-positivist forms of research, participatory and action researchers seek to "mobilize oppressed people to act on their own behalf" rather than to act for them (Maguire, 1996, p. 29). Feminisms introduce a number of critical questions into this movement-building agenda, including, for example, whether a feminist perspective on participatory and action research challenges researchers to rethink the organization and community-building aspects of these research methodologies. These questions, and others summarized in our discussion of crosscutting issues, are fundamentally about power and the need not only to redistribute power but also to interrogate traditional understandings of power and to transform the praxis of power. We argue here, as suggested by Maguire (1996), that a feminist-infused participatory and action research "re-conceptualize[s] the very notion of power" (p. 29).

Specifically, power, a term of relationality, is often conceptualized as "power over" or possessing the resources and authority to impose one's will on individuals or groups with fewer resources. Power is typically associated with domination and vested in the state, religion, rulers, or other authorities. However, PAR, AR, and PR suggest alternative formulations, focusing frequently on power as the "capacity to." Many social scientists, feminists, and development workers embrace the language of "empowerment." Yet the term *empowerment*, about which there is now a significant body of theory and research (see, e.g., Rappaport, 1987; Zimmerman, 1995, 2000), suggests that someone is handing power over to a less powerful person or group. If power is the potential for an increased sense of an individual's or a community's capacity or ability to act for herself, himself, or itself and is the result of people's involvement in participatory or action research projects, then it cannot be given, but must be appropriated or taken. Thus, greater equity among coresearchers, a principle of participatory and action research processes, translates through shared action to enhanced or transformed equality within the research process and beyond, that is, in the wider community or in the world at large. From this perspective, "a popular people's organization [could be] a necessary prerequisite or a hoped-for outcome of PR" (Maguire, 1996, p. 29).

Research at the interface of feminisms and PAR, AR, and PR is, thus, complex. Many have argued that it is more likely for participatory and action researchers in educational, health, and community contexts to ignore gender or recapitulate traditional gendered relations than to enact transformative praxis alongside of women in ways that help them move from margin to center. As suggested previously, many of the initiatives designed to facilitate change fail to equip women with the resources necessary to engage in the complex new relations that are envisioned. To sustain a developing transformative collaboration, feminist, participatory, and action researchers must challenge themselves to think critically about their roles in the research endeavor. By explicitly shifting research participants from objects of study to agents or actors, feminist and participatory and action research implicitly concerns itself with issues of power and relationship. The work discussed here suggests just a few of the risks faced in engaging traditional dynamics of domination or control that, at a broader social level, constitute the situations coresearchers aim to change. Not surprisingly, many of the programs and projects described in this chapter fall short of transforming the power relations of inequality or of building a movement toward that end.

In this final section, we explore the ways in which, despite transformative goals and a discourse of change, feminist-informed participatory and action researchers sometimes reify rather than redress existing systems of power and control and fail to reduce the social injustices that are so carefully and critically described and analyzed through their work. We offer these concluding remarks both as cautionary tales and also to reflect, through our praxis, the underlying assumption articulated herein, that is, that feminist-infused participatory and action research is continuously iterative, not an endpoint.

Interrogating Power: Status, Functions, and Ideology

The issues of power already described hold particular resonance for feminist researchers in the academy, who, once among the population of the oppressed, now increasingly find themselves in positions of relative power and "gatekeeping." Social mobility may thus allow them vantage points as insiders *and* outsiders, challenging them "to continue to question the sources of [their] power, how it cannot be separated from the politics and the ideological position of the user, and how power [over] functions even within communities committed to social justice" (Unger, 1996, p. 177).

University-based external researchers often serve as "catalysts" asked to perform multiple roles as technical adviser, participant, and link to power sources, depending upon the context. This role as "catalyst" or "external change agent" can cause tensions in movement building, especially when a project becomes a group undertaking or collective process rather than one housed in the world of the "catalyst" (Martin, 1996; McDonald, 2003). McDonald (2003) discusses this tension in feminist participatory and action research—the disjuncture between demands that leadership be a driving force behind a project and feminist ideals of collaboration. Specifically, she discussed challenges in shifting or transforming the collective understanding of the project from "her project" to "our project" (McDonald, 2003, p. 77).

The researcher may struggle with navigating group dynamics and encouraging equitable participation by all while acknowledging that she is being treated as an expert, being deferred to by the group but also, in many ways, excluded from the group process. Yet she may also yield to a desire to utilize her status as a tool, exercising control or "power over" in order to keep the research project "on a comfortable course" progressing toward "her goals." Her "expert status" may also complicate basic decision making in participatory research endeavors; for

example, the researcher may hold important knowledge regarding the suitability of specific methods although the ideals of the project dictate that the decision about methodology be made collectively rather than executively by the researcher (Martin, 1996). Ospina et al. (2004) argue that "[f]or groups to function both effectively and democratically each member must feel authorized by the group and they must take up their own authority in the service of the group" (p. 65). Attention should be paid to understanding multiple forms of leadership, different leadership styles, and strategies for transferring control of a project to the participants or the community prior to the beginning of any project. Moreover, researchers are challenged to be transparent about these processes, each of which is frequently negotiated with partners external to the research process (e.g., funding agents, universities) that, nonetheless, exercise powerful influence at different points in the process.

Cautionary Tales From Participatory Development Work

Although not widely read by teachers, social science researchers, or health workers in the Northern Hemisphere, participatory and action research with and for women in the global South in development contexts offers important insight for feminist-infused participatory and action research that aspires explicitly toward social and transformative change.

Gender Issues in Participatory Development

Irene Guijt and Meera Kaul Shah (1998) report on a wide range of field experiences, particularly in the English-speaking majority world and, more specifically, in parts of Africa and India, and they discuss the promise—and limitations—of transformative AR, PR, and PAR projects. The case studies in this edited volume are preceded by seven theoretical chapters that discuss a range of challenges confronting researchers who seek to destabilize gender assumptions in a diverse range of participatory projects aimed at facilitating local communities' interrogation of the causes of power inequalities that impede development processes. The editors challenge those engaged in participatory processes who are committed to redressing power inequalities to deconstruct the local community functions of maleness and femaleness and to extend their focus on consciousness-raising to include the transformation of structural or institutional systems of oppression (see, e.g., Cornwall, 1998; see also, Cornwall, 2000, 2003). Yet, despite the growing involvement of women as participants in such projects, Heaven Crawley (1998) argues that "[f]or many involved in participatory research or action, gender is a footnote, rather than a place from which to begin the analysis" (p. 25) and that gender as a critical aspect of power relations is ignored in this work.

Dawn Currie (1999) challenges development theoreticians and practitioners to transform or "indigenize" knowledge. Her goal is to "develop a methodology that links social change to the experiences and needs of women as defined by women, and for social justice for women" (Currie, 1999, p. 99). She draws on the work of Kate Young (1993), who differentiated women's practical needs from their strategic interests in political and social struggles for equality. Young (1993) situates the construct of "women's needs" within a framework often overlooked by many, that is, amidst cultural and social realities in which women lack a sense of having rights or needs. She suggests further that "women's lack of access to information about their own societies, and the range of debate about political and economic matters is often a key element in their hesitancy about change" (Young, 1993, p. 157). Her work contributes importantly to participatory researchers who seek to develop a community-based process wherein participants develop their capacities to identify and share their needs and, from that base, begin to develop change processes. Finally, Andrea Cornwall (2003) cautions that the essentialist axes of difference that characterize much of development research and action with women—for example, "women in development" (WID), "women and development" (WAD), "women and sustainable development" (WED), and "gender and development" (GAD; Currie, 1999, p. 99)—obscure complex and deeply contextualized constructions of power and powerlessness within local communities.

Participation and Empowerment: New Forms of Colonial Power?

Despite their reflexive self-awareness and their commitment to transformative change, many participatory development practitioners and researchers have been criticized as only involving "local people taking part in other people's projects, according to agendas set by external interests" (Cornwall, 1996, p. 95). Participation, a *sine qua non* of action research, is highly structured, frequently yoked to democratic group processes, and often described as in the service of empowerment. Thus, participation carries with it expectations of public speech or group sharing, activities with varied meanings for women in the majority world. PAR researchers rarely interrogate the values underlying norms of participation or the parameters that define and characterize what constitutes participation. Cooke and Kothari (2001) have argued that it is critical to interrogate the discourse of participation itself, what they describe, somewhat provocatively, as the "tyranny of participation." Among other cautions, they suggest that the particular forms of "democratic participation" championed in action research and in development work and, we would argue, by feminists, shape particular identities that facilitate engagement in "the modern sector of developing societies" (p. 13), mapping and codifying local knowledge, thereby marginalizing indigenous ways of knowing that might challenge a newly developing status quo or be "messy" or unmanageable. The recently published edited volume by Andrea Cornwall (2011) contributes importantly to this ongoing dialogue about the multiple understandings of and experiences with participation.

Exposing Difference

Moreover, as Andrea Cornwall (1998) notes, "there may be aspects of women's lives and livelihoods which are especially important to conceal from fellow traders, worshippers or from family members that might be shared with others" through a participatory research methodology (p. 55). In southwestern Nigeria, for example, women meet in various fora, including market associations, prayer groups, and lineage groups, all of which have different communication dynamics and goals, which are specific to the women involved and to the nature of the meeting group (Cornwall, 1998). Moreover, Parpart (2000) argues that in Java, women's ability to control their speech and public behavior is equated with empowerment. This local understanding reflects a concept of empowerment that, in its implementation, may be at odds with Euro-American feminist conceptualizations and PAR goals.

Of equal concern are the possible risks to participants of exposing differences or private matters in group or public fora, strategies endorsed by participatory and action research. Moreover, "care needs . . . to be taken to ensure that the use of group fora, which emphasize group consensus, do not mask intra-group differences" (Kindon, 1998, p. 160). Consider, for example, a discussion group meeting of a men's *dusun* (the smallest administrative unit of a government village in Bali), a meeting facilitated as part of a community-based participatory process. About this meeting, researcher Sara Kindon (1998) noted that, due to the presence of a high-caste man (Brahmin) in a group of mid- to lower-caste men, the lower-caste men did not openly challenge the Brahmin's statements "for fear of losing face." Kindon (1998) concluded that "the group's consensus to follow such status-related codes of conduct masked considerable disagreement with this particular man's views" (p. 160). Others have suggested that participatory tools or techniques are sometimes used as devices to achieve technical outcomes rather than as principles that inform or transform political or social realities (see, e.g., Baker Collins, 2005; Guijt & Shah, 1998).

These experiences underscore the ways in which cultural specificities importantly inform and transform feminist discourse and praxis. As importantly, they suggest that conflict management and facilitation may be significant resources for increasing the likelihood for the best representation of the less powerful in participatory and action research projects undertaken from a feminist or gender-analytical perspective.

Inter- and Cross-Cultural Feminist Dialogue?

Feminist researchers are often based in Euro-American academic circles and grounded in modes of discourse, ideology, analysis, and action that may not be considered relevant to the individuals or cultures of the communities with whom they work, both in the West and beyond. For example, in an action research project with Black and white women in a Michigan drug treatment program, Dorothy Jo Henderson (1994) found that activism was not necessarily a method of change to which the participants could relate. Or, at the Medica Women's Centre established in Central Bosnia following the Balkan conflicts, Cockburn (1998) found that women held varied perspectives on feminism, some scoffing at Euro-American theories of feminism and International Women's Day—the former considered a luxury of women without families, the latter a disingenuous display of "flowers and flattery." Moreover, women in many majority world societies place great value on the opportunities for social and political influence that exist due to their roles as wives and mothers. Euro-American feminism's emphasis on challenging patriarchy and traditional gender roles may be seen as threatening to such women's cultural traditions, and as devaluing contributions they perceive to be grounded in and based on their traditional gender roles within their culture.

More locally, sociologist Nancy Naples's attempts to develop a feminist-based dialogue with a fellow survivor of childhood incest led her to the realization that "Emily [her coresearcher, a native Iowan, mother, and community activist] does not see the immediate relevance of academic discourse and feminist methodology for her goals [of empowering victims of sexual violence to tell their stories]" (Naples, 2003, pp. 192–193). Despite Naples's expectations of the ability of PR to "[generate] survivor-centered discourses that could broaden our understanding of the myriad forces contributing to violence against women" (p. 187) through dialogue and community outreach with adult survivors of sexual abuse and other survivors of violence, "the final product [of the efforts] was inevitably more an extension of [her] concerns than of [coresearcher] Emily's" (Naples, 2003, pp. 192–193).

CONCLUSION

Despite the critical contributions of explicitly feminist praxis, with its critique of power and gender asymmetries, it sometimes sits uneasily within the participatory norms of participatory and action research. Others have argued that these participatory norms fail to challenge gendered hierarchies or to transform traditional relations that oppress women. Moreover, much participatory and action research emphasizes local issues, dynamics, and change and does not directly address larger political and economic structures. Participants may choose not to work on social change at the level of state or national power structures—either because it is not a priority or because they are not confident that they have the power to achieve that change. Who *does* participate is, in many cases, who *can* participate. Specifically, the duration of an action project (i.e., more hours than a participant can spare from minimum-wage work or day work), its location at a distance from the duties of participants (e.g., away from the field or one's children), and participants' lack of skills to contribute to the report writing and analyses required of some participatory and action research are all obstacles that may have a negative impact on the ability of community members to participate (Parpart, 2000).

Participatory and action researchers working from a feminist standpoint articulate a commitment to challenge systems of power and to redress social injustice. Thus, at least implicitly, they have committed to challenging local, national, and global power structures that maintain local systems of inequality and oppression, and, despite multiple challenges, feminist-infused participatory and action research processes and outcomes have transformative potential. In a report written for the Centre of African Studies at the University of Copenhagen, Jane Parpart articulates certain requirements for rethinking and implementing anew participation and empowerment techniques for action researchers and participatory development projects. She challenges action researchers and feminists

> to develop a more nuanced and sophisticated analysis of power. . . . [that] incorporate[s] an analysis of the way global and national power structures impact on the local, the character and resilience of local power structures, the link between knowledge/discourse and power; and the complex ways people seek to ensure their well-being in the world. . . . Participatory empowerment techniques will have to pay more attention to the way national and global power structures constrain and define the possibilities for change at the local level. (Parpart, 2000, p. 18)

Many of the projects described in this chapter share a desire for change that supports movement building and social transformation. The group and community processes are designed to open spaces wherein women—and men—address gender relations and consider new approaches to struggles that they face in their ever-widening circles of relationality. The liberatory aspects of feminist and participatory and action research seek to raise awareness regarding oppressive forces at work in daily life. Through this experience, and the equitable power dynamic of the research process itself, the collaborative project identifies and works to transform power imbalances that contribute to the maintenance of systems of oppression. When coresearchers take the knowledge and momentum of these collective and community-based processes forward into the society at large for the purpose of addressing other, larger power imbalances, feminist-infused participatory and action research processes reach toward the creation of social and transformative change.

Discussion Questions

1. Compare and contrast the three iterations of feminist-infused participatory and action research, that is, research that (1) repositions gender, race, and class; (2) excavates indigenous cultural knowledges and generates voices; and (3) deploys intersectionality as an analytic tool for transformation.

2. How would you characterize a feminist-infused participatory and action research project that is transformative?

3. Is feminist-infused participatory and action research gender specific; that is, must it be done exclusively or mainly with, by, and for women or girls?

Online Resources

PARticipatory FEMinism (PARFEM)

http://www.einaudi.cornell.edu/parfem/parfem.asp

This site is an online participatory feminist resource where co-learners can contribute materials and ideas and carry on dialogue. The site includes an online bibliography, case studies, and live events such as presentations and discussions that can be downloaded.

Institute of Development Studies

http://www.ids.ac.uk/go/home

The Institute of Development Studies is a leading global, nongovernmental organization committed to research, teaching, and communications on international development. Its purpose is to understand and explain the world, and to try to change it—to influence as well as to inform.

Highlander Research and Education Center

http://www.highlandercenter.org/index.html

Highlander serves as a catalyst for grassroots organizing and movement building in Appalachia, the South, and beyond. Through popular education, participatory research, and cultural work, it develops leadership and helps create and support strong, democratic organizations that work for justice, equality, and sustainability.

Relevant Journals

Action Research

Feminism & Psychology

Feminist Studies

International Journal of Qualitative Studies in Education

Women's Studies International Forum

Notes

1. Within this chapter, the term *coresearcher* will henceforth refer to all engaged in the research endeavor, both those traditionally labeled *researchers* (also referred to as outsiders, facilitators, and catalysts) and those traditionally labeled *participants* (also referred to as insiders, coresearchers, and community members).

2. Rather than the terms *third world* or *developing world*, we use the terms *majority world* or *global South* to refer to countries outside the North American, European, and Northern Hemisphere orbit. These countries have a majority of the world's population and occupy a majority of the earth's land surface or geographical space, excluding China.

3. *La violencia,* literally "the violence," is used by most rural Mayan peasants to describe the nearly 36-year armed conflict that destroyed many of their communities and was later characterized as genocide by the United Nations. It represents these experiences while obscuring much of their horror and silencing the speaker's protagonism or victimization in the conflict.

References

Acker, J., Barry, K., & Esseveld, J. (1996). Objectivity and truth: Problems in doing feminist research. In H. Gottfried (Ed.), *Feminism and social change: Bridging theory and practice* (pp. 60–67). Urbana and Chicago: University of Illinois Press.

Adelman, C. (1993). Kurt Lewin and the origins of action research. *Educational Action Research, 1*(1), 7–24.

Allen, D., & Hutchinson, T. (2009). Using PAR or abusing its good name? The challenges and surprises of PhotoVoice and PAR in a study of chronic illness. *International Journal of Qualitative Methods, 8*(2), 116–128.

Arratia, M., & de la Maza, I. (1997). Grounding a long-term deal: Working with the Aymara for community development. In S. E. Smith, D. G. Williams, & N. A. Johnson (Eds.), *Nurtured by knowledge: Learning to do participatory action research* (pp. 111–137). New York: The Apex Press.

Baker Collins, S. (2005). An understanding of poverty from those who are poor. *Action Research, 3*(1), 9–31.

Balcazar, F. E., Garcia-Iriarte, E., & Suarez-Balcazar, Y. (2009). Participatory action research with Colombian immigrants. *Hispanic Journal of Behavioral Sciences, 31,* 112–127.

Bartunek, J. M., & Louis, M. R. (1996). *Insider/outsider team research* (Qualitative Research Methods Series, 40). Thousand Oaks, CA: Sage.

Boston Women's Health Book Collective. (1973). *Our bodies, ourselves: A book by and for women.* New York: Simon & Schuster.

Brabeck, K. M., Lykes, M. B., & Hershberg, R. (2011). Framing immigration to and deportation from the United States: Guatemalan and Salvadoran families make meaning of their experiences. *Community, Work & Family, 14*(3), 275–296.

Brabeck, K. M., & Xu, Q. (2010). The impact of detention and deportation on Latino immigrant children and families: A quantitative exploration. *Hispanic Journal of Behavioral Sciences, 32*(3), 341–361.

Bradbury, H. (2001). Learning with *The Natural Step:* Action research for sustainable development. In P. Reason & H. Bradbury (Eds.), *Handbook of action research: Participative inquiry and practice* (pp. 307–313). Thousand Oaks, CA: Sage.

Brydon-Miller, M. (2004). The terrifying truth: Interrogating systems of power and privilege and choosing to act. In M. Brydon-Miller, P. Maguire, & A. McIntyre (Eds.), *Traveling companions: Feminism, teaching, and action research* (pp. 3–20). Westport, CT: Praeger.

Brydon-Miller, M., & Greenwood, D. (2003). Why action research? *Action Research, 1*(1), 9–28.

Brydon-Miller, M., & Maguire, P. (2009). Participatory action research: Contributions to the development of practitioner inquiry in education. *Educational Action Research, 17*(1), 79–93.

Brydon-Miller, M., Maguire, P., & McIntyre, A. (2004). *Traveling companions: Feminism, teaching, and action research.* Westport, CT: Praeger.

Bunster, X., & Chaney, E. M. (1989). Epilogue. In X. Bunster & E. M. Chaney, *Sellers and servants: Working women in Lima, Peru* (pp. 217–233). Granby, MA: Bergin & Garvey Publishers, Inc.

Cammarota, J., & Romero, A. (2010). Participatory action research for high school students: Transforming policy, practice, and the personal with social justice education. *Educational Policy, 20*(10), 1–19.

Cancian, F. (1996). Participatory research and alternative strategies for activist sociology. In H. Gottfried (Ed.), *Feminism and social change: Bridging theory and practice* (pp. 187–205). Urbana and Chicago: University of Illinois Press.

Chavez, V., Duran, B., Baker, Q., Avila, M., & Wallerstein, N. (2003). The dance of race and privilege in community-based participatory research. In M. Minkler & N. Wallerstein (Eds.), *Community-based participatory research for health* (pp. 81–97). San Francisco: Jossey Bass.

Christinansen, E. D. (2010). Adolescent Cape Verdean girls' experiences of violence, incarceration, and deportation: Developing resources through participatory community-based groups. *International Journal of Intercultural Relations, 34*(2), 127–140.

Cockburn, C. (1998). *The space between us: Negotiating gender and national identities in conflict.* New York: Zed Books, Ltd.

Coker-Appiah, D. S. (2009). In their own voices: Rural African American youth speak out about community-based HIV prevention interventions. *Progress in Community Health Partnerships: Research, Education, Action, 3*(4), 301–312.

Collins, P. H. (1990). *Black feminist thought: Knowledge, consciousness, and the politics of empowerment.* Boston: Unwin Hyman.

Collins, P. H. (1996). What's in a name? Womanism, Black feminism, and beyond. *The Black Scholar, 26*(1), 9–17.

Collins, P. H. (1998). *Fighting words: Black women and the search for justice.* Minneapolis: University of Minnesota Press.

Commission for Historical Clarification (CEH). (1999). *Guatemala: Memory of silence* (Report of the Commission for Historical Clarification). Retrieved May 10, 2005, from http://shr.aaas .org/guatemala/ceh/report/english/recs1.html

Cooke, B., & Kothari, U. (Eds.). (2001). *Participation: The new tyranny?* London and New York: Zed Books, Ltd.

Cornwall, A. (1996). Towards participatory practice: Participatory rural appraisal (PRA) and the participatory process. In K. de Koning & M. Martin (Eds.), *Participatory research in health: Issues and experiences* (pp. 95–107). Johannesburg, South Africa: Zed Books Ltd.

Cornwall, A. (1998). Gender, participation, and the politics of difference. In I. Guijt & M. K. Shah (Eds.), *The myth of community: Gender issues in participatory development* (pp. 46–57). London: Intermediate Technology Publications.

Cornwall, A. (2000). *Making a difference? Gender and participatory development* (IDS Discussion Paper No. 378). Brighton, UK: Institute of Development Studies.

Cornwall, A. (2003). Whose voices? Whose choices? Reflections on gender and participatory development. *World Development, 31*(8), 1325–1342.

Cornwall, A. (2011). *The participation reader.* London: ZED Books.

Crawley, H. (1998). Living up to the empowerment claim? The potential of PRA. In I. Guijt & M. K. Shah (Eds.), *The myth of community: Gender issues in participatory development* (pp. 24–34). London: Intermediate Technology Publications.

Crosby, A. (2009). Anatomy of a workshop: Women's struggles for transformative participation in Latin America. *Feminism & Psychology, 12*(3), 343–353.

Currie, D. (1999). Gender analysis from the standpoint of women: The radical potential of women's studies in development. *Asian Journal of Women's Studies, 5*(3), 99–144.

Davis, A. (1981). *Women, race, and class.* New York: Vintage Books.

Debbink, G., & Ornelas, A. (1997). Cows for campesinos. In S. E. Smith, D. G. Willms, & N. A. Johnson (Eds.), *Nurtured by knowledge: Learning to do participatory action research* (pp. 13–33). New York: The Apex Press.

Denzin, N. K., & Lincoln, Y. S. (Eds.). (2000). *Handbook of qualitative research* (2nd ed.). Thousand Oaks, CA: Sage.

Dick, B. (2004). Action research literature: Themes and trends. *Action Research, 2*(4), 425–444.

Drolet, C. (2008). Female youth social empowerment through educational technology: Digital film as critical language of transcendence. *An educational adventure: Active learning through media literacy.* Retrieved June 14, 2011, from http://drofilm1 .edublogs.org/artifacts-2/article-empowering-women-in-ed-tech/

Du Bois, B. (1983). Passionate scholarship: Notes on value, knowing, and method in feminist social science. In G. Bowles & R. D. Klein (Eds.), *Theories of women's studies* (pp. 105–116). London: Routledge & Kegan Paul.

Dyrness, A. (2008). Research for change versus research as change: Lessons from a *mujerista*

participatory research team. *Anthropology & Education Quarterly, 39*(1), 23–44.

Ecumenical Women's Team Visit. (1992). *Rape of women in war.* Geneva: Author.

Eikeland, O. (2001). Action research as the hidden curriculum of the western tradition. In P. Reason & H. Bradbury (Eds.), *Handbook of action research: Participative inquiry and practice* (pp. 145–156). Thousand Oaks, CA: Sage.

Evans, S. M. (1979). *Personal politics: The roots of women's liberation in the civil rights movement and the new left.* New York: Vintage.

Fals-Borda, O. (1985). *Knowledge and people's power: Lessons with peasants in Nicaragua, Mexico, and Colombia.* New Delhi: Indian Social Institute.

Fals-Borda, O. (1991). *Some basic ingredients.* New York: Apex Press.

Fals-Borda, O. R., & Rahman, M. A. (Eds.). (1991). *Action and knowledge: Breaking the monopoly with participatory action research.* New York: Apex Press.

Fine, M. (1992). *Disruptive voices: The possibilities of feminist research.* Ann Arbor: University of Michigan Press.

Fine, M. (1994). Dis-stance and other stances: Negotiation of power inside feminist research. In A. Gitlin (Ed.), *Power and method: Political activism and educational research* (pp. 13–35). New York: Routledge.

Fine, M., Roberts, R. A., Torre, M. E., Bloom, J., Burns, A., Chajet, L., Guishard, M., & Payne, Y. (2004). *Echoes of Brown: Youth documenting and performing the legacy of Brown v. Board of Education.* New York: Teacher's College Press.

Fine, M., & Ruglis, J. (2009). Circuits and consequences of dispossession: The racial realignment of the public sphere for U.S. youth. *Transforming Anthropology, 17*(1), 20–33.

Fournier, B., Mill, J., Kipp, W., & Walusimbi, M. (2007). Discovering voice: A participatory action research study with nurses in Uganda. *International Journal of Qualitative Methods, 6*(1), 1–19.

Freeman, J. (Ed.). (1975). *Women: A feminist perspective.* Oxford, UK: Mayfield.

Freire, P. (1970). *Pedagogy of the oppressed.* (M. B. Ramos, Trans.). New York: Continuum.

Friedan, B. (1963). *The feminine mystique.* New York: W. W. Norton.

Frisby, W., Maguire, P., & Reid, C. (2009). The "f" word has everything to do with it: How feminist theories inform action research. *Action Research,* *7*(1), 13–29.

Gluck, S. B., & Patai, D. (Eds.). (1991). *Women's words: The feminist practice of oral history.* New York: Routledge.

Gorelick, S. (1996). Contradictions of feminist methodology. In H. Gottfried (Ed.), *Feminism and social change: Bridging theory and practice* (pp. 23–45). Urbana and Chicago: University of Illinois Press.

Greenwood, D., & Levin, M. (1998). *Introduction to action research: Social research for social change.* Thousand Oaks, CA: Sage.

Guijt, I., & Shah, M. K. (Eds.). (1998). *The myth of community: Gender issues in participatory development.* London: Intermediate Technology Publications.

Gustavsen, B. (2001). Theory and practice: The mediating discourse. In P. Reason & H. Bradbury (Eds.), *Handbook of action research: Participative inquiry and practice* (pp. 17–26). Thousand Oaks, CA: Sage.

Harding, S. (1986). *The science question in feminism.* Ithaca, NY: Cornell University Press.

Harvey, I., Shulz, A., Israel, B., Sand, S., Myria, D., Lockett, M., Weir, S., & Hill, Y. (2009). The healthy connections project: A community-based participatory research project involving women at risk for diabetes and hypertension. *Progress in Community Health Partnerships: Research, Education, and Action, 3*(4), 287–300.

Henderson, D. J. (1994). *Feminist nursing participatory research with black and white women in drug treatment.* Unpublished doctoral dissertation, University of Michigan School of Nursing, Ann Arbor, MI.

Hergenrather, K. C., Rhodes, S. D., & Bardhoshi, G. (2009). PhotoVoice as community-based participatory research: A qualitative review. *American Journal of Health Behavior, 33*(6), 686–698.

Hesse-Biber, S. (Ed.). (2007). *Handbook of feminist research: Theory and praxis.* Thousand Oaks, CA: Sage.

hooks b. (1981). *Ain't I a woman: Black women and feminism.* Boston: South End Press.

hooks, b. (1984). Black women: Shaping feminist theory. In b. hooks, *Feminist theory: From margin to center* (pp. 1–15). Boston: South End Press.

hooks. b. (1990). *Yearning: Race, gender, and cultural politics.* Boston: South End Press.

Hope, A., & Timmel, S. (1984–2000). *Training for transformation: A handbook for community workers* (Vols. 1–4). London: Intermediate Technology Publications.

Khanna, R. (1996). Participatory action research (PAR) in women's health: SARTHI, India. In K. de Koning & M. Martin (Eds.), *Participatory research in health: Issues and experiences* (pp. 62–71). Johannesburg, South Africa: Zed Books Ltd.

Kindon, S. (1998). Of mothers and men: Questioning gender and community myths in Bali. In I. Guijt & M. K. Shah (Eds.), *The myth of community: Gender issues in development* (pp. 152–164). London: Intermediate Technology Publications.

Kralik, D., Koch, T., & Eastwood, S. (2003). The salience of body: Transition in sexual identity for women living with multiple sclerosis. *Journal of Advanced Nursing, 42,* 11–20.

Lennie, J. (2002). Rural women's empowerment in a communication technology project: Some contradictory effects. *Rural Society, 12*(3), 224–245.

Lorde, A. (1984). *Sister outsider: Essays and speeches.* Berkeley, CA: Crossing Press.

Lykes, M. B. (1994). Terror, silencing, and children: International, multidisciplinary collaboration with Guatemalan Maya communities. *Social Science and Medicine, 38*(4), 543–552.

Lykes, M. B. (2010). Silence(ing), voice(s), and gross violations of human rights: Constituting and performing subjectivities through PhotoPAR. *Visual Studies, 25*(3), 238–254.

Lykes, M. B., & Mallona, A. (2008). Towards transformational liberation: Participatory action research and activist praxis. In P. Reason & H. Bradbury (Eds.), *The SAGE handbook of action research II* (pp. 260–292). London: Sage.

Lykes, M. B., Mateo, A. C., Anay, J. C., Caba, A. L., Ruiz, U., & Williams, J. W. (1999). Telling stories—rethreading lives: Community education, women's development, and social change among the Maya Ixil. *International Journal of Leadership in Education: Theory and Practice, 2*(3), 207–227.

Lykes, M. B., Terre Blanche, M., & Hamber, B. (2003). Narrating survival and change in Guatemala and South Africa: The politics of representation and a liberatory community psychology. *American Journal of Community Psychology, 31*(1/2), 79–90.

Maguire, P. (1987). *Doing participatory research: A feminist approach.* Amherst: Massachusetts Center for International Education, University of Massachusetts.

Maguire, P. (1996). Proposing a more feminist participatory research: Knowing and being embraced more openly. In K. de Koning & M. Martin (Eds.), *Participatory research in health: Issues and experiences* (pp. 27–29). Johannesburg, South Africa: Zed Books Ltd.

Maguire, P. (2001). *Uneven ground: Feminism and action research.* Thousand Oaks, CA: Sage.

Maguire, P. (2004). Reclaiming the f-word: Emerging lessons from teaching and feminist-informed action research. In M. Brydon-Miller, P. Maguire, & A. McIntyre (Eds.), *Traveling companions: Feminisms, teaching, and action research* (pp. 117–136). Westport, CT: Praeger.

Marecek, J., Fine, M., & Kidder, L. (2001). Working between two worlds: Qualitative methods and psychology. In D. L. Tolman & M. Brydon-Miller (Eds.), *From subjects to subjectivities: A handbook of interpretive and participatory methods* (pp. 29–44). New York: New York University Press.

Martin, M. (1996). Issues of power in the participatory research process. In K. de Koning & M. Martin (Eds.), *Participatory research in health: Issues and experiences* (pp. 82–93). London: Zed Books.

Mazowiecki, T. (1993). *United Nations Commission on Human Rights: Situation of human rights in the territory of the former Yugoslavia.* New York: United Nations.

McDonald, S. (2003). Answering questions and asking more: Reflections on feminist participatory research. *Resources for Feminist Research, 30*(2), 77–95.

McIntyre, A. (1997). *Making meaning of whiteness: Exploring racial identity with white teachers.* Albany, NY: SUNY Press.

McIntyre, A., Chatzopoulos, N., Politi, A., & Roz, J. (2007). Participatory action research: Collective reflections on gender, culture, and language. *Teaching and Teacher Education, 23,* 748–756.

McIntyre, A., & Lykes, M. B. (2004). Weaving words and pictures in/through feminist participatory action research. In M. Brydon-Miller, P. Maguire, & A. McIntyre (Eds.), *Traveling companions: Feminism, teaching, and action research* (pp. 57–77). Westport, CT: Praeger.

McTaggart, R. (Ed.). (1997). *Participatory action research: International contexts and consequences.* Albany: State University of New York Press.

Merton, R. K. (1972). Insiders and outsiders: A chapter in the sociology of knowledge. *American Journal of Sociology, 78,* 9–47.

Minkler, M., & Wallerstein, N. (2003). Introduction to community based participatory research. In M. Minkler & N. Wallerstein. (Eds.), *Community based participatory research for health* (pp. 3–26). San Francisco: Jossey-Bass.

Mitchell, C., & Reid-Walsh, J. (2002). *Researching children's popular culture: The cultural spaces of childhood.* New York: Routledge.

Mohanty, C. T. (2003). *Feminism without borders: Decolonizing theory, practicing solidarity.* Durham, NC: Duke University Press.

Molestane, R., Mitchell, C., de Lange, N., Stuart, J., Buthelezi, T., & Taylor, M. (2009). What can a woman do with a camera? Turning the female gaze on poverty and HIV and AIDS in rural South Africa. *International Journal of Qualitative Studies in Education, 22*(3), 315–331.

Moraga, C., & Anzaldúa, G. (1983). *This bridge called my back: Writings by radical women of color.* New York: Kitchen Table, Women of Color Press.

Naples, N. A. (2003). *Feminism and method: Ethnography, discourse analysis, and activist research.* New York: Routledge.

Naples, N. A., & Clark, E. (1996). Feminist participatory research and empowerment: Going public as survivors of childhood sexual abuse. In H. Gottfried (Ed.), *Feminism and social change: Bridging theory and practice* (pp. 160–186). Urbana and Chicago: University of Illinois Press.

ODHAG/Oficina de Derechos Humanos del Arzobispado de Guatemala [Office of Human Rights of the Archdiocese of Guatemala]. (1998). *Nunca más: Informe proyecto interdiocesano de recuperación de la memoria histórica* [Never again: Report of the inter-diocescan project on the recovery of historic memory] (Vols. 1–5). Guatemala: Author.

Okigbo, C., Reierson, J., & Stowman, S. (2009). Leveraging acculturation through action research: A case study of refugee and immigrant women in the United States. *Action Research, 7*(2), 127–142.

Ospina, S., Dodge, J., Godsoe, B., Minieri, J., Reza, S., & Schall, E. (2004). From consent to mutual inquiry: Balancing democracy and authority in action research. *Action Research, 2*(1), 47–69.

Parpart, J. L. (2000). *The participatory empowerment approach to gender and development in Africa: Panacea or illusion?* (Occasional Paper). Copenhagen: Centre of African Studies University of Copenhagen.

Patai, D. (1994). When method becomes power (Response). In A. Gitlin (Ed.), *Power and method: Political activism and educational research* (pp. 61–73). New York: Routledge.

Personal Narratives Group. (1989). *Interpreting women's lives: Feminist theory and personal narratives.* Bloomington: Indiana University Press.

Post-Deportation Human Rights Project (PDHRP). (2009). *Keeping families connected: Annual Report, 2008–2009.* Chestnut Hill, MA: Center for Human Rights and International Justice at Boston College. Retrieved July 12, 2011, from http://www.bc.edu/content/dam/files/centers/humanrights/pdf/PDHRPAnnualReport.pdf

Post-Deportation Human Rights Project (PDHRP). (2010). *Annual report, 2009–2010.* Chestnut Hill, MA: Center for Human Rights and International Justice at Boston College. Retrieved July 12, 2011, from http://www.bc.edu/content/dam/files/centers/humanrights/pdf/PDHRPAnnualReport.pdf

Rahman, A. (2004). Globalization: The emerging ideology in the popular protests and grassroots action research. *Action Research, 2*(1), 9–23.

Rappaport, J. (1987). Terms of empowerment/exemplars of prevention: Toward a theory for community psychology. *American Journal of Community Psychology, 15*(2), 121–148.

Reason, P., & Bradbury, H. (2001). Introduction: Inquiry and participation in search of a world worthy of human aspiration. In P. Reason & H. Bradbury (Eds.), *Handbook of action research: Participative inquiry and practice* (pp. 1–14). Thousand Oaks, CA: Sage.

Reason, P., & Bradbury, H. (2008). *Handbook of action research: Participative inquiry & practice* (2nd ed.). London: Sage.

Reid, C., & Frisby, W. (2008). Continuing the journey. Articulating dimensions of feminist participatory action research. In P. Reason & H. Bradbury (Eds.), *Handbook of action research: Participative inquiry & practice* (2nd ed., pp. 93–105). London: Sage.

Reinharz, S. (1992). *Feminist methods in social research.* New York: Oxford University Press.

Rhodes, S. D., Hergenrather, K. C., Arceo, R., Remnitz, I. M., Montaño, J., & Alegría-Ortega, J. (2007). Exploring Latino men's HIV risk using community-based participatory research. *American Journal of Health Behavior, 31*(2), 146–158.

Roberts, H. (1981). *Doing feminist research.* Boston: Routledge & Kegan Paul.

Rosen, R. (2000). *The world split open: How the modern women's movement changed America.* New York: Penguin Putnam.

Sánchez, P. (2009). Chicana feminist strategies in a participatory action research project with transnational Latina youth. *New Directions for Youth Development, 123,* 83–97.

Sandoval, C. (2000). *Methodology of the oppressed.* Minneapolis: University of Minnesota Press.

Sleeter, C., Torres, M. N., & Laughlin, P. (2004). Scaffolding conscientization through inquiry in teacher education. *Teacher Education Quarterly, 31*(1), 81–96.

Smith, D. E. (1987). *The everyday world as problematic: A feminist sociology.* Boston: Northeastern University Press.

Smith, D. E. (1991). *The conceptual practices of power: A feminist sociology of knowledge.* Boston: Northeastern University Press.

Spelman, E. V. (1988). Gender in the context of race and class: Notes on Chodorow's "Reproduction of Mothering." In E. V. Spelman, *Inessential woman: Problems of exclusion in feminist thought* (pp. 80–113). Boston: Beacon.

Stacey, J. (1996). Can there be a feminist ethnography? In H. Gottfried (Ed.), *Feminism and social change: Bridging theory and practice* (pp. 88–101). Urbana and Chicago: University of Illinois Press.

Stern, S. P. (1998). Struggle over schooling in an African American community. In N. Naples (Ed.), *Community activism and feminist politics: Organizing across race, class, and gender* (pp. 107–127). New York: Routledge.

Swiss, S., & Giller, J. E. (1993). Rape as a crime of war: A medical perspective. *Journal of the American Medical Association, 270,* 612–615.

Themba, M. N., & Minkler, M. (2003). Influencing policy through community-based participatory research. In M. Minkler & N. Wallerstein (Eds.), *Community-based participatory research for health* (pp. 349–370). San Francisco: Jossey-Bass.

Torre, M. E. (2008). Participatory action research and critical race theory: Fueling spaces for *nos-otras* to research. *Urban Review, 41,* 106–120.

Torre, M. E., & Fine, M. (2003). Youth reframe questions of educational justice through participatory action research. *The Evaluation Exchange, 9*(2), 6–22.

Trinh, T. Minh-ha. (1989). *Woman, native, other: Writing post-coloniality and feminism*: Bloomington: Indiana University Press.

Umrungi, J. P., Mitchell, C., Gervaise, M., Ubalijoro, E., & Kabarenzi, V. (2008). PhotoVoice as a methodological tool to address HIV and AIDS and gender violence amongst girls on the streets in Rwanda. *Journal of Psychology in Africa, 18*(3), 413–420.

Unger, R. K. (1996). Using the master's tools: Epistemology and empiricism. In S. Wilkinson (Ed.), *Feminist social psychologies: International perspectives* (pp. 165–181). Milton Keynes, UK: Open University Press.

UNICEF. (2005). Patterns in conflict: Civilians are now the targets. *Information: Impact of armed children in conflict*. Retrieved May 25, 2005, from http://www.unicef.org/graca/patterns.htm

Walker, Λ. (1983). *In search of our mothers' gardens*. New York: Harcourt, Brace Jovanovich.

Wang, C. (1999). Photovoice: A participatory action research strategy applied to women's health. *Journal of Women's Health, 8*(2), 185–192.

Wang, C., Burris, M., & Xiang, Y. (1996). Chinese village women as visual anthropologists: A participatory approach to reaching policymakers. *Social Science & Medicine, 42*(10), 1391–1400.

Welbourne, A. (1998). Gender, participation and HIV: A positive force for change. In I. Guijt & M. K. Shah (Eds.), *The myth of community: Gender issues in participatory development* (pp. 131–140). London: Intermediate Technology Publications.

Whyte, W. F. (Ed.). (1991). *Participatory action research*. Newbury Park, CA: Sage.

Williams, J. W., & Lykes, M. B. (2003). Bridging theory and practice: Using reflexive cycles in feminist participatory action research. *Feminism & Psychology, 13*(3), 287–294.

Williams, P., & Chrisman, L. (Eds.). (1994). *Colonial discourse/political theory*. New York: Columbia University Press.

Women of PhotoVoice/ADMI & Lykes, M. B. (2000). *Voces e imágenes: Mujeres Mayas Ixiles de Chajul/Voices and images: Mayan Ixil women of Chajul*. Guatemala: MagnaTerra.

Worthen, M., Veale, A., McKay, S., & Wessels, M. (2010, January 19). "I stand like a woman": Empowerment and human rights in the context of community-based reintegration of girl mothers formerly associated with fighting forces and armed groups. *Journal of Human Rights Practice*, pp. 1–22.

Wu, K., Burris, M., Li, V., Wang, Y., Zhan, W., Xian, Y., Yang, K., & Wang, C. (Eds.). (1995). *Visual voices: 100 photographs of village China by the women of Yunnan Province*. Yunnan: Yunnan People's Publishing House.

Young, K. (1993). *Planning with women: Making a world of difference*. London: MacMillan.

Zeichner, K. (2001). Educational action research. In P. Reason & H. Bradbury (Eds.), *Handbook of action research: Participative inquiry and practice* (pp. 273–284). Thousand Oaks, CA: Sage.

Zimmerman, M. A. (1995). Psychological empowerment: Issues and illustrations. *American Journal of Community Psychology, 23*(5), 581–599.

Zimmerman, M. A. (2000). Empowerment theory: Psychological, organizational, and community levels of analysis. In J. Rappaport & E. Seidman (Eds.), *Handbook of community psychology* (pp. 43–63). Dordrecht, The Netherlands: Kluwer Academic Publishers.

17

NARRATIVES AND NUMBERS

Feminist Multiple Methods Research

ELIZABETH R. COLE AND ABIGAIL J. STEWART

In this chapter, we draw on insights we gleaned while co-teaching, along with our colleague David Featherman, a yearlong graduate seminar introducing students to feminist social science research that integrated qualitative and quantitative methods. The goal of the seminar was to move beyond a conflict about the value of these two approaches that has been characterized as a debate (sometimes known as the QQD; Rabinowitz & Weseen, 1997) or even a war (Tashakkori & Teddlie, 2003). Like some other scholars currently working in this area, we felt the distinctions between the two approaches were commonly overstated (Hanson, 2008), and we sought to transcend this stale debate in order to give our students the opportunity to take advantage of the strengths of both methods while overcoming the limitations of either approach

(Gelo, Braakmann, & Benetka, 2008). Without advocating any particular methods, we aimed to examine the obstacles and benefits associated with combining and integrating qualitative and quantitative methods and to encourage students to become skilled in the use of both approaches.

Our syllabus began with readings that outlined ideal approaches for combining methodologies (Newman & Benz, 1998; Tashakkori & Teddlie, 1998, 2003); with these as a backdrop, the remainder of the course was a series of invited lectures by researchers from across the United States whose research programs used both qualitative and quantitative methods. Over the academic year, we learned a great deal about the ways that researchers called on these two approaches to address their research questions. The combinations reflected a wish to gain

Authors' Note: We are grateful to the Rackham Graduate School at the University of Michigan for a Rackham Interdisciplinary Seminar Grant to develop and teach a graduate course entitled "Narratives and Numbers" with our colleague David Featherman. We owe a great deal to David Featherman, to the guest visitors to the course, and to the students in the seminar for providing such a stimulating opportunity to think about these issues. Thanks also to Amal Fadlalla for her suggestions about combining qualitative and quantitative methods in the field of anthropology. Finally, we appreciated thoughtful and helpful feedback on an early draft of this chapter from Christa McDermott, Perry Silverschanz, Cynthia Torges, and the editor.

knowledge about a phenomenon unconstrained by methodological preconceptions, and, at the same time, they were almost always pragmatic, often innovative, and even occasionally based on serendipity or the resources at hand.

In this chapter, we aim to distill some of what we learned from this teaching experience, thereby sharing it with a broader audience. Our reflections have led us to generate a typology of approaches based not on ideal types but on combinations of strategies actually used by researchers whose work addresses women, gender, and sexuality. In order to cast our net widely, we have used a broad definition of feminist research in this chapter: we are interested in work that takes gender or sexuality as a central focus or category of analysis. But this endeavor, as we've defined it, begs two larger questions. First, is feminist mixed methods research different from that undertaken by any other researcher, and, if so, how? Here we are in agreement with Harding (1987): feminist research is distinguished not so much by its methods, that is, the procedures through which information or observations are collected, but by its methodology, that is, the underlying theory about how research should be conducted and what its aims should be. Harding argues that feminist researchers typically ground their research questions in the experience of women, with the goal of understanding women's experience and improving women's lives, and, in doing so, many attempt to equalize the hierarchy in the traditional relationship between "researchers" and "subjects."

The second question asks, why should any social scientist attempt to combine these methods, methods that, some would argue, are based on fundamentally different assumptions about epistemology and ontology (Guba & Lincoln, 1994)?[1] Perhaps the most commonly offered answer to this question is that different methods suit different questions or aspects of questions. Courses in research methods typically represent the research process as composed of two sequential phases: the context of discovery, in which hypotheses are generated, and the context of justification, in which they are tested. In this tradition, qualitative methods are often presented as subjective, unsystematic, and inherently unreliable, and thus only appropriate for the context of discovery.[2] In contrast, the strengths of quantitative methods are held to be reliability, replicability, and generalizability. They therefore hold sway over the context of justification. However, Ann Lin (1998) has cogently challenged this binary, arguing that, although many believe qualitative and quantitative approaches are divided by an underlying divergence in their epistemological assumptions (which she terms interpretivist and positivist, respectively), this characterization is misleading. Lin argues that positivist approaches aim to identify relationships between variables that are generalizable to different contexts; in contrast, interpretivist methods are designed to reveal mechanisms that underlie these relationships in particular cases or contexts. She argues that qualitative methods can be used in research with both types of epistemological aims, and she demonstrates this with examples from public policy research.

For example, both Stack (1974) and Edin (1991) used qualitative methods to study how poor women survive on very limited incomes. Stack's now-classic project, an interpretivist one, demonstrated how women share resources within social networks even when doing so comes at personal costs to individuals. Stack studied the norms and sense of obligation among women in one kin network, richly documenting the particularity of this social context. In contrast, Edin used the qualitative methods of in-depth interviews and ethnography to construct a detailed accounting of her respondents' household budgets, finding that women often used family gifts and undocumented work to make ends meet. Because the gap between the cost of living and welfare payments is similar in different parts of the country, Edin argued that it was appropriate to generalize these findings. Thus, Lin's insights suggest that one of the most commonly given justifications for combining qualitative and quantitative methods in a single project may unnecessarily constrain researchers; a researcher with both interpretivist and positivist aims could also choose to design a pair of qualitative studies to address these research questions. Proponents of mixing qualitative and quantitative methods also argue that this approach can increase our confidence in the robustness of a finding when the relationship appears to hold using a variety of research approaches (this represents a form of replication or cross-validation, and is often termed triangulation). However, as Lin's work reminds us, this particular strength of the multiple methods approach could be accomplished using any combination of methods and does not necessitate the combination of quantitative and qualitative approaches.

Among social scientists, feminist scholars have been vocal in arguing for the value of mixed methods research approaches, though for a variety of reasons (see especially Fine & Gordon, 1989; Jayaratne & Stewart, 1991; Peplau & Conrad, 1989; Reinharz, 1992; however, see Giddings & Grant, 2007, for a caution). First, because feminist scholars often begin from a posture of critique of existing social science findings and recognize that social science research has often "left out" or ignored aspects of phenomena that they care about, they are much less inclined to believe that a single method is the "royal road" to understanding. Thus, feminist scholars have often embraced pluralism partly as a strategy that might be less likely to produce a narrow and selective picture of human experience (Jayaratne & Stewart, 1991; Rabinowitz & Weseen, 1997; Sherif, 1979/1987; Unger, 1981; Weisstein, 1971).

Feminist scholars are also specifically impressed by the dangers of false generalization in formulating research questions. Sapiro (1995) noted, of political science, that "in the early days most work was of the 'add women and stir' or compensatory variety, taking conventional questions in different fields, but especially political behavior and political theory, and asking, 'what about the women?'" (p. 291). Smith (1987) made a parallel argument about sociological studies of the family and education—that they began from the standpoint of men, even when they included attention to women and children. Similarly, feminist scholars commented that, until the late 1960s, much of psychology was in fact a generalization from research on male college sophomores (Lykes & Stewart, 1986; Wallston, 1981; Weisstein, 1971). Because of their recognition of this early false generalization from men, or even male college sophomores, to "people," feminist scholars were sensitive to the importance of care in defining and describing samples, as well as specific measures (Morawski, 1994).

For example, one early target of feminist critique was the notion of "achievement motivation," which was based on a model of male-male competition that was clearly too narrow to cover all kinds of achievement even for men, much less for women (see, e.g., Horner, 1972). To many feminist scholars, utilization of multiple measures helps ensure a more valid operationalization of the phenomenon (with different definitions and techniques of assessment), and this added breadth seems likely to increase validity as well as generalizability (see, e.g., Ÿllo, 1988, on studying marital rape).

Alternatively, of course, a deeper reflection on the nature of generalizability can be an outgrowth of this preoccupation. Instead of worrying about ensuring generalizability, many feminist scholars instead urged greater specificity about the nature of the generalizability that could be claimed (Morawski, 1994). For example, Fine and Weis (1998) found that groups of women of different ethnic backgrounds viewed and responded to domestic violence differently because of the specific relationships of their ethnic group with social institutions such as the police. These differences were systematic, but they also mean that one cannot make broad generalizations about how women—even poor women—respond to domestic violence.

Because feminist scholars are often interested in phenomena that are studied in different social science disciplines (e.g., women's labor market experience, breast-feeding, sexual harassment), their reading tends to cut across fields. This exposure to interdisciplinary theory and evidence inevitably exposes feminist scholars to alternative habits and ways of thinking about methods. For example, feminist psychologists may be drawn to ethnographic or historical methods (Dottolo & Stewart, 2008; Hurtado, 2000; Stewart, 2003), while feminist sociologists may consider interpreting psychological tests (Martin, 1996) and feminist political scientists may decide to include experimental treatments in their surveys (Harris-Lacewell, 2001; Huddy et al., 1997). In short, exposure to a wide range of methods in the literatures that feminist scholars study nearly inevitably produces an increased temptation to borrow methods from neighboring disciplines. Indeed, recently, some have argued that mixed methodology has evolved into an academic field in its own right, cutting across disciplinary divides (Tashakkori & Creswell, 2008).

Equally, because feminist scholars tend to read across disciplinary boundaries, they are also inclined to theorize about problems that are new to their own disciplines. Thus, for example, feminist psychologists are increasingly studying issues that arise in the "workplace" (such as sexual harassment and incivility), historically the province of sociologists (see, e.g., Cortina, Magley, & Williams, 2001; Ragins, 2004), while feminist political scientists are increasingly noticing that individuals' family lives (traditionally the domain of sociology and psychology) have implications for their political behavior and civic engagement (see, e.g., Burns, Schlozman, & Verba, 1997; Hodgkin, 2008). Anthropologists who study culturally based conceptualizations of health and fertility may use the tools of demography to complement ethnographic methods (Bledsoe, 2002). There is an intellectual energy and excitement that occurs as feminist scholars identify and theorize these new questions, and their new theories demand methods that are often new to the field of study.

The same impulses (the wish to study phenomena that may or may not fit within traditional boundaries and the willingness to study them with unfamiliar tools) often result in a desire to speak to new and different audiences, audiences who may find different methods persuasive. Thus, feminist scholars may find that, because they want to use a theoretical concept such as "intersectionality" to study multiple social categories (e.g., gender and race or class at the same time; see, e.g., Bowleg, 2008), they want to address not only audiences across disciplines and methods but also scholars of race and class and gender, and not only one of these. The need to address different audiences in turn often reinforces the use of multiple methods because different audiences are likely to be persuaded by different kinds of evidence—evidence that is familiar within "their" paradigm.

Finally, feminist scholars' intellectual commitments may lend themselves to combine methods in new ways that differ from the formulas advocated by texts touting the virtues of "multiple methods" (e.g., Newman & Benz, 1998; Tashakkori & Teddlie, 1998). For example, an interest in postmodern and post-structuralist theory is likely to lead researchers to greater comfort with paradox and complexity, with seeming contradiction, even with "messiness" (Gergen, 2001; Stewart, 1994). Some argue that these pragmatist approaches can be particularly well suited to research with liberatory aims (Mertens, 2007), goals that are the impetus and center of much feminist work.

Alternatively, the habit of reflexivity—of continually revisiting and reframing questions in light of knowledge produced or insight gained— may support an iterative rather than a linear process. Reflexivity is a central tenet of feminist scholarship, which has long held that any claims of neutrality or objectivity made on behalf of any standpoint are in fact a smoke screen for privilege. Studies based on this kind of process may deviate radically from conventional notions that separate "contexts of discovery" from "contexts of justification." Instead they may seem to circle around and around a phenomenon, with the goal of clarifying its nature and features as they do so (Tolman & Szalacha, 1999).

Thus, we argue that there can be no prescriptive typology for combining qualitative and quantitative methods (although some methods texts have aimed to develop them; see, for example, Morgan, 1998, or Newman & Benz, 1998). Instead, in the following sections, we turn to a review of the research literature in order to identify projects that we feel have fruitfully combined "narratives and numbers," and, in this way, we generate a necessarily partial and preliminary list of suggested approaches for those considering mixing quantitative and qualitative methods.

MODELS FOR INTEGRATING "NARRATIVES AND NUMBERS"

There are many ways to integrate "narratives," or qualitative data, with "numbers," or quantitative data, in a single study. Each approach requires different resources and assets of a research project, and each offers different benefits to a study or a researcher. In this section, we examine diverse strategies for combining these two kinds of data in a project or research program. In most cases, we will refer to studies conducted by researchers who explicitly identify themselves as having feminist perspectives or aims; however, in some cases, we will discuss research that may not have an explicitly feminist perspective but that focuses on women's or girls' experiences or on gendered phenomena.

Systematic Transformation of Qualitative Data Into Quantitative Data

Perhaps the most common and the least controversial approach is to gather narrative or qualitative data in the course of a research project and then to transform it (usually via systematic content analysis) into quantitative data that can be analyzed (see, e.g., Boyatzis, 1998; Smith, 1992). Feminist scholars who have developed longitudinal studies of women's lives have often adopted this strategy (see Hulbert & Schuster, 1993, for a compendium of such studies). Frequently, they argue that including material that is articulated freely by women in their own terms enables a larger, generally quantitative project to represent women's experience more adequately (Hulbert & Schuster, 1993, pp. 12–13; see also chapters in Hulbert & Schuster by Helson, by Stewart & Vandewater, and by Tangri & Jenkins, among others, for examples). Often, researchers adopting this strategy develop systematic content analysis strategies— reflecting either a priori themes or emergent themes from the data gathered—to transform the qualitative data gathered into presence-absence codes or ratings, both of which can be treated as "numbers" in data analysis. Thus, for example, the Ginzberg-Yohalem study (see Yohalem, 1993, for a summary) included an open-ended question about missed opportunities: "Were there any attractive opportunities for career or other long-range activities that you did not pursue? Why did you not pursue them? Any regrets?" (See Ginzberg & Associates, 1966, p. 206.) Yohalem (1993) quotes one woman from their study of women who earned graduate degrees at Columbia in the late 1940s:

> Having children before finishing a Ph.D. made the pursuit of the highest degree impractical for me. Not getting a Ph.D. has made the salary range I command smaller. I regret not having had the opportunity to finish that work as a

younger woman. The competing demands of family and career can make a woman's choice very difficult, especially if she marries after 30 as I did. (p. 149)

Data like these enriched the project's ability to represent not only the choices women made but also the ways in which those choices felt constrained and reverberated over the years of their lives. In addition, though, by collecting data like these, researchers were able to develop "codes" that can be used in statistical analyses. This process involves coding themes as present or absent, or sometimes as reflecting an underlying scale (e.g., from positive through neutral to negative). This kind of quantification is not particularly valued by some qualitative researchers who view quantification as oversimplifying the rich complexity of qualitative data (see, e.g., Mishler, 1990). For our purposes, this kind of coding enables analyses (e.g., comparing people with and without certain kinds of regrets) that are otherwise impossible. Stewart and Vandewater (1999) developed a measure of regrets about career and family decisions, which they used to code data collected in two different longitudinal studies that asked the same questions that Ginzberg and Yohalem had (as well as some different ones). By categorizing women's responses to capture the nature of their regrets, they were able to show that women who expressed regrets about making more "traditional" role choices (not to acquire education or pursue careers) had lower scores on well-being indicators (e.g., life satisfaction) and higher scores on indicators of distress (such as depressive symptoms and anxiety) in middle age. However, if they made life changes in the direction of remedying those regrets, their subsequent scores on well-being and distress indicators were equivalent to those of women who had no regrets of that sort. More recently, Torges, Stewart, and Miner-Rubino (2005) looked at related issues in an older sample and found that it was possible to code qualitative data to capture whether individuals have "come to terms" with their regrets internally or not. They also found that not coming to terms at that later age was associated—as was regret itself—with poorer health outcomes. Collecting the qualitative data (as Ginzberg did in 1951) and recognizing the important and variable life experiences it might be capturing (as later scholars could) allowed researchers to assess an aspect of these people's lives for which no standard measures exist.

Working with two data sets, Duncan and Agronick (1995) were able to explore the differential impact of social experiences occurring at different stages in women's lives by coding the qualitative data in one data set to render it roughly equivalent to the quantitative data in another. In one of the data sets, drawn from graduates of Radcliffe College, Stewart and Healy (1989) had gathered quantitative ratings of the impact on women of a list of social events; Helson had asked an open-ended question along the same lines in her study of Mills College graduates, but there were no ratings available in her sample from a slightly—and crucially—different birth cohort (see Helson, 1993, for an overview). In a creative and imaginative approach, Duncan and Agronick (1995) coded Helson's data and conceptually replicated their findings from quantitative data from the Radcliffe sample, using the coding of qualitative data in the Mills sample. Doing this strengthened confidence in the finding (or its validity) both because it held up in two different samples and cohorts and because it held up when assessments were made in such different ways. This kind of approach—in which a phenomenon is assessed with multiple measures, and its relations with other phenomena are also multiply assessed—is sometimes referred to as *triangulation* (see, e.g., Tashakkori & Teddlie, 1998).

In these examples, qualitative data are used to investigate questions that can be addressed—if they are recognized and assessed—with quantitative data. In contrast, Tolman and Szalacha (1999) provide an example of a study in which qualitative data may be the best or even the only way actually to assess the phenomenon under study because of the pervasive silence surrounding the issue—adolescent girls' experience of sexual desire. Tolman and Szalacha (1999) argued that collecting "in-depth narrative and descriptive data from girls on their thoughts about and subjective experiences of sexuality, including sexual desire, sexual pleasure, feeling

sexy, and sexual fantasies, during private, one-on-one, semi-structured clinical interviews" itself constitutes a feminist intervention because "one of the primary tools of oppression of women is the maintenance of silence about their experiences and perspectives" (pp. 12–13). Through an iterative process, they used the data they collected to address three different research questions.

First, they simply described girls' experiences of sexual desire based on the qualitative data. Despite social pressures to the contrary, most girls described an intense, urgent, and powerful experience of sexual desire. At the same time, they also expressed doubt and confusion about what their feelings implied. The qualitative analysis indicated that girls from urban versus suburban backgrounds articulated very different reasons that desire must be countered by self-control. Urban girls felt that sexual expression carried many practical risks or dangers; in contrast, suburban girls viewed the issue as one of internal self-image, commenting, for example, "I don't like to think of myself as feeling really sexual" (Tolman & Szalacha, 1999, p. 16).

Once they had generated this distinction in the qualitative analysis, Tolman and Szalacha were interested in assessing the degree to which this distinction characterized girls' experiences. They coded 128 narratives (produced by 30 girls) for expressions of vulnerability and of pleasure, thus transforming the girls' narratives into data that could be analyzed quantitatively. They found urban girls were somewhat more likely to express vulnerability in their narratives compared with suburban girls. On the other hand, suburban girls were much more likely to express pleasure than were urban girls. The researchers further considered the role of sexual abuse in association with these themes and found that suburban girls who had experienced abuse expressed themes similar to those articulated by urban girls (whose narratives did not differ as a function of their sexual abuse experience).

In a third iteration, the researchers returned to the original qualitative data to explore in detail the different sexual experiences of these four groups of girls (suburban or urban; abused or not). This study demonstrates how readily qualitative data can be pressed into service to provide a richer understanding of a phenomenon or to test a relatively narrowly specified hypothesis. In the hands of flexible and creative researchers, qualitative data can be used to do both, allowing a single study with a relatively small sample to provide us with a solid base for further research on adolescent girls' sexuality.

In an ongoing program of research, Diamond has examined the development and relinquishment of different sexual identities among women, using systematic content analysis of interview data collected longitudinally over 10 years (see Diamond, 1998, 2000, 2003, 2008). At each time point, she conducted scripted, face-to-face interviews with the women in the sample. Interviews began with this question: "How do you currently label your sexual identity to yourself, even if it's different from what you might tell other people? If you don't apply a label to your sexual identity, please say so" (Diamond, 2008, p. 8). Diamond examined whether bisexual identification in young adulthood represents a third sexual orientation, a tendency toward sexual fluidity, or merely a stage on the way to lesbian identity. In the most recent wave (2008), she reported that, 10 years out, two-thirds of the sample had changed the label they chose to describe their sexual orientation at the study's inception, suggesting that, among sexual minority women, identity change rather than stability is the norm. Interestingly, changes in self-labeling were not associated with age at time 1, family history, or the experience of sexual stigma. Instead, based on her content coding of the patterns of sexual attraction that women described in their interviews, she concluded that women changed their labels to reflect their own experiences of sexual desire and behavior.

We have seen, then, that generating quantitative indicators out of qualitative data allows researchers to create new measures for previously unmeasured variables (as in the case of types of regrets and responses to regret), to replicate findings with other measures (as in the study of the impact of political events), to assess the frequency of newly identified features of phenomena (as in the study of adolescent girls' sexual experiences), and to tap change over time in the link between self-labeling and autobiographical experience (as in the study of sexual minority women's self-labeling).

Using Quantitative Data to Contextualize or Frame Issues Raised by Qualitative Data

One approach taken by multimethods scholars is to employ quantitative data as a way to frame and contextualize findings from a qualitative study. Researchers who do qualitative studies with interpretive or constructivist aims may be hesitant to generalize those findings to other settings or populations (Lin, 1998). In these cases, findings from a more positivist-based quantitative study can provide a context in which the qualitative findings may be better understood.

Raffaelli and Ontai's (2004) study of gender socialization in Latino/a families provides a paradigmatic case. They conducted in-depth interviews with a small sample of adult Latinas regarding their experiences of socialization about sexuality within their families of origin, as well as their early sexual and romantic experiences. They used multiple coders to identify emergent themes in the interview transcript. This process revealed three main themes of parental behavior: differential treatment of boys and girls, enforcement of feminine behavior among girls, and restriction of girls' freedom of activity. Based on these interviews, survey items were developed tapping each of these themes, and a larger sample of both women and men were asked to rate the extent to which their mothers and fathers had encouraged these behaviors. These survey data confirmed the qualitative analysis, as men and women reported the expected differences in their gender socialization. Quantitative analyses also revealed reliable patterns of gender socialization for parents with different backgrounds; for example, mothers who were more acculturated to the United States were more likely to encourage tomboy behavior in their daughters. The utilization of both qualitative and quantitative approaches within this study allowed the researchers to gauge how typical the results from the qualitative study were and to develop a quantitative measure that is likely to have a high degree of ecological validity.

Pattillo-McCoy (1998) shows us a slightly different approach to this type of multimethod strategy. She conducted an in-depth ethnography of a black middle-class neighborhood, a study whose methods included her participation in the social networks of the community as well as interviews with community leaders and residents; the research was undertaken over several years. Much of the interpretive power of her analysis of these interviews, however, comes from the way she contextualized this community using census data. She demonstrated that this community was surrounded by neighborhoods with higher rates of poverty and crime; comparable white middle-class neighborhoods were much less likely to be found in close geographical proximity to neighborhoods facing such high levels of crime and poverty. Her ethnography confirmed that this spatial proximity fostered a social proximity as well, which engendered costs and benefits: links between gang members and more stable members of the community provided a form of social control while, simultaneously, making it impossible to eradicate gangs and drugs from the community. This work suggests that combining qualitative and quantitative data in this way is a means of understanding a phenomenon at multiple levels of causality.

Similarly, Cohen (1999) combined qualitative and quantitative methods to understand at multiple levels the African American community's limited and late response to the HIV/AIDS crisis. In her award-winning book *The Boundaries of Blackness*, she used content coding to chart the incidence of coverage of HIV/AIDS stories in both mainstream and black media. Her analysis of coverage in the *New York Times* between 1983 and 1994 is a good example. During this period, the rate of AIDS cases among African Americans grew steeply, as did the coverage of AIDS stories in general, but stories concerning HIV among blacks were scarce until a sharp uptick in 1991 when Magic Johnson announced his diagnosis. Indeed, only 38% of the reporting on African Americans and HIV/AIDS during this time concerned anyone other than Johnson and Arthur Ashe. This discrepancy in media coverage was made even more stark by her finding that African Americans comprised 32% of all AIDS cases

during this time, while only 5% of *Times* stories were devoted to this group. Cohen (1999) asserted that these analyses revealed a pattern of marginalization, a contention that was bolstered by her more finely grained analysis of the way that the AIDS crisis and the black community's response to it was framed in these stories. Importantly, her larger argument is that practices of marginalization take place at multiple levels and change over time. Later chapters used interviews to explore how black political and religious leaders chose not to define AIDS as a threat to African Americans because they did not want to acknowledge gay people and users of intravenous drugs as part of the black community, framing AIDS instead as a problem to be blamed on "bad behavior" by individuals. Taken together, these multiple levels of analysis, employing both qualitative and quantitative methodology as appropriate, paint a picture of how narrow identity politics led to social conservatism, exclusion of certain segments of the black community, and, ultimately, a public health crisis.

Finally, Hodson (2004) used quantitative analyses to generalize from qualitative research in a very unusual way, conducting a meta-analysis of ethnographies aimed at understanding the role played by gender and race in shaping experience in workplaces. Rather than averaging effect sizes, as a traditional meta-analysis would, Hodson systematically coded 120 book-length ethnographies. This method allowed him to capitalize on the strengths of the ethnographic method—the opportunity to draw on many observations of a social system and to analyze these observations in great depth—while avoiding its greatest drawback, which is that the ethnographer brings this depth and range to only a very small number of social systems, often only one. Hodson noted that several ethnographies had characterized women as dutiful, acquiescent, and, thus, relatively complacent workers (particularly in contrast to men). Thus, he expected the meta-analysis to confirm this finding by uncovering that women have higher job satisfaction; however, the opposite was true. Nevertheless, in the United States men were more likely to express their dissatisfaction by engaging in confrontational behavior such as infighting and strikes. However, among people of color and workers outside the United States, men were actually more acquiescent. Clearly, the breadth of these findings was beyond the scope of a single ethnography to address.

These examples of using quantitative data to frame qualitative findings suggest that this approach offers a way to magnify the strengths of qualitative methods, for example, their depth, validity, and descriptive and interpretive power, either by leveraging the qualitative findings into a more generalizable set of findings or by helping to understand them as one piece of a complex system working at many levels.

Use of Ethnographic or Interview Narratives to Illuminate Issues Raised by Quantitative Findings

Another way that researchers often combine quantitative and qualitative methods is through the use of a qualitative study as a follow-up to clarify or explain findings from the quantitative analysis. This approach is consistent with Lin's (1998) distinction between the epistemological standing of *positivist methods*, which can establish relationships among variables, and *constructivist methods*, which can demonstrate causal mechanisms. The approach of using qualitative methods to illuminate issues raised by quantitative findings is one of the more common ways of combining the two; this is noteworthy because it challenges the conventional wisdom so often transmitted in traditional research methods courses (Bernard, 1865/1927; Hempel, 1965), which frequently teach that qualitative methods are most appropriate for the context of discovery. Findings revealed in such a discovery-oriented qualitative study, so the classical argument goes, should be validated through the context of justification, usually involving a more positivist and usually quantitative study.

Carr's (2004) research on the retrospective career reflections of mid-life women who came of age in the 1950s provides a prototypical example of a study in which qualitative analysis was used to help illuminate quantitative findings. Based on a large-scale longitudinal survey of nearly 500 predominantly white women with daughters, Carr's research found that mothers who felt that their daughters were more occupationally successful than they themselves had

been suffered no decrement in self-acceptance if the mothers took a great deal of credit for their daughters' success. Because this outcome contradicted the predictions made by social comparison theory, Carr turned to qualitative data to understand how mothers could maintain self-esteem even when making an upward comparison between themselves and their daughters. Interviews with a subsample of original respondents revealed that mothers who rated their daughters as more successful often explained their attainment in terms of social changes that gave their daughters more choices, but many also cited the additional stress that combining roles contributed to their daughters' lives. She concluded that these attributions protected mothers' self-esteem. Interestingly, Carr (2004) argued that this portion of the project "seek[s] to explore and generate hypotheses—not to test hypotheses—about the ways social comparisons are made, explained, and interpreted" (p. 138). Thus, she carefully framed her project within the traditional parameters of the contexts of discovery and justification—an interesting move given that her qualitative analysis was subsequent to her quantitative analyses.

Guinier, Fine, Balin, Bartow, and Stachel (1997) similarly designed their qualitative inquiry to illuminate the findings of their quantitative analysis. Interestingly, they wrote that the initial survey emerged from Bartow's desire to make a film documenting her personal experiences of gender bias in law school. Bartow approached Guinier to supervise the project, who suggested that she begin by surveying her classmates to learn whether her experiences were typical. The original impetus for the project, thus, was the desire to learn whether the personal was indeed reflective of a larger political context. The research team began by examining student records obtained from the law school. They learned that, although women entered with comparable qualifications to their male peers, women's grades were consistently lower through all three years, and women were much less likely to achieve honors. Results of Bartow's survey revealed other, perhaps more disturbing, patterns: first-year women students reported a systematic pattern of bias against women, including exclusion, disregard, and even sexist comments in the classroom. By the third year, it appeared that either such experiences had decreased or that women became more tolerant of such behaviors, as fewer of these incidents were reported. At the same time, this cross-sectional comparison indicated that women entered with greater interest in public interest law, but, by the third year, they were no more interested in pursuing this area than were men. In these ways, the authors argue that law schools force women to "become gentlemen." The qualitative data, based on open-ended survey questions and interviews, suggest the cost of this transformation. Women students reported feeling alienated, outraged, and silenced in law school. Sadly, many internalized these feelings, looking for counseling and support from women peers to address what they felt were personal shortcomings. Most reported that, to overcome these feelings and the obstacles they posed to success in the law school, they had to suppress and repress their feelings.

Thus, although women have been allowed access to legal education, these results indicate that late in the 20th century, women had not yet truly won equality in this setting. Instead, first-year law students entered an environment in which "a gender system is established, legitimated, and subtly internalized" (Guinier et al., 1997, p. 61). This analysis would not have been possible based only on the data from the registrar and the survey; indeed, the findings generated from such methods might have been more likely to be interpreted in terms of women students' inadequacies. The qualitative data allowed Guinier et al. (1997) access to understand the context in which the outcomes described in the quantitative data emerged. This example clearly illustrates Lin's distinction between the strength of positivist methods to demonstrate relationships among variables and that of interpretivist methods to demonstrate causal processes.

Using Quantitative and Qualitative Methods in "Parallel"

Some researchers find that quantitative and qualitative methods enable them to address *different* research questions rather than to explore the same ones in different ways. In these cases, the particular constraints on interpretation or inference imposed by different methods can be offset by parallel use of both approaches. Most often, qualitative methods are used in these research programs to unearth or identify issues or themes, while quantitative methods are used to answer questions about frequency and association that often cannot be addressed by quantitative methods.

Cortina, in the context of a larger program of research on gender in the workplace, provides one model in her research on Latinas' experiences of sexual harassment. She aimed to develop a fuller understanding of how the phenomenon of "sexual harassment," typically defined in terms of white women's experience in the United States, might be different for Latinas—both because of differences in the way that people treat them and because of differences in the social context or cultures they bring to their experience.

In the first study, Cortina (2001) conducted focus groups with 45 Latinas recruited through a public adult vocational school in San Diego. The focus group facilitator was "a native Spanish-speaking Mexican American woman who understood the culture and life experiences of the participants, spoke both English and Spanish fluently, and possessed the skills necessary to guide focus group discussions" (p. 167). Cortina examined the transcripts (transcribed by a bilingual researcher and in both languages twice) and noted "specific behavioral examples of harassing behaviors" and "references to categories of harassing behaviors" (p. 167). She then compared the terms generated from the focus group discussions with a standard measure developed on the basis of the experiences of white women. This comparison yielded six items, two of which regarded unique verbal behavior not covered (or not covered in the same way) in the standard measure. For example, one item was "addressed you informally when a more formal manner of address was more appropriate (for example, used *tú* rather than *usted*)" (Cortina, 2001, p. 170). In addition, four of the new items addressed non-verbal behaviors, such as "gave you a sexual 'look' that made you feel uncomfortable or dirty." Finally, five new items addressed a sense of the intersection of sexual harassment with ethnic or racial harassment; Cortina termed this "sexual racism." Examples of these items included "called you insulting names that referred to your gender and ethnicity (for example, 'Mexican bitch')" and "said they expected you to behave certain ways because you are a Latina woman (for example, expecting you as a Latina woman to wear sexy clothes)" (Cortina, 2001, p. 170).

Cortina then used these new items, along with the "standard" ones, with a large sample of Latinas recruited in a similar way. Using a process of the double translation of items, she gave participants the option to complete the survey in Spanish or English. Analyses of these data aimed at identifying the common and unique features of sexual harassment experiences of Latinas and white women. This strategy yielded important insights: both the focus group and the survey data suggested that Latinas were more inclined than the research samples comprised predominantly of white women to infer sexual intentions from nonsexual behavior. She quoted one woman as saying,

> What I've seen is that [white women] are more open . . . if it's something sexual they'll laugh and giggle about it, and I would take that offensively. And they wouldn't, because they're like more open to sexual stuff than Mexican or Hispanic ladies are. (Cortina, 2001, p. 176)

Interestingly, though there were clear examples of sexual racism reported in the focus groups, the quantitative study provided little support for the importance of this construct. Nevertheless, Cortina (2001) pointed out that the likely explanation is not that sexual racism is unimportant; rather, "the relative absence of racial harassment in participants' workplaces [can be attributed to the fact that]. . . . the great majority of participants did *not* work in environments dominated by non-Latinos—who would be most likely to racially harass Latinos" (p. 177). Thus, she weighted the qualitative data equally with the quantitative and concluded by advocating for more research on Latinas' workplace experiences in environments dominated by Anglos. In subsequent research, Cortina and her colleagues (Cortina, 2004; Cortina, Fitzgerald, & Drasgow, 2002) have used the revised version of the standard measure created for Latinas (the Sexual Experiences Questionnaire—Latina) to study the impact of sexual harassment on Latinas,

while paying close attention to features of Latino culture and processes of acculturation. Notably, Cortina did not jettison the qualitative findings because the quantitative data did not support them; rather, she reflected on the discrepancies revealed, regarding the discrepancy as a legitimate subject for future research in this area.

Sigel (1996), a political scientist, offers a model that is both similar and different in her study of *Ambition and Accommodation: How Women View Gender Relations*. Like Cortina, Sigel employed both focus groups and surveys, but she was not interested in the development of measures as a result of this research. Instead, she was interested in knowing both "what the population-at-large (or a given segment of the population) thinks about an important issue" and "a great deal about each individual and how she or he comes to hold these thoughts or sentiments" (Sigel, 1996, p. 24). Thus, she was interested in both the generalizability of findings and the depth and complexity of the material that could be obtained.

Her telephone surveys indicated that American women in general show high levels of awareness of discrimination and express a great deal of anger about the discrimination they encounter. However, few of the women in her sample either advocated or took part in political action to redress these problems. Indeed, in focus-group interviews, Sigel found women were quick to describe examples of gender discrimination that they themselves or women they knew had experienced, but few women advocated collective action to address their problems, instead suggesting that women look for solutions at the level of the individual. This seeming paradox turned out to be the central question of her book.

Sigel (1996) conceded that, although her initial expectation was that the focus groups would be mainly "guides to questionnaire construction, it soon became obvious that they had an independent contribution to make" (p. 34). She stressed that the focus group data did, in fact, guide the development of the survey protocol and that they also were used to help interpret the survey findings. She said,

> Listening to men and women in the groups actually helped shape my sensitivity to the role the topic [gender] played in the daily lives of the

public. I felt as though I became privy to some of their frustrations as well as gratifications, and most of all, I learned what mattered to them and what did not when they thought about gender. (Sigel, 1996, p. 35)

Using Diverse Materials as Data

Often those who wish to describe the challenge posed by multiple methods research are particularly concerned about the difficulty of combining qualitative and quantitative data due to opposing epistemological assumptions underlying each approach (Tashakkori & Teddlie, 2003); quantitative methods are thought to reflect positivist assumptions, while qualitative analyses rely on an interpretivist frame (see Lin, 1998, for a nuanced rethinking of this common assumption). However, as this section will show, the work of some feminist researchers transcends this simple dichotomy to incorporate data from unusual sources, for example, photographs or other visual media, material from historical archives, or even literature, often combining these less often used types of data with more commonly used sources, such as responses to interviews or surveys. Some who employ these creative data sources also draw on innovative methods to analyze these data.

We will begin with an example that represents a fairly common approach: scholars within communications studies often pair a close reading of a media text with an audience reception study of that same text. One such example is Press and Cole's (1999) examination of how social class and position on abortion as a political issue shape women's readings of prime-time entertainment television depictions of women facing abortion decisions. Drawing on the work of Condit (1994), they reviewed entertainment television depictions of abortion decisions, arguing that television offers a limited pro-choice position in which legal abortion is seen as necessary but undesirable unless the woman faces extreme hardship, including extreme financial hardship or blocked opportunities for moving up out of poverty. Focus group interviews showed that pro-choice women viewed these narratives very differently. Middle-class women, who often claimed to be very critical of television as a medium, were very accepting of

the rationales proffered by the working-class heroines seeking abortions in the shows. In contrast, many working-class women did not accept the heroine's protests that they had no option but abortion; many working-class viewers could offer stories in which they faced similar obstacles and overcame them. By pairing the textual analysis of television shows with the qualitative analysis of women's responses to them, Press and Cole (1999) were able to identify an important rift within the pro-choice movement.

Metzl, a psychiatrist and cultural critic, has similarly employed methods from both the humanities and social sciences in his attempt to understand how the gendered meanings associated with clinical depression have shifted over time in relation to changes in psychiatric opinion on how the disease is best treated. In his book *Prozac on the Couch* (2003), he subjected to a close interpretive reading news and fashion periodicals and popular literature (such as memoirs and novels) dealing with psychotropic drugs and, more recently, with selective serotonin reuptake inhibitors (SSRIs) such as Prozac and Zoloft. Through the sort of close reading of text and images commonly employed in the humanities, Metzl persuasively demonstrated that notions of gender informed by psychoanalysis are pervasive even within the realm of scientific, biologically based psychiatry. In a subsequent paper, Metzl and Angel (2004) adopted standard social science methods to approach the same research question in a very different way: systematic content analysis of a random sample of popular representations of depression appearing between 1985 and 2000. These data showed that, as the SSRIs gained in social acceptance and visibility, conditions that had previously been viewed as normative for women (such as emotional disturbances associated with menstruation, childbirth, or menopause) became conceptualized as biologically based, pathological, and treatable. Side by side, these two projects could be viewed simply as the triangulation of methods, long recommended even in mainstream thinking on methodology (e.g., see Jick, 1979). Yet, by freely drawing on two very disparate traditions of scholarship, Metzl makes an important contribution to current thinking about medicine and mental health and illness, and he continues a tradition of ardent conversation between the humanities and social sciences, one that has been taking place in women's studies programs since their inception in the early 1970s.

Clearly, this approach to combining qualitative and quantitative approaches is particularly fruitful for those who are interested in popular culture and visual imagery. Moreover, by expanding traditional social science notions of what constitutes "data," this approach could open new avenues of inquiry and may be a particularly promising approach for the study of individuals and groups that are not literate (for innovative examples of such qualitative work, see Cooper & Yarbrough, 2010; Killion & Wang, 2000).

Bringing Together Qualitative and Quantitative Researchers in a Team

Some projects address the issue of bridging qualitative and quantitative research methods by bringing together teams of researchers with different dispositions, backgrounds, and talents (obviously these researchers do not, and cannot, view the epistemological barriers to this kind of collaboration as insurmountable). Most often, studies using this approach have fairly substantial resources that permit them to involve researchers who will impose quite different design and measurement constraints and who may operate both independently and collaboratively within the study.

One study that deliberately set out to draw on both types of methods is the New Hope Project, which is an evaluation study of a large-scale poverty intervention program (Huston et al., 2001). The intervention employed a true experimental design and aimed to assess the relative benefits for working poor families of a comprehensive support package including a wage supplement, subsidies for health insurance, child care vouchers, and a job opportunity program (Duncan, Huston, & Weisner, 2007; Huston et al., 2004). Of course many of the key outcomes for the program were quantitative (e.g., actual income, assessed performance of all family members in many social arenas), and many of the collaborators on the project were primarily quantitative researchers (for example, psychologists Huston and McLoyd and economist Duncan). However, the project also included an anthropologist (Weisner), who set up a fieldwork team of seven ethnographers to work in the Milwaukee, Wisconsin, areas of the project. The aim was to use ethnographic data collected from a stratified random sample of cases

> to assist in gaining a richer, more detailed understanding of the impact of New Hope on participating families than could be gained from the . . . survey alone. The ethnographic study was also linked closely to the quantitative data from the surveys and child assessment data, with ongoing conversations among the group. (Lieber, Weisner, & Presley, 2003)

Several New Hope Project collaborators were impressed by the power of the qualitative data to reveal phenomena that had not been guessed at from the outset of the study but that could be confirmed with the larger quantitative survey. In their valuable consideration of these issues, Gibson and Duncan (2005) report that Gibson and Weisner (2002) found (using the qualitative data) that the family participants in the study valued the elements of the program in vastly different ways (e.g., some in cost-benefit terms and others because it served some personal preferences; see also Romich & Weisner, 2000). These different values in turn guided service use. Basing her analyses on these insights, Gibson used the survey data to confirm the importance of this heterogeneity in shaping the program's impact on families.

In a more complicated example of the iterative relationship between the qualitative and the quantitative findings, quantitative researchers noted that the New Hope experimental boys, but not the girls, were rated as significantly higher achieving than controls (see Gibson & Duncan, 2005). The qualitative data helped researchers recognize that, in fact, parents tended to view their male rather than their female children as more "at-risk," so they tended to channel more of the program's resources to their sons than to their daughters. Armed with this insight, quantitative researchers were able to examine other aspects of national survey data and to show that parents with both sons and daughters who live in "bad" neighborhoods systematically direct time and other resources toward boys rather than girls (Romich, 2000).

On a project like this, it is critical, then, for the dialogue between qualitative and quantitative researchers to be continual and respectful. It is clear that, in that context, the New Hope Project benefited greatly from its own successful mixed method collaborative environment. Attempting this kind of collaboration does not, though, guarantee its success: one can easily imagine a project in which insights and findings would be on parallel tracks and would never meet. Moreover, even when successful, this sort of effort exacts a high cost in communication labor.

The Fragile Families and Child Wellbeing Study is another umbrella project involving many collaborators and including both qualitative and quantitative researchers working on a variety of narrower subprojects. In fact, two feminist sociologists with different backgrounds (England, a quantitative researcher, and Edin, a qualitative researcher) joined forces with several other collaborators (including the economist McLanahan) on a subproject within that study that aims to understand "why some couples with very young children break up while others remain together, [and] why some fathers remain actively involved in their parental role while others do not" (Bendheim-Thoman Center for Research on Child Wellbeing, 2011). The Time, Love, Cash, Care, and Children Study (TLC3) was set up to examine a subsample of 75 low- to moderate-income couples drawn from the larger Fragile Families study (of nearly 5,000 families). In this project, qualitative and quantitative researchers actually joined together to examine qualitative findings in the context of quantitative data and quantitative findings in the context of qualitative data. For example, Gibson, Edin, and McLanahan (2003) began by noting that quantitative data suggest that the Fragile Families couples who are unmarried have positive views of marriage and say they plan to marry. Yet few did. Gibson, Edin, and McLanahan (2003) used qualitative data from the TLC3 data to explore this contradiction and argued that the qualitative data suggest that, actually, the views these couples held of marriage were so positive that they felt they did not qualify for it. They believed that they had to reach a variety of economic and achievement milestones in order to justify marriage. In another paper, England, Edin, and Linnenberg (2003) found that the couples—particularly the women—struggled

in relatively unsatisfying nonmarital relationships with their children's fathers because they believed that financial independence and stability were prerequisites for marriage and these achievements had eluded them.

It is clear that this kind of collaborative project has remarkable potential to leverage the insights gained from both quantitative and qualitative data to account for and validate the results gleaned from each method, and to enrich our understanding of the meaning of these results. That potential is only realized, though, to the extent that these projects engage researchers with both kinds of gifts and training, scholars who are willing and able to collaborate. Feminist research—which often aims to excavate key voices and perspectives that are relatively silent, powerless, or subordinated—is particularly likely to benefit from this sort of collaboration.

Building a Narrative Account From a Quantitative Description

The final strategy we encountered for combining quantitative and qualitative methods is perhaps the least often employed. It involves researchers taking quantitative indicators—for an individual or group of individuals—and constructing a qualitative analysis on the basis of those indicators. Perhaps the most straightforward example of this approach involves identifying an individual outlier or a group of people who score very high (or low) on some dimension and then conducting a case study of those individuals or that group. Helson, Mitchell, and Hart (1985) did this when they studied the "lives of women who became autonomous." They selected the seven women in Helson's longitudinal study who scored at the autonomous stage on Loevinger's (1976) measure of ego development at middle age, and they conducted a group "case study," in which they hoped to identify the personality and life experiences that might underlie successful personality achievement. Specifically, they wanted to evaluate both Levinson's (1978) model of male development and Gilligan's (1982) model of female development. They found that the theories were uneven in their applicability and that different paths led to successful ego development. They were struck, though, that, "to an unusual degree, the seven sought out the challenges and suffered the hardships particular to their time in history" (p. 283). They concluded that "it may still be true that *autonomous* ways of thinking and behaving are so much discouraged in women that only those who have known pain or marginality develop a high ego-level, and those who have a high ego-level are unlikely to live a conventional life" (p. 284). This emphasis on both suffering and unconventionality offered new insight into the pathway toward the highest levels of ego development.

Peterson (1998) used a similar strategy in his study of women who were high in different forms of midlife generativity. By selecting 12 women and grouping them according to whether they scored high on both measures, on one measure or the other, or on neither measure, he hoped to identify the characteristics of women who are high (and low) in generativity realization or generativity motivation or both. With three women in each of the four groups, he hoped to avoid being distracted by highly idiosyncratic details and instead to identify some patterns across the women within each cell—patterns that differentiated them from the women in the other three cells. His analysis pointed to the centrality of life's disappointments and ongoing preoccupations (rather than specific personality qualities or life experiences) as differentiating the groups from each other. Thus, the women who were high on both forms of generativity were currently engaged in generative activities, but (unlike the group low in realization but high in motivation) they did not report frustration or disappointment with past generative efforts. The group with the reverse pattern (high in realization and low in motivation) was not actively focused on generative activities in the present at all, though they also reported no frustrations or disappointments in that domain. Finally, the group low in both was also low in well-being and quite distressed. These midlife portraits certainly "fit" the pattern of scores (and Peterson's account is, of course, much richer than this summary), but they also extend our understanding of how two related but separate personality characteristics may interact to produce distinctive patterns.

Finally, Singer and Ryff (2001; see also Singer, Ryff, Carr, & Magee, 1998) have pioneered a person-centered method that goes further. They actually prepared a narrative account of the individuals in their studies based on the quantitative data about their lives. They then use this narrative as data, constructing taxonomies of life histories or profiles that reflect different pathways to a range of health outcomes. There is no doubt room for more inventive efforts along these lines.

CONCLUSIONS

Our hope in presenting alternate models to our students, and to the readers of this chapter, is that it is both stimulating and empowering to consider a range of alternative ways to conduct research. Our view, then, is frankly pragmatic and thereby finesses one of the key debates among some feminist scholars. Tashakkori and Teddlie (1998) outline in detail the ways in which positivism and postpositivism (normally philosophical positions promoted by quantitative methodologists), on the one hand, and constructivism (a position often promoted by qualitative methodologists), on the other, have resisted reconciliation. They detail six important differences in the assumptions made by researchers adopting one or the other position (assumptions about the nature of reality, the relationship of the knower to the known, the role of values in inquiry, the nature of generalizations, the possibility of establishing cause and effect, and the importance of induction or deduction). This polarized debate has been reproduced in a slightly different form among feminist scholars, for whom an additional issue is salient: which kind of method produces knowledge compatible with feminist goals (Jayaratne & Stewart, 1991; Peplau & Conrad, 1989)? Even to consider combining narrative and numbers in a single study, one must refuse this binary framing and proceed instead from something like the assumption associated with pragmatism that there is no essential link between epistemology and method (see the exposition by Tashakorri & Teddlie, 1998, pp. 11–13).

Because social scientists and feminist researchers have been so preoccupied with the incompatibilities between these kinds of methods, certain developments have been quite uneven. For example, we have well-developed criteria for evaluating validity in quantitative research. Though there have been increasing efforts along these lines with regard to qualitative methods (e.g., Parker, 2004), criteria are not yet consensual among qualitative researchers, much less widely disseminated among all researchers. Even more, we have virtually no established criteria for assessing the success of any given combined or integrated use of both kinds of methods. Such criteria can only be developed successfully if we have more models of successful combinations and integrations. We will all benefit—in our own research and in our efforts to equip students for the future—when there are many more models of individuals and projects that have brought narratives and numbers together in a fruitful way on many different topics.

Discussion Questions

1. There are a number of terms and concepts that the proponents of qualitative and quantitative methods invoke to privilege their approaches. For example, qualitative researchers speak of their approaches as being "grounded" and as "giving voice" to participants. In contrast, quantitative researchers claim their methods guard against "bias" and result in "rigor" and even "objectivity." How can mixed methods interrogate these assumptions? For example, do qualitative methods always "give voice"? Can quantitative methods ever "give voice"? What conditions are necessary to "give voice" in any research? And what assumptions about power are implicit in the idea that voice can be "given"?

2. Qualitative researchers often discuss the importance of reflexivity at length. Less obviously (and thus perhaps more importantly), how do mixed methods illuminate the importance of reflexivity in quantitative research?

3. This chapter offers four different models for integrating qualitative and quantitative approaches. How would you characterize each of the four approaches? What do you see as the strengths and weaknesses of each model?

4. Now that we have considered four models for integrating qualitative and quantitative methods, we can revisit the "politics" of our choices of research methods. What strategies for generating knowledge are considered "legitimate?"

Giddings and Grant (2007) warned that mixed methods can be a "Trojan horse" for positivism. Can you identify features of mixed methods approaches that guard against this tendency?

Online Resource

Bridges: Mixed Methods Network for Behavioral, Social, and Health Sciences

http://www2.fiu.edu/~bridges/

This website provides access to a variety of resources, including relevant textbooks and course syllabi and a glossary of terms and concepts.

Relevant Journal

Journal of Mixed Methods Research

Notes

1. Epistemology is concerned with the study of knowledge and how it is possible to make knowledge claims. Sprague and Zimmerman (1993) argue that positivism, which holds that definitive knowledge can only be obtained through the systematic and objective observation of observable phenomena, has been the dominant epistemology since the mid-nineteenth century. Ontology refers to the metaphysical study of existence.

2. The context of discovery refers to the creative or even intuitive phase of the research process in which ideas are generated; in contrast, the context of justification involves testing these ideas using the stringent and objective principles of the scientific method.

References

Bendheim-Thoman Center for Research on Child Wellbeing. (2011). Study design: Collaborative. *Fragile Families and Child Wellbeing Study*. Retrieved June 23, 2011, from http://www.fragilefamilies.princeton.edu/collaborative.asp

Bernard, C. (1927). *An introduction to the study of experimental medicine*. New York: Macmillan. (Original work published 1865)

Bledsoe, C. H. (2002). *Contingent lives: Fertility, time, and aging in West Africa*. Chicago: University of Chicago Press.

Bowleg, L. (2008). When black + lesbian + woman ≠ black lesbian woman: The methodological challenges of qualitative and quantitative intersectionality research. *Sex Roles, 59*, 312–325.

Boyatzis, R. E. (1998). *Transforming qualitative information: Thematic analysis and code development.* Thousand Oaks, CA: Sage.

Burns, N., Schlozman, K., & Verba, S. (1997). The public consequences of private inequality: Family life and citizen participation. *American Political Science Review, 9*, 373–389.

Carr, D. (2004). "My daughter has a career; I just raised babies": The psychological consequences of women's intergenerational social comparisons. *Social Psychology Quarterly, 67*, 132–154.

Cohen, C. J. (1999). *The boundaries of blackness: AIDS and the breakdown of black politics.* Chicago: University of Chicago Press.

Condit, C. (1994). *Decoding abortion rhetoric: Communicating social change.* Urbana: University of Illinois Press.

Cooper, C., & Yarbrough, S. (2010). Tell me—show me: Using combined focus group and photovoice methods to gain understanding of health issues in rural Guatemala. *Qualitative Health Research, 20*, 644–653.

Cortina, L. M. (2001). Assessing sexual harassment among Latinas: Development of an instrument. *Cultural Diversity and Ethnic Minority Psychology, 7*, 164–181.

Cortina, L. M. (2004). Hispanic perspectives on sexual harassment and social support. *Personality and Social Psychology Bulletin, 30*, 570–584.

Cortina, L. M., Fitzgerald, L. F., & Drasgow, F. (2002). Contextualizing Latina experiences of sexual harassment: Preliminary tests of a structural model. *Basic and Applied Social Psychology, 24*, 295–311.

Cortina, L. M., Magley, V. J., & Williams, J. H. (2001). Incivility in the workplace: Incidence and impact. *Journal of Occupational Health Psychology, 6*(1), 64–80.

Diamond, L. (1998). Development of sexual orientation among adolescent and young adult women. *Developmental Psychology, 34*, 1085–1095.

Diamond, L. (2000). Sexual identity, attractions, and behavior among young sexual-minority women over a two-year period. *Developmental Psychology, 36*, 241–250.

Diamond, L. (2003). Was it a phase? Young women's relinquishment of lesbian/bisexual identities over a 5-year period. *Journal of Personality and Social Psychology, 84*, 352–364.

Diamond, L. (2008). Female bisexuality from adolescence to adulthood: Results from a 10-year longitudinal study. *Developmental Psychology, 44*, 5–14.

Dottolo, A., & Stewart, A. (2008). "Don't ever forget now, you're a Black man in America": Intersections of race, class, and gender in encounters with the police. *Sex Roles, 59*(5–6), 350–364.

Duncan, G. J., Huston, A. C., & Weisner, T. S. (2007). *Higher ground: New hope for the working poor and their children.* New York: Russell Sage.

Duncan, L., & Agronick, G. (1995). The intersection of life stage and social events: Personality and life outcomes. *Journal of Personality and Social Psychology, 69*, 558–568.

Edin, K. (1991). Surviving the welfare system: How AFDC recipients make ends meet in Chicago. *Social Problems, 38*, 462–474.

England, P., Edin, K., & Linnenberg, K. (2003, September 4–5). *Love and distrust among unmarried parents.* Paper presented at the National Poverty Center Conference on Marriage and Family Formation among Low-Income Couples, Washington, DC.

Fine, M., & Gordon, S. M. (1989). Feminist transformations of/despite psychology. In M. Crawford & M. Gentry (Eds.), *Gender and thought* (pp. 146–174). New York: Springer-Verlag.

Fine, M., & Weis, L. (1998). *The unknown city: Lives of poor and working-class young adults.* Boston: Beacon.

Gelo, O., Braakmann, D., & Benetka, G. (2008). Quantitative and qualitative research: Beyond the debate. *IPBS: Integrative Psychological & Behavioral Science, 42*, 266–290.

Gergen, M. (2001). *Feminist reconstructions in psychology: Narrative, gender, and performance.* Thousand Oaks, CA: Sage.

Gibson, C. M., & Duncan, G. J. (2005). Qualitative/quantitative synergies in a random-assignment program evaluation. In T. S. Weisner (Ed.), *Discovering successful pathways in children's development: New methods in the study of childhood and family life* (pp. 283–304). Chicago: University of Chicago Press.

Gibson, C. M., Edin, K., & McLanahan, S. (2003). *High hopes but even higher expectations: The retreat from marriage among low-income couples*

[Working Paper No. 03-06-FF]. Princeton, NJ: Center for Research on Child Wellbeing.

Gibson, C. M., & Weisner, T. (2002). "Rational" and ecocultural circumstances of program take-up among low-income working parents. *Human Organization, 61*, 154–167.

Giddings, L. S., & Grant, B. M. (2007). A Trojan horse for positivism? A critique of mixed methods research. *Advances in Nursing Science, 30*, 52–60.

Gilligan, C. (1982). *In a different voice.* Cambridge, MA: Harvard University Press.

Ginzberg, E., & Associates. (1966). *Educated American women: Life styles and self-portraits.* New York: Columbia University Press.

Guba, E. G., & Lincoln, Y. S. (1994). Competing paradigms in qualitative methods. In N. Denzin & Y. Lincoln (Eds.), *Handbook of qualitative research* (pp. 105–117). Thousand Oaks, CA: Sage.

Guinier, L., Fine, M., Balin, J., Bartow, A., & Stachel, D. L. (1997). Becoming gentlemen: Women's experiences at one Ivy League law school. In L. Guiner, M. Fine, & J. Balin (Eds.), *Becoming gentlemen: Women, law school, and institutional change.* Boston: Beacon Press.

Hanson, B. (2008). Wither qualitative/quantitative? Grounds for methodological convergence. *Quality & Quantity, 42*, 97–111.

Harding, S. (1987). Is there a feminist method? In S. Harding (Ed.), *Feminism and methodology: Social science issues* (pp. 1–14). Bloomington: Indiana University Press.

Harris-Lacewell, M. (2001). No place to rest: African American political attitudes and the myth of black women's strength. *Women, Politics & Policy, 23*, 1–33.

Helson, R. (1993). The Mills classes of 1958 and 1960: College in the fifties, young adulthood in the sixties. In K. D. Hulbert & D. T. Schuster (Eds.), *Women's lives through time: Educated American women of the twentieth century* (pp. 190–210). San Francisco: Jossey-Bass.

Helson, R., Mitchell, V., & Hart, B. (1985). Lives of women who became autonomous. *Journal of Personality, 53*, 257–285.

Hempel, C. (1965). *Aspects of scientific explanation.* New York: Free Press.

Hodgkin, S. (2008). Telling it all: A story of women's social capital using a mixed methods approach. *Journal of Mixed Methods Research, 2*, 296–316.

Hodson, R. (2004). A meta-analysis of workplace ethnographies: Race, gender, and employee attitudes and behaviors. *Journal of Contemporary Ethnography, 33*, 4–38.

Horner, M. S. (1972). Toward an understanding of achievement-related conflicts in women. *Journal of Social Issues, 28*, 157–176.

Huddy, L., Billig, J., Bracciodieta, J., Heoffler, L., Moynihan, P. J., & Pugliani, P. (1997). The effect of interviewer gender on the survey response. *Political Behavior, 19*, 197–220.

Hulbert, K. D., & Schuster, D. T. (Eds.). (1993). *Women's lives through time: Educated American women of the twentieth century.* San Francisco: Jossey-Bass.

Hurtado, A. (2000). "La cultura cura": Cultural spaces for generating Chicana feminist consciousness. In L. Weis & M. Fine (Eds.), *Construction sites: Excavating race, class, and gender among urban youth* (pp. 274–289). New York: Teachers College Press.

Huston, A. C., Duncan, G. J., Granger, R., Bos, J., McLoyd, V. C., Mistry, R., Crosby, D., Gibson, C., Magnuson, K., Romich, J., & Ventura, A. (2001). Work-based anti-poverty programs for parents can enhance the school performance and social behavior of children. *Child Development, 72*, 318–336.

Huston, A. C., Miller, C., Richburg-Hayes, L., Duncan, G. J., Eldred, C. A., Weisner, T. S., Lowe, E., McLoyd, V. C., Crosby, D. A., Ripke, M. N., & Redcross, C. (2004). *New hope for families and children: Five-year results of a program to reduce poverty and reform welfare.* New York: MDRC.

Jayaratne, T. E., & Stewart, A. J. (1991). Quantitative and qualitative methods in the social sciences: Current feminist issues and practical strategies. In M. M. Fonow & J. A. Cook (Eds.), *Beyond methodology: Feminist scholarship as lived research* (pp. 85–106). Bloomington: Indiana University Press.

Jick, T. D. (1979). Mixing qualitative and quantitative methods: Triangulation in action. *Administrative Science Quarterly, 24*, 602–611.

Killion, C. M., & Wang, C. C. (2000). Linking African American mothers across lifestage and station through photovoice. *Journal of Health Care for the Poor and Underserved, 11*, 310–325.

Levinson, D. J. (1978). *The seasons of a man's life.* New York: Knopf.

Lieber, E., Weisner, T. S., & Presley, M. (2003). EthnoNotes: An Internet-based field note management tool. *Field Methods, 15*, 405–425.

Lin, A. C. (1998). Bridging positivist and interpretivist approaches to qualitative methods. *Policy Studies Journal, 26*, 162–179.

Loevinger, J. (1976). *Ego development*. San Francisco: Jossey-Bass.

Lykes, M. B., & Stewart, A. J. (1986). Evaluating the feminist challenge to research in personality and social psychology, 1963–1983. *Psychology of Women Quarterly, 10*, 393–412.

Martin, K. A. (1996). *Puberty, sexuality, and the self: Girls and boys at adolescence*. New York: Routledge.

Mertens, D. M. (2007). Transformative paradigm: Mixed methods and social justice. *Journal of Mixed Methods Research, 1*, 212–225.

Metzl, J. M. (2003). *Prozac on the couch: Prescribing gender in the era of wonder drugs*. Durham, NC: Duke University Press.

Metzl, J. M., & Angel, J. (2004). Assessing the impact of SSRI antidepressants on popular notions of women's depressive illness. *Social Science and Medicine, 58*, 577–584.

Mishler, E. G. (1990). Validation in inquiry-guided research: The role of exemplars in narrative studies. *Harvard Educational Review, 60*, 415–442.

Morawski, J. G. (1994). *Practicing feminisms, reconstructing psychology*. Ann Arbor: University of Michigan Press.

Morgan, D. L. (1998). Practical strategies for combining qualitative and quantitative methods: Applications to health research. *Qualitative Health Research, 8*, 362–376.

Newman, I., & Benz, C. (1998). *Qualitative-quantitative research methodology: Exploring the interactive continuum*. Carbondale: Southern Illinois Press.

Parker, I. (2004). Criteria for qualitative research in psychology. *Qualitative Research in Psychology, 1*, 95–106.

Pattillo-McCoy, M. E. (1998). Sweet mothers and gangbangers: Managing crime in a black middle-class neighborhood. *Social Forces, 76*, 747–774.

Peplau, L. A., & Conrad, E. (1989). Beyond nonsexist research: The perils of feminist methods in psychology. *Psychology of Women Quarterly, 13*, 379–400.

Peterson, B. E. (1998). Case studies of midlife generativity: Analyzing motivation and realization. In D. P. McAdams & E. de St. Aubin (Eds.), *Generativity and adult development* (pp. 101–131). Washington, DC: American Psychological Association.

Press, A. L., & Cole, E. R. (1999). *Speaking of abortion: Television and authority in the lives of women*. Chicago: University of Chicago Press.

Rabinowitz, V. C., & Weseen, S. (1997). Elu(ci)d(at)ing impasses: Re-viewing the qualitative/quantitative debates in psychology. *Journal of Social Issues, 53*(4), 605–630.

Raffaelli, M., & Ontai, L. L. (2004). Gender socialization in Latino/a families: Results from two retrospective studies. *Sex Roles, 50*, 287–299.

Ragins, B. R. (2004). Sexual orientation in the workplace: The unique work and career experiences of gay, lesbian, and bisexual workers. *Research and Human Resources Management, 23*, 35–120.

Reinharz, S. (1992). *Feminist methods in social research*. New York: Oxford University Press.

Romich, J. (2000, March 25). *To sons and daughters: Gender, neighborhood quality, and resource allocation in families*. Paper presented at the annual meeting of the Population Association of America, Los Angeles, CA.

Romich, J., & Weisner, T. (2000). How families view and use the EITC: Advance payment versus lump sum delivery. *National Tax Journal, 53*, 1245–1265.

Sapiro, V. (1995). Feminist studies and political science—and vice versa. In D. Stanton & A. J. Stewart (Eds.), *Feminisms in the academy* (pp. 291–310). Ann Arbor: University of Michigan Press.

Sherif, C. W. (1987). Bias in psychology. In S. Harding (Ed.), *Feminism and methodology* (pp. 37–56). Bloomington: Indiana University Press. (Original work published 1979)

Sigel, R. (1996). *Ambition and accommodation: How women view gender relations*. Chicago: University of Chicago Press.

Singer, B., & Ryff, C. D. (2001). Person-centered methods for understanding aging: The integration of numbers and narratives. In R. H. Binstock (Ed.), *Handbook of aging and the social sciences* (pp. 44–65). San Diego: Academic Press.

Singer, B., Ryff, C. D., Carr, D., & Magee, W. J. (1998). Linking life histories and mental health: A person-centered strategy. In A. Raftery (Ed.), *Sociological methodology* (pp. 1–51). Washington, DC: American Sociological Association.

Smith, C. P. (1992). *Motivation and personality: Handbook of thematic content analysis*. New York: Cambridge University Press.

Smith, D. E. (1987). *The everyday world as problematic: A feminist sociology*. Toronto, ON: University of Toronto Press.

Sprague, J., & Zimmerman, M. K. (1993). Overcoming dualisms: A feminist agenda. In P. England (Ed.), *Theory on gender/feminism on theory* (pp. 255–280). New York: Aldine de Gruyter.

Stack, C. (1974). *All our kin: Strategies for survival in a black community*. New York: Harper and Row.

Stewart, A. J. (1994). Toward a feminist strategy for studying women's lives. In C. Franz & A. J. Stewart (Eds.), *Women creating lives: Identities, resilience, and resistance* (pp. 11–35). Boulder, CO: Westview.

Stewart, A. J. (2003). Gender, race, and generation in a Midwest high school: Using ethnographically informed methods in psychology—The 2002 Carolyn Wood Sherif Award Address. *Psychology of Women Quarterly, 27*, 1–11.

Stewart, A. J., & Healy, J. M. (1989). Linking individual development and social changes. *American Psychologist, 44*, 30–42.

Stewart, A. J., & Vandewater, E. A. (1993). The Radcliffe Class of 1964: Career and family social clock projects in a transitional cohort. In K. D. Hulbert & D. T. Schuster (Eds.), *Women's lives through time: Educated American women of the twentieth century* (pp. 235–258). San Francisco: Jossey-Bass.

Stewart, A. J., & Vandewater, E. A. (1999). "If I had it to do over again . . . ": Midlife review, midcourse corrections, and women's well-being in midlife. *Journal of Personality and Social Psychology, 76*, 270–283.

Tangri, S. S., & Jenkins, S. R. (1993). The University of Michigan Class of 1967: The Women's Life Paths Study. In K. D. Hulbert & D. T. Schuster (Eds.), *Women's lives through time: Educated American women of the twentieth century* (pp. 259–281). San Francisco: Jossey-Bass.

Tashakkori, A., & Creswell, J. W. (2008). Mixed methodology across disciplines. *Journal of Mixed Methods Research, 2*, 3–6.

Tashakkori, A., & Teddlie, C. (1998). *Mixed methodology: Combining qualitative and quantitative approaches*. Thousand Oaks, CA: Sage.

Tashakkori, A., & Teddlie, C. (Eds.). (2003). *Handbook of mixed methods in social and behavioral research*. Thousand Oaks, CA: Sage.

Tolman, D. L., & Szalacha, L. A. (1999). Dimensions of desire: Bridging qualitative and quantitative methods in a study of female adolescent sexuality. *Psychology of Women Quarterly, 23*, 7–39.

Torges, C., Stewart, A. J., & Miner-Rubino, K. (2005). Personality after the prime of life: Men and women coming to terms with regrets. *Journal of Research on Personality, 39*, 148–165.

Unger, R. K. (1981). Sex as a social reality: Field and laboratory research. *Psychology of Women Quarterly, 5*, 645–653.

Wallston, B. (1981). What are the questions in the psychology of women? A feminist approach to research. *Psychology of Women Quarterly, 5*, 597–617.

Weisstein, N. (1971). *Psychology constructs the female or, the fantasy life of the male psychologist*. Boston: New England Free Press.

Ÿllo, K. (1988). Political and methodological debates in wife abuse research. In K. Ÿllo (Ed.), *Feminist perspectives on wife abuse* (pp. 28–50). Newbury Park, CA: Sage.

Yohalem, A. (1993). Columbia University graduate students: The vanguard of professional women. In K. D. Hulbert & D. T. Schuster (Eds.), *Women's lives through time: Educated American women of the twentieth century* (pp. 140–157). San Francisco: Jossey-Bass.

18

FEMINISM, GROUNDED THEORY, AND SITUATIONAL ANALYSIS REVISITED

Adele E. Clarke

Simply finding grounded theory was not self evident. It meant walking a twisted path, full of contingency and accidental proximities. . . . In bringing both contingencies and commitments to explicit, overt analysis, one creates the chance to . . . include the heart of method as a part of lived experience. . . . The growing community of analysts, critics, and students is my ground of reflection, and we give each other the courage to go on.

—Susan Leigh Star
(2007, pp. 79, 91)

Grounded theory (hereafter GT), developed by Barney Glaser and Anselm Strauss (1967), has become such a

leading method in qualitative research transnationally that it now merits its own hefty *Handbook of grounded theory* (Bryant & Charmaz, 2007); a major new text (Charmaz, 2006); and a four-volume reader in the SAGE Benchmarks in Social Research Methods series, titled *Grounded Theory and Situational Analysis* (Clarke & Charmaz, forthcoming), which is due out circa 2013. Interestingly, in the new book devoted to the diversity of approaches *within* GT generated by the second generation of scholars (Morse et al., 2009), all of those scholars are women, most if not all feminists.

GT merits such ambitious works especially because of its transnational and transdisciplinary travels (e.g., Morse et al., 2009, pp. 254–256; Schutze, 2008; Tarozzi, 2008). It is renowned today not only in sociology (e.g., Clarke & Charmaz, forthcoming; Strauss & Corbin, 1997)

Author's Note: In sorrow I dedicate this chapter to the memory of a superb feminist grounded theorist, Susan Leigh Star, mentor, colleague, friend (Star, 2007; Clarke, 2010b). For comments on this and related work, I thank Leigh, Monica Casper, Kathy Charmaz, Carrie Friese, and Virginia Olesen. I cite the grounded theory and situational analysis literatures lightly because of space, and I omitted many citations found in my earlier version (Clarke, 2007a). See also bibliographies in Bryant and Charmaz (2007) and at www.situationalanalysis.com.

and nursing (e.g., Kearney, 2007; Plummer & Young, 2010; Schreiber & Stern, 2001; Stern, 2007), where it was originally taught, but also in organization and management studies (e.g., Dougherty, 2005; Locke, 2001; Pearse & Kanyangale, 2009; Suddaby, 2006); education (e.g., Cresswell, 2007); library science (e.g., Star & Bowker, 2007); counseling psychology (e.g., Fassinger, 2005); computer and information science (Bryant, 2006; Urquhart, 2007); social work (e.g., Gilgun, forthcoming; Padgett, 2008); public health (e.g., Dahlgren, Emmelin, & Winkvist, 2007), science, technology, and medicine studies (e.g., Clarke & Star, 2008); and queer studies (e.g., Plummer, 2005). GT has been quite well elaborated over the years by a number of scholars, most especially Charmaz.[1] Situational analysis (hereafter SA), which I developed, is an extension of GT inspired in part by Donna Haraway's (1991) concept of "situated knowledges" and by Norm Denzin's (1970/1989) early efforts at situating research in his book *The Research Act*. It integrates post-structural assumptions with those of GT and strong feminist emphases on elucidating differences, the analysis of power, and including documentary, historical, and visual discourses (Clarke, 2003, 2005, forthcoming).

Feminisms here are approaches fundamentally provoking research toward improving the heterogeneous situations of women and promoting social justice. The feminisms I have been involved in seek to elucidate the dynamics of sexism, racial and ethnic discrimination, classism, homo- and queer-phobias, discrimination against the disabled, looksism, and ageism—and their complex interrelations are often theorized as intersectionality (e.g., Collins, 2004; Dill & Zambrana, 2009; Schulz & Mullings, 2006; Weber, 2010). In addition to this broad research agenda, feminist practices—praxis—matter. Feminisms also affect *how* we go about research (and other aspects of life). Pushing ourselves and others to be open to new ways of seeing and knowing, to legitimate and promote epistemic diversity (knowledge production by differently situated producers), and to work against epistemic violence that erases or silences minor voices and perspectives are each and all important. In sum, I share with Dorothy Smith (2007) her goal of opening her feminism "from a sociology for women to a sociology for people."

In terms of feminism(s) and GT and SA, there exist vast numbers of citations from multiple disciplines and recent reviews (Olesen, 2007, 2011). My goal here is to examine a range of selected research using GT and SA vis-à-vis their contributions to feminist research and praxis.[2] It is requisite to remember that no one method can do everything that feminists might want to do. Fonow and Cooke (2005), for example, assert that "there has never been one correct feminist epistemology generating one correct feminist methodology" (p. 213), and I would add, there never will be.

I first elucidate what GT is and specify the ways in which GT has always already been *implicitly* feminist in its pragmatist epistemology/ontology. I then turn to the feminist GT literature and demonstrate how scholars have to date made GT more *explicitly* feminist through using it in feminist projects. Next I discuss what SA is, how it, too, is also always already implicitly feminist, and some feminist research using it to date. In conclusion, I frame my hopes for the feminist futures of both GT and SA.

WHAT IS GROUNDED THEORY?

> Social phenomena are complex. Thus they require complex grounded theory. (Strauss, 1987, p. 1)

GT and SA are both first and foremost modes of *analysis* of qualitative research data. That is, neither claims to offer a fully elaborated methodology from soup to nuts—from project design to data collection to final write-up. Many elements of a full-blown methodology are offered by both, and situational maps can be especially useful for design stages. But analysis is their core goal. Building on traditional GT, which is usually used with field data or in-depth interviews, SA explicitly extends analysis to discursive data including narrative and historical documents and visual materials. Across many disciplines, there has been a dramatic increase in multisite research projects that generate many kinds of data. Both GT and SA can be used across heterogeneous data sources and are thus excellent for such projects.

GT and SA are both deeply *empirical* approaches to the study of social life. The very term *grounded theory* means data-grounded theorizing. In the words of Atkinson, Coffey, and Delamont (2003), "Grounded theory is not a description of a kind of theory. Rather it represents a general way of generating theory (or, even more generically, a way of having ideas on the basis of empirical research)" (p. 150). The theorizing is generated *abductively* by tacking back and forth between the nitty-gritty specificities of empirical data and more abstract ways of thinking about them.[3] In doing SA, too, the analyst relentlessly returns to the crudest of the maps to remind herself of the palpability and heterogeneity of the data and their interconnections.

In using or doing GT, the analyst initially codes the qualitative data (open coding)—word by word, segment by segment—and gives temporary labels (codes) to particular phenomena. Over time, the analyst determines whether codes generated through one data source also appear elsewhere, and elaborates their properties. Related codes that seem robust through the ongoing coding process are then densified into more enduring and analytically ambitious "categories" (Charmaz, 2006). Memos are written about each designated code and category: What does it mean? What are the instances of it? What is the variation within it in the data? What does and doesn't it seem to "take into account" (Lempert, 2007)? Ideally, the categories generated and deemed robust are ultimately integrated into a theoretical analysis of the substantive area of the current research project. Thus, a "grounded theory" of a particular phenomenon is composed of the analytic codes and categories generated abductively in the analysis and *explicitly integrated* to form a theory of the substantive area. The analyst generates an empirically based "substantive theory" (Strauss, 1987). In traditional GT, over time, after the researchers have generated multiple substantive theories of a particular broad area of interest through an array of empirical research projects, so the argument went, more "formal theory" could be developed (see Glaser, 2007; Kearney, 2001, 2007; Moore, 2007; Strauss, 1995). Formal theory was originally used here in the modernist sense of social theory, aiming at "Truth," and I return to this point later.

What remains relatively unique and very special to this approach is first GT's requiring that analysis begin as soon as there are data. Coding begins immediately, and theorizing based on that coding does as well, however provisionally (Glaser, 1978). Second, there are at least two kinds of sampling involved in doing grounded theory research. First is the usual sampling driven by attempts to be "representative" of some social body or population and its heterogeneities—to examine a full array of persons and sites of the phenomenon. Second is "theoretical sampling" guided explicitly by *theoretical* concerns that have emerged in the provisional analysis. Such "theoretical sampling" focuses on finding *new data sources* (persons and/or things—and *not* theories) that are excellent for explicitly addressing specific theoretically interesting facets of the emergent analysis. Theoretical sampling has been integral to GT from the outset, remains a fundamental strength of this analytic approach, and is also crucial for SA.[4]

In fact, it can be argued that precisely what is to be studied *emerges* from the analytic process over time, rather than being designated a priori: "The true legacy of Glaser and Strauss is a collective awareness of the heuristic value of developmental research designs [through doing theoretical sampling] and exploratory data analytic strategies, not a 'system for conducting and analyzing research'" (Atkinson et al., 2003, p. 163). I see this emergence as implicitly feminist in that it tries to build an adequate "database" for a project through expanding the data to be collected "as needed" analytically and also through researchers' mining their own reflexivity. This is a much more modest than arrogant approach to the production of new knowledge—assuming that we learn as we go (Haraway, 1997). Thus it takes "experience" into account in all its densities and complexities (Scott, 1992)—especially the experiences of the researchers with their project and their reflexivity about it (Charmaz, 2006).

Most research using GT has relied on fieldwork to generate interview or ethnographic data through which to analyze human action (e.g., Strauss & Corbin, 1997). Conventional GT has focused on generating the "basic social process" occurring in the data concerning the phenomenon of concern—the basic form of human *action*. The key or basic social process is typically articulated in gerund form connoting ongoing action at an abstract level. Studies have been done, for example, on *living with* chronic illness (Charmaz, 2010), *classifying* and its consequences (Lampland & Star, 2009), *producing* accountability in hospitals (Wiener, 2000), *explaining* suspicious deaths at the morgue (Timmermans, 2006), *creating* a new social actor—the unborn patient—via fetal surgery (Casper, 1998), and *disciplining* the scientific study of reproduction (Clarke, 1998).

Around this basic process, the analyst then constellates the particular and distinctive conditions, strategies, actions, and practices engaged in by the human and nonhuman actors involved. For example, the subprocesses of disciplining the scientific study of reproduction include *formalizing* a scientific discipline, *establishing* stable access to research materials, *gleaning* fiscal support for research, *producing* contraceptives and other technoscientific products, and *handling* the social controversies the science provokes, for example, regarding the use of contraceptives (Clarke, 1998). Many excellent projects have been done using basic GT, and this action-centered approach will continue to be fundamentally important analytically (Clarke & Charmaz, forthcoming).

GROUNDED THEORY AS ALWAYS ALREADY IMPLICITLY FEMINIST

There are several ways in which I and others such as Susan Leigh Star[5] have long understood GT to have been always already *implicitly* feminist: (1) its roots in American symbolic interactionist sociology and pragmatist philosophy emphasizing actual experiences and practices—the lived doingness of social life; (2) its use of George Herbert Mead's concept of perspective that emphasizes partiality, situatedness, and multiplicity; (3) its assumption of a materialist social constructionism; (4) its foregrounding deconstructive analysis and multiple simultaneous readings; and (5) its attention to range of variation as featuring of difference(s) (Clarke, 2005; Star, 2007).

First and foremost here are what I and other feminists see as the roots of GT in symbolic interactionist sociology and pragmatist philosophy.[6] This was not always the case. Historically, Glaser and Strauss (1967), Glaser (1978), and

Schatzman and Strauss (1973) argued that GT as a methodological approach could be effectively used by people from a variety of theoretical as well as disciplinary perspectives. That is, they initially took a "mix and match" approach. Their challenge—which they ably met—was to articulate a new qualitative methodology in the belly of the haute positivist quantitative sociological beast of the 1960s (Bryant & Charmaz, 2007; Olesen, 2007). They sought to do so through a systematic approach to analyzing qualitative research data.[7] Their emphases in the early works cited were on taking a *naturalistic* approach to research, having initially *modest* (read, substantively focused) theoretical goals, and being *systematic* in what we might today call the interrogation of qualitative research data in order to work against what they and others then saw as the *distorting subjectivities* of the researcher in the concrete processes of interpretive analysis (discussed further later).[8]

In considerable contrast, it can be argued that GT is rooted in American pragmatist philosophy and the approach to sociology generated through it—symbolic interactionism (e.g., Blumer, 1969; Strubing, 2007). That is, grounded theory/symbolic interactionism can be seen as constituting a theory/methods package that is implicitly feminist. Star framed such theory/methods packages as including a set of epistemological and ontological assumptions along with concrete practices through which a set of practitioners go about their work, including relating to and with one another and the various nonhuman entities involved in the situation. This concept of a theory/methods package focuses on the ultimately nonfungible aspects of ontology and epistemology—viewing these as co-constitutive (Star, 2007; Clarke & Star, 2008). Vis-à-vis symbolic interactionism, this features researching the meanings held by the actors themselves—an implicitly feminist stance (Clarke, 2005).

Specifically, I and others have argued that GT is a methodology inherently predicated on various forms of symbolic interactionist theoretical and philosophical ontology (e.g., Charmaz, 2006; Locke, 2001; Olesen, 2007). "Method, then, is not the servant of theory: method actually grounds theory" (Jenks, 1995, p. 12). Historically, as GT grew in stature and began to be used more and more widely, and as the implications of

Berger and Luckmann's (1966) *The Social Construction of Reality* began to be taken up more explicitly, more and more practitioners of GT began tugging GT in constructionist and postmodernist directions (e.g., Charmaz, 2000; Locke, 2001; Strauss, 1987). The second generation of GT scholars (Bowers, Charmaz, Clarke, Corbin, Morse, and Stern) agree that Strauss but not Glaser moved in such directions (Morse et al., 2009). Significantly, such directions are requisite if GT is to continue to be a useful method for feminist research.[9]

The second way in which GT has been always already implicitly feminist is its rootedness in George Herbert Mead's concept of perspective. Much of symbolic interactionism has always been perspectival, fully compatible with producing through research what are today understood as situated knowledges (Haraway, 1991, 1997; McCarthy, 1996). Perspective involves the commitment to representing those we study on their own terms, through their own perspectives. That is, the groundedness of good grounded theorizing lies deeply in the seriousness of the analyst's commitment to representing *all* understandings, all knowledges and actions of those studied—as well as the analyst's own—as perspectival. Feminists have often come to grasp such partialities through considerable pain (Star, 2007).

Thus, the interactionist concept of perspective can be deployed to complicate—to make analyses more radical, democratic, and transgressive. Representing the full multiplicity of perspectives in a given situation (from the heterogeneous "powers that be" to the prisoners of various kinds of panopticons, "minority" views, "marginal" positions, "subjugated knowledges," and/or the "other(s)"/alterity) disrupts the *representational* hegemony that usually privileges some and erases others (Clarke, 2005, pp. 58–60; Denzin, Lincoln, & Smith, 2008). Representing *is* intervening (Hacking, 1983). This, of course, has been at the heart of many feminist projects (e.g., Lather & Smithies, 1997). (It also links to the concept of implicated actors, discussed later.)

Third, I would argue that GT is always already feminist (at least vis-à-vis my grasp of feminisms) because an interactionist constructionism is a *materialist* social constructionism (Law, 1999). That is, many people (mis)interpret social constructionism as concerned only with the ephemeral or ideological or symbolic. But the material world is itself constructed—materially produced, interpreted, and given meanings—by us and by those whom we study. It is *what* we study. The material world, including the nonhuman and our own embodiment, is present and to be accounted for in our interpretations and analyses. This materialism, this importance of things, this sociality of things was also argued by Mead (1934/1962, p. 373), as Blumer (1969, pp. 10–11) and McCarthy (1984) have most elegantly demonstrated.

The fourth way in which GT can be viewed as always already feminist lies in its foregrounding of a deconstructive mode of analysis via open coding. Open coding connotes just that—data are open to multiple simultaneous readings or codes. Many different phenomena and many different properties can be named, tracked, and traced through reams of all different kinds of data. There is no one right reading. All readings are temporary, partial, provisional, and perspectival—themselves situated historically and geographically (e.g., Haraway, 1991; McCarthy, 1996).

When analyzing, we can ourselves attempt to "read" the data from different perspectives and for different purposes. Strauss's concrete practice to produce multiple readings was working data analysis groups that take up members' project data. Multiple readings are routinely and explicitly sought and produced through such group efforts. Such group work is also the usual pedagogical tradition for teaching and learning GT—to bring multiple perspectives together so that you can more easily produce multiple readings, multiple possible codes. In this way of working, the analyst is constantly banging into and bouncing off the interpretations of others. Of course, this further enhances and legitimates the capacity of the analyst to come up with multiple possible readings on his or her own and to abandon ideas about "right" and "wrong" readings. I would characterize such analytic working groups as "consciousness raising" because they use the same basic social process of laying out multiple experiences and interpretations.[10]

The fifth way in which GT is always already tacitly feminist concerns difference as range of variation. Variation has always been attended to in GT, but the attention has, I argue, been too scant. Strauss (1993) returned to this point in his capstone book and emphasized it as follows:

> [Social science activity] is directed at understanding the entire range of human actions, of which there are so many that the dictionary can scarcely refer to them all. That is, an interactionist theory of action should address action generally and be applicable to specific types of action, so that in effect the theory can also help us understand the incredibly variegated panorama of human living. (p. 49)

Through SA (discussed later) I seek to further shift the emphasis in GT from attending primarily to commonalities to attending to this "incredibly variegated panorama of human living," to mapping and analyzing differences of all kinds. Making differences more visible and making silences speak (also often about difference) are two of the explicit goals of SA.

Yet, for all its implicit feminisms, there were and continue to be problems for feminists with traditional forms of GT. These include a lack of reflexivity, tendencies toward oversimplification, the interpretation of data variation as "negative cases" rather than differences worthy of understanding, and, for some, a search for fundamental(ist) "purity" and "Truth" through GT (Clarke, 2005, pp. 11–18). Charmaz's (2006) constructionist GT actively works against these problems.

Making Grounded Theory More Explicitly Feminist

Many scholars have forged GT into explicitly feminist tools for qualitative research over the past 40 or so years (Clarke, 2007a; Olesen, 2007). The range of feminist usages of GT is staggeringly broad, and it is truly impossible to review this vast literature here. Instead, I highlight several clusters of contributors who have made GT explicitly feminist in important

and enduringly valuable ways: nurse researchers; sociologists; and science, technology, and medicine scholars. Issues of diversity crosscut disciplinarity, and I also discuss both Glaser's and Strauss's positions vis-à-vis gender and race in GT research.

Feminist GT Nursing Research

It comes as no surprise that nurse researchers comprised the first group of scholars to adopt GT. Strauss and Glaser were faculty in the School of Nursing at UC San Francisco (UCSF) in the 1960s when they conceived the GT method and published their book, and Strauss remained on the faculty until his death in 1996. Virginia Olesen was also on the faculty and introduced feminist theory and feminist social science perspectives on women's health to sociology and nursing curricula beginning in 1973.[11]

The earliest wave of feminist nursing GT scholarship was undertaken by Holly Wilson, Sally Hutchinson, Phyllis Noerager Stern, Ellen O'Shaughnessy, June Lowenberg, Barbara Bowers, Susan Kools, Ellen Schumacher, and others.[12] It was generally more tacitly rather than explicitly feminist. That is, the research topics often featured concerns particular to girls and women and to caregiving, and they centered on giving voice to ill people and their families, noting gender. Explicitly gendered analyses such as the problematization, production, or performance of gendered identities were rare. Nor did this early work pursue the intersectionalities of gender identities with race and class issues, as feminist research often does (more in what follows).

More recently, many nurse scholars have extended their efforts in more explicitly feminist directions. Among these is Margaret Kearney, whose research on pregnant African American women using crack cocaine was groundbreaking (e.g., Kearney, 2001). An array of studies led to her GT-based *Understanding Women's Recovery From Illness and Trauma* (Kearney, 1999). Suellen Miller (1996) did feminist research on how new mothers developed career reentry strategies. Her and Kearney's (Kearney, Murphy, Irwin, & Rosenbaum, 1995) GT integrative analytic diagrams are among the best in print, superb for teaching theoretical integration. Benoliel (2001) edited a special issue of *Health Care for Women International* on "Expanding Knowledge About Women Through Grounded Theory." Marcellus (2005) offers a review of GT in maternal-infant research and practice (see also Olshansky, 2003). Other feminist work has focused on nursing interventions for domestic violence (Ford-Gilboe, Wuest, & Merritt-Gray, 2005) and foster care (Kools & Kennedy, 2003). Much, if not most, of this work has clear advocacy, intervention, and policy aims, and all would be of interest to feminists across the disciplines focusing on such topics.

Nurse researchers have also written extensively on GT as method. Recent work addresses the shift from traditional to postmodern GT (Kools, 2008; Mills, Chapman, Bonner, & Francis, 2007). It also focuses on dimensional analysis as a form of GT (Bowers & Schatzman, 2009; Kools, 2008); taking GT beyond psychological process (Kearney, 2009); GT sampling and reflexivity (Morse, 2007; Neill, 2006); how "people change and methods change" (Corbin, 2009; Corbin & Strauss, 2008); the development of formal theory (Kearney, 2001, 2007); and debates between the Straussian and Glaserian approaches (see note 9). Schumacher (2008) offers an account of her two decades of GT research on family caregiving. She is especially insightful about the conundrums confronted in a sustained research program, such as whether to handle one's own earlier research conclusions and theorizing with the dubiousness generally accorded to "received theory" in GT work. Kearney (2008) compared the GT research trajectories of a nurse and a sociologist both studying depression. The nurse began with more applied concerns and, over the years, moved into theorizing, while the sociologist's trajectory was just the reverse.

Looking to the future of GT in nursing research, Kushner and Morrow (2003) elucidated relations with interactionist, feminist, and critical theories. They found several useful commonalities, including a special focus on vulnerable groups, the explication of researchers' standpoints, respect for participant expertise within the research process, and emancipatory intent. Plummer and Young (2010) argue that GT is especially compatible with feminist inquiry for research on women.

Feminism, Glaser, Strauss, and American Sociology

In terms of the advent of feminism in GT nursing research, Susan Kools (2008) notes that many of the early generation of GT nurse scholars were trained before the postmodern turn by the white men at the University of California, San Francisco. The same was true for early GT sociologists. Both Glaser and Strauss, as well as Schatzman, had serious problems with the explicit feminist approaches to knowledge production that began circulating in the 1970s. For example, Glaser (2002b), at the request of nurse scholars, wrote on "Grounded Theory and Gender Relevance," reasserting his earlier arguments that gender, like race and other "face sheet data," needs to "earn [its] way into" a GT analysis rather than "forcing" it (p. 789; see also Bryant, 2003; Glaser, 2002a). He ignores how, over the past 40 years, gender and race/ethnicity have become central to the American sociological enterprise. They have been theorized as fundamental social aspects of being and action that are learned, performative, variegated, enculturated, and situated. They are of intrinsic and nonfungible sociological importance, though precisely *how* they may "matter" in any situation remains an empirical question. Moreover, to allow such issues to "earn their way" into GT analysis would require data to be collected that are capable of addressing them, rather than just waiting for them to appear. Pursuing such data—and then analyzing it— would both make researchers more accountable and the feminisms and antiracisms engaged more explicit (see Clarke, 2005, pp. 73–78).

At the request of French feminists editing a volume about how major social theorists engaged or did not engage gender, I wrote an article about Strauss's unease both with the concept of gender and with addressing gender- or sex-based and race/ethnicity-based inequities in research (Clarke, 2008, 2010a). Through the lifelong commitment of his wife Fran Strauss to the American Civil Liberties Union and his ongoing engagement with Blumer's (1958) and other interactionists' work on race (e.g., Duster, 1990/2003; Omi and Winant, 1994), Strauss saw both sets of issues routinely "on his table." He engaged them in limited fashion. That is, while sex/gender and race/ethnicity issues were rarely explicitly theorized in his work, they were tacitly constitutive elements of some of the situations he studied, methods and analytic strategies he developed, and theories he generated. For example, certain ways of doing GT scholarly work, such as the small working groups and teams, were and remain deeply congruent with feminist precepts. Many threads of Strauss's work have also been taken up and elaborated in explicitly feminist and antiracist ways by his students, in ways that echo the reparative work of feminist Foucauldians (Clarke, 2008; Star, 2007).

My main assertion here is that neither Glaser's nor Strauss's versions of *formal* social theory could legitimately include sex/gender or race/ethnicity perspectives (Clarke, 2008, 2010a). In mid-twentieth-century mainstream American sociology, such "identity" issues were understood as sources of *bias*. They had to be *made* sociological (e.g., DuBois, 1993; Blumer, 1958; this volume). Today, they are viewed as fundamental aspects of social organization and stratification, not only integral to but *requisite for* adequate theorizing—nationally *and* transnationally. For nearly 30 years, feminist standpoint theories have further argued that those positioned in the margins actually have clearer perspectives on certain phenomena (Star, 2007; see this volume). Moreover, in the United States today, it is theoretically necessary to *simultaneously* consider issues of race/ethnicity along with sex/gender as these are historically deeply entwined, along with other identity issues, in ways that are increasingly understood as intersectional (e.g., Collins, 2004; Dill & Zambrana, 2009; Schulz & Mullings, 2006; Weber, 2010). Schwalbe, Goodwin, Schrock, Thompson, and Wolkomir (2000) superbly frame generic processes in the reproduction of inequality. An impressive chapter in the new *Handbook of Grounded Theory* by Green, Creswell, Shope, and Plano Clark (2007) lays out strategies for enhancing diversity in GT research, and Charmaz (2005, 2011) strategizes using GT methods for social justice research.

Social theory no longer precludes addressing differences; rather, it demands it.

Feminist Sociological and Other GT Research

Turning to recent feminist GT sociological research, we find a number of projects explicitly pursuing diversity goals. Wingfield (2007) used GT in a fascinating paper on intersectionality titled "The Modern Mammy and the Angry Black Man: African American Professionals' Experiences With Gendered Racism in the Workplace." The professionals she interviewed often had to combat such gendered images from historical racist discourse—or be dealt with stereotypically themselves (see also Settles, Pratt-Hyatt, & Buchanan, 2008). Anthropologist Maternowska and colleagues (2010) analyzed reproductive decision making among recent Mexican migrants in California. They found that migrants' marginalization and isolation along with economic challenges and new access to contraceptives were together changing familial relationships and reproductive decision making.

Taking GT into feminist queer studies, sociologist Laura Mamo (2007) used GT at the intersection of lived experience and technology studies to explore how both cultural discourses and assisted reproduction are used by lesbian-identified women seeking pregnancy through technoscientific means. Mamo argues that lesbians both follow given technological scripts and create their own interpretations of the technologies, thus subverting the expectations of developers, marketers, and service providers. Berkowitz and Marsiglio (2007) studied how gay men who had fathered children outside of heterosexual intercourse negotiated procreative, father, and family identities. Finding change across these gay men's life spans, they note that the men's procreative consciousness was strongly shaped by institutions (such as adoption and fertility agencies) and by ruling relations (such as assumptions about gay men). Negotiation was a major social process in constructing "out" gay and lesbian parent families "beyond the closet"—navigating residual heterosexual dominance in institutions such as schools and in personal interactions—despite greater acceptance at least in some places (Ryan & Berkowitz, 2009). For lesbians frequenting bars, another GT study found trade-offs associated with bar patronage regarding the psychosocial importance of the bar for individual reasons and for a sense of community and the relationship between minority stress and alcohol use (Gruskin, Byrne, & Kools, 2006).

Emotion work (Hochschild, 1969) and intimate care work (Boris & Parrenas, 2010) have long been of interest to feminists. Wolkomir and Powers (2007) used GT in their thoughtful study of the challenges of emotional labor in an abortion clinic. They found that the workers needed to balance helping women and protecting themselves, and they did so by classifying patients in terms of their different needs and personal styles. Clinic workers then generated effective strategies to handle these differences, including boundary setting to buffer what they viewed as inappropriate demands upon them as providers of care. Schrock and Padavic (2007) also use GT to study a challenging workplace—a batterer intervention program. They found that hegemonic masculinity was both produced (in terms of the men's setting boundaries to maintain their "patriarchal dividend") and negotiated (in terms of their taking some responsibility and choosing nonviolence). The distinctive partialities of "success" were fascinating.

Invisible work and the also invisible burdens of doing it have also long been of interest to feminists and others (e.g., Star, 1991, 2007). Landstedt, Asplund, and Gådin (2009) explored teens' perceptions of what is significant for mental health in Sweden, applying a gender analysis. Boys' more positive mental health appeared to be associated with their low degree of responsibility taking and beneficial positions relative to girls. Girls were at greater risk for mental health problems, due, in large part, to the weight of the invisible work of being more responsible in interactions and performatively. I am unhappily reminded of the classic feminist article "Why I Want a Wife" (Syfers, 1971). *Plus ça change . . .*

Janet Shim's (2005, forthcoming) ambitious research combines the lived experiences tradition with feminist science, technology, and medicine studies approaches in GT research. She focuses on two different sets of people concerned with cardiovascular diseases (CVDs) in the United States today: epidemiologists and related researchers who study racial, ethnic, sex/gender, social class, and other distributions of CVDs in populations and people of color diagnosed as having CVDs. Shim's explicitly comparative approach centers on the *meanings* of race, class, and sex vis-à-vis CVDs— constructed by the epidemiologists, on the one hand, and by the people of color diagnosed and living with CVDs, on the other (see also Schwalbe et al., 2000). Shim's work demonstrates the fruitfulness of doing feminist GT with a comparative design and then teasing out comparisons both within and between emerging categories (Kathy Charmaz, personal communication, October 2005). Clarke, Mamo, Fosket, Fishman, and Shim's (2010) edited volume *Biomedicalization: Technoscience, Health, and Illness in the U.S.* offers an array of technoscience studies, many of which utilize grounded theory approaches on gender-related topics.

Last, feminist economists have challenged traditional economic theory by developing a gendered reconceptualization of social indicators based on the use of GT with focus-group data (Austen, Jefferson, & Thein, 2003). Such new indicators can be used to reorganize how economic analyses are done in ways that, quite radically even today, include gender.

I must end this section with an apology. While I discuss some works pursued in "faraway places," my "lite" review here emphasizes work done by nurses and sociologists who trained at UCSF. I certainly do not mean to imply that these works are in any way "better" than others. Rather, I merely know them better myself. I will discuss the limitations of GT and SA below, before concluding.

What Is Situational Analysis?

In the extension of GT I developed called situational analysis (Clarke, 2003, 2005), *the situation of inquiry itself broadly conceived is the key unit of analysis.*[13] This is radically different from traditional GT, which focuses on the main social processes—human action—in the area of inquiry. In SA, the situation of inquiry is empirically constructed through the making of three kinds of maps and by following through with analytic work and memos of various kinds.

The first maps are *situational maps* that lay out the major human, nonhuman, discursive, historical, symbolic, cultural, political, and other elements in the research situation of concern (Figure 18.1). The goals of this map are first to enhance research design by laying out everything about which at least some data should be gathered. Downstream in the research, situational maps are used to provoke analysis of relations among the different elements. Working *against* the usual simplifications (Star, 1983) in particularly postmodern and feminist ways,

these maps capture and provoke discussion of the many and heterogeneous elements and the messy complexities of the situation (see Clarke, 2005, pp. 83–123).

Second, the *social worlds/arenas maps* lay out all of the *collective* actors and the arenas of commitment within which they are engaged in ongoing discourse and negotiations. Such maps offer meso-level interpretations of the situation, taking up its social organizational, institutional, and discursive dimensions. They are distinctively postmodern in their assumptions: we cannot assume directionalities of influence; boundaries are open and porous; negotiations

Figure 18.1 Messy Abstract Situational Map

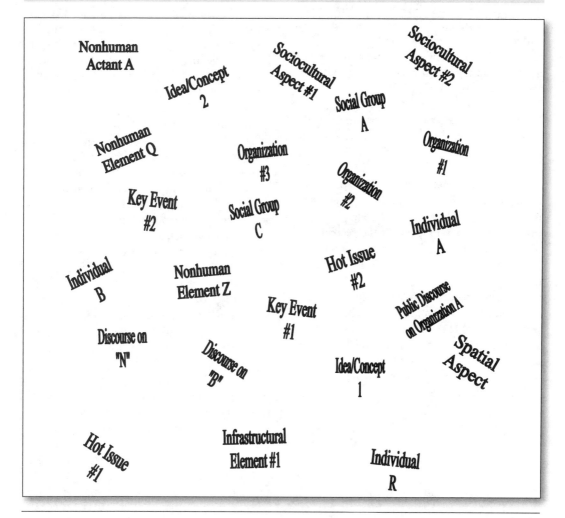

are fluid; discourses are multiple and potentially contradictory. *Negotiations* of many kinds from coercion to bargaining are the "basic social processes" that construct and constantly destabilize the social worlds/arenas maps (Strauss, 1993). Things could always be otherwise—not only individually but also collectively, organizationally, institutionally, and discursively, and these maps portray such postmodern possibilities (see Clarke, 2005, pp. 109–124).

Third, *positional maps* lay out the major positions taken, and *not* taken, in the data vis-à-vis particular axes of variation and difference, focus, and controversy found in the situation of concern. Perhaps most significantly, positional maps are *not* articulated with persons or groups but rather seek to represent the full range of *discursive* positions on key issues. They allow multiple positions and even contradictions within both individuals and collectivities to be articulated. Complexities are themselves heterogeneous, and we need improved means of representing them (see Clarke, 2005, pp. 125–136). I see this as explicitly feminist as well.

Significantly, SA takes the nonhuman in the situation of inquiry very seriously. The nonhuman can include things, animals, technologies, discourses, and so forth. In doing initial situational maps, the analyst is asked to specify the nonhuman elements in the situation, thus making pertinent materialities and discourses visible from the outset. The flipside of the second kind of map, the social worlds/arenas maps, are discourse/arenas maps. Social worlds are "universes of discourse" routinely producing discourses about elements of concern in the situation. Such discourses can be mapped and analyzed. Last, positional maps open up the discourses per se by analyzing positions taken on key axes. Discourses can thereby be disarticulated from their sites of production, decentering them and making analytic complexities visible.

SITUATIONAL ANALYSIS AS ALWAYS ALREADY IMPLICITLY FEMINIST

SA is always already feminist both in the ways discussed previously as characteristic of GT (since SA is an extension of GT after the postmodern turn) and also in (at least) the following ways:

1. Acknowledging researchers' embodiment and situatedness

2. Grounding analysis in the lived material and symbolic situation itself

3. Conceptually foregrounding complexities and differences in the data

4. Mapping *all* the actors and discourses in the situation regardless of their power in that situation

First, while traditional GT historically and occasionally today may have a foot in the positivist domain that assumes the possibility of "scientific objectivity" and "Truth," constructivist GT and SA do not. That is, neither constructivist GT nor SA assumes that there is a singular transcendent "Truth" in the Enlightenment scientific sense of being True at all times and places. Rather, both assume that different epistemologies—different modes of knowledge production—will produce different "truths" that are congruent with the assumptions and practices involved in producing them and that are historically and geopolitically located (Charmaz, 2006; Clarke, 2005). There are no global verities. Instead, constructivist GT and SA not only assume but explicitly acknowledge the embodiment and situatedness of knowledge producers—both us (the researchers) and them (who and what we are studying)—as we collaborate in the production of new knowledge, which is assumed to be partial (Haraway, 1991, 1997; Lather, 2007, 2008; McCarthy, 1996). Second, SA is always already feminist in its overall analytic focus on the situation itself as the unit of analysis that transforms "objects of study" and their "contexts" into a single ultimately nonfungible unit by refusing the object-context binary. The important so-called contextual elements are not constellated somehow *around* the objects of study but, instead, are actually *inside the situation itself.* They are *constitutive* of it (Figure 182).

The concept situation is feminist in part in terms of its *gestalt*—how a situation is always greater than the sum of its parts because it includes their relationality in a particular temporal

Figure 18.2   Clarke's Situational Matrix

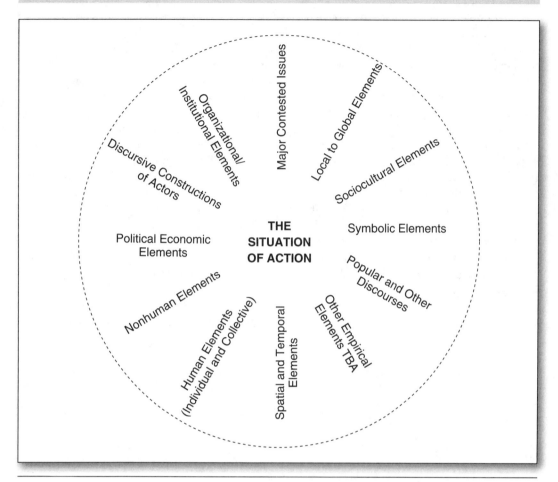

and spatial moment. A gestalt understanding of situations as generating "a life of their own" offers a very post-structuralist reading, granting a kind of agency to the situation per se similar to the agency discourses have or are in Foucauldian terms. Such agency is most important in understanding SA. Relationalities and situatedness have long been central to feminisms.

A third way that SA is always already feminist concerns the assumptions and representational strategies of focusing on normativity or homogeneity versus focusing on differences, complexities, or heterogeneities. The capacity of GT techniques to fracture data and permit multiple analyses is a key contribution. SA features

and enhances this capacity. Foundationally, this involves analyzing *against* the assumptions of the normal curve, the conceptual default drive of Western science, black-boxed inside the hardware of knowledge production and inside the software of social science training. Please visualize a normal curve. The normal curve is a high modern concept embodying Enlightenment thinking and thereby producing knowledge that fits its orderly classificatory preconceptions (e.g., Lampland & Star, 2009). Although the fringes or margins of the normal curve are literally contiguous with the center, we are led to assume they are *not* constitutive of the "normal." In sharp contrast, it is the boundaries/margins that *produce* the center, the peripheries/colonies that *constitute* the core/metropole (Said, 1978). Moreover, in narrowly focusing on what is construed as "the normal," the broader situation in which the phenomenon has been historically and otherwise located recedes to the point of invisibility.

SA replaces such metaphors of normal curves and normativity with relational metaphors of ecology and cartography. Figure 18.3 displays (in two dimensions but please imagine three) a wide variety of differently situated positions: P1, P2, . . . P10, and so on. This messy positional map conceptually replaces modernist unidimensional normal curves with a postmodern multidimensional representation of the variety of positionalities and human and nonhuman activities and discourses within a lived situation. We need to move seriously *toward* complexity and heterogeneity rather than away from them, instead of seeking simplification. Otherwise, we merely continue performing recursive classifications that ignore the empirical world (Lampland & Star, 2009). For example, we cannot fathom biodiversity without ambitious sciences of plants and animals and the situated ecologies of their relations. The same holds for humans living on this complex planet.

Such relational modalities of representation do not concern themselves with frequency. Instead, they attend intently to positions and their distribution across situational or topographical maps that do the work of helping us to "see" the full range of positions. In doing SA, one draws maps to help make known, understand, and represent the heterogeneity of positions taken in the situation under study and/or within given (historical and/or visual and/or narrative) discourses in that situation.

The main goal of SA vis-à-vis differences is not only to enhance their *empirical* study but also to describe them more richly. That is, we cannot assume what any kinds of differences mean to those in a given situation, and we need more and

Figure 18.3 Mapping Positionality

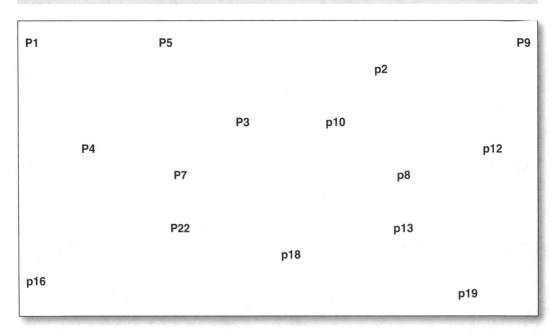

Note: In your mental image, please make this figure three-dimensional.

better methods to explore the existence, meanings, and consequences of differences within concrete social practices. This may include studying the production and consumption of discourses as practices (e.g., Schwalbe et al., 2000). We need to grasp variation *within* data categories, the range of variation within data, complexities, contradictions, multiplicities, and ambivalences that manifest individually, collectively, and discursively. The situational maps are each and all designed to do precisely this de-essentializing feminist work.

The fourth and last way I would argue that SA is always already feminist is that it requires mapping of *all* the actors and discourses in the situation regardless of their power in that situation. This can be both a feminist and a democratizing move. Many contemporary modes of analysis, including those of Foucault (e.g., 1975) and Latourian actor-network theory (e.g., Law & Hassard, 1999), center on the analysis of (those in/discourses in) power. In sharp contrast, SA goes beyond what could be called "the master discourse" (Hughes, 1971). By *not* analytically recapitulating the power relations of domination, SA analyses that represent the full array of actors and discourses turn up the volume on lesser but still present discourses, lesser but still present participants, the quiet, the silent, and the silenced.

Such analyses can amplify not only differences but also resistances, recalcitrance, and sites of rejection. The concept of *implicated actors* is important here. These are actors explicitly constructed and/or addressed by a social world and for whom the actions of that world may be highly consequential—*but* who are either not present or not allowed to be fully agentic in the actual doings of that world. The actions taken "on behalf of" implicated actors are often supposedly "for their own good." Individuals and social groups with less power in situations tend to be implicated rather than fully agentic actors (Clarke, 2005, pp. 46–48; Clarke & Montini, 1993). They often tend to be female or otherwise "othered," possibly including the nonhuman. SA focuses on making the less powerful, silent, and silenced more visible and more analytically central.

In sum, the goal of SA is not prediction but vivid descriptions and strong analytic insights.

Theorizing should make thick description and thick interpretation possible. SA studies also seek to specify what has gone and goes unstudied— that which may not be seen or perceived or which may be refused—and is worthy of note regardless (Star, 2007). Thus, making the heretofore invisible visible is a goal congruent with ongoing feminist analytics, and one that takes feminism beyond gender relations when gender relations are not enough (Collins, 2009; Smith, 2007; Weber, 2010).

MAKING SITUATIONAL ANALYSIS MORE EXPLICITLY FEMINIST

SA has been increasingly taken up since it first appeared in 2005 (Clarke, 2005). Studies using situational mapping along with grounded theory have often done so to better grasp what has usually been understood as the broader social context. For example, Mills, Francis, and Bonner's (2008) "Getting to Know a Stranger— Rural Nurses' Experiences of Mentoring: A Grounded Theory" addressed the problems of recruiting and retraining nurses. In rural areas, they are often the sole health care providers for large geographic regions. The project explored how experienced nurses cultivated novices through recognizing their potential and teaming up in critical situations. In contrast, another study focused on enhancing access to mental health services for potential patients who are culturally diverse. Schnitzer, Loots, Escudero, and Schechter (2009) examined the quite limited help seeking of ultraorthodox Jewish parents in a Belgian city, which was both highly gendered and framed predominantly in spiritual and religious ways. Mothers largely dealt with daughters' educational and health needs and problems (both mental and physical) and fathers with sons'. They suggest culturally sensitive ways to enhance the accessibility of services, which also need, at times, to be gender specific for this population.

The concepts of social worlds and arenas were developed by Strauss and elaborated by me prior to making them part of SA via mapping them (Clarke, 1991, 1998; Clarke & Montini, 1993; Strauss, 1978, 1993). In brief, social worlds are groups with shared commitments to certain activities, sharing resources of many kinds to achieve their goals and building shared ideologies about how to go about their business. They are interactive units, worlds of discourse, bounded not by geography or formal membership but by the limits of effective communication. Social worlds are fundamental "building blocks" of collective action and the main units of analysis in such studies. In arenas, all the social worlds come together that focus on a given issue and are prepared to act in some way. Clarke and Montini (1993) is an especially accessible exemplar. The article analytically places the technology RU486 in the center and then moves through the specific perspectives taken on it by each of the major social worlds involved in the broader abortion and reproduction arena. By attending to diversities *within* worlds, the paper also demonstrates that social worlds are not monolithic.

Moore's (2007) book, *Sperm Tales: Social, Cultural, and Scientific Representations of Human Semen,* uses GT and SA to analyze representations of sperm from different social worlds/arenas—reproductive sciences, the Internet, children's "facts of life" books, forensic transcripts, sex workers' narratives, and personal expertise. Semen representations, she finds, are distinctively related to the changing social positions of men, masculinities, and constructions of male differences in the different arenas and beyond. Moore (2007) also offers a sophisticated methods appendix with an account of more than a decade of research on these different arenas and of her strategies of triangulation to produce a formal grounded theory (pp. 155–164).

Kohlen (2009) offers an extended SA in *Conflicts of Care: Hospital Ethics Committees in the USA and Germany.* Although such committees were initiated in the United States in the 1980s, only in recent years have German hospitals followed suit. Kohlen compares three different hospitals, finding differences in the committees due to institutional structures, local cultures, and histories. As in the United States, nurses (mostly women) are particularly committed to such work, seeking "real rather than symbolic" engagement toward improving patient care. The nurses framed moral understandings of and standards for patient care that too often were an "elusive quest" in ways similar to

accountability in U.S. hospitals (Wiener, 2000). Kohlen (2009) also used SA to identify silences and exclusions in the discourse, finding that nurses did *not* discuss *nursing* problems of care in the ethics committees, not wanting to expose "not only the dying patient in utmost vulnerability, but also the work of nursing including its messy necessities" (pp. 228–229).

Science, technology, and medicine studies continue to draw feminist GT and SA researchers. Clarke and Star (2008) offer an ambitious overview of the social worlds/arenas approach as a theory-methods package, and they review recent work in the field. Although a number of studies have used positional mapping, other than Kohlen's (2009) book, discussed already, to date they have not been feminist projects.

LIMITATIONS OF GROUNDED THEORY AND SITUATIONAL ANALYSIS

All methodologies feature advantages and pose limitations. Both GT and SA are distinctively *analytic* approaches to taking data apart. GT does this by coding, integrating codes and categories, and generating a substantive theory of action that characterizes the common social processes in the situation. Situational maps do it by abstracting all the elements in the situation and mapping them. Social worlds/arenas maps parse the meso-level organizations and institutions in the situation. Positional maps analyze the contested discourses in the situation, seeking especially to analyze silences.

But the idea of deconstruction is even stronger here. GT and other *analytic* approaches have been criticized for "fracturing" data, for "violating" the integrity of participants' narratives, and for "pulling apart" stories, for example by Riessman (2008, p. 79). I see this not as a weakness or problem but instead as the key to GT's *analytic,* rather than *re-representational,* strength. Analysis and re-representation are two deeply different qualitative research approaches. Re-representation usually centers on the lived experiences of individuals (occasionally on those of collectivities). Analysis centers instead on elucidating *processes* of social phenomena—action. Feminist research needs both—and more (e.g., Riessman, 2008, p. 209n24).

GT can certainly be used to understand and explain individuals' lived experiences per se (e.g., Charmaz, 2010). And, through social worlds analysis, GT and SA help theorize social action at the collective level (e.g., Casper, 1998; Clarke, 1998). But while both attend to the social setting, neither centers on generating rich ethnography, institutional or other. Finally, neither method explicitly targets understanding long-term politico-economic and related change. However, a group of now former students and I theorized the rise of medicine, medicalization, and biomedicalization by generating a historical database (Clarke, Shim, Mamo, Fosket, & Fishman, 2003; Clarke et al., 2010). And I offered methodological strategies for theorizing biomedicalization in its transnational travels, utilizing local and regional historical and visual materials (Clarke, 2010c).

CONCLUSION

With Lather, I am seeking "a fertile ontological space and ethical practice in asking how research-based knowledge remains possible after so much questioning of the very ground of science . . . gesturing toward the science possible after the critique of science" (Lather, 2007, pp. viii, ix). In feminist hands, both GT and SA can help generate such fertile spaces and ethical practices. Further, "The work of grounded theorists will be enhanced with . . . [greater] recognition, so deeply rooted in the symbolic interactionist bones of GT, that researcher and participant are mutually imbedded in the social context of the research and that data are co-created" (Olesen, 2007, p. 427). And reading and teaching widely in our feminist community of discourse will nurture, sustain, and provoke us both intellectually and politically. This volume is a major resource for such practices.

In terms of future feminist research using GT, my hopes are for more explicitly feminist projects, especially research that questions the very grounds of traditional disciplinary categories and conventions and opens up possible new avenues for enhancing social justice. Here, I am thinking of Austen and colleagues' (2003) exciting deconstruction of "social indicators" in the discipline of economics, which for decades remained impenetrable by feminist perspectives. Another exemplar, especially of epistemic diversity, is Shim's (2005, forthcoming) nuanced study of the meanings of "race," "class," and "gender" to epidemiologists and people of color with CVDs. While much epidemiology rotely pursues "the usual suspects," the people of color she studied produced their own insightful understandings of how racism, sexism, and class-based discrimination were making their heart conditions worse. Shim hopes that policies in health care, epidemiology, and beyond will be built on such subjugated knowledges toward alleviating health inequalities.

What other kinds of feminist-informed knowledges exist and how might they be channeled by good research into improving social policies and reducing inequalities? Resources toward such goals include Charmaz's (2005, 2011) work on using GT toward social justice ends, Olesen's (2005, 2007) papers on feminist research, and Denzin and colleagues' (2008) book on decolonizing methods. My paper on doing transnational research on biomedicalization, including feminist and gender issues, encourages the use of historical, visual, and other discursive materials (Clarke, 2010c).

I particularly recommend using SA in feminist studies where import is placed on elucidating differences, making silences speak, and revealing contradictions within positions and within social groups. Samik-Ibrahim (2000) has argued that GT methodology is especially useful in less-developed countries and settings. The same holds true for SA; hence there is potential utility for both in feminist postcolonial studies. SA would be especially valuable where (nonhuman) infrastructural elements of situations are quite different (availability of roads, water, health care, traditional and changing gender arrangements, and divisions of labor). Researchers need to take such differences into *explicit* account to generate policy recommendations and programmatic interventions (Clarke, 2010c). An example here is local needs assessment research in which the desire is to grasp *both* the specifics of the local situation materially *and* the perspectives of local people on their own needs—remembering that these may well be multivocal, gendered, and contradictory. Thus, SA should be helpful in feminist postcolonial studies and transnational studies wherein the particularities of situatedness are of special import.

I also hope for feminist research using GT and SA in the study of discourses—historical, visual, and narrative—and in multisite research that combines studies of discursive data with interviews and ethnographic work. I have framed how this can be pursued via integrative mapping (all data sources analyzed together) and comparative mapping (data sources analyzed separately) (Clarke, 2005, pp. 176–177). I would argue also that the time has come for more comparative work, explicitly contrasting the positions articulated in public discourses with those produced by the various sets of actors active in and implicated by those discourses (Lather & Smithies, 1997; Shim, 2005, forthcoming).

Following in Anselm Strauss's (1987) proto-feminist footsteps, I particularly advocate researchers' participation in working groups of various kinds to provoke analysis by having to come to grips with other perspectives, other interpretations of data, commentary on preliminary incarnations of integrated analyses, and so on. Strauss believed so strongly in the working group process that in his 1987 GT book, he actually provides transcripts of the sessions of such groups. Groups explicitly focused on feminist research would further echo consciousness raising and further provoke discussions of feminist theoretical developments and needs (e.g., Lather, 2007). Using GT and SA in such groups can be done in actual collaborative research (e.g., Lather & Smithies, 1997) or with independent research projects using such groups as analytic worksites (e.g., Lessor, 2000; Wiener, 2007).

Beyond actually using GT and SA in feminist research, my major recommendation for making them—or any other approach—more explicitly feminist is to engage with the work of exciting feminist and other theorists, methodologists, and researchers. Feminist qualitative research is itself, as demonstrated by this volume and its impressive predecessor, a lively community of ongoing discourses. It is a widely distributed and very heterogeneous arena that can be a source of wondrous provocation. It exceeds "conversations" and "collaborations," and it too has a gestalt that is greater than the sum of its parts. For me, reading Patti Lather, whom I see

as a theorist of feminist methodologies, always ruptures my taken-for-granted-ness. She vividly portrays dilemmas, conundrums, partialities, contradictions, ethics—the agonies and ecstasies of research. She reminds us that we are merely *trying* to be feminist at this historical moment, "getting lost" along the way, knowing we grasp and acknowledge only a few of the shortfalls of our work. But we go on.

Discussion Questions

1. Discuss the major emphases of feminist GT studies.

2. Discuss the major emphases of feminist SA studies.

3. What are some of the key differences between GT and SA?

4. Why is studying difference and differences so important to feminists?

5. Why is studying silences and who and what is invisible so important to feminists?

6. What are some of the main limitations of GT? Of SA?

Online Resources

Situational Analysis

http://www.situationalanalysis.com

This is the only website devoted to SA. It offers lists of publications using SA, upcoming conferences and workshops, bibliographies, and more.

Anselm Strauss

http://sbs.ucsf.edu/medsoc/anselmstrauss

This site focuses on the work of Anselm Strauss, including his grounded theory work. It includes unpublished essays, topical bibliographies, and more.

Relevant Journals

Gender & Society

International Journal of Qualitative Methods

International Review of Qualitative Research

Qualitative Health Research

Qualitative Inquiry

Qualitative Research

Qualitative Sociology

Symbolic Interaction

NOTES

1. See especially Glaser (1978, 2002a, 2007), Glaser and Holton (2004), Strauss (1987, 1995), Strauss and Corbin (1990, 1994, 1998), Charmaz (2000, 2006, 2008a, 2009), Bryant and Charmaz (2007), Clarke (2003, 2005, 2007a, 2007b, 2009), Corbin and Strauss (2008), and Locke (2001).

2. On feminist research, see, e.g., this volume and its first edition (Hesse-Biber, 2007). See also Hekman (2007), Lather (2007, 2008), Naples (2003), Olesen (2005, 2007, 2011), and Smith (2007).

3. The concept of abduction is, appropriately, from pragmatist philosophy where the roots of symbolic interaction and GT also lie (e.g., Locke, 2007; Reichertz, 2007; Richardson & Kramer, 2006; Strubing, 2007; Timmermans & Tavory, in review). I have recently extended the concept in theorizing anticipation as our current modus operandi (Adams, Murphy, & Clarke, 2009).

4. See, on theoretical sampling, Glaser and Strauss (1967, pp. 45–77), Glaser (1978, pp. 36–54), Strauss (1987, pp. 38–39), Strauss and Corbin (1998, pp. 201–215), Clarke (2005, especially pp. 31–35), Charmaz (2006, pp. 96–122), and Morse (2007).

5. At an early National Women's Studies Association conference, held in Bloomington, Indiana, in 1980, there was a panel on "Qualitative Methods and Feminism" (www.nwsaconference.org/archives .html). On the panel, according to Star, were Sandra Harding, Pauline Bart, and herself. Star's presentation was predicated on the dissertation research of Barbara DuBois at Harvard in clinical psychology, which used GT to analyze women's experiences (DuBois, 1983; Star, 2007).

6. In the United States, there has long been what I see as a misuse of the term *pragmatic* largely to equal *expedience* based in the logics of homo economicus, with some form of capitalism as the only reasonable path. In sharp contrast, pragmatists like Dewey referred to the pragmatic as what would work or be feasible to do, *given the conditions of the situation*. As such, it is

more closely akin to Foucault's "conditions of possibility" (Foucault, 1975), elucidating what needs to be taken into account to answer his question, "What is to be done?" (Foucault, 1991, p. 84).

7. See also Atkinson et al. (2003, pp. 148–152) and Denzin (2007). Glaser (1978, 2002a) and Glaser and Holton (2004) argue that GT could also be used with quantitative research.

8. Issues of trust vis-à-vis research have changed. In the mid-twentieth century, neither researchers nor respondents (now called participants) were deemed reliable or trustworthy—generating a vast literature on reliability. Today, we are much more publicly skeptical, exhibiting profound distrust in governments, media, science, corporations, professions—and in research. In feminist literatures, the question of trust is often argued in terms of accountability (e.g., Haraway, 1991, 1997; Hesse-Biber, 2007; Lather, 2007, 2008).

9. The debate between Glaser and Strauss and Corbin, which has implications for feminist research, is extensively taken up in Bryant and Charmaz (2007) and in Morse et al. (2009, here and there). Morse et al. (2009) include a dialogue among the second generation that ends up asserting that today there are different kinds of GT (pp. 236–247). Denzin (2007) describes Glaserian GT as objectivist, the Strauss and Corbin version as systematic, the Charmaz version as constructivist, and Clarke's as situationist. I think these terms work well. See also Charmaz (2000, 2006, 2008a, 2008b, 2009), Clarke (2005, pp. 12–18; 2007), Glaser (2002a, 2007), Glaser and Holton (2004), Locke (2001), Morse (2009), and Walker and Myrick (2006).

10. Strauss so much believed in this process that he incorporated transcripts of group analysis sessions into one of his major methods books (Strauss, 1987). See Star (2007) on feminist issues and Wiener (2007) and Lessor (2000) on working groups.

11. See the Anselm Strauss website at www.ucsf .edu/anselmstrauss. See Glaser's website at www .groundedtheory.com. On Virginia Olesen (2005, 2007, 2011), see http://nurseweb.ucsf.edu/www/ffolesv.htm.

12. Stern (2007, 2009), Bowers and Schatzman (2009), Kools (2008), and Schumacher (2008) all provide accounts of this era. Benoliel (1996) analyzed GT nursing research published from 1980 to 1994.

13. After publication of my book, I discovered several other methods also called "situational analysis." What this means in terms of electronic searching for my version of "situational analysis" is that it needs to be done with "AND grounded theory."

REFERENCES

Adams, V., Murphy, M., & Clarke, A. E. (2009). Anticipation: Technoscience, life, affect, temporality. *Subjectivity, 28,* 246–265.

Atkinson, P., Coffey, A., & Delamont, S. (2003). *Key themes in qualitative research: Continuities and change.* Walnut Creek, CA: AltaMira Press/Rowman and Littlefield.

Austen, S., Jefferson, T., & Thein, V. (2003). Gendered social indicators and grounded theory. *Feminist Economics, 9*(1), 1–18.

Becker, H. S. (1963). *Outsiders: Studies in the sociology of deviance.* New York: Free Press.

Becker, H. S. (1970). Whose side are we on? In H. S. Becker, *Sociological work: Method and substance* (pp. 123–134). New Brunswick, NJ: Transaction Books.

Benoliel, J. Q. (1996). Grounded theory and nursing knowledge. *Qualitative Health Research, 6*(3), 406–428.

Benoliel, J. Q. (2001). Expanding knowledge about women through grounded theory: Introduction. *Health Care for Women International, 22*(1–2), 7–9.

Berger, P., & Luckmann, T. (1966). *The social construction of reality: A treatise in the sociology of knowledge.* Garden City, NJ: Doubleday.

Berkowitz, D., & Marsiglio, W. (2007). Gay men: Negotiating procreative, father, and family identities. *Journal of Marriage and the Family, 69,* 366–381.

Blumer, H. (1958). Race/ethnicity prejudice as a sense of group position. *Pacific Sociological Review, 1,* 3–8.

Blumer, H. (1969). *Symbolic interactionism: Perspective and method.* Englewood Cliffs, NJ: Prentice Hall.

Boris, E., & Parrenas, R. S. (Eds.). (2010). *Intimate labors: Cultures, technologies and the politics of care.* Stanford, CA: Stanford University Press.

Bowers, B., & Schatzman, L. (2009). Dimensional analysis. In J. M. Morse, P. N. Stern, J. M. Corbin, K. C. Charmaz, B. Bowers, & A. E. Clarke, *Developing grounded theory: The second generation* (pp. 86–106). Walnut Creek, CA: Left Coast Press.

Bryant, A. (2003). A constructive/ist response to Glaser. *FQS: Forum for Qualitative Social Research, 4*(1). Retrieved August 2010, from http://www.qualitative-research.net/index.php/fqs/article/view/757

Bryant, A. (2006). *Thinking informatically: A new understanding of information, communication, and technology.* Lampeter, Ceredigion, UK: Edwin Mellen.

Bryant, A., & Charmaz, K. (Eds.). (2007). *Handbook of grounded theory.* London: Sage.

Casper, M. J. (1998). *The making of the unborn patient: A social anatomy of fetal surgery.* New Brunswick, NJ: Rutgers University Press.

Charmaz, K. (2000). Grounded theory: Objectivist and constructivist methods. In N. Denzin & Y. Lincoln (Eds.), *Handbook of qualitative research* (2nd ed., pp. 509–536). Thousand Oaks, CA: Sage.

Charmaz, K. (2005). Grounded theory in the 21st century: Applications for advancing social justice studies. In N. K. Denzin & Y. S. Lincoln (Eds.), *The SAGE handbook of qualitative research* (3rd ed., pp. 507–536). Thousand Oaks, CA: Sage.

Charmaz, K. (2006). *Constructing grounded theory: A practical guide through qualitative analysis.* London: Sage.

Charmaz, K. (2008a). Grounded theory as an emergent method. In S. N. Hesse-Biber & P. Leavy (Eds.), *The handbook of emergent methods* (pp. 155–170). New York: Guilford.

Charmaz, K. (2008b). The legacy of Anselm Strauss in constructivist grounded theory. *Studies in Symbolic Interaction, 32,* 127–142.

Charmaz, K. (2009). Shifting the grounds: Constructivist grounded theory methods. In J. M. Morse, P. N. Stern, J. M. Corbin, K. C. Charmaz, B. Bowers, & A. E. Clarke, *Developing grounded theory: The second generation* (pp. 127–155). Walnut Creek, CA: Left Coast Press.

Charmaz, K. (2010). Studying the experience of chronic illness through grounded theory. In G. Scambler & S. Scambler (Eds.), *New directions in the sociology of chronic and disabling conditions: Assaults on the lifeworld* (pp. 8–36). London: Palgrave.

Charmaz, K. (2011). Grounded theory methods in social justice research. In N. K. Denzin & Y. S. Lincoln (Eds.), *The SAGE handbook of qualitative research* (4th ed., pp. 359–380). Thousand Oaks, CA: Sage.

Clarke, A. E. (1991). Social worlds/arenas theory as organizational theory. In D. R. Maines (Ed.), *Social organization and social process: Essays in honor of Anselm Strauss* (pp. 119–158). New York: Aldine De Gruyter.

Clarke, A. E. (1998). *Disciplining reproduction: Modernity, American life sciences, and the "problem of sex."* Berkeley: University of California Press.

Clarke, A. E. (2003). Situational analyses: Grounded theory mapping after the postmodern turn. *Symbolic Interaction, 26*(4), 553–576.

Clarke, A. E. (2005). *Situational analysis: Grounded theory after the postmodern turn.* Thousand Oaks, CA: Sage.

Clarke, A. E. (2007a). Feminisms, grounded theory, and situational analysis. In S. Hesse-Biber (Ed.), *Handbook of feminist research: Theory and praxis* (pp. 345–370). Thousand Oaks, CA: Sage.

Clarke, A. E. (2007b). Grounded theory: Conflicts, debates and situational analysis. In W. Outhwaite & S. P. Turner (Eds.), *Handbook of social science methodology* (pp. 838–885). Thousand Oaks, CA: Sage.

Clarke, A. E. (2008). Sex/gender and race/ethnicity in the legacy of Anselm Strauss. *Studies in Symbolic Interaction, 32,* 161–176.

Clarke, A. E. (2009). From grounded theory to situational analysis: What's new? Why? How? In J. M. Morse, P. N. Stern, J. M. Corbin, K. C. Charmaz, B. Bowers, & A. E. Clarke, *Developing grounded theory: The second generation* (pp. 194–233). Walnut Creek, CA: Left Coast Press.

Clarke, A. E. (2010a). Anselm Strauss en heritage: Sexe/genre et race/ethnicite. In D. Chabaud-Rychter, V. Descoutures, A. Devreux, & E. Varikas (Eds.), *Questions de genre aux sciences sociales "normâles"* (pp. 245–259). Paris: La Découverte.

Clarke, A. E. (2010b). In memorium: Susan Leigh Star, 1954–2010. *Science, Technology, and Human Values, 35*(5), 1–20.

Clarke, A. E. (2010c). Thoughts on biomedicalization in its transnational travels. In A. E. Clarke, L. Mamo, J. R. Fosket, J. R. Fishman, & J. K. Shim (Eds.), *Biomedicalization: Technoscience, health, and illness in the U.S.* (pp. 380–405). Durham, NC: Duke University Press.

Clarke, A. E. (In preparation). Situational analysis: A Haraway-inspired feminist approach to qualitative research.

Clarke, A. E., & Charmaz, K. (Eds.). (Forthcoming). *Grounded theory and situational analysis* (SAGE Benchmarks in Social Research Series, Vols. 1–4). London: Sage.

Clarke, A. E., & Friese, C. (2007). Situational analysis: Going beyond traditional grounded theory. In A. Bryant & K. Charmaz (Eds.), *Handbook of grounded theory* (pp. 694–743). London: Sage.

Clarke, A. E., Mamo, L., Fosket, J. R., Fishman, J. R., & Shim, J. K. (Eds.). (2010). *Biomedicalization: Technoscience, health, and illness in the U.S.* Durham, NC: Duke University Press.

Clarke, A. E., & Montini, T. (1993). The many faces of RU486: Tales of situated knowledges and technological contestations. *Science, Technology, and Human Values, 18*(1), 42–78.

Clarke, A. E., Shim, J. K., Mamo, L., Fosket, J. R., & Fishman, J. R. (2003). Biomedicalization: Technoscientific transformations of health, illness, and U.S. biomedicine. *American Sociological Review, 68*(2), 161–194.

Clarke, A. E., & Star, S. L. (2008). Social worlds/arenas as a theory-methods package. In E. Hackett, O. Amsterdamska, M. Lynch, & J. Wacjman (Eds.), *Handbook of science and technology studies* (2nd ed., pp. 113–137). Cambridge, MA: MIT Press.

Collins, P. H. (2004). *Black sexual politics: African Americans, gender, and the new racism.* New York: Routledge.

Collins, P. H. (2009). Emerging intersections: Building knowledge and transforming institutions. In B. T. Dill & R. E. Zambrana (Eds.), *Emerging intersections: Race, class, and gender in theory, policy, and practice* (pp. vii–xiii). New Brunswick, NJ: Rutgers University Press.

Corbin, J. (2009). Taking an analytic journey. In J. M. Morse, P. N. Stern, J. M. Corbin, K. C. Charmaz, B. Bowers, & A. E. Clarke, *Developing grounded theory: The second generation* (pp. 35–54). Walnut Creek, CA: Left Coast Press.

Corbin, J., & Strauss, A. (2008). *Basics of qualitative research: Grounded theory procedures and techniques* (3rd ed.). Thousand Oaks, CA: Sage.

Creswell, J. W. (2007). *Qualitative inquiry and research design: Choosing among five traditions* (2nd ed.). London: Sage.

Dahlgren, L., Emmelin, M., & Winkvist, A. (2007). *Qualitative methodology for international public health.* Umea, Sweden: International School of Public Health, Umea University.

Denzin, N. (1989). *The research act: A theoretical introduction to sociological methods.* Chicago: Aldine. (Original work published 1970)

Denzin, N. (2007). Grounded theory and the politics of interpretation. In A. Bryant & K. Charmaz (Eds.), *Handbook of grounded theory* (pp. 454–472). London: Sage.

Denzin, N. K., & Lincoln, Y. S. (Eds.). (2005). *The SAGE handbook of qualitative research* (3rd ed.). Thousand Oaks, CA: Sage.

Denzin, N., Lincoln, Y., & Smith, L. T. (Eds.). (2008). *Handbook of critical and indigenous methodologies.* Thousand Oaks, CA: Sage.

Dill, B. T., & Zambrana, R. E. (2009). *Emerging intersections: Race, class, and gender in theory, policy, and practice.* New Brunswick, NJ: Rutgers University Press.

Dougherty, D. (2005). Grounded theory research methods. In J. A. C. Baum (Ed.), *The Blackwell companion to organizations* (pp. 849–866). Oxford, UK: Blackwell.

DuBois, B. (1983). Passionate scholarship: Notes on values, knowing, and method in feminist social sciences. In G. D. K. Bowles & R. Duelli-Klein (Eds.), *Theories of women's studies* (pp. 105–117). London: Routledge & Kegan Paul.

DuBois, W. E. B. (1993). *W.E.B. DuBois reader.* New York: Scribner.

Duster, T. (2003). *Backdoor to eugenics.* New York: Routledge. (Original work published 1990)

Fassinger, R. E. (2005). Paradigms, praxis, problems, and promise: Grounded theory in counseling psychology research. *Journal of Counseling Psychology, 52*(2), 156–166.

Fonow, M. M., & Cook, J. A. (2005). Feminist methodology: New applications in the academy and public policy. *Signs: Journal of Women in Culture and Society, 30*(4), 211–236.

Ford-Gilboe, M., Wuest, J., & Merritt-Gray, M. (2005). Strengthening capacity to limit intrusion: Theorizing family health promotion in the aftermath of woman abuse. *Qualitative Health Research, 15*(4), 477–501.

Foucault, M. (1975). *The birth of the clinic: An archeology of medical perception.* New York: Vintage/Random House.

Foucault, M. (1991). Questions of methods. In G. Burchell, C. Gordon, & P. Miller (Eds.), *The Foucault effect: Studies in governmentality* (pp. 73–86). Chicago: University of Chicago Press.

Gilgun, J. F. (Forthcoming). Hand into glove: Grounded theory, analytic induction and social work research. In W. Reid & R. Miller (Eds.), *Qualitative methods in social work* (2nd ed.). New York: Columbia University Press.

Glaser, B. G. (1978). *Theoretical sensitivity: Advances in the methodology of grounded theory.* Mill Valley, CA: Sociology Press.

Glaser, B. G. (2002a). Constructivist grounded theory? *FQS Forum: Qualitative Social Research, 3*(3). Retrieved August 2010, from http://www.qualitative-research.net/index.php/fqs/article/view/825

Glaser, B. G. (2002b). Grounded theory and gender relevance. *Health Care for Women International, 23*(8), 786–793.

Glaser, B. G. (2007). Doing formal theory. In A. Bryant & K. Charmaz (Eds.), *Handbook of grounded theory* (pp. 97–113). London: Sage.

Glaser, B. G., & Holton, J. (2004). Remodeling grounded theory. *Forum for Qualitative Social Research, 5*(2). Retrieved August 2010, from http://www.qualitative-research.net/index.php/fqs/article/view/607

Glaser, B. G., & Strauss, A. L. (1967). *The discovery of grounded theory: Strategies for qualitative research.* Chicago: Aldine.

Green, D. O., Creswell, J. W., Shope, R. J., & Plano Clark, V. L. (2007). Grounded theory and racial/ethnic diversity. In A. Bryant & K. Charmaz (Eds.), *Handbook of grounded theory* (pp. 472–492). London: Sage.

Gruskin, E., Byrne, K., & Kools, S. (2006). Frequenting the lesbian bar. *Women's Health, 44*(2), 103–120.

Hacking, I. (1983). *Representing and intervening: Introductory topics in the philosophy of natural science.* Cambridge, UK: Cambridge University Press.

Haraway, D. (1991). Situated knowledges: The science question in feminism and the privilege of partial perspectives. In D. Haraway, *Simians, cyborgs, and women: The reinvention of nature* (pp. 183–202). New York: Routledge.

Haraway, D. (1997). Modest_Witness@Second_Millenium. In D. Haraway, *Modest_Witness@ Second_Millenium. FemaleMan© Meets_Onco Mouse™: Feminism and technoscience* (pp. 23–48). New York: Routledge.

Hekman, Susan. (2007). Feminist methodology. In W. Outhwaite & S. P. Turner (Eds.), *Handbook of social science methodology* (pp. 534–546). Thousand Oaks, CA: Sage.

Hesse-Biber, S. N. (Ed.). (2007). *Handbook of feminist research: Theory and praxis.* Thousand Oaks, CA: Sage.

Hochschild, A. (1969). Emotion work, feeling rules, and social structure. *American Journal of Sociology, 85,* 551–575.

Hughes, E. C. (1971). *The sociological eye.* Chicago: Aldine Atherton.

Jenks, C. (1995). The centrality of the eye in Western culture: An introduction. In J. A. Walker & S. Chaplin (Eds.), *Visual culture: An introduction* (pp. 1–16). London: Routledge.

Kearney, M. H. (1999). *Understanding women's recovery from illness and trauma.* Thousand Oaks, CA: Sage.

Kearney, M. H. (2001). Enduring love: A grounded formal theory of women's experience of domestic violence. *Research in Nursing & Health, 24,* 270–282.

Kearney, M. H. (2007). From the sublime to the meticulous: The continuing evolution of grounded formal theory. In A. Bryant & K. Charmaz (Eds.), *Handbook of grounded theory* (pp. 127–150). London: Sage.

Kearney, M. H. (2008). Inconstant comparisons: A nurse and a sociologist study depression using grounded theory. *Studies in Symbolic Interaction, 32,* 143–160.

Kearney, M. H. (2009). Taking grounded theory beyond psychological process [Editorial]. *Research in Nursing & Health, 32,* 567–568.

Kearney, M. H., Murphy, S., Irwin, K., & Rosenbaum, M. (1995). Salvaging self: A grounded theory of pregnancy on crack cocaine. *Nursing Research, 44*(4), 208–213.

Kohlen, H. (2009). *Conflicts of care: Hospital ethics committees in the USA and Germany.* Frankfurt and New York: Campus Verlag.

Kools, S. B. (2008). From heritage to postmodern grounded theorizing. *Studies in Symbolic Interaction, 32,* 73–86.

Kools, S. B., & Kennedy, C. (2003). Foster child health and development: Implications for primary care. *Pediatric Nursing, 29*(1), 39–46.

Kushner, K. E., & Morrow, R. (2003). Grounded theory, feminist theory, critical theory. *Advances in Nursing Science, 26*(1), 30–43.

Lampland, M., & Star, S. L. (Eds.). (2009). *Standards and their stories: How quantifying, classifying,* and formalizing practices shape everyday life. Ithaca, NY: Cornell University Press.

Landstedt, E., Asplund, K., & Gådin, K. (2009). Understanding adolescent mental health: The influence of social processes, doing gender and gendered power relations. *Sociology of Health and Illness, 31*(7), 962–978.

Lather, P. (2007). *Getting lost: Feminist efforts toward a double(d) science.* Albany: State University of New York Press.

Lather, P. (2008). (Post) Feminist methodology. *International Review of Qualitative Research, 1*(1), 55–64.

Lather, P., & Smithies, C. (1997). *Troubling the angels: Women living with HIV/AIDS.* Boulder, CO: Westview Press.

Law, J. (1999). After ANT: Complexity, naming, and topology. In J. Law & J. Hassard (Eds.), *Actor-network theory and after* (pp. 1–19). Malden, MA: Blackwell.

Lempert, L. B. (2007). Asking questions of the data: Memo writing in the grounded theory tradition. In A. Bryant & K. Charmaz (Eds.), *Handbook of grounded theory* (pp. 245–264). London: Sage.

Lessor, R. (2000). Using the team approach of Anselm Strauss in action research: Consulting on a project on global education. *Sociological Perspectives, 43*(4), S133–S147.

Locke, K. (2001). *Grounded theory in management research.* Thousand Oaks, CA: Sage.

Locke, K. (2007). Rational control and irrational free-play: Dual-thinking modes as necessary tension in grounded theorizing. In A. Bryant & K. Charmaz (Eds.), *Handbook of grounded theory* (pp. 565–579). London: Sage.

Mamo, L. (2007). *Queering reproduction: Achieving pregnancy in the age of technoscience.* Durham, NC: Duke University Press.

Marcellus, L. (2005). The grounded theory method and maternal-infant research and practice. *Journal of Obstetrical, Gynecological, and Neonatal Nursing, 34*(3), 349–357.

Maternowska, C., Westrada, F., Campero, L., Herrera, C., Brindis, C. D., & Vostrejs, M. M. (2010). Gender, culture and reproductive decision-making among recent Mexican migrants in California. *Culture, Health and Sexuality, 12*(1), 29–43.

McCarthy, D. (1984). Towards a sociology of the physical world: George Herbert Mead on physical objects. *Studies in Symbolic Interaction, 5,* 105–121.

McCarthy, D. (1996). *Knowledge as culture: The new sociology of knowledge.* New York: Routledge.

Mead, G. H. (1962). *Mind, self, and society* (C. W. Morris, Ed.). Chicago: University of Chicago. (Original work published 1934)

Miller, S. (1996). Questioning, resisting, acquiescing, balancing: New mothers' career reentry strategies. *Health Care for Women International, 17,* 109–131.

Mills, J., Chapman, Y., Bonner, A., & Francis, K. (2007). Grounded theory: A methodological spiral from positivism to postmodernism. *Journal of Advanced Nursing, 58*(1), 72–79.

Mills, J., Francis, K., & Bonner, A. (2008). Getting to know a stranger—rural nurses' experiences of mentoring: A grounded theory. *International Journal of Nursing Studies, 45*(4), 599–607.

Moore, L. J. (2007). *Sperm tales: Social, cultural, and scientific representations of human semen.* New York: Routledge.

Morse, J. M. (2007). Sampling in grounded theory research. In A. Bryant & K. Charmaz (Eds.), *Handbook of grounded theory* (pp. 229–244). London: Sage.

Morse, J. M. (2009). Tussles, tensions, and resolutions. In J. M. Morse, P. N. Stern, J. M. Corbin, K. C. Charmaz, B. Bowers, & A. E. Clarke, *Developing grounded theory: The second generation* (pp. 13–23). Walnut Creek, CA: Left Coast Press.

Morse, J. M., Stern, P. N., Corbin, J. M., Charmaz, K. C., Bowers, B., & Clarke, A. E. (2009). *Developing grounded theory: The second generation.* Walnut Creek, CA: Left Coast Press.

Naples, N. A. (2003). *Feminism and method: Ethnography, discourse analysis, and activist research.* New York: Routledge.

Neill, S. J. (2006). Grounded theory sampling: The contribution of reflexivity [Review]. *Journal of Research in Nursing, 11*(3), 253–260.

Olesen, V. L. (2005). Early millennial feminist qualitative research: Challenges and contours. In N. K. Denzin & Y. S. Lincoln (Eds.), *The SAGE handbook of qualitative research* (3rd ed., pp. 235–278). Thousand Oaks, CA: Sage.

Olesen, V. L. (2007). Feminist qualitative research and grounded theory: Complexities, criticisms, and opportunities. In A. Bryant & K. Charmaz (Eds.), *Handbook of grounded theory* (pp. 417–435). London: Sage.

Olesen, V. L. (2011). Feminist qualitative research in the millennium's first decade: Developments, challenges, prospects. In N. K. Denzin & Y. S. Lincoln (Eds.), *The SAGE handbook of qualitative research* (4th ed., pp. 129–146). Thousand Oaks, CA: Sage.

Olshansky, E. (2003). A theoretical explanation for previously infertile mothers' vulnerability to depression. *Journal of Nursing Scholarship, 35*(3), 263–268.

Omi, M., & Winant, H. (1994). *Racial formation in the United States: From the 1960s to the 1990s.* New York: Routledge.

Padgett, D. K. (2008). *Qualitative methods in social work research.* Thousand Oaks, CA: Sage.

Pascale, C. M. (2008). Talking about race: Shifting the analytical paradigm. *Qualitative Inquiry, 14*(5), 723–741.

Pearse, N., & Kanyangale, M. (2009). Researching organizational culture using the grounded theory method. *The Electronic Journal of Business Research Methods, 7*(1), 67–74.

Plummer, K. (2005). Critical humanism and queer theory: Living with the tensions. In N. Denzin & Y. Lincoln (Eds.), *Handbook of qualitative research* (3rd ed., pp. 357–373). Thousand Oaks, CA: Sage.

Plummer, M., & Young, L. E. (2010). Grounded theory and feminist inquiry. *Western Journal of Nursing Research, 32*(3), 305–321.

Reichertz, J. (2007). Abduction: The logic of discovery of grounded theory. In A. Bryant & K. Charmaz (Eds.), *Handbook of grounded theory* (pp. 214–228). London: Sage.

Richardson, R., & Kramer, E. H. (2006). Abduction as the type of inference that characterizes the development of a grounded theory. *Qualitative Research, 6*(4), 497–513.

Riessman, C. K. (2008). *Narrative methods for the human sciences* (2nd ed.). Thousand Oaks, CA: Sage.

Ryan, M., & Berkowitz, D. (2009). Constructing gay and lesbian families "beyond the closet." *Qualitative Sociology, 32,* 153–172.

Said, E. (1978). *Orientalism.* New York: Random House.

Samik-Ibrahim, R. M. (2000). Grounded theory methodology as the research strategy for a developing country. *Forum: Qualitative Social Research, 1*(1), Art. 19. Retrieved June 15, 2011, from http://www.qualitative-research.net/index.php/fqs/article/viewArticle/1129/2511

Schatzman, L., & Strauss, A. (1973). *Field research.* Englewood Cliffs, NJ: Prentice Hall.

Schnitzer, G., Loots, G., Escudero, V., & Schechter, I. (2009). Negotiating the pathways into care in a globalizing world: Help-seeking behaviour of ultra-orthodox Jewish parents. *International Journal of Social Psychiatry, 57*(2), 153–165.

Schreiber, R. S., & Stern, P. N. (Eds.). (2001). *Using grounded theory in nursing.* New York: Springer.

Schrock, D. P., & Padavic, I. (2007). Negotiating hegemonic masculinity in a batterer intervention program. *Gender & Society, 21,* 625–649.

Schulz, A. J., & Mullings, L. (Eds.). (2006). *Gender, race, class, and health: Intersectional approaches.* San Francisco: Jossey-Bass.

Schumacher, K. (2008). Twenty years of grounded theorizing about family caregiving: Accomplishments and conundrums. *Studies in Symbolic Interaction, 32,* 87–102.

Schutze, F. (2008). The legacy in Germany today of Anselm Strauss's vision and practice of sociology. *Studies in Symbolic Interaction, 32,* 103–126.

Schwalbe, M., Goodwin, D. H., Schrock, S., Thompson, S., & Wolkomir, M. (2000). Generic processes in the reproduction of inequality: An interactionist analysis. *Social Forces, 79,* 419–452.

Scott, J. W. (1992). Experience. In J. Butler & J. W. Scott (Eds.), *Feminists theorize the political* (pp. 22–40). New York: Routledge.

Settles, I. H., Pratt-Hyatt, J. S., & Buchanan, N. T. (2008). Through the lens of race: Black and white women's perceptions of womanhood. *Psychology of Women Quarterly, 32,* 454–468.

Shim, J. K. (2005). Constructing "race" across the science-lay divide: Racial projects in the epidemiology and experience of cardiovascular disease. *Social Studies of Science, 35*(3), 405–436.

Shim, J. K. (Forthcoming). *Embodied inequalities: Heart disease and the politics of knowledge.* New York: NYU Press.

Smith, D. E. (2007). Institutional ethnography: From a sociology for women to a sociology for people. In S. Hesse-Biber (Ed.), *Handbook of feminist research: Theory and praxis* (pp. 409–418). Thousand Oaks, CA: Sage.

Star, S. L. (1983). Simplification in scientific work: An example from neuroscience research. *Social Studies of Science, 13,* 208–226.

Star, S. L. (1991). The sociology of the invisible: The primacy of work in the writings of Anselm Strauss. In D. R. Maines (Ed.), *Social organization and social process: Essays in honor of Anselm Strauss* (pp. 265–283). Hawthorne, NY: Aldine de Gruyter.

Star, S. L. (2007). Living grounded theory: Cognitive and emotional forms of pragmatism. In A. Bryant & K. Charmaz (Eds.), *Handbook of grounded theory* (pp. 75–94). Thousand Oaks, CA: Sage.

Star, S. L., & Bowker, G. (2007). Enacting silence—residual categories as a challenge for ethics, information systems, and communication technology. *Ethics and Information Technology, 9,* 273–280.

Star, S. L., & Strauss, A. L. (1998). Layers of silence, arenas of voice: The ecology of visible and invisible work. *Computer Supported Cooperative Work: The Journal of Collaborative Computing, 8,* 9–30.

Stern, P. N. (2007). On solid ground: Essential properties for growing grounded theory. In A. Bryant & K. Charmaz (Eds.), *Handbook of grounded theory* (pp. 114–126). London: Sage.

Stern, P. N. (2009). Glaserian grounded theory. In J. M. Morse, P. N. Stern, J. M. Corbin, K. C. Charmaz, B. Bowers, & A. E. Clarke, *Developing grounded theory: The second generation* (pp. 55–85). Walnut Creek, CA: Left Coast Press.

Strauss, A. L. (1978). A social world perspective. *Studies in Symbolic Interaction, 1,* 119–128.

Strauss, A. L. (1987). *Qualitative analysis for social scientists.* Cambridge, UK: Cambridge University Press.

Strauss, A. L. (1993). *Continual permutation of action.* New York: Aldine de Gruyter.

Strauss, A. L. (1995). Notes on the nature and development of general theories. *Qualitative Inquiry, 1*(1), 7–18.

Strauss, A. L., & Corbin, J. (1990). *Basics of qualitative research: Grounded theory, procedures, and techniques.* Newbury Park, CA: Sage.

Strauss, A. L., & Corbin, J. (1994). Grounded theory methodology: An overview. In N. Denzin & Y. Lincoln (Eds.), *Handbook of qualitative research* (pp. 273–285). Thousand Oaks, CA: Sage.

Strauss, A. L., & Corbin, J. (Eds.). (1997). *Grounded theory in practice.* Thousand Oaks, CA: Sage.

Strauss, A. L., & Corbin, J. (1998). *The basics of qualitative analysis: Grounded theory procedures and techniques* (2nd ed.). Thousand Oaks, CA: Sage.

Strubing, J. (2007). Research as pragmatic problem-solving: The pragmatist roost of empirically-grounded theorizing. In A. Bryant & K. Charmaz

(Eds.), *Handbook of grounded theory* (pp. 580–602). London: Sage.

Suddaby, Roy. (2006). What grounded theory is not. *Academy of Management Journal, 49*(4), 633–642.

Syfers, J. (1971). Why I want a wife. *Ms Magazine, 1*(1).

Tarozzi, M. (2008). *Che cos'è la grounded theory.* Rome: Carocci.

Timmermans, S. (2006). *Postmortem: How medical examiners explain suspicious deaths.* Chicago: University of Chicago Press.

Timmermans, S., & Tavory, I. (In review). *Theory construction in qualitative research: Grounded theory and the logic of abduction.*

Urquhart, Cathy. (2007). The evolving nature of grounded theory method: The case of the information systems discipline. In A. Bryant & K. Charmaz (Eds.), *Handbook of grounded theory* (pp. 339–362). London: Sage.

Walker, D., & Myrick, F. (2006). Grounded theory: An exploration of process and procedure. *Qualitative Health Research, 16*(4), 547–559.

Weber, L. (2010). *Understanding race, class, gender, and sexuality: A conceptual framework* (2nd ed.). New York: Oxford University Press.

Wiener, C. (2000). *The elusive quest: Accountability in hospitals.* New York: Aldine de Gruyter.

Wiener, C. (2007). Making teams work in conducting grounded theory. In A. Bryant & K. Charmaz (Eds.), *Handbook of grounded theory* (pp. 293–310). London: Sage.

Wingfield, A. H. (2007). The modern mammy and the angry black man: African American professionals' experiences with gendered racism in the workplace. *Race, Gender & Class, 14*(1–2), 196–212.

Wolkomir, M., & Powers, J. (2007). Helping women and protecting the self: The challenge of emotional labor in an abortion clinic. *Qualitative Sociology, 30,* 153–169.

19

FEMINIST PERSPECTIVES ON SOCIAL MOVEMENT RESEARCH

SARAH MADDISON AND FRANCES SHAW

INTRODUCTION: THE FIELD OF SOCIAL MOVEMENT RESEARCH

The field of social movement studies has, at least in part, been characterized by intense debates about the validity and usefulness of various theoretical approaches. For some scholars, this conflict has amounted to nothing more than "theory bashing" (see, e.g., Lofland, 1993). However, in their collection devoted to methods of social movement research, Bert Klandermans and Suzanne Staggenborg (2002, p. ix) argue that this conflict has in fact served to advance the study of social movements, particularly where an openness to new approaches has been accompanied by a willingness to test new ideas in the field. Importantly in this context, feminist social movement scholars such as Verta Taylor (2000; also Rupp & Taylor, 1987; Staggenborg & Taylor, 2005; Taylor & Rupp, 2002), Myra Marx Ferree (1987; also Ferree & Gamson, 2003; Ferree & Martin, 1995; Ferree & Merrill, 2000), Nancy Whittier (1995), Nancy Naples

(2003), Mary Margaret Fonow (2003), and Belinda Robnett (1997), among others, have brought a lively empirical rigor to the field, in ways that have provided an important critique of the gendered assumptions underpinning much previous social movement research.

To some extent, empirical studies of social movements have mirrored the much-discussed conflicts between the European and North American schools of theory. Methods developed in Europe include Alberto Melucci's (1989, 1996) emphasis on videotaped focus group discussion and Alain Touraine's (1981, 2000) highly innovative "intervention sociologiques." A sociological intervention as outlined by Touraine involves the researcher providing analytical feedback and even direction to social movement groups based on their observations of the group's activities. This method of direct intervention is designed to "bring actors to 'discover' the highest possible meaning of their own action" (Touraine, 2000, p. 905). Although this method has been used to produce compelling results by scholars such as Kevin McDonald in his study of young people's "struggles for subjectivity" (see McDonald, 1999), these methods have not gained wide acceptance among North American social movement researchers (Johnston, 2002, p. 83).

Similarly, methods that were developed by resource mobilization and political process scholars, such as Shorter and Tilly's (1974) method of "protest event analysis," have not been taken up by researchers working in the European "new" social movement approach. Protest event analysis uses newspapers, police files, and reports of press agencies as data sources in which the protest event itself is the unit of analysis (Klandermans & Staggenborg, 2002, p. xii). The focus of protest event analysis is on the "quantification of many properties of protest, such as frequency, timing and duration, location, claims, size, forms, carriers, and targets, as well as immediate consequences and reactions" (Koopmans & Rucht, 2002, p. 231). The macro-dimensional focus of the North American scholars and the micro-dimensional focus of much European scholarship saw research on the two continents take divergent paths.

Other differences have emerged as, over time, scholars' attitudes toward social movements have changed, and theoretical developments have created a range of different "lenses" through which these phenomena may be observed and interpreted (Goodwin & Jasper, 2003, p. 5). James Jasper (1997) describes some of these lenses:

> Quantitative approaches may give special attention to resources, the most measurable dimension. Historical approaches might recommend closer attention to political structures and the strategic interactions by which they are created and transformed. Ethnographic and participant research allow more than a crude reckoning of explicit beliefs. (p. 334)

One outcome of these differences is that the field of social movement scholarship remains refreshingly free of "methodological dogmatism" (Klandermans & Staggenborg, 2002, p. xii). Although David Meyer (2002) advocates

greater connection between scholars researching social movements to create a "larger whole" that is as "inherently collective" as the object of our study (p. 3), it would seem that, given the multifaceted complexity of social movements as an empirical phenomenon, a plurality of methodological approaches must remain an imperative.

Our research, as outlined in this chapter, takes a feminist cultural approach to the study of social movements. We consider it crucial that the field of social movement studies should involve activists—as the subjects of our research—both in the research process and as a critical audience. Such involvement will inevitably focus our attention on our "local knowledge" rather than our "general knowledge" (Jasper, 1997, p. 377) as it develops in dialogue with the activists themselves, from their perspective and giving them a voice in the process. The cultural lens brings into focus a far wider range of social movement activity, including those activities that take place quietly, "behind the scenes," and yet without which no publicly visible movement could be possible. Such focus, on what Melucci (1985, p. 800) calls "submerged networks," constitutes social movement actors as "diffuse and decentralized" (Taylor, 2000, p. 222) and takes account of periods away from the public spotlight.

Moreover, such a perspective does much to explain the continuity and survival of social movements around the world. For example, in their study of the survival of the women's movement in the United States and the United Kingdom, Joyce Gelb and Vivien Hart (1999) argue that the maintenance of "networks of women [that] have been sustained locally and nationally and also across differences of ethnicity, nationality, sexuality, and class" (p. 181) has been vital for movement continuity. This perspective recognizes that social movements need to adopt different "structural forms and strategies" at different periods depending on whether they are "in a stage of formation, success, continuation and survival or decline" (Rupp & Taylor, 1987, p. 9).

This chapter discusses our approach to the study of social movements as one that is feminist, cultural, constructivist, and grounded in standpoint theory. Our perspective is one that begins by acknowledging and privileging what we have termed an *activist standpoint*. In explaining this approach, we will consider the intersections between feminist standpoint theory and the idea of social movement collective identity *as a process*. In the following sections, we will consider the importance of feminist theory to social movement research and argue for the importance of an activist standpoint in the study of movements. We will then outline our own methods for researching activism from this perspective, specifically through the case studies of two submerged networks of contemporary young feminist activists in Australia (Sarah) as well as the case study of a feminist blogging network in Australia (Frances), considering the ways in which feminism has influenced our approach to these methods.

These two research projects have in common a methodological approach that combines feminist standpoint epistemology with a cultural constructivist approach to social movement studies. In addition, because our research covers both offline and online activist groups, we discuss the relevance of social movement studies to online activist communities. Staggenborg and Taylor (2005) identify the Internet as the site of a development of new tactics to which a feminist approach to social movement research should pay attention. They argue that the Internet "has contributed to the vitality of the women's movement" because it has facilitated the sharing of "advice, reading lists, rants, and calls for action" (p. 47). The Australian feminist blogging community is an example of such a case. Along with Twitter, Tumblr, LiveJournal, and other backchannels, blogs have facilitated discussions between feminists all over Australia and the world. These actions take place at the level of "discursive and performative" social movement activity (Staggenborg & Taylor, 2005, p. 47). In this sense, the use of feminist standpoint epistemology for the study of online activist groups is an important development in feminist approaches to social movement research, particularly given the significant lack of research into online activism in the field of social movement studies more generally.

FEMINIST SOCIAL MOVEMENT RESEARCH

A feminist approach to the study of social movements remains a challenging and important enterprise. Verta Taylor and Nancy Whittier (1998) argue that

> analyzing social movements as simultaneously political and gendered raises sweeping and exciting challenges for both fields. Scholars grounded in social movements and gender have begun to bring together the concerns and analytical approaches of the two fields. . . . Feminist reconceptualizations of the state, cultural hegemony, discourse, identity, and organization challenge social movement approaches that treat these institutions as gender neutral. (p. 622)

We concur with Taylor and Whittier's (1998, p. 622) suggestion that a feminist approach that takes account of gender, along with its intersections with race, class, ethnicity, and sexuality, and places these concerns at the center of social movement analysis "poses unresolved questions" that suggest considerable challenges to previous understandings of social movement processes. Staggenborg and Taylor's (2005) survey of alternative perspectives on social movements advocates that the study of women's movements requires a broader conception of social movements themselves. Aside from the more visible aspects of social movements, such as women's movement organizations and public protest, there is also institutionalized feminism, as well as feminist culture and collective identity and the tactical repertoires that feminists have developed (Staggenborg & Taylor, 2005, pp. 41–45). Indeed, as Armstrong and Bernstein (2008) point out, the aspects of social movement research that privilege visible, state-focused activism tend to "reproduce the marginal status of movements that target society" (p. 80), including the women's, LGBTI (lesbian, gay, bisexual, transgender, and intersex), and peace movements. A desire to challenge gender-neutral assumptions about social movements has been one of the important factors in shaping our own research practices.

A considerable amount of feminist scholarship has considered social research methods in light of feminist epistemological understandings (see, e.g., Fonow & Cook, 1991; Stanley, 1990; among others). Indeed, questions of method and methodology continue to engage feminist scholars such as Anne Byrne and Ronit Lentin (2000), Caroline Ramazanoğlu and Janet Holland (2002), Jane Ribbens and Rosalind Edwards (2009), and Anna Jónasdóttir and Kathleen Jones (2009), among others. Shulamit Reinharz (1992, p. 240) suggests certain themes that are present in much discussion of feminist social research—specifically, feminism is a perspective, not a research method; feminist research uses a multiplicity of research methods and involves an ongoing criticism of nonfeminist scholarship guided by feminist theory; feminist research may be transdisciplinary; feminist research aims to create social change and strives to represent human diversity; feminist research includes the researcher as a person and frequently attempts to develop special relations with the people studied (in interactive research); and, finally, feminist research frequently defines a special relation with the reader.

That Reinharz (1992) specifically claims that feminist research aims to create social change underscores the importance and usefulness of considering feminist approaches to the study of activism. Feminist research methodologies are often "impelled by a concern with social justice" and therefore "are designed to reveal the gender problematic through prioritising women's lived experience of the social, telling this experience 'in their own voice'" (Byrne & Lentin, 2000, p. 7). Iris Marion Young (1997) also argues that feminism is "a mode of questioning, an orientation and set of commitments" that entails "a commitment to ameliorating . . . harms and disadvantages" that women experience (p. 3). Young also points out, however, that applying this commitment to feminist scholarship should not be understood as implying "a claim to common attributes, circumstances or harms that all women share" (p. 6). In other words, describing a commitment to social justice through feminist research and scholarship should not be read as a universalizing claim regarding women's needs or lived experiences. Nevertheless, this commitment to social justice suggests that feminist approaches to research have much to contribute to the field of social movement research more generally.

As Jennifer Somerville (1997) points out, "Feminism as a social movement is rich in descriptive, historical accounts" (pp. 673-674), but these accounts have generally been "atheoretical," and very few use the concept of social movement "analytically." With few exceptions, past studies of Australian feminist activism (such as Bulbeck, 1997; Kaplan, 1996; Lake, 1999) start from the assumption that the women's movement is a defined object for study that can be explored in terms of history, goals, and achievements. According to Alberto Melucci (1995), however, this approach is inadequate because it can never

> answer the questions of how social actors come to form a collectivity and recognise themselves as being part of it; how they maintain themselves over time; how acting together makes sense for the participants in a social movement; or how the meaning of collective action derives from structural preconditions or from the sum of individual motives. (p. 42)

Constructivist "new" social movement theory offers an approach to answering these questions, for both activists and researchers. Melucci (1996) argues that by shifting from a "monolithic and metaphysical idea of collective actors" (p. 43) to a more "processual" approach that uses the concept of collective identity as an analytical tool, we are able to better understand how collective mobilization can occur and be sustained in complex societies (Melucci, 1995, 1996).

Common Ground: Feminist Epistemologies and Collective Identity as a Process

Our approach to the study of social movements is—first and foremost—informed by feminist epistemological assumptions. In other words, we begin with the assumption that knowledge and the production of knowledge are inherently gendered. Furthermore, we remain convinced that feminist epistemologies have enormous potential to subvert and transgress traditional, disciplinary knowledge, creating new spaces for theory and research practice (Randall, 2010; Reinharz, 1992). There seems a very obvious and important link to be made between the subversive potential of feminist *thinking* and the subversive potential of social movement *activism*. Feminist social movement research has an outstanding capacity to draw these links in ways that can only enrich the field of social movement studies.

Despite feminist (and other) challenges, there is still considerable faith in the universal, sex-neutral subject and in neutral, transparent methodologies and techniques whereby the product (i.e., knowledge) is also considered value neutral (Longino, 1993). These assumptions operate to maintain belief in a "reality" or a "truth" that can be discovered through rational knowledge and thus create a hegemony of all aspects of knowledge: what it is, how it is made, and who can make it. These assumptions do not recognize that knowledge *does things;* it is an activity, not just thought and reflection (Grosz, 1993). Given this implicit, but often unrecognized, control over knowledge production, it is hardly surprising that the types of knowledges that have been produced, particularly about gender (and in this case gender and activism), have reinforced and reified the same paradigms within which they were made.

The feminist maneuver of valorizing experience is a radical departure from these terms and these ways of validating knowledge. This "reversal strategy" assumes that women's experience is drastically different from academic knowledges and that it potentially offers a critique of these knowledges (Waldby, 1995, p. 16). However, these methodological departures have been criticized for making certain assumptions about the nature of experience, which, it is argued by critics, should not be understood as either transparent or unequivocal. This is not the same criticism as the rationalist dismissal of experience as being entirely perspectival and without objective merit. Rather, it points to the fact that choosing to validate a particular standpoint as epistemologically privileged requires social theory in order to understand social positioning and powerlessness and thus grant this privilege (Longino, 1993). Here the site of epistemic privilege shifts from the group as defined objectively (i.e., women) to the group defining itself subjectively as a collective political agent or as holders of a particular form of political consciousness (in this case,

feminists). The claim is not to a universal "women's standpoint" but to a politicized and partial "feminist standpoint."

If a feminist standpoint can be described as being "derived from a committed feminist exploration of women's experiences of oppression" (Stanley & Wise, 1990, p. 27), we are proposing that an *activist standpoint* can be conceived as a transformative exploration of activists' experiences of *resistance* to oppression. Bernstein's (2005) review of approaches to the study of identity politics argues that feminist standpoint theory has done much to explain that the development of a standpoint is part of political activism, without relying on essentialism to explain this standpoint. Activists are motivated to act in response to oppression as a result of a collective interpretation and analysis of their experiences (Bernstein, 2005, p. 60). In this theoretical context, Alberto Melucci's (1995, 1996) processual approach to understanding movement collective identity can allow for the standpoints of feminist and other activists to be revealed through an analysis of the ways in which they construct their own experiences and understandings. Melucci's approach offers a theory and method that can, in turn, illuminate standpoint theory, revealing the processes behind the articulation of a politicized collectivity.

The process of collective identity is one of the most significant and yet most misunderstood elements of the "new" social movement approach to analyzing collective action. In large part, the misunderstandings surrounding the term arise from the use of the word *identity* with its psychological overtones, and a problem arises when scholars overly psychologize the concept of collective identity[1] rather than acknowledge its fundamentally political character. As Stacey Young (1997) points out, this "misses the efforts of movements (particularly the feminist and lesbian/bisexual/gay movements) to analyse in social and political terms oppression and resistance grounded in identity" (p. 20). In similar terms, Aldon Morris (1992, pp. 360–372) argues that differing forms of what he terms "political consciousness" arise from different standpoints or real experiences of particular forms of domination: racial consciousness as a response to racial domination, gender consciousness as a response to male domination, and so on.

Collective identity should not be understood as a "thing to be studied" (Melucci, 1995, p. 46) but rather as a tool for understanding processes that produce a set of reflexively constructed and negotiated definitions regarding the "field of opportunities and constraints offered to collective action" (Melucci, 1985, p. 793). These processes, which occur in specific contexts, organizations, and locations (Whittier, 2002, p. 298) that may or may not constrain diversity, are "experienced [by movement participants] as an action rather than a situation" (Melucci, 1995, p. 51), in that they constitute an important function in and of themselves. Collective identity in this sense is "fluid and relational," involving acts of "perception and construction" (Polletta & Jasper, 2001, p. 298). Understanding processes of collective identity in this way allows us to "get at" the ways in which social movements determine such issues as membership and activities (Laraña, Johnston, & Gusfield, 1994) or agree on the fundamental question of "who they are" (Taylor & Whittier, 1992, p. 105), while also allowing for the constantly debated and contested nature of these agreements. As Whittier (1995) points out,

> In the process of constructing a collective identity, challenging groups adopt labels for themselves (such as "feminist"), draw lines between insiders and outsiders, and develop interpretive frameworks, a political consciousness through which members understand the world. Of course "collective identities" exist only as far as real people agree upon, enact, argue over, and internalise them; group definitions have no life of their own, and they are constantly changing rather than static. (p. 15)

Ultimately, the fact that we are able to observe the action of social movements in the form of organizational structures *presupposes* processes of collective identity and is therefore a goal in its own right (Gamson, 1992; Melucci, 1995).

Conflict and disagreement play an important role in these processes of collective identity. Jodi Dean (1997) argues that in feminist politics, for example, differences between women have often been "experienced as conflicts that threatened both the integrative role of the groups and the individual woman's sense of self" (p. 245). To many participants, these experiences of conflict appeared to clash with notions of unity, solidarity,

and sisterhood that were deemed essential to successful feminist praxis, and therefore, the conflicts themselves were repressed or smothered wherever possible. Attempts to repress conflict, however, do not recognize its significance as a creative force in social movement processes of collective identity. In the case of the women's movement, Dean (1997) argues that

> there is no "feminism" to be defined and solidified once and for all. Instead, it is always in process, the continuing accomplishment of our discussions and reflections. So, rather than viewing criticism as potentially disruptive, a solidarity of differences employs it to further our recognition of each other. (p. 254)

In other words, through conflicts over differences to do with identity ("race," class, sexuality, and age), meaning, goals, and strategy, movement actors are able to conceive of new forms of social existence and produce new understandings of social, cultural, and political life that have implications beyond the movement itself. It is in the reflexive processes of collective identity that these conflicts are able to occur. Furthermore, these conflicts indicate a movement's continued relevance and vitality and, as such, should be seen as both productive and integral to movement survival, rather than as something to be resolved and put aside. It is our contention that this attention to conflict as a constituent component of feminist and other processes of collective identity goes some way toward overcoming the perceived problem with the feminist standpoint, that being the failure of such a perspective to acknowledge the existence of multiple standpoints. Any collective identity developed in any movement must make space for a range of standpoints, which may in turn be debated and contested as a part of these processes. This process makes women's experiences explicit and offers a lens for revealing not only the differences between women but also the ways in which these differences and conflicts can work to produce a collective—yet continually contested—identity.

David Snow (2001) is critical of this focus on social movement processes over what he perceives as the end result or "product" of these processes. Snow argues that it is "both questionable and unnecessary to contend that the process is more fundamental than the product to understanding the character and functionality of collective identity" (p. 3). However, this perspective implies that, over time, processes of collective identity may produce an identity that is a stable and homogeneous "social object," allowing Snow to argue that

> although collective identities can congeal in various aggregations and contexts, they appear not to do so on a continuous basis historically. Instead, their emergence and vitality appear to be associated with conditions of sociocultural change or challenge, socio-economic and political exclusion, and political breakdown and renewal, thus suggesting that they cluster historically in social space. (p. 4)

Such a claim only can be made, however, if one views collective identity as an *object.* As a *process,* collective identity can be seen as "vital" (if not "emerging" in the sense of being publicly visible), even in times of movement decline or abeyance and in between-the-waves moments such as the one in which the contemporary Australian women's movement is currently located. While this claim may not be true of all social movements all of the time, an understanding of collective identity as a process does not restrict the study of it to periods of high-profile social movement activism. In the case studies discussed below, we have studied low-profile, small-scale activist groups to understand the processes of collective identity at play, highlighting the ways in which these processes keep the movement "vital."

Whittier (1995, p. 24) argues that the concept of collective identity is crucial to understanding "new" social movements, such as the women's movement, that are engaged in politics beyond institutional transformation. It is this lens that allows researchers to recognize movement continuity and to identify struggles that occur in culture and everyday life. Melucci (1995) outlines the processes of collective identity as requiring the following factors:

1. "Cognitive definitions concerning the ends, means, and field of action" and that these definitions are constructed through interaction and compromise

2. "A network of active relationships" of which styles of organization, leadership and communication are constitutive parts

3. "A degree of emotional investment, which enables individuals to feel like part of a common unity" (Melucci, 1995, pp. 44–45)[2]

It is through a reflexive engagement with these factors that social movements are able to present an empirical unity. But Melucci (1995) emphasizes that this apparent unity should be considered a "result rather than a starting point, a fact to be explained rather than evidence" (p. 43). Continued debate over these factors is an indication of a movement's ongoing vitality and relevance or that the collective identity in question, such as "feminist," still "means something" (Whittier, 1995, p. 18). Collective identity suggests that structural position is not enough to mobilize a group's members, but rather it is the continual reformulation and discussion in groups over "sameness and difference, homogeneity and diversity" that determine the "central questions" of personal, social, and political action (Whittier, 1995, pp. 56–58).

RESEARCHING CONTEMPORARY FEMINIST ACTIVISM

The research projects that we focus on for the remainder of this chapter emerged from Sarah's desire to begin documenting the types of activism being practiced by young women in the contemporary Australian women's movement (see Maddison, 2008). Frances's case study of contemporary online feminism builds on the findings from Sarah's study. In the mid- to late 1990s, the Australian women's movement, like the women's movements in the United States and the United Kingdom, had been consumed by suggestions of intergenerational warfare. Questions had been raised about the presence and visibility of young women in the movement, and assertions that some forms of feminist praxis were "good" and some were not began to undermine the value of the important work being done in this "between-the-waves" moment. Sarah's hope was that by developing an understanding of what young women are doing *now,* we might begin to conceptualize what a resurgence of highly visible feminist activism might look like in the future. She hoped this knowledge would assist both older and younger feminists to recognize their points of connection and similarity as well as their points of difference.

Sarah's project posed a number of specific research questions:

1. What role are young women playing in constructing and maintaining the contemporary Australian women's movement?

2. How do social movements sustain themselves during periods without highly visible activism?

3. How can we distinguish processes of social movement continuity from the failure or demise of a movement?

4. What role does conflict between women have in feminist processes of collective identity?

5. How do these processes facilitate social movement continuity?

From the outset, it was clear that this would be a qualitative study. Sarah wanted to know how certain groups of young women were constructing themselves as a collectivity within the Australian women's movement and also how they dealt with conflict as a part of their processes of collective identity. Bringing a feminist standpoint to the study of collective identity would facilitate a unique qualitative methodological approach to answering these questions, specifically by seeking to understand "political actors as conscious social beings who shape the world of politics as well as being shaped by it" (Devine, 2002, p. 198). Fiona Devine (2002) suggests that qualitative methods "capture meaning, process and context" and are most appropriately used in research where the aim is to "explore people's subjective experiences and the meanings they attach to those experiences" (p. 199). Devine also suggests that qualitative methods are appropriate in the study of processes, thereby making them appropriate to our concern with activists' processes of collective identity. Minichiello, Aroni, Timewell, and Alexander (1995, p. 10) add that qualitative research allows for an understanding of how experience, feelings, meaning, and process in turn influence the *actions* of research participants.

With this in mind, Sarah chose two case studies for this research, in very different locations, with two very different groups of young women. The first was a campus-based group, the Cross Campus Women's Network (CCWN), operating primarily in metropolitan Sydney, and second was the Young Women Who Are Parents Network (YWWAPN), operating from a women's health center in an economically disadvantaged suburb on Sydney's southwestern outskirts. The two groups represented different strands and trajectories of the Australian women's movement. The CCWN represented the strand of the women's movement that both grew out of, and remains a constituent part of, the student movement. Both the CCWN and the student movement consider themselves to be a part of the broad left in Australia and work in coalition with other groups and movements across a range of issues. By contrast, the YWWAPN represented the strand of the movement that developed into the women's health movement and remains concerned with service provision and local community development with women. Both groups were highly politicized but in relation to very different issues. The ages of the women in both groups ranged from 17 to 23. The two cases provided interesting comparative material due to the differing socioeconomic status of the participants and the diverse range of issues that concern them. As "critical cases" (Snow & Trom, 2002, p. 158), they suggest particular features that are of empirical significance rather than being seen as in any way typical or representative of young women in the contemporary Australian women's movement.

Frances's research into the discursive legacy of the women's movement focuses on the uses of the Internet by contemporary Australian feminists. The Australian feminist blogging community that forms the case study for Frances's research is a loose-knit and informal network of bloggers that link to one another, list each other on "blogrolls," and engage in debate and discussion from feminist and progressive perspectives (Bruns, 2006, p. 16; Boyd, 2009; Lovink, 2008; Rettberg, 2008). Rather than being defined by membership or attendance, as with other social movement groups, the blogging community is defined by networks of attention—the relationships that have developed between different bloggers (Boyd, 2009). The community also connects with the international feminist blogging network and various other progressive and minority blogging communities all over the world (particularly New Zealand and the United States). This community was chosen for the study of discursive feminist activism in Australia because it is engaging in feminist activism in new ways, using new strategies for engagement with and criticism of mainstream public debate. The individual bloggers' understanding and experience of the community itself are varied.

The following sections detail the research methods in these case studies.

Feminist Case Study Methodology

In considering the role of qualitative methods in the study of social movements, Kathleen Blee and Verta Taylor (2002) suggest that these methods are often used to "uncover the essential features of a case or number of cases" and that these cases may then be used to exemplify "more general theoretical processes pertaining to social movements" (p. 111). David Snow and Danny Trom (2002) suggest that case studies should not be understood as a research method but rather as "a research strategy that is associated with a number of data-gathering methods or procedures" (p. 151). Snow and Trom provide a workable and clear definition of a case study as including

> (a) investigation and analysis of an instance or variant of some bounded social phenomenon that (b) seeks to generate a richly detailed and "thick" elaboration of the phenomenon studied through (c) the use and triangulation of multiple methods or procedures that include but are not limited to qualitative techniques. (p. 147)

The aim of case study research should be to produce "a holistic—that is, a richly or thickly contextualized and embedded—understanding of the phenomenon or system under investigation" (Snow & Trom, 2002, p. 150). This goal and the definition above nicely summarize our approach to the case studies in this project. In addition, as Reinharz (1992) points out, "Case studies are important for putting women on the map of social life" (p. 174). One of the goals of

both of these research projects was to put contemporary young feminist activists and feminist Internet activists on the "map" of the Australian women's movement.

Feminist interest in case study research stems in part from a desire to document women's experiences and achievements "for future secondary analysis and future action on behalf of women" (Reinharz, 1992, p. 171). Where the subject of the research is the women's movement itself, a case study approach is particularly appropriate given the often dispersed nature of movement organizations and groups. As Nancy Whittier (1995) points out in her study of the radical women's movement in the United States, the fact that the movement has traditionally been based in "grassroots, loosely organized groups" means that "any study of radical feminism is thus, by necessity, a local case study" (p. 5). Similarly, in Australia, no centralized organization can claim to constitute the women's movement, nor has such an organization ever really existed.[3] Furthermore, the questions with which this research was concerned arose largely from the apparent invisibility of groups of young feminist activists to the broader women's movement. These case studies, therefore, were an effort to increase the visibility of young women and women bloggers in the movement by documenting the work that they were doing. In addition, the case study documenting online feminist activism addresses both the absence of women from many discussions of blogging culture (Bahnisch, 2006; Gregg, 2006) and the absence of online activism from studies of social movements.

Participant Observation

To build a suitably holistic and "thick" elaboration of these cases, Sarah chose to engage in participant observation with two groups of young women she was studying, while Frances, although not in a face-to-face sense, engaged in participant observation within an online feminist community. While there is, as Paul Lichterman (2002, p. 119) notes, "more than one way to do participant observation," the general intention is for researchers to "immerse" themselves into the social setting of their field site, thereby "observing people in their own milieux and participating in their activities" (Devine, 2002). Participant observation "opens a window on lived experience" (Lichterman, 2002, p. 121) providing a unique source of research data. Lichterman (2002) describes it as follows:

> Listening to people talking in their own settings, on their own time, participant-observers have the opportunity to glean the everyday meanings, tacit assumptions, ordinary customs, practical rules of thumb that organize people's everyday lives. (p. 138)

As Nancy Whittier (1995) notes, it is through the observable "concrete lived experience of organizing a challenge together, not an abstract 'spirit of the times'" that processes of collective identity are revealed to a researcher and through which movement participants negotiate their "shared worldview" (p. 17). Of particular importance to this study was the fact that participant observation allowed for a unique perspective on the influence of social movements over time. As Lichterman (2002) argues, through participant observation, social movement researchers can observe the "enduring influence of a movement on everyday life, years after the movement's height of visibility and political influence" (p. 141).

Sarah engaged in participant observation with both groups in her study over a 12-month period during 2001 and into early 2002. In the case of the CCWN, she attended their fortnightly meetings and participated in other activities such as mail-outs and planning meetings. She also attended the annual Network of Women Students Australia (NOWSA) conference, appropriately titled "Which Way Forward for Women's Liberation?" in which she participated by giving a paper and through discussion on the conference floor and in workshops. In addition, Sarah participated on the e-mail lists for both the CCWN and NOWSA, which were active sites of contestation to do with the group's processes of collective identity. In the case of the YWWAPN, she spent one day a week in Campbelltown, where she attended network meetings and engaged more informally with the young women in the program. Over the course of the year, Sarah participated with both staff and young women in the program through activities such as working with the young women to produce an orientation

booklet for new members, conducting program evaluation, and running a workshop on "gender issues" as a part of their "Opportunities and Choices" training course. Through participant observation, she also identified key informants who were invited to participate in in-depth interviews toward the end of the research process.

Frances engaged in participant observation in an online community as part of her research into the uses of the Internet for contemporary Australian feminists. Her project used a similar research methodology and triangulated approach to Sarah's, although with some necessary differences arising from the online location of the community being studied. Online participant observation, while still possible, is qualitatively different from participant observation in offline organizations because the researcher's presence is virtual and lacks the physical "arrival" traditionally associated with ethnographic research (Hine, 2000, pp. 43–45). As Baym and Markham (2009, p. xviii) argue, the role of the researcher is relatively uncharted in Internet research, particularly in participant observation, because a researcher can observe unnoticed online in ways that he or she cannot in face-to-face interaction. Therefore, the necessity for authentic self-representation, trust building, respecting privacy, and obtaining consent is all the more imperative in online research (Baym & Markham, 2009, p. xviii; Hine, 2000, p. 48; Wilson & Peterson, 2002, p. 461).

The blogging community provided an excellent case study for research into discursive activism in online politics. While the medium is new, many of the tools used within the feminist blogging community echo the strategies of other feminist activists. Consciousness-raising and linguistic interventions, for example, form part of the discursive work of the community (Katzenstein, 1995). Feminist bloggers are also developing new and innovative methods of discursive politics specific to Internet spaces. Furthermore, the Australian community is engaged in transnational networks through their connections with the international feminist blogging network and various other progressive and minority blogging communities all over the world (particularly New Zealand and the United States). The focus in this study, however, was on Australian feminist writers. Through reading and participating in blog conversations, Frances identified key informants to be invited to participate in in-depth interviews.

In-Depth Interviewing

Lichterman (2002) argues that participant observation evidence and interview evidence can be combined "judiciously to create a richer account of lived experience" (p. 141). According to Blee and Taylor (2002), an interview is simply "a guided conversation," but the difference between an interview and other forms of conversation is the need on the part of the interviewer to "elicit specific kinds of information" (p. 92). It is important to note the distinct difference in method between structured or survey interviews that are used in quantitative research and the type of qualitative, unstructured interviews conducted in the fieldwork for these projects. Feminists such as Ann Oakley (1981) suggest that structured interviews rest on positivist assumptions about research and can be disempowering for participants. In contrast, feminists have written extensively on the benefits of unstructured interviews for providing "access to people's ideas, thoughts and memories in their own words rather than in the words of the researcher," which can be seen as an important historical corrective to the marginalization of women's voices in traditional research (Reinharz, 1992, p. 19). Minichiello et al. (1995) argue that this type of interviewing "empowers participants in the same way as other forms of participatory research" (p. 7).

In contrast to the use of structured interviews in the study of social movements, Blee and Taylor (2002) suggest that unstructured or semistructured interviews "provide greater breadth and depth of information [and] the opportunity to discover the respondent's experiences and interpretations of reality" (p. 92). They argue that the unstructured form of such interviews allows respondents to "generate, challenge, clarify, elaborate or recontextualize understandings of social movements based on earlier interviews, documentary sources, or observational methods" (p. 94). Fontana and Frey (2003, pp. 90–91) describe unstructured interviews as a "negotiated text" in which interviewer and interviewee together create shared meanings. In Sarah Maddison's study, the amount of time that she had already spent as a participant observer prior to conducting the interviews served to locate these conversations in a relational context of existing shared meanings. In Frances Shaw's study, interviews were also located in a context of shared meanings drawn from mutual interactions in the feminist blogosphere, but because the picture of the feminist online community differs for every blogger located within it, understandings of the community varied quite broadly. This is most likely a result of bloggers choosing to some extent their own readership and reading matter, which varies considerably in both volume and subject matter. Compared with a community that functions more like an organization, all feminist bloggers are rarely "in the same room," even in the most popular discussion spaces. Despite this, convergence of meaning and identity does occur in the community as a whole.

The two research methods worked to complement one another extremely well, enhancing the breadth and depth of the findings. Blee and Taylor (2002) also suggest that this type of interviewing can allow researchers to

> gain insight into the individual and collective visions, imaginings, hopes, expectations, critiques of the present, and projections of the future on which the possibility of collective action rests and through which social movements form, endure, or disband . . . [Interviews] can illuminate how activists are mobilized or politically sustained during periods of relative quiescence or abeyance. (p. 95)

The women Sarah interviewed for her project were astonishingly thoughtful and reflexive in their consideration of these issues, and these qualities added greater richness and depth to the case studies.

Sarah conducted three in-depth interviews with women who were associated with the CCWN that were supplemented by e-mail discussion and interviews with six other women who had attended the NOWSA conference. At the YWWAPN, she selected three key staff members and three long-term network members to participate in interviews. As "key informants," these participants were chosen from both groups because of their particular experiences in the movement organizations, rather than because they were necessarily representative of the wider membership of their groups (Blee & Taylor, 2002, p. 100). As Blee and Taylor (2002) point out, the criteria for selecting key informants are different from the criteria needed to select a representative sample of interviewees. For key informant selection, the crucial consideration is "the amount of knowledge [the informant] has about a topic and his or her willingness to communicate with the researcher" (p. 105).

The interviews in both studies ranged in length from one to two and a half hours and were unstructured in their form. Due to Sarah's (by then lengthy) involvement with each organization, the interviews felt like a continuation of ongoing conversations with the participants. For Frances, the change in context from online to offline meant that most interviews were the first face-to-face meetings and therefore often had very different dynamics to previous online conversations. For some participants, direct online conversations had not taken place between interviewer and interviewee until the interview request. For many others, most previous direct or indirect conversation had taken place in back channels such as Twitter, a quite ephemeral and informal method of communication.

For Sarah's project, each interview ranged over a wide variety of themes. While there was some variation in these themes for each organization, the following themes were almost always present:

- The history of each interviewee's involvement with that particular organization and with activism more broadly
- The interviewee's reflection on what it meant to "be a feminist"
- The challenges and problems that each interviewee had experienced in her activism
- The interviewee's thoughts about the role of organizational location, structure, and processes in determining the scope and focus of her activism
- The challenges that the interviewees had experienced as arising from differences and conflict between women in the movement to do with ideology, goals, and strategy
- The challenges to feminist activism that each interviewee had experienced in trying to organize around intersections of "race," class, sexuality, and so on

- The interviewee's views about the future possibilities for feminist activism in Australia

Lichterman (2002, p. 126) argues for the importance of being clear about one's position as a researcher from the very beginning. For this reason, Frances has a research blog and various research-specific Internet profiles, in order to be seen as participating as a researcher rather than as an everyday Internet user. Her methodology draws on the reflexive approach to Internet research advocated by Internet ethnographers, in which conversations about people's experience of online discursive activism inform her theory (Baym, 2000, 2006; Hine, 2000; Markham, 1998; Senft, 2008; Sundén, 2003; Turkle, 1995). These ethnographic research practices inform Frances's methods, particularly in terms of online participant observation and analysis of messages, but also the combination of text analysis and accounts of online experience gained through interviews. Face-to-face interviews helped to contextualize the research and provided further opportunities to gain the perspectives of community members about their role in and experience of this community (Baym, 2006, p. 85; Orgad, 2009, p. 39).

In Frances's research, the themes and structure of the interviews evolved over the course of interviews in response to what interviewees were saying. However, every interview covered many or all of these main themes:

- The history of each person's blogging practices, how they have changed over time, and the reasons for those changes, if any
- The interviewee's experience of community in the blogosphere and her experience of conflict, if any
- The relationship between the identity of the interviewee and the feminist blogging community and whether the community has changed or otherwise affected the interviewee's identity
- The history of the interviewee's political involvement more generally and how this relates to her blogging practice
- Their relationships with other bloggers and things that affect those relationships, such as location, identity markers, and offline or backchannel social contact

- Discussion of how blogging and being part of the blogging community have affected their everyday life and personal-political practice
- Discussion of the motivation to write particular blog posts and engage in particular discussions. What do bloggers get out of writing their blogs that keeps them involved and engaged?

Triangulation and Textual Analysis

Despite this emphasis on participant observation and in-depth interviewing, our research strategy in these projects should more accurately be described as one of triangulation or multiple-methods research, so that the textual analysis that forms an important part of our analysis is not overlooked. As Reinharz (1992) argues, "Multimethod research creates the opportunity to put texts or people in contexts, thus providing a richer and far more accurate interpretation" (p. 213). The inclusion of textual material is entirely compatible with the activist standpoint approach. The primary textual material that informed Sarah's research included historical interview and autobiographical texts that allowed her to trace feminist processes of collective identity from the 1970s to the present, along with the organizational documents that she studied during her time in the field. These organizational documents included minutes from meetings, newsletters, annual reports, planning and evaluation reports, conference proceedings, research reports, and publicity or information materials for the general public. Similarly, in Frances's research in online communities, textual material forms a large part of the data for analysis. The detail in these documents allows researchers to supplement and verify the information gathered from participant observation and interviewing. This approach is not unusual in the study of social movements, as Blee and Taylor (2002, p. 111) point out, because triangulation significantly increases the amount of detail researchers can bring to their analysis. Blee and Taylor argue that

> the combination of participant observation or document analysis with semi-structured interviewing can be a useful means of analysing the specific contexts within which participants in social movements construct their understandings of these movements. (p. 112)

In relation to both feminist bloggers and young women in the contemporary Australian women's movement, a significant part of this context is the contentious history of the women's movement itself. Second-wave Australian feminism has generated a significant quantity of auto/biographical material that has not been subject to any significant analysis. Material by Susan Mitchell (1984), Jocelynne Scutt (1987), and Jan Bowen (1998) provides fairly raw interview material, while autobiographies from Zelda D'Aprano (1995), Anne Summers (1999), Susan Ryan (1999), and Wendy McCarthy (2000), among others, contribute to a growing body of literature that allows feminists to speak in their own words and is fertile ground for social movement analysis. Online blog-based texts, particularly in personal blogs written by feminists, can also have this function, allowing contemporary feminist writers to frame their own experiences in ways of their own choosing. In the context of these research projects, all such texts are considered "documents of interaction" (Angrosino, 1989, p. 4), a category that covers biography, autobiography, life history, and personal narratives, and refers to the fact that "the interaction between the individual reliving and reinterpreting life experiences and the individual whose *active* responses to that telling become an integral part of its process of creation" (Angrosino, 1989, p. 4). For online-based autobiographical text, this process of interactive creativity is enhanced through the use of comments and off-blog responses and links. Inherent to this perspective is the understanding that interview and autobiographical material, as acts of sharing, presuppose an interested audience and therefore primarily include deliberately chosen facets of an individual's experience. We cannot, therefore, analyze this material uncritically as a historical "truth" (Angrosino, 1989, pp. 5–8).

Margaret Henderson (2002) has been critical of feminist autobiographies because she feels that they represent a version of feminist activism that has been "made comprehensible and palatable to the mainstream." Henderson argues that if we were to rely on these accounts alone, then the second wave of the Australian women's movement "should be renamed the 'tidiest revolution'" (p. 181). For the purposes of Sarah's study, however, these documents were useful as individualistic accounts that, taken together, provided richly personal data entirely suitable for an activist standpoint analysis and certainly did not reveal the "tidiness" of these women's experiences of feminist activism in the 1970s. When analyzed in relation to feminist processes of collective identity and the scholarly histories of the period, what is most apparent are the confusion and difficulty that many of these women experienced in dealing with conflict between their "sisters." The contemporary texts of the Australian feminist blogging community tell us similar stories of conflict and frustration as important components of feminist collective identity processes.

PRIVILEGING AN ACTIVIST STANDPOINT

Together these research methods generate a wealth of data. Both Sarah and Frances emerged from their fieldwork with extensive field notes from participant observation, interview transcripts, organizational documents, historical material, and records from e-mail discussion lists. Using the analytic method described in the first half of this chapter, they were then able to consider the processes of collective identity that the young activists and online activists in the networks were engaged in and to situate these processes in the historical context of the Australian women's movement. Their analysis was derived from the "activist standpoint" described earlier in the chapter. Both Sarah and Frances privileged the perspectives of the women themselves as knowing, politicized subjects who articulated their processes of collective identity through their feminist discourse and action. Such an approach is dependent on a certain humility, what Cynthia Kaufman (2003) describes as "a sense that no matter how much we know, other people have experiences and perspectives that we have much to learn from" (p. 4). A humble approach to research and analysis, from an activist perspective, provides the space and opportunity to "give the voice back to the protestors we study" (Jasper, 1997, p. 379). An analysis of processes of collective identity from this perspective can allow researchers the opportunity to observe and document what Chela Sandoval (2000) describes as the "differential

mode of consciousness," which "depends on a form of agency that is self-consciously mobilized" (p. 58). This consciousness, which Sandoval describes as "processual and differential," bears striking parallels with Melucci's processes of collective identity. Both suggest the fluid and strategic nature of collective identity and reveal that any such identity is itself created from social and political struggle (Taylor & Whittier, 1992, p. 110).

For the women who participated in these research projects, these struggles are a part of their everyday experiences as activists. The women in the CCWN, for example, often experience their activism to be frustrating, isolating, and paralyzing. They battle continuously with ideological and strategic dilemmas, as well as issues of inclusion and coalition that would sound very familiar to many feminists of the second wave. This is echoed in the Australian feminist blogosphere, where intersectionality and social inclusion are areas of important discursive activism and, as part of this, form ideological points of contention between online feminist bloggers. With little support, the women in these networks struggle to find ways of making their actions seem meaningful to a broad category of women, while their heightened awareness of debates around difference and inclusion and exclusion sometimes threatens to silence them altogether. The pressure that some of the women place on themselves is, at times, quite extraordinary. For example, in an e-mail communication with Sarah, "Fiona"[4] expressed the view that while she is active on a personal level, she feels guilty that she does not "do more" and "would like to be more active on a political level." She then went on to describe her activism as including

> Nike blockades each week and I am involved in mass protests, like S11 and M1. I expect to go on Reclaim the Night. I go to Critical Mass (a bike rally), do volunteer work at a food co-op and tutor a young woman in literacy once a week. I think that volunteer work in my local community is very important and has more of a connection than just big rallies. I'm vegetarian and choose to shop at the co-op and local IGA. I don't use plastic bags and try to buy organic food. . . . Other consumer choices include not consuming much, and when

I do I choose not to spend money with companies that have bad human-rights records [such as] Nestle, Nike, Sussan, Shell . . . I think that self-education is important. I choose to live with queer women and spend time in the women's department at uni. This gives me strength and inspiration. I hope to become more active as Bloody Feminists starts up again on campus. I'm also running as women's officer next year. My honours thesis (in linguistics) is on a gender issue and I try to live my political commitments every day.

This commitment to incorporating feminist politics into all aspects of their daily lives is typical of the young women who participated in this research, and as in the case of Fiona, it is hard to imagine many of them having any time left to become *more* politically active.

And yet this sense of inadequacy is a theme for the young women in the CCWN. In her end-of-year report as convenor for 2001, Pru expressed her feeling that she has "probably disappointed many comrades" by not achieving more during the year and expresses the hope that her colleagues understand that "even the revolution goes on holiday." There is a constant tension for Pru in wanting to always "be active where I'm at in my everyday life" and the recognition that there are also other things she wants to do with her life, including activism on other issues. These activists have a strong sense of responsibility to the broader women's movement, especially in terms of maintaining a feminist political space.

For Pru, however, one of the difficulties is that campus activism is so "insular" and yet the demands on young feminists seem so great:

It's hard because you want to sort of look beyond the square you're in but at the same time taking on the world is really difficult when there's no base for doing that. . . . So we need to learn from what we've been doing and sort of look at other movements a bit as well, seeing where they're going. It's just hard. It's really difficult . . . I know so many feminists who are . . . depressed in a clinical sense and I think one of the issues there is that women's lives are just so hectic.

In the more supported environment of the YWWAPN, the challenges of feminism are different, primarily due to the different social location of the young women involved. The older women who work to support the young women's program have an enormous sensitivity about the disturbing, and often distressing, effects that developing a feminist consciousness can have on the young, working-class women in the program. This experience is one that is common to many women, as program director Maggie explains:

It's profoundly disturbing I think when any of us start to realise how oppressed women are. Profoundly disturbing. It shakes the way you look at the world and the way you see the world. And once you do that there is absolutely no going back. And I think it's the same for these women; it questions their relationships, how they've been treated and the future they've pictured for themselves or had painted for them. It's huge.

Maggie also explains that the program prepares for the potential effects of this new awareness and "take[s] into account the fact that the participants are going to be profoundly shaken up."

Kerry is one young woman in the YWWAPN who experienced these personal challenges of "coming to feminism":

It was a really traumatic time in my life. I was searching for who am I outside of being my partner's girlfriend and my child's mother. I didn't even realise I was supposed to be someone outside of these other roles. That's when I started learning and reading about what was happening in the world with women and the roles that women play in men's lives. This radar came up and I felt really naked and exposed and really aware of what was going on around me—it was really scary.

Kerry's new knowledge about herself and the world is also tainted by a sense of confusion about why so many people in the community reject feminism:

When people say you're a feminist they can mean it in such horrible ways. Like we're some really weird thing. I'm not saying *they're* weird, I'm just saying I can't understand why they're not saying what we're saying. It's out there every day and they're just so blind to it.

The bloggers that Frances spoke to also recognized that their actions as bloggers were political and that this gave them a particular responsibility to write in an informed way and to maintain a safe space for feminist discourse. As one participant argued,

I don't have any sort of pretensions about . . . its national importance but yes, I think . . . it is political for a woman to choose not to be nice, and the thing is that I will continue to be nice in my day to day stuff, but I think even carving out a space in which to talk back and giving other people a space in which they can say things or they can laugh about things that it wasn't really okay to say before. . . . And I think it comes up a fair bit in blogging but . . . the personal is political.

Another blogger explained her frustrations with people's attitudes toward political discourse online, as though it wasn't real politics.

[People sometimes say] if you really cared about this why aren't you out marching in the streets? And some of us are saying well, this is the streets now, mate.

She identified her experience of blogging as an action within a political community to which she had a responsibility to contribute. Bloggers see value both in finding others who think in similar ways to them and in creating new discourses and exposing others to new ideas. Part of this comes from challenging the assumptions that are present in media representations of gender relations and other social inequalities:

I would love to look at the bigger picture. A lot of the time I hope I'm trying to do that, because that's what's so valuable with blogging. Sure, it's not journalism or whatever, [but] it's where you get together threads of the things you see in daily life and things that you read and things that you hear and say "Hey, look, there's a bit of a pattern emerging here." And we do get continually shouted down and that's what I find exhausting.

Another woman explains the way these two motivations—to expose other people to different ideas and to build community—come together on her blog:

One of the really positive things that come out of blogging for me I think is that it's that kind of outlet so if I do feel outraged by something I can express that and I hope that some people read it and concur. Or some of the people I know in real life might read it and go oh I never really thought about that. I think [because] my background is teaching, . . . all I want to do is educate people.

However, bloggers do express frustration that the discourses used within the community do not have a broader reach and appeal in Australian society:

It's still basically only somebody who wants to come and find out about feminism, it's not a lot of people going out and saying we've actually got some important ideas here that are not just about a lot of people with hairy armpits sort of thing, this is actually. . . . Some of this stuff matters to everybody all the time, and I don't think there's a lot of that kind of reach out going on.

This blogger expressed the opinion that the community holds a supportive function for her personally and is not always about creating change in broader society:

I've just found that it keeps me constantly stimulated with new material and new ideas and new challenges to my thought. And rather than being complacent about some idea of mine, having those challenged is quite good. It's also good in terms of not feeling alone as a feminist activist, because in this world it's so hard often to find people who you can be in alignment with in your thinking, and who won't constantly put that down or put women down, so having people there to affirm that I'm okay and I'm doing alright, that's been quite good.

Sometimes collective identity processes within the community, as well as some aspects of online behavior, can have an emotional impact on community members that is frustrating or draining:

There's been blog drama after blog drama, and I've mostly not been in those but the ones I've had, it's been quite distressing. But I try to remember that it's gonna happen again and again and I need to just stay focused on doing the valuable work that we need to do and be in community with these people, because we can't all get along but most of the time we can, so that's what I'm trying to do.

These small vignettes from our research reveal a great deal about the deep commitment that these women bring to their activism. In their struggles over processes of collective identity, they consistently demonstrate an ethic of care for the work that they do that illuminates the importance of their work both for broader feminist struggles and in social movement communities more generally. Of course, the relationship that we had mutually constructed meant that, in some senses, neither we nor the women in the projects could be truly "themselves" or be "objective" about the research experience. The nature of research means that the sort of action and interaction that they were participating in, observing, and documenting was itself somewhat artificial in character. However, this acknowledgment that research does not "mirror 'true' reality" (Melucci, 1996, p. 390) is not intended to invalidate the research findings or undermine the importance of the activist standpoint. Rather, this acknowledgment brings us closer to a recognition of what research actually is: "namely, that it is a social activity, a self-reflexive process constructed within the possibilities and constraints of a social field" (Melucci, 1996, p. 390). Furthermore, acknowledging the constructed nature of the research process is ultimately beneficial, as it can provide both the researcher and the research participants with a "welcome space for reflection" (Lichterman, 2002, p. 127)—on the research process itself and on the broader context of social movement activism.

CONCLUSION

Both Sarah and Frances intended that, through the research process, the women in their case studies would have an opportunity to reflect on and develop their local practices and strategies that would assist them to achieve their goals for feminist social and political change. Their goal was to give these feminists a greater voice of their own in conceptualizing, theorizing, and organizing the social conditions in which their activism may flourish and be recognized. More broadly, however, we again agree with Melucci

(1996) when he suggests that "analysis of movements provides insights that point behind the back of the collective actors as empirical facts" (p. 380). Behind the women who participated in this study is a diversity of young feminist and online feminist praxis that deserves a wealth of scholarly attention.

Alain Touraine (1985) has argued that the concept of social movement should be centrally important to sociological inquiry because it can act as a "bridge between the observation of new technologies and the idea of new forms of political life" (p. 782). Melucci (1996) goes further by suggesting that the sort of focus on the "plurality and tensions constituting collective life" that we have advocated in this chapter can "contribute to a practice of freedom" (p. 397). To layer a feminist perspective on this project once more, as researchers, we must remember that "the aim of feminist research is liberation" (Fonow & Cook, 1991, p. 6). As David Meyer (2002) reminds us, in the study of social movements,

> It is too easy to forget the critical importance of what we study. The people who make social movements are trying to change the world, trying to promote their visions of peace, justice, and social progress—sometimes at great personal risk. This means that we start with subjects invested with emotion, import, conflict, and tension from the outset. I hope that the work of scholars can be more clearly animated by the importance of such commitments, treating the puzzles of collective action with the passion employed by activists about their own efforts. (p. 20)

Considering the study of social movements from an activist standpoint can give activists, including online activists, a voice in articulating their commitment, highlighting their strategic and fluid engagement with a differential consciousness and revealing the processes by which they construct their collective identities. In these humble researchers' opinion, the rest of us have much to learn.

Discussion Questions

1. Social movements are complex social phenomena that have generated a rich field of research. What does feminism/feminist theory bring to this field of research?

2. How does feminist standpoint theory inform/ transform the study of collective identity?

3. What role does conflict play in processes of collective identity?

4. How can feminist standpoint theory and theories of social movement collective identity contribute to research into online feminist activism?

Online Resources

Mapping the Australian Women's Movement

http://cass.anu.edu.au/research_projects/mawm

This website provides information about the wider context of some of the research discussed in this chapter and its outcomes.

Qualitative Research Guidelines Project

http://www.qualres.org/index.html

This website identifies and describes a broad range of qualitative research methods.

Women's Movements and Feminist Sites

http://culturalpolitics.net/social_movements/ women

Here the reader will find a list of historical resources and links on the women's movement from a social movement studies perspective, including historical information, contemporary websites, and further reading.

Relevant Journals

Australian Feminist Studies

Mobilization

Social Movement Studies

NOTES

1. For a discussion of the ways in which collective identity is considered analytically distinct from both individual and public identity, see Laraña, Johnston, and Gusfield (1994).

2. The study of emotion as a vital component of social movement processes has seen something of a return to favor after the dominance of studies of structure and rationality in the field in recent decades. In a recent collection devoted to this task, Jeff

Goodwin, James Jasper, and Francesca Polletta (2001) express their hope that "[e]motions, properly understood, may prove once again to be a central concern of political analysis" (p. 2).

3. The closest thing to a national or centralized organization in the women's movement that Australia has seen was the Coalition of Australian Participating Organisations of Women (CAPOW!), which was formed in 1991. CAPOW! was an attempt by a range of organizations in the Australian women's movement to form a national networking coalition. While CAPOW! played an important coordinating role in the lead-up to the United Nations Conference for Women in Beijing in 1995, it was the first women's organization to be defunded by the Howard government in 1996. The death of Helen Leonard (CAPOW! convenor and one of Australia's most active feminists) in 2001 has meant that the organization continues to exist in name only.

4. This respondent's name has been changed as she chose not to be identified in this research. Other respondents chose to be identified.

REFERENCES

Angrosino, M. V. (1989). *Documents of interaction: Biography, autobiography, and life history in social science perspective.* Gainesville: University of Florida Press.

Armstrong, E. A., & Bernstein, M. (2008). Culture, power and institutions: A multi-institutional politics approach to social movements. *Sociological Theory, 26*(1), 74–99.

Bahnisch, M. (2006). The political uses of blogs. In A. Bruns & J. Jacobs (Eds.), *Uses of blogs* (pp. 139–150). New York: Peter Lang.

Baym, N. K. (2000). *Tune in, log on: Soaps, fandom, and online community.* Thousand Oaks, CA: Sage.

Baym, N. K. (2006). Finding the quality in qualitative research. In D. Silver & A. Massanari (Eds.), *Critical cyberculture studies* (pp. 79–87). New York: New York University Press.

Baym, N. K., & Markham, A. N. (2009). Introduction: Making smart choices on shifting ground. In A. N. Markham & N. K. Baym (Eds.), *Internet inquiry: Conversations about method* (pp. vii–xix). Thousand Oaks, CA: Sage.

Bernstein, M. (2005). Identity politics. *Annual Review of Sociology, 31,* 47–74.

Blee, K. M., & Taylor, V. (2002). Semi-structured interviewing in social movement research. In B. Klandermans & S. Staggenborg (Eds.),

Methods of social movement research (pp. 92–117). Minneapolis: University of Minnesota Press.

Bowen, J. (1998). *Feminists fatale: The changing face of Australian feminism.* Pymble, NSW, Australia: HarperCollins.

Boyd, D. (2009). A response to Christine Hine. In A. N. Markham & N. K. Baym (Eds.), *Internet inquiry: Conversations about method* (pp. 26–32). Thousand Oaks, CA: Sage.

Bruns, A. (2006). The practice of news blogging. In A. Bruns & J. Jacobs (Eds.), *Uses of blogs* (pp. 11–22). New York: Peter Lang.

Bulbeck, C. (1997). *Living feminism: The impact of the women's movement on three generations of Australian women.* Cambridge, UK: Cambridge University Press.

Byrne, A., & Lentin, R. (2000). (Eds.). *(Re)searching women: Feminist research methodologies in the social sciences in Ireland.* Dublin: Institute of Public Administration.

D'Aprano, Z. (1995). *Zelda.* North Melbourne, Australia: Spinifex Press.

Dean, J. (1997). The reflective solidarity of democratic feminism. In J. Dean (Ed.), *Feminism and the new democracy: Re-siting the political* (pp. 244–263). London: Sage.

Devine, F. (2002). Qualitative analysis. In D. Marsh & G. Stoker (Eds.), *Theory and methods in political science* (2nd ed., pp. 197–215). London: Macmillan.

Ferree, M. M. (1987). Equality and autonomy: The women's movements of the United States and West Germany. In C. Mueller & M. Katzenstein (Eds.), *The women's movements of the United States and Western Europe* (pp. 172–195). Philadelphia: Temple University Press.

Ferree, M. M., & Gamson, W. (2003). The gendering of governance and the governance of gender: Abortion politics in Germany and the USA. In B. Hobson (Ed.), *Recognition struggles and social movements* (pp. 35–63). New York: Cambridge University Press.

Ferree, M. M., & Martin, P. M. (Eds.). (1995). *Feminist organizations: Harvest of the new women's movement.* Philadelphia: Temple University Press.

Ferree, M. M., & Merrill, D. (2000). Hot movements, cold cognition: Thinking about social movements in gendered frames. *Contemporary Sociology: A Journal of Reviews, 29,* 454–462.

Fonow, M. M. (2003). *Union women: Forging feminism in the United Steelworkers of America.* Minneapolis: University of Minnesota Press.

Fonow, M. M., & Cook, J. A. (1991). Back to the future: A look at the second wave of feminist epistemology and methodology. In M. M. Fonow & J. A. Cook (Eds.), *Beyond methodology: Feminist scholarship as lived research* (pp. 1–15). Bloomington: Indiana University Press.

Fontana, A., & Frey, J. (2003). The interview: From structured questions to negotiated text. In N. K. Denzin & Y. S. Lincoln (Eds.), *Collecting and interpreting qualitative materials* (2nd ed., pp. 61–106). Thousand Oaks, CA: Sage.

Gamson, W. (1992). The social psychology of collective action. In A. D. Morris & C. M. Mueller (Eds.), *Frontiers in social movement theory* (pp. 53–76). New Haven, CT: Yale University Press.

Gelb, J., & Hart, V. (1999). Feminist politics in a hostile environment: Obstacles and opportunities. In M. Guigni, D. McAdam, & C. Tilly (Eds.), *How social movements matter* (pp. 149–181). Minneapolis: University of Minnesota Press.

Goodwin, J., & Jasper, J. M. (2003). Editors' introduction. In J. Goodwin & J. M. Jasper (Eds.), *The social movements reader: Cases and concepts* (pp. 3–8). Malden, MA: Blackwell Publishing.

Goodwin, J., Jasper, J. M., & Polletta, F. (2001). *Passionate politics: Emotions and social movements.* Chicago: University of Chicago Press.

Gregg, M. (2006). Posting with passion: Blogs and the politics of gender. In A. Bruns & J. Jacobs (Eds.), *Uses of blogs* (pp. 151–160). New York: Peter Lang.

Grosz, E. (1993). Bodies and knowledges: Feminism and the crisis of reason. In L. Alcoff & E. Potter (Eds.), *Feminist epistemologies* (pp. 187–216). New York: Routledge.

Henderson, M. (2002). The tidiest revolution: Regulative feminist autobiography and the defacement of the Australian women's movement. *Australian Literary Studies, 20*(3), 178–191.

Hine, C. (2000). *Virtual ethnography.* London: Sage.

Jasper, J. (1997). *The art of moral protest: Culture, biography and creativity in social movements.* Chicago: University of Chicago Press.

Johnston, H. (2002). Verification and proof in frame and discourse analysis. In B. Klandermans & S. Staggenborg (Eds.), *Methods of social movement research* (pp. 62–91). Minneapolis: University of Minnesota Press.

Jónasdóttir, A., & Jones, K. (2009). *The political interests of gender revisited: Redoing theory and research with a feminist face.* Tokyo: United Nations University Press.

Kaplan, G. (1996). *The meagre harvest: The Australian women's movement 1950s–1990s.* St. Leonards, Australia: Allen & Unwin.

Katzenstein, M. (1995). Discursive politics and feminist activism in the Catholic Church. In M. M. Ferree & P. Y. Martin (Eds.), *Feminist organizations: Harvest of the new women's movement* (pp. 35–52). Philadelphia: Temple University Press.

Kaufman, C. (2003). *Ideas for action: Relevant theory for radical change.* Cambridge, UK: South End Press.

Klandermans, B., & Staggenborg, S. (Eds.). (2002). *Methods of social movement research.* Minneapolis: University of Minnesota Press.

Koopmans, R., & Rucht, D. (2002). Protest event analysis. In B. Klandermans & S. Staggenborg (Eds.), *Methods of social movement research* (pp. 231–259). Minneapolis: University of Minnesota Press.

Lake, M. (1999). *Getting equal: The history of Australian feminism.* St. Leonards, Australia: Allen & Unwin.

Laraña, E., Johnston, H., & Gusfield, J. R. (Eds.). (1994). *New social movements: From ideology to identity.* Philadelphia: Temple University Press.

Lichterman, P. (2002). Seeing structure happen: Theory-driven participant observation. In B. Klandermans & S. Staggenborg (Eds.), *Methods of social movement research* (pp. 118–145). Minneapolis: University of Minnesota Press.

Lofland, J. (1993). Theory-bashing and answer-improving in the study of social movements. *The American Sociologist, 24*(2), 37–58.

Longino, E. H. (1993). Subjects, power and knowledge: Description and prescription in feminist philosophies of science. In L. Alcoff & E. Potter (Eds.), *Feminist epistemologies* (pp. 101–120). New York: Routledge.

Lovink, G. (2008). *Zero comments: Blogging and critical Internet culture.* New York: Routledge.

Maddison, S. (2008). *Collective identity and Australian feminist activism: Conceptualising a third wave.* Berlin: VDM.

Markham, A. N. (1998). *Life online: Researching real experience in virtual space.* Walnut Creek, CA: AltaMira Press.

McCarthy, W. (2000). *Don't fence me in.* Milsons Point, NSW: Random House Australia.

McDonald, K. (1999). *Struggles for subjectivity, identity, action and youth experience.* Cambridge, UK: Cambridge University Press.

Melucci, A. (1985). The symbolic challenge of contemporary movements. *Social Research, 52*(4), 789–815.

Melucci, A. (1989). *Nomads of the present: Social movements and individual needs in contemporary society.* Philadelphia: Temple University Press.

Melucci, A. (1995). The process of collective identity. In H. Johnston & B. Klandermans (Eds.), *Social movements and culture* (pp. 41–63). London: UCL Press.

Melucci, A. (1996). *Challenging codes: Collective action in the information age.* Cambridge, UK: Cambridge University Press.

Meyer, D. S. (2002). Opportunities and identities: Bridge-building in the study of social movements. In D. S. Meyer, N. Whittier, & B. Robnett (Eds.), *Social movements: Identity, culture and the state* (pp. 3–24). New York: Oxford University Press.

Minichiello, V., Aroni, R., Timewell, E., & Alexander, L. (1995). *In-depth interviewing: Principles, techniques, analysis* (2nd ed.). South Melbourne, Australia: Addison Wesley Longman.

Mitchell, S. (1984). *Tall poppies.* Melbourne, Australia: Penguin.

Morris, A. (1992). Political consciousness and collective action. In A. Morris & C. Mueller (Eds.), *Frontiers in social movement theory* (pp. 351–373). New Haven, CT: Yale University Press.

Naples, N. (2003). *Feminism and method: Ethnography, discourse analysis, and activist research.* New York: Routledge.

Oakley, A. (1981). Interviewing women: A contradiction in terms. In H. Roberts (Ed.), *Doing feminist research* (pp. 30–61). London: Routledge and Kegan Paul.

Orgad, S. (2009). How can researchers make sense of the issues involved in collecting and interpreting online and offline data? In A. N. Markham & N. K. Baym (Eds.), *Internet inquiry: Conversations about method* (pp. 33–53). Thousand Oaks, CA: Sage.

Polletta, F., & Jasper, J. M. (2001). Collective identity and social movements. *Annual Review of Sociology, 27,* 283–305.

Ramazanoğlu, C., & Holland, J. (2002). *Feminist methodology: Challenges and choices.* London: Sage.

Randall, V. (2010). Feminism. In D. Marsh & G. Stoker (Eds.), *Theory and methods in political science* (3rd ed., pp. 114–135). Basingstoke, UK: Palgrave Macmillan.

Reinharz, S. (1992). *Feminist methods in social research.* New York: Oxford University Press.

Rettberg, J. W. (2008). *Blogging.* Cambridge, UK: Polity.

Ribbens, J., & Edwards, R. (Eds.). (2009). *Feminist dilemmas in qualitative research: Public knowledge and private lives.* London: Sage.

Robnett, B. (1997). *How long? How long? African American women in the struggle for civil rights.* New York: Oxford University Press.

Rupp, L. J., & Taylor, V. (1987). *Survival in the doldrums: The American women's rights movement, 1945 to the 1960s.* New York: Oxford University Press.

Ryan, S. (1999). *Catching the waves: Life in and out of politics.* Sydney, Australia: HarperCollins.

Sandoval, C. (2000). *Methodology of the oppressed.* Minneapolis: University of Minnesota Press.

Scutt, J. (Ed.). (1987). *Different lives: Reflections on the women's movement and visions for its future.* Melbourne, Australia: Penguin.

Senft, T. M. (2008). *Camgirls: Celebrity & community in the age of social networks.* New York: Peter Lang.

Shorter, E., & Tilly, C. (1974). *Strikes in France, 1830–1968.* Cambridge, UK: Cambridge University Press.

Snow, D. (2001). *Collective identity and expressive forms.* Irvine, CA: Center for the Study of Democracy. http://www.democ.uci.edu/democ/papers/snow.htm

Snow, D. A., & Trom, D. (2002). The case study and the study of social movements. In B. Klandermans & S. Staggenborg (Eds.), *Methods of social movement research* (pp. 146–172). Minneapolis: University of Minnesota Press.

Somerville, J. (1997). Social movement theory, women and the question of interests. *Sociology, 31*(4), 673–695.

Staggenborg, S., & Taylor, V. (2005). Whatever happened to the women's movement? *Mobilization, 10*(1), 37–52.

Stanley, L. (Ed.). (1990). *Feminist praxis: Research, theory, and epistemology in feminist sociology.* London: Routledge.

Stanley, L., & Wise, S. (1990). Method, methodology and epistemology in feminist research processes. In L. Stanley (Ed.), *Feminist praxis: Research, theory, and epistemology in feminist sociology* (pp. 20–60). London: Routledge.

Summers, A. (1999). *Ducks on the pond: An autobiography 1945–1976.* Ringwood, Victoria, Australia: Viking.

Sundén, J. (2003). *Material virtualities: Approaching online textual embodiment.* New York: Peter Lang.

Taylor, V. (2000). Mobilizing for change in a social movement society. *Contemporary Sociology, 29*(1), 219–230.

Taylor, V., & Rupp, L. (2002). Loving internationalism: The emotion culture of transnational women's organizations. *Mobilization, 7*(2), 141–158.

Taylor, V., & Whittier, N. (1992). Collective identity in social movement communities: Lesbian feminist mobilization. In A. D. Morris & C. M. Mueller (Eds.), *Frontiers in social movement theory.* New Haven, CT: Yale University Press.

Taylor, V., & Whittier, N. (1998). Guest editors' introduction. *Gender & Society, 12*(6), 622.

Touraine, A. (1981). *The voice and the eye.* Cambridge, UK: Cambridge University Press.

Touraine, A. (1985). An introduction to the study of social movements. *Social Research, 52*(4), 749–787.

Touraine, A. (2000). A method for studying social actors. *Journal of World Systems Research, 1*(3), 900–918.

Turkle, S. (1995). *Life on the screen: Identity in the age of the Internet.* New York: Simon & Schuster.

Waldby, C. (1995). Feminism and method. In B. Caine & R. Pringle (Eds.), *Transitions: New Australian feminisms* (pp. 15–28). Sydney, Australia: Allen & Unwin.

Whittier, N. (1995). *Feminist generations: The persistence of the radical women's movement.* Philadelphia: Temple University Press.

Whittier, N. (2002). Meaning and structure in social movements. In D. S. Meyer, N. Whittier, & B. Robnett (Eds.), *Social movements: Identity, culture and the state* (pp. 289–307). New York: Oxford University Press.

Wilson, S. M., & Peterson, L. C. (2002). The anthropology of online communities. *Annual Review of Anthropology, 31,* 449–467.

Young, I. M. (1997). *Intersecting voices: Dilemmas of gender, political philosophy, and policy.* Princeton, NJ: Princeton University Press.

Young, S. (1997). *Changing the wor(l)d: Discourse, politics and the feminist movement.* New York: Routledge.

20

FEMINIST RESEARCH AND ACTIVISM TO PROMOTE HEALTH EQUITY

LYNN WEBER AND JENNIFER CASTELLOW

To provide effective solutions to the deeply embedded structured inequalities that characterize the 21st century, social policy must derive from what feminist scholarship has come to understand about the ways in which race, class, gender, sexuality, nation, and other systems of inequality intersect. These systems are complex, pervasive, persistent, mutually constituted, and socially constructed power relationships (see Collins, 2000a; Dill & Zambrana, 2009; Weber, 1998, 2010). Without taking into account the complex nexus of systemic inequalities within which these relationships are embedded, trying to understand women's lives and to develop social policy to redress women's oppression is like trying to clean the air on one side of a screen door.[1]

Feminists have long sought to promote just social policies through their scholarship and activism. These scholar-activists have emphasized the need to combine macro-level policies with a localized and complex understanding of people's lives—eschewing both an expert-centered approach that fails to engage the people

and a grassroots approach that fails to engage the broader structural environment for macro-level policies (see Naples, 2003). But even though feminist scholarship has influenced public policies and advanced understanding of social inequalities of gender and its intersections, it has done so largely outside the mainstream of public funding for research and outside legitimized avenues for shaping social policy that have become increasingly dominated by corporate, moneyed interests. In health research, for example, the biomedical paradigm and its social science offshoots solidly dominate major research funding, prestigious publications, and public policy (for discussions, see Braithwaite, 2008; Hankivsky et al., 2010; Inhorn, 2006; Institute of Medicine [IOM], 2002; Lewis, 2007; Rogers, 2006; Weber, 2006).

The hegemony of the biomedical paradigm is particularly problematic because it conceives of gender not as a social construction but as a fixed category and a biological fact, and that conception is deeply embedded in the dominant structures of health research and practice. As a consequence, women's health has historically been equated with reproductive health, so much so that other major threats to women's health receive scant attention (Carpenter & Casper, 2009; Collins, 2009; Hankivsky et al., 2010; Hyams, 2010). For example, federal funding for lung cancer research—which takes more women's lives every year than breast, ovarian, and uterine cancers combined—was recently estimated at 21 times less than funding for breast cancer and 13 times less than funding for prostate cancer (Hyams, 2010). Furthermore, the narrow attention to individual bodies conceived in isolation from their environments is narrowing even further—increasingly turning to the microscopic aspects of bodies such as genes and biomarkers (see Office of Research on Women's Health [ORWH], 2010). These emphases carry important political and economic consequences because they shift national health resources away from health education, prevention, and primary care—efforts that benefit a much wider array of women—and to more expensive, highly technical, and less available secondary and tertiary care health interventions.

Since 2007, major feminist health policy efforts in the United States have concentrated on bringing feminist approaches and concerns to the health care reform process. The Patient Protection and Affordable Care Act of 2010 portends the most sweeping change in the U.S. health care system since the advent of Medicare in the 1960s, and feminist scholar activists were intimately involved in working to affect that legislation. Their efforts succeeded in helping to garner important new systems to protect the health of women and their families yet failed in efforts to achieve inclusion for all in the health care system. Activists were also unsuccessful in their efforts to alter the health care system in a way that would challenge the domination of for-profit health care—a system that is destabilizing the national economy and the lives of many in subordinated groups (Avery Institute for Social Change [AISC], 2008; Mishel, Bernstein, & Shierholz, 2009; Pearson, 2010; Raising Women's Voices [RWV], 2010b; Uttley, Avery, Allina, Pandit, & Pearson, 2010).

In this chapter, we suggest some ideas for and highlight new work aimed at directing feminist health scholarship so that it becomes situated more solidly in the foreground of social science and becomes more central in the dialogue and debate that constitutes the public policy process. New directions for feminist scholarship and activism will obviously derive from

- the interplay of the social, economic, and political forces shaping the policy context
- an awareness of and dialogue about the strengths and limitations of the feminist intersectional paradigm, other alternative paradigms, and conventional positivist paradigms addressing social inequalities
- the efficacy of efforts to strengthen the scholarship/activism connection in ways that shape policies to promote social justice.

To contextualize the broader arguments about ways to increase the impact of feminist scholarship on social policy, a useful case to examine is the arena of women's health and health disparities of race, ethnicity, nation, gender, and social class.[2] First, health research is the best-funded research in all of academia. Second, the positivist biomedical paradigm solidly dominates the intellectual terrain of women's health and health disparities scholarship and policy, so much so that the social science of health has largely evolved as an emulation of that paradigm—despite its nominal effectiveness at reducing health disparities (Baum, Begin, Houweling, & Taylor, 2009; Rogers, 2006; Weber & Parra-Medina, 2003). Third, despite the hegemony of the positivist biomedical paradigm, the women's health movement—integrally tied to the development of second-wave feminism—has had a significant impact on women's health policy, health care institutions, a wide variety of medical practices, and feminist theory, particularly intersectional theory (Lekan, 2009; Morgen, 2002, 2006; Ruzek, 1978; Ruzek & Becker, 1999). Finally, in part because of the drain on the economy and on individual lives brought about by several decades of rising costs, health care in the United States has become the landscape for a bitter and protracted policy struggle intensely engaging corporate, professional, and grassroots activists, including feminists. And while extensive reform legislation was signed into law on

March 23, 2010, the struggle continues to shape its implementation and to reconsider the perceived limitations of that bill (Kaiser Family Foundation, 2010; RWV, 2009, 2010a, 2010b).

To further the impact of feminist scholarship on health policy, feminist scholars and activists must

- sharpen our critique of status quo research and policy, documenting its limitations in addressing the diversity of women's health experiences
- improve our research theory and practice by explicating power relationships, clarifying the strengths and limits of various methods, and specifying the links between research and action for social change
- develop new and solidify existing alliances and principled coalitions for change.

SHARPENING OUR CRITIQUE OF STATUS QUO RESEARCH AND POLICY

Building effective social policy requires that feminist scholars continually monitor and seek to understand the macro-level shifts in social conditions that shape fundamental social inequalities and thus the contexts within which social policy is constructed. In recent years, such processes include globalization and attendant wealth concentration, the global economic crisis, the growth of fundamentalist movements, increased class and race divides between professionals and the working class and poor populations whose lives the professionals shape, in part through the social policy process, and the aging of the U.S. population amid the relative youth of non-Western nations (see Mishel et al., 2009; Mullings, 2005; Ruzek, 2004; Ruzek & Becker, 1999).

All of these trends have evolved over a long period of time; contribute to increased gender, race, class, and national inequality; and will likely persist as fundamental challenges to a just social order for years to come. In this context, the need for perspectives on health that recognize the complexities and differences in women's life circumstances becomes even more apparent (Hankivsky et al., 2010; Hankivsky & Cormier, 2009; Lekan, 2009; Schulz & Mullings, 2006; Zoller, 2005). Yet despite increased public awareness and outcry, concern among

researchers and government funding agencies, and years of funding social science research on health inequalities, there is very little evidence that health disparities across race and ethnicity, class, and gender have abated (Adler & Rehkopf, 2008; Braveman, 2006; Commission on Social Determinants of Health [CSDH], 2008a; IOM, 2009, 2010; U.S. Department of Health and Human Services [USDHHS], 2009). One clear culprit in this failure has been the positivist biomedical paradigm and its hegemony over the research and policy landscape.

Nearly a decade ago, the prestigious Institute of Medicine (IOM) of the National Academies of Science,[3] for example, recognized the failure of existing models and the need for new approaches to public health and health disparities. In *The Future of the Public's Health in the Twenty-First Century* (2002), the IOM pointed to the dominance of the biomedical paradigm as a *cause* of the gap between U.S. health-related expenditures—then roughly 13% of our gross domestic product, more than any other industrialized nation—and our health status, which lags behind that of many nations:

> The vast majority of health care spending, as much as 95 percent by some estimates, is directed toward medical care and biomedical research. However, there is strong evidence that behavior and environment are responsible for over 70 percent of avoidable mortality and that health care is just one of several determinants of health. (p. 2)

Even though more recent reports from the IOM and the U.S. Department of Health and Human Services (USDHHS) have not restated the biomedical paradigm as *the cause* of the gap, they have reiterated the failure of existing approaches to significantly reduce the disparities and have called for developing new models for addressing health disparities, recognizing health equity as an essential element in health care quality, improving health measurement, identifying data needs, training providers, raising awareness, and forming partnerships to identify and test solutions (Graham & Spengler, 2009; IOM, 2009, 2010; USDHHS, 2009). Furthermore, in a landmark report in 2008, *Closing the Gap in a Generation: Health Equity Through Action on the Social Determinants of*

Health, the World Health Organization (WHO) directly addressed social inequalities as causes of health disparities and their elimination as an "ethical imperative" (CSDH, 2008a, 2008b).

Yet the hegemony of the biomedical paradigm makes it difficult to successfully address the social hierarchies of race, class, gender, sexuality, and nation that produce different health outcomes. The paradigm itself obscures the social bases of health and facilitates the shift of national resources away from the fundamentals of health and toward an over-medicalized, highly technical, and socially unequal health care system that works well for the privileged few (Baum et al., 2009; CSDH, 2008a, 2008b; Hankivsky & Christoffersen, 2008; Inhorn, 2006; Rogers, 2006; Weber & Fore, 2007). Women, especially poor, working-class, immigrant, and racial/ethnic women, remain instead at equal risk with women in many Third World countries in such basic health indicators as infant mortality, human immunodeficiency virus (HIV) infection, cardiovascular disease and stroke, obesity, diabetes, and other chronic diseases (Braveman, 2006; Centers for Disease Control and Prevention [CDC], 2010; CSDH, 2008a, 2008b; Mishel et al., 2009; USDHHS, 2009; Weber & Fore, 2007).

How the biomedical paradigm could be a part of the problem of unequal health in the United States becomes somewhat clearer when we compare the epistemologies, methodologies, and theoretical premises of a feminist intersectional paradigm—which emerged from a social justice impulse—to those of the positivist biomedical paradigm, which views advocacy as antithetical to science. In so doing, we not only sharpen our critique of status quo research paradigms and policy and highlight weaknesses in our own approaches; we also uncover arenas of potential convergence with other alternative paradigms that may catalyze future collaborations and alliances for change.

Feminist Intersectional and Positivist Biomedical Paradigms

Although important variations exist among them, mainstream social science studies of health disparities typically employ standards reflecting the ideals of a positivist biomedical paradigm and share common assumptions, conceptualizations, and methodologies. Below, we summarize key differences in positivist biomedical (PB) and feminist intersectional (FI) approaches to the study of health disparities across race, class, gender, and other dimensions of inequality (RCG).

Motivation	PB—Knowledge accumulation
	FI—Social justice
Researcher stance	PB—Affective neutrality; researcher "expert" controls research
	FI—Engaged subjectivity, reflexivity; researcher collaborates with researched
Methodology	PB—Emphasizes measurement, quantification; individuals as units; surveys and randomized controlled trials
	FI—Emphasizes holistic representation of meaning in individual lives and institutional arrangements in social context; multimethod
Inequality measures	PB—Resource differences among individuals (e.g., levels of education, income)
	FI—Power relations of dominance and subordination between groups at macro- and micro levels
Goal of analysis	PB—Separate independent effects of RCG on health outcomes; identify more proximate causes (e.g., stress, health behaviors) between social inequality and health
	FI—Explicate interconnected nature of RCG at macro-systemic and micro-individual levels
Change strategies	PB—Interventions designed to change proximate causes
	FI—Interventions designed to change broad systems of RCG, including those outside health (e.g., economy, jobs, education, law) that shape health (for a more complete comparison of these paradigms, see Weber, 2006; Weber & Parra-Medina, 2003).

The strengths of a feminist intersectional approach to understanding and developing effective policies to challenge health disparities rest precisely in the ways this approach contrasts with the dominant biomedical paradigm. Sandra Morgen (2006) demonstrated the strengths of an intersectional paradigm for addressing health disparities by contrasting two reports on the issue: an IOM report, *Unequal Treatment: Confronting Racial and Ethnic Disparities in Health Care* (Smedley, Stith, & Nelson, 2003), published by the National Academy of Sciences, and a publication prepared for the National Colloquium on Black Women's Health (NCBWH), an event and publication cosponsored by the National Black Women's Health Project (NBWHP), the Congressional Black Caucus Health Brain Trust, and the U.S. Senate Black Legislative Staff Caucus ((NBWHP, 2003). The IOM report clearly approaches the question of health disparities from the positivist biomedical framework while the Colloquium on Black Women's Health takes a feminist intersectional approach.

Directly comparing the two approaches, Morgen (2006) shows clearly the limitations of the IOM report as a guide for research to address health disparities. She notes three critical problems with the positivist biomedical paradigm in the IOM report, each of which distinguishes it from an intersectional approach:

> (1) the extraction of race/ethnicity from the complex matrix of power relations that characterize and shape inequality in the United States; (2) the reduction of structural/systemic inequalities to individual-level problems of bias, stereotyping, and discriminatory behavior; and (3) framing issues in a putatively objective, scientific manner that also tends to mute the urgency and mask the human costs of injustice. (p. 408)

In contrast, the NCBWH focused on the intersectional character of black women's health and on the macro-structural conditions of racism, sexism, and classism and promoted an activist goal of eliminating inequalities in health care and the health status of multiply oppressed groups. In so doing, the NCBWH was able to identify such key factors in black women's health as the historical convergence of a variety of social policies—eugenics, family planning, welfare "reform," different opportunities for access to health care coverage—that represent the institutional mechanisms of race, class, gender, and religious inequalities in black women's lives and that directly affect their health. As Morgen (2006) notes, the impact of these policies on health disparities is rarely mentioned in the IOM report because they are deemed to be outside its purview.

Morgen's approach demonstrates that one method for sharpening our critique of status quo research and policy is to engage critically with dominant paradigms—in this case, the positivist biomedical paradigm—by direct comparison with a feminist intersectional approach. Unfortunately, this process has been one that feminist scholars have often eschewed. As Patricia Hill Collins notes (2000b), "Mainstream science operates as such a powerful discourse and set of social practices that, to many, it appears to be invincible" (p. 275). It is so powerful and ubiquitous, in fact, that even many feminist scholars whose work is deeply critical of mainstream science unwittingly contribute to its dominance by simply rejecting science out of hand and refusing to engage in dialogue at all. Postmodernist theories, for example, have become popular in feminist circles in part because by minimizing the importance of science's power over the intellectual landscape, these theories simultaneously avoid addressing the role of power relationships in shaping feminists' own critical knowledge (Collins, 2000b). In the end, while comfortably isolating postmodernist scholars from critical self-reflection on the role of class, race, sexuality, gender, and national power in shaping their own theories and research, these approaches do little to challenge science for its biases. As Collins's reflection on science and postmodernist feminism implies, one benefit of engaging with the dominant science paradigm is that doing so suggests avenues for strengthening feminist scholarship and practice by highlighting its weaknesses and, for example, demanding greater clarity in definitions of constructs, in theories of social change, and in delineating the limits of its applicability.

Improving Feminist Intersectional Scholarship

Two avenues seem particularly important for moving feminist intersectional scholarship into the foreground of health disparities research and policy:

- Explicating power relationships and the mechanisms of oppression
- Improving research methods and practices

Explicating Power Relationships and the Mechanisms of Oppression

Incorporating an explicit analysis of race, class, and gender as power relationships into the larger domain of health disparities scholarship is at once perhaps the most challenging and the most important contribution that intersectional and other critical scholarships can make to health research and policy (see Dill & Zambrana, 2009; Hankivsky et al., 2010; Hofrichter, 2003; Lewis, 2007; Minkler & Wallerstein, 2008). Identifying the linkages between the privilege of some and the disadvantage of others is particularly difficult when both the dominant culture and biomedical science routinely avoid the question of who benefits from particular social arrangements, instead seeing the disadvantaged—their bodies, behaviors, resources, and mental states—as the primary, if not sole, source of evidence for understanding health disparities.

Yet as the complex experiences of movement scholar activists demonstrate, recognizing *that* power relations are a central dynamic in race, class, and gender structures is not the same as demonstrating *how* power relations are co-constructed, maintained, and challenged. And explicating how these systems operate—the *mechanisms* that constitute and connect them—is a critical challenge before feminist and other scholars (Hankivsky & Cormier, 2009; Mullings, 2005; Naples, 2003; Reskin, 2003). Recognizing, for example, the persistence of race- and gender-based workplace discrimination in the presence of formal legal structures prohibiting it, Reskin (2003) argued that scholars need to shift attention away from the *motives* for discrimination and to its *mechanisms*. We

should not ask *why* allocators (people in positions of power) in the workplace produce inequality by making decisions that produce unequal outcomes for women and people of color (i.e., their motives) but instead ask *how* their actions produce inequality—stated otherwise, *what* actions or processes produce the inequalities (i.e., the mechanisms). Conversely, we should also ask what actions produce equitable outcomes (e.g., blind assessments, formalization of reward systems).

Much like the traditional research on workplace discrimination that focused on changing the motives of individual allocators (e.g., through diversity training), research emerging from a biomedical paradigm tends to focus on changing the values, behaviors, cognitions, or even biochemical processes of individuals. Understanding the mechanisms of power relationships enables us to entertain different kinds of interventions by shifting the balance of power away from the biomedical paradigm with its focus on medical care and biomedical research to the social contexts of and prerequisites for health[4]—away from the health of individual bodies to the health of communities.

In recent years, this push to understand and address the social contexts and determinants of health and to focus on community health has gained momentum in more mainstream venues, as typified by the WHO's report of the Commission on Social Determinants of Health (CSDH, 2008a, 2008b). But while recognizing the commission as "an unprecedented global effort to understand the extent and nature of social inequities in health worldwide and what is needed to ameliorate them" (Bates, Hankivsky, & Springer, 2009, p. 1002), intersectional feminist scholars have critiqued the report for its static and unidimensional approach to gender and its intersections, for the absence of men and masculinities and therefore of a complex view of power relations, and for its advocacy of gender mainstreaming policies that have also contributed to inequalities among women (Bates et al., 2009; CSDH, 2008a, 2008b, 2008c).

Feminist intersectional approaches centered in power complicate dichotomous notions of dominance and subordination, oppressor and oppressed, so that we can see diversity within monolithically conceived dominant groups such as "men" and interrogate relations among multiple hierarchies of men as well as of women. In so doing, our analysis and the policies and programs deriving from it can be more complex and effective.

Following are two examples of intersectional analyses and theorizing that complicate traditional understandings of gender and health by exploring multiple dimensions of power relations. The first, by Higgins, Hoffman, and Dworkin (2010), reconsiders power relations among multiple groups of women and men by focusing on *disadvantaged heterosexual men's* vulnerability to HIV as a result of their structural position, biological factors, and gender relations, including sexual relations with HIV-infected women. The second, by Carpenter and Casper (2009), explores *inequalities between women in different nation-states and regions* as they are reinscribed through the dynamic interplay between the powerful forces of U.S.-driven and -funded nongovernmental organizations (NGOs) focused on global women's health and pharmaceutical companies in their push to promote worldwide administration of the vaccine for human papillomavirus (HPV), a sexually transmitted infection, and to link its administration to HIV efforts by the same entities.

Men, Masculinity, and HIV. Research by Higgins et al. (2010) complicates understandings of HIV transmission by focusing not solely on power relations between presumably dominant men and subordinate women but also on men and women in multiple relations of power. The researchers aim to reframe the prevailing public health explanations for women's vulnerability to HIV, which sees women's vulnerability as primarily a function of biological susceptibility to infection and men's sexual power and privilege. These researchers reexamine data about heterosexual men's sexual behaviors, women's sexual agency and behaviors, and prevalence rates among groups in high-epidemic countries (e.g., in South Africa, Kenya, Cameroon) and in high-incidence groups in low-epidemic countries (e.g., U.S. black and Latino men).

Recent evidence of high rates of long-term concurrent sex partners among both women and men and low rates of male circumcision suggests a much greater contribution from women's partnership behaviors to the high HIV prevalence in these generalized epidemics than previously thought. Research on heterosexual couples in these settings now documents that in 30% to 40% of the cases where only one partner is HIV positive, the woman—not the man—is HIV infected. In short, heterosexual men and women are infecting each other at far more similar rates than the women's vulnerability paradigm has suggested (Higgins et al., 2010).

Traditional intervention programs based on the women's vulnerability framework focus solely on women—on relationship empowerment workshops, access to female-initiated prevention methods, and structural policy efforts to increase women's access to education and microfinance opportunities. Men's roles were undertheorized—focusing on sociocultural constructions of masculinity that are associated with men's risk-taking behaviors, pleasure seeking, lack of interest in their own health, and denial or discomfort with homosexuality. And men's contributions to HIV transmission were attributed to adherence to masculine norms or moral failings associated with a presumably unstoppable sex drive. As a consequence, men were viewed as the problem and unchangeable while women were seen as needing help. Prevention programs provided few tools to help men deal with their vulnerability to HIV. And yet many contextual power-driven factors heighten socially disenfranchised men's risk of HIV—residential segregation, unstable housing and homelessness, unemployment, migratory work, and, in the United States especially, high rates of incarceration among men of color.

Higgins et al. (2010) conclude, "The vulnerability paradigm fails to address how masculinity and the intersection of various structural forces (e.g., class, race, and global inequalities) shape heterosexual men's HIV risk" (p. 441). When men's power is problematized as well as women's, more complex analyses of complex problems emerge. Masculinity and men's power shape both men's and women's health, and men can and must be involved in prevention efforts as well. Higgins et al. also note, however, that much more work needs to consider the difficult question of how to embrace men's susceptibility to HIV while simultaneously addressing their gender privileges—the kind of question that an intersectional framework foregrounds.

Women, Nation-States, and the HPV Vaccine. Carpenter and Casper (2009) explore the impact of a new technology, the HPV vaccine, on the emergence and consolidation of NGOs' focus on women's sexuality and reproduction and the ways that the technology builds on, reinforces, and challenges unequal relations across gender, race, class, age, citizenship status, geopolitical zones, and nation-states. The authors trace the efforts of the Alliance for Cervical Cancer Prevention (ACCP), a collaborative of five international public health NGO partners focused on promoting women's health in resource-poor settings—four of which are located in the United States—to introduce the HPV vaccine in these settings.

Ninety-nine percent of cervical cancers and their precursors are linked to HPV, a genital infection. Two U.S.-based drug companies, Merck and GlaxoSmithKline, have developed vaccines, Gardasil and Cervarix, which have been effective in clinical trials and stand to garner billions for the companies in the United States alone—an average treatment course costs $375. Estimates of annual U.S. sales are at $3.2 billion (Allen, 2007). Heavily funded by the Bill and Melinda Gates Foundation, ACCP is collaborating with Big Pharma, Merck and GlaxoSmithKline, to "innovate" the HPV vaccine transnationally, with the promise of preventing 70% of cervical cancers (Carpenter & Casper, 2009).

Deaths from cervical cancer (CC), while largely eliminated by extensive screenings in the United States among privileged populations of women, remain high in less developed nations (constituting 80% to 85% of worldwide cervical cancer deaths) and among racial minorities and women of low socioeconomic status in the United States. The high rates in both cases reflect disadvantaged women's limited access to health care and preventive technologies (WHO, 2006).

Bringing a critical feminist perspective to the global CC effort, Carpenter and Casper (2009) point out that structural inequalities (e.g., political will, adequate health infrastructure, provider training, funding, and the means to identify,

screen, and follow up target populations) already complicate widespread access to screening, the most effective current prevention effort. The vaccine can't improve access to screening—which remains especially critical since the impact of the vaccine, once administered, won't be realized for a decade—and it also can't improve the overall status of the most vulnerable women, which is dependent on so many other factors. Carpenter and Casper further raise the question of the many possible impacts of efforts centered in the West, which are devised without the input of Third World women, who so clearly stand to benefit from Western corporate medicine. The authors also note the ways that the HPV vaccine and the cervical cancer threat have been co-opted by NGOs already focused on HIV/AIDS prevention, a form of "technology transfer" that can also reinscribe varying hierarchical constructions of women and sexuality across nations and regions.

In short, this technology, while an obvious benefit to some, can leave intact the underlying material, ideological, and political structures of inequality that threaten women's health in resource-poor nations and regions. Carpenter and Casper (2009) state:

> Biopolitical strategies and techniques are resource dependent; they are shaped by and in turn sustain social inequities, particularly in the global South. In the absence of widespread social change to improve women's lives, technological efforts that promise a "quick fix" may be of limited value. Technologies designed to improve women's health often reflect the narrow definitions of *"women's health,"* based on assumptions about female sexuality and reproduction that prevail in many settings. For women to truly benefit from public health efforts and new technologies, notions of women's health need to be reconfigured to recognize women as whole people with complex health needs and embodied desires. Yet . . . the HPV vaccine is routinely framed in ways that position women as means to an end. (p. 92)

Conclusions. Ostensibly "progressive" contemporary practices (e.g., introducing the HPV vaccine) may overlay less progressive agendas and have less progressive impacts, including reinforcing inequality among women through traditional gender framings that, for example, see Third World women as "always and already reproductive" and thus viable and homogeneous biopolitical targets (Carpenter & Casper, 2009, p. 95). Because First World/U.S.-based corporations and NGOs direct these technologically driven interventions and because local women's voices in subordinate locales are not motivating, defining, or guiding the health practices or interventions, public health practices intended to decrease cervical cancer or prevent the spread of HIV/AIDS may simultaneously reinforce gender inequality among women in different positions of power as a result of their national or regional, race and ethnic, and social class positions.

The question of the potential deleterious impact of externally driven health interventions echoes a statement by Patricia Hill Collins (2009) about a fundamental tenet of intersectionality:

> Seemingly inclusionary knowledge produced in exclusionary contexts remains suspect, no matter how well intentioned the practitioners might be. (p. xii)

When social inequalities are viewed as power relationships, the ways in which dominant groups benefit from denying others medical access, adequate child care, and so on or from imposing externally driven definitions of health problems and solutions on subordinate groups become a focus of attention. So changes that might alter the balance of power—a living wage; shifts in workplace control; universal, affordable, quality child care; accessible public transportation; safe, affordable housing; equal access to quality education; and universal prevention-focused health care—become the preferred interventions. While the biomedical paradigm may change the lives of those involved in targeted programs, an intersectional approach is more likely to effect the changes needed to significantly reduce health disparities.

Improving Research Methods and Practice

Recent reviews of feminist methodology affirm the now common assumption in feminist

scholarship that no single methodology is uniquely feminist even though qualitative methodologies have heavily dominated feminist research generally and intersectional research specifically (Cole, 2009; Fonow & Cook, 2005; Hankivsky, 2011; Maynes, Pierce, & Laslett, 2008; Naples, 2003; Stewart & Cole, 2007; Weber & Parra-Medina, 2003). Furthermore, both the intersectional and interdisciplinary thrusts of feminist research have spawned new methods such as intertexuality (Fonow & Cook, 2005), intercategorical complexity (McCall, 2005), and strategic singularity (Luft, 2009) and encouraged the use of multiple methods for critically analyzing systems of inequality.

As a result, today's methodological challenges lie not in making a simple choice between qualitative and quantitative approaches but in selecting a variety of methods from among the many at our disposal—many of which blur the distinction between quantitative and qualitative research. Yet our selections of methods are complicated by the very power dynamics and value conflicts that shape the broader terrain of knowledge production (Maynes et al., 2008).

In *Feminism and Method: Ethnography, Discourse Analysis, and Activist Research,* for example, Nancy Naples (2003) complicates the rather straightforward and seemingly uncomplicated argument in most social science methods texts that research methods should be chosen that are appropriate for the research questions asked. While not disagreeing with that statement, Naples (2003) points out:

> The methods we choose are not free of epistemological assumptions and taken-for-granted understandings of what counts as data, how the researcher should relate to the subjects of research, and what are the appropriate products of a research study. Furthermore, seldom do the authors of traditional methods books acknowledge that the questions researchers ask are inevitably tied to particular epistemological understandings of how knowledge is generated. (p. 5)

When social activism and social policy are the goals, researchers value strategies such as dialogue and consciousness raising that are designed to minimize the inequities in the knowledge production process and to enable a critical assessment of the ways that dominant discourses infuse our own understandings of what counts as data and whose voices are privileged in our ethnographic accounts (Maynes et al., 2008; Naples, 2003). Egalitarian research practices are increasingly common in public health research. Community-based participatory action research (CBPAR), for example, received greater legitimation in health disparities research in 2005 when the National Institutes of Health's (NIH's) National Center for Minority Health and Health Disparities (NCMHHD) established its Office of Community-Based Participatory Research and Outreach. Having the NCMHHD itself raised to institute status within NIH as a part of the Patient Protection and Affordable Care Act of 2010 will significantly improve its ability to direct and to fund research endeavors primarily centered in health disparities. Furthermore, as a complement to the micro-focus of CBPAR, many public health and feminist scholars now call for research that is multilevel and multisite, even engaging communities and scholars transnationally (e.g., to trace the impact of globalization on women workers) (Barndt, 2002; Fonow & Cook, 2005; Kazanjian & Hankivsky, 2008; ORWH, 2008).

Feminist activist research that employs multiple methods inevitably invites tough questions about the limits and uses of particular methods, and these limits must be examined in light of the power inequities in the structure of dominant knowledge producing institutions (Fonow & Cook, 2005). Blee (2004) argues, for example, that rethinking the relationship between qualitative and quantitative research is in order. She notes that the traditional view of qualitative research—that it is an appropriate prelude wherein hypotheses are developed and relationships examined on a small scale that can actually be tested with quantitative research—places qualitative research in the role of a "maidservant" to the more powerful quantitative master. But beyond this traditional role, qualitative research can also be used to interrogate more fully systematic empirical relationships revealed in quantitative studies. And this use of qualitative research was what Reskin (2003) concluded is necessary to uncover the mechanisms of discrimination. Specifically, she argued that *seeing patterns* of

discrimination requires research at the firm and organizational levels but that *revealing the mechanisms at work* requires qualitative and ethnographic research. Reskin's call was affirmed by a National Science Foundation report on the scientific foundations of qualitative research (Ragin, Nagel, & White, 2004) and by IOM and NIH reports (Hankivsky, 2011; Smedley & Syme, 2000; NIH, 2001; Smedley et al., 2003).

Awareness of the relative power attached to the use of qualitative and quantitative methods is especially critical for feminist policy studies in the United States because traditional, narrowly construed "scientific" research designs remain highly valued in U.S. policy arenas. Many other countries rely more on qualitative and consensus studies in setting their public policy agendas and enacting corresponding legislation (Fonow & Cook, 2005; Maynes et al., 2008).

The power imbalance between qualitative and quantitative research is one that feminist scholars must continue to challenge directly by critically assessing the strengths and weaknesses of both dominant and feminist research approaches and by asking how we can use multiple methods together effectively without privileging one method and thus one set of research questions (Hankivsky & Cormier, 2009; Hankivsky, 2011). Biomedical health research, for example, can become so fixed on measurement and quantification that it impedes actions to eliminate hierarchies of health—actions that themselves can lead to a better understanding of these hierarchies. In contrast, intersectional scholarship's heavy reliance on qualitative methodologies has too often focused primarily on revealing the meaning, mechanisms, and experience of social inequalities without documenting or assessing the efficacy of different approaches to social change (DeVault, 1999).

As more scholars have employed an intersectional framework in their health research, the very practical questions of how to resolve these dilemmas in the context of particular research projects are increasingly being raised and engaged. Hancock (2007) contends that "one area of research that remains underexplored within intersectionality is the development of research designs and methods that can capture effectively all the tenets of intersectionality theory" (p. 79). Hankivsky et al. (2010) suggest five reasons why translating intersectionality theory into methodological practice in health research is not easy—either for critical feminist intersectional scholars or for those operating from more traditional frameworks:

- a disconnect between intersectional scholarship and mainstream conceptualizations of research questions and designs
- a lack of certainty about how, when, and where intersectional frameworks can be applied—in part fueled by researchers' own blind spots about ways of (re)framing their research in light of multiple intersecting inequalities
- the particular difficulty of applying intersectionality to quantitative research designs
- the difficulty of determining which systems of inequality and intersections are relevant in any given project and which may be most salient
- a lack of pertinent health information on multiple groups.

Hankivsky et al. (2010) call for more explicit attention to how intersectionality can inform research design, evidence production, and knowledge translation as well as how researchers can engage in "reflexive, critical, and accountable feminist inquiry" (Davis, 2008, p. 79).

Addressing the value of intersectionality to research in psychology, Elizabeth Cole (2009) cautions that researchers employing quantitative methods must do more than merely include interactions of race and gender in statistical models but instead must reconsider the ways that race, gender, and other social categories are deployed and given meaning in particular contexts. She contends that intersectional analyses must take seriously the cultural and political history of groups and the ways these socially constructed categories not only take meaning in light of each other but also jointly produce outcomes. She suggests three questions for researchers to ask about the social categories of difference they examine:

- Focusing attention on the diversity within categories—Who is included in the category?
- Drawing attention to the roles of power and privilege in all aspects of social life—What role does inequality play?
- Looking for commonalities in groups viewed as different—Where are there similarities?

To strengthen research practice, we need to explicate our theories of change, our epistemological assumptions, their connections with various methods, and our assessments of change. Transnational, multilevel, multisite, participatory action research can be a solid foundation for developing and implementing policies and practices that promote social justice. Effective research that challenges the hegemony of traditional approaches, especially in the policy arena, also requires that we develop and sustain coalitions with others working for justice from multiple perspectives.

DEVELOPING ALLIANCES AND PRINCIPLED COALITIONS FOR CHANGE

The social movements of the civil rights era have demonstrated the possibility of both change for justice and the long-range difficulty of sustaining and building on that change (see Morgen, 2002, 2006; Mullings, 2005; Naples, 2003). One clear message that has emerged from intersectional scholars' understandings of this history and their involvement in activist scholarship is that effective scholarship and policy for the future—in health and other arenas—will depend on our ability to develop strong, principled alliances and coalitions (Collins, 2000a; Morgen, 2002, 2006; Ruzek, 2004; Schulz & Mullings, 2006; Weber, 2006).

If we hope to develop a more equitable and engaged scholarship and practice to eliminate health disparities, we must promote a more inclusive intellectual landscape to support dialogue and collaboration across intersectional, critical public health, and biomedically derived paradigms.

These coalitions will involve scholars with a justice agenda who may be working from different disciplinary approaches as well as community-based organizations whose engagement we need to sharpen our critique of the status quo, to improve our own scholarship, and to identify paths to effective activism and change (Baum et al., 2009; Graham & Spengler, 2009; Hankivsky & Cormier, 2009; Hankivsky et al., 2010; Lewis, 2007; Rogers, 2006).

The call for alliances is, in fact, so widespread that the critical question today is not *should* we develop alliances for change but *how* do we go about bridging our differences to effectively promote change that furthers social justice? What are the processes we should engage? With whom is it most fruitful to engage? And how do we know when those differences are unbridgeable or, if bridged, might impede or divert rather than promote social justice?

In this section, we address three areas that show promise for building and sustaining effective, principled coalitions for social justice.

- Promising areas of convergence in health research
- Methodological advances in bridging disciplinary and social boundaries
- Development of bridging organizations and outlets

Promising Areas of Convergence in Health Research

Although different in approach from feminist intersectional approaches, several recent reports of the IOM, CDC, WHO, and NIH call for changes to the traditional biomedical paradigm in health research, policy, and education— changes that converge with key elements of both intersectional and other critical public health paradigms:

- Ecological, systems, social determinants, and fundamental cause approaches to health research, policy, and education that incorporate "upstream" factors such as social contexts and public policies even in sectors beyond health that nonetheless shape it, such as law, economy, education, and media
- Community engaged collaborative research
- Multilevel, multimethod (including qualitative and quantitative methods), interdisciplinary research and intervention (Agency for Healthcare

Research and Quality [AHRQ], 2009; Baum et al., 2009; CSDH, 2008a, 2008b; Graham & Spengler, 2009; IOM, 2003, 2009, 2010; Rashid et al., 2009)

These reports reflect growing recognition among scholars both critical of and immersed within the biomedical paradigm that understanding and reducing or eliminating health disparities require new directions. A review of traditional social psychological research on health disparities, for example, highlights the historical and place-specific contexts of disparities:

> Socioeconomic position and race/ethnicity are constituted within mesolevel environments that give them salience and meaning. By implication, the processes through which they have effects will vary across cultural, geographic, and historical contexts and cannot be neatly separated from them. (Schnittker & McLeod, 2005, pp. 93–94)

And in a more progressive tradition, the WHO's (CSDH, 2008a) report on the social determinants of health calls for a shift away from individual bodies to the environment—in communities and nations across the globe. The report calls for being aware of the role of power in the production of health and for recognizing a range of types of evidence, the gender bias in research processes, and the added value of globally expanded knowledge networks.

To some extent, these calls reflect the impact on dominant health research institutions of feminist and other alternative, justice-oriented public health approaches to health disparities that differ in significant ways from the biomedical paradigm: ecological and systems (Parra-Medina & Fore, 2004; Van Wave, Scitchfield, & Honoré, 2010); technoscience (Carpenter & Casper, 2009; Clarke & Olesen, 1999; Shim, 2002); social capital, social determinants, and fundamental cause (Baum et al., 2009; Phelan & Link, 2005; Phelan, Link, & Tehranifar, 2010; Song & Lin, 2009); community-based participatory research (Minkler & Wallerstein, 2008); and social justice (Braithwaite, 2008; Braveman, 2006; CSDH, 2008a, 2008b; Hofrichter, 2003).

One common theme in these alternative approaches is that they shift the focus of attention away from individual bodies as primary loci of health and from biomedical research as the sole or best way to understand and to improve a nation's health. Instead, they attend to the social production of health and illness; to social equity in access to health care, education, and other determinants of health; and to the power dynamics shaping knowledge production and health promotion institutions.

Yet even when we agree on some of the elements critical to a more robust research process and framework, even when we are clear about the underlying causal factors, the mechanisms producing inequality, and the goals for change—all essential elements in producing effective change—we have not yet arrived. We have only some of the pieces of the process of producing health equity. And, unfortunately, many mainstream and even critical health approaches too often stop here.

Even more progressive and forthright groups, such as WHO, calling for systemic change are not exempt. In the conclusion to its report on social determinants of health, WHO states,

> This is a long term agenda, requiring investment starting now, with major changes in social policies, economic arrangements, and political action. At the centre of this action should be the empowerment of people, communities, and countries that currently do not have their fair share. . . . What is needed now is the *political will* to implement these eminently difficult but feasible changes. (CSDH, 2008a, p. 23)

Yes, political will—but how do we get it? How do we enact those changes we know can work? How do we challenge those fundamental causes? What can we do? These are the questions that cry out for an answer, one that feminist scholars have demonstrated depends on learning how to bridge differences in alliances to achieve health equity.

Methodological Advances in Bridging Disciplinary and Social Boundaries

To build successful partnerships and alliances for change across the unequal power relations that structure research and social life, intersectional and other critical, justice-oriented scholars contend that we need to engage in what is variously labeled "border work," "boundary crossing," "bridging," and "trans-ing" social and disciplinary divides and of doing so by inhabiting "in-between spaces" or "outsider-within locations" (Collins, 2009; Dill, 2002; Dill & Zambrana, 2009; Pryse, 2000; Yuval-Davis, 1997). Many feminist communities, both here and across the globe, have sought to identify ways to bridge race, class, gender, sexuality, and disciplinary boundaries to achieve truly interdisciplinary thought and effective social action. As Ruzek, Clarke, and Olesen (1997) described it, "The challenge is to find new ways to grow beyond our differences while not evading or ignoring them" (p. 83). Identifying and refining strategies for initiating and nurturing these principled coalitions or "multivocal" alliances is one of the most difficult challenges for feminist research.

Israeli feminist Nira Yuval-Davis, for example, calls for "transversal politics" as a method for bridging these barriers. In transversal politics, participants bring with them the ROOTING in their own social location and identity and at the same time try to SHIFT in order to put themselves in a situation of exchange with others who have different social locations and identities. By focusing the process of *shifting* to understand and incorporate the views of others in a *rootedness* born of a critical self-awareness of our race, gender, class, nation, discipline, and other sources of identity and by employing the "shifting" skills that intersectional scholars develop as they seek to work across disciplinary boundaries, we have the potential to develop what Collins (2000a) calls principled coalitions. Such coalitions are based not on the exploitation of power differentials but on self-awareness, self-respect, and a genuine appreciation of others (Hankivsky et al., 2010; Hankivsky & Cormier, 2009).

Ester Shapiro (2005), for example, describes the rooting and shifting skills that enable U.S. Latina immigrants working in health promotion to make distinctive contributions to transnational and transversal approaches to feminist activism through their ongoing associations with global Third World feminisms. As the coordinating editor of *Nuestros Cuerpos, Nuestras Vidas* (*NCNV*), the Spanish cultural adaptation of *Our Bodies, Ourselves,* the now-classic women's health resource book, Shapiro demonstrates how including U.S. Latina perspectives helped to revision the text's relationship to transnational feminist movements (Boston Women's Health Book Collective, 1998, 2000).

By conducting interviews with feminist activists engaged in coalition building, psychologist Elizabeth Cole (2008) identified two themes characterizing their narratives that are key elements in social change processes: the challenge of defining similarity in order to draw members of diverse groups together—to find common ground—and the need to directly address power differentials—to maintain a working alliance. Because all alliance building requires a delicate balancing act—between finding common interests while maintaining a sensitivity to the limits of those interests—the activists' narratives questioned the assumption that "natural" affinity groups exist.

Rachel Luft and Jane Ward (2009) employ their experiences in academia and as researchers and organizers in feminist, queer, racial, and economic justice movements to identify four general challenges to intersectional practice, defined as an activity aimed at intersectional, sustainable social justice outcomes. They argue that each of these challenges emanates from various ways of misidentifying the concept of intersectionality—as solely feminist, ignoring its racial roots and tensions; as diversity or diversity management, without challenging the institutions within which they are embedded; as multiple jeopardy or several simultaneous oppressions, not a more fluid, mutually constitutive process; and as solely focused on the vulnerable and oppressed, not on the systems of power relations between the privileged and oppressed. Thus, intersectionality is challenged on these fronts:

- Appropriation—using the term as a shorthand for difference, power, or justice, unconnected to intersectional practice aimed at social transformation
- Institutionalization—especially in corporate and nonprofit service organizations, showing appreciation for diversity and teaching tolerance while not challenging white middle-class

norms and underlying systems of structured inequality

- Reification—using the intersecting metaphor to the point that it obscures the processes of change and the shifting nature of these inequalities
- Operationalization—operationalizing intersectionality in the context of social movements without compromising facets of identity, reproducing oppressive patterns, or sabotaging long-term movement goals. Can short-term singularity of focus (e.g., on gender or racial justice alone), for example, be a viable basis for broader, enduring movement alliances?

Addressing each of these challenges is critical to enacting intersectionality in ways that remain true to its roots in the racial and gender justice movements and to the unique angle of vision on power and oppression provided by groups, such as women of color, who live at the intersection of multiple hierarchies of oppression.

In all of the research addressing ways of bridging disciplinary and social boundaries, scholars conclude that creating and maintaining an inclusive vision is necessary to achieve far-reaching social change. Cole (2008) describes the process succinctly:

> For such a broad agenda to be effective, we must struggle to recognize social categories as specific, historically based, contextualized, intersecting and constructed through power while simultaneously remembering that our common heritage is that we share the experience of life within this web of intersections. (p. 451)

Continued work to improve existing methods and to develop new methods for bridging the researcher-researched, race, class, gender, nation, and disciplinary divides is key to increasing the effectiveness of our activism and the impact of feminist scholarship on public policy.

Development of Bridging Organizations and Outlets

Today, many feminist policy and other activist organizations and communication and publication outlets are working to support and to promote alliances and coalitions that seek social justice.

The National Council for Research on Women, a member organization of more than 3,000 individuals and organizations and 120 research, policy, and advocacy centers, focuses on advocacy for women and girls. The Institute for Women's Policy Research conducts research, publishes policy reports, and organizes scholar–activist–policy maker meetings to promote understanding and collaborations to advance progressive social change. *Women, Politics and Policy,* coedited by Heidi Hartman and Carol Hardy-Fanta, is a scholarly journal that highlights policy developments in Europe, Latin America, and the United States around a variety of issues, including citizenship, elections, social capital, human rights, and women's roles in policy implementation.

In the women's health arena, both long-standing grassroots organizations and more recently developed professional health equity organizations populate the policy landscape. The Boston Women's Health Book Collective, Federation of Feminist Women's Health Centers, Avery Institute for Social Change, DES Action, Incite! Women of Color Against Violence, National Women's Health Network, National Black Women's Health Project, National Latina Health Organization, National Asian Women's Health Organization, and Native American Women's Health Education Resource Center are just some of the many grassroots women's health advocacy groups whose work has shaped women's health and public policy.

Women's health organizations were better organized than ever to collaborate in the national health care reform process that culminated in the Patient Protection and Affordable Care Act of 2010. One particularly expansive and effective feminist alliance is Raising Women's Voices (RWV), a national initiative striving to bring women's voices to the fore of the health care policy-making process. Founded by the Avery Institute for Social Change, the National Women's Health Network, and the MergerWatch Project, RWV put forth in 2008 a vision of what we must do to attain inclusive, feminist health care reform:

- provide affordable and available health care coverage
- develop acute, preventative, chronic, and supportive health care services

- eliminate health disparities based on race, ethnicity, gender, class, immigration status, disability, or sexuality through research, policy, and culturally competent services
- develop a transparent and user-friendly health care system
- provide the highest attainable health standard for women, families, and communities through a holistic, comprehensive approach that includes considering community as well as individual health. (AISC, 2008)

RWV (2009) is well organized with

- an advisory board representing 28 diverse feminist organizations, including, for example, the National Asian Pacific American Women's Forum and Black Women for Reproductive Justice
- 22 regional coordinators
- many partners, including the Feminist Majority Foundation, the CommonWealth Fund, Planned Parenthood, and the National Women's Law Center.

Comprising feminist researchers, advocates, health providers, and a variety of organizations, RWV organizes and disseminates information to stakeholders involved in health care reform. It informs the public by highlighting areas of concern in reform and its implementation—budget cuts threatening the new Public Health and Prevention Funds, coverage of abortions, contraception, and preventive health care—and describes actions that individuals and groups can take to affect public policy. It publishes comprehensive review papers that are written in an accessible and yet not simplistic manner, and through regional coordinators, it also arranges for public presentations and community meetings (RWV, 2009, 2010a, 2010b).

RWV's efforts were clearly important in helping to shape the legislation that ultimately included improved women's health services, Medicaid coverage for 16 million more people, extension until age 26 of health coverage for adult children on parents' insurance plans, eliminating gender rating (charging women more than men for the same policy), eliminating the possibility of denied coverage for preexisting conditions or lifetime limits on coverage, increased access to affordable health insurance, increased availability of screening and preventive services, expansion of community health centers, and increased funding for health disparities research (Kaiser Family Foundation, 2010; RWV, 2010b; Uttley et al., 2010).

At the same time, feminist aims were thwarted and even regressed in important areas: failure of a single-payer system or for a public insurance option to compete with for-profit insurance companies, increased restrictions on abortion coverage, denial of health care coverage for undocumented immigrants, and inclusion of a "conscience clause" that protects health providers or payers who oppose abortion but not those who provide this legal health service (RWV, 2010a; Uttley et al., 2010). But despite the lack of national attention to the issue of health reform since the passage of health care reform, these activist groups along with many others continue in their efforts to improve the health policy terrain for diverse groups of women, as well as their families and children (see RWV, 2009).

CONCLUSION

Feminist intersectional scholars must continue to develop our intellectual base and critique of the status quo, our methodological expertise, and our organizational strategies to bridge the divides of race, class, gender, nation, discipline, and organization. Our success in these ventures will determine how effective we can be at placing our work more solidly in the center of health disparities research and policy and in promoting health equity and social justice in the years ahead.

Discussion Questions

1. Why is it important to consider both dominant and grassroots perspectives when addressing health disparities?

2. What are some of the limitations of using a traditional positivist analysis, such as the biomedical paradigm, when exploring health disparities? What details are overlooked?

3. Why is the exploration of power dynamics so important to feminist research? How does a researcher explicate mechanisms of oppression using this power analysis?

4. In what ways does a mixed-method approach that incorporates both qualitative and quantitative analyses improve on single-method approaches?

5. According to Weber, what are the benefits of engaging in multidisciplinary research? What are some of the processes involved in working in a coalition?

6. How have feminist researchers and advocates succeeded in informing health care policy? How have they failed?

Online Resources

National Council for Research on Women (NCRW)

www.ncrw.org

NCRW is a network of 120 leading national and international research, policy, and advocacy centers dedicated to improving the lives of women and girls. NCRW provides "the latest news, analysis and strategies needed to ensure fully informed debates, effective policies and inclusive practices."

Raising Women's Voices for the Health Care We Need

http://www.raisingwomensvoices.net/

This coalition is a collaborative network of feminist scholars dedicated to informing health care reform policy in a way that sufficiently acknowledges and addresses women's health issues.

National Women's Health Network

http://nwhn.org

This website is dedicated to improving the overall health of women by critically analyzing health issues to encourage discussion that informs consumers of health services and affects public policy.

Relevant Journals

Annual Review of Public Health

Critical Public Health

*Feminist Formations (*formerly the *NWSA Journal)*

International Journal for Equity in Health

Social Science & Medicine

Women's Health Issues

NOTES

1. This analogy was inspired by Jean Anyon's (1997, p. 168) statement on fixing inner-city schools.

2. *Health disparities* is the terminology used by the government and medical establishment to refer to differences in the incidence, prevalence, mortality, and burden of diseases and other adverse health conditions that exist among specific population groups in the United States (for an extended discussion, see Braveman, 2006).

3. The IOM, solidly entrenched in the positivist biomedical paradigm, is designed to provide scientific advice for policy development. In its own words, "The Institute provides unbiased, evidence-based, and authoritative information and advice concerning health and science policy to policy-makers, professionals, leaders in every sector of the society, and the public at large" (http://www.iom.edu/about.asp).

4. The World Health Organization, which proposes a much broader definition of health than the biomedical paradigm, defines the prerequisites of health as freedom from the fear of war; equal opportunity for all; satisfaction of basic needs for food, water, and sanitation; education; decent housing; secure work and a useful role in society; and political will and public support (for a detailed discussion, see Downie, Fyfe, & Tannahill, 1990).

REFERENCES

Adler, N., & Rehkopf, D. (2008). U.S. disparities in health: Descriptions, causes, and mechanisms. *Annual Review of Public Health, 29,* 235–252. doi:10.1146/annurev.publhealth.29.020907.090852

Agency for Healthcare Research and Quality (AHRQ). (2009). *National healthcare disparities report.* Rockville, MD: U.S. Department of Health and Human Services. Retrieved May 15, 2010, from http://www.ahrq.gov/qual/nhdr09/nhdr09.pdf

Allen, T. J. (2007). Merck's murky dealings: HPV vaccine lobby backfires. *Corp-Watch.* Retrieved June 17, 2010, from http://www.corpwatch.org/article.php?id=14401

Anyon, J. (1997). *Ghetto schooling: A political economy of urban educational reform.* New York: Teachers College Press, Columbia University.

Avery Institute for Social Change (AISC), MergerWatch Project of Community Catalyst, & National Women's Health Network. (2008). A women's vision for quality, affordable health care for all. In *Raising women's voices for the health care we need.* Retrieved May 24, 2010, from http://www.raisingwomensvoices.net/storage/pdf_files/RWV-Principles-4.07.08.pdf

Barndt, D. (2002). *Tangled routes: Women, work, and globalization on the tomato trail.* Lanham, MD: Rowman & Littlefield.

Bates, L., Hankivsky, O., & Springer, K. (2009). Gender and health inequities: A comment on the Final Report of the WHO Commission on the Social Determinants of Health. *Social Science & Medicine, 69,* 1002–1004. doi:10.1016/j.socscimed.2009.07.021

Baum, F. E., Begin, M., Houweling, A. J., & Taylor, S. (2009). Changes not for the fainthearted: Reorienting health care systems toward health equity through action on the social determinants of health. *American Journal of Public Health, 99*(11), 1967–1974.

Blee, K. M. (2004). Evaluating qualitative research. In C. Ragin, J. Nagel, & P. White (Eds.), *Workshop on scientific foundations of qualitative research* (pp. 55–57). Washington, DC: National Science Foundation.

Boston Women's Health Book Collective. (1998). *Our bodies, ourselves.* New York: Simon & Schuster.

Boston Women's Health Book Collective. (2000). *Nuestros cuerpos, nuestras vidas* [Our bodies, ourselves]. New York: Siete Cuentos Editorial.

Braithwaite, K. (2008) Health is a human right? *American Journal of Public Health, 98*(Suppl. 1), S5–S7.

Braveman, P. (2006). Health disparities and health equity: Concepts and measurement. *Annual Review of Public Health, 2,* 167–194. doi: 10.1146/annurev.publhealth.27.021405.102103

Carpenter, L., & Casper, M. (2009). Global intimacies: Innovating the HPV vaccine for women's health. *Women's Studies Quarterly, 37*(1–2), 80–100.

Centers for Disease Control and Prevention (CDC). (2010). Basic information about health disparities in cancer. *Cancer Prevention and Control.*

Retrieved May 15, 2010, from http://www.cdc. gov/cancer/healthdisparities/basic_info/index.htm

Clarke, A., & Olesen, V. (Eds.). (1999). *Revisioning women, health, and healing: Feminist, cultural, and technoscience perspectives.* New York: Routledge.

Cole, E. (2008). Coalitions as a model for intersectionality: From practice to theory. *Sex Roles, 59*(5–6), 443–453.

Cole, E. (2009). Intersectionality and research in psychology. *American Psychologist, 64*(3), 170–180.

Collins, P. H. (2000a). *Black feminist thought* (2nd ed.). New York: Routledge.

Collins, P. H. (2000b). Moving beyond gender: Intersectionality and scientific knowledge. In M. M. Ferree, J. Lorber, & B. Hess (Eds.), *Revisioning gender* (pp. 261–284). Lanham, MD: Rowman & Littlefield.

Collins, P. H. (2009). Knowledge and transforming institutions. In B. Dill & R. Zimbrana (Eds.), *Emerging intersections: Race, class, and gender in theory, policy, and practice* (pp. vii–xvii). New Brunswick, NJ: Rutgers University Press.

Commission on Social Determinants of Health (CSDH). (2008a). *Closing the gap in a generation: Health equity through action on the social determinants of health* (WHO Pub. No. 9789241563703_eng). Geneva, Switzerland: World Health Organization. Retrieved June 28, 2010, from http://whqlib doc.who.int/publications/2008/9789241563703_ eng.pdf

Commission on Social Determinants of Health (CSDH). (2008b). *Final reports and additional documents from the knowledge networks.* Geneva, Switzerland: World Health Organization. Retrieved from http://www.who.int/social_deter minants/knowledge_networks/final_reports/en/ index.html

Commission on Social Determinants of Health (CSDH). (2008c). Gender equity. In *Closing the gap in a generation: Health equity through action on the social determinants of health* (WHO Pub. No. 9789241563703_eng, pp. 145–153). Geneva, Switzerland: World Health Organization. Retrieved June 28, 2010, from http://whqlibdoc.who.int/ publications/2008/9789241563703_eng.pdf

Davis, K. (2008). Intersectionality as a buzzword: A sociology of science perspective on what makes a feminist theory successful. *Feminist Theory, 9*(1), 67–85.

DeVault, M. L. (1999). *Liberating method: Feminism and social research.* Philadelphia: Temple University Press.

Dill, B. T. (2002). *Work at the intersections of race, gender, ethnicity and other dimensions of identity in higher education.* College Park: University of Maryland, Consortium for Research on Race, Gender, and Ethnicity.

Dill, B., & Zambrana, R. (2009). *Emerging intersections: Race, class, and gender in theory, policy, and practice.* New Brunswick, NJ: Rutgers University Press.

Downie, R. S., Fyfe, C., & Tannahill, A. (1990). *Health promotion models and values.* New York: Oxford University Press.

Fonow, M. M., & Cook, J. A. (2005). Feminist methodology: New applications in the academy and public policy. *Signs: A Journal of Women in Culture and Society, 30*(4), 2211–2236.

Graham, G. N., & Spengler, R. E. (2009). Collaborating to end health disparities in our lifetime. *American Journal of Public Health, 99*(11), 1930–1932.

Hancock, A. (2007). When multiplication doesn't equal quick addition: Examining intersectionality as a research paradigm. *Perspectives on Politics, 5*(1), 63–79.

Hankivsky, O. (2011). *Intersectionality health research in Canada.* Vancouver: University of British Columbia Press.

Hankivsky, O., & Christoffersen, A. (2008). Intersectionality and the determinants of health: A Canadian perspective. *Critical Public Health, 18*(3), 271–283.

Hankivsky, O., & Cormier, R. (2009). *Intersectionality: Moving women's health research forward.* Vancouver: Women's Health Research Network.

Hankivsky, O., Reid, C., Cormier, R., Varcoe, C., Clark, N., Benoit, C., et al. (2010). Exploring the promises of intersectionality for advancing women's health research. *International Journal for Equity in Health, 9*(5), 1–15.

Higgins, J., Hoffman, S., & Dworkin, S. (2010). Rethinking gender, heterosexual men, and women's vulnerability to HIV/AIDS. *American Journal of Public Health, 100*(3), 435–445.

Hofrichter, R. (2003). The politics of health inequities: Contested terrain. In R. Hofrichter (Ed.), *Health and social justice: Politics, ideology, and inequity in the distribution of disease* (pp. 1–56). San Francisco: Jossey-Bass.

Hyams, T. S. (2010, May). The hidden women's cancer. *Women's Health Activist Newsletter.* National

Women's Health Network. Retrieved October 10, 2010, from http://nwhn.org/hidden-womens-cancer

Inhorn, M. C. (2006). Defining women's health: A dozen messages from more than 150 ethnographies. *Medical Anthropology Quarterly, 20*(3), 345–378.

Institute of Medicine (IOM). (2002). *The future of the public's health in the 21st century.* Committee on Assuring the Health of the Public in the 21st Century. Washington, DC: National Academy of Sciences.

Institute of Medicine (IOM). (2003). *From neurons to neighborhoods: The science of early childhood development.* Washington, DC: National Academy of Sciences.

Institute of Medicine (IOM). (2009). *Race, ethnicity, and language data: Standardization for health care quality improvement.* Washington, DC: National Academy of Sciences. Retrieved May 15, 2010, from http://www.iom.edu/~/media/Files/Report%20Files/2009/RaceEthnicityData/Race%20Ethnicity%20report%20brief%20FINAL%20for%20web.ashx

Institute of Medicine (IOM). (2010). *Future directions for the national healthcare quality and disparities reports.* Washington, DC: National Academy of Sciences. Retrieved May 15, 2010, from http://www.iom.edu/~/media/Files/Report%20Files/2010/Future-Directions-for-the-National-Healthcare-Quality-and-Disparities-Reports/Future%20Directions%20AHRQ%20Quality%20Disparities%20Reports%202010%20%20Report%20Brief.ashx

Kaiser Family Foundation. (2010). Summary of new health reform law. In *Focus on health reform.* Retrieved June 14, 2010, from http://www.kff.org/healthreform/upload/8061.pdf

Kazanjian, A., & Hankivsky, O. (2008). Reflections on the future of women's health research in a comparative context: Why more than sex and gender matters. *Women's Health Issues, 18*(5), 343–346. doi:10.1016/j.whi.2008.06.002

Lekan, D. (2009). Sojourner syndrome and health disparities in African American women. *Advances in Nursing Science, 32*(4), 307–321.

Lewis, B. (2007). The new global health movement: Rx for the world? *New Literary History, 38*(3), 459–477.

Luft, R. (2009). Intersectionality and the risk of flattening difference: Gender and race logics, and the strategic use of antiracist singularity.

In M. T. Berger & K. Guidroz (Eds.), *The intersectional approach: Transforming the academy through race, class, & gender* (pp. 100–117). Chapel Hill: University of North Carolina Press.

Luft, R. E., & Ward, J. (2009). Toward an intersectionality just out of reach: Confronting challenges to intersectional practice. *Advances in Gender Research: Special Volume: Intersectionality, 13,* 9–37.

Maynes, M. J., Pierce, J. L., & Laslett, B. (2008). *Telling stories: The use of personal narratives in the social sciences and history.* Ithaca, NY: Cornell University Press.

McCall, L. (2005). The complexity of intersectionality. *Signs: Journal of Women in Culture and Society, 30*(3), 1771–1800.

Minkler, M., & Wallerstein, N. (Eds.). (2008). *Community-based participatory research for health* (2nd ed.). San Francisco: Jossey-Bass.

Mishel, L., Bernstein, J., & Shierholz, H. (2009). *The state of working America 2008/2009.* Ithaca, NY: Cornell University Press.

Morgen, S. (2002). *Into our own hands: The women's health movement in the United States 1969–1990.* New Brunswick, NJ: Rutgers University Press.

Morgen, S. (2006). Movement-grounded theory: Gender, race, class, and health. In L. Mullings & A. Schulz (Eds.), *Race, class, gender and health* (pp. 394–423). San Francisco: Jossey-Bass.

Mullings, L. (2005). Interrogating racism: Toward an antiracist anthropology. *Annual Review of Anthropology, 34,* 667–693.

Naples, N. (2003). *Feminism and method: Ethnography, discourse analysis, and activist research.* New York: Taylor & Francis.

National Black Women's Health Project. (2003). *National colloquium on black women's health.* Washington, DC: Congressional Black Caucus Health Brain Trust and U.S. Senate Black Staff Legislative Caucus.

National Institutes of Health (NIH)/Office of Behavioral and Social Science Report. (2001). *Towards higher levels of analysis: Progress and promise in research on social and cultural dimensions of health: Executive summary* (NIH Pub. No. 21-5020). Washington, DC: Author.

Office of Research on Women's Health (ORWH). (2008). *Interdisciplinary research and career development programs in women's health: Initiatives to promote sex and gender research and career development.* Bethesda, MD: Author.

Office of Research on Women's Health (ORWH). (2010). *Moving into the future with new dimensions and strategies: A vision for 2020 for women's health research.* Retrieved October 10, 2010, from http://www.womenspolicy.org/site/DocServer/ORWH_Strategic-Plan_Vol_1_508.pdf?docID=3701

Parra-Medina, D., & Fore, E. (2004). Behavioral studies. In B. M. Beech & M. Goodmand (Eds.), *Race and research* (pp. 101–112). Washington, DC: American Public Health Association.

Pearson, C. (2010). Building on what we can get to get to what we really want. In *National Women's Health Network: A voice for women, a network for change.* Retrieved June 17, 2010, from http://nwhn.org/building-what-we-can-get-get-what-we-really-want

Phelan, J. C., & Link, B. G. (2005). Controlling disease and creating disparities: A fundamental cause perspective. *Journal of Gerontology, Social Sciences, 60B,* 27–33.

Phelan, J. C., Link, B. G., & Tehranifar, P. (2010). Social conditions as fundamental causes of health inequalities: Theory, evidence, and policy implications. *Journal of Health and Social Behavior, 51*(Suppl.), S28–S40.

Pryse, M. (2000). Trans/feminist methodology: Bridges to interdisciplinary thinking. *NWSA Journal, 12*(2), 105–118.

Ragin, C., Nagel, J., & White, P. (Eds.). (2004). *Workshop on scientific foundations of qualitative research.* Washington, DC: National Science Foundation.

Raising Women's Voices (RWV). (2009). *Raising women's voices for the healthcare we need.* Retrieved June 28, 2010, from http://www.raisingwomensvoices.net/

Raising Women's Voices (RWV). (2010a). Health reform and reproductive health: Positive and negative effects. In *Raising women's voices for the health care we need.* Retrieved June 14, 2010, from http://www.raisingwomensvoices.net/storage/RWV%20on%20Health%20Reform%20and%20Reproductive%20HealthFINAL3.30.10.pdf

Raising Women's Voices (RWV). (2010b). What health reform will do for women and families. In *Raising women's voices for the health care we need.* Retrieved June 14, 2010, from http://www.raisingwomensvoices.net/storage/pdf_files/RWVHealth%20reform%20benefits%20for%20women3.21.10.pdf

Rashid, J. R., Spengler, R. F., Wagner, R. M., Melanson, C., Skillen, E. L., Mays, R., et al. (2009). Eliminating health disparities through transdisciplinary research, cross-agency collaboration, and public participation. *American Journal of Public Health, 99*(11), 1955–1961.

Reskin, B. (2003). Presidential address: Including mechanisms in our models of ascriptive inequality. *American Sociological Review, 68*(1), 1–21.

Rogers, W. A. (2006). Feminism and public health ethics. *Journal of Medical Ethics, 32*(6), 351–354.

Ruzek, S. (1978). *The women's health movement.* New York: Praeger.

Ruzek, S. (2004). How might the women's health movement shape national agendas on women and aging? *Women's Health Issues, 14,* 112–114.

Ruzek, S., & Becker, J. (1999). The women's health movement in the U.S: From grassroots activism to professional agendas. *Journal of American Medical Women's Association, 54*(1), 4–8, 40.

Ruzek, S., Clarke, A., & Olesen, V. (1997). What are the dynamics of difference? In S. Ruzek, V. Olesen, & A. Clarke (Eds.), *Women's health: Complexities and differences* (pp. 51–95). Columbus: Ohio State University Press.

Schnittker, J., & McLeod, J. D. (2005). The social psychology of health disparities. *Annual Review of Sociology, 31,* 75–103.

Schulz, A., & Mullings, L. (Eds.). (2006). *Race, class, gender and health.* San Francisco: Jossey-Bass.

Shapiro, E. R. (2005). Because words are not enough: Latina re-visionings of transnational collaborations using health promotion for gender justice and social change. *NWSA Journal, 17*(1), 141–172.

Shim, J. (2002). Understanding the routinised inclusion of race, socioeconomic status and sex in epidemiology: The utility of concepts from technoscience studies. *Sociology of Health and Illness, 24*(2), 129–150.

Smedley, B. D., Stith, A. Y., & Nelson, A. R. (Eds.). (2003). *Unequal treatment: Confronting racial and ethnic disparities in health care.* Washington, DC: National Academy Press.

Smedley, B. D., & Syme, S. L. (Eds.). (2000). *Promoting health: Intervention strategies from social and behavioral research.* Washington, DC: National Academy Press.

Song, L., & Lin, N. (2009). Social capital and health inequality: Evidence from Taiwan. *Journal of Health and Social Behavior, 50*(2), 149–163.

Stewart, A., & Cole, E. (2007). Narratives and numbers: Feminist multiple methods research. In S. Hesse-Biber (Ed.), *Handbook of feminist research* (pp. 327–344). Thousand Oaks, CA: Sage.

U.S. Department of Health and Human Services (USDHHS). (2009). *National healthcare disparities report.* Rockville, MD: Agency for Healthcare Research and Quality. Retrieved May 15, 2010, from http://www.ahrq.gov/qual/nhdr09/nhdr09.pdf

Uttley, L., Avery, B., Allina, A., Pandit, E., & Pearson, C. (2010). Statement in response to the House of Representatives votes in support of the Patient Protection and Affordable Care Act and the Health Care and Education Affordability Reconciliation Act. In *Raising women's voices for the health care we need.* Retrieved May 24, 2010, from http://www.raisingwomensvoices.net/storage/pdf_files/RWV%20Statement.HCR%20Bill%20Passage%203.21.10.pdf

Van Wave, T., Scitchfield, F., & Honoré, P. (2010). Recent advances in public health systems research in the United States. *Annual Review of Public Health, 31,* 283–295. doi:10.1146/annurev.publhealth.012809.103550

Weber, L. (1998). A conceptual framework for understanding race, class, gender, and sexuality. *Psychology of Women Quarterly, 22,* 13–32.

Weber, L. (2006). Reconstructing the landscape of health disparities research: Promoting dialogue and collaboration between the feminist intersectional and positivist biomedical traditions. In L. Mullings & A. Schulz (Eds.), *Race, class, gender and health* (pp. 21–59). San Francisco: Jossey-Bass.

Weber, L. (2010). *Race, class, gender, and sexuality: A conceptual framework.* New York: Oxford University Press.

Weber, L., & Fore, E. (2007). Race, ethnicity, and health: An intersectional framework. In H. Vera & J. Feagin (Eds.), *Handbook of the sociology of racial and ethnic relations* (pp. 191–218). New York: Springer.

Weber, L., & Parra-Medina, D. (2003). Intersectionality and women's health: Charting a path to eliminating health disparities. In V. Demos & M. T. Segal (Eds.), *Advances in gender research: Gender perspectives on health and medicine* (pp. 181–230). Amsterdam: Elsevier.

World Health Organization (WHO). (2006). *Preparing for the introduction of HPV vaccines: Policy and programme guidance for countries.* Geneva, Switzerland: Author. Retrieved June 28, 2010, from http://www.rho.org/files/WHO_HPV_vac_intro_2006.pdf

Yuval-Davis, N. (1997). Women, ethnicity and empowerment: Towards transversal politics. In *Gender and nation* (pp. 116–133). Thousand Oaks, CA: Sage.

Zoller, H. (2005). Women caught in the multi-causal web: A gendered analysis of Healthy People 2010. *Communication Studies, 56*(2), 175–192. doi:10.1080/00089570500078809

21

JOINING THE CONVERSATION

Social Work Contributions to Feminist Research

STÉPHANIE WAHAB, BEN ANDERSON-NATHE,
AND CHRISTINA GRINGERI

Despite engagement with women's issues since the mid-1800s, social work has been notably absent from broader social science conversations about feminist research. We believe that social work has something to offer as well as gain from joining these conversations, and we engage both these topics throughout this chapter. We build on our previous work (Gringeri, Wahab, & Anderson-Nathe, 2010) that mapped the landscape of contemporary feminist social work research to highlight what we believe is some of the exemplary feminist research in our discipline. We discuss praxis as social work's central contribution to broader feminist social science projects, as well as encourage social work colleagues to deepen our engagement with theory so that social work may enhance and trouble its knowledge base, as well as disrupt binaries that all too often frame our theoretical lenses and interventions.

SOCIAL WORK AND FEMINISMS

Social work as a profession and academic discipline in the United States has long centered on women and issues of concern to women (suffrage, reproductive rights, labor rights, equal rights, violence, poverty, etc.). In fact, the social work profession was started by and maintained in large part by women and has been home to several generations of feminists, starting with recognized first-wave feminists, including Jane Addams, Octavia Hill, and Mary Richmond. Numerous scholars (Collins, 1986; Gould, 1987; Nes & Iadicola, 1989; Swigonski, 1994; Van Den Bergh & Cooper, 1986; Wetzel, 1986) have discussed the compatibility between feminist theory and social work, citing common interests such as the importance of diversity, the inherent worth and dignity of all individuals,

Authors' Note: Portions of this chapter have been integrated from Christina E. Gringeri, Stéphanie Wahab, and Ben Anderson-Nathe (2010). "What Makes It Feminist? Mapping the Landscape of Feminist Social Work Research," *Affilia, 25*(4), 390–405.

the value of considering individuals within the context of their environments, and the valuing of process. Also central to both feminisms and social work has been the attention to power (personal and political) and the various ways power, in all its dimensions (interpersonal, intrapersonal, social, political, economic, spiritual, etc.), informs individual and collective experiences. Perhaps the most salient of these similarities, however, is the centrality of social change within social work and feminisms, particularly social change focused on challenging systems and institutions that perpetuate power inequities, privilege, and oppression. Nevertheless, discussions of feminism within social work have remained largely contained by the disciplinary boundaries of the profession; as a group, social work feminists have not engaged with others in the broader social science feminist discourse. Consequently, social work has been late and reluctant to take up the strands of critical and third-wave feminist thought, despite the central role feminisms have played in the social work tradition.

While some have suggested that feminisms' influence on social work practice, teaching, and research has been "almost breathtaking" (Shaw, 1999, p. 114), others have commented that social work lacks an appreciation for and engagement with the complexities of feminisms, calling for a deeper engagement with feminist theories (Orme, 2003; Sands & Nuccio, 1992). Even though social work has engaged with the three feminist waves to different degrees, some have suggested that social work discourse and theory have been more influenced by the liberal, radical, and postmodern feminisms (Freeman, 1990; Nes & Iadicola, 1989) that characterized feminism's second wave than by third-wave feminist discourses of cultural studies, postfeminism, and postcolonial feminist theory (see Baines, 1997; Barnoff & Moffatt, 2007; Orme, 2003; Sands & Nuccio, 1992).

Baines (1997) provides powerful examples of the ways in which some of the pivotal principles of feminist social work theory and practice unintentionally reproduce marginalization and oppression. For example, within the role as a pediatric social worker in an inner-city hospital, Baines noticed that the central feminist social work ideal of "equalizing power in the

intervention," in part through self-disclosure, created greater distance between herself and the clients (mostly poor women and mothers of color). Baines theorized that the practice of self-disclosure, taught as a mechanism to normalize clients' experiences and to demystify the social work practice relationship, is rooted in notions of sameness that do not recognize the role of racism and classism in people's lives.

> Although women of different races and classes may experience similar trauma, the meaning accorded to these experiences differs greatly, depending on the woman's location in the matrix of domination. . . . Rather than normalize a client's experience, self-disclosure may revictimize poor women and women of color by reemphasizing an unattainable, oppressive, hegemonic, White middle-class standard. (p. 306)

Barnoff and Moffatt's (2007) study of an anti-oppression approach in feminist social service agencies in Canada exposes contradictory tensions when feminist members of oppressed communities perceived their particular form of oppression unattended to within an anti-oppression approach. Their research suggests that when complicated analyses of identity, power, and difference are not engaged with, members of oppressed groups may experience anti-oppression approaches to social work practice and organization as replicating "the invisibility they have experienced in the past" (p. 56). Consequently, they recommend being conscious about difference when talking about oppression, rather than assuming that the different forms of oppression (or identity, for that matter) are experienced similarly across or within groups.

At the heart of such tensions lie social workers' relationships with categories, particularly around axes of difference. On one hand, categories help social workers fulfill our mission to interrupt oppression as categories support us to organize with and advocate for marginalized populations. On the other hand, categories can function as stagnant (rather than fluid) labels and consequently promulgate oppression in their superficiality (Sands & Nuccio, 1992).

> If there is no commonly held definition of "woman," how are women's psychological issues, special

needs, and vulnerabilities to be located? If feminist social workers give up their advocacy for special programs adapted to the needs of women (for example, women-centered substance abuse programs), will women clients find themselves in "humanist" programs that are adapted to the needs of men? How can diversity and specificity be preserved simultaneously? (p. 493)

Indeed, our own research associated with mapping the landscape of feminist social work research (Gringeri et al., 2010) certainly supports the notion that social work has been more engaged with second-wave feminisms than with third-wave feminisms, as we discuss below.

The Dominance of Radical Feminism in Social Work: A Case in Point

The social work literature associated with female commercial sex work provides a clear example of the predominance of second-wave feminist theories, specifically radical feminism, and their influence on practice and research. Despite a plethora of feminist positions and theories (liberal, Marxist, radical, black feminist thought, radical sexual pluralist) on sex work or prostitution (the framing typically depends on one's feminist orientation), social work literature and research associated with sex work are overwhelmingly informed by radical feminist constructions of "prostitution" that equate sex work with violence and abuse (S. Bell, 1994; Nagel, 1997; Sloan & Wahab, 2000; Zatz, 1997).

MacKinnon (1987), a leading radical feminist against pornography and sex work, argued that female sexuality is constructed entirely as an object of male desire: "Women's sexuality is, socially, a thing to be stolen, sold, bought, bartered, or exchanged by others. . . . Women never own or possess it" (p. 59). According to MacKinnon and others, it is impossible for women to have agency in and desire for sexual acts. In fact, many anti–sex work radical feminists argue that sex work is inherently oppressive and violent and serves the purpose of asserting male dominance and power over women. Accordingly, sex work institutionalizes women's dependence on men and is therefore inherently exploitative. Proponents of this construction vehemently deny the notion that sex

work is labor and consequently object to (and refuse to use) the term *sex work,* preferring the term *prostitution.* Advocates often use the term *female sexual slavery,* coined by Barry (1979), or a more contemporary term, *trafficking,* to refer to sex work and argue for the abolition of sex work.

On the other end of the feminist sex work theorizing spectrum (the feminist "sex wars" around prostitution are unfortunately highly polarized) are radical sexual pluralist feminists (Califia, 1994; Rubin, 1984), postcolonial feminists (Kempadoo & Doezema, 1998), and advocates in support of sex workers' rights who may or may not identify as feminists (L. Bell, 1987; Nagel, 1997; Jenness, 1990; Pheterson, 1989), who all reject the universal construction of sex worker as victim. These feminists and advocates consider sex work a legitimate form of labor, advocate for the decriminalization of prostitution, suggest that some women choose to engage in sex work and feel empowered by it, and argue that sex workers are political and sexual persons able to make decisions for themselves about how they use their bodies, emotions, and labor. Feminists in support of sex workers' rights reject the notion that female heterosexuality perpetuates male privilege and men's dominance over women (Jenness, 1990). Many sex workers believe that all women are empowered when female sex workers charge men (clients) for what men expect all women to provide for free (Jenness, 1990). This stance, marginalized within many social work circles, conflicts with the radical feminist view that sex work perpetuates men's belief in their right to sexual access to all women (Barry, Bunch, & Castley, 1984; Dworkin, 1987; MacKinnon, 1987).

As evidenced by the policy statement on *Prostituted People, Commercial Sex Workers, and Social Work Practice* by the National Association of Social Workers (NASW; 2009),[1] prostitution is framed as "involuntary or forced sexual activity in exchange for remuneration" (p. 273). Consequently, the statement equates prostitution with exploitation and violence and confounds language of prostitution, sex work, and trafficking (for further discussion about problems with the trafficking discourse, see Capous Desyllas, 2007; Kempadoo, Sanghera, & Pattanaik, 2005; Soderlund, 2005). Guided by this policy statement, social work practices and interventions associated with sex work therefore overwhelmingly favor approaches informed by radical feminist theory (for additional discussion, see Sloan & Wahab, 2000). Unfortunately, the near hegemony of radical feminist approaches to social work with sex workers obscures and denies the rich, complicated, and diverse feminist theorizing associated with commercial sex work. We use this example to underscore the predominance of second-wave feminisms in social work, as well as Orme's (2003) suggestion that social work needs a deeper and more critical engagement with feminist theory.

Social Work Research and Feminisms

Much has been written about the contested relationship between science and politics. As Harding (1991) and numerous others have previously noted, feminism and science are social constructs shaped within political struggles and remain "contested terrains" (p. 298). We agree with Mies (1991) that feminist research must be explored and understood as "part of the historical movement of which it has emerged" (p. 64). Consequently, discussions and critiques of what constitutes feminist research are largely informed by their respective place and point in time, as well as subjectivities that articulate them. It is impossible to address "feminist research" without invoking feminisms and the politics associated with feminisms, as demonstrated throughout this handbook.

> It is important to recognize that knowledge production is continually dynamic—new frames open which give way to others which in turn open again and again. Moreover, knowledges are only partial. Some may find these views discomfiting and see in them a slippery slope of ceaseless constructions with no sure footing to action of whatever sort. It is not that there is no platform for action, reform, transformation or emancipation, but that the platforms are transitory. (Olesen & Clarke, 1999, p. 356)

Many have written about what constitutes feminist research, but few have written about what constitutes feminist social work research.

Writing on feminist social work research and power, Davis (1986, p. 37), quoting Mies (1979), suggested that one of the goals of "female methodology" was to establish a relationship between the researcher and "subject" "characterized by egalitarian involvement" (Mies, 1979, p. 15), where the researcher(s) and study participant(s) are equal partners. The meaning of being equal partners and how that is operationalized in feminist research is central to many contested spaces within feminist scholarship both in and out of social work. Mason (1997), a social worker, also posed the question, "Is there a feminist social work method?" and argued that while feminist researchers tend to agree on feminist principles to be included or addressed in research, disagreements exist about the application of these principles. These principles include "the use of women's experiences as a resource for research, the improvement of women's lives through research, and the reconceptualization of power" (p. 12). As in the broader social science feminist research, recently published feminist social work research further articulates and troubles this reconceptualization of power, as we discuss later.

Issues of shared concern to feminist researchers and social workers (we do not suggest that the two are mutually exclusive) include attention to power, authority, ethics, reflexivity, praxis, and difference. Nevertheless, we must keep in mind that although these features surface across diverse social work feminist projects, they represent contested, dynamic, and often controversial spaces within feminist research as well as social work practice and teaching.

Locating Ourselves

We, the authors, agree with feminist scholars Cummerton (1986), Davis (1986), Swigonski (1993), and Mason (1997) that while there are no uniquely feminist research methods or feminist social work research methods, feminist ideas, principles, and tenets can be brought to the inquiry process to create feminist social work research. In a previous study (Gringeri et al., 2010), which was informed by Olesen's (2005) map of the landscape of feminist qualitative research, we reviewed 50 feminist social work research articles published from 2000 to 2008 to better understand and map the landscape of feminist social work research. Our primary motivation for engaging in such a project emerged as we noticed that social work has been notably absent from broader social science feminist research conversations (Olesen, 2005).

In our review of these articles, we found that by and large, while some contemporary feminist research in social work is critically engaged with feminisms and tensions associated with feminist research (as discussed later on), social work offerings engage a somewhat limited array of feminisms. As a result, much feminist social work research defines feminism as "by, about, and for women." In doing so, these works both accept and reinforce essential and binary gender categories, rather than engage theoretical work such as Butler's (1990), for example, to help conceptualize gender as fluid and performative. Orme (2003) characterizes the social work discipline as generally resistant to theory, thus limiting the theoretical scope and explanatory power of the research. This may be due to social work developing as a practice-centered and pragmatic discipline, and thus the research tends to follow suit by emphasizing professional practice issues; social work researchers more often anchor their work in theories examining the intra- and interpersonal, rather than in broader, socially critical explanations.

In the present work, our aim is to challenge both our discipline and our feminist social science colleagues to see the ways in which both parties benefit from social work's participation in feminist social science conversations. Consequently, we locate our work within the realm of "future directions in feminist theory, research, and pedagogy" (Hesse-Biber, 2007) that engage the politics of difference.

SOCIAL WORK'S CONTRIBUTION: PRAXIS

Given social work's explicit commitment to and engagement in practice (many think of social work as a profession rather than a discipline) with individuals, couples, families, groups, and communities—particularly practice associated with social change, quality of life, and social justice—feminist social work researchers are well poised to engage and contribute to broader feminist social science projects concerned with oppression and liberation. Jane Addams, considered one of the founding mothers of social work, defined social justice–oriented social work at the intersection of our "sympathies" and "trained intelligence."

> Those who believe that Justice is but a poetical longing within us, the enthusiast who thinks it will come in the form of a millennium, those who see it established by the strong arm of a hero, are not those who have comprehended the vast truths of life. The actual Justice must come by trained intelligence, by broadened sympathies toward the individual man or woman who crosses our path; one item added to another is the only method by which to build up a conception lofty enough to be of use in the world. (Addams, 1910/1961, p. 38)

Through our daily engagement in the lives of individuals and communities, we witness, create, and participate in the perpetuation and interruption of oppression and social change. Feminist social work researchers, with our direct connections to (particularly marginalized) people and their lived experiences, and through access to systems designed to "help" those in need, bring a deep grounding in praxis to broader feminist social science conversations about feminist research.

Still, feminist social work researchers do not merely stand to contribute to the broader social science discourse associated with feminist research, but our own field also stands to benefit from its inclusion in such a discourse. Social work has for too long engaged in feminist discussion only within its own disciplinary borders, which may have contributed to the field's reluctance to pick up the threads of third-wave feminist discourse. By engaging and dialoguing with social science feminist researchers, feminist social work researchers will be better positioned to engage with more complicated and sophisticated theories and issues associated with feminist research.

THE RESEARCH PROCESS

Our reflections on the contributions social work can offer the larger feminist research discourse, as well as what our field can gain, emerged from a research project investigating the state of feminist social work research. The project's first phase drew heavily from Olesen's (1994, 2000, 2005) classification of the threads and trends in feminist research outside the social work tradition. On the basis of this classification, we conducted a content analysis of 50 randomly selected feminist research studies published between 2000 and 2008 in 35 high-impact social work and related journals to map the landscape of contemporary social work research (Gringeri et al., 2010). This first phase of the project highlighted exemplary feminist social work research while also drawing attention to areas in which social work, as a discipline, may lag behind other social sciences in engaging the discourse of contemporary critical feminisms. This chapter reflects the second phase of our project, in which we build on the earlier analysis (discussed in more depth below) to discuss and critique feminist social work research from 2000 to 2010 that critically engaged the central threads of third-wave feminist work.

Data Collection and Analysis

To generate a sample of feminist social work studies for both phases of the project, we used the Web of Science to identify high-impact journals read by social workers, even if not explicitly focused on social work. Although they were not listed in the high-impact journals, we also included *Critical Social Work* and *Qualitative Social Work,* due to their likelihood of publishing feminist social work research. In addition, we searched the broader social science literature for feminist research on topics of potential interest to social workers, using keywords *feminism* or *feminist* and *social work,* resulting in the inclusion of social work–related articles from *Signs: Journal of Women in Culture and Society, Family Relations, Feminist Criminology,* and similar publications.

From the journals listed in the Web of Science, we collected citations for all research-based articles containing the keyword *feminist* or *feminism* covering a period from 2000 to early 2010 (through 2008 in the first phase, 2009 to March 2010 in the second). Using these search terms resulted in a sample of articles in which the authors explicitly claimed feminism in some way in their work; the term could appear in the

title, abstract, keywords, text, or references. While this is a starting point for identifying feminist social work and social work–related research, it is not all-inclusive, particularly of those researchers who may be doing feminist work without specifically claiming feminism.

Phase One. In the first phase (mapping the landscape of feminist social work research), the article search generated a total of 84 individual articles, of which 50% were published in *Affilia: Journal of Women and Social Work.* Each article was assigned a number, and using a random number generator, 50 articles were selected for inclusion in the content analysis. Of these, we subsequently removed from the sample five papers that did not present findings from research studies. Using the random number generator, replacements were selected from the original pool.

Informed by Olesen's (2005) map of the landscape of feminist qualitative research, we developed a review template (see Figure 21.1) to organize and analyze salient data from each article in the sample. In addition to collecting identifying information for each paper, we used the template to record the article's purpose, treatment of the gender binary, indication of the study's underlying theoretical frame, research methods, data collection strategies, and the degree to which the paper incorporated the issues in feminist research identified by Olesen (2005): complexities, approaches to research, and enduring issues in research. In keeping with our iterative analytical process, we revised the template several times before arriving at its final form, each refinement reflecting our conversations and insights about the data.

After using the template to review the first 20 articles in the sample, we conducted a preliminary analysis of the findings as one step in the process of refining our instrument. This preliminary analysis revealed that several categories and items on the template were seldom evidenced in the papers comprising this first set. Indeed, it became clear that the social work and social work–related articles we had reviewed did not attend to many of Olesen's (2005) organizing characteristics. Few papers demonstrated, for instance, attention to enduring issues such as reflexivity, validity and trustworthiness, representation, and research ethics in research with

Figure 21.1 Feminist Research Review Template

Citation

Female author(s)   ☐ Yes   ☐ No   ☐ Unknown   Based on: ☐ Name   ☐ Author(s)' self-disclosure

Specific groups

Purpose

Treatment of gender binary (range of poss.)

Theory informed?   ☐ Yes
☐ Unknown/unclear

Complexity *(Note which strand(s) of complexity are addressed in the paper, and offer clarifying notes in the text box)*

☐ Researcher/participant epistemology or roles

☐ Deconstructing traditional concepts

☐ Destabilizing insider/outsider *(researcher membership)*

☐ Sex/sexuality

☐ Other

☐ Unremitting whiteness

☐ Difference *(tensions among sim/diff within and among identities)*
☐ Gender

☐ Oppression/social justice

☐ Other

(Continued)

Figure 21.1 (Continued)

Approaches *(Note which approaches/orientations are evidenced in the paper, and offer clarifying notes in the text box)*

□ Postcolonial feminist thought
  □ Implicit □ Explicit

□ Standpoint theory *(essential & universal meanings)*
  □ Implicit □ Explicit

□ Poststructuralist theory *(soc. constr.: lang = reality)*
  □ Implicit □ Explicit

□ Globalization *(focuses on global economy/markets)*
  □ Implicit □ Explicit

□ Postmodern theory *(social constr. not only language)*
  □ Implicit □ Explicit

□ Other feminist approaches
  □ Implicit □ Explicit

Enduring Issues in Research *(Note which research issues are articulated in the paper, and offer clarifying notes in the text box)*

□ Bias/objectivity

□ Participants' voices/reflexivity

□ Research ethics *(IRB+ – privacy, consent, deception, & "big" ques. of epist, meth, etc)*

□ Making feminist work count

□ Quality/rigor/validity

□ Representation *(partic. voice in context, attention to how voices are presented)*

□ Transforming the academy *(central focus on problematizing the academy)*

□ Other

Strategies/Methods (Note which research methods are reported in the paper, and offer clarifying notes in the text box)

☐ Qualitative, nonspecific

☐ Autoethnography

☐ Phenomenology or narrative inquiry (specify)

☐ Case study

☐ Quantitative

☐ Ethnography or autoethnography (specify)

☐ Performance art

☐ Grounded theory

☐ Participatory action research

☐ Other

Data Collection (Note which data collection strategies are reported in the paper, and offer clarifying notes in the text box)

☐ Interviews (specify structured, semi-, or non-)

☐ Questionnaires

☐ Life history/narrative (journals, diaries, logs)

☐ Film/art

☐ Dialogue

☐ Field research/observations (specify)

☐ Focus groups

☐ Length of time in data collection, if known

sufficient depth to warrant keeping the range of indicators included on the template. Likewise, few articles in the sample engaged postcolonial theories or post-structuralism. While we developed the template as an expansion of Olesen's map of feminist qualitative research and hoped that it would help us articulate the complexity of feminist social work research, this preliminary content analysis revealed that the feminist social work research landscape has not yet developed a critical treatment of feminisms for such a template to be truly beneficial.

Consequently, we revised the template substantially based on its preliminary application. Recognizing that the individual illustrations of Olesen's (2005) components of feminist research were not represented in the papers we reviewed—therefore limiting the utility of the template overall—the broad categories nevertheless remained central to our investigation. Ultimately, we distilled four dominant questions from our content analysis that broadly encapsulated the categories of the original instrument: (1) What makes this paper feminist? (2) How does the paper treat binary (essentialized) thinking? (3) To what degree is the paper clearly grounded in theory? and (4) How does the paper treat its discussion of methodology?

All articles in the sample were analyzed around specific dimensions of each of the four questions. For the first question, these dimensions included how authors made explicit theoretical or methodological claims of feminism(s), as well as whether claims of feminism resurfaced in the methods, findings, or discussions sections of the paper. We used the second question, related to the paper's treatment of binary thought, to evaluate how authors reinforced or troubled essentialized categories such as gender, sexual orientation, religion, race, insider-outsider, and developed-underdeveloped nationhood, among others. To evaluate the paper's attention to the third question, related to a clear grounding in theory, we examined whether and how authors provided explicit theoretical foundations for their research questions or implications. Did authors directly name and articulate the theoretical traditions from which they drew their questions, within which they conducted their methodology, or according to which they structured their findings and implications? Finally, for the fourth

question, papers were evaluated for the ways authors discussed issues identified by Olesen (2005) as central to feminist research, including praxis, ethics, and reflexivity.

The first five papers were read by all three authors, and each subsequent article was reviewed by at least two authors. Direct quotes were also recorded to add context and clarity to the observations we recorded on the template. Each author's completed template, including explicit indications of the paper's treatment of the four questions, was then compared with that of the other reviewer, giving rise to discussion over points of agreement and disagreement in our interpretations. All three authors participated in these conferences, allowing the third author (who had not reviewed the article in question) to offer commentary and seek clarification related to points of concern for each article.

On the basis of these conferences, we developed a thematic summary for each article, articulating how the paper addressed each of the four questions and including central quotes or text blocks from the original paper. This process revealed a continuum of feminist social work and social work–related research across a broad range. One group of papers contained a fairly conventional treatment of gender, feminism, and binary thinking and lacked a clear articulation of theory or attention to Olesen's (2005) enduring issues in feminist research methods. Moving along the continuum, another group of papers demonstrated solid and critical attention to one of the four questions, despite little or no attention to the others; with few exceptions, these papers attended most solidly to the treatment of theory and less frequently highlighted another of our four questions, and thus we classified these as "theory informed." A smaller cluster of papers demonstrated broader and more inclusive feminist research, containing critical responses and attention to all four of our central questions. Papers in this cluster were identified as exemplary, demonstrating the best of contemporary feminist social work research.

Phase Two. The second phase of this project builds on the first phase in two key ways: expanding the date range of the first project to include social work studies through the first quarter of 2010 (resulting in the addition of 27 articles to the original sample) and focusing a deeper analysis on those feminist social work research papers that emerged as exemplars from the combined samples (12 in total), representing the best of feminist social work research from 2000 to 2010.

Using a similar process as the first phase, the second phase of this project generated 27 feminist social work or social work–related articles (this search, however, only used the high-impact journals from the Web of Science plus *Critical Social Work* and *Qualitative Social Work;* non–social work journals, including *Signs: Journal of Women in Culture and Society,* were omitted from the search). All 27 papers were subjected to the analytic process used in the first phase, focusing on how each paper addressed our four central questions. Since this part of the project sought only to feature the contributions feminist social work can bring to the larger feminist social science discourse, those papers that demonstrated conventional treatments of feminism, gender, and binary thinking, as well as those that were "theory informed" but failed to address our other questions, were subjected to no further analysis. Consistent with our findings in the first phase of the project, the majority of research articles fell into these categories, with five exemplars emerging from the expanded sample.

We expanded our preliminary analysis of the five exemplars by assessing not only whether they addressed all four of our questions but also the breadth and depth of how they treated specific features of each of the four questions. These papers were then combined with the seven exemplars that emerged during the first phase of the project, resulting in a total of 12 research articles that demonstrated critical, grounded, and complex treatments of feminism in the social work tradition. Our subsequent thematic analysis focused on identifying commonalities among how authors attended to each question's central features. Taken as a whole, these commonalities not only illustrate the best of what social work has to offer the broader feminist social science discourse but also point to opportunities for feminist discourse and research in our own discipline to deepen as a result of more deliberate integration with the social sciences.

SOCIAL WORK EXEMPLARS

The following discussion articulates how social work exemplars engaged our four questions and uses excerpts and examples from the articles themselves to illustrate how feminist social work researchers attended to issues central to critical feminist theory and methods. Certainly, these questions reflect larger principles with significant overlap among them; it would be naive to treat them as entirely distinct from one another. Despite their potential overlap, the questions offer a useful framework for presenting the features of exemplary social work research. By presenting exemplary critical feminist research from within our own discipline, we hope to make clear the contributions social workers may offer the larger feminist social science discourse.

Claims of "Feminism"

Claims of feminism in social work research address how scholars engage feminist tenets and principles, articulate theory, and attend to issues of power, reflexivity, praxis, and social justice in research. Although constructions of feminism in social work too often rely on the taken-for-granted and essentialized understandings of feminism as being "for women, by women, about women," exemplary scholarship has emerged that attends directly to bringing social work into the critical feminist discourse evident in other disciplines.

Authors' claims to feminisms in their projects were articulated in a variety of ways, such as a deep anchoring in feminist theory, critical focus on women and/or women's issues, critical understanding of gender and/or multiple social identities, or willingness to explore, reflect on, and critique the research process itself from a feminist perspective. All 12 exemplary articles, for example, clearly focused on various aspects of sex/gender, as well as women's issues/lives/ experiences. The substantive topics included mothers' experiences of early childhood violence, teen mothers' intimate relationships, gender and homelessness, gender and disabilities in the Middle East, identity and refugee women, and intimacy and violence. While focusing on these topics alone certainly does not guarantee that the project is feminist, the researchers' critical stance with respect to gender, difference, power, ethics, social identity, and research grounds the more persuasive feminist claims in research.

Articles that explicitly engaged all four questions noticeably made feminist claims in their research methods. For example, Canadian authors McKinnon, Davies, and Rains (2001) framed their work by stating that "feminist theorists and activists have challenged the ideology of the monolithic family and the social construction of motherhood" (p. 80). They acknowledged feminists' priority in "attending to differences among women, mediated by women's experiences of race, class, ethnicity, sexuality, age and ability." Later, they discussed postmodern theory and gender relations, noting that postmodernism moves feminism beyond "essentialist conceptualizations of women" and that it "rejects fixed categories, such as women and men," challenging "feminist assumptions about power, difference, knowledge, gender and subjectivity" (p. 81). Martha Kuwee Kumsa (2002), an Oromo woman born in Ethiopia and located at a Canadian school, explicitly staked feminist claims:

> Some feminists have challenged the notion of autonomous self, claiming relational identity. Others have disputed both autonomous/relational and self/structure binaries. I join them in claiming relational autonomy and expounding the process of identity construction as the interplay between self and social structures. (p. 473)

Andrea Daley (2010) unequivocally linked a critical feminist approach to anti-oppressive social work by addressing context, positionality, and subjectivity via critical reflexivity:

> A critical feminist approach, for example, positions the research process in time, place, culture, and situation and promotes the use of researchers' reflexivity and critical reflection to recognize and respond to power structures and relations in the research process, in general, and the interviewing relationship, in particular. (p. 68)

Daley (2010) explained the link between critical feminism and anti-oppressive social work practice: "Although reflexivity and critical reflection are positioned by feminist researchers as integral to the development of liberatory and transformative research approaches, they are similarly positioned in the social work literature as critical skills in anti-oppressive approaches in social work practice" (p. 69). These authors made feminist claims for their works that go beyond "women's issues" or adding gender as a category of analysis; their work questioned the essentialist categories upon which earlier feminist work is built. Of equal importance, these authors approached feminist research in ways that connect and extend their commitments to professional practice and the values of social work.

Treatment of Binary Thought

How authors treated binaries and dualistic thinking in their research was of much interest given our critical feminist leanings and the tensions within feminist research associated with difference. Based on an understanding of critical feminisms rooted in the commitment to disrupting binary thinking, how exemplary articles treated dualisms was (not surprisingly) closely related to their feminist claims. Examples of how social work exemplars troubled binary thinking included disrupting gender categories and associations between gender and bodies, questioning subject-object relationships, and critiquing commonly held polemic constructions in social work practice such as layperson-expert and perpetrator-victim.

We noted McKinnon et al.'s (2001) critique of gender and masculinities and Kumsa's (2002) challenge of the global-local binary, which gives rise in the work to the term *glocal*. Ristock's (2003) work examined violence in lesbian relationships and acknowledged "affirming real people who live their lives as lesbian, gay, bisexual, transgendered while rejecting the simplistic notion that such labels represent a set of natural categories that accurately describe people and distinguish them from each other" (p. 332). Daley (2010) challenged the dualisms of subject-object and knower-known in research where participants self-identified as lesbian/queer users of a mental health system: "Her question had the effect of shifting me from the subject position of researcher to that of participant (interviewee) while subordinating whatever 'expert' knowledge I considered myself to have as a lesbian-identified social worker" (p. 75). Daley later reflected,

> My awareness of the possibility that women may experience the interview process as reproducing traditional power relations between "patient" and "provider" and the need to adopt strategies to reduce the social distance between women and me was particularly relevant, given that the interview protocol included assessing the women's capacity to give informed consent. I conceptualized the process of assessing capacity to consent as an inherent tension (i.e., repathologizing or further marginalizing the participants) within a research context that sought to "give voice" to and empower women who have traditionally been marginalized within research and knowledge-production processes. . . . I became cognizant of fluid and shifting power relations as I reflexively engaged with the ways in which some women unsettled operations of power during the interview process through "talking back." (p. 75)

Through this critically reflexive process, Daley's troubling of the social work patient-provider binary illustrated how disrupting such dualisms in the research endeavor can open up spaces to see and engage participants as experts, subjects, and directors of the research.

Catlett, Toews, and Walilko (2010) examined the gendered ways men perceived and understood intimate partner violence; however, rather than view men as one half of a dichotomous variable (perpetrator-victim), they problematized gender by focusing on masculinities. In doing so, they acknowledged that males occupy different social positions with widely varying access to privileges. Engaging masculinities allowed the authors to account for within-group diversity; using masculinities as a broad category avoided assumptions about men based on binary constructions. Thus, moving beyond binary thinking allows feminist researchers to observe, listen to, and participate in more complex realities, thus contributing to less reductionist epistemologies that reinscribe marginalization and oppression. Given social work's (and feminist social work research's) commitment to respecting individuals' self-determination,[2] it is imperative that we engage epistemologies that

support us to view people as complex, fluid, and self-determining.

Anchoring in Theory

Given Orme's (2003) claims that social work generally lacks deep and critical engagement with theory, including feminist theories, we studied articles to understand how they engaged theory in their research. Our exemplary papers presented theory not only as a framework but also as a set of guiding principles throughout data analysis and the discussion. In the process of reviewing articles, we looked to see if authors named and discussed theory to help conceptualize their work, the ways in which they applied theory to examine and critique social categories, and whether theory was used to inform findings and discussions. Beck and Britto (2006) used the works of Jaggar (1983) and Gilligan (1982) as a theoretical and practical lens in developing the protocol to interview capital offenders' family members from a restorative justice perspective. Few, Stephens, and Rouse-Arnett (2003) pulled together an eclectic theoretical lens based on black feminist theory, symbolic interactionism, social ecology, and critical science and critical race theory to examine the challenges black women researchers encounter in field research with black women. In these types of articles, theory was not an add-on to the work but an integral and complex scaffolding that organized and integrated the entire piece.

Ristock (2003) used theories from community psychology, feminism, and postmodernism to highlight the limitations of binary thinking relative to interpersonal violence in lesbian relationships. Ristock wrote that the "'victim gets constructed' as 'the one who did not start it' regardless of her subsequent actions or intentions. This then reinforces the dichotomies of victim/perpetrator; passive/active; innocent/evil that underlie gendered discourses of violence and mask complexities" (p. 338). In addition, Ristock questions the ways in which female-male dichotomies "remain unproblematized and homogenize women's experiences." Later, Foucault's notion of "regimes of truth" regarding interpersonal violence is applied to question the ways in which social services "obscure, delegitimize or subjugate certain knowledges or subjects while legitimizing or normalizing others" (p. 338). Ristock used theories to probe the findings in order to understand the ways in which underlying complexities and unquestioned assumptions shaped the services that are delivered to lesbians experiencing relationship violence.

Catlett et al. (2010) grounded their study in feminist-informed gender theory, in which gender is seen as a routine accomplishment that is reinforced by daily interaction, and masculinities and femininities are best understood as gendered projects. They noted that "an exploration of the social construction of multiple masculinities holds the potential to link our understanding of men's creation and maintenance of gendered selves with our understanding of the ways in which gender influences power relations and perpetuates inequalities" (p. 110). The authors used feminist-informed gender theory to open the space wherein gender moves away from a dichotomous variable to a social construct with multiple, overlapping, and interacting meanings and weaved that theoretical understanding through their analysis, discussion, and implications to produce a rich and nuanced construction of the gendered use of power in intimate relationships. This work helps move social workers beyond simplistic notions of males as perpetrators of violence to understand violence as articulations of masculinities, consequently providing a more useful map for considering interventions that target structural and individual change. As we suggest that macro-level interventions for intimate partner violence merit additional attention, we also recognize the significant challenges associated with both creating services for individuals who are survivors of intimate partner violence and simultaneously creating macro-level interventions that perhaps do away with constructions of males as perpetrators and females as victims. One particular challenge that many domestic violence communities across the United States have experienced is associated with re-envisioning and creating shelters for survivors of intimate partner violence that do not discriminate based on gender identity.

Discussion of (Feminist) Methodology

Our fourth evaluative question helped us examine the ways in which authors dealt with notions of feminist research methods. In particular, we looked for authors' articulation of ethical issues beyond institutional review board approval, such as power, voice, authority, and representation; we also looked for attention to praxis and reflexivity. Few et al. (2003) explicitly questioned and critically articulated the researcher-participant relationship by framing the connections between these relationships as knowledge production. They used black feminist thought to critique themselves and their research, pointing out that researchers need to know our locations and the effects of our presence, becoming more aware of the situated researcher-self. They also offered readers five steps to ensure reflexivity. Foster (2007) presented an engaging discussion focused on feminist research in which the insider-outsider researcher relationship is destabilized, examined researcher-participant epistemologies and roles, and dealt with reflexivity and representation. Foster, citing Riessman (1993), offered a useful corrective to qualitative researchers in particular, writing that "we cannot give voice but we do hear voices that we record and interpret. Representational decisions cannot be avoided; they enter at numerous points in the research process, and qualitative analysts including feminists must confront them" (p. 370). Beck and Britto (2006) presented a reflective and transparent self-interrogation of the research protocol they developed and how they implemented that protocol with attention to capital offenders' family members' experiences, voice, and care. They embedded this work in a critical awareness of power, specifically the power endemic in the research relationship, demonstrating a spirit of deep caring and respect for the participants.

Andrea Daley (2010) reflected deeply on the presentation of self-identity in the study about the psychiatric and mental health service experiences of lesbian and queer women, noting, for example, that one participant challenged the use of *lesbian* rather than *queer,* the term preferred by the participant. Daley shifted her work to include the term *queer* as they continued the interview but later reflected,

> Contesting the use of the term lesbian and introducing the term queer suggested a potential difference

between us that was based on sexual identity politics. I responded to the perceived shift in power relations by attempting to narrow the social distance between us through the inclusion of the term *queer* in the remainder of the interview. (p. 72)

Daley (2010) saw social distancing as an outcome of unequal power between researchers and participants and sought to minimize that in the work, while simultaneously reflecting on the inherent tensions:

[These tensions] may be interpreted as the material effect of structural power as represented by the degree to which heteropatriarchal and feminist and consumer/survivor ways of knowing about women, sexuality, and mental disorder inform agencies' and organizations' philosophy, policy, and practices. (p. 78)

Daley (2010) saw that in research, we may reinforce and/or reproduce the power relations of social institutions, particularly those that "serve" marginalized women, and that the challenge and obligation of feminist researchers is to reflect on and analyze those practices with the aim of transforming them into new practices that are empowering for both researchers and participants. In this process, feminist researchers not only hope to transform organizational practices, policies, and philosophies but are also open to personal transformation.

DISCUSSION

Our aim in this project was twofold; we examined exemplary feminist social work research to begin to discuss the ways in which social work as a profession and discipline can participate in feminist social science research discussions and to explore how social work stands to gain from participating in these scholarly conversations. We now discuss the ways in which our findings respond to each of these aims.

We recognize praxis as the central contribution of social work to the feminist social science research discourse. As previously noted, the social work profession has a historical grounding in praxis. Praxis, understood as a constant action and reflection process (Freire, 1973), is defined

by Kieffer (1984) as "the circular relationship of experience and reflection through which actions evoke new understandings, which then provoke new and more effective actions. . . . Involvement generates insight which in turn promotes more knowing participation" (p. 26).

Unlike in other professions or disciplines, praxis in social work is uniquely concerned with the interactive and reflexive relationship between research, theories, practice, and social action. Social work praxis is a spiral in which research and practice contribute to new theories and refine old ones, as well as direct interventions for purposes of social change. Social work's professional code of ethics compels practitioners to ongoing engagement with praxis:

Social workers challenge social injustice. Social workers pursue social change, particularly with and on behalf of vulnerable and oppressed individuals and groups of people. Social workers' social change efforts are focused primarily on issues of poverty, unemployment, discrimination, and other forms of social injustice. These activities seek to promote sensitivity to and knowledge about oppression and cultural and ethnic diversity. Social workers strive to ensure access to needed information, services, and resources; equality of opportunity; and meaningful participation in decision making for all people. (NASW, 1996)

By foregrounding praxis in feminist research and underscoring feminist contributions to social change, social work can contribute information about context and process associated with the lived experiences of those who are often at the center of feminist social science research. Grounding research in lived experiences while considering structural realities can support us to engage research participants and the issues relevant to their lives in complicated terms while engaging them as co-creators of knowledge and partners in social change.

As noted in the above excerpt, our profession articulates an explicit value for and commitment to applying social justice principles for the purpose of social change, which also informs our research. Social workers have a daily proximity to the topics and problems central to feminist research agendas, not only in terms of the problems and issues experienced by women but also in terms of the impacts of gendered structures on women, men, transgendered people, children, families, and communities nationally and internationally. Social workers in the fields of intimate partner violence, sex work, poverty, employment and discrimination, health and mental health, community organizing, and welfare policies and programs daily witness and participate in the ways in which gender, difference, and social identities shape human experiences, potential, conflicts, and resolutions. Grounded in these experiences, feminist social work researchers can strengthen the social justice aspect of feminist research in the social sciences.

The daily proximity social workers have with oppression and privilege positions us well to deconstruct taken-for-granted binary assumptions. We noted above Kumsa's (2002) questioning of the local-global binary, based on her work with Oromo refugee women in Canada. Kumsa's multiple roles as social worker, researcher, and immigrant sharpened the attention to the stories of young refugee women and helped create a space where local-global binaries could be questioned. Other feminist social work researchers questioned binaries with respect to insider-outsider, both in the research process and in cultural contexts; privilege-oppressed; masculinities-femininities; social work's resistance-reinscription of oppression; and subject-object in research (Catlett et al., 2010; Daley, 2010; Hulko, 2009; Zufferey, 2009).

Social work offers a third contribution that stems from its commitment to social justice, social change, and proximity to lived experiences: the ability to strengthen and extend feminist researchers' engagement in participatory action models of social research. As cogs in the wheel of oppressive systems, we (social workers) also seek to change and are positioned—via our complex relationships with individuals, families, communities, organizations, and social structures—to implement and support feminist participatory action research. Consequently, our professional identity and work exist in tension with and can challenge the oppressor–change agent binary in the service of feminist research projects.

In return, we argue here that feminist social science conversations have a great deal to offer social work. Social work needs the impetus and support from other feminist social science scholars to deepen and broaden our engagement with feminist theories, particularly critical feminisms. Participation in such scholarly conversations will challenge us to pay more deliberate attention to theory and thus strengthen the research basis for professional practice. The presence and space created by an explicitly feminist/womanist journal, *Affilia: Journal of Women and Social Work,* is important to acknowledge, as it has allowed feminisms in social work to make the progress noted up to this point. Over the past decade, 12 articles met our review standards of "exemplary" feminist research, and the majority of those articles have been published in *Affilia.* This relatively small number also suggests to us that our discipline's flagship feminist journal has somewhat institutionalized "second-wave" feminisms within social work. Thus, participation in scholarly conversations with other feminist social science researchers could serve as a "call to action" to social work to continue to challenge its engagement with multiple, diverse, and critical feminisms.

This feminist research, informed by critical feminist theories in particular, pulls back the covers so that power dynamics within structural, institutional, political, social, and personal relationships may be exposed, better understood, and ideally transformed in service of social justice and knowledge creation. As Roof (2007) argues, "Feminist research in general believes in the power of critique and inquiry to change materially the structures of culture and the lives of individuals" (p. 426). As feminism itself is a critique of "the ways power and authority are distributed in relation to the gendered structures of patriarchy" (p. 426), feminist researchers are committed to taking the precarious position of disrupting power inequalities while simultaneously engaging in the projection of power through knowledge claims. Ackerly and True (2008), for instance, have suggested that attention to power in feminist research surfaces in several key aspects of inquiry, including (1) attention to the power of knowledge and epistemology; (2) boundaries, marginalization, and silences; (3) relationships and their power relationships; and (4) our situatedness as researchers.

Given this articulation of critical feminist approaches to research outside social work, implications for deepening social work's framing of feminism are significant. First, a critical feminist orientation to social work research brings greater consonance with the values of the social work profession, specifically with regard to the application of a power analysis as one tool for interrupting social injustices and affirming the individual's right to self-determination. Second, by adopting critical feminist discourse more resonant with that evident in the broader social science literature, feminist social work researchers can be better positioned to shed dualistic frames of reference and appreciate the intersectionality operating in the lived experiences of our research participants. Finally, as a field, social work can benefit from joining the social science feminisms discourse in that this discourse offers a number of frameworks for conceptualizing feminist research itself. That is, by participating in the broader conversation of feminist research, social work researchers can further develop and refine strategies for research itself, including frameworks for attending to issues of reflexivity, praxis, and critical focus on ethics in the research process.

CONCLUSION

The nexus of social work and critical feminist research helps academics to promote the centrality of a critical understanding of gender and difference in social work research and practice. Social work has historically relied heavily on binary understandings of gender, difference, and diversity (and "isms" in general) and has based professional practice on those conceptualizations. We call upon feminist social work researchers to join other feminist social science researchers engaged in these dialogues to challenge binary categories and refocus gender-related projects around multifaceted femininities and masculinities, foregrounding work on the intersectionalities of identities. We are not arguing for the elimination of gender, nor do we suggest that it has declined in significance; rather, we suggest that, as researchers, we unpack the construct of gender so we can see and question the many links between gender and other social categories shaping identity. By "being at the table," social work could be challenged to revisit and critique those binary understandings

that limit our research and practice to expand our scholarly agendas as feminists and more deeply and thoughtfully develop our anti-oppressive practices.

Discussion Questions

1. How does social work praxis inform feminist social work research? How can feminist social work research inform and influence social work praxis?

2. In what ways is feminist research consonant with the values of social work associated with the NASW code of ethics?

3. How can social work benefit from third-wave feminisms?

4. How does binary thinking restrict emancipatory social work practice and research?

Online Resources

Southwest Institute for Research on Women (SIROW)

www.sirow.arizona.edu

Housed within the University of Arizona's Women's Studies Department, SIROW conducts action research and offers resources through collaborative relationships with educational, social service, and advocacy organizations across the Southwest.

INCITE! Women of Color Against Violence

http://www.incite-national.org/

This radical feminist organization focuses on advocacy and activism to address violence and related issues of concern for women of color. Its community forum, blog, and other resources call attention to points of intersection between critical feminisms and features of social work practice emphasizing social justice.

The State of Feminist Social Work

http://www.amazon.com/State-Feminist-Social-Work/dp/0415328438

White's (2006) book lays out a critical analysis of feminisms within social work, including explorations of feminist social work identity, critiques of egalitarian relationships and empowerment, issues of identity and stance within social work, and more.

Relevant Journals

Affilia

Critical Social Work

Journal of Progressive Human Services

Qualitative Inquiry

Qualitative Social Work

Notes

1. Previously titled *Commercial Sex Workers and Social Work Practice* (NASW, 2006) before being overturned (as a policy statement) and rewritten by anti–sex work radical feminist social workers.

2. "Social workers respect and promote the right of clients to self-determination and assist clients in their efforts to identify and clarify their goals. Social workers may limit clients' right to self-determination when, in the social workers' professional judgment, clients' actions or potential actions pose a serious, foreseeable, and imminent risk to themselves or others" (NASW, 1996, Code of Ethics, 1.02).

References

Ackerly, B., & True, J. (2008). Reflexivity in practice: Power and ethics in feminist research on international relations. *International Studies Review, 10*(4), 693–707.

Addams, J. (1961). *Twenty years of Hull House.* New York: New American Library. (Original work published 1910)

Baines, D. (1997). Feminist social work in the inner city: The challenges of race, class and gender. *Affilia, 12*(3), 297–317.

Barnoff, L., & Moffatt, K. (2007). Contradictory tensions in anti-oppression practice in feminist social services. *Affilia, 22*(1), 56–70.

Barry, K. (1979). *Female sexual slavery.* Englewood Cliffs, NJ: Prentice Hall.

Barry, K., Bunch, C., & Castley, S. (Eds.). (1984). *International feminism: Networking against female sexual slavery.* New York: International Women's Tribune Centre.

Beck, E., & Britto, S. (2006). Using feminist methods and restorative justice to interview capital offenders' family members. *Affilia, 21,* 59–70.

Bell, L. (Ed.). (1987). *Good girls, bad girls.* Seattle, WA: Seal.

Bell, S. (1994). *Reading, writing and rewriting the prostitute body.* Bloomington: Indiana University Press.

Butler, J. (1990). *Gender trouble: Feminism and the subversion of identity.* New York: Routledge.

Califia, P. (1994). *Public sex: The culture of radical sex.* Pittsburgh: Cleis Press.

Capous Desyllas, M. (2007). A critique of the global trafficking discourse and global policy. *Journal of Sociology & Social Welfare, 34*(4), 57–79.

Catlett, B., Toews, M. L., & Walilko, V. (2010). Men's gendered constructions of intimate partner violence as predictors of court-mandated batterer treatment drop out. *American Journal of Community Psychology, 45*(1–2), 107–123.

Collins, B. G. (1986). Defining feminist social work. *Social Work, 31,* 214–219.

Cummerton, J. M. (1986). A feminist perspective on research: What does it help us see? In N. Van Den Bergh & L. B. Cooper (Eds.), *Feminist visions for social work* (pp. 80–100). Silver Spring, MD: National Association of Social Workers.

Daley, A. (2010). Reflections on reflexivity and critical reflection as critical research practices. *Affilia, 25*(1), 68–82.

Davis, L. V. (1986). A feminist approach to social work research. *Affilia, 1*(1), 32–46.

Dworkin, A. (1987). *Intercourse.* New York: Free Press.

Few, A. L., Stephens, D. P., & Rouse-Arnett, M. (2003). Sister-to-sister talk: Transcending boundaries and challenges in qualitative research with black women. *Family Relations, 52,* 205–216.

Foster, V. (2007). "Ways of knowing and showing": Imagination and representation in feminist participatory social research. *Journal of Social Work Practice, 21,* 361–376.

Freeman, M. (1990). Beyond women's issues: Feminism and social work. *Affilia, 5,* 72–89.

Freire, P. (1973). *Education for critical consciousness.* New York: Seabury Press.

Gilligan, C. (1982). *In a different voice: Psychological theory and women's development.* Cambridge, MA: Harvard University Press.

Gould, K. H. (1987). Feminist principles and minority concerns: Contributions, problems, and solutions. *Affilia, 2,* 6–19.

Gringeri, C., Wahab, S., & Anderson-Nathe, B. (2010). What makes it feminist? Mapping the landscape of feminist social work research. *Affilia, 25*(4), 390–405.

Harding, S. (1991). *Whose science? Whose knowledge?* Ithaca, NY: Cornell University Press.

Hesse-Biber, S. N. (Ed.). (2007). *Handbook of feminist research: Theory and praxis.* Thousand Oaks, CA: Sage.

Hulko, W. (2009). The time- and context-contingent nature of intersectionality and interlocking oppressions. *Affilia, 2*(1), 44–55.

Jaggar, A. (1983). *Feminist politics and human nature.* Totowa, NJ: Rowman & Allenheld.

Jaggar, A. (1991). Prostitution. In A. Soble (Ed.), *Philosophy of sex: Contemporary readings* (pp. 348–368). Savage, MD: Rowman & Littlefield.

Jenness, V. (1990). From sex as sin to sex as work: COYOTE and the reorganization of prostitution as a social problem. *Social Problems, 37,* 403–420.

Kempadoo, K., & Doezema, J. (1998). *Global sex workers: Rights, resistance, and redefinition.* New York: Routledge.

Kempadoo, K., Sanghera, J., & Pattanaik, B. (2005). *Trafficking and prostitution reconsidered: New perspectives on migration, sex work and human rights.* Boulder, CO: Paradigm.

Kieffer, C. (1984). Citizen empowerment: A developmental perspective. *Prevention in Human Services, 3*(2/3), 9–36.

Kumsa, M. K. (2002). Negotiating intimacies in a globalized space: Identity and cohesion in young Oromo refugee women. *Affilia, 17,* 471–496.

MacKinnon, C. A. (1987). *Feminism unmodified: Discourses on law and life.* Cambridge, MA: Harvard University Press.

Mason, S. (1997). Social work research: Is there a feminist method? *Affilia, 12*(1), 10–32.

McKinnon, M., Davies, L., & Rains, P. (2001). Taking account of men in the lives of teenage mothers. *Affilia, 16,* 80–99.

Mies, M. (1979). *Toward a methodology for feminist research.* Occasional paper No. 77. The Hague, The Netherlands: Institute of Social Studies.

Mies, M. (1991). Women's research or feminist research? The debate surrounding feminist science and methodology. In M. G. Fonow & J. A. Cook (Eds.), *Beyond methodology: Feminist scholarship as lived research* (pp. 60–84). Bloomington: Indiana University Press.

Nagel, J. (1997). *Whores and other feminists.* New York: Routledge.

National Association of Social Workers (NASW). (1996). *Code of ethics.* Washington, DC: NASW Press.

National Association of Social Workers (NASW). (2006). *Commercial sex workers and social work practice.* Washington, DC: NASW Press.

National Association of Social Workers (NASW). (2009). *Prostituted people, commercial sex workers, and social work practice.* Washington, DC: NASW Press.

Nes, J. A., & Iadicola, P. (1989). Towards a definition of feminist social work: A comparison of liberal, radical, and socialist models. *Social Work, 34,* 12–21.

Olesen, V. (1994). Feminisms and models of qualitative research. In N. K. Denzin & Y. S. Lincoln (Eds.), *Handbook of qualitative research* (pp. 158–174). Thousand Oaks, CA: Sage.

Olesen, V. (2000). Feminisms and qualitative research at and into the millennium. In N. K. Denzin & Y. S. Lincoln (Eds.), *The handbook of qualitative research* (pp. 215–256). Thousand Oaks, CA: Sage.

Olesen, V. (2005). Early millennial feminist qualitative research: Challenges and contours. In N. K. Denzin & Y. S. Lincoln (Eds.), *The handbook of qualitative research* (pp. 235–278). Thousand Oaks, CA: Sage.

Olesen, V. L., & Clarke, A. E. (1999). Resisting closure, embracing uncertainties, creating agendas. In A. E. Clarke & V. L. Olesen (Eds.), *Revisioning women, health and healing: Feminist cultural studies and technoscience perspectives* (pp. 355–357). New York: Routledge.

Orme, J. (2003). "It's feminist because I say so!" *Qualitative Social Work, 2*(2), 131–153.

Pheterson, G. (1989). *A vindication of the rights of whores.* Seattle, WA: Seal.

Riessman, C. K. (1993). *Narrative analysis.* Thousand Oaks, CA: Sage.

Ristock, J. L. (2003). Exploring dynamics of abusive lesbian relationships: Preliminary analysis of a multisite, qualitative study. *American Journal of Community Psychology, 31*(3–4), 329–342.

Roof, J. (2007). Authority and representation in feminist research. In S. Hesse-Biber (Ed.), *Handbook of feminist research: Theory and praxis* (pp. 425–442). Thousand Oaks, CA: Sage.

Rubin, G. (1984). Thinking sex. Notes for a radical theory on the politics of sexuality. In C. Vance (Ed.), *Pleasure and danger: Exploring female sexuality* (pp. 267–319). London: Routledge.

Sands, G. R., & Nuccio, K. (1992). Postmodern feminist theory and social work. *Social Work, 37*(6), 489–494.

Shaw, I. (1999). Seeing the trees for the wood: The politics of evaluation in practice. In B. Broad (Ed.), *The politics of social work research evaluation* (pp. 109–126). Birmingham, AL: Venture Press.

Sloan, L., & Wahab, S. (2000). Feminist voices on sex work: Implications for social work. *Affilia, 15*(4), 457–479.

Soderlund, G. (2005). Running from the rescuers: New U.S. crusades against sex trafficking and the rhetoric of abolition. *NWSA Journal, 17*(3), 64–87.

Swigonski, M. (1993). Feminist standpoint theory and the question of social work. *Affilia, 8*(2), 171–183.

Swigonski, M. E. (1994). The logic of feminist standpoint theory for social work theory. *Social Work, 39,* 387–395.

Van Den Bergh, N., & Cooper, L. B. (1986). *Feminist visions for social work.* Silver Spring, MD: National Association of Social Workers.

Wetzel, J. W. (1986). A feminist world view conceptual framework. *Social Casework, 67,* 166–173.

White, V. (2006). *The state of feminist social work.* New York: Routledge.

Zatz, N. (1997). Sex work/sex act: Law, labor, and desire in constructions of prostitution. *Signs: Journal of Women in Culture and Society, 22,* 277–308.

Zufferey, C. (2009). Making gender visible: Social work responses to homelessness. *Affilia, 24*(4), 382–293.

22

WRITING FEMINIST RESEARCH

KATHY CHARMAZ

Feminist researchers have stood at the forefront of changing academic writing conventions and have advanced current trends to produce good writing. Feminist perspectives inform a rich research literature and inspire innovative ideas about reporting research. Numerous feminist researchers aim to make their writing clear, crisp, engaging, and effective—all criteria for good writing. Their writing unites perspective and writing practice. Yet how they meet these criteria remains invisible.

Epistemological challenges about scientific roles and the representation of subjects have had fundamental consequences for writing feminist research. Increasingly, we appear in our texts as thinking, acting—and feeling—participants rather than as disembodied reporters of collected facts. Lines between the subjective and objective blur. Feminist research and writing ranges on a continuum from seemingly external examinations of specific topics that affect women such as job discrimination or caregiving to authors' autobiographical reflections in which they themselves become the object of inquiry and of the examined text. Numerous studies at both objective and subjective ends of the continuum provide significant contributions—and other studies produce mundane statements.

- What does a feminist perspective bring to writing research reports?
- What makes feminist research compelling to read?
- How do feminist researchers construct their writings?
- How can feminist researchers use writing strategies to advance their work?

To address these questions, we can study feminist research reports and explicate the writing practices embedded in them. These reports reflect if, when, how, and where their authors enter the research scene, as well as the views and values they bring with them. Thus, I take a short step back and discuss entering the scene before analyzing how feminist researchers adopt literary conventions and writing strategies to express their thoughts. Throughout the chapter, I explore how taken-for-granted use of language imparts meanings and messages and explicate how several reports exemplify writing strategies, whether or not their authors consciously invoked these strategies. In short, I emphasize how these authors write instead of what they write. Last, I conclude the chapter with some advice for writing and for managing to write.

By developing a strong authorial voice, offering fresh metaphors, interrogating taken-for-granted metaphors, and adopting writers' strategies and rhetorical devices—what David L. Carroll (2000) calls a "writers' tricks"—authors construct memorable arguments. We can blend a repertoire of writer's tricks with social scientific data and reasoning to strengthen our writing and to expand our audiences. This approach broadens the discourse about writing feminist research, challenges taken-for-granted assumptions about writing and research, and suggests ideas for handling writing projects.

Effective writing necessitates balancing the author's style with the audience's desire for clarity, usefulness, and insight. True, not all writing is effective. Captive, rather than captivated, audiences permit some academic authors to forgo clarity. Academic fiefdoms allow imposing an arcane language on novices confined within the castle towers. Both ruling authorities and their underlings living in the castle lose touch with ordinary language and discourse beyond the castle moat. Not everyone, however, can afford to let her or his writing remain obscure and opaque.[1] Researchers who wish to reach new or broader audiences, including the people they studied, must spark readers' interest, kindle their curiosity, and ignite their imaginations, and do so with clarity. Aiming for clarity does not mean reducing theoretical ideas to simplistic description. It does mean stating these ideas in the most simple, direct terms possible and providing readers with an analytic path to understand them. Precise definitions, solid evidence, and sound reasoning construct this analytic path. By using writers' strategies, researchers can increase the power and significance of their writing.

Might feminist researchers attend more closely to the writing process than their nonfeminist counterparts? Many feminist researchers do. Does feminist writing differ from other forms of writing? Not always. Must we claim subjectivist proclivities in our writing? Not necessarily. We can take a middle ground between the objectivist reporter and the subjectivist narrator. Feminist researchers have challenged conventional positivistic assumptions about speaking with and speaking for research participants. Yes, we place ourselves in the research process and try to maintain allegiances as we create images of those we study and represent their situations in words, tables, or diagrams. In keeping with Patti Lather (2001), feminist researchers understand complexity, acknowledge partial truths, and recognize multiple subjectivities—and we can write them into our research narratives.

Before we embark on our scrutiny of feminist writing, we need to consider gender. Contested, contingent, and reconstructed notions of gender shape or underlie feminist inquiry (Glenn, 2002; Olesen, 2005). Gender is more than a variable. It is a way of seeing and experiencing the world. As evident in Judith A. Howard and Jocelyn A. Hollander's (1997) book, a gender lens illuminates interactional patterns and institutional practices and sharpens our view of power, privilege, and priorities. Although we may shift the lens and change its focus, gender provides a powerful tool in research and analysis, and often addresses marginalized populations (Kleinman, 2007; Maynes, Pierce, & Laslett, 2008). Adopting a gender lens can bring race, class, age, and embodiment into focus. A gender lens brings women into the center of analysis focusing on women's—and men's—lives, concerns, and the institutional arrangements that affect them.

A gender lens makes diverse standpoints visible—the researcher's as well as the research participants' (Clarke, 2005; Clarke & Friese, 2007; Harding, 1991; Hartsock, 1998; Kleinman, 2007; Smith, 1987, 1999, 2005; Sprague, 2005). This lens has enabled feminist researchers to examine how their own standpoints spawn beliefs and practices. Subsequently, they have attempted to push beyond taken-for-granted middle-class, white, heterosexist, age, and able-bodied assumptions embedded in earlier feminist writings. An initial focus on gender opened scrutiny of multiple embedded assumptions in researchers' standpoints. This focus on gender, then, can be significant for all researchers because it prompts them to examine a range of taken-for-granted standpoints. Those who do not recognize their standpoints risk reproducing the assumptions given in their standpoints in their writing (Charmaz, 2005, 2006).

Entering the Research Scene

Feminist ethnographers increasingly write about how they entered their research scene and what their personal experience has been within it. This trend has spread throughout feminist research but takes a different tack than traditional social research. Social scientists have long acknowledged and sometimes advocated that researchers pursue topics of personal interest in their empirical studies. John Lofland, David Snow, Leon Anderson, and Lyn Lofland (2006) urge novice qualitative researchers to draw on their experiences and thus title their first chapter "Starting Where You Are."

Many feminist researchers start where they are but subject this starting point to rigorous empirical scrutiny. Increasingly, as feminists, we position ourselves, lives, and goals in relation to the topic, particularly in books.[2] In the preface of her study of manic depression, Emily Martin (2008) points out the self-doubt most writers have when drafting a new work. Then she discloses experiencing bi-polar symptoms:

> That kind of a self-doubt was a familiar feeling to me, too. But this time something different happened: whenever I tried to write, I felt a sinister figure, a cold gray gargoyle, perched tenaciously on my shoulder, looking at what I was writing . . . and muttering a devastatingly negative commentary about what it read there. Obscene and inescapable, the creature knew me intimately and did not wish me well. (p. xv)

Martin positions herself in her study but warns against rash disclosures of this stigmatized diagnosis. Speaking as an accomplished author from a prestigious institution bestows protections that others are unlikely to have. Still, new scholars may reveal their situations to their research participants and readers. Carla Rice (2009) writes of the quandaries she faced while gathering data and writing about the body images of 81 overweight and disabled women. Rice's quandaries have multiple implications for what feminist researchers learn from their research participants, how they represent them in their writings, and what an embodied reflexivity can mean. Among other knotty questions, she asked, "How can critical researchers cultivate ethical relationships that incorporate our subjectivities yet refrain from centering our experiences or irresponsibly interpreting those of participants?" (p. 246). Rice described herself as a fat woman when she began the research and viewed her weight as fostering her early research participants' identification with her. She ended the research at an average weight, which she saw as repositioning her relationship with them. She received some harsh questions about why an attractive woman would want to conduct this research. Although startled by the questions, Rice realized that her other body secrets remained hidden, questioned her silence about them, and later theorized how her own "bodily privilege and abjection" (p. 246) affected her interpretations. Rice's article brings complex new questions about "the possibilities and perils of traversing the space between self and other, and 'other in the self', within feminist research" (p. 247).

Feminist positioning typically means acknowledging values and ideological positions. Such positioning is becoming prerequisite in feminist scholarly studies and may also appear in methodological treatises. In both types of writing, feminist allegiances may be understood but not necessarily fully articulated because they permeate the entire structure of the work (see, e.g., Clarke, 2005; Shrock & Padavic, 2007). For example, in her methodological treatise that extends grounded theory, Adele E. Clarke (2005) expresses her appreciation of participating in a special research group on "feminist epistemologies and methodologies." She says, "We focused on research methods and feminist scholarship, informing my earliest work on this book" (p. xix) without specific iteration of how this scholarship contributed to her reconstruction of grounded theory.

Authors who reveal their starting points and standpoints—and concerns and commitments—permit readers to assess both their approach and the quality of their content. These starting points and standpoints may be theoretical or ideological or both, as well as methodological. In their study of narrating trauma in post-conflict Karachi, Lubna Nazir Chaudhry and Corrine Bertram (2009) positioned themselves as emphasizing "the multiplicity and interconnectedness of oppressions," and relied on research assistants who spoke Urdu (p. 299). An articulated position such as these authors took becomes an anchor point for the observations and interpretations that follow. Readers can then place the narrative into perspective and delineate the boundaries of generalizations within it.

Certain topics—particularly those that address hierarchical relations in organizations—result in taking sides. As feminist researchers, we often position ourselves and our work with the underdog. Such positioning is not new; some ethnographers have long taken it as prerequisite for obtaining certain types of data rather than for endorsing ethical preferences or claiming political allegiances. Erving Goffman (1989), for example, argues that to understand life at the bottom of a hierarchy, ethnographers must align themselves with the people there and live as they do. Researchers may have present or potential privileges that their research participants will never enjoy, such as health, education, and opportunities. Feminist researchers seldom live as participants do, but we often align ourselves with people at the bottom of an organizational hierarchy—and write from this position. In her book, *Women Without Class: Girls, Race, and Identity,* Julie Bettie (2003) states,

> Because I am narrating a story largely through the eyes of students and simply because I am performing a critical analysis, I "other" teachers at times, and I apologize for this necessary betrayal. . . . My analysis is not meant to be critical of individual people, but of the social systems, processes, and ideologies present in our culture to recruit individual actors and inform their actions. (p. x)

Similar positioning is necessary in other studies that entail insider-outsider relationships. Feminist researchers may study a topic from the position they are or once were at. Exploring topics of profound subjective meaning can illuminate how difficult experiences have shaped researchers as well as research participants' lives. Knowing that the author holds a personal stake in the topic once marked research as biased. Increasingly, however, readers see a personal stake as a mark of authorial credibility instead of bias, particularly when authors conduct thorough research on the topic.

A researcher's positioning of herself in the study may be explicit as in Martin's (2008) and

Rice's (2009) studies or less visible until after she has accomplished specific goals. Adina Nack (2008) brought readers inside the studied experience. She began her study of women with incurable sexually transmitted diseases (STDs) by portraying a 20-year-old undergraduate's thoughts when she learned that she might have an STD:

> How could this have happened to me? I'm not a slut: I've only had sex with three guys and always used condoms. I talked with both my ex-boyfriends and current boyfriend before we ever had sex—they told me about their sexual histories and sexual health. These guys had all tested negative for HIV, so they were "safe"—healthy and trustworthy—right? (p. 1)

In the appendix of the book, Nack reveals that this story was her own. Feminist writers who share the experience that they research often feel honor bound to disclose it to their participants. Nack found that her experience as a sexual health educator and, moreover, of having an STD eased her access to research participants and legitimized her research objectives. As part of her ethical responsibility to self-disclose, Nack wrote an autoethnography of her travails with having an STD, because her experience had sparked her motivation to conduct the interview study.

Pressures to position oneself in relation to the studied experience can arise from other sources than self or colleagues. Editors may request it. Readers identify with an author who has shared the studied experience. For trade and crossover books, such positioning may serve to establish the author's voice in the narrative and add to the book's market appeal.

Researchers' experiences during their studies may force them to reexamine their values and grapple with multiple views and actions. If so, their openness to challenge likely increases their credibility. When she wrote her award-winning study about fetal surgery, Monica J. Casper (1998) stated, "My politics and intellectual assumptions have been shaken time and again" (p. 25). In her 2007 reflection about this study, she revisited the negative response her study received from surgeons, despite her sharing of their concern for fetal health. She wrote:

> Surely we were roughly on the same side. Yet I had also positioned myself as an advocate for

pregnant women, arguing for their safety, care, and autonomy while challenging many aspects of the procedure itself. In the end, I realized that my book had become caught up in the very politics about which I had written. (Casper, 2007, p. 25)

Like Casper, feminist researchers increasingly talk about *how* their perspectives become entangled in the research process rather than hiding underneath a scientific mantle. *Which* topic we choose, how we study it, and what sense we make of our subsequent data are not neutral decisions. Rather, a feminist perspective in research commits scholars to reveal circumstances in women's—and, increasingly, men's—lives and to create knowledge that can improve them. Feminist research often arises from concerns about embodiment (Dworkin & Wachs, 2009; Fingerson, 2006; Rice, 2009; Smith, 1987, 1999), honors stories (Riessman, 2008), opens silences (Charmaz, 2009; Clarke, 2005), and brings hidden institutional practices into view (Smith, 1987, 2005).

Feminist researchers have been at the forefront of epistemological developments during the past 40 years and now write of their emotions and experiences during the research process (see, e.g., Kleinman & Copp, 1993; Rice, 2009). The objective, disinterested, neutral observer resides in the past. We are part of the research process; we are intertwined with what we study and how we study it (Charmaz, 2005, 2006). Any study occurs under specific historical, cultural, and situational conditions. Whether we study small groups, historical documents, questionnaire results, or people in natural settings, we bring our perspectives not only into the research process but also into how we write our research products. Our words and concepts suggest who we are, as does the subject matter we choose to write about.

Rethinking Titles, Abstracts, and Metaphors

Titles Talk

A title can tell more than what a paper or book is about. A title may reveal the author's point of view, political stance, and tribal connections, as well as current disciplinary trends. The wording

of a title may indicate a feminist approach, which is the case in "Recasting Global Feminisms: Toward a Comparative Historical Approach to Women's Activism and Feminist Scholarship" (Lal, McGuire, Stewart, Zaborowska, & Pas, 2010). Both Wang Zheng and Ying Zhang's (2010) article, "Global Concepts, Local Practices: Chinese Feminism Since the Fourth UN Conference on Women," and Mire Koikari's (2008) book, *Pedagogy of Democracy: Feminism and the Cold War in the U.S. Occupation of Japan*, make feminism an object of historical study. Julie Hemment's (2007) title, *Empowering Women in Russia: Activism, Aid, and NGOs*, states the topic and takes an active stance toward it, and Sharlene Nagy Hesse-Biber's (2007) title, *The Cult of Thinness,* suggests feminist inquiry of experiences with weight and a critique of cultural prescriptions about it.

What makes a title work? Effective titles reflect contemporary concerns and reproduce common parlance, if these titles are clear and concrete.[3] Arlie Hochschild's titles, *The Time Bind: When Work Becomes Home and Home Becomes Work* (1997) and *The Second Shift: Working Parents and the Revolution at Home* (1989), both still work years after their original publication dates. These titles reflect problematic situations that readers share. A 40-hour workweek has become a distant memory for many North Americans. Work hours and workweeks have stretched as full-time jobs increasingly require a second unpaid shift, and many men and women who cannot find full-time work piece together part-time jobs. In such cases, family work goes to a third shift. Note that these titles each imply a point of view—that something is amiss. *The Time Bind* also asserts that social change is happening and *The Second Shift* announces that an upheaval has occurred. Ironic titles invite a further look and also impart a point of view.

Shaping a title that works requires rethinking as you revise. Gayle Sulik's (2010) initial main title, *Under the Pink*, alluded to the pink ribbons designed to raise awareness of breast cancer, the women who had cancer, and the organizations seeking funds for it. Her original subtitle, *Breast Cancer Culture in the United States*, explained the title, but offered no perspective on it. Changing the main title to *Pink Ribbon Blues* stated the topic precisely, suggested Sulik's point of view, and sharpened the imagery. Sulik's new subtitle,

How Breast Cancer Culture Undermines Women's Health, underscores her point of view, advances her argument, and foretells action. Adding the words "blues" and "undermines" infuses the title with feeling and ties the pink ribbon culture to women's actual experience of having breast cancer. Yet having cancer is not the sole reason for "having the blues." Rather, the pink ribbon culture itself can spawn having "the blues." The new subtitle tells us that we will learn about the ways this culture works and understand its concrete consequences for living with and dying from breast cancer. In short, Sulik's new title not only implies that readers will learn of the hidden story behind breast cancer culture but also of its implications for health care and women's travails with cancer and this culture.

Ronnee Schreiber's (2008) title, *Righting Feminism: Conservative Women and American Politics,* simultaneously points out the ironic twist in conservative women's contemporary political participation and announces what the book is about. The title of Jennifer Dunn's (2003) book, *Courting Disaster: Intimate Stalking, Culture, and Criminal Justice,* is also ironic. Her main title takes a stronger point of view than Schreiber's title, but its triple entendre is initially more cryptic to readers unfamiliar with the topic. For those who read beneath the surface, courtship is a disaster; the situation is inviting trouble for everyone involved, and stalking cases can turn out to be a disaster in the courtroom. Dunn's subtitle clarifies and counters the allusions in the main title. Her explicit subtitle positions the book in the specific topic, context, social institution, and field of study.

Many authors play on words in their titles. Deborah A. Sullivan (2001) adopts a straightforward title but plays on words in the subtitle: *Cosmetic Surgery: The Cutting Edge of Commercial Medicine in America.* The book designer underscored the point by putting "cutting edge" in boldface on the cover and by inserting a picture of a man and woman, each with idealized bodies. Some titles play on readers' taken-for-granted assumptions. Creating surprise invites a browser to read further. Verta Taylor and Leila J. Rupp's (2005) article title, for example, catches readers' attention: "When the Girls Are Men: Negotiating Gender and Sexual Dynamics in a Study of Drag Queens."

Titles reflect trends. Used carefully, a trend can help authors to position their work—in the title and throughout the narrative. Attempts to be trendy, however, rapidly date a book or article as fads rise and fall. Some authors ride fads to heights of fame; other authors crash with a falling fad. What started out as an innovative direction can become a convenient peg on which an author hangs his or her work. In the 1970s, studies with the term "identity" in the title gained popularity. More recently, the phrase "race, class, and gender" took hold of considerable theorizing and book titles throughout the social sciences and humanities. Jennifer Crewe (2007), the editorial director at Columbia University Press, recounts:

> A few years ago the words *race, class, and gender* graced the title or sub-title of almost four hundred submissions I received in a single year in literary studies. Some of these scholars even seemed to have forced consideration of race or class into a book that actually had a largely different focus. A couple of years later *postcoloniality* was the term in the vast majority of titles of books submitted to me in this field. Ten years before that, almost every submission had a portion of a word in the title in parentheses or featured a slash or two. . . . As you can imagine, these books all sound alike to an editor after the first dozen or so. Our eyes glaze over and we're inclined to reject the book right away. (pp. 136–137)[4]

Titles that bored Crew touted trends and tribal connections. Titles designed to capture the point of the research may also be ineffective when they are ambiguous, incomplete, or misleading. Many of us have a string of misguided titles trailing behind us.

Adopting and twisting a pointed cliché, common term, or familiar metaphor can make a snappy title. Dana Rosenfeld (2003) adopts "the changing of the guard" as the main title of her book. She aims to theorize generational change by examining discontinuous identity cohorts among gay and lesbian elders and, hence, offers a subtitle: *Lesbian and Gay Elders, Identity, and Social Change.*

Titles are growing longer. Howard S. Becker (2003) points out that titles have grown longer, advertise more keywords, and frequently consist of two "colon-ized" clauses (p. iv), one catchy, one scientific. Becker contends that this trend emerged because hiring and career decisions rest on citation counts. Thus, he absolves authors of blame for overloading their titles. (Becker's 29-word title of his three-page editorial underscores his point.)

Subtitles can clarify what the piece is about and pick up analytic slack in their respective titles. Like keywords, subtitles have become increasing important for electronic searches and impact factors (computations that assess an article or journal's influence on its field). Authors, journal editors, and publishers grant considerable significance to impact factors, and academic careers can hang on publishing in high impact journals. The impact of a journal may rest, in part, on whether it resides in accessible large databases for which universities have contracts.

In addition, marketing directors may add an explanatory subtitle or change a title to fit their conceptions of market demand, but these marketing concerns may not coincide with prescriptions for good writing. Researchers may choose a title that alludes to the purpose of the book or their position on the topic. Publishers aim to maximize the market and, thus, may advocate a general, recognizable—and mundane—title. Such titles identify the topic but flatten the content. A crisp, catchy title may have worked better. When choosing a title, authors are well advised to consider what kind of title will work best for their articles and books and their audiences at—and beyond—the time of publication.

Instructive Abstracts and Keywords

Why fuss over abstracts and keywords when the work itself is what counts? The obvious answer lies in a publication reaching its intended audience. Article titles, abstracts, and keywords all serve as signals to readers who decide whether to read and use an article. The less obvious answer speaks to the veiled role that abstracts, in particular, play in academic publishing. Reviewers form their first impression of your manuscript from the relative strength and clarity of your abstract. Editors of journals with numerous submissions heavily rely on reviewers to make their final decisions about your manuscript. In turn, when reviewing submissions in a subfield, editors of high impact journals call on the same pool of senior scholars to serve as reviewers—and exhaust them. After reading your abstract, these reviewers may decide whether to write a dismissive or constructive review.

Researchers who write chapters and books also cannot afford to be cavalier about abstracts. A proposal for an edited volume may rest on the collective strength of a set of chapter abstracts. In addition, effective book proposals rely on skills similar to those necessary for writing good abstracts. Prospective book authors should be able to deliver a succinct exegesis about their manuscript during a fleeting conversation with an editor or employer. This short, persuasive statement amounts to having a sparkling abstract.

What is an effective abstract? How do you construct one? Consider the following two examples, one from criminology and the other from social psychology.

"Colonialism and Carceral Motherhood: Native Hawaiian Families Under Corrections and Child Welfare Control" by Marilyn Brown and Barbara E. Bloom

This article uses data from Hawai'i as a case study to illustrate overlapping, racialized, and gendered regimes of state power in the contemporary post-welfare, neo-liberal political environment. Native Hawaiian families, as a legacy of colonialism, are especially at risk as targets of this control due to strategies of regulation and control coincident with the rise of neo-liberal politics. In this policy environment, penal and welfare practices attempt to shift the responsibility for structural disadvantage onto individuals in marginalized populations, while extending the state's power to police families among a broader network of kin. This article contributes to the literature on gendered state regulation and neo-liberal governance by illustrating patterns of criminalization and expanding child welfare control in this marginalized population. (Brown & Bloom, 2009, p. 151)

"Mothers and Mastery: The Consequences of Perceived Neighborhood Disorder" by C. André Christie-Mizell and Rebecca J. Erickson

Using longitudinal data from a nationally representative sample of mothers, we specify the conditions under which the neighborhood context shapes the experience of mastery. In so doing, we extend the work of others who have shown that neighborhood perceptions influence one's sense of personal control over and above the effects of sociodemographic and objective neighborhood characteristics. Specifically, we demonstrate that the benefits to mastery generally afforded to mothers through marital status, household income, physical health, and living in a higher-income neighborhood are diluted by perceptions of neighborhood disorder. These findings suggest the importance of including measures of proximal experiences when attempting to link objective components of social structure with individual and family-level outcomes. Providing further support for the emphasis placed on these proximate mechanisms by the social structure and personality framework, our analyses indicate that failing to consider negative community perceptions suppresses the significant impact that central city residence and race have on mothers' sense of personal control. (Christie-Mizell & Erickson, 2007, p. 340)

These abstracts are both striking because of their clarity, coverage, conciseness, and suitability for their respective journals and audiences. Brown and Bloom's abstract spotlights their macro-level argument and connects it with current criminal justice and welfare practices that extend state control over already marginalized families. They present a complex argument in direct terms and state its contribution. Note that they do not specify details of their data in the abstract. Instead they use the data to support their critical analysis. Christie-Mizell and Erickson, in contrast, state the source of the data first and move right to their purpose.

Both abstracts contain specialized language. Is it jargon? The answer depends on your point of view. Brown and Bloom's concepts locate their article theoretically, and Christie-Mizell and Erickson locate theirs in an empirical literature about a sense of personal mastery and measures of it. The language of each abstract speaks to the audience its respective authors aim to reach. Should they wish to address broader audiences, they would need to rewrite

their abstracts—and their studies—in simple, direct terms.

Several suggestions can help you improve your abstract:

- State your purpose and argument as soon as your disciplinary conventions allow.
- Tell how this paper is significant—for example, by indicating that it addresses a new area, challenges existing ideas, offers new data, reexamines old problems from a new perspective, or extends current knowledge.
- Specify what's new in this paper.
- Include your concepts and conclusions.
- Revise the abstract for each successive draft of your manuscript.

Creating Original Metaphors and Similes

Original metaphors and similes can make a piece distinctive. A metaphor makes an implicit comparison by taking a term that ordinarily has one meaning and using it to designate another. A simile compares and likens two fundamentally dissimilar things. Writers construct original metaphors and similes to serve specific purposes, including evoking a particular response from readers.

What makes a metaphor work? How does it help you make a point? How have feminist researchers used original metaphors and similes to advance their ideas? Rosanna Hertz (2002) evokes a powerful simile in her study of single mothers who chose to have known or unknown donors father their child. How can the sociologist portray this relationship? What images does the donor dad evoke? To what can his presence be likened? Hertz (2002) creates a compelling simile in the following way:

The known donor's image is as a negative of a photograph. On a negative, light and shadow are the reverse of the positive generated from it. The negative offers a glimpse of a person who was there but missing. The child knows his or her genetic identity, but the man remains in shadow socially. Ironically, the mother knows him as a whole person (the positive print) because of a shared past relationship. The child still must imagine what it would be like to have a dad, even if the mother's history and memory form the basis of talk with the child about her imagined father. . . . The known donor appears visible on the unprinted negative, forming an image for the child but not as the developed self of the dad. (p. 17)[5]

By likening the donor's image to the negative of a photograph, Hertz's simile reproduces the ambiguity of the child's relationship to his or her donor father. She draws a picture for the reader using outline and shadow. Depth and detail blur in the image of the photographic negative, as in the child's relationship to the donor dad. The blurred image reveals the father's phantom presence but conceals the quirks and qualities that would enliven his image and make him real. This simile works because it captures the problematic and ambiguous relationship in condensed form. It evokes an image the reader can grasp and envision and melds this image in Hertz's narrative. The simile extends the analysis and deepens the narrative.

Hertz's simile does more than provide an intriguing image. Rather, the shadow image of the donor then becomes a metaphor for the child-father relationship. Hertz uses the metaphor of the ambiguous negative to intrigue the reader and to build her argument. She thus informs and locates the reader's knowledge of the ambiguous role of the blurred dad as well as of the child's understanding about what a family is. The child learns that traditional forms of family roles and boundaries do not hold in his or her family.

All kinds of metaphors and similes reside in research narratives. It matters whether authors construct metaphors and similes with forethought or invoke them unwittingly. Hertz constructs the simile to clarify her analysis. Writers create metaphors to reveal a deeper meaning, a hidden truth. They invoke metaphors unwittingly when they assume that the metaphor *is* the truth. Metaphor and reality merge.

In her classic unveiling of metaphors, Emily Martin (2008) conveys an exquisite awareness of the power of taken-for-granted metaphors and creates an original metaphor to depict them. Martin points out that literary conventions refer to "dead" metaphors, but she finds "sleeping metaphors in science" and challenges feminists to "awaken" them (p. 25). These metaphors appear in the writing of scientific text but

lie hidden within the content. Martin uses sleep and wakefulness as metaphors for our language use and narrative understanding. Words that are asleep still lie there seemingly inert, but they have not died.

Sleeping metaphors wield power precisely because they remain tacit: They shape the text and, moreover, our conceptions of the realities it addresses. Such metaphors shape *what* we see and *how* we see it, and they contain hidden reasons that explain, justify, and perpetuate *why* we see it that way.

Uncovering Taken-for-Granted Metaphors

Writers invoke taken-for-granted metaphors when they say one thing *means* or *symbolizes* another. These metaphors merge separate entities such as masculinity and aggressiveness or take one characteristic of a process or an object as the whole, such as saying "aging is deterioration." We can extend Martin's (2007) concept of sleeping metaphors to include all those metaphors we take for granted. Implicit meanings embedded in these metaphors slip by as they become an unexamined part of everyday discourse. How are taken-for-granted metaphors used? When do research participants and writers invoke them? To what extent are they shared throughout a group or setting? How do they influence what we do? We all use metaphors—often unconsciously. Uncovering hidden and not so hidden metaphors reveals perspectives and shows how they inform practices.

Metaphors not only shape images of specific phenomena but also persuade audiences. Martin (2007) found that metaphors of women's bodies in medical and popular texts shape the very way we see women's bodies. After examining the language authors adopt, Martin takes the diffuse images and information found throughout the texts and re-presents them in condensed conceptualized form. See how Martin articulates implied metaphors and makes them visible in the following example of medical writing about menopause:

> In both medical texts and popular books, what is being described is the breakdown of a system of authority. The cause of ovarian "decline" is the

"decreasing ability of the aging ovaries to respond to pituitary gonadotropins." At every point in this system, functions "fail" and falter: Follicles "fail to muster the strength" to reach ovulation. As functions fall, so do the members of the system decline: "breasts and genital organs gradually atrophy," "wither," and become "senile." (p. 293)[6]

By garnering evidence and presenting it systematically, Martin transforms conventional images and descriptions, assembles them, and creates an impressive argument.

> Many criticisms have been made of the medical propensity to see menopause as a pathological state. I would like to suggest that the tenacity of this view comes not only from negative stereotypes associated with aging women in our society, but as a logical outgrowth of seeing the body as a hierarchical information-processing system in the first place. (Martin, 2007, p. 292)[7]

Martin traces the language flowing from these metaphors, and this language, in turn, gives rise to more metaphors including "unresponsive" ovaries that "regress" and then become "senile," a hypothalamus "addicted" to estrogen that gives "inappropriate orders," and a system that "fails" (p. 293). By bringing these sleeping metaphors to life, she shows how the texts impart a fundamentally gendered analysis.

Sleeping metaphors shape consciousness without our knowing it. Common, unambiguous metaphors may permeate it more than we realize. In both circumstances, metaphors frame our understandings of experience, and, thus, we may not see beyond these frames. Sulik (2010) examines the war metaphor in cancer culture, specifies its uses in breast cancer advertising, and relates it to the war metaphor in medicine. The war metaphor works in subtle as well as overt ways. It is ubiquitous and unambiguous, and thus some women may transcend its conventional meanings. However, simultaneously, the very generality of the metaphor and its power to shape care, culture, and individual consciousness can ensnare women. Sulik (2010) explicates meanings of a pivotal word in the metaphor of war, "survivor," and excavates its implications:

> The merit of survivorship comes from being a real survivor: that is, one who has suffered through the ordeal of breast cancer to come out on the other side, not necessarily unscathed but better off for having had the experience. The image of the triumphant survivor sets the bar of suffering high, making the glory of triumph that much sweeter and deserving of others' admiration. Rather than validating the full range of experience, the survivor model constructs a misery quotient. Did I suffer enough to be called a survivor? Did others suffer more than me? Am I worthy of the sisterhood? (p. 319)

Troubling meanings of being a genuine survivor, worthy of the heroism bestowed upon her, become apparent in Sulik's analysis. She intentionally invoked words that recalled the suffering and glory of war—"unscathed," "ordeal," "glory," "triumph," " merit," and "admiration"— to show how ubiquitous these terms are and the images of having breast cancer that they evoke. Sulik also used the words "setting the bar high" and "misery quotient" to remind the reader of the similar use of sporting language to infuse the war on cancer with competition and fortitude.[8]

Making Memorable Arguments

Invoking Metaphors as Markers and Measures

The best writers construct arguments we remember. How might they craft an argument through telling an analytic story? What role might metaphor play in telling an analytic story and in advancing an argument?

Early in her book on intimate stalking, Dunn (2003) invokes an old metaphor in a new way. This metaphor crystallizes both her point of view and purpose after she lays out the logic of her argument and gives it punch. The women she studied

> must "accomplish" victimization (Holstein and Miller 1990) through complicated processes of identity work. However, they encounter their crucial and critical audiences not simply as potential stalking victims, but as women and as victims of domestic violence, two further identities that shape

interpretive frameworks. In order to make their claims heard and to be believed, women who are being stalked must prove that they are truly victims of a crime and that they play no part in its initiation or recurrence. This requires much of them; every move they make will be scrutinized and there is almost nothing they do that is not subject to multiple interpretations, many of them unfavorable. It is like walking a tight rope held at one end by an enemy over an abyss, toward a destination presenting worse yet hazards. (Dunn, 2003, p. 30)

In one short paragraph, Dunn first provides the logic of her argument and then foreshadows the subsequent story by invoking a metaphor that infuses the logic of her study with plot and process, and does so with imagery. Will the woman be able to cross the tightrope? Will she fall into the abyss below? What does it take to cross the tightrope without experiencing lasting harm?

Writers can also tell a story with a fresh metaphor or simile that simultaneously marks their work and makes it distinctive. The story serves as a means of setting the stage for the argument to come, and, when it is successful, does so with a fresh twist. Hochschild (1997) tells a story about an incident in the company's day care center where she was observing. She moves from dialogue to explanatory description as she takes the reader into four-year-old Cassie's relationship with her mother, Gwen Bell, and into the day care center. In Hochschild's story, Gwen arrives late with an unkempt Cassie in tow. Cassie has already wheedled Gwen into giving her a fudge bar and now pleads with Gwen to take her with her. Through Hochschild's description of the incident, readers learn of Gwen's discomfort about leaving Cassie during long workdays and Cassie's successful bargaining to get a fudge bar as recompense for being left.

Hochschild gives adversarial bargaining a new twist: it proceeds from taken-for-granted assumptions about children's rights to have their parents' sustained attention and parental obligations to give it. From this perspective, Gwen fails Cassie, and Cassie knows it. Then Gwen and Cassie reveal their tensions and contests about time bargaining at the day care center. Hochschild writes,

As Gwen Bell later explained to me, she continually feels that she owes Cassie more time than she actually gives her. She has a time-debt to her daughter. If many busy parents settle such debts on evenings or weekends when their children eagerly "collect" promised time, Cassie insists on a morning down payment, a fudge bar that makes her mother uneasy but saves her the trouble and embarrassment of a tantrum. (Hochschild, 1997, p. 5)

Hochschild (1997) weaves fresh metaphors and creates similes in her description and punctuates them with familiar metaphors. Debts take the form of time. The fudge bar symbolizes a hard bargain. Hochschild treats adversarial bargaining as a dominant metaphor and slips it into her narrative through the description itself. She adopts related metaphors that measure this bargaining when she tells of a "hard bargain," "time-debt," "defeat," and "down payment." Throughout the anecdote about Gwen and Cassie, Hochschild's words convey the struggles between them. Cassie "pleads," is "resigned," makes a "deal," "keeps her mother to it," and "insists on a morning down payment." Gwen "owes" more time but trades an "uneasy" bargain and "saves" herself "trouble." The metaphor of bargaining shapes and unifies the narrative.

Hochschild "represents" each actor in the scene, but she does so through describing the incident. Her even style and tone make her voice creditable and the story believable. She stands in the scene but does not enter the story. As Hochschild presents the scenario at the day care center, she represents Cassie and Gwen. Does Hochschild retell everything that occurred during this incident? Probably not. More likely, she distills the incident to bare essentials. She lets Gwen and Cassie speak in their own voices—*while they deliver their most revealing lines* in a dialogue of only four sentences. No irrelevant small talk disrupts the tale. Hochschild's voice forms the rest of the anecdote, as quoted above. Yet readers gain a sense of who Cassie and Gwen are and what their respective actions mean through Hochschild's rendering of the scene.

A few deft sentences paint images of the actors in the scene; however, their actions take precedence and shape this story. In turn, the story tells a larger tale than the idiosyncratic actions of individuals. Readers understand that

Cassie's payoff results from the bargaining about Gwen's time bind. Hochschild describes the incident with concrete details, rather than relating it in general terms. Readers gain a sufficient sense of the actors and the scene to accept her portrayal of it.

The balance between dialogue and description permits Hochschild to use her research participants' direct statements without usurping their meaning. Meaning lies in the action and scene, as well as in the research participants' statements. The story of the incident allows us to locate their statements because of how Hochschild tells the tale. As she creates and connects images in this story, Hochschild constructs and strengthens her analytic narrative. Later, Hochschild (1997) brings the reader back to Gwen Bell's time bind: "Cassie still stands at the front door holding her fudge bar like a flag, the emblem of a truce in a battle over time" (p. 11). A fudge bar flags the truce but marks the battle.

Offering Surprising Examples

Surprising examples catch and capture readers' interest. On the first pages of the preface of her book *You Were Always Mom's Favorite! Sisters in Conversation Throughout Their Lives,* Deborah Tannen (2009) asserts that women's relationships with their sisters hold lifelong significance (pp. 3–4). She next introduces the extraordinary power of a sister's disapproval. Tannen buttresses her point by including a direct statement from a woman who felt that her sister was inextricably part of her. This woman advanced Tannen's argument because she explained how her bonds with her sister caused her to feel the force of her sister's disapproval in ways that did not occur with other people. Subsequently, Tannen (2009) underscores her point with the following surprising example:

> "You know Sadie doesn't approve of me sometimes," said Bessie Delany of her older sister. "She frowns at me in her big-sister sort of way." When she said this, Bessie was 101 while Sadie was 103. Sadie said "I told Bessie that if she lives to 120, then I'll just have to live to 122 so I can take care of her." (p. 4)

Tannen catches the reader's attention when she mentions Bessie and Sadie's respective ages. In addition, this surprising example does much more narrative work. Bessie and Sadie's brief quotations are apt selections to follow the book's plaintive title and Tannen's opening personal anecdote about looking like her elder sister's identical twin in a family photograph. Sadie's poignant statement about taking care of Bessie as her reason for living reveals their enduring bond and underscores Tannen's thesis about sisters. This example becomes a means of introducing more voices into the narrative and extending readers' views of sisters. Bessie and Sadie show readers what being sisters over long decades can mean and thus frame and foretell Tannen's analysis in the body of the book. By introducing this example early in the preface, Tannen sets a brisk pace for the chapters to follow.

Quantitative and mixed methods researchers can use a surprising statistical finding to accomplish similar goals and may organize an entire article around this finding. C. André Christie-Mizell and Rebecca J. Erickson (2007) discovered several surprising findings when they linked mothers' perceptions of relative neighborhood disorder with their sense of personal control. These authors found that high-status married women reported a lower sense of personal mastery when they believed that they lived in a disordered neighborhood. Christie-Mizell and Erickson (2007) also found that studying the perceptions of relative neighborhood disorder revealed other surprising effects:

> The "true" effects of living in the inner city and being African American were suppressed until we included perceived neighborhood disorder in our estimation of mastery. In fact, we find that both central city residents (compared to suburbanites) and African American mothers (compared to European American mothers) experience higher levels of mastery. (p. 359)

Christie-Mizell and Erickson use these findings to form their argument about the significance of mothers' perception of neighborhood disorder. In presenting their surprising findings, they simultaneously make a new argument and refine and extend knowledge about an individual's sense of personal mastery.

Using Rhetorical Devices

Good writers of all kinds use a variety of rhetorical devices to interest their readers and to make memorable arguments. Hochschild (1997) used the narrative quoted previously to establish her idea of the time bind and to launch her argument about it. Although Hochschild does not enter the narrative, she brings a persuasive authorial voice to it. Authors of quantitative reports can also build a strong authorial voice into their narratives and use rhetorical devices to further their objectives. They too build images but with numbers and explanations. They can ask rhetorical questions and provide unexpected answers.

Instead of starting with a strong thesis sentence, as writing handbooks prescribe, Michelle J. Budig and Paula England (2001) begin their article with a provocative question: "Does motherhood affect an employed woman's wages?" (p. 204). This question sparks interest and brings readers into the article. The authors then state a clear purpose for the article and list five possible explanations for the finding that motherhood does seem to be connected with lower wages:

We provide evidence of a penalty for the cohort of American women currently in their childbearing years, and we investigate its causes. Five explanations for the association between motherhood and lower wages have been offered. First, many women spend time at home caring for children, interrupting their job experience, or at least interrupting full-time employment. Second, mothers may trade off higher wages for "mother-friendly" jobs that are easier to combine with parenting. Third, mothers may earn less because the needs of their children leave them exhausted or distracted at work, making them less productive. Fourth, employers may discriminate against mothers. Finally, perhaps the association is not really a penalty *resulting* from motherhood and its consequences at all. What appears in cross-sectional data to be a causal effect of having children may be a spurious correlation; some of the same unmeasured factors (such as

career ambition) that discourage childbearing may also increase earnings. (p. 204)

Observe Budig and England's trenchant wording of their finding and how they use it to frame the purpose for this article. They do not waste words or time. After listing four one-sentence possible explanations, they state the fifth and most contentious explanation. By placing this explanation last and giving it the most space, Budig and England create rhythm and balance in the paragraph, provide a logical ordering of the explanations, and set the stage for juxtaposing their argument against these explanations.

Before delving into their analysis, Budig and England argue that readers should care about this wage penalty because of gender inequality. Instead of stating this argument in general terms, they introduce novel ideas:

Good parenting, for example, increases the likelihood that a child will grow up to be a caring, well-behaved, and productive adult. This lowers crime rates, increases the level of care for the next generation, and contributes to economic productivity. Most of those who benefit—the future employers, neighbors, spouses, friends, and children of the person who has been well-reared—pay nothing to the parent. Thus, mothers pay a price in lowered wages for doing childrearing, while most of the rest of us are "free riders" on their labor. (Budig & England, 2001, p. 205)

Readers share Budig and England's starting premise. Their outline of the benefits of good parenting extends our agreement. Then they spring the real economic point on us—most beneficiaries pay nothing. By interjecting a surprising fact into their reasoning, they rivet our attention. While we absorb this surprising news, Budig and England tweak us further by calling us "free riders." We have taken a place in the argument; it no longer merely refers to a category of people out there somewhere. Budig and England enter the narrative and bring their argument home—to us.

In a short paragraph, Budig and England catch their potential adversaries and force them to rethink if not reverse their views. Because they do not exempt themselves from the free rider label, they simultaneously establish a link to their readers and give us a glimpse of who they are. Then they recede from view.

More often, writers align themselves with their readers through the topic, personal experience, and voice. In her book *Passing By*, Carol Brooks Gardner (1995) uses each as she opens her narrative and charts its course. She begins by mentioning a harmless flirtation and then recounts an incident that occurred while she was traveling. A young male attendant teased her when she was paying for gas by holding her credit card out to her but retracting it as she reached for it. Readers understand Gardner's experience in a public place and accept her view of the public realm as a particular site in which

> rituals—sometimes argued by women and men alike to be innocuous, even flattering, or explained away as the province only of the lower classes or the youthful—can be transformed into full-fledged verbal abuse or can escalate into unambiguous physical assault, even rape. . . . For women and those in other social categories who are disadvantaged in public places, even these routine pleasures will be experienced with knowledge of what *can* occur. (Gardner, 1995, p. 2)

Note that Gardner says that women may experience pleasures in public places but realize what can occur. She offers this woman's story:

> About a year ago, I was aerobic-walking near a mall, for exercise. It wasn't very late, just past dusk. It was the summertime. It was nice out. As I went by one of the stores, a man standing outside said hello to me, and just to be polite, I smiled and said hello back. Then he started to follow me, keeping talking to me. I was only a few blocks away from home, so I started to run. The man started to run too, and he caught me and raped me. At gunpoint. They never caught him. (p. 2)[9]

Within public places, trivial incidents are linked with terrifying events. Gardner foreshadows the last incident with progressive intensity by moving from innocuous flirtation to an irritating gender game to sexual assault. She gives us warnings. Like a novelist, Gardner foreshadows the impending violence by the intensifying

force of her terms. Her verbs shift from a neutral to a foreboding tone. Telling verbs build momentum and add suspense. Certain incidents can be "explained away," but ritual public harassment can "escalate." Then, by defining the outcomes of escalation—"unambiguous physical assault, even rape"—Gardner establishes the seriousness of her topic and underscores it with how "the knowledge of what can occur" casts an ominous cloud over women in public.

Gardner introduces another voice, another view with her informant's story. It simultaneously magnifies all that precedes and shrinks the shift from innocuous interaction to horrific assault. Does Gardner's skillful foreshadowing prepare us for the rape? Not entirely. The narrative still imparts an element of shock and horror. The innocence of the woman's voice magnifies her innocent action, and, for a moment, we feel disarmed. Then we sense the full meaning of her story as she says, "He caught me and raped me. At gunpoint."

Rhetorical devices can help researchers serve several simultaneous goals. The following excerpts are from my paper "Views From the Margins: Voices, Silences, and Suffering" (Charmaz, 2007), which served as a keynote address and a research report. I aimed to bring both the listening and reading audiences into the topic. The conference organizers had invited me to talk about the marginalization of people with chronic illnesses and disabilities. Rather than assuming a definition of marginalization, I built one from an inductive analysis of my empirical materials. The first few paragraphs read as follows:

> To begin our discussion of marginalization, consider the story of an adventurous 46-year-old woman whose chronic illness took her from the thick of social life to the margins of American society. In her earlier years, Marilyn Raymer had attended college far from home, volunteered at a kibbutz in Israel, worked in a plastics factory, and later became an indispensable—and affluent—manager in a thriving family business. After a new company bought the business, Marilyn left. She traveled, attended school, and then worked in a wildlife rescue center cleaning up birds from oil spills. Nine months after her first clean up, Marilyn developed inexplicable symptoms.

Months of nagging symptoms and negative medical tests followed. Marilyn recalled receiving her diagnoses:

> My husband was diagnosed with inoperable lung cancer on the same day that I was diagnosed with chronic fatigue syndrome and fibromyalgia, and he died a few weeks later. And I've been thinking he was the luckier one of the two of us.

The past forms the backdrop for Marilyn's story. The crucial day when she received the news became a symbolic marker that divided her life—the time before everything changed and the time after. Marilyn wanted the interviewer to know who she was before illness marginalized her as well as whom she has become in its aftermath. Marilyn contrasted her present unending saga of illness with stories of her past successes.

> I did a lot of things that were very challenging, and, you know, I used to work 50, 60 hours a week, and made good money and had great benefits, and had a life and all of that stuff changed one year—really abruptly in one year. And since then, everything is gone—from the financial to memory to—and everything in between.

Like most people who have serious chronic conditions early in life, Marilyn searches the past to make sense of her present (Charmaz, 1991; Roberts, 2004). The diagnoses form a connection between past and present but an incomplete one. What else might account for the distance she has traveled between health and illness? What could have caused her current disturbing symptoms? (Charmaz, 2007, p. 7)

What did these paragraphs accomplish? The initial description invites readers into the forthcoming analysis and informs them of the topic. Marilyn's poignant statement startles the reader, sets the tone, and builds tensions in the narrative. The subsequent analytic paragraph picks up the melancholy event and juxtaposes past and present. Marilyn's story anchors the analytic story, which, in turn, suggests looking at marginalization as a process that occurs to real people. Marginalization is more than a category that researchers apply to faceless groups.

Readers conjure images of Marilyn and identify with her. Their involvement in her story encourages their engagement in mine.

I used the phrase, "before illness marginalized her" to begin to weave my analysis of marginalization together. As the paper progresses, I shift the reader's attention to this analysis. The phrase "like most people" signals that Marilyn's tale illuminates a collective story. I add other voices but weave Marilyn's statements into the collective story throughout the paper. Her statements contribute to the depth and coherence of the analysis and form an implicit link to other people's stories in the paper and in the reader's imagination.

ATTENDING TO LANGUAGE

Writers who attend to their research participants' language—and their own—have the makings of a memorable argument. Key terms that participants use to describe their actions and each other reveal divisions between groups, ideologies, and practices. Writers can use their analyses of these terms to frame their studies and present the terms as compelling evidence. Jennifer Dunn (2010) focuses on the language of advocates, victims, and scholars to show how they construct images of victims and survivors. These images draw on words suffused with emotions and evaluations such as "blame-worthy, ideal, pathetic, and admirable" (p. 193). Anne Arnett Ferguson (2000) looks at the meanings and consequences of African American schoolboys being "at risk," "inappropriate," and "educable" and exhibiting "needy behavior" and links them to the social structure of the school. These links allow Ferguson to see beyond and through school officials' views of the boys' behavior as identifying them as troubled and troublesome. She says of one boy, "So Donel is marked as 'inappropriate' through the very configuration of self that school rules regulate: bodies, language, presentation of self" (p. 92).

Like Ferguson, we can attend to our research participants' language and portray them through their words. Building the analysis on participants' words encourages both writer and reader to sense or see implicit meanings. This approach also can resolve two other writing problems that feminist researchers face. First, a researcher's commitments to social justice can spawn nagging questions about representing research participants: "How can I do justice to their experience? How can I find words to express it?" An artful weaving of participants' words in the research narrative shows the rhythm, grace, and expressiveness of their voices and the passion in their words. They speak for themselves; the writer creates the stage and focuses the spotlight. Second, studying research participants' language illuminates how they make sense of their situations and, in some cases, explains how they may perpetuate disadvantages that affect them (Kleinman, 2007; Lively, 2001; Murray, 2000). Michelle Wolkomir (2006) finds that her gay and ex-gay research participants' ideological maneuvering enabled them to resolve their Christian beliefs with their homosexuality but not without costs. These men's ideological maneuvering left the structures that oppressed them unchanged. She writes:

> If marginalized groups retain their beliefs in the legitimacy of dominant ideas, then they are apt to use these ideas as building blocks in their attempts to revise oppressive ideologies. Doing so might remodel outer appearance, but the fundamental dominant structure remains intact. Using the master's tools to facilitate social change is thus likely to result in the building not of a new house but of more comfortable servants' quarters, albeit with perhaps better amenities than previous structures. (Wolkomir, 2006, p. 197)

CONCLUSION

Feminist researchers are not all alike. Our relative access to time, privileges, and resources varies enormously. How can feminist researchers with heavy workloads maintain a writing agenda despite isolation and lack of resources? What helps feminist researchers become accomplished and published writers? What distinguishes good writing from mundane reporting? How can feminist researchers improve their work?

Advice books for scholarly writers seldom address their readers' situations and hence offer acontextual prescriptions, impose general standards of success, and individualize blame for problems in making progress (see, e.g., Zerubavel, 1999). Similarly, advice from senior scholars may reflect their circumstances of long ago and current privileges, not your situation. A heavy workload may vitiate usual prescriptions such as "Write every day." Is it possible?

Writing every day is sound advice if you can do it but leads to guilt and frustration when you cannot. The structure of your day—and night—alone may squash hopes of writing when long hours of meetings, organizational housekeeping, classes, and office hours fill your days and endless grading, preparation, e-mails, and clerical tasks consume your nights and weekends. Kathleen Kendall-Tackett (2007) says that writing every day makes her "super-productive" but discloses, "The problem is that I've never been able to make it work for me long term; my life keeps getting in the way" (p. 46). Organizational deskilling has serious consequences for aspiring writers and differentially affects those who already have little time. Perhaps you can simplify or eliminate some tasks, but perhaps not. The common prescription to squeeze in 15 minutes of writing here and there works for didactic pieces and departmental business—anything you can treat as straightforward and routine. This prescription rarely works when you struggle with ambiguous meanings and theoretical interpretations. So how do you manage to write?

Two recommendations may help. First, make writing a collaborative venture, whether or not you collaborate on writing projects. Writing is an inherently social act. We build on past works and write for specific readers. Make some of those readers local and immediate through finding a writing partner or forming a supportive writing group. Then be accountable to each other for giving and receiving constructive critiques. Accountability will get you started; accountability with caring will keep you going—and keep *you* caring about your research. Second, learn to take full advantage of the times you can write: develop a writing rhythm, a way of immersing yourself in the task so the words flow from you. Having a writing rhythm increases your comfort with writing and helps you to resume your work after periods when daily demands precluded writing. Studying your schedule—and your writing practices—helps, too. You can discern when and how you compose new ideas and what encourages you to return to old drafts. Rather than struggling to compose complex ideas in those scarce minutes you carve out, revising and editing may make more productive use of your time.

Writing teachers have long known that writing consists of two phases: a learning phase and a revising phase (Ede, 2007; Elbow, 1998, 2000). In the learning phase, you make discoveries as you compose. During the revising phase, you clarify, organize, and tighten your writing for an audience, although new ideas may surface (Cheney, 2005). Granted, ready-made disciplinary templates outline traditional research reports, but learning and innovation emerge within the content. In any form of writing, the location, concentration, and amount of time that you require for composing and revising may differ. Awareness of such differences can help you construct realistic time projections and schedules. Learning *how* you write will help you manage *to* write.

Last, I offer some writing strategies to help you improve your writing:

- Study effective writing
- Critique other writers' works in progress
- Write for yourself first
- Write in the active voice
- Use strong, descriptive nouns and verbs
- Show, don't just tell your reader
- Provide concrete evidence
- Impose organization after composing a draft
- Revise for clarity and power
- Eliminate needless words, sentences, and passages
- Revise for your specific audience
- *Enjoy the process!*

Discussion Questions

1. How do you invite a reader into your manuscript? What keeps a reader involved in it?

2. How do metaphors frame the reader's thinking about a topic? How can a writer make good use of metaphors and similes?

3. What makes your writing work? Which strategies will help you improve your writing?

Online Resources

American Psychological Association: LifeTools

http://search.apa.org/publications?query=&facet=subject:LifeTools Book Series&section=subject&pubtype=books

The American Psychological Association offers a "LifeTools" section that includes a series of useful books and guides for navigating professional life, including writing and publishing.

SAGE: Academic and Student Resources

http://www.sagepub.com/productSearch.nav?course=Course13&sortBy=defaultPubDate desc

SAGE Publications has an "Academic and Student Resources" listing that contains helpful books on scholarly writing and publishing. Also look in this publisher's specialized lists, such as the one for qualitative research, for helpful guides on writing.

The Writer's Digest: Conferences/Events

http://www.writersdigest.com/conferences-events/

The Writer's Digest website provides ready access to the organization's many events and publications that take up the craft of writing and the pragmatics of getting published.

Relevant Journals

Feminism & Psychology

Gender & Society

Writer's Digest

Written Communication

NOTES

1. Mentors who published their doctoral dissertations decades ago may be unaware of what their students need to do today. These mentors may offer their students poor advice about submitting manuscripts for publication review, such as sending a dissertation off to a publishing house without revising it (Charmaz, 2006). Standards for writing have risen, as has competition to publish in good venues.

2. Researchers now make candid statements about how their race, social class, age, and, when they deem relevant, sexual orientation influence the direction and content of their studies. Positioning oneself in relation to one's research could affect present or potential employment and has affected certain feminist researchers in both explicit and elusive ways. When employers welcome diversity, stating one's positions and standpoints may help an author. Still, how potential colleagues and administrators interpret these positions and standpoints can vary and can remain elusive. For example, acknowledging invisible disability and chronic illness may have unforeseen negative consequences.

3. The emphasis on contemporary concerns is not limited to social scientists and professionals interested in pressing problems. Historians' titles often reflect contemporary interests or current foci but may document and explain its historical emergence or its significance in a particular time and place. See, for example, Erika Kuhlman (2008), *Reconstructing Patriarchy After the Great War: Women, Gender, and Postwar Reconciliation Between Nations.*

4. Permission granted by the University of California Press. Jennifer Crewe, "Caught in the Middle: The Humanities," in *Revising Your Dissertation: Advice From Leading Editors*, edited by Beth Luey. © 2007 by the Regents of the University of California. Published by the University of California Press.

5. Permission granted from the University of California Press. Rosanna Hertz, "The Father as an Idea: A Challenge to Kinship Boundaries by Single Mothers," in *Symbolic Interaction* vol. 25, no. 1, pp. 1–31. © 2002 by The Society for the Study of Symbolic Interaction. Published by the University of California Press.

6. *The Woman in the Body*, by Emily Martin. Copyright © 1987, 1992 by Emily Martin. Reprinted by permission of Beacon Press, Boston.

7. *The Woman in the Body*, by Emily Martin. Copyright © 1987, 1992 by Emily Martin. Reprinted by permission of Beacon Press, Boston.

8. Personal communication with Gayle Sulik, September 23, 2010.

9. Permission granted from the University of California Press for these two excerpts. Carol Brooks Gardner, *Passing By: Gender and Public Harassment*. © 1995 by the Regents of the University of California. Published by the University of California Press.

ACKNOWLEDGEMENTS

I thank Sharlene Hesse-Biber for her interest in my work and Molly Ashe for help with seeking permissions.

REFERENCES

Becker, H. S. (2003). Guest Editorial: Long-term changes in the character of the sociological discipline: A short note on the length of titles submitted to the *American Sociological Review* during the year 2002. *American Sociological Review, 68*(3), iii–v.

Bettie, J. (2003). *Women without class: Girls, race, and identity.* Berkeley: University of California Press.

Brown, M., & Bloom, B. E. (2009). Colonialism and carceral motherhood: Native Hawaiian families under corrections and child welfare control. *Feminist Criminology, 4*(2), 151–169.

Budig, M. J., & England, P. (2001). The wage penalty for motherhood. *American Sociological Review, 66*, 204–225.

Caraway, T. E. (2007). *Assembling women: The feminization of global manufacturing.* Ithaca, NY: Cornell University Press.

Caron, S. M. (2008). *Who chooses? American reproductive history since 1830.* Gainesville, FL: University Press of Florida.

Carroll, D. L. (2000). *A manual of writer's tricks.* New York: Paragon House.

Casper, M. J. (1998). *The making of the unborn patient: A social anatomy of fetal surgery.* New Brunswick, NJ: Rutgers University Press.

Casper, M. J. (2007). Fetal surgery then and now: There is too much emphasis on the fetus and not enough on the woman. *Conscience, 28*(3), 24–27.

Charmaz, K. (2005). Grounded theory in the 21st century: Applications for advancing social justice studies. In N. K. Denzin & Y. S. Lincoln (Eds.), *Handbook of qualitative research* (3rd ed., pp. 507–535). Thousand Oaks, CA: Sage.

Charmaz, K. (2006). *Constructing grounded theory: A practical guide through qualitative analysis.* London: Sage.

Charmaz, K. (2007). Views from the margins: Voices, silences, and suffering. *Qualitative Research in Psychology, 5*(1), 7–18.

Charmaz, K. (2009). Stories and silences: Disclosures and self in chronic illness. In D. E. Brashers &

D. J. Goldstein (Eds.), *Communicating to manage health and illness* (pp. 240–270). New York: Routledge.

Chaudhry, L. N., & Bertram, C. (2009). Narrating trauma and reconstruction in post-conflict Karachi: Feminist liberation psychology and the contours of agency in the margins. *Feminism & Psychology, 19*(3), 293–312.

Cheney, T. A. R. (2005). *Getting the words right: 39 ways to improve your writing* (2nd ed.). Cincinnati, OH: Writer's Digest Books.

Christie-Mizell, C. A., & Erickson, R. J. (2007). Mothers and mastery: The consequences of perceived neighborhood disorder. *Social Psychology Quarterly, 70*(4), 340–365.

Clarke, A. E. (2005). *Situational analysis: Grounded theory after the postmodern turn*. Thousand Oaks, CA: Sage.

Clarke, A. E., & Friese, C. (2007). Situational analysis: Going beyond traditional grounded theory. In A. Bryant & K. Charmaz (Eds.), *Handbook of grounded theory* (pp. 694–743). London: Sage.

Crewe, J. (2007). Caught in the middle: The humanities. In B. Luey (Ed.), *Revising your dissertation: Advice from leading editors* (2nd ed., pp. 131–147). Berkeley: University of California Press.

Dunn, J. (2003). *Courting disaster: Intimate stalking, culture, and criminal justice*. New York: Aldine de Gruyter.

Dunn, J. (2010). *Judging victims: Why we stigmatize survivors, and how they reclaim respect*. Boulder, CO: Lynne Rienner.

Dworkin, S. L., & Wachs, F. L. (2009). *Body panic: Gender, health, and the selling of fitness*. New York: New York University Press.

Ede, L. (2007). *The academic writer*. Boston: Bedford/St. Martin's.

Elbow, P. (1998). *Writing with power* (2nd ed.). New York: Oxford University Press.

Elbow, P. (2000). *Everyone can write: Essays toward a hopeful theory of writing and teaching writing*. New York: Oxford University Press.

Ferguson, A. A. (2000). *Bad boys*. Ann Arbor: University of Michigan Press.

Fingerson, L. (2006). *Girls in power: Gender, body, and menstruation in adolescence*. Albany: State University of New York Press.

Gardner, C. B. (1995). *Passing by*. Berkeley: University of California Press.

Glenn, E. N. (2002). *Unequal freedom: How race and gender shaped American citizenship and labor*. Cambridge, MA: Harvard University Press.

Goffman, E. (1989). On fieldwork. *Journal of Contemporary Ethnography, 18,* 123–132.

Harding, S. (1991). *Whose science, whose knowledge?* Ithaca, NY: Cornell University Press.

Hartsock, N. C. M. (1998). *The feminist standpoint revisited and other essays*. Boulder, CO: Westview Press.

Hemment, J. (2007). *Empowering women in Russia: Activism, aid, and NGOs*. Bloomington: Indiana University Press.

Hertz, R. (2002). The father as an idea: A challenge to kinship boundaries by single mothers. *Symbolic Interaction, 25,* 1–31.

Hesse-Biber, S. N. (2007). *The cult of thinness*. New York: Oxford University Press.

Hochschild, A. (1989). *The second shift: Working parents and the revolution at home*. New York: Viking.

Hochschild, A. (1997). *The time bind: When work becomes home and home becomes work*. New York: Metropolitan Books.

Hochschild, A. (2003). *The commercialization of intimate life: Notes from home and work*. Berkeley: University of California Press.

Howard, J. A., & Hollander, J. A. (1997). *Gendered situations, gendered selves: A gender lens on social psychology*. Thousand Oaks, CA: Sage.

Johnson, J. E. (2009). *Gender violence in Russia: The politics of feminist intervention*. Bloomington: Indiana University Press.

Kendall-Tackett, K. A. (2007). *How to write for a general audience: A Guide for academics who want to share their knowledge with the world and have fun doing it*. Washington, DC: American Psychological Association.

Kleinman, S. (2007). *Feminist fieldwork analysis*. Thousand Oaks, CA: Sage.

Kleinman, S., & Copp, M. (1993). *Emotions and fieldwork*. Newbury Park, CA: Sage.

Koikari, M. (2008). *Pedagogy of democracy: Feminism and the cold war in the U.S. occupation of Japan*. Philadelphia: Temple University Press.

Kuhlman, E. (2008). *Reconstructing patriarchy after the Great War: Women, gender, and postwar reconciliation between nations*. New York: Palgrave MacMillan.

Lal, J., McGuire, K., Stewart, A. J., Zaborowska, M., & Pas, J. M. (2010). Recasting global feminisms:

Toward a comparative historical approach to women's activism and feminist scholarship. *Feminist Studies, 36*(1), 13–39.

Lather, P. (2001). Postmodernism, post-structuralism and post(critical) ethnography: Of ruins, aporias and angels. In P. Atkinson, A. Coffey, S. Delamont, J. Lofland, & L. Lofland (Eds.), *Handbook of ethnography* (pp. 477–492). London: Sage.

Lather, P. (2007). *Getting lost: Feminist efforts toward a double(d) science.* Albany: State University of New York.

Lively, K. J. (2001). Occupational claims of professionalism: The case of paralegals. *Symbolic Interaction, 24,* 343–366.

Lofland, J., Snow, D., Anderson, L., & Lofland, L. H. (2006). *Analyzing social settings: A guide to qualitative observation and analysis* (4th ed.). Belmont, CA: Wadsworth/Thomson Learning.

Martin, E. (2007). Medical metaphors of women's bodies: Menstruation and menopause. In K. Charmaz & D. Paterniti (Eds.), *Health, illness, and healing: Society, social context, and self* (pp. 292–293). New York: Oxford.

Martin, E. (2008). *Bipolar expeditions: Mania and depression in American culture.* Princeton, NJ: Princeton University Press.

Maynes, M. J., Pierce, J. L., & Laslett, B. (2008). *Telling stories: The use of personal narratives in the social sciences and history.* Ithaca, NY: Cornell University Press.

McCorkel, J., & Myers, K. (2003). What difference does difference make? Position and privilege in the field. *Qualitative Sociology, 26*(2), 199–231.

Murray, S. B. (2000). Getting paid in smiles: The gendering of child care work. *Symbolic Interaction, 23,* 135–160.

Nack, A. (2008). *Damaged goods? Women living with incurable sexually transmitted diseases.* Philadelphia: Temple University Press.

Neal, D. G. (2008). *The masculine self in late medieval England.* Chicago: University of Chicago Press.

Olesen, V. (2005). Early millennial feminist qualitative research: Challenges and contours. In N. K. Denzin & Y. S. Lincoln (Eds.), *Handbook of qualitative research* (3rd ed., pp. 235–278). Thousand Oaks, CA: Sage.

Pangsapa P. (2007). *Textures of struggle: The emergence of resistance among garment workers in Thailand.* Ithaca, NY: Cornell University Press.

Rice, C. (2009). Imagining the other? Ethical challenges of researching and writing women's embodied lives. *Feminism & Psychology, 19*(2), 245–266.

Riessman, C. K. (2008). *Narrative methods for the human sciences.* Thousand Oaks, CA: Sage.

Rosenfeld, D. (2003). *The changing of the guard: Lesbian and gay elders, identity, and social change.* Philadelphia: Temple University Press.

Schreiber, R. (2008). *Righting feminism: Conservative women and American politics.* New York: Oxford University Press.

Shrock, D. P., & Padavic, I. (2007). Negotiating hegemonic masculinity in a batterer intervention program. *Gender & Society, 21,* 625–649.

Smith, D. E. (1987). *The everyday world as problematic: A feminist sociology.* Boston: Northeastern University Press.

Smith, D. E. (1999). *Writing the social: Critique, theory and investigations.* Toronto, ON: University of Toronto Press.

Smith, D. E. (2005). *Institutional ethnography: A sociology for people.* Walnut Creek, CA: AltaMira Press.

Sprague, J. (2005). *Feminist methodologies for critical researchers: Bridging differences.* Walnut Creek, CA: AltaMira Press.

Sulik, G. A. (2010). *Pink ribbon blues: How breast cancer culture undermines women's health.* New York: Oxford University Press.

Sullivan, D. A. (2001). *Cosmetic surgery: The cutting edge of commercial medicine in America.* New Brunswick, NJ: Rutgers University Press.

Tannen, D. (2009). *You always were mom's favorite! Sisters in conversation throughout their lives.* New York: Random House.

Taylor, V., & Rupp, L. J. (2005). When the girls are men: Negotiating gender and sexual dynamics in a study of drag queens. *Signs: The Journal of Women in Culture & Society, 30,* 2115–2139.

Wang, Z., & Zheng, Y. (2010). Global concepts, local practices: Chinese feminism since the Fourth UN Conference on Women. *Feminist Studies, 36*(1), 40–70.

Zerubavel, E. (1999). *The clockwork muse: A practical guide to writing theses, dissertations, and books.* Cambridge, MA: Harvard University Press.

23

PUTTING FEMINIST RESEARCH PRINCIPLES INTO PRACTICE

KRISTEN INTEMANN

Over the past several decades, feminist scholars have advocated for a variety of research principles that aim to increase scientific objectivity and promote more socially just science. While rejecting traditional conceptions of objectivity that require scientists to perform the impossible task of stripping away all of their own values, interests, experiences, and assumptions while conducting research, feminists have offered a variety of recommendations to help minimize the negative effects of problematic biases (Harding, 1991; Longino, 1990). The idea is to structure scientific communities and practices in ways that encourage the identification and critical evaluation of background assumptions, theories, and models (including those that are sexist, racist, or Eurocentric) while producing research that challenges, rather than reinforces or ignores, oppression.

Despite the fact that these recommendations have emerged from diverse feminist approaches and theoretical frameworks (such as feminist empiricism, standpoint feminism, and postcolonial feminism), there is much overlap in terms of the kinds of principles endorsed for directing feminist research. In particular, several have argued that scientific communities ought to

1. include researchers with diverse experiences, social positions, interests, and values (Harding, 2008; Longino, 2002; Rolin, 2006; Solomon, 2006);

2. provide multiple opportunities for the scrutiny and criticism of methods, assumptions, models, values, and interpretations of data by inquirers with equality of intellectual authority (Anderson, 2006; Longino, 1990, 2002; Nelson, 1990);

3. investigate scientific phenomena from the perspectives, interests, and conditions of marginalized stakeholders potentially affected by the research (Collins, 1991; Harding, 2004, 2008; Kourany, 2003; Wylie, 2003); and

4. encourage and produce a plurality of models and theoretical frameworks for understanding scientific phenomena (Longino, 2002; Solomon, 2001).

Yet more work is needed to determine what exactly these recommendations would require and the epistemic and social benefits they would yield in specific research contexts.

In this chapter, I will focus on the epistemological and social benefits that feminist research principles could yield in the context of climate change research. This area of research is particularly fruitful for applying and identifying these principles for several reasons. First, climate change research shapes global public policy. That is, the aim of the research is not just to describe climate change but also to generate knowledge that can be used to guide action and evaluate various public policy options. Because of this, such research has the potential to promote (or fail to promote) issues of social justice. For example, many of the models currently used in climate research have been criticized as failing to capture adequately how marginalized groups will be impacted, despite the fact that they are likely to be the most affected by and least responsible for global warming (for examples of critiques, see Argawal, 2002; Schneider, Kuntz-Duriseti, & Azar, 2000). Second, climate change research involves generating predictions from complex models that must make a multitude of assumptions in the face of uncertainties. Thus, there is a vast web of background assumptions that researchers rely on, many of which are made implicitly and unconsciously. This opens up the possibility that some assumptions have not received sufficient scrutiny and may be unjustified or may reflect the experiences and values of the relatively homogeneous group of researchers building climate models. Moreover, because climate change is a politically charged topic, many climate scientists and environmental economists have defended the objectivity of their research by maintaining that their analyses are "value-free" or neutral with respect to social, ethical, and political values (e.g., Lomborg, 2007). As a result, value-laden assumptions and internal disagreements between scientists may be masked or downplayed so as to protect scientific authority and expertise (Beatty, 2006). Thus, climate research faces epistemological challenges that are deeply connected with issues of social justice, making it a fruitful area in which to apply feminist research principles.

The purpose of this chapter is twofold. First, to show that current climate change research faces three problems or limitations that feminist research principles are well suited to address. As a result, incorporating feminist principles would produce both epistemic and social benefits in climate science. Second, to demonstrate how feminist research principles would apply in the context of climate change research so as to increase our understanding of what these principles require as well as why they are beneficial. I will begin by outlining some of the current problems and challenges in climate change research. In the sections that follow, I will show how each of the feminist research principles can offer resources for addressing these problems.

CHALLENGES IN CLIMATE CHANGE RESEARCH

Climate change research has focused, broadly speaking, on two central projects. First, some climate research has examined the rate and magnitude at which average global temperature is increasing and the causes for those changes. Such research aims to make predictions about what changes we might expect depending on the level of CO_2 equivalents in the atmosphere and other factors that can exacerbate or lessen the greenhouse effect, such as aerosols, cloud formation, and water vapor feedback. Second, some research aims to predict and measure the *impacts* of climate changes on ecosystems and human communities, including the impacts of potential policy strategies for slowing global warming or adapting to changes created by a warmer global climate. Both areas of research involve a wide range of disciplines and, as is the case with virtually all scientific research, have faced a variety of challenges, limitations, and criticisms. Examining some of the main challenges and limitations of current climate research will help clarify aspects about the nature of climate science that feminist research principles might enhance.

My intent is *not* to encourage skepticism about climate change or to undermine our confidence in climate science. There is broad scientific consensus that human carbon emissions are a significant cause of increasing average global temperature, and this consensus seems justified by a convergence of evidence (though I will not defend this evidence here). Yet research practices can, to greater or lesser degrees, promote or obscure knowledge production. Thus, for any area of scientific research, it is important to examine how research practices might be improved to better promote epistemic goals.

Moreover, there are different ways of producing knowledge about a phenomenon, and some of these will be more or less useful depending on how we hope to use that information (Cartwright, 2006; Shrader-Frechette, 2007). For example, complex climate models that are highly accurate but that will take decades to run will probably not be helpful in generating predictions that will help prevent dangerous climate change, as we simply would not have access to the data in a timely manner. Thus, it is also important to examine how research might be enhanced so as to achieve the sort of knowledge or evidence that will also promote the social aims of the research. What follows, then, is a discussion of three main problems or limitations that I believe are present in current climate change research. As we will see, these problems are precisely the sorts of concerns that feminist research principles aim to address.

Lack of Recognition of Implicit Value Judgments

There are several ways that climate research implicitly relies on value-laden assumptions that are not acknowledged by researchers and, as a result, are not critically examined by a broader group of stakeholders. One way results from uncertainties that arise in climate research. Empirical research aimed at measuring and predicting climate changes has utilized general circulation models (GCMs), which are used to simulate the effects of increasing atmospheric (equivalent) CO_2 concentrations. A central challenge in building GCMs is that there is a significant amount of uncertainty about several variables that can influence global warming. For example, there are large ranges of interactive processes that contribute to cloud formation and cloud-radiation interaction, and these can produce "feedbacks" with either warming effects or cooling effects. Because there is a high degree of uncertainty about how clouds will form and interact, experts disagree about the extent to which clouds will contribute to amplifying or mitigating warming (Intergovernmental Panel on Climate Change [IPCC], 2007; Weare, 2000a, 2000b). In its most recent assessment report, the IPCC maintains that cloud feedbacks remain the largest source of uncertainty (IPCC, 2007, p. 38). Water vapor feedbacks are also a significant source of uncertainty.

Water vapor in the atmosphere is itself a greenhouse gas that can have a warming effect on global climate. In fact, changes in water vapor represent the greatest feedback affecting net changes in global mean near-surface air temperature that would result from a doubling of CO_2 equivalents (IPCC, 2007, p. 38). Some studies have found that water vapor feedback could cause twice as much warming as would occur if water vapor were held fixed (Cess et al., 1990; Hall & Manabe, 1999; Held & Soden, 2000; Schneider, Kirtman, & Lindzen, 1999). Again, however, there is uncertainty about the amount and distribution of water vapor that will likely be in the atmosphere as CO_2 increases over the next 100 years. Because cloud processes also affect the water vapor pattern and moisture distribution, uncertainty about cloud processes has thus also led to difficulties in modeling water vapor feedback (IPCC, 2001, p. 267).

Yet, although there is a significant amount of uncertainty regarding variables that can strongly affect average global temperature, these variables must be parameterized or quantified in GCMs in order to run the model simulation and generate predictions about the effects of increasing atmospheric CO_2. Assumptions must be built into models about cloud formation and water vapor feedback. Such decisions, however, presuppose implicit value judgments about the sort of errors that are most acceptable in generating predictions. No matter what assumptions are made about cloud feedback there is a risk of being wrong and these errors would have social consequences. Falsely assuming cloud conditions that amplify warming could lead to the overregulation of CO_2, as well as to wasting resources on unnecessary mitigation strategies. At the same time, falsely assuming cloud conditions that lessen warming could lead to the underregulation of CO_2 and could lead to greater climate change impacts than predicted. This assumption, then, could have potentially devastating and irreversible consequences for biodiversity, human health, food production, habitats, and economic systems. Which assumptions should be adopted depends partly on which risks of error are judged to be most acceptable (Biddle & Winsberg, 2010; Douglas, 2000, 2007). This choice relies on ethical value judgments about whether it is *worse* to risk overregulating or underregulating.

Climate impacts research can also involve implicit value judgments. Climate change impact models aim to measure the costs and benefits of various potential policy options, as well as of unconstrained climate change. It may be tempting to think that cost-benefit analyses merely describe the physical and economic conditions that result from various scenarios. Indeed, most of the disagreements in climate impacts research appear to focus on empirical disagreements about which scenarios are most probable or whether a policy would indeed produce a certain consequence (Schneider, 2002). But cost-benefit analyses are not value-free assessments (Shrader-Frechette, 2007). They rest on value judgments about, for example, what counts as a "cost" or a "benefit." These judgments reflect what we take to be important or of significant value. For example, most models measure costs such as loss of GDP or human lives. The impacts to other potential goods, such as biodiversity or quality of health, are not represented. As a result, existing models reflect implicit value judgments about what we take to be important "costs" and "benefits."

Climate and climate change impact models also make value-laden assumptions about *whose* impacts deserve consideration. Should climate modelers consider impacts to nonhuman animals, ecosystems, or future generations of human beings? Or should models focus on only those impacts that are likely to be experienced by living humans? Answers to these questions depend on judgments about the beings or entities that we take to be deserving of moral consideration. Modelers implicitly assume whose interests deserve consideration in the selection of impacts that they choose to measure. For example, at this point, most GCMs do not make predictions past 2100 (IPCC, 2007). Yet, if we have an obligation to consider impacts to future generations, then duration of models may need to be extended to determine more long-term policy consequences. Determining the extent of our ethical obligations seems particularly important insofar as future generations are likely to suffer the most significant impacts without having contributed to the problem.

Thus, there are a variety of value judgments that operate as background assumptions in both climate change and climate change impact modeling. The problem is that this circumstance goes unacknowledged by most researchers. Climate scientists, like most scientists, tend to deny that their research is in any way value laden, as they fear admitting this necessity would imply their research is subjective. This view persists among many scientists despite the fact that much literature has shown that such values can be compatible with and may even enhance scientific objectivity (e.g., Harding, 1998; Kourany, 2008; Longino, 1990, 2002; Solomon, 2001). Consequently, throughout scientific training, scientists are discouraged from endorsing any social, ethical, or political values because of the worry that doing so will lead to bias. The commitment to value neutrality is also reflected in the lack of training that scientists receive in identifying or evaluating the ethical and social implications of their research.

In the context of climate modeling, value judgments are implicitly presumed in the models adopted by researchers without any explicit discussion about which value judgments should be endorsed. This method is problematic because it renders such assumptions less visible or available for critical evaluation by a wider group of stakeholders. The worry, then, is that the value judgments implicitly built into climate models may be unsupported or may, inadvertently, reflect only the interests of modelers.

Homogeneity of Models

A second potential problem in climate change research is that, in certain respects, the models employed are homogeneous. For example, as mentioned before, climate impact research tends to rely solely on cost-benefit analyses to assess the impacts of various mitigation and adaptation policies. Some have argued that such models are limited in important ways (Graves, 2007). First, such models tend to focus on measuring costs that can be more easily quantified, such as the number of lives lost, the dollar amount of property damage, and the GDP loss from a doubling of atmospheric CO_2 equivalent concentrations (Schneider & Kuntz-Duriseti, 2002). This focus, however, excludes costs that are not easily quantifiable but may be incredibly important, such as the loss of cultural traditions, decreased biodiversity, the increased dependence of developed countries on developing countries, or reductions in quality of life and health (Argawal, 2002; Schneider et al., 2000; Schneider, Rosencranz, & Niles, 2002). Second, it is not clear that the costs being quantified are commensurable (Graves, 2007). Suppose, for example, one mitigation policy decreases GDP but increases the number of species saved, while a second policy option increases GDP but decreases the number of species saved. Which policy should be preferred? Although these two outcomes might be quantified, it is not clear they can be quantified in a way that makes them commensurable. How much of a loss in GDP is the equivalent of losing five species? These are not goods that appear to share a single scale of value. Thus, researchers' singular reliance on cost-benefit analyses results in homogeneity and is vulnerable to the same sorts of limitations.

Similarly, climate modelers have tended to deal with practical or logistical challenges in exactly the same ways. For example, modelers are constrained by the technological capabilities and resources that are available for building GCMs. The greater the complexity of a climate model, the longer it can take to run. The longer a model takes to run, however, the less useful it will be in terms of generating predictions that can inform policies capable of preventing or mitigating dangerous climate change. Of course, the more focused modelers are on building GCMs with faster computational times, the more such models would be idealized simplifications that will not accurately capture the complex processes and interactions that are likely to occur in the real world. There is a trade-off here between simplicity and accuracy.

Because the climate modelers generally face similar logistical constraints, they often make the same sort of trade-offs. This decision, however, can produce models that share certain assumptions that are not highly confirmed. For example, most models assume that the climate will respond to increased CO_2 equivalents slowly and at the same rate over time (Schneider & Thompson, 2000). In reality, climate change may be erratic and may produce "climate surprises" (or sudden rapid events), which could have very different effects than steady climate change. Of course, models that assume slow and stable climate change are simpler and may be preferable on

pragmatic grounds. Nonetheless, the lack of models that address climate surprises also limits what we know and how impacts are measured.

Another source of homogeneity in climate models is the representation of aerosols. Aerosols can have a net cooling effect; thus, the concentration and distribution of aerosols and aerosol precursor emissions (such as sulfur dioxide, black carbon, and organic carbon) represented in climate models can also influence the magnitude of warming effects. In all of the GCMs used for the IPCC's fourth assessment report (2007), aerosol properties and processes were highly simplified using simulations that do not capture the various interactions between aerosols and other variables, such as clouds and precipitation (Rind, Yu, Schwartz, & Halthore, 2009). While aerosol models may be improving (Ghan & Schwartz, 2007; Koch, Schmidt, & Field, 2006; Rind et al., 2009), it is clear that current GCMs represent aerosols in ways that are likely to be inaccurate. Moreover, this likelihood has provided ammunition to climate skeptics who argue that problematic assumptions about aerosols contribute to the exaggeration of the extent and impact of global warming (e.g., Ball, 2010). Thus, the concern is that climate modelers may deal with logistical constraints and uncertainties in similar ways that produce shared, but not highly confirmed, assumptions or practices.

Inadequate Representation of the Interests of Those Most Likely Affected

A further set of problems is that many models fail to address adequately the interests and needs of those most likely to be adversely affected by climate change. This is so for a number of reasons. First, as stated earlier, because climate impact research relies heavily on cost-benefit analyses, the impacts that are measured are ones that can be more easily quantified. This focus on the quantifiable, however, tends to exclude the sorts of impacts that might matter most to those in developing countries, where the effects of climate change are likely to be the greatest. Current models fail to consider impacts such as loss of cultural traditions or increased dependence on developed countries (Argawal, 2002; Schneider et al., 2000).

Second, most climate impact models measure only aggregate costs and benefits for the entire planet and not the distribution of costs and benefits among particular regions or countries (Schiermeier, 2010; Schneider et al., 2000). This method of measurement does not allow us to determine whether the distribution of costs and benefits under a particular policy option is fair or equitable. There may be policies that increase overall net utility in ways that provide the greatest benefits to those who are the most well off while those who are already the least well off face a disproportionate burden of the costs. For example, some argue that, although there are areas where agriculture would be affected adversely by unconstrained climate change, this effect would be offset by areas where agricultural production would increase. Farmland in Bangladesh may be ruined by increased salinity caused by rising sea levels, but warmer temperatures in northern parts of North America and Europe will increase their food production such that the global food supply will remain essentially the same. Of course, the benefits in this scenario accrue mostly to those in northern countries, while those in southern countries would be the most impacted by the loss of local food production and agricultural economies. Thus, while the aggregate costs of unconstrained climate change may be small with respect to agriculture, the distribution of those costs seems unjust. Yet most climate models do not measure this.

In addition to examining the distribution of costs and benefits between developed and developing countries, there may be other populations within a particular geographical region who are impacted differently by climate change. For example, it might turn out that climate changes will affect women and men very differently. Suppose that agricultural work tended to be done largely by female workers in certain areas that were likely to be highly impacted by climate change. In this case, impacts to agriculture might impact women in ways that are not directly experienced by men. It could even have the potential effect of making women more economically dependent on men in their families. Similarly, individuals from lower socioeconomic classes are likely to be impacted differently than those in higher ones. Wealthier families are more

likely than lower-income families to have homes that are located and designed to withstand extreme weather events. Thus, current models that only measure aggregate impacts fail to capture how certain populations are disproportionately affected by certain policies.

Presumably, however, not every conceivable population is important in measuring the distribution of costs and benefits within climate policy scenarios. We are not interested in, for instance, how costs are distributed between right-handed and left-handed individuals because handedness does not appear to be a salient category of analysis with respect to climate change. So, the question is, which categories of analyses *are* salient and should be adopted in measuring the distribution of costs and benefits? The answer will depend on which categories we take to be relevant to promoting social justice. Most climate researchers, however, do not engage in a discussion about which populations (or *whose* impacts) are important to measure.

To summarize, I have identified three areas of concern in climate change research:

- Implicit value judgments that go unrecognized and unscrutinized
- Homogeneity in climate modeling that leads to systematic limitations
- Inadequate representation of the interests of those most likely to be affected

These areas of concern are, of course, interconnected. All three problems are related to the fact that there are a host of background assumptions that climate researchers implicitly adopt, many of which are value judgments and some of which may be problematic or unconfirmed. Because many of these assumptions and values are widely shared by those currently conducting climate research, an unintended cumulative effect occurs—models are homogeneous and limit our knowledge of climate impacts in systematic ways. Moreover, it appears that one systematic limitation of current climate impact models is that they fail to account adequately for the interests of those who are likely to be most affected by climate change.

This list is not intended to be exhaustive of the potential challenges to climate change research or to climate change impact models, but it provides a good starting place for examining how feminist research principles might apply to and enhance climate research. Of course, this is not to say that feminist research principles, by themselves, would be sufficient for addressing all of these problems completely. Nonetheless, the next sections will consider how feminist research principles might provide useful resources for dealing with the challenges that climate researchers face or, at the very least, how these principles can lessen the problematic consequences of these challenges.

How Feminist Research Principles Might Enhance Climate Change Research

Feminist research principles aim to help decrease problematic biases that result from sexism and other forms of oppression while promoting more socially just science. I will focus on four feminist principles for governing research communities that would be particularly useful in climate change research. Specifically, communities of inquirers should

1. be comprised of inquirers with diverse experiences, interests, and values;

2. provide multiple opportunities for the scrutiny and criticism of methods, assumptions, models, values, and interpretations of data by inquirers with equality of intellectual authority;

3. "study from the margins out" or begin investigations of phenomena from the perspectives and conditions of marginalized stakeholders potentially affected by the research; and

4. produce a plurality of models that can provide a range of alternatives when dealing with significant uncertainties.

I take these to be "feminist" research principles because they emerged to advance two important feminist aims in research. First, these principles aim to increase the objectivity of research communities by preventing or reducing the negative epistemic effects of gender bias and sexist oppression (as well as other forms of bias and oppression). Second, such principles also aim to promote socially just science that undermines rather than reinforces existing systems of oppression. This is not to say that these are exclusively feminist principles or that all and only feminists hold them, nor are they intended to be exhaustive of research principles that feminists might advocate. They jointly provide, however, a fruitful starting place to consider how feminist epistemic and social aims might be advanced in specific research contexts in ways that enhance research. I will now develop each of the four feminist research principles in more detail and explain how they apply and yield both epistemic and social benefits in climate change studies.

Establishing Diverse Research Communities

As we have seen, a main problem with climate change research is that such research must make a host of complex background assumptions, some of which are value judgments. To the extent that these are not recognized or evaluated, there is a risk that they arbitrarily reflect the experiences, interests, and values of those who happen to be conducting the research. For example, assumptions about what counts as a "cost" in measuring climate impacts are informed by what researchers take to be important goods. The fact that such assumptions are informed by the experiences, values, and interests of researchers is not necessarily a problem, so long as those assumptions are justified or consistent with the experiences, values, and interests of a broader group of stakeholders.

Yet it can be very difficult for researchers to recognize all of the background assumptions being employed in a particular research context. One reason these are difficult to recognize, even for conscientious researchers, is that when the assumptions are consistent with one's values and experiences or widely held by those in a research group, they are taken for granted and more difficult to recognize (Longino, 2002). When scientific communities are comprised of researchers with diverse life experiences and interests, however, a fuller range of experiential evidence can be brought to bear on critically evaluating background assumptions. A diverse research group increases the chances that any problematic background assumptions will be identified (Longino, 2002, p. 51). When assumptions conflict with one's own experiences, values, or interests, they are easier to recognize. Thus, a scientific community comprised of individuals with diverse life experiences, values, and interests will be more likely to identify and critically evaluate problematic assumptions and value judgments operating in theories, models, experiments, explanations, or interpretations of data. Such a community will also be more likely to generate a fuller range of hypotheses and alternative models. As a result, diverse research communities will be more objective than a community of researchers with homogeneous experiences and values in the sense that background assumptions will be more likely to be justified and less likely to reflect the idiosyncratic biases of individual researchers. In this way, communities, rather than individuals, are the locus of objectivity (Code, 1991; Nelson, 1990).

What sort of diversity is necessary for accomplishing this sort of objectivity? Some have argued that it is diversity of values and interests that is important (Longino, 1990, 2002) while others have argued that it is diversity of social position (Haraway, 1988; Harding, 1991; Rolin, 2006) or diversity of ideas (Solomon, 2001). In part, the sort of diversity that is epistemically beneficial depends on the type of research being conducted. The potential epistemic benefits of diversity are related to identifying and evaluating problematic background assumptions and generating a fuller range of hypotheses, explanations, and models. The kind of diversity that would help generate these benefits depends on the sorts of experiences that would be relevant to evaluating the content of the background assumptions at stake (Intemann, 2009). In addition, particular types of diversity may be particularly important insofar as certain interests and experiences have been historically underrepresented or ignored (Harding, 1991; Rolin, 2006). Thus, the types of diversity that would be useful can depend on the context of the research.

In climate change research, it is important to have a community of researchers that reflects the diversity of the stakeholders affected by climate policies. Therefore, it will be important to involve researchers from different geographical areas (e.g., from developing countries in the Southern Hemisphere as well as from developed countries) who will be in a better position to evaluate whether climate models or policies address the needs and interests of populations in those areas. Researchers from developing countries, for example, would be better situated to realize when certain impacts that are salient to those in the global South are being neglected. It will also be beneficial to involve researchers with diverse expertise in a variety of relevant fields (such as economics, political science, atmospheric science, and sociology). Neither an atmospheric scientist nor an economist may have the expertise needed to be able to consider whether there are interests, such as loss of cultural traditions, that should be measured or how to do so. A sociologist or anthropologist, however, might be useful in this regard. It may also be important to involve researchers with a variety of social positions and life experiences (e.g., different ethnicity, class, or gender). Those from different social positions would be more likely to have experiences that would make them concerned about how climate change impacts populations differently, and they would see the need for certain categories of analysis. The aim is to have a community of inquirers that is likely to have diverse values, interests, life experiences, and expertise—a community comprised of members whose individual differences will be relevant to seeing the limitations of and problems associated with the assumptions being made by other researchers. Although the IPCC has attempted to include researchers from a variety of countries and regions, the disproportionate majority of climate scientists (including those who are IPCC authors or reviewers) are males from Europe and North America (Argawal, 2002; IPCC Secretariat, 2008). Of the 40 scientists who comprised the core writing team for IPCC's Fourth Assessment Report, 6 were female, 3 were from countries in Africa, and 3 were from South America (IPCC, 2007). Moreover, although there is some disciplinary diversity within the working groups of the IPCC, there are no social scientists (other than economists) with expertise relevant to conducting research on the more qualitative aspects of climate change impacts. Thus, greater diversity may be useful in achieving the greater scrutiny of background assumptions, as well as in the development of new alternative models.

Of course, merely having a diverse community of inquirers is not enough to ensure that individual researchers will be able to challenge problematic value judgments successfully or the other background assumptions operating in research. It must also be the case that individuals have the opportunity and resources to evaluate climate research critically and to have those criticisms taken seriously by researchers.

Equality of Intellectual Authority and Opportunities for Criticism

To promote the identification, evaluation, and revision of problematic background assumptions, researchers must provide opportunities for criticizing research. In fact, the objectivity of the research may be enhanced by providing not only opportunities for criticism from within the larger scientific community (i.e., peer review) but also opportunities for criticism from those outside of that community that are affected by the research (Harding, 2008; Longino, 2002). Because research communities often share many assumptions in virtue of their training, recognizing problematic background assumptions may be better accomplished by those outside of the community.

In the case of the IPCC, there has been a conscious effort to solicit feedback on its reports from governments as well as experts (IPCC, 2008). The IPCC has established multiple rounds of review, and all of the review comments made by experts and governments are made available to everyone participating in the review process during that process (see Figure 23.1). Furthermore, those review comments are publicly available for at least five years after a report is published (IPCC, 2008, p. 3).

Yet, despite these efforts, it is not clear that the mechanisms for feedback in climate research

Figure 23.1 IPCC Review Procedures

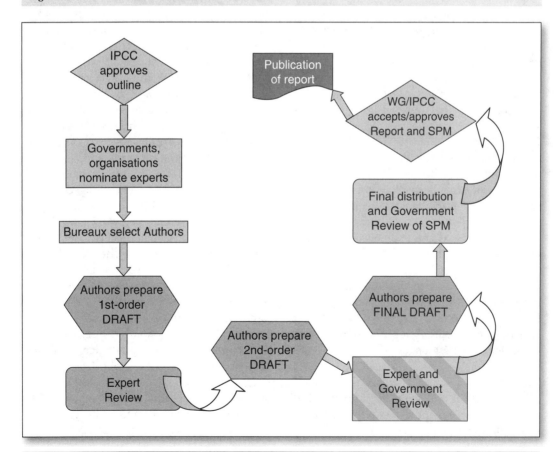

Source: Reprinted by permission of the Intergovernmental Panel on Climate Change (IPCC; 2010).

are adequate. First, the IPCC relies on a host of already published climate change studies to produce its assessment reports and summaries for policy makers. Thus, although the synthesized reports may undergo multiple review processes, the studies used to produce those reports have not necessarily had the same rigorous scrutiny. In fact, the IPCC has acknowledged that it relies on "selected non-peer reviewed literature produced by other relevant institutions including industry" (IPCC, 2010).

Second, even peer-reviewed scientific literature does not undergo any review by those outside of the scientific community until, perhaps, after publication. This circumstance puts the burden on members of the public without scientific expertise to read a technical paper and attempt to criticize it. In contrast, climate scientists might work with organizations or stakeholder representatives to receive feedback on assumptions they are making (such as what constitutes an "impact" or which risks are most acceptable) before research is conducted or published.

Third, opportunities for critical transformative discourse can only be successful when there is a certain degree of transparency of methods, reasoning, and assumptions. In some cases, however, details about methodology or about the assumptions made in data collection and interpretation are not apparent in a manuscript submitted for publication (de Melo-Martín & Intemann, 2009). Climate researchers might increase transparency of methods and assumptions by publishing these in greater detail. Some journals, for example, allow more detailed descriptions of methodology to be published in online versions of the journal. Making assumptions and methods more explicit creates more opportunity for evaluation.

Finally, in order for a process of critical evaluation to be successful, those involved in the process must be treated as having equal intellectual authority or the power to have their criticisms heard and taken seriously regardless of their social position or political influence (Longino, 2002, p. 131; Nelson, 1990). The idea here is that a consensus produced through processes of critical evaluation should be reached because of the epistemic merits of the arguments made—it should *not* be the result of exercising political or social power to exclude or ignore dissenting perspectives. Recognizing equality of intellectual authority means that researchers must engage with the criticisms raised to their research and respond to them—either by defending their methodologies, reasoning, and assumptions or by making revisions to account for the criticism—until a broad consensus is reached among researchers with diverse experiences and interests.

There are worries that, despite opportunities for the critical evaluation of climate change research, intellectual equality has not been fully achieved. Although the IPCC involves governments in reviewing its reports, it is not clear that the comments of all governments are given the same weight, irrespective of their economic and political power. In addition, maintaining equality of intellectual authority is generally helped when members of the research community are not aware of *who* is making the criticism (Wallington & Moore, 2005). That way, they are less likely to dismiss someone who may be less well known or from a certain geographical location. The double-blind review of manuscripts is not always followed by peer-reviewed journals. Nor is it included in the IPCC review process.

Promoting equality of intellectual authority can be difficult, however, particularly in climate change research where some dissent has been deliberately generated to create doubt and confusion over the state of climate science (Oreskes & Conway, 2010). Must climate scientists take seriously and respond to *every* criticism that is raised to their research? Longino has suggested two constraints on the equality of intellectual authority (Longino, 2002, pp. 133–134). First, individuals may lose their claim to equality of intellectual authority if they are repeating criticisms that have already been made while ignoring the replies that have been given. That is, those participating in criticism also have a responsibility to treat the targets of their criticism with equal intellectual authority by taking seriously the responses that they have offered. Second, Longino argues that recognizing equality of intellectual authority does not require granting equality of cognitive authority to all participants (Longino, 2002, p. 133). Intellectual authority is the capacity to participate in critical discussion and contribute to critical understanding. Recognizing this capacity, however, is compatible with recognizing that some will have higher cognitive authority or will have more knowledge of certain areas in which they have received more training or education. Thus, although everyone must be treated with the same rights and be acknowledged as having the capacity to participate in cognitive discourse, this does not mean that every criticism will have the same weight. Longino suggests that it is appropriate to give more weight to experts when the matter is a technical one relevant to their area of expertise (Longino, 2002, p. 133).

By promoting equality of intellectual authority and enhancing opportunities for criticism, climate researchers could increase the rigor of scrutiny brought to bear on their research. As a result, the assumptions they rely upon are more likely to be justified and inclusive of the interests and needs of those most affected by climate change.

Studying From the Margins Out

A third feminist research principle is to "study from the margins out"—to begin investigations of phenomena from the perspectives, interests, and conditions of marginalized stakeholders who are most potentially affected by the research (Crasnow, 2006; Harding, 1991, 2004; Kourany, 2003; Wylie, 2003). This principle of giving voice to those silenced has a long tradition in standpoint theory, but it can also be found more generally in calls to make marginalized social categories "visible" in relation to research problems (Longino, 1996; Wylie & Nelson, 2007). Grounding research in the experiences of those most affected by it requires researchers to identify marginalized populations whom a particular scientific problem will impact (when this is the case) and to examine the ways in which their marginalization may contribute to or be affected by the problem. This approach is particularly relevant in areas of research that will be used to generate public policy, interventions, or new technologies aimed at addressing some social problem. When the interests and needs of marginalized populations are not taken into account, even well-intentioned science may lead to policies and interventions that reinforce

rather than address existing social inequalities (Harding, 2008; Intemann & de Melo-Martín, 2010; Lacey, 2005).

There are both ethical and epistemic motivations for studying from the margins. As stated earlier, one central aim of feminist research is to investigate phenomena in ways that help challenge or undermine systems of oppression rather than in ways that reinforce or ignore oppression altogether. Attending to both oppressive structures and the perspectives of those oppressed is one mechanism for producing research that gives priority to the needs of marginalized groups. At the same time, this approach can also have the epistemic benefit of revealing features or aspects of the object of scientific study that were previously obscured. For example, as female archaeologists began to ask how women contributed to the evolution of tool use, they revealed new lines of evidence and artifacts that had previously been ignored (Wylie, 2001). Similarly, examining how particular health problems affect women in developed countries differently than women in developing countries can reveal crucial nuances in the causal mechanisms of disease and disease transmission (Intemann & de Melo-Martín, 2010).

In the context of climate change research, studying from the margins requires investigating how marginalized groups might be impacted by climate changes as well as considering various adaptation and mitigation strategies. This approach involves using certain relevant social groupings, such as gender, class, ethnicity, and geographical location, as categories for analyzing climate change impacts. Researchers should attempt to make gender, for example, "visible" by asking how women and men might be impacted differently by climate change. How might climate impacts manifest or be experienced differently by those with less political or economic power? How might climate change or various policy options affect marginalized populations given their material conditions and the legacies of oppression? To what extent are the interests of marginalized groups represented in current climate models? Answering this last question involves determining what members of marginalized groups take to be valuable and evaluating how various policies might work given the social, economic, and political barriers that such groups face.

Of course, not all marginalized individuals (or marginalized groups) share the same values and interests. But, by working directly with marginalized populations, researchers can become more aware of the range of interests at stake and better identify whether current models adequately address them. Thus, a commitment to attending to the perspectives of those who are potentially most affected by climate change also requires research to be directed by marginalized populations and organizations that advocate for such populations. Because this approach requires determining the interests of members of these groups, it necessitates that investigators work closely with them in addition to securing the participation of researchers who have experiences or knowledge of what life is like in those contexts.

Moreover, determining the interests of particular populations will require that researchers acquire additional knowledge about social, political, cultural, biological, and economic factors that might be relevant to how climate change will impact certain populations. Given that neither economists nor climate scientists can be expected to have all of the relevant expertise, studying from the margins calls for scientists, social scientists, ethicists, and policy makers to work collaboratively in determining the features that a successful climate policy would need to have, deciding what will count as costs and benefits, and so on.

How might approaching climate change research using this feminist principle help address some of the challenges faced by climate researchers? As with some of the other principles discussed, studying from the margins allows for the identification and evaluation of background assumptions by involving the participation of a greater number of stakeholders. Moreover, by placing particular importance on the needs and interests of marginalized groups, this approach can reveal features and aspects of a scientific phenomenon that have been previously obscured or neglected. For example, it may help researchers determine if women in developing countries may be affected by climate change in ways that are different from men or women in developed countries. This evidence, in turn, helps better inform policy

makers so that the policies adopted are less likely to further disadvantage marginalized groups unintentionally.

Promoting Pluralism of Models

A final feminist research principle is to encourage and promote the production of a plurality of models for understanding or studying scientific phenomena (Longino, 2002; Parker, 2006; Solomon, 2001). This principle provides resources for addressing the problem of homogeneity in models, so that we do not end up with a group of models that are systematically limited in similar ways. For example, as we have seen, some of the challenges in climate modeling result from areas of significant uncertainty, such as cloud and water vapor feedback. Producing a plurality of models that represent different assumptions would allow us to observe and measure impacts for a greater range of scenarios. Similarly, we have seen that there are limitations to the dominant models and frameworks used in climate research, such as the cost-benefit analysis. Promoting different methodological approaches to climate research, for example, including methods that examine aspects of climate impacts that are difficult to quantify, could provide new insight into the sorts of impacts that could be expected. In this way, although any singular model might be viewed as "biased" or "limited" in the assumptions that it makes, a diverse group of models as a whole can convey a range of possibilities that may help better inform policy making.

To some extent, this pluralism already happens in global climate computer simulation models. Climate scientists use a variety of models to help account for uncertainties in how best to represent the climate system, as well as to investigate disagreements about the relative merits of complex models (Parker, 2006). Economists could also endeavor to contribute to model pluralism as well as examine a full range of models when making policy recommendations. Granting agencies might also provide incentives for doing so.

Although additional work is needed to further examine how these four research principles might apply in other research contexts, I have argued that they would help in addressing several key challenges in climate change research. To the degree that these four recommendations are met, climate researchers are more likely to produce studies and models that are epistemically adequate as well as socially responsible. These principles jointly work to promote the adoption of background assumptions (including value judgments) that are well supported. Also, diversity and pluralism increase the range of hypotheses and models that are likely to be developed and pursued. As a result, our knowledge of climate change is less likely to be limited or obscured in systematic ways. Finally, studying from the margins out and ensuring that value judgments are justified helps produce research that is more responsive to the needs and interests of marginalized groups. This approach also helps ensure that the knowledge generated will be useful in promoting the social and policy aims of the research.

Conclusion

I have argued that feminist research principles can have epistemic benefits and help produce more socially just climate change research. In particular, they can help identify and facilitate more rigorous scrutiny of background assumptions in climate modeling, particularly those that are value-laden. The research principles discussed do not aim to *eliminate* value judgments from climate research. Indeed, these principles themselves presuppose that scientific research should aim to promote social justice and address, rather than reinforce or ignore, systems of oppression when possible.

This chapter also does not imply that climate research is radically subjective or "just a reflection of politics." So long as we think that ethical and social value judgments can be critically evaluated, defended, and revised, they are not unlike other background assumptions that operate in science. Like any background assumption, such judgments may turn out to be wrong, or there may be disagreement. With mechanisms to manage individual biases and increase the likelihood that value judgments will be well supported and democratically endorsed by a broad group of stakeholders, the

resulting theories, models, and policy recommendations will be more objective, or less distorted and partial, than they would otherwise be.

Objectivity, then, should not be understood as requiring freedom from values or value neutrality. An objective research community is not one that refrains from making value judgments. Rather, an objective research community is one that is *responsible or fair* in representing phenomena, building models, interpreting data, adopting value judgments, and making policy recommendations. On this account, objectivity comes in degrees (rather than as an all or nothing property). Research communities can be more objective or less objective to the extent that they are successfully able to meet the four recommendations discussed in this chapter.

Research communities guided by feminist principles will be more responsible in identifying, evaluating, and revising problematic assumptions in research. They will be more likely to provide checks and balances against idiosyncratic individual biases. They will be more open to revising theories and models, and to proposing a full range of new alternatives. To the extent that there are value judgments involved in research, feminist research communities will be more likely to endorse value judgments that are well grounded and widely supported.

This is not to say that value judgments are *always* relevant or appropriate in research. Whether it is legitimate to rely on value judgments will depend on the content of the judgment and how it is being relied on in the research (whether it is relevant to the methodological decision being made). But, if scientists continue to maintain that their research is value free or value neutral, a discussion of which values should be endorsed and whether they are operating in legitimate ways cannot even begin.

Discussion Questions

1. What are some of the central challenges in climate change research, and why might these be particularly troubling from a feminist perspective?

2. What are the potential epistemic and social benefits to increasing diversity among climate change researchers?

3. What is required by "studying from the margins out," and how might this approach enhance climate research?

4. Feminist research principles have often been advocated for use in a variety of social science research contexts. Are there compelling reasons to think that such principles might also be useful in the natural or physical sciences?

Online Resources

The Intergovernmental Panel on Climate Change

http://www.ipcc.ch/

This site provides all IPCC working group and task force reports, synthesis reports, summaries for policy makers, and other publications.

The Copenhagen Diagnosis

http://www.copenhagendiagnosis.org/download/default.html

At this URL is a downloadable update on climate science research since the last IPCC report was released in 2007. It provides a summary of peer-reviewed scientific studies that have been done on climate change, its impacts, and possible mitigation strategies prior to the next IPCC report due out in 2013.

Assessments of Impacts and Adaptations to Climate Change (AIACC) in Multiple Regions and Sectors

http://www.aiaccproject.org/aiacc.html

AIACC is a global initiative developed in collaboration with the IPCC, the United Nations Environment Programme, and the Third World Academy of Sciences in order to expand understanding of how developing countries are impacted by climate change and increase the number of developing country researchers participating in climate research.

Relevant Journals

Episteme: A Journal of Social Epistemology

Hypatia: A Journal of Feminist Philosophy

Journal of Climate

Social Epistemology

REFERENCES

Anderson, E. (2006). The epistemology of democracy. *Episteme, 3,* 9–23.

Argarwal, A. (2002). A southern perspective on curbing global climate change. In S. H. Schneider, A. Rosencranz, & J. O. Niles (Eds.), *Climate change policy: A survey* (pp. 375–391). Washington, DC: Island Press.

Ball, T. (2010, April 4). Atmospheric aerosols: Another major IPCC omission. *Canada Free Press.* Retrieved April 5, 2010, from http://www.canadafreepress.com/index.php/article/21674

Beatty, J. (2006). Masking disagreement among experts. *Episteme: A Journal of Social Epistemology, 3,* 52–67.

Biddle, J., & Winsberg, E. (2010). Value judgments and the estimation of uncertainty in climate modeling. In P. D. Magnus & J. Busch (Eds.), *New waves in philosophy of science* (pp. 172–197). Hampshire, UK: Palgrave Macmillan.

Cartwright, N. (2006). Well-ordered science: Evidence for use. *Philosophy of Science, 73*(5), 981–990.

Cess, R. D., Potter, G. L., Blanchet, J. P., Boer, G. J., Del Genio, A. D., Déqué, M., et al. (1990). Intercomparison and interpretation of climate feedback processes in 19 atmospheric general circulation models. *Journal of Geophysics Research, 95,* 16601–16615.

Code, L. (1991). *What can she know? Feminist theory and construction of knowledge.* Ithaca , NY: Cornell University Press.

Collins, P. H. (1991). *Black feminist thought: Knowledge, consciousness, and the politics of empowerment.* New York: Routledge.

Crasnow, S. (2006). Feminist anthropology and sociology: Issues for social science. In S. Turner & M. Risjord (Eds.), *Handbook of the philosophy of science: Vol. 15. Philosophy of anthropology and sociology* (pp. 827–861). Amsterdam: Elsevier.

de Melo-Martín, I., & Intemann, K. (2009). How do conflict of interest policies fail? Let us count the ways. *Federation of American Societies for Experimental Biology Journal, 23,* 1638–1642.

Douglas, H. (2000). Inductive risk and values in science. *Philosophy of Science, 67*(4), 559–579.

Douglas, H. (2007). Rejecting the ideal of value-free science. In H. Kincaid, J. Dupré, & A. Wylie (Eds.), *Value free science? Ideals and illusions* (pp. 120–139). Oxford , UK: Oxford University Press.

Ghan, S. J., & Schwartz, S. E. (2007). Aerosol properties and processes. *Bulletin of the American Meteorological Society, 88,* 1059–1083.

Graves, P. (2007). *Environmental economics: A critique of benefit-cost analysis.* Lanham, MD: Rowman & Littlefield Publishers, Inc.

Hall, A., & Manabe, S. (1999). The role of water vapor feedback in unperturbed climate variability and global warming. *Journal of Climate, 12,* 2327–2346.

Haraway, D. (1988). Situated knowledges: The science question in feminism and the privilege of partial perspective. *Feminist Studies, 14,* 575–599.

Harding, S. (1991). *Whose science? Whose knowledge? Thinking from women's lives.* Ithaca, NY: Cornell University Press.

Harding, S. (1998). *Is science multicultural? Postcolonialism, feminism, and epistemologies.* Bloomington: Indiana University Press.

Harding, S. (2004). A socially relevant philosophy of science? Resources from standpoint theory's controversiality. *Hypatia, 19*(1), 25–47.

Harding, S. (2008). *Sciences from below: Feminisms, postcolonialities, and modernities.* Raleigh, NC: Duke University Press.

Held, M., & Soden, B. J. (2000). Water vapor feedback and global warming. *Annual Review of Energy and the Environment, 25,* 441–475.

Intemann, K. (2009). Why diversity matters: Understanding and applying the diversity component of the NSF's broader impacts criterion. *Social Epistemology, 23*(3–4), 249–266.

Intemann, K., & de Melo-Martín, I. (2010). Social values and evidentiary standards: The case of the HPV vaccine. *Biology and Philosophy, 25*(2), 203–213.

IPCC. (2001). *Climate change 2001: Impacts, adaptation, and vulnerability* [Contribution of Working Group II to the Third Assessment Report of the Intergovernmental Panel on Climate Change]. Cambridge, UK: University of Cambridge Press.

IPCC. (2007). *Climate change 2007: Synthesis report.* Geneva, Switzerland: Author.

IPCC. (2008). Procedures for the preparation, review, acceptance, adoption, approval, and publication of IPCC reports. *Appendix A to the Principles Governing IPCC Work.* Retrieved June 23, 2010, from http://www.ipcc.ch/pdf/ipcc-princi ples/ipcc-principles-appendix-a.pdf

IPCC. (2010). Publications and data. *IPCC.* Retrieved June 23, 2010, from http://www.ipcc.ch/publi cations_and_data/publications_and_data.htm

IPCC Secretariat. (2008, April). Future of the IPCC. *Compiled comments from governments, authors, organizations, and bureau members: Twenty-eighth session, Budapest, 9–10 April 2008* (IPCC Document No. XXVII/INF.1 [6.III.2008]). Geneva, Switzerland: Author.

Koch, D., Schmidt, G. A., & Field, C. V. (2006). Sulfur, sea salt, and radionuclide aerosols in GISS Model E. *Journal of Geophysical Research, 111,* D06206, doi:10.1029/2004JD005550

Kourany, J. (2003). A philosophy of science for the twenty-first century. *Philosophy of Science, 70,* 1–14.

Kourany, J. (2008). Replacing the ideal of value-free science. In M. Carrier, D. Howard, & J. Kourany (Eds.), *The challenge of the social and the pressure of practice: Science and values revisited* (pp. 87–111). Pittsburgh, PA: University of Pittsburgh Press.

Kourany, J. (2009). The place of standpoint theory in feminist science studies. *Hypatia, 24*(4), 209–218.

Lacey, H. (2005). *Values and objectivity in science.* Lanham, MD: Rowman & Littlefield Publishers.

Lomborg, B. (2007). *Cool it: The skeptical environmentalist's guide to global warming.* New York: Alfred A. Knopf.

Longino, H. (1990). *Science as social knowledge.* Princeton, NJ: Princeton University Press.

Longino, H. (1996). Cognitive and non-cognitive values in science: Rethinking the dichotomy. In L. H. Nelson & J. Nelson (Eds.), *Feminism, science, and the philosophy of science* (pp. 39–58). Dordrecht, The Netherlands. Kluwer Academic Publishers.

Longino, H. (2002). *The fate of knowledge.* Princeton, NJ: Princeton University Press.

National Science Foundation. (2007). Merit review broader impacts criterion: Representative activities. *Broader Impacts Review Criterion.* Retrieved June 23, 2010, from http://www.nsf.gov/pubs/ gpg/broaderimpacts.pdf

Nelson, L. H. (1990). *Who knows? From Quine to a feminist empiricism.* Philadelphia: Temple University Press.

Oreskes, N., & Conway, E. M. (2010). *Merchants of doubt: How a handful of scientists obscured the truth on issues from tobacco smoke to global warming.* London: Bloomsbury.

Parker, W. (2006). Understanding pluralism in climate modeling. *Foundations of Science, 11,* 349–368.

Rind, D., Yu, H., Schwartz, S .E., & Halthore, R. N. (2009). The way forward. In M. Chin, R. A. Khan, & S. E. Schwartz (Eds.), *Atmospheric aerosol properties and climate impacts: A report by the U.S. Climate Change Science Program and the Subcommittee on Global Change Research* (pp. 85–90). Washington, DC: National Aeronautics and Space Administration.

Rolin, K. (2006). The bias paradox in feminist standpoint epistemology. *Episteme, 1*, 125–136.

Schiermeier, Q. (2010). The real holes in climate science. *Nature, 463*, 284–287.

Schneider, E. K., Kirtman, B. P., & Lindzen, R. S. (1999). Tropospheric water vapor and climate sensitivity. *Journal of Atmospheric Sciences, 36*, 1649–1658.

Schneider, S. H. (2002). Modeling climate change impacts and their related uncertainties. In R. N. Cooper & R. Layard (Eds.), *What the future holds* (pp. 123–155). Cambridge, MA: MIT Press.

Schneider, S. H., & Kuntz-Duriseti, K. (2002). Uncertainty and climate change policy. In S. H. Schneider, A. Rosencranz, & J. O. Niles (Eds.), *Climate change policy: A survey* (pp. 53–88). Washington, DC: Island Press.

Schneider, S. H., Kuntz-Duriseti, K., & Azar, C. (2000). Costing non-linearities, surprises, and irreversible events. *Pacific and Asian Journal of Energy, 10*(1), 81–106.

Schneider, S. H., Rosencranz, A., & Niles, J. O. (2002). *Climate change policy: A survey.* Washington DC: Island Press.

Schneider, S. H., & Thompson, S. L. (2000). A simple climate model used in economic studies of global change. In S. J. DeCanio, R. B. Howarth, A. H. Sanstad, S. H. Schneider, & S. L. Thompson (Eds.), *New directions in the economics and integrated assessment of global climate change* (pp. 59–80). Washington, DC: Pew Center on Global Climate Change.

Shrader-Frechette, K. (2007). *Taking action, saving lives: Our duties to protect environmental and public health.* Oxford, UK: Oxford University Press.

Solomon, M. (2001). *Social empiricism.* Cambridge, MA: MIT Press.

Solomon, M. (2006). Norms of epistemic diversity. *Episteme, 1*, 23–36.

Wallington, T. J., & Moore, S. A. (2005). Ecology, values, and objectivity: Advancing the debate. *Bioscience, 55*(10), 873–878.

Weare, B. C. (2000a). Insights into the importance of cloud vertical structure in climate. *Geophysics Research, 27*, 907–910.

Weare, B. C. (2000b). Near-global observations of low clouds. *Journal of Climate, 13*, 1255–1268.

Wylie, A. (2001). Doing social science as a feminist: The engendering of archaeology. In A. N. H. Creager, E. Lunbeck, & L. Schiebinger (Eds.), *Feminism in twentieth century science, technology, and medicine* (pp. 23–45). Chicago: University of Chicago Press.

Wylie, A. (2003). Why standpoint matters. In R. Figueroa & S. Harding (Eds.), *Science and other cultures: Issues in philosophies of science and technology* (pp. 26–48). New York: Routledge.

Wylie, A., & Nelson, L. H. (2007). Coming to terms with the values of science: Insights from feminist science studies scholarship. In H. Kincaid, J. Dupré, & A. Wylie (Eds.), *Value-free science: Ideals and illusions* (pp. 58–86). Oxford, UK: Oxford University Press.

PART III

FEMINIST ISSUES AND INSIGHTS IN PRACTICE AND PEDAGOGY

24

CHALLENGES AND STRATEGIES IN FEMINIST KNOWLEDGE BUILDING, PEDAGOGY, AND PRAXIS

SHARLENE NAGY HESSE-BIBER AND ABIGAIL BROOKS

In Part II of the *Handbook*, we observed how research methods in the hands of feminists become flexible and fluid. Feminist researchers bend their methods in order to answer a range of new questions, sometimes finding that they need to combine methods or create emergent methods to get at subjugated knowledge. Feminist research and the epistemologies, theories, and practices that inform it continue to disrupt, modify, and trouble dominant categories of knowledge and traditional approaches to knowledge building. As feminists apply and develop new and diverse methods to more accurately reflect women's knowledge and experiences, they also encounter epistemological challenges across the spectrum of their research practices. In Part III, the authors confront issues of truth and knowledge, authority and ethics, power and representation, and diversity and difference at all stages of the research process. These epistemological dimensions are conceptualized and problematized through a feminist lens and in the context of specific feminist research practices and pedagogies.

FEMINIST STRATEGIES IN KNOWLEDGE BUILDING: AUTHORITY, REPRESENTATION, AND REFLEXIVITY

In "Authority and Representation in Feminist Research," Judith Roof illuminates the diverse ways that feminist researchers, scholars, and activists—across the first, second, and third waves of feminism—apply and rework traditional Western models of knowledge building and construct new methods and models all together to uncover gender-based power imbalances, biases, and exclusions; expose and correct false gendered assumptions and stereotypes; "give voice" to women's accomplishments, knowledge, and experiences; and achieve gender equity and gender justice. In and through her synthesis of feminists' corrective, expansive, and innovative contributions to the pursuit of knowledge throughout the 20th and into the 21st century, Roof also highlights several key questions, tensions, conflicts, and contradictions that continue to surface in light of feminists' knowledge projects.

Roof foregrounds the "fine and self-critical line" that feminists necessarily walk between the "attractions of the authorized, universal subject wielding both Enlightenment logics and authoritarian rhetoric and the insights feminist research itself has gained by attending to the subjective, the instinctive, and the disempowered" (Roof, Chapter 25, this volume); yet she also outlines feminists' successful application of these different modes of inquiry to produce new knowledge. Roof highlights the contributions of "second wave" feminists, such as Virginia Woolf and Simone de Beauvoir, who utilize a combination of personal experience and observation and who deploy "traditional modes of reason" to uncover the flaws in traditional modes of reason and to show how these modes have been misused to explain and justify women's unequal capacities and roles in society. Roof also focuses on the work of Betty Friedan, who (like Woolf and de Beauvoir) presents convincing evidence and arguments as to the social, cultural, and historical *construction* of women's inferior role in society. Indeed, as Roof points out, it is Friedan's use in *The Feminine Mystique* of personal experience, observation, and interviews with everyday women that helped to inspire the "personal is political" and the "authority of the personal" as effective models for women-centered social activism and social change.

Roof urges feminist scholars, researchers, and activists to practice a "self-conscious disciplinarity" as they apply traditional modes of inquiry; she also calls on feminists to be reflexive about their own positionality and to "speak with care of experiences and cultural sites not their own" (Roof, Chapter 25, this volume). The attendance to difference among and across women's experiences—Roof reminds us—cannot be overemphasized. As feminists of color, both nationally and globally, continue to illuminate, women do not share one lived experience or position but experience multiple social, economic, cultural, and racial realties. Women's diverse experiences continue to be articulated and theorized in the writing and scholarship of feminists of color—Angela Davis, Alice Walker, Gloria Hull, Sonia Sanchez, Nikki Giovanni, Audre Lorde, and Gloria Anzaldúa, to name only a very few—in new branches of feminist standpoint theory, in new feminist theories of the body that explore women's diverse subjectivities and ways of knowing through their bodies, and in new feminist artistic work whereby art becomes a "means of community building" and a "marker of separatist difference" (Roof, Chapter 25, this volume).

Alison Wylie continues the conversation in "The Feminism Question in Science: What Does It Mean to 'Do Social Science as a Feminist?'" Wylie is interested in exploring what it means "to do science as a feminist," taking us through the tensions of feminist practice. She acknowledges the reservations Noretta Koertge grappled with in Part I of this volume and notes, "The anxiety that haunts these discussions is that if research is guided by explicitly feminist values, its epistemic credibility is irrevocably compromised" (Wylie, Chapter 26, this volume). Wylie provides in her commentary a set of specific practices and examples of how feminists have addressed these epistemic concerns. Additionally, she believes a reformulation of standpoint theory can also serve to counteract these critiques of feminist inquiry, suggesting that new formulations of the feminist standpoint can be a "pivotal" tool by providing a "transformative critique."

Integrating reflexivity into the research process certainly improves the capacity for "transformative critique." In their chapter, "The Feminist Practice of Holistic Reflexivity," Sharlene Hesse-Biber and Deborah Piatelli describe the practice of reflexivity as a potentially "transformative process for researchers, participants, and the larger community of knowledge builders" (Hesse-Biber & Piatelli, Chapter 27, this volume). Through tracing feminist reflexivity in practice, Hesse-Biber and Piatelli demonstrate its effectiveness as a "methodological tool for deconstructing power and cocreating knowledge throughout the entire research process" (this volume). Whether practicing reflexivity takes the form of critical self-reflection and conversations within the self (on the part of the researcher self or the participant self) or of active dialogue and discussions between researcher and participant, identities are unhinged. Reflexive interrogation shakes up the boundaries between researcher and participant, as well as the taken-for-granted role of the researcher as a questioner of others. Roles are exchanged—researcher as participant and participant as researcher. And this fluidity, this crossing of boundaries and borders, creates a potential common space for knowledge building.

Practicing reflexivity can lead to a heightened awareness of the differences between participant and researcher, to transformation on the part of the researcher or the participant or both, and to the construction of common ground between them. The practice of reflexivity requires an acknowledgment that there is an aspect of lived experience that is invisible to those "who possess neither the language nor the cultural equipment either to elicit or understand that experience" (Rhodes, 1994, p. 549, cited in Hesse-Biber & Piatelli, Chapter 27, this volume).

FEMINIST ETHICS AND THE KNOWLEDGE BUILDING PROCESS

Attending to the relationship between researcher and participant continues to be a fundamental aspect of feminist research. According to Judith Preissle and Yuri Han, more feminist researchers are "taking relationship into account in their research goals than was the case 30 years ago" (Preissle & Han, Chapter 28, this volume). In their chapter, "Feminist Research Ethics," Preissle and Han argue that this attention to the researcher-researched relationship reflects a unique set of feminist ethics—an ethics of care versus an ethics of principle—a "situated ethics" versus a "detached ethics" (Vivat, 2002, cited in Preissle & Han). Preissle and Han draw from the work of feminist psychologist Carol Gilligan (1982) and feminist philosopher Nell Noddings (1984) to articulate a cogent feminist ethics framework. Gilligan's research reveals that, for women, morality is characterized by actively caring for others, by connected networks and webs or reciprocities. Similarly, Noddings argues that women engage in a practical ethics that is focused on relationships with others as opposed to the adherence to universal principles of morality or reason. This practical ethics, or "ethics of care," is motivated not by the pursuit of some universal principle but by an active and ongoing commitment to "the development of another" (Noddings, 1984, as paraphrased by Preissle & Han, Chapter 28, this volume).

Preissle and Han do not suggest that feminists ignore the relevance of universal principles, such as justice, nor do they deny that feminists also draw on the ethics of principle as a rationale for their research. However, it is the ethics of care—attending to the researcher-participant relationship and responding to the goals of participants—Preissle and Han argue, that motivates many feminist researchers and makes feminist research unique. But integrating an ethics of care into the research process is a complex and challenging task, and, in some respects, an ethics of care is more demanding than an ethics of principle. Greater value placed on the relationship between the researcher and participant requires greater responsibility—in short, an ethics of care does not "eliminate our ethical dilemmas" (Preissle & Han, Chapter 28, this volume).

Taking an ethics of care seriously means being receptive to the "*situation-specific* quality of human relationships" (Preissle & Han, Chapter 28, this volume). There is no one answer, universal principle, or set of questions that teaches us how to cultivate the researcher-researched relationship or how to attend to the well-being, goals, and needs of participants. Different approaches, methods, questions, and decisions may be required in different contexts and with different communities of participants. Researchers must evaluate each case based upon its particular and situated location—an approach to cultivating a respectful relationship between the researcher and her participant may succeed in one community but alienate another. For example, some feminist researchers engage in self-reflexive critique (see the following cited by Preissle & Han, Chapter 28, this volume: Ellis, 2007; Fine, 1994; Visweswaran, 1994), share their own experiences with respondents (see Seibold, 2000, cited by Preissle & Han, Chapter 28, this volume), and actively collaborate with respondents and include their voices and interpretations in research texts (see Blakeslee, Cole, & Conefrey, 1996, cited by Preissle & Han, Chapter 28, this volume). On the other hand, feminist researchers may decide not to share data with participants in order to protect their physical safety, psychological well-being, and privacy (see the following cited by Preissle & Han, Chapter 28, this volume: Hopkins, 1993; Robertson, 2000).

DIFFERENCE MATTERS: FEMINIST RESEARCH CONTRIBUTIONS TO DIFFERENCE RESEARCH

We provide insight into the feminist practice of difference and research across difference in three additional chapters in Part III. The 1980s and 1990s were characterized by a turn toward difference among feminist researchers:

> feminists working in and across many disciplines began developing new ways of thinking about, writing about, and researching women and their lives. For example, in the late 1980s and early 1990s, sociologist Patricia Hill Collins . . . began uncovering black women's subjugated knowledge when she created a black women's epistemological standpoint she termed the "outsider within." With this epistemology, she criticized the while middle-class feminists who overgeneralized without reference to the diversity of women's lives. (Hesse-Biber & Yaiser, 2004, p. 101)

Early efforts on the part of feminists to conceptualize difference served more to stereotype and generalize "the other." In the introduction to their volume, *Feminist Approaches to Theory and Methodology*, Hesse-Biber, Gilmartin, and Lydenberg (1999) commented on this aspect of the difference conundrum as follows:

> Efforts to represent difference . . . often fell into stereotypes and generalizations that . . . obscured the specificity of difference. Mohanty describes, for example, the "discursive colonization" by which "material and historical heterogeneities" of third-world women's experiences were lost in Western feminists' construction of a "composite, singular Third World Woman." (pp. 4–5)

The postmodern turn (e.g., Butler, 1993) transformed our understanding of the category of gender as a socially constructed and not fixed category of analysis and brought feminists face to face with the political aspects of

embracing difference: If feminists cannot accept that the category of gender is based on women's lived experience, then what is the "'essence' of feminist praxis" (see Hesse-Biber et al., 1999, p. 4)?

The authors who address issues of difference find common ground with each other in acknowledging the importance of difference in understanding women's lives, and they underscore their concerns about how to bridge the divide between theory and praxis of difference; but each comes to feminist research from a different approach. In "Transgender, Transsexualism, and the Queering of Gender Identities: Debates for Feminist Research," Katherine Johnson looks at key debates in the field of transgender, transsexual, and queer movements and important considerations in these areas for the feminist researcher. Her chapter argues for ethical and political coalitions to promote the solidarity that trans and non-trans feminists need in order to engage constructively with one another in the research process and critically analyze our own identity positions.

Diane Reay expands the conversation to the broader issue of researching difference in "Future Directions in Difference Research: Recognizing and Responding to Difference in the Research Process" by considering the primary example of social class differences, as well as others. Reay looks at the implications and difficulties of difference for feminist research theory and practice, using a broad range of research examples: "the challenge is to build towards an understanding of the complex of differences as both a set of dynamic relationships and operating within specific contexts." She concludes by advocating "the 3Rs . . . recognition, respect, and response."

Further issues in working with difference arise as feminists attempt to develop an empowered feminist community of researchers across transnational space and reach out across their own differences to begin to globalize their understanding of the standpoint of women and of women's oppression. Feminists discussing this conundrum are in agreement on the importance of expanding this vision globally. Most disagreement centers on the questions feminists should be asking regarding globalization, as well as on how to carry out research on a global scale and for what ends. Some feminists advocate a research agenda that is political and activist; others are more cautious in their approach, seeking to gather knowledge locally without necessarily drawing on its more global and political ramifications.

Postcolonial feminists study relations of power and knowledge within a global context paying specific attention to differences among women that result from what Patricia Hill Collins (2000) terms a "matrix of domination." Feminist theorist Jacqui Alexander states that the "conception of the international [in international feminism] has been the notion of a universal patriarchy operating in a trans historical way to subordinate all women" (Alexander & Mohanty, 1997, p. xix). She stresses the need for rethinking international feminism, not as a global essential sisterhood but as one that encompasses a "transnational" feminism. A transnational feminist perspective traverses boundaries of nationality and geographical region; it rejects binary thinking and stresses the need to understand women's experiences through acknowledging their different degrees of disadvantage and privilege in an unequal, historically created system of oppression.

Patricia Hill Collins (2000) envisions a transnational perspective on empowerment by noting that "we must find common differences that characterize an intercontinental movement, one that responds to intersecting oppressions that are differently organized via a global matrix of domination" (p. 238). Quoting Angela Miles, Collins (2000) goes on to say that we must find "shared political issues that constitute a potential basis for common political struggle" and that "[g]lobal feminisms are the result of this common struggle grounded in diverse local realities" (p. 240). Collins (2000) suggests that developing a "transversal politics," one that "emphasizes coalition building that takes into account the specific positions of 'political actors,'" empowers women's issues and concerns (p. 245).

How do we begin to move toward a transnational feminism and develop a new mode of consciousness—one that erases boundaries and empowers and unites people in common struggles against oppression? In their chapter, "Feminizing Global Research/Globalizing Feminist Research: Methods and Practice Under Globalization," Jennifer Bickham Mendez and Diane Wolf ask whether feminists can realign the ways in which they theorize and practice research with a more expanded awareness of globalization. How can a global understanding of women's issues and concerns catalyze a rethinking of analytical categories, such as the concept of "place" and "community," as well as impact how feminists practice their research? Expanding our vision globally enables us to see the interconnections among and between women suffering under globalized systems of oppression. Power and resistance become "multisited, ever shifting, and 'situated and contextualized within particular intersubjective relationships' (Bloom, 1998, p. 35)," thereby opening up new research alliances among and between transnational feminists (see Mendez & Wolf, Chapter 31, this volume). Acknowledging how globalization changes the meaning of "place" and "community" complicates the notion of insider/outsider yet, at the same time, offers feminists multiple spaces for dialogue and collaboration.

FEMINIST PERSPECTIVES ON PEDAGOGY IN THE WOMEN'S AND GENDER STUDIES CLASSROOM

In the final three chapters of the *Handbook*, we ask these questions: How can feminists convey the range of women's scholarship that differentiates it from the charge that women's studies scholarship conveys only ideology, not knowledge? Has women's studies drifted away from activism, and should there be a place for activism in the women's studies classroom? To what extent is there dialogue across differences within the women's studies classroom?

In this last section, we take up feminist pedagogy as praxis, both looking at practical issues of teaching women's studies and also aiming to address some of the controversial issues that are often left out of more mainstream pedagogical discussions, including the lived experiences of teachers within the women's studies classroom and where feminist research and theory meet the road of the lived classroom experience.

Debra Kaufman and Rachel Lewis's commentary, "From Course to Dis-course: Mainstreaming Feminist Pedagogical, Methodological, and Theoretical Perspectives," relates their pedagogical experiences in teaching and learning feminist methodology. At the outset, they declare their pedagogy to be "as political as it was academic." They raise the question of politics and research this way: "In what ways, we asked our students, are we historical and political subjects when *we* do our research? How do our life histories and stage of career affect our choice of topic and how we formulate research problems" (see Kaufman & Lewis, Chapter 32, this volume, emphasis in the original)? Kaufman relates her own research journey, undertaken to gather insights for her book *Rachel's Daughters*. On this journey, she confronted issues of political difference when she conducted ethnographic research on Orthodox Jewish women who embrace Jewish fundamentalism and its opposition to equality between women and men. Kaufman's research leads her to ask a number of crucial questions about how to study and teach about difference: "How do we 'do' research on those whose identity politics are different from ours? Or, put another way, how do I do socially committed work as a feminist activist and still respect the integrity of my respondents who differ from me politically" (Kaufman & Lewis, Chapter 32, this volume)? Kaufman and Lewis remind us that to make one's scholarship more subject to rigor requires facing our own values and attitudes and dealing with them up front, both in our own research and in the teaching of women's studies scholarship.

Daphne Patai, in "Feminist Pedagogy Reconsidered," views a conflict between feminist politics, research, and teaching. She notes, "The political engagement underlying feminism in the academy is bound to set up a highly tendentious model for research and teaching, a paradigm most feminists would hardly accept were its objectives contrary to their own" (Patai, Chapter 33, this volume). She does not agree with feminist arguments that knowledge building of the past has been exclusively male biased and exclusive of women's concerns and interests, an overgeneralization used to advance the "feminist agenda . . . as a corrective," in her view. From Patai's perspective, introducing the term "feminist" in the classroom has become "a patently political project," and teaching needs to return to a neutral context in which knowledge is valued

over political agenda and neither feminist nor masculinist perspectives are promoted.

Patai's article is an important critique of feminists whose research and teaching practices often assume a tight link between knowledge and politics. From Patai's perspective, even if all knowledge building of the past were male biased, it does not behoove feminism to do the same and err in the opposite direction. At its core, Patai's chapter asks whether or not feminism is compatible with scientific inquiry when it is unable to adequately critique its own "pet ideas." We must ask whether there is any common ground on which to dialogue across the range of feminist perspectives on knowledge building. What is the best course of action for feminists of different persuasions to take when they don't agree?

Debjani Chakravarty, Judith Cook, and Mary Margaret Fonow end this section with their commentary, "Teaching, Techniques, and Technologies of Feminist Methodology: Online and on the Ground." They point to the fluid and ever changing aspects of feminist knowledge building. They note, "We are often asked to define and defend feminist methodology as a unique methodology, and we have always resisted giving a precise response because we do not want to foreclose new avenues of inquiry and discovery" (Chakravarty et al., Chapter 34, this volume). Their teaching of feminist methodology is guided by a set of principles that can apply to a range of qualitative and quantitative methods and strives to ensure "that students understand how to select and defend their choices in the design, collection, representation, and interpretation and of data" (Chakravarty et al., Chapter 34, this volume). They describe Cook's experience training feminist policy researchers and provide a look at feminist research and new technologies, particularly the opportunities of the Internet, for transnational, inclusive, activist, and interdisciplinary research.

It is our hope that the final three chapters in this section will inspire dialogue between and across different points of view and lay bare a range of feminist thoughts and approaches to pedagogy. bell hooks (1994) stresses the importance of dialogue and describes it as "one of the simplest ways we can begin as teachers, scholars, and critical thinkers to cross boundaries, the barriers that may or may not be erected by race, gender, class, professional standing, and a host of other differences" (p. 130). Through dialoguing, we express our beliefs and uncertainties, as well as gain better insight into other viewpoints. Dialogue's purpose is not necessarily to shift our beliefs but to shift our mode of communication by creating conversational practices that prevent unnecessary and destructive debate and, instead, foster a constructive exchange of ideas and collaboration.

To gain legitimacy within the feminist community of theory and practice as well as pedagogy means having an openness to critique. To what extent are feminists responsive to each other's versions of reality? To what extent do feminists envision themselves as a community of knowledge builders? And to what extent are these communities inclusive of differing points of view?

Conclusion

Part III articulates some important principles of feminist praxis and pedagogy that underscore what it means to engage in feminist research. These "feminist principles of praxis" can sometimes find their way into mainstream research endeavors, but the feminist roots and origins of these principles are often neglected. Judith Preissle and Yuri Han's articulation of feminist ethics sheds light on what makes research feminist *without* reducing all feminist research to a limited category with a finite set of characteristics. Although a feminist ethic demands that we attend to the researcher-researched relationship, each relationship, Preissle and Han remind us, is "situation-specific." For Hesse-Biber and Piatelli, tending to and respecting the researcher-researched relationship means incorporating reflexivity into all stages of the research process. To practice reflexivity is to break down power differentials between researchers and participants. But practicing reflexivity can manifest in a myriad of ways and incorporate a diverse range of outcomes—from a heightened awareness of the differences and commonalities between the researcher and participant to a change or transformation on the part of the researcher, participant, or both. Preissle's emphasis on the situated

aspect of feminist ethics also finds resonance with Judith Roof's illumination of the knowledge contained within women's situation-specific and personal experiences.

The authors in this section interrogate epistemologies of truth and knowledge, power and authority, ethics and representation, and diversity and difference from a feminist perspective. The traditional meanings of these terms are challenged, reworked, and reinvented as the authors explore their implications for *feminist research praxis*. In and through the practice of feminist research, truth is transformed from universal applicability to situated location, knowledge from objectivity and value neutrality to lived experience and personal perspective. Personal experience becomes a source of authenticity rather than a contaminant, and, by honestly acknowledging her situated perspective, the researcher increases the validity and legitimacy of her research project. Morality shifts from the realm of abstract principles to that of living, human relationships, and issues of power and representation are problematized throughout all stages of the research process.

Feminists' perspectives on these epistemological issues are multiple and complex, however, and feminists continue to engage in dialogue and debate on how best to address, confront, and translate issues of truth, knowledge, and power into their research practices. And as feminists reconceptualize these epistemological meanings and work them into their research practices, new questions, demands, and challenges arise. Practicing feminist ethics, for example, requires acute attention to the "situation-specific" quality of each researcher-researched relationship, and the practice of reflexivity alternatively involves sharing, collaboration, and a heightened sensitivity to difference. Further, if knowledge and truth are based in personal experience and situated perspective, is there any room for seeking commonalities and shared knowledge between and across these experiences and situations? And if authenticity is rooted in situated perspective and personal experience, what happens if perspectives and experiences change? The authors in this section begin to tackle these kinds of questions by illuminating the importance of recognizing difference *and* by embracing "diversity as a means"—dialogue and constructive critique across and among diverse perspectives bring potential change and transformation.

The authors' contributions in Part III remind us that there is no one feminist point of view on feminist inquiry. Feminist researchers continue to wrestle with key epistemological challenges and themes and to confront how best to reinvent and incorporate these themes into the practice of feminist research. Feminists engage and dialogue with each other, sometimes in contentious discussion; and it is through these interactions that the landscape of feminist theory, praxis, and teaching are ever evolving.

Parting Reflection

A feminist approach to research challenges the status quo and the dominant paradigm of positivism. Early on, philosopher Thomas Kuhn (1962) noted that these types of challenges often create a "crisis" in science that provides space for social change to occur. Our intention in this *Handbook* has been to explore, interrogate, and transform the interconnections of epistemology, methodology, and methods in the hope of furthering knowledge building on behalf of women and other oppressed groups. Put differently, this text's goal is to move research toward what Thomas Kuhn (1962) terms a reevaluation of dominant epistemological frameworks, to create a "crisis" and the movement toward a "revolution" in the study of women and society.

There is no *one* feminist viewpoint that defines feminist inquiry. As we have gleaned from the chapters in the *Handbook*, feminists continue to engage in and dialogue across a range of diverse approaches to theory, praxis, and pedagogy. Judith Roof's chapter also reminds us that, as feminist scholars, researchers, and activists move forward, they will still confront the contradictions and tensions between, on the one hand, the potential utility of traditional modes of logic and inquiry for dismantling the sex-gender system and its inequities and, on the other, the association between these modes and the patriarchal status quo (Roof, Chapter 25, this volume). Indeed, Roof states, this "discomfort" about the "utility of a potentially biased tradition" must

necessarily "persist throughout feminist thought even as feminists employ the scientific method and linear logics to gain their own insights" (Roof, Chapter 25, this volume); it is this discomfort that also pushes feminists to continue to interrogate, and be mindful of, the biases within traditional modes of inquiry, and to be mindful of their own positionality as well. Indeed, if feminist knowledge building is to move forward toward the creation of a truly liberatory research movement, one in which social change for women and other oppressed groups is the goal, ongoing communication and dialogue across difference—seeking alliances and building coalitions while respecting difference—must *necessarily* inform all practices and strategies of the research process.

References

Alexander, M. Jacqui, & Mohanty, Chandra Talpade. (1997). *Feminist genealogies, colonial legacies, democratic futures.* New York: Routledge.

Butler, Judith. (1993). *Bodies that matter: On the discursive limits of "sex."* New York: Routledge.

Collins, Patricia Hill. (2000). *Black feminist thought: Knowledge, consciousness, and the politics of empowerment* (2nd ed.). New York: Routledge.

Fonow, Mary Margaret, & Cook, Judith A. (1991). *Beyond methodology: Feminist scholarship as lived research.* Bloomington: Indiana University Press.

Hesse-Biber, Sharlene Nagy, Gilmartin, Christina, & Lydenberg, Robin. (Eds.). (1999). *Feminist approaches to theory and methodology: An interdisciplinary reader.* New York: Oxford University Press.

Hesse-Biber, Sharlene Nagy, & Yaiser, Michelle L. (2004). Difference matters: Studying across race, class, gender, and sexuality. In Sharlene Nagy Hesse-Biber & Michelle L. Yaiser (Eds.), *Feminist perspectives on social research* (pp. 101–120). New York: Oxford University Press.

hooks, bell. (1994). *Teaching to transgress: Education as the practice of freedom.* New York: Routledge.

Kuhn, Thomas. (1962). *The structure of scientific revolutions.* Chicago: University of Chicago Press.

Ritzer, George. (1975). *Sociology: A multiple paradigm science.* Boston: Allyn & Bacon.

25

AUTHORITY AND REPRESENTATION IN FEMINIST RESEARCH

JUDITH ROOF

Feminist research is an invention of the twentieth century. As such, it participates in the assumptions and methods of (primarily Western) thought that dominate the era, which include empirical scientific methods of showing various sex/gender functions and inequities (sociology, biology, anthropology) and more abstract philosophical and linguistic-based interrogations of sex/gender focused on various aspects of representation (images of woman and gender, the gender bias of underlying assumptions in the arts, literature, film, theatre, and culture broadly speaking). The first set is considered "objective" and scientific, and assumes the transparency of all representations (words and people mean what they say). The second set, the humanistic, investigates the ways structures, organizations, ideologies, and representations are anything but transparent, exploring the various ways both cultural material and our ways of thinking about such material already depend upon assumptions about and evaluations of gender—and at the same time continually construct notions of gender. In these two different approaches, authority derives from the slightly different bases by which "truth" is discerned. Science asserts fact and method as the basis for its authority. The humanities derive authority from the logical power of arguments and insights as well as from specific understandings of rhetoric, images, and self-representation. In both cases, an investigator's authority is augmented by many factors: the soundness of method, the clarity and certainty of facts, the persuasive elegance of argument, the professional reputation of the speaker, the effectiveness of rhetoric, and the identitarian affiliations (gender, race, ethnicity, class, national origin, age, religion) of speakers themselves. Finally, authority and power depend on historical circumstances—on how timely an argument is and how ready audiences are to hear it.

Feminist research is also in itself a set of representations, both in the ways in which research is communicated and in its presentation of the experiences of individual women, identifiable interest groups, and general populations. The presentation of research usually follows the prescribed modes of various disciplines—empirical reportage in the sciences, analysis and critique in the humanities. But it also begins to devise distinctly feminist formulations of communication, including producing work cooperatively, personalizing modes of argumentation, and mixing genres (empirical research and autobiography, testimony and statistics, life writing and criticism). Feminist experiments in representing work often serve as ways of enacting the "personal is political" assumptions of a feminist program, enacting new modes of cooperative inquiry, showing the need to treat different subjects (women, non-Western perspectives) differently and illustrating the advantages of thinking about issues through multiple disciplines. Feminist researchers and writers generally demonstrate that modes of communicating research are inextricable from the research they present.

That feminist research often calls for multiple discourses in its representations points to the ways feminism itself requires a mixing of disciplines. Although empirically based studies and the humanities deploy incommensurate methodologies with conflicting assumptions, feminist research has often combined the two, seeing that neither in itself can account for the complex difficulties presented by the pervasive sex/gender asymmetries underwriting human cultures. In addition, feminist researchers have questioned the possible "objectivity" of either approach, suggesting that what we regard as objective or universal veils the privileges of patriarchal organizations and male speakers. Because feminism is itself a critique of the ways power and authority are distributed in relation to the sex/gendered structures of patriarchy, feminist research and renditions of it have had to walk a fine and self-critical line between the attractions of the authorized universal subject wielding both Enlightenment logics and traditional authoritarian rhetoric and the insights feminist research itself has gained by attending to the subjective, the instinctive, and the disempowered.

As feminist researchers often judiciously deploy multiple modes of inquiry with conflicting assumptions, the practices of feminist interrogations are also complicated by the association between traditional modes of logic and a patriarchal status quo. As Audre Lorde famously queried, can feminists build their own systems of thought using "the master's tools"? To what extent do traditional modes of inquiry lead inevitably to traditional, gender-biased conclusions? Have the traditional scientific methods and assumptions of philosophy produced the gender asymmetries of Western culture and their attendant disparities of power and authority, or are these methods gender neutral and thus useful in feminist projects by which the sex/gender system and its inequities might be dismantled? This discomfort about the utility of a potentially biased tradition persists throughout feminist thought even as feminists employ the scientific method and linear logics to gain their own insights.

Power and authority in feminist research has seemed to exist, thus, in a set of complex paradoxes, trading between the authority of science and the power of experience, working with traditional modes of inquiry it simultaneously questions. In addition, although we tend to assume that power and authority follow one from the other, the projects of feminist research have critiqued the intrinsic gender biases of that relation, have shown various ways in which authority may be gained without power, have empowered alternative modes of authority, have devised alternative distributions of power, and have offered alternative visions of what might constitute research itself. These projects represent multiple approaches to the problems of (1) wielding authority while questioning it, (2) deploying scientific approaches or critical theories to critique gendered practices of power and authority, (3) developing convincing alternative theories and methods of inquiry, and (4) devising new techniques of persuasion. What is clear is that feminist research in general believes in the power of critique and inquiry to change materially the structures of culture and the lives of individuals.

QUESTIONING THE BASES OF AUTHORITY

Although feminist pioneers such as Mary Wollstonecraft, Charlotte Perkins Gilman, and Susan B. Anthony observed the unhappy effects of patriarchy on women of all classes, it was not until Virginia Woolf (1929) wrote her famous *A Room of One's Own* that the observation of inequality was joined by a systematic interrogation of the conditions and assumptions by which gender inequities are produced and sustained. Woolf's queries, followed and deepened in her 1938 exposition *Three Guineas*, began the unraveling of privilege, authority, and material conditions premised upon and alibied by sex/gender myths. *A Room of One's Own* is famous for its concluding proposition that, with a yearly income of £500 and a room of her own, a woman might be as inquiring, creative, and authoritative as a man. The essay is, however, also an insightful exploration of the assumptions and presumptions grounding patriarchal authority itself.

Looking to the wisdom of male writers, sociologists, historians, and critics, Woolf finds a universal misogyny seemingly established only through the angry repetition of cultural assumptions. The sex/gender bias of male thinkers, she realizes, becomes the means of such experts' assumption of authority. She counters these forays into the masculinist universe of scholarly inquiry with insights gained from her own observations about the effects material conditions have upon an individual's ability to indulge in scholarly or creative activities. Noting that women in general rarely have the education, income, or opportunity to write or create, Woolf describes the institutional and material disadvantages of women—like those of Shakespeare's apocryphal sister—which prevent them from easily exploring their own talents. Her recommendation of privacy and sustenance depends, finally, on the experiential observation that the hungry, overworked, and dispossessed can hardly be expected to be the equals of their much better fed and institutionally equipped male counterparts.

Combining the experience and observation of a woman with a rhetoric of open-minded exploration, *A Room of One's Own* commences nearly a century of feminist critique of the unchallenged alignment of authority, power, masculinity, privilege, and wealth. Woolf's project, furthered by her own insights in *Three Guineas*, precedes Simone de Beauvoir's (1949) extended inquiry into the theoretical and methodological bases of women's oppression, an

inquiry published as *The Second Sex*. Trained as a philosopher, de Beauvoir systematically addresses every mode of post-Enlightenment analysis, from the empiricisms of biology and sociology to the theoretical interventions of psychoanalysis and Marxism. Like Woolf, de Beauvoir deploys traditional modes of reason to show the flaws in the ways such reasoning has traditionally been used. De Beauvoir's investigation is divided into two parts: "Book One" is an interrogation of the "Facts and Myths" through which the category "woman" has been understood in biological, historical, sociological, anthropological, literary, psychoanalytic, and Marxist terms. De Beauvoir's mode of analysis is a critical interrogation of the ways these discourses and methods assume, depend upon, naturalize, and reproduce specific myths of the inferiority, inabilities, and patriarchal dispositions of women. Her authority is based on her ability to demonstrate a consistent inconsistency in the way all of these disciplines understand "woman"—is based, in other words, on the persuasiveness of her analysis combined with the pervasiveness of her findings.

Showing the systematic bias of multiple disciplines provides de Beauvoir with the platform from which she can launch the argument of "Book Two" of her project, "Woman's Life Today," which more exhaustively than Woolf's essays presents the category "woman" as a cultural production. "One is not born," she says, "but rather becomes, a woman" (de Beauvoir, 1949, p. 249). This second section, like the first, is an exhaustive counter-reading of cultural myths and attitudes, engaging alike expert opinion and popular fantasy. De Beauvoir devises the position from which she speaks as a combination of her own perspective and the rapier incisiveness of a perceptive, penetrating observer. Her rhetoric constructs a commanding, authoritative voice and knowing subject whose mustering of facts, phenomena, and argument displays an estimable intelligence.

Woolf and de Beauvoir both employ the persona of the brilliant and capable woman to counteract myths about women's ability to do what each accomplishes in her books. This representational strategy combines analysis, rhetoric, and the performance of an authoritative persona, humble in the case of Woolf and masterful in the case of de Beauvoir, but both in the position of an observer of sex/gender inequities from a more reasoned, less biased perspective than had previously been available. Because a large portion of their work shows that the perspective of patriarchal culture is indeed skewed, they position their own observations as less biased correctives.

During the 1960s and 1970s, de Beauvoir's works grounded the "second wave" of feminist examinations of the biases inherent in patriarchal authority and of the illogical inequality of women in Western culture. Many of the influential works that follow in this vein—for example, Betty Friedan's (1963) *The Feminine Mystique*, Germaine Greer's (1971) *The Female Eunuch*, Jill Johnston's (1973) *Lesbian Nation*, and Kate Millet's (1970) *Sexual Politics*—continue the process of demythologizing myths about women through reasoned counter-analysis. Friedan grounds her authority in being a representative— the spokeswoman for a large underrepresented group of women. Beginning her exploration with an evocation of women's daily lives, Friedan uses her own experience, glossed in a quasi-objective interviewing method, as a way to organize and dismantle literary, historical, and cultural myths about the proper roles and abilities of women. Although Friedan occasionally cites studies from sociology, her arguments are based on an appeal to the comments of real people, comments she gathered through interviews with women who may, it is implied, have been more willing to talk to Friedan than to male researchers. For example, Friedan (1963) begins her chapter on sexuality with the following nod to the sources of her authority: "I did not do a Kinsey study, but when I was on the trail of the problem that has no name, the suburban housewives I interviewed would often give me an explicitly sexual answer to a question that was not sexual at all" (p. 247).

Although very few of Friedan's conclusions are based on the opinions she gathered, her appeal to the disenfranchised masses augments her authority as analyst and pits experience against traditional logic. Her elevation of experience as valid evidence not only picks up the strain of the personal from Woolf's work but also establishes a gendered set of epistemologies that become difficult to escape in feminist analyses: a

feminist reliance on the personal as both political and authoritative as opposed to what becomes the increasingly suspicious modes of "male" theorizing and analysis. The inherent gendering of experiential evidence versus more traditional modes of reasoning has the effect of locating women on the side of the subjective, personal, and, occasionally, insubstantial side of experience while relegating logical analyses and abstract thinking to the realm of men. This bifurcation holds sway through the 1970s during a period when women are becoming widely conscious of the effects of patriarchy. Valorizing experience, however, also reinscribes the sex/gender system in the terms feminism tries to escape. When women have always been perceived as the subjective and the personal, relegating feminist knowledge to those realms threatens to reproduce the status quo. In addition, it is difficult to argue with personal experience, especially in populations accustomed to being disenfranchised generally. The effect of this, which persists even into the 21st century, is yet another unresolved tension in the methods of feminist analysis and persuasion in which the experiential and the logical might simultaneously enable new insight or come to an impasse.

Less dependent than Friedan on testimony about experience, Millett, Greer, and Johnston all perform extended analyses of social practices, institutions, and discourses designed to demonstrate the pervasiveness of misogyny as a condition of social existence. Their various analyses depend upon the performance and representation of insightful counter-reading made persuasive through the persona of the writer and the trenchancy of her observations. They all share in the combination of empirical methodologies (i.e., survey facts, interviews, other sociological texts) and the kinds of critical analyses practiced by de Beauvoir, as deftly managed by an insightful critic whose first imprimatur of authority consists in her mastery of argument and style. Because each of these figures is among the first to argue publicly for radical feminist analyses, they also gain power through our perception of them as brave and pioneering. At the same time, the power of their analyses also comes from their readers' recognition that someone is finally describing their own experience of the world. In this latter sense, such analyses gain their authority from the burgeoning feminist interest in "consciousness raising" as a counter-mode of authority based in experience. These works and others pave the way for contemporaneous kinds of analyses that deploy critical and disciplinary strategies to make visible the endemic sexism of both methodologies and fields of knowledge.

THE POWER OF FEMINIST CRITIQUE

The power of feminist critique derives from the masterful deployment of critical and disciplinary methodologies, first, to discern and correct the systematic omission of women and, second, to correct the sexist and misogynist practices and assumptions associated with specific modes of research. Almost all of this work represents a moment in which political necessity makes analysis relevant and desirable across a range of disciplines—from the recovery projects of feminist history, sociology, anthropology, philosophy, and literary studies to the discipline-based analyses of sex/gender in culture as performed by sociologists, historians, political scientists, anthropologists, philosophers, and literary, media, and cultural theorists as well as the extended feminist critiques of such discourses as philosophy, social policy, law, psychology and psychoanalysis, and medicine. All of these projects base their authority on the responsible, reasoned, and expert practice of disciplinary methodologies. All gain power from the timing of their appearance in the late 1970s to mid-1980s, the quality of their inquiry, the persuasiveness of their argument, and the effectiveness of their rhetoric. In other words, as correctives and critiques, they premise authority on the very same qualities by which such authority has been traditionally granted, with the difference being that these analyses are focused on women and presented primarily (though not exclusively) by women in explicit relation to issues of gender and sexuality.

Although critiques of disciplinary assumptions rely less on experience than on reason, recovery projects in which the omitted or underrepresented experiences of women are made visible do presume the authoritative presence of alternative perspectives. In fact, the reason for collecting them, apart from providing a more balanced view of humanity, is to demonstrate the previous bias of scholarly inquiry, which had omitted both the accomplishments of influential women and the women's meaningful participation in larger cultural processes. Endeavors to collect and present lost women's traditions in history, sociology, anthropology, culture, literature, and film began in the early 1970s and continue even now as feminist projects become more global and work to devise ways to incorporate and speak across national, ethnic, religious, and class divisions to women and to make their role in histories, societies, and cultures visible. In so doing, such projects establish an alternative set of perspectives based on the asymmetries of the sex/gender system, perspectives that assume both the difference and the validity of another side to issues of aesthetics, experience, and truth.

The impetus of feminist recovery projects is corrective. Its authority derives from a belief in the bias of traditional disciplines as well as from the sheer quantity of material these projects exhume. That there were numerous important and influential women in history justifies and empowers the project of finding them. Building an archive of previously ignored historical figures, writers, and artists produces a counter-history in which the rediscovered figures also speak for themselves. Like most historical scholarship, feminist recovery projects depend upon the authority of historical texts, basing any claims about the value and importance of women figures on what the figures themselves have said and done. Incorporating this rediscovered material, which comes increasingly from an enlarged, more global reserve, revises understandings of the historical, political, social, and literary contexts in which they were produced. Newer understandings of context invite further investigation, so that what might appear to be simply the authority garnered through the corrective rediscovery of lost women figures is in fact a complicated renegotiation of entire fields where power and authority rest equally on the presentation of new material and the reinterpretation of the old in light of the new.

Often, though not always, these recovery projects have been undertaken by women scholars, presumed by an incipient identity politics (which assumes a naturalized, identificatory link between subjective identity and the objects of study) to be especially interested in the process. Such endeavors undertaken by male scholars increasingly came under suspicion as appropriative, preemptive, or dismissive. The tendency to associate the sex/gender of authors with their "right" to wield an authority marks the incipient stages of the kinds of identity politics that became pronounced in the 1980s as guaranteeing authority in themselves.

Although all of these recovery projects were implicitly political insofar as the idea of finding lost women's traditions assumes and acts upon women's previous exclusion, some are more overtly feminist than others, combining an analysis of women's oppression with the process of bringing women's roles and achievements to light. Juliet Mitchell's (1971) *Women's Estate* and Vivian Gornick and Barbara Moran's (1971) *Woman in Sexist Society* both reread history as an analysis of distributions of power and disadvantage. Elizabeth Janeway's (1971) *Man's World, Woman's Place* provides a rereading and analysis of gender relations in social history, following the much earlier work of Anna Spencer's (1925) *Women's Share in Social Culture*. Sociologists and political scientists begin to focus on accounts of women's roles in social and political processes. Feminist collectives begin to ameliorate the dearth of information available about women's health in forms accessible to women in the landmark *Our Bodies, Ourselves*, first published in 1971 and continually expanded and updated (Boston Women's Health Book Collective, 1971). Early 1970s feminist literary criticism splits its energies between rediscovering lost or underappreciated women authors such as Aphra Behn, Virginia Woolf, Charlotte Perkins Gilman, and Gertrude Stein and forging a critical practice that takes gender as its central concern (Brown & Olson, 1978; Cornillon, 1972; Spacks, 1975).

The authority of these texts comes from their construction of a specific female viewpoint understood as perceiving women differently and more accurately than that of traditional male scholars. The sense, too, that many women scholars put their careers on the line to engage in studies about women lends these projects the credibility of bravery and sacrifice. In addition, producing explicitly women's texts, especially as *Our Bodies, Ourselves* does in a collective, low-budget, straightforward way, elicits the sway of the credible friend who has no motive other than the philanthropy of feminist activism grounding the project. In other words, the power and authority of these earlier projects derives from the politicized circumstances of their very production as a feminist act. Their modes of representing knowledge as accessible, friendly, and familiar produce a style of feminist representation that enacts a democratization of knowledge and a sense of communal sharing. Their persuasiveness is produced by their appeal to the practical.

Just as the process of recovery has been itself simultaneously a political action and a political critique, so too does it accompany a reevaluation of the various disciplinary methods and assumptions by which women and their accomplishments were initially excluded. This process occurs in every discipline, though various factors, such as the traditional presence of women in the field, the relative influence of the area, and the extent to which traditional forms of inquiry and method were entrenched, influenced how quickly disciplines accepted feminist correction and critique. History, sociology, and literature participated in the earliest recovery projects, while the method-centered fields of science, philosophy, and psychology attracted analyses correcting the assumptions by which their disregard of women and gender as a category had produced skewed studies and theories. In these latter fields, knowing disciplinary assumptions and methodology became the primary basis for critiquing omissions and conclusions. Continuing the work of Simone de Beauvoir, Mary Daly (1973) examines the concatenation of religions and patriarchy in *Beyond God the Father: Toward a Philosophy of Women's Liberation*. Other feminist philosophers such as Marilyn Frye, Sarah Hoagland, and Alison Jaggar continued the examination of the presumptions of Western metaphysics as well forging a specifically feminist philosophy (Frye, 1983; Hoagland, 1988; Jaggar, 1984). This philosophy focused on issues of ethics and epistemology as the specific sets of questions by which patriarchal and sexist assumptions might be challenged and altered.

Philosophy exudes the authority of metaphysics, of a reasoning process presumably untainted by specific content or bias. The same is true of "hard" science, which, like philosophy, was challenged as a set of methods and an epistemology by feminist philosophers and scholars of science. The interrogation of the sex/gender bias of scientific methods and science's exclusion of women came later, however, than a set of inquiries into the status of women in science, which occurred through the 1970s and early 1980s. The initial work on women and science was concerned with the relative absence of women working as scientists, assuming that fuller participation by women would correct some of the field's sexist biases. Thus bypassing issues of method in favor of the gender identity of researchers, early surveys of women in science identified the problem as literally a problem of women's absence from scientific fields (Cole, 1979; Fausto-Sterling & English, 1985; Haas & Perrucci, 1984; Rossiter, 1982; Schilling & Hunt, 1974).

By the early 1980s, however, feminist scholars began to question the sex/gender bias of science's assumptions and methods. Deploying a mode of feminist critique that reads "across" a discipline's own assertions and claims, feminist critics merged an authority premised on a thorough knowledge of a field with the power of feminist critique, especially focusing on the way such a critique made visible the sexist assumptions and exclusions of scientific thought and practice. Biology was a natural first target insofar as it deals most directly with issues of sex. Ruth Bleier's (1984) *Science and Gender: A Critique of Biology and Its Theories* commenced a series of feminist interrogations of science in general, which included Evelyn Fox Keller's (1985) *Reflections on Women in Science*, Sandra Harding's (1986) *The Science Question in Feminism*, Donna Haraway's (1989) *Primate Visions: Gender, Race, and Nature in the World of Modern Science*, Nancy Tuana's (1989) collection of essays entitled *Feminism and Science*, and Mary Jacobus and Sally Shuttleworth's (1990)

anthology *Body/Politics: Women and the Discourses of Science.*

More recently, the feminist interrogation of the hard sciences has turned to the arena dubbed "posthumanist"—an endeavor that questions the assumption that humans are the central and only significant vantage in a world perceived more ecologically and systemically in a context of cyber and information technologies. If sex/gender biases clearly swayed the presumed objectivity of scientific inquiry, what bias has been exercised by a humanist presumption? In part, posthumanism has emerged from an extension of the same presumptions made by feminist work: traditional vantage points are skewed toward those who deploy them. There is an advantage to be gained from recognizing the disenfranchised. The work of Donna Haraway (1989, 1991, 1997, 2005) provided crucial analyses that helped inaugurate posthumanism, including her *Primate Visions* and continuing in her *Simians, Cyborgs, and Women: The Reinvention of Nature, Modest_Witness@ Second_Millenium.FemaleMan©_Meets_ OncoMouse™: Feminism and Technoscience,* and, most recently, in *When Species Meet.*

Feminist critics' engagement with posthumanist questions such as, on the one hand, animal rights and, on the other, the possibilities and effects of the cyberworld have spawned significant inquiries that have focused the methods of feminist critique on issues produced by an expanded vision of intellectual terrain. From the ecofeminist concerns of the 1980s and 1990s, collected in such anthologies as Greta Gaard and Patrick Murphy's (1998) *Ecofeminist Literary Criticism: Theory, Interpretation, Pedagogy*, to considerations of science, bodies, and ethics, as presented in Paul Brodwin's (2000) *Biotechnology and Culture: Bodies, Anxieties, Ethics*, to more recent and now international feminist considerations of science, technology, and media, as in Anneke Smelik and Nina Likke's (2008) *Bits of Life: Feminism at the Intersections of Media, Bioscience, and Technology*, feminist critical interventions envision a field of multiple intersecting discourses understood as already deriving partially from and reflecting a feminist point of view. The posthumanist intersectionality of science, sex/gender, and media also became the concern of such feminist philosophers as Elizabeth

Grosz (2005) in *Time Travels: Feminism, Nature, Power* and Kelly Oliver (2009) in *Animal Lessons: How They Teach Us to Be Human.*

A similar questioning of exclusion and method in tandem with a gradually enlarging terrain of investigation occurred contemporaneously in the social sciences. Less concerned with the absence of female researchers, political scientists and sociologists also began questioning the gender bias of disciplinary assumptions. Susan Okin's (1979) *Women in Western Political Thought* was followed by Judith Evans's (1986) *Feminism and Political Theory* and Diana Coole's (1988) *Women in Political Theory: From Ancient Misogyny to Contemporary Feminism*; all texts interrogate the gendered biases of political thinking. Sociological methodologies and assumptions were queried by Nancy Fraser (1989) in *Unruly Practices: Power, Discourse, and Gender in Contemporary Social Theory*, while Henrietta Moore's (1988) *Feminism and Anthropology* approaches similar problems in anthropology. Kathleen Weiler's (2001) collection, *Feminist Engagements: Reading, Resisting, and Revisioning Male Theorists in Education and Cultural Studies*, questions the sexist assumptions of education and cultural studies.

Like scholars in the hard sciences, social scientists expanded the breadth of their critique crucially to find ways to engage with more global perspectives. The trend toward globalism occurred simultaneously in both the social sciences and the humanities, but it appeared first as a set of overtly social and political concerns coming from multiple perspectives. Paralleling the humanities' interest in the voices of disenfranchised women, a consciousness of the global character of sex and gender struggles emerged in the persuasive writings of Gayatri Spivak and Chandra Mohanty: see, for example, *In Other Worlds: Essays in Cultural Politics* (Spivak, 1988) and *Feminism Without Borders: Decolonizing Theory, Practicing Solidarity* (Mohanty, 2003). Concerns about feminist politics in a global perspective became a central part of a feminist critical endeavor in which issues of ethics, positionality, and inclusion became a new version of feminist recovery and disciplinary critique. Anthologies such as *Transitions,*

Environments, Translations: Feminism in International Politics by Joan W. Scott, Cora Kaplan, and Debra Keates (1997) bring the Western character of feminist politics into question, while Cynthia Enloe's (2001) *Bananas, Beaches, and Bases: Making Feminist Sense of International Politics* and Robin Riley, Chandra Mohanty, and Minnie Brice Pratt's (2008) *Feminism and War: Confronting U.S. Imperialism* bring a feminist critical perspective to bear on global issues. The more recent global focus of feminist political critique has resulted in attempts to forge ways of understanding feminist praxis as an issue of universal rights, as illustrated by the work in such collections as Myra Ferree and Aili Tripp's (2006) *Global Feminism: Transnational Women's Activism, Organizing, and Human Rights*, Wendy Hesford and Wendy Kozol's (2005) *Just Advocacy: Women's Human Rights, Transnational Feminisms, and the Politics of Representation*, and Manisha Desai's (2009) *Gender and the Politics of Possibilities: Rethinking Globalization.*

Generally, the projects of recovery and disciplinary critique draw their authority from the disciplines themselves, entering and altering the field's own conversations. At the turn of the twenty-first century, this authority again turns to the evidentiary experience of testimony, as feminist critique engages with its own Western bias. At the same time, however, both the interrogated disciplines and the inclusion of previously disenfranchised voices begin to reconstitute the field of women's studies from which they gain an additional institutional authority. Although all of the scientific, social, and humanities disciplines interrogated by feminist scholars have constructed themselves in one way or another through the exclusion of women and a reliance upon gender-biased assumptions, most feminist critique itself derived from one of two sets of assumptions about authority itself. While we may map the disciplines according to whether we understand their endeavors as empirical or representational, science or humanism, the basic sets of questions applied derive either from a belief in the defining capacities of human psychology or from the credibilities attributed to historical circumstances and material conditions. For this reason, the discourses of psychoanalysis and historical materialism have occupied a central place as both modes and objects of feminist critique.

AUTHORIZING ASSUMPTIONS: PSYCHOANALYSIS AND THE FEMINIST SUBJECT

Psychoanalysis is the study of the human subject with an eye toward treating mental illness. As Sigmund Freud formulated his understandings of how the human psyche formed and functioned, gender and sexuality constituted a large part of the subject's conscious and unconscious mental structure. Although credited with the line "Biology is destiny," Freud saw very clearly that individual bodies and desires did not necessarily align into neat binaries. His formulations about gender and sexuality, however, assumed a male subject as his unquestioned model. Although a significant portion of Freud's work on sexuality focused on femininity and female sexuality, he was never able to theorize either adequately. Because psychoanalysis—and particularly Freudian psychoanalysis—seemed to have a profound influence on the normativizing impetuses of analysts, medical practitioners, and social policy makers and because it was so overtly focused on gender and sexuality, it was one of the first targets of feminist critique. From the earliest moments, however, that critique was ambivalent, accepting the idea of a subjective structure and the unconscious while trying to expose and revise the sexist assumptions of such founding fathers as Freud and Havelock Ellis.

After Simone de Beauvoir devotes a chapter to "The Psychoanalytic Point of View" in *The Second Sex*, feminist thinkers such a Kate Millett (1970), Betty Friedan (1963), and Phyllis Chesler (1972) take on its authority by showing the intrinsic patriarchalism of some of Freud's conclusions. Both Millett and Friedan blame Freud for providing a new and scientized authority for traditional beliefs about the second-class status of women. Pointing to such formulations as "anatomy is destiny" and "penis envy," Millett and Friedan demystify Freudian psychoanalysis as thinly veiled patriarchal ideology, especially in the apparent sexism of its more publicly bruited conclusions. Understanding psychoanalysis itself as an authority to be defeated if women were to achieve any measure of equality, feminists attacked Freud's theories.

Freud and psychoanalysis were not, however, without their feminist defenders. Scholars such as Juliet Mitchell, Jacqueline Rose, Ellie Ragland, Teresa Brennan, Jane Gallop, and others saw in Freudian psychoanalysis a mode of analysis and an understanding of the subject that left room for a much more sophisticated and open understanding of the relations among subjects, genders, and sexualities (Brennnan, 1989; Gallop, 1982; Mitchell, 1975; Mitchell & Rose, 1985; Ragland-Sullivan, 1986; Rose, 1986). This kind of work, which began with Mitchell's (1975) *Psychoanalysis and Feminism,* continued through the 1980s as feminist scholars argued that the various psychoanalytic methods might become a mode of authority for feminist work. Certainly, most understandings of textual analysis are derived from a psychoanalytic model in the first place—a model in which one reads a text's symptoms to discern its operation and less obvious meanings. Feminist modes of reading across and against texts depended upon understanding this kind of analysis as something that showed a text's underlying assumptions and enabled both critique and revision.

The authority of psychoanalysis as wielded by feminist thinkers was increased by the dissemination of the thought of Jacques Lacan, whose understandings of sexuation, sexuality, and subjectivity engaged more contemporary theories of language and image. Although feminist thinkers charged Lacan with the same kind of patriarchalism as Freud's, many literary, film, and feminist psychoanalytic scholars such as Rose, Ragland, Kaja Silverman, Laura Mulvey, Brennan, Gallop, Elizabeth Grosz, and Judith Butler saw Lacan's insights as opportunities for a more feminist and less patriarchal understanding of the dynamics of gender, sexuality, and the development of various forms of the female subject (Brennan, 1993; Butler, 1990; Gallop, 1985; Grosz, 1990; Mulvey, 1989; Ragland-Sullivan, 1986; Rose, 1986; Silverman, 1983). This understanding depended on seeing the dynamics of process as more important than the sometimes sexist conclusions derived therefrom. This meant that psychoanalytic ideas, assumptions, and methods could be turned to a feminist use, along with the authority psychoanalysis connoted.

As a discourse that provides tools to understand both the sex/gender system and the constitution of a subject with an unconscious, psychoanalysis provides feminist criticism with a set of concepts that enable an understanding of gender and sexuality as a joint construction of culture and the psyche, while also bringing the reliability of any kind of experiential testimony into question. This second unlooked-for effect of psychoanalytic concepts introduced another tension into the conflicting practices of feminist critique. On the one hand, the critique of the personal as itself an effect of subjective psychology offered a valuable corrective to the occasional feminist overreliance on experience. On the other hand, such a conclusion continued to raise questions about the inherent biases of psychoanalysis itself, as it appeared again to discount alternative perspectives. One solution to this dilemma was to deploy the models offered by psychoanalysis from a specifically feminist perspective to read against patriarchal texts.

While textual and film critics developed a feminist psychoanalytic method of criticism, others, such as Carol Gilligan, Nancy Chodorow, and Jessica Benjamin, devised new psychological theories of female development. Still premised upon the methods and assumptions of psychoanalysis, these female-centered theories considered a different set of influences and values that might account for and to some extent liberate possibilities for female subjects. Both Chodorow's (1978) *The Reproduction of Mothering* and Gilligan's (1982) *In a Different Voice: Psychological Theory and Women's Development* provided new bases for feminist authority over the female subject. At the same time, feminist psychologists such as Sue Cox and Jessica Benjamin developed specifically feminist understandings of female psychology, and others, such as Anica Mander and Anne Rush, devised modes of feminist clinical practice (Benjamin, 1988; Cox, 1976; Mander & Rush, 1974).

Because psychoanalytic understandings of gender were so closely allied to issues of sexuality,

feminist researchers also took on their own examination of the otherwise under-considered realm of female sexuality. Nancy Friday gathered specifically women's sexual fantasies in her 1973 publication *My Secret Garden,* and Shere Hite, a sex researcher, published her landmark study of female sexuality, *The Hite Report: A Nationwide Study on Female Sexuality*, in 1976. The development of a feminist psychology and of studies of female sexuality, though derived from the insights of psychoanalysis, also depended largely on collecting the experiences of women. These begin a shift toward women's experience as a primary basis for the authority of feminist research, especially in areas of social and psychological study. Representations of this research mixed accounts of women's experience with more empirical arguments and analyses.

AUTHORIZING ASSUMPTIONS: HISTORICAL MATERIALISM

A psychoanalytic focus on the subject, however, did not address other possible theories for the conditions within which women lived. While psychoanalytic theorists saw the ways we think about gender, sexuality, and the subject itself as correctible vectors of oppression, historical materialists sought the reasons for sexism in the class divisions and material conditions of women's lives. As she did with psychoanalysis, Simone de Beauvoir recommences this kind of analysis in *The Second Sex*, though she picks up a debate begun earlier by Emma Goldman in her monthly periodical *Mother Earth*, published from 1906 to 1917, and in her writings collected later in *The Traffic in Women and Other Essays* (Goldman, 1970). Although, as de Beauvoir points out, Marxism itself does not address gender directly, its analysis of the oppressive effect of class relations provides a model for understanding the interrelations among gender, class, and capitalist practices that provide women with a very different material experience of the world than is provided to men. Women become cheap labor in a system in which patriarchy is wed to capitalism.

The study of the material conditions of women's lives stems from this understanding and provides another kind of authority for feminist analyses based on the material conditions of women as a class. Considering women within a structure of class relations provides another motive for recovering and documenting the lives and experiences of women. Making visible and accessible the lives of otherwise unrepresented women changes the way we might conceive of gender relations as well as the stakes involved in social change. Seeing, for example, the ways women are the objects of exchange between men, as Luce Irigaray and Gayle Rubin do, situates gender relations as market relations, women as objects instead of subjects, and reveals the masculinist and homosocial bases of Western culture (Irigaray, 1977; Rubin, 1996). Such critics as Lillian S. Robinson, Judith Newton, and Rosemary Hennessy present a materialist feminist view of both Western representations of women and feminist practice itself, premising their analyses on Marxist insights about class (Hennessy, 2000; Newton, 1978; Robinson, 1978). Feminism's more recent engagement in global issues also depends upon an assumption that material conditions both produce and define women's perspectives, and it brings into question the material bases upon which Western feminist inquiry is premised.

The processes of feminist recovery and the critique of existing discourses locate authority in the ability of feminist critics to wield traditional disciplinary assumptions and methods both to make visible the women's lives, experience, and accomplishments that have been ignored and to point out and correct the sexist assumptions of traditional fields. Adding women to various fields of inquiry has the effect of changing the ways that disciplines such as biology, history, sociology, anthropology, and literary studies conceive of their subject matter as well as the ways they understand their own methods. The power of considering women's points of view as both a subject and method of inquiry alters the ways such inquiries are conducted, but also raises additional questions about the value and effect of different kinds of experience, the ethics of using traditional methodologies, and the modes of communicating thought to feminist audiences. Enlarging the field of feminist inquiry to the global, although reverting to an authority

recognized as experiential, also questions the sex/gender binaries upon which Western feminism has relied.

AUTHORIZING ASSUMPTIONS: EXPERIENCE, PERSPECTIVE, AND INCLUSION

In an influential essay titled "The Master's Tools Will Never Dismantle the Master's House," poet and critic Audre Lorde raises the question of what the relation might be between traditional modes of thinking and science. How, in other words, might feminists "use the master's tools" to build anything other than the master's house? Or what other tools, ways of thinking, and modes of representation might feminist researchers employ that would have persuasive power and authority? Experience as represented by nontraditional, nonmainstream, or disenfranchised women has become an extension of one of feminism's original mantras: "The personal is political." Blurring the assumptions of both humanities' critiques of language and materialist objectivity, experience is a third authorizing assumption. Personal experience is neither empirical nor critical of its subjective potential; nonetheless, this notion of the "voice" undergirds a feminist notion of inclusion that itself authorizes feminist analysis and politics as that which, by definition, must challenge the impersonal conclusions of traditional scholars. Experience provides the perspectives that authorize feminist accounts of the world, breaking down oppressive stereotypes and patriarchal conclusions of uniformity and forging a theory based on the imagined practicalities of women's existence. Personalizing theory meant making it real, practical, and immediate. It also meant making it less universalized, which both enabled a different mode of more personal argument and allowed more broadly accessible forms of representation that often involved group projects (e.g., the Combahee River Collective) or personal essays such as Lorde's own collection or Gloria Anzaldúa's *Borderlands: The New Mestiza* or, more recently, collecting and reproducing the perspectives of women in developing nations.

In the 1960s, the American women's movement declared that the "personal is political," an idea that not only made relevant previously trivialized aspects of women's lives but also empowered their speech as if from a new kind of subject. This new liberationist subject became immediately expert about her own experience and was encouraged to recognize her difficulties, trials, and frustrations as a more profound version of truth than the cultural ideologies of feminine domesticity by which those perceptions had been dismissed as neurotic, spoiled, weak, or imaginary. The authority of the personal was encouraged by the emergence of consciousness-raising groups where women got together, talked, and found that their experiences often contradicted the lauded happiness of suburbia, the securities of happy marriage, or the myths of survival in the business world. It was also encouraged by an incipient flood of popular press material such as Friedan's *The Feminine Mystique* that put those frustrations and contradictions in print.

Spurred by a new sense of communal vigor and support, women began working with other women to address issues such as rape, incest, battery, poverty, exploitation, racism, job discrimination, and sexual frustration—all problems previously ignored or suppressed by mainstream culture. The consciousness-raising group gave women a place to voice their problems, uncertainties, and fears, and women often found there others whose experience ratified their own. These groups of women, then, whose perceptions of the world were reinforced by one another's experiences, enabled the more public dissemination of what Friedan calls "the problem that has no name" and culminated in the form of feminist activism focused on rendering women's lives and problems visible. While publication and popular media attention cultivated an audience of women liberated through self-recognition (or women devoutly hunkered in defense and denial), personal testimony became a primary source of power and authority for women's liberation. Women talking to other women became an effective catalyst for female enlightenment.

One collection of personal experiences and analysis, Robin Morgan's (1970) *Sisterhood Is Powerful*, had a profound effect on the burgeoning women's movement by showing that women's voices and experiences are indeed valuable, catalyzing forces for change. Morgan's collection

was joined by an increasing number of small press publications and periodicals by and for women: *The Ladder* (1956–1972), *Voice of the Women's Liberation Movement* (1968–1969), *Off Our Backs* (1970–), *It Ain't Me Babe* (1970–1971), *Battle Acts* (1970–1974), *The Way We See It* (1970), *Womankind* (1971–1973), *Mother Lode* (1971–1973), *The Furies* (1972–1973), *Lavender Woman* (1971–1976), and *Amazon Quarterly* (1972–1975). These continued the promulgation of women's experiences and the analyses of various forces of oppression. By providing publication opportunities, small presses and alternative journals and comics provided a site of empowerment for feminist researchers who had a better way to reach audiences and whose work and ideas were less likely to be censored in these venues than in mainstream modes of publication.

The mainstream itself, however, picked up on this new market of women interested in women's issues. With Random House's publication of *Sisterhood Is Powerful*, women authors found new and effective outlets for their work. *Ms.* magazine began its mainstream publication in 1972. Nancy Friday, Marilyn French, Erica Jong, and Rita Mae Brown began publishing fiction focused on women's experiences, and poets Nikki Giovanni, Judy Grahn, Audre Lorde, and Adrienne Rich gained a new visibility and wider audience. Women artists such as Judy Chicago made quite visible the differences in perception and aesthetics that emerge from women's experiences. All of this production authorized a continued exploration of women's expression. The more evident presence of women-centered art in turn authorized an expanding field of women artists and writers who themselves made women's experience and vision the subject and aesthetic of their works.

This burgeoning artistic activity fed into developing women's studies programs at universities, which, defined already by their recovery projects, found new terrain for feminist scholarship. The link between feminist community activities such as rape crisis centers, women's newspapers and book stores, women's concerts, women's centers, and women's studies programs and other women-centered endeavors not only produced a system of mutual support but also authorized and empowered women's political initiatives, such as the fight for the ERA and reproductive rights and lobbying for more protective domestic relations laws, fairer social security and other benefits, child care programs, and better health care for women. Women's studies programs began national conferences in 1977, and music festivals such as the Michigan Womyn's Music Festival started in the same year to bring women together from all over the United States.

Politically, such public conversations among women produced action groups such as the National Organization for Women (NOW), begun in 1966 by Betty Friedan and others. NOW lobbied first for the Equal Rights Amendment, then for reproductive rights and against discrimination. Other "official" women-centered activities such as the International Women's Year in 1975 brought attention to the plight of women in nonindustrialized countries. The national organization, visibility, and public endorsement of women's perspectives additionally authorized feminist research as respectable and almost mainstream. As a mode of authority, visibility was central in the 1970s, especially as women's difficulties had been convincingly presented by Friedan and others as partly a problem of anonymity and invisibility. In addition, the increasing importance of media visibility in general in the 1970s, as television became more central and pervasive, made media attention necessary to certify the significance of events and causes.

As the consolidation of feminist communities brought together women of different backgrounds, classes, and races, so, too, did differences among women and their experiences become more evident. If experience could authorize speech, community, and political action, it also showed disparate needs, interests, and perspectives. Thus, as a mode of representative authority, experience was a two-edged sword. On the one hand, it countered more overtly ideological versions of women's truth and enabled the development of communities of individuals with common problems, anxieties, and experiences that seemed to support the truth of lived experience. On the other hand, the different experiences of women also demonstrated that the category itself was full of variations and even clashes in class, opportunity, race, sexualities, regional and ethnic interests, religious

affiliations, and understandings of the relative importance of gender itself. In other words, presenting feminist issues as personal demonstrated not only how representative experiences might be but also how idiosyncratic and unrepresentative they often were. Experiences of gender oppression itself differed for women of different races, ages, sexualities, and classes as did ideas about the urgency and proper mode of addressing sexism. Trying to subsume all under the rubric of "women" became, thus, increasingly difficult as feminists began to perceive the pervasiveness of oppressions, especially in the intersections of issues of race, class, ethnicity, and sexual orientation.

OTHER WOMEN AS OTHER: THE AUTHORIZING IMPETUS OF THE DISENFRANCHISED

African American women, often already engaged in the ongoing civil rights movement, readily pointed out the disparities among women, questioning assumptions about the universality of women's experience of oppression. Most often, African American women's objections were themselves based on experience, one inflected with an acute understanding of the effects of racism. Already in the early 1970s, African American women made their perspectives clear. Angela Davis called for antiracist activism in her letter from prison (1971), while such writers as Gloria Hull, Sonia Sanchez, and Alice Walker published poetry and stories and Toni Cade Bambara edited a collection of essays and stories about black women (Bambara, 1970; Davis, 1971). As experience itself became more obviously complex and contradictory, its authorizing aegis was defined more and more in relation to imagined degrees of oppression. Privileged white women began to feel less authorized to speak from their own experience in light of the more difficult lives of other women. If oppression was ultimately the subject of feminist research and if the experience of oppression was a primary mode of authorization, then less oppressed women experienced a species of de-authorization. In addition, the practice of academic authority, perceived as universalizing and exclusive, was discredited by some as itself oppressive to women.

The recognition of women's vastly different experiences, then, led to the development of new modes of feminist authority, representation, and rhetoric. Experience became a matter of subject position in a politics of identity in which one's experience and insights were linked to categories of race, ethnicity, class, and sexuality. Traditional academic theories were examined for more than their sexist bias; they became suspect for some as intrinsically oppressive, catalyzing the development of specifically feminist theories or the adoption of approaches that seemed less authoritative, universalist, and expert and more experiential, democratic, and accessible. The valorization of identity as determining experience resulted in identity politics and standpoint epistemologies, on the one hand, while suspicion and critique of the intrinsic sexist bias in theorizing led to alternative ways of theorizing, on the other.

Some feminists, such as those deploying psychoanalytic or Marxist analyses, understand experience as simultaneously individual and an effect of social organizations such as patriarchy or capitalism. For these scholars, the individual becomes the nexus of conflicting forces, and, though neither mode of analysis posits that individual experience represents broader truth, they, as well as many feminists, regard personal experience as a mode of authority. The value of this experience as a mode of authorizing lies more in its imagined authenticity than in any representative capability. Those who testify about their experiences as women speak bravely from a site of oppression about events and feelings only women in their position can understand and communicate. They are imagined to speak from the heart, although, of course, their testimony has no more claim to truth than that of anyone else. Situating such testimony as unassailable displaces issues of authority into the identities of those often deemed to be "other." Despite the fact that making explicit the fantasy subtending this idea of authenticity produces an inevitable hint of cynicism, the fantasy nonetheless underwrites many populist conceptions of the unassailable value of testimony based on experience (as with victims of the Holocaust) and powerlessness, defined as differences in relation to a middle-class, white, Christian majority.

These experiences are deemed not only to be authoritative in themselves but also to testify on behalf of the sociocultural position of the speaker. What began as testimony about individual experience is transformed into a speech representing grids of sociocultural presence defined in terms of those categories believed to be oppressed in and of themselves. Nonwhite speakers, for example, inevitably speak as oppressed racial others, lower class people as oppressed poor people. The experience of individuals is subsumed by the position from which they are imagined to speak, and this position becomes what authorizes and authenticates their testimony. The equation of individuals and subject positions has the effect of erasing idiosyncrasy while appealing to difference and diversity. At the same time, it encourages individual responsibility for a consciousness of the effects of sociocultural positioning on beliefs, experience, and authority. It suggests that only those approaching social phenomena from a specific position may speak from and for that position. It suggests, in other words, that the distribution of authority through culture is not only inequitable; it is also appropriative, dismissive, and dependent on the invisibility of those whom it oppresses to secure its power.

IDENTITY POLITICS

That the relations between a speaker's "identity" and the status and authority of what she says represent in themselves a set of problems, however, might also be an inevitable conclusion of feminist theorizing. If patriarchy depends upon an oppressed class of gendered others whose speaking for themselves might begin their liberation, then this same model works for other situations of oppression. Displacing the locus of authority from experience to the schematized categories of economic, racial, and ethnic intersection from which individuals are imagined to speak dissolves individual experiences into the truths of the political theories of oppression. This conflation of witness and oppression is then understood to combat the universalizing erasure of other perspectives. One's speech is not only testimony but also the inevitable product of a subject position. This set of connections suggests that individuals can only speak authoritatively from their own subject positions. In addition, however, this positioning process also suggests that some subject positions are more "positioned" to see the truth of oppression than others. In other words, those who are understood as more oppressed are more likely to see this oppression than those located on the side of the oppressors. If subject positions are imagined in relation to their imagined access to power (i.e., in relation to economic, social, racial, and ethnic regimes of privilege), then those more enfranchised to speak perceptively about oppression are those in positions of less advantage.

The problem with this approach is that it both represents and depends upon the same modes of oppression that it tries to critique. On the one hand, seeing authority in relation to oppression enables many to speak powerfully. On the other, this mode of enfranchisement assumes rather than questions the bases by which certain subject positions are constructed as well as the terms through which both oppression and concepts of the subject itself are understood. Only certain kinds of difference and oppression are acknowledged; the theoretical bases by which these positions are constructed remain fairly invisible or are themselves authorized by the ratifying self-identifications of subjects who understand *themselves* to occupy those positions. Finally, position, understood in terms of a few categories of social oppression such as race, class, gender, and ethnicity, becomes coterminous with identity. Group politics become a matter of sorting individuals by identity category. Although acknowledging that different groups and subject positions represent very different experiences that should be included in any feminist analysis, some feminists argue that, without reconsidering the framework of such inclusions, these tend to repeat a structure of dominance and repression within feminism that can be antithetical to productive politics. On the other hand, as more recent work on global feminism has demonstrated (compare Mohanty, 2003), such inclusions might also reinvigorate thinking about feminism's underlying categories.

STANDPOINT EPISTEMOLOGY

Obviously, any notion of identity premised primarily on stereotyped categorization reiterates the power disparities feminist theorists have

long critiqued, as does the assumption that all members of categories share similar experiences. The reduction of authorization to a semaphore of identity categories became a way of short-circuiting individual experience in favor of the imaginary authorizations of particular theories of relative oppression. The idea that individuals perceive the world itself according to these identity categories produces a notion of a "standpoint epistemology," a way of knowing the world from a specific, identifiable point defined as the intersection of certain kinds of socially relevant categories such as race, class, and gender. Discussions about the validity of standpoint epistemologies took center stage in the early 1990s, as the idea of standpoint epistemology represents both the apotheosis of the logic of identity politics and a delimiting factor for any universalizing practices. Collections such as Judith Roof and Robyn Wiegman's (1995) *Who Can Speak? Authority and Critical Identity* and Linda Alcoff and Elizabeth Potter's (1993) *Feminist Epistemologies* identify and explore the complex issues of identity, ethics, authority, and representative speech.

Standpoint epistemologies eventually became a matter of an ethical recognition of both the differences of others and one's own production as subject in relation to cultural forces. At the same time, standpoints have been increasingly collapsed into bodies themselves as sites that indicate subjective standpoint. Shane Phelan's (1994) *Getting Specific* argues for a thorough and responsible accounting for differences, while feminist theories of the body provide a different kind of challenge to the systems of thought by which identity categories are produced in the first place.

Just as feminist challenges to the theoretical bases of authority push feminist researchers toward personal experience as one mode of validation, so, too, do they push feminist researchers to devise explicitly feminist theories. As bodies define sociocultural and political positions, and as familial and economic organizations such as patriarchy and capitalism depend upon the same subjugation of bodies, the site of the body, the family, and economies seem the most propitious sites for feminist interventions. If, for example, we believe that ways of knowing come from the subject's experience of her body, then feminist thinkers employ the female body as the place from which a different way of knowing might be authorized. French feminist theorists such as Julia Kristeva, Luce Irigaray, and Hélène Cixous all devised counter-theories of subjectivity, epistemology, and aesthetics from the female body as providing a distinctly different experience of the world. Kristeva (1984) devised an understanding of poetics in relation to the different relation between female bodies and language (*Revolution in Poetic Language*), while Irigaray (1977, 1985) assails psychoanalysis and Western philosophy from an assumption that women's bodies experience existence as essentially more multiple and decentered than do male bodies (see *This Sex Which Is Not One* and *Speculum of the Other Woman*). Cixous devises alternative theories of literature and aesthetics based on an understanding of the different relation between women's bodies, language, and aesthetics (Cixous, 1994; Cixous & Clément, 1986). Straddling the material and the imaginary, analyses of women and the body locate the body as a site of oppressive operations as well as empowerments, as in the work of Judith Butler (1993) in *Bodies That Matter: On the Discursive Limits of "Sex,"* Elizabeth Grosz (1994) in *Volatile Bodies: Toward a Corporeal Feminism*, and Rose Weitz (2009) in *The Politics of Women's Bodies: Sexuality, Appearance, and Behavior*.

Feminist Art, Authority, and Experience

Feminist artists and aesthetic theorists likewise devise new understandings of a feminist aesthetic based on the differences in perception and bodily experiences of women. Judy Chicago's exhibitions, such as *The Dinner Party* (1974–1979) and *The Birth Project* (1980–1985), and other writing by women authors, artists, playwrights, and filmmakers have devised theories of feminist praxis whose power is specifically womanist—addressing and appealing to women. On the basis of this rich new tradition of feminist artistic work, feminist theorists devise different ways of understanding a feminist aesthetics, premised on the works' foregrounding of styles, colors, themes, and stories associated with and focusing on women, women's

bodies, and women's experiences. Understood as multiple, dispersed, tactile, often crafts-based, and nonobjectifying, women's art is formulated in feminist theories of women's art as a medium of communication, a mode of authority, a site of both individual and group self-representation, a means of community building, and, occasionally, a marker of separatist difference, speaking to women only or primarily and eschewing both the supposed universalism and rebellious oedipality of mainstream artistic production. Like works deriving their authority from the body or the identitarian speaker, feminist art is often imagined to speak from beyond the structure of oppression as sincere, perceptive, heart-felt, and true. Of course, like all other modes of sincere or presumably "unmediated" communication, artistic expression constitutes a mode of critique and self-expression that often represents the perspective of many while simultaneously effecting an individual vision. Its authority lies in its appeal to the senses and the visceral, while its power lies in its ability to capture and express what appear to be the insights of individual and group experience.

Understanding art as a mode of communal authority requires some reconsideration of the function of art itself as well as adjusting and valorizing a specifically womanist or feminist aesthetic practice, one that simultaneously envisions and critiques, expresses, and enables a different kind of vision understood specifically as female. This retheorizing of the aesthetic occurs in all media: music (e.g., Sally MacArthur's [2002] *Feminist Aesthetics in Music* and Sally MacArthur and Cate Poynton's [1999] *Music and Feminisms*), theater (e.g., *Theatre and Feminist Aesthetics*, edited by Karen Laughlin and Catherine Schuler [1995]), film (e.g., Mary Gentile's [1985] *Film Feminisms: Theory and Practice*), and plastic arts (e.g., Griselda Pollock's [2003] *Vision and Difference: Femininity, Feminism, and Histories of Art*). Others have developed more general feminist aesthetic theories; see, for example, Gisela Ecker's (1985) *Feminist Aesthetics*, Peg Brand and Carolyn Korsmeyer's (1995) *Feminism and Tradition in Aesthetics*, and Tuzyline Allen's (1995) *Womanist and Feminist Aesthetics*. Other edited collections in this field include the following: *Aesthetics in Feminist Perspective*, edited by Hilde Hein and Carolyn

Korsmeyer (1993); *The Power of Feminist Art: The American Movement of the 1970s, History and Impact*, edited by Norma Broude and Mary Garrard (1994); *Women Making Art: Women in the Visual, Literary, and Performing Arts Since 1960*, edited by Deborah Johnson and Wendy Oliver (2001); *Art and Feminism*, edited by Helena Reckitt (2001); and *Reclaiming Female Agency: Feminist Art History After Postmodernism*, edited by Norma Broude and Mary Garrard (2005). Florence Ebila and Florence Muhanguzi's (2006) *Women, Culture, and Creativity* globalizes the scope of this inquiry into feminine aesthetics and enlarges traditional notions of creativity, and *Doing Gender in Media, Art, and Culture*, edited by Rosemarie Buikema and Iris van der Tuin (2009), reviews and reconsiders the power of feminist theories in more contemporary media and art.

Digital culture, too, has become another matrix for the development and extension of feminist theorizing and self-expression. Digital culture becomes itself a medium for feminist expression, as considered in Bracha Ettinger's (2006) *The Matrixial Borderspace* and Kim Toffoletti's (2007) *Cyborgs and Barbie Dolls: Feminism, Popular Culture and the Posthuman Body*. Constituting a new medium for feminist art, digital culture promises another vector for women's communication, a site of individual and group self-representation, a means of community building, and a technology that might level the differences among women of various ages, classes, and privileges. The technologies of cyberspace have enabled the dissemination of a new "girl" (or "grrl") culture in which identities are no longer grounded in bodies but can morph, emerge, and disappear as creatures of discursive acts. This apparent power—extolled in such collections as Mary Ann O'Farrell and Lynne Vallone's (2000) *Virtual Gender: Fantasies of Subjectivity and Embodiment*, Anita Harris's (2004) *All About the Girl: Culture, Power, and Identity*, Theresa Senft's (2008) *Glamgirls: Celebrity and Community in the Age of Social Networks*, Mary Sheridan-Rabideau's (2008) *Girls, Feminism, and Grassroots Literacies: Activism in the GirlZone*, and Emilie Zaslow's (2009) *Feminism, Inc.: Coming of Age in Girl Power Media Culture*—locates a democratizing authority in the possibilities of digital culture in which feminist ideas are disseminated and young women are both communally and creatively empowered by the digital platform's provision of a transnational community. At the same time, digital culture has its dangers, including the extension of patriarchal ideologies, as Anne Balsamo (1995) warns in her early critique of cyber technologies, *Technologies of the Gendered Body: Reading Cyborg Women*. In *Global Obscenities: Patriarchy, Capitalism, and the Lure of Cyberfantasy*, Zillah Eisenstein (1998) points to both the dangers and the potentials of cyber fantasy worlds, while Lisa Nakamura critiques the persistence of racist, ethnic, and essentialist ideologies in cyberspace in both *Cybertypes: Race, Ethnicity, and Identity on the Internet* and *Digitizing Race: Visual Cultures of the Internet*, published in 2002 and 2007, respectively.

THE AUTHORITY OF ALTERNATIVE RELATIONS

Just as the body provides a site upon which different theories of feminist epistemology, political practice, and artistic expression might be premised, privileging the maternal offers a challenge to patriarchal dominance in thought and social organization. Modeled on mother-daughter relations, woman-to-woman relations enable feminists to reconceive relations among women and envision a more generous, selfless culture based on sharing and nurturing instead of selfishness and single-minded ego. Mother-daughter relations ground Nancy Chodorow's (1978) theory of female psychological development in *The Reproduction of Mothering*, as well as understandings of literary and artistic production. Marianne Hirsch (1989), for example, deploys the maternal model as a way of reading women's literature in *The Mother/Daughter Plot*, and Madelon Sprengnether (1990) begins from the mother as a way of rereading Freud in *The Spectral Mother: Freud, Feminism, and Psychoanalysis*. Understanding the maternal as an ethic of selfless interrelation, feminist theories often read women's interrelations, particularly relations among generations, as maternal. This produces a critical practice in which earlier generations become sites of empathy and admiration, and ideas are shared and nurtured among many. This utopian and often separatist ideal gains its authority from the alternative to patriarchy it seems to offer, especially as most such theories ignore maternal difficulties and mother-daughter strife, dismissing both as effects of patriarchy.

Matriarchy also encompasses social organizations in which the singularity of patriarchal nuclear families gives way to expansive, cooperative communities, imagined at least in literature such as Monique Wittig's (1975) *The Lesbian Body* or Rita Mae Brown's (1978) *Six of One*. Feminist social theorists undertake rethinking the family along these lines (see Barrie Thorne and Marilyn Yalom's [1982] *Rethinking the Family: Some Feminist Questions*), while ecofeminists deploy a feminist ethic of sharing and coexisting in re-envisioning the relations among humans, spirits, and the world (see, e.g., Carol Adams [1993], *Ecofeminism and the Sacred*; Carolyn Merchant [1992], *Radical Ecology*; Irene Diamond and Gloria Feman Orenstein [1990], *Reweaving the World: the Emergence of Ecofeminism*; and Greta Gaard [1993], *Ecofeminism: Women, Animals, Nature*).

Finally, some feminist thinkers ground an alternative ethic in an appeal to a different cosmology, which is governed by female principles and the goddess. This specifically feminist spirituality authorizes practices of generosity and sharing as well as witchcraft, womanist rituals, and empowering transformations. As in all religions, the power of feminist spirituality lies in its appeal to a truth beyond proof—to feeling, sensing, and communing with something beyond. Feminist spirituality avoids the patriarchal imperatives of monotheisms by countering with a more pervasive, nourishing spirit world: see, for example, Wendy Griffin (2000), *Daughters of the Goddess: Studies of Healing, Identity, and Empowerment*; Wendy Roberts (1998), *Celebrating Her: Feminist Ritualizing Comes of Age*; and Carol Christ (1997), *Rebirth of the Goddess: Finding Meaning in Feminist Spirituality*.

TECHNIQUES OF PERSUASION

This expanded range of authorizing structures empowers a rethinking of patriarchal culture and of the assumptions about women's lives, the ways of reading culture, and our presumptions about ethics and justice. The "master's tools," however, still dominate actual practices of empowerment, especially modes of public persuasion. Logics, theories, and rhetorical practices conform to familiar patterns as a part of their persuasive operation. Even if feminist thinkers bring alternative theories to light, communicating those theories—outside of feminist artistic practices—becomes difficult within traditional conventions of argumentation.

Virginia Woolf's presentation of the difficulties faced by creative women took the form of personal essays in which the protagonist sought out most of the forms of traditional authority in her quest to understand why there have not been more women artists and thinkers. In *A Room of One's Own*, Woolf (1929) contrasts conventional "authorities" with her own experience and that of other women to forward her theory that poor material conditions and lack of personal freedom make it difficult for women to be artists. Using a first person narrator to contrast an experience of pinching poverty with the misogynistic pronouncements of pampered experts, Woolf deploys the personal as a most influential mode of persuasion in these essays.

Woolf's use of the personal model has become a persuasive trope for feminist writers and researchers. If women's experience and insight have been omitted in favor of a universalizing masculinist view, what better way to begin to correct the situation than through the very voices and experiences that have been squelched? Not simply an overlooked and ignored resource, personal experience becomes a rhetorical guarantee of authenticity not easily countermanded. Who, after all, can argue with a person's experience? Experience thus occupies an ambivalent position in feminist representation. Situated simultaneously as an unquestionable authority and the product of cultural forces, experience both grounds feminist epistemologies and is open to question. Experience is an unresolved point of contestation in feminist thought, but a point whose value is rarely openly contested because doing so appears to disenfranchise those whom feminism champions.

Because of the ambivalent status of experience, feminist persuasion also bolsters experience with the expert practice of disciplinary conventions for argument, evidence, and objectivity.

Feminist researchers rarely conform to disciplinary conventions without also signaling their consciousness of the potentially nonobjective character of those conventions. In other words, feminist researchers often practice a self-conscious disciplinarity in which they can use the persuasive techniques of fields of study while indicating their own positions as researchers and their knowledge that techniques and methods may incorporate power disparities.

The simultaneous feminist use and critique of disciplinary methods and assumptions occurs in most disciplines: in history (e.g., Scott, 1999), literary history and criticism (e.g., Gilbert & Gubar, 1979), anthropology and folklore (e.g., Behar & Gordon, 1995), philosophy (e.g., Frye, 1983), psychoanalysis (e.g., Rose, 1986), and science (e.g., Harding, 1986). Like de Beauvoir, contemporary feminist theorists and critics straddle the line between disciplinary "soundness" and responsibility and disciplinary critique as itself a mode of feminist authority. In this way, feminist criticism accomplishes a double labor. Not only does it attend to a more comprehensive disciplinary study that includes previously elided viewpoints and subjects, but it also demonstrates the assumptions and practices that have enabled the exclusion and mischaracterization of women for so long.

One crucial disciplinary authorizing technique is the citation of the work and ideas of predecessors. Although in traditional disciplines that precedent often reflects the sexist ideologies of the field, feminist researchers deploy alternative and often previously ignored work by pioneering women and others. Establishing a feminist history has been important not only as a way to recover lost experiences and lives but also as a way to support the insights of more contemporary thought. The work of other feminist thinkers serves as well to produce a burgeoning field of expertise that begins to authorize itself.

The personalizing impetus in much feminist research is also related to the exigencies of identity politics, as positionality itself becomes a primary mode of authorizing. When the personal is the political, then the positional aspects of the personal become authorizing categories of an insight as well as expertise about the lives of variously oppressed groups or of groups engaged in alternative or nontraditional modes of life. Researchers must speak with care of experiences and cultural sites not their own. Positioning oneself as a part of a ritual of writing becomes a preliminary mode of self-authorization.

CONCLUSION

Feminist persuasion changes with the circumstances within which it is produced. A "first wave" of feminist work, which occurred in the nineteenth and early twentieth centuries, deployed traditional modes of reasoning refocused through the vantage of a woman writer, such as Woolf or de Beauvoir. "Second wave" feminist modes of authority, which began in the 1960s, developed from a two-pronged approach: examining the biases of traditional modes of thinking and collecting and celebrating the work of women writers, artists, and thinkers that had previously been ignored. During this second wave, rhetorical techniques such as the insertion of autobiographical detail and experience, the ritual self-positioning of authors, and references to sets of preeminent feminist thinkers became shorthands for authority. Power, however, continued to derive as well from clarity, timeliness, generosity, and care. More recent "third wave" feminist thought, beginning in the 1990s, illustrates even more convincingly that the power and authority of feminist theory and criticism come from feminist thinkers' willingness always to reconsider and retool their own assumptions and practices. Susan Gubar's (2006) *Rooms of Our Own*, for example, rethinks questions of authority and feminist scholarship in the new global, digital contexts of contemporary feminist praxis, while Phyllis Chesler (2005) theorizes feminism's future in *The Death of Feminism*. Third wave feminism, defined and discussed by the contributors to *Third Wave Feminism: A Critical Exploration*, edited by Stacy Gillis, Gillian Howie, and Rebecca Munford (2004), represents both an extension of the earlier primarily Western arena of feminist thought and a renewed hope in the tactics of inclusion, as suggested by Naomi Zack (2005) in *Inclusive Feminism: A Third Wave Theory of Women's Commonality*, and in intersectionality, as explored by the contributors to *Emerging Intersections: Race, Class, and Gender in Theory, Policy, and Practice*, edited by Bonnie Dill and Ruth Zambrana (2009). As third wave feminism continues its hope of change, it becomes clear that, in its most recent incarnations, the power and authority of feminist theory and criticism reside in feminism's ability to adjust its assumptions, preserve its ideals, and continue its battle.

Discussion Questions

1. In what ways can feminist thinkers use traditional modes of reasoning without adopting some of their sexist biases?

2. Are traditional modes of reasoning necessarily gender biased? In what ways?

3. What are the arguments for and against the use of personal experience as a form of evidence or authority?

4. What are the relations between what one says and how one says it?

5. Can a feminist thinker deploy both empirical and humanist assumptions at the same time? What are those assumptions?

Online Resources

Women & Gender Studies Section

http://libraries.mit.edu/humanities/WomensStudies/Culture2.html

This page, which is part of the WSSLinks project developed and maintained by the Association of College and Research Libraries, provides an annotated list of websites that specialize in various aspects of women in literature, the history of women's literature, and women's writing.

ArtWomen.org

http://artwomen.org/

This omnibus website contains descriptions and images of women's art, current exhibits, women's art news, and critical topics of interest to women artists.

Feminism and Philosophy

http://www.cddc.vt.edu/feminism/phi.html

This "Feminism and Philosophy" website, hosted by the Center for Digital Discourse and Culture at Virginia Tech University, contains a bibliography and links to major feminist philosophers.

Relevant Journals

CALYX: A Journal of Art and Literature by Women

Camera Obscura: Feminism, Culture, and Media Studies

differences: A Journal of Feminist Cultural Studies

Genders (Online only)

Hypatia: A Journal of Feminist Philosophy

n.paradoxa

Tulsa Studies in Women's Literature (TSWL)

Women & Performance: A Journal of Feminist Theory

References

Adams, C. (Ed.). (1993). *Ecofeminism and the sacred.* New York: Continuum.

Alcoff, L., & Potter, E. (1993). *Feminist epistemologies.* New York: Routledge.

Allen, T. (1995). *Womanist and feminist aesthetics.* Athens: Ohio University Press.

Amazon quarterly. (1972–1975). Oakland, CA: Amazon Press.

Anzaldúa, G. (1987). *Borderlands/La frontera.* San Francisco: Aunt Lute Books.

Balsamo, A. (1995). *Technologies of the gendered body: Reading cyborg women.* Durham, NC: Duke University Press.

Bambara, T. (1970). *The black woman.* New York: Penguin.

Battle acts. (1970–1974). New York: Women of Youth Against War and Fascism.

Behar, R., & Gordon, D. (Eds.). (1995). *Women writing culture.* Berkeley: University of California Press.

Benjamin, J. (1988). *The bonds of love: Psychoanalysis, feminism, and the problem of domination.* New York: Pantheon.

Bleier, R. (1984). *Science and gender: A critique of biology and its theories.* New York: Pergamon Press.

Boston Women's Health Book Collective. (1971). *Our bodies, ourselves*. Boston: New England Free Press.

Brand, P., & Korsmeyer, C. (Eds.). (1995). *Feminism and tradition in aesthetics*. University Park: Penn State University Press.

Brennan, T. (Ed.). (1989). *Between feminism and psychoanalysis*. New York: Routledge.

Brennan, T. (1993). *History after Lacan*. New York: Routledge.

Brodwin, P. (Ed.). (2000). *Biotechnology and culture: Bodies, anxieties, ethics*. Bloomington: Indiana University Press.

Broude, N., & Garrard, M. (Eds.). (1994). *The power of feminist art: The American movement of the 1970s, history and impact*. New York: H. N. Abrams.

Broude, N., & Garrard, M. (Eds.). (2005). *Reclaiming female agency: Feminist art history after postmodernism*. Berkeley: University of California Press.

Brown, C., & Olson, K. (Eds.). (1978). *Feminist criticism: Essays on theory, poetry, and prose*. Metuchen, NJ: Scarecrow.

Brown, R. M. (1978). *Six of one*. New York: Harper and Row.

Buikema, R., & van der Tuin, I. (Eds.). (2009). *Doing gender in media, art, and culture*. New York: Routledge.

Butler, J. (1990). *Gender trouble: Feminism and the subversion of identity*. New York: Routledge.

Butler, J. (1993). *Bodies that matter: On the discursive limits of "sex."* New York: Routledge.

Chesler, P. (1972). *Women and madness*. Garden City, NY: Doubleday.

Chesler, P. (2005). *The death of feminism: What's next in the struggle for women's freedom*. New York: Palgrave Macmillan.

Chicago, J. (Artist). (1974–1979). *The dinner party* [Ceramic, porcelain, textile]. (Available at the Brooklyn Museum, 2000 Eastern Parkway, Brooklyn, NY 11238-6052)

Chicago, J. (Artist). (1980–1985). *The birth project* [Multimedia art]. (More information available from the Through the Flower website: http://throughtheflower.org/page.php?p=12&n=2)

Chodorow, N. (1978). *The reproduction of mothering: Psychoanalysis and the sociology of gender*. Berkeley: University of California Press.

Christ, C. (1997). *Rebirth of the goddess: Finding meaning in feminist spirituality*. Reading, MA: Addison-Wesley.

Cixous, H. (1994). *The Hélène Cixous reader* (S. Sellers, Trans. & Ed.). New York: Routledge.

Cixous, H., & Clément, C. (1986). *The newly born woman* (B. Wing, Trans.). Minneapolis: University of Minnesota Press.

Cole, J. (1979). *Fair science: Women in the scientific community*. New York: Free Press.

Combahee River Collective. (1986). *The Combahee River Collective statement: Black feminist organizing in the seventies and eighties*. New York: Kitchen Table Women of Color Press.

Coole, D. (1988). *Women in political theory: From ancient misogyny to contemporary feminism*. Sussex, UK: Wheatsheaf Books.

Cornillon, S. (Ed.). (1972). *Images of women in fiction: Feminist perspectives*. Bowling Green, OH: Bowling Green University Press.

Cox, S. (1976). *Female psychology: The emerging self*. Chicago: Science Research Associates.

Daly, M. (1973). *Beyond God the father: Toward a philosophy of women's liberation*. Boston: Beacon Press.

Davis, A. (1971). *A letter from Angela to Ericka*. New York: New York Committee to Free Angela Davis.

de Beauvoir, S. (1949). *The second sex* (H. M. Parshley, Trans.). New York: Knopf.

Desai, M. (2009). *Gender and the politics of possibilities: Rethinking globalization*. New York: Rowman and Littlefield.

Diamond, I., & Orenstein, G. (Eds.). (1990). *Reweaving the world: The emergence of ecofeminism*. San Francisco: Sierra Books.

Dill, B., & Zambrana, R. (Eds.). (2009). *Emerging intersections: Race, class, and gender in theory, policy, and practice*. New Brunswick, NJ: Rutgers University Press.

Ebila, F., & Muhanguzi, F. (Eds.). (2006). *Women, culture, and creativity*. Kampala: Women and Gender Studies.

Ecker, G. (Ed.). (1985). *Feminist aesthetics* (H. Anderson, Trans.). London: Women's Press.

Eisenstein, Z. (1998). *Global obscenities: Patriarchy, capitalism, and the lure of cyberfantasy*. New York: New York University Press.

Enloe, C. (2001). *Bananas, beaches, and bases: Making feminist sense of international politics*. Berkeley: University of California Press.

Ettinger, B. (2006). *The matrixial borderspace*. Minneapolis: University of Minnesota Press.

Evans, J. (1986). *Feminism and political theory.* London: Sage.

Fausto-Sterling, A., & English, L. (1985). *Women and minorities in science: An interdisciplinary course.* Wellesley, MA: Wellesley College Center for Research on Women.

Ferree, M., & Tripp, A. (Eds.). (2006). *Global feminism: Transnational women's activism, organizing, and human rights.* New York: New York University Press.

Fraser, N. (1989). *Unruly practices: Power, discourse, and gender in contemporary social theory.* Minneapolis: University of Minnesota Press.

Friday, N. (1973). *My secret garden: Women's sexual fantasies.* New York: Pocket Books.

Friedan, B. (1963). *The feminine mystique.* New York: Dell.

Frye, M. (1983). *The politics of reality: Essays in feminist theory.* Trumansburg, NY: Crossing Press.

The furies. (1972–1973). Washington, DC: The Furies Collective.

Gaard, G. (1993). *Ecofeminism: Women, animals, nature.* Philadelphia: Temple University Press.

Gaard, G., & Murphy, P. (Eds.). (1998). *Ecofeminist literary criticism: Theory, interpretation, pedagogy.* Urbana: University of Illinois Press.

Gallop. J. (1982). *The daughter's seduction: Feminism and psychoanalysis.* Ithaca, NY: Cornell University Press.

Gallop, J. (1985). *Reading Lacan.* Ithaca, NY: Cornell University Press.

Gentile, M. (1985). *Film feminisms: Theory and practice.* Westport, CT: Greenwood Press.

Gilbert, S., & Gubar, S. (1979). *The madwoman in the attic.* New Haven, CT: Yale University Press.

Gilligan, C. (1982). *In a different voice: Psychological theory and women's development.* Cambridge, MA: Harvard University Press.

Gillis, S., Howie, G., & Munford, R. (Eds.). (2004). *Third wave feminism: A critical exploration.* New York: Palgrave Macmillan.

Goldman, E. (Ed.). (1906–1917). *Mother earth.* New York: Emma Goldman.

Goldman, E. (1970). *The traffic in women and other essays on feminism.* New York: Times Change Press.

Gornick, V., & Moran, B. (Eds.). (1971). *Woman in sexist society.* New York: Basic Books.

Greer, G. (1971). *The female eunuch.* New York: McGraw-Hill.

Griffin, W. (2000). *Daughters of the goddess: Studies of healing, identity, and empowerment.* Walnut Creek, CA: AltaMira Press.

Grosz, E. A. (1990). *Jacques Lacan: A feminist introduction.* New York: Routledge.

Grosz, E. A. (1994). *Volatile bodies: Toward a corporeal feminism.* Bloomington: Indiana University Press.

Grosz, E. A. (2005). *Time travels: Feminism, nature, power.* Durham, NC: Duke University Press.

Gubar, S. (2006). *Rooms of our own.* Urbana: University of Illinois Press.

Haas, V., & Perrucci, C. (1984). *Women in scientific and engineering professions.* Ann Arbor: University of Michigan Press.

Haraway, D. (1989). *Primate visions: Gender, race, and nature in the world of modern science.* New York: Routledge.

Haraway, D. (1991). *Simians, cyborgs, and women: The reinvention of nature.* New York: Routledge.

Haraway, D. (1997). *Modest_Witness@Second_ Millenium.FemaleMan©_Meets_OncoMouse™: Feminism and technoscience.* London: Taylor and Francis.

Haraway, D. (2005). *When species meet.* Minneapolis: University of Minnesota Press.

Harding, S. (1986). *The science question in feminism.* Ithaca, NY: Cornell University Press.

Harris, A. (2004). *All about the girl: Culture, power, and identity.* New York: Routledge.

Hein, H., & Korsmeyer, C. (Eds.). (1993). *Aesthetics in feminist perspective.* Bloomington: Indiana University Press.

Hennessy, R. (2000). *Profit and pleasure: Sexual identities in late capitalism.* New York: Routledge.

Hesford, W., & Kozol, W. (Eds.). (2005). *Just advocacy: Women's human rights, transnational feminisms, and the politics of representation.* New Brunswick, NJ: Rutgers University Press.

Hirsch, M. (1989). *The mother/daughter plot.* Bloomington: Indiana University Press.

Hite, S. (1976). *The Hite report: A nationwide study on female sexuality.* New York: Macmillan.

Hoagland, S. (1988). *Lesbian ethics: Toward a new value.* Palo Alto, CA: Institute of Lesbian Studies.

Irigaray, L. (1977). *Ce sexe qui n'en est pas un.* Paris: Editions de Minuit.

Irigaray, L. (1985). *Speculum of the other woman* (G. Gill, Trans.). Ithaca, NY: Cornell University Press.

It ain't me babe. (1970–1971). Berkeley, CA: W.L.P.B. Collective.

Jacobus, M., & Shuttleworth, S. (Eds.). (1990). *Body/politics: Women and the discourses of science*. New York: Routledge.

Jaggar, A. (1984). *Feminist frameworks: Alternative theoretical accounts of the relations between men and women*. New York: McGraw-Hill.

Janeway, E. (1971). *Man's world, woman's place*. New York: Morrow.

Johnson, D., & Oliver, W. (Eds.). (2001). *Women making art: Women in the visual, literary, and performing arts since 1960*. New York: Peter Lang.

Johnston, J. (1973). *Lesbian nation*. New York: Simon and Schuster.

Keller, E. F. (1985). *Reflections on women in science*. New Haven, CT: Yale University Press.

Kristeva, J. (1984). *Revolution in poetic language* (M. Waller, Trans.). New York: Columbia University Press.

The ladder. (1956–1972). New York: Arno Press.

Laughlin, K., & Schuler, C. (1995). *Theatre and feminist aesthetics*. Madison, NJ: Fairleigh Dickinson University Press.

Lavender woman. (1971–1976). Chicago: Lavender Woman Collective.

Lorde, A. (1984). *Sister outsider: Essays and speeches*. Trumansburg, NY: Crossing Press.

MacArthur, S. (2002). *Feminist aesthetics in music*. Westport, CT: Greenwood Press.

MacArthur, S., & Poynton, C. (1999). *Music and feminisms*. Sydney, NSW: Australian Music Centre.

Mander, A., & Rush, A. (1974). *Feminism as therapy*. New York: Random House.

Merchant, C. (1992). *Radical ecology*. New York: Routledge.

Millett, K. (1970). *Sexual politics*. Garden City, NY: Doubleday.

Mitchell, J. (1971). *Women's estate*. New York: Pantheon.

Mitchell, J. (1975). *Psychoanalysis and feminism*. New York: Penguin.

Mitchell, J., & Rose, J. (1985). *Feminine sexuality: Jacques Lacan and l'école Freudienne*. New York: Norton.

Mohanty, C. (2003). *Feminism without borders: Decolonizing theory, practicing solidarity*. Durham, NC: Duke University Press.

Moore, H. (1988). *Feminism and anthropology*. Cambridge, MA: Polity.

Morgan, R. (Ed.). (1970). *Sisterhood is powerful*. New York: Vintage.

Mother lode. (1971–1973). San Francisco: Mother Lode.

Mulvey, L. (1989). *Visual and other pleasures*. Bloomington: Indiana University Press.

Nakamura, L. (2002). *Cybertypes: Race, ethnicity, and identity on the Internet*. London: Taylor and Francis.

Nakamura, N. (2007). *Digitizing race: Visual cultures of the Internet*. Minneapolis: University of Minnesota Press.

Newton, J. (1978). *Women, power, and subversion: Social strategies in British fiction, 1778–1860*. Athens: University of Georgia Press.

O'Farrell, M. A., & Vallone, L. (Eds.). (2000). *Virtual gender: Fantasies of subjectivity and embodiment*. Ann Arbor: University of Michigan Press.

Off our backs. (1970–). Washington: Off Our Backs.

Okin, S. (1979). *Women in Western political thought*. Princeton, NJ: Princeton University Press.

Oliver, K. (2009). *Animal lessons: How they teach us to be human*. New York: Columbia University Press.

Phelan, S. (1994). *Getting specific: Postmodern lesbian politics*. Minneapolis: University of Minnesota Press.

Pollock, G. (2003). *Vision and difference: Femininity, feminism, and histories of art*. London: Routledge.

Ragland-Sullivan, E. (1986). *Jacques Lacan and the philosophy of psychoanalysis*. Champaign: University of Illinois Press.

Reckitt, H. (2001). *Art and feminism*. New York: Phaidon.

Riley, R., Mohanty, C., & Pratt, M. B. (Eds.). (2008). *Feminism and war: Confronting U.S. imperialism*. London: Zed.

Roberts, W. (1998). *Celebrating her: Feminist ritualizing comes of age*. Cleveland, OH: Pilgrim Press.

Robinson, L. (1978). *Sex, class, and culture*. Bloomington: Indiana University Press.

Roof, J., & Wiegman, R. (1995). *Who can speak? Authority and critical identity*. Champaign: University of Illinois Press.

Rose, J. (1986). *Sexuality in the field of vision*. London: Verso.

Rossiter, M. (1982). *Women scientists in America: Struggles and strategies to 1940*. Baltimore: Johns Hopkins University Press.

Rubin, G. (1996). The traffic in women: Notes on the "political economy" of sex. In J. Scott, *Feminism and history* (pp. 105–151). New York: Oxford University Press.

Schilling, G. F., & Hunt, M. K. (1974). *Women in science and technology*. Santa Monica, CA: Rand.

Scott, J. (1999). *Gender and the politics of history*. New York: Columbia.

Scott, J., Kaplan, C., & Keates, D. (Eds.). (1997). *Transitions, environments, translations: Feminism in international politics*. London: Taylor and Francis.

Senft, T. (2008). *Glamgirls: Celebrity and community in the age of social networks*. New York: Lang.

Sheridan-Rabideau, M. (2008). *Girls, feminism, and grassroots literacies: Activism in the GirlZone*. Albany: State University Press of New York.

Silverman, K. (1983). *The subject of semiotics*. New York: Oxford University Press.

Smelik, A., & Likke, N. (Eds.). (2008). *Bits of life: Feminism at the intersections of media, bioscience, and technology*. Seattle: University of Washington Press.

Spacks, P. (1975). *The female imagination*. New York: Knopf.

Spencer, A. (1925). *Women's share in social culture*. Philadelphia: Lippencott.

Spivak, G. (1988). *In other worlds: Essays in cultural politics*. New York: Routledge.

Sprengnether, M. (1990). *The spectral mother: Freud, feminism, and psychoanalysis*. Ithaca, NY: Cornell University Press.

Thorne, B., & Yalom, M. (Eds.). (1982). *Rethinking the family: Some feminist questions*. New York: Longman.

Toffoletti, K. (2007). *Cyborgs and Barbie dolls: Feminism, popular culture and the posthuman body*. London: I. B. Taurus.

Tuana, N. (Ed.). (1989). *Feminism and science*. Bloomington: Indiana University Press.

Voice of the women's liberation movement. (1968–1969). Chicago: Voice of the Women's Liberation Movement.

The way we see it. (1970). Springfield, MA: Springfield Women's Liberation.

Weiler, K. (Ed.). (2001). *Feminist engagements: Reading, resisting, and revisioning male theorists in education and cultural studies*. New York: Routledge.

Weitz, R. (2009). *The politics of women's bodies: Sexuality, appearance, and behavior*. New York: Oxford University Press.

Wittig, M. (1975). *The lesbian body* (D. LeVay, Trans.). Boston: Beacon Press.

Womankind. (1971–1973). Chicago: Chicago Women's Liberation Union.

Woolf, V. (1929). *A room of one's own*. London: Hogarth.

Woolf, V. (1938). *Three guineas*. London: Hogarth.

Zack, Naomi. (2005). *Inclusive feminism: A third wave theory of women's commonality*. Lanham, MD: Rowman and Littlefield.

Zaslow, E. (2009). *Feminism, Inc.: Coming of age in girl power media culture*. New York: Palgrave Macmillan.

26

THE FEMINISM QUESTION IN SCIENCE

What Does It Mean to "Do Social Science as a Feminist"?

ALISON WYLIE

From the time feminists turned a critical eye on conventional practice in the social sciences, they have asked what it would mean to do better, more inclusive research. For many, initially the challenge was to counteract sexist, androcentric erasure and bias in mainstream social science. Practical guidelines and handbooks proliferated, such as Eichler's (1988) *Nonsexist Research Methods,* codifying principles many of which are now widely accepted. But for others, the challenge was to think beyond conventional practice: What forms of social science do we need to develop to be effective in addressing questions that have largely been left out of account, questions that particularly matter for understanding, with precision and explanatory force, the systems of social differentiation and conditions of life, the forms of experience and identity, that are, to varying degrees and in diverse ways, oppressive for those categorized as women or

as sex/gender variant? These issues became the focus of sustained discussion through the 1980s and early 1990s in the context of the feminist method debate: the "feminism question in science," as I will refer to it, inverting the question Harding (1986) poses in *The Science Question in Feminism.*

I focus here on two broad strategies of response: Longino's discussion of what it means to "do science as a feminist" and a distillation of the guidelines for practice proposed by feminist social scientists. I then consider examples of feminist research that both exemplify and put epistemically consequential pressure on these principles. The anxiety that haunts these discussions is that if research is guided by explicitly feminist values, its epistemic credibility is irrevocably compromised. The methodological principles I will consider illustrate how this worry is countered in practice; I conclude with an argument for a reformulation of feminist standpoint theory that captures the wisdom implicit in this practice.

METHODOLOGICAL ESSENTIALISM AND THE VALUE(S) OF SCIENCE

One family of answers to my central question has long been highly contentious: that feminists must seek a distinctive form of practice, a uniquely "feminist science," because conventional modes of research in the social sciences are inherently patriarchal and cannot be recuperated.[1] This is a view more often attributed to feminists than exemplified by their practice, but those who might be interpreted as holding such a position include feminist social scientists of the late 1970s and early 1980s who were intransigent critics of the scientism they found dominant in mainstream social science. Smith (1978), for example, saw these fields as one node in a network of "ruling practices" that operate by systematically "eclipsing" women's roles and contributions, marginalizing their experience, and trivializing their self-understanding, while Mies (1983) and Stanley and Wise (1983b) objected that a positivist rhetoric of objectivity and value neutrality compounds the problem, obscuring the highly partial, context-specific interests that animate the social sciences (Mies, 1983; Stanley & Wise, 1983a). Although none of these feminist social scientists advocate wholesale abandonment of the tools of social research,[2] for epistemically conservative critics, it seems a short step from the antipathy they express for scientific modes of practice to the conclusion that they must endorse the quest for distinctively feminist forms of practice. And this they reject out of hand on grounds that the very idea of "feminist science" is a contradiction in terms. These lines of argument will be familiar from well-worn patterns of debate characteristic of the science wars (e.g., Gross & Levitt, 1994, pp. 107–147; contributors to "Feminisms" in Gross, Levitt, & Lewis, 1996, pp. 383–441). To take one prominent example, Haack (1993, 2007) objects that any intrusion of gender-specific interests into the sciences can only compromise their integrity. To advocate a feminist methodology or a feminist science is to abandon "honest inquiry"—inquiry inspired by a "genuine desire to find out how things are"—in favor of a dogmatic commitment to "make a case for a foregone conclusion"; it can be nothing more than "sham" research (Haack, 1993). For Haack and her fellow travelers (e.g., Pinnick, Koertge, & Almeder, 2003), the quest for a feminist mode of inquiry must presuppose an untenable gender essentialism: that women qua women must share a distinctively female or feminine "way of knowing" (perhaps of the kind made famous by Belenky, Clinchy, Goldberger, & Tarule, 1986) and that women scientists must rely on feminine forms of intuition and (non) reason that have been, in their view, rightly ignored by traditional theories of knowledge and marginalized within mainstream science.

In fact, feminists were among the earliest and most uncompromising critics of gender essentialism, and some of the sharpest challenges to the quest for a distinctively feminist method came from advocates of feminist practice in the social sciences. One catalyst for the feminist method debate was the question, "Why limit feminist initiatives to one particular set of methods or research strategy" (Jayaratne, 1983)? By the early 1990s, Reinharz (1992a) could identify feminist uses of virtually every research method and methodology available in the social sciences, and in the mid-1990s, Gottfried (1996) concluded that feminist practitioners had made a decisive "move from singularity to plurality" (p. 12). Parallel arguments had been made a decade earlier by Harding (1987) and Longino (1987), who argued that there is no brief for positing "a distinctive female way of knowing"; why should feminists allow methodological commitments to define in advance the scope of their research agenda? Was this not simply to re-entrench at the core of feminist research programs the mystification of method that feminists found so debilitating in the sciences they hoped to reform (Harding, 1987, p. 19)? Longino (1987) urged that questions about the nature and direction of feminist research be reframed: We should ask not what it means to build or to do "feminist science" but what is involved in "doing science as a feminist" (p. 53). By extension, we should be prepared to recognize that what "doing research as a feminist" means in practice will be as diverse as what it means to be a feminist and as situationally specific as the fields in which feminists have undertaken to "do science."

While Haack and like-minded critics might be reassured by this repudiation of essentialism, they would no doubt find the pluralism characteristic of feminist social science at least as worrisome, predicated as it is on the conviction that scientific inquiry is always relative to context.[3] But, far from being a marginal extreme, the arguments for a pragmatic, contextualist turn in thinking about the sciences—for recognizing that the sciences are historically contingent and deeply structured by context-specific interests and values—are by now generic to the philosophy of science (Lloyd, 1995).[4] The point of departure for contextualist arguments includes canonical philosophical theses as the underdetermination of theory by evidence, the inescapably theory-laden nature of evidence, and Quine-Duhem holism (the thesis that hypotheses never stand alone but face the tribunal of evidence as a web of interlinked claims). Taken together, these establish that cognitive, evidential, and logical factors rarely, if ever, determine theory choice: "whatever grounds for knowledge we have, they are not sufficient to warrant the assertion of claims beyond doubt" (Longino, 1994, p. 472). Crucially, this is not just a matter of the underdetermination of content, such that contextual factors must take up the slack in determining the significance of empirical data as evidence (Intemann, 2005). It is, in addition, a matter of second-order (meta-) underdetermination: The cognitive and epistemic values that constitute well-functioning (unbiased, objective) science are themselves underdetermined as guidelines for practice. The practical import of such widely cited principles as a commitment to maximize the empirical adequacy, predictive and explanatory power, intertheoretic consistency, and internal coherence of scientific theories is by no means obvious; they require interpretation and typically cannot be simultaneously maximized. These arguments were made by Kuhn himself (Kuhn, 1977, p. 322) and by early commentators

on the implications of his contextualism (e.g., Doppelt, 1988), and they have since been developed by a number of feminist commentators (Longino, 1995; Wylie, 1995; see especially Intemann [2001, 2005] on the "gap" argument). What counts as meeting a requirement of empirical adequacy, for example, is by no means given by the facts themselves or by abstract ideals of rationality. Standards of empirical adequacy are context specific and evolve within distinct research traditions, in response to goals and interests that are external to inquiry as well as to internal theoretical and technical considerations. And when epistemic values come into conflict, as when a commitment to formal idealization (e.g., to expand explanatory and predictive scope) requires a trade-off of localized empirical adequacy, the question of which constitutive value should take precedence must generally be settled by appeal to the noncognitive goals and values that inform the research program.[5]

Doing (social) science as a feminist is a matter, then, of insisting that we be accountable for the values and interests that shape not just our choice of research questions but also the whole range of decisions and conventions that constitute our research practice. Far from seeing this pragmatism as grounds for despair or for outrage (in the case of Haack), I join a growing contingent of social epistemologists and science studies theorists who argue that we should regard the role played by contextual values not as a source of compromising contamination but as a crucial condition for the success of the sciences (Wylie & Nelson, 2007).

The Feminist Question in (Social) Science

Consider, then, two ways in which feminists have articulated a mandate for "doing research as a feminist": Longino's philosophical account of the community values that inform the research undertaken by feminists in the sciences generally and the methodological guidelines developed by feminist social scientists.

Longino has identified six community values—or "theoretical virtues"—as characteristic of the work of feminist scientists (Longino,

1987, 1990, 1994; Wylie, 1995). There is some ambiguity about the status of these virtues: whether they describe what feminist practitioners actually do (in an unspecified range of sciences) or are intended to capture what feminists could or should do. And they are strikingly free of any explicit feminist content. They cluster around three focal concerns:

1. Epistemic values: Longino finds feminists committed, first and foremost, to a fundamental requirement of empirical adequacy and to a preference for novel hypotheses (Longino, 1994, p. 476; Longino, 1995, p. 386).

2. Ontological: She identifies, as well, a preference for hypotheses that take full account of diversity in the objects of study—that allow "equal standing for different types"—and that treat "complex interaction as a fundamental principle of explanation" (Longino, 1994, pp. 477–478; see also Longino, 1995, pp. 387–388).

3. Normative and pragmatic values: She finds feminist research animated by a commitment to use the tools of scientific inquiry to generate knowledge that is "applicab[le] to current human needs" (Longino, 1994, p. 476; Longino, 1995, p. 389) and to democratize the production of knowledge in ways that foster an "equality of intellectual authority" (Longino, 1990, pp. 78–81; Longino, 1993a, 1993b; Longino, 1995, p. 389).

Even this last, most explicitly normative commitment is warranted on Longino's account not because it makes scientific practice a site for institutional change along lines advocated by feminists in other contexts but because it provides for a redistribution of power and resources within the sciences that Longino (1990, pp. 76–80) believes will enhance the epistemic integrity of inquiry. It counteracts the reification of epistemic authority, expanding the range of perspectives brought to bear on conventional assumptions; it reinforces a recognition that knowledge production is a pluralistic enterprise that serves divergent goals ("cognitive needs"), engaging dissent seriously and fostering if not an idealized "view from everywhere," at least "views from many wheres" (Longino, 1993b, p. 113).[6]

The sense in which these community values are feminist is that they embody what Longino (1994) describes as a "bottom-line" feminist commitment. They have the effect of "prevent[ing] gender from being disappeared," and in this they are evaluative standards that "mak[e] gender a relevant axis of investigation" (p. 481). So, for example, the preference for novelty counteracts the conservative, gender-disappearing effects that can be expected to follow from the more typical directive to maximize consistency with other well-established theories (given that these are likely to be predicated on just the kinds of gender-conventional wisdom feminists are intent on challenging). The preference for ontological and causal complexity likewise counters conventions of practice that privilege the sorts of simplifying idealization Smith (1978) found responsible for the "eclipsing" of women's (gendered) experience. And a commitment to democratize scientific practice, while justified on gender-neutral epistemic grounds, puts the onus on the scientific community to ensure that marginal voices are not systematically silenced, including the voices of women. Longino (1994) adds to these principles and the "bottom-line" maxim one further meta-principle: epistemic provisionalism. Each of the other community values must be held open to revision in light of what feminists learn from practice (p. 483).

In the context of feminist social science, Longino's community values find their clearest articulation in the guidelines for nonsexist research mentioned at the outset, where the goal is to improve research by conventional standards. Feminist interests and values serve as a resource; they draw attention to gaps and distortions in conventional research and to aspects of the subject domain and explanatory possibilities that have been overlooked. In practice, however, feminist research has been animated by much more explicitly feminist goals than these; the principles articulated in the context of the method debate are broadly consistent with Longino's community values but go well beyond them. I identify four widely shared commitments around which the overlapping systems of general principles, ideals, maxims, and guidelines for feminist research have coalesced since the early 1980s (see Potter, Wylie, & Bauchspies, 2010, Section 4).

The principle to which feminist social scientists typically give priority is a specification of explicitly feminist goals: The "human needs" that feminist researchers should be concerned to address when they practice as feminists are those of women and, more generally, those oppressed by sex/gender systems of inequality. Sometimes these feminist goals have been articulated as a requirement that feminist research should be "movement generated"; not only should it expose the sexism inherent in extant institutions—"muckraking research" (Ehrlich, 1975, p. 10)—but it should also generate strategies for changing these institutions (p. 13). Any more specific guidelines should be articulations of how best to realize feminist goals, however these are defined.

The second principle is a directive to ground feminist research in women's experience: to take "as our starting point" women's experience and everyday lives (Harding, 1993a, 1993b; Harding, 2006, pp. 83–85; Smith, 1974; Smith, 1987, p. 85). In effect, Longino's (1994, p. 481; 1995, p. 391) "bottom-line maxim" is reframed as a commitment, not just to ensure that gender is "not disappeared" but also to treat gendered experience and self-understanding as a crucial resource in developing a systematic understanding of the gendered dimensions of community life and institutions, systems of belief, social differentiation, and inequality. Sometimes this principle counters the second, ontological cluster of values Longino (1994, pp. 477–478; 1995, pp. 387–388) identifies: Rather than advocate ontological heterogeneity and multidirectional causality as desirable in themselves, it suggests that feminists should build into their theories whatever degree of complexity (or simplification) is necessary to do justice to women's experience and the sex/gender systems that structure their lives.

A third cluster of principles specifies ethical commitments that give further content to Longino's (1994, p. 478; 1995, p. 389) normative and pragmatic values: Feminists are accountable to research subjects and to those affected by their research. At the very least, the research process should not oppress or exploit research subjects; ideally, it should empower them, particularly when they are themselves oppressed by sex/gender systems. Feminist practitioners often insist, more ambitiously, that they should make research practice a site for instituting feminist social and political values: They should deliberately counteract the hierarchical structures that make social science a "ruling practice" and implement egalitarian, participatory forms of knowledge production. Here, a general argument for democratizing research practice is specified as a commitment to break down the (gendered) hierarchies of power and authority that operate in much conventional research; in the ideal, research subjects and those affected by research should play an active, collaborative role at all stages of research design, data collection, analysis, and authorship, on the model of engaged social science practice long established by traditions of participatory action research and community-based participatory research (e.g., Fortmann, 2008; Hickey & Mohan, 2004).

Fourth, virtually every set of published guidelines for feminist research in the social sciences emphasizes the importance of cultivating a stance of sustained and critical reflexivity. As Narayan (1988) put it, "One of the most attractive features of feminist thinking is its commitment to contextualizing its claims" (p. 32). At the very least, this requires feminist social scientists "to state their premises rather than hide them" (Reinharz, 1992b, p. 426). On stronger formulations, it requires that feminists, qua feminists, take into account the various ways in which their own social location, their interests and values, are constitutive of the research process and of the understanding it produces (e.g., Cook & Fonow, 1986; Fonow & Cook, 1991; Mies, 1983). Standpoint theorists specify what this involves in terms of a requirement for "strong objectivity": The tools of jointly empirical and conceptual inquiry should be applied (reflexively) to the research process itself (Harding, 1993a, 1993b; Harding, 2006, pp. 50–65; Wylie, 2008, pp. 206–208). With this, Longino's (1994, p. 483) principle of "methodological provisionalism" is reframed as a requirement, not just that feminists should be willing to revise orienting principles but that they should subject them, actively and continuously, to conceptual and empirical scrutiny.

DOING SOCIAL SCIENCE AS A FEMINIST, IN PRACTICE

The research projects that most straightforwardly realize these principles and that stood as an ideal for much early feminist social science were various forms of community self-study: research undertaken by women, on women, for women (Gorelick, 1991, p. 459; e.g., Jacobson, 1977). Here, women's experience gives rise directly to the questions asked; inquiry is motivated by explicitly activist objectives and designed with the aim of leveling the hierarchy of authority inherent in traditional "expert" forms of social scientific research. The use of qualitative, participatory methods of inquiry (e.g., oral history, ethnography, discourse analysis) serves not only to engage research subjects directly in the research process but also to resituate women's experience and self-understanding at the center of inquiry, counteracting the "eclipsing" of this experience and its assimilation to gender-conventional categories of description and analysis (Smith, 1974, 1978). In some cases, these projects were directly inspired by consciousness-raising practice conceived as a matter of "grasp[ing] the collective reality of women's condition from within the perspective of that experience" (MacKinnon, 1982, p. 536), bearing witness to the particularities of women's lives and critically situating these in the frame of broader patterns of gender politics and gendered institutions (Wylie, 1992, p. 237; Wylie, 2011). A classic example is the grassroots research on workplace environment issues—the "chilly climate" that women encounter in academia and other traditionally male-dominated professions—that proliferated in the late 1970s and 1980s (Chilly Collective, 1995). In these projects, the four methodological principles I have identified are given a literal interpretation and are mutually reinforcing.

At the same time, however, those who pioneered contemporary traditions of feminist research in the social sciences explored a range of questions and research strategies that quickly pointed at ambiguities inherent in the interpretation of these principles and showed how they might come into conflict with one other. Consider, specifically, some examples that put pressure on a literal reading of the directive to ground feminist research in women's experience—the most contentious of the four principles where worries about epistemic integrity and objectivity are concerned.

The Subject of Research

First, and perhaps most obviously, if the goal of feminist research is to address questions that are relevant for understanding and ultimately changing gendered systems of oppression, it does not follow that women must always be the primary subject of feminist inquiry. For an early example, consider the case made by Stanley and Wise (1979, 1983a, 1983b) that if feminists are to understand the hostility to women that underpins patriarchal culture, it will be necessary to study the attitudes and behaviors of sexist and misogynist men; this was the rationale for their early work on obscene telephone calls. A complementary example comes from the tradition of grassroots activist research on workplace environment issues that took shape in the 1980s and 1990s (Wylie, Jakobsen, & Fosado, 2007). A recurrent theme in these "chilly climate" studies is that the gendered dimension of subtle, often unintended "micro-inequities" comes into focus only as a "shock of recognition," when women have an opportunity to compare experiences they thought were idiosyncratic (e.g., Aisenberg & Harrington, 1988, p. ix). By extension, it is the comparison with the experience and career trajectories of male peers that makes clear just how powerfully small-scale differences in recognition and support coalesce into systematic patterns of marginalization, reproducing systemic gender inequality in outcomes for women on a large scale (see, e.g., Sonnert & Holton's [1995, pp. 147–163] comparisons of career timetables and styles of research in the sciences).

But beyond changing the subject, feminist practitioners often draw on women's experience as a source of research questions and interpretive insight rather than taking it as a direct subject of inquiry. This opens space for feminist research in fields where the experiential dimensions of social life are often inaccessible, as in archaeology (Wylie, 2001), or where the subject of inquiry is projectively gendered, as in primatology (Fehr, 2011; Strum & Fedigan, 2000). It also throws into relief the potentially radical implications of a thoroughgoing commitment to epistemic provisionalism. Those who undertake research as feminists routinely discover that what they most need to understand, to address a problem initially identified in gender terms, are the dynamics of class formation or the emergence and maintenance of systemic racism, along with myriad other forms of social differentiation that are mutually constitutive of contemporary sex/gender systems. The lessons from queer theory and transnational feminisms make it especially clear that a sophisticated understanding of gender inequality cannot be expected to arise from research that focuses narrowly on gendered institutions, roles, and identities. Far from dogmatically recapitulating foregone conclusions, the substantive results of feminist research frequently destabilize—even "disappear"—the categories that originally gave it impetus and direction.

Critiques of Experientialism

Even when women and gender are the primary subject of analysis, there are two further reasons to resist a literal reading of the directive to ground research in women's experience. One targets an early construal of the "grounding" requirement that took it to be a proscription against questioning women's experience, as when Stanley and Wise (1983a, 1983b) insisted that, in countering sexist assumptions about the credibility and significance of women's self-reports—in treating women as authorities about their own experience—feminist researchers must never "go beyond" women's experience. The pitfalls of such "experientialism" became an immediate focus of attention in the feminist method debate (e.g., Brunsdon, 1978; Grant, 1987). In her classic article, "The Evidence of Experience," Scott (1991) objects that "when experience is taken as the origin of knowledge, the vision of the individual subject becomes the

bedrock on which explanation is built," foreclosing questions about "the constructed nature of experience, about how subjects are constituted different in the first place, about how one's vision is structured" (p. 776). "Giving voice is not enough" (Gorelick, 1991, pp. 463, 477), even when the goal of research is to bear witness to forms of community life and experience that have been systematically marginalized in a sexist, heteronormative society.

The practical implications of this critique of experientialism are evident, for example, in the care with which Kennedy and Davis (1993) scrutinize their subjects' recollections of a working-class lesbian community that took shape in Buffalo in the 1940s and 1950s. They worry about the vagaries of memory, where interviewees were asked to recall events and conditions of life from 30 or 40 years earlier, and about the impact on these memories of fundamental changes in social and cultural conceptions of what it means to be a lesbian that had emerged in the intervening years. They employ a strategy of triangulation, systematically cross-checking interviewees' accounts to ensure the factual accuracy of the historical ethnography they constructed. It is precisely because they respect their subjects and the larger community they represent that Kennedy and Davis insist on the need to treat these experiential accounts judiciously, not disrespectfully, but with critical caution.

Similar principles are operative in the context of feminist research that is explicitly designed as a form of therapeutic and activist intervention. The staff of the Battered Women's Advocacy Center (BWAC) in London (Ontario, Canada) developed a standardized intake form that made it possible to collect information about the demography, family histories, experiences of violence, and strategies of response reported by the women who made use of BWAC's services. While this form provided crucial support for the research mandate of the agency, the frontline advocates and counselors found that it also served an important counseling function (Greaves, Wylie, & the Staff of the BWAC, 1995). Sometimes questions about particular aspects of a recent violent episode or about long-term patterns of physical and collateral forms of abuse (economic control, social isolation, psychological abuse) would elicit an overall picture that was starkly at odds with an interviewee's initial self-report. The standardized questionnaire reflected the experience reported by other women, so specific questions that drew attention to some hitherto unacknowledged or unspoken aspect of a woman's experience made it palpably clear that, however unique a woman might think her own experience of violence, it is often by no means idiosyncratic. In short, "going beyond" our experience—questioning it, rethinking it, putting it in perspective, asking how and why it arises—is a crucial part of coming to terms with sex/gender oppression in a heteronormative society.

A second, related concern often raised about strong experientialist readings of the second principle is that any directive to "ground feminist research in women's experience" must be articulated with some care if it is not to prove perniciously parochial, reproducing and reifying precisely the conditions of oppression that feminists ought to challenge. In *White Women, Race Matters,* Frankenberg (1993) reads her subjects' testimony against the grain with an eye to discerning the contours of race privilege, including the privileges of ignorance, that define the lives of white women. She focuses on contradictions inherent in first-person accounts that reveal the unacknowledged "racial geography" of her interviewees' lives. These themes are powerfully developed by a number of contributors to *Feminist Epistemologies of Ignorance* (Tuana & Sullivan, 2006; e.g., Ortega, 2006; see also Daukas, 2006). Critiques published since the early 1990s generalize the methodological point implicit here, drawing attention to the inherent elitism of inquiry grounded in the experience of those relatively privileged women who are most likely to be in a position to undertake systematic empirical research (Mohanty, 1991) or to be recruited as research subjects (Cannon, Higginbotham, & Leung, 1991). Women's experience may offer a crucial corrective to the systems of common sense and scientific knowledge that render it invisible and inauthoritative, but it is always intersectionally partial, and in this, it offers, at most, a point of departure, not an end point for feminist inquiry (Bannerji, 1991, p. 67; Smith, 1974, pp. 12–13).[7]

The upshot is that the liberatory goals of feminist research—articulated as the first principle—put considerable pressure on any literal or essentialist reading of the second principle (the requirement for experiential grounding). Effective activism depends on understanding accurately and in detail how "specific form[s] of oppression originated, how [they have] been maintained and all the systemic purposes [they] serve" (Narayan, 1988, p. 36). This, in turn, requires that feminists go substantially beyond women's experience and self-understanding in a number of senses. They must expand the range of experience on which they ground social research, on the principle that all experience reflects the partiality of location. They must be prepared to critically interrogate this experience, on the principle that it is often the opacity of social institutions and practices that makes them effective in conditioning our self-understanding. And they must contextualize it, on the principle that we need to grasp "how [the world of everyday experience] is put together," to posit the socioeconomic order that lies "in back" of and that makes possible and organizes immediate experience (Gorelick, 1991, pp. 463–466; Smith, 1974, pp. 12–13).

Crucially, it is not only the subjects' gendered experience that must be situated, read against the grain, and treated as a point of departure and not a destination; it is also the researcher's own experience and self-understanding that require scrutiny in all these ways. What practitioners rely on when they do social science are, therefore, the resources of a feminist standpoint, not just a gendered social location (Wylie, 2011).

CONCLUSION

Two epistemic implications follow from these observations about feminist practice in the social sciences. First, far from illustrating a sad decline into cynical dogmatism—a state in which, Haack (1993) feared, "foregone conclusions" would dictate not only the goals but also the outcomes of research—the dominant effect of feminist community values has been to mobilize transformative critique (Longino, 1990, pp. 73–76). Time and again, feminist commitments have catalyzed much more critical scrutiny of the presuppositions of research—including those that inform feminists' practice as well as the conventions they challenge—than conventional epistemic virtues had done or faith in the self-correcting capacity of scientific method seems likely to do (Anderson, 2006; Wylie & Nelson, 2007). It is, in short, one especially compelling example of the kind of critical engagement that Longino, among others, identifies as the hallmark of well-functioning epistemic communities (see Longino's account of procedural objectivity [Longino, 2002, pp. 128–131]).

Second, the feminist standpoint that, as I have suggested, is pivotal to this enterprise need not be construed in essentialist terms or be accorded any automatic epistemic privilege—the key features of feminist research programs that worry critics such as Haack (1993).[8] Central to the conception of a feminist standpoint is a situated knowledge thesis: What we experience and understand, the differential strengths and liabilities we develop as epistemic agents, are systematically shaped by our location in hierarchically structured systems of power relations, the material conditions of our lives, the relations of production and reproduction that shape our social interactions, and the conceptual resources we rely on to interpret and represent these relations. Gender is one dimension along which our lives are structured in epistemically consequential ways. What feminist standpoint theory adds to this account of situated knowledge is an inversion thesis. Those who are subject to structures of domination that systematically marginalize and oppress them may in fact have substantial (contingent) epistemic advantage relative to those who are comparatively privileged (and who enjoy a presumption of epistemic authority on this basis); they may have access to an expanded range of evidence and interpretive heuristics, as well as a critical perspective on otherwise unacknowledged framework assumptions, by virtue of what they typically experience and how they understand their experience (Fehr, 2011; Wylie, 2003, 2011).

Two points follow where the specifics of "doing social science as a feminist" are concerned. First, the directive to ground feminist research in women's experience should be construed, in standpoint terms, as a recommendation to treat the situated knowledge of gendered subjects as a resource (not a foundation) for understanding the form and dynamics of the sex/gender systems that shape their lives. Second,

Longino's (1994, 1995) principle of epistemic provisionality should be framed as a substantive requirement to develop an explicitly feminist standpoint on knowledge production; as feminist social scientists have long recognized, it is crucial to build into research a critical consciousness of our social locations and the difference these make epistemically. Anderson (2004b) makes a particularly compelling case for the constructive, corrective value of a reflexive stance not just in general terms but as a methodological principle of epistemic accountability that informs the specifics of research design and practice in the social sciences.

In short, far from signaling an abdication of epistemic responsibility, these guidelines for doing research as a feminist effectively raise the epistemic bar; they constitute a demand for "strong" self-critical objectivity. They represent a commitment to empirical and conceptual rigor that takes account of, and makes social scientists accountable for, the situated partiality of their research practice. More specifically, they direct feminists to make discerning use of contingent epistemic advantages that may accrue to them by virtue of their gendered social locations and hard-won feminist standpoint.

Discussion Questions

1. What does it mean to do social science as a feminist: to you and to key contributors to the "feminist method" debate?

2. How and why does "starting from women's lives" make a difference to social research?

3. Do the guidelines, norms of practice, and goals identified in this chapter capture what you find most distinctive and important about feminist research programs in the social sciences?

Online Resources

The Association for Feminist Epistemologies, Methodologies, Metaphysics and Science Studies (FEMMSS)

http://femmss.org/

FEMMSS is a professional organization that sponsors conferences, projects, and publications designed to support interdisciplinary work that has the potential to influence research and foster global justice in the public sphere.

Feminist Epistemology and Philosophy of Science

http://plato.stanford.edu/entries/feminism-epistemology/

In the *Stanford Encyclopedia of Philosophy,* Elizabeth Anderson provides a sustained discussion of feminist epistemology and the philosophy of science and Potter, Wylie, and Bauchspies provide an overview of "Feminist Perspectives on Science."

Relevant Journals

Hypatia

Journal of Women's History

Signs: Journal of Women in Culture and Society

NOTES

1. This represents one end of a spectrum of feminist perspectives on science, characterized in more detail by Potter, Wylie, and Bauchspies (2010).

2. As indicated, however uncompromising their challenges to the positivist presuppositions of much mainstream social science, Smith, Mies, and other feminist social scientists writing in the 1970s and 1980s argued that their critiques did not call for a wholesale rejection of empirical social research. Rather, they made the case for the discerning and selective application to feminist questions of a range of research strategies—typically qualitative, participatory methods—that had been marginalized within mainstream social science and that seemed especially well suited to the task of countering the entrenched sex/gender biases of conventional research (Hesse-Biber, Leavy, & Yaiser, 2004, p. 14; Naples, 2003; Smith, 1974, p. 8; Smith, 1987, pp. 61–69).

3. Note that this claim of context specificity does not necessarily entail a commitment to "relativism," as Hesse (1980, p. 181) made clear early in the debate about the implications of sociological science studies.

4. Indeed, there are good reasons to regard Haack's (1993, and later 2007) diatribe against cynical critics of the authority of science as a sustained argument against a straw opponent, predicated on an implausibly narrow view of the range of epistemic positions that reasonably may be taken by those who reject the Enlightenment ideals she defends

(Anderson, 1995, pp. 34–42; Anderson, 2004a; Wylie, 1995, p. 347; Wylie, 2000, pp. 171–174).

5. These arguments for recognizing the pragmatic, contextual nature of methodological judgment need not entail commitment to a corrosive relativism or anti-realism (as suggested in Note 3). See, for example, Tulodziecki's (2007, in press) recent reassessment of arguments from underdetermination. She makes the case that judgments about how to apply methodological principles are themselves empirically grounded (and in this sense carry epistemic weight), inasmuch as that they embody the wisdom of successful research practice.

6. Longino (2002, pp. 128–135) later elaborates this epistemic rationale for more democratic, inclusive modes of practice in her account of the jointly social/cognitive norms that are conditions for procedural objectivity. For an especially compelling analysis and refinement of these social/cognitive norms, see Lloyd's (2005, pp. 241–255) extended critique of the inherent sexism of selectionist explanations for human female orgasm.

7. For a general analysis of the contours of "epistemic injustice" that underpin these patterns of inattention and bias in the social sciences, see Fricker (2007).

8. I summarize here an argument that is developed in more detail in "Why Standpoint Matters" (Wylie, 2003) and applied to research on workplace environment issues, in "What Knowers Know Well" (Wylie, 2011).

REFERENCES

Aisenberg, Nadya, & Harrington, Mona. (Eds.). (1988). *Women of academe: Outsiders in the sacred grove.* Amherst: University of Massachusetts Press.

Anderson, Elizabeth. (1995). Knowledge, human interests, and objectivity in feminist epistemology. *Philosophical Topics, 23,* 29–58.

Anderson, Elizabeth. (2004a). Review of Cassandra Pinnick, Noretta Koertge, and Robert Almeder, eds., Scrutinizing Feminist Epistemology. *Metascience, 13,* 395–399. (An extended critical notice is available at www-personal.umich.edu/%7 Eeandersn/hownotreview.html)

Anderson, Elizabeth. (2004b). Uses of value judgments in science: A general argument, with lessons from a case study of feminist research on divorce. *Hypatia, 19*(1), 1–24.

Anderson, Elizabeth. (2006). The epistemology of democracy. *Episteme, 3*(1–2), 8–22.

Bannerji, Himani. (1991). But who speaks for us? Experience and agency in conventional feminist paradigms. In Himani Bannerji, Linda Carty, Kari Dehli, Susan Heald, & Kate McKenna (Eds.), *Unsettling relations: The university as a site of feminist struggle* (pp. 67–108). Toronto, ON: Women's Press.

Belenky, Mary F., Clinchy, Blythe M., Goldberger, Nancy R., & Tarule, Jill M. (1986). *Women's ways of knowing.* New York: Basic Books.

Brunsdon, Charlotte. (1978). It is well known that by nature women are inclined to be rather personal. In Women's Studies Group, Centre for Cultural Studies, University of Birmingham (Ed.), *Women take issue: Aspects of women's subordination* (pp. 18–34). London: Hutchinson.

Cannon, Lynn Weber, Higginbotham, Elizabeth, & Leung, Marianne L. A. (1991). Race and class bias in qualitative research on women. In Mary Margaret Fonow & Judith A. Cook (Eds.), *Beyond methodology: Feminist scholarship as lived research* (pp. 107–118). Bloomington: Indiana University Press.

Chilly Collective. (Ed.). (1995). *Breaking anonymity: Anonymity: The Chilly Climate for Women Faculty.* Waterloo, ON: Wilfrid Laurier Press.

Cook, Judith A., & Fonow, Mary Margaret. (1986). Knowledge and women's interests: Issues of epistemology and methodology in feminist sociological research. *Sociological Inquiry, 56,* 2–29.

Daukas, Nancy. (2006). Epistemic trust and social location. *Episteme, 3*(1–2), 109–124.

Doppelt, Gerald D. (1988). The philosophical requirements for an adequate conception of scientific rationality. *Philosophy of Science, 55*(1), 104–133.

Ehrlich, Carol. (1975). *The conditions of feminist research* (Research Group One Report No. 21). Baltimore: Vacant Lots Press.

Eichler, Margrit. (1988). *Nonsexist research methods: A practical guide.* Boston: Allen & Unwin.

Fehr, Carla. (2011). What is in it for me? The benefits of diversity in scientific communities. In Heidi Grasswick (Ed.), *Feminist epistemology and philosophy of science: Power in knowledge* (pp. 133–155). New York: Springer.

Fonow, Mary Margaret, & Cook, Judith A. (1991). Back to the future: A look at the second wave of feminist epistemology and methodology. In Mary Margaret Fonow & Judith A. Cook (Eds.), *Beyond methodology: Feminist scholarship as lived research* (pp. 1–15). Bloomington: Indiana University Press.

Fortmann, Louise. (2008). Doing science together. In Louise Fortman (Ed.), *Participatory research in conservation and rural livelihoods* (pp. 1–17). Oxford, UK: Wiley-Blackwell.

Frankenberg, Ruth. (1993). *White women, race matters: The social construction of whiteness.* Minneapolis: University of Minnesota Press.

Fricker, Miranda. (2007). *Epistemic injustice: Power and the ethics of knowing.* Oxford, UK: Oxford University Press.

Gorelick, Sherry. (1991). Contradictions of feminist methodology. *Gender & Society, 5,* 459–477.

Gottfried, Heidi. (Ed.). (1996). *Feminism and social change: Bridging theory and practice.* Urbana: University of Illinois Press.

Grant, Judith. (1987). I feel therefore I am: A critique of female experience as the basis for a feminist epistemology. *Women and Politics, 7*(3), 99–114.

Greaves, Lorraine, Wylie, Alison, & the Staff of the Battered Women's Advocacy Clinic. (1995). Women and violence: Feminist practice and quantitative method. In Sandra D. Burt & Lorraine Code (Eds.), *Changing methods: Feminists transforming practice* (pp. 301–326). Peterborough, ON: Broadview Press.

Gross, Paul R., & Levitt, Norman. (1994). *Higher superstition: The academic left and its quarrels with science.* Baltimore: Johns Hopkins University Press.

Gross, Paul R., Levitt, Norman, & Lewis, Martin W. (Eds.). (1996). *The flight from science and reason.* New York: New York Academy of Sciences Press.

Haack, Susan. (1993). Knowledge and propaganda: Reflections of an old feminist. *Partisan Review, 60,* 556–565. (Reprinted in *Scrutinizing feminist epistemology: An examination of gender in science,* pp. 7–19, by Cassandra Pinnick, Noretta Koertge, & Robert Almeder, Eds., 2003, New Brunswick, NJ: Rutgers University Press.)

Haack, Susan. (2007). *Defending science—within reason: Between scientism and cynicism.* New York: Prometheus.

Harding, Sandra. (1986). *The science question in feminism.* Ithaca, NY: Cornell University Press.

Harding, Sandra. (1987). The method question. *Hypatia, 2,* 19–36.

Harding, Sandra. (1993a). Rethinking standpoint epistemology: What is "strong objectivity"? In Linda Alcoff & Elizabeth Potter, *Feminist epistemologies* (pp. 49–82). New York: Routledge.

Harding, Sandra. (1993b). *Whose science? Whose knowledge? Thinking from women's lives.* Ithaca, NY: Cornell University Press.

Harding, Sandra. (2006). *Science and social inequality: Feminist and postcolonial issues.* Chicago: University of Illinois Press.

Hesse, Mary. (1980). In defense of objectivity. In *Revolutions and reconstructions in the philosophy of science* (pp. 167–186). New York: Harvester Press.

Hesse-Biber, Sharlene Nagy, Leavy, Patricia, & Yaiser, Michelle L. (2004). Feminist approaches to research as a process: Reconceptualizing epistemology, methodology, and method. In Sharlene Nagy Hesse-Biber & Michelle L. Yaiser (Eds.), *Feminist perspectives on social research* (pp. 3–26). New York: Oxford University Press.

Hickey, Sam, & Mohan, Giles. (2004). Towards participation as transformation: Critical themes and challenges. In Sam Hickey & Giles Mohan (Eds.), *Participation: From tyranny to transformation?* (pp. 3–24). London: Zed Books.

Intemann, Kristen. (2001). Science and values: Are value judgments always irrelevant to the justification of scientific claims? *Proceedings of the Philosophy of Science, 68,* S506–S518.

Intemann, Kristen. (2005). Feminism, underdetermination, and values in science. *Philosophy of Science, 72,* 1001–1012.

Jacobson, Helga E. (1977). *How to study your own community: Research from the perspective of women.* Vancouver, BC: Vancouver Women's Research Centre.

Jayaratne, Toby Epstein. (1983). The value of quantitative methodology in feminist research. In Gloria Bowles & Renate Duelli Klein (Eds.), *Theories of women's studies* (pp. 140–162). London: Routledge & Kegan Paul.

Kennedy, Elizabeth Lapovsky, & Davis, Madeline D. (1993). *Boots of leather, slippers of gold: The history of a lesbian community.* New York: Penguin.

Kuhn, Thomas. (1977). Objectivity, value judgment, and theory choice. In *The essential tension: Selected studies in scientific tradition and change* (pp. 320–339). Chicago: University of Chicago Press.

Lloyd, Elisabeth. (1995). Objectivity and the double standard for feminist epistemologies. *Synthese, 104*(3), 351–381.

Lloyd, Elisabeth. (2005). *The case of the female orgasm: Bias in the science of evolution.* Cambridge, MA: Harvard University Press.

Longino, Helen. (1987). Can there be a feminist science? *Hypatia, 2*(3), 51–64.

Longino, Helen. (1990). *Science as social knowledge: Values and objectivity in scientific inquiry.* Princeton, NJ: Princeton University Press.

Longino, Helen. (1993a). Feminist standpoint theory and the problems of knowledge. *Signs: Journal of Women in Culture and Society, 19,* 201–212.

Longino, Helen. (1993b). Subjects, power and knowledge: Description and prescription in feminist philosophies of science. In Linda Alcoff & Elizabeth Potter (Eds.), *Feminist epistemologies* (pp. 101–120). New York: Routledge.

Longino, Helen. (1994). In search of feminist epistemology. *The Monist, 77*(4), 472–485.

Longino, Helen. (1995). Gender, politics, and the theoretical virtues. *Synthese, 104,* 383–397.

Longino, Helen. (2002). *The fate of knowledge.* Princeton, NJ: Princeton University Press.

MacKinnon, Catherine. (1982). Feminism, Marxism, method and the state: An agenda for theory. *Signs: Journal of Women in Culture and Society, 7,* 515–544.

Mies, Maria. (1983). Towards a methodology for feminist research. In Gloria Bowles & Renate Duelli Klein (Eds.), *Theories of women's studies* (pp. 117–139). London: Routledge & Kegan Paul.

Mohanty, Chandra Talpade. (Ed.). (1991). Under Western eyes: Feminist scholarship and colonial discourses. In *Third World women and the politics of feminism* (pp. 51–80). Bloomington: Indiana University Press.

Naples, Nancy A. (2003). *Feminism and method: Ethnography, discourse analysis, and activist research.* New York: Routledge.

Narayan, Uma. (1988). Working together across difference: Some considerations on emotions and political practice. *Hypatia, 3*(2), 31–48.

Ortega, Mariana. (2006). Being lovingly, knowingly ignorant: White feminism and women of color. *Hypatia, 21*(3), 56–74.

Pinnick, Cassandra, Koertge, Noretta, & Almeder, Robert. (Eds.). (2003). *Scrutinizing feminist epistemology: An examination of gender in science.* New Brunswick, NJ: Rutgers University Press.

Potter, Elizabeth, Wylie, Alison, & Bauchspies, Wenda K. (2010). *Feminist perspectives on science: Stanford encyclopedia of philosophy.* Stanford, CA: Stanford University. http://plato.stanford.edu/entries/feminist-science/

Reinharz, Shulamit. (1992a). *Feminist methods in social research.* New York: Oxford University Press.

Reinharz, Shulamit. (1992b). The principles of feminist research: A matter of debate. In Cheris Kramarae & Dale Spender (Eds.), *The knowledge explosion: Generations of feminist scholarship* (pp. 423–437). New York: Teachers College Press.

Scott, Joan W. (1991). The evidence of experience. *Critical Inquiry, 17,* 773–797.

Smith, Dorothy E. (1974). Women's perspective as a radical critique of sociology. *Sociological Inquiry, 44,* 7–13.

Smith, Dorothy E. (1978). A peculiar eclipsing: Women's exclusion from man's culture. *Women's Studies International Quarterly, 1,* 281–295. (Reprinted in Smith, 1987)

Smith, Dorothy E. (1987). *The everyday world as problematic: A feminist sociology.* Toronto, ON: University of Toronto Press.

Sonnert, Gerhard, & Holton, Gerald. (1995). *Who succeeds in science? The gender dimension.* New Brunswick, NJ: Rutgers University Press.

Stanley, Liz, & Wise, Sue. (1979). Feminist research, feminist consciousness and experiences of sexism. *Women's Studies International Quarterly, 2,* 359–374.

Stanley, Liz, & Wise, Sue. (1983a). "Back into the personal" or: Our attempt to construct "feminist research." In Gloria Bowles & Renate D. Klein (Eds.), *Theories of women's studies* (pp. 192–209). London: Routledge & Kegan Paul.

Stanley, Liz, & Wise, Sue. (1983b). *Breaking out: Feminist consciousness and feminist research.* London: Routledge & Kegan Paul.

Strum, Shirley C., & Fedigan, Linda M. (Eds.). (2000). *Primate encounters: Models of science, gender, and society.* Chicago: Chicago University Press.

Tuana, Nancy, & Sullivan, Shannon. (Eds.). (2006). Feminist epistemologies of ignorance [Special issue]. *Hypatia, 21*(3).

Tulodziecki, Dana. (2007). Breaking the ties: Epistemic significance, bacilli, and underdetermination. *Studies in History and Philosophy of Science Part C: Studies in History and Philosophy of the Biological and Biomedical Sciences, 38*(3), 627–641.

Tulodziecki, Dana. (In press). Epistemic equivalence and epistemic incapacitation. *British Journal for the Philosophy of Science.*

Wylie, Alison. (1992). Reasoning about ourselves: Feminist methodology in the social sciences. In Elizabeth Harvey & Kathleen Okruhlik (Eds.), *Women and reason* (pp. 225–244). Ann Arbor: University of Michigan Press.

Wylie, Alison. (1995). Doing philosophy as a feminist: Longino on the search for a feminist epistemology. *Philosophical Topics, 23*(2), 345–358.

Wylie, Alison. (2000). Feminism in philosophy of science: Making sense of contingency and constraint. In Miranda Fricker & Jennifer Hornsby (Eds.), *The Cambridge companion to feminism in philosophy* (pp. 166–184). Cambridge, UK: Cambridge University Press.

Wylie, Alison. (2001). Doing social science as a feminist: The engendering of archaeology. In Angela Creager, Elizabeth Lunbeck, & Londa Schiebinger (Eds.), *Feminism in twentieth century science, technology, and medicine* (pp. 23–45). Chicago: University of Chicago Press.

Wylie, Alison. (2003). Why standpoint matters. In Robert Figueroa & Sandra Harding (Eds.), *Philosophical explorations of science, technology, and diversity* (pp. 26–48). New York: Routledge.

Wylie, Alison. (2008). Social constructionist arguments in Harding's *Science and Social Inequality. Hypatia, 23*(4), 202–211.

Wylie, Alison. (2011). What knowers know well: Women, work and the academy. In Heidi Grasswick (Ed.), *Feminist epistemology and philosophy of science: Power in knowledge* (pp. 157–181). New York: Springer.

Wylie, Alison, Jakobsen, Janet R., & Fosado, Gisela. (2007). *Women, work and the academy: Strategies for responding to "post–civil rights era" gender discrimination.* New York: Barnard Center for Research on Women.

Wylie, Alison, & Nelson, Lynn Hankinson. (2007). Coming to terms with the values of science: Insights from feminist science studies scholarship. In Harold Kincaid, John Dupré, & Alison Wylie (Eds.), *Value-free science? Ideals and illusions* (pp. 58–86). Oxford, UK: Oxford University Press.

27

THE FEMINIST PRACTICE OF HOLISTIC REFLEXIVITY

Sharlene Nagy Hesse-Biber
and Deborah Piatelli

Sharlene

I am conducting participant observations and interviews with African American girls between the ages of 11 and 18 at an inner-city community center that houses an after-school program for youth. What is it like for young teens to "come of age" in their community? I have been hanging out at the center for over a month now, meeting with the girls once or twice a week. Sometimes they ask me to join them in playing basket-ball, or I watch them practice their "step-ping" routines. I tutor the younger children once a week.

The neighborhood surrounding the center had several drive-by shootings, and, last week, one of the girls mentioned that a male youth was recently shot outside the center's back door. One girl told me she rarely goes out after school except when she comes to the community center. What is it like for young girls to have their day-to-day mobility so restricted? How does violence in their community affect

Deb

Upon entering my research with a peace and justice network, I considered myself both an insider and outsider to this community of activists. I shared their perspectives and values, yet I was not a part of this community. Although I anticipated sharing many of the cultural and structural experiences of these activists, the majority of whom were white, middle-class women, there would be a number of activists with whom I would not find an apparent commonality. Equipped with the insights from feminist researchers, I entered the field acknowledging that there would be differences in our lived experiences. I was prepared to share openly my research interests, my background, and my commitment and to work through any power imbalances that arose during the research process. I understood that, because I was working across differences, there would be many moments when I would need to listen more and talk less.

peer group interactions? How do girls cope with the high levels of violence so close to their doorsteps?

Today, Nora, my research assistant, and I are the only two white people in the entire community center, and I have been dealing with feelings of being on the margins, concerned that my whiteness and my difference in age and social class are impacting my ability to listen to the girls. How can I bridge the differences divide? Do I expect too much of myself? Of them?

I usually stay in my car before pulling out of the community center driveway. I have a tape recorder to capture my reflections. The following are reflections on a meeting Norah and I had with the girls one Friday afternoon.

Norah: I think the girls were more open this time. I don't know if it was just because we bought them pizza, but I think that it was the fact that they have seen a lot of us and we are showing interest in the boys there as well, and I felt that they were open to talking about things like discrimination and white people, and I didn't feel like there was as much tension around us being white.

Sharlene: I really felt the girls opened up to me today. I think that one of the keys, it kind of fell into our laps, was that, by not excluding the boys who happened to walk into our room today, we gave legitimacy to the girls being there with us, because the boys wanted to be there as well. I think it made it an important thing that day. In a crazy way, the boys legitimized the whole thing.

As I reflected on my conversation with Norah, I realized that I had not thought about what our presence at the center meant for the boys that were also there. Our talking exclusively to the girls served to "de-center" the boys, and they became quite curious about what we were doing there. In fact, our openness to having the boys hang out with all of us for a brief time allowed them to know us a little, and it opened up an opportunity for us to ask them if we could talk with them as well at a later point in our visit. There were things that the girls would say about the boys, especially around issues of body image and appearance, and this gave us an opportunity to see how their perceptions matched up to

Despite this reflexive work, my access and initial conversations were problematic. Members responded negatively to my attendance at meetings and requests for interviews. My activist identity and the desire to collaborate and produce a useful product for this community did not seem to be enough to gain the trust of these members. I began to take their refusals to meet and the distancing at meetings personally until I attended a workshop as part of a forum that this community sponsored. The purpose of the workshop was to bring academics and activists in conversation with each other. What transpired within the first 20 minutes of that session revealed to me the invisible barrier I was facing in my own work. I began to see myself through the eyes of these activists, and I did not like what I witnessed. I began to understand their resistance to trusting academics.

As is customary in many community and academic settings, we went around the room and introduced ourselves. Thirty-five of the 44 people in the room identified themselves as academics first, activists second. Eight identified themselves solely as activists. I followed suit—officially, I was not yet an academic; rather I was an activist and graduate student. Two academics facilitated the session. We went around the room once again, and each of us was asked to identify an issue plaguing the Left. However, what began as a participatory conversation quickly came to a halt as several academics began constructing "research questions" appropriate for academics to undertake in order "to help activists." One woman (an activist) raised her hand and said, "Those questions are great, but if you really want to help us, come do the work." One of the academic facilitators responded by saying "Well, that's what we're trying to do. We [academics] have the intellectual skills and the resources, and so our time is best spent researching these issues and telling you how to solve them." The eight self-identified activists stood up and walked out. The academics looked puzzled; however, they continued on with their conversation. I was horrified.

I wondered—was this the way I was being perceived and identified in the community, as *how the boys felt about what they found attractive in a female.*

One of the issues I was hoping the girls would bring up was that of what it meant to be a black female within their community. Today, one of the girls actually talked about this issue. It came up when one of the girls touched on what it meant be an African American female. This moment provided me with an opportunity to ask the girls directly what being black and being female meant to them and whether they felt that one identity was first and the other second. I reflected on this interview moment.

Sharlene: I found it interesting that all the girls said they considered themselves black first and female second. In most cases, they responded that, above all, they were black. They attributed this feeling to the fact that being black fundamentally shaped their sense of self and the way in which others perceived them, much more so than their gender. Related to this is the way in which the girls equated being black with a sense of strength. Many of the girls indicated that a defining factor of African American womanhood was strength, not only for each woman's self but also for her family and the community.

I also reflected on what it meant for a white researcher to ask this question. What assumptions was I making concerning race and gender? Would I ask such a question if my respondents were white? How does my own positionality reflect my agenda?

a disconnected intellectual not willing to do the dirty work of organizing while suggesting that I had the solutions to their problems? A few days later I was invited to speak briefly at one of the network's weekly planning meetings. I discussed my experience in the workshop, but, instead of professing my sincerity and commitment, I listened to their interpretations of my experience. By dialoguing about the workshop and not specifically about my access, individuals more freely expressed their concern with the role of academics in activist communities. Through this conversation, I was able to view myself reflexively through their eyes and better understand what I needed to do in order to gain their trust.

After 18 months in the field, I am neither insider nor outsider. My researcher identity remains and interacts with my other identities, sometimes acting as an asset and other times as a hindrance. Although I spend much time reflecting about my social location, the power I hold as a researcher, and how I present myself in the field, I also consider the power others have in defining who I am, why I am there, and how much access I am allowed. By extending reflexivity outward, I am able to shift the angle of vision from analyzing my own self-presentation to also considering how I am being defined and why. My positionality continues to be both the subject and object of study.

Reflexivity exposes the exercise of power throughout the *entire* research process. It questions the authority of knowledge and opens up the possibility for negotiating knowledge claims and introducing counter-hegemonic narratives, as well as holding researchers accountable to those with whom they research. Reflexivity addresses two central questions that concern feminist researchers: What can be known, and how do we know it? These epistemological and ontological questions about power and knowledge have long been the subject matter for social theorists. Although reflexivity is not a new concept, feminist researchers bring a unique perspective to the understanding and practice of reflexivity. In the following pages, we explore the historical discourse from which contemporary feminist conceptualizations of reflexivity have emerged. Using the insights and practices of feminist researchers that have greatly impacted our approach to research, we illustrate how reflexivity can serve as a methodological tool for deconstructing power and cocreating knowledge throughout the entire research process. Moreover, we consider the "context" of reflexivity, discussing both researcher and participant reflexivity as well as the complexity online environments bring to the practice of reflexivity. Last, drawing from the practice of "experience sampling,"[1] we suggest a practical method of *reflexivity sampling* that allows researchers to experience sample their own reflexive moments as well as those of the research participants. Experiencing and practicing *reflexivity in the moment*,[2] as demonstrated in the excerpts of our field notes above, can uncover new angles of vision, reveal invisible barriers of power or ethical concerns, and lead to greater understandings, less hierarchical relationships, and more authentic, socially transformative research.

FEMINIST CONTRIBUTIONS: BUILDING ON HISTORICAL DISCOURSE

A Reflexive Methodology

Reflexivity is a holistic process that takes place along all stages of the research process—from the formulation of the research problem and the shifting positionalities of the researcher and participants through to interpretation and writing. A reflexive methodology offers the opportunity for raising new questions, engaging in new kinds of dialogue, producing transformative knowledge, and organizing different kinds of social relations (Collins, 1998, 2000; Harding, 1991, 1993; Smith, 1987). For the feminist, reflexive researcher, the process of reflection begins prior to entering the field. Reflexivity, at one level, is a self-critical action whereby the researcher finds that the world is mediated by the self—what can be known can only be known through oneself, one's lived experiences, and one's biography. Through self-critical action, reflexivity can help researchers explore how their theoretical positions and biographies shape what they choose to be studied and their approach to studying it. Reflexivity is also a communal process that requires attentiveness to how the structural, political, and cultural environments of the researcher and participants and the nature of the

> "It [reflexivity] permeates every aspect of the research process, challenging us to be more fully conscious of the ideology, culture, and politics of those we study [with] and those whom we select as our audience" (Hertz, 1996, p. 5).

study affect the research process and product. Reflexivity at this level fosters sharing, engaged relationships, and participatory knowledge-building practices, hence producing less hierarchical and more ethical, socially relevant research. The practice of reflexivity, by both the researcher and participants, can bring alternative forms of knowledge into public discourse. The reflexive researcher acknowledges that "all knowledge is affected by the social conditions under which it is produced and that it is grounded in both the social location and the social biography of the observer and the observed" (Mann & Kelley, 1997, p. 392). A methodology that is reflexive can be a transformative process for researchers, participants, and the larger community of knowledge builders.

A reflexive methodology challenges the status quo of scientific inquiry—inquiry that rests on the foundation of positivism. A positivist methodology has been critiqued by those supporting alternative paradigms such as an interpretative approach, critical theory, and constructivism (Denzin & Lincoln, 2000; Guba & Lincoln, 2000).

> Reflexivity can lead to the "development of critical consciousness of both researcher and participants, improvement of the lives of those involved in the research process, and transformation of fundamental societal structures and relationships" (Maguire, 1987, p. 29).

In addition to bringing forward criticisms of an ontological nature, these alternative paradigms have challenged the positivist model's commitment to replication and neutrality. Feminists have also challenged positivism and argue that its principles of objectivity, detachment, value neutrality, and universality are rooted in a historical, gendered, scientific paradigm that results in unequal power relations between the researcher and the participants involved in the inquiry (Harding, 1991, 1993; Hartsock, 1998; Reinharz, 1992; Smith, 1987). A feminist epistemology questions the proposition that the social world is one fixed reality that is external to individual consciousness and suggests that this world is socially constructed, consisting of multiple perspectives and realities. To propose that an objective social reality exists is to deny that reality is humanly and socially constructed within a historical context. It also denies the importance of human subjectivity and consciousness as part of knowledge creation. Without considering democratic values and interests, a positivist methodology can produce distorted research and exclude the problems, the knowledge, and the voices of those on the receiving end of relations of the ruling.[3]

> "The idea of a social world to be known implies a knower; the knower is the expert, and the known are the objects of someone else's knowledge, not, most importantly, of their own" (Oakley, 1998, p. 710).

Moving Toward a "Stronger Science"[4]

Objectivity implies a separation of ideology and science, an observation of the world without the infectivity of political and individual beliefs. In order to study the social, feminists argue for a reflexive science or, as Sandra Harding (1986) suggests, a "stronger science." This reflexive science is one that better reflects the world around us and one that acknowledges that researchers bring their biographies, experiences, and knowledge into the field of research. As theorists of reflexivity and reflexive researchers grapple with their social biography and its role in the research process, they find that ideological and personal beliefs muddy the waters of knowledge production. Separation of science and ideology becomes impossible and theoretically untenable, a fact that many theorists have accepted and articulated. Pierre Bourdieu (1993) stepped away from the more rigid definitions of objective knowledge. He argues that there are objects of knowledge to be understood by the sociologist but also that the sociologist is an active participant within these objects and fields of knowledge, which are the patterns of habitus. Reflexive researchers and writers are responsible for and indebted to the very texts that they shape, as it is the text that externalizes the reflexive self, taking on a material life of its own. Within Bourdieu's analysis, there is a deep sense that power is "relational or process oriented . . . [that it] is a function of relations between subjects and so . . . must be seen to function through a multiplicity of relations" (Everett, 2002, p. 57). The destructive force of objectivity can be contrasted with the potential for a transcendent force of reflexivity, through which the world could be transformed by transforming its representation (Everett, 2002, p. 74). If we accept with Bourdieu that the social world of interactions and meanings is directly linked to the cognitive knowing of this world, then, through the symbolic world of language and representation, the known world is dominated, subordinated, and controlled. However, to work and aim to be a critical theorist, one must, according to Bourdieu, examine "one's relation to the research object" (Everett, 2002, p. 71). In other words, researchers must reflect the scientific gaze back upon themselves, upon the objectifying gaze of sociology. Feminists, most notably Harding (1993), argue that the scientific model of objectivity needs to be replaced by a *strong objectivity,* an objectivity that can be found in feminist epistemologies. From her grounding aim of strong objectivity, Harding (1993) moves reflexivity in a slightly different direction, describing *strong reflexivity* where the researcher or theorist's own conceptual framework is the subject of critique. Additionally, strong objectivity can be achieved not by removing oneself from the world but by acknowledging our situated location and being reflexive of our position within it. Harding's (1993) conceptualization of strong objectivity goes beyond what has been critiqued as confessional discourse and toward a more potent form of objectivity. Strong objectivity is built upon the sustainable desire for critical self-reflection and an attempt at liberatory social change, starting from women's lives. Harding (1992) speaks of reflexivity as "self criticism in the sense of criticism of the widely shared values and interests that constitute one's own institutionally shaped research assumptions" (p. 569). Harding (1992) turns her own gaze toward the critique of the social sciences just as Bourdieu (1993) turns the sociological gaze back upon itself. Harding (1993) sees that "the grounds for knowledge are fully saturated with history and social life rather than abstracted from it" (p. 57). The singularity and universality of truth is in question here, for, when the door is open to the interpretation of knowledge and facts, a single truth cannot be obtained. The purpose of research is not to validate a truth, but to enable different forms of knowledge to challenge power. Multiple truths and diverse knowledges become the actual product of research when the subjectivity, location, and humanness of the knower are included. Dorothy Smith (1987) asks that we not wrestle with notions of truth but more with how to "write a sociology that will lay out for people how our everyday worlds are organized and how they are shaped and determined by relations that extend beyond them" (p. 121). A stronger, reflexive science becomes one that reconstructs or reorganizes the social relations of building knowledge (Harding, 1986; Smith, 1987).

Interrogating the Self or Selves

Alfred Schutz (1964) argued that both experience and biography play a direct role in the knowing of the social world. Bringing one's "own being in the world"[5] to the research endeavor can redirect positivist conceptualizations of objectivity. Like Schutz (1964), feminists ask that researchers be critically self-reflexive of personal and cultural biases in the formation of their theoretical perspectives of the social world. However, feminists push researchers further and ask them not only to bring the individual self into the research but also to acknowledge that "we cannot rid ourselves of the cultural self we bring with us into the field any more than we can disown the eyes, ears, and skin through which we take in our intuitive perceptions about the new and strange world we have entered" (Olesen, 1998, pp. 314–315). One phase of reflexivity is the methodological interrogation of the researcher's positionality, namely that of insider or outsider.[6]

In the early twentieth century, traditional ethnographic researchers positioned themselves as the detached observer, Schutz's "stranger"[7]—some standing outside the culture gazing upon it and others submersing themselves in the culture.

Whether or not one was a professional stranger or had simply gone native,

"I, the human being, born into the social world, and living my daily life in it, experience it as built around my place to it, as open to my interpretation and action, but always referring to my actual biographically determined situation" (Schutz, 1964, p. 314).

the ethnographer was expected to "maintain a polite distance from those studied and to cultivate rapport, not friendship; compassion, not sympathy; respect, not belief; understanding, not identification; admiration, not love" (Tedlock, 2000, p. 457). At the end of the day, the lone ethnographer transformed his or her observations of the other into text, and this text became the authoritative representation of the other. Shaped by the legacy of colonialism, classic ethnographic writing became the inscription of an observed other.

Many critics have raised concerns about the positionality of the objective observer or the immersed native. Robert Merton (1972) questioned the epistemic privilege claims of the "insider doctrine" and argued that researchers "unite" their insider/outsider identities and "consider their distinctive and interactive roles in the process of truth seeking" (p. 36). Although Merton (1972) recognized the multiplicity of the "contrasting statuses" that each individual holds, feminists have argued that he did not acknowledge the fluid and shifting nature of these identities, a fluidity based on a multitude of reasons such as one's social location and in-the-moment knowledge of participants, issues, and organizational culture. Moreover, not only do we as researchers attempt to define our role, but others also do so on a shifting basis (Acker, 2000; Kondo, 1990; Marx, 2000). Feminists have pointed to the danger of self-identifying as an insider or outsider prior to entering the research setting, arguing that researchers can only come to understand themselves as subjects and objects, insiders and outsiders, by reflexively examining the continuously shifting nature of their role in the field. Power relations occur between the researcher and research participants, and exploitative processes bound forth. Hence, the reflexive researcher must examine not only her or his own biography but also the unequal power relationship between the knower and the known. In considering positionality, we must not take for granted that we are insiders as we may make false assumptions, blind ourselves to important insights and viewpoints, or simply ask the wrong questions. However, if we stand back and distance ourselves, positioning ourselves as outsiders, we are in danger of producing the very barriers we wish to deconstruct (Anderson, 1998; Edwards, 1990; Riessman, 1987). Interrogating

"Immersion may be a useful strategy to attempt to view a culture from within, and it may position the researcher in a way that differs from a more distant participant-observer, but it does not basically alter the researcher's positionality, which remains part of her in the field and to which she returns in full when she is finished. Changing locations does not fundamentally alter one's positionality or the situatedness of one's knowledge" (Wolf, 1996, p. 10).

the self or selves is more than just examining one's social location and its effect on the field; rather, this reflexive process also involves negotiating one's positionality and recognizing the shifting nature of power relations from site to site.

In writing on her research experience in Iowa, Nancy Naples (1996, 2003) draws our attention to the importance of continuous self-reflection and the duality of the insider-outsider phenomenon. Naples describes her feelings of outsider status upon entering the research setting. She was an urban type, not familiar with the rural way of life. However, as she progressed through her fieldwork she found that she was also considered an insider by community members who felt alienated from their community. Furthermore, Naples (1996, 2003) found varying degrees of insiderness and outsiderness among community members based on shifting power relations and patterns of inequality in these small towns. It is the multiple aspects of our identity, she says, not necessarily the insider-outsider perspective, that shape our research experience, and this identity continuously shifts throughout the research process. Researchers are never fully insiders or outsiders. By allowing herself to reflect on and experience the fluidity of her positionality throughout the research process, Naples was able to gain greater insight about her own biases and assumptions as well as to explore the similarities and differences between herself and the community members she encountered.

In her ethnography of young Indian women's experiences of reading Western romance novels and of the meanings these women give to the texts, postcolonial feminist scholar Radhika Parameswaran (2001) stresses the importance of examining our positionality within the research setting, whether we are studying within our own culture or whether we have stepped outside the familiar boundaries of our identities. Although comfortable within the boundaries of sharing her Indian heritage with her participants, Parameswaran (2001) found this insider identity worked against her when she spoke with male "gatekeepers," who questioned her research and position, and with the parents of some of the women, who accused her of generating problems for them and their daughters. She also found that she was vulnerable to the parents and relatives of her informants, who wanted to manipulate her for their own purposes. To deal with issues of power and authority, she continuously had to negotiate both her identity and positionality. Parameswaran (2001) reminds us that concepts such as "insider and outsider," "native and Western," "self and other" are not binary concepts; rather, they are fluid and are subject to negotiation within the research setting. Like Naples (1996, 2003), the researcher can be an insider in one time and place and an outsider in another.

Negotiating Power and Co-Constructing Knowledge

An array of interlocking identities such as race, gender, and class influence the research process, and insider-outsider positionalities become more complicated as the researcher ventures into relationships across difference. Therefore, assuming commonality based on a single dimension of identity is detrimental to the project of deconstructing power relations and co-constructing knowledge (Anderson, 1998; Beoku-Betts, 1994; Collins, 2000; Dunbar, Rodriguez, & Parker, 2000; Edwards, 1990; Riessman, 1987). To minimize power differentials in knowledge construction, one must acknowledge difference. Acknowledging difference involves reflecting about one's situatedness in a complicated, shifting *matrix* of social locations and conversing openly with the research participants about that difference (Collins, 2000; Edwards, 1990). In her experience interviewing Afro-Caribbean women, Rosalind Edwards (1990) found that assuming commonality based on gender and shared experience as a mother or student was not conducive to building rapport across difference.

Her privilege as a white, middle-class woman clearly offered her a different mothering and academic experience than that of her participants. She states,

> I realized that rapport was easier after I had signaled not a nonhierarchical, nonexploitative, shared-sex relationship, but rather an acknowledgement that I was in a different structural position to them with regard to race and did not hold shared assumptions on that basis. My placing was not just as a woman but as a white woman. (Edwards, 1990, p. 486)

By acknowledging difference rather than similarity in their experiences, Edwards found that the women in her study were open to meeting with her and spoke more freely during their conversations. Similarly, Margaret Anderson (1998) found that by reflexively interrogating her own privilege as a white researcher and the barriers this placed upon her relationships, she was able to more easily enter the research site and build relationships with the women of color in her study. Placing a conventional methodological approach aside, Anderson (1998) engaged in open, dialogical conversations with participants, exchanging and co-constructing knowledge by revealing her own biography, experiences, and opinions.

Acknowledging difference also involves understanding that there is an aspect of lived experience that is invisible to those "who possess neither the language nor the cultural equipment either to elicit or understand that experience" (Rhodes, 1994, p. 549). However, this inability to readily unveil the invisible does not translate into a failure to study across difference. What this implies is that a researcher must undertake a reflexive project and navigate the research process through her or his own shifting positionality as well as that of the participants in order to produce relationships that are less hierarchical and research that is more inclusive

> *"A researcher can overcome the structural constraints of power by negotiating a role consistent with the respondent's level of power, both improving the quality of interactions and enriching the research process" (Marx, 2000, p. 132).*

and less distorted. Working across difference depends not only on possessing common language and cultural knowledge but also on establishing trust and engaging in dialogical relationships (Collins, 2000; Rhodes, 1994). Difference mediates the meaning of questions that are asked and how those questions are answered and interpreted. In her study on overt and perceived racism on a college campus, Dalia Rodriguez describes "the reflexive interplay between background knowledge derived ethnographically and experientially and the personal narratives generated by way of interview questions" (Dunbar et al., 2000, p. 285). By reflexively drawing from and sharing her own experiences, Rodriguez was able to find common experiential ground with the people of color she engaged with, but, at the same time, she vocalized the differences in their experiences (Dunbar et al., 2000). Utilizing her knowledge of the "racialized subject," which she acquired "experientially and ethnographically," she was able to place the participants' experiences into social context, thereby better informing her listening skills, choice of language and questions, and interpretation of the experiences of these students of color (Dunbar et al., 2000). Moreover, by reflexively engaging with the experiential knowledge she had gained outside the interview setting, Rodriguez was better able to notice and interpret the silences and to find alternative approaches for engaging participants (Dunbar et al., 2000). Similarly, Helen Ralston (2001) drew on her experiential knowledge as a white, middle-class, British-colonized Australian who had migrated to Canada when she interviewed urban, middle-class South Asian women from the Indian subcontinent about their experiences of migration to Canada, Australia, and New Zealand. Although she shared class and immigrant status with these women, Ralston was attentive to how differing skin color and language shaped their experiences. Ralston (2001) used her experiential knowledge, but reflexively placed it within a political, structural, and

> *"Taking the standpoint of the immigrant woman involves an initial and ever developing awareness of the personal and structural barriers and boundaries of the interviewer and interviewee" (Ralston, 2001, p. 221).*

cultural context in order to bring into view the institutional and structural barriers that these women faced in their lives. By doing so, Ralston (2001) was better able to appropriately "record the stories of their lived experience from their standpoint" (p. 219).

Acknowledging difference can always be difficult, but it can also become even more complicated when participants assume commonality where none exists. For instance, in her research with white, middle-class women on organizing practices among differing racial and class-based groups, Piatelli (2009) found that several of these women made the assumption that they shared similar experiences and beliefs based on their commonality of "whiteness." These assumptions made it more difficult to share perspectives, particularly on the matter of white privilege, for fear of shutting down the interview or damaging any rapport that had been built. Piatelli (2009) found that, by fostering a safe environment that encouraged participants to be reflexive about their white identities, she was able to encourage participants to rethink how their whiteness (and class) influenced their worldviews and organizing practices.

Researchers who encourage participant reflexivity throughout the research process have found success in introducing counter-hegemonic narratives, reducing power imbalances, and reaching new understandings (Dodson & Schmalzbauer, 2005; Dodson, Schmalzbauer, & Piatelli, 2007; Gallagher, 2000, 2008; Piatelli, 2009; Riach, 2009; Smith, 2006).

Marjorie DeVault (1990) argues that, oftentimes, words are not available to describe lived experience and that researchers must "develop methods for listening around and beyond words" (p. 101). DeVault stresses the importance of collecting embodied texts—texts that are grounded in lived experiences and produced physically as well as verbally. Christopher Dunbar relates his own experiences of interviewing persons of color across class and calls attention to the importance of "observing facial expressions, vernacular voice intonations, nonverbal cues, and other forms of body language" when interviewing across difference (Dunbar et al., 2000, p. 293). Attentiveness to physical cues can alert the researcher to hidden feelings or culturally sensitive questions that are not apparent in the ordinary course of the conversation.

Sharlene

How does one really listen? How do I listen in a way that the girls feel they are being heard? How do I listen to them across our many differences?

I remember walking into the community center feeling "the outsider" as a white, middle-class researcher. My concerns centered on trying very hard not to have a strict agenda—a set of prepackaged questions I would ask all of them, reminiscent of a survey where there is little room for the voices of those I interview to be heard outside of my own agenda of questions. I also wanted to position myself in the setting so that I would be able to break down, somewhat, the power and authority that is often inherent in the researcher-researched relationship.

As that Friday afternoon progressed, the girls talked about their feelings of being "black girls" and the racial discrimination they experience. At one point, Tasha expressed how difficult it was to be a black female and

---

Deb

As a peace activist and a scholar of social movements, I approached my research project holding the belief that sustained collective action around an antiwar agenda would eventually force a change in U.S. intervention around the world. Although committed to supporting an antiwar agenda, I also understood the links between militarism and domestic policy and that U.S. foreign policy was racist in that its prey was overwhelmingly people of color. Furthermore, I agreed with many critics of the peace movement that, in order to fulfill its agenda, the movement needed to shed its white, middle-class identity and work to become more diverse. In my fieldwork, I was interested in learning exactly how activists within a particular peace and justice network were attempting to do just that. However, through reflexive listening, I have shifted my views and, in turn, my research and consciousness.

to keep the fiber of the black community together. Racial discrimination is a constant issue the girls bring up, for example, being watched when they go into a predominately white downtown mall. Tasha comments, "Society is in my face, in front, in back, on the side, telling me how I should be. It won't let me be, ya know? They said you are gonna steal from this store and we're here to prevent you from doing it; it's not we're here to welcome you."

Listening to Tasha, Norah and I reflected on our own white privilege and on living our lives in predominately white middle-class communities.

Norah: I cannot imagine that these girls are only 13, 14, 15, and 16, and I almost felt like they have lived more of a life than mine. They have so much more experience and knowledge. I didn't have to worry about things like going to the mall because I grew up in white suburbia; my parents had money. I was with white people everywhere I went, so I never experienced those things; it wasn't a problem.

Sharlene: White women don't have to deal with our whiteness. We don't have to feel the eyes of white surveillance on a daily basis.

As my car began to pull out of the driveway of the center, I realized that the world in which these girls lived was less than five miles from my house. The children in my neighborhood don't have to leave their homes, as one of the girls I interviewed put it, "looking to the left and then to the right" to make sure a bullet was not coming her way. I wanted to delve deeper into the impact of violence on the girls' lived experience. We began to touch on some of these issues in my conversations with them, but the girls were guiding me to ask deeper questions on issues of community violence as well as the overall impact of discrimination on their day-to-day lives.

During my conversations in the field, I began to note that people spoke about peace work and approached organizing in very different ways. Initially, I thought it was simply because people had different political experiences and that these experiences led them to different forms of organizing. However, by listening more closely, openly sharing biographies, and encouraging participants to question my beliefs, I began to understand that people's understanding of peace work shaped their approaches to organizing and that these beliefs and practices were products of different structural, lived experiences in a racialized, classed, and gendered society.

Through these reflexive relationships, I was challenged to examine my own social biography—not just how it shaped what I asked and how I heard others but also how my social location, my white privilege in particular, shaped my views. Through this different angle of vision, I began to construct an alternative definition of peace work, one that began to see the limited gains an antiwar agenda can make in constructing a more democratic, just society. I began to realize that working across difference has to do not only with deconstructing individual barriers but also with interrogating one's social biography and with becoming conscious of how one's knowledge is shaped. Examining my own privilege as a white, middle-class woman facilitated the transformation of my worldview, my activism, and the research project. No longer was the research focused simply on organizational practices that could hinder or foster work across difference, but rather it began to consider the broader structural and cultural forces shaping differing worldviews and hence our efforts to build relationships and alliances across differences. Practicing reflexive listening across the entire research process asks that the researcher not only interrogate her or his positionality and social location but also engage in a dialogical practice of sharing with others. A dialogical relationship can identify points of connection that can cultivate changes in thinking, leading to actions and experiences that can alter consciousness.

In reflexive relationships, the researcher experiences a moment or moments during the conversation when an exchanging of roles occurs—the researcher as participant, the participant as researcher. This fluidity of roles in the process of constructing knowledge occurs when the researcher is reflexive about the interview relationship and the social conditions that affect the conversation. Because we carry our biographies and presumptions into the interview setting, we must problematize all positions, whether shared or not, in order to create a nonhierarchical environment conducive to sharing. In the previous excerpts, we suggest that, by reflexively listening and engaging in dialogical relationships with our participants, we can bring the blind field into view and radically change the way we know and what we know. Working across difference requires entering another's personal space. By entering either experientially, like Rodriquez (Dunbar et al., 2000) or Ralston (2001), or by finding innovative ways of listening and interpreting, like DeVault (1990) or Dunbar et al. (2000), or by encouraging participant reflexivity as did Piatelli (2009) or Riach (2009), the researcher must not only reflexively interrogate his or her positionality but also engage in the communal processes of crossing borders and boundaries and creating a common space for building knowledge.

> *"The researcher is transformed in the process of research—influenced and taught by her respondent-participants as she influences them"* (Gorelick, 1991, p. 469).

Authenticating Voice

> As ethnographers we want to learn about our informants but as reflexive ethnographers we also learn about our own lives in the process of grasping how the lives of others could teach us something about all lives. Here lies that potential for change inherent in the reflexive stance—the learning itself is viewed as empowering the scholar while the recording is a political task and thus may help change the informants' lives. (Wasserfall, 1993, p. 23)

Negotiating power is not simply changing the relationship between researcher and researched. Feminist researchers value and bring alternative forms of knowledge to the forefront of public discourse and argue that the ultimate goal of sociology is the creation of a more just society (Collins, 2000; Harding, 1992; Mertens, 2003; Reinharz, 1992). Socially just research can foster changed consciousness, encourage collective empowerment, and transform both researcher and participants in the research process. A reflexive methodology seeks to describe reality within its multiple contexts, to encourage interaction between the researcher and participants, and to minimize power differentials during the research process (Eichler, 1997; Harding, 1991). Reflexive researchers acknowledge that "knowledge is not neutral but is influenced by human interests, that all knowledge reflects the power and social relationships within society, and that an important purpose of knowledge construction is to help people improve society" (Mertens, 2003, p. 139). Whether transforming sociology, methods, or people's lives, a reflexive methodology works to create a more democratic, just society. Although diverse in approaches and aims, reflexive researchers are socially engaged, committed activists in their own disciplines and in society at large.

Dorothy Smith (1987) and Patricia Hill Collins (2000) utilize the concept of bifurcated consciousness when discussing the life experience of subjugated individuals. Smith's (1987) *insider sociology* and Collins' (2000) *outsider within* perspectives both suggest that subjugated knowledge is produced from a different angle of vision that reveals certain aspects of power relations. Rooted in Marxian theory, feminist standpoint epistemology privileges the knowledge of persons whose standpoints arise from positions of intense subordination in the intersection of the vectors of oppression. Smith (1987) states that a woman's location and experience is distinctive, and Collins (2000) suggests that the lived experience of the "other" can shape a consciousness that is counter-hegemonic because it is from a special vantage point—the lived experience of the dominated rather than the dominant. However, although subjugated knowledge provides critical insight into understanding how oppressive social relations operate, we must acknowledge that each unique, situated standpoint is only a partial perspective, as there is not one way, but many ways, of knowing (Collins, 2000; Haraway, 1988; Hartsock, 1993; Smith, 1987). Although it is tempting to claim that the most subjugated voices have a more accurate view of oppression, we must not rank human oppression (Collins, 2000). Instead, we must consider the subjugated voices from every group, their unique standpoints and their own partial and situated knowledges. Validating and legitimizing the knowledge that emerges from the everyday life experiences of *outsiders within* and moving subjugated knowledge *from the margin to the center* of social inquiry are just two of the ways in which feminism has broadened the theorizing of reflexivity (Collins, 2000; hooks, 1984). Nancy Hartsock (1993) states that "we [researchers] need to develop our understanding of difference by creating a situation in which hitherto marginalized groups can name themselves, speak for themselves, and participate in defining terms of interaction, a situation in which we can construct an understanding of the world that is sensitive to difference" (p. 545). The purpose of research, then, is not to construct grand generalizations but to work closely with people, maintaining an inclusive reality, open and flexible, consisting of a diversity of perspectives and enhancing their understanding and ability to control their own reality.

While reflexive practices uncover subjugated knowledge, engaging participants in reflexivity can also uncover hidden discourses of privilege. In his study on white identity, Charles Gallagher (2000, 2008) argues that researchers, particularly those engaging in critical white studies, have a responsibility not only to document privileged discourse but also to offer new ways of thinking to disrupt it. He states, "My experiences suggest that when white respondents are given counterarguments that demonstrate that racial inequality still exists they modify many of their positions" (Gallagher, 2000, p. 84). Gallagher encourages researchers to provoke participant reflexivity by purposefully crafting the questions we ask so that participants are forced to think of the structural advantages and

how they have shaped their experiences, thereby adding deeper reflection upon interpretations of those experiences. Sometimes, challenging participants to consider their own privilege can often occur through open reflection. Other times, however, it requires more creative ways of unearthing this discourse. We discuss some of these processes in the next paragraphs.

Participatory action research is one example of social inquiry that reflexively seeks to authenticate the voices of those with whom researchers study (Lykes & Hershberg, Chapter 16, this volume; Maguire, 1987; Reason, 1998; Stringer, 1996). Participatory action research is an iterative process that combines dialogue, reflection, and action. Participants assess their situation, analyze data they have collected themselves, and act on the findings. Participatory research results in action at the local level and seeks to involve people as active participants in the research process. It aims to "promote collective processes of inquiry that expose the ideological, political, and social processes underlying and permeating systems of inequality" (Lykes & Hershberg, Chapter 16, this volume). The participatory action researcher is neither an observer nor an external consultant but an engaged participant who works as an interactive partner with community members. Researchers encourage participation, promote dialogue, and foster relationships. Process is as important as product, and, through these participatory processes, people explore the ways in which their lives are shaped and constrained by extra-local processes and find ways to either change or work within them (Lykes, 1997; Lykes & Hershberg, Chapter 16, this volume; Maguire, 1987; Reason, 1998; Stringer, 1996).

REPRESENTING THE SOCIAL—
INTERPRETATION AND WRITING

From the moment the researcher engages in the research project through the steps of probing and asking questions and transcribing field notes, the voices of the participants have already been interpreted. Even when employing participatory methods, the researcher ultimately holds authority over the interpretation and writing of the final research product. Can the researcher, during the process of interpretation and writing, find ways to share power as well as to better represent people's lives? Gaining an understanding of the reality of people's lives within their structural and cultural contexts was at the center of Max Weber's (1921) inquiry. His concept of *verstehen* was a significant contribution to the methodology of contemporary sociology. However, whether or not the researcher has the ability to know another's experience or has the authority to give voice to it continues to remain the subject of debate within methodological discourse across disciplines. Can we really know another's experience or are we simply able to just "hear voices that we record and interpret" (Riessman, 1993, p. 8)?

> Verstehen: "We cannot understand what people do without some sense of how they subjectively interpret their own behavior" (Weber, 1921).

In her much-cited essay, Judith Stacey (1991) draws our attention to the multiple ways in which the researcher holds power over the participants in the research process and argues that critical self-reflection is not enough to ease the power difference between researcher and participant. Stacey (1991) argues that the highly personalized relationship between ethnographer and participant masks actual differences in power, knowledge, and structural mobility and places research subjects at grave risk of manipulation and betrayal by the ethnographer. Even though a researcher may wish to establish an egalitarian relationship with participants, the researcher has the power to determine what is recorded and what is not as well as how things are interpreted. Furthermore, participants become extremely vulnerable and trust becomes an issue when they feel encouraged by researchers to share the most intimate and confidential details of their lives (Kirsch, 1999; Pini, 2004). The published ethnography becomes an "intervention into the lives and relationships of its subjects" (Stacey, 1991, p. 114). Although innovative approaches to interpretation and writing attempt to deconstruct the author's authority, the research product is ultimately that of the researcher, whether it is coauthored by the participant or not. Researcher power over what is written (or not written) is unavoidable. Similarly, Carol Warren (2000) states that the danger for exposure of both the other and the self begins with the writing of our field notes. She points to the tension between the need for thick description and the desire to protect the identity of both the research setting and the participants. She asks us to consider how much the altering of the site's and participants' identifying information distorts the meaning of people's lived experiences. Moreover, Warren (2000) argues that, in writing the other, we also write the self. She asks how researchers can resolve the tension between "revelation and concealment" of one's identity—how can one inscribe the self, without erasing the voice of the participant? Jayati Lal (1996) speaks of the problems of self-reflexivity in that it can give more voice to the author and less to the subject. She argues that the researcher should attempt to employ both narrative and reflexivity but, at the same time, not selectively choose participants' voices to buttress the researcher's arguments:

> Researchers contributing to debates in feminist methodology and experimental ethnography point to the strategies of polyvocality and suggest giving research subjects a voice in a move to decolonize the subject, yet we often fail to take account of the challenges to modes of representations and contestations for meaning by research subjects who provide their own self presentations. We need to acknowledge this agency, to treat the researched as subjects with whom we are engaged in a mutual, though unequal power-charged social relation of conversation. (Lal, 1996, p. 205)

Reflexive Interpretive Processes

Interpretation involves translation, as researchers do not have direct access to another's experience. The reflexive researcher must not only listen for "the everyday processes of translation" that are a part of their participants' speech but also convert that speech into readable text (DeVault, 1990, p. 102). Catherine Riessman (1993) argues that there are at least five levels of representation in the research process: attending to experience or the choice in what you notice and select to tell, telling, transcribing, analyzing, and reading. Researchers, then, are interpreting and creating texts at every juncture of the process. DeVault (1990) further describes the process of translation as listening, editing, and writing.

In her research on the work of feeding a family, DeVault (1990) reflexively drew on her own personal experiences as a resource for listening to how women searched for and used "close enough" language to describe their everyday experiences. She was attentive to preserving the "messiness of everyday talk," an approach that enhanced her ability to hear participants in new ways and enabled her to extend beyond presumptions and focus on what was said as well as on what was not (DeVault, 1990). In her research on chronic illness, Kathy Charmaz (2000) found that a research relationship that honors respect for emotionality and fosters an environment that is conducive to sharing can provide greater insight on the part of both the researcher and participant. Through reflexive listening and approaching interviews as "contextualized conversations" (Stage & Mattson, 2003), DeVault (1990) and Charmaz (2000) were able to better understand the experiences of their participants.

Language is embedded in cultural contexts. The work of translation becomes further complicated when working across languages and cultures. Bogusia Temple (1997) discusses the problems that might arise when researchers rely on interpreters or even do the work of language translation themselves. She cautions researchers to question the familiar as they label and name experience, as words and concepts "have a history specific to the society they originate from" (p. 611). When researchers translate, she suggests that they engage in examining and sharing their "intellectual autobiographies" to explore the different perspective individuals bring to the process of translation. Dealing with interpretive conflict is an issue many researchers confront in the processes of translation and interpretation.

Gesa Kirsch (1999) relates her experience negotiating with a participant over the interpretation of her experience. Although she attempted to negotiate her interpretation with that of the participant, they both remained polarized in their interpretations.

> Intellectual autobiography: "An analytic (not just descriptive) concern with the specifics of how we come to understand what we do, by locating acts of understanding in an explication of the grounded contexts these are located in and arise from" (Stanley, 1990, p. 62).

Kirsch (1999) was faced "with the dilemma of interpreting another woman's experience and presuming interpretive powers that transcended hers" (p. 49). In her text, Kirsch (1999) decided to place the interpretations side by side, allowing readers to evaluate the two different readings.

Researchers working with vulnerable populations have been required to find innovative ways to do the work of translation. Building on more conventional methods of focus groups and member checking, Lisa Dodson and Leah Schmalzbauer (2005) use an innovative method of "interpretive focus groups" to give greater understanding to the voices and experiences of people in their studies.[8] In their work with women in low-income communities, oftentimes across languages and cultures, Dodson and Schmalzbauer (2005) utilize a collaborative, communitarian, participatory methodology in their research. Seeking "co-analysis, not confirmation of data previously gathered," interpretive focus groups engage community members who have not participated in the data-gathering phase to fulfill the role of expert interpreter (Dodson & Schmalzbauer, 2005, p. 949). Vulnerable populations tend to hide the real experiences of their everyday lives and rightly so. These "habits of hiding" show up as silences, contradictions, or selective telling in conversations (Dodson & Schmalzbauer, 2005; Dodson, Schmalzbauer, & Piatelli, 2006, 2007; Scott, 1990). Dodson and Schmalzbauer (2005) embarked on their research in order to provide accurate descriptions of the experiences of low-income families in America, decentering the distorted visions that affect social policy on a daily basis. Respecting the right of these women to disclose or not disclose their private experiences, Dodson and Schmalzbauer found that interpretive focus groups enabled participants to bring their experiences safely into discourse without causing them harm or having them risk exposure. Interpretive focus groups (IFGs) seek a "communitarian approach to analysis and multivocal representation of the meaning of data" (Dodson & Schmalzbauer, 2005, p. 949).

Deb Piatelli (2009) found that the IFG method was also useful in revealing the hidden discourses of the privileged population of a peace and justice network in her research study on privilege, difference, and organizing practices. In this study, simply raising the issue of white privilege often shut down the conversation, as some white participants were unwilling to discuss it or preferred to retreat into colorblind discourse. This reluctance is understandable as there are risks in exposing one's vulnerability. Interpretive focus groups provided a way to diminish the risk in telling and uncover the racialized discourse operating within this network and how it affects the selection and definition of issues and organizing practices.

Deb

In one particular community group, I facilitated an educational session on my research to date. Educational sessions were viewed as nonconfrontational learning experiences during which people could learn about different topics. On this date, there were two people of color and 10 white individuals in attendance. I began by presenting my overall findings on the differing approaches to organizing I had witnessed within the network. This presentation produced good conversation, and I saw it as an opportunity to introduce an emergent theme in my analysis—privilege—to see how the conversation would unfold. I presented my observations and excerpts from the conversations I had had with members from other groups about working across race and class. The atmosphere in the focus group was much more comfortable than in the personal interviews, as people were more open in speaking about privilege when interpreting other white people's actions and words as opposed to their own. There was a distancing from the privilege that provided a safe environment within the focus-group setting. This dialogue provided great insight as members began to construct possible reasons that some members behaved in certain ways. "They're used to controlling the agenda," "they want to be the leaders," and "they don't have any experience being around people of color" were some of the various reasons offered as to why some whites might be working in an exclusive manner. However, as the conversation turned to the group's specific practices, the atmosphere shifted. As a few of the white members began to interrogate their own privileges, experiences, and beliefs, other whites retreated into defensive, color-blind discourse in order to avoid any accusations that they were part of the problems being raised by the rest of the group. One white woman asked,

> Why are you making me apologize for being a white, middle-class activist? Why aren't people of color reaching out to us? Why do we have to do the reaching out? Maybe they're racist.

And another, a white male, said, "Let's just do our work and then see who wants to join us. If we end up being white, so what?" At this point, a black male joined the conversation and voiced his experience of working in a predominately white context:

> I feel silenced all the time. White people don't seem to want to get into conversations about race or even class. But I think we need to talk about it if we're seriously going to talk about ending war.

The conversation continued for a few moments and then turned toward a discussion on why (and if) it was important to work across race and class. Through these conversations, I learned that people's definitions of what it meant to be white were directly related to how they defined peace and, in turn, approached alliance building. I also learned how volatile and difficult it is to acknowledge and address privilege. Following the interpretive focus group, a number of members decided to have a series of educational sessions on racism and white privilege. Several months later, I began to see a shift in the process of issue formulation and meeting structure, as many members began to reach out and support the agendas of low-income people and people of color in their community and develop educational sessions around community-centered issues.

Many researchers have found ways to bring participants into the interpretation process. Jonathan Smith (2006) engaged participants in his study on identity change during the transition to motherhood as "fully self-reflexive co-researchers." In his own version of interpretive analyses, Smith offered the women in his study the opportunity to perform a reflexive analysis upon his interpretations of their experiences. Kathleen Riach (2009), in her study exploring organizational age inequalities and aging identities, experimented with what she termed a "participant-centred reflexivity" analysis. She argued that researchers can move beyond encouraging participant reflexivity during the data collection process and perform a "participant-centred reading of interview transcripts" (p. 358) whereby the researcher mines the transcripts for reflexive moments when the participant steps outside the traditional interview protocol (p. 361). For example, Riach noted that participants often made interjections about the context of their knowledge and experience during the interview process, and these interjections added greater insight into the meaning participants had created about their lives. Moreover, Riach provides examples whereby participants questioned her ability to understand their experiences due to generational differences, which in turn provoked more questioning of their own interpretations of their thoughts and experiences. Hence, Riach (2009) argues that researchers should listen for reflexive moments during the analysis process to glean more understanding and context.

Writing the Reflexive

In their controversial 1986 text, *Writing Culture: The Poetics and Politics of Ethnography,* James Clifford and George Marcus raised the question of the researcher's power and authority over ethnographic representation. Influenced by the writings of the French post-structuralists, Clifford and Marcus questioned the reproduction of culture and knowledge by the objective social researcher. Ethnographic writing is not simply cultural reporting; it is "always caught up in the invention, not the representation of cultures" (Clifford & Marcus, 1986, p. 2). They called for ethnographers to "avoid a detached posture of neutral observation, and acknowledge their subjects as collaborators in a project that the researcher can never fully control" (Stacey, 1991, p. 115). They argue that the other can never be fully experienced; hence, any interpretive work will always be a partial truth (Marcus, 1994). These writings raised important questions about the validity and existence of a "true," complete ethnographic account. Reflexivity, then, became a tool for critical self-reflection in the writing process.

Feminists had addressed issues of power and representation long before this new critique of ethnography surfaced. Dating back to the nineteenth century, feminists were rejecting the disinterested and omniscient observer and calling for researchers to reveal the social location from which they spoke, share their emotional responses to the field experience, and engage in analytical dialogue with their participants (Cooper, 1892; Martineu, 1836/1837; Perkins-Gilman, 1898; Tristan, 1844/2007). Speaking from their position as the other, these first wave feminists questioned the construction of the woman as the other in experience, language, and discourse. In her autobiographical work *A Voice From the South by a Black Woman From the South*, Anna Julia Cooper (1892), an African American woman and associate of W. E. B. DuBois, called for the necessity of hearing the black woman's voice in order to understand the raced, classed, and gendered nature of American society (Lemert, 1998). Cooper (1892) argued, "Only the Black woman can say when and where I enter, in the quiet, undisputed dignity of my womanhood, without violence and without suing on special patronage, then and there the whole Negro race enters with me" (Cooper, quoted in Lemert, 1988, p. 63). For these women, the role of the researcher was not an objective, value-neutral one; it was engaged, rooted in everyday life experiences, and it gave voice to those who had been silenced. Contemporary feminist writings on the woman as other can be traced back to the early 1950s with Simone de Beauvoir's (1953) *The Second Sex*, which called for women to speak for and claim themselves as subject (Mascia-Lees, Sharpe, & Cohen, 1989). Attention to voice and representation was a primary focal point for second wave feminists.

This self-critical reflexive turn in ethnographic writing, an "experimental moment in the human sciences," resulted in a reexamination of the writing of ethnography and produced a genre of scholars calling for researchers to experiment with alternative forms of representation by employing a polyvocality in their writing and performing a critical self-analysis of their experiences in the field (Marcus & Fischer, 1999). Early ethnographic texts or realist tales took the form of a dispassionate, third-person narration (Van Maanan, 1988, p. 45). These realist tales performed what Donna Haraway (1988) called the "god trick," writing the other from nowhere, and they reflected the textual authority of the researcher. In these texts, the other's words, experiences, and behaviors were called upon to verify or validate the researcher's interpretations. This literary format produced and re-produced, when read by others, the power imbalance inherent in ethnographic research. At the other extreme, confessional tales were considered "highly personalized styles" and "self-absorbed" texts (Van Maanen, 1988, p. 73). These self-reflective writings positioned the self front and center and described the decisions and dilemmas of the fieldwork experience and the impact that the field had on the researcher. Confessionals were often written in addition to the realist account, as attempts to reveal the biases and biography of the researcher in order to allow the reader to evaluate the validity of the text. Although produced to deconstruct the power of the researcher, these texts actually rendered the other more invisible.

More experiential forms of writing have attempted to bring researcher and participant together in representational form. These texts pay attention to critical self-reflection as well as multiplicity and partiality instead of singularity and universality. They range in form from the literary to the coauthorship of research texts.[9] These texts are

> messy because they insist on an open-endedness, an incompleteness, and an uncertainty about how to draw a text/analysis to a close. Such open-endedness often marks a concern with an ethics of dialogue and partial knowledge that a work is incomplete without critical, and differently positioned, responses to it by its (one hopes) varied readers. (Marcus, 1994, p. 567)

These new forms are concerned with exposing the power relations embedded in ethnographic writing. A reflexive text attempts to deconstruct power relations between the researcher and participants by decentering the authority of the researcher's voice.

Writing is biographical work. At the moment of inscription, the other becomes vulnerable, and, when we write the other, we also write the self (Coffey, 1999; Fine, 1998; Warren, 2000). Amanda Coffey (1999) draws our attention to the relationship between the self and the field and asks researchers to write reflexively by interrogating their own biographies. We must ask not only how our presence has affected the field but also how the field has affected us. The central concern for the reflexive writer is deconstructing power: Who has it, how is it used, and for what purposes? Although new ethnographic writing or what is sometimes referred to as the *literary turn* in ethnographic writing allows for writing the self into the text in a new way, we are always writing and have always written the self because our biography shapes what we see and hear, how we interpret, and how we choose what to write. Typically ethnographers have kept personal field notes separate from their ethnographic observations and interactions and have carried this forward in their writings. Coffey offers field notes, partial autobiographical accounts, and tales of the self as alternatives to writing the self into an ethnography. Writing in the self can be a good practice in reflexivity. Reflexivity, she says, is "having an ongoing conversation experience while simultaneously living in the moment; while voice is presenting the author's self while simultaneously writing the respondents' accounts and representing their selves" (Coffey, 1999, p. 132). The boundaries between self-indulgence and reflexivity are blurred. There will always be a struggle in determining how much to reveal or silence.

How does one bear witness and accurately represent people's lives? One form of writing is the testimonio,[10] in which the researcher brings the voices of those who are silenced and marginalized into public discourse by creating a text told in the first person voice of those being researched. The uniqueness of the form of the testimonio is the presence of "an 'I' that demands

"The presence of the voice, which the reader is meant to experience as the voice of a real rather than fictional person, is the mark of a desire not to be silenced or defeated, to impose oneself on an institution of power and privilege from the position of the excluded, the marginal, the subaltern" (Beverly, 2000, p. 556).

to be recognized, that wants or needs to stake a claim on our attention" (Beverly, 2000, p. 556). The narrator is the "real protagonist or witness of the events she or he recounts," and the testimonio is constructed with limited interpretive interference by the researcher through the tape-recording, transcription, and editing of an oral account (Beverly, 2000, p. 555). The testimonio subdues the presence and authority of the author and instead affirms the authenticity of lived experience within political, social, and cultural contexts. The testimonio allows the subaltern to speak in his or her own unique voice and on his or her own terms (Spivak, 1988).

Transforming Lives— Transforming the Social

As discussed earlier, many feminist researchers see the ultimate goal of sociology as the creation of a more just society, a goal we can move toward through reflexive methodology in the construction of knowledge. For instance, institutional ethnography has radically transformed the practice of social research by providing "the empirical investigation of linkages among local settings of everyday life, organizations, and translocal processes of administration and governance" (DeVault & McCoy, 2000, p. 751). Beginning with people's everyday lives, institutional ethnography "problematizes the social relations and organization that extend beyond experience," looking to "discover how what we experience locally is shaped by what we cannot know directly" (Smith, 2007, p. 409). By uncovering how extra-local relations organize people's lives, institutional ethnography can expand local knowledge, empower local change strategies, and reveal the interconnectedness of translocal communities (Campbell &

Manicom, 1995; DeVault & McCoy, 2000; Smith, 1987, 2002, 2007).

Reflexive researchers continue to seek innovative techniques to negotiate power, minimize harm, and illuminate and transform the social structures that oppress people on a daily basis. A reflexive methodology can allow the researcher to "become aware of, and diminish the ways in which domination and repression are reproduced in the course of research and in the products of their work" (Naples, 2003, pp. 37–38). However, power cannot be entirely eliminated from the research process. Differences of culture, ethnicity, race, and class place strains on the research process. Although the practice of reflexivity can enable researchers to become more sensitive to power relations and see how their own social location shapes the research process, it cannot completely eradicate power differences between the researcher and participants or between participants in the study (Stacey, 1991; Wasserfall, 1993; Wolf, 1996). Adopting a reflexive perspective in practice often involves the researcher becoming both insider and outsider, taking on a myriad of different standpoints, and negotiating these identities simultaneously. This is aptly expressed by Trinh T. Minh-ha's (1991) concept of multiple subjectivities:

> Working right at the limits of several categories and approaches means that one is neither entirely inside or outside. One has to push one's work as far as one can go: to the borderlines, where one never stops, walking on the edges, incurring constantly the risk of falling off one side or the other side of the limit while undoing, redoing, modifying this limit. (p. 218)

Attention to doing necessary "border work" has been at the forefront of feminist practice, most notably in postcolonial feminist research (Anzaldúa, 1987; Parameswaran, 2001; Patai & Gluck, 1991; Spivak, 1988; Trinh, 1991). This "border work" also requires attention to and reassessment of our own disciplinary practices and consideration of how tightly bound each one of us might have become to the specific methodological practices and conceptual definitions of our own disciplines.

HOLISTIC REFLEXIVITY AND NEW TECHNOLOGIES

Feminist researchers often look to new technologies in order to ask new questions and interpret their data, and this process exposes them to a range of new and emergent methods (Hesse-Biber & Leavy, 2008). These emergent technologies and methods have implications for how feminists practice holistic reflexivity across the research process.

The availability and use of computer-mediated communications (CMC) such as Web 2.0 and newly emergent mobile technologies are on the rise. As of 2010, an estimated 1.5 billion users are currently online, approximately 22 percent of the world's population (Kozinets, 2010, p. 15). In 2010, the U.S. household Internet access rate was 77.3% (Internet World Statistics, 2010), and the frequency of access ranged from weekly to daily contact (Horrigan, 2007). Social scientists are increasingly using emergent technologies to collect new forms of data sources from social networking sites such as Facebook. These new technologies are especially important for locating hidden populations, and they enable researchers to explore new research questions, especially with regard to online user behaviors and attitudes. Computer-mediated communications also fundamentally change traditional research practices such as survey research, ethnography, and intensive interviewing, as these traditional methods undergo transformation in their praxis when they are applied as online data-gathering instruments (Dicks & Mason, 2011; James & Busher, 2010; Robinson & Schulz, 2011).

The growth in online technologies is matched by an equally impressive increase in the use of traditional online technologies in their crossover to other disciplines. Geographic integrated systems (GIS), a mapping technology used by geographers, is one technology that is crossing over into the social sciences, the arts, and the humanities. In addition, new mobile technologies in the form of mobile phones with global positioning systems (GPS) are providing the researcher with a new tool for gathering user behaviors in real time and geographical space (Cope & Elwood, 2009).

New Technologies' Challenges for Holistic Reflexivity

As researchers begin to employ newly emergent computer-mediated technologies and refashion old methods in the process of doing online research, some important issues are raised regarding the practice of holistic reflexivity. One important challenge is the lack of visual cues in many online environments, which usually offer the researcher fewer ways to observe linguistic and extralinguistic behavior than are found in off-line, face-to-face interactions. Actually being in the same place together with participants can provide the researcher with further contextual understanding of their lived experiences (Mann & Stewart, 2000). For example, in an online environment, a research participant may decide to veil (or alter) her or his gender, race, class, age, and other characteristics. This decrease in the ability to collect "embodied texts" (DeVault, 1990) can impact the researcher's ability to be reflexive about the full meaning conveyed in interactions with a participant as well as about the researcher's own positionality and how that affects communications and interpretations. Moreover, the inability to hear how things are said (and not said) can distort interpretations and cause a researcher to miss important meanings. New technologies such as the webcam may help to alleviate some of these concerns, but, often, a research participant may not have access to these computer peripherals that allow for face-to-face interaction in cyberspace.

As researchers begin to access different modes of research—combining off-line with online modes—these new forms of interaction may also impede the researcher's practice of reflexivity. For example, the extent to which data collection happens at the same time (synchronous) or different times (asynchronous) can impact *how* a participant answers a researcher's queries (Mann & Stewart, 2000). How does a researcher assess the degree of participant comfort when participants are answering questions posed to them via e-mail, and they can take the time to develop their response asynchronously? What happens to the process of co-constructing knowledge? Does synchronous interaction increase or decrease the researcher's ability to assess the participant's comfort with the research process and hence the trustworthiness of the data? Would a synchronous more instant response time mean that a participant would reply in a more subconscious manner?

Gathering data online may also impact participant reflexivity as the researcher loses the ability to relay visual and linguistic cues that can often spur reflexive participant moments. Moreover, the online environment produces challenges in developing the trust and rapport that can further encourage both researcher and participant reflexivity. Although synchronous online communications can resemble the ebb and flow of naturalistic conversation, the loss of body language and spoken word can distort interpretations of what is being "said." Combining online with off-line research may also impact the ability of a researcher to practice holistic reflexivity. Doing research in synchronous virtual time may cut down on the ability of the researcher to take notes on the fly, and online research may require researchers to shift gears regarding how they reflect on their research, so as to take into account the (possibly invisible) spatial location of their research participants.

Geographical spatial mapping technologies in the form of GIS as well the use of mobile technologies that employ GPS can resolve many of the challenges resulting from a loss of real-time observation. These technologies can enable researchers to gain a more "context-rich" understanding of the lived experiences of their participants, thereby increasing the possibilities for a more reflexive understanding of these experiences. Mobile technologies allow respondent data to be collected in an ongoing manner because GPS systems collect streaming data that is gathered over time, enabling a researcher to discern micro-changes in a participant's attitudes, behaviors, and social context. For example, a researcher can track participants' movements in space—looking at whom they interact with over their mobile or smart phones and those significant others in their peer phone network who may be present in their immediate physical environment

(Eagle, 2011; Visser & Mulder, 2011). In addition, a researcher can interact with participants as they go about their daily round by sampling their experiences—their actions, thoughts, and feelings throughout the day or week or month. Such was the case in a recent study on what makes people happy (Killingsworth & Gilbert, 2010). Researchers using smart phone technologies sampled participants' feelings throughout their daily activities by having them respond at random intervals to inquiries about their level of happiness and what they were doing and thinking at that time. Those research participants who were engaged in a focused activity rather than in a "mind-wandering" activity appeared to have the highest self-reported happiness.

Gathering this type of streaming data, however, can lead to data overload, which may begin to impact the researcher's ability to reflect on the meaning contained in such vast amounts of data and also make it hard to determine what data are important, not to mention the ethical issues that arise from the gathering of such data.

Ethical Issues and New Technologies

Emergent technologies trouble the waters between public and private information. New technologies also impact ethics practices in social research (see Collste, 2011; Winston & Edelbach, 2009). The possibilities for gathering a range of very personal research data via the Internet present some difficult ethical issues about which researchers also need to reflect. For example, social networking sites such as Facebook contain personal online information that is available to the general public. When a participant gives his or her "informed consent" to participate in a study, that person may have already been selected for the study based on personal information researchers acquired online. Is it ethical to collect and analyze this "public" but personal data?

What is clear even from this brief discussion is that new technologies will continue to challenge the researcher's practice of reflexivity across the research process. As discussed throughout this chapter, feminist researchers are attentive to the ways in which power influences the research process, and online communications present many challenges for the reflexive feminist researcher to consider. Issues of confidentiality and informed consent are challenged in the online environment (Collste, 2011; Mann & Stewart, 2000; Winston & Edelbach, 2009), and power relations between researcher and participant (and other participants) become more complex in that environment too. Differences in technological cultural capital can contribute to researcher status and enable a researcher to dominate interactions, complicating the negotiation of power between researcher and participant. Moreover, the ambiguity over public and private space in the virtual research environment can impede the creation of safe spaces conducive to sharing.

Conclusion

Drawing on the feminist research examples and discussions of reflexivity we have presented in this chapter, we end by offering some useful tips to promote holistic reflexive praxis:

- Know your standpoint prior to entering the research project.[11] To what extent do you recognize, examine, and comprehend how your own socioeconomic background and assumptions about the researched affect the type of questions you seek to ask and the questions you choose not to ask? What particular biases do you bring to or impose upon your research? How does your epistemology impact both the types of questions you ask and how you intend to approach the research process? For whom are you doing this research?
- Examine your positionality and role in the field. To what extent do you make visible your own social locations and identities during the research process? How does your positionality shift from site to site, participant to participant, and why?
- Monitor your relationship with participants. To what extent do you interact with participants? How often did you answer a question from the participants or share a piece of your social biography? What is the quality of rapport you have developed between yourself and the participants?
- Listen to your participants. Are you providing an environment in which participants can express their attitudes and feelings freely? Are there silences or hesitations? Is a participant expressing discomfort with the conversation?

Are you attentive to participants' probes for information? Do you provide an environment for participants to engage in reflexivity?
- Listen to yourself. Are you confused or unclear about something the participant said or didn't say? Why? Are you feeling personal discomfort? Why?
- Be attentive to difference. What are the differences that matter, given your research question? Are you making assumptions based on your perceptions of how similar to or different from participants you are? Are you conversing openly with the research participants about that difference? Are you considering political, social, and cultural contexts as you converse and observe? Are you awarding epistemic privilege to any particular group?
- Reflexively interrogate your data. What are your specific analytic and social biases? How do you respond emotionally and intellectually to this data? Are there ways to bring participants into the interpretation of the data? The writing of the report?

Discussion Questions

1. In what ways do your own values and beliefs shape your research? Why is it important to consider your own standpoint as a researcher in the research process?

2. How have feminist scholars engaged with the concept of reflexivity? More specifically, cite three ways in which feminists have engaged with reflexivity.

3. Why is it important to consider the power differentials within the various stages of the social research process? Provide one example of how feminists have engaged with differences in power differentials between the researcher and the researched.

4. What are the various ways in which the feminist practice of reflexivity becomes "holistic"?

Online Resources

Isis International

http://www.isiswomen.org/

This is the website of Isis International, an organization that "advocates for the realisation of women's human rights in the struggle against patriarchal and fundamentalist forces by documenting feminist visions, creating critical communications, and strengthening social movements. Working primarily with women's groups and networks that use communications for women's empowerment, Isis employs feminist analyses, multimedia production, advocacy, networking, and capacity-building strategies."

Sociological Research Online

http://www.socresonline.org.uk/6/4/letherby.html

This article, "Claims and Disclaimers: Knowledge, Reflexivity and Representation in Feminist Research," published by *Sociological Research Online*, is a doctoral student's personal reflections on reflexivity and representation in conducting her feminist sociological doctoral research project.

Relevant Journals

Gender & Society

Reflective Practice: International and Multi-disciplinary Perspectives

Sex Roles

Notes

1. For more information on the history and method of experience sampling, see Conner and Bliss-Moreau (2006).

2. See Guillemin and Gillam (2004) for their important reflections and insights on reflexivity and ethically important moments.

3. The feminist contributions and critiques of positivism are too numerous to mention here, but most notably are Harding (1986, 1991, 1993); Hartsock (1998); Oakley (1998); Reinharz (1992); and Smith (1987).

4. See Harding (1986).

5. See Schutz (1964).

6. We highlight in this chapter some of the most influential writings on the insider/outsider concept in our work: Acker (2000); Collins (1998); Cook and Fonow (1986); Griffith (1998); Naples (1996); Reinharz (1992); and Stanley and Wise (1993).

7. See Schutz (1964).

8. Lisa Dodson developed this method of interpretive focus groups during the many years she has worked with low-income women. See Dodson (1998).

Leah Schmalzbauer utilized this method in her study of survival strategies of poor Honduran transnational families. See Schmalzbauer (2005).

9. There are many examples of innovative writing techniques. Of particular note: Anzaldúa (1987), Behr (1993, 1996), Ellis and Bochner (2000), Lather and Smithies (1997), Richardson (2000), and Wolf (1992).

10. See Beverly (2000) for citations of exemplary forms of testimonios.

11. Kirk and Miller (1986) suggest that, in addition to Type I and Type II errors (false positives and negatives) found in quantitative research, there is another type of error—Type III, which they define as the researcher just asking the *wrong* research question. One important guard against this type of error is for each researcher to be reflexive about her or his own standpoint.

References

Acker, Sandra. (2000). In/out/side: Positioning the researcher in feminist qualitative research. *Resources for Feminist Research Journal, 28*(1/2), 189–208.

Anderson, Margaret. (1998). Studying across difference: Race, class, and gender in qualitative research. In Maxine Baca Zinn, Pierette Hondagneu-Sotelo, & Michael A. Messner (Eds.), *Through the prism of difference: Readings on sex and gender* (pp. 70–85). Boston: Allyn & Bacon.

Anzaldúa, Gloria. (1987). *Borderlands/la Frontera: The new mestiza.* San Francisco: Aunt Lute.

Behr, Ruth. (1993). *Translated woman: Crossing the border with Esperanza's story.* Boston: Beacon Press.

Behr, Ruth. (1996). *The vulnerable observer: Anthropology that breaks your heart.* Boston: Beacon Press.

Beoku-Betts, Josephine. (1994). When black is not enough: Doing field research among Gullah women. *NWSA Journal, 6*(3), 413–433.

Beverly, John. (2000). Testimonio, subalternity, and narrative authority. In Norman K. Denzin & Yvonna S. Lincoln (Eds.), *Handbook of qualitative research* (2nd ed., pp. 555–565). Thousand Oaks, CA: Sage.

Bourdieu, Pierre. (1993). Structures, habitus, practices. In Charles Lemert (Ed.), *Social theory: The multicultural and classical readings* (pp. 434–440). Boulder, CO: Westview Press.

Campbell, Marie, & Manicom, Ann. (Eds.). (1995). *Knowledge, experience, and ruling relations: Studies in the social organization of knowledge.* Toronto, ON: University of Toronto Press.

Charmaz, Kathy. (2000). Grounded theory: Objectivist and constructivist methods. In Norman K. Denzin & Yvonna S. Lincoln (Eds.), *Handbook of qualitative research* (pp. 217–285). Thousand Oaks, CA: Sage.

Clifford, James, & Marcus, George E. (Eds.). (1986). *Writing culture: The poetics and politics of ethnography.* Berkeley: University of California Press.

Coffey, Amanda. (1999). *The ethnographic self: Fieldwork and the representation of identity.* Thousand Oaks, CA: Sage.

Collins, Patricia Hill. (1998). *Fighting words: Black women and the search for justice.* Minneapolis: University of Minnesota Press.

Collins, Patricia Hill. (2000). *Black feminist thought* (2nd ed.). New York: Routledge.

Collste, Göran. (2011). Under my skin: The ethics of ambient computing for personal health monitoring. In Sharlene Nagy Hesse-Biber (Ed.), *The handbook of emergent technologies in social research* (pp. 89–110). New York: Oxford University Press.

Conner, Tamlin, & Bliss-Moreau, Eliza. (2006). Sampling human experience in naturalistic settings. In Sharlene Nagy Hesse-Biber & Patricia Leavy (Eds.), *Emergent methods in social research* (pp. 109–129). Thousand Oaks, CA: Sage.

Cook, Judith, & Fonow, Margaret. (1986). Knowledge and women's interests. *Sociological Inquiry, 56*(4), 2–29.

Cooper, Anna Julia. (1892). *A voice from the south by a black woman from the south.* Xenia, OH: Aldine.

Cope, Meghan, & Elwood, Sarah. (2009). *Qualitative GIS: A mixed methods approach.* London: Sage.

de Beauvoir, Simone. (1953). *The second sex.* New York: Knopf.

Denzin, Norman K., & Lincoln, Yvonna S. (2000). Introduction: Entering the field of qualitative research. In Norman K. Denzin & Yvonna S. Lincoln (Eds.), *Handbook of qualitative research* (pp. 1–17). Thousand Oaks, CA: Sage.

DeVault, Marjorie. (1990). Talking and listening from women's standpoint. *Social Problems, 37*(1), 96–116.

DeVault, Marjorie, & McCoy, Lisa. (2000). Institutional ethnography: Using interviews to investigate ruling relations. In Jaber F. Gubrium & James A. Holstein (Eds.), *Handbook of interview research: Context and method* (pp. 751–776). Thousand Oaks, CA: Sage.

Dicks, Bella, & Mason, Bruce. (2011). Clickable data: Hypermedia and social research. In Sharlene Nagy Hesse-Biber (Ed.), *The handbook of emergent technologies in social research* (pp. 133–157). New York: Oxford University Press.

Dodson, Lisa. (1998). *Don't call us out of name: The untold lives of women and girls in poor America.* Boston: Beacon Press.

Dodson, Lisa, & Schmalzbauer, Leah. (2005). Poor mothers and habits of hiding: Participatory methods in poverty research. *Journal of Marriage and Family, 67*, 949–959.

Dodson, Lisa, Schmalzbauer, Leah, & Piatelli, Deborah. (2006). Behind the scenes: A conversation about interpretive focus groups. In Sharlene Nagy Hesse-Biber & Patricia L. Leavy (Eds.), *Feminist research practice: A primer* (pp. 174–182). Thousand Oaks, CA: Sage.

Dodson, Lisa, Schmalzbauer, Leah, & Piatelli, Deborah. (2007). Researching inequality through interpretive collaborations: Shifting power and the unspoken contract. *Qualitative Inquiry, 13*(6), 808–820.

Dunbar, Christopher J., Rodriguez, Dalia, & Parker, Laurence. (2000). Race, subjectivity, and the interview process. In Jaber F. Gubrium & James A. Holstein (Eds.), *Handbook of interview research: Context and method* (pp. 279–298). Thousand Oaks, CA: Sage.

Eagle, Nathan. (2011). Mobile phones as sensors for social research. In Sharlene Nagy Hesse-Biber (Ed.), *The handbook of emergent technologies in social research* (pp. 492–521). New York: Oxford University Press.

Edwards, Rosalind. (1990). Connecting methods and epistemology: A white woman interviewing black women. *Women's Studies International Forum, 13*(5), 477–490.

Eichler, Margrit. (1997). Feminist methodology. *Current Sociology, 45*(2), 9–36.

Ellis, Carolyn, & Bochner, Arthur. (2000). Autoethnography, personal narrative, reflexivity: Researcher as subject. In Norman K. Denzin & Yvonna S. Lincoln (Eds.), *Handbook of qualitative research* (2nd ed., pp. 733–768). Thousand Oaks, CA: Sage.

Everett, Jeffery. (2002). Organizational research and the praxeology of Pierre Bourdieu. *Organizational Research Methods, 5*(1), 56–80.

Fine, Michelle. (1998). Working the hyphens: Reinventing self and other in qualitative research. In Norman K. Denzin & Yvonna S. Lincoln (Eds.), *The landscape of qualitative research* (pp. 70–82). Thousand Oaks, CA: Sage.

Gallagher, Charles A. (2000). White like me? Methods, meaning, and manipulation in the field of white studies. In France Winddance Twine & Jonathan W. Warren (Eds.), *Racing research, researching race: Methodological dilemmas in critical race studies* (pp. 67–92). New York: NYU Press.

Gallagher, Charles A. (2008). The end of racism as the new doxa: New strategies for researching race. In Tukufu Zuberi & Eduardo Bonilla-Silva (Eds.), *White logic, white methods: Racism and methodology* (pp. 163–178). Lanham, MD: Rowman & Littlefield.

Gordon, Deborah. (1988). Writing culture, writing feminism: The poetics and politics of experimental ethnography. *Inscriptions, 3/4,* 7–24.

Gorelick, Sherry. (1991). Contradictions of feminist methodology. *Gender & Society, 5*(4), 459–477.

Griffith, Alison I. (1998). Insider/outsider: Epistemological privilege and mothering work. *Human Studies, 21,* 361–376.

Guba, Egon, & Lincoln, Yvonna S. (2000). Competing paradigms in qualitative research. In Norman K. Denzin & Yvonna S. Lincoln (Eds.), *Handbook of qualitative research* (pp. 105–117). Thousand Oaks, CA: Sage.

Guillemin, Marilys, & Gillam, Lynn. (2004). Ethics, reflexivity, and "ethically important moments" in research. *Qualitative Inquiry, 10*(2), 261–280.

Haraway, Donna. (1988). Situated knowledges: The science question in feminism and the privilege of partial perspective. *Feminist Studies, 14*(3), 575–599.

Harding, Sandra. (1986). *The science question in feminism.* Ithaca, NY: Cornell University Press.

Harding, Sandra. (1991). *Whose science? Whose knowledge? Thinking from women's lives.* Ithaca, NY: Cornell University Press.

Harding, Sandra. (1992). After the neutrality ideal: Science, politics, and "strong objectivity." *Social Research, 59*(3), 567–587.

Harding, Sandra. (1993). Rethinking standpoint epistemology: What is strong objectivity? In Linda Alcoff & Elizabeth Potter (Eds.), *Feminist epistemologies* (pp. 49–81). New York: Routledge.

Hartsock, Nancy. (1993). Foucault on power: A theory for women. In Charles Lemert (Ed.), *Social theory: The multicultural and classic readings* (pp. 545–554). Boulder, CO: Westview Press.

Hartsock, Nancy. (1998). *The feminist standpoint revisited.* Boulder, CO: Westview Press.

Hertz, Rosanna. (1996). Introduction: Ethics, reflexivity, and voice. *Qualitative Sociology, 19*(1), 3–9.

Hesse-Biber, Sharlene Nagy, & Leavy, Patricia. (Eds.). (2008). *The handbook of emergent methods.* New York: Guilford Press.

hooks, bell. (1984). *Feminist theory: From margin to center.* Boston: South End Press.

Horrigan, John. (2007, February 25). Wireless Internet access. *Pew Internet and American life project.* Retrieved July 1, 2011, from http://www.pewinternet.org/Reports/2007/Wireless-Internet-Access/Data-Memo.aspx

Internet World Statistics. (2010). *United States of America Internet usage and broadband usage report.* Retrieved July 1, 2011, from http://www.internetworldstats.com/am/us.htm

James, Nalita, & Busher, Hugh. (2010). *Online interviewing.* London: Sage.

Killingsworth, Matthew A., & Gilbert, Daniel T. (2010, November 12). A wandering mind is an unhappy mind. *Science, 330,* 932.

Kirk, Jerome, & Miller, Marc L. (1986). *Reliability and validity in qualitative research.* Newbury Park, CA: Sage.

Kirsch, Gesa. (1999). *Ethical dilemmas in feminist research: The politics of location, interpretation, and publication.* Albany: State University of New York Press.

Kondo, Dorinne K. (1990). *Crafting selves: Power, gender, and discourses of identity in a Japanese workplace.* Chicago, IL: University of Chicago Press.

Kozinets, Robert V. (2010). *Netnography: Doing ethnographic research online.* London: Sage.

Lal, Jayati. (1996). Situating locations: The politics of self, identity, and other in living and writing the text. In Diane Wolf (Ed.), *Feminist dilemmas in fieldwork* (pp. 185–214). Boulder, CO: Westview.

Lather, Peggy, & Smithies, Chris. (1997). *Troubling the angels: Women living with HIV/AIDS.* Boulder, CO: Westview.

Lemert, Charles, & Bahn, Esme. (Eds.). (1998). *The voice of Anna Julia Cooper*. Baltimore: Rowman and Littlefield.

Lykes, M. Brinton. (1997). Activist participatory research among the Maya of Guatemala: Constructing meanings from situated knowledge. *Journal of Social Issues, 53*(4), 725–746.

Maguire, Patricia. (1987). *Doing participatory research*. Amherst: University of Massachusetts.

Mann, Chris, & Stewart, Fiona. (2000). *Internet communication and qualitative research: A handbook for researching online*. Thousand Oaks, CA: Sage.

Mann, Susan A., & Kelley, Lori. (1997). Standing at the crossroads of modernist thought: Collins, Smith, and the new feminist epistemologies. *Gender & Society, 11*(4), 391–408.

Marcus, George E. (1994). What comes (just) after "post"? The case of ethnography. In Norman K. Denzin & Yvonna S. Lincoln (Eds.), *Handbook of qualitative research* (pp. 563–574). Thousand Oaks, CA: Sage.

Marcus, George E., & Fischer, Michael M. J. (Eds.). (1999). *Anthropology as cultural critique* (2nd ed.). Chicago: The University of Chicago Press.

Martineau, Harriet. (1836/1837). *Society in America*. New York: Saunders and Otley.

Marx, Marcia. (2000). Invisibility, interviewing, and power. *Resources for Feminist Research, 28*(3/4), 131–155.

Mascia-Lees, Frances, Sharpe, Patricia, & Cohen, Colleen Ballerino. (1989). The postmodernist turn in anthropology: Cautions from a feminist perspective. *Signs: Journal of Women in Culture and Society, 15*(1), 7–33.

Mertens, Donna M. (2003). Mixed methods and the politics of human research: The transformative-emancipatory perspective. In Abbas Tashakkori & Charles Teddlie (Eds.), *Handbook of mixed methods* (pp. 135–164). Thousand Oaks, CA: Sage.

Merton, Robert. (1972). Insiders and outsiders: A chapter in the sociology of knowledge. *American Journal of Sociology, 78*(1), 9–47.

Naples, Nancy A. (1996). The outsider phenomenon. In Carolyn D. Smith & William Kornblum (Eds.), *In the field: Readings of the field research experience* (pp. 139–159). Westport, CT: Praeger.

Naples, Nancy A. (2003). *Feminism and method: Ethnography, discourse analysis, and activist research*. New York: Routledge.

Oakley, A. (1998). Gender, methodology and people's way of knowing: Some problems with feminism and the paradigm debate in social science. *Sociology, 32*(4), 707–731.

Olesen, Virginia. (1998). Feminisms and models of qualitative research. In Norman K. Denzin & Yvonna S. Lincoln (Eds.), *The landscape of qualitative research: Theories and issues* (pp. 300–332). Thousand Oaks, CA: Sage.

Parameswaran, Radhika. (2001). Feminist media ethnography in India: Exploring power, gender, and culture in the field. *Qualitative Inquiry, 7*(1), 69–103.

Patai, Daphne, & Gluck, Sherna B. (Eds.). (1991). *Women's words: The feminist practice of oral history*. New York: Routledge.

Perkins-Gilman, Charlotte. (1898). *Women and economics*. Boston: Small and Maynard.

Piatelli, Deborah. (2009). *Stories of inclusion? Power, privilege, and difference in a peace and justice network*. Lanham, MD: Lexington Books.

Pini, Barbara. (2004). On being a nice country girl and an academic feminist: Using reflexivity in rural social research. *Journal of Rural Studies, 20*(2), 169–179.

Ralston, Helen. (2001). Being a white Australian-Canadian feminist doing research with South Asian women of color in the diaspora: Crossing borders and boundaries, creating spaces. *Advances in Gender Research, 5*, 213–231.

Reason, Peter. (1998). Three approaches to participative inquiry. In Norman K. Denzin & Yvonne S. Lincoln (Eds.), *Strategies of qualitative inquiry* (pp. 261–291). Thousand Oaks, CA: Sage.

Reinharz, Shulamit. (1992). *Feminist methods in social research*. New York: Oxford University Press.

Rhodes, P. J. (1994). Race-of-interviewer effects in qualitative research. *Sociology, 28*(2), 547–558.

Riach, Kathleen. (2009). Exploring participant-centred reflexivity in the research interview. *Sociology, 43*(2), 356–370.

Richardson, Laurel. (2000). Writing a method of inquiry. In Norman K. Denzin & Yvonna S. Lincoln (Eds.). *Handbook of qualitative research* (2nd ed., pp. 923–948). Thousand Oaks, CA: Sage.

Riessman, Catherine. (1987). When gender is not enough: Women interviewing women. *Gender & Society, 1*(2), 172–207.

Riessman, Catherine. (1993). *Narrative analysis*. Thousand Oaks, CA: Sage.

Robinson, Laura, & Schulz, Jeremy. (2011). New field-sites, new methods: New ethnographic opportunities. Sharlene Nagy Hesse-Biber (Ed.), *The handbook of emergent technologies in social research* (pp. 190–198). New York: Oxford University Press.

Schmalzbauer, Leah. (2005). *Striving and surviving: A daily life analysis of Honduran transnational families*. New York: Routledge.

Schutz, Alfred. (1964). *Collected papers* (Arvid Brodersen, Ed.). The Hague The Netherlands: Martinus Nijhoff.

Scott, James C. (1990). *Domination and the arts of resistance: Hidden transcripts*. New Haven, CT: Yale University Press.

Smith, Dorothy. (1987). *The everyday world as problematic: A feminist sociology*. Boston: Northeastern University Press.

Smith, Dorothy. (2002). Institutional ethnography. In Tim May (Ed.), *Qualitative methods in action* (pp. 17–52). Thousand Oaks, CA: Sage.

Smith, Dorothy. (2007). Institutional ethnography: From a sociology for women to a sociology for people. In Sharlene Nagy Hesse-Biber (Ed.), *Handbook of feminist research: Theory and praxis* (pp. 409–416). Thousand Oaks, CA: Sage.

Smith, Jonathan A. (2006). Towards reflexive practice: Engaging participants as co-researchers or co-analysts in psychological inquiry. *Journal of Community & Applied Social Psychology, 4*(4), 253–260.

Sonn, Christopher C. (2008). Educating for anti-racism: Producing and reproducing race and power in a university classroom. *Race, Ethnicity, and Education, 11*(2), 155–166.

Spivak, Gayatri Chakravorty. (1988). Can the subaltern speak? In Cary Nelson & Lawrence Grossberg (Eds.), *Marxism and the interpretation of culture* (pp. 271–313). Urbana: University of Illinois Press.

Stacey, Judith. (1991). Can there be a feminist ethnography? In Daphne Patai & Sherna B. Gluck (Eds.), *Women's words: The feminist practice of oral history* (pp. 111–120). New York: Routledge.

Stage, Christina W., & Mattson, Marifran. (2003). Ethnographic interviewing as contextualized conversation. In Robin Patric Clair (Ed.), *Expressions of ethnography: Novel approaches to qualitative methods* (pp. 97–105). Albany: State University of New York Press.

Stanley, Liz. (1990). Moments of writing: Is there a feminist auto/biography? *Gender and History, 2,* 58–67.

Stanley, Liz, & Wise, Sue. (1993). *Breaking out again: Feminist ontology and epistemology*. New York: Routledge.

Stringer, Ernest. (1996). *Action research: A handbook for practitioners*. Thousand Oaks, CA: Sage.

Tedlock, Barbara. (2000). Ethnography and ethnographic representation. In Norman K. Denzin & Yvonna S. Lincoln (Eds.), *Handbook of qualitative research* (2nd ed., pp. 445–487). Thousand Oaks, CA: Sage.

Temple, Bogusia. (1997). Watch your tongue: Issues in translation and cross-cultural research. *Sociology, 31*(3), 607–618.

Trinh, T. Minh-ha. (1991). *Framer framed*. New York: Routledge.

Tristan, Flora. (2007). *The workers' union* (Beverly Livingston, Trans.). Urbana: University of Illinois Press. (Original work published 1844)

Van Maanen, John. (1988). *Tales of the field: On writing ethnography*. Chicago: The University of Chicago Press.

Visser, Albertine, & Mulder, Ingrid. (2011). Emergent technologies for assessing social feelings and experiences. In Sharlene Nagy Hesse-Biber (Ed.), *The handbook of emergent technologies in social research* (pp. 369–393). New York: Oxford University Press.

Warren, Carol A. B. (2000). Writing the other, inscribing the self. *Qualitative Sociology, 23*(2), 183–199.

Wasserfall, Rahel R. (1993). Reflexivity, feminism, and difference. *Qualitative Sociology, 16*(1), 23–41.

Weber, Max. (1921). *Economy and society*. Totowa, NJ: Bedminster Press.

Winston, Morton E., & Edelbach, Ralph D. (Eds.). (2009). *Society, ethics, and technology* (4th ed.). Belmont, CA: Thompson.

Wolf, Diane. (1996). Situating feminist dilemmas in fieldwork. In Diane L. Wolf (Ed.), *Feminist dilemmas in fieldwork* (pp. 1–55). Boulder, CO: Westview.

Wolf, Margery. (1992). *A thrice-told tale: Feminism, postmoderism, and ethnographic responsibility*. Stanford, CA: Stanford University Press.

28

FEMINIST RESEARCH ETHICS

JUDITH PREISSLE AND YURI HAN

Helen was dying of breast cancer. Facing her own mortality uncertainly, she struggled with how to help her young children through this experience. A few miles away, a research ethics board hesitated about approving a study of the relationship between dying mothers and young children. Approaching people at what some board members thought to be a most vulnerable time to request consent to study them and their family seemed crass. How could the risk of intrusion and the compromise of privacy possibly balance any benefit from what might be learned? Other board members objected to what seemed to be a paternalistic assumption that these mothers could not make their own competent decisions—that their presumed vulnerable state would open them to coercion to comply with researcher requests.

Ethics and moral theory are about making judgments, especially judgments informed by some explicit framework. Ethics, or the judgment of actions and experiences as good or bad by some criteria, is a universal human phenomenon. All societies designate some activities as right, desirable, or even prescribed while others are wrong, undesirable, and proscribed (see Singer, 1991, for a compendium of ethical principles from around the world). These judgments are commonly based on values, what people see

as important and unimportant; the values that undergird a society or social group compose part of the group's folk philosophy (Kilby, 1993). Philosophers vary in whether they distinguish ethics, morality, and moral theory. When they do, they consider morality to be the specific proscriptions and prescriptions shared as conventions by a group of people, for example, the directive to do no harm. Doing harm is immoral and avoiding harm is moral. Moral theories, on the other hand, are the more general principles that underlie such directives. The directive to do no harm has been considered part of a consequentialist or utilitarian moral theory where the anticipated results of a decision are central to a judgment of whether the decision is good or bad. Ethics, finally, is the study of and reflection on our moralities and moral theories (Hinman, 2003).

Moral choices and ethical decision making in all groups are challenging because, in any given situation, multiple values are relevant, and decisions must be based on priorities among values. In his introduction to ethics for the U.S. public, Kidder (1995) comments that most people readily distinguish the good choice from the bad choice, even when they opt for the bad choice. What makes decision making difficult is when people are faced with selecting among competing goods or choosing which of several bad choices are the least aversive. Even people who share the same moral framework may disagree about which standard should have priority in any given situation. Ethics in our global world and multicultural societies is further complicated by variations in sets of values and thus in the content of the standards of right and wrong people use and assume. Social scientists disagree about whether any particular standard can be considered universal, but they do agree that all human groups have standards, and many believe that it is these sets of competing standards that cause dissension and conflict among groups.

Feminism and the varieties of feminisms themselves constitute moral and ethical frameworks because they each represent value positions on the experiences and places of women around the world. We agree with the pragmatist feminist Charlene Haddock Seigfried (1996) that all feminisms seek to improve the lot of women. Making gender a basic category of analysis, of course, also revalues women in relationship to men and leads to interrogating the categories of sex and gender themselves (Butler, 1990). As Tong (1998) emphasizes, feminisms vary in how women's revaluation, empowerment, and emancipation ought to be formulated, accomplished, and assessed. Liberal feminists are said to advocate social reform of existing social arrangements so that social organizations operate more justly and so that all individuals' rights are respected (see Grimshaw, 1991, for the centrality of justice and individual rights to the ethics of some 19th-century feminists). Socialist, communitarian, and Marxist feminists advocate restructuring society and the social relationships within it. Here, a more dialogic and communal ethic is the priority, with a goal of ensuring all members of a group access to adequate resources and equitable decision making while affirming human dignity and solidarity (for elaborations, see Benhabib, 1992; Denzin, 1997). Thus, different feminisms assume a variety of ethical-moral positions, based on differing ethical-moral premises.

In this chapter, we explore the development of feminist research ethics over the past several decades in the context of two influences: the increasing worldwide attention to responsible conduct of research and feminist ethics more generally. Feminist ethics developed in part as an explicit challenge to conventional patterns of Western epistemology and ethics and thus has its roots in two feminist projects. The first is the 20th-century work by psychologists such as Carol Gilligan and philosophers such as Nel Noddings who have formulated an *ethic of care* believed to better characterize the moral decision making of females than the modernist variety of Western moral theories centered in abstract principles or *ethics of principle.* The *ethics of care* project posits differences between how men and women conceptualize and practice ethics and morality, and we summarize this subsequently.

The second feminist project, discussed more fully in other chapters in this handbook and treated only tangentially here, is work by feminist social theorists and philosophers who have contributed to the efforts of post-structuralists, postcolonialists, and postmodernists to challenge the epistemological assumptions of modern scientific practice. Calling into question presuppositions about the nature of human beings, about the efficacy of positivist and postpositivist research models, and about the relationship of knower to known, these feminist thinkers propose alternative ways to define, create, and assess human knowledge. Among these alternatives are more tightly connecting knowledge with who makes it and how they do so. In response to challenges to the morally neutral and epistemologically objective presuppositions of conventional scientific scholarship, feminists and others have been exploring what it means to acknowledge that research and the creation of knowledge are always done by individuals with their particular perspectives and worldviews (see Bordo, 1987; Nagel, 1986). Whether implicitly or explicitly, we select topics to study because we believe pursuing them is a good thing to do, we conduct ourselves as scholars with some ideas of integrity, we interact with research participants according to some model of how to treat others decently, and the results of our studies are reviewed according to standards of various areas. Taking this as our premise, we begin this chapter by sharing who we are and how we have come to speak of feminist research ethics.

How Can They Judge?

With apologies to Lorrain Code (1991) for adapting the title of her cogent consideration of feminist epistemology, we offer here our own positions in the array of feminisms and the approach we took in developing a chapter on ethics in feminist research. Because positions are highly individual, we two authors offer our positions individually.

Jude's Positioning

Where do I, Jude Preissle, position myself as a feminist? At times I must admit to an eclectic feminism because my positioning has varied by time, place, circumstances, and people. Having grown up in a conventional 1950s, upwardly mobile, European American family, I have lived an adulthood that some of those family members still consider unconventional: 45 years a teacher, 35 years an academic, childless, divorced twice, and married thrice. In my role as an educational anthropologist, I aspire to be a multicultural and global feminist. In my role as a qualitative research methodologist, this feminism blends with critical and postmodern perspectives and philosophical pragmatism. Educated as a progressive teacher in the 1960s and radicalized by women's liberation in the 1970s, I view change and continuity as the result of the dynamic dialectic among individuals in their ongoing and ever-changing groups, communities, and collectivities.

How does any of this qualify me to comment on feminist research ethics and to make feminist ethical judgments? My preparation as a scholar was in educational research from an anthropological and ethnographic perspective. I have been conducting and teaching qualitative research from a feminist perspective—sometimes explicit and other times tacit—for 35 years. For the past 20 of those 35 years, I have served on my university's institutional review board, the human subjects research review committee for U.S. universities, the same board that decided to approve the study of dying mothers and their young children. At the start of the new century, I won a year's support to study philosophy, working principally with a feminist ethicist and an epistemologist with feminist leanings. Studying the topic of feminist research ethics has provided me an opportunity to synthesize several literatures: feminist theory, feminist social research, feminist research methods, qualitative research methods and design at its many intersections with feminism, general research ethics, feminist ethics within the general area of ethics, and moral theory from philosophy. The material that we cite throughout the chapter reflects both general reading in these areas and the results of specific searches on feminist research ethics.

Finally, I offer some comments about what I think I have learned about ethics over the years. First, ethics at best are frameworks that guide decision making. They are not rules, regulations, or laws. Even ethicists who claim absolute values struggle with how those values apply in any given situation. What makes ethical decisions difficult is that several competing "goods" may be at stake or several simultaneous "bads" are to be avoided. I may arrive at an adequate answer, but it is rarely ideal. I use good and bad here not as a mere dichotomy but as representing all the states of well-being and all the varieties of harm people experience. Some states may be considered dichotomous such as alive (good) and dead (bad), but recent medical advances have led to situations where parts of bodies are functioning or alive and other parts are not functioning: People are now considered sometimes "brain dead" despite their strong and beating hearts. Goods and bads then are not merely dichotomous; they do not always lay out neatly on a continuum. They are qualities, sometimes with quantitative dimensions, that represent what we aspire to and what we avoid in our conduct with others. Finally, ethicists agree that moral decisions involve choosing the good and avoiding the bad, but how goods and bads are formulated depends on the moral theory being used and the meta-ethical assumptions underlying the theory.

Second, a review of a research plan for protection of human participants provides only input from other researchers on obvious problematic issues; it does not guarantee that the researcher will have no further ethical challenges. Third, feminist values of whatever kind provide us with ethical frameworks for our decision making, but we must still prioritize those values and decide how they are at play in any given situation. In the 21st century, those situations are complex, layered, and always global, as my coauthor exemplifies.

Yuri's Positioning

What is my positionality? I am a single Korean woman in her mid-30s, the oldest daughter in my family, with a mother and a sister. With over 10 years of work experience in Korea, I am currently pursuing a doctoral degree in the United States. Others, especially Koreans, often assume that I am a strong-willed woman who feels comfortable in going her own way. In fact, as I was growing up, I tried not to stand out. I believed that staying in the mainstream would guarantee happiness, but then I started to ask, "Why do I feel like I am being pushed by invisible others?" I constantly found myself defending my sometimes unconventional decisions, such as postponing marriage for graduate study abroad, and other choices that went against what the majority of Koreans consider normal.

I try to find answers for my life from my scholarship. Counseling psychology helps me to see the inner self; qualitative research broadens my perspectives from the self to the society where I belong; adult learning confirms that I should continue learning throughout my life to develop my potential; and feminist care ethics teaches me the importance of maintaining genuine, healthy relationships based on empathy and respect for others. Most of all, I try to be mindful of my responsibility as a researcher to go beyond academics and to follow feminist research ethics as a valuable guide in times of complexity and moral confusion.

Our Summary

As colleagues, we have compared and contrasted the experiences of women in different societies around the globe. Most recently, we examined how being female affects immigrant education in the United States and Korea (Preissle & Han, 2009). In the rest of this chapter, we present the challenges other feminist scholars have faced in considering what is good and bad, what is right and wrong in pursuit of life and of research on the human experience.

As we have emphasized previously, although ethicists disagree heatedly on what constitutes good and bad and right and wrong and how they should be conceptualized, they do agree that these qualities define ethical and moral decision making. Caputo (1993), in his rejection of simplistic moral conventions, nevertheless formulates what is desirable in human conduct:

> We are all children of the same dark night, inhabited by the same demons, haunted by the same specters. We are all equally beset by the inscrutability of what happens, and none of us, philosophers or analysts, have a hotline which feeds us special information about [what] is behind what is happening. . . . What we have to offer one another is our voice, our healing hand, our laughter, ourselves. . . . That is the feminine operation. It is not a question of finding an answer to the night of truth but of sitting up with one another through the night, of dividing the abyss in half in a companionship that is its own meaning. (pp. 243, 244)

FEMINISM AND ETHICS

Feminism as it developed in the Western world was grounded in the moral and ethical theories of the European Enlightenment. Women defended their demands for better treatment in society on the basis of several ethical principles: Because of their common humanity with men, women are entitled to the same fundamental *rights;* these rights depend on a system of equitable *justice;* women are thus owed the same respect and *duty* as men; women must also be included in considering *consequences,* or the good and ill, of actions taken. Rights, justice, duty, and consequences are principles 19th- and 20th-century feminists depended on in their fights for equity in education, in citizenship, in legal status, and in economic position. They remain central to feminist moral and ethical decision making today, and they have become the foundation of the research ethics framing much scholarly practice worldwide.

What feminist scholars have added to what has come to be called principle-based ethics is a concern for human relationships in making moral decisions (Tong, 1993). What is good and bad or right and wrong is more than conformation to principles. Such decisions are social and take place in a specific time and place among particular individuals who connect to one another in some relationship. Two scholars, Carol Gilligan and Nel Noddings, epitomize the challenge of 20th-century feminism to modernism's principle-based frameworks of moral theory.

In her 1982 text, the psychologist Gilligan challenged the model of moral development, organized around ascending levels of abstract principles, advocated by her mentor Lawrence Kohlberg (1981; Colby & Kohlberg, 1987). She insisted that women's most sophisticated moral decision making was based on the value for relationship, not the value for principle. Contingencies such as gender challenge the possibility of universality in human behavior and thus may undermine expectations for certainty and predictability in human activity. Gilligan concludes that balancing rights and duties is the challenge for all adults, male and female, but that men and women formulate these values and how to prioritize them differently. Individuals learn that the ideals of care and fairness can never be achieved fully for everyone in any particular decision, but that care, responsibility, fairness, and rights all enter the mix when autonomous choices are to be made.

Gilligan argued against privileging the abstract over the concrete, the principle over relationship, the absolute over the relative, the universal over the particular, the objective over the subjective, and the cognitive over the affective. She discussed real people in their material worlds, making decisions by trying to achieve multiple values and seeking wise choices for satisfying lives. These decisions undermined such assumed binaries as objective and subjective or even absolute and relative and reveal them more as ideal, if contradictory, states to which we aspire but which we never reach. Such challenges to philosophical premises embedded in Gilligan's work were approached more directly by philosopher Nel Noddings (1984, 2003).

The feminine approach to ethics Noddings endorses is rooted in the relationship of caring and being cared for. Although caring is a feeling accessible to all, judgments based on caring are particular to a given situation and may not be applicable to other situations where the

particulars are different. Noddings, however, rejects the binary of objectivity versus relativism by noting how both may operate in any given circumstances. Likewise, she says that she depends on intuitionism and emotivism as well as rationality to build her case for the ethic of caring—an eclectic mix that refuses only absolutism. Caring, according to Noddings, is a commitment to the development of another. An ethic of care begins with what Noddings believes is common to all humans, "a longing for goodness" (Noddings, 1984, p. 27). It relies on the capacity for empathy, receptiveness to the experience of another, requiring both affective and cognitive capacities.

Thus, both Noddings and Gilligan shift the focus of ethics from principles and argumentation to relationships and exploration of particulars. Neither gives up principles and arguments because consideration of both is necessary for deciding what is in the best interest of those in the relationship and for weighing the conditions and particulars that contribute to competing priorities. The traditions of principle-based, Western ethical thought are present in the feminist approach to ethics exemplified by these two scholars, but they are framed differently. These traditions contribute to alternative ways of formulating what is positive in a relationship, rather than as standards to emulate in decision making. Similar to the epistemological contributions of such philosophers as Bordo (1987) and Code (1991), Noddings's philosophical assumptions are inclusive and multidimensional, resisting such binaries as objective and subjective, absolute and relativistic, for a more faceted consideration of what is at play in the assumptions about how we experience the world and develop knowledge that underlie how we make ethical choices (see the chapters in Part I). Noddings's work is grounded in the existentialist emphasis on relationships (Noddings, 2002) and in the philosophical pragmatists' concerns with purpose and relationships between means and ends (Noddings, 1995). She supports truth while rejecting Truth. She believes that rationality and logic should be informed by emotions.

Noddings and Gilligan together offer a feminist ethic based in relationship that challenges the domination of ethical thought and moral theory by the principles of rights, justice, consequences, and such. Both scholars recognize the contributions of constructs such as rights and justice to improving the well-being of women and girls in some parts of the world, but both insist that these are insufficient for understanding how most women and girls make their own moral decisions. Moral and ethical decisions are not merely rational acts. They are grounded in human emotions and occur in the context of human relationships. Noddings and Gilligan have been criticized by some for essentialist assumptions that reduce human behavior to the unchangeable determinism of genetic sex typing: Women depend on an ethics of relationship and men on an ethics of principle (cf. Fuss, 1989, for an antiessentialist argument on the positive contributions of essentialism to feminist thought). However, both scholars argue that patterns of difference need not mean mutually exclusive thinking and action; both also emphasize the complicated and socially embedded nature of moral decision making (cf., however, Lloyd's [1996] challenge to the dichotomy underlying the separation of thought from emotion, of reason from intuition, in both conventional ethics and relational ethics). Their formulations of an ethic of care have since been refined and elaborated by others (e.g., Brabeck, 1989).

But how does their thinking contribute to feminist *research* ethics? To address this question, we first summarize the development of a tradition of ethics for research practice. Our focus on the United States is intended as one case among the cases worldwide of concerns for ethical research practice, not as the only way societies and scholars have developed research ethics. We argue later that the principled orientation to research ethics as it has developed in the United States in the past quarter century has been challenged and, in some cases, has been reformulated by feminist ethics—by the concern with relationship, particularity, constraint, and inclusion.

RESEARCH ETHICS IN THE UNITED STATES

Throughout the 20th century, a collection of established status hierarchies was challenged, and in many cases the authority of these structures

was overturned. Political colonialism was dismantled; ethnic and racial civil rights movements around the world won civil liberties and political participation for many; and various worldwide women's movements challenged and even overturned patriarchal structures. In Western societies, one of the hierarchies so challenged was the subject-researcher relationship. An ethic of authority, where researchers decided what was best for those they studied, has been replaced by a participatory ethic, where researchers' plans are scrutinized by colleagues before being reviewed by potential participants, who are expected to make their own free and informed decisions about consenting to the research.

Consequently, most discussions of ethics in social science and professional research focus on who is being studied—the human subjects, participants, or coresearchers. How people are sought, studied, and recompensed for research studies became such a crucial ethical issue in the 20th century that nations such as the United States developed federal guidelines regulating government-funded research on human beings. The relationship between the studied and the studier, between the inquirer and those inquired about, is a defining attribute of research in the human, social, and professional sciences, but it has been abstract principle rather than caring that frames most conventional thought about this relationship (e.g., National Research Council, 2003). In this section, we address the ethical problems and controversies that ongoing human relationships pose, but we add to this the ethical implications of formulating research goals and of representing those studied in research reports. Of course, goals, relationships, and representations are not mutually exclusive categories of research conduct; they are all interacting facets of the research experience. We separate them for heuristic purposes to ensure that the ethical implications of each are addressed directly.

Ethics of Research Purpose

What is the value of conducting research with human beings? Why should we do this at all? What is right and wrong about studying people? What is intrinsically moral and ethical about inquiry into human endeavors, and how do we make that decision? Why should feminists distract themselves from more important tasks to conduct research? Our argument is that, although different feminists may find different values in their research purposes, all feminists understand that research itself is value laden rather than value neutral and hence are attempting to realize some value through their research.

Some have addressed the question of research value by claiming that knowledge is superior to ignorance—that understanding by itself has intrinsic value. The normative codes adopted by professional research organizations in the United States such as the American Anthropological Association (1998), the American Educational Research Association (2000), the American Psychological Association (2002), and the American Sociological Association (1997) prescribe knowledge generation as good.

Many feminists likewise value knowledge over ignorance. Much of the initial feminist research in the 1970s, for example, focused on differential patterns of experience and behavior among men and women (e.g., Goetz, 1978; Goetz & Grant, 1988) to demonstrate that scholarship on men could not be assumed to represent knowledge about women. Gilligan's (1982) work in women's moral development exemplifies this pattern.

Another justification for research appeals to nature. Our animal physiology and development revolve around sensing the environment, storing and using the information acquired, and learning from this process. We could argue that, as particular kinds of beings, we are predisposed genetically to seek information, to know, to understand. Although this natural law justification frames much of 19th-century feminist demand for equality of treatment (Traina, 1999), most feminist thought is ambivalent about appeals to biology. This may be changing with such feminist challenges to conventional evolutionary theory as that of Gowaty (1997) and Waage and Gowaty (1997), whose genetic research disputes sexist assumptions about biology in the notion of biology as destiny (cf. Haraway, 1989; Harding, 1998).

Most cultures around the world incorporate in their ideology, their belief systems, some presumption of an intrinsic value of knowledge—knowledge is good. Here it is a virtue, and that

becomes its justification. Or because knowledge is taken as inherently good, we can understand it as a duty to pursue. The Western scientific movement (Harmon, 1996) that arose during the European Enlightenment was based on the idea that knowledge is freeing—that it provides an alternative to superstition, to religious orthodoxy, and to feudal authority. This assumption of the intrinsic value of knowledge is deeply embedded in feminist thought. Around the world, women's access to knowledge and to education provides the means to improving their lives (Bloom, 1998; Martin, 1985; Sexton, 1976). DeVault (1999), in her survey of feminism and social research, stresses the value of revealing hitherto invisible knowledge. Throughout her text, she emphasizes not only neglected experiences but also corrective research—studies that provide views of women's experiences that are alternatives to gender-insensitive portrayals.

Nevertheless, cultures often offer the antithesis of knowledge being good as a second attribute. Knowledge can be bad—it can be painful, disillusioning, frightening, and destructive. Fonow and Cook (1991) briefly acknowledge how the intimate and personal nature of what many participants reveal in feminist research may generate knowledge that they and other women might prefer to avoid. This suggests that the intrinsic nature of knowledge may be neither good nor bad—but good or bad according to its content and the purposes to which it is put, in context and in relation to the knower and the known. Knowledge per se then becomes integral to other values, and knowledge as inherently political is a fundamental claim of 20th-century Western feminisms (e.g., Harding, 1987; Stanley & Wise, 1993).

The idea of an intrinsic value of knowledge is related to the view of knowing and the search for truth as constituting a form of worship. In revealing the mystery of life and of others, the knower is affirming a value beyond self—god, nature, community, group, or cosmos. However the value is conceptualized, the search is a way of respecting and honoring god, nature, community, cosmos, or other value beyond self. Among feminists, Mary Daly's (1978) mystical formulation of an essential, natural female beingness provides such an ethical purpose for the inquirer. Daly's work, generally grouped with radical feminism, embraces gender separatism as best promoting the interests of women, solidarity with other women being the value beyond self. Needless to say, this is a position some other feminists find objectionable. Such profound disagreements prompt the question of what values are served by the quest for knowledge because the values beyond self are multiple and sometimes competing or even contradictory.

During the Enlightenment, the religious premise—service to god—became a service to the human community, and the idea was transformed into the consequentialist philosophy of right action being what benefits the community. Here, what made knowing and inquiry good were more or less direct consequences—study is good because it promotes more effective behavior or better solutions to human problems (Reason, 1996). Seeing knowledge that fosters social change and the transformation of societies into better places for women to live, where they may "liberate themselves from oppression" (Tong, 1998, p. 280), is arguably one of the common threads among many feminisms. Bloom and Sawin (2009), for example, emphasize the ethical responsibility of feminist activist researchers to make a positive improvement in the lives of women in poverty. In her characterization of feminist research, Reinharz (1992, p. 240) likewise includes "creation of social change" as one of 10 common themes. However, the question of who benefits from research requires that we also ask who may be harmed by the inquiry and the knowledge produced and what benefits are privileged at the cost of alternative goods. Feminist researchers vary in how they conceptualize harms and benefits and thus how they frame their studies (see Hesse-Biber & Leckenby, 2004, for commonalities among the diversity of feminist social research).

Addressing the cost-benefit issue requires consideration of relationships of power. How power and the distribution of resources are considered among feminists varies, of course. Among Marxist, socialist, and postmodern feminists, concern for power differentials is commonly integrated into research goals (Naples, 2003), often with the intention of disturbing or dismantling conventional arrangements of power, as Fine (1992) has attempted in a number of her research endeavors and as many

standpoint theorists advocate (e.g., Harding, 2004). For ethical research on international relations, Ackerly and True (2008) stress the necessity of noticing and destabilizing the power of epistemologies, especially the power of privileged ones, through which researchers claim the authority of knowledge they produce. The call for research to serve women's interests has come from many feminist scholars, and justifications for feminist research are as diverse as feminism itself, or feminisms themselves. Eichler (1988) proposes nonsexist inquiry, including women's perspectives to achieve a more representative knowledge of humanity, a goal reflecting issues of fairness or justice. However, Du Bois (1983) has sought research that would "address women's lives and experience *in their own terms,* to create theory grounded in the actual experience and language of women" (p. 108), moving the emphasis from creating balance to valuing research on women for its own sake. Here, a concern for justice or fairness, in Eichler's rationale, becomes care for or interest in the particular. In Smith's (1987) formulation, women's positions, experiences, and views of the world are standpoints that lack cultural representation:

> The issue is more than bias. It is more than simply an omission of certain kinds of topics. It involves taking up the standpoint of women as an experience of being, of society, of social and personal process that must be given form and expression in the culture, whether as knowledge, as art, or as literature or political action. (p. 36)

Smith and other standpoint theorists (e.g., Harding, 2004) insist that research is always carried out by someone in a particular position and that understanding the purpose of a study requires understanding the position of the researcher.

Like Du Bois and Smith, Lather (1991, 2007) denies neutrality in research. She calls for "research as praxis," or research to serve the purposes of social justice, for a feminist research to put gender at the center of inquiry. The intent is both to make the gendered facet of human identity clear in any study of humans and to redress implicit and explicit gender inequities. Lather proposes that, to ensure awareness of choice in the values directing any study, feminist researchers must consider and reconsider their own purposes and approaches in the self-reflexive Derridian critique of "a feminist doubled science" (cf. Doucet & Mauthner, 2002). Collins (1990) elaborates the feminist agenda by cautioning that studying gender without concern for race and class merely privileges some experiences of marginality without addressing the complexities of human oppression. Longino (1994) likewise compares racial and gender biases in her discussion of how researchers' assumptions, questions, procedures, and conceptualization of data reflect social values that prejudice the knowledge generated. Roman and Apple (1990) offer a set of questions for feminist researchers to consider in assessing how well their endeavors serve the integrity and purposes of their participants (cf. Grossman et al., 1997; Massat & Lundy, 1997). Finally, Allen and Baber (1992) summarize the limitations of goals, such as those voiced by feminists, that seek to transform the lives of others—risks of homogenizing diversity among women, of co-opting or subverting others' visions of themselves and goals for themselves, of losing public relevance in overemphasizing the personal, of trading the universal for the particular. Acker, Barry, and Esseveld (1991), for example, in their study of women's entry and reentry into the labor force, found that women participants do not always share researchers' desires for their emancipation.

Feminist researchers from a variety of disciplines have tried to ensure that their studies serve women's purposes by including participants in the formulation, planning, conduct, and analysis of the work. Some scholars may formulate this as a kind of feminist participatory action research (PAR), but others consider it integral to the feminism they practice (Tolman & Brydon-Miller, 2001). Fine (1992), for example, builds a strong case that conventional and interpretive research, however much influenced by a feminist perspective, cannot relieve women's oppression as effectively as does activist participatory feminist research.

Participatory feminist research has had mixed success, depending on research participants' interest in and commitment to the endeavor. As might be expected, this varies greatly. For example, Seibold's (2000) study of the experience of menopause of single midlife women was assured some value for women because she herself had experienced menopause as a single middle-aged woman and because participant concerns guided her selection, collection, and analysis of information. Paradis (2000), on the other hand, had not experienced the homelessness she wanted to study in an urban setting, and she details the variety of issues that feminist professionals face when trying to plan a study both *on* and *for* homeless women. McGraw, Zvonkovic, and Walker (2000) increased interest in their study of work and family life among Northwest fishing families by adding to their objectives a goal specified by their female participants that could be construed as antifeminist by some. However, both this study and another by Skelton (2001) of female youth in Wales indicate how researchers must prioritize even feminist goals. Both studies show researchers focusing on how women want to view goals they themselves formulate, regardless of how well these goals fit a particular feminist agenda. These examples also highlight inevitable contradictions in any ethical system. On one hand, feminists want women to make decisions about their own lives. On the other hand, feminists prefer some decisions to others. The challenge for researchers in these situations is to choose their priorities, and these are likely to vary by situation.

Ironically, feminist principles or policies may or may not foster feminist care. Patai (1991) believes that the undeniable and inevitable inequities between researchers and those they study make unavoidable a certain level of exploitation in research. She counsels humility in our claims to benefit others and courage to continue research that is ethical enough without being ethically perfect (cf. Gillies & Alldred, 2002).

In this section, we have explored what we have called the ethics of research purpose. Feminist scholars from the spectrum of feminisms have formulated their research purposes for the values they seek to realize, and these are ethical choices. The ethics of principle, especially social justice, and the ethics of care have been the predominant rationales used by feminist researchers to justify their endeavors. Feminist research in the 1970s and 1980s, with its focus on sex differences, was more explicitly concerned with equity per se. We sought to expose inequalities in resources and power and to discredit claims that women were somehow lesser men. More recent feminist research, informed by Gilligan, Noddings, and others, has been more preoccupied with a responsive research that attends to the goals of participants.

However, the goals and objectives of research are only one facet of the ethical issues in research. Feminists and other emancipatory theorists share additional concerns. What interests are served and what are ignored or imperiled in a particular study? Who will have access to the knowledge produced, who decides this, and how is it decided? Who gets to be the inquirer and who is the inquired about? What balances of resources and decision making do these roles represent? These questions are addressed in part by consideration of the researchers' roles and interactions with those researched. Feminists have been at the forefront of challenging conventional researcher roles and interactions with those researched, just as they have been at the forefront of challenging the neutrality of research purpose.

Ethics of Research Roles and Conduct

In the past 30 years, ethical codes provided by the U.S. government and various U.S. professional groups have regulated the participation of people in research studies. Such codes have set parameters for the conduct of research that constrain all scholars, and the codes themselves may be challenged by emerging feminist practices. The current professional standards of research conduct toward study participants have been influenced by transgressions of human rights, neglect of respect for others, and violations of conventional standards of decency in the United States and elsewhere (Mello & Wolf, 2010; Reverby, 2009; Skloot, 2010; War Crimes Tribunal, 1947; World Medical Association, 1975). The Kantian ethical imperative (Tong, 1993) that people be treated as ends, rather than as means, has been ignored in the name of research time and again by scholars around the world.

The National Research Act, a U.S. law passed in 1974, resulted in the development of a set of principles, summarized in the Belmont Report, governing human participation in research studies: respect for persons, beneficence, and justice

(National Commission for the Protection of Human Subjects of Medical and Behavioral Research, 1979). These principles frame a code of conduct requiring informed consent of those studied, assessment of the balance of risk to benefit in any research, and fairness in selection of human participants. This is the guide used across the United States by the institutional review boards (IRBs) charged with the protection of human subjects of research by reviewing and approving research proposals (Mazur, 2007). Its focus is on what happens during the period when data are collected. Although beneficence requires researchers to consider the morality of the research itself—Will the presumed benefits outweigh any harm to participants?—the emphasis is on the people directly involved. Likewise, the justice principle is often interpreted to mean justice for those involved, rather than justice more broadly; this may be changing as concerns have increased about funding for offshore research in circumstances less regulated than in the United States.

Much of the initial feminist commentary on research relationships occurred within the same timeframe—the 1980s and into the early 1990s—that IRBs were being set up around the United States. We believe that feminist researchers were responding, in part, to the same climate of criticism of conventional research practice and policy (Barnbaum & Byron, 2001) that prompted governmental intervention: concern over a proliferation of research studies that manipulated and endangered people.

One feminist response to protection based on principle is a challenge to the assumed division between who is the researcher and the knower and who is the researched or the known. The principles themselves may be inoffensive, even desirable, given our history of research abuses, but they assume a relationship and an ethics governing relationship that many feminist scholars have found problematic (e.g., Edwards & Mauthner, 2002; England, 1994; Robertson, 2000). An initial challenge to the researcher as detached, protective expert is Oakley's (1981) classic comment on interviewing. In a study of expectant mothers, Oakley found herself restricted by expectations of distance and detachment from her participants and especially hampered by the asymmetry of the interviewer as the questioner and the respondent as the answerer. She found these expectations contradictory to her commitment to caring about the women as individuals, to establishing authentic relationships with them, and to offering whatever she knew that might improve their lives (cf., however, Oakley's [2000] reconsideration of the deeper gender assumptions underlying such dichotomies as qualitative and quantitative research). Stacey (1991) took this argument further, finding that fieldwork requires researchers to misrepresent themselves and to manipulate participants. Her second issue with a feminist ethnography is that the product, the ethnography, is a representation of participants and their lives that is ultimately controlled by the researcher. We elaborate on the latter concern in a later section.

In 1981, Oakley found the conventional research *relationship* unfeminist, but a decade later, Stacey questioned whether conventional research itself might be unfeminist (however, cf. Kirsch, 1999, pp. 42–43, for how the vagaries of ordinary relationships are inevitable in research relationships too, and D. L. Wolf, 1996, for how research conventions may be used to further feminist efforts in fieldwork). Between these positions are endeavors of many feminist researchers to reform the exploitative hierarchy of the researcher and the researched, and these efforts have affected a generation of feminist practice (Romyn, 1996). Fisher (2000), for example, endorses a process that brings research participants into the moral decision making such that the ethics of any study may be considered not only by researchers and peer review boards but also by those to be studied. In her hospital-based video ethnography of clinician learning, Carroll (2009) shares the researcher-edited video footage with participants and values their inputs as experts' knowledge. Carroll also explains the power shifts that occurred in video reflexivity sessions when her position moved from the observer, who has a control over videoing, to the observed by letting herself be recorded with other participants in front of the camera.

What else happens when feminist researchers strive to put these policies of reciprocity into practice? As might be expected, this varies. Gatenby and Humphries (2000), in their PAR

with Maori participants in higher education, report a level of success that may have been fostered by a study of women educating themselves in ways they themselves selected. Knight (2000) similarly engaged members of an education community to improve and to document her work with diverse communities and thus drew on participants' own aspirations in framing her research. Guimaraes (2007) reports that, in her interviews with abused women about their interactions with police in Brazil, she once intervened to provide advice to a participant, but she later discarded this case as contaminated data because she believed she had failed to maintain the objective role of interviewer. However, on subsequently reexamining these data, she realized that her intervention had been appropriate in that it was her moral responsibility as a feminist to support women in need. In contrast, Morris-Roberts (2001) was challenged to maintain equity in her relationships with the teenage girls she was studying when she began to observe some of them bullying others, and she felt impelled to intervene. In another study of young women, Morris, Woodward, and Peters (1998) also report being challenged for their affiliation among the participants in the study.

These studies suggest that reducing the ethical tensions of unequal status may only open the way to the ethical dilemmas of living among peers. Choices in affiliation are complicated further when the researcher is operating across levels of institutional status, as Weinberg (2002) reports in a study of a facility for single mothers in Ontario. She was pressed to balance her allegiance between the female clients and the female staff. How ethical decisions may vary according to the differing interests of diverse research participants and the variety of contexts researchers may encounter is illustrated well by Vivat's (2002) ethnographic study of a hospice in Scotland; Vivat uses the notion of "situated ethics" as a contrast with a principle-based "detached ethics."

As ethicist Hinman summarizes (2003), traditional principled ethics seeks universality, generality, disinterestedness, impartiality, and publicity. Situated ethics (not to be confused with situational ethics, a Christian framework; see Fletcher, 1966), in contrast, recognizes how moral and ethical decisions occur in a time, place, and context that are inevitably unique and derive from the positions of the research participants. This is a facet of relational ethics, recognizing that ethical choices always occur within a situation involving particular relationships. Drawing on Haraway's (1988) construct of situated knowledge, Vivat (2002) says that

> situated ethics . . . [is] characterized by the agent paying attention to the particular situation and to the consequences for the relations between those involved, and by an absence of interest in making universal claims, although the agent may still appeal to abstract principles of both justice and care. (p. 240)

Robertson's (2000) study of bulimia among adult women indicates other issues when studying individuals from an assumed position of equality. First, as a recovered bulimic, she notes the researcher's care of self as part of a responsibility to protect everyone in a research endeavor, echoing both Gilligan's and Noddings's emphasis on self-care as an indication of maturity. Second, she found that sharing data and results with some participants put them at risk of psychological distress that contributing information had not. Third, a request from a participant to interview the researcher about her own experience with bulimia permitted Robertson a view of her ethical practice she had not previously had. Finally, like Patai (1991), Robertson emphasizes the ethical considerations in ending the research relationship. This is yet another power difference between researchers and their participants.

Intimate, equitable relationships pose ethical dilemmas that distant, hierarchical relationships may avoid (see Avis, 2002). Birch and Miller (2002) and Duncombe and Jessop (2002) report experiences with attempting to put their feminist principles into practice that indicate the pitfalls and hazards of all human relationships. Bingley (2002) suggests incorporating approaches from psychotherapy, such as directly exploring people's feelings about experiences, into research practice so as to better address these pitfalls and hazards. De Laine (2000) provides extensive examples of the assault on a researcher's psyche such difficulties create. D. L. Wolf (1996) discusses the disadvantages

that fieldworkers who are members of a field community encounter because of the conflicts between their insider role and their researcher role, and she stresses what she considers power differentials between researchers and participants that complicate friendships in the field. What all these examples suggest is that moving from a codified and principle-based set of ethical standards to an ethic of care does not prevent or even reduce ethical dilemmas.

The principle-based ethics of respect for persons, beneficence, and justice helps researchers to consider those they are studying as fellow human beings with their own goals, priorities, and agendas. They aid feminist researchers, for example, in balancing feminist agendas with those claimed by the women we may be studying. What principle-based ethics does not do is address the situation-specific quality of human relationships and interactions. The ethic of care provides a systematic model for an engaged and reciprocal relationship with research participants. It gives us a set of priorities for decision making that takes into account the specifics of who we are while we study ourselves and our similar-to-different others (Gluck & Patai, 1991a; Sultana, 2007). Constant questioning and reflection on ethical decisions required during research bring about an awareness of this kind of relational ethics (Ellis, 2007). Nevertheless, feminist ethnographer Bell (1993), who summarizes her development over a period of years from a "naïve feminist empiricist stance" to an appreciation of how the politics of feminism and power differentials operate in field situations, cautions that "feminist ethnography opens a discursive space for the 'subjects' of the ethnography and as such is simultaneously empowering and destabilizing" (p. 31).

Although the ethic of care permits us to judge the quality of our researcher roles and human interactions in a research study, it does not eliminate our ethical dilemmas. The challenges of research remain; the asymmetries created by the different interests of researchers, participants, and even researcher-participants are inevitable; and unanticipated issues may plague researchers who have added new sets of expectations to their notions of ideal research practice. The principle of respect for persons that we discussed previously as guiding informed consent may be a less demanding ethical precept for research conduct than is the ethic of care, which requires that we acknowledge a relationship of whatever kind we seek. Miller and Boulton (2007, p. 2204), on the basis of four studies conducted over the past 35 years, stress that a concept of informed consent should reflect a "fluid and multi-faceted" researcher-participant relationship in which potential participants have personal as well as professional expectations of researchers, such as ready access to researchers' own knowledge, and in which people have more control over research in resisting and negotiating their participation. To the extent that an ethic of care becomes the major influence on our research conduct, our responsibilities are much greater (Gluck & Patai, 1991b). These responsibilities are no less complicated when relationships are mediated by technology, as they are in the increasing use of research in Internet venues.

Internet Research Ethics

Researchers' ethical roles and conduct are critical not only in face-to-face settings but also in online research as worldwide distribution of the Internet and its unique characteristics has opened wholly new opportunities for scholars. For example, researchers now have better access to participants who are in dangerous or prohibited areas such as war zones, centers of criminal and illegal activity, and plague-ridden sites (Mann & Stewart, 2002). Different areas of the Internet—bulletin boards, e-mail, gaming, instant messaging services, social networking sites, listservs, multiuser domains (MUDs), object-oriented domains (MOOs), online chatrooms, USENET newsgroups, and Web logs (blogs)— enable researchers to easily collect ready-made data and observe online users anonymously as "lurkers." Online research is also cost-effective compared with fieldwork for which researchers have to travel to their sites and spend considerable time to gather data.

However, these advantages in online research entail risks and ethical problems. First, the distinct characteristics of online space where users can remain invisible, use pseudonyms, or sometimes have multiple identities make it hard for researchers to get informed consent, to trace

original sources for citations, and to debrief participants (Hewson, 2008; Jolly, 2008). Second, lack of cultural understanding of the targeted online communities can offend users to the extent of provoking animosity toward researchers (Chen, Hall, & Johns, 2004; Hall, Frederick, & Johns, 2004). Third, reckless use of participants' online nicknames and postings in the results of a study jeopardizes their privacy because individuals' online aliases may be their online identities, "function[ing] similarly to real names, and [they] should be treated in the same way one treats real names" (Bruckman, 2002, p. 229). Fourth, researchers themselves are subject to potential harm by receiving distressful information from anonymous participants (Eynon, Fry, & Schroeder, 2008).

Furthermore, researchers' stances on online research ethics vary. Some researchers regard online venues as public space, and they assume that Internet users are capable of making rational decisions when posting their opinions or works on the Internet. Those researchers protect participants' privacy less strictly than other researchers who consider online venues private space and, therefore, are attentive to feminist research ethics to protect Internet users from potential harm as research subjects (Chen et al., 2004). One of the criteria generally used for the public/private debate is the expectation Internet users bring to the venues where they interact. Widely accessed information open to the public without membership requirements, and with purposes of publicity or advocacy, can be treated as less sensitive than information shared only with registered members for private interests (Salmons, 2010). However, considering various forms of interactions occurring in the Internet space, it behooves researchers to see the public/private issues as a continuum rather than a dichotomy and to take proper actions to protect a research participant's privacy and confidentiality (Bruckman, 2002; Kanuka & Anderson, 2007).

Currently, technological development and interdisciplinary approaches to study have led to challenges for Internet researchers who are required to protect human subjects' rights on a global scope where different cultures and nations have different standards. In an effort to clarify and resolve frequent ethical problems at the institutional level, ethicists and researchers from 11 countries developed the AoIR (Association of Internet Researchers) ethics statement (Ess & Jones, 2004). The AoIR ethics statement promotes "ethical pluralism" and "cross-cultural awareness" to guide researchers to a greater awareness and better understanding of different ethical frameworks, such as deontology, consequentialism, and feminist ethics, which can be applied differently in multiple contexts across the globe when working through ethical conflicts (Ess & Jones, 2004, pp. 28–29).

Other scholars have offered additional recommendations for online research. For example, using "netiquette," etiquette on the Internet, is crucial to build rapport between the researcher and online community members because the researcher's oversights, such as the improper use of the community-specific language and the researcher's insufficient self-identification, can panic the community members and seriously and quickly damage, and sometimes end, their relationship with the researcher (Hall et al., 2004; Mann & Stewart, 2002). Franklin (2004) states the need to acknowledge asymmetric power relations between observer and observed because "the voice that predominates after the fact is that of the Observer" (p. 14). Also, the importance of considering feminist communitarian ethics proposed by Denzin (1997), discussed previously in the chapter, encouraging researchers to actively pursue developing and benefitting communities beyond just informing the members of the research results, applies to research in online communities just as in any field research (e.g., Chen et al., 2004; Hall et al., 2004).

Nevertheless, these suggestions of the AoIR ethics working committee and other scholars are merely guidelines for practice; no easy answers avoid potential ethical problems online, just as nothing prevents them face-to-face. Making ethical decisions in online research is complicated because ethical standards that are too lax might endanger participants' privacy and human rights, whereas standards that are too rigid might hinder scholars from the knowledge afforded by large-scale and globally distributed data from the Internet (Bruckman, 2002). Therefore, rather than adhering to rule-based solutions, researchers

are required to weigh potential advantages of online research against costs and risks when they deal with each case (Ess, 2007).

The Internet has provided new opportunities to study various human interactions. However, relationships through the monitor in the Internet space keep researchers from making the most of their senses and intuitions during the research process and thus keep them from using the fundamental tool, researchers themselves. Therefore, Internet researchers can benefit from feminist research ethics, which allows researchers to be fully aware of their positionality and to apply situated ethics to maximize their research results, while minimizing intrusions of online users' human rights. The bottom line is that researchers should use discretion and consider the perspectives of participants in making ethical judgments in all decision processes in online research just as they do in face-to-face encounters. Because publishing and otherwise presenting or disseminating the research adds to the levels of complexity in both online and face-to-face ethical decision making, we turn to this next.

Ethics of Representation

The ethics of representation is the good or ill that results from how participants are represented in publications, presentations, and other reports of research. Feminists have a particular stake in the ethics of representation because of what many of us believe to have been misrepresentations of women and our experiences. The androcentric scholarship that feminist thinkers such as Code (1991, 1995) find so objectionable both ignores and distorts women's lives and views (cf. Richardson, 1997). Feminists have led the way in challenging how people are represented in the human and professional sciences. Will research participants be distressed when they learn how they are described, characterized, and interpreted? Will they agree with how they are represented? Will individuals be placed at risk from others in their situation or from the general public by how they are presented? Although presentation of self is a concern of all human beings, distortions from conventional gender expectations make this a central issue for feminists. Will other people—other teenagers, others suffering from bulimia, other single mothers, or other online gamers, for example—face difficulties in their lives because of how those who share their attributes are represented?

The feminist ethic of care provides moral justification for the concern expressed by scholars such as Hopkins (1993) for relationships with research participants and for researchers' desires to support their pride and avoid embarrassing them. Another ethical challenge to feminist representations has been the assumption of homogeneity among women whose points of view and experiences vary considerably by race, ethnicity, class, religion, sexual orientation, and ability-disability conditions. Having objected to being portrayed as no different than men in social science research, white women scholars have been challenged by scholars of color, by queer theorists, and by others with divergent points of view to honor, respect, and celebrate the diversity of women's experiences and views of the world (e.g., hooks, 1984; Lewin, 1995). Although by the 21st century feminist scholarship may have become more welcoming of diversity among women, debates continue as feminism is taken up by more groups around the world. An example of this in the current century is discussions among Islamic feminists about women's views among Muslims (Badran, 2002).

In a now-classic formulation about representing others in what we write and present about them, Fine (1994) struggles with the conventions, positioning, and hierarchies that produce a mostly offstage author writing a tidy image of players. The writing itself, who writes whom, creates imbalances in power and an inevitable "othering" of participants. Fine advocates addressing this issue by "working the hyphens." She does this by presenting material that defies stereotypes and conventional images of people, material that critiques those who create these conventional images, and material that calls for direct action to rectify inequities. She struggles to address our multiple, interacting identities as women, individuals whose abilities, ethnic and racial backgrounds, religious affiliations, and sexual orientations vary. She advocates studying the powerful as well as the powerless.

Fine (1994) stresses that, although our identities are fluid and changeable, they nevertheless associate us more with some in our communities than with others. These groups and affiliations can be caricatured and stereotyped in ways that hamper and hurt both individuals and communities. Even more important is positioning of self and other at what Fine calls "the hyphen." This metaphor invites the reader to reflect on the self as other and the other as self. We challenge one another with questions such as this: "How might I write differently about my experiences with my research participants if I write about *we* or if I write about an *I and thou* relationship?" The ethics of relationships provides models of connections with those we study. These sources and the other strategies Fine suggests permit us to work the hyphen, to problematize rather than to assume the relationships between researcher and researched (cf. Alldred & Gillies, 2002). Thus, Robertson (2000) is working the hyphen when she agrees to be interviewed by a research participant about her own struggle with bulimia. Stacey (1991) works the hyphen by insisting that feminist ethnographers take responsibility for an ethically imperfect research practice. Rice (2009), in her study on women's perceptions of their physical appearances, works the hyphen by critically reflecting on her embodied subjectivity before creating meanings of participants' experiences.

M. Wolf's (1992) representation of a young mother's unconventional behavior in a village in Taiwan through three different genres—field notes, a conventional ethnographic report, and a short story—was intended to illustrate many of the complications of the ethics of representation. She discusses the "double responsibility" of "feminists doing research on women," responsible both to their women participants and to the broader world of women whose lives we hope to improve. She cautions that power is not merely held by researchers over participants but also by participants who make their own decisions about what to share with, withhold from, or distort for investigators. Having shown the multiple and competing views of one woman's interactions with her neighbors, Wolf nevertheless worries about the academic consequences to feminist scholars of being forthright about acknowledging the power that participants may exert. She is concerned that feminist arguments may be viewed as less convincing to other researchers if feminists indicate forthrightly the limitations imposed on their material by participant control over knowledge about their own experiences. Although such control has come to be expected when researchers are studying powerful people in society (see Nader, 1974, for example), it has been discussed less frequently for those assumed to have little power.

Some feminist researchers attempt to address the ethics of representation by limiting their studies to collaborative research or PAR or to such personal endeavors as autoethnography (Ellis, 2009) and experimental ethnography (Visweswaran, 1994). Others ask research participants to "vet" or otherwise edit or approve data and even interpretations that involve them. Disputed material may be omitted, or disagreements about material may be included in reports. Reports and presentations may be composed so as to include multiple voices and commentators—researcher, researched, and other stakeholders (Blakeslee, Cole, & Conefrey, 1996). Researchers Kirsch (1999) and Mortensen and Kirsch (1996) examine the multiple ways researchers have struggled with the moral and ethical issues of representation and conclude that every alternative has its strengths and limitations.

In a study of women activists on both sides of the abortion debate, Ginsburg (1993) considers the issue of representation as broader than the particular individuals directly involved in her study; she uses the notion of polyphony, developed by the Russian literary scholar Mikhail Mikhailovich Bakhtin, to generate a multifaceted and heterogeneous presentation of her research. Zeni, Prophete, Cason, and Phillips (2001) similarly apply Collins's (1990) analysis of African American feminists to represent multiple perspectives held by individuals in diverse communities. In contrast, Mills (2002) finds the authentic representation of even a single individual to pose a challenge to the skills and knowledge of researchers—how to move from autobiography to biography in a way faithful to and respectful of the subject. Jacobs (2004) recounts a different issue of representation in

her study of the experiences of females during the Holocaust where the death of those she studies does not relieve her sense of ethical obligation to them. The tension expressed by all these researchers is underscored by their relationships to those they study. In representing their participants, they are also representing themselves and facets of themselves that they share with the participants. Similarity and difference merge, and the ethics of research becomes the ethics of everyday life.

CONCLUSION

What we have tried to do in this chapter, first, is show the connections and disconnections between the Western approach to ethics developed in academic philosophy, especially as it applies to women, and the challenge to that ethics posed in the 20th century by feminist ethicists. Carol Gilligan, Nel Noddings, and their successors have challenged the privileging of principle-based decision making, and they reconceptualized moral theory to include the ethics of relation. Second, we have linked this to general research ethics as applied by many social scientists and to ethical practices developed among researchers using an explicitly feminist approach. Although many feminist researchers continue to be guided by such ethical principles as justice, most have integrated an ethic of care and relationship into their conduct of research. In this chapter, we have examined how these two frameworks play out in how we feminists formulate our research purposes, how we work with others in the research, how we are adapting our studies for online environments, and how we represent those we study in our research reports.

However, feminist ethics does not resolve moral dilemmas in research. Women studying women, about women or with women, for the purpose of relieving women's oppression and reconfiguring androcentric knowledge into a more inclusive understanding of "huwomanity," complicates the research process. This is the pattern attested to by many of the feminist researchers we have cited here. Feminist ethics likely generates as many issues as it may help either avoid or address. This is particularly evident in trading a detached, distant, and hierarchical stance for an intimate, close, and equitable position. Distance and intimacy create their own problems.

Even within sets of coherent guidelines lie troubling tensions. The feminist project is deeply grounded in the principle of justice. Women's rights have traditionally been justified by the values of equity and equality. The ethic of care and relationship does not preclude consideration of principle but may provide a parallel formulation of human rights and responsibilities to one another. Nevertheless, philosophers such as Jean Grimshaw (1991) caution feminists about the implications of claiming an ethics of care that may place women back into a gendered ghetto by suggesting that women operate by a different, inevitably lesser standard of decision making. Our own view, however, is that the care ethic has been taken up as a welcome framework for accounting for affect, emotion, and relationship in moral choices.

We believe that the ethics of relationship complements the ethics of principle in ways that support scholars and researchers in moral decision making. Using the two together better represents the challenges we face in ethical choices. How the two frameworks play out in practice and which has priority in what situations varies according to the situation and research concerned (see Held, 1995, for further discussions of justice and care together). Frameworks are resources to help us think through our decisions. They do not provide answers but rather suggest alternatives to consider. Feminists' ongoing concerns with the status of women and girls around the world (Porter, 1999) are enriched by this dual framework.

Discussion Questions

1. How do feminist commitments influence the moral and ethical decisions researchers make?

2. What are some of the different ethical and moral premises influencing decisions that feminist researchers make?

3. How are ethical decisions in feminist research similar to and different from ethical decisions in ordinary, daily life?

4. How do ethical decisions online compare and contrast with ethical decisions in other situations?

5. How may people be harmed by reports of research on their activities?

Online Resources

Association for Feminist Ethics and Social Theory

http://www.afeast.org/

"Feminist Ethics and Social Theory is a professional organization dedicated to promoting feminist ethical perspectives on philosophy, moral and political life, and public policy. Through meetings, publications, and projects, [members] hope to increase the visibility and influence of feminist ethics, as well as feminist social and political theory, and to provide support to emerging scholars from diverse and underrepresented populations."

Ethics Updates: Gender and Sexism

http://ethics.sandiego.edu/Applied/Gender/index.asp

This website from the University of San Diego provides a range of resources related to gender and ethics.

Relevant Journals

American Journal of Bioethics

Hypatia

Journal of Global Ethics

Signs: Journal of Women in Culture and Society

Women's Studies International Forum

References

Acker, J., Barry, K., & Esseveld, J. (1991). Objectivity and truth: Problems in doing feminist research. In M. M. Fonow & J. A. Cook (Eds.), *Beyond methodology: Feminist scholarship as lived research* (pp. 133–153). Bloomington: Indiana University Press.

Ackerly, B., & True, J. (2008). Reflexivity in practice: Power and ethics in feminist research on international relations. *International Studies Review, 10,*

693–707. http://www3.interscience.wiley.com/cgi-bin/fulltext/121520314/PDFSTART

Alldred, P., & Gillies, V. (2002). Eliciting research accounts: Re/producing modern subjects? In M. Mauthner, M. Birch, J. Jessop, & T. Miller (Eds.), *Ethics in qualitative research* (pp. 146–165). London: Sage.

Allen, K. R., & Baber, K. M. (1992). Ethical and epistemological tensions in applying a postmodern perspective to feminist research. *Psychology of Women Quarterly, 16*(1), 1–15.

American Anthropological Association. (1998). *Code of ethics of the American Anthropological Association.* http://www.aaanet.org/committees/ethics/ethcode.htm

American Educational Research Association. (2000). *Ethical standards of AERA.* http://www.aera.net/aboutaera/?id=222

American Psychological Association. (2002). *Ethical principles of psychologists and code of conduct.* http://www.apa.org/ethics/code2002.html

American Sociological Association. (1997). *Code of ethics.* http://www.asanet.org/about/ethics.cfm

Avis, H. (2002). Whose voice is that? Making space for subjectivities in interviews. In L. Bondi, H. Avis, R. Bankey, A. Bingley, J. Davidson, R. Duffy, et al. (Eds.), *Subjectivities, knowledges, and feminist geographies: The subjects and ethics of social research* (pp. 191–207). Lanham, MD: Rowman & Littlefield.

Badran, M. (2002, January 17–23). Islamic feminism: What's in a name? *Al-Ahram Weekly Online,* Issue No. 569. http://weekly.ahram.org.eg/2002/569/cu1.htm

Barnbaum, D. R., & Byron, M. (2001). *Research ethics: Text and readings.* Upper Saddle River, NJ: Prentice Hall.

Bell, D. (1993). Yes, Virginia, there is a feminist ethnography: Reflections from three Australian fields. In D. Bell, P. Caplan, & W. J. Karim (Eds.), *Gendered fields: Women, men and ethnography* (pp. 28–43). London: Routledge.

Benhabib, S. (1992). *Situating the self: Gender, community and postmodernism in contemporary ethics.* New York: Routledge.

Bingley, A. (2002). Research ethics in practice. In L. Bondi, H. Avis, R. Bankey, A. Bingley, J. Davidson, R. Duffy, et al. (Eds.), *Subjectivities, knowledges, and feminist geographies: The subjects and ethics of social research* (pp. 208–222). Lanham, MD: Rowman & Littlefield.

Birch, M., & Miller, T. (2002). Encouraging participation: Ethics and responsibilities. In M. Mauthner, M. Birch, J. Jessop, & T. Miller (Eds.), *Ethics in qualitative research* (pp. 91–106). London: Sage.

Blakeslee, A. M., Cole, C. M., & Conefrey, T. (1996). Constructing voices in writing research: Developing participatory approaches to situated inquiry. In P. Mortensen & G. E. Kirsch (Eds.), *Ethics and representation in qualitative studies of literacy* (pp. 134–154). Washington, DC: National Council of Teachers of English.

Bloom, L. R. (1998). *Under the sign of hope: Feminist methodology and narrative interpretation.* Albany: State University of New York Press.

Bloom, L. R., & Sawin, P. (2009). Ethical responsibility in feminist research: Challenging ourselves to do activist research with women in poverty. *International Journal of Qualitative Studies in Education, 22*(3), 333–351. doi:10.1080/09518390902835413

Bordo, S. R. (1987). *The flight to objectivity: Essays on Cartesianism and culture.* Albany: State University of New York Press.

Brabeck, M. M. (Ed.). (1989). *Who cares? Theory, research, and educational implications of the ethic of care.* New York: Praeger.

Bruckman, A. (2002). Studying the amateur artist: A perspective on disguising data collected in human subjects research on the Internet. *Ethics and Information Technology, 4,* 217–231. http://www.springerlink.com/content/t01630466t132246/fulltext.pdf

Butler, J. (1990). *Gender trouble: Feminism and the subversion of identity.* New York: Routledge.

Caputo, J. D. (1993). *Against ethics: Contributions to a poetics of obligation with constant reference to deconstruction.* Bloomington: Indiana University Press.

Carroll, K. (2009). Outsider, insider, alongside: Examining reflexivity in hospital-based video research. *International Journal of Multiple Research Approaches, 3*(3), 246–263.

Chen, S. S., Hall, G. J., & Johns, M. D. (2004). Research paparazzi in cyberspace: The voices of the researched. In M. D. Johns, S. S. Chen, & G. J. Hall (Eds.), *Online social research: Methods, issues, & ethics* (pp. 157–175). New York: Peter Lang.

Code, L. (1991). *What can she know? Feminist theory and the construction of knowledge.* Ithaca, NY: Cornell University Press.

Code, L. (1995). How do we know? Questions of method in feminist practice. In S. Burt & L. Code (Eds.), *Changing methods: Feminists transforming practice* (pp. 13–44). Peterborough, ON: Broadview Press.

Colby, A., & Kohlberg, L. (1987). *The measurement of moral judgment: Vol. 1. Theoretical foundations and research validation.* Cambridge, UK: Cambridge University Press.

Collins, P. H. (1990). *Black feminist thought: Knowledge, consciousness, and the politics of empowerment.* London: HarperCollins Academic.

Daly, M. C. (1978). *Gyn/ecology, the metaethics of radical feminism.* Boston: Beacon Press.

de Laine, M. (2000). *Fieldwork, participation and practice: Ethics and dilemmas in qualitative research.* London: Sage.

Denzin, N. K. (1997). *Interpretive ethnography: Ethnographic practices for the 21st century.* Thousand Oaks, CA: Sage.

DeVault, M. L. (1999). *Liberating method: Feminism and social research.* Philadelphia: Temple University Press.

Doucet, A., & Mauthner, M. (2002). Knowing responsibly: Linking ethics, research practice and epistemology. In M. Mauthner, M. Birch, J. Jessop, & T. Miller (Eds.), *Ethics in qualitative research* (pp. 123–145). London: Sage.

Du Bois, B. (1983). Passionate scholarship: Notes on values, knowing and method in feminist social science. In G. Bowles & R. D. Klien (Eds.), *Theories of women's studies* (pp. 105–116). London: Routledge & Kegan Paul.

Duncombe, J., & Jessop, J. (2002). "Doing rapport" and the ethics of "faking friendship." In M. Mauthner, M. Birch, J. Jessop, & T. Miller (Eds.), *Ethics in qualitative research* (pp. 107–122). London: Sage.

Edwards, R., & Mauthner, M. (2002). Ethics and feminist research: Theory and practice. In M. Mauthner, M. Birch, J. Jessop, & T. Miller (Eds.), *Ethics in qualitative research* (pp. 14–31). London: Sage.

Eichler, M. (1988). *Nonsexist research methods: A practical guide.* New York: Routledge.

Ellis, C. (2007). Telling secrets, revealing lives: Relational ethics in research with intimate others. *Qualitative Inquiry, 13*(1), 3–29. doi:10.1177/1077800406294947

Ellis, C. (2009). *Revision: Autoethnographic reflections on life and work.* Walnut Creek, CA: Leftcoast Press.

England, K. V. L. (1994). Getting personal: Reflexivity, positionality, and feminist research. *Professional Geographer, 46*(1), 80–89.

Ess, C. (2007). Internet research ethics. In A. Joinson, K. McKenna, T. Postmes, & U. D. Reips (Eds.), *The Oxford handbook of Internet psychology* (pp. 485–500). http://www.socialnetresearch.org/wp-content/uploads/2008/02/ess-chap31_internetresearchethics.pdf

Ess, C., & Jones, S. (2004). Ethical decision-making and Internet research: Recommendations from the AoIR ethics working committee. In E. A. Buchanan (Ed.), *Readings in virtual research ethics: Issues and controversies* (pp. 27–44). Hershey, PA: Information Science Publishing.

Eynon, R., Fry, J., & Schroeder, R. (2008). The ethics of Internet research. In N. Fielding, R. M. Lee, & G. Blank (Eds.), *The SAGE handbook of online research methods* (pp. 23–41). London: Sage.

Fine, M. (1992). *Disruptive voices: The possibilities of feminist research.* Ann Arbor: University of Michigan Press.

Fine, M. (1994). Working the hyphens: Reinventing self and other in qualitative research. In N. K. Denzin & Y. S. Lincoln (Eds.), *The handbook of qualitative research* (pp. 70–82). Thousand Oaks, CA: Sage.

Fisher, C. B. (2000). Relational ethics in psychological research: One feminist's journey. In M. M. Brabeck (Ed.), *Practicing feminist ethics in psychology* (pp. 125–142). Washington, DC: American Psychological Association.

Fletcher, J. (1966). *Situation ethics: The new morality.* Philadelphia: Westminster Press.

Fonow, M. M., & Cook, J. A. (1991). Back to the future: A look at the second wave of feminist epistemology and methodology. In M. M. Fonow & J. A. Cook (Eds.), *Beyond methodology: Feminist scholarship as lived research* (pp. 1–15). Bloomington: Indiana University Press.

Franklin, M. I. (2004). *Postcolonial politics, the internet, and everyday life: Pacific traversals online.* London: Routledge.

Fuss, D. (1989). *Essentially speaking: Feminism, nature & difference.* New York: Routledge.

Gatenby, B., & Humphries, M. (2000). Feminist participatory action research: Methodological and ethical issues. *Women's Studies International Forum, 23*(1), 89–105.

Gillies, V., & Alldred, P. (2002). The ethics of intention: Research as a political tool. In M. Mauthner,

M. Birch, J. Jessop, & T. Miller (Eds.), *Ethics in qualitative research* (pp. 32–52). London: Sage.

Gilligan, C. (1982). *In a different voice: Psychological theory and women's development.* Cambridge, MA: Harvard University Press.

Ginsburg, F. (1993). The case of mistaken identity: Problems in representing women on the right. In C. B. Brettell (Ed.), *When they read what we write: The politics of ethnography* (pp. 163–176). Westport, CT: Bergin & Garvey.

Gluck, S. B., & Patai, D. (1991a). Introduction. In S. B. Gluck & D. Patai (Eds.), *Women's words: The feminist practice of oral history* (pp. 1–5). New York: Routledge.

Gluck, S. B., & Patai, D. (1991b). Part I: Language and communication. In S. B. Gluck & D. Patai (Eds.), *Women's words: The feminist practice of oral history* (p. 9). New York: Routledge.

Goetz, J. P. (1978). Theoretical approaches to the study of sex-role culture in schools. *Anthropology and Education Quarterly, 9*(1), 3–21.

Goetz, J. P., & Grant, L. (1988). Conceptual approaches to studying gender in education. *Anthropology and Education Quarterly, 19*(2), 182–196.

Gowaty, P. A. (1997). Sexual dialectics, sexual selection, and variation in mating behavior. In P. A. Gowaty (Ed.), *Feminism and evolutionary biology* (pp. 351–384). New York: Chapman & Hall.

Grimshaw, J. (1991). The idea of a female ethic. In P. Singer (Ed.), *A companion to ethics* (pp. 491–499). Oxford, UK: Blackwell.

Grossman, F. K., Gilbert, L. A., Genero, N. P., Hawer, S. E., Hyde, J. S., & Maracek, J. (1997). Feminist research: Practice and problems. In J. Worell & N. G. Johnson (Eds.), *Shaping the future of feminist psychology: Education, research, and practice* (pp. 73–91). Washington, DC: American Psychological Association.

Guimaraes, E. (2007). Feminist research practice: Using conversation analysis to explore the researcher's interaction with participants. *Feminism & Psychology, 17*(2), 149–161. doi:10.1177/0959353507076547

Hall, G. J., Frederick, D., & Johns, M. D. (2004). "NEED HELP ASAP!!!": A feminist communitarian approach to online research ethics. In M. D. Johns, S. S. Chen, & G. J. Hall (Eds.), *Online social research: Methods, issues, & ethics* (pp. 239–252). New York: Peter Lang.

Haraway, D. (1988). Situated knowledges: The science question in feminism and the privilege of partial perspective. *Feminist Studies, 14*(3), 575–599.

Haraway, D. (1989). *Primate visions: Gender, race, and nature in the world of modern science.* New York: Routledge.

Harding, S. (1987). Conclusion: Epistemological questions. In S. Harding (Ed.), *Feminism and methodology: Social science issues* (pp. 181–190). Bloomington: Indiana University Press.

Harding, S. (1998). *Is science multicultural? Postcolonialisms, feminisms, and epistemologies.* Bloomington: Indiana University Press.

Harding, S. (2004). Introduction: Standpoint theory as a site of political, philosophical, and scientific debate. In S. Harding (Ed.), *The feminist standpoint theory reader: Intellectual and political controversies* (pp. 1–15). New York: Routledge.

Harmon, W. W. (1996). The shortcomings of Western science. *Qualitative Inquiry, 2*(1), 30–38.

Held, V. (Ed.). (1995). *Justice and care: Essential readings in feminist ethics.* Boulder, CO: Westview.

Hesse-Biber, S. N., & Leckenby, D. (2004). How feminists practice social research. In S. N. Hesse-Biber & M. L. Yaiser (Eds.), *Feminist perspectives on social research* (pp. 209–226). New York: Oxford University Press.

Hewson, C. (2008). Internet-mediated research as an emergent method and its potential role in facilitating mixed methods research. In S. N. Hesse-Biber & P. Leavy (Eds.), *Handbook of emergent methods* (pp. 543–570). New York: Guildford Press.

Hinman, L. M. (2003). *Ethics: A pluralistic approach to moral theory* (3rd ed.). Belmont, CA: Thomson Wadsworth.

hooks, b. (1984). *Feminist theory: From margin to center.* Boston: South End Press.

Hopkins, M. C. (1993). Is anonymity possible? Writing about refugees in the United States. In C. B. Brettell (Ed.), *When they read what we write: The politics of ethnography* (pp. 121–129). Westport, CT: Bergin & Garvey.

Jacobs, J. L. (2004). Women, genocide, and memory: The ethics of feminist ethnography in Holocaust research. *Gender & Society, 18*(2), 223–238.

Jolly, M. (2008). *In love and struggle: Letters in contemporary feminism.* New York: Columbia University Press.

Kanuka, H., & Anderson, T. (2007). Ethical issues in qualitative e-learning research. *International Journal of Qualitative Methods, 6*(2), Article 2. http://www.ualberta.ca/~iiqm/backissues/6_2/kanuka.pdf

Kidder, R. M. (1995). *How good people make tough choices: Resolving the dilemmas of ethical living.* New York: Fireside.

Kilby, R. W. (1993). *The study of human values.* Lanham, MD: University Press of America.

Kirsch, G. E. (1999). *Ethical dilemmas in feminist research: The politics of location, interpretation, and publication.* Albany: State University of New York Press.

Knight, M. G. (2000). Ethics in qualitative research: Multicultural feminist activist research. *Theory Into Practice, 39*(3), 170–176.

Kohlberg, L. (1981). *Essays on moral development: Vol. 1. The philosophy of moral development: Moral stages and the idea of justice.* New York: Harper & Row.

Lather, P. (1991). *Getting smart: Feminist research and pedagogy with/in the postmodern.* New York: Routledge.

Lather, P. (2007). *Getting lost: Feminist efforts toward a double(d) science.* Albany: State University of New York Press.

Lewin, E. (1995). Writing lesbian ethnography. In R. Behar & D. A. Gordon (Eds.), *Women writing culture* (pp. 322–335). Berkeley: University of California Press.

Lloyd, G. (1996). The man of reason. In A. Garry & M. Pearsall (Eds.), *Women, knowledge, and reality: Explorations in feminist philosophy* (pp. 149–165). New York: Routledge.

Longino, H. (1994). Gender and racial biases in scientific research. In K. Shrader-Frechette (Ed.), *Ethics of scientific research* (pp. 139–151). Lanham, MD: Rowman & Littlefield.

Mann, C., & Stewart, F. (2002). Internet interviewing. In J. F. Gubrium & J. A. Holstein (Eds.), *Handbook of Internet research: Context & method* (pp. 603–627). Thousand Oaks, CA: Sage.

Martin, J. R. (1985). *Reclaiming a conversation: The ideal of the educated woman.* New Haven, CT: Yale University Press.

Massat, C. R., & Lundy, M. (1997). Empowering research participants. *Affilia: Journal of Women and Social Work, 12*(1), 33–56.

Mazur, D. J. (2007). *Evaluating the science and ethics of research on humans: A guide for IRB members.* Baltimore: Johns Hopkins University Press.

McGraw, L. A., Zvonkovic, A. M., & Walker, A. J. (2000). Studying postmodern families: A feminist analysis of ethical tensions in work and family research. *Journal of Marriage and Family, 62*(1), 68–77.

Mello, M. M., & Wolf, L. E. (2010, June 9). The Havasupai Indian Tribe case—Lessons for research involving stored biologic samples. *New England Journal of Medicine Online First.* doi:10.1056/NEJMp1005203. http://content.nejm.org/cgi/reprint/NEJMp1005203v1.pdf

Miller, T., & Boulton, M. (2007). Changing constructions of informed consent: Qualitative research and complex social worlds. *Social Science & Medicine, 65,* 2199–2211. doi:10/1016/j.socscimed.2007.08.009

Mills, E. (2002). Hazel the dental assistant and the research dilemma of (re)presenting a life story: The clash of narratives. In W. C. van den Hoonaard (Ed.), *Walking the tightrope: Ethical issues for qualitative researchers* (pp. 107–123). Toronto, ON: University of Toronto Press.

Morris, K., Woodward, D., & Peters, E. (1998). "Whose side are you on?" Dilemmas in conducting feminist ethnographic research with young women. *Social Research Methodology, 1*(3), 217–230.

Morris-Roberts, K. (2001). Intervening in friendship exclusion? The politics of doing feminist research with teenage girls. *Ethics, Place & Environment, 4*(2), 147–153.

Mortensen, P., & Kirsch, G. E. (Eds.). (1996). *Ethics and representation in qualitative studies of literacy.* Washington, DC: National Council of Teachers of English.

Nader, L. (1974). Up the anthropologist—Perspectives gained from studying up. In *Reinventing anthropology* (pp. 284–311). New York: Vintage Books.

Nagel, T. (1986). *The view from nowhere.* New York: Oxford University Press.

Naples, N. A. (2003). *Feminism and method: Ethnography, discourse analysis, and activist research.* New York: Routledge.

National Commission for the Protection of Human Subjects of Medical and Behavioral Research. (1979).

The Belmont report: Ethical principles and guidelines for the protection of human subjects of research. Washington, DC: Department of Health, Education, and Welfare. http://ohsr.od.nih.gov/guidelines/Belmont.html.

National Research Council. (2003). *Protecting participants and facilitating social and behavioral sciences research.* Washington, DC: Author.

Noddings, N. (1984). *Caring: A feminine approach to ethics and moral education.* Berkeley: University of California Press.

Noddings, N. (1995). *Philosophy of education.* Boulder, CO: Westview Press.

Noddings, N. (2002). *Starting at home: Caring and social policy.* Berkeley: University of California Press.

Noddings, N. (2003). *Caring: A feminine approach to ethics and moral education* (2nd ed.). Berkeley: University of California Press.

Oakley, A. (1981). Interviewing women: A contradiction in terms. In H. Roberts (Ed.), *Doing feminist research* (pp. 30–61). London: Routledge & Kegan Paul.

Oakley, A. (2000). *Experiments in knowing: Gender and method in the social sciences.* New York: New Press.

Paradis, E. K. (2000). Feminist and community psychology ethics in research with homeless women. *American Journal of Community Psychology, 28*(6), 839–858.

Patai, D. (1991). U.S. academics and Third World women: Is ethical research possible? In S. B. Gluck & D. Patai (Eds.), *Women's words: The feminist practice of oral history* (pp. 137–153). New York: Routledge.

Porter, E. (1999). *Feminist perspectives on ethics.* London: Longman.

Preissle, J., & Han, Y. (2009, November 6). *Gender and the demographics of immigrant education.* A presentation for the Friday Speaker Series of the Institute for Women's Studies, University of Georgia, Athens, GA.

Reason, P. (1996). Reflections on the purposes of human inquiry. *Qualitative Inquiry, 2*(1), 15–28.

Reinharz, S. (1992). *Feminist methods in social research.* New York: Oxford University Press.

Reverby, S. M. (2009). *Examining Tuskegee: The infamous syphilis study and its legacy.* Chapel Hill: University of North Carolina Press.

Rice, C. (2009). Imagining the other? Ethical challenges of researching and writing women's embodied lives. *Feminism & Psychology, 19*(2), 245–266. doi:10.1177/0959353509102222

Richardson, L. (1997). *Fields of play: Constructing an academic life.* New Brunswick, NJ: Rutgers University Press.

Robertson, J. (2000). Ethical issues and researching sensitive topics: Mature women and "bulimia." *Feminism & Psychology, 10*(4), 531–537.

Roman, L. G., & Apple, M. W. (1990). Is naturalism a move away from positivism? Materialist and feminist approaches to subjectivity in ethnographic research. In E. W. Eisner & A. Peshkin (Eds.), *Qualitative inquiry in education: The continuing debate* (pp. 38–73). New York: Teachers College Press.

Romyn, D. M. (1996). Problems inherent in the epistemology and methodologies of feminist research. In J. F. Kikuchi, H. Simmons, & D. Romyn (Eds.), *Truth in nursing inquiry* (pp. 140–149). Thousand Oaks, CA: Sage.

Salmons, J. (2010). *Online interviews in real time.* Thousand Oaks, CA: Sage.

Seibold, C. (2000). Qualitative research from a feminist perspective in the postmodern era: Methodological, ethical and reflexive concerns. *Nursing Inquiry, 7*(3), 147–155.

Seigfried, C. H. (1996). *Pragmatism and feminism: Reweaving the social fabric.* Chicago: University of Chicago Press.

Sexton, P. C. (1976). *Women in education.* Bloomington, IN: Phi Delta Kappa Educational Foundation.

Singer, P. (Ed.). (1991). *A companion to ethics.* Oxford, England: Blackwell.

Skelton, T. (2001). Girls in the club: Researching working class girls' lives. *Ethics, Places, and Environment, 4*(2), 167–173.

Skloot, R. (2010). *The immortal life of Henrietta Lacks.* New York: Crown.

Smith, D. E. (1987). *The everyday world as problematic: A feminist sociology.* Boston: Northeastern University Press.

Stacey, J. (1991). Can there be a feminist ethnography? In S. B. Gluck & D. Patai (Eds.), *Women's words: The feminist practice of oral history* (pp. 111–119). New York: Routledge.

Stanley, L., & Wise, S. (1993). *Breaking out again: Feminist ontology and epistemology.* London: Routledge.

Sultana, F. (2007). Reflexivity, positionality and participatory ethics: Negotiating fieldwork dilemmas in international research. *ACME: An*

International E-Journal for Critical Geographies, 6(3), 374–385. http://www.acme-journal.org/v016/FS.pdf

Tolman, D. L., & Brydon-Miller, M. (Eds.). (2001). *From subjects to subjectivities: A handbook of interpretive and participatory methods.* New York: New York University Press.

Tong, R. (1993). *Feminine and feminist ethics.* Belmont, CA: Wadsworth.

Tong, R. (1998). *Feminist thought: A more comprehensive introduction* (2nd ed.). Boulder, CO: Westview Press.

Traina, C. L. H. (1999). *Feminist ethics and natural law: The end of the anathemas.* Washington, DC: Georgetown University Press.

Visweswaran, K. (1994). *Fictions of feminist ethnography.* Minneapolis: University of Minnesota Press.

Vivat, B. (2002). Situated ethics and feminist ethnography in a west of Scotland hospice. In L. Bondi, H. Avis, R. Bankey, A. Bingley, J. Davidson, R. Duffy, et al. (Eds.), *Subjectivities, knowledges, and feminist geographies: The subjects and ethics of social research* (pp. 236–252). Lanham, MD: Rowman & Littlefield.

Waage, J., & Gowaty, P. A. (1997). Myths of genetic determinism. In P. A. Gowaty (Ed.), *Feminism and evolutionary biology* (pp. 585–613). New York: Chapman & Hall.

War Crimes Tribunal. (1947). *The Nuremberg code.* http://www.hhs.gov/ohrp/references/nurcode.htm

Weinberg, M. (2002). Biting the hand that feeds you, and other feminist dilemmas in fieldwork. In W. C. van den Hoonaard (Ed.), *Walking the tightrope: Ethical issues for qualitative researchers* (pp. 79–94). Toronto, ON: University of Toronto Press.

Wolf, D. L. (1996). Situating feminist dilemmas in fieldwork. In D. L. Wolf (Ed.), *Feminist dilemmas in fieldwork* (pp. 1–55). Boulder, CO: Westview Press.

Wolf, M. (1992). *A thrice told tale: Feminism, postmodernism, and ethnographic responsibility.* Stanford, CA: Stanford University Press.

World Medical Association. (1975). *World Medical Association Declaration of Helsinki: Ethical principles for medical research involving human subjects.* http://www.wma.net/en/30publications/10policies/b3/17c.pdf

Zeni, J., Prophete, M., Cason, N., & Phillips, M. (2001). The ethics of cultural invisibility. In J. Zeni (Ed.), *Ethical issues in practitioner research* (pp. 112–113). New York: Teachers College Press.

29

TRANSGENDER, TRANSSEXUALISM, AND THE QUEERING OF GENDER IDENTITIES

Debates for Feminist Research

KATHERINE JOHNSON

Feminist politics needs to speak to (and be spoken by) many more subjects than women and men, heterosexual women and lesbians. How—in theory and in practice— should feminism engage bisexuality, intersexuality, transsexuality, transgender, and other emergent identities that reconfigure both conventional and conventionally feminist understandings of sex, gender, and sexuality?

—C. Heyes (2003, p. 1093)

Feminism has a contentious history with regard to transgender, transsexual, and queer movements that seek to shake certainty in our understandings of sex, gender, and sexuality. It is, of course, impossible to speak of "feminism" in a single breath without fleshing out the nuanced investments that

underpin it as a political movement, academic discipline, and personal identity. Nevertheless, it can be argued that the questions trans identities and communities raised for second-wave feminism were crucial in precipitating the shift from identity politics to a "third-wave" feminism that bases itself on the "politics of gender performativity, choice, personal power, and individualism" (Pfeffer, 2010, p. 178). This shift has not been seen as positive in some sectors of feminism, particularly for those who see transgender as a threat to lesbian subjectivity (e.g., Jeffreys, 2003), but theoretical and empirical accounts of transgender subjectivity produced by trans and non-trans scholars (e.g., Hines, 2007; Rubin, 2003) have emerged to challenge some of the earlier lesbian-feminist critiques of transsexual and transgender practices (e.g., Raymond, 1980, 1994). Despite this, not all transsexuals have welcomed the tendency to celebrate transgender subjectivity as a queer vanguard for the deconstruction of gender (e.g., Bornstein, 1994; Halberstam, 1998; Hines, 2007) and have established their own critiques of feminist and queer theorists who promote this perspective (e.g., Namaste, 2005; Prosser, 1998), and the way this has led to a division between transsexual and transgender subjectivities. Here, they lament the way transsexualism has been aligned with the conservative practices of maintaining the binary gender system, while transgender has been celebrated as a playful means of disrupting gender normativity. This critique has found sympathetic support within some feminist accounts (e.g., Elliot, 2009) where feminists are urged to consider how we might work alongside trans people to undo hierarchies of gender. Elsewhere, other feminist theorists have drawn on transgender studies to argue for a rethinking of a feminist ethics of self-transformation outside of pathologizing discourses or conflicting ideological approaches to identity politics that recognizes solidarity with some of the body projects that trans and non-trans feminists are caught up in (Heyes, 2003, 2007). It is these debates that we consider in the next four sections before concluding with a reflection on the political usefulness of trans feminist and queer coalitions for promoting social justice and challenging broad structures of gender oppression.

What Is in a Name? Relational Definitions and the Use of Gender Terminology

A plethora of terms circulate in the literature that relates to transgender. It is not uncommon to see authors use the labels *transsexualism, transgenderism, queer,* or *gender variance,* and sometimes this will occur within the same article. In this section I will attempt to unpack the increasingly complex relationship they have with one another while reflecting on how language use can also be used to position feminist research in the context of wider theoretical and political debates over the status of gender claims. Transsexualism originated from the clinical literature that defined it as a diagnostic category (Benjamin, 1966) before replacing it with the diagnosis "gender identity disorder" (American Psychiatric Association, 2000) to distinguish between the

identity (transsexual) and the disorder (gender dysphoria). In contrast, *transgender* was originally formulated as a term to resist the pathologizing associations with an identity that emerged out of psychiatric diagnostic practices and to imply gender nonconformity without biomedical intervention. Virginia Prince (1976, p. 145) is credited with pioneering the terms *transgenderist* and *transgenderal* to refer to people who live full-time in the gender opposite to their biological sex but do not seek sex/gender reassignment surgery (Ekins & King, 1999, p. 581).

During the 1990s, the distinction between transgender and transsexual became played out in relation to the burgeoning influence of queer politics and theory. Here, transgender became aligned or even, as some have argued (e.g., Prosser, 1998), co-opted by queer theory as a transgressive and radical practice, which involved reinventing oneself outside of the normative gender system. In contrast, transsexualism was seemingly relegated to the inferior position of reinforcing the binary gender system, as it was perceived to be based on the practice of transitioning to live as either male or female. Despite this controversy, some researchers have suggested that all nonnormative gender identities (such as transsexualism, transgender, cross-dresser, intersex, transvestite, drag king or queen, and other queer performances of gender transgression) can exist under the umbrella term *transgender,* while others maintain the distinction between transsexuals and other forms of transgenderism on the basis of their engagement in biomedical techniques that transform the body via hormones and surgery (e.g., Namaste, 2000). The encompassing umbrella term is one that became popular in the "transgender community" and often stretched further to include partners, families, and professions working in the field (Ekins & King, 1999). Yet, there is no clear agreement about whether transgender should be seen as a distinct category because of a refusal to engage with biomedical practices or whether it is a label that can incorporate transsexual men and women who have had hormonal and surgical interventions, as well as other gender nonconformists.

In a more recent twist, the abbreviation of both transsexual and transgender to the term *trans* has become more commonplace within community settings (e.g., Lim & Browne, 2008), particularly as we see the expansion of the LGBTQIU (lesbian, gay, bisexual, trans, queer, intersex, unsure) banner to incorporate those who may affiliate with, but not identify as, lesbian, gay, or bisexual. The motivation for this could be couched in terms of simplifying the language games that have permeated trans communities in the past 15 years, but it also enables researchers, practitioners, and policy makers to avoid some of the problematic assumptions that definitions of transgender and transsexualism raise in terms of their varying relationship to clinical and medical practice.

Thus, if feminist researchers are looking for carefully defined labels that stipulate where individuals might be in their own transgender journey, the terms people use to define their identities may not be the most appropriate form of analysis. Transitioning is something that always necessitates some form of movement across or between the socially established binary genders, but it must be acknowledged that when theorists or individuals refer to the collective *trans,* they may mean different things in terms of both identities and practices. Richard Ekins and Dave King's (1999) position on this is to take a flexible and inclusive stance where "transgendering refers BOTH to the idea of moving across (transferring) from one pre-existing category to the other (either temporarily or permanently), AND to the idea of transcending or living 'beyond gender' altogether" (pp. 581–582). In fact, their position has been increasingly strengthened by a focus on the processes of transition rather than identities (see Ekins & King, 2006). However, forms of self-labeling are important as they can serve particular functions by enabling individuals to position themselves in relation to discursive constructions of gender, irrespective of how their identity might fit with gender practice.

For example, from my own experience of conducting research in the field, I found that participants do not fit simply into preconceived identity categories. I discovered this when I set out to investigate how people who self-identified as transsexual or transgendered constructed their identity (Johnson, 2001). When the project commenced, I purposefully sought to recruit people who met the clinical account that defined "transsexual" in terms of having begun, or completed,

transition to live full-time as the other gender (Bockting & Coleman, 1992), rather than those who might be classified as "transgendered," in terms of not engaging with hormonal and surgical interventions (Prince, 1976). What rapidly became clear during the research process was how difficult it was to draw a clear distinction between the ways these two "trans" identities were used by participants to self-define. While 13 of the 14 participants I interviewed fitted neatly into my working definition of *transsexual,* many strongly resisted using this term to describe themselves, preferring to use the term *transgender.* The reasons for this varied between participants. For some, the use of the term *transgender* enabled them to align themselves with the notion that the practice of transition was a transgressive act, underpinned by the then popular theoretical account of gender performativity (Butler, 1993) that had vitalized queer studies. To be transgendered also enabled them to sidestep the feminist critique that their practice of gender transition was a conservative act that upheld and reinforced the binary gender system (e.g., Jeffreys, 2003; Wilton, 2000). In contrast, for other participants, the identity "transsexual" implied a state of living "in between," serving as a painful reminder that they were not simply male or female. For these participants, the purpose of transitioning was to become male or female, not to become a transsexual. These accounts echoed the sentiments of Jay Prosser (1998), who has argued that identifying as transsexual (or even transgender) may be necessary to recoup understandings of trans people's experiences and to transform transsexuals from medical objects of study to active subjects partaking in the construction of their own subjectivity, however this shift has occurred at the personal cost of giving up on the "realness" of their male or female identities. There are few feminist or trans researchers in the field who would simply accept a self-definition of a trans person as "male" or "female" as it would make invisible the specificity of the trans experiences they are trying to understand. In this context, the researcher would at the very least wish to mark the participant as a "transman" or "transwoman," while others would seek to denote the direction of transition through references to abbreviations of male-to-female (e.g., MTF, M-t-F, or M2F) or female-to-male (e.g., FTM, F-t-M, F2M). While this aids in the empirical validity of knowledge we wish to produce, it is important to also be aware of the ethical implications of either applying or rejecting certain gender identifications.

The practice of labeling also tells us something about some feminist and trans academics' political goals, as well as their theoretical orientation. For instance, in the work of lesbian-feminist Sheila Jeffreys (2003), we find numerous references to trans academics in terms of the pronoun of their gender at birth. For example, when discussing the ideas of trans activist and law professor Stephen Whittle, Jeffreys refers to him as "her" and "she." This act can be interpreted in two ways depending on our own political and theoretical affiliations. For Jeffreys, the reinscription of Whittle's "factual" birth sex enables her to reclaim FTM trans subjectivity as one of butch lesbianism. Her argument is predicated on the judgment that transsexualism and the surgical reassignment associated with it are an attempt to eradicate homosexuality. In contrast, other feminists, inspired by post-structuralist theory, might critique Jeffreys's stance as an injurious speech act predicated on an essentialist claim that, for instance, transmen "really" are butch lesbians seeking to reappropriate and promote masculine values. Here they would argue (e.g., Elliot, 2009) that research with transmen shows that their engagement with masculinity is more complex than a reenactment of patriarchal values (e.g., Johnson, 2007a; Rubin, 2003). Certainly normative accounts of masculinity can be found in transmen's narratives, but empirical data also illustrate that they are reflexively engaged with constructing alternative forms of masculinity. These may have the possibility to subvert aspects of "dominant masculinity" and denaturalize the relationship between maleness and power (Halberstam, 1998). Furthermore, they argue that it is the very history of sharing a relationship with feminism and lesbian communities that drives this desire to form alternative masculinities and "redefine the meaning of being a man" (Rubin, 2003, p. 124; Johnson, 2007a). Less comfortable for non-trans feminists might be the argument that "dis-identifying" from women and butch lesbians in particular is a necessary part of their "identity project" when forming a masculine

identity (Rubin, 2003, p. 126), particularly if they once lived as a lesbian or identify as a heterosexual transman. However, Patricia Elliot (2009) argues that it is the complexity of these practices of desire that require greater attention in feminist research, rather than "reducing such desires to a question of bad politics" (p. 27).

An alternative method to help avoid fixing people into ill-fitting identity categories is to use the term *gender variance. Gender variance* is increasingly used to refer to a variety of practices that constitute movement across gender identities and has growing feminist support to describe those individuals who live outside of normative sex/gender configurations (e.g., Elliot, 2009). Here there is also a marked attempt to replace the use of *transgender* as a catch-all "umbrella" term because it can "erase transsexual subjectivity" (Namaste, 2000). Instead, gender variance can be used to capture the range of practices that are associated with the more established identity categories, with the perceived benefit that it also avoids the hierarchical judgment that transgender is somehow better—an assumption that has emerged when using transgender as an alternative category to transsexual over the past 15 years (Elliot, 2009).

Finally, feminists should also be ready to revisit the labels they apply to their own gender identities when conducting research in the field with trans or gender-variant others. For example, one criticism that has been directed at feminist scholars from trans academics is that feminists are quick to question the purpose and legitimacy of trans identities, while leaving their own gender identity claims intact. When non-trans feminists are about to embark on research in this field, it is worth reflecting on the impassioned account of Henry Rubin (1998):

> Nontranssexuals assume the coherent legibility of their gendered embodiment or their identities and are not expected to carry a share of the revolutionary burden of over throwing gender or imagining what to replace it with. They do not walk around, as they seem to be asking us to do, without gender identities or legible bodies. . . . They are not called upon to account for the fact that their gender is something they achieve. Somehow it has become our responsibility alone as transsexuals to shatter these norms. Somehow these

critics think that because we "know the rules" we should be the vanguard in charge of breaking them. It disappoints them that we have not made this connection between our knowledge and their program. (p. 273)

Recently, work has emerged out of transgender studies that attempts to return the labeling gaze onto those who proclaim normalized gender identities. For instance, the terms *bio-woman* and *bio-man* can be used to demarcate the identity of non-trans individuals' gender identity by illustrating that their "gender assignment at birth matches their gender identity" (Scott-Dixon, 2006, p. 242). Other terms that might be used are *genetic girl* or *natal female/male,* but as Krista Scott-Dixon (2006) points out, "these terms are sometimes seen as *biocentric,* or overly focused on biological markers as definitive of reality." Scott-Dixon also sets out the definition for another term that can be attributed to non-trans people, *cisgender.* This is "a synonym for non-trans that highlights normative gender presentation and congruence with biological sex. The 'cis' prefix plays on chemistry terminology: a 'cis' molecule configuration is the opposite of 'trans'" (p. 243). Others have coined new terms such as *hir* and *s/he* to help make transgendered people recognizable, definable, and visible in a gender system that relies on the binary she/he (Pershai, 2006). Elsewhere, the term *zie* or *ze* is used to represent those who wish to be recognized as living beyond the male/female gender system and has received attention following the legal case of norrie mAy-Welby in Australia (Fae, 2010). To paraphrase Heyes (2003, p. 1093), these labeling practices are useful because they remind us that a feminist engagement with transgender needs to entail an ongoing critical reflection with both conventional and unconventional understandings of sex, gender, and sexuality.

This raises certain considerations for the feminist researcher about the impact of gender labeling as well as the need to reflect on the preconceptions we might bring to our field of study and how we negotiate these with participants. If we are conducting research with or about trans-identified people, allowing participants to self-identify or giving voice to the way trans academics represent themselves can reveal new insights that unsettle established boundaries between particular identity categories. Thus, we should be mindful of the way labels and labeling strategies reveal as much about our own positions, personally, politically, and theoretically, as they do about others. For the purpose of this chapter, I primarily use the inclusive terms *transmen* and *transwomen* except when I am exploring theorists' arguments or personal accounts that wish to draw a distinction between the specificity of transsexualism and transgenderism. As we move on to consider how the figure of the transsexual has been used as a conceptual motif in feminist debates about the social construction of gender, I try to stay as true as possible to the authors' usage of gender labels. However, my own position that wishes to see more affiliation between trans and non-trans feminists as well as less hierarchal divisions between transsexuals and transgenderists will inevitably bleed into some of my interpretations.

Epistemological Challenges and the Purpose of Transgender Research

One of the primary issues for feminists working in the field of transgender research is whether or not claims to gender categories should be grounded in essentialist or social constructionist terms. The essentialism versus constructionism question was central to second-wave feminism sparking debate in theory, politics, and practice. Feminist post-structuralism, aroused by Simone de Beauvoir's (1949/1953) now infamous declaration "one is not born a woman," inspired a generation of scholars and activists to call for recognition of the socially constructed nature of gender. However, shaking the epistemological foundations of gender also raised significant challenges for those feminists who rejected transsexualism on political grounds. While social constructionism was seen as useful for arguing that the social roles ascribed to women were not based in nature, this argument readily came unstuck if it permitted others, who had been born male, to lay claim to the social identity "woman." This was and still is something of a conundrum for feminist researchers. In this section, I examine the importance that the "figure" of the transsexual played in driving feminist accounts that sought to demonstrate the socially constructed nature of gender and reflect on the way this theory clashed with feminist perspectives motivated by political goals that rely on essentialist claims to gender realness. To do this, we examine feminist accounts that use ethnomethodological and post-structuralist approaches before evaluating the criticism that feminists have been too interested in using "transsexualism" as a concept to support their own theoretical challenges to the binary gender system, rather than using their insights to develop a broader understanding of the specificities of trans people's lives.

In an early empirical account based on an ethnomethodological analysis of transsexualism, Suzanne Kessler and Wendy McKenna (1978/1985) argued for a radical shift from the gender theorists of the day by suggesting that both sex and gender were social constructs. It could seem that these two feminists preempted the developments of queer theory by almost a decade. Years before Moira Gatens (1983/1996), Gayle Rubin (1984), or Judith Butler (1990) began the task of critiquing the sex/gender distinction, Kessler and McKenna proposed that

> the constitutive belief that there are two genders not only produces the idea of gender role, but also creates a sense that there is a physical dichotomy . . . gender is a social construction, that a world of two "sexes" is a result of the socially shared, taken-for-granted methods which members use to construct reality. (p. xi)

Their research represented a significant shift away from traditional studies of transsexualism that focused on etiology (e.g., Stoller, 1968, 1975), social deviance (e.g., Feinbloom, 1976), or treatment (e.g., Benjamin, 1966) yet also avoided the moralistic diatribe that dominated critiques such as that of radical feminist Janice Raymond (1980). Rather, their prime focus was to investigate "what transsexualism can illuminate about the day-to-day social construction of gender by all persons" (Kessler & McKenna, 1978/1985, p. 112). Their ethnomethodological analysis of interviews with 15 transsexuals produced six beliefs that focused on practices of

"passing" that contributed to the "naturalization of gender." They suggested that by rarely referring to themselves as "transsexual" and by claiming to have always been one gender, transsexuals, like all of us, reinforced the "natural" binary gender system. However, the transsexual has to consciously employ particular techniques for "passing" as this gender, which include creating gender attributes, general talk, public physical appearance, the private body, and the personal past.

To expand on the concept of "passing," Kessler and McKenna (1978/1985) drew upon the theoretical work of Garfinkel (1967), who suggested that passing is an *ongoing* practice. However, they proposed an amendment to Garfinkel's thesis that most of the gender "work" in order to "pass" needs to be done by the displayer, rather than the perceiver. Instead, they suggested that

> in short, there is little that the displayer needs to do once he/she has provided the initial information, except maintain the sense of "naturalness" of her/his gender. Passing is an ongoing practice, but it is practiced by both parties. Transsexuals become more "natural" females or males and less self-consciously transsexuals when they realize that passing is not totally their responsibility. (p. 137)

In this context, like the rest of us, trans people can rely on the fact that the perceiver tends to stick to his or her original gender reading, unless it is seriously challenged. However, the task of maintaining their own narration of gender coherence must be seen as more problematic, particularly with reference to the last "passing" technique, "the personal past."

> Gender is historical. In concrete terms this involves talking in such a way that we reveal ourselves to have a history as a male or female. Transsexuals must not only conceal their real past (in most cases), but they must also create a new past. (Kessler & McKenna, 1978/1985, p. 132)

These techniques for "passing" (denying a different gender history and moving through the identity category transsexual to man or woman) were, at the time, central to the clinically managed process of a successful gender transition.

In more recent years, these practices have been increasingly challenged by transgendered scholars and activists (e.g., Stone, 1991; Stryker, 1994), who argue for the necessity of "coming out" in order to gain greater recognition of the specificity of transsexual subjectivity. Thus, there appears to have been a shift in the past 20 years where refusing to "pass" not only allows for a greater understanding of the embodied subjectivity of trans people but also demonstrates how trans identifications can contribute to a day-to-day *de*naturalization of gender. Kessler and McKenna's (1978/1985) feminist project must be acknowledged for the role it has played in this, despite their own motivation for understanding transsexuals for the purpose of interrogating the socially constructed nature of categories "sex" and "gender."

However, within feminist debates on transsexualism and transgenderism, Kessler and McKenna's (1978/1985) work was often overlooked (Lungren, 2000). Others produced deliberations over the ontological status of "woman" based on essentialist claims that transwomen cannot lay claim to the identity "woman" because they will never feel or experience what it is "to be a woman" (e.g., Grosz, 1994; Jeffreys, 2003; Raymond, 1980). A good example of this can be found in an acerbic critique by the well-known feminist Germaine Greer. In a chapter titled "Pantomime Dames," Greer (1999) concludes that

> whatever else it is gender reassignment is an exorcism of the mother. When a man decides to spend his life impersonating his mother (like Norman Bates in *Psycho*) it is as if he murders her and gets away with it, proving at a stroke that there was nothing to her. His intentions are no more honourable than any female impersonator's; his achievement is to gag all those who would call his bluff. When he forces his way into the few private spaces women may enjoy and shouts down their objections, and bombards the woman who will not accept him with threats and hate mail, he does as rapists have always done. (p. 74)

Despite being keen to promote social constructionist views of gender elsewhere in order to free women politically from stereotypical gender roles, Greer (1999) reverts to "gender essentialism" to negate the claim of transwomen to the category "woman." Undoubtedly, she is making some tacit reference to the dispute that ensued after the appointment of a transwoman at her Cambridge college and may have led to her own resignation. Here, transwomen are constructed as the bastard of the feminist movement: infiltrating and penetrating female spaces, impersonating and annihilating their mothers, not just in a "weird" or "freakish" sense, but in the fashion of the ultimate psychopath—Norman Bates. These types of representations of transwomen echo the now infamous ideas of Janice Raymond (1980) expressed in *The Transsexual Empire* and, more recently, repeated by Sheila Jeffreys (2003) in *Unpacking Queer Politics*. In this latter text, the ideas of Raymond are updated in order to defend lesbian feminism against queer theory and politics. Here, Jeffreys's central concern is that gender reassignment surgery is a technique to eradicate homosexuality. Certainly the power differentials of gender relationships will be involved in expressions of sexual desire, and likewise, Western societies are predominantly heteronormative; however, Jeffreys's thesis does not stand up when presented with the evidence that as many as 50% of transwomen go on to identify as lesbian (Nataf, 1996, p. 32). This might create debates over whether lesbian-identified transwomen should have access to lesbian- or women-only spaces, the critique that Raymond (1980) promoted and others have rejected (e.g., Koyama, 2006), but it certainly does not support an explanation of gender reassignment as a flight from homosexuality. Furthermore, other feminists have argued (perhaps against their own grain) that opening up membership to the category "lesbian" could be politically useful in terms of challenging gender oppression (e.g., Wilton, 1995), while the category "lesbian not-woman" (Calhoun, 1996) might also provide a comfortable identity for transwomen, particularly those who may not achieve an embodiment that enables them to "pass" in all interactions. For some, falling short of the ideals of femininity is one way of unsettling gender assumptions, and therefore it appears that rather than rejecting transsexuals, there is the possibility for greater affiliation between lesbians and transwomen and more reflection on the fragility of all our identity claims to the category "woman" (Johnson, 2007b).

What this conflict between various feminist threads illustrates is the emotive topic that transsexualism and transgenderism can be for feminist researchers. It is worth remembering that those who worked in radical feminist perspectives were seeking to challenge patriarchal values and gender oppression, as well as create safe spaces for women, some of whom had suffered from violence and discrimination often perpetrated by men. However, the response to the plight of trans-identified people by feminists such as Raymond and Jeffreys diminishes the importance of broader social institutions in maintaining gender inequality and oppression, while laying blame at the feet of minorities who have their own struggles to construct what Butler (2004) refers to as a livable life. As Gayle Rubin argued as long ago as 1984,

> Transsexuals are as likely to exhibit sexist attitudes or behavior as any politically random social grouping. But to claim that they are inherently anti-feminist is sheer fantasy. A good deal of current feminist literature attributes the oppression of women to graphic representations of sex, prostitution, sex education, sadomasochism, male homosexuality and transsexuality. Whatever happened to the family, religion, education, child-rearing practices, the media, the state, psychiatry, job discrimination, and unequal pay? (p. 302)

In more recent years, post-structuralist informed feminist accounts of transsexualism and transgenderism have prevailed over radical feminist critiques. Yet, the figure of the transsexual for gender theory, rather than the specificity of transsexual or transgendered subjectivity, has continued to drive much feminist research (e.g., Garber, 1992; Hausman, 1995; Wilton, 2000). Here, feminist theorists have focused on produced sociocultural analyses of transsexualism as a medical construct in order to comment on the political consequences for gender. For example, in a Foucauldian-inspired framework, Bernice Hausman (1995) argues that the notion "changing sex" helps regulate a binary gender. While her analysis of transsexualism as a technology of the body and as a medical phenomenon has found some support, her thesis has been criticized by other feminists for foreclosing the possibility of resistance by

transsexual subjects to the "medical-technological complex" (Heyes, 2007, p. 49). Likewise, the trans academic Henry Rubin (1998) cites Hausman's critique of transsexualism as one that relegates the transsexual to a passive subject position who, as Rubin describes, "should somehow know better than to 'believe' in gender (while letting nontranssexuals off the hook)" (p. 271). Tamsin Wilton (2000) provides another example of a post-structuralist informed analysis that draws a distinction between discourse and subjectivity. In "Out/Performing Our Selves," she begins by professing that

> this article is not "about" transsexual *people,* but about medicalized *discourses* of MTF transsex and, although I recognize that such discourses both produce and are produced by transpeople, it is the discourses themselves and their wider effects on the gendered politics of sexuality that I am interrogating (p. 237)

But we might question the usefulness of isolating a specific set of discourses for understanding "the gendered politics of sexuality," particularly when attention to other discourses and material practices could easily unpack or counteract the claimed effects. Seemingly aware of this, Wilton (2000) goes on to note,

> It is important to acknowledge that claims of "being in the wrong body" mark only one strand of the many which currently characterize the transsexual/transgender experience. In recent years the performativities of those for whom attributed sex is at odds with their sense of self have proliferated beyond the always-fragile bounds of the medical model of trans-sex, to incorporate gender-transience, blurring and other transitionalities. Such strategies . . . do not concern me here. (p. 238)

Similarly, her "focus also excludes female-to-male trajectories, although FTM accounts complicate the politics of sexuality in intriguing ways" (Wilton, 2000, p. 238). Thus, the problem with Wilton's account for feminists who *are* interested in moving beyond conceptual accounts of transsexualism is obvious. While she acknowledges that trans subjectivity is not simply produced by medical discourses, she avoids engaging with those aspects of trans experience that will disturb the professed effects of medical discourses upon the politics of gendered sexuality. It is precisely the complexities and inconsistencies in the narrated accounts of transmen and transwomen that have the ability to *unsettle* the medical discourses that attempt to regulate the binary gender system and heteronormativity. Hence, while Wilton focuses on the medical discourses of transsexualism rather than "transsexual *people*," other feminist researchers have sought to explore the way trans people negotiate these discourses (e.g., Elliot & Roen, 1998; Hines, 2007; Johnson, 2001, 2005) in order to flesh out understandings of trans subjectivities as well as interrogate the intersections of sex, gender, and sexuality. A feminist post-structuralist interrogation of only medical discourses of transsexualism will do little more than reinforce binary assumptions about gender transition. However, if feminists incorporated a narrative engagement with the multiplicity of trans subjective experience into their methodological approaches, it would enable a feminist research praxis that offers the possibility of gender critique and potentially highlight shared experiences of gender oppression.

For example, in my research (Johnson, 2007b), participants did not speak of an easy relationship to the category "male" or "female," with many expressing a conscious fragility in their claims to a new gender identity as the following extract illustrates:

> We're not in the case of male-to-female, we're not natural born women nor will we ever be so and the kind of sense and feeling of womanhood is the closest approximation to how we are ourselves rather than actually being a woman (K: right) and so from that context I kind of feel that . . . we should as a body kind of accept and understand ourselves as transsexual rather than necessarily as women . . . because we're never quite there and you know, I can't tell you what it feels like to be a woman, all I know is that's the closest association umm in rigid gender terms (Emily, transwoman, age 33). (p. 124)

One of the most salient problems that many feminists have with trans women is the practical issue that they have not been socialized as "women" and therefore should not have access to women-only space (Gottschalk, 2009). Emily (a pseudonym) acknowledges the tenuous claim that she and other transwomen have to the identity category "woman" but turns our attention to the idea that while the dominant gender order is in the form of a binary system, "woman" is the closest approximation to her sense of gendered self.

This raises several issues for the relationship between feminist theory and praxis. First, if we are drawing on a theoretical orientation that promotes anti-essentialist, post-structuralist accounts of gender, then we must acknowledge that *all* women have a tenuous claim to the identity category woman. Second, if a primary political goal of feminism is to challenge gender oppression, we must be mindful of how our own theoretical and empirical endeavors contribute to the political oppression and silencing of other minorities. For instance, if we reject transwomen's claims to the identity categories "woman" or "lesbian" or refuse them access to women's services or women's spaces on the basis of their ontological claims to that gender identity, do we not take part in another form of gender oppression? If we listen to the accounts of transwomen and transmen, we see that their identificationary practices are restricted and constrained by the institutional forces that continue to support a binary gender system, and we need to reflect on how our own engagement with transgender and transsexual experience might contribute to their marginalization in a society that only recognizes men and women.

If feminist researchers heed the lessons from these debates, we can see that it is not enough to use the transsexual or the transgendered subject as a metaphorical figure, or motif, for the singular purpose of making theoretical or political points. Feminist arguments will be strengthened and our own ideological values challenged by a deeper engagement with the specificities of trans experiences and the multiple and competing ways these simultaneously support and undermine the binary gender system. While trans subjects may be complicit with certain discourses of gender, non-trans people also need to reflect on how our identities do little to challenge or reinvent new modes of being. In the next section, we will examine further the influence of queer/feminist theory on the emergence of accounts of transsexual and transgender subjectivity and critically evaluate the claim that these accounts have contributed to the growing hierarchy between them. We also consider the limitations of queer/feminist accounts and review the way some trans and feminist theorists have drawn on phenomenological and psychoanalytic concepts to address the question of trans embodiment.

QUEER DISRUPTIONS AND THE MAKING OF TRANS SUBJECTIVITIES

Despite the 1980s being well documented in the social sciences and humanities as ushering in the "cultural turn" where social constructionist ideas were used to challenge essentialist thinking, it was the dramatic impact that Judith Butler's *Gender Trouble* (1990) and, later, *Bodies That Matter* (1993) had in the field of gender studies that precipitated the emergence of a new field of transgender studies. In *Gender Trouble,* Butler formulated a challenge to the ontological status of gender, arguing that "being" is reducible to the form of "appearing." Using an analysis of drag, Butler argued that there is no ontological "truth" to being male or female; rather, every aspect of gender is performed. In *Bodies That Matter,* she readdressed the notion of gender construction by focusing on the materialization of "sex." Here, Butler (1993) argued that the process of materialization *"stabilizes over time to produce the effect of boundary, fixity, and surface we call matter"* (p. 9). Thus, there is no "real" male or female body, only an unattainable ideal to aspire to become. This ideal is maintained through the iteration and embodiment of gender norms cemented together by heterosexuality.

Following Butler's contention that all of our claims to "be male" or "be female" are a fiction, it could be argued that transmen and transwomen are embroiled in much the same process of attaining a "sex" as non-trans identified men and women. Namely, we are all striving for the effect of "realness" in the ongoing process of *becoming* male or female—although trans people are also required to undo the gender they wish to reject (Johnson, 2007a). While criticisms (e.g., Martin, 1992/1996) of Butler's apparent failure to acknowledge the limitations of the body, as well as its potential, are well documented in feminist accounts, it has also been possible to argue that "it was precisely *because* of her failure to sufficiently theorise the body that the space was created for the emergence of a wide variety of non-pathologising accounts of gender and sex transgression" (Johnson, 2005, p. 36). However, feminist researchers should also be aware that the importance of Butler's work in trans academic circles is of some contention. Some (e.g., Namaste, 2000) have vociferously lamented the way Butler's work has seemingly contributed to the hierarchical division between the newly celebrated "transgenderist" and the relegated "transsexual." Others (e.g., Rubin, 1998), including non-trans feminists (e.g., Elliot & Roen, 1998; Johnson, 2007a), have highlighted that citational methods alone are insufficient for accounting for the way trans subjectivities are lived and have turned to phenomenological and psychoanalytic accounts to better theorize trans embodiment. It is the strength and limitations of these approaches that we examine here.

In the early 1990s, key trans theorists and activists such as Susan Stryker (1994, 1998), Kate Bornstein (1994), and Riki Anne Wilchins (1995) embraced the language of "performativity" to dispute essentialist, radical feminist critiques of transsexualism and promote accounts of transgender subjectivity predicated on a "coming-out" discourse. As Stryker proposed, at least two pronounced sets of factors determined the academy's growing interest in "transgender." The first she describes as the "postmodern condition"; the second, she suggested, was in part due to the proliferation of individuals who "lay claim to some form of transgender identity" within "cultural zones where postmodern representational systems are well established" (Stryker, 1998, p. 147). Both provided new configurations of discourses for critical theorists to dissect. Accordingly, Stryker (1998) argued,

> Transgender phenomena have achieved critical importance (and critical chic) to the extent that they provide a site for grappling with the problematic relation between the principles of *performativity* and a *materiality* that, while inescapable, defies stable representation, particularly as experienced by embodied subjects. (p. 147, emphasis added)

Mary Brown Parlee (1996) averred that the new representations of gendered embodiment that emerged from the discourses of the "transgender liberation" movement (Leslie Feinberg's [1993] term) are "strikingly different from psychological theories of gendered embodiment emanating from the academy" (p. 633). Parlee suggests that activists who are committed to accounting for the variety in transgendered persons' embodied subjectivities have had to move beyond such bedrock concepts as "man," "woman," "male," "female," "lesbian," "gay," and "straight." To do this, Parlee draws upon the writings of Riki Anne Wilchins, founder of the activist group Transsexual Menace, to illustrate how transgender activists have been engaged in "rethinking—re-theorizing—sex and gender categories, developing new terms" (p. 633). Wilchins states,

> I don't believe in "male" and "female" or "man" and "woman" either. Certainly I believe in them as political accomplishments, cultural categories instituted to cause us to read the body in a specific way: promoting and sustaining the imperative that the most important thing bodies can do is reproduce. But I don't view them as the so-called "natural facts" they are interminably and predictably proposed to represent. . . . The point is all these names reflect the political aims of a cultural regime which produces certain gender "realities" for its own changing, and historically specific, needs. . . . So, if we are to disrupt the regime, we must take control of language, take control of (corrupt) the definitions, disturb the structure. This brings us to a number of terms coming into increasing coinage in the "gender community," such as "gendertrash," one "S" transsexuals, "genderqueer" etc. (cited in Parlee, 1996, p. 635)

The influence of queer strategies and Judith Butler's work in particular is apparent here, and inevitably, Wilchins goes on to make this explicit. As such, it can be argued that Butler's work provided the discursive means by which transgendered individuals could begin to express and direct their "rage," as Susan Stryker (1994) would describe it, at the medical and scientific discourses that had sought to create uniformity in or annihilation of their embodied gendered subjectivities. Certainly, in the exciting and edifying days of early queer politics, the political climate was ripe for the emergence of a transgender activism that threatened to tear up gender norms. But this activism, as well as the radical challenge it endeavored to make, was also dependent on the articulations of "queer" feminist theorists such as Judith Butler.

Sandy Stone (1991) was another key voice to reposition transgender as a radical, transformative practice. In her exciting and exuberant article "The Empire Strikes Back," Stone was one of the first transgender academics to draw on Judith Butler's work. Employing Butler's concept of *cultural intelligibility,* Stone suggested that in the case of the transsexual, "the varieties of performative gender, seen against a culturally intelligible gendered body *which is itself a medically constituted textual violence,* generate new and unpredictable dissonances" (p. 296). These dissonances would be created by juxtaposing the transsexual's "refigured body" with conventional gender discourse that, Stone argued, would result in the fragmentation and reconstitution of gender into new and unexpected fields. Thus, she suggested that transsexuals should not be constituted as a class or "third gender" but

> rather as a *genre*—a set of embodied texts whose potential for *productive* disruption of structured sexualities and spectra of desire has yet to be explored. (p. 296)

However, in order for this to take effect, it would require transsexual subjects to make themselves *visible,* which in turn has serious implications for the narration of gender transition. As we have seen from the work of Kessler and McKenna (1978/1985), the one factor that best indicates a successful transition is to "pass." Yet, "passing" requires what Stone (1991) has described as the "effacement of the prior gender role," the construction of a plausible history, and ultimately has been attributed to the practice of those who wish to fit into the binary gender system. Here, we see the impact of queer/feminist theory beginning to shape the transsexual/transgender distinction that aligns transsexual with a conservative gender practice of passing and transgender with the celebratory model of "coming out." While Stone is sympathetic to "passing" transsexuals, on a personal level, she is critical of the seeming acceptability of "wrong body" as an adequate descriptive category for transsexual experience. As she says, "In fact 'wrong body' has come, virtually by default, to *define* the syndrome," and while academics, clinicians, and trans people continue to "ontologize both sexuality and transsexuality in this way, we have foreclosed the possibility of analyzing desire and motivational complexity of individual lived experience" (p. 297).

However, the way Butler's work was promoted by some transgender activists often included a misreading of the notion of gender performativity. "It's an exciting time here at the beginning of a movement," declared self-proclaimed "gender outlaw" Kate Bornstein (1994) in one of the best examples of a misreading of Butler's notion of "gender performativity." In a style more celebratory than Stone's and less empathetic to the plight of most transsexuals, Bornstein embarked upon an enthusiastic and deconstructive assault on the "rules" of the gender system where

> gender fluidity is the ability to freely and knowingly become one or many of a limitless number of genders, for any length of time, at any rate of change. Gender fluidity recognizes no borders or rules of gender. (p. 52)

Although Bornstein's (1994) *Gender Outlaw: On Men, Women, and the Rest of Us* possesses an energy that makes it fun to read, many of her theoretical goals are problematic for both feminists and trans subjects. For example, one of Bornstein's principal concerns is to distinguish between those transsexual or transgendered individuals who appear to contest the gender system: "gender outlaws," such as herself, and those individuals who appear to uphold the gender order, "gender defenders." As such, transsexuals who "pass" are devalued because in appearing to conform to gender rules, they reinstate the very rules that their act of transition undid. But as Patricia Elliot and Katrina Roen (1998) correctly point out, "The opposition Bornstein constructs for the purpose of privileging the outlaws denies the complexity and fluidity of identity she hopes to affirm and denies the possibility of a sexual politics that might find support in either group" (p. 239).

A second related problem with Bornstein's (1994) account concerns how she perceives the relationship between the body and gender fluidity. Bornstein argues that the body has no limit on gender signification, that gender identities can be taken on at will and are in no way dependent on the physical manifestation of the body. But can gender identities simply be taken on in isolation from others' readings of our body? Even if this were the case, one might wonder why Bornstein was compelled to construct a female body, to signify to others her female identity. I should add that after reading her radical thesis, which divides the world between gender defenders and gender outlaws, I was interested to see how this "gender outlaw" manifested physically—how she performed "gender outlaw" in an embodied manner. However, from the photograph on the back cover of the book, my reading of her was as a white, straight female. Unless, of course, she comes out as "Kate Bornstein, the MtF transgenderist, lesbian, performance artist" in every transient interaction, how are others to know she is a "gender outlaw"? Despite this, she criticizes, as many feminists do, those she constructs as seeking to "pass" on a daily basis for reinstating the binary gender system. I think that perhaps the most disappointing aspect of Bornstein's thesis is that these claims are made retrospectively. She *has* transitioned and does manifest to all intents and purposes as female, despite her claim to be a gender outlaw. Yet, she begins to argue against those who, for what must be a variety of social, psychological, and economic factors, try to live their lives within the structures of a binary gender system. Unfortunately, Bornstein's work, while admirable for attempting to provide an account of transgender experience outside of sociomedical discourses, feeds into the divisive tendency for the "transgenderist" to be valorized over and above the transsexual.

In a contrasting account that also demarcates the split between proposals for transgender and transsexual visibility, Jay Prosser (1998) agrees with Stone that the "wrong body formula" has become the nub of transsexual rhetoric deployed in order to obtain access to hormones and surgery. Yet, he argues that the proliferation of the wrong body figurative cannot be attributed singularly to its discursive power and cohesion with medical narratives. Instead, he suggests that many transsexuals continue to use this aphorism simply because it gives a very good representation of their feelings of *dis*embodiment. As he states,

> If the goal of transsexual transition is to align the feeling of gendered embodiment with material body, body image—which we might be tempted to align with the imaginary—clearly already has a material force for transsexuals. The image of being trapped in the wrong body conveys this force. . . . The image of wrong embodiment describes most effectively the experience of pretransition (dis)embodiment: the feeling of a sexed body dysphoria profoundly and subjectively experienced. (p. 69)

This sentiment resonates with some of the accounts I found in my own research with people who identified as transsexual or transgendered (Johnson, 2001). For example, one participant, Caroline (a pseudonym), could not be couched as a passive dupe of medical discourses (as some feminists have claimed); rather, she knowingly described the general suspicion of the "wrong body" discourse but supports it as a means to explain the affective and embodied sense of being transsexual:

> This is going to sound so clichéd you know the thing about the woman trapped in a man's body, it is the biggest cliché under the sun but it's true. It's the only way you can really describe it and it's not until you start going through the whole process of changing over that you realize that. (Caroline, transwoman, age 29) (Johnson, 2001, p. 118)

Thus, in turning away from performativity, Prosser (1998) highlights the particular concern for transsexual subjects with the correspondence between material body surface and body image or, to paraphrase, the feeling of being at home in one's skin. For Prosser, skin appears as an organ both illustrating and enabling the "psychic/corporeal interchange of subjectivity." Thus, subjectivity cannot be said to be only about having a physical skin; rather, subjectivity is a matter of "psychic investment of self in skin" (p. 73). Furthermore, Prosser is also critical of the claim

that queer studies enabled the representation of transgendered subjectivity. In contrast, Prosser suggests "queer studies *has made the transgendered subject,* the subject who crosses gender boundaries, a *key queer trope*" (p. 5, emphasis added). While acknowledging that "transgender would not be of the moment if not for the queer moment" (p. 6), Prosser argues that queer theory has elevated the transgendered subject above and beyond the transsexual subject. This, he suggests, is the result of queer theory's particular interest in those who cross gender lines, rather than in those who cross the lines of sex. Thus, Prosser attempts to redress what he sees as queer theory's omission of embodiment—in favor of gender performativity—by concentrating on transsexual narratives. He suggests that "transition," in queer theory, may be explored in order to evidence the sex/gender system as a construction and thus indicate the impossibility of identity. However, for transsexualism, in contrast, "transition" may be "the very route *to* identity and bodily integrity" (Prosser, 1998, p. 6, emphasis added).

Prosser's project is an important one. Having himself transitioned from female to male, his position is both sentient and sensitive to the experience of being transsexual. As such, he questions the growing trend for transsexuals to give up on "passing," to "come out," which he posits as an effect of the transsexual community engagement with transgendered politics. Prosser acknowledges that a politically driven "coming-out" rhetoric is important for creating both transgendered and transsexual as specific and, importantly, allied subjectivities. However, Prosser argues that rather than revealing gender categories as a fiction, as most "queer" accounts would assert, *both* transsexual and transgendered narratives, to paraphrase, produce the sobering realization of the ongoing functional power that the categories of man and woman still carry for a sense of cultural belonging (Prosser, 1998, p. 11). Thus,

> While coming out is necessary for establishing subjectivity, for transsexuals the act is intrinsically ambivalent. For in coming out and staking a claim to representation, the transsexual *undoes the realness* that is the conventional goal of this transition. These narratives return us to the complexities and

difficulties that inevitably accompany real-life experiences of gender crossing and to the personal costs of not simply being a man or a woman. In accounts of individual lives, outside its current theoretical figuration transition often proves a barely livable zone. (Prosser, 1998, pp. 11–12, emphasis added)

Similarly, in an empirical study with trans-women and transmen, Elliot and Roen (1998) recorded that some participants had difficulties with notions that were being promoted by transgender theorists. These difficulties included "the desire to pass as the other gender, the demand for anatomical congruity with gender through surgical intervention, and the reluctance to politicize what is also an intensely personal experience" (Elliot & Roen, 1998, p. 257). In a particularly poignant excerpt taken from an interview with Babe, who was born with a female anatomy but identifies as a man, the authors describe how he has to negotiate a range of contradicting and powerful discourses:

It is possible to perceive Babe as being caught painfully among these opposing discourses: medical discourses that hold out a promise of surgery that might never actually be available; transgender discourses that challenge him to live as a man, or better, as a transgendered person, without relying on the promise of surgery; and the Christian discourses of his home and family, which encourage him to love and respect his (female) body as a creation of God. It is little wonder that the Cartesian view of oneself as "trapped in the wrong body" is of greatest comfort and therefore of immediate use to Babe. (Elliot & Roen, 1998, p. 250)

Thus, a number of trans and feminist scholars are skeptical of many postmodern or post-structuralist informed accounts that promote celebratory notions of transgender border crossings at the expense of theorizing transsexual embodiment, particularly the exigent feelings of *dis*embodiment that constitute much of transsexual lived experience. Elliot and Roen (1998) argue that while it is important to be "critical of medical approaches to the body and to transsexuality," they support Martin's (1992/1996) view that "the 'complex relations between the body and psyche (must not) disappear.' That is treating

the body as a manipulative thing suggests there are no psychic investments in it that require consideration." Furthermore, they reject theories that "read gender identities and bodies as effects of historically specific constructions or that valorize crossing as a way to escape historical constructions" (Elliot & Roen, 1998, p. 243). Accordingly, they turn their attention to psychoanalytic concepts to enrich their analysis of transgendered embodiment. In a critique of the views of Judith Butler, they suggest that despite Butler's claim that psychoanalysis "is the best account of the psyche—and psychic subjection—that we have," she is unable "to escape the cultural determinism she explicitly hopes to avoid." Consequently, they suggest that

when the major concern of feminist, queer, or transgender theorists is with the ways in which a given society stigmatizes, oppresses, or excludes its nonnormative others, it is necessary to employ a sociological or historical analysis. What poses problems . . . is that sexuality and psychic life cannot be understood with historical tools alone. To do so is to produce a limited reading that cannot adequately theorize a given subject's relation to his/her own embodiment, to unconscious desire, and to the particular history of a subject's own psychic life. (Elliot & Roen, 1998, p. 246)

It is for this precise reason that Henry Rubin (1998) suggests that phenomenology provides a framework for making sense of transsexualism in a way that also attends to and recognizes transsexual agency and embodiment:

Phenomenology recognizes the circumscribed agency of embodied subjects who mobilize around their body image to sustain their life projects. A phenomenological method works to return agency to us as subjects and to return authority to our narratives. It justifies a turn to the self-reports of transsexual subjects as a place to find counterdiscursive knowledge. (p. 271)

Rubin's (2003) thesis also signaled another "strike back" from the *Transsexual Empire* (Stone, 1991) by highlighting the growing gulf between the way many feminists and queer theorists have expected "transgender" not only to represent an *occasion* for gender transgression but to actually break down and demolish the existing binary gender system. This posed a stark comparison with the lived experience of many of those who might actually describe themselves as transgendered or transsexual. From Kessler and McKenna[1] (1978/1985), via Raymond (1980) and Wilton (2000), to Hausman (2001), and with many others in between, feminist authors have frequently lamented that transsexuals reaffirm rather than transgress the binary gender system, while leaving their own normative, congruent gender identities and sexed bodies unexamined.

As I have noted previously, this practice forecloses the possibility of collaboration between feminist and trans academics, despite the potential for sharing the common goal of challenging practices of gender oppression. More recently, Viviane Namaste (2005) has stated emphatically what she sees as at stake in the polarization of feminist, queer, and transgender accounts of transsexuality. In an insightful summary, the non-trans feminist scholar Patricia Elliot (2009) outlines four substantial critiques Namaste makes of the way transsexual identities have seemingly been co-opted by feminist/queer theorists for the purpose of challenging the binary gender system. First, by assuming transsexualism within the umbrella "transgender," Namaste argues this makes transsexual subjectivity invisible. For Namaste, there is something markedly different between transgender and transsexual in that "the transgender emphasis on gender identity obscures transsexuals' concern with the social and political processes involved in becoming and living as the other sex" (Elliot, 2009, p. 8). Second, Namaste is critical of the transgender discourse that elevates transgender practices to a higher moral ground while relegating transsexual practices to the realms of political conservatism. Of particular concern is the way this hierarchy overlooks the history of transsexual politics that have sought legal protection and the right to live and work as transsexuals, as well as undermining their contribution to gender politics more generally. Third, Namaste, like Prosser, points out that most transsexuals do not seek to transgress gender categories but rather embody them, and this has little to do with queer identities. Here, Elliot points out that Namaste's reading is based on the interpretation of queer as specifically aligned with lesbian, gay, and bisexual orientations, rather than as a

performative strategy for disrupting normative ideals. As such, Elliot (2009) resists Namaste's reluctance to engage with the possibility of "queer" because

> although the queer transgendered perspective may place greater emphasis on the visible crossing of gender boundaries that interrupts taken-for-granted views of congruence between sex and gender, there is also something queer about the transsexual claim that their identity is not (obviously) grounded in their birth sex, and that for them, the desired congruence must be created. (p. 11)

Finally, Namaste (2005) has accused transgender theorists and Judith Butler in particular of "contempt" for failing to engage with transsexual theorists' responses that reject queer interventions. Her critique goes further to claim that not only are transsexual lives ignored and hidden by a focus on identity and rights; transsexuals are also prevented from understanding or critiquing the institutional dimensions of their lives (Namaste, 2005, p. 17, in Elliot, 2009, p. 12). Namaste's work focuses on transsexual lives that are seen as marginalized in terms of race and class and also at risk of health and substance misuse problems. These accounts can seem a long way from the privilege of the academy and the application of queer theory in order to dismantle gender. Yet, Elliot (2009) is unwilling to accept Namaste's critique outright. Instead, she suggests that Namaste could produce a critique that points to the need for greater voice to be given to those most marginalized, rather than promoting the view of "the intransigent privileged minority that is unable to think beyond its own boundaries" (p. 13). In Elliot's considered conclusion, she states that feminists need to reflect not on the "good" and "bad" politics of transgender and transsexual accounts but on "how gender variance is to be supported by non-trans feminists, especially since this rift originates in competing desires, needs and goals" (p. 27). While the queering of transsexualism has created the possibility for more gender expressions, it has also created a detrimental hierarchy between transgender and transsexual. Thus, questioning the position of Butler (2004), Elliot (2009) states, "What needs undoing is not gender, but hierarchies of transgender. . . . For non-trans feminists, the value placed on both transsexual and transgender expressions of gender variance may be measured by our support for this undoing" (p. 27).

ETHICAL COALITIONS AND TRANS FEMINIST POTENTIALS

In this final section, we consider whether it is possible to formulate coalitions across various identity borderlines, including trans and non-trans feminist, which might undo these hierarchies. Here we consider the argument for feminist solidarity based on shared ethical and political goals, and whether trans feminism might offer an alternative to "queer" for forging "inessential coalitions" (Lloyd, 2005) to promote social justice along gender lines.

In the excellent text *Self-Transformations: Foucault, Ethics, and Normalized Bodies,* Cressida Heyes (2007) argues for a feminist solidarity that recognizes that the ethical and political questions that concern trans and non-trans feminists may not be as different as some theorists have claimed. Here, she provides a detailed analysis of transgender oppression (Feinberg, 1993) and draws comparisons to feminist concerns with body modification practices such as dieting and cosmetic surgery (e.g., Davis, 1995). Heyes (2007) is mindful of falling into the trap of suggesting that reassignment surgery is the same as other cosmetic interventions (e.g., Halberstam, 1994) but attempts to promote feminist solidarity through a middle ground where an "ethics of self-fashioning" might flourish. As she states,

> I am not arguing for a one-size-fits-all theory of embodied identities, or minimizing the grave emotional and pragmatic implications of moving in the world with a sexed body at odds with one's gender. Often the psychic battles of those considering diets and cosmetic surgeries are not accessible to others as embodied dissonances; they have the dubious luxury of seeming "normal," and the steps they take to transform themselves are usually less dramatic and can be part of a less disjointed life story. Nonetheless, we all feel the weight of culture where identities and bodies are supposed to line up, and despite our deep differences we share the goal of making our existence as gendered critics of gender livable, while opening possibilities for new kinds of lives. (p. 62)

Similarly, in my research (Johnson, 2007b), I have also argued for greater affiliation between those who crisscross the axes of gender and sexuality. The narrative accounts of those who come to identify as either transgender or transsexual illustrate rich variety in feelings toward identities lost and found. However, empirical studies show that the messy tales of gender and sexuality transition do not sit well with attempts to demarcate identity borderlines about who can claim to be male or female and who cannot, because once lesbians, gays, transsexuals, women, and so forth begin to tell their stories, it is clear how enmeshed they are: by historical and medical discourses, by media sensationalism and misunderstanding, and by violence and discrimination. Yet identity borderline battles continue, and I would argue this has as much to do with psychic health as with political affiliation. Our identities matter to us as ways of feeling we belong and as means of positioning ourselves in relation to social and political conditions. However, essentialist notions of identity that underpin "identity politics" have not delivered the forms of transformation they promised often because action has been stifled by debilitating internal debates over the precise status of the "identity" they purport to represent.

An alternative approach to transformative action can be promoted through coalition politics, and several attempts have been made to forge these by feminist collectives (e.g., Anzaldúa & Keating, 2002). In studies of the everyday lives of trans-identified people, we find stories of acute social and economic marginalization, violence, health, and mental health difficulties (e.g., Namaste, 2005). My aim here is not to simply position these trans people as "victims" but to point to the opportunity for feminists to work alongside trans community members to address how these issues fit into the larger picture of gender inequality and oppression. Transformation of this type will not be achieved through theoretical reflection alone but might be effected by drawing on methods such as participatory action research (e.g., Paxton, Guentzel, & Trombacco, 2006; Billies, Johnson, Murungi, & Pugh, 2009). This approach requires genuine collaboration and deep personal reflection on our values and assumptions, a willingness to learn from and be challenged by others, while tackling goal-related questions that are relevant to community issues. Within these types of actions, it may be possible to configure coalitions between trans and non-trans feminists that join forces in political struggles for wider social justice. For example, Paxton et al. (2006) describe a number of lessons learned from developing a research partnership with the transgender community. Working through a participatory action research framework, they outline the knowledge exchange process between "Diana," an African American transwoman with a wealth of experience working in trans communities on HIV prevention, and "Carla," an African American, biological, heterosexual woman who worked as an academic researcher in clinical/community psychology. The two formed a collaborative relationship when Diana was hired as a research associate and requested Carla to work with her in the transgender community. The study outlines both their journeys as they reflect on their identity differences and similarities and how these can be a barrier to and facilitator of personal and social transformation. While the study presents highly individual narratives of change, it demonstrates the importance of reflexivity for feminist praxis when working with those who might be seen as "other." It also promotes the value of collaborative projects that focus on social and health inequalities, as partaking in these can break down stereotypical assumptions and heighten understandings of shared gender experiences.

Trans feminism is another such coalition that has sought to debate the differences between trans people and non-trans feminists, acknowledge the importance of feminism to trans theory and politics, and explore points of commonality. In *The Transfeminist Manifesto,* Emi Koyama (2001) defines "transfeminism" as

primarily a movement by and for trans women who view their liberation to be intrinsically linked to the liberation of all women and beyond. [It] is not about taking over existing feminist institutions. Instead it extends and advances feminism as a whole though our own liberation and coalition work with others. It stands up for trans and non-trans women alike, and asks non-trans women to stand up for trans women in return. *Transfeminism* embodies feminist coalition politics in which women from different backgrounds stand up for each other, because if we do not stand for each other, nobody will. (pp. 1–2)

One of the strengths of the trans feminism coalition is that it showcases the way many trans people have historically been engaged with similar political battles as non-trans feminists and that non-trans feminists also have a history of working alongside trans people to challenge perceptions and promote equality. Scott-Dixon (2006) draws together these perspectives in an edited collection that broadens trans-feminist voices to include transmen and non-trans feminists to ask the following questions:

What ideas, struggles and experiences do trans and feminist political projects share, what related concerns do they raise and how might insights from one area benefit the other? How might trans and feminist ideas inform future struggles for social justice and the enhancement of human dignity, and how might we build solidarity in order to improve people's lives? (p. 12)

While this offers a promising beginning, key points of contention need to be debated and reconsidered. For instance, the feminist movement is challenged by trans feminists to examine its "own biases and internalized oppressions" (Koyama, 2001, p. 1) and to "acknowledge its own complicity with the biological essentialisms at the core of the sex/gender system" (Noble, 2006, p. 102). However, if non-trans feminists, quite rightly, need to give up on some of their assumed gender certainty, trans feminists also need to sacrifice the narrative of coalition based on their own authentic claim to the identity category "woman." As Dan Irving (2008) has argued, in a review of *Trans/forming Feminisms,* for trans feminism to offer a productive relationship, there is a

need to create a space to challenge trans narratives without being dismissed as "transphobic" . . . the cultivation of solidarity demands that trans/ feminists challenge each other rigorously. This relation of "mutual respect" will be based not on a politics of identity but on shared goals of social justice and equity for all. (p. 367)

This returns me to the political possibility of "queer," not as an identity category but as an organizing label that resists the essentialist claims that are more likely to emerge from a movement that promotes coalitions around a stake in the identity category woman. We have seen that queer disruptions have not always been well received by trans academics because of the perceived role that feminist/queer theory played in constructing a hierarchical division between transgender and transsexual. However, elsewhere it has been argued that queer has the potential to signify "inessential coalitions" (Lloyd, 2005) in the political field and can offer a strategy that seeks to unsettle both gender and sexuality definitions and practices. While some versions of trans feminism might also look to include trans and non-trans identified others, Koyama's (2001) original definition implies trans feminism is more orientated toward transwomen than transmen. This approach risks introducing new hierarchal divisions, not between transgender and transsexual but between transmen and transwomen, where the purpose of trans feminism is to create change primarily for "women." However, others have argued that transmen often have a rich history of engagement with feminism, having previously shared the social spaces of women and often lesbians prior to transition and after transition, many seek to produce new forms of masculinity (Johnson, 2007a). The emergence of trans feminism has the potential to challenge and disrupt our gender assumptions across trans and non-trans feminist divisions, but it could also return us to debates about essentialism, authenticity, and hierarchal divisions of inclusion. Rather than falling back into debates over individual identity claims, a mutual and continuous critical engagement with sex, gender, and sexuality practices and the ethical and political implications of these may be a workable route toward an inclusive, inessential trans feminist solidarity that is beneficial for all.

CONCLUSION

In this chapter, I have illustrated how a new academic discipline has arisen in an attempt to gain a greater understanding of transsexual subjectivity. The disagreements between those promoting a transgender agenda, where they argue for a rejection of "passing" and in some cases the refusal of bodily alteration (e.g., Bornstein, 1994; Stone, 1991), and those who embrace and

theorize the experiences of those who do transition, perhaps even investing in a return to identity and essence (e.g., Prosser, 1998), have pushed forward the project of understanding embodied "trans" subjectivities. Transsexualism has so often been theorized conceptually in an attempt to grasp the relationship between sex, gender, and sexuality. These new debates not only are of benefit for those feminists seeking knowledge of transsexualism and transgenderism but should also yield a more nuanced understanding of the embodied gendered subjectivities of us all. Empirical research into transsexual subjectivity that is sensitive to the lived experiences of transsexual and transgendered people will reveal that the material grounding of their new gender experiences can also unravel the certainty of particular pervasive discourses. As such, the notion of "changing sex" may help to regulate a binary gender system, but the subsequent state of gender ambiguity in which many trans people reside, exemplified through the risk of not "passing," challenges, threatens, and undoes gender certainty for us all (Johnson, 2005). While significant debate remains over the usefulness of queer as a theoretical and political intervention in the field, some do argue that it can help forge new "inessential" coalitions across sexual and gendered positions (e.g., Lloyd, 2005). To do this will require effort to avoid focusing on internal identity borderline battles while simultaneously recognizing that identity conflict can emerge over subject positions that carry psychological investment for the individuals involved. Feminist, transgender, and queer theorists all have different dialogues with the term *queer,* and it is these types of distinctions that need to be embraced rather than rejected. As Lloyd (2005) argues, "Humans cannot escape the differential relations that mark out subject positions; this is the ontological ground of existence. They can, however, try to create the conditions in which the Other is no longer viewed as an enemy that must be eradicated (or excluded) but is transformed into an adversary or a counterpart" (p. 165). It is these words that we might heed when forming "ethical coalitions" for producing research in the field of transgender that acknowledges the everyday life experiences of those marginalized by institutional gender discrimination and evidenced in accounts of violence, poverty, and poor health. Here, non-trans feminists might work alongside trans feminists to produce and partake in gender projects that promote understanding and lead to personal and social transformation. However, there is always the ongoing need to transform the social structures of gender oppression by producing, transgressing, and embodying new forms of gender expression. To do this, we need to engage in political practices that acknowledge our cultural impurity, as well as the psychological investments we hold for a range of identity positions.

Discussion Questions

1. What are your personal, political, and theoretical orientations toward transsexualism and transgenderism?

2. What are the strengths and limitations of the impact of feminist/queer theory for understanding trans subjectivities?

3. How might the hierarchy between transgender and transsexualism be undone through feminist research and praxis?

4. What potential is there for sustaining a widely inclusive trans-feminist coalition and what might be the barriers to this?

Online Resources

Gender Across Borders

http://www.genderacrossborders.com

Gender Across Borders is a global feminist blog that critically examines issues of gender, race, sexuality, and class to promote positive gender relations worldwide. This includes regular posts on transgender as well as issues of race, sexuality, and social class.

Trans-Academics

http://www.trans-academics.org/

Trans-Academics.org is a U.S.-based website that focuses on discussion of gender theory, the trans community, and gender identities in the context of both academic and everyday life. It covers information on trans studies programs and trans syllabi, and it has an excellent reference library.

TransgenderZone

http://www.transgenderzone.com/

TransgenderZone is a U.K. Internet forum that seeks to educate, communicate, and inform. It is a useful resource for those who are transgendered as well as others interested in learning more and provides a wealth of information via its library.

Relevant Journals

Feminism & Psychology

GLQ: A Journal of Lesbian and Gay Studies

International Journal of Sexuality and Gender Studies

International Journal of Transgenderism

Journal of Bisexuality

Journal of Gay and Lesbian Issues in Education

Journal of Gender Studies

Journal of Sex Research

Psychology & Sexuality

Sexualities

NOTE

1. They acknowledge this oversight in a recent reappraisal of *Gender: An Ethnomethodological Approach* (Kessler & McKenna, 2000).

REFERENCES

American Psychiatric Association. (2000). *Diagnostic and statistical manual of mental disorders* (4th ed., text revision). Washington, DC: Author.

Anzaldúa, G., & Keating, A. (Eds.). (2002). *This bridge we call home: Radical visions for transformation*. London: Routledge.

Benjamin, H. (1966). *The transsexual phenomenon*. New York: Julian Press.

Billies, M., Johnson, J., Murungi, K., & Pugh, R. (2009). Naming our reality: Low-income LGBT people documenting violence, discrimination and assertions of justice. *Feminism & Psychology, 19*(3), 375–380.

Bockting, W. O., & Coleman, E. (1992). A comprehensive approach to the treatment of gender dysphoria. *Journal of Psychology and Human Sexuality, 5*(4), 131–155.

Bornstein, K. (1994). *Gender outlaw: On men, women, and the rest of us.* New York: Vintage/Random House.

Butler, J. (1990). *Gender trouble: Feminism and the subversion of identity.* New York: Routledge.

Butler, J. (1993). *Bodies that matter: On the discursive limits of "sex."* New York: Routledge.

Butler, J. (2004). *Undoing gender.* London: Routledge.

Calhoun, C. (1996). The gender closet: Lesbian disappearance under the sign "woman." In M. Vicinus (Ed.), *Lesbian subjects: A feminist studies reader* (pp. 209–232). Bloomington: Indiana University Press.

Davis, K. (1995). *Reshaping the female body: The dilemma of cosmetic surgery.* London: Routledge.

de Beauvoir, S. (1953). *The second sex* (H. M. Parshley, Ed. & Trans.). Harmondsworth, UK: Penguin. (Original work published 1949)

Ekins, R., & King, D. (1999). Towards a sociology of transgendered bodies. *Sociological Review, 47,* 580–602.

Ekins, R., & King, D. (2006). *The transgender phenomenon.* London: Sage.

Elliot, P. (2009). Engaging trans debates on gender variance: A feminist analysis. *Sexualities, 12*(5), 5–32.

Elliot, P., & Roen, K. (1998). Transgenderism and the question of embodiment: Promising queer politics. *GLQ: A Journal of Lesbian and Gay Studies, 4*(2), 231–261.

Fae, J. (2010, March 11). Australia is first to recognise "non-specified" gender. *Pink News.* Retrieved February 9, 2010, from http://www.pinknews.co.uk/2010/03/11/australia-is-first-to-recognise-non-specified-gender/

Feinberg, L. (1993). *Stone butch blues.* Ithaca, NY: Firebrand.

Feinbloom, D. H. (1976). *Transvestites and transsexuals: Mixed views.* New York: Dell.

Garber, M. (1992). *Vested interests: Cross-dressing and cultural anxiety.* London: Penguin.

Garfinkel, H. (1967). *Studies in ethnomethodology.* Englewood Cliffs, NJ: Prentice Hall.

Gatens, M. (1996). A critique of the sex/gender system. In *Imaginary bodies: Ethics, power and corporeality* (pp. 3–28). London: Routledge. (Original work published 1983)

Gottschalk, L. H. (2009). Transgendering women's space: A feminist analysis of perspectives from Australian women's services. *Women's Studies International Forum, 32,* 167–178.

Greer, G. (1999). *The whole woman.* London: Doubleday.

Grosz, E. (1994). *Volatile bodies: Toward a corporeal feminism.* Bloomington: Indiana University Press.

Halberstam, J. (1994). F2M: The making of female masculinity. In L. Doan (Ed.), *The lesbian postmodern.* New York: Columbia University Press.

Halberstam, J. (1998). *Female masculinity.* Durham, NC: Duke University Press.

Hausman, B. L. (1995). *Changing sex: Transsexualism, technology, and the idea of gender.* Durham, NC: Duke University Press.

Hausman, B. (2001). Recent transgender theory. *Feminist Studies, 27*(2), 465–490.

Heyes, C. (2003). Feminist solidarity after queer theory: The case of transgender. *Signs: Journal of Women in Culture and Society, 28*(4), 1093–1120.

Heyes, C. J. (2007). *Self-transformations: Foucault, ethics, and normalized bodies.* Oxford, UK: Oxford University Press.

Hines, S. (2007). *Transforming gender: Transgender practices of identity, intimacy and care.* Bristol, UK: Policy Press.

Irving, D. (2008). Book review: Trans/forming feminisms: Trans-feminist voices speak out. *Journal of International Women's Studies, 9*(3), 363–368.

Jeffreys, S. (2003). *Unpacking queer politics: A lesbian feminist perspective.* Cambridge, UK: Polity Press.

Johnson, K. (2001). *Being transsexual: Self, identity and embodied subjectivity.* Unpublished doctoral dissertation, Middlesex University, UK.

Johnson, K. (2005). From gender to transgender: 30 years of feminism. *Social Alternatives, 24*(2), 36–39.

Johnson, K. (2007a). Changing sex, changing self: Transitions in embodied subjectivity. *Men and Masculinities, 10*(1), 54–70.

Johnson, K. (2007b). Fragmented identities, frustrated politics: Transsexuals, lesbians and "queer." *Journal of Lesbian Studies, 11*(1–2), 123–141.

Kessler, S., & McKenna, W. (1985). *Gender: An ethnomethodological approach* (2nd ed.). Chicago: University of Chicago Press. (Original work published 1978)

Kessler, S., & McKenna, W. (2000). Retrospective response. *Feminism & Psychology, 10*(1), 66–72.

Koyama, E. (2001). *The transfeminist manifesto.* Retrieved February 11, 2010, from http://eminism.org/readings/pdf-rdg/tfmanifesto.pdf

Koyama, E. (2006). Whose feminism is it anyway? The unspoken racism of the trans inclusion debate. In S. Stryker & S. Whittle (Eds.), *The transgender studies reader.* London: Routledge.

Lim, J., & Browne, K. (2008). Senses of gender. *Sociological Research Online, 14*(1), 6. Retrieved June 30, 2010, from http://www.socresonline.org/14/1/6.html

Lloyd, M. (2005). *Beyond identity politics: Feminism, power and politics.* London: Sage.

Lungren, E. (2000). Ahead of their time, children of their time, in and out of step 20 years later. *Feminism & Psychology, 10*(1), 55–61.

Martin, B. (1996). Sexualities without genders and other queer utopias. In *Femininity played straight.* London: Routledge. (Original work published 1992)

Namaste, V. (2000). *Invisible lives: The erasure of transsexual and transgendered people.* Chicago: University of Chicago Press.

Namaste, V. (2005). *Sex change, social change: Reflections on identity, institutions, and imperialism.* Toronto, ON: Women's Press.

Nataf, Z. I. (1996). *Lesbians talk transgender.* London: Scarlet Press.

Noble, B. (2006). Our bodies are not ourselves: Tranny guys and the racialized class politcs of embodiment. In K. Scott-Dixon (Ed.), *Trans/forming feminisms: Trans-feminist voices speak out.* Toronto, ON: Sumach Press.

Parlee, M. B. (1996). Situated knowledges of personal embodiment: Transgender activists' and psychological theorists' perspectives on "sex" and "gender." *Theory and Psychology, 6*(4), 625–645.

Paxton, C. K., Guentzel, H., & Trombacco, K. (2006). Lessons learned in developing a research partnership with the transgender community. *American Journal of Community Psychology, 37,* 349–356.

Pershai, A. (2006). The language puzzle: Is inclusive language a solution? In K. Scott-Dixon (Ed.), *Trans/forming feminisms: Trans-feminist voices speak out.* Toronto, ON: Sumach Press.

Pfeffer, C. A. (2010). "Women's work"? Women partners of transgender men doing housework and emotion work. *Journal of Marriage and Family, 72,* 165–183.

Prince, V. (1976). *Understanding cross-dressing.* Los Angeles: Chevalier.

Prosser, J. (1998). *Second skins: The body narratives of transsexuality.* New York: Columbia University Press.

Raymond, J. G. (1980). *The transsexual empire.* London: The Women's Press.

Raymond, J. (1994). The politics of transgender. *Feminism and Psychology, 4,* 628–633.

Rubin, G. (1984). Thinking sex: Notes for a radical theory of the politics of sexuality. In C. Vance (Ed.), *Pleasure and danger: Exploring female sexuality* (pp. 267–320). London: Routledge.

Rubin, H. (1998). Phenomenology as method. *GLQ: A Journal of Lesbian and Gay Studies (The Transgender Issue), 4*(2), 262–281.

Rubin, H. (2003). *Self-made men: Identity and embodiment among transsexual men.* Nashville, TN: Vanderbilt University Press.

Scott-Dixon, K. (Ed.). (2006). *Trans/forming feminisms: Trans-feminist voices speak out.* Toronto, ON: Sumach Press.

Stoller, R. J. (1968). *Sex and gender.* London: Hogarth Press.

Stoller, R. J. (1975). *Sex and gender: Vol. II. The transsexual experiment.* New York: Jason Aronson.

Stone, S. (1991). The empire strikes back: A posttranssexual manifesto. In J. Epstein & K. Straub (Eds.), *Body guards: The cultural politics of gender ambiguity* (pp. 280–304). London: Routledge.

Stryker, S. (1994). My words to Victor Frankenstein above the village of Chamounix: Performing transgender rage. *GLQ: A Journal of Lesbian and Gay Studies, 1,* 237–254.

Stryker, S. (1998). The transgender issue: An introduction. *GLQ: A Journal of Lesbian and Gay Studies, 4*(2), 145–148.

Wilchins, R. A. (1995). What's in a name? The politics of genderspeak. *Transgender Tapestry, 4,* 46–47.

Wilton, T. (1995). *Lesbian studies: Setting an agenda.* London: Routledge.

Wilton, T. (2000). Out/performing our selves: Sex, gender and Cartesian dualism. *Sexualities, 3*(2), 237–254.

30

FUTURE DIRECTIONS IN DIFFERENCE RESEARCH

Recognizing and Responding to Difference in the Research Process

DIANE REAY

T his chapter focuses on differences among women and the tensions that are generated within feminist research that attempts to address differences. It draws on existing feminist research that engages with a range of differences. While the chapter has a particular emphasis on social class as a marginalized but enduring difference, it also examines differences of ethnicity, political commitment, sexuality, and age and their consequences, not only for feminist methodology but also for actual research processes and practices. All too often, the high moral ground of feminist theory is lost in the messy realities of fieldwork as some of the differences so neatly captured in our texts become far more difficult to make sense of in the field. While I would see the commitment to positioning difference as something that needs to be consciously recognized and considered empathetically as integral to feminist research, fieldwork practice often renders the ideals of feminist research more difficult to enact. The chapter

looks at feminist accounts that have, with varying degrees of success, attempted to deal with differences within the field, drawing on research projects where the salient differences were identified from the outset but also those where some key differences only emerged during the course of the fieldwork. And of course it is important to recognize that even when potential differences are deliberately identified from the outset of the research, differences that later prove to be salient may still be overlooked. The chapter concludes by suggesting some research practices that support feminist research in bridging theory and praxis and by mapping out feminist ways of working in the field for the 21st century.

As Loraine Gelsthorpe (1992) notes, "Women are never just women"—we have a class, a sexuality, an ethnicity, often national, religious, and cultural affiliations, and all these, and many other aspects of difference, affect our situation and views. Historically, feminism has been overshadowed by a neglect of difference. While notions of

627

difference have long constituted important issues for feminist theory, politics, and practice, the overriding preoccupation with sexism has far too often resulted in feminists ignoring differences of race, class, ethnicity, age, dis/ability, sexuality, and nationality. For example, second-wave Western feminists prioritized sex/gender relations and inequalities, arguing against the conceptualization of women as other in relation to a male norm. One consequence in both the United States and the United Kingdom has been that the histories of the feminist movement have been fraught with racism, homophobia, and exclusionary practices (Ahmed, 2009; Bhavnani & Coulson, 2005; Torrey, 2008). As Bhavnani and Coulson (2005) point out, feminist accounts have frequently erased, denied, ignored, or tokenized the contradictory and conflicting interests that women have. But as the examples discussed in the second half of the chapter show, even feminist research that consciously sets out to position difference as a central focus of research can struggle to do so in ways that are sensitive to and valuing of those differences.

In response to accusations of homogenizing women as a group and neglecting the differences among them, feminists increasingly moved to an engagement with the power differentials and inequalities that exist between women. Particularly influential has been Haraway (1988), who argues for an engagement with difference that enshrines responsibility and accountability. She stresses the importance of feminists being "answerable for what we learn to see" (p. 583). So recognizing differences is a vital first step but a wholly inadequate one on its own. Too often faced with the impossibility of addressing the complex range of permutations of difference, feminists have resorted to "the mantra approach" to difference—reeling them off and then relegating most of them to the sidelines of the research endeavor. Cealey Harrison and Hood-Williams (1998) criticize the notion that we as researchers could possibly work with all the differences out in the research field. After arguing that sexuality, dis/ability, age, gender, social class, and ethnicity are the relevant forms of social classification in the current sociological lexicon, they continue,

> Given that these groups themselves contain a greater number of different subject positions within them (perhaps only two for sexual orientations, perhaps as many as nine for ethnicity) and that it is possible to belong to any combination of groups, the total combinatory of positions created by intersections that are fundamental to a full understanding is actually likely, at a conservative estimate, to be around 288. Depending on the "intersections" one defines and the variant forms of positionality within them there is no mathematical limit to the social divisions thus produced. (pp. 2–3)

Cealey Harrison and Hood-Williams clearly underestimate the different subject positions within sexuality and ethnicity, but factoring more subject positions into the feminist research landscape only serves to reinforce their original point. How can we do more than pay lip service to difference if we play a numbers game? The additive model of addressing difference ignores the myriad ways in which experience is transformed by identity factors (Francis, 2001).

So at the beginning of the second decade of the 21st century, feminism is struggling to understand patterns of inequalities in a context of a heightened awareness of individual and multiple differences. In particular, the rise of postmodernism and the deconstruction of grand narratives within feminist theorizing have granted theoretical prominence to notions of difference and the multiplicity of identities and inequalities (Francis & Skelton, 2008) but left us bereft of any guidance on vital theoretical and methodological issues facing feminist thought. For instance, how do we understand and theorize feminist solidarity if the supposedly inclusive "we" of feminism is revealed to be partial and excluding (Craig & Hurt, 2008)? The vexing problem of feminist exclusions Susan Bordo (1990) identified in 1990 is still with us. Then, as now, the issue was one of how feminists could theorize difference without losing the analytic force of gender analysis. I would argue that the challenge is to respect cultural difference and diversity while still recognizing cross-cultural categories such as gender. But that has become a difficult enterprise within contemporary feminisms in particular because of the power of postmodern theorizing and its influence on feminist thought.

A further confounding factor has been the rapid development in digital, virtual, online, and mobile technologies that have added a further layer of complication to the conundrum of difference for feminist research. As Anna Markham (2007) asserts, "Good research, online or off, is good research. At the same time, Internet research has highlighted some of the weaknesses of research practice in general, including its ethical regulation" (p. 43). For one, the possibilities that Internet samples include those who are assuming other identities points to the potential complexity of exploring not only issues of gender but those of other aspects of identity in online spaces. Feminists need to be attuned to the fine nuances and diverse shades of meaning new technologies have for different groups, particularly how differences are configured by new technologies. As a bottom line, this entails both understanding and knowledge of technological innovations, on one hand, and personal experience and awareness of the possibilities they generate for new forms of interaction, on the other. However, beyond informed personal engagement, feminists need to be aware of the ways in which new technologies, despite their liberatory potential, can continue to reinscribe existing inequalities. So, for instance, a growing body of feminist research on mobile technologies (Green & Singleton, 2009; Singleton & Green, 2007; Wallis, 2008) shows how they are reifying gender differences rather than democratizing them.

IMPLICATIONS OF DIFFERENCE FOR FEMINIST THEORIZING

It may seem that we are stuck in a feminist quagmire, but there are ways forward. One positive direction is to work toward new conceptual frameworks. We require analytic concepts that allow us to examine how any one difference is affected by and affects all of the other aspects of difference in multiple ways. The challenge is to build toward an understanding of the complex of differences as both a set of dynamic relationships and operating within specific contexts. We need to understand how we can simultaneously be an insider, outsider, both, and neither in the research endeavor (Bahkru, 2008; Sultana, 2007). Hesse-Biber and Yaiser (2004) stress the importance of recognizing that differences are contextual, emphasizing

that they are constantly undergoing change "as the economy changes, politics shifts, and new ideological processes, trends and events occur" (p. 108). They argue that researchers and feminist academics need to work with dynamic fluid definitions and theories that are a reflection of society and include political, historical, and social significance. Similarly, Candice West and Sarah Fenstermaker (2002) argue against the additive approach to differences, positing a view of differences as ongoing accomplishments that cannot be understood apart from the context in which they are accomplished. As I illustrate later in relation to both others' and my own research, different differences are stressed or muted depending on the social context.

Susan Heckman argues (1999) that it is time for feminists to stop arguing about differences and get on with the task of devising a theory for understanding differentiation. She goes on to argue,

> An epistemology of differences must develop a conception of subjectivity that defines differences as constitutive rather than marginal. The defining feature of the Cartesian subject is the stability of its identity, it assumes a universal human essence. By contrast the subject of difference is unstable— its identity varies according to an array of differences, only one of which is gender. (p. 42)

This is similar to Kathy Ferguson's (1993, p. 153) argument that feminists need to conceive of subjectivity as mobile—temporal, relational, and shifting, yet enduring, ambiguous, messy, and multiple. Such understandings complement those of Hesse-Biber and Yaiser (2004). Different aspects of the researcher's self become more prominent in some contexts than in others. Our social class positioning, age, ethnicity, and sexuality are foregrounded in some interactions and localities but remain muted in others. So, for example, working-class students often become hyperaware of their class background in elite universities where upper-class accents and dispositions are the norm (Reay, Crozier, & James, 2011), while black visitors to predominantly white rural areas are constantly reminded of their blackness, something that would happen far less frequently in multicultural urban locales. Similarly, gender can become particularly salient in certain contexts, as young women often find out if they walk through a construction site, but is relatively unimportant in other contexts, for example, visiting an art museum.

This is no fragmentary postmodern approach to difference. In my own and the research of many other post-structural feminists, categorical differences such as gender remain central to our analyses. In particular, I and many other feminists have no desire to lose sight of the term *woman* and wish to revitalize feminist politics. But the feminist politics of the 1970s and 1980s that neglected the range of differences within the category of gender and too often treated women as if they were all the same oversimplified the issues at stake in feminist politics. It is important to recognize the complexities of feminist subjectivities and the myriad competing interests and loyalties we endlessly struggle with. To state it baldly—differences operate differently in different contexts, and we have to develop analytic tools to make sense of this.

Instead of separating out a multiplicity of differences, one approach is to draw difference in as an expression of a relationship, moving beyond description to "an analysis of the forces producing those differences and relationships and the dynamic structure of which they are a changing part" (Gorelick, 1996, p. 41). Gorelick (1996) draws on the example of the concept of compulsory heterosexuality, arguing that

> when Adrienne Rich moved beyond complaining about the exclusion of lesbians from feminist writing to analysing "compulsory heterosexuality," lesbians—and indeed feminism itself—moved beyond discussing "difference" to analyzing the determinants of lesbian existence. More than that: The concept of compulsory heterosexuality examines not only lesbianism but also heterosexuality as a set of institutions and ideological practices. (p. 41)

So theory building is vital to the feminist enterprise of addressing differences. Adrienne Rich's (1980) concept of compulsory heterosexuality has spoken to the experience of both lesbians and heterosexual women. There have been further key conceptual developments that address other aspects of difference. For example, Beverley Skeggs's (2004) feminist reworking of

Marxist use and exchange value has progressed feminist understandings of the mediation of social class on gender. Both Rich's and Skeggs's concepts meet Patricia Hill Collins's (2008) criteria that any feminist analyses must remain rooted in how differences are put to use in defending unequal power relations. This means for Collins that power relations and material inequalities must be kept firmly in the feminist research frame. The theoretical challenge for feminisms remains one of how to hold together conceptions of difference and structural inequalities. Feminisms need to continue to develop and expand insights in relation to both epistemology and methodology but always keeping power relations in view.

WORKING IN THE FIELD WITH DIFFERENCES

I have discussed the difference differences make to feminist methodology and theorizing. I now want to focus on how differences play out in more mundane everyday research processes and practices. As we know so well from mainstream academic theorizing and research practice, there is far too often a chasm between what we write and theorize about and our actual practice. Key questions for feminist research are how and to what extent does our research deal with differences within the research encounter, particularly the power differentials that these differences generate.

This is not just an issue of recognizing differences within fieldwork, analysis, and writing up but a much more holistic concern that spans the affective as well as the intellectual, encompassing concerns with philosophical issues of ethics and morality. Such a concern stretches from theory to the mundane everyday micro-details of fieldwork—what data do we include and exclude in our analyses and why? Who do we like and dislike in our interactions in the field, and how do we deal with our affective responses? To engage with the consequences of differences for everyday research processes and practices, in the next three sections, I look at three feminist accounts of research that attempt to deal with differences in the field. Although all three studies included men as well as women, they were all guided by feminist principles, giving particular attention to "issues of power, authority, reflexivity, ethics, and difference" (Hesse-Biber, 2007, p. 15), and were underpinned by a commitment to creating a fairer, more socially just world not only for women but also for other oppressed groups. I conclude by drawing on the insights from these studies to suggest some research practices that support feminist research in bridging theory and praxis.

The first project, directed by Louise Archer (2004), focused on identity construction among British Muslim male and female students ages 14 to 15 in urban northeast England and was carried out with the assistance of two Asian female researchers. While there were clear differences of ethnicity and culture between Louise and the young Asian students she was researching, differences were far more masked between her Asian co-researchers and the researched. Molly Andrews's (2002) research is a narrative account of the lives of senior activists and political campaigners. What emerges powerfully from her study are differences of values and attitudes and how these more "individual" differences, despite being frequently overlooked in research accounts, are just as salient as categorical differences for feminist research. In my own research with white middle-class parents choosing urban state schools (Reay, 2008; Reay et al., 2008), my own positioning as a white middle-class mother who made similar choices for her children comes powerfully into play but not always as a source of strength and empathy as I had anticipated.

Taking Up Different Positions Within the Research Relationship

In Louise Archer's (2004) study, focus group interviews were carried out by Louise, who is British and white, and two British Asian female researchers. Sixteen focus groups were conducted, including eight single-sex male and eight female focus groups. Four male and four female group interviews were conducted by Louise and four female and four male group interviews by one of the two Asian researchers. In the study, difference was deliberately worked into the research design. In addition to exploring

how the young people understood and constructed their ethnic and gendered identities, Archer and her co-researchers encouraged the young people to talk about the possible impact of the interviewer's race and gender within the discussions and how or if they thought the discussions may have been different with an Asian or white, male or female interviewer.

In her reflexive account of the research process, Louise Archer draws on her experience of interviewing young Asian students to illustrate the utility of Brah's (1999) application of the Urdu terms *ajanbi, apna,* and *ghair.* Brah uses the three terms to capture emotional relations of difference across structural locations of difference. While ajanbi is "a stranger; a newcomer but one who holds the promise of friendship, love and intimacy, apna is 'one of our own'" (p. 19). In contrast, ghair walks the tightrope between insider/outsider. It is a form of irreducible, opaque difference. Archer (2004) fruitfully draws on Brah's conceptual terminology to make sense of complex and shifting differences within the research relationship. She identified herself as initially occupying an ajanbi or ghair position in relation to her young Asian respondents but describes how, as the research developed and the young respondents gained in confidence, shifting power relations and in particular the opening up of herself for interrogation by the respondents meant she moved between ajanbi, ghair, and apna positions. Points of commonality were forged by respondents and the interviewer sharing experiences of bullying in school and the extent to which the interviewer knew about and had participated in Asian cultural practices through a previous partner. Relatedly, one of her Asian co-researchers' positioning as apna "was sometimes disrupted as psychosocial/emotional differences were opened up in terms of her own differing religious identification, lifestyle choices and/or gendered sexual values" (p. 464). As a consequence, she moved between apna and ghair positions over the course of the fieldwork. However, Archer, as a white woman, had to deal with the difficult evidence in a later feedback session that the young Asian men and women who participated in her study were almost unanimous in their construction of an Asian woman as the "ideal" interviewer. There are issues here of context and temporality in which different aspects of difference such as religious affiliation become more salient in different research contexts and at different times but also, in the case of this particular research project, of the power of shared ethnicity to create a sense of empathy and mutual understanding.

DEALING WITH THE SEDUCTIONS OF "KNOWING BETTER"

Molly Andrews (2002) addresses a difference that is rarely articulated in feminist research—the difference between feminists and non- and anti-feminists (although see also Schreiber, 2008). She conducted what she terms an in-depth narrative analysis of the ways in which political belief is developed and sustained in the lives of 15 U.K. activists, both male and female. We are talking about not only key differences of age and generation (the participants were all older than age 60 while Andrews was a young doctoral student [Andrews, 1991]) and, in some cases, gender but also political differences of consciousness, beliefs, and values where feminist researchers confront very different problems to those usually posed through difference research. For nearly all her participants, regardless of their sex, feminism had been negligible in their lives. Contrary to Andrews's own academic and activist concerns, feminist issues were viewed as a distraction by most of the respondents. Gender was not perceived to be a salient social categorization. Unlike for Andrews herself, gender consciousness was not part of their political consciousness and, as she laments, was actually seen by some to undermine political consciousness.

Her research raises the issue of how feminist researchers can maintain a commitment simultaneously to the expressed viewpoint of participants and the causes of feminisms in general. Andrews faced what Rizq (2008) identifies as the troubling issue of what we do when our understandings and interpretations of what participants tell us is in tension with their own narrative accounts and, as a result, represent a form of challenge or threat to their perceptions and coping strategies. The majority of Andrews's

female respondents rejected feminist identification, and those who did accept it were liberal feminists pushing for progress within existing systems. For Andrews, there was a continual tension between her interpretation of her respondents' experiences and the meaning the participants themselves tended to attribute to their experience since the majority of them did not analyze these experiences in terms of patriarchy or sex-gender systems but considered them to be individualized, or as "just something that had to be coped with." Andrews's work reminds us that the seductions of "knowing better" rather than knowing differently are ever present but also provides us with a way of rethinking differences that does not lapse into hierarchy. Andrews draws on Nancy Chodorow's (1996) work in order to generate a productive tension in her research in relation to difference. For Chodorow (1996, p. 24), differences in women's interpretation of a situation need to be understood within a historical cultural and generational context. Following Chodorow, Andrews develops an analysis in which both knowledge and gender are situated:

> Gender is a situated phenomenon, both in itself, as it can be more or less salient in different arenas or at different times of life, and in respect to other aspects of social and cultural categorisation and identity. (Chodorow, 1996, p. 43)

As a result, cultural and historical processes as well as social situations make certain conceptualizations and not others probable (Chodorow, 1996). Chodorow's theoretical insight allows Andrews to understand the low level of gender salience among her respondents not as a failure within them but as a tool for understanding their worldview. Andrews's research highlights the importance of context for consciousness, as she recognizes that not only are the views of her respondents historically and culturally situated but so are her own. However, we can extend and develop Chodorow's insights about the importance of context and situatedness to all other aspects of difference. All aspects of our identity become more salient in some contexts than in others. I draw on an example of the difficulties inherent in foregrounding some aspects of our female identity such as our ethnicity or social class at the expense of others such as our political commitments and moral beliefs by examining my own fieldwork with white middle-class parents.

THE PERILS OF ASSUMED COMMONALITIES

Even when feminists are sensitized to difference, there still remain the perils of assumed commonalities—the hidden differences we often don't want to see. Joanne Braxton (1989), in describing her responses to other black women's texts, writes, "I read every text through my own experience, as well as the experiences of my mother and my grandmothers" (p. 1). The affirmation of finding yourself at the core of other women's accounts contains enormous power. We can read our centrality where previously there had only been partiality. However, as well as strengths there are also the hazards of neglecting the salience of more mundane everyday differences. As we can see from Andrews's research, these small, more individual differences of perspective, position, disposition, and beliefs are just as important as the macro-categorical and group differences of race, sexuality, nationality, and class. However, while for Andrews, the differences in opinion and perspective between herself and the women she interviewed were always evident, in my own research, a sense of difference would suddenly emerge in sharp contrast to the commonalities that predominated throughout much of the fieldwork. In particular, the study participants' attitudes to classed others threatened my sense of sameness. They would generate a desire to distance myself from the very women who only moments before I had been strongly identifying with.

I have written about the frequently overlooked anxieties, conflicts, desires, defenses, and ambivalences within white middle-class identities (Reay et al., 2007; Reay et al., 2008) but never about the tensions that have frequently simmered near the surface of my own psyche during my periods in the field. In a recently published book (Reay et al., 2011), myself and two colleagues wrote of the white middle classes who send their children to socially diverse urban schools:

> These white middle classes are managing deeply felt and unresolved tensions in relation to their children's schooling. There were strong signs of Bourdieu's "divided habitus" (Bourdieu 1999: 511). The white middle-class subject produced through "acting against the normative middle-class grain" is split, divided between the acquisitive self-interested self and a more altruistic, public spirited self and has to live with the tensions generated through the contradictory interplay of cooperation and competition, consumerism and welfarism. (p. 106)

These white middle-class parents were dealing with difficult differences around social class in a national context where the white working classes are seen to have a problematic influence on middle-class children's achievement if both are sharing the same educational space. They had positioned themselves in much closer proximity to their class and ethnicity other than was the norm for most white middle classes, who tend to choose more selective or even private schooling, but the consequences were evident in their high levels of anxiety. They attempted to empathize with and understand their working-class "others" while at the same time trying to ensure their own children avoided what they often perceived to be "bad" influences. Classism has been an articulated concern in research far less often than racism and sexism (for two recent examples, see McDowell & Fang, 2009; Shpungin & Lyubansky, 2006), but the often classist attitudes of the white middle-class parents, and in particular a frequently articulated sense of superiority, became difficult for me to deal with both emotionally and politically. Their struggles with uncomfortable differences became mirrored in my own struggles to identify with aspects of their attitudes and actions while disidentifying with others. Far more often than I could ever have anticipated, I experienced "frustrated expectations and bewilderment toward the ways through which research participants depicted themselves" (Viladrich, 2005, p. 384) and others. As Erica Townsend-Bell (2009) points out, "It is not simply the subjects that we study, but us as well who have to negotiate sometimes sticky issues of race, class, gender, nationality and so forth" (p. 311).

There were moments when I experienced a strong visceral reaction during fieldwork that made it difficult to maintain a sense of empathy with respondents, as when Tricia, a London mother, told me about the white working-class community living adjacent to her daughter's school. She said,

> They are really an indigenous community and have long histories of being servants to the military and now that military has gone, everything has crumbled around them. They don't have so many jobs. The army has just kind of left them and that's actually an erosion of 100s of years of history. You may not like the attitudes, you may not like the lack, you know, the quite aggressive culture, the racism in that culture, you may not like it, but to pretend that it never existed and that it is unimportant is only to create problems for yourself. And the problems that you deal with schools, are the only places, I think, the only places, where you actually confront those issues, because particularly state schools are pulling in everybody.

At the time we were analyzing the data using Bourdieu's conceptual framework, and his theory of identity formation focuses on habitus as the internalization of hierarchical social relations, an internalization that produces dispositions that reflect the individual's position in the social hierarchy. And Tricia's microscopic analysis, her privileged view from above, displayed the classic middle-class habitus (Reay et al., 2011). We can also see in Tricia's words Layton's (2008) "failure of empathy." Tricia epitomizes the attitudes and affective responses of many of the parents and children in our study to the working classes, particularly the white working-class other. On one level, they are to be pitied, and Tricia stresses the importance of knowing and understanding their situation intellectually. But there is also the emotional impossibility of putting yourself in the position of those who are defined in the middle-class imaginary through

"their lack," "their aggression," and above all "their racism" (Haylett, 2001). Rather than developing any empathetic understanding, the challenge is to learn about and understand the working classes as a problem to be dealt with. Despite their left-leaning, communitarian impulses, these parents and their children had complex and difficult feelings toward their classed other, ranging from ironic distaste to more ambivalent but still defended response. Dealing with the discomforts of privilege in disadvantaged contexts all too often results in varying degrees of repression, sublimation, and dis-identification (Skeggs, 1997). They were attempting to do class distinction work under conditions of anxious proximity (Raisborough & Adams, 2008) to working-class groups they feared might have a detrimental impact on their own children's educational performance.

This reluctant recognition of the implicit sense of superiority of the white middle classes left me in an impossible position, straddled between two irreconcilable spaces—the space of the now-privileged white middle-class academic and the space—often hidden but always simmering beneath the surface—of the once white working-class girl. So I felt myself to be in a place of heavy conflict, tussling simultaneously with identifying and dis-identifying, embodying both commonality and difference with my sample. Too often over the course of the fieldwork, antipathies superseded affinities. I was frequently in danger of the "failure of empathy" I had identified in my respondents. One negative consequence was the constant risk of representing the respondents less favorably in the analysis because I found it difficult at times to sympathize with their concerns.

Camilla, a young Londoner, was of all those we interviewed the most transparent about the difficult feelings that class differences can arouse. Now in her mid-20s, she reflects on how when she was at secondary school, "there was an element of being embarrassed about being middle class." She explains that this was especially so as secondary school was the first time in her life that she was confronted with people she describes as "having a lot less than anyone I had ever met." Her recollections of her secondary school experiences illuminate difficult tensions between empathy and desires to distance herself. On one hand, she describes how she was

> quite upset to see it though and I remember feeling really sorry for the working class kids because although I knew it happened and I knew it was an issue, you know, until you actually see it for yourself you don't actually think about it. And then knowing that we had so much more and knowing that when I came back after my first day my mum was going to ask me how it went. And there were so many kids there whose parents obviously probably didn't have hardly anything and you know weren't going to ask or didn't care sort of thing and that was quite sad.

However, on the other hand, permeating her sense of empathy and embarrassment at her own privilege was a countervailing sense of superiority. Her words also poignantly reveal her need to defend against a sense of inferiority in relation to her parents who are both senior academics:

> I think they looked up to me to a certain extent and I didn't sort of consciously think it but I subconsciously felt slightly superior to them in that I had everything that they didn't have. You know everything that my mum and dad had given me and I was more intelligent than they were and there was more going for me than there was for them. And I think also because my mum and dad had achieved so much I think I probably felt quite second rate to them and being friends with these people made me feel like the one you know who was achieving you know and was superior to them.

Camilla's uncomfortably honest account of her own struggles to deal with class difference allowed me a better understanding of what was at play in the claiming of intellectual superiority by the vast majority of our participants. I would argue that the norm among the sample was to take refuge in what Freud terms "splitting." Freud (1949) argued that when faced with a traumatic situation that calls into question one's integrity, the ego often deals with what appears to be an irreconcilable dilemma through processes of disavowal that lead to a splitting of the ego. What is seen to be shameful—in this case, any responsibility for very visible inequalities—is split off and projected onto subordinate groups. But as Layton (2009) asserts, "The split polarities that result from the shaming instantiation of oppressive social structures such as sexism or racism—and I would add, classism—proliferate in the dark" (p. 106).

Recognition of the splitting endemic among the sample forced me to an uneasy awareness of the splitting I too was investing in. There was a powerful tension between the morally "pure" egalitarian, the committed socialist feminist, who would spurn such elitist action, and the white middle-class woman who, like those I was interviewing, has to live out invidious structural inequalities of race and class on an everyday basis and inevitably makes compromises very similar to those made by the parents in the sample.

So on being confronted with extensive evidence of their internal struggles, I then had to deal with what this recognition of an internal struggle between the acquisitive self-interested self and a more altruistic, public-spirited self meant for me as a white middle-class academic who had made almost identical choices to those of the parents in the sample. Their articulated conflict raised complex and contradictory reactions in myself. Defensive distancing is common even in feminist research (Hollway & Jefferson, 2000), but how do you deal with differences when those difficult differences are a buried part of the self? My sample were mostly mothers from very similar backgrounds to my own who were making hard decisions very like the ones I had made in relation to my own children. Tamara Mose Brown and Erynn Masi de Casanova (2009) argue that we feminists enter the field not only as gendered, raced, and classed individuals but also as members of families and (sometimes) as mothers. Having motherhood in common with the women I interviewed did on the whole lead to a strong sense of rapport. But it was also an unexpected source of difference and dis-identification in relation to those women who expressed a strong sense of entitlement, and sometimes superiority, in relation to their children and their education. So, for example, Catherine, whose parents and grandparents attended university, talked about how it was essential to avoid the danger of sending children to schools where "there are too many working classes." As a consequence, I spent concerted periods of time in the field disassociating myself from them and their attitudes. Many of these parents still considered private schooling for their children as a last resort while I was clear morally and ethically that this was not a choice I would ever have contemplated for my own children. The moral high ground was an ever-present seduction. The proximity I had initially thought would be an asset in the field turned out instead to be a minefield. Recent research has addressed the difficulties that sameness between the researcher and the researched may present (Mand & Wilson, 2006; Ramji, 2008), but no one has critically explored the discomforts, tensions, and antipathies that can arise when unexpected and troubling differences break through the comforting veneer of sameness. Yet, there is an ever-present danger that such discomforts, tensions, and antipathies can lead to judgmental portrayals of respondents in research papers and reports. It is difficult to avoid a sense of betrayal when those we assume are "people like us" reveal unwelcome differences.

Barbara du Bois (1983) succinctly captures the seductions of sameness:

> The closer our subject matter to our own life and experience, the more we can probably expect our own beliefs about the world to enter into and shape our work—to influence the very questions we pose, our conceptions of how to approach those questions, and the interpretations we generate from our findings. (p. 105)

But my research dilemma was even messier than du Bois's scenario. Identification and dis-identification can follow fast on each other's heels, leading at one moment to empathy and in another moment to antipathy. What I have learned from my own experiences is that empathy and identification with respondents can be rapidly superseded by dis-identification and antipathy in the course of a single interview. Commonalities of class, gender, and ethnicity can still be overwhelmed by differences in political and moral values. As a feminist, the challenge is to ensure that those moments of negative reaction and judgment do not influence the analysis of the data, and that empathetic understanding and reflexive

questioning take the place of the moralistic "knowing better" stance I assumed at points in the fieldwork. We can try to overlook the differences we don't want to see, but they still bubble under the surface, and if we do not own and deal with them, they can invidiously influence our analyses in unanticipated ways. This brings me back to the point I made earlier, in relation to Molly Andrews's research, about context and the salience of different aspects of our identities in different social situations. In interviews with middle-class women expressing negative views about the working classes, my working-class background suddenly became salient in a way that it has largely ceased to be in most middle-class contexts. While this can be a strength, it can also, as I have tried to show, be a liability, especially if it results in a blindness about my own current privilege. Feminist reflexivity is in knowing the difference between the two. In response to the cultural hierarchies the respondents often constructed, I too constructed my own moral hierarchy of "knowing better" just as Molly Andrews had done. The irony was that while Molly Andrews's "knowing better" was constructed in relation to women who identified as "anti-feminist," many of the women that I interviewed would have seen themselves, like me, as feminists. In such circumstances "the creativity and knowledge building that lies within the tensions of difference" (Hesse-Biber, 2007, p. 3) disappears. Although there is no magic solution for ensuring our prejudices and judgmental attitudes disappear, like Andrews, I found Chodorow's injunction to always maintain a strong focus on the broader macro-context within which women are operating helpful.

As I have touched on earlier, the notion of the insider/outsider has been a recurrent concern within feminist research (Naples, 2003). Like Bahkru (2008), "I was in varying instances, simultaneously both insider and outsider in relation to my research subject" (p. 207). But this sense of insider-ness or outsider-ness could shift significantly over the course of a single interview. While there are clearly direct consequences in terms of empathizing and sympathetically understanding respondents' perspectives at times in the interview but not at others, there are also more far-reaching consequences for analysis and interpretation. We risk reaching judgmental conclusions in relation to what we cannot understand and empathize with. Guarding against this requires a feminist vigilance, a sensitive and emotionally attuned reflexivity.

In this section, I have examined three very different feminist attempts to address differences in the field. In Archer's work, beyond the focus on context for feminist research, we gain a sense of the importance of temporality, of differences that shift and transform over time as well as space. Andrews's research suggests a means of thinking difference in nonhierarchical ways through a focus on the situatedness of both gender and knowledge. Both studies work with strong boundaries and easily recognized differences in the research field. In contrast, my own research interrogates commonalities and reveals the ways in which differences are always at play regardless of how much we apparently share in common with our respondents. It also raises powerful ethical issues about how we as feminists should deal with what we perceive to be inequalities in other women's attitudes and practices. In my own research, one potential way of dealing with these was to incorporate a critical analysis of the structural context and dominant discourses that frame individuals' understandings of themselves and others alongside an explicit articulation of power dynamics (Reay et al., 2011). But, across these differences of approach and emphasis, in diverse ways, all three bodies of work alert us to the difficulties of dealing with difference for feminist research.

Conclusions

Perversely after criticizing the "counting" approach to difference at the beginning of this chapter, I want to argue for what I call the 3Rs approach to feminist research. But whereas the 3Rs usually conjure up images of the basics, the 3Rs I have in mind—recognition, respect, and response—ensure that inherent complexities, the broader context, and issues of temporality within feminist research are all addressed. First we need to recognize differences within the research field, not only the multiple differences among women but also the difference our own differences make. This entails a particular kind of feminist vigilance, the hard work of

constant scrutiny and socio-awareness. While social justice research more generally is about ethical scrutiny and conscious efforts to reduce inequalities both in fieldwork interaction and in representations of our respondents, feminist research is alert to the workings of oppression and committed to unmasking and countering it, specifically in the area of gender but also in relation to all other areas of difference. That is why recognition of the many aspects of identity that constitute us is so important.

There also needs to be a response that comes from respecting the differences between the researcher and the women she is researching. Commitment to feminisms means a commitment to respecting the ways in which women who are different both experience and describe their lives (Collins, 2008). So I am arguing for a very particular ethic of reflexivity akin to the feminist vigilance I mentioned earlier. This ethic should also embrace a focus on the differences within as well as without. It also requires an attention to the internally complex nature of subjectivity and how this manifests itself at the level of self-understanding and practice. As I demonstrate in the examples from my own research and that of Louise Archer, certain aspects of self become far more salient at particular times and in specific contexts. It is important to be attuned to these psychic shifts and changes if we are to be reflexive feminist researchers.

Reflexivity has become a commonplace requirement for social justice research. On a fundamental level, reflexivity is about giving as full and honest an account of the research process as possible, in particular explicating the position of the researcher in relation to the research. However, there is a paradox implicit in reflexivity. We explicate the processes and positions we are aware of being caught up in. But inevitably some of the influences arising from aspects of social identity remain beyond the reflexive grasp.

There is always a need for continuous interrogation. The 3Rs I elaborated earlier are not discrete stages of research or targets to be achieved. Rather, they are complex and constantly shifting processes requiring constant monitoring and reevaluation, a feminist vigilance that recognizes, respects, and responds to differences in a process of continuous interrogation of the self and others.

Discussion Questions

1. Cite three ways in which reflexivity is a research tool to assist researchers with studying across differences.

2. What are some specific ways researchers can get in touch with their own positionality in the research process?

3. In what way(s) has conducting research using online technologies helped or hindered the ability of the researcher to practice reflexivity?

Online Resources

British Educational Research Association

http://www.bera.ac.uk/critical-approaches-in-qualitative-educational-research/perspective-reflexivity-and-bias/

This website provides a short introduction to reflexivity across the research process from the British Education Research Association (BERA).

"On Becoming a Qualitative Researcher: The Value of Reflexivity"

http://www.nova.edu/ssss/QR/QR12–1/watt.pdf

"On Becoming a Qualitative Researcher: The Value of Reflexivity," by Diane Watt, appeared in *The Qualitative Report* (Volume 12, Number 1, March 2007, pp. 82–101). The author's use of her first-person journal account allows the reader to track her reflections on her research project, showing how she makes the connections between theory and praxis.

Relevant Journals

Gender & Society

Qualitative Report

Qualitative Sociology

References

Ahmed, S. (2009). Embodying diversity: Problems and paradoxes for Black feminists. *Race, Ethnicity and Education, 12*(1), 41–52.

Andrews, M. (1991). *Lifetimes of commitment.* Cambridge, UK: Cambridge University Press.

Andrews, M. (2002). Feminist research with non-feminist and anti-feminist women: Meeting the challenge. *Feminism & Psychology, 12*(1), 55–77.

Archer, L. (2004). Re/theorizing "difference" in feminist research. *Women's Studies International Forum, 27,* 459–473.

Bahkru, T. (2008). Negotiating and navigating the rough terrain of transnational feminist research. *Journal of International Women's Studies, 10,* 198–216.

Bhavnani, K., & Coulson, M. (2005). Transforming socialist feminism: The challenge of racism. *Feminist Review, 80*(1), 87–97.

Bordo, S. (1990). Feminism, postmodernism and gender-scepticism. In L. Nicholson (Ed.), *Feminism/postmodernism* (pp. 133–176). New York: Routledge.

Bourdieu, P., & Champagne, P. (1999). The contradictions of inheritance. In P. Bourdieu, A. Accardo, G. Balazs, S. Beaud, F. Bonvin, E. Bourdieu, et al. (Eds.), *The weight of the world.* Cambridge, UK: Polity.

Brah, A. (1999). The scent of memory: Strangers, our own and others. *Feminist Review, 61,* 4–26.

Braxton, J. (1989). *Black women writing autobiography: A tradition within a tradition.* Philadelphia: Temple University Press.

Cealey Harrison, W., & Hood-Williams, J. (1998). More varieties than Heinz: Social categories and sociality in Humphries Hammersley and beyond. *Sociological Research Online, 3*(1). www.socresearchonline.org.uk/3/1/contents

Chodorow, N. (1996). Seventies questions for thirties women: Some nineties reflections. In S. Wilkinson (Ed.), *Feminist social psychologies: International perspectives* (pp. 21–50). Milton Keynes, UK: Open University Press.

Collins, P. H. (2008). *Black feminist thought: Knowledge, consciousness and the politics of empowerment.* New York: Routledge.

Craig, L., & Hurt, E. (2008). Theory and praxis: The feminist solidarity group at UT Austin. *Thirdspace: A Journal of Feminist Theory and Culture, 8*(1).

du Bois, B. (1983). Passionate scholarship: Notes on values, knowing and method in feminist social science. In G. Bowles & R. Klein (Eds.), *Theories of women's studies* (pp. 105–116). London: Routledge & Kegan Paul.

Ferguson, K. (1993). *The man question: Visions of subjectivity in feminist research.* Berkeley: University of California Press.

Francis, B. (2001). Commonality and difference? Attempts to escape from theoretical dualisms in emancipatory research in education. *International Studies in Sociology of Education, 1*(2), 157–172.

Francis, B., & Skelton, C. (2008). "The self-made self": Analyzing the potential contribution to the field of gender and education of theories that disembed selfhood. *Discourse, 29*(3), 311–323.

Freud, S. (1949). *An outline of psychoanalysis.* London: Hogarth Press.

Gelsthorpe, L. (1992). Response to Martyn Hammersley paper on feminist methodology. *Sociology, 26*(2), 213–218.

Gorelick, S. (1996). Contradictions of feminist methodology. In H. Gottfried (Ed.), *Feminism and social change: Bridging theory and practice* (pp. 23–45). Champaign: University of Illinois Press.

Green, E. E., & Singleton, C. (2009). Mobile connections: An exploration of the place of mobile phones in friendship relations. *Sociological Review, 57*(1), 125–144.

Haraway, D. (1988). Situated knowledges: The science question in feminism and the privilege of partial perspective. *Feminist Studies, 14,* 575–599.

Haylett, C. (2001). Illegitimate subjects? Abject whites, neoliberal modernisation and middle-class multiculturalism. *Environment and Planning D: Space and Society, 19*(3), 351–370.

Heckman, S. (1999). *The futures of differences: Truth and method in feminist theory.* Cambridge, UK: Polity.

Hesse-Biber, S. (2007). Feminist research: Exploring the interconnections of epistemology, methodology, and method. In S. Nagy Hesse-Biber (Ed.), *Handbook of feminist research* (pp. 1–28). Thousand Oaks, CA: Sage.

Hesse-Biber, S., & Yaiser, M. (2004). Difference matters: Studying across race, class, gender and sexuality. In S. Hesse-Biber & M. Yaiser (Eds.), *Feminist perspectives on social research* (pp. 101–120). New York: Oxford University Press.

Hollway, W., & Jefferson, T. (2000). *Doing qualitative research differently.* London: Sage.

Layton, L. (2008). What divides the subject? Psychoanalytic reflections on subjectivity, subjection and resistance. *Subjectivity, 22,* 60–72.

Layton, L. (2009). "Who's responsible?" Our mutual implication in each other's suffering. *Psychoanalytic Dialogues, 19*(2), 105–120.

Mand, K., & Wilson, S. (2006, June). *Ambivalent positions: Ethnicity and working in our own communities.* Paper presented at "Britain: From Anti-Racism to Identity Politics to . . . ?" University of Surrey, Surrey, UK.

Markham, A. (2007). Ethic as method, method as ethic: A case for reflexivity in qualitative ICT research. *Journal of Information Ethics, 15*(2), 37–54.

McDowell, T., & Fang, S. (2009). Feminist-informed critical multiculturalism: Considerations for family research. *Journal of Family Issues, 20*(4), 549–566.

Mose Brown, T., & Masi de Casanova, E. (2009). Mothers in the field: How motherhood shapes fieldwork and researcher-subject relations. *Women's Studies Quarterly, 37*(3–4), 42–57.

Naples, N. (2003). *Feminism and method: Ethnography, discourse analysis and activist research.* New York: Routledge.

Raisborough, J., & Adams, M. (2008). Mockery and morality in popular cultural representations of the white, working class. *Sociological Research Online.* http://www.socresonline.org.uk/13/6/2.html

Ramji, H. (2008). Exploring commonality and difference in in-depth interviewing: A case-study of researching British Asian women. *British Journal of Sociology, 59*(1), 99–117.

Reay, D. (2008). Psycho-social aspects of white middle-class identities: Desiring and defending against the class and ethnic "other" in urban multiethnic schooling. *Sociology, 42*(6), 1072–1088.

Reay, D., Crozier, G., & James, D. (2011). *White middle class identities and urban schooling.* London: Palgrave.

Reay, D., Crozier, G., James, D., Hollingworth, S., Williams, K., Jamieson, F., et al. (2008). Reinvigorating democracy? White middle class identities and comprehensive schooling. *Sociological Review, 56*(2), 236–255.

Reay, D., Hollingworth, S., Williams, K., Crozier, G., James, D., Jamieson, F., et al. (2007). A darker shade of pale: Whiteness, the middle classes and multi-ethnic inner city schooling. *Sociology, 41*(6), 1041–1060.

Rich, A. (1980). Compulsory heterosexuality and lesbian existence source. *Signs: Journal of Women in Culture and Society, 5*(4), 631–660.

Rizq, R. (2008). The research couple: A psychoanalytic perspective on dilemmas in the qualitative research interview. *European Journal of Psychotherapy & Counselling, 10*(1), 39–53.

Schreiber, R. (2008). *Righting feminism: Conservative women and American politics.* Oxford, UK: Oxford University Press.

Shpungin, E., & Lyubansky, M. (2006). Navigating social class roles in community research. *American Journal of Community Psychology, 37*(3–4), 2227–2235.

Singleton, C., & Green, E. E. (2007). Mobile selves: Gender, ethnicity and mobile phones in the everyday lives of young Pakistani-British women and men. *Information Communication & Society, 10*(4), 506–526.

Skeggs, B. (1997). *Formations of class and gender.* London: Sage.

Skeggs, B. (2004). *Class, self, culture.* London: Routledge.

Sultana, F. (2007). Reflexivity, positionality and participatory ethics: Negotiating fieldwork dilemmas in international research. *ACME: An International E-Journal for Critical Geographies, 6*(3), 374–385.

Torrey, J. (2008). Racism and feminism: Is women's liberation for whites only? *Psychology of Women Quarterly, 4*(2), 281–293.

Townsend-Bell, E. (2009). Being true and being you: Race, gender, class and the fieldwork experience. *Political Science & Politics, 42,* 311–314.

Viladrich, A. (2005). "You just belong to us": Tales of identity and difference with populations to which the ethnographer belongs. *Cultural Studies, Critical Methodologies, 5*(3), 383–401.

Wallis, C. (2008). *Technomobility in the margins: Mobile phones and young rural women in Beijing.* Unpublished doctoral dissertation, University of Southern California, Los Angeles.

West, C., & Fenstermaker, S. (2002). Doing difference. In S. Fenstermaker & C. West (Eds.), *Doing gender, doing difference* (pp. 55–80). New York: Routledge.

31

FEMINIZING GLOBAL RESEARCH/GLOBALIZING FEMINIST RESEARCH

Methods and Practice Under Globalization

JENNIFER BICKHAM MENDEZ AND DIANE L. WOLF

Increased awareness of global and transnational connectivities of people and places around the world has prompted a critical reevaluation of notions of place, community, and "the local." The study of global processes has altered feminist thinking, creating a new wave of scholarship that enriches our theoretical, analytical, and empirical understandings of the interactions between global processes and gendered structures. Feminists have explored and raised questions about global economic, social, and cultural impacts on women in different localities by race and ethnicity, and they have explored what globalization has meant for gendered ideologies, practices, and political organizing. Despite these important efforts, a parallel rethinking of feminist methods in a globalized political economy has only recently gotten under way (see Thayer, 2010, and Mendez, 2009).

The gendered dimensions of globalization compel us to reconsider some of the main issues in feminist methods and research. Recent scholarship and our own research demonstrate how globalization may offer possibilities for expanding and reconceptualizing feminist research projects. For example, transnational collaborations, coalitions, and alliances among organizations and researchers offer new sites of intervention and possibilities for feminist researchers.

In this chapter, we envisage how an approach to research that recognizes the localized dynamics of global processes can inform and address issues related to feminist methods and praxis. We consider the following questions: How does globalization affect the contradictions, dilemmas, and possibilities of feminist research practices? What does this imply for future research? How might we conceptualize new modes of praxis for future scholars?

Our own backgrounds as politically minded, feminist academics situate our critical approach not only to methods but also to epistemological issues and those related to positionality. Jennifer's research has centered on the dynamics of gender and globalization as they are implicated in labor organizing in the maquila factories of postrevolutionary Nicaragua and, more recently, as they unfold in the experiences of recent immigrants from Mexico and Central America to a site much "closer to home," Williamsburg, Virginia. Over the course of her work, she has come to see her "field sites" as "transnational spaces" in which global political and economic processes and power differentials shape social relations (Mendez, 2009). This insight has been brought home to her particularly in her work with and about Latino/a immigrants. For example, transnational processes such as the effects of the North American Free Trade Agreement (NAFTA) on corn prices in Central Mexico were a major factor stimulating emigration from Mexican farming communities. Immigrants from rural localities must adapt to new rhythms of life in Williamsburg where "car culture" reigns, given the dispersed organization of public space.

The contradictions inherent in Diane's dissertation and post-dissertation research in Java, Indonesia, on gender and family dynamics among young women working in what we now call global sweatshops (Wolf, 1992) led her to write her essay and edit the volume *Feminist Dilemmas in Fieldwork* (Wolf, 1996). Attempting to engage in a more activist-academic endeavor, she ran a project at UC Davis with Jennifer's help that brought third world women activists to Davis in order to interact with academics, students, and each other and to study and work on a project of their choosing. Despite good intentions, the same kinds of hierarchies persisted and were reproduced in this transnational feminist work (Mendez & Wolf, 2001).

Diane has continued her focus on the links between gender and family dynamics amidst global transformations, such as those experienced by Southeast Asian immigrants and refugees to California and by Jewish families in post–World War II Holland, after genocide (Wolf, 2007). To some extent, both the inequalities inherent in doing research among poor families coupled with the politics of being a white, Western, middle-class woman working in a poor third world setting steered Diane toward researching "her own" (e.g., Jews) where the relationships are more lateral. This positioning can still be problematic, conflict laden, and confrontative but in ways that are less politicized than doing research about poverty-stricken people.

A generation of feminist theory has shown that there is no singular feminism but a multitude of ways to think, be, and act feminist. This insight, as well as our own experiences as feminist researchers, leads us to see the development of globalized feminist research methods as a continually evolving "strategy" that involves balancing a series of issues related to methodologies, accountability, and feminist principles (DeVault, 2004, p. 227).

In our discussion of the implications of globalization for feminist research, we maintain that a conceptualization of power as a zero-sum game in which research by first world feminists *always* victimizes third world respondents is overly simplistic and, indeed, inaccurate. Rather, we envisage power as multisited, ever shifting, and "situated and contextualized within particular intersubjective relationships" (Bloom, 1998, p. 35). Such a conceptualization moves us away from a unidirectional view of power and assumptions that seriously underestimate the capacity of people in the global South to mobilize discursive tools of resistance and political capital, while also mischaracterizing first world feminist researchers as constituting a homogeneous category (Blacklock & Crosby, 2004, p. 57).

In our view, collaborative, nonhierarchical relationships between researcher and researched, while important to pursue, on their own cannot change broader power relations. Nonetheless, just as there are multiple feminisms, globalized feminist research methods must take multiple forms if they are to be effective tools for generating knowledge and contributing to social transformation (Lather, 1991). Thus, global feminist research projects, like all feminist research, must be premised not only on a recognition of how research relations are constituted within particular structures that constrain and dominate but also with the understanding that participants are not merely the "objects" of research. Rather, the design of feminist research

practices must take into account that participants from poor and disadvantaged groups in
the global South hold the capacity to navigate
actively the newly emerged transnational social
spaces and the relationships within them.[1] In such
cases, poor women forge new solidarities as well
as challenge and dispute representations featured
in academic research. Indeed, they may increasingly demand accountability from northern-
based, feminist researchers (Thayer, 2010).

We argue that designing and implementing
globalized feminist research must involve a strategic awareness of the contradictions and problems embedded in research relationships that are
constituted within transnational social spaces, as
they are molded and shaped by shifting hegemonies and intersecting power structures. In our
final section, we highlight sophisticated research
that has contributed to the field both as models
of what we consider exemplary global feminist
scholarship and as springboards for future
endeavors.

Globalization's Challenge to Research Methods

As both a process and an analytical concept,
globalization has a vast scope. Its purported
extension to all domains of social and economic
life make it difficult to grasp in its complexity.
For the sake of conceptual clarity, in this chapter,
globalization refers to the historical, economic,
social, and cultural processes through which
individuals, groups, and institutions are increasingly interconnected on a worldwide scale. Thus,
the term *globalization* has implied an idea of
social, cultural, and political economic processes
that occur largely without reference to specific
national, territorial, or local boundaries.

Taken in this way, globalization disrupts
underlying assumptions of what constitutes a
society, traditionally defined as the confines of
nation-states, and destabilizes embedded notions
of "place" and "community." Thus, globalization may challenge researchers to reconfigure
their units of analysis for scholarly inquiry and
rethink methodologies (Albrow, 1997; Gille &
Ó Riain, 2002; Marcus, 1995).

Despite the implication that "global flows"
occur without reference to specific localities, a
wide range of interdisciplinary research has
clearly shown the multiple and complex ways in
which place continues to matter in a context of
globalization.[2] Indeed, far from giving rise to a
"borderless" world, the promotion of open markets and the free flow of capital across national
borders that is so central to neoliberal globalization has been accompanied by the systematic
and oppressive social control of often displaced
and marginalized peoples through the militari-
zation of national, territorial boundaries. Thus
the "debordering" of economies also involves
"rebordering" in the form of the redrawing and
re-enforcement of racial-ethnic boundaries
within and across nation-states and the reterritorialization of nation-states through intensified
immigration control (Spener & Staudt, 1998). In
a related process, even as neoliberal policies
transfer state power upward to global institutions (such as the WTO), the responsibility for
social welfare has fallen increasingly to localities, resulting in deep structures of exclusion
that fracture local communities.

Under globalization, new dialectical articulations of race, class, and gender emerge, and
these are enacted in culturally and place-specific
ways. A generation of feminist scholarship has
recognized the ways in which gendered and
racialized ideologies and power structures that
devalue women and their work are foundational
to the inner workings of the global economy.
Women from the global South constitute the
bulk of cheap labor that continues to serve transnational capital, which seeks a young and "docile" labor force. Under the global hegemony of
neoliberalism and in a context of globally circulating commodities, women have increasingly
taken on breadwinner capacities in ways that
both draw on and undermine traditional gender
roles (Peterson & Runyan, 1999, pp. 130–147).
Women workers in the global economy embrace
new global modes of consumption in an expanding arena and are exposed to new desires, yearn-
ings, and dreams in ways that disrupt the
boundaries and understandings of social class
and "actively reconfigure the forms and meanings of work and self amid neoliberal globalization" (Freeman, 2010, p. 580).

Given their substantive focus on people's
movement across borders and incorporation
into new societies, migration scholars have been

prominent in advancing understandings of the local dynamics of globalization processes. Feminist scholars have been particularly influential in theorizing the ways shifting racialized and gendered structures shape the experiences of migration (see Hirsch, 2003; Hondagneu-Sotelo, 2001). In the current global context, women make up a large proportion of migrants, setting up transnational families and leaving their children behind in order to work abroad and send remittances home (Parreñas, 2001). Care work has also gone transnational. Sometimes facilitated through state-sponsored labor brokerage, women from economically disadvantaged countries leave homes and families to fill a demand for labor to care for children or the elderly in wealthier countries (Hondagneu-Sotelo, 2001; Rodriguez, 2010).

Transnational migration is structured, regulated, and even brokered by nation-states in gendered and racially specific ways with dramatic implications for models of sovereignty and citizenship and forms of social belonging. Newly emerging governing strategies draw upon and contribute to the construction of racialized and gendered categories of social membership within nations, with differing rights and privileges accorded to distinct groups. Such governing strategies are exemplified by the recent trend of local immigration enforcement initiatives in localities across the United States, often enacted in communities that have only recently become destinations for immigrant newcomers. Thus, the imperatives of neoliberalism dovetail with local restrictionist projects, especially in new migrant destinations, creating unchartered borders of gendered and racial social belonging. Such social borders are "patrolled" in various realms of public life, not only by police but also by private citizens and government workers such as landlords, hospital staff, school officials, and social workers (Kretsedemas, 2008). While immigrant men are seen as a dangerous economic and criminal threat whose activities should be policed and scrutinized by law enforcement, "border enforcement" that limits immigrant women's participation in new societies occurs through restrictions on the services, supports, and economic opportunities that correspond to their social reproductive roles as

caregivers for their families (Deeb-Sossa & Bickham Mendez, 2008; Schmalzbauer, 2009).

Public expressions of nativism; intensified anti-immigrant sentiments voiced by political pundits, media personalities, and ordinary people in geographic contexts around the world; and the emergence of vigilante, anti-immigrant groups are fueled by "controlling images" that circulate in the globalized mainstream media against which immigrants are challenged to define themselves. "Controlling images" discursively demarcate boundaries of social belongings and are "major instrument[s] of power" in that they create and maintain race, class, and gender oppression (Collins, 2000, p. 68). In the context of the United States, xenophobic discourses and representations as propagated by the media represent "acceptable forms" (Chavez, 2008) of what has been termed "color-blind" racism (Bonilla-Silva, 2010; Collins, 2005). In a subsequent section of this chapter, we turn to a discussion of the increased influence of racially based media representations and the possibilities of new media technologies for contributing to global feminist research projects.

FEMINIST RESEARCH METHODS

Feminist researchers have interrogated and analyzed how hierarchies of power and authority shape the research process, revealing how the privilege of the powerful to speak and be heard can be reproduced in scholarship (Hesse-Biber & Leckenby, 2004, pp. 209–210; Naples, 2003, pp. 4–5). Rather than claiming the position of the "objective observer," whose presence goes unexamined, feminist researchers analyze their own social locations and the ways in which power differentials can reinforce and reproduce inequalities. Feminist epistemologies challenge the assumptions of positivism. In endeavoring to construct projects "by, for, and about women," they have struggled to develop research methods that challenge and break down "the dualities between 'theory' and 'praxis,' researcher and researched, subject and object" (Richardson, 1997, p. 55). Some feminist researchers approach their methods and resultant research relations as feminist practice in and of itself, as action with the potential to facilitate respondents' gaining a deeper understanding of their situations through self-reflection that might lead to their seeking change in their lives—that is, as consciousness raising.

By challenging assumptions about knowledge production and by raising questions about the purpose of research and whose voices are privileged in the production of scholarship, feminist writings have undoubtedly opened important dialogues. Feminist scholars have experimented with new methodological approaches and forms of representation that seek to decenter the interpretative authority of the researcher and generate polyvocal texts through which the "researched" present their perspectives (Wolf, 1996). Feminist researchers have used reflective strategies to promote awareness of and minimize the ways in which hierarchies of power and domination are reproduced through the course of research, but it is less clear whether they have succeeded in designing research methodologies that overcome the contradictions that stem from race, class, nationality, and other differences within their projects. Scholars continue to address this Achilles' heel in feminist research by striving to develop research practices that reflect feminist principles. For example, in her recent book on transnational feminisms and women's organizations in Brazil, Millie Thayer (2010) includes an e-mail dialogue with a leader of a rural women's organization that she studied who takes issue with some of her findings. The leader's responses are critical and direct, but, to her credit, Thayer includes these reactions in an effort to address issues of the asymmetries within struggles over representation in a context of transnational connections.

Some feminists have promoted research models that inform and are informed by transformative struggles, calling for methodologies that emphasize political engagement and collaboration with movements for social change (Maguire, 1987, 2001; Mies, 1978). Where such types of projects have been carried out (Rappaport, 2007; Richards, 2006; Speed, 2006; Thayer, 2010), collaboration has taken many shapes and involved varied levels of working together to accomplish such tasks as formulating research questions, developing interview or survey questions, interpreting "data," and even writing final research "products" (compare Wolf, 1996, p. 27). Researchers may also draw on their "data" to prepare briefs or provide expert testimony in court proceedings to document human rights abuses (Hernandez-Castillo, 2006; Sanford, 2006).

FEMINIZING POLITICALLY ENGAGED RESEARCH IN THE GLOBAL SPHERE

"Politically engaged" or "action" research is a general rubric that refers to a messy array of scholarly approaches, schools of thought, and methods. Other labels include "activist scholarship," "participatory" or "collaborative" research, "civic engagement," and public intellectual work (see Burawoy, 2005; Hale, 2008; Sanford, 2006). The unifying goal of this type of work, however, is a reconfiguration of knowledge production so as to shift power and control into the hands of the poor, oppressed, or marginalized, thereby creating a space for the expression of "subjugated knowledges" (Collins, 2000) and, in so doing, transforming oppressive social structures (Brydon-Miller, Hall, & Jackson, 1993; Fals-Borda & Rahman, 1991; Maguire, 1987; Park, 1993; Stoecker, 1999).

Although feminist and politically engaged research both seek to expose the myth of value-free knowledge production through the pursuit of positive social change, the literatures on and practices of action research have not always included women, gender issues, or feminist orientations (Maguire, 1996, 2001). As Maguire so astutely points out, feminist perspectives are in fact integral to action research in that they highlight not just the power in the social construction of knowledge but the ways in which power is multifaceted and intersectional, shaped by race, class, gender, and other dimensions. Feminisms have called attention not only to whose voices are missing or marginalized from knowledge production but to how categories like "community," "the oppressed," or "the poor" might obfuscate differences of power and perspective.

Feminist advocates for research in the service of social justice argue for incorporating (multiple) feminist perspectives—including the second wave feminist principle that the personal is political—into research models, raising questions about who exactly in the community is empowered by this kind of work (Maguire, 1996, p. 111; Naples, 2003). Researchers place emphasis on the *process* of collective endeavors as empowering and more than simply a means to an end. As Hesse-Biber and Leckenby (2004) point out, "This positions feminist research at the crossroads of intellectual endeavors within a community of academics and social change endeavors within a community of activists" (p. 223).

Both feminist critics and globalization theorists have challenged notions of bounded, homogeneous "local" communities (see Burawoy, 2000, and Maguire, 2001). Globalization's disruption of simplistic notions of community "belonging" adds new dimensions to the power issues confronted by activist researchers, such as the multiple power differentials that cross-cut organizations and communities and the consequences of research in communities to which one belongs as opposed to those in which the researcher is a "foreigner" or outsider. For example, economic globalization has resulted in the "third-worlding" of urban and even suburban areas in the United States and Europe. Thus, the "third world" becomes a process, not a fixed geographical location. Corporations can outsource jobs to "third world" locations in order to reduce labor costs, or, in the case of industries such as the meatpacking and hotel industries in the United States, they can "import" third world workers and work conditions.

In an era of globalization, interactions with respondents are complicated by transnational dimensions, often in unanticipated ways. Jennifer's recent research with Latino/a immigrants in Williamsburg, Virginia, is a case in point. In this next section, Jennifer discusses the complex ways in which local power dynamics articulate with global relations of power within a collaborative research project.

Enacting Feminist Research in a New Destination for Latino/a Immigrants

My recent research on Latino/a migration to Williamsburg, Virginia, has involved collaborations with the Program for Integral Community Health (PICH),[3] a nonprofit organization that seeks to improve low-income families' access to public services and medical care. Although at first glance the scope of this organization's mission might appear to be quite local, neoliberal globalization is relevant for its work, having prompted new transnational migratory processes that have resulted in a demographic shift in the people who receive its services. Over the last 15 years, the population that PICH serves has shifted to include a large proportion of immigrants from Central America and Mexico who do not speak English. In the early 2000s, PICH's staff members worked to broaden their understandings of the issues that these families face and adapted their outreach and support efforts to meet the particular needs of this new "clientele." Their efforts involved adjusting to cultural and language differences as well as understanding other issues particular to the immigrant community. Such issues range from the economic hardships that stem from supporting family members left in home communities to the difficulties experienced in accessing medical care as undocumented immigrants. Finally, PICH and its staff came face-to-face with the effects of growing local and national anti-immigrant public sentiments and policies.

My collaboration with PICH began when the organization sought my help in these efforts. The program's director asked me to facilitate a support group for Spanish-speaking families. This group, which usually included between 15 and 22 mothers (and sometimes one or two fathers), was a space for immigrants to meet and share stories and information in their own language, building a sense of solidarity as they reflected on their lives in their new surroundings. I also volunteered to work with PICH outreach workers, serving as an interpreter for Spanish-speaking immigrants at doctor and social service appointments.

In collaboration with PICH, I designed a research project with the goal of documenting and exploring Latina immigrants' experiences of exclusion, economic survival, and integration based on narratives about their experiences and the realities that they faced. My students and I developed a series of research questions that emerged from the parent group meetings, and we conducted intensive interviews with recent immigrants. In dialogue with community leaders and a network of organizations that formed in Williamsburg to address issues facing Latin American immigrants in the community, we sought out different ways to convey the results of this study to the broader community. Our goal was to help make visible immigrants' obstacles to inclusion, including the misconceptions and negative representations about them; we shared our findings at community workshops, forums, and training for staff at social services and other organizations that provide services to immigrants.

Not surprisingly, the dynamics of power that underlay my collaborations with PICH's professional staff, as well as with the organization's "clients," varied considerably in ways that illustrated the research's embeddedness in different and intersecting global and local power structures. My role in PICH was unique in that the multiple positions that I occupied, as an academic professional, Spanish speaker, researcher, and volunteer, allowed me to cross borders of hierarchy, status, and culture, although not always with total success. Dramatic asymmetries in cultural and social capital flavored my relationships with the Latina women who received services from PICH. I clearly possessed useful cultural knowledge, not only in the form of English but regarding how to navigate "the system" and tap economic and social resources in the community, evidenced when I accompanied them as an interpreter on doctors' visits and appointments with social services and legal services and when I helped connect them to English as a second language (ESL) resources. The challenge that presented itself was that, through collaborations with PICH, I became positioned as a "service provider" with the potential to be seen as someone who "does for" and not "with"—a patron-client-like relationship that would seem to reproduce rather than dismantle power inequities.

I established a level of rapport with many of the women of the parent group, and, because of my (then) marriage to a Nicaraguan, I became a kind of cultural "insider" as contrasted with the professional staff from the nonprofit who did not speak Spanish or engage in direct interactions with PICH clients. My close relationships with a number of mothers led to my undertaking two research trips to Mexico where I visited the home communities of these women and interviewed their family members. These trips enabled me not only to explore and observe the social ties that linked immigrants to their families and communities across the U.S. border but also to bring a transnational perspective to my understanding of their lives and experiences. In a sense, I came to develop a greater cultural and experiential understanding of the daily realities of PICH's immigrant clients than PICH program directors and administrators.

From the point of view of the administrative staff at PICH, my position vacillated between "insider," a community partner and ally, and "outsider," potentially part of the controlling gaze of the larger "community." And, although the administration frequently recognized my involvement, featuring my work in the parent group and as an advocate in its reports and highlighting my attendance at community meetings, PICH program directors and administrators had the power to deny or restrict my research activities if they perceived them to be inappropriate or not in keeping with the organization's policies or mission.

NEW SPACES AND TECHNOLOGIES IN GLOBALIZED FEMINIST RESEARCH

As illustrated by the example above, globalization has added complexities to feminist research practices. But global processes have also created some new and exciting possibilities for unsettling systems of domination, including "cross-race and cross-national projects, feminist movements, anticolonial struggles, and politicized cultural practices" (Lowe & Lloyd, 1997, p. 25).

Global forces have sparked the growth of increasingly transnational public spheres. The explosion of nongovernmental organizations (NGOs) onto the political stage represents an important element of this process. Reflecting what has become a globalized civil society, these increasingly active groups have undertaken a wide array of social, political, and even economic functions. Indeed, NGOs are significant actors in transnational politics and have successfully deployed transnational strategies to gain influence in national as well as international political circles (Keck & Sikkink, 1998).

Globalization has given rise to shifts in relations between civil societies and nation-states. Despite these changes, nation-states remain extremely powerful regulators and continue to exert a great deal of control over their national populations. Scholars like Aihwa Ong (2006) have explained how neoliberal globalization has set the stage for newly emerging forms of sovereignty and for governing strategies in which the state manages different segments of the population differently.

And yet, governing strategies that differentiate between distinct groups at the national level have occurred in a context of the emergence of a global and universalized set of international norms and rules. Based on liberalism and the notion that individuals are the bearers of unalienable rights, these norms have transformed the sphere of international political activity. In addition, the globalized discourse of human rights has become a crucial idiom for disenfranchised groups as they frame their claims and demands. Although this language of rights converges with the discursive frameworks of neoliberal state regimes and multilateral donor organizations, it holds radically different meanings for social movements who posit alternative conceptions of citizenship, even as they use the same language as state and other powerful actors (Schild, 1998).

Globalized norms and discourses surrounding rights and citizenship have been important tools for women's transnational political networks (Keck & Sikkink, 1998). The strategies and collaborations of groups within such alliances have been facilitated by the emergence of telecommunications technologies and the dramatic decrease of transportation costs, both of which have stimulated the circulation of ideas, discourses, resources, and people across national, regional, and international sites (Appadurai, 1996). Organizations seeking social change use diffuse, transnational links with organizations in other national contexts (often through the use of communication technologies) to transmit information and reach other national or transnational public spheres and "foreign reference publics" (Keck & Sikkink, 1998). The practices involved in such politics include negotiation, lobbying, and media campaigns with the goal of exerting impact through persuasion and

changing perceptions and values by challenging the meaning of democracy under global capitalism (Schild, 1998).

Feminist discourses and practices now move through increasingly globalized circuits and through transnational linkages among feminists. Regional and "world" conferences have resulted in "the multiplication . . . of the spaces and places in which women who call themselves feminists act" (Alvarez, 1998, p. 294) and in the emergence of what Thayer (2010) terms "transnational feminist counterpublics." Heterogeneous and fractured by contradictory power inequities, these counterpublics are transnational, oppositional political spaces in which networks, organizations, and individuals may engage with each other collaboratively or conflict with one another. Despite contradictions of power, the fabric of transnational connections and relationships among women's movement participants and feminists creates a hybrid social arena where oppositional perspectives can be articulated, debated, constructed, and shared. And given the potential for these counterpublics to be spaces of solidarity and democratic participation across power differentials and differences of class, nationality, and race, they represent logical spaces for globalized feminist research to contribute to projects of social change. Examples include dialogue, interaction, and engagements that occur through relationships within transnational networks of women's and feminist organizations (Hernández Castillo, 2010; Mendez, 2005; Thayer, 2010); the World Social Forum (De Sousa Santos, 2008); cross-border organizational initiatives for workers' rights in maquila factories (Bandy, 2004); and the transnational indigenous rights movement (Brysk, 2000). Spaces that permit and foster solidarity and exchange and in which groups and individuals link local issues, grievances, and even identities to an understanding of global processes provide fertile ground for forging counter-hegemonies and developing alternatives to the dominant neoliberal paradigm.

Neoliberal globalization produces problems that manifest themselves locally but have implications that are not always readily observable to people on the ground. Throughout the late 1990s and into the 2000s, transnational coalitions that addressed the injustice, abuses, and work conditions in export processing "sweat-shops" emerged. Supported by an array of trans-national solidarity organizations, coalitions such as the Network of Central American Women in Solidarity with Maquila Workers and the Coalition for Justice in the Maquilas, as well as networks of transnational supporters, have engaged in community and labor organizing, litigation, and lobbying efforts to install "codes of conduct." Beyond these strategies, organiza-tional members of these networks have sought to empower communities by raising conscious-ness about local and global economic problems and by promoting economic justice and human rights—from the home to the global economy. Such initiatives illustrate the potential for trans-national cultures of solidarity that can create a space for dialogue and exchange across barriers of national origin, race, gender, and class (Bandy & Bickham Mendez, 2003). But they also reveal how gender, along with power relations of race, ethnicity, and nation, "fracture the space of transnational civil society and constrain opposi-tion to neoliberalism" (Bandy & Bickham Mendez, 2003, p. 174).

Within transnational spaces of dialogue and engagement, feminist researchers could collabo-rate with locally engaged organizations and activ-ists to make explicit the global-local connections in women's lives, allowing "for the subversive possibility of women seeing beyond the local to the global" (Eisenstein, 1997, p. 147). This prac-tice is in keeping with broadly defined feminist principles, mirroring consciousness-raising—linking personal transformation to broader issues of gender inequalities—and predicated on the feminist notion that the means and ends of strug-gle are interrelated (Eschle, 2001, p. 96).

Increasingly internationally accessible and rapidly developing communication and media technologies have played an important role in facilitating the formation of transnational polit-ical strategies and the generation of transna-tional feminist counterpublics. At the same time as such technology has demonstrated emanci-patory potential and has facilitated the develop-ment of solidarities across geographic place, the media's increased influence has been cen-tral in propagating controlling images and rep-resentations that have fueled xenophobia and "moral panics" regarding the "threat," often to

the sovereign nation, of criminalized, "othered" groups of outsiders. This is particularly the case in a post-9/11 context in which media represen-tations of what "terrorists look like" have helped justify the racial profiling of Muslims as well as of various groups of immigrants.

In this context, counter-hegemonies and alternative images and representations of mar-ginalized groups become highly significant cul-tural components of social justice struggles. Recently, one of Jennifer's undergraduate stu-dents undertook a research project in which she explored the potential for visual production as a tool for "community engagement." On a research trip and educational delegation to the region of Tucson, Arizona, and Nogales, Sonora, on the border between the United States and Mexico, she produced a documentary featuring the voices of humanitarian organizations, art-ists, and activists on both sides of the border. Her aim was to "uncove[r] the way our com-munities are built around lines of inclusion and exclusion" and to demonstrate that "border issues register in places far from the geographic border" (Chung, 2009a). She purposefully did not include representations of the migrants themselves, given issues of power and control over such depictions. Instead she struggled with how to make the "invisible" visible in a way that could promote community dialogue about immigration issues, not just along the U.S.-Mexico border but also back in Williamsburg, Virginia, where social borders of exclusion also affect recent immigrants from Latin America.

As she edited the short documentary, Sewon Chung made her work public in a variety of local and transnational spheres of interaction. She developed a blog to dialogue with other activist-researchers who are devising ways to put visual media to the service of community empowerment. She screened the documentary in multiple public venues in Williamsburg, including at a community forum attended by social workers, law enforcement officers, and members of the general public as well as for a group of ESOL tutors. Finally, she posted the documentary on YouTube and another video-sharing site (Chung, 2009b).

One interesting outcome occurred when the documentary was screened and used as a tool for discussion in a popular education program at

La Comisión Provincial por la Memoria. This social justice organization, located in La Plata, Argentina, promotes public reflection and discussion about authoritarianism and democracy through popular education programs and the preservation of a public archive of police files from the "Dirty War." The graduate student interns and popular educators from La Comisión later visited the U.S.-Mexico border and participated in an educational delegation. This project illustrates the potential of alternative media as a vehicle for creating and promoting counter-hegemonic images and narratives that could support social justice initiatives.

This example also highlights how globalization holds important implications for constructing a "politics of accountability with those with whom we work" (Blacklock & Crosby, 2004, p. 69). In today's world of global technologies, research respondents increasingly have access to the worlds of feminist researchers. Indeed, in a context of transnational links among women's organizations and the reliance of groups in the South on funding and support from NGOs in the North, women in the South rightly perceive that the stakes of control are increasingly high over representations of themselves and their work in the research of first world academics, given the potential of these representations to jeopardize relationships with potential donors (Thayer, 2010; see also Mendez, 2005). And, consequently, organizers in the South may actively seek to limit the most well-meaning researcher's access to information or activities, as they recognize that they have little control over how the information may be used or presented once it reaches a transnational public sphere.

For the "global ethnographer" (Burawoy, 2000), "the field" becomes an ever more politicized arena, and departure from her geographical "field site" does little to extract her from the political implications of her research or from engagement with the political issues that she analyzes. In the case of transnational, feminist, and activist projects, academics are not the only ones who travel within transnational circuits. And researchers may unexpectedly come into contact with "respondents" at conferences or in other forums. Respondents are more likely than before to read our writings or at least hear about something that we communicated in a public forum due to transnational social and activist networks.

In some ways, globalization and transnational communications and networks enforce accountability, making researchers more aware than ever of the political implications of their research. This is especially the case for feminist activist-researchers who collaborate with and study social justice movements. In these cases, transnational communications and activism have given a voice to activists in the South who can engage in dialogue with the researcher about the findings of the research as well as its political implications, which clearly represents a positive step toward more accountability and equality within research relationships. At the same time, such enforced accountability also opens up new dilemmas and questions. Feminist activist researchers who work with transnational feminist struggles must decide what to do when their analytical interpretations do not match those of their respondents or when participants disagree with researchers' findings. In some cases, negotiations about access or publications might be crystal clear, but in others the waters are muddier. At best, researchers run the risk of committing a political faux pas. At worst, researchers could unintentionally damage an organization's chances at securing funding or even undermine the political strategy of a movement.

Emerging Research Topics in Global Feminist Research

Much of the feminist research related to globalization focuses on emergent configurations of work and gender and the ideologies that develop alongside these changes. The best examples of scholarship in this area reflect a deep understanding of these shifting and often contradictory ideologies and how they play out in the daily lives and practices of those involved (Freeman, 2000; Lee, 1999). Still, the global assembly line remains a vivid site for feminist research (Collins, 2003; Mendez, 2005; Salzinger, 2002), and the so-called "sweatshop" issue is a compelling one for transnational political activism.

The issues seem straightforward and easily bifurcated into what's right—better wages and work conditions for workers producing brand-name apparel—and what's wrong—purchasing the goods that workers produce under poor work conditions while receiving "sweatshop" wages.

However, feminist research has also uncovered how important these jobs are for women despite low and exploitative wages. In some cases, women's incorporation into the labor force, a process facilitated by the globalization of the economy, has empowered them economically and has even provided them with "the means to generate solidarity across class and gender lines" (Giles & Hyndeman, 2004, p. 303). Given other available alternatives in the labor market, for women workers who are the only breadwinners in their large families, the maquila industry often presents them with the best survival strategy. Boycotts by well-meaning students and labor organizers in the North could end up hurting the very workers they are trying to help by contributing to factory closures and moves to ever cheaper locales. As Kabeer (2004) notes, boycotting campaigns are "blunt instruments" that leave little room for "nuanced, balanced and differentiated accounts of ground-level realities in low-income countries" (p. 179).

The deleterious effects on women workers of this kind of earnest activism need to be acknowledged. Likewise transnational labor movements cannot ignore the fact that the majority of workers in free trade zones are, in fact, brown, black, or Asian women whose gendered responsibilities as caretakers of the home contribute to their facing harsh realities that obligate them to accept dangerous and substandard work conditions (Kabeer, 2004, p. 187). Although women in Southeast and East Asia have been prominent in research on factory labor as well as the sex trade, another area has brought the effects of globalization into focus—that of the export of women for marriage and for domestic work. The globalized marriage market (Constable, 2003) draws from women in China, the Philippines, and elsewhere, for example, the former Soviet Union, to fulfill both Western ideologies of romance and a traditional sexual division of labor. Tens of thousands of Filipina

women constitute an extremely lucrative state export for yet another niche and are in demand in many advanced industrial economies around the globe—as servants (Parreñas, 2001; Rodriguez, 2010). Up until now, Hong Kong, Italy, and the United States have been studied, but important sites such as Taiwan, Japan, Israel, and other countries in the Middle East have not yet been mined.[4] It would be extremely useful to understand the interactions between Filipina domestics and different state-society configurations.

Women's labor in sex work, factories, and domestic service has been perhaps the main focus thus far of the majority of research in the field of gender and globalization. Another body of scholarship that has received recent attention is in the area of advanced reproductive technologies. Rene Almeling's study of egg and sperm donations in her book *Sex Cells* (2011) demonstrates the highly gendered division of emotional labor in these endeavors. Women who donate eggs are encouraged by clinic staff to develop feminized emotions such as giving, empathy, and caretaking for the intended couple. The egg donors develop relationships with the intended couple even though they are unlikely to meet (Haylett, 2010). They are encouraged to think about the "gift" they are giving the couple, which may be a tactic not only to keep them on the very potent drug regime they must follow but also to keep them from trying to push for more remuneration. Sperm donors are viewed in a very different way: they come to the clinic, do their "job" (donate sperm), and get paid for their work. While egg donors are notified when a live birth occurs, sperm donors are not. In the United States, reproductive technologies are not regulated, leaving important medical and ethical decisions to doctors who stand to benefit from facilitating the use of these technologies. This lack of regulation leaves decision makers with a tremendous potential to exploit the labor and bodies of poor minority women.

Surrogacy represents another emerging area of research that captures global-local gender dynamics. Teman's (2010) award-winning and powerful ethnography about the relationship between the surrogate and the intended mothers in Israel brilliantly depicts how surrogate mothers detach from the bodily experience of housing someone else's baby. The intended mother accompanies the surrogate mother to checkups; the women are seen together, and both names appear in their medical files. During sonograms, intended mothers watch the screen while surrogate mothers look away, reinforcing their detachment from the being they are incubating for someone else. While Teman's work is national in its focus, the emotional dynamics of distancing and detachment are relevant for transnational surrogacy relationships.

Teman found that, although the surrogates tended to be from a lower class than the intended mothers, the relationship between the two women is complicated and much more nuanced beyond a simplistic notion of the exploiter and the exploited. Indeed, the two women tend to bond and develop almost a love relationship during the pregnancy, ignoring their male partners. Teman elucidates how some of the surrogates miss the close relationship with and attention from the intended mothers once the baby is born.

On the other hand, in Amrita Pande's (2010) ethnography of transnational surrogate relationships in a clinic in India, the economic and emotional divisions are very clear. Poor women who might have considered selling an organ carry a pregnancy for couples from wealthier countries (Japan, Europe, the United States, Israel) and are housed together in a dorm-like setting for the full term of their pregnancy. As mother-workers, their labor is quite literally "reproductive," as their movement and bodily functions are surveilled and controlled. Their relationships with intended mothers are more varied and uneven than in Teman's case, which is not surprising given that the greater differences of class are compounded by national and linguistic differences. Pande (2009) found more bodily claims than did Teman in that the Indian women felt that their "blood" went into making the baby.

The reproductive warehouses depicted in Pande's work represent an emergent form of the labor of third world women revealing striking paradoxes, not unlike those uncovered in research on "global factory work." Without question, these women constitute cheap, reproductive labor for couples from advanced industrial countries. Like the *domésticas* whom Pierrette Hondagneu-Sotelo (2001) describes in Los Angeles, these Indian women leave behind their own children in order to incubate babies belonging to wealthier people. At the same time and unlike *domésticas*, the women undergoing these nine-month stints in a central location, while surveilled and controlled, can rest and briefly escape the anxieties and demands of feeding their families, perhaps for the first and last time. They receive significant compensation that enables them to better ensure their families' economic survival.

Thus, transnational mothering now covers a myriad of relationships, from Filipina domestics and nannies, to Mexican *domésticas* who are forced to leave behind their own children to care for those of wealthier women, to poor third world women who incubate babies for economically advantaged foreigners. A focus on global motherhood presents new opportunities to further feminist theorizing on shifting relations concerning culture and consumption within the global economy. Carla Freeman (2010) writes about the importance of "a purposeful engagement with culture/economy not as dual spheres—as they are often portrayed—but rather as mutually constitutive forces, and domains of practice and meaning" (p. 578). This approach is particularly important when we consider how economically advantaged mothers may engage in active class reproduction through particular kinds of consumption that directly involve the labor of poorer women.

Globalization has affected the desire for consumption and presentation of self among all classes; fulfilling these desires and dreams, however, is limited to those with means. Studies on culture and consumption tap into what we might call the sociology of emotions, on all sides—the haves, the have-some-but-not-a-lots, and the have-nots. The struggles of poor mothers within a context of the global economy starkly contrast with the kind of intensive mothering and "concerted cultivation" practiced by middle- to upper-middle-class mothers in the United States (Hays, 1998; Hochschild, 2003; Lareau, 2003). The labor of poor women from the developing world enables first world women to engage in concerted cultivation and balance the gendered "double-bind" of work and family life. Poor women must often separate from their children in order to ensure the daily and generational maintenance of the nuclear families of wealthier women in the first world, whose children benefit through gaining the resources and social capital that enable them to maintain their class position—at the expense of the children of their "nannies." Thus, cross-cultural and transnational studies of motherhood that interrogate and study these political-economic relationships and their important emotional components would be welcome additions to the literature on gender and the family.

Gender and nationalism, war, and the military have been the focus of feminist scholarship over the last two decades, but since 9/11 and the so-called "war on terrorism," these topics merit yet another look through feminist lenses, particularly in regard to the Middle East, in order to further our understanding of international politics, neocolonialism, and the militaristic turn (Lentin, 2000). A focus on gender and war has zeroed in on (1) women as warriors and soldiers, (2) women's bodies as the site of war, and (3) the effects of war and genocide on women and their families (Sancho, 1997). The current wars in Iraq and Afghanistan, especially the sexual abuse of male prisoners at Abu Ghraib, invite a feminist analysis of this particular mélange of power, sexualities, gender and the body, and imperialism.[5] We have recently seen another version of this abuse featuring a female Israeli soldier posing with Palestinian prisoners. The topic of gender and war or genocide in sites such as Bosnia-Herzegovina (Boric, 1997), Rwanda, Sudan, Palestine, and elsewhere deserves more attention and should rank high on the feminist agenda. A focus on war and genocide leads to other topics, such as immigration, flight, displacement, asylum, and the plight of refugees in camps and in exile. Again, feminists have turned their lens to this topic with regard to refugees (Julian, 1997) and refugee camps (Hans, 2004; Hyndman, 2004), but the subject of gender and war invites much more scholarship. Indeed, the gendered aspects of exile, memory, and diaspora have not been sufficiently mined (Rose, 2005). One exception is the recent emergence of writings by Iranian women in exile, such as Marjane Satrapi's (2003, 2004) series *Persepolis I* and *II*, welcomed

contributions that can and should be connected to scholarly works on gender, nationalism, and exile.

CONCLUSIONS

What is a feminist ethnography? Perhaps the best way to describe a feminist ethnography is to define what it is not. A feminist ethnography is not certain, institutional, unchallenged, contained, uncomplicated, or value free. It does not "give voice" but hopefully opens up spaces for the contestation of oppositionally defined identities and of how voices are not only represented but accessed and interpreted. (Smith, 2004)

What do we tell our feminist students, neophyte researchers who want to venture into a world that is much more complicated and contradictory than ever before and clearly more challenging to those with a critical and feminist approach? The demands on feminist researchers to be ever conscious about issues of accountability, their self-presentation, and the dynamics of exploitation and power within research relationships may be overwhelming. We would stress the following: First, process is as important as results, and the search for a "pure" feminist methodology with "absolute" transformative potential is a fruitless one. Researchers should approach the design of feminist methods as neither theory nor practice but as a strategy constructed out of political engagement within global and grounded, local contexts. If we choose to design and implement methods that involve collaborations with community organizations, then we must do so strategically with an awareness of the contradictions and problems embedded in these relationships, and we must do so guided by a set of principles established through dialogue and exchange with our collaborators. We should avoid the trap of an idealized notion of "grassroots" communities as homogeneous entities free from power differentials and detached from a global context. Researchers should endeavor to engage in dialogue about research as part of a grounded, political strategy that includes mechanisms for researcher accountability to those studied.

Second, although the "demands" of global feminist research outlined in this chapter may be daunting, it is also important to remember that this is a new frontier for feminists engaged in global research with more possibilities than ever before. There is perhaps more room for yet unimagined global linkages and connections as well as for creative interweavings of resources, organization, strategies, and perspectives. Feminist theory and scholarship give us tools to confront different, ever-shifting situations while engaged in global feminist research. We must use our critical faculties to recognize power in its multiple forms, not just as an "external" force present in global capitalism but also as constituted within intersubjective relations and micro-level dynamics that involve the specific ways in which global and local power structures interact.

In the tradition of feminism, we must endeavor to connect theory and practice by applying our theoretical findings about the way that power works to situational analyses in order to engage in dialogue with our respondents about their perspectives and in order to build strategies for social change. By connecting feminist insights about multiple ways to be and act feminist with what we know about how global processes and the gendered experiences of men and women are lived on the ground, we can confront the challenges that will emerge in the field. We cannot expect to know how to "do feminism" or for that matter "feminist research" as disconnected from grounded situations, but we can build on the work of those who came before us and be open to dialogue and future imaginings of what feminist research could look like if it were to embody feminist principles within a context of globalization.

Discussion Questions

1. In considering globalized, feminist research methods, Audre Lorde's well-known quotation comes to mind: "For the master's tools will never dismantle the master's house" (Lorde, 1984, p. 112). Do you think that research can contribute to social change? In what ways do you think its potential for the transformation of global injustice is limited?

2. What makes a particular research method or practice "feminist"? What distinguishes "feminist" methods from other types of research designs? Is it possible for a man to practice "feminist" research methods? Why or why not?

3. In what ways do you think that communication technologies, social networking sites such as Facebook and YouTube, and other digital media have affected research and how it is conducted? Have they affected your awareness of events and people in other countries?

4. Consider the ways in which poor people's labor is connected with your and your family's lifestyle—for example, housecleaning, babysitting, food, clothing, and services of which you and your family make use, such as restaurants, clothes cleaners, or gardening. How does the paid labor of others, both domestically and globally, affect your daily life? What would occur if that labor were not available, or if it cost a lot more?

Online Resources

Global Exchange

http://www.globalexchange.org/

Global Exchange is "an international human rights organization dedicated to promoting social, economic, and environmental justice around the world." The site features great informational resources about social issues in the global economy, including democracy and economic justice, climate change, migration, and fair trade. The site has a new multimedia center with a photo and video gallery featuring clips of interviews with activists in the global justice movement and other media.

Sociological Images: Inspiring Sociological Imaginations Everywhere

http://thesocietypages.org/socimages/

Sociological Images is an online forum and blog dedicated to promoting the exercise and development of sociological imaginations through public discussions about visual images. Users can contribute images for public comment, and discussions and commentary revolve around issues related to gender, the global economy, race, and other social themes.

Relevant Journals

Gender & Society

Gender, Place, and Culture

Globalizations

Identities

Signs: Journal of Women in Culture and Society

Notes

1. See, for example, the work of Hernández Castillo (2010) and Speed and Hernández Castillo (2006) for a discussion of the ways in which indigenous women in Latin America have articulated new, alternative versions of feminism, claiming indigenous epistemologies as spaces of resistance and then transnationalizing "indigenous feminist" practices and ideas through international networks of indigenous women.

2. The work of Saskia Sassen (2000, 2001) is worthy of mention as is a wide range of scholarship in the field of human and social geography, which has been particularly influential in this regard. See, for example, Harvey (2006). See also "transnational studies," which have largely focused on the study of migration (Glick Schiller, 1999; Schiller & Çağlar, 2009; Smith & Bakker, 2007; Smith & Guarnizo, 1998).

3. PICH is a pseudonym. For a more detailed account of this project and the methodological and ethical issues that it involved, see Mendez (2009).

4. Most Filipinas who immigrated to the United States after 1965 were educated professionals and did not become domestic servants; thus the United States is most likely not the most profitable research site for this focus.

5. Though not a specifically feminist analysis, Lisa Hajjar's (2005) penetrating ethnography of Israeli military courts deals almost entirely with males—both as Israeli soldiers and as Palestinian prisoners. Applying Lentin's more critical feminist and postcolonialist analysis to Hajjar's data and topic would be but a small step.

References

Albrow, Martin. (1997). *The global age: State and society beyond modernity.* Stanford, CA: Stanford University Press.

Almeling, Rene. (2011). *Sex cells: The medical market in eggs and sperm.* Berkeley: University of California Press.

Alvarez, Sonia. (1998). Latin American feminisms "go global": Trends of the 1990s and challenges for the new millennium. In Sonia E. Alvarez, Evelina Dagnino, & Arturo Escobar (Eds.), *Culture of politics/Politics of cultures: Re-visioning Latin American social movements* (pp. 293–324). Boulder, CO: Westview Press.

Bandy, Joe. (2004). Paradoxes of transnational civil society: The coalition for justice in the maquiladoras and the challenges of coalition. *Social Problems, 51*(3), 410–431.

Bandy, Joe, & Bickham Mendez, Jennifer. (2003). A place of their own? Women organizers negotiating the local and transnational in the maquilas of Nicaragua and Northern Mexico. *Mobilization, 8*(2), 173–188.

Basch, Linda G., Schiller, Nina Glick, & Blanc, Cristina Szanton. (Eds.). (1994). *Nations unbound: Transnational projects, postcolonial predicaments and deterritorialized nation-states.* Langhorne, PA: Gordon & Breach.

Bonilla-Silva, Eduardo. (2010). *Racism without racists: Color-blind racism and the persistence of racial inequality in the United States.* New York: Rowman and Littlefield.

Brysk, Allison. (2000). *From tribal village to global village: Indian rights and international relations in Latin America.* Palo Alto, CA: Stanford University Press.

Burawoy, Michael. (2000). Introduction: Reaching for the global. In Michael Burawoy, Joseph A. Blum, Sheba George, Zsuzsa Gille, Teresa Gowan, Lynne Haney, Maren Klawiter, Steven H. Lopez, Sean Ó Riain, & Millie Thayer. *Global ethnography: Forces, connections, and imaginations in a postmodern world.* Berkeley: University of California Press.

Burawoy, Michael. (2005). 2004 presidential address: For public sociology. *American Sociological Review, 70*(1), 4–28.

Burawoy, Michael, Blum, Joseph A., George, Sheba, Gille, Zsuzsa, Gowan, Teresa, Haney, Lynne, Klawiter, Maren, Lopez, Steven H., Ó Riain, Sean, & Thayer, Millie. (2000). *Global ethnography: Forces, connections, and imaginations in a postmodern world.* Berkeley: University of California Press.

Chavez, Leo. (2008). *The Latino threat: Constructing immigrants, citizens, and the nation*. Stanford, CA: Stanford University Press.

Chung, Sewon. (2009a). *The borderlands: A short documentary*. Retrieved December 15, 2010, from http://vimeo.com/groups/journalists/videos/8243652

Chung, Sewon. (2009b). *Visual sociology*. Retrieved December 10, 2010, from http://openwound.wordpress.com/about/

Collins, Jane L. (2003). *Threads: Gender, labor, and power in the global apparel industry*. Chicago: University of Chicago Press.

Collins, Patricia Hill. (2000). *Black feminist thought: Knowledge, consciousness, and the politics of empowerment*. New York: Routledge.

Collins, Patricia Hill. (2005). *Black sexual politics: African Americans, gender, and the new racism*. New York: Routledge.

Deeb-Sossa, Natalia, & Bickham Mendez, Jennifer. (2008). Enforcing borders in the *Nuevo* South: Gender and migration in Williamsburg, VA and the research triangle, NC. *Gender & Society, 22*(5), 613–638.

De Sousa Santos, Boaventura. (2008). The World Social Forum and the global left. *Politics & Society, 36,* 247–270.

DeVault, Marjorie L. (2004). Talking and listening from women's standpoint: Feminist strategies for interviewing and analysis. In Sharlene Nagy Hesse-Biber & Michelle L. Yaiser (Eds.), *Feminist perspectives on social research* (pp. 227–250). New York: Oxford University Press.

Eisenstein, Zillah. (1997). Women's publics and the search for new democracies. *Feminist Review, 57,* 140–167.

Eschle, Catherine. (2001). *Global democracy, social movements, and feminism*. Boulder, CO: Westview Press.

Fals-Borda, Orlando. (1991). Some basic ingredients. In Orlando Fals-Borda & Mohammad Anisur Rahman (Eds.), *Action and knowledge: Breaking the monopoly with participatory action research* (pp. 3–12). New York: The Apex Press.

Fals-Borda, Orlando, & Rahman, Mohammad Anisur. (Eds.). (1991). *Action and knowledge: Breaking the monopoly with participatory action research*. New York: The Apex Press.

Fantasia, Richard. (1988). *Cultures of solidarity: Consciousness, action, and contemporary American workers*. Berkeley: University of California Press.

Freeman, Carla. (2000). *High tech and high heels in the global economy: Women, work and pink-collar identities in the Caribbean*. Durham, NC: Duke University Press.

Freeman, Carla. (2010). Analyzing culture through globalization. In John Hall, Laura Grindstaff, & Ming-Cheng Lo (Eds.), *Handbook of cultural sociology* (pp. 577–587). New York: Routledge Press.

Gaventa, John. (1993). The powerful, the powerless, and the experts: Knowledge struggle in an information age. In Peter Park, Mary Brydon-Miller, Budd Hall, & Ted Jackson (Eds.), *Voices of change: Participatory research in the United States and Canada* (pp. 21–40). Westport, CT: Bergin and Garvey.

Gille, Zsuzsa, & Ó Riain, Sean. (2002). Global ethnography. *Annual Review of Sociology, 28,* 271–295.

Glick Schiller, Nina. (1999). Transmigrants and nation-states: Something old and something new in the U.S. immigrant experience. In Charles Hirschman, Philip Kasinitz, & Josh Dewind (Eds.), *The handbook of international migration: The American experience* (pp. 94–119). New York: Russell Sage Foundation.

Guidry, John A., Kennedy, Michael D., & Zald, Mayer N. (2000). Globalizations and social movements. In John A. Guidry, Michael D. Kennedy, & Mayer N. Zald (Eds.), *Globalizations and social movements: Culture, power, and the transnational public sphere* (pp. 1–32). Ann Arbor: University of Michigan Press.

Hale, Charles R. (Ed.). (2008). *Engaging contradictions: Theory, politics, and methods of activist scholarship*. Berkeley, CA: UCIAS Press.

Harper, Caroline. (2001). Do the facts matter? NGOs, research, and international advocacy. In Michael Edward & John Gaventa (Eds.), *Global citizen action* (pp. 247–258). Boulder, CO: Lynne Rienner Press.

Harvey, David. (2006). *Spaces of global capitalism: Towards a theory of uneven geographical development*. London: Verso.

Haylett, Jennifer. (2010). *One woman helping another: Family and motherhood in egg donor narratives*. Unpublished qualifying paper, Department of Sociology, University of California Davis.

Hays, Sharon. (1998). *The cultural contradictions of motherhood*. New Haven, CT: Yale University Press.

Hernández Castillo, Aida. (2010). The emergence of indigenous feminism in Latin America. *Signs: Journal of Women in Culture and Society, 35*(3), 539–545.

Hesse-Biber, Sharlene Nagy, & Leckenby, Denise. (2004). How feminists practice social research. In Sharlene Nagy Hesse-Biber & Michelle L. Yaiser (Eds.), *Feminist perspectives on social research* (pp. 209–226). New York: Oxford University Press.

Hesse-Biber, Sharlene Nagy, & Yaiser, Michelle L. (2004). Feminist approaches to research as a *process:* Reconceptualizing epistemology, methodology, and method. In Sharlene Nagy Hesse-Biber & Michelle L. Yaiser (Eds.), *Feminist perspectives on social research* (pp. 3–26). New York: Oxford University Press.

Hirsch, Jennifer. (2003). *A courtship after marriage: Sexuality and love in Mexican transnational families.* Berkeley: University of California Press.

Hondagneu-Sotelo, Pierrette. (2001). *Doméstica: Immigrant workers cleaning and caring in the shadows of affluence.* Berkeley: University of California Press.

Kabeer, Nalia. (2004). Labor standards, women's rights, basic needs: Challenges to collective action in a globalizing world. In Lourdes Benería & Savitri Bisnath (Eds.), *Global tensions: Challenges and opportunities in the world economy* (pp. 173–192). New York: Routledge.

Keck, Margaret, & Sikkink, Kathryn. (1998). *Activists beyond borders: Transnational advocacy networks in international politics.* Ithaca, NY: Cornell University Press.

Kretsedemas, Philip. (2008). Immigration enforcement and the complication of national sovereignty: Understanding local enforcement as an exercise in neoliberal governance. *American Quarterly, 60*(3), 553–573.

Lareau, Annette. (2003). *Unequal childhoods: Class, race, and family life.* Berkeley: University of California Press.

Lowe, Lisa, & Lloyd, David. (1997). Introduction. In Lisa Lowe & David Lloyd (Eds.), *The politics of culture in the shadow of capital* (pp. 1–32). Durham, NC: Duke University Press.

Maguire, Patricia. (1987). *Doing participatory research: A feminist approach.* Amherst: Center for International Education, School of Education, University of Massachusetts.

Maguire, Patricia. (1996). Considering more feminist participatory research: What's congruency got to do with it? *Qualitative Inquiry, 2*(1), 106–118.

Maguire, Patricia. (2001). Uneven ground: Feminisms and action research. In Peter Reason & Hilary Bradbury (Eds.), *Handbook of action research* (pp. 59–69). London: Sage.

Marchand, Marianne H., & Runyan, Anne Sisson. (Eds.). (2000a). *Gender and global restructuring: Sightings, sites, and resistances.* New York: Routledge Press.

Marchand, Marianne H., & Runyan, Anne Sisson. (Eds.). (2000b). Introduction. In Marianne H. Marchand & Anne Sisson Runyan (Eds.), *Gender and global restructuring: Sightings, sites, and resistances.* New York: Routledge Press.

Marcus, George E. (1995). Ethnography in/of the world system: The emergence of multi-sited ethnography. *Annual Review of Anthropology, 24,* 95–117.

Mendez, Jennifer Bickham. (2005). *From the revolution to the maquiladoras: Gender, labor and globalization in Nicaragua.* Durham, NC: Duke University Press.

Mendez, Jennifer Bickham. (2009). Globalizing feminist research. In Martha Huggins & Marie-Louise Glebbeek (Eds.), *Women fielding danger: Gender, ethnicity, and ethics intersecting in social science research* (pp. 67–97). New York: Rowman and Littlefield.

Mendez, Jennifer Bickham, & Wolf, Diane L. (2001). Where feminist theory meets feminist practice: Outcomes and processes in a transnational feminist organization in academia. *Organization: Interdisciplinary Journal of Organization, Theory, and Society, 8*(4), 723–750.

Naples, Nancy A. (2003). *Feminism and method: Ethnography, discourse analysis, and activist research.* New York: Routledge Press.

Naples, Nancy A. (2004). The outsider phenomenon. In Sharlene Nagy Hesse-Biber & Michelle L. Yaiser (Eds.), *Feminist perspectives on social research* (pp. 373–381). New York: Oxford University Press.

Ong, Aihwa. (2006). *Neoliberalism as exception: Mutations in citizenship and sovereignty.* Durham, NC: Duke University Press.

Pande, Amrita. (2009). "It may be her eggs but it's my blood": Surrogates and everyday forms of kinship in India. *Qualitative Sociology, 32*(4), 379–405.

Pande, Amrita. (2010). Commercial surrogacy in India: Manufacturing a perfect "mother-worker." *Signs: Journal of Women in Culture and Society, 35*(4), 969–992.

Park, Peter. (1993). What is participatory research? A theoretical and methodological perspective. In Peter Park, Mary Brydon-Miller, Budd Hall, & Ted Jackson (Eds.), *Voices of change: Participatory research in the United States and Canada* (pp. 1–21). Westport, CT: Bergin and Garvey.

Parreñas, Rhacel Salazar. (2001). *Servants of globalization: Women, migration, and domestic work.* Stanford, CA: Stanford University Press.

Peterson, V. Spike, & Runyan, Anne Sisson. (1999). *Global gender issues.* Boulder, CO: Westview Press.

Rodriguez, Robyn Magalit. (2010). *Migrants for export: How the Philippine state brokers labor to the world.* Minneapolis: University of Minnesota Press.

Salzinger, Leslie. (2002). *Gender in production: Making workers in Mexico's global factories.* Berkeley: University of California Press.

Sanford, Victoria, & Angel-Ajani, Asale. (Eds.). (2006). *Engaged observer: Anthropology, advocacy, and activism.* New Brunswick, NJ: Rutgers University Press.

Sassen, Saskia. (2000). *Cities in a world economy* (2nd ed.). Thousand Oaks, CA: Pine Forge Press.

Sassen, Saskia. (2001). Spatialities and temporalities of the global: Elements for a theorization. In Arjun Appadurai (Ed.), *Globalization* (pp. 260–278). Durham, NC: Duke University Press.

Schild, Veronica. (1998). New subject of rights? Women's movements and the construction of citizenship in the "new democracies." In Sonia E. Alvarez, Evelina Dagnino, & Arturo Escobar (Eds.), *Culture of politics/Politics of cultures: Re-visioning Latin American social movements* (pp. 93–117). Boulder, CO: Westview Press.

Schmalzbauer, Leah. (2009). Gender on a new frontier: Mexican migration in the rural mountain west. *Gender & Society, 23,* 747–767.

Smith, Michael Peter, & Bakker, Matt. (2007). *Citizenship across borders: The political transnationalism of el migrante.* Ithaca, NY: Cornell University Press.

Smith, Michael Peter, & Guarnizo, Luis Eduardo. (Eds.). (1998). *Transnationalism from below.* New Brunswick, NJ: Transaction Publishers.

Smith, Tracy. (2004, June 15). Final paper for a seminar on gender and globalization. Presented at the University of California Davis, Davis, CA.

Speed, Shannon. (2006). Indigenous women and gendered resistance in the wake of Acteal: A feminist activist research perspective. In Victoria Sanford & Asale Angel-Ajani (Eds.), *Engaged observer: Anthropology, advocacy, and activism* (pp. 170–188). New Brunswick, NJ: Rutgers University Press.

Speed, Shannon, R., Castillo, Aida Hernandez, & Stephen, Lynn M. (2006). *Dissident women: Gender and cultural politics in Chiapas.* Austin, TX: University of Texas Press.

Staudt, Kathleen, & Spener, David. (1998). A view from the frontier: Theoretical perspectives undisciplined. In David Spener & Kathleen Staudt (Eds.), *The U.S.-Mexico border: Transcending divisions, contesting identities* (pp. 3–34). Boulder, CO: Lynne Rienner.

Stoecker, Randy. (1999). Are academics irrelevant? Roles for scholars in participatory research. *American Behavioral Scientist, 42*(5), 840–854.

Teman, Elly. (2010). *Birthing a mother: The surrogate body and the pregnant self.* Berkeley: University of California Press.

Thayer, Millie. (2004). *Negotiating the global: Northeast Brazilian women's movements and the transnational feminist public.* Unpublished doctoral dissertation, University of California, Berkeley.

Thayer, Millie. (2010). *Making transnational feminism: Rural women, NGO activists and northern donors.* New York: Routledge.

Wolf, Diane Lauren. (1992). *Factory daughters: Gender, household dynamics, and rural industrialization in Java.* Berkeley: University of California Press.

Wolf, Diane Lauren. (Ed.). (1996). *Feminist dilemmas in fieldwork.* Boulder, CO: Westview Press.

Wolf, Diane Lauren. (2007). *Beyond Anne Frank: Hidden children and postwar families in Holland.* Berkeley: University of California Press.

32

FROM COURSE TO DIS-COURSE

Mainstreaming Feminist Pedagogical, Methodological, and Theoretical Perspectives

DEBRA RENEE KAUFMAN AND RACHEL LEWIS

When asked to rewrite my original chapter for this revised text, I, Debra Kaufman, knew immediately that I wanted to include the work of one of my graduate students who had recently taken my course in feminist theory. In her fine paper written for the course, Rachel Lewis called herself a "feminist pedagogue." Her thinking about feminist pedagogy aligned nicely with some of the themes developed in my original chapter for this text. I am delighted that she agreed to write and share her thinking. Her insights add an interdisciplinary component, as she is a teaching fellow in the English Department at Northeastern University and I am a sociologist.

This chapter has been rewritten as a dialogue between the two of us. This dialogue is meant to reflect the kind of pedagogy we assert is at the base of a feminist teaching and learning. When writing, we use the personal pronoun, I, as a way of reflecting not only the dialogue between us but also the self-reflexive approach we understand as the foundation for feminist methodological and pedagogical perspectives.

The dialogue between us also represents the dialogue we each have had with the texts we have incorporated into the chapter. We are hopeful that this encourages the reader to enter into the conversation as we make explicit our own developmental journey about mainstreaming pedagogical, methodological, and theoretical feminist perspectives. By using a narrative structure in the first person, we attempt to generate a connection between the real world of personal practice and the academic classroom. Similarly, the journal essays and discussions so critical to Rachel's classroom were also in the first person voice, once again in an attempt to connect the personal and the academic works of the poets, writers, and scholars covered in the classroom assignments. For us, first person narrative texts are a focal point for multiple standpoints and perspectives, adding not only a diversity to the classroom but an opportunity to move beyond personal experiences to competing theoretical explanations about the very texts and issues we examine. For us, reflexivity means maintaining an ongoing open conversation among faculty and students about our personal and disciplinary perspectives, as we share and refine our responses to the texts we read together. We have introduced each section of dialogue with our names, as is sometimes done in feminist theory texts that present a discussion among and between several authors as they respond to each other and write for a reading audience.

BUILDING FEMINIST PEDAGOGY AS AN INTERDISCIPLINARY TOOL

Debra: If the past is prologue to the future, then my many years of experience as a teacher of feminist methodologies[1] may prove useful in contemplating whether feminist methodological, theoretical, and pedagogical perspectives will be accepted into mainstream disciplinary analyses or, as with many other critical views, be relegated to the margins of the disciplines. Currently in my discipline, sociological analysis is statistically driven and technologically sophisticated. Although statistics and technology are not inherently inimical to feminist modes of analyses, logical positivism's insistence on the separation of moral concerns, value commitments, and the researcher from scientific inquiry emphatically is.[2] The questions we ask (or do not ask) and the moral imperatives that provoke that inquiry are as important to feminist scholars and teachers as are the answers we find. As feminists, we are committed to the dictum that *how* we study determines *what* we know. If the feminist perspective is to have any academic base, it is vital that feminist methodological and theoretical perspectives survive as a critical part of every curriculum.

Some years ago I was asked to write a piece for the *Journal of Radical Education and Cultural Studies* (1996) about feminist pedagogy. In that piece, I argued that we must "trouble" our disciplinary categories by de-centering the theories and methodologies that reproduce scholarship according to a white male normative model, a model that neglects and devalues the female experience. My politics were clear. We were to make room for women not only as scholars within the academy but also as subjects known on their own terms, in their own voices,

and through their own experiences. Although the initial formulation was naive, since I had failed to specify whose experiences, whose voices, and whose agency represented the categories of women and men, I had little doubt that the ideas formulated in the academy needed to be placed in touch with the outside world. Our theories and methodologies were tied to real-life policies, experiences, and applications. It is the tie between the "real" world and the world of the academic that the now hundreds of students I have encountered in feminist classes find so compelling and simultaneously vexing. The first task for those of us teaching feminist methodologies is to rethink, reflect, and, eventually, rewrite the texts that lie at the very foundations of our specific disciplines.

Although sociology, my own discipline, had a history of self-conscious critique, especially between the functionalists and conflict theorists, it was the work of feminist thinkers, particularly outside the social sciences, that gave me the language to formulate a critique of positivist social science. Until then, "I had been operating (albeit freely) within the boundaries of established paradigmatic parameters. With feminism, I learned not only to 'cross the borders' but to dissolve the boundaries between them" (Kaufman, 1996, pp. 166–167). The first feminist methodology course I taught was called "Feminist Methodologies: New Ways of Knowing and Doing." Reading and reflecting on the writings of leading feminist thinkers from disciplines both within and outside of the social sciences helped me and my co-teacher, Christine Gailey, an anthropologist, design our syllabus to challenge and rework the disciplinary assumptions within each of our academic fields. The classroom itself was designed to examine assumptions about the relationship between private and public, between the classroom and the community, and between the teacher and the student. The pedagogy was informed by feminist methodological assumptions about the social world and the way in which we were to study it as feminists. Traditional binaries were questioned, and established hierarchies were flattened. For instance, because feminist inquiry asserts that all research, all scholarship is value laden, some of our first questions were these: For whom was the curriculum designed, and for what purpose? Whose voice, whose text, and whose interests predominated? And, implicitly, what and who were missing?

Since feminist inquiry insists that all scholarship or research is a social process filled with power dimensions, we structured the classroom in ways that helped eliminate the distance between teacher and student. We sat in a circle, and we called each other by our first names. Because feminist inquiry demands that the researcher and the "researched" are mutually constitutive, we redesigned some of the syllabus and added texts as we discovered students' interests and concerns. Just as feminist researchers recognize the importance of social position, power, and control in research practice, we were aware of the very same issues in the classroom. As teachers, we tried to position ourselves as experienced readers of the material and as experienced scholars, but not as authoritarian experts. We understood that the very class we were teaching had a historical place in feminist scholarship within our university and within the larger context of feminist inquiry. We raised consciousness about the very politics that made or unmade the teaching of feminist methodology. We were all actors in this project of discovery.

The multidisciplinary representation of faculty and students (our classes served male and female students from outside our disciplines as well) led to a classroom rife with assumptions about, and explanations for, almost every topic under investigation. No term could be understood at face value. No topic was off limits for investigation. The only rule that applied across topics and disciplines was the need to historically locate and critically scrutinize the assumptions about gender within each investigation and the ideas that supported it. Because our disciplines often led us to focus on different issues in the presentation of material, Christine and I often differed in our points of emphasis and in our interpretations. "Our best discussions (according to the students)," I wrote, "came when we [Christine and I] disagreed with each other's interpretations of the readings, thereby setting the stage for one of the key principles of feminist pedagogy: the notion of de-centering authority by presenting multiple voices and therefore multiple interpretations" (Kaufman, 1996, p. 169). In this way, "we were able to lay bare the assumptions deeply embedded in our own feminist understanding(s) of our disciplinary texts and the methods they used" (Kaufman, 1996, p. 169). Because our classroom was filled with students from a variety of ethnic and racial backgrounds, "voice" became an important dimension of our classroom discussions. We self-consciously raised the issues of race, class, and gender as positional markers in the social process called feminist inquiry.

Our pedagogy was as political as it was academic. We wished to develop a future audience for, as well as active scholars of, feminist scholarship and research. In what ways, we asked our students, are we historical and political subjects when *we* do our research? How do our life histories and stage of career affect our choice of topic and how we formulate research problems?

Since "good" feminist methodology and "good" methodology in general require that we be self-reflexive from the beginning to the end of our research journeys, students often asked us how we had come to our research. They wanted us to give them the "insider" information about the trials and tribulations of doing feminist research. How had our feminist concerns become one with our intellectual interests? Often, such retrospection elicited issues we had either forgotten or long repressed.

Rachel: Similarly, I have attempted various forms of consciousness-raising in my class on college writing, a mandatory composition class at Northeastern University. While feminist texts repeatedly appear on my syllabus, feminist thinking is not a requirement of the course curriculum; rather, feminist thinking represents the influence of my politics over my pedagogical practice. The goal of my class is to raise my students' consciousness as to how meanings are forged within both their own writing and that of others. I've found feminist pedagogy helpful in this task—discussing gender as an open-ended question in the classroom has assisted my students in opening the "debate over the meaning or subversive possibilities" of their multiple subjectivities in their writing and in their lives (Butler, 1990/2008, p. 91). Just as Debra Kaufman found it useful to study the ways that methodologies are made and unmade, discovering how meanings and text are made and unmade often shows how the subjectivities of the writers are created and re-created. Much of the knowledge I gained in Debra Kaufman's feminist theory course was applicable to my own classroom.[3] I became particularly interested in the relevance of feminist standpoint theory (Harding, 2004; Hartsock, 2004; Hirschmann, 2004) and postmodern feminist theory (Butler, 1990/2008; Trinh, 1989) to my own classroom of student writers. I began to explore the ways in which my own pedagogy reflected these theories and how I, too, might be able to foster future audiences for, and producers of, feminist scholarship. Like Robbin Crabtree and David Alan Sapp (2003), I sought to "define feminist pedagogy as a set of classroom practices, teaching strategies, approaches to content, and relationships grounded in critical pedagogical and feminist theory" (p. 131).

I typically assign readings from Susan Bordo's *Unbearable Weight* or Alice Walker's "Beauty: When the Other Dancer Is the Self" to my class of first-year students, two narrative pieces in which the authors transparently integrate theory and commentary into their own stories of lived experience. Susan Bordo uses the concept of "subject position" to illustrate how her own experience with advertising reflects the "situation" of our interpretation of advertisements. Alice Walker tells a story about her disfigurement from gun violence and how this influenced her body image and, consequently, her subject position as a woman and mother. Occasionally, I will accompany our discussion of these readings with an exercise wherein students engage part of the writing process under the imagined circumstance that they occupy a different subject position than that with which they generally identify. In doing this, I am practicing the theory that my students have access to multiple identities and ways of knowing, although they have frequently been taught to utilize only one way of knowing and identifying. While I always receive a few parodies, many of my students choose to imagine

switching gender while they write, sometimes quite seriously addressing their "masculine" or "feminine" selves. Eventually, the students are able to *theorize* this practice, realizing that, through these ways of feeling and knowing, they have the ability to access the idea of subject positions other than their own. Simultaneously, however, they realize that they do not have the permission of their culture to easily do so. The connection between our lived experiences and the theories we craft from them parallel the connections between methodology and theory. I found that the concepts of Debra Kaufman's feminist theory class could be shifted to the practices of teaching college writing. For instance, the use of "privileged knowledges" as epistemological (Hartsock, 2004, p. 245) was useful in my understanding of sociological theory and in my teaching of the literary concept of subjectivity in a written text. Privileging a way of knowing that is typically marginalized or "othered" reinforces that our feminist research and my writing class's discussions do not take place in a vacuum of objectivity. Rather, both occur in a hierarchy of knowledge that, as a student of feminist theory and as a teacher of feminist pedagogy, I am working to upend.

Because we were conscious of the ways in which knowledge is privileged and structured, practicing feminist pedagogy allowed me and my students a renewed understanding of the ways the particular classroom can go against the grain of the general expectations of authority in the university. We were able to observe how (and theorize why) the multiple knowledges in the classroom and the academy were "colonized" and "contested" (Mohanty, 2003, p. 170). Although watching students make their own discoveries in the classroom is gratifying, allowing oneself to make discoveries as a teacher carries its own set of institutional risks. Recognizing that knowledge is situated in both narrative and methodology, students become conscious of how particular knowledges and truths have been privileged, while others have been marginalized. Writing on the hegemonic hold of science and technology in the academy, Haraway (2004) claims that this attention to the "situatedness" of knowledge disrupts the "truth claims of hostile science by showing the radial historical specificity, and so contestability, of every layer of the onion of scientific and technological constructions" (p. 83). Switching subject positions through writing in the composition classroom also practices the disruption of "truth claims." Asking students to engage in aspects of their writing—and their selves—that I could not manage or predict made a place for situated knowledge within the classroom. For a group of students who have typically engaged with broad, Enlightenment-based definitions of knowledge, discovering multiple and partial ways of thinking can be an alarming deviation from the canonical ideal of knowledge. But their responses—serious and playful, oppositional and cooperative, liberated and anxious—(re)formed the ways I thought about the work of the classroom as an educator. A new understanding of how knowledge is made in the university challenged how they unconsciously made knowledge through their own lives and their own standpoints. My students and I created the critical relationship between theory and practice in the moment of the classroom. This collaboration reinforces the fact that individual classrooms practicing feminist methodology are a means for generating the institutional expectations of critical thinking, original writing, and new avenues through which students can conduct their "search for knowledge" (to borrow language from Northeastern University's mission statement).

Locating our concepts of "knowledge" in our lived experiences produces a self-reflexive process of simultaneously acknowledging and questioning our standpoints within the feminist classroom. Debra, as noted earlier, calls this not only "'good' feminist methodology but 'good' methodology in general" because it requires "that we be self-reflexive from the beginning to the end of our research journeys." A focus on the situation of the researcher, the teacher, and the students aids in mainstreaming feminist practice both in the classroom and in wider realms of scholarship. "Teaching," according to Baiada and Jensen-Moulton (2006), "tends to walk hand in hand with the creation of scholarly works and is, in fact, the arena in which we can make the greatest contributions to the preservation and growth of feminism in both academia

and society [. . .] through our students, female and male" (p. 288).

In my feminist theory class with Debra, the practice of feminist theory was, as she describes it, twofold: we were both the producers of research and the audiences of each other's research. Although my own classroom focuses explicitly on reading and writing, I find that the teaching of composition necessitates critical conversations about gender and subjectivities. Feminist theory can be transported from my graduate sociology class to the pedagogy of my undergraduate writing class. Feminist methodology can be implemented into the very process of my teaching in the humanities, demonstrating the links between feminist social scientists and the pedagogical practices of the humanities. The mobility of feminist theory, through its methodological practices, is essential to its ability to mainstream across the disciplines of the university. This mobility means that students will begin to see methodology and pedagogy as an intentional practice of feminism. Crawley, Lewis, and Mayberry (2008) refer to this interdisciplinary practice of feminist methodology as "a way of orienting to academic work that is attuned to power relations, both within the academy and within knowledge construction itself" (p. 2). Our emphasis is on the processes made available through the practice of feminist theory, rather than on the product alone. Many students in humanities classes have the perception that "feminist theory" is a set of universal principles. I put forth a definition of feminist theory that, through pedagogical practice, emphasizes the processes incurred in continuously shaping and thinking about feminist theory.

Another methodological approach that I employ in the making of a feminist pedagogy is heightening the awareness of feminist thinking in conjunction with traditional texts in the composition classroom. When the class reads an excerpt from Michel Foucault's *Discipline and Punish,* I often pair our discussion of Foucault's "docile bodies" with an excerpt from feminist philosopher Sandra Lee Bartky. Bartky's analysis of Foucault's "self-discipline" focuses on dieting and eating disorders in women from a perspective unique in its focus on women's studies. Reading Bartky after Foucault allows students to observe the situated nature of both authors' presentations. Additionally, this juxtaposition aids in our understanding that information presented as objective and value neutral still follows masculine social norms. The absence of women in Foucault's text calls attention to the process that went into choosing and excerpting the essay itself; such considerations further our ability to understand the standpoints and power dynamics involved in reading and writing in the academy. Reading Foucault and Bartky together led students to a greater consciousness about gender and a wider range of writing about the body. Additionally, students became interested in the arc of their curriculum, noting, at the end of the course, what could be accomplished through the varied standpoints we examined as a class. After a required screening of Jean Kilbourne's *Killing Us Softly 3*, a critique on the use of the female body in advertising, one male student ("Abe") remarked that he felt this video, although it related to the concepts of discipline in Foucault's excerpt, would have "worked better" with Alice Walker's "Beauty: When the Other Dancer Is the Self" (R. Lewis, personal communication, March 22, 2010). Abe felt that a study of women in advertising "worked better" in the context of "beauty standards" rather than within a discussion of the power structures that create those standards.

Over time, this conversation with Abe grew into a dialogue regarding the place of "women's issues" (shorthand, perhaps, for "women's studies" and the even more stigmatized term "feminism") in the academic space of the classroom *and* the university. Why did the example of the disciplinary effect of power structures on women's bodies automatically become about "beauty standards" or a "female" concern? Why would it fit better with a narrative discussion of social norms than with an analysis of the very structures that make those norms? While I did not (and did not expect) to agree completely with Abe, consensus was beside the point. By incorporating a consciousness of gender into the text, we were able to engage in a discussion that questioned the categorization within institutional expectations of whose experiences and whose standpoints are recognized as normative and which are considered too particular to have

a real place in academic spaces. The "otherness" and marginalization often ascribed to texts that take up the subject—and subject position—of female was made visible in our conversations.

PRAXIS IN THE CLASSROOM AND FEMINIST RESEARCH

Debra: Just as Rachel has, I have relied on analyses of the subject and subject position—the relationship between the researcher and the researched, the writer and the reader, the student and the teacher—as key pedagogical tools in the making and maintaining of a feminist classroom. In the early 1990s, I wrote *Rachel's Daughters*, a book about the "return" to Jewish Orthodoxy during the closing decades of the 20th century by once secular, highly assimilated, highly educated, middle-class, white, Jewish women. Perhaps no research is better positioned to touch on the knottiest of feminist methodological issues than the exploration of women, religion, and politics. The early works on fundamentalist and presumably "antifeminist" women are perhaps even more intriguing today than they were some 15 years ago. Consider, for a moment, what we "knew" or thought we knew about the attitudes, behaviors, and everyday experiences of Religious-Right women at that time. Questions, primarily taken from quantitative surveys, were aimed at "objectively" measuring the attitudes, values, and behaviors associated with patriarchal living. What we knew about women who had turned to the Right, we knew primarily from their activities in antifeminist contexts. We knew very little about them in their own voices and even less about their everyday lives as religious women. Indeed, there was little in the feminist lexicon, beyond vague references to "false consciousness" and monolithic models about patriarchy and oppression, that could help us to explain this phenomenon.

The study of women who embrace and advocate for patriarchal religious traditions presents several interrelated problems for us as feminist empirical researchers and a plethora of questions for our students. It provokes the most basic pedagogical question: How do we "do" research on those whose identity politics are different from ours? Or, put another way, how do I do socially committed work as a feminist activist and still respect the integrity of my respondents who differ from me politically? Feminist practice demands we make the lived experiences of women visible. When we study women who advocate and support fundamentalist traditions, we help to make vocal and visible the narratives of those whose politics we do not share. This dilemma was not lost on students.

The women I wrote about in *Rachel's Daughters* had embraced the denomination of Judaism most opposed to equality between men and women at the very same time that such inequalities were breaking down within other denominations in Judaism as well as in the secular world. As a committed Jewish feminist, I wished to know more about the ways in which feminism, and especially Jewish feminism, had failed them. The return in their young adult years of many once-feminist women, or indeed any women, to the most traditional arm of Judaism surprised, perplexed, and worried me. Children of the New Left and inheritors of a nascent Jewish feminist movement, these women had turned away from the very social forces that had pulled me into the women's movement and later into feminist academic work. I was anything but a neutral observer or agent in this research process. Several key issues facing us when we teach our students how to "do" feminist research emerge when we look at empirical data from the "inside," as my students refer to it.

Rachel: I have also found that supporting, restructuring, and questioning texts not only provides an opportunity to bring feminist material into the classroom but supports the practice of feminist inquiry itself. Rather than presenting the primary text as the sole source for the making of meaning, we open multiple conversations with one another, using the multivoiced nature of the classroom to consider a variety of meanings. Just as students are encouraged to embrace the multiplicity of their own subjectivities in the classroom, they are enabled, because of the diversity within the classroom itself, to share different aspects of knowledge. Students and

teachers actively engage and challenge the seemingly unmovable "truths" of institutional study. As we name the institutional, literary, and gendered structures in place around our educational space, we understand how "truths" and "texts" are made. If students can observe the processes by which these "truths" are created, then they can speak to these ideas with greater understanding.

Because the norms within which we are positioned are invisible, we can make them visible and show their complexities by naming them and situating our multiple, discordant voices within them. In this sense, it is indeed possible to "teach" feminist pedagogy in the composition classroom, as well as in the sociology classroom. Students and teachers can simultaneously practice the methodological practice of transparency and visibility across disciplines. Take, for example, this excerpt from my teaching journal:

> Today, as class was about to start, Jennifer began teasing Chris about the fact that his girlfriend "does all his laundry." Chris responded that he didn't make her do it but that she liked to, so he went along with it. "She likes doing it," he said. "She just loves doing laundry, maybe because she's a girl." Guiltily, he looked up and caught my eye, not sure about what I would think—I do not frequently discuss explicit feminist positions I hold (or, for that matter, my laundry habits) with my students, but we had just read an essay by Susan Bordo in class, and Chris knew enough to wonder what I would say to such an obvious application of gender dynamics. "I guess Bordo wouldn't like that," he said cautiously, "but she really does want to do it. Hey, you're not going to give me a bad grade on my Bordo essay because of this, right?"

Although his last comment was meant humorously, Chris struggled with both the clashing of political, academic, and institutional power dynamics and the discomfort of making invisible norms explicit. He was not only implicitly identifying me as the teacher and as the authoritative voice of the classroom but also as a voice with specific values and experiences that would affect an interpretation of his words. In such moments, teachers may seize on their (limited) institutional power to create a didactic teaching moment or choose to focus on the feminist processes the student was already implementing. Ellen Carillo (2007) maintains that authority in the feminist classroom remains "a problematic issue" due to its potential as a site of power for the teacher (p. 34). Since power is often used to express "truth" or "dominance," it can be difficult to recognize the steps Chris had already taken. He had recognized his own experience as discursive and textual, he had inscribed the ideology of gender practices onto his own narrative experience, and he had jokingly destabilized the relationship of these elements to the institutional consequence of "grading." Chris and I were able to use a nonauthoritarian approach to discuss assessment and grading as part of the same structures that shape our work and as being parallel to the hierarchies that create conventional gender practices.

As such, I want to suggest that feminist pedagogy is more than teaching the lines of inquiry practiced within feminist methodology. Rather, I propose that the classroom itself is a site of feminist methodology. What we teach as feminist teachers and what we do as feminist scholars are intrinsically related through the practices of situating our discourses and continually questioning what is included (and excluded) from the academy and who we are and how we speak in the academy. Understanding the methodology of self-construction and reflexivity is just as important to the exploratory classroom as it is to exploratory scholarship.

Classroom practices can inform our methodological practices. The classroom represents a bounded, experimental place where particular pedagogical moments can interact with the more "universal" (less particularistic) methods of feminist inquiry—in fact, without the multivoiced classroom, methodological practices would be stripped of some of the many processes that initially gave rise to them. Hirschmann (2004) claims that a multiplicity of standpoints contributes to "feminism" as "the product of ongoing political negotiation" (p. 320). In other words, the feminist processes of engaging and negotiating multiple standpoints for the formation of theory depend on conversations within classroom communities and the multiple narrations possible in those discursive spaces. It is

worth noting, of course, that this interpretation of Hirschmann's theory heightens the need for classrooms that incorporate standpoints across the lines of race, religion, class, gender, sexuality, and ability. The narrative space of the classroom allows different stories and standpoints to emphasize shared and interpreted experiences—and the persistence of these experiences tests and stretches methodological practices in and out of the classroom.

Debra: Rachel's examples and commentary are excellent reminders of the complicated interplay among and between feminist methodological, theoretical, and pedagogical perspectives. For instance, "doing" feminist research raises many of the issues important to the feminist classroom. If how we study determines what we know, then several pedagogical issues bear repeating. First, no investigation is value neutral. What is in need of an explanation is always a problem of interest to someone, to some class of people, or to some nation. As I noted earlier, work on Religious-Right women is laden with issues about the value and possibility of "neutral" science. What surprised many of us doing feminist research on fundamentalist women in the early 1990s was the way in which our most basic assumptions were often offset by how our subjects formulated issues about family and gender relations. For instance, many of the interviewees in my study of Orthodox Jewish women used feminist rhetoric and a woman-centered focus in their narratives about life as Religious-Right women, presenting perspectives not unlike those of the domestic feminists of the late 19th century and/or of some contemporary feminists (Kaufman, 1993). Judith Stacey (1990) coined the term *protofeminist* to describe the Pentecostal women she studied.

A second pedagogical issue raised is that the way we theorize our research often shapes the way in which we do our research. Because in the early 1990s we knew little about fundamentalist women apart from their antifeminist activities, many of us assumed a priori that such women were assuredly antifeminists. In a chapter I wrote some years ago about feminist methodology and family theory, I argued against making a priori assumptions about what is or is not feminist, arguing for a feminist interpretive sociology:

Feminist-interpretive methodology, developed from theoretical assumptions about grounding theory in the actual lives women lead, insists that we not limit the world to male images of women nor that we assume that the parameters of women's experiences are set by male exploitation alone. (Kaufman, 1990, p. 126)

If we do so, we "transform women's history into a subcategory of the history of male values and behavior" (Smith-Rosenberg, 1980, p. 56). In a sophisticated rendering of her distinction between a priori categories substituting for interpersonal relations, Chandra Mohanty (1988) suggests that, if we assume that women are a unified, powerless group prior "to the historical and political analysis in question," then we have specified "the context after the fact" (p. 68). She writes that such women "are now placed in the context of the family, or in the workplace, or within religious networks, almost as if these systems existed outside the relations of women with other women, and women with men" (p. 68). Abstract or political designations cannot substitute for "voice" and lived experience.

The third feminist methodological lesson is that we often must go beyond our disciplinary boundaries to put into context the lives we wish to explore. For instance, for me, Jewish feminists' *theological* conclusions about the oppression of Orthodox women posed the beginning of important *sociological* feminist questions. Do women experience Orthodoxy in the ways in which they are theologically described? Using a feminist methodological framework, I wanted to move beyond abstract claims in describing these women's lives (what Leacock [1977] refers to as unwarranted teleology) to the actual and complex lives women lead. All empirical work must be placed within a specific political, historical, and sociological context. This often demands the insights and tools of an interdisciplinary perspective.

The fourth pedagogical lesson is that those we research are agents in the making of their worlds as much as they are subjects. Feminist methodology cautions that we are never just observers when we do our research. It is also clear that those under scrutiny are never just subjects. In my analysis, for instance, Orthodox Jewish women were not passive, unthinking

recipients of theological discourse and patriarchal structure. Despite their "antifeminist" attitudes, many of the women I interviewed used the rhetoric of feminism when offering a direct critique of male, secular normative models to explain their choice of Jewish Orthodoxy. They compared a male normative secular world of individualistic and competitive striving with the spiritual, modest, "feminine," and communally oriented world of Jewish Orthodoxy. Because they came to their Orthodoxy as young adults, they were able to offer critiques of *both* the secular and the religious worlds, analyses that resonated with feminist rhetoric and criticism. One woman claimed that she preferred the "patriarchal devils" within Orthodoxy to those outside of it (Kaufman, 2002).

The fifth lesson to be learned from my research narrative was that all research is historically specific. The "return to Jewish Orthodoxy" for these women came within a specific sociohistorical moment. It was a time of turning inward, a time of great upheaval in gender dynamics and institutional organization, and a time when we were experiencing a "turn to the right," both politically and religiously. What were the specifics of the relationships, at both the personal and institutional level, that maintained and sustained these women in their Orthodoxy? How did these women compare to and differ from 19th-century domestic feminists who argued strenuously for a woman-centered world in contrast to a world gone awry with male values? How did these women compare to and differ from women living in other contemporary, sex-segregated religious communities in different geographic, class, and racial contexts? How did they disrupt the categories of patriarchy, motherhood, and sex segregation in ways both familiar and unfamiliar? How did their narratives compare with those of contemporary radical lesbian feminists who extol the virtues of women's bodies and sexuality, as did these women? In short, how did the specific historical and political contexts of their embracing Jewish Orthodoxy affect their "patriarchal" experiences?

If we do not differentiate by time, place, and politics, we end up disguising rather than explaining the effects of the structure of patriarchy on religious discourses about gender relations. Elizabeth Brusco (1986), for instance, discovered that the growth of Evangelicalism among Colombian women was, in part, a way these "born-again" women held "impious men" to "pious" rules through adherence to the religious dictates of the church not to smoke, drink, or gamble. It serves as an important lesson in the meaning and measure of patriarchy. In part, the growth of Protestant fundamentalism was a way, argues Brusco, to combat the "machismo" of the Catholic Church. We also learn the way in which patriarchal rule varies between two equally patriarchal churches.

FEMINIST PEDAGOGY AND MULTICULTURAL FEMINISM

Debra: Uma Narayan (1989) warns that patriarchal resolutions and strategies vary. She suggests that what might be good within Western countries may backfire in non-Western ones. She cautions that "it may be politically counterproductive for nonwestern feminists to echo uncritically the terms of western feminist epistemology that seeks to restore the value of a woman's experience" because it only values woman's place "as long as she keeps to the place prescribed" (p. 259). She continues her warning by noting that she is "inclined to think that in nonwestern countries feminists must still stress the negative sides of the female experience within that culture" (p. 259). The time for a more sympathetic evaluation is not, in her words, "quite ripe" (p. 259).

In my more than 20 years teaching feminist methodology courses at Northeastern University, I have co-taught only once with a woman of color, a black social psychologist. Increasingly, the lack of a multicultural base either in the curriculum or within the mix of teachers and students has been of some concern across many universities. When I joined the faculty of the Graduate Consortium on Women's Studies at Radcliffe, I found a more diverse faculty with whom to teach feminist methodology courses. I was forced to address the ways in which the feminist curriculum had (or had not) responded to a growing critique from within. Although multiculturalism was the new buzzword in feminist teaching and research, Narayan (2000) warned us of the pitfalls of such analyses as

well. She advised us not to replace gender essentialism with "culture-specific essentialist generalizations" (p. 81), such as Western women and non-Western women. Such categories, she argues, "conflate the abstract, socially dominant norms in operation within any one culture," for the reality of practices within each. As such, the "social construction of culture, its history, and politics" are lost in our theoretical and methodological models (p. 84). She further argues, as I did earlier with reference to much of the scholarly work done (or, more precisely, not done) on "born-again" women, that cultural essentialism promotes the discovery of differences a priori, before the "kind and quality of real differences" can emerge (p. 85). We are caught in the dilemma of trying to capture experience before theory constructs it (Kaufman, 1990).

A series of essays in response to Susan Okin's (1999) lead essay in *Is Multiculturalism Bad for Women?* raises controversial issues, at both the theoretical and empirical levels, for the feminist study of multiculturalism. It certainly raised many questions among my students. Whose voice and whose everyday experiences do we investigate, theorize about, and value in our inquiries? Okin's challenge to reconcile egalitarian principles with cultural and religious diversity is parallel to feminist debates about reconciling feminism and the politics of universalistic and particularistic claims. The questions Okin poses bring into focus the theoretical issues critical to the development of a feminist practice that is able to form alliances across class, race, national, and international boundaries (and, as noted earlier, disciplinary boundaries). Her choice of what she sees as the most blatant of gender inequalities—child marriages, forced marriages, divorce systems biased against women, polygamy, and clitoridectomy—present some of the most heated debates I have experienced within the classroom.

For many, especially Western-trained students, there are clear directives. We must put all our efforts into eliminating such inequalities and oppressive practices. For others, we must locate the *specific* historic and political context within which such practices take place and salvage that which can be maintained as central components of cultural identity without being inimical to women. A feminist approach, as Narayan (2000) suggests, can discover the historical and political processes that make culturally dominant norms of femininity central components of cultural identity and, thereby, can uncover how dominant groups misuse, romanticize, reinvent, or present cultural practices as unchanging to their own advantage.

Feminist historical and political inquiries can make clear how radically changed cultural practices (often quite inimical to women) can remain hidden under the label of cultural preservation (Narayan, 2000). Theoretical questions about the meaning of epistemic advantage and the place of women's everyday experience and language are critical to this balancing act. Perhaps the most troubling of the issues raised in these multicultural debates is the possibility of ever being able to generalize beyond the particular set of voices under consideration. If we are unable to speak of women as a category, how do we act on women's political behalf? Similarly, if we are unable to speak of a culture, how can we make claims for equity among its members? Narayan (2000) offers a not altogether satisfying response. She writes,

> I believe that antiessentialism about gender and about culture does not entail a simple-minded opposition to *all generalizations,* but entails instead a commitment to examine both their empirical accuracy and their political utility or risk. It is seldom possible to articulate effective political agendas, such as those pertaining to human rights, without resorting to a certain degree of abstraction, which enables the articulation of salient similarities between problems suffered by various individuals and groups. On the other hand, it seems arguably true that there is no need to portray female genital mutilation as an "African cultural practice" or dowry murders and dowry related harassment as a "problem of Indian women" in ways that eclipse the fact that not *all* "African women'" or "Indian women" confront them in identical ways, or in ways that efface local contestations of these problems. (Narayan, 2000, pp. 97–98)

Multicultural debates evoke many questions from students. How might we find a common ground for a "practice" politics, which honors the particular without othering or romanticizing

it? Need we throw out the liberal baby with the Western bathwater? Robert Post (1999, p. 67) suggests that liberal multiculturalism both sustains and constrains individual freedom. The struggle, both within the classroom and outside of it, to distinguish between enabling and oppressive cultural norms demands that all cultural and institutional structures be placed within *their own historical evolution.* The classroom then becomes the place where we struggle to move beyond the "Western/non-Western" dichotomy and to find the balance between particular integrity and universal solidarity, the place where the universal and the particular meet (Kaufman, 2002).

Teaching with colleagues from different disciplinary perspectives parallels many of the issues raised when addressing multiculturalism and feminist scholarship and practice. How do we understand the "other" when teaching with colleagues and to students from disciplines other than our own? Often a multidisciplinary teaching team creates tensions similar to those created by a multicultural set of voices within our texts and empirical research. Each discipline poses its own hierarchy of values and concerns that dictates the choice of materials to be taught and the "voice" from which it will be taught. Students face similar issues in placing their teachers' comments in a perspective that is compatible with the values and issues they have come to recognize as disciplinarily important to them. The multicultural issues raised by Okin (1999) are particularly exacerbated when we combine humanists, scientists, and social scientists in the same classroom. Students are frequently caught between competing claims and different levels of analysis in coming to terms with feminist policy on gender patterns not only in cultures different from theirs but also from different disciplinary perspectives.

CONCLUSION

Rachel: Several important issues have emerged in our integrated narrative. My interests have been in the intersection between the broader, "universal" structures that shape our particular selves and the construction of the subject within a feminist pedagogy. The contrast between

Dorothy Smith, a sociologist, and Trinh T. Minh-ha, a writer and filmmaker, is useful in understanding how the individual student subject is shaped by institutional norms, and vice versa. Woman as a sociological subject, says Smith (2004), is complicated by the fact that there is a "contradiction" between the disciplinary structure of sociology and a woman's own experience (p. 27). She writes, "The lived experiences of women fall outside the perceptions of masculine reality" (p. 31). However, Smith cautions against the imposing of female experience as an absolute reality in response to this exclusion. Instead, we must allow for multiple experiences and realities to be expressed, intertwined, and validated, while simultaneously understanding their gendered nature. In the classroom, theories of intersecting and overlapping standpoints are put into practice when we work in spaces that bring together diverse student bodies. Writing about intersectionality and the subject, Trinh (1989) notes the following: "The pitting of anti-racist and anti-sexist struggles against one another allows some vocal fighters to dismiss blatantly the existence of either racism or sexism within their lines of action, as if oppression only comes in separate, monolithic forms" (p. 104). Diversifying our classrooms and our feminisms is an avenue for opening and restructuring the very systems of "reality" that would pit the oppressed against the oppressed, rather than against the oppression.

Thus, Debra's question regarding how subjectivity plays out in the classroom—how do I do socially committed work as a feminist activist and still respect the integrity of my respondents who differ from me politically?—applies to the construction of the subject in the classroom. Our own biases and prejudices as teachers are typically "invisible." Openly acknowledging our position within those structures sets a model for our students to do the same. Trinh, like Smith, recognizes the difficulty of constructing the female subject within a discipline—and a world—that seeks repeatedly to establish that subjectivity for and through them. In the words of Judith Butler (1990/2008), "The subjects regulated by such structures are, by virtue of being subjected to them, formed, defined, and reproduced in accordance with the requirements of those structures" (p. 3). How can we criticize and challenge the ways we have been taught to be and know without invalidating the importance of our standpoints in the classroom and in the university?

Teaching against the very systems that have taught us ways of learning, being, and seeing can feel like an impossible task. Accomplishing Smith's multiple spaces for a variety of subjectivities necessitates that we engage both the "master's tools" and our own. Feminist pedagogies, as Smith suggests, need not replicate patriarchal pedagogies in their dominant, often exclusive wielding of power. The lived experiences of the other, while they are mappable and describable, must function as "an unconditional datum." As feminist teachers, we can, as we have done as feminist theorists, see the limits of one kind of "knowledge" as a point for further exploration. This is a pedagogical model we must engage if we are to embrace Smith's goal of becoming "capable of explicating and analyzing the properties of the experienced world rather than administering it" (Smith, 2004, p. 30).

While we certainly cannot escape the structures that have shaped our identities, our classrooms allow for valuable places to discuss how subjects are constructed—and, in my case, how the subject is written in the classroom. Since, as Debra says, the way we theorize our research often shapes the way in which we do our research, categorization and intersectionality intentionally practiced in the classroom shape the ways we students and teachers express ourselves in the classroom and in our essays. Critical pedagogy indicates that students become actors in the world when they begin to grasp their historical moment in the classroom. Students' awareness of their roles as actors of history, actors with and against cultural norms, and actors within structures that shape their subjectivities in terms of their identities can help them refer to other ways of knowing through situating their own. Resistance becomes a vital piece of agency. In addition to seeing themselves as products of invisible, dominant social structures, students can see the shaping of their subjectivities through those structures. Increased awareness of how and why they know what they know leads to a deeper understanding of the intersection of identity and experience. This kind of search yields its own kind of education, fostering, as bell hooks (1994) says, "yearning as a way to know" (p. 92).

Debra: All methodological choices have consequences. That recognition is critical to a feminist consciousness. The issues raised in this chapter move beyond feminist methodologies and raise questions about the power politics inherent in academic life and in the making of knowledge. They raise questions about the price we pay for leaving the safety of our disciplines and for making "cutting edge" choices. For whom and to whom do we write and teach as feminists? At times, I am at a loss to answer this question. I often feel that I have lost my academic compass; I'm not quite sure for whom I am writing or, more important, for whom my writing is important.

As teachers and scholars, we must see ourselves as historical and political subjects. We must make explicit how we have come to our topics of inquiry and the disciplinary tools we choose or, even more important, disregard in our scholarly journeys. We must be self-reflexive in our research process and aware of its political repercussions—not only within our disciplines but also within the very communities we are investigating. For whom is our research important? Have we built a wide enough audience, both within the academy and outside of it, to ensure a place for future feminist scholars? Does multidisciplinary teaching and interdisciplinary inquiry open new audiences for our work, or does it muddy the process whereby we can mainstream our scholarship and teaching? Feminist pedagogy is a key component in mainstreaming feminist methodological and theoretical perspectives.[4]

We have come full circle to my question at the beginning of this chapter. Will feminist methodological, theoretical, and pedagogical perspectives ever be accepted into mainstream, disciplinary analyses, or, as with other critical views, will they be relegated to the margins of the disciplines? Need they remain marginal to traditional disciplinary inquiry to evoke an epistemological revolution? What will happen should feminism find its way to the center of disciplinary traditions?

There is little to indicate that feminism will be brought into the mainstream of most disciplinary discourses any time soon. Mohanty (1988) claims that "feminist scholarly practices exist within relations of power—relations which they counter, redefine, or even implicitly support" (p. 62). The future promises no easy resolution of these inherent tensions but rather a continuing dialogue and a lively set of debates among and between feminists, our students, and the academy.

Discussion Questions

1. What are some current pedagogical practices used or considered important in feminist classrooms, and how might they be used across disciplines and media? How do they reflect feminist theories?

2. Feminist considerations and perspectives can often be dismissed in classrooms because the structure of the university is hierarchical. How might we give credence and value to feminist standpoints without necessarily relying on the institutional authority of the professor?

3. What is multicultural, postcolonial feminism, and how might we successfully practice it within our classrooms and our scholarship? Do opportunities exist for the exploration of "identity politics" across disciplines and across feminist standpoints?

4. Is it possible to mainstream feminist practices through pedagogy, and, if so, how do we maintain variation and multiplicity in the standpoints and pedagogies we use in the classroom?

Online Resources

Gender and Technology Bibliography

http://www.umbc.edu/cwit/pdf/gendertechbib.pdf

Originally compiled for the unpublished paper *Gender and Technology: A Research Review* (Sanders, 2005), this bibliography documents a number of sources helpful to teachers considering the introduction of technology into a gender-conscious classroom.

Women's Studies Librarian's Office

http://womenst.library.wisc.edu/

The University of Wisconsin's Women's Studies Librarian's Office provides helpful advice on where and how to conduct research on gender in education; it includes a list of public access websites.

Feminist Teacher

http://www.press.uillinois.edu/journals/ft.html

Feminist Teacher, a periodical, provides discussions of varied topics, including multicultural, postcolonial, and interdisciplinary education within a feminist context.

Feminist Teaching

http://feministeaching.wordpress.com/

Feminist Teaching is the website that reports on the newly started symposium on Feminist Pedagogy, Diversity and Social Justice Education. Besides information on the conference's planning, the site also offers several resources for feminist teaching, activism, and curriculum planning (primarily through blogs and other personal, but accessible, forms of media).

Relevant Journals

Feminist Teacher

Interdisciplinary Journal of Problem-Based Learning

Journal of Radical Education and Cultural Studies

Journal of the Scholarship of Teaching and Learning

Radical Teacher

Notes

1. The study of the organizing principles and underlying rules fundamental to our research and scholarship (methodology) is different from the methods (tools) we use to do that work (but of course they are related). As I wrote in the syllabus for my feminist inquiry course, "Doing feminist research involves rethinking disciplinary assumptions and methodologies, developing new understandings of what counts as knowledge, seeking alternative ways of understanding the origins of problems/issues, and redefining the relationship between subjects and objects of study."

2. It is important to note here, however, that positivism is not the only source of critical concern for feminists and that it may present a different set of issues for third world women (see Narayan, 1989).

3. It should be mentioned here that the reciprocity between theory and methodology was heavily emphasized in this course; as such, applying a course on theory to the practice of my own classroom happened very fluidly during my own research for the class.

4. Through a cursory exploration, Rachel and I found that among the top education schools in the country there are a growing number of gender courses, and we found one course explicitly named "feminist pedagogy" at UCLA.

References

Arroyo, Sarah J. (2005). Playing to the tune of Electracy: From post-process to a pedagogy otherwise. *JAC, 25*, 683–715.

Baiada, Christa, & Jensen-Moulton, Stephanie. (2006). Building a home for feminist pedagogy. *Women's Studies Quarterly, 34*(3/4), 287–290.

Bartky, Sandra Lee. (1988). Foucault, femininity, and the modernization of patriarchal power. In I. Diamond & Lee Quinby (Eds.), *Feminism and Foucault: Reflections and resistance* (pp. 61–86). Boston: Northeastern University Press.

Brusco, Elizabeth. (1986). Colombian Evangelicalism as a strategic form of women's collective action. *Feminist Issues, 6*(2), 3–13.

Bunch, Charlotte, & Pollack, Sandra. (Eds.). (1983). *Learning our way: Essays in feminist education.* Trumansburg, NY: The Crossing Press.

Burghardt, Deborah, & Colbeck, Carol L. (2005). Women's studies faculty at the intersection of institutional power and feminist values. *The Journal of Higher Education, 76*(3), 301–330.

Butler, Judith. (2008). *Gender trouble.* New York: Routledge. (Original work published 1990)

Carillo, Ellen. (2007). "Feminist" teaching/Teaching "feminism." *Feminist Teacher, 18*(1), 28–40.

Crabtree, Robbin D., & Sapp, David Alan. (2003). Theoretical, political, and pedagogical challenges in the feminist classroom: Our struggles to walk the walk. *College Teaching, 51*(4), 131–140.

Crawley, Sara L., Lewis, Jennifer E., & Mayberry, Maralee. (2008). Introduction—Feminist pedagogies in action: Teaching beyond disciplines. *Feminist Teacher, 19*(1), 1–12.

Culley, Margo, & Portuges, Catherine. (Eds.). (1985). *Gendered subjects: The dynamics of feminist teaching.* London: Routledge & Kegan Paul.

Ferguson, A. (1982). Feminist teaching: A practice developed in undergraduate courses. *Radical Teacher, 20*, 26–29.

Freire, Paulo. (1993). *Pedagogy of the oppressed.* London: Continuum Intl Pub Group.

Gonzales, Sylvia. (1980). Toward a feminist pedagogy for Chicana self-actualization. *Frontiers, 5*(2), 48–51.

Gray-Rosendale, Laura, & Harootunian, Gil. (Eds.). (2003). *Fractured feminisms: Rhetoric, context, and contestation.* Albany: State University of New York Press.

Greenbaum, Andrea. (2001). "Bitch" pedagogy: Agonistic discourse and the politics of resistance. In Andrea Greenbaum (Ed.), *Insurrections: Approaches to resistance in composition studies* (pp. 151–168). Albany: State University of New York Press.

Haraway, Donna. (2004). Situated knowledges: The science question in feminism and the privilege of partial perspective. In S. Harding (Ed.), *Feminist standpoint theory reader* (pp. 81–102). London: Routledge.

Harding, Sandra. (2004). *Feminist standpoint theory reader.* London: Routledge.

Hartsock, Nancy. (2004). Comment on Hekman's "Truth and method: Feminist standpoint theory revisited": Truth or justice? In S. Harding (Ed.), *Feminist standpoint theory reader* (pp. 243–246). London: Routledge.

Helmers, Marguerite. (2006). Objects, memory, narrative: New notes toward materialist rhetoric. In K. Ronald & J. Ritchie (Eds.), *Teaching rhetorica: Theory, pedagogy, practice* (pp. 114–130). Portsmouth, NH: Boynton/Cook Publishers.

Hirschmann, Nancy. (2004). Feminist standpoints as postmodern strategy. In S. Harding (Ed.), *Feminist standpoint theory reader* (pp. 317–333). London: Routledge.

Hoffman, Nancy. (1977). White woman, black woman: Inventing an adequate pedagogy. *Women's Studies Newsletter, 5*, 21–24.

hooks, bell. (1994). *Teaching to transgress.* New York: Routledge.

hooks, bell. (2010). *Teaching critical thinking: Practical wisdom.* New York: Routledge.

Jensen, Elizabeth J., & Owen, Ann L. (2001). Pedagogy, gender, and interest in economics. *The Journal of Economic Education, 32*(4), 323–343.

Kaufman, Debra Renee. (1990). Engendering family theory. In Jetse Sprey (Ed.), *Fashioning family theory* (pp. 107–135). Newbury Park, CA: Sage.

Kaufman, Debra Renee. (1993). *Rachel's daughters: Newly orthodox Jewish women.* New Brunswick, NJ: Rutgers University Press.

Kaufman, Debra Renee. (1996). Rethinking, reflecting, rewriting: Teaching feminist methodology. *Journal of Radical Education and Cultural Studies, 181*, 165–174.

Kaufman, Debra Renee. (2002). Better the devil you know and other contemporary identity narratives: Orthodoxy and reform Judaism. In Dana Evan Kaplan (Ed.), *Platforms and prayer books: Theological and liturgical perspectives on reform Judaism* (pp. 251–260). Lanham, MD: Rowman & Littlefield.

Kirsch, Gesa. (1993). *Women writing the academy: Audience, authority, and transformation.* Carbondale: Southern Illinois University Press.

Lauer, Janice M. (1995). The feminization of rhetoric and composition studies? *Rhetoric Review, 13*(2), 276–286.

Leacock, E. (1977). The changing family and Levi-Strauss, or whatever happened to fathers. *Sociological Research, 44*, 235–289.

Lewis, Magda Gere. (1993). *Without a word: Teaching beyond women's silence.* New York: Routledge.

Love, Meredith A., & Helmbrecht, Brenda M. (2007). Teaching the conflicts: (Re)engaging students with feminism in a postfeminist world. *Feminist Teacher, 18*(1), 41–58.

Luke, Carmen, & Gore, Jennifer. (Eds.). (1992). *Feminisms and critical pedagogy.* New York: Routledge.

Mohanty, Chandra Talpade. (1988). Under Western eyes: Feminist scholarship and colonial discourses. *Feminist Review, 30*, 61–88.

Mohanty, Chandra Talpade. (2003). *Feminism without borders: Decolonizing theory, practicing solidarity.* Durham, NC: Duke University Press.

Narayan, Uma. (1989). The project of feminist epistemology: Perspectives from a non-Western feminist. In Alison Jaggar & Susan Bordo (Eds.), *Gender/body/knowledge* (pp. 256–269). Princeton, NJ: Rutgers University Press.

Narayan, Uma. (2000). Essence of culture and a sense of history: A feminist critique of cultural essentialism. In Uma Narayan & Sandra Harding (Eds.), *Decentering the center: Philosophy for a multicultural, postcolonial, and feminist world* (pp. 80–100). Bloomington: Indiana University Press.

Okin, Susan Moller. (Ed.). (1999). *Is multiculturalism bad for women?* Princeton, NJ: Princeton University Press.

Olson, Gary A. (1999). Toward a post-process composition: Abandoning the rhetoric of assertion. In T. Kent (Ed.), *Post-process theory: Beyond the writing-process paradigm* (pp. 7–15). Carbondale: Southern Illinois University Press.

Omolade, B. (1987). A black feminist pedagogy. *Women's Studies Quarterly, 15,* 32–39.

Orr, Catherine, & Lichtenstein, Diane. (2004). The politics of feminist locations: A materialist analysis of women's studies. *NWSA Journal, 16*(3), 1–17.

Post, Robert. (1999). Between norms and choices. In Susan Moller Okin (Ed.), *Is multiculturalism bad for women?* (pp. 65–68). Princeton, NJ: Princeton University Press.

Sanders, Jo. (2005). *Gender and technology: A research review.* Retrieved June 20, 2011, from http://www.josanders.com/educators.html

Shrewsbury, Carolyn M. (1993). What is feminist pedagogy? *Women's Studies Quarterly, 21*(3/4), 8–16.

Siebler, Kay. (2008). *Composing feminisms: How feminists have shaped composition theories and practices.* Cresskill, NJ: Hampton Press.

Smith, Dorothy. (2004). Women's perspective as a radical critique of sociology. In S. Harding (Ed.), *Feminist standpoint theory reader* (pp. 21–34). London: Routledge.

Smith-Rosenberg, C. (1980). Politics and culture in women's history: A symposium. *Feminist Studies, 6*(1), 55–64.

Stacey, J. (1990). *Brave new families.* New York: Basic Books.

Stenberg, Shari. (2006). Making room for new subjects: Feminist interruptions of critical pedagogy rhetorics. In K. Ronald & J. Ritchie, *Teaching rhetorica: Theory, pedagogy, practice* (pp. 131–146). Portsmouth, NH: Boynton/Cook Publishers.

Thompson, Martha. (1987). Diversity in the classroom: Creating opportunities for learning feminist theory. *Women's Studies Quarterly, 15*(3/4), 81–89.

Trinh, T. Minh-ha. (1989). *Woman, native, other: Writing postcoloniality and feminism.* Indianapolis: Indiana University Press.

Wallace, Miriam L. (1999). Beyond love and battle: Practicing feminist pedagogy. *Feminist Teacher, 12*(3), 184.

33

FEMINIST PEDAGOGY RECONSIDERED

Daphne Patai

Established in 1977, [the National Women's Studies Association] . . . provides critical support for members pursuing bold goals on their campuses and in their communities by challenging existing power structures and working to create a world built upon principles of social justice.

—National Women's Studies Association (n.d.)

Something has changed drastically in American higher education in recent years. In many academic departments and even entire universities, education has become an insufficient objective. Instead, there is a growing emphasis on "social justice," and this is no longer confined to social work programs and schools of education.[1]

Nor is the emphasis on "social justice" found merely in programs explicitly driven by identity politics. By now, this emphasis has gone mainstream, recasting teaching and research in tendentious ways. Consider, for example, three positions advertised in October 2010 by Oregon State University's School of Language, Culture, and Society (comprising departments of anthropology, ethnic studies, foreign languages and literatures, and women's studies):

> These three positions reflect the School of Language, Culture, and Society's developing emphasis in social justice and diversity. The aim of this cohort is to strengthen the School's academic offerings and engaged scholarship in social justice and to build upon our commitments to creating a welcoming and inclusive environment for an increasingly diverse student body. (Women's Studies List, wmst-l@listserv.umd.edu, October 5, 2010)

Details of the three advertised positions indicate that "social justice" is central to each. Furthermore, the very term is treated as self-explanatory. The association of "social justice" with the familiar feminist focus on the "intersections" of, or "specialization in," race, ethnicity, gender, nation, class, and so on will apparently, somehow, eventually result in the much sought-after "social justice." And what decent person could possibly object to official commitments to such a lofty goal?

As for the term *engaged scholarship* (high-lighted above in the school's self-description), that language, too, is increasingly popping up in academe. At the University of Massachusetts Amherst, where I teach, the Faculty Senate Outreach Committee organized a faculty forum in November 2010 on "The Practice of Engaged Scholarship" to "discuss how engagement with external organizations and community partners facilitates vital and dynamic scholarship." The aim of the forum was clear: to devise ways in which "engaged scholarship can be documented, either in the Annual Faculty Review, or in other materials used for tenure and promotion" (e-mail received by D. Patai on October 3, 2010).

Since "scholarship," especially in research universities, is already a major measure of faculty achievement (and in fact is the primary rationale for university teachers' small course loads), it is evidently not scholarship itself that is at issue. As with *feminist scholarship,* the term *engaged scholarship* can only be a subset of scholarship, perhaps intended to shift emphasis from "scholarship" to the "engaged" efforts made on its behalf, for it is explicitly the engagement that this faculty forum wishes to see rewarded.

ACADEMIC FEMINISM

Academic feminism has, of course, been the crucial precursor of all such efforts. As innumerable women's studies mission statements, course descriptions, and websites attest (for examples, see Patai & Koertge, 2003, chaps. 10–11), the adjective *feminist* adds and is intended to add a very specific purpose to whatever nouns it modifies—namely, a project of political advocacy. The activist design underlying women's studies has been present since its earliest days four decades ago, when the new field was defined as "the academic arm of the women's movement," but its expression has grown ever more blatant over the years. Feminist scholars usually retort to their critics that there are "many feminisms," not one, and that it is an innovative and constantly developing field. All this may be true, and new debates may evolve, typically resulting from conflicts among different or newly emerging identity groups, each making

the familiar claim to having been rendered "invisible" or "silent" hitherto. A recent feminist essay characteristically defends the importance of intersectionality (which has replaced the earlier "integrated analysis" offered by women's studies), labels it an "emerging paradigm" of feminism, and argues that it enables the pursuit of "an activist agenda of social justice" (Dill, McLaughlin, & Nieves, 2007, p. 636). Thus, the prevailing orthodoxy regarding what feminism in the academy is intended to achieve continues into its fifth decade.

Little doubt accompanies the conventional, if vague, feminist rhetoric about women's studies' unique ability to bring about a better world, as is apparent in the introduction to a 2009 collection of essays titled *Feminist Pedagogy.* Originally published in the *NWSA Journal* between 1988 and 2002, the essays in this volume are offered as examples with which to fortify the ongoing practice of feminist pedagogy, here labeled "inclusive, antioppressive, and transformative." The focus on gender alone may have been extended to encompass ever more groups—the famed "complex intersectional analysis of race, class, sexuality, and gender"—but the fundamental assumptions about feminism's unique ability to inform and inspire correct political activism continue undaunted (Crabtree, Sapp, & Licona, 2009, p. 17).

The notion that "feminism" transforms everything it touches is equally alive in the inaugural issue of *Feminist Formations* (the new incarnation of what was formerly called the *NWSA Journal*), which includes essays on such themes as "feminist hospitality" and "feminist love," while everywhere tropes relating to "positionality" and "intersectionality" are on display. The editors summarize their aim for the renamed journal in this way: "We hope you find this and future issues of *Feminist Formations* useful in fueling your scholarship and activism" (Ropers-Huilman, 2010).

The problem with all these statements is that they celebrate the very thing that should give one pause in an educational setting: the commitment to essentially political aims, at the service of which higher education is placed. And as with other grandiose political rhetoric, clarity or agreement about the real content of these goals is largely absent, as is serious discussion of how to attain them. To assume they are self-evident—that we all know and agree about what "social justice" is and how "oppression" can be ended—and to make them the objective of teaching and research is to allow politics to override education. Furthermore, anyone acquainted with history—especially the history of the 20th century—should view the imposition of political objectives on education with suspicion, if not alarm. And that is so even leaving aside the relevant questions of whether political indoctrination is indeed the purpose of higher education and what consequences it entails for free inquiry.

Yet the political advocacy defining women's studies from its very inception has rarely been the object of reflection within the field. Even today, for example, a common occurrence at feminist events is public confession, as feminists themselves announce their "complicity" in the dreaded *isms* (racism, heterosexism, classism, ablism, etc.), but as for questioning the appropriate place of politics in education? No; on this matter, there is broad general agreement, as women's studies own statements make abundantly clear. Instead, what the field is called, not what its agenda is, has been a cause of great controversy.

Starting in the late 1990s and increasingly in the past decade, numerous women's studies programs have changed their name. By incorporating references to "gender" and "sexuality," currently the odds-on favorites, "women's studies" programs have become "women, gender, sexuality studies" or some variation thereof.[2] This rebranding has itself been the object of heated debate, with some feminists complaining that "gender studies" erases "women" by implicitly denying the importance of women as a category, while others see the original name as a white, middle-class, heteronormative holdover. The latter group argues that the focus on "women" was always exclusionary and is now outdated and that the renaming is essential to defending the field and presenting it as broader, more inclusive, and more fitting for our time (for more on renaming, see Halberstam, 2005; in Canada: Carlson, 2010).

Notwithstanding some new rhetoric, however, feminism in the classroom expresses itself in the familiar way: at the least, as a commitment to "the goal of educational and social transformation" (Ropers-Huilman, 2009), involving fundamental feminist tenets and teaching practices typically described as collaborative, student centered, and activist. Is such an orientation problematic to conscientious teaching and research? Not inevitably, perhaps, but very likely. And that is because the political engagement underlying feminism in the academy is bound to set up a highly tendentious model for research and teaching, a paradigm most feminists would hardly accept were its objectives contrary to their own. In addition, one cannot pursue an overarching political agenda in education without curtailing free speech and academic freedom.[3] But rather than confront these dilemmas directly, feminists in academe usually opt for other tactics.

To justify and defend the introduction of *feminist* as a legitimate modifier of their *teaching* and *research,* feminists have had to emphasize and greatly exaggerate the flaws of the pre- or nonfeminist models they are contesting. They insist that in the routine practices of the old dispensation, teaching and research always were and in many cases still are biased, exclusionary, and inimical to the interests of women. In short, they are "masculinist." To many feminists, this is a decisive claim, for only when previous academic procedures can be portrayed in such starkly negative terms can the feminist agenda appear as a corrective: legitimate, appropriate, fair, salutary, and urgently necessary. The continued stress on this deplorable history is thus built into the field's self-definition.

One example of this distorted vision is the assertion put forth by some feminist scholars in the United States that "the academy remains an essentially single sex institution. It is male-dominated, and that domination exerts itself in both numbers and power" (Scollay & Bratt, 1997, p. 274). More recent incarnations of such claims play from the same script. Thus, the editors of a volume published in 2009 on their very first page defend the need for feminist pedagogy, defined as "a movement against hegemonic educational practices that tacitly accept or more forcefully reproduce an oppressively gendered, classed, racialized, and androcentric social order" (Crabtree et al., 2009, p. 1).

This view of the situation of women in academe should probably not be ascribed to an inability to recognize the profound changes and improvements that have occurred over the past few decades. More likely, it is a tactical necessity for feminist faculty, endlessly circling the wagons around their purportedly vulnerable little programs. Yet young women, somehow, are not getting the message. Instead, for several decades now, women have stubbornly insisted on attending universities in higher numbers than men and receiving an ever greater percentage of degrees. The latest U.S. Department of Education statistics, for example, reveal that the change has now reached graduate education as well:

> Between 1997–98 and 2007–08, the percentage of degrees earned by females fluctuated between 60 and 62 percent for associate's degrees and between 56 and 58 percent for bachelor's degrees, while the percentage of master's degrees earned by females increased from 57 to 61 percent. The percentage of first-professional degrees and doctoral degrees earned by females also increased during this period. In 1997–98, females earned 43 percent of first-professional degrees and 42 percent of doctoral degrees; in 2007–08, the respective percentages were 50 and 51 percent. (U.S. Department of Education, 2010)

True, despite this astonishing success, gender discrepancies still exist in specific academic fields and not only among students. In faculty positions overall, women have not yet reached parity with men. The *NEA 2010 Almanac of Higher Education* (National Education Association, 2010) tells us that over the past 10 years (through 2008–2009), women's share of positions at the lower levels—instructors and lecturers—has held steady, at 59% and 56%, respectively. At higher ranks, women in 2008–2009 constituted 43% of associate professors (up from 37%) and 32% of professors (up from 23% in 1997–2008). At the assistant professor rank, women in 2008–2009 constituted just under 50% of faculty overall. But as with salary issues, aggregate data do not tell us enough to understand the situation (see Furchtgott-Roth, 2010).

There is considerable feminist disinclination to plain talk about the possible reasons for persisting gender disparities in higher education. The crucial contention of feminists, however, as

of other political activists, is that disparity necessarily equals discrimination. So entrenched is this position that even as notable a figure as Lawrence H. Summers, while he was president of Harvard University, could be cowed by feminist critics into abject apologies (though these did not save him from losing his job) merely for wondering, at a conference on diversifying the science and engineering workforce, if innate differences and personal choices might explain why fewer women than men pursue careers in science and math (see Goldin & Katz, 2005).

Insisting that disparity (wherever it exists in men's favor) equals injustice is an important move from the perspective of attaining political power while economizing on effort, for the inevitable conclusion is that feminist activism in the university is as necessary today as ever. The unceasing struggle against oppression can then be used to justify the introduction into the classroom of what is a patently political project, the project of *feminist* transformation. This project has a broad range of objectives—from the basic pedagogical goals of "liberal feminism" or "equality for women," which are often derided and dismissed by some feminists, to the extreme views associated with such figures as Catharine MacKinnon, who treats the concept *liberal* as a disguise for the exercise of patriarchal privilege. MacKinnon titled one of her books *Feminism Unmodified* (1987) precisely to stress her belief that her own brand of feminism alone is the genuine article and therefore tolerates no qualifier.

If we start, however, with a different set of assumptions—namely, the suppositions that teaching and research are not, and ought not to be, either feminist or masculinist and that, despite the historical exclusion of women, the substance of a liberal education and the ideals on which it rests have not been always and inherently flawed—the adjective *feminist* begins to look less like a salutary and perpetually needed corrective and more like the calamitous imposition of a political agenda. Why calamitous? Because it undermines the most valuable aspect of the modern university: to provide that rare space in which emphasis can be on *how* to think, not *what* to think, and on acquiring intellectual tools, not accepting hand-me-down political doctrines. To assert that indoctrination is what men have in fact traditionally perpetrated in all fields, and that it is now the turn of women to do the same, even if it were not a caricature, is a feeble defense (as well as a self-destructive one) since it would merely turn the feminist program into a replica of a practice considered defective and even malevolent. Surely the appropriate response to whatever are deemed the shortcomings of traditional teaching is not simply to reverse the biases of the past but rather to surpass them.

To avert the consequences of this conundrum, feminists have resorted to the proposition that "all teaching is political,"[4] a claim that allows them to represent feminist academic activism as no less legitimate than earlier academic practices that were, so the argument goes, similarly tainted. For if all these activities are inherently political, and they have been so in a way that has oppressed women (and other groups), then the feminist-inspired activist classroom is a corrective demanded by both justice and fairness. This is the argument that anchors and justifies the feminist position on education (see Letherby, 2003). It is the typical rejoinder also made by well-established defenders of leftist indoctrination (which includes but is not limited to feminism) in the classroom. Marilyn Cochran-Smith and her four coauthors, for example, in their recent essay "Teacher Education for Social Justice: Critiquing the Critiques," rest their defense essentially on the charge "you do it too":

> We argue that although the critiques claim to be apolitical and value-free, they are, in fact, neither. Rather, many of the critiques of teacher education for social justice are part of a larger political ideology based on a narrow view of learning, an individualistic notion of freedom, and a market-based perspective on education that substitutes accountability for democracy. What most of the critics want is not a value-free teacher education, but one that matches their values, not an apolitical teacher education, but one with a more hegemonic and therefore invisible politics. (Cochran-Smith, Barnatt, Lahann, Shakman, & Terrell, 2008, p. 625)

Ironically, such a defense would seem to be self-refuting since it is typically made by people teaching in those much despised "liberal" societies that nonetheless have left considerable space for challengers to make their case—and even earn a good living for doing so. After all, actual societies disdaining "individualistic notions of freedom" and openly embracing political indoctrination in the classroom hardly have a great track record. But no doubt feminist educators and other left-wing academics would dismiss the liberal tradition in secular education, with its emphasis on open inquiry and freedom of expression, by referring to some version of Marcuse's notion of "repressive tolerance." For decades, this notion has been a handy intellectual tool for discrediting the very values that allow "non-hegemonic" ideas and work (whether homegrown or produced by exiles from totalitarian regimes) to reach the public sphere in the first place.

Nonetheless, it is important to address directly the claim that all education and research are "political" and at best (or worst) manage to conceal their biases. Certainly in particular cases, a political slant may be demonstrated, but it seems absurd to insist that this distortion is omnipresent and leftist academics alone have the honesty to face up to it (or, like women's studies professors, bravely embrace it). Only by turning itself into mere triviality can the assertion that "all education is political" survive scrutiny, regardless of the ease with which most anything can be shown to have *some* political aspect or implication, however remote. But to paint all past knowledge with such a broad brush is merely a gross caricature, one that requires purposeful ignorance of the differences between a liberal and a totalitarian education, sweeps away meaningful distinctions, and promotes a blinkered view of intellectual, social, and political issues. None of this bodes well for education.

FEMINIST CRITIQUES OF SCIENCE

In fact, in some cases, the feminist critique is irrelevant. I made this very point on an online "chat" sponsored by the *Chronicle of Higher Education,* countering the argument that "everything is political" with the example of the periodic table (Patai, 2000; see Boghossian, 2001, pp. 6–8). Where exactly, I wondered, is the "unacknowledged political agenda" (mentioned by one of the discussants) inherent in the periodic table? I received an answer from one women's studies professor:

> Doesn't the teaching of the Periodic Table imply that "man's" appropriate relationship with "nature" is one of dominance? And that we should search for the meaning of existence through science? Since when are such humanist assertions free from political implications? (http://userpages .umbc.edu/~korenman/wmst/patai1.html)

Here we find the confusion routinely warned against by philosophers of science—namely, the logical fallacy of confounding the *content* of science with the *context* in which scientific work is done and disseminated. But this attitude toward science—indeed toward knowledge generally—seems actually to be a requisite of much feminist pedagogy. The philosopher of science Noretta Koertge (2003) has explained why taking on science has been a particularly important goal of feminists:

> Scientific inquiry embodied all of the so-called masculine virtues that feminism most wanted to challenge—objectivity (vs. subjectivity), the power of reason (instead of intuition), problem solving through logical analysis and the weighing of evidence (vs. conflict resolution through empathy and plumbing the depths of oppression).[5] (p. 321)

If feminists could demonstrate that even science—supposedly the most rational human pursuit—is at its core political and that claims to objectivity are always fraudulent, they could then justify similar critiques of other domains of knowledge a fortiori and thus undergird their own legitimacy. And for that very reason, hostility to science, as it emerges from a host of feminist writings and teaching materials (see Koerber & Lay, 2002; Rice & Waugh, 2001; Walker, Geertsema, & Barnett, 2009), is in my view an important criterion for judging the intellectual integrity that feminists bring—or fail to bring—to the classroom.

Is the charge that feminism is hostile to science a mere caricature? A predictable part of the "backlash" against feminism? To answer these questions, I turn to the evidence of discussions about sex taking place in women's studies classes everywhere. Women's studies programs and the books on their reading lists treat as a matter of orthodoxy the view that gender differences are always socially constructed. However, unlike earlier second-wave feminist work that attempted to distinguish between gender (social) and sex (biological), many women's studies teachers these days have extended social constructionism to the point where it engulfs biology altogether.[6]

Some years ago, on the Women's Studies e-mail list (WMST-L), which began in 1991 and by 2005 had about 5,000 subscribers, I questioned the utility of spending much class time on Anne Fausto-Sterling's work, extremely popular to this day in women's studies courses, which argues that there are more than two sexes (Fausto-Sterling, 2000, p. 20). The existence of a very small percentage of infants born with sexual anomalies, I stated, in no way challenges the reality of sexual dimorphism as a biological fact. This comment sparked a multitude of denunciations, one of which even accused me of attacking the civil rights of minorities. But more than the tone, what startled me about these responses was the categorical insistence that Fausto-Sterling demonstrates that our very bodies are "socially constructed" as binary, the apparent underlying assumption being that "biology" itself is somehow inimical to feminist interests and has to be reconceived. This conviction led to some astonishing messages, accusing me of reiterating *with no evidence* that sexual dimorphism is indeed a biological fact (see Kane, 2001; "Policing the Academy" in Patai & Koertge, 2003). At last, a biologist (Masaracchia, 2001), who was also directing a women's studies program, wrote in to say that she was appalled at the lack of basic knowledge of biology demonstrated in the discussion. Offering to explain the reality of sexual dimorphism, she asked,

> So where would you like to start—dimorphism in utero, chromosomes and chromosomal diversity, differentiation and development? I will try to be succinct but I will also provide some facts that many of you (based on your comments) aren't going to like.

Few people took her up on the offer. Instead, she was denounced in short order for claiming to have expertise (apparently an affront to feminist egalitarianism), and she soon decided to leave the list. The issue came up yet again on the WMST-L in 2008, when it was once more asserted that the "biologically-based concept of 'women'" is a myth. I replied,

> Unfortunately, the "biologically-based concept" *is* what unites all women. It is far from "mythical." There is such a thing as biological sexual dimorphism, period. The social/historical construction of what it means to be a woman is a separate issue, but the biology is very real.
>
> Hard to believe one wants to teach one's students from a starting point that is patently false. As I've commented many times before on this list, the existence of biological anomalies does not change the fundamental facts, and I don't see it as a service to our students to attempt to deny those facts. If we begin from such patently ideological denials of reality, those are pretty good grounds for students to wonder about the validity of what we teach them in general. (WMST-L posting by D. Patai on September 12, 2008)

I recount these episodes to convey the mood and characteristic attitudes found among faculty members most involved in teaching women's studies, those who regularly participate on the WMST-List, which provides a fascinating portrait of the attitudes and postures prevalent in women's studies. But it is important to add here that even while being mostly denounced on the list, I have over the years received quite a few "behind-the-scenes" messages of support from women's studies faculty members and graduate students, who tell me privately that they share my concerns and are made uneasy by the dogma of social constructionism or other favored tenets of women's studies but feel unable to say so openly for fear of jeopardizing their careers.

The result is that while progress occurs in many other fields, consequent on the extraordinary scientific and sociopolitical advances of our time, many teachers of women's studies, like other ideologues, prefer the more economical route of dismissing opinions they see as threatening to their narrow worldview. In *The*

Riddle of Gender: Science, Activism, and Transgender Rights, Deborah Rudacille (2005) argues against the social constructionist orthodoxy so prevalent in the past few decades. "Today," she writes, "the pendulum in gender research is slowly swinging back to biology. Hormones acting under the influence of genes are now thought to be the primary architects of gender identity" (pp. 138–139), although the exact developmental mechanisms are not yet clear. As Rudacille puts it, "Nature may provide the architecture of gender, but culture does the decorating," and although her work aims to promote tolerance for transgendered people, she has no trouble asserting that "as seems increasingly certain, [gender identity] is hardwired into the brain at birth" (p. 292).

The difficulty feminist academics evidently have in modifying their core beliefs, no matter how anachronistic they have become, is readily apparent when one turns to publications on science in the field of women's studies. Mary F. Rogers and C. D. Garrett (2002), in their book *Who's Afraid of Women's Studies? Feminisms in Everyday Life,* for example, flatly state that "sexual identities have been culturally constructed" (p. 49). Another book, *Feminist Science Studies: A New Generation* (Mayberry, Subramaniam, & Weasel, 2001), similarly reveals the feminist desire to dismiss science and put in its place politically agreeable notions. The latter book purports to present the latest thinking in the burgeoning field of feminist science studies, described by the three editors as committed to exploring "situated knowledges," in which the relationship between feminism and science and "the intersections between race, class, gender, and science and technology" are examined, the goal being a "disruption of the dichotomy between scientific inquiry and policy" (pp. 5, 6). As the introduction explains, *Feminist Science Studies* aims at nothing less than to provide "progressive, positive readings of science, and of reconstructions of science consistent with feminist theories, ideals, and visions" (p. 10). The extraordinary nature of this objective seems not to trouble the field of feminist science studies, nor has it hindered the uncritical adoption of articles in this field in the "multidisciplinary" women's studies courses typically taught by nonscientists.

Martha Whitaker (2001), in her essay in *Feminist Science Studies,* affirms that Anne Fausto-Sterling's (2000) work has been of special importance "in helping me to understand that scientists' analyses and quantification of earth and natural processes *are* social and political processes" (p. 49)—a perfect expression, this, of the reigning approach to science among feminists. Still another contributor (Subramaniam, 2001) aims to go beyond feminist science studies' penchant for "taking apart the visible workings of science to highlight the invisible factors that shaped the interconnections between nature and culture, science and society." Her project is "one of reconstruction—to use [the] insights of deconstruction to rebuild a practice that was scientifically rigorous but also informed by the rigors of feminist politics and scholarship" (p. 57)—as if the problem were not precisely that the "rigors" of these different endeavors are hardly to be compared (see Tallis [2000] for a telling description of the crucial distinction between these two modes of inquiry).

Particularly revealing is an article by Rebecca M. Herzig (2001) describing her Introduction to Women's Studies course at Bates College. Hoping to dispel students' notion that biology exists "outside the effects of culture and history," Herzig provides her class with "modules" complete with guided readings designed to help students "query received knowledge about 'the female body.'" While this appears to be an unobjectionable aim, Herzig's true goals are apparent in her tendentious module on "Sexual Dimorphism," which relies heavily on readings by Fausto-Sterling and a few others that emphasize the existence of intersexed humans. Here is how the module presents the problem:

> Lurking in most contemporary discussions about gender and sexuality in the United States is a presumption of the universal, timeless dimorphism between human males and females. How empirically sound are these dualistic categories? What evidence has been presented for and against universal human sexual dimorphism? How might cross-cultural ethnographic evidence challenge biomedical assumptions of a strict two-sex model? How does the presumption of sexual dimorphism inform our understandings of human sexuality? (pp. 183–192)

The module's very phrasing gives the agenda away: It is important to attack the notion of biological dimorphism because the fact of dimorphism is essential to our history of sexual reproduction. And sexual reproduction, from a biological point of view, confirms the normalcy, indeed the ordinariness, of heterosexuality, which is the very thing—now relabeled "heteronormativity"—that academic feminists routinely identify as the institution at the root of women's oppression. Biology thus presents a particularly intractable problem for feminist analysis, and it is not surprising that many feminists spend considerable energy arguing that biology is merely one more ingredient in the formidable ideology sustaining patriarchy. Contradictions in this critique of biology arise when some feminists who denounce the existence of biological "facts" also promote essentialist (and always negative) characterizations of "males" and their intrinsic nature. The result is that today positions that used to be identified with radical feminism (see, e.g., Echols, 1989) often appear institutionalized within women's studies programs.

There is, then, a deep and—for many feminists—vital link between challenging the biology of sex differences and undermining the "institution" of heterosexuality, seen as the linchpin of male dominance. I have documented elsewhere this salient tendency within much contemporary feminism.[7] But lest readers think that arguments against biology come from only a few doctrinaire radical feminists now perhaps out of fashion, even standard reference works have for some time now presented as fact what was once thought to be controversial within feminism. In the Houghton Mifflin *Reader's Companion to U.S. Women's History,* the entry on "Heterosexuality" (Trimberger, 1998) states,

> Sexuality is not private, but is political and related to power. "Compulsory heterosexuality" is part of a power structure benefiting heterosexual males at the expense of women and homosexuals. This inequity is justified by an ideology that sees heterosexuality as natural, universal, and biologically necessary, and homosexuality as the opposite. The system also is reinforced by legal sanctions and violence against women (rape, battering, incest,

and murder) and against lesbians, gays, and trans-gendered persons (verbal harassment, physical assault, and murder). (p. 255)

The author spells out why it is important for feminists to press such an argument: "If our sexuality is socially constructed it can also be de- and reconstructed"—a clear indication of feminism's urgent need to reconstitute every-thing about men's and women's lives that is perceived to hinder its particular vision of social transformation. A recent discussion on the WMST-List (WMST-L, July 13–15, 2011), ostensibly about "forced" marriage, once again insisted that students must be made to question the distinction between "forced" and "free," and between the West's supposedly "progressive" societies and other, more "traditional" ones. The overt objective is to denounce ethnocentrism and any vestige of "us" versus "them" thinking; the thinly disguised one, however, is to dismiss the notion that women might actually experi-ence and seek to act on their own interest in and attraction to men.

CHALLENGING KNOWLEDGE

Beyond feminism's immediate political objec-tive lies a broader attack on knowledge, which by now has spread to other countries as well and become ever more extreme. Consider, for exam-ple, the PhD dissertation written by Maria Suárez Toro at La Salle University in Costa Rica (2006), which contains 26 chapters designed to constitute a "major epistemological critique of patriarchy," by highlighting women's neglected contributions to every conceivable field. According to the website she co-founded, Toro protests the "Newtonian paradigm," which, together with capitalism and patriarchy, is "responsible for the atomization of knowledge and the de-legitimization and 'invisibilization' of oppressed people's experiences and subjec-tivities in the construction of knowledge." As an example, she argues that "the scientific 'discovery' of quantum physics at the turn of the last cen-tury is what feminism and women already knew from their experiences, science and conscience: That all knowledge is relative to the subject who

constructs it." Yet, Toro asserts, "Little or no credit was given to feminism for its contribution to that central 'discovery.'" Toro's challenge to feminism is to escape from the logic of the Newtonian paradigm and develop an "Emerging Vital Paradigm."[8]

If, even in relation to science, feminist edu-cators do not shrink from their tendentious argu-ments, what should we expect as feminists endeavor to reshape other, more fuzzy areas? It should be, but is not, needless to say that the integrity of education is always in danger when politics or ideology supersedes rational inquiry and the careful consideration of evidence. Twentieth-century history has demonstrated this peril in abundance, and it is distressing that aca-demic feminists have not taken these disastrous examples to heart.

Nonetheless, does it really matter that offi-cial feminist pedagogy rests on the belief that teaching is invariably political? That feminists hold fairness and claims of objectivity in research to be mere illusions, if not outright frauds? It does matter, because teachers who embrace such views are unlikely to even attempt to question their own biases, let alone transcend them. And, worse yet, they are programmati-cally committed to propagating their biases in the "feminist classroom." Thus, women's stud-ies teachers openly declare their objective to make students (depending on their identity, of course) confront their own privilege, in its many possible forms, and to recognize the "institu-tional" causes of their status. And in the name of multi- or interdisciplinarity, these "engaged" teachers pass on to their students all manner of research, the merits of which they may be unable to evaluate but which are accepted or rejected on political grounds. In such classes, students rarely encounter criticisms of feminist-inspired work, nor are they encouraged to develop the capacity for independent judgment and appraisal that might challenge the feminist presuppositions on which their courses rest.[9]

Challenges have, of course, occurred for decades now to the feminist program in aca-deme, and some feminist pedagogues have come up with creative tactics for avoiding con-structive engagement with criticism. A striking example is Annette Kolodny's proposal of the category of "antifeminist intellectual harassment." Kolodny identifies antifeminist intellectual harassment as "a serious threat to academic freedom" and then, borrowing from sexual harassment regulations, outlines three very broad categories of offense, culminating in the assertion that antifeminist intellectual harassment occurs "when any policy, action, statement, and/or behavior creates an environment in which research, scholarship, and teaching pertaining to women, gender, or gender inequities are devalued, discouraged, or altogether thwarted" (Kolodny, 1998b, p. 9). Such a concept is obviously designed to shield feminism, (almost) uniquely in the university world, from any and all criticism.

BACKLASH OR LEGITIMATE CRITIQUE?

Having written about these issues for the past two decades, I am aware that the usual response to criticisms of this type—and often merely to raising these issues—is to dismiss the critic with labels such as "conservative," "right wing," or "reactionary." Whole books have been devoted to attempting to prove that criticisms of women's studies are merely examples of "backlash" (see Rogers & Garrett, 2002). Indeed, the very word *backlash* has acquired a sacramental aura in feminist circles, obviating even the possibility of a reasoned response to the specific criticisms that have been voiced.

Despite this predictable response, even some well-known senior scholars closely associated with feminism in the academy have eventually felt moved to object to the politicizing of education. In the summer 2000 issue of *Signs: Journal of Women in Culture and Society,* devoted to dozens of essays on feminism and the academy, Elaine Marks, a widely recognized lesbian scholar who, until her death in late 2001, was Germaine Brée Professor of French and Women's Studies at the University of Wisconsin, Madison, complained that she was beginning to feel "isolated in Women's Studies," where she had come to be perceived as "a closet conservative." Why? Because she deplored the prevalence of identity politics in literature courses and now agreed with Harold Bloom (1994): "to read in the service of any

ideology is not, in my judgment, to read at all" (p. 29). Marks confessed that she herself used to have politically correct responses—the kind that seek, in any work of literature, traces of the dreaded *isms* (sexism, racism, etc.)—but she was no longer satisfied with such approaches. Hence, she decided to air in public some of what she considered to be "feminism's perverse effects" in the academy.

"It is no simple matter," Marks (2000) concluded, "in this millennial fin de siècle, to criticize certain tendencies in cultural studies or Women's Studies or ethnic studies without being accused of participating in a conservative political agenda" (p. 1163). And she is right. In the topsy-turvy world of academe, to call for an education *not* bound to a political agenda is tantamount to being "conservative." Moreover, the fact that *conservative* has become a label of instant dismissal in academe exemplifies the ideological rigidity that now disfigures the one arena that was supposed to fearlessly and openly explore ideas and knowledge claims on their own merits (see, e.g., the reactions to David Horowitz's [2003] *Academic Bill of Rights,* discussed below).

More recently, intellectual gadfly and provocateur Stanley Fish has written against politicizing education. His arguments have at least been taken somewhat seriously and addressed, for example, in the volume *Debating Moral Education: Rethinking the Role of the Modern University* (Kiss & Euben, 2010). Fish now states that a line should indeed be drawn between academic and nonacademic activities and that faculty members should refrain from any sort of partisan activity. If you are an academic, he now asserts (as some of us have argued for many years), you're being paid to dissect ideas, not to advocate them, and this is true whether those ideas are political, moral, or ethical (Fish, 2010, p. 77). He explains this by what he terms (drawing on the legal theorist Ernest Weinrib) "the distinctiveness of tasks," noting that if education is indistinguishable from other tasks such as politics, character formation, or nation building, there is no rationale for giving it "a room of its own, not to mention a budget and a vast machinery by which its practitioners are produced and credentialed" (p. 78). For his trouble, of course, he is charged with advocating "passivity" and acting like a "good German" (p. 86).

A more substantive—and earlier—analysis of the problems of politicizing education has been clearly set forth by the philosopher Susan Haack, whose work should be indispensable reading for every feminist who aspires to scholarly integrity. Haack's book *Manifesto of a Passionate Moderate: Unfashionable Essays* is filled with challenges to the notion that a "feminist" perspective strengthens intellectual work, the sorts of challenges routinely ignored in women's studies classrooms. To Haack (1998b), "The politicization of inquiry, . . . whether in the interests of good political values or bad, is always epistemologically unsound" (p. 119).[10] She further argues that "the rubric 'feminist epistemology' is incongruous on its face, in somewhat the way of, say, 'Republican epistemology'" (Haack, 1998a, p. 124; see also Koertge, Chapter 6, this volume). Haack (1998a) explains,

> The profusion of incompatible themes proposed as "feminist epistemology" itself speaks against the idea of a distinctively female cognitive style. But even if there were such a thing, the case for feminist epistemology would require further argument to show that women's "ways of knowing" . . . represent better procedures of inquiry or subtler standards of justification than the male. And, sure enough, we are told that insights into the theory of knowledge are available to women which are not available, or not easily available, to men. (p. 126)

Dismissing "the egregious assumption that one thinks with one's skin or one's sex organs," Haack (1998b) in another essay stresses that

> this form of argument, when applied to the concepts of evidence, truth, etc., is not only fallacious; it is also pragmatically self-undermining. . . . For if there were no genuine inquiry, no objective evidence, we couldn't know what theories are such that their being accepted would conduce to women's interests, nor what women's interests are. (p. 118)

Reflecting on the disinclination of many feminist scholars to confront the contradictions of their own positions, Haack has no trouble recognizing what drives "the new, imperialist feminism," as she calls it. It is, she says, quite simply a determination "to colonize epistemology." She then makes the telling comment: "There would be a genuinely feminist epistemology if the idea could be legitimated *that feminist values should determine what theories are accepted*" (Haack, 1998a, p. 128). And, indeed, precisely such an effort is regularly embraced and celebrated in women's studies circles, where few seem to notice that it will in the end undermine the ground of their own pedagogy.

In recent years, I have not seen any evidence that women's studies teachers have modified their antagonism toward claims to positive knowledge in particular and scientific reasoning in general. And, not surprisingly, they are now finding themselves in some company they may not choose to keep. As "creation science," recast these days as "intelligent design," extends its reach and threatens the teaching of basic science (reduced to a competing ideology) in the United States, its defenders make comments about the status of evolution—that it is "just a theory," for example, though one that claims for itself a privileged status—that are remarkably similar to the feminist depreciation of science.[11] Like creationists, many feminists have shown contempt for evidence when it did not support their preconceptions. They may misunderstand science (perhaps intentionally), denounce its procedures, and ignore its commitment to self-correction—all in order to be able to characterize it as ideology and not even as honest a one as their own ideology, which proudly acknowledges its political interests.

But the rejection of the ideals of objective knowledge (however imperfectly attainable) and the deployment of the admitted limitations of knowledge as a weapon with which to dismiss the work of patriarchal dead white men gain feminists only an illusory victory. For, although disdaining standards of evidence and logic may leave feminists free—for the moment—to defend and promote their agenda, it also renders them vulnerable to ignorant or politically motivated calumnies directed against them. For how will feminists respond when, with the next cultural turn, we are once again told that the blood of menstruating women causes milk to curdle? Aren't standards of evidence and unbiased investigation crucial to all women (to all people) as they attempt to combat prejudice and ignorance? But feminists who spend their energy arguing that Einstein's theories were really produced by his first wife (see http://www.esterson.org/milevamaric.htm) or, alternatively, that they have to be dismissed as sexist (see Irigaray, 1982; and the discussion of her claim in Sokal & Bricmont, 1998), will have no weapons with which to challenge equally unsound claims aimed at them.

Because I have often observed feminists veering from one line of argument to another (e.g., resorting to biological determinism when denouncing men while insisting on social constructionism—still the official feminist orthodoxy—most of the time), I have concluded that caring more about achieving "feminist" goals than about meeting the obligations of scrupulous teaching and research leads to an opportunistic intellectual stance in the academy and—most harmfully—in the classroom. Society has changed, but feminist activists seem determined to repeat old stereotypes about academic hostility to women, male violence and female victimization and oppression, and the unique contributions of feminism in academe as though they were startling insights (see Fisher, Daigle, & Cullen, 2010; Pilcher & Whelehan, 2004).

Ironically, women's studies seems to have learned little from its own criticisms of what happens when education is governed by political agendas. Nor do many feminist teachers appear to have grasped the implications of such illuminating 20th-century cases as Lysenkoism in the USSR, a stellar example of science "reconstructed" so as to be "consistent with" a reigning political ideology—the overt goal, as we saw earlier, of the volume *Feminist Science Studies* (Mayberry et al., 2001). Embracing, as feminism in the academy does, the principle that all education is political and declining to explore just how this might be true, to what extent, in what circumstances, and at what costs, makes it impossible for women's studies and other politically inspired programs to respond convincingly to political pressures from the other side. It also forces disingenuous misrepresentations of challenges to current orthodoxies. Thus, David Horowitz's (2003) *Academic Bill of Rights* (*ABOR*), for example, with its demand for political diversity in the name of academic freedom, is routinely charged by multicultural/feminist/left-liberal professors

with being a thinly disguised effort to enforce his own (conservative) politics. Despite his careful delineation of his proposal, Horowitz is constantly depicted as attacking academic freedom in that hitherto pristine bastion of intellectual exploration, the modern university.

But those who claim that all education is political hardly have grounds for objecting to the inclusion of political views not currently fashionable in the academic world. If feminists really believe their characterization of nonfeminist education, why are they (like many academic organizations) in a panic over initiatives such as the *ABOR*? The fact is that Horowitz has stolen the high ground from those who might now, opportunistically, wish to reclaim it. For while the campus left, including feminists, has affirmed that all education is political, Horowitz is relying on definitions of academic freedom that have a long and distinguished lineage—including statements made generations ago by the American Association of University Professors. And, even worse, when feminists themselves, in an effort to combat their critics, are forced to switch gears and suddenly attack the notion of politics in education, they stand revealed as hypocritical opportunists.

Furthermore, if feminists and other politically committed teachers are worried about being sued by students disgruntled with their one-sided representations of knowledge (as a bill introduced in Florida would have allowed), why haven't they objected to the nationwide adoption of harassment policies and speech codes in academe, which have already made major inroads into free inquiry and expression on campus? Where are the feminist professors objecting to the censure, loss of job, and legal actions taken against their colleagues because a student (usually a woman) was offended by, say, a professor's nonfeminist discussion of abortion or rape? I have not seen women's studies teachers rush to protect academic freedom and uninhibited class discussion for those whose views contradict their own. The reality is quite the contrary, as I have documented at length (see Patai, 1998; Patai & Koertge, 2003, chaps. 10 and 11).

Where, one might well ask, will feminists be able to go in this struggle over which and whose ideas should be protected in the academy?

Many feminists would respond that *their* ideas are true or better, but to sustain this claim, they would be forced to resort to high standards of evidence, rigorous logic, and fair evaluation not in thrall to political predispositions—in short, the very procedures they have so often attacked. In combating other ideologues and their claims, the feminist promotion of subjectivity, value-laden theory, or standpoint epistemology—all still very much in vogue—will not serve them well. For their own practice has helped create an educational environment with no rules, merely competing political passions.

As many commentators have observed, feminism itself could not even have gotten started without embracing claims resting on supposedly unbiased research believed to accurately assess the situation of women vis-à-vis men. In light of feminism's path, therefore, the present assertions of feminist pedagogy seem not only tendentious but disingenuous. The feminist promotion of subjectivity, of standpoint epistemology, and of the paradigm that "everything is political" is, it turns out, at best situational. It hardly justifies the pedagogy that has grown up around it and which by now has descended to K–12 education as well.

The scholarly and educational function of the university is, de facto, undergoing redefinition. One would have thought that teaching the young is itself of value, obviously contributing to "the community" and certainly involving "outreach." But the insistence on these additional terms reveals that the work usually done by faculty members is these days seen as woefully inadequate and hence requires renewed justification. And that justification has to be sought outside the university, in something other than what faculty members routinely do, which is teach and learn. Clearly, "higher education" has become so debased a concept that only by redefining it can it be defended.

Women's studies is not alone in promoting these habits, though perhaps it deserves considerable credit—or blame—as a successful precursor. As contradictory as it may seem, it is not merely academic activism that is the problem. Postmodernist fashions, too, have made a variety of vulnerable intellectual and pedagogical approaches acceptable and widely used. And this is the case even among feminist critics of postmodernism who, while decrying its alienating and pretentious vocabulary and its distance from everyday political struggles, nonetheless adopt its practices whenever they prove convenient. Postmodernism's indiscriminate rejection of significant distinctions, its obsession with power, and its habit of dogmatic assertion (the very thing, ironically, that postmodernism claims to "interrogate") have influenced feminist academics' own critiques, though, of course, this at times contravenes an agenda that would be meaningless without some firm convictions about the real world and our ability to obtain and convey knowledge of it.

CONCLUSIONS

Feminist pedagogues by their own accounts indulge in a series of wide-ranging self-destructive habits. They inconsistently dismiss logic as so much phallocentric baggage; celebrate emotion and intuition and, at the same time, communal values and groupthink, as if there were no pertinent historical examples of what actually happens when a society attempts to re-create itself according to such values; and assume that identity politics tells us most of what we need to know for adjudicating among competing views and knowledge claims. (How this can happen within the context of a postmodernism that has challenged the very notion of a stable identity is not clear, but the problem dissolves once logic and coherence are rejected as "masculinist.") Feminist pedagogues also welcome and defend "local knowledges" in relation to Third World "others" but rigidly resist them when they come from disapproved groups within Western societies.[12] Distinctions fall by the wayside: Ear piercing and breast implants are equivalent to clitoridectomy; high-heeled shoes hardly differ from Chinese footbinding. Honor killings in the Muslim world are no different from "domestic violence" in the West, and to say otherwise is to engage in "racism" (see Patai, 2008, pp. 10–11). Double standards prevail. The "authority of experience," so praised by feminists in their struggle to have women's voices heard (logocentrism notwithstanding), is subjected to cynical deconstruction when the proclaimed experience is not one that suits the feminist causes of the moment or when the "identity" of the speaker can be attacked. What all this means in practice is that opportunism lies at the heart of feminist pedagogy today.

Teaching and the research on which it rests are noble pursuits. To commit oneself to fostering the intellectual development of one's students is no small or unworthy task. And, contrary to what many feminists believe, this task requires something other than political passion and advocacy. Only professors dedicated more to their teaching than to their politics—and able to tell the difference—provide us with reason for hope. Although feminist pedagogues typically refuse to recognize the fact, there are vital distinctions to be drawn between teaching that is conscientious and not subservient to politics and teaching that attempts to persuade students to sign onto a particular political vision—the vision proudly announced by feminist teachers, programs, and even entire institutions. The important role of educators is precisely not to deny but to embrace these distinctions, to observe them, and indeed to cherish them.

Discussion Questions

1. What concerns and practices does the addition of the word *feminist* bring to research and teaching?

2. How valid is the underlying argument made by feminists that prior researchers and teachers were just as political as academic feminists are today in their own teaching and research?

3. What would be the likely consequences if a widespread feminist restructuring of research and teaching were to occur in all aspects of education and intellectual life?

4. Alternatively, what would education look like were all academic programs to adopt their own (not necessarily feminist) overtly political agendas?

Online Resources

Women's Studies E-mail List

listserv@listserv.umd.edu

Joan Korenman, a pioneer in using the Internet to promote women's studies, founded and maintains a number of extremely informative online resources relating to women's studies. The most widely subscribed one is the Women's Studies e-mail list (WMST-L), established in 1991. It is described on its home page as "an electronic forum for Women's Studies teaching, research, and program administration." The list (in English) currently has more than 5,200 subscribers in 47 countries, although most active participants are concentrated in the United States.

Women's Studies/Women's Issues Resource Sites

http://userpages.umbc.edu/~korenman/wmst/links.html

Another important endeavor of Korenman's is the Women's Studies/Women's Issues Resource Sites, described as "a selective, annotated, highly acclaimed listing of web sites containing resources and information about women's studies/women's issues, with an emphasis on sites of particular use to an academic women's studies program."

National Women's Studies Association (NWSA)

http://www.nwsa.org/about/index.php

The National Women's Studies Association (NWSA), established in 1977, describes itself as "leading the field of women's studies in educational and social transformation." Its mission is as follows: "Our members actively pursue a just world in which all persons can develop to their fullest potential—one free from ideologies, structures, or systems of privilege that oppress or exploit some for the advantage of others."

The above three sources promote women's studies and feminism in academe. By contrast, the following resources defend intellectual and educational endeavors from politicization and promote informed and unbiased work not subject to academic orthodoxies.

Relevant Journals

Butterflies and Wheels

Feminist Collections

Minding the Campus

Philosophy and Literature

Notes

1. Johnson (2009) has extensively criticized "social justice" criteria in schools of social work and education (i.e., criteria demanding currently approved political positions on race, class, gender, sexuality, etc.). "Dispositions theory" is the pretext by which faculty can evaluate their students' professional suitability on personal (read: political) rather than academic grounds. Johnson himself had to undertake a legal battle to combat Brooklyn College's denial of tenure to him on the grounds of his deficient "collegiality." His offense was to criticize hiring and promotion criteria based on race and sex rather than on academic qualifications (see Johnson, 2003).

2. This is the new name of the program at the University of Massachusetts Amherst, where I teach. In addition to an undergraduate major and minor, the program offers a "Graduate Certificate in Advanced Feminist Studies." The certificate requires a final research paper described as follows: "Whatever the field of study, the research paper must focus on the intersection of race, class, gender, sexuality and, if relevant, transnational issues" (see University of Massachusetts Amherst, n.d.).

3. As Susan Sontag famously said, "When you want to change everything, you're forced to oppress" (Poague, 1995, p. 103).

4. For recent examples of this position from various English-speaking countries, see Women's Studies e-mail list at wmst-1 @listserv.umd.edu, August 22–25, 2005. The posting by J. L. Tallentire (2005; then a Canadian graduate student in history and women's studies, now a professor) is a particularly clear exposition of the feminist claim as it is absorbed by students: "Anyone who complains about the proselytizing in some classrooms but not others is simply mistaken about the nature of teaching. Feminists have seen fit to face it and embrace it, because we recognize that politics has *always* been in the classrooms we attended—a politics that left women and marginalized peoples out, usually—and we needed to get our own in there too."

5. Koertge (2003) goes on to analyze three books (including Anne Fausto-Sterling [2000], discussed below) that represent some of the most widely known feminist works on science, demonstrating the faulty research strategies each engages in. In an earlier chapter, Koertge and I analyze the very popular book *Women's Ways of Knowing* and its profound impact on feminist teaching (Patai & Koertge, 2003). Cassandra L. Pinnick (2000), in her review essay "Feminist Philosophy of Science: High Hopes," takes on the claim made by feminists that feminist science is better than ordinary science.

6. Noretta Koertge and I refer to this predilection in women's studies as "biodenial" (Patai & Koertge, 2003, chap. 6). For an intriguing and amusing critique of the zealous embrace of social constructionism, see Ian Craib (1997, pp. 10, 11), who asks what anxieties might give rise to comforting collective beliefs not open to rational debate and suggests that extreme social constructionism (which he calls a "manic psychosis") allows us to fantasize control over change, which in fact we do not possess.

7. See Patai (1998), from which some passages in the present essay are adapted.

8. See Toro at http://www.alasdemariposa .org/p_eng/02history.htm, retrieved on October 14, 2010. My thanks to Allen Esterson for introducing me to Toro's work.

9. For an interesting example of a women's studies reader that does register a bit of criticism of the field while attempting to inoculate its readers against that criticism, see Sheila Ruth (1998). For a recent example of how higher education in general has absorbed and imposed (or tried to) politically correct perspectives on students, see http://thefire.org/ case/752. The Foundation of Individual Rights in Education (FIRE) had to intervene to undo a mandatory indoctrination program in the residence halls at the University of Delaware. The program forced the 7,000 students living in residence halls to attend sessions aimed at instilling attitudes and views the university considered correct on questions of race, politics, sexuality, the environment, and a number of other such issues. See FIRE's website, thefire.org, where accounts of scores of similar cases are archived.

10. For an example of work that incorporates critiques of science without falling prey to what she calls the "New Cynicism," see Haack (2003).

11. See, for example, PBS's *NewsHour With Jim Lehrer* ("Evolution Debate," 2005). For a thorough analysis of the flaws of the controversy surrounding the teaching of intelligent design, which, in my view, has implications for the feminist attack on "positive" knowledge generally, see Jerry Coyne (2005).

12. For an analysis of the retrograde effects on less developed countries of anti-Western, antiscience,

and postmodernist fashions (including feminist critiques of science), see the important work of Meera Nanda (1998, 2003).

REFERENCES AND ADDITIONAL READING

Bauerlein, M. (2010, April 26). Teach social justice—or else. *Minding the Campus.* Retrieved September 22, 2010, from http://www.mindingthecampus.com/forum/2010/04/teach_social_justiceor_else.html

Bloom, H. (1994). *The Western canon: The books and school of the ages.* New York: Harcourt Brace.

Boghossian, P. A. (2001, February 23). What is social construction? Flaws and contradictions in the claim that scientific beliefs are "merely locally accepted." *Times Literary Supplement,* pp. 6–8.

Boyer, E. (1990). *Scholarship reconsidered: Priorities of the professoriate.* Princeton, NJ: Carnegie Foundation for the Advancement of Teaching.

Carlson, K. B. (2010, January 4). Women's studies R.I.P. *National Post.* Retrieved September 20, 2010, from http://www.nationalpost.com/news/story.html?id=2480860#ixzz10YQKJ07Z

Clery, S. B., & Christopher, B. L. (2009). Faculty salaries: 2008–2009. In *The NEA 2010 Almanac of Higher Education* (pp. 7–28). Retrieved October 3, 2010, from http://www.nea.org/home/38294.htm

Cochran-Smith, M., Barnatt, J., Lahann, R., Shakman, K., & Terrell, D. (2008). Teacher education for social justice: Critiquing the critiques. In W. Ayers, T. Quinn, & D. Stovall (Eds.), *The handbook of social justice in education* (pp. 625–639). Philadelphia: Taylor & Francis.

Connelly, J., & Grüttner, M. (Eds.). (2005). *Universities under dictatorship.* University Park: Pennsylvania State University Press.

Cook, P. W. (1997). *Abused men: The hidden side of domestic violence.* Westport, CT: Praeger.

Coyne, J. (2005, August 22). The faith that dare not speak its name. *The New Republic.* Retrieved May 19, 2006, from www.tnr.com/doc.mhtml?i=20050822&s=coyne082205

Crabtree, R. D., Sapp, D. A., & Licona, A. C. (Eds.). (2009). *Feminist pedagogy: Looking back to move forward.* Baltimore: Johns Hopkins University Press.

Craib, I. (1997). Social constructionism as a social psychosis. *Sociology, 31*(1), 1–15.

Davis, D. R. (2010). Unmirroring pedagogies: Teaching with intersectional and transnational methods in the women and gender studies classroom. *Feminist Formations, 22*(1), 136–162.

Dill, B. T., McLaughlin, A. E., & Nieves, A. D. (2007). Future directions of feminist research: Intersectionality. In S. N. Hesse-Biber (Ed.), *Handbook of feminist research: Theory and praxis* (pp. 629–637). Thousand Oaks, CA: Sage.

Echols, E. (1989). *Daring to be bad: Radical feminism in America, 1967–1975.* Minneapolis: University of Minnesota Press.

Esterson, A. (2010, April 18). Scholarly standards in feminist science studies. *Butterflies and Wheels.* Retrieved September 24, 2010, from http://www.butterfliesandwheels.org/2010/scholarly-standards-in-feminist-science-studies/

Evolution debate. (2005, March 28). *NewsHour With Jim Lehrer.* Retrieved May 19, 2006, from http://www.pbs.org/newshour/bb/education/jan-june05/creation_3–28.html

Fausto-Sterling, A. (2000). *Sexing the body: Gender politics and the construction of sexuality.* New York: Basic Books.

Fish, S. (2008). *Save the world on your own time.* New York: Oxford University Press.

Fish, S. (2010). I know it when I see it. In E. Kiss & J. P. Euben (Eds.), *Debating moral education: Rethinking the role of the modern university* (pp. 76–81). Durham, NC: Duke University Press.

Fisher, B. S., Daigle, L. E., & Cullen, F. T. (2010). *Unsafe in the ivory tower: The sexual victimization of college women.* Thousand Oaks, CA: Sage.

Furchtgott-Roth, D. (2010, November 11). The 77% income fallacy. *Realclearmarkets.* Retrieved November 13, 2010, from http://www.realclearmarkets.com/articles/2010/11/11/the_77_of_income_fallacy_98754.html

Ginsberg, A. E. (Ed.). (2008). *The evolution of American women's studies: Reflections on triumphs, controversies, and change.* New York: Palgrave Macmillan.

Goldin, C., & Katz, L. F. (2005, January 23). Summers is right. *Boston Globe.*

Haack, S. (1998a). Knowledge and propaganda: Reflections of an old feminist. In *Manifesto of a passionate moderate: Unfashionable essays.* Chicago: University of Chicago Press.

Haack, S. (1998b). Science as social?—Yes and no. In *Manifesto of a passionate moderate: Unfashionable essays.* Chicago: University of Chicago Press.

Haack, S. (2003). *Defending science—within reason: Between scientism and cynicism.* Amherst, NY: Prometheus.

Halberstam J. (2005, May 9). The death of English. *Insidehighered.* Retrieved September 24, 2010, from http://www.insidehighered.com/views/2005/05/09/halberstam

Halfin, I. (2009). *Stalinist confessions: Messianism and terror at the Leningrad Communist University.* Pittsburgh: University of Pittsburgh Press.

Hatten, J. (2005, August 24). Message posted to Women's Studies electronic mailing list. Archived at www.wmst-1 @listserv.umd.edu

Herzig, R. M. (2001). What about biology? Building sciences into introductory women's studies curricula. In M. Mayberry, B. Subramaniam, & L. H. Weasel (Eds.), *Feminist science studies: A new generation* (pp. 183–192). New York: Routledge.

Horowitz, D. (2003). *Academic bill of rights.* Retrieved May 19, 2006, from www.students foracademicfreedom.org

Irigaray, L. (1982). Le sujet de la science est-il sexué? [Is the subject of science sexed?]. *Les Temps modernes, 9*(436), 960–974.

Jiménez, I. (2009). Feminist teacher [Web log post]. Retrieved September 28, 2010, from http://feministteacher.com/about-feminist-teacher/

Johnson, K. C. (2003). My Brooklyn College tenure battle. *History News Network.* Retrieved October 15, 2010, from http://hnn.us/articles/1470.html

Johnson, K. C. (2009, October 20). The slippery use of "social justice." *Minding the Campus.* Retrieved September 22, 2010, at http://www.mindingthecampus.com/forum/2009/10/by_kc_johnson_for_educational.html

Kane, S. (2001, February 24). Message posted to Women's Studies electronic mailing list. Archived at www.wmst-1 @listserv.umd.edu

Kiss, E., & Euben, J. P. (Eds.). (2010). *Debating moral education: Rethinking the role of the modern university.* Durham, NC: Duke University Press.

Koerber, A., & Lay, M. M. (2002). Understanding women's concerns in the international setting through the lens of science and technology. In M. M. Lay, J. Monk, & D. S. Rosenfelt (Eds.), *Encompassing gender: Integrating international studies and women's studies* (p. 82). New York: Feminist Press.

Koertge, N. (2003). Feminists take on science: Tilting at the evil empire. In D. Patai & N. Koertge (Eds.), *Professing feminism: Education and indoctrination*

in women's studies (Rev. ed., pp. 321–362). Lanham, MD: Lexington Books.

Kolodny, A. (1998a). *Failing the future: A dean looks at higher education in the twenty-first century.* Durham, NC: Duke University Press.

Kolodny, A. (1998b). Paying the price of antifeminist intellectual harassment. In V. Clark, S. N. Garner, M. Higgonet, & K. H. Katrak (Eds.). *Antifeminism in the academy* (pp. 3–33). New York: Routledge.

Letherby, G. (2003). *Feminist research in theory and practice.* Buckingham, UK: Open University Press.

MacKinnon, C. A. (1987). *Feminism unmodified: Discourses on life and law.* Cambridge, MA: Harvard University Press.

MacNabb, E. L., Cherry, M. J., Popham, S. L., & Prys, R. P. (Eds.). (2001). *Transforming the disciplines: A women's studies primer.* New York: Haworth.

Marks, E. (2000). Feminism's perverse effects. *Signs: Journal of Women in Culture and Society, 25*(4), 1161–1166.

Masaracchia, R. (2001, March 1). Message posted to Women's Studies electronic mailing list. Archived at wmst-1 @listserv.umd.edu

Mayberry, M., Subramaniam, B., & Weasel, L. H. (2001). Adventures across natures and cultures: An introduction. In M. Mayberry, B. Subramaniam, & L. H. Weasel (Eds.), *Feminist science studies: A new generation* (pp. 1–11). New York: Routledge.

Musial, J. (2005, August 23). Message posted to Women's Studies electronic mailing list. Archived at wmst-1 @listserv.umd.edu

Nanda, M. (1998). The epistemic charity of the social constructivist critics of science and why the Third World should refuse the offer. In N. Koertge (Ed.), *A house built on sand: Exposing postmodernist myths about science* (pp. 286–311). New York: Oxford University Press.

Nanda, M. (2003). *Prophets facing backward: Postmodern critiques of science and Hindu nationalism in India.* New Brunswick, NJ: Rutgers University Press.

National Education Association. (2010). *NEA 2010 almanac of higher education.* Washington, DC: Author. Retrieved October 12, 2010, from http://www.nea.org/home/38294.htmp

National Women's Studies Association. (2010). *Mission statement.* Retrieved October 3, 2010, from http://www.nwsa.org/govern/policy.php

National Women's Studies Association. (n.d.). Home page. Retrieved September 25, 2010, from http://www.nwsa.org/index.php

Patai, D. (1998). *Heterophobia: Sexual harassment and the future of feminism.* Lanham, MD: Rowman & Littlefield.

Patai, D. (2000). The state of women's studies. *Chronicle of Higher Education.* Retrieved May 19, 2006, from http://chronicle.com/colloquylive/transcripts/2000/10/20001004patai.htm

Patai, D. (2001, August 5). Biology and silence. Message posted to Women's Studies electronic mailing list. Archived at wmst-1 @listserv.umd.edu

Patai, D. (2008). The fading face of humanism. In *What price utopia? Essays on ideological policing, feminism, and academic affairs* (pp. 1–11). Lanham, MD: Rowman & Littlefield.

Patai, D., & Koertge, N. (2003). *Professing feminism: Education and indoctrination in women's studies* (Rev. ed.). Lanham, MD: Lexington Books.

Pilcher, J., & Whelehan, I. (2004). *Fifty key concepts in gender studies.* London: Sage.

Pinnick, C. L. (2000). Feminist philosophy of science: High hopes. *Metascience, 9*(2), 257–266.

Poague, J. (Ed.). (1995). *Conversations with Susan Sontag.* Jackson: University of Mississippi Press.

Rice, P., & Waugh, P. (Eds.). (2001). *Modern literary theory: A reader* (4th ed.). London: Arnold.

Ristock, J. L. (2002). *No more secrets: Violence in lesbian relationships.* New York: Routledge.

Rogers, M. F., & Garrett, C. D. (2002). *Who's afraid of women's studies? Feminisms in everyday life.* Walnut Creek, CA: AltaMira Press.

Ropers-Huilman, R. (2009). Editorial introduction. *NWSA Journal, 21*(1), vii.

Ropers-Huilman, R. (2010). Editorial introduction. *Feminist Formations, 22*(1), vii. http://www.cehd.umn.edu/feminist-formations/

Rudacille, D. (2005). *The riddle of gender: Science, activism, and transgender rights.* New York: Pantheon.

Ruth, S. (Ed.). (1998). *Issues in feminism: An introduction to women's studies* (4th ed.). London: Mayfield.

Sax, L. (2002). How common is intersex? A response to Anne Fausto-Sterling. *Journal of Sex Research, 39*(3), 174–179. Retrieved May 20, 2006, from http://www.findarticles.com/p/articles/mi_m2372/is_3_39/ai_94130

Scollay, S. J., & Bratt, C. S. (1997). Untying the Gordian knot of academic sexual harassment. In B. R. Sandler & R. J. Shoops (Eds.), *Sexual harassment on campus: A guide for administrators, faculty, and students* (pp. 261–277). Boston: Allyn & Bacon.

Scott, J. W. (Ed.). (2008). *Women's studies on the edge.* Durham, NC: Duke University Press.

Slagter, J. T., & Forbes, K. (2009). Sexual harassment policy: Bureaucratic audit culture, and women's studies. *NWSA Journal, 21*(2), 144.

Sokal, A., & Bricmont, J. (1998). *Fashionable nonsense: Postmodern intellectuals' abuse of science.* New York: Picador.

Subramaniam, B. (2001). And the mirror cracked! Reflections of natures and cultures. In M. Mayberry, B. Subramaniam, & L. H. Weasel (Eds.), *Feminist science studies: A new generation* (p. 57). New York: Routledge.

Tallentire, J. L. (2005, August 24). Message posted to Women's Studies electronic mailing list. Archived at www.wmst-1 @listserv.umd.edu

Tallis, R. (2000). Evidence-based and evidence-free generalisations. In M. Grant (Ed.), *The Raymond Tallis reader* (pp. 309–329). Hampshire, UK: Palgrave.

Trimberger, E. K. (1998). Heterosexuality. In W. Mankiller, G. Mink, M. Navarro, B. Smith, & G. Steinem (Eds.), *Reader's companion to U.S. women's history* (p. 255). Boston: Houghton Mifflin.

University of Massachusetts Amherst. (n.d.). *What is women, gender, sexuality studies?* Retrieved November 5, 2010, from http://www.umass.edu/wost/aboutus.htm

U.S. Department of Education. (2010). *The condition of education 2010* (NCES 2010-028). Washington, DC: National Center for Education Statistics. Retrieved September 28, 2010, from http://nces.ed.gov/programs/digest/d09/

Walker, D. L., Geertsema, M., & Barnett, B. (2009). Inverting the inverted pyramid: A conversation about the use of feminist theories to teach journalism. *Feminist Teacher, 19*(3), 177–178.

Whitaker, M. P. L. (2001). Oases in a desert: Why a hydrologist meanders between science and women's studies. In M. Mayberry, B. Subramaniam, & L. H. Weasel (Eds.), *Feminist science studies: A new generation* (p. 49). New York: Routledge.

Winter, B. (2005, August 23, 25). Message posted to Women's Studies electronic mailing list. Archived at www.wmst-1 @listserv.umd.edu

34

TEACHING, TECHNIQUES, AND TECHNOLOGIES OF FEMINIST METHODOLOGY

Online and on the Ground

Debjani Chakravarty, Judith A. Cook, and Mary Margaret Fonow

O ur ideas about feminist methodology have evolved since we first published *Beyond Methodology: Feminist Scholarship as Lived Research* (Fonow & Cook, 1991) and, later, reflected on these ideas and identified newer developments in feminist methodology in a special issue of *Signs: Journal of Women in Culture and Society* devoted to the dilemmas of feminist research practices (Fonow & Cook, 2005). Our commentary here will focus more directly on teaching feminist methodology to graduate students and training feminist policy researchers in a range of virtual and online settings and contexts including seminars, workshops, conferences, and research and training institutes. One important change since our original essay appeared in the first edition of the *Handbook of Feminist Research* (Hesse-Biber, 2007) is the rapid growth of new technologies that affect both the object and mode of feminist inquiry. Because this development has important implications for how we teach feminist

methodology and train policy researchers, we invited Debjani Chakravarty, a doctoral student in gender studies at Arizona State University and a former student in Fonow's feminist methodology graduate seminar, to reflect on these new technological developments and what they might mean for feminist scholars.

We are often asked to define and defend feminist methodology as a unique methodology, and we have always resisted giving a precise response because we do not want to foreclose new avenues of inquiry and discovery. Feminist methodology, we believe, involves the description, explanation, and justification of techniques used in feminist research and scholarship and is an abstract classification that refers to a variety of methodological stances, conceptual approaches, and research strategies. Feminist methodologies include epistemological arguments on how to apprehend the social; the evaluation of specific research techniques and practices; the formulation of research questions and designs that capture the historical,

693

intersectional, and transnational dimensions of women's lives and gender relations; attention to the ethical and policy implications of research; acknowledgment of the representational quality of research and scholarship; and attention to the outcomes of research including the development of multiple strategies for the dissemination of research findings.

A GRADUATE SEMINAR ON FEMINIST METHODOLOGY

In 2001, Fonow and Lather, her colleague at Ohio State, designed a feminist methodology course for the graduate curriculum in women's studies at Ohio State University. Lather (2001, 2007; Lather & Smithies, 1997) is a professor of cultural studies in education and an international expert on critical and feminist methodology. We did not intend the course to be a practical, "how-to" course but rather a course that used feminist insights to theorize about the conduct of inquiry and, in the process, open new paths of discovery. We sought to establish an interdisciplinary feminist plane from which we could analyze research practices in women's studies and in education and make informed decisions about our individual projects. Readings for the course focus on the methodological implications of feminist epistemologies; the ethical dilemmas and politics of feminist inquiry; the strategies involved in collecting, interpreting, and analyzing primary material; reflexivity; and issues in representation. We use texts that include methodological reflections and analysis of race, class, gender, nation, and sexuality in the production of social and cultural knowledge.

The seminar explores the pleasures and anxieties of doing research through exercises and activities that afford students the opportunity to visit the backstage of knowledge production. We demystify the research process by inviting researchers to share early versions of their own work and by sharing our early drafts, by having students deconstruct a published text by feminist scholars, and by staging a mini-conference at the end of the course, which re-creates a typical professional meeting, complete with organizers and discussants and with each student presenting her or his final paper.

One particularly fruitful exercise is to have students deconstruct a published monograph written by a feminist scholar. The purpose of the exercise is to provide students with examples of the type of methods and interpretative approaches they might use in their own work, and we ask them to read as much for what is missing as for what is included. They answer the following set of questions about the exemplar and share answers with the rest of the class:

- What is the book's object of inquiry?
- What are the key research questions?
- What materials, data, and primary sources are used?
- What methodological approach does the author employ? Why is it feminist? How is the choice justified?
- What specific methods, techniques, or interpretative strategies are used?
- Is it interdisciplinary and why?
- If you could interview the author, what questions would you ask about her or his methodological choices?

In another exercise, we ask students to select one feminist academic journal from a list provided by us and write a profile of that journal. The purpose of the exercise is to familiarize students with the publishing process and with the topics and methods being used by feminist scholars. They are often surprised to see how little explicit attention is given to methodological discussions in published journal articles. We use this opportunity to explain the peer-review process and to share with them the various stages our own work has passed through on the way to final publication. The profile consists of the history and focus of the journal, the nature of the editorial board, the journal's intended audience and circulation, acceptance rate, and impact factor. Students choose two issues of the journal and describe topics, epistemological characteristics, and methodological strategies and techniques and analyze what makes it feminist scholarship. We ask them to pay particular attention to how researchers validate their knowledge claims and use writing as a tool of analysis.

The seminar situates feminist methodology within the context of early feminist critiques of science, particularly the critiques of positivism. To make the debates about positivism intelligible to students, we show the 1965 film *Obedience*, a documentary about the famous Milgram laboratory experiments that were conducted at Yale. The grainy, black-and-white film features a researcher in a white lab coat who tells subjects to administer electrical shocks to research confederates when they make a mistake in matching pairs of nonsense words. We use the film as a springboard to discuss the logic of experimental design (e.g., sampling, conceptualization, operationalization, cognitive authority, norms of science) and to discuss the ethical implications of human subject research and the university's Human Subject Review process. Next, the course introduces some of the epistemological issues associated with feminist methodology. We view epistemology at the most general level as the framework for specifying the generation of knowledge: How does the knower come to understand and interpret the nature of reality? We see the domain of epistemology as concerned with larger philosophical questions: What is knowledge? Who can know and by what means? How do we recognize, validate, and evaluate knowledge claims? Women of color have raised important questions concerning the epistemologies of the oppressed: Do oppressed people, by virtue of their knowledge of both the oppressor's views of reality and that of their own subjugated groups, have access to truer or better knowledge of reality? Who is privileged in an epistemological sense—feminists, women of color, lesbians, working-class women, postcolonials? Who can speak for whom (Fonow & Cook, 2005)?

The actual methods we cover vary and are chosen more to reflect the general principles of feminist methodology than a comprehensive review of all the possibilities. Graduate students are encouraged to seek broad training in research methods through research seminars and other methodology courses in historiography, visual and textual analysis, survey, ethnography, and so on. We are concerned that students understand how to select and defend their choices in the design, collection, representation, and interpretation of data. We ask them to consider the following questions: What methods will help you to answer your research question, and what is your rationale for selecting this approach? How are you, as the researcher,

situated in this project? What ethical safeguards are you planning for your study and how do they reflect feminist ethics? What are your responsibilities as a feminist researcher? How does your approach address difference (marked and unmarked)? Will research subjects play a role in the research, and what are some of the dilemmas of involving research subjects? How do you plan to represent your findings, and what are the politics involved in such a representation?

We no longer teach at the same university, but we continue to exchange ideas for the course and keep each other informed about new developments and resources. For example, the *Handbook of Feminist Research* is a new resource that did not exist when we originally designed the course, and it does a good job of organizing many of the debates and exemplars of feminist research in one convenient place. Consequently, I have assigned it as either the main text or a supplement. Increasingly, feminist journals such as *Signs: Journal of Women in Culture and Society, Frontiers: A Journal of Women Studies,* and *Feminist Theory* have devoted special issues to the topic of feminist methodology, and I use selections from each (see Campbell & Fonow, 2009; Harding & Norberg, 2005; "Intimate Public Practices," 2009). In addition, there is a proliferation of online resources (see the list at the end of this chapter) that serve as rich resources for course materials and are discussed more fully below in the section titled "New Technologies."

I begin the course with critiques of normative social science as a way to move toward more complex epistemological and ontological discussions about the nature of inquiry, including critiques, revisions, and innovations in feminist approaches. I emphasize that, although feminists acknowledge that research is messy and that there are some things we simply cannot know (at least at this time), we can, and in fact must, proceed to create feminist knowledge. To get them to embrace the messiness of doing and undoing research and not be stymied, I assign Lather's *Getting Lost* (2007). For Lather, there is value in loss: loss of control, comprehension, and comfort. Students warm up to the idea that they, too, are like Lather and her research subjects—"unreliable narrators" struggling with the "unreadability" of experience. The students begin to come to terms with the value of "rigorous confusion," but it is confusion all the same. They vacillate between moments of total loss and moments of clarity as they struggle with the indeterminacy of language and the meaning of deconstruction, detachment, and data. Students grapple with questions such as these: How does "post" enable ethnography with a new criticality? How is failure an enabling device? How can loss be central to a radical feminist epistemology? What should praxis embrace—solution or identification? "Doing" feminist research can never be the same after we struggle with Lather's utterly maddening yet immensely engaging accounts of textwork, headwork, and fieldwork.

Reading about how others do feminist research is important, but students need an opportunity to try out various approaches, methods, and techniques of data collection and analysis, and I now incorporate more hands-on research exercises in the seminar. I try to avoid the quantitative-qualitative distinction since most of the students I teach are PhD students in women and gender studies or students from the humanities or social sciences who are pursuing a graduate certificate in gender studies. They are interested in interdisciplinary research tools that will allow them to address research questions that bridge the old divides within the social sciences as well as the divides between the social sciences, the humanities, and, increasingly, the natural sciences—particularly science and environmental studies. The certificate students are interested in research approaches that they cannot find in their own programs and welcome unorthodox feminist ideas about knowledge construction. For example, a doctoral student in social work who wanted to develop a measure of transphobia discovered that the conventional training in her field did not prepare her for the complexity of the task but that feminist approaches to measurement grounded in queer theory and lived "experience" did. Another student from the humanities who is conducting research on sex trafficking discovered ways she could apply her training in discourse analysis in the English department to ethnographic interview data. Our own students in women and gender studies benefit from the exchanges with the certificate students, and we encourage them to take methods courses in other programs. In addition to my

course, our PhD students are required to take a research design course and two additional methods courses related to their dissertations (although the term *methods* is broadly defined and the courses can be from anywhere on campus). One doing a dissertation about gender and the urban garden movement has taken courses at the Arizona State University's School of Sustainability, the first in the country.

It is a tall order to cover specific methods that will resonate across such an eclectic group—but well worth the effort. To give students practice using different methodological tools, I developed an exercise based on Adele Clarke's (2005) situational analysis (SA). I treat SA as a heuristic device or strategy for organizing, collecting, and analyzing evidence or data regardless of topic. It provides students with the opportunity to explore the link between theory and method and to learn how to use a variety of methods, including discourse analysis, observation, mapping, and interviewing. As a class, we visit a very large discount mall that is divided up into smaller, discrete shopping neighborhoods. Students observe a specific neighborhood first as individuals and then in teams. They take notes on their observations and construct three types of empirical maps; situational maps, social world maps, and positional maps. Next, they devise a questionnaire from their observations and maps and conduct an interview with one of the social actors from the mall's social world— for example, a teen shopper, security guard, buyer, or clerk. We then map out each neighborhood in relationship to the mall as a whole. The maps help students see the relationships between various elements in the field and various positions taken and not taken in the data vis-à-vis their situation of concern. SA helps students make connections between the human and the nonhuman, between the material and the symbolic, and to understand how discourses function to render some actors and situations more visible than others. The students gather their data on social worlds from the messy maps and ordered maps and go on to explore processes, discourses, and people that flow through the mall.

For example, Chakravarty focused on the mobile semipermanent or temporary kiosks or carts that are placed in the passageways between entrances of larger permanent stores as spaces of queerness and contradictions, ambivalence and cognitive dissonance. She interviewed kiosk clerks who represented under-researched social groups or individuals: for example, legal immigrants working illegally and a queer single mother who fell through the Temporary Assistance for Needy Families (1997) safety net for not fulfilling all the "responsibility requirements" and getting a job in time. The kiosks represented a safe space where there is safety in transience and anonymity, but they are unsafe in their inability to generate steady income for those that work there. The kiosks are also situated in what Clarke (2007) designates as the "boundaries or margins that produce the center," and they exemplify spaces where the "alternative relational modality of representation does not concern itself particularly with frequency but instead with positions and their distribution across some kinds of situational or topographical maps that do the work of helping us to 'see' the range of positions" (p. 356). Chakravarty's work, briefly outlined here, demonstrates the complex and sophisticated research possible when seminar members work through theoretical discussions on methods, analyze the actual "products" of feminist research, and "do" the research.

In spite of the successes of my students, the more I teach the seminar, the more I see what is missing. Fortunately, there are a number of recent and forthcoming publications that go a long way to fill in the gaps. Just when I thought no one would ever come clean about various aspects of the research process, we have several recent publications to guide us, including Kristin Luker's (2008) *Salsa Dancing Into the Social Sciences: Research in an Age of Info-Glut*, Eszter Hargittai's (2008) *Research Confidential: Solutions to Problems Most Social Scientists Pretend They Never Have*, and Ramsey, Sharer, L'Eattenier, and Mastrangelo's (2010) *Working in the Archives: Practical Research Methods for Rhetoric and Composition*. Luker believes that the way we teach about methods has not caught up with post-Foucauldian notions about the nature of social reality. Many people teaching about methods to graduate students came of age in the pre-Foucauldian age when researchers believed that there was an unmediated reality "out there" that we could apprehend if we just had the right method, when there was

a scarcity of information compared with today's glut, and when the logic guiding our world was more linear than the hypertext one inhabited by our students today. Luker provides an honest gut check about her own methodological advice to graduate students and recommends that we also deal more honestly with our own students. She uses salsa dancing as a metaphor for how to practice research in the post-Foucauldian era. Salsa dancing, like social research, requires the practice of structured moves but provides space for improvisation. Luker (2008) writes,

> As your shoes trace new patterns on the dance floor and your hips start to swivel, a different part of your mind takes over and you find yourself drifting into new intellectual areas, making connections across boundaries and even across disciplines. You suddenly find yourself knowing things you didn't know you knew. (p. 2)

Flexible thinking in our information-saturated social world is required if we ever hope to address the types of complex issues we desire to understand. Luker (2008) details her own struggles with trying to make canonical methods fit her research questions and demonstrates how to be inventive while still attending to the concerns that have preoccupied conventional methods, such as sampling, validity, reliability, empirical generalizations, and data reduction and analysis. She gives practical advice, shows how she solved many different dilemmas, covers specific methods, and gives tips on how to navigate the rich minefield of the Internet. This book will help students gain confidence in their own research judgments.

The essays in *Research Confidential*, edited by Hargittai (2008), are written by younger scholars whose memories of their own struggles to produce a dissertation are still fresh in their minds. Hargittai is an associate professor in communications at Northwestern University who also writes a career advice column for *Inside Higher Ed*, and she has excellent rapport with young scholars. The book provides a behind-the-scenes examination of conducting empirical research with the goal of confronting head-on the obstacles less seasoned researchers often encounter in the early phases of their careers, when the pressure to publish is most keenly felt. The project was born from Hargittai's own frustration as a graduate student and later as a junior faculty member, a frustration stemming from her effort to learn how to do research from textbooks that were too general or from published results that were too polished. Hidden from view was the practical advice she needed to overcome the ordinary obstacles most researchers face but never talk about, at least in public, things like how many subjects you need to contact before you find someone willing to talk to you or how long it may take to get institutional review board (IRB) approval. The book covers a broad range of topics with a special emphasis on new technologies: how to use them for research and how to research the technologies themselves.

Another excellent practical research guide for feminist scholars is *Working in the Archives* (Ramsey et al., 2010). Although designed specifically for researchers in rhetoric and composition, it is a valuable resource for anyone doing archival research. The essays, many written by feminists, cover a wide range of topics including archival theory, the use of hidden or digital archives, search tools, locating and using letters and photographs, how to get the most out of an archive, and even the joys of building your own archive. The emphasis of the collection is on the created nature of all archives, and the text focuses on what is included as well as what is excluded, as its opening quotation from Carol Steedman (2002) demonstrates: "The Archive is made from selected and consciously chosen documentation from the past and also from the mad fragments that no one intended to preserve and that just ended up there" (p. 68). I coupled readings from *Working in the Archives* with a field trip to the archive at my university and a workshop on using virtual archives.

Finally, we have a how-to feminist research textbook, *Doing Feminist Research in Political and Social Science,* by Brooke Ackerly and Jacqui True (2010). They guide students through the research process in a way that reveals the underlying methodological structure of feminist research praxis. They argue, "Making a feminist research project accessible to a non-feminist academic audience is not about concealing its feminism: it is about revealing its theoretical and methodological rigor" (Ackerly & True, 2010, p. 4). Each chapter contains key concepts, boxed inserts with useful research tips, and suggestions for further reading. There is also a website associated with the text that hosts other supporting material and resources, such as practical research exercises, a glossary of terms, examples for ongoing feminist research projects, and the authors' own lived experience as feminist researchers. The book was explicitly created to help students develop their own practice of feminist research and is very useful for both advanced undergraduates and graduate students.

TRAINING FEMINIST POLICY RESEARCHERS

As a feminist sociologist whose professional life has been spent in the realm of policy research in the field of mental health disability, Cook has been successful in obtaining and maintaining significant national funding regardless of the political climate. We, as feminist researchers at various stages in our careers, believe that feminists engaged in policy research, especially in organizations that rely on external funding, must be both methodologically rigorous and politically astute in order to assure that their results can be heard by policy makers and that their findings are given the appropriate weight.

It is important for policy researchers to begin with a thorough understanding of the policy being studied. Feminist policy researchers must be able to read and understand policy material written in bureaucratic language that is often tedious and repetitive. Here are questions useful for analyzing policies: How does the language of the law read? How have federal or state agencies interpreted the law? What do regulations or directives based on the law require? How are local administrators using them? What has been the impact on the individuals with whom the feminist researcher is concerned—for example, a mentally ill woman not permitted to stay at a homeless shelter because it is funded as "transitional" even though there is no low-income housing to which she can transition? The next step involves a review of the previous research used to construct the policy you are concerned with—its quality, who conducted it and why, how it was conducted, and what the findings were. This step is important whether the researcher respects or agrees with the research, the researcher, or the findings or believes that the prior research came from a nonfeminist ideological standpoint. In the case of an unfair policy the researcher wants to see changed, it is often very important to see why and how the supporters of the current policy used the earlier research. The feminist researcher should keep in mind that research used to support a policy may not have been designed to be policy research; nevertheless, as soon as it is used to set policy, it has become policy research.

Externally funded research comes with built-in challenges: funding agents may not want to support long-term studies, and policy makers may not be able to wait for a longitudinal study. The researcher will have to balance what the policy makers need with the knowledge that the methods possible in that time frame may not be ideal. When reviewing prior research, the researcher may want to remember that quick-and-dirty techniques may have been used and may not provide a sound foundation for the policy.

Sometimes, reviewing the primary documents and past research is not sufficient, and the researcher may have to contact individuals—individuals who do not necessarily support the researcher's perspective—to gain a better understanding of the policy and its intended purpose. Careful preparation will be required because some individuals are not accustomed to and will not welcome such interviews. Another approach is to find a mentor who knows the policy and can guide the researcher's interpretation, someone who can say, for example, what Congress meant when the law was written or who can describe what is happening on the ground now that regulations are out. Researchers must be aware of not only their own bias but also the bias an informant may bring to any interpretation of the policy and of its aims and realities.

Once the policy is thoroughly understood, the researcher can begin to frame questions that elucidate the policy and its outcomes and to design methodological approaches. Researchers should be careful in thinking about policy questions because their findings can have implications for other policies; the research must answer the primary question, but the researcher should think in advance about other implications of the findings. Sometimes, research findings around the primary question do not support the policy's goal, but the research may show unintended positive consequences. For example, a government-funded preschool intervention program did not lead to higher test scores, but it had other positive outcomes: the children's parents were more active at the school and the home lives of these children were more stable. The positive family results may be enough to support ongoing funding, and the agency providing the program can now seek ways to use the family benefits to lead to increased test scores.

It is often useful to employ multiple methods when conducting policy research. The choice of methods should be guided by knowledge of how policy makers are likely to use the research results. Sometimes, a policy maker is less persuaded by numbers than by personal stories, but that is an individual question; if researchers have not used quotations from interviews, a policy maker may not be open to qualitative approaches. Qualitative approaches alone may be persuasive when the findings are egregious or unanimous. For example, if in-depth interviews with 25 single-mother welfare recipients revealed that every one cited some form of coercion by her caseworker, although the researcher cannot hypothesize about the prevalence of coercion overall, the finding may warrant further investigation by the policy makers. Sometimes, policy makers are able to use the stories gleaned from qualitative research to convince their constituencies that a change is needed.

Large data sets frequently remain untapped as resources, yet interesting or radical stories may be hiding in these data. Sometimes, large data sets are the sole source of information on a problem, and, if researchers understood the data better, they could demonstrate findings that no prospective data collection can. Feminists may be able to effect policy change by analyzing large data sets to see whether counterarguments can be made, by using the data set to answer new questions, or by thinking about new ways to use the data.

Feminists engaged in policy research have an opportunity to change the minds of policy makers in a positive direction; however, change usually cannot be accomplished using theory that is too abstract or by a direct request to adopt a contradictory policy that may threaten the stakeholders of the status quo. The policy researcher must understand the position of those supporting the current policy and the research that helps them maintain their position. Then, the researcher can do similar research with similar methods and determine whether the initial findings hold.

Sometimes, it is possible to impact policy makers by noting that the research covers only a few years of follow-up. The researcher may propose extending the timeline to show that better outcomes could be achieved. Creative researchers look for opportunities, for example, to fund long-term research or to include a different population in the research. Even policy makers who have drawn their "line in the sand" may support policy changes if the researcher provides the evidence to support a different approach. If your research shows that women who have mental health disabilities do not require additional costly health care or social services as long as problems with existing services are rectified, a policy maker may be able to make a fiscal argument to justify a policy change.

Several pitfalls await the unprepared policy researcher. Most policy makers prefer a simple, useful answer, but research findings seldom provide one central finding and may often be complex or ambiguous. We train our graduate students to develop complex research designs, and, although this training is a good thing, we must also train them to think about how policy makers can make use of such complex findings. A related pitfall is presenting too much research to policy makers or presenting research with the kind of hedging that is appropriate for a scholarly journal but not for policy makers. The latter need to know what, overall, is the effect of the policy on the constituencies the policy addresses.

When training feminist scholars, one must pay considerable attention to the ethical issues involved in conducting policy research. Researchers must be able to recognize their investment in the research and manage both their biases and sometimes their disappointment in results.

Feminist researchers often care deeply about the issues and the research participants; nevertheless, it is critical to be reflective about how this level of caring might influence the inquiry or the way findings are presented. The researcher may have difficulty in knowing whether her or his bias is present.

Management of disappointment is also important for policy researchers. A study's findings may provide evidence for an unfair policy's status quo when the researcher expected the opposite. In such situations, a multimethod approach often saves the day by providing qualitative evidence of the policy's negative effects on women that were not apparent when global outcomes were analyzed quantitatively. For example, imagine that a researcher's data find equivalent work outcomes for an employment program designed to assist both men and women, even though it is widely recognized that program services are designed around the needs of men and are difficult for women to access. By using quotations from interviews with women describing how lack of child care and transportation made it difficult to access services, the researcher can clarify how gender inequities exist side by side with equivalent work outcomes for men and women.

In presenting findings, one must remember that most policy makers are well-educated, bright individuals. Thus, it may be unnecessary to report findings with extensive interpretation. Instead, the researcher can present factual information in such a way that the facts lead to obvious policy conclusions. One research project, for example, showed the unemployed impacted by a certain policy that had the unintended consequence of discouraging rather than encouraging employment. Had the report stated outright that the policy was motivating people to remain unemployed, the policy makers might not have agreed. The report was therefore structured to lead deductively to that conclusion without having to state it. In this case, the policy makers concluded that they were actually paying people not to work. The well-prepared researcher can help policy makers reach their own understanding.

When a research topic is controversial or has political implications, as do HIV, reproductive choice, and welfare reform, the researcher should anticipate how study findings can be used or abused and prepare for news media attention. When interview requests are made, the well-prepared researcher will learn who the journalist is (newspaper, TV, freelance?), the vehicles and audiences for which he or she writes (*Good Housekeeping* or the *Washington Post?*), and the nature of his or her perspectives or possible biases. Preparing sound bites is helpful to avoid being misunderstood or misquoted. For example, suppose the findings show that people with mental health disabilities have a high quit rate in their first job but that, over time, they stay longer at subsequent jobs and earn higher salaries. Stating the finding chronologically may lead the press to emphasize the quit rate. Instead, the researcher can prepare a sound bite to read, "People with mental health disabilities go on to longer term, better paid employment if allowed to 'try out' one or two jobs beforehand." Such a sound bite accurately reflects the research findings while it helps the media select the more positive results. Finally, researchers should think about what to do if findings are abused, which often occurs when the media report one part of a study's results. Some strategies include seeking a correction, talking to other media to obtain accurate coverage, and contacting related organizations that can refute the abusive statements, for example, by quoting the rest of your results. The findings of policy research can often be used to support a number of arguments; researchers must recognize this and be prepared to handle such issues.

Policy research is quite complex, and it will be difficult to help students conduct research in one semester. Curriculum redesign may be required to allow students enough time to experience a truly feminist policy methodology. One example is a policy internship that lasts more than a quarter or a semester. We also recommend that courses teach multiple methods to increase the versatility of students. Requiring the use of both quantitative and qualitative methods allows students to experience the limitations of using one or the other exclusively. If a student is new to a policy area, using multiple methods can be an effective way to be introduced to a topic. We discussed large data sets earlier, and we recommend teaching the skills needed to do data mining. Students should be able to read policy and related material, conduct interviews, and collect, digest, and analyze both quantitative and qualitative data. Students also benefit from increasing their research-related creativity, for example, by using two additional data sets with the usual approach to find new results. They should have examples that show how different statistical approaches lead to different findings, that demonstrate how effects seen in a smaller data set may shrink when doing policy research on a large scale, and that teach them techniques for the statistical control of the "messiness" in real-world data. Ideally, courses will guide them through different stages of policy research and expose them, through the use of case examples of different policy studies, to typical issues in the design, execution, and interpretation of this research. For example, students may be assigned to look for bias in how a question was phrased. We require students to produce a policy report, an executive summary, and a presentation of findings. We can also benefit our students greatly by introducing them to the special realities of externally funded policy research, such as how to stand out when the researcher is unknown or when the findings or approach are not notable, and the importance of understanding the sponsors' culture and worldview in order to understand their likely responses, objections, and concerns. These are aspects that do not influence the methodologies and yet are important to obtaining and maintaining resources.

Most policy researchers learn best by doing. Internships and pro bono support to organizations are two ways to begin to do policy research. Students might intern at a state agency or in Washington, D.C., to become familiar with the sources of data and types of research and to see how findings are used by political decision makers. Or they could identify and volunteer at organizations that do policy research. Examples include the research divisions of departments of health that are impacting policy, for example, around HIV prevention. Municipal, federal, and state courts often have staff that collect data to assist the judges. Local nonprofit organizations and nongovernmental organizations (NGOs) can provide fruitful internships and can be good places to learn about the need for evaluation and the data they use. Remember, too, that some policy research goes by other names: program evaluation research or needs assessment is often conducted to support policy.

After three decades of conducting research as feminist sociologists in a variety of contexts, we have come to the realization that training students and young policy researchers is an ongoing endeavor. Feminist methodology can be taught in courses and in workshops, but much of it only makes sense when the researcher is in the thick of conducting research. We know the future will involve preparing researchers to think about gender in an increasingly complex world, and, although this will be challenging work, we don't have to do it alone—and we don't have to start from scratch.

NEW TECHNOLOGIES

Technology represents a cutting-edge tool of feminist research and provides the organizing principle and enabling structures for cyberfeminism, a new form of feminist intervention that uses the "cyberspace" for feminist politics. In the hands of feminist researchers and activists, technology can create political identities and strengthen participatory research (Campbell, 2004; Eubanks, 2004; Hawthorne & Klein, 1999), but, in different hands, it can also be a tool for the co-optation of and opposition to feminist goals (McPherson, 2009). The Internet (cyberspace) is both a tool of research and a "field" of inquiry, and, sometimes, these two roles of technology coalesce, creating conceptual confusion. For activists, it signifies a connected way of being, a new form of networked subjectivity, a kind of democratic agency. It might also signify imagined transnational communities and active local ones, inclusion as well as exclusion, and, with feminisms, the cocreation of a powerful methodology.

Internet research methods can advance the interdisciplinary mission of feminist research by opening up research pathways into previously inaccessible or elusive spaces. Cyberspace can allow for multisite, multimethodological, interdisciplinary investigations into issues of representation, identity formation, governmentality, development, policy, and epistemology, to name just a few areas. Interdisciplinarity is imperative because the virtual space that is being studied or made use of as a habitus, field, lifeworld, or resource is not a docile space: it is a space of constant interaction, engagement, and change. Using narrative or content analysis to understand web narratives or using approaches from literary or film criticism to understand visual representations will not be sufficient. Theories of mass communication, political science, or sociology alone will not explain, for example, religious fundamentalism on the web, which turns an online experience or technological innovation into a site of global religious conflict and a persuasive project of ideological domination. Analysis must take into account the exchange of meanings and experience, the immediacy of the accelerated back-and-forth nature of discourse generation, and the real and symbolic conditions of technological and epistemological production, and this will require interdisciplinary approaches.

For example, Haas (2009), in her study of online infertility support communities, brings together the theories and approaches of rhetoric, the sociology of health, history, and cultural and feminist studies to analyze issues of infertility, issues spanning reproductive technologies, medicalization, public policy, and the management of self and subjectivities. Haas examines the online communities where empowerment takes the form of information exchange and sisters (community members) become "cysters" narrating experiences—seeking and giving support. Interdisciplinary approaches that reconfigure conventional approaches from conventional disciplines produce insights that quantitative research on infertility or qualitative research (featuring interviews with "affected" couples or health care professionals) might not be able to generate. The Internet also opens up spaces of engagement that cannot often be subsumed under familiar notions of "cyberfeminism" or "support networks" but that have to be studied using approaches from network analysis and game theory, phenomenology, and critical discourse analysis. Because the Internet represents at the same time a methodological and a substantive realm of research, feminist interdisciplinary online research methods can effectively research gendered lives, experiences, ideational categories, knowledge, relationships and inequalities. Interdisciplinarity in online feminist research creates new concepts such as "cyberfigurations" (Matrix, 2002) and "cyber conduits"

(Pierce, 2007), concepts that enrich academic feminism and redefine the notion of hybridity, borders, and queerness.

Intervention is central to feminist methodology, whether as "active radical listening to create knowledge and policy questions" or as full-fledged action research that can include transformative participatory evaluation, placing the research knowledge generated in the service of the research subjects, contributors, or coresearchers (Brisolara & Seigart, 2007; Hesse-Biber & Piatelli, 2007). Cyberspace has been designated as an activist space by many feminist scholars, a space that allows the formation of virtual kinships for anticapitalist and other forms of struggles, reinvigorates feminist pedagogy, resists gender hierarchy in the realm of technology, and creates conditions for transnational feminisms (Blair, Gajjala, & Tulley, 2009; Eubanks, 2004; Mohanty, 2002; Zukic, 2009). The Internet provides a space and context of feminist activism, advocacy, and action research. Campbell (2004) considers information and communication technology (ICT) to be radically changing the participatory research design, turning methodological principles of participatory research "inside out." Talking about the research project undertaken by her and Eubanks with women in transitional circumstances at the YWCA of Troy-Cohoes, she states that, because it "privileges social learning, redistributes the risks and benefits of research, facilitates scale change, provides methodological flexibility, and offers a problem-posing rather than problem-solving orientation, popular technology [ICT] is well-suited to exploring forms of critical technological citizenship necessary for attainment of social justice in an age of rapid technological change" (Campbell, 2004, p. 72). Campbell describes how a practice of collaborative inquiry can tap the experiences and existing knowledge of research participants (both the knowledge imbricated in the project and that extant in broader shared social contexts) and positions participants as "asset bearing" individuals rather than "skills-deficient" learners of information technology and passive providers of research data. Speaking of the same project, Eubanks (2007), in consultation with her research participants, states that a bridge over the digital divide is an inadequate metaphor of equity: it

creates strapping binaries of haves and have-nots, learners and teachers, reifying the divide and connecting only *two points* instead of looking at the underlying structures of inequality in the political and information economy.

Another example of using popular technology to research gendered social realities is "Blank Noise," an activist project in India that deals with issues of sexual harassment. Blank Noise maintains that calling sexual harassment "Eve teasing" (the popular name for street sexual harassment in India) does not make it any less offensive or illegal. In a society smarting under the burden of globalization where women are negotiating identities between patriarchies and postfeminisms, sexual harassment laws are in place but rarely executed, especially when such harassment happens in crowded streets or on public transportation, where the physical proximity of women's bodies for want of space is exploited by men to satisfy their sexual desires. Blank Noise is an activist blog (supplemented by off line activist interventions), which researches and raises awareness about "Eve teasing" and covers its legal, sociological, historical, and cultural aspects. Activists ask site users to send in their experiences, perspectives, and pictures (of perpetrators, the space where violations occurred, the clothes worn by the woman who was harassed because the overwhelmingly popular conception in India still seems to be that the harassed women wore provocative clothes or otherwise provoked the sexual criminal in some way). User accounts, not just of harassment but also of activism and intervention, are also encouraged. Users complete surveys that are used as data for research. The site provides resources for activism and awareness raising and serves as a platform for debates and discussions, busting popular myths (that make their way into legal interpretations and executions), such as that women "ask for it" or that providing separate "safe spaces" (e.g., on public transportation) for women would solve or contain the problem. Blank Noise exemplifies "imbrication," an inside-out methodology of participatory practice in which subjects are considered expert in their own lives, as explained by Campbell (2004). For Blank Noise, imbrication and intersubjectivity together constitute the normative central organizing principle of participatory research using ICT.

The Internet gives people the opportunity to speak up against injustices such as state and religious violence and other forms of domination that they might not challenge in a face-to-face, extra-virtual world context. The reasons may range from personal discomfort to structural or political threats. Cyberspace provides a safer space for online community formation, and, although this safety is often illusory in the present era of pervasive surveillance, online blogs, forums, and spaces for comments often generate narratives that represent the complex realities of a globalized world. A recent women's studies dissertation completed by Teresa Pierce (2007) explains how the "hypermodern" cyberspace can be harnessed as a feminist methodology that reconfigures usual feminist methods. Her work on Afghan, Iranian, and Iraqi women bloggers demonstrates the use of feminist cybermethods to understand how some women in authoritarian religious societies have found a relatively safe space to represent their everyday lives to the world. However, Pierce (2007) makes an underlying assumption in considering the blogosphere as a chosen site of research:

> Gender online is not an imitation of offline gender. Rather, life online and life offline are different contexts that influence everyday life and the stories we tell about it. And, in their own ways, each of the bloggers reinforced, subverted, and challenged their enculturated gender identities. (p. 242)

Pierce engages in textual analysis of the informal hypertext narratives in personal weblogs by looking at live versions of these blogs, user interactions (comments, discussions), and blog archives. She reconfigures discourse analysis, technical media narrative analysis, and the analysis of personal narratives to suit a feminist investigation of the political web sphere framework. She uses the blogs as an integral part of her case study of cyberspace as a political space, and she presents a "feminist interpretation" of personal narratives and hypertext narratives:

> [I]n weblogs, . . . the structure emerges in the performances and interaction. Both the storyteller and her audience co-produce the story. Moreover, this co-production changes with every interaction, and random access is important. There are

no pre-programmed assets to follow in a weblog, and the story emerges in spontaneous interactivity. In both formal and informal hypertextual narratives, the audience no longer sits in the dark theatre watching the plot evolve; they become part of the plot. (Pierce, 2007, p. 162)

Pierce's subjects challenge the political order (through critiquing the Islamic republic) and the symbolic order (the mainstream civil society— the press, the public spaces of protest and gathering) through inhabiting the virtual sphere where their presence cannot be ignored and cannot be restricted easily. And the researcher, as the audience, can (and did) interact with the writers to interpret and expand the meanings and significations produced by the writing, an interaction that rearranges the Derridean notion of "*différance*." The idea of identity as performatively constituted forms the basis of her argument about the ambiguous identities of her webloggers, problematic identities that subvert cultural categories. In the digital world, the idea of a physical body is not as important as the notion of embodied subjectivity. Pierce explains the nature of communication on the Internet, with the user as both subject and object relying upon multiplicity and differences to form connections. The women bloggers are cyberconduits who engage in subversive politics. Each blogger is "both dynamic and interactive, producing and reproducing her maps while living in political areas mapped by government agreements and, at the same time, subverting state borders by re-mapping . . . physical worlds using digital technology" (Pierce, 2007, p. 344). Pierce suggests that the Internet can be used as an effective public political tool, especially in physical conflict-torn places, where democracy has been repressed. Rather than reaching solid conclusions, Pierce, as another participant in the virtual world, as a reader of the blogs, explores how the bloggers perform gender in virtual spaces (weblogs) that are simultaneously public and private.

In terms of the performance of gender, the Internet provides a kind of queer, hybrid intersubjective space of mediation where the self or selves exist as textual body, taking on a virtual identity, becoming what Butler (1987) calls "subjects of desire" emerging within discourses that do not always follow the rules of conventional epistemic production. Ashford (2009) believes technology heightens our awareness of the fluidity of identity, provides a space and context for interpretive-qualitative analysis marked by an intersubjective consciousness, and presents the possibilities of reducing as well as magnifying the deferral and difference that constitutes "*différance*" in the creation of discourses.

Some scholars argue that the Internet accords opportunities to multiply oppressed groups embodying composite raced, sexed, classed, gendered, and religious identities to interact, network, and create selves (Ashford, 2009; Zukic, 2009). Cyberspace also creates what Gajjala (2004) terms "cyborg diaspora," online communities of postcolonial (trans) nationals. Researching high-risk intersectional identity communities often becomes easier on the Internet and provides benefits to subjects or coresearchers and researchers or coparticipants (Campbell, 2004; Walstrom, 2004). If intersectionality is understood as an approach to analyze how social and cultural roles, identities, and categories intertwine to produce multiple axes of oppression, then cyberspace can provide a rich field of analysis, in both heavily and sparsely connected societies. The intersection of "real" and virtual, digital, and social networked and isolated subjectivities, especially from a feminist intersectional perspective, is an under-researched realm. Studies of social informatics often surprisingly overlook issues of gender, race, and class. Those that do not tend to overlook the issue of intersectionality, using singular identity variables instead. We argue that an intersection of feminist and online methodologies can enrich not just feminist research but also media studies and policy studies by incorporating a fresh new understanding of composite and hybrid identities occupying the fringes and luminal spaces of a globalized neoliberal market society.

While cyberspace can become a liberating space for marginalized groups, activists, feminist researchers, and feminisms, it also presents grave socio-ethical questions. Websites can be used as weapons against feminism (e.g., anti-abortion websites or religious fundamentalist websites), and the same anonymity that frees and empowers marginalized voices can be used to stifle these voices. Comments on video-sharing websites such as YouTube or on new websites such as NYTimes.com, certain groups formed on social networking websites such as Facebook, and numerous other blogs, forums, and chatting websites represent some of the staunchest and most violent articulations of racism, sexism, and ethnocentrism. The Internet also embodies anomie, a lack of social values and norms (embodied in the proliferation of expressions associated with stark individualism, free expression, desire for financial gain, belief in equal opportunity) that translate into hostility toward marginalized groups such as "illegal immigrants" or "welfare moms." The opportunity for undeterred free speech and infinite dissemination of hypertexts (in spite of legal and user-generated deterrents such as moderator activities) can amount to symbolic violence and the swaying of public beliefs against feminism and other social justice issues. The disembodied experience of the Internet threatens the cohesive community structure and collective consciousness conventionally associated with social movements.

There's also the issue of access and the digital divide. The latest Pew data show that more than 80% of the American society has regular online access, but technology adoption within lower income and racial minority communities remains lower with a slow rate of growth. The rate of technology integration in global South countries such as India or in strife-torn nations such as Afghanistan is even lower, and although in the former, Internet use is picking up, in the latter, it still remains elusive, especially for women. Thus, while considering technological empowerment, we should keep in mind the social, economic, and political situatedness of the concept (Blair et al., 2009).

Another problem is the issue of misrepresentation. Gajjala (2004) contends that the Internet, specifically cyber diasporas, can slip into becoming postcolonial hegemonic agents and native informers, creating monolithic categories of a certain kind of women and their experiences. Thus, the issue of epistemic injustice and homogenization must be kept in mind while doing feminist research about the Internet or while using the Internet in this research. Feminist ethnography and feminist media studies are powerful realms of investigation and intervention, but they demand the same or perhaps an increased level of reflexivity on the part of researchers in their dialogic encounters with the "researched." The issues of the power and the material and cultural privilege of the researcher must be inserted into the project, negotiated, troubled. Walstrom (2004) advances an "engaged research approach" that makes the researcher emotionally and interactionally invested in the research of online communities that ultimately benefits the communities in some way (p. 174). Campbell (2004) calls for a similar approach of imbrications and engagement. Hine (2005) reminds researchers that technology is not what makes online research unique; it is the nature of the interaction, the new rules of communication. It is important to pay attention to the political and material conditions of such communication and to the processes of cyber formation—to go beyond what a website or forum says in order to understand the process of formation of these spaces.

Access to technology and "ease" of use remain seminal issues to consider when we look at the role of ICT in feminist research. Eubanks (2000) contends that the trend of simplifying technology for women, making it more user-friendly, is dangerously exclusionary. The Internet displays a "frontier rhetoric," which dictates the logic of technology integration. Here is an explication:

> American frontier rhetoric, in both its historical and contemporary incarnations, is both deeply contradictory and shockingly consistent. On one hand, it professes the ideals of self-determination, democracy, individual freedom, universal possibility, and connectivity. On the other, it authorizes selfishness, profiteering, lack of community responsibility, colonialism, and violent conquest. This two-faced rhetoric was deployed to justify many of the gross injustices of the geographical frontier; my concern is that it is justifying similar (albeit more subtle) behavior on the Internet. (Eubanks, 2000, ¶ 17)

In spite of all the issues outlined, the Internet continues to remain a space of powerful feminist intervention, represented by some feminists as the new feminist "e-criture" or what Kristeva (1986) theorized as the herethics of feminist writing. The Internet can become the site of "unrepresentable power" and subversion that mocks the rigid grammatical structure of language and turns the "lack" in feminine, as theorized in psychoanalysis, to something empowering. Cyberspace can open up spaces for transnational feminist engagements and preserve, promote, and protect the voices of those whose "speech" and "speakability" have been compromised historically by structures of colonialism, capitalism, epistemology, and technology.

Conclusion

Feminist methodology has not lost its ability to inspire a new generation of young feminist researchers or to continue to engage more seasoned researchers. Some are located in academia, and some are located in policy institutes, in government, and in nongovernmental agencies and organizations. Some are more familiar with the new technologies than others, yet they are researching some of the most challenging questions of our time. We know that methodological training and education is a lifetime proposition. It is encouraging to us that so many young scholars continue to produce new ideas about the role of research and new techniques and technologies for doing feminist research. They challenge us, and they ignite our passion for knowledge—the passion that motivates us to want to change the world.

Discussion Questions

1. What are some of the major dilemmas faced by feminist researchers, and what are some of the ways to address them?

2. Feminist methodology has gained a lot of currency in other disciplines and fields of research. What does this phenomenon mean for the corpus of feminist methodology? Will it expand the interpretive and interventional space of feminist research? Will it change other fields?

3. How is feminist policy research different from other forms of policy studies? What are some of the key issues and questions that must form a part of feminist policy research?

4. What is the double bind in using technology in feminist research and researching gendered technology? How does technology alter the feminist research imaginary? What are some ethical issues involved?

Online Resources

Engendering the Archive

http://www.socialdifference.org/projects/archives

This site, hosted by the Center for the Critical Analysis of Social Difference at Columbia University, is an interdisciplinary project that focuses on the "archive" as a repertoire of social and political memory products and discourses. It investigates the gendered nature of archives and archival research and provides resources and a platform to discuss feminist methodological and epistemological issues.

Gender Evaluation Methodology (GEM)

http://www.apcwomen.org/gem/

GEM is a guide to integrate gender analysis in research using information and communication technology (ICT). The GEM guide covers three phases: (1) integrating gender analysis, (2) gathering information using gender and ICT indicators, and (3) putting evaluation results to work. This website provides a comprehensive overview of GEM and is a resource for feminist researchers, especially those working in development and policy.

Gender Analysis Framework

http://www.gdrc.org/gender/framework/framework.html

This website, provided by the Global Development Research Center (GDRC), provides practical assistance in using gender as a category of analysis in research. It features analytical tools such as the Gender Analysis Matrix and the Access and Activity Profile.

Realities, Part of the ESRC National Centre for Research Methods

http://www.socialsciences.manchester.ac.uk/realities/aboutus/index.html

This is a website of the University of Manchester that has ongoing projects on innovative qualitative

and mixed methodologies. The focus is on intergenerational dynamics, memory as method, and "critical associations."

Relevant Journals

Feminist Theory

Forum: Qualitative Social Research (Online only)

Frontiers: A Journal of Women Studies

Signs: Journal of Women in Culture and Society

The Scholar and Feminist (S & F) Online

References

Ackerly, B. A., & True, J. (2010). *Doing feminist research in political and social science.* New York: Palgrave/Macmillan.

Ashford, C. (2009). Queer theory, cyber-ethnographies, and researching online sex environments. *Information and Communications Technology Law, 18*(3), 297–314.

Blair, K. B., Gajjala, R., & Tulley, C. (2009). *Webbing cyberfeminist practice: Communities, pedagogies, and social action.* Cresskill, NJ: Hampton Press.

Bloom, L. R. (1998). *Under the sign of hope: Feminist methodology and narrative interpretation.* Albany, NY: SUNY Press.

Brisolara, S., & Seigart, D. (2007). Feminist evaluation research. In S. N. Hesse-Biber (Ed.), *Handbook of feminist research* (pp. 277–295). Thousand Oaks, CA: Sage.

Butler, J. P. (1987). *Subjects of desire: Hegelian reflections in twentieth-century France.* New York: Columbia University Press.

Campbell, N. (2004). Making sense of imbrication: Popular technology and "inside-out" methodologies. *Proceedings of the Eighth Conference on Participatory Design—Artful Integration: Interweaving Media, Materials, and Practices, 1,* 65–73.

Campbell, N. D., & Fonow, M. M. (Eds.). (2009). Knowledge that matters: Feminist epistemology, methodology, and science [Special issue]. *Frontiers: A Journal of Women Studies, 30*(1).

Clarke, A. (2005). *Situational analysis: Grounded theory after the postmodern turn.* Thousand Oaks, CA: Sage.

Clarke, A. (2007). Feminisms, grounded theory, and situational analysis. In S. Nagy Hesse-Biber (Ed.), *Handbook of feminist research* (pp. 345–370). Thousand Oaks, CA: Sage.

Cook, J. A., & Fonow, M. M. (2005). Feminist methodology: New applications in the academy and public policy. *Signs: Journal of Women in Culture and Society, 30*(4), 2211–2236.

DeVault, M. L. (1999). *Liberating method: Feminism and social research*. Philadelphia: Temple University Press.

Eubanks, V. (2000). Paradigms and perversions: A women's place in cyberspace. *The CPSR Newsletter, 18*(1). Retrieved June 24, 2011, from http://cpsr.org/prevsite/publications/newsletters/issues/2000/Winter2000/eubanks.html

Eubanks, V. (2004). Cyberfeminism meets NAFTAzteca: Recoding the technotext. In R. Eglash, J. L. Croissant, G. Di Chiro, & R. Fouché (Eds.), *Appropriating technology: Vernacular science and social power* (pp. 151–162). Minneapolis: University of Minnesota Press.

Eubanks, V. (2007). Trapped in digital divide: The distributive paradigm in community informatics. *The Journal of Community Informatics, 3*(2). Retrieved June 24, 2011, from http://www.ci-journal.net/index.php/ciej/article/view/293/318

Fonow, M. M., & Cook, J. (1991). *Beyond methodology: Feminist scholarship as lived research*. Bloomington: Indiana University Press.

Fonow, M. M., & Cook, J. (2005). Feminist methodology: New applications in the academy and public policy. *Signs: Journal of Women and Culture in Society, 30*(4), 2211–2236.

Gajjala, R. (2004). *Cyber selves: Feminist ethnographies of South Asian women*. Walnut Creek, CA: AltaMira Press.

Generett, G., & Jeffries, R. (Eds.). (2003). *Black women in the field: Experiences understanding ourselves and others through qualitative research*. Cresskill, NJ: Hampton Press.

Gottfried, H. (Ed.). (1996). *Feminism and social change: Bridging theory and practice*. Urbana: University of Illinois Press.

Haas, A. (2009). Wired wombs: A rhetorical analysis of online infertility support communities. In K. Blair, R. Gajjala, & C. Tulley (Eds.), *Webbing cyberfeminist practice: Communities, pedagogies, and social action* (pp. 61–84). Cresskill, NJ: Hampton Press.

Halse, C., & Honey, A. (2005). Unravelling ethics: Illuminating the moral dilemmas of research ethics. *Signs: Journal of Women in Culture and Society, 30*(4), 2141–2162.

Harding, S., & Norberg, K. (Eds.). (2005). Methodologies [Special issue]. *Signs: Journal of Women in Culture and Society, 30*(4).

Hargittai, E. (Ed.). (2008). *Research confidential: Solutions to problems most social scientists pretend they never have*. Ann Arbor: University of Michigan Press.

Hawthorne, S., & Klein, R. (1999). Cyberfeminism: Introduction. In S. Hawthorne & R. Klein (Eds.), *Cyberfeminism: Connectivity, critique, and creativity* (pp. 1–16). N. Melbourne, Australia: Spinifex Press.

Hesse-Biber, S. N. (Ed.). (2007). *Handbook of feminist research: Theory and praxis*. Thousand Oaks, CA: Sage.

Hesse-Biber, S. N., & Piatelli, D. (2007). From theory to method and back again: The synergistic praxis of theory and method. In S. Nagy Hesse-Biber (Ed.), *Handbook of feminist research* (pp. 143–153). Thousand Oaks, CA: Sage.

Hesse-Biber, S. N., & Yaiser, M. L. (2004). *Feminist perspectives on social research*. New York: Oxford University Press.

Hine, C. (2005). *Virtual methods: Issues in social research on the Internet*. Oxford, UK: Berg Publishers.

Hunter, L. (1999). *Critiques of knowing: Situated textualities in science, computing, and the arts*. New York: Routledge.

Intimate public practices [Special issue]. (2009). *Feminist Theory, 10*(3).

Jacobs, M. (Ed.). (2002). *Is anyone listening? Women, work, and society*. Toronto, ON: Women's Press.

Kirsch, G. E. (2005). Friendship, friendliness, and feminist fieldwork. *Signs: Journal of Women in Culture and Society, 30*(4), 2163–2172.

Kristeva, J. (Ed.). (1986). Stabat Mater. In T. Moi (Ed.), *The Kristeva reader* (pp. 160–186). New York: Columbia University Press.

Lather, P. (2001). Postbook: Working the ruins of feminist ethnography. *Signs: Journal of Women in Culture and Society, 27*(1), 199–228.

Lather, P. (2007). *Getting lost: Feminist efforts toward a double(d) science*. Albany, NY: SUNY Press.

Lather, P., & Smithies, C. (1997). *Troubling the angels: Women living with HIV/AIDS*. Boulder, CO: Westview.

Letherby, G. (2003). *Feminist research in theory and practice*. Buckingham, UK: Open University Press.

Luker, K. (2008). *Salsa dancing into the social sciences: Research in an age of info-glut*. Cambridge, MA: Harvard University Press.

Matrix, S. (2002). Cyberfigurations: Constructing cyberculture and virtual subjects in popular media. *Dissertation Abstracts International, 63A*(12), 4502.

McCall, L. (2005). The complexity of intersectionality. *Signs: Journal of Women in Culture and Society, 30*(3), 1771–1800.

McPherson, T. (2009). "Resisting" the utopic-dystopic binary. In K. Blair, R. Gajjala, & C. Tulley (Eds.), *Webbing cyberfeminist practice: Communities, pedagogies, and social action* (pp. 379–384). Cresskill, NJ: Hampton Press.

Mohanty, C. T. (2002). "Under Western Eyes" revisited: Feminist solidarity through anticapitalist struggles. *Signs: Journal of Women in Culture and Society, 28*(2), 499–535.

Naples, L. H. (1990). *Who knows? From Quine to a feminist empiricism*. Philadelphia: Temple University Press.

Parker, L., Deyhle, D., & Villenas, S. (Eds.). (1999). *Race is. . . race isn't: Critical race theory and qualitative studies in education*. Boulder, CO: Westview.

Pierce, T. T. (2007). Women, weblogs, and war: Digital culture and gender performativity. Three case studies of online discourse by Muslim cyberconduits of Afghanistan, Iran, and Iraq. *Dissertation Abstracts International, 68A*(03), 3255020.

Ramazannoglu, C., & Holland, J. (2002). *Feminist methodology: Challenges and choices*. London: Sage.

Ramsey, A. E., Sharer, W. B., L'Eplattenier, B., & Mastrangelo, A. S. (2010). *Working in the archives: Practical research methods for rhetoric and composition*. Carbondale: Southern Illinois University Press.

Sandoval, C. (2000). *Methodology of the oppressed*. Minneapolis: University of Minnesota Press.

Smith, D. (1998). *Writing the social: Critique, theory, and investigations*. Toronto, ON: University of Toronto Press.

Smith, D. (2005). *Institutional ethnography: Sociology for people*. Lanham, MD: AltaMira Press.

Smith, L. T. (1999). *Decolonizing methodologies: Research and indigenous peoples*. London: Zed Press.

Steedman, C. (2002). *Dust: The archive and cultural history*. New Brunswick, NJ: Rutgers University Press.

St. Pierre, E. A., & Pillow, W. S. (Eds.). (2000). *Working the ruins: Feminist poststructural theory and methods in education*. New York: Routledge.

Tuana, N., & Morgen, S. (Eds.). (2001). *Engendering rationalities*. Albany, NY: SUNY Press.

Twine, F. W., & Warren, J. W. (Eds.). (2000). *Racing research/Researching race: Methodological dilemmas in critical race studies*. New York: New York University Press.

Valerie, L. (1996). *Granny midwives and black women writers: Double-Dutched readings*. New York: Routledge.

Walstrom, M. K. (2004). Ethics and engagement in communication scholarship: Analyzing public, online support groups as researcher/participant-experiencer. In E. A. Buchanan (Ed.), *Readings in virtual research ethics: Issues and controversies* (pp. 174–200). Hershey, PA: Information Science Publishing.

Zukic, N. (2009). Sehakia's voices: Realigning the zone of the speakable in cyberspace. In K. Blair, R. Gajjala, & C. Tulley (Eds.), *Webbing cyberfeminist practice: Communities, pedagogies and social action* (pp. 287–308). Cresskill, NJ: Hampton Press.

AUTHOR INDEX

SUBJECT INDEX

SAGE Research Methods Online

The essential tool for researchers

An expert research tool

- An **expertly designed taxonomy** with more than 1,400 unique terms for social and behavioral science research methods

- **Visual and hierarchical search tools** to help you discover material and link to related methods

- Easy-to-use navigation tools
- Content organized by complexity
- Tools for citing, printing, and downloading content with ease
- Regularly updated content and features

A wealth of essential content

- The most comprehensive picture of quantitative, qualitative, and mixed methods available today

- More than **100,000 pages of SAGE book and reference material** on research methods as well as editorially selected material from SAGE journals

- More than **600 books** available in their entirety online

Launching 2011!

SAGE research methods online